For Students

MEANINGFUL HELP AND FEEDBACK

- Personalized interactive learning aids for point-of-use help and immediate feedback. These learning aids include:
  - "Help Me Solve This" walks students through solving an algorithmic version of the questions they are working, with additional detailed tutorial reminders. These informational cues assist the students and help them understand concepts and mechanics.
  - "Accounting Simplified" videos give students a 3- to 5-minute lesson on concepts. Our new videos are engaging whiteboard animations that help illustrate concepts for students.
  - eText links students directly to the concept covered in the problem they are working on.
  - Homework and practice exercises with additional algorithmically generated problems for further practice and mastery.

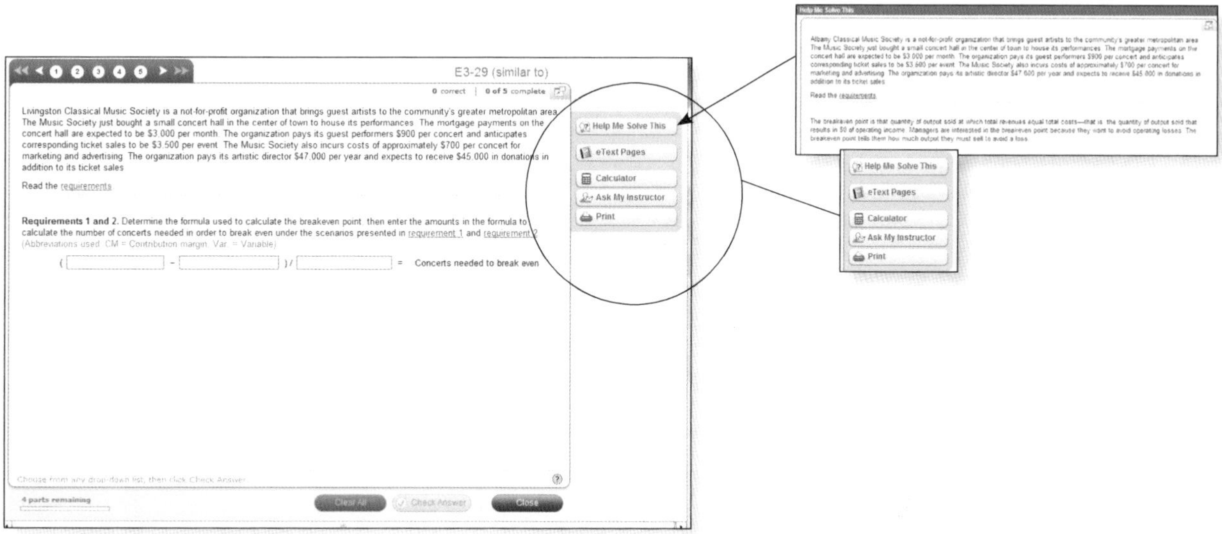

PERSONALIZED STUDY PATH

- Assists students in monitoring their own progress by offering them a customized study plan based on Homework, Quiz, and Test results.
- Includes regenerated exercises with unlimited practice and the opportunity to prove mastery through Quizzes on recommended learning objectives.

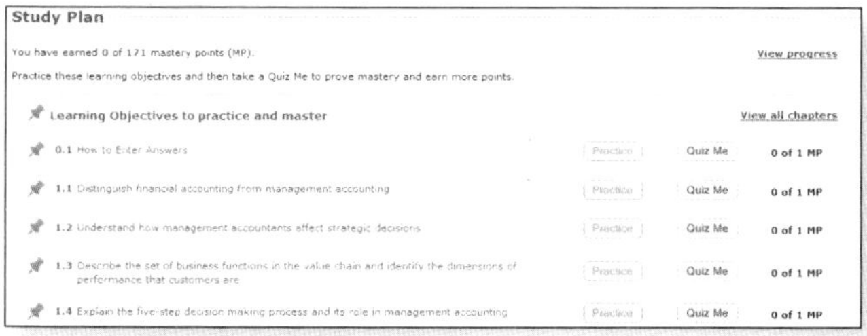

Managerial Accounting

Making Decisions and Motivating Performance

Srikant M. Datar

Madhav V. Rajan

PEARSON

Boston Columbus Indianapolis New York San Francisco Upper Saddle River
Amsterdam Cape Town Dubai London Madrid Milan Munich Paris Montreal Toronto
Delhi Mexico City Sao Paulo Sydney Hong Kong Seoul Singapore Taipei Tokyo

Editor in Chief: Donna Battista
Acquisitions Editor: Ellen Geary
VP/Director of Development: Stephen Deitmer
Development Editors: Deepa Chungi, Lena Buonanno
Editorial Project Manager: Nicole Sam
Editorial Assistants: Jane Avery, Lauren Zanedis
Director of Marketing: Maggie Moylan Leen
Marketing Manager: Alison Haskins
Director of Production: Erin Gregg
Managing Editor: Jeffrey Holcomb
Associate Managing Editor: Karen Carter
Senior Operations Supervisor: Evelyn Beaton
Senior Operations Specialist: Carol Melville
Art Director: Anthony Gemmellaro
Interior Design: Studio Montage
Cover Design: Anthony Gemmellaro
Permissions Specialist: Jill C. Dougan
Image Lead: Rachel Youdelman
Full-Service Project Management: Laserwords
Printer/Binder: LSC Communications
Cover Printer: LSC Communications
Text Font: Minion Pro 10/12

Credits and acknowledgments borrowed from other sources and reproduced, with permission, in this textbook appear on the appropriate page within text.

Library of Congress Cataloging-in-Publication Data

Datar, Srikant M.
Managerial Accounting : Making Decisions and Motivating Performance / Srikant M. Datar, Madhav Rajan. — First edition.
pages cm
Includes index.
ISBN-13: 978-0-13-702487-2
ISBN-10: 0-13-702487-8
1. Managerial accounting. I. Rajan, Madhav V. II. Title.
HF5657.4.D37 2014
658.15'11—dc23

2012040618

PEARSON

ISBN 10: 0-13-702487-8
ISBN 13: 978-0-13-702487-2

Dedication

To our grandparents, parents, in-laws, and siblings for their boundless love and support

Table of Contents

14 Strategy, Balanced Scorecard, and Strategic Profitability Analysis 583

15 Transfer Pricing 624

About the Authors

Srikant M. Datar is the Arthur Lowes Dickinson Professor at Harvard University. A graduate with distinction from the University of Bombay, he received gold medals upon graduation from the Indian Institute of Management, Ahmedabad, and the Institute of Cost and Works Accountants of India. A chartered accountant, he holds two master's degrees and a doctoral degree from Stanford University.

Cited by his students as a dedicated and innovative teacher, Dr. Datar received the George Leland Bach Award for Excellence in the Classroom at Carnegie Mellon University and the Distinguished Teaching Award at Stanford University.

Dr. Datar has published his research in leading accounting, marketing, and operations management journals, including *The Accounting Review, Contemporary Accounting Research, Journal of Accounting, Auditing and Finance, Journal of Accounting and Economics, Journal of Accounting Research,* and *Management Science.* He has also served on the editorial board of several journals and presented his research to corporate executives and academic audiences in North America, South America, Asia, Africa, Australia, and Europe.

Dr. Datar is a member of the board of directors of HCL Technologies Ltd., ICF International, Novartis A.G., and Stryker Corporation, and has worked with many organizations, including Apple Computer, AT&T, Boeing, DuPont, Ford, General Motors, HSBC, Hewlett-Packard, Morgan Stanley, PepsiCo, TRW, Visa, and the World Bank. He is a member of the American Accounting Association and the Institute of Management Accountants.

Madhav V. Rajan is the Robert K. Jaedicke Professor of Accounting and Senior Associate Dean for Academic Affairs and head of the MBA program at Stanford University's Graduate School of Business.

Dr. Rajan received his undergraduate degree in commerce from the University of Madras, India, and his MS in accounting, MBA, and PhD degrees from the Graduate School of Industrial Administration at Carnegie Mellon University. In 1990, his dissertation won the Alexander Henderson Award for Excellence in Economic Theory.

Dr. Rajan's primary area of research interest is the economics-based analysis of management accounting issues, especially as they relate to internal control, cost allocation, capital budgeting, quality management, supply chain, and performance systems in firms. He has published his research in leading accounting and operations management journals including *The Accounting Review, Review of Financial Studies, Journal of Accounting Research,* and *Management Science.* In 2004, he received the Notable Contribution to Management Accounting Literature Award.

Dr. Rajan has served as the Departmental Editor for Accounting at *Management Science,* as well as associate editor for both the accounting and operations areas. From 2002 to 2008, Rajan served as an editor of *The Accounting Review.* Dr. Rajan has twice been a plenary speaker at the AAA Management Accounting Conference.

Dr. Rajan has won several teaching awards at Wharton and Stanford, including the David W. Hauck Award, the highest undergraduate teaching honor at Wharton. He has taught in a variety of executive education programs including the Stanford Executive Program and the National Football League Program for Managers, as well as custom programs for firms including nVidia, Genentech, and Google.

Dr. Rajan is a Director of iShares, Inc. and a Trustee of the iShares Trust.

Preface

Some of your students will become entrepreneurs who create new products or services. Other students will become managers for a range of organizations—from a small business to a large multinational corporation. We developed this book to provide future managers and business owners with the core skills they need to become integral members of their company's decision-making teams. We avoid distracting students with the details of the accounting process and instead emphasize how to understand cost structures, ask intelligent questions about costs, make budgeting decisions, and manage and motivate employee performance.

While the book speaks primarily to the unique needs of management accounting courses in MBA programs, it can also be used in undergraduate management accounting courses for business and accounting majors.

Our Approach

In the last few years, we have received repeated requests from instructors to abridge and focus our book *Cost Accounting: A Managerial Emphasis* for future managers rather than accountants. *Managerial Accounting: Making Decisions and Motivating Performance* aims to fulfill this need. Each chapter highlights decisions that managers make and emphasizes why the management accounting information presented in the chapter is critically important to making those decisions. For example, Chapter 7 discusses decisions managers make about customers and how customer-profitability analysis provides managers with the necessary insights to make wise decisions.

I have been looking for a text just like this. You have hit it on the head. A text really written for MBAs, not an undergrad text adjusted slightly. A book written from the "how to use," not the "how to do" viewpoint.

Alan Czyzewski, Indiana State University

We wrote this book for future managers, appreciating the fact that they do not always need to study accounting details. Our treatment of relevant costs and performance management, for example, focuses on the manager's point of view and omits accounting details. In other topics, however, such as job, process, or product costing, we use simple T-accounts because it helps students understand the flow of costs within a costing system. Future managers need to understand these systems to distinguish inventoriable costs from period costs and to make decisions about pricing, production, and inventory.

In recent years several critics of management education have argued that students are taught theories and frameworks ("knowing") but not the skills, capabilities, and techniques of management practice ("doing") nor the values, attitudes, and beliefs, the preferred treatment of others, and the behaviors that typify integrity, honesty, and fairness ("being"). In this book, we present not just the theories but the implementation methods for topics ranging from activity-based costing to budgeting. We also discuss behavioral issues that arise when managers use management accounting systems to control the activities of a company. Management accounting is more than just learning the technical details. Many times, human factors are crucial to successfully implementing management accounting principles.

I like the focus on managerial decision making.

Paul A. San Miguel, Western Michigan University

The assignment materials reinforce this theme by asking students to think about managerial issues beyond the numbers. At the end of the book, we provide suggestions and approaches for field-based projects where students have the opportunity to learn about the challenges of applying what they have learned in class to real-world settings.

Structural Overview of the Book

We highlight three features of cost accounting and cost management across a wide range of applications and develop these ideas throughout the book: (1) calculating cost of products, services, and other cost objects; (2) analyzing relevant information for making decisions; and (3) obtaining information for planning and control and performance evaluation.

Calculating Cost of Products, Services, and Other Cost Objects

Chapters 4, 5, 6, and 7 describe systems such as job costing, process costing, and activity-based costing. In these chapters, we discuss how managers use these systems to calculate total costs and unit costs of products and services. The chapters also show how managers use this information to formulate strategy and make pricing, product-mix, and cost-management decisions.

> I really like this Chapter 9, just as it is. Everything covered in the chapter is important to a decision maker. In accounting, we provide information that is IMPORTANT to the decision maker, and this book hits it right on target. The way you have the book structured, this chapter slots right in perfectly.
>
> Benny Zachry, Tulane University

Analyzing Relevant Information for Making Decisions

To make decisions about strategy design and strategy implementation, managers must understand which revenues and costs to consider and which ones to ignore.

- Chapter 3 analyzes how operating income changes with changes in units sold and focuses on how managers use this information to make resource allocation decisions.
- Chapter 8 describes methods to estimate the fixed and variable components of costs.
- Chapter 9 applies the concept of relevance to decision making in various situations and describes methods managers use to maximize income given the resource constraints they face.
- Chapter 10 introduces the relevant revenues and costs of quality, inventory, and time.
- Chapter 11 identifies relevant revenues and costs for capital investment decisions.

Obtaining Information for Planning and Control and Performance Evaluation

To execute strategy and implement decisions, managers need to plan actions and monitor outcomes.

- Chapter 12 describes budgeting, the most commonly used tool for planning and control. A budget forces managers to look ahead, to translate strategy into plans, to coordinate and communicate within the organization, and to provide a benchmark for evaluating performance. Budgeting often plays a major role in affecting behavior and decisions because managers strive to meet budget targets.
- Chapter 13 discusses variance analysis. At the end of a reporting period, managers compare actual results to planned performance. The manager's tasks are to understand why variances between actual and planned performances arise and to use the information provided by these variances as feedback to promote learning and future improvement.
- Chapter 14 introduces the balanced scorecard as a tool for implementing strategy.
- Chapter 15 describes the benefits and costs of decentralization and the use of transfer prices to coordinate the actions of different managers.
- Chapter 16 presents various measures for evaluating performance designed to align the interests of managers and owners.

Throughout the book, we use some common pedagogical approaches to present management accounting concepts. We describe these next.

> Information provided in the chapters is very informative and easy to read and follow. Examples are all real companies in the world and students would identify themselves with the companies and issues discussed in each chapter.
>
> Mehmet Kocakulah, University of Southern Indiana

Emphasis on Managerial Decision Making

We build each chapter around an extended real-world example that illustrates a challenge that a manager or management team faces. These examples help students build the decision-making skills they will need to pursue managerial careers. Such examples include:

- Chapter 2, "An Introduction to Cost Terms and Purposes," uses the example of managers making decisions at a BMW plant. What are the alternative ways for managers to define and classify costs? Why is it important for managers to use sound judgment to classify costs?
- Chapter 3, "Cost–Volume–Profit Analysis," follows an entrepreneur who wants to sell a test preparation book and software package. What decisions should she make to ensure a profit?
- Chapter 9, "Decision Making and Relevant Information," considers a strategic decision facing managers at Precision Sporting Goods, a manufacturer of golf clubs: Should it reorganize its manufacturing operations to reduce manufacturing labor costs?

- Chapter 12, "Master Budget and Responsibility Accounting," uses the example of budgeting at Pace, a United Kingdom–based manufacturer of electronic products. How do managers work with individual departments within the company and their supply chain partners to ensure timely production?

Integrating Modern Topics with Traditional Coverage

Many core concepts in management accounting, such as job costing and variance analysis, developed several years ago still have great relevance today. Other concepts such as activity-based costing and lean accounting are more recent. We combine modern topics with traditional coverage in several parts of the book to develop a comprehensive view of the management accounting tools and techniques used by managers today. For example:

- Chapter 4 discusses job costing while Chapter 6 describes circumstances when managers need to implement activity-based costing systems. Chapter 7 then describes how job costing systems can be designed to focus on customers.
- Chapter 9 describes the core ideas of relevant costs. Chapter 10 applies these ideas to modern practices such as managing quality, timeliness, and just-in-time inventory by introducing ideas like value streams and lean accounting.
- Chapter 13 presents traditional variance analysis to monitor and manage operations, as practiced by many corporations around the world. Chapter 14 presents modern approaches to variance analysis used to strategically analyze income statements. It expands the financial focus of variance analysis to nonfinancial measures and the balanced scorecard.

The Practice of Management Accounting

Every chapter emphasizes how the concepts presented in the chapter play out in practice. What are the challenges of implementing the ideas? Why might the information be difficult to obtain? What are the incentives of various parties to do or not to do something?

- Chapter 2 explores the advantages of producing products for inventory, even though the products cannot be sold, and then considers various approaches to controlling such behavior.
- Chapter 8 describes why managers may not take actions that are in the best interests of the company because the decision model conflicts with the performance-evaluation model.
- Chapter 10 presents the challenges of measuring the financial benefits of higher quality and lower inventory.
- Chapter 13 cautions against using variance analysis to allocate blame rather than to learn and improve.

The assignment material for every chapter closes with a case. The cases are designed to help students begin to see the gaps between textbook knowledge and the application of this knowledge in practice. The field-based assignments take this learning one step further. They are specifically designed to reduce the knowing–doing gap by helping students learn that the real challenges of management accounting are not computational but the insufficiency, unavailability, and interpretation of data.

Behavioral Aspects of Management Accounting

This book emphasizes that successful managers pay particular attention to behavioral aspects of management accounting because management accounting is not a mechanical tool. Implementing management accounting techniques requires an understanding of human behavior, persuasion, and intelligent interpretation. For example:

- Chapter 1 discusses ethics and values and the behaviors and judgments needed to lead and motivate people.
- Chapter 12 examines the psychology of stretch targets and why these targets may motivate superior performance.
- Chapter 16 describes the elements of management control systems designed to prevent risky and unethical behavior.

Clarity of Presentation

We have paid particular attention to clarity of presentation, specifically centering on the needs of managers. For example, we have included accounting ideas, such as T-accounts, only when they support the discussion. We have balanced simplicity and detail to help students understand the material without the burden of excessive information.

The majority of cases at the end of the chapters make the text attractive.

Paul A. San Miguel, Western Michigan University

Cases That Emphasize the Managerial Decision-Making Process

Every chapter closes with a case study that reinforces the concepts of the chapter. Each case describes a company, presents a challenge facing the managers, and explores how the managers address the challenge. The case questions test students' understanding of the chapter's concepts and their creativity in applying them. The cases come from a varied group of sources, including the Harvard Business School.

Cases include:

- *Colorscope, Inc.*, from Harvard Business School, explores a graphic arts firm (Chapter 4, "Job Costing").
- *Wilkerson, Inc.*, from Harvard Business School, explores a manufacturer of water purification equipment (Chapter 6, "Activity-Based Costing and Activity-Based Management").
- *To Trim or Not to Trim: That is the Question,* from Harvard Business School, explores Novartis Pharmaceuticals (Chapter 9, "Decision Making and Relevant Information").
- *Liquid Chemical Company,* adapted from Darden Business Publishing, explores the container department of a high-grade chemical manufacturing company (Chapter 11, "Capital Investments").

Features

Concepts in Action Feature

Each chapter includes two or more Concepts in Action boxes that cover real-world cost accounting issues across a variety of industries including retailing, manufacturing, health care, and entertainment. Examples include:

- Home Depot Undergoes an Inventory Management "Fix-It" (Chapter 4, "Job Costing")
- Hybrid Costing for Mi Adidas Customized Sneakers (Chapter 5, "Process Costing and Cost Allocation")
- Hospitals Use Time-Driven Activity-Based Costing to Reduce Costs and Improve Care (Chapter 6, "Activity-Based Costing and Activity-Based Management")
- After the Encore: Just-in-Time Live Concert Recordings (Chapter 10, "Quality, Inventory Management, and Time")

The authors have used some high-profile companies that the students will be familiar with, that is always a plus. I particularly liked that they used some automobile companies in Chapter 3 ... one of my favorite industries to follow and use examples from.

Benny Zachry, Tulane University

Keys to Success Boxes

The Keys to Success boxes filter the key concepts in a chapter through a managerial prism. Scattered throughout the chapters, the Keys to Success focus students on how to apply these concepts in practice.

Assignment Materials

Building managerial decision-making skills requires practice. To provide students with the opportunity to apply and practice what they have learned, each chapter has an extensive array of assignment materials: 10 Questions, 10–12 Exercises, 10–12 Problems, and one case study. Many of the problems contain managerial questions that require students to interpret the numbers they have calculated and recommend plans of action.

Students can complete these and additional exercises on **MyAccountingLab,** get tutorial help, and receive instant feedback and assistance on exercises they answered incorrectly.

Resources

The following resources are available for students:

- MyAccountingLab
- Companion Website—www.pearsonhighered.com/datar

The following resources are available for instructors:

- Solutions Manual
- Test Item File and TestGen
- Instructor's Manual
- PowerPoint Presentations
- Image Library
- Instructor's Resource Center—www.pearsonhighered.com/datar

Acknowledgments

As is customary, we reserve our deepest thanks for our families. Swati (Srikant's wife) and Gayathri (Madhav's wife) have been a source of great strength and solace during the hectic days we spent working on this book. Their love, support, and encouragement kept us going. Radhika, Gayatri, and Sidharth (Srikant's children) and Sanjana and Anupama (Madhav's children) kept us in good spirits by reminding us about the important things in our lives.

Our grandparents, parents, in-laws, and siblings have meant much to us. Srikant thanks Dr. and Mrs. Pandit for the values they instilled, Capt. and Mrs. Datar for the inspiration they provided, Dr. and Mrs. Chaphekar for their warmth and kindness, and Gautam for being special and bringing endless joy and fun. Madhav thanks Dr. and Mrs. Vasantharajan and Mrs. Raghunathan for their gentle encouragement and enduring optimism. For these reasons and many others, we dedicate this book to them.

We are indebted to many people for their ideas and assistance. Our primary thanks go to the many academics and practitioners who have advanced our knowledge of cost accounting. The package of teaching materials we present is the work of skillful and valued team members developing some excellent end-of-chapter assignment material.

Tommy Goodwin, Richard Saouma (University of California Los Angeles), and Shalin Shah (University of California Berkeley) provided outstanding research assistance on technical issues and current developments. We would also like to thank the dedicated and hard-working supplements author team and Laserwords. The book is much better because of the efforts of these colleagues.

In shaping this edition, we would like to thank a group of colleagues who worked closely with us and the editorial team.

Reviewers

Alan B. Czyzewski, Indiana State University

Mehmet Kocakulah, University of Southern Indiana

Paul A. San Miguel, Western Michigan University

Benny R. Zahry, Tulane University

Contributors

Molly Brown, James Madison University

Shannon Charles, University of Utah

Lisa Johnson, Centura College

Accuracy Checkers

Alan Czyzewski, Indiana State University

Victoria Kaskey, Ashland University

Charles J. Russo, Towson University

The Manager and Management Accounting

1

Learning Objectives

1. Distinguish financial accounting from management accounting
2. Understand how management accountants support strategic decisions
3. Describe the set of business functions in the value chain and identify the dimensions of performance that customers are expecting of companies
4. Explain the five-step decision-making process and its role in management accounting
5. Describe three guidelines management accountants follow in supporting managers
6. Understand how management accounting fits into an organization's structure
7. Understand what professional ethics mean to management accountants

All businesses are concerned about revenues and costs. In today's dynamic global business environment, managers at companies small and large must understand how revenues and costs behave or risk losing control. Managers use cost accounting information to make decisions about research and development, budgeting, production planning, pricing and the products or services to offer.

By studying management accounting, you will learn how successful managers run their businesses and prepare yourself for leadership roles. Many large companies, such as Constellation Energy, Nike, and the Pittsburgh Steelers, have senior executives with accounting backgrounds.

The Chapter at a Glance previews key features of management accounting and how it creates value for a company.

Chapter at a Glance

- Managers use management accounting information to make strategic decisions by identifying how a company creates value for its customers as distinct from its competitors.
- Managers implement strategy and add value to customers via six primary business functions: research and development (R&D), design of products and processes, production, marketing, distribution, and customer service.
- The outcome of value creation is improved cost and efficiency, quality, timeliness, and/or innovation.
- To create value, managers use a five-step decision-making process: (1) identify the problem, (2) obtain information, (3) make predictions, (4) choose among alternatives, and (5) implement the decision.
- To guide decision making, managers and management accountants weigh the costs and benefits of different decision alternatives, consider how decisions affect behavior, calculate different costs for different decision purposes, and act in keeping with the highest ethical standards.

Learning Objective 1

Distinguish financial accounting

. . . reporting on past performance to external users

from management accounting

. . . helping managers make decisions

Financial Accounting and Management Accounting

As many of you have already seen in your financial accounting class, accounting systems take economic events and transactions, such as sales and materials purchases, and process the data into information helpful to managers, sales representatives, production supervisors, and others. Processing any economic transaction means collecting, categorizing, summarizing, and analyzing. For example, costs are collected by category, such as materials, labor, and shipping. These costs are then summarized to determine total costs by month, quarter, or year. Accountants analyze the results and together with managers evaluate, say, how costs have changed relative to revenues from one period to the next. Accounting systems provide the information found in the income statement, the balance sheet, the statement of cash flow, and in performance reports, such as the cost of serving customers or running an advertising campaign. Managers use accounting information to make decisions about the activities, businesses, or functional areas they oversee. For example, a report that shows an increase in sales of laptops and iPads at an Apple store may prompt Apple to hire more salespeople at that location. Understanding accounting information is essential for managers to do their jobs.

Individual managers often require the information in an accounting system to be presented or reported differently. Consider, for example, sales order information. A sales manager at Porsche may be interested in the total dollar amount of sales to determine the commissions to be paid. A distribution manager at Porsche may be interested in the sales order quantities by geographic region and by customer-requested delivery dates to ensure timely deliveries. A manufacturing manager at Porsche may be interested in the quantities of various products and their desired delivery dates, so that he or she can develop an effective production schedule. To simultaneously serve the needs of all three managers, Porsche creates a database, sometimes called a data warehouse or infobarn, consisting of small, detailed bits of information that can be used for multiple purposes. For instance, the sales order database will contain detailed information about product, quantity ordered, selling price, and delivery details (place and date) for each sales order. The database stores information in a way that allows different managers to access the information they need. Many companies are building their own enterprise resource planning (ERP) systems, single databases that collect data and feed it into applications that support the company's business activities, such as purchasing, production, distribution, and sales.

Financial accounting and management accounting have different goals. As you know, **financial accounting** focuses on reporting financial information to external parties such as investors, government agencies, banks, and suppliers. It measures and records business transactions and provides financial statements that are based on Generally Accepted Accounting Principles (GAAP). The most important way that financial accounting information affects managers' decisions and actions is through compensation, which is often, in part, based on numbers in financial statements.

Management accounting measures, analyzes, and reports financial and nonfinancial information that helps managers make decisions to fulfill the goals of an organization. Managers use management accounting information to:

1. develop, communicate, and implement strategy
2. coordinate product design, production, and marketing decisions and to evaluate performance

Management accounting information and reports do not have to follow set principles or rules. The key questions are always (1) how will this information help managers do their jobs better, and (2) do the benefits of producing this information exceed the costs?

Exhibit 1-1 summarizes the major differences between management accounting and financial accounting. Note, however, that reports such as balance sheets, income statements, and statements of cash flows are common to both management accounting and financial accounting.

We frequently hear businesspeople use the term *cost management.* Unfortunately, that term does not have a set definition. We use **cost management** to describe the approaches and activities of managers to use resources to increase value to customers and to achieve organizational goals. Cost management decisions include decisions such as whether to enter new markets, implement

Exhibit 1-1

Major Differences Between Management and Financial Accounting

	Management Accounting	Financial Accounting
Purpose of information	Help managers make decisions to fulfill an organization's goals	Communicate organization's financial position to investors, banks, regulators, and other outside parties
Primary users	Managers of the organization	External users such as investors, banks, regulators, and suppliers
Focus and emphasis	Future-oriented (budget for 2013 prepared in 2012)	Past-oriented (reports on 2012 performance prepared in 2013)
Rules of measurement and reporting	Internal measures and reports do not have to follow GAAP but are based on cost-benefit analysis	Financial statements must be prepared in accordance with GAAP and be certified by external, independent auditors
Time span and type of reports	Varies from hourly information to 15 to 20 years, with financial and nonfinancial reports on products, departments, territories, and strategies	Annual and quarterly financial reports, primarily on the company as a whole
Behavioral implications	Designed to influence the behavior of managers and other employees	Primarily reports economic events but also influences behavior because manager's compensation is often based on reported financial results

new organizational processes, and change product designs. Information from accounting systems helps managers to manage costs, but the information and the accounting systems themselves are not cost management.

Cost management has a broad focus and is not only about reduction in costs. Cost management includes decisions to incur additional costs—for example, to improve customer satisfaction and quality and to develop new products—with the goal of enhancing revenues and profits.

Strategic Decisions and the Management Accountant

Learning Objective 2

Understand how management accountants support strategic decisions

. . . they provide information about the sources of competitive advantage

Strategy specifies how an organization matches its own capabilities with the opportunities in the marketplace to accomplish its objectives. In other words, strategy describes how an organization will compete and the opportunities its managers should seek and pursue. Businesses follow one of two broad strategies. Some companies, such as Southwest Airlines and Vanguard (the mutual fund company), follow a cost leadership strategy. They have been profitable and have grown over the years on the basis of providing quality products or services at low prices by judiciously managing their costs. Other companies such as Apple (the computer, phone, and tablet company) and Johnson & Johnson (the pharmaceutical giant) follow a product differentiation strategy. They generate their profits and growth because they offer differentiated or unique products or services that appeal to their customers and are often priced higher than the less-popular products or services of their competitors.

Deciding between these strategies is a critical part of what managers do. Management accountants work closely with managers in various departments to formulate strategies by providing information about the sources of competitive advantage, such as (1) their company's cost, productivity, or efficiency advantage relative to competitors or (2) the premium prices a company can charge relative to the costs of adding features that make its products or services distinctive. **Strategic cost management** describes cost management that specifically focuses on strategic issues.

Management accounting information helps managers formulate strategy by answering questions such as the following:

- *Who are our most important customers, and how can we be competitive and deliver value to them?* After Amazon.com's success in selling books online, management accountants at Barnes and Noble presented senior executives with the costs and benefits of several alternative approaches for building its information technology infrastructure and developing the capabilities to also sell books online. A similar cost-benefit analysis led Toyota to build flexible computer-integrated manufacturing plants that enable it to use the same equipment efficiently to produce a variety of cars in response to changing customer tastes.
- *What substitute products exist in the marketplace, and how do they differ from our product in terms of price, cost, and quality?* Hewlett-Packard, for example, designs, costs, and prices new printers after comparing the functionality and quality of its printers to other printers available in the marketplace.
- *What is our most critical capability? Is it technology, production, or marketing? How can we leverage it for new strategic initiatives?* Kellogg Company, for example, uses the reputation of its brand to introduce new types of cereals with high profit margins.
- *Will adequate cash be available to fund the strategy, or will additional funds need to be raised?* Proctor & Gamble, for example, issued new debt and equity to fund its strategic acquisition of Gillette, a maker of shaving products.

The best-designed strategies and the best-developed capabilities are useless unless they are effectively executed. In the next section, we describe how management accountants help managers take actions that create value for their customers.

Learning Objective 3

Describe the set of business functions in the value chain and identify the dimensions of performance that customers are expecting of companies

. . . R&D, design, production, marketing, distribution, and customer service supported by administration to achieve cost and efficiency, quality, time, and innovation

Value-Chain and Supply-Chain Analysis and Key Success Factors

Customers demand much more than just a fair price; they expect quality products (goods or services) delivered in a timely way. The entire customer experience determines the value a customer derives from a product. In this section, we explore how a company goes about creating this value.

Value-Chain Analysis

Value chain is the sequence of business functions in which customer usefulness is added to products. Exhibit 1-2 shows six primary business functions: research and development (R&D), design of products and processes, production, marketing, distribution, and customer service. We illustrate these business functions with Sony Corporation's television division.

1. **Research and development (R&D)**—Generating and experimenting with ideas related to new products, services, or processes. At Sony, this function includes research on alternative television signal transmission and on the picture quality of different shapes and thicknesses of television screens.
2. **Design of products and processes**—Detailed planning, engineering, and testing of products and processes. Design at Sony includes determining the number of component parts in a television set and the effect of alternative product designs on quality and manufacturing costs. Some representations of the value chain collectively refer to the first two steps as technology development.[1]
3. **Production**—Procuring, transporting and storing ("inbound logistics"), coordinating, and assembling ("operations") resources to produce a product or deliver a service. Production of a Sony television set includes the procurement and assembly of the electronic parts, the cabinet, and the packaging used for shipping.
4. **Marketing (including sales)**—Promoting and selling products or services to customers or prospective customers. Sony markets its televisions at trade shows, via advertisements in newspapers and magazines, on the Internet, and through its sales force.
5. **Distribution**—Processing orders and shipping products or services to customers ("outbound logistics"). Distribution for Sony includes shipping to retail outlets, catalog vendors, direct sales via the Internet, and other channels through which customers purchase new televisions.

[1] M. Porter, *Competitive Advantage* (New York: Free Press, 1985).

Exhibit 1-2

Different Parts of the Value Chain

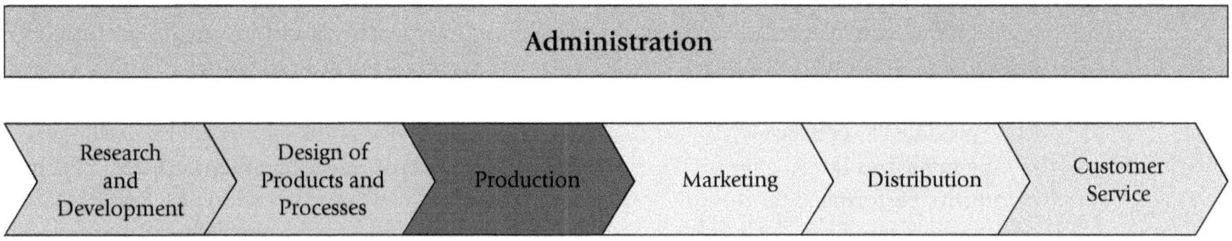

6. **Customer service—**Providing after-sales service to customers. Sony provides customer service on its televisions in the form of customer-help telephone lines, support on the Internet, and warranty repair work.

In addition to the six primary business functions, Exhibit 1-2 shows an administrative function, which includes accounting and finance, human resource management, and information technology, that supports the six primary business functions. When discussing the value chain in subsequent chapters of the book, we include the administrative function within the primary functions. For example, included in the marketing function is the function of analyzing, reporting, and accounting for resources spent in different marketing channels, while the production function includes the human resource management function of training front-line workers.

Each of these business functions is essential to companies satisfying their customers and keeping them satisfied (and loyal) over time. To implement their corporate strategies, companies such as Sony and Procter & Gamble use **customer relationship management (CRM),** a strategy that integrates people and technology in all business functions to deepen relationships with customers, partners, and distributors. CRM initiatives use technology to coordinate all customer-facing activities (such as marketing, sales calls, distribution, and after-sales support) and the design and production activities necessary to get products to customers.

Different companies create value in different ways—cost and efficiency at Lowe's (the home-improvement retailer); quality at Toyota Motor Company; fast response times at eBay (the online auction giant); innovation at Genentech (the biotechnology leader); and building a consumer brand at Gucci. As a result, at different times and in different industries, one or more of these functions is more critical than others. For example, a company such as Genentech, which develops innovative new biotechnology products, will emphasize R&D and design of products and processes, while a company such as Gucci in the consumer goods industry will focus on marketing, distribution, and customer service to build its brand.

Exhibit 1-2 depicts the usual order in which different business-function activities physically occur. Do not, however, interpret Exhibit 1-2 as implying that managers should proceed sequentially through the value chain when planning and managing their activities. Companies gain (in terms of cost, quality, and the speed with which new products are developed) if two or more of the individual business functions of the value chain work concurrently as a team. For example, inputs into design decisions by production, marketing, distribution, and customer service managers often lead to design choices that reduce total costs for the company.

Managers track the costs incurred in each value-chain category. Their goal is to reduce costs and to improve efficiency. Management accounting information helps managers make cost–benefit tradeoffs. For example, is it cheaper to buy products from outside vendors or to do manufacturing in-house? How does investing resources in design and manufacturing reduce costs of marketing and customer service?

Keys to Success

Managers use management accounting information to create value for their customers via six primary business functions: research and development, design of products and processes, production, marketing, distribution, and customer service.

Supply-Chain Analysis

The parts of the value chain associated with producing and delivering a product or service—production and distribution—are referred to as the *supply chain*. **Supply chain** describes the flow of goods, services, and information from the initial sources of materials and services to the delivery of products to consumers, regardless of whether those activities occur in the same organization or in other organizations. Consider Coke and Pepsi, for example; many companies play a role in bringing these products to consumers. Exhibit 1-3 presents an overview of the supply chain. Cost management emphasizes integrating and coordinating activities across all companies in the supply chain, to improve performance and reduce costs. Both the Coca-Cola Company and Pepsi Bottling Group require their suppliers (such as plastic and aluminum companies and sugar refiners) to frequently deliver small quantities of materials directly to the production floor to reduce materials-handling costs. Similarly, to reduce inventory levels in the supply chain, Walmart is asking its suppliers, such as Coca-Cola, to be responsible for and to manage inventory at both the Coca-Cola warehouse and Walmart.

Key Success Factors

Customers want companies to use the value chain and supply chain to deliver ever-improving levels of performance regarding several (or even all) of the following:

- **Cost and efficiency**—Companies face continuous pressure to reduce the cost of the products they sell. To calculate and manage the cost of products, managers must first understand the tasks or activities (such as setting up machines or distributing products) that cause costs to arise. They must also monitor the marketplace to determine prices that customers are willing to pay for products or services. Management accounting information helps managers calculate a target cost for a product by subtracting the operating income per unit of product that the company desires to earn from the "target price." To achieve the target cost, managers eliminate some activities (such as rework) and reduce the costs of performing activities in all value-chain functions—from initial R&D to customer service (see Concepts in Action: Trader Joe's Recipe for Cost Leadership).

  Increased global competition places ever-increasing pressure on companies to lower costs. Many U.S. companies have cut costs by outsourcing some of their business functions. Nike, for example, has moved its manufacturing operations to China and Mexico, and Microsoft and IBM are increasingly doing their software development in Spain, Eastern Europe, and India.
- **Quality**—Customers expect high levels of quality. **Total quality management (TQM)** is an integrative philosophy of management for continuously improving the quality of products and processes. Managers who implement TQM believe that the quality of products and processes is the responsibility of everyone throughout the value chain. The goal of TQM is to deliver products and services that exceed customer expectations. Using TQM, companies design products or services to meet customer needs and wants, to make these products with zero (or very few) defects and waste, and to minimize inventories. Managers use management accounting information to evaluate the costs and revenue benefits of TQM initiatives.

Exhibit 1-3

Supply Chain for a Cola Bottling Company

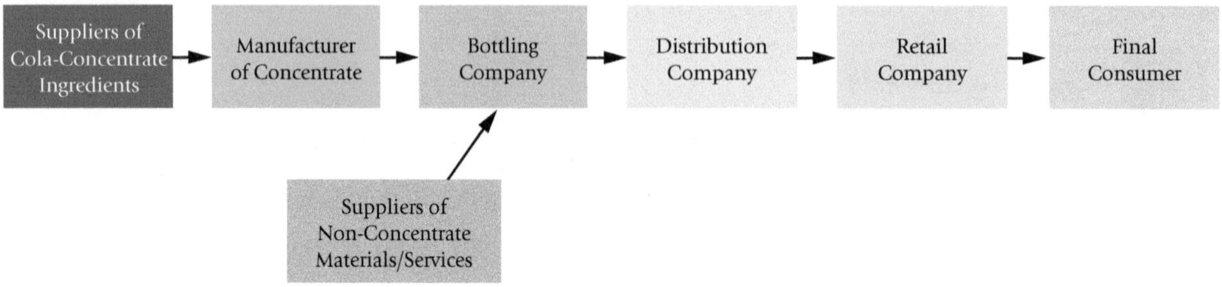

- **Time**—Time has many dimensions. Two of the most important dimensions are new-product development time and customer-response time. New-product development time is the time it takes for companies to create new products and bring them to market. The increasing pace of technological innovation has led to shorter product life cycles and more rapid introduction of new products. To make product and design decisions, managers need to understand the costs and benefits of a product over its life cycle.

  Customer-response time describes the speed at which an organization responds to customer requests. To increase customer satisfaction, organizations need to reduce delivery time and reliably meet promised delivery dates. The primary cause of delays is bottlenecks that occur when the work to be performed on a machine, for example, exceeds available capacity. To deliver the product on time, managers need to increase the capacity of the machine to produce more output. Management accounting information helps managers quantify the costs and benefits of relieving bottleneck constraints.
- **Innovation**—A constant flow of innovative products or services is the basis for ongoing company success. Managers rely on management accounting information to evaluate alternative investment and R&D decisions.

Keys to Success

Managers aim to please customers by delivering low-cost, innovative, and high-quality products and services in a timely way.

Concepts in Action: Trader Joe's Recipe for Cost Leadership

Trader Joe's has a special recipe for cost leadership: delivering unique products at reasonable prices. The grocery store chain stocks its shelves with low-cost, high-end staples (cage-free eggs and organic blue agave sweetener) and exotic, affordable luxuries (Belgian butter waffle cookies and Thai lime-and-chili cashews) that are distinct from what traditional supermarkets offer. Trader Joe's can offer these items at everyday low prices by judiciously managing their costs.

Source: Michael Nagle/Getty Images

At Trader Joe's, customers swap selection for value. The company has relatively small stores with a carefully selected, constantly changing mix of items. While typical grocery stores carry 50,000 items, Trader Joe's sells only about 4,000 items. About 80% of the stock bears the Trader Joe's brand, and management seeks to minimize costs of these items. The company purchases directly from manufacturers, which ship their items straight to Trader Joe's warehouses to avoid third-party distribution costs. With small stores and limited storage space, Trader Joe's trucks leave the warehouse centers daily. This encourages precise, just-in-time ordering and a relentless focus on frequent merchandise turnover.

This winning combination of quality products and low prices has turned Trader Joe's into one of the hottest retailers in the United States. Its stores sell an estimated $1,750 in merchandise per square foot annually, which is more than double Whole Foods, its top competitor.

Sources: Based on Beth Kowitt, "Inside the Secret World of Trader Joe's," *Fortune* (August 23, 2010); Christopher Palmeri, "Trader Joe's Recipe for Success," *Businessweek* (February 21, 2008); and Mark Mallinger and Gerry Rossy, "The Trader Joe's Experience: The Impact of Corporate Culture on Business Strategy," *Graziadio Business Review* (2007, Volume 10, Issue 2).

Sustainability

Companies are increasingly applying the key success factors of cost and efficiency, quality, time, and innovation to promote **sustainability**—the development and implementation of strategies to achieve long-term financial, social, and environmental performance. For example, the sustainability efforts of Japanese copier company Ricoh focuses on energy conservation, resource conservation, product recycling, and pollution prevention. By designing products that can be easily recycled, Ricoh simultaneously improves efficiency, cost, and quality. Interest in sustainability appears to be intensifying.

Recently, many companies, such as General Electric, Poland Springs, and Hewlett-Packard, have placed increased importance on sustainability in their decision making. Sustainability performance is important to these companies for several reasons:

- More and more investors care about sustainability. These investors make investment decisions based on a company's financial, social, and environmental performance, and raise questions about sustainability at shareholder meetings.
- Companies that emphasize sustainability find that sustainability goals attract and inspire employees.
- Customers favor products of companies with good reputations for sustainability and boycott products of companies with poor sustainability records.
- Society, and in particular activist nongovernmental organizations, monitor the sustainability performance of different companies and act against companies with weak sustainability and environmental records by initiating legal action against them. Already, government regulations in countries such as China and India are encouraging companies to develop and report on their sustainability initiatives.

Besides tracking the economic and sustainability performance of their own companies, management accountants help managers track performance of competitors on the key success factors. Competitive information serves as a *benchmark* and alerts managers to market changes. These benchmarks motivate companies to *continuously improve* their operations. These improvements include on-time arrival for Southwest Airlines, customer access to online auctions at eBay, and cost reduction on home-improvement products at Lowe's. Sometimes, more fundamental changes in operations, such as redesigning a manufacturing process to reduce costs, may be necessary. However, successful strategy implementation requires more than value-chain and supply-chain analysis and execution of key success factors. The decisions that managers make help them to develop, integrate, and implement their strategies. Good decision-making processes, such as the planning and control systems at General Electric, support sustained long-term value creation.

Learning Objective 4

Explain the five-step decision-making process

. . . identify the problem and uncertainties; obtain information; make predictions about the future; make decisions by choosing among alternatives; implement the decision, evaluate performance, and learn

and its role in management accounting

. . . planning and control of operations and activities

Decision Making, Planning, and Control

We illustrate a five-step decision-making process using the example of the *Daily News*, a newspaper in Boulder, Colorado. Subsequent chapters of the book describe how managers use this five-step decision-making process to make many different types of decisions.

The *Daily News* differentiates itself from its competitors by using (1) highly respected journalists who prepare in-depth analyses of news, (2) color to enhance attractiveness to readers and advertisers, and (3) a Web site that delivers up-to-the-minute news, interviews, and analyses. The newspaper has the following resources to deliver on this strategy: an automated, computer-integrated, state-of-the-art printing facility; a Web-based information technology infrastructure; and a distribution network that is one of the best in the newspaper industry.

To keep up with steadily increasing production costs, Naomi Crawford, manager of the *Daily News*, needs to increase revenues. To decide what she should do, Naomi works through the five-step decision-making process.

1. **Identify the problem and uncertainties.** Naomi has two main choices: (a) increase the selling price of the newspaper or (b) increase the rate per page charged to advertisers. The key uncertainty is the effect on demand of any increase in prices or rates. A decrease in demand could offset price or rate increases and lead to lower overall revenues.
2. **Obtain information.** Gathering information before making a decision helps managers gain a better understanding of uncertainties. Naomi asks her marketing manager to talk to some representative readers to gauge their reaction to an increase in the newspaper's selling price.

She asks her advertising sales manager to talk to current and potential advertisers to assess demand for advertising. She also reviews the effect that past price increases had on readership. Ramon Sandoval, management accountant at the *Daily News,* presents information about the effect of past increases or decreases in advertising rates on advertising revenues. He also collects and analyzes information on advertising rates competing newspapers and other media outlets charge.

3. **Make predictions about the future.** On the basis of this information, Naomi makes predictions about the future. She concludes that increasing prices would upset readers and decrease readership. She has a different view about advertising rates. She expects a marketwide increase in advertising rates and believes that increasing rates will have little effect on the number of advertising pages sold.

   Naomi recognizes that making predictions requires judgment. She looks for biases in her thinking. Has she correctly judged reader sentiment or is the negative publicity of a price increase overly influencing her decision making? How sure is she that competitors will also increase advertising rates? Is her thinking in this respect biased by how competitors have responded in the past? Have circumstances changed? How confident is she that her sales representatives can convince advertisers to pay higher rates? After retesting her assumptions and reviewing her thinking, Naomi feels comfortable with her predictions and judgments.

4. **Make decisions by choosing among alternatives.** When making decisions, strategy is a vital guidepost. Many individuals in different parts of the organization at different times make decisions. Consistent strategies bind individuals and timelines together and provide a common purpose for disparate decisions. Aligning decisions with strategy enables an organization to achieve its goals.

   Consistent with the product differentiation strategy, Naomi decides to increase advertising rates by 4% to $5,200 per page in March 2013 but not to increase the selling price of the newspaper. She is confident that the *Daily News*'s distinctive style and Web presence will increase readership, creating value for advertisers. She communicates the new advertising rate schedule to the sales department. Without this alignment, decisions will be uncoordinated, pull the organization in different directions, and produce inconsistent results. Ramon estimates advertising revenues of $4,160,000 ($5,200 per page × 800 pages predicted to be sold in March 2013).

   The Concepts in Action: The iTunes Charts describes Apple's decision to increase prices on its most popular songs.

Steps 1 through 4 are collectively referred to as *planning.* **Planning** comprises selecting organization goals and strategies, predicting results under various alternative ways of achieving those goals, deciding how to attain the desired goals, and communicating the goals and how to achieve them to the entire organization. Management accountants serve as business partners in these planning activities because they understand the key success factors and what creates value.

The most important planning tool when implementing strategy is a *budget.* A **budget** is the quantitative expression of a proposed plan of action by management and is an aid to coordinating what needs to be done to execute that plan. For March 2013, budgeted advertising revenue equals $4,160,000. The full budget for March 2013 includes budgeted circulation revenue and the production, distribution, and customer-service costs to achieve sales goals; the anticipated cash flows; and the potential financing needs. Because the process of preparing a budget crosses business functions, it forces coordination and communication throughout the company, as well as with the company's suppliers and customers.

5. **Implement the decision, evaluate performance, and learn.** Managers at the *Daily News* take actions to implement the March 2013 budget. Management accountants collect information to follow through on how actual performance compares to planned or budgeted performance (also referred to as scorekeeping). Information on actual results is different from the *predecision* planning information Naomi collected in Step 2, which enabled her to better understand uncertainties, to make predictions, and to make a decision. The comparison of actual performance to budgeted performance is the *control* or *postdecision* role of information. **Control** comprises taking actions that implement the planning decisions, deciding how to evaluate performance, and providing feedback and learning to help future decision making.

   Measuring actual performance informs managers how well they and their subunits are doing. Linking rewards to performance helps motivate managers. These rewards are both intrinsic (recognition for a job well done) and extrinsic (salary, bonuses, and promotions linked to performance). We discuss this in more detail in a later chapter (Chapter 16). A budget serves as much as a control tool as a planning tool. Why? Because a budget is a benchmark against which actual performance can be compared.

Consider performance evaluation at the *Daily News*. During March 2013, the newspaper sold advertising, issued invoices, and received payments. The accounting system recorded these invoices and receipts. Exhibit 1-4 shows the *Daily News*'s performance report of advertising revenues for March 2013. This report indicates that 760 pages of advertising (40 pages fewer than the budgeted 800 pages) were sold. The average rate per page was $5,080, compared with the budgeted $5,200 rate, yielding actual advertising revenues of $3,860,800. The actual advertising revenues were $299,200 less than the budgeted $4,160,000. Observe how managers use both financial and nonfinancial information, such as pages of advertising, to evaluate performance.

The performance report in Exhibit 1-4 spurs investigation and **learning,** which involves examining past performance (the control function) and systematically exploring alternative ways to make better-informed decisions and plans in the future. Learning can lead to changes in goals, strategies, the ways decision alternatives are identified, and the range of information collected when making predictions, and sometimes can lead to changes in managers.

The performance report in Exhibit 1-4 would prompt the management accountant to raise several questions directing the attention of managers to problems and opportunities. Is the strategy of differentiating the *Daily News* from other newspapers attracting more readers? In implementing the new advertising rates, did the marketing and sales department make sufficient efforts to convince advertisers that, even with the higher rate of $5,200 per page, advertising in the *Daily News* was a good buy? Why was the actual average rate per page of $5,080 instead of the budgeted rate of $5,200? Did some sales representatives offer discounted rates? Did economic conditions cause the decline in advertising revenues? Are revenues falling because editorial and production standards have declined? Are more readers getting their news online? Answers to these questions could prompt the newspaper's publisher to take subsequent actions, including, for example, adding

Concepts in Action: The iTunes Charts: Downloads Are Down, but Apple's Profits Are Up

Source: Iain Masterton/Alamy

Can selling less of something be more profitable than selling more of it? In 2009, Apple changed the pricing structure for songs sold through iTunes from a flat fee of $0.99 to a three-tier price point system of $0.69, $0.99, and $1.29. The top 200 songs in any given week make up more than one-sixth of digital music sales. Apple now charges the higher price of $1.29 for these hit songs by artists like Taylor Swift and the Black Eyed Peas.

After the first 6 months of the new pricing model in the iTunes store, downloads of the top 200 tracks were down by about 6%. While the number of downloads dropped, the higher prices generated more revenue than before the new pricing structure was in place. Since Apple's iTunes costs—wholesale song costs, network and transaction fees, and other operating costs—do not vary based on the price of each download, the profits from the 30% increase in price more than made up for the losses from the 6% decrease in volume.

Apple has also applied this new pricing structure to movies available through iTunes, which range from $14.99 for new releases to $9.99 for most other films.

Sources: Based on Anthony Bruno and Glenn Peoples, "Variable iTunes Pricing a Moneymaker for Artists," *Reuters* (June 21, 2009); Glenn Peoples, "The Long Tale?" *Billboard* (November 14, 2009); Eric Savitz, "Apple: Turns Out, iTunes Makes Money Pacific Crest Says; Subscription Services Seems Inevitable," *Barron's* "Tech Trader Daily" blog (April 23, 2007); and Apple, Inc. "Frequently Asked Questions (FAQ) for Purchased Movies." Accessed September 23, 2011.

Exhibit 1-4

Performance Report of Advertising Revenues at the *Daily News* for March 2013

	Actual Result (1)	Budgeted Amount (2)	Difference: (Actual Result – Budgeted Amount) (3) = (1) – (2)	Difference as a Percentage of Budgeted Amount (4) = (3) ÷ (2)
Advertising pages sold	760 pages	800 pages	40 pages Unfavorable	5.0% Unfavorable
Average rate per page	$5,080	$5,200	$120 Unfavorable	2.3% Unfavorable
Advertising revenues	$3,860,800	$4,160,000	$299,200 Unfavorable	7.2% Unfavorable

more sales personnel, making changes in editorial policy, or putting more resources into expanding its presence online and on mobile devices. Good implementation requires the marketing, editorial, and production departments to work together and coordinate their actions.

The management accountant could go further by identifying the specific advertisers that cut back or stopped advertising after the rate increase went into effect. Managers could then decide when and how sales representatives should follow up with these advertisers.

The planning and control activities must be flexible enough so that managers can seize sudden opportunities unforeseen at the time the plan is formulated. In no case should control mean that managers cling to a plan when unfolding events (such as a sensational news story) indicate that actions not encompassed by that plan (such as spending more money to cover the story) would offer better results for the company (from higher newspaper sales).

The left side of Exhibit 1-5 provides an overview of the decision-making processes at the *Daily News*. The right side of the exhibit highlights how the management accounting system aids in decision making.

Exhibit 1-5

How Accounting Aids Decision Making, Planning, and Control at the *Daily News*

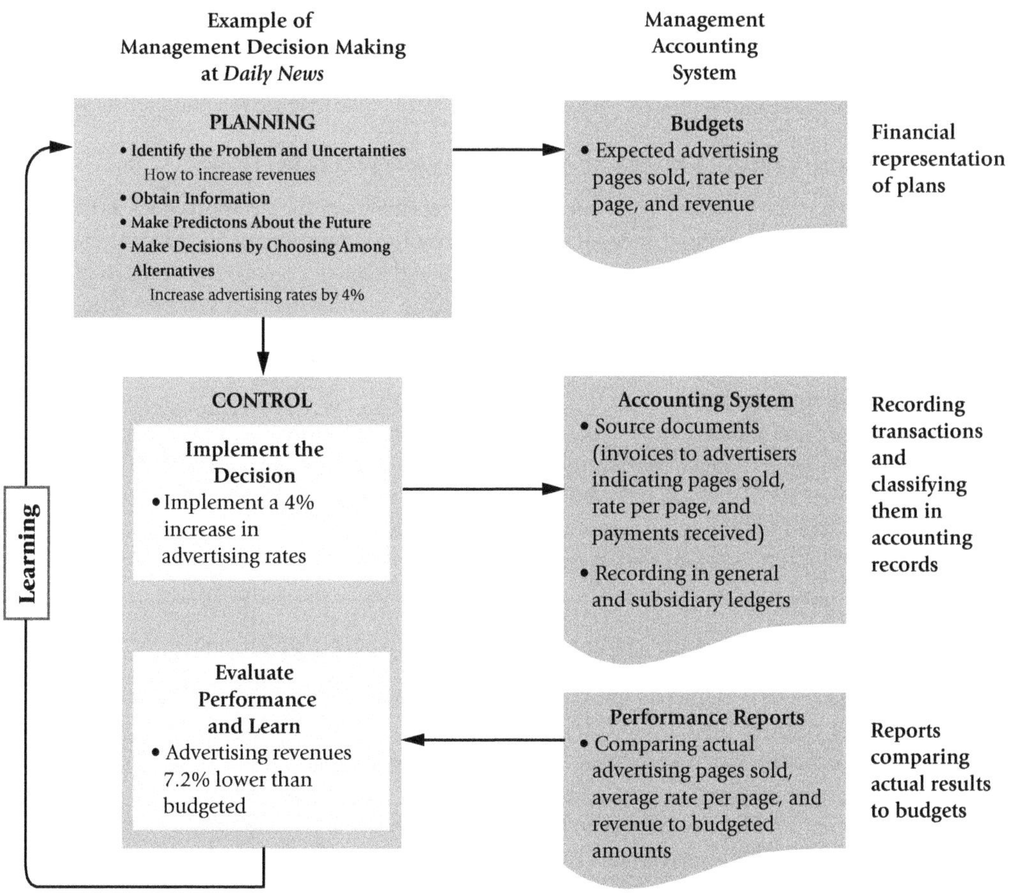

Keys to Success

Managers make decisions using a five-step decision-making process: (1) identify the problem and uncertainties; (2) obtain information; (3) make predictions about the future; (4) make decisions by choosing among alternatives; and (5) implement the decision, evaluate performance, and learn. Management accounting information is a key input in these decisions.

Learning Objective 5

Describe three guidelines management accountants follow in supporting managers

. . . employing a cost-benefit approach, recognizing behavioral as well as technical considerations, and calculating different costs for different purposes

Key Management Accounting Guidelines

Three guidelines help management accountants provide the most value to their companies in strategic and operational decision making: (1) employ a cost–benefit approach, (2) give full recognition to behavioral and technical considerations, and (3) use different costs for different purposes.

Cost–Benefit Approach

Managers continually face resource-allocation decisions, such as whether to purchase a new software package or hire a new employee. They use a **cost–benefit approach** when making these decisions. Managers should spend resources if the expected benefits to the company exceed the expected costs. Managers rely on management accounting information to quantify expected benefits and expected costs (although all benefits and costs are not easy to quantify).

Consider the installation of a consulting company's first budgeting system. Previously, the company used historical recordkeeping and little formal planning. A major benefit of installing a budgeting system is that it compels managers to plan ahead, compare actual to budgeted information, learn, and take corrective action. These actions lead to different decisions that improve performance relative to decisions that would have been made using the historical system, but the benefits are not easy to measure. On the cost side, some costs, such as investments in software and training, are easier to quantify. Others, such as the time spent by managers on the budgeting process, are more difficult to quantify. Regardless, senior managers compare expected benefits and expected costs, exercise judgment, and reach a decision, in this case to install the budgeting system.

Behavioral and Technical Considerations

The cost–benefit approach is the criterion that helps managers make certain decisions, such as whether or not they should install a proposed budgeting system or continue to use an existing historical system. In making such decisions, senior managers keep technical and behavioral considerations in mind.

The technical considerations help managers make wise economic decisions by providing them with the desired information (for example, costs in various value-chain categories) in an appropriate format (for example, actual results vs. budgeted amounts) and at the preferred frequency (for example, weekly or quarterly).

Both managers and management accountants should always remember that management is not confined to technical matters. Management is primarily a human activity that should focus on encouraging individuals to do their jobs better. Budgets have a behavioral effect by motivating and rewarding employees for achieving organization goals. When workers underperform, however, behavioral considerations suggest that managers discuss with workers ways to improve performance rather than just sending them a report highlighting their underperformance.

Different Costs for Different Purposes

This book emphasizes that managers use alternative ways to compute costs in different decision-making situations because there are different costs for different purposes. A cost concept used for the external-reporting purpose of accounting may not be an appropriate concept for internal, routine reporting to managers.

Consider the advertising costs associated with Microsoft Corporation's launch of a major product with a useful life of several years. For external reporting to shareholders, television advertising costs for this product are fully expensed in the income statement in the year they are incurred. Generally Accepted Accounting Principles (GAAP) require this immediate expensing for external reporting. For internal purposes of evaluating management performance, however, the television advertising costs could be capitalized and then amortized or written off as expenses over several years. Microsoft could capitalize these advertising costs if it believes doing so results in a more accurate and fairer measure of the performance of the managers that launched the new product.

Keys to Success

When designing management accounting systems, managers use a cost-benefit approach, recognize behavioral as well as technical considerations, and compute different costs for different purposes.

We now discuss the relationships and reporting responsibilities among managers and management accountants within a company's organization structure.

Organization Structure and the Management Accountant

Learning Objective 6

Understand how management accounting fits into an organization's structure

. . . for example, the responsibilities of the controller

We focus first on broad management functions and then look at how the management accounting and finance functions support managers.

Line and Staff Relationships

Organizations distinguish between line management and staff management. **Line management,** such as production, marketing, and distribution management, is directly responsible for achieving the goals of the organization. For example, managers of manufacturing divisions may target particular levels of budgeted operating income, certain levels of product quality and safety, and compliance with environmental laws. Similarly, the pediatrics department in a hospital is responsible for quality of service, costs, and patient billings. **Staff management,** such as management accountants and information technology and human-resources management, provides advice, support, and assistance to line management. A plant manager (a line function) may be responsible for investing in new equipment. A management accountant (a staff function) works as a business partner of the plant manager by preparing detailed operating-cost comparisons of alternative pieces of equipment.

Increasingly, organizations such as Honda and Dell are using teams to achieve their objectives. These teams include both line and staff management so that all inputs into a decision are available simultaneously.

The Chief Financial Officer and the Controller

The **chief financial officer (CFO)**—also called the **finance director** in many countries—is the executive responsible for overseeing the financial operations of an organization. The responsibilities of the CFO vary among organizations, but they usually include the following areas:

- **Controllership**—provides financial information for reports to managers and shareholders and oversees the overall operations of the accounting system
- **Treasury**—oversees banking and short- and long-term financing, investments, and cash management
- **Risk management**—manages the financial risk of interest-rate and exchange-rate changes and derivatives management
- **Taxation**—plans income taxes, sales taxes, and international taxes
- **Investor relations**—communicates with, responds to, and interacts with shareholders

An independent internal audit function reviews and analyzes financial and other records to attest to the integrity of the organization's financial reports and to adherence to its policies and procedures.

The **controller** (also called the *chief accounting officer*) is the financial executive primarily responsible for management accounting and financial accounting. This book focuses on the controller as the chief management accounting executive. Modern controllers have line authority over only their own departments. Yet the modern concept of controllership maintains that the controller affects the entire company. By reporting and interpreting relevant data, the controller influences the behavior of all employees and exerts a force that impels line managers toward making better-informed decisions as they implement their strategies.

Exhibit 1-6

Nike: Reporting Relationship for the CFO and the Corporate Controller

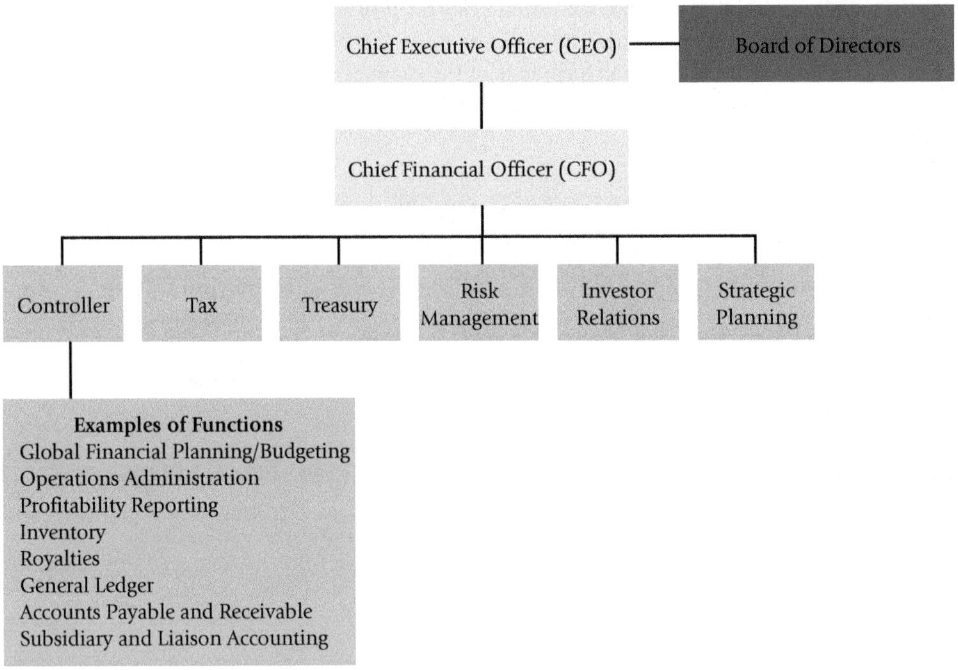

Exhibit 1-6 is an organization chart of the CFO and the corporate controller at Nike, the leading footwear and sports apparel company. The CFO is a staff manager who reports to and supports the chief executive officer (CEO). As in most organizations, the corporate controller at Nike reports to the CFO. Nike also has regional controllers who support regional managers in the major geographic regions in which the company operates, such as the United States, Asia Pacific, Latin America, and Europe. Regional controllers report to the regional manager rather than the corporate controller because the regional controller supports the activities of the regional manager, for example by managing budgets or analyzing costs. Regional controllers have a functional (often called a dotted-line) responsibility to the corporate controller to align accounting policies and practices. Individual countries sometimes have a country controller. Organization charts such as the one in Exhibit 1-6 show formal reporting relationships. In most organizations, there also are informal relationships that must be understood when managers attempt to implement their decisions. Examples of informal relationships are friendships among managers (friendships of a professional or personal kind) and the personal preferences of top management about the managers they rely on in decision making.

Think about what managers do to design and implement strategies and the organization structures within which they operate. Then think about the management accountants' and controllers' roles. It should be clear that the successful management accountant must have technical and analytical competence *as well as* behavioral and interpersonal skills.

Management Accounting Beyond the Numbers[2]

To people outside the profession, it may seem like accountants are just "numbers people." It is true that most accountants are adept financial managers, yet their skills do not stop there. The successful management accountant possesses several skills and characteristics that reach well beyond basic analytical abilities.

Management accountants must work well in cross-functional teams and as a business partner. In addition to being technically competent, the best management accountants work well in teams, learn about business issues, understand the motivations of different individuals, respect the views of their colleagues, and show empathy and trust.

[2] Sources: Based on Eric Dash and Andrew Ross Sorkin, "Government seizes WaMu and sells some assets," *New York Times*, September 25, 2008; Wendy Garling, "Winning the Transformation Battle at the Defense Finance and Accounting Service," *Balanced Scorecard Report*, May–June 2007; Kalama Gollakota and Vipin Gupta, "WorldCom Inc.: What went wrong," Richard Ivey School of Business Case No. 905M43. London, ON: The University of Western Ontario, (c) 2007; and Mark Green, Jeannine Garrity, Andrea Gumbus, and Bridget Lyons, "Pitney Bowes Calls for New Metrics," *Strategic Finance*, May 2002.

Management accountants must promote fact-based analysis and make tough-minded, critical judgments without being adversarial. Management accountants must raise tough questions for managers to consider, especially when preparing budgets. They must do so thoughtfully and with the intent of improving plans and decisions. In the case of the 2012 $4 billion (or more) loss at JP Morgan, controllers should have raised questions about whether the company's bet on improving economic conditions overseas had significant risks.

They must lead and motivate people to change and be innovative. Implementing new ideas, however good they may be, is difficult. When the United States Department of Defense (DoD) began consolidating more than 320 finance and accounting systems into a common platform, the accounting services director and his team of management accountants held meetings to make sure that everyone in the agency understood the goal for such a change. Ultimately, DoD aligned each individual's performance with the transformative change and introduced incentive pay to promote adoption and drive innovation within this new framework.

They must communicate clearly, openly, and candidly. Communicating information is a large part of a management accountant's job. Pitney Bowes Inc. (PBI), a $4-billion global provider of integrated mail and document management solutions, implemented a reporting initiative to give managers feedback in key areas. The initiative succeeded because it was clearly designed and openly communicated by PBI's team of management accountants.

They must have a strong sense of integrity. Management accountants must never succumb to pressure from managers to manipulate financial information. They must always remember that their primary commitment is to the organization and its shareholders. At WorldCom, under pressure from senior managers, members of the accounting staff concealed billions of dollars in expenses. Part of the reason WorldCom declared bankruptcy was because the accounting staff lacked the integrity and courage to stand up to and report corrupt senior managers. Some members of the accounting staff and the senior executive team served prison terms for their actions.

Professional Ethics

Learning Objective 7

Understand what professional ethics mean to management accountants

. . . for example, management accountants must maintain integrity and credibility in every aspect of their job

At no time has the focus on ethical conduct been sharper than it is today. Corporate scandals at Arthur Andersen, a public accounting firm; Countrywide Financial, a home mortgage company; Enron, an oil and gas company; Lehman Brothers, an investment bank; and WorldCom, a telecommunications company, have seriously eroded the public's confidence in corporations. All employees in a company, whether in line management or staff management, must comply with the organization's—and more broadly, society's—expectations of ethical standards.

Ethics form the basic foundation of any well-functioning economy. When ethics are weak, suppliers bribe executives to win supply contracts rather than invest in improving quality or lowering costs. Subsequently, customers have very little confidence in the quality of products produced, reducing their willingness to buy and causing markets to fail. Costs are higher because of higher prices paid to suppliers and fewer products being produced. Investors are unsure about the integrity of financial reports, affecting their ability to make investment decisions, resulting in a reluctance to invest and misallocation of resources. The scandals at Ahold, an international supermarket operator, and Tyco International, a diversified global manufacturing company, and others make clear that value is quickly destroyed by unethical behavior.

Institutional Support

Accountants have special ethical obligations, given that they are responsible for the integrity of the financial information provided to internal and external parties. The Sarbanes–Oxley legislation in the United States was passed in 2002 in response to a series of corporate scandals. The act focused on improving internal control, corporate governance, monitoring of managers, and disclosure practices of public corporations. These regulations call for tough ethical standards and criminal penalties on managers and accountants and provide a process for employees to report violations of illegal and unethical acts (these employees are called whistleblowers).

The Sarbanes–Oxley Act requires CEOs and CFOs to certify that the financial statements fairly represent the results of operations. In order to increase auditor independence, the act empowers the audit committee of the board of directors, composed exclusively of independent directors, to hire, compensate, and terminate the public accounting firm to audit a company. The act limits audit firms from providing consulting, tax, and other advisory services to audit clients to reduce financial dependency on individual clients. It authorizes the Public Company Accounting Oversight Board to oversee, review, and investigate the work of the auditors.

Professional accounting organizations, which represent management accountants in many countries, promote high ethical standards. Each of these organizations provides certification programs indicating that the holder has demonstrated the competency of technical knowledge required by that organization in management accounting and financial management, respectively.

In the United States, the Institute of Management Accountants (IMA) has also issued ethical guidelines. Exhibit 1-7 presents the IMA's guidance on issues relating to competence, confidentiality, integrity, and credibility. To provide support to its members to act ethically at all times, the IMA runs an ethics hotline service. Members can call professional counselors at the IMA's Ethics Counseling Service to discuss their ethical dilemmas. The counselors help identify the key ethical issues and possible alternative ways of resolving them, and confidentiality is guaranteed. The IMA is just one of many institutions that help navigate management accountants through what could be turbulent ethical waters.

Keys to Success

Managers must always act ethically and with integrity. In many countries, this is also a legal responsibility. Management accountants have ethical responsibilities that relate to competence, confidentiality, integrity, and credibility.

Typical Ethical Challenges

Ethical issues can confront management accountants in many ways. Here are two examples:

- **Case A:** A division manager has concerns about the commercial potential of a software product for which development costs are currently being capitalized as an asset rather than being shown as an expense for internal reporting purposes. The manager's bonus is based, in part, on division profits. The manager argues that showing development costs as an asset is justified because the new product will generate profits but presents little evidence to support his argument. The last two products from this division have been unsuccessful. The management accountant disagrees but wants to avoid a difficult personal confrontation with the boss, the division manager.
- **Case B:** A packaging supplier, bidding for a new contract, offers the management accountant of the purchasing company an all-expenses-paid weekend to the Super Bowl. The supplier does not mention the new contract when extending the invitation. The accountant is not a personal friend of the supplier. The accountant knows cost issues are critical in approving the new contract and is concerned that the supplier will ask for details about bids by competing packaging companies.

In each case, the management accountant is faced with an ethical dilemma. Ethical issues are not always clear-cut. Case A involves competence, credibility, and integrity. The management accountant should request that the division manager provide credible evidence that the new product is commercially viable. If the manager does not provide such evidence, expensing development costs in the current period is appropriate.

Case B involves confidentiality and integrity. The supplier in Case B may have no intention of raising issues associated with the bid. However, the appearance of a conflict of interest in Case B is sufficient for many companies to prohibit employees from accepting "favors" from suppliers. Exhibit 1-8 presents the IMA's guidance on "Resolution of Ethical Conflict." The accountant in Case B should discuss the invitation with his or her immediate supervisor. If the visit is approved, the accountant should inform the supplier that the invitation has been officially approved subject to following corporate policy (which includes maintaining information confidentiality).

Most professional accounting organizations around the globe issue statements about professional ethics. These statements include many of the same issues discussed by the IMA in Exhibits 1-7 and 1-8. For example, the Chartered Institute of Management Accountants (CIMA) in the United Kingdom identifies the same four fundamental principles as in Exhibit 1-7: competency, confidentiality, integrity, and credibility.

Exhibit 1-7

Ethical Behavior for Practitioners of Management Accounting and Financial Management

Practitioners of management accounting and financial management have an obligation to the public, their profession, the organizations they serve, and themselves to maintain the highest standards of ethical conduct. In recognition of this obligation, the Institute of Management Accountants has promulgated the following standards of ethical professional practice. Adherence to these standards, both domestically and internationally, is integral to achieving the Objectives of Management Accounting. Practitioners of management accounting and financial management shall not commit acts contrary to these standards nor shall they condone the commission of such acts by others within their organizations.

IMA STATEMENT OF ETHICAL PROFESSIONAL PRACTICE

Practitioners of management accounting and financial management shall behave ethically. A commitment to ethical professional practice includes overarching principles that express our values and standards that guide our conduct.

PRINCIPLES

IMA's overarching ethical principles include: Honesty, Fairness, Objectivity, and Responsibility. Practitioners shall act in accordance with these principles and shall encourage others within their organizations to adhere to them.

STANDARDS

A practitioner's failure to comply with the following standards may result in disciplinary action.

COMPETENCE

Each practitioner has a responsibility to:

1. Maintain an appropriate level of professional expertise by continually developing knowledge and skills.
2. Perform professional duties in accordance with relevant laws, regulations, and technical standards.
3. Provide decision support information and recommendations that are accurate, clear, concise, and timely.
4. Recognize and communicate professional limitations or other constraints that would preclude responsible judgment or successful performance of an activity.

CONFIDENTIALITY

Each practitioner has a responsibility to:

1. Keep information confidential except when disclosure is authorized or legally required.
2. Inform all relevant parties regarding appropriate use of confidential information. Monitor subordinates' activities to ensure compliance.
3. Refrain from using confidential information for unethical or illegal advantage.

INTEGRITY

Each practitioner has a responsibility to:

1. Mitigate actual conflicts of interest. Regularly communicate with business associates to avoid apparent conflicts of interest. Advise all parties of any potential conflicts.
2. Refrain from engaging in any conduct that would prejudice carrying out duties ethically.
3. Abstain from engaging in or supporting any activity that might discredit the profession.

CREDIBILITY

Each practitioner has a responsibility to:

1. Communicate information fairly and objectively.
2. Disclose all relevant information that could reasonably be expected to influence an intended user's understanding of the reports, analyses, or recommendations.
3. Disclose delays or deficiencies in information, timeliness, processing, or internal controls in conformance with organization policy and/or applicable law.

Source: IMA Statement of Ethical Professional Practice, Institute of Management Accountants, www.imanet.org. Reprinted with permission.

Exhibit 1-8

Resolution of Ethical Conflict

In applying the Standards of Ethical Professional Practice, you may encounter problems identifying unethical behavior or resolving an ethical conflict. When faced with ethical issues, you should follow your organization's established policies on the resolution of such conflict. If these policies do not resolve the ethical conflict, you should consider the following courses of action:

1. Discuss the issue with your immediate supervisor except when it appears that the supervisor is involved. In that case, present the issue to the next level. If you cannot achieve a satisfactory resolution, submit the issue to the next management level. If your immediate superior is the chief executive officer or equivalent, the acceptable reviewing authority may be a group such as the audit committee, executive committee, board of directors, board of trustees, or owners. Contact with levels above the immediate superior should be initiated only with your superior's knowledge, assuming he or she is not involved. Communication of such problems to authorities or individuals not employed or engaged by the organization is not considered appropriate, unless you believe there is a clear violation of the law.
2. Clarify relevant ethical issues by initiating a confidential discussion with an IMA Ethics Counselor or other impartial advisor to obtain a better understanding of possible courses of action.
3. Consult your own attorney as to legal obligations and rights concerning the ethical conflict.

Source: IMA Statement of Ethical Professional Practice, Institute of Management Accountants, www.imanet.org. Reprinted with permission.

Problem for Self-Study

Campbell Soup Company incurs the following costs:

a. Purchase of tomatoes by a canning plant for Campbell's tomato soup products
b. Materials purchased for redesigning Pepperidge Farm biscuit containers to make biscuits stay fresh longer
c. Payment to Backer, Spielvogel, & Bates, the advertising agency, for advertising work on the Healthy Request line of soup products
d. Salaries of food technologists researching feasibility of a Prego pizza sauce that has minimal calories
e. Payment to Safeway for redeeming coupons on Campbell's food products
f. Cost of a toll-free telephone line used for customer inquiries about using Campbell's soup products
g. Cost of gloves used by line operators on the Swanson Fiesta breakfast-food production line
h. Cost of handheld computers used by Pepperidge Farm delivery staff serving major supermarket accounts

Required

Classify each cost item (**a–h**) as one of the business functions in the value chain in Exhibit 1-2 (page 5).

Solution

a. Production
b. Design of products and processes
c. Marketing
d. Research and development
e. Marketing
f. Customer service
g. Production
h. Distribution

Decision Points

The following question-and-answer format summarizes the chapter's learning objectives. Each decision presents a key question related to a learning objective. The guidelines are the answer to that question.

Decision	Guidelines
1. How is financial accounting different from management accounting?	Financial accounting reports to external users on past financial performance using GAAP. Management accounting provides future-oriented information in formats that help managers (internal users) make decisions and achieve organizational goals.
2. How do management accountants support strategic decisions?	Management accountants contribute to strategic decisions by providing information about the sources of competitive advantage.
3. How do companies add value, and what are the dimensions of performance that customers are expecting of companies?	Companies add value through research and development (R&D), design of products and processes, production, marketing, distribution, and customer service. Customers want companies to deliver performance through cost and efficiency, quality, timeliness, and innovation.
4. How do managers make decisions to implement strategy?	Managers use a five-step decision-making process to implement strategy: (1) identify the problem and uncertainties; (2) obtain information; (3) make predictions about the future; (4) make decisions by choosing among alternatives; and (5) implement the decision, evaluate performance, and learn. The first four steps are the planning decisions, which include deciding on organization goals, predicting results under various alternative ways of achieving those goals, and deciding how to attain the desired goals. Step 5 is the control decision, which includes taking actions to implement the planning decisions and deciding on performance evaluation and feedback that will help future decision making.
5. What guidelines do management accountants use?	Three guidelines that help management accountants increase their value to managers are (a) employ a cost–benefit approach, (b) recognize behavioral as well as technical considerations, and (c) identify different costs for different purposes.
6. Where does the management accounting function fit into an organization's structure?	Management accounting is an integral part of the controller's function in an organization. In most organizations, the controller reports to the chief financial officer, who is a key member of the top management team.
7. What are the ethical responsibilities of management accountants?	Management accountants have ethical responsibilities that relate to competence, confidentiality, integrity, and credibility.

Terms to Learn

Each chapter will include this section. Like all technical terms, accounting terms have precise meanings. Learn the definitions of new terms when you initially encounter them. The meaning of each of the following terms is given in this chapter and in the Glossary at the end of this book.

budget (p. 9)
chief financial officer (CFO) (p. 13)
control (p. 9)
controller (p. 13)
cost–benefit approach (p. 12)
cost management (p. 2)
customer relationship management (CRM) (p. 5)
customer service (p. 5)
design of products and processes (p. 4)
distribution (p. 4)
finance director (p. 13)
financial accounting (p. 2)
learning (p. 10)
line management (p. 13)

Assignment Material

Questions

1-1 "Management accounting should not fit the straitjacket of financial accounting." Explain and give an example.

1-2 How can a management accountant help formulate strategy?

1-3 Describe the business functions in the value chain.

1-4 "Management accounting deals only with costs." Do you agree? Explain.

1-5 Describe the five-step decision-making process.

1-6 Distinguish planning decisions from control decisions.

1-7 As a new controller, reply to this comment by a plant manager: "As I see it, our accountants may be needed to keep records for shareholders and Uncle Sam, but I don't want them sticking their noses in my day-to-day operations. I do the best I know how. No bean counter knows enough about my responsibilities to be of any use to me."

1-8 Where does the management accounting function fit into an organization's structure?

1-9 Name the four areas in which standards of ethical conduct exist for management accountants in the United States. What organization sets forth these standards?

1-10 What steps should a management accountant take if established written policies provide insufficient guidance on how to handle an ethical conflict?

Exercises

1-11 Value chain and classification of costs, computer company. Dell Computers incurs the following costs:

a. Electricity costs for the plant assembling the Inspiron computer line of products
b. Transportation costs for shipping the Inspiron line of products to a retail chain
c. Payment to an independent design firm for design of the Inspiron 14R laptop
d. Salary of computer scientist working on the next generation of minicomputers
e. Cost of Dell employees' visit to a major customer to demonstrate Dell's ability to interconnect with other computers
f. Purchase of competitors' products for testing against potential Dell products
g. Payment to television network for running Dell advertisements
h. Cost of cables purchased from outside supplier to be used with Dell printers

Required Classify each of the cost items (**a–h**) into one of the business functions of the value chain shown in Exhibit 1-2 (page 5).

1-12 Value chain and classification of costs, pharmaceutical company. Pfizer, a pharmaceutical company, incurs the following costs:

a. Cost of redesigning blister packs to make drug containers more tamperproof
b. Cost of videos sent to doctors to promote sales of a new drug
c. Cost of a toll-free telephone line used for customer inquiries about drug usage, side effects of drugs, and so on
d. Equipment purchased to conduct experiments on drugs yet to be approved by the government

e. Payment to actors for a television infomercial promoting a new hair-growth product for balding men
f. Labor costs of workers in the packaging area of a production facility
g. Bonus paid to a salesperson for exceeding a monthly sales quota
h. Cost of Federal Express courier service to deliver drugs to hospitals

Required Classify each of the cost items (**a–h**) as one of the business functions of the value chain shown in Exhibit 1-2 (page 5).

1-13 Value chain and classification of costs, fast-food restaurant. McDonald's, a hamburger fast-food restaurant, incurs the following costs:

a. Cost of oil for the deep fryer
b. Wages of the counter help who give customers the food they order
c. Cost of costumes for McDonald's television commercials
d. Cost of children's toys given away free with kids' meals
e. Cost of the posters indicating the special "two cheeseburgers for $2.50"
f. Costs of frozen onion rings and French fries
g. Salaries of the food specialists who create new sandwiches for the restaurant chain
h. Cost of "to-go" bags requested by customers who could not finish their meals in the restaurant

Required Classify each of the cost items (**a–h**) as one of the business functions of the value chain shown in Exhibit 1-2 (page 5).

1-14 Key success factors. Dominic Consulting has issued a report recommending changes for its newest manufacturing client, Casper Engines. Casper Engines currently manufactures a single product, which is sold and distributed nationally. The report contains the following suggestions for enhancing business performance:

a. Add a new product line to increase total revenue and to reduce the company's overall risk.
b. Increase training hours of assembly-line personnel to decrease the currently high volumes of scrap and waste.
c. Reduce lead times (time from customer order of product to customer receipt of product) by 20% in order to increase customer retention.
d. Reduce the time required to set up machines for each new order.
e. Benchmark the company's gross margin percentages against its major competitors.

Required Link each of these changes to the key success factors that are important to managers.

1-15 Key success factors. Morten Construction Company provides construction services for major projects. Managers at the company believe that construction is a people-management business, and they list the following as factors critical to their success:

a. Provide innovative tools to simplify and enhance the construction process.
b. Foster cooperative relationships with suppliers that allow for more frequent deliveries as and when products are needed.
c. Integrate tools and techniques that reduce errors in construction projects.
d. Provide continuous training for employees on new tools and equipment.
e. Benchmark the company's gross margin percentages against its major competitors.

Required Match each of the above factors to the key success factors that are important to managers.

1-16 Planning and control decisions. Cranfield Corporation makes and sells brooms and mops. It takes the following actions, not necessarily in the order given.

Required For each action (**a–e**) state whether it is a planning decision or a control decision.

a. Cranfield asks its marketing team to consider ways to get back market share from its newest competitor, Swiffer.
b. Cranfield calculates market share after introducing its newest product.
c. Cranfield compares costs it actually incurred with costs it expected to incur for the production of the new product.

d. Cranfield's design team proposes a new product to compete directly with the Swiffer.

e. Cranfield estimates the costs it will incur to sell 30,000 units of the new product in the first quarter of the next fiscal year.

1-17 Five-step decision-making process, manufacturing. Tadeski Foods makes frozen dinners that it sells through grocery stores. Typical products include turkey, pot roast, fried chicken, and meatloaf. The managers at Tadeski have recently proposed a line of frozen chicken pies. They take the following actions to help decide whether to launch the line.

a. Tadeski performs a taste test at a local shopping mall to see if consumers like the taste of its proposed new chicken pie product.

b. Sales managers estimate they will sell more meat pies in their northern sales territory than in their southern sales territory.

c. Managers discuss the possibility of introducing a new chicken pie.

d. Managers compare actual costs of making chicken pies with their budgeted costs.

e. Costs for making chicken pies are budgeted.

f. The company decides to introduce a new chicken pie.

g. To help decide whether to introduce a new chicken pie, the purchasing manager calls a supplier to check the prices of chicken.

Required Classify each of the actions (**a–g**) as a step in the five-step decision-making process (identify the problem and uncertainties; obtain information; make predictions about the future; make decisions by choosing among alternatives; implement the decision, evaluate performance, and learn). The actions are not listed in the order they are performed.

1-18 Five-step decision-making process, service firm. Brook Exteriors is a firm that provides house-painting services. Richard Brook, the owner, is trying to find new ways to increase revenues. Mr. Brook performs the following actions, not in the order listed.

a. Mr. Brook calls Home Depot to ask the price of paint sprayers.

b. Mr. Brook discusses with his employees the possibility of using paint sprayers instead of hand painting to increase productivity and thus revenues.

c. The workers who are not familiar with paint sprayers take more time to finish a job than they did when painting by hand.

d. Mr. Brook compares the expected cost of buying sprayers to the expected cost of hiring more workers who paint by hand, and estimates profits from both alternatives.

e. The project scheduling manager confirms that demand for house-painting services has increased.

f. Mr. Brook decides to buy the paint sprayers rather than hire additional painters.

Required Classify each of the actions (**a-f**) according to its step in the five-step decision-making process (identify the problem and uncertainties; obtain information; make predictions about the future; make decisions by choosing among alternatives; implement the decision, evaluate performance, and learn).

1-19 Professional ethics and reporting division performance. Maria Mendez is division controller and James Dalton is division manager of the Hestor Shoe Company. Mendez has line responsibility to Dalton, but she also has staff responsibility to the company controller.

Dalton is under severe pressure to achieve the budgeted division income for the year. He has asked Mendez to book $200,000 of revenues on December 31. The customers' orders are firm, but the shoes are still in the production process. They will be shipped on or around January 4. Dalton says to Mendez, "The key event is getting the sales order, not shipping the shoes. You should support me, not obstruct my reaching division goals."

Required

1. Describe Mendez's ethical responsibilities.
2. What should Mendez do if Dalton gives her a direct order to book the sales?

Problems

1-20 Planning and control decisions, Internet company. PostNews.com offers its subscribers several services, such as an annotated TV guide and local-area information on weather, restaurants, and movie theaters. Its main revenue sources are fees for banner advertisements and fees from subscribers. Recent data are as follows:

Month/Year	Advertising Revenues	Actual Number of Subscribers	Monthly Fee per Subscriber
June 2011	$ 415,972	29,745	$15.50
December 2011	867,246	55,223	20.50
June 2012	892,134	59,641	20.50
December 2012	1,517,950	87,674	20.50
June 2013	2,976,538	147,9251	20.50

The following decisions were made from June through October 2013:

a. June 2013: Raised subscription fee to $25.50 per month from July 2013 onward. The budgeted number of subscribers for this monthly fee is shown in the following table.

b. June 2013: Informed existing subscribers that from July onward, monthly fee would be $25.50.

c. July 2013: Offered e-mail service to subscribers and upgraded other online services.

d. October 2013: Dismissed the vice president of marketing after significant slowdown in subscribers and subscription revenues, based on July through September 2013 data in the following table.

e. October 2013: Reduced subscription fee to $22.50 per month from November 2013 onward.

Results for July–September 2013 are as follows:

Month/Year	Budgeted Number of Subscribers	Actual Number of Subscribers	Monthly Fee per Subscriber
July 2013	145,000	129,250	$25.50
August 2013	155,000	142,726	25.50
September 2013	165,000	145,643	25.50

Required

1. Classify each of the decisions (**a–e**) as a planning or a control decision.
2. Give two examples of other planning decisions and two examples of other control decisions that may be made at PostNews.com.

1-21 Strategic decisions and management accounting. Consider the following series of independent situations in which a firm is about to make a strategic decision.

Decisions

a. Pedro Phones is about to decide whether to launch production and sale of a cell phone with standard features.

b. Flash Computers is trying to decide whether to produce and sell a new home computer software package that includes the ability to interface with a sewing machine and a vacuum cleaner. There is no such software currently on the market.

c. Celine Cosmetics has been asked to provide a "store brand" lip gloss that will be sold at discount retail stores.

d. Nicholus Meats is considering developing a special line of gourmet bologna made with sun-dried tomatoes, pine nuts, and artichoke hearts.

Required

1. For each decision, state whether the company is following a cost leadership or a differentiated product strategy.
2. For each decision, discuss what information the management accountant can provide about the source of competitive advantage for these firms.

1-22 Strategic decisions and management accounting. Consider the following series of independent situations in which a firm is about to make a strategic decision.

Decisions

a. A popular restaurant is considering hiring and training inexperienced cooks. The restaurant will no longer hire experienced chefs.

b. An office supply store is considering adding a delivery service that its competitors do not have.

c. A regional airline is deciding whether to install technology that will allow passengers to check themselves in. This technology will reduce the number of desk clerks required inside the airport.

d. A local florist is considering hiring a horticulture specialist to help customers with gardening questions.

Required

1. For each decision, state whether the company is following a cost leadership or a differentiated product strategy.
2. For each decision, discuss what information the managerial accountant can provide about the source of competitive advantage for these firms.

1-23 Management accounting guidelines. For each of the following items, identify which of the management accounting guidelines applies: cost–benefit approach, behavioral and technical considerations, or different costs for different purposes.

1. Analyzing whether to keep the billing function within an organization or outsource it.
2. Deciding to give bonuses for superior performance to the employees in a Japanese subsidiary and extra vacation time to the employees in a Swedish subsidiary.
3. Including costs of all the value-chain functions before deciding to launch a new product, but including only its manufacturing costs in determining its inventory valuation.
4. Considering the desirability of hiring an additional salesperson.
5. Giving each salesperson the compensation option of choosing either a low salary and a high-percentage sales commission or a high salary and a low-percentage sales commission.
6. Selecting the costlier computer system after considering two systems.
7. Installing a participatory budgeting system in which managers set their own performance targets, instead of top management imposing performance targets on managers.
8. Recording research costs as an expense for financial reporting purposes (as required by U.S. GAAP) but capitalizing and expensing them over a longer period for management performance-evaluation purposes.
9. Introducing a profit-sharing plan for employees.

1-24 Management accounting guidelines. For each of the following items, identify which of the management accounting guidelines applies: cost–benefit approach, behavioral and technical considerations, or different costs for different purposes.

1. Analyzing whether to produce a component needed for the end product or to outsource it.
2. Deciding whether to compensate the sales force by straight commission or by salary.
3. Including costs related to administrative function to evaluate the financial performance of a division, but including only controllable costs in evaluating the manager's performance.
4. Considering the desirability of purchasing new technology.
5. Basing bonus calculations on financial measures such as return on investment, or basing bonus calculations on delivery time to customer.
6. Deciding whether to buy or lease an existing production facility to increase capacity.
7. Determining the loss in future business because of poor quality but including only estimated scrap and waste as potential loss on the budgeted financial statements.

1-25 Role of controller, role of chief financial officer. George Jimenez is the controller at Balkin Electronics, a manufacturer of devices for the computer industry. The company may promote him to chief financial officer.

Required

1. In this table, indicate which executive is *primarily* responsible for each activity.

Activity	Controller	CFO
Managing accounts payable		
Communicating with investors		
Strategic review of different lines of businesses		
Budgeting funds for a plant upgrade		
Managing the company's short-term investments		
Negotiating fees with auditors		
Assessing profitability of various products		
Evaluating the costs and benefits of a new product design		

2. Based on this table and your understanding of the two roles, what types of training or experience will George find most useful for the CFO position?

1-26 Budgeting, ethics, pharmaceutical company. Chris Jackson was recently promoted to Controller of Research and Development (R&D) for BrisCor, a *Fortune* 500 pharmaceutical company that manufactures prescription drugs and nutritional supplements. The company's total R&D cost for 2013 was expected (budgeted) to be $5 billion. During the company's midyear budget review, Chris realized that current R&D expenditures were already at $3.5 billion, nearly 40% above the midyear target. At this current rate of expenditure, the R&D division was on track to exceed its total year-end budget by $2 billion!

In a meeting with CFO Ronald Meece later that day, Jackson delivered the bad news. Meece was both shocked and outraged that the R&D spending had gotten out of control. Meece wasn't any more understanding when Jackson revealed that the excess cost was entirely related to research and development of a new drug, Vyacon, which was expected to go to market next year. The new drug would result in large profits for BrisCor, if the product could be approved by year-end.

Meece had already announced his expectations of third-quarter earnings to Wall Street analysts. If the R&D expenditures weren't reduced by the end of the third quarter, Meece was certain that the targets he had announced publicly would be missed and the company's stock price would tumble. Meece instructed Jackson to make up the budget shortfall by the end of the third quarter using "whatever means necessary."

Jackson was new to the controller's position and wanted to make sure that Meece's orders were followed. Jackson came up with the following ideas for making the third-quarter budgeted targets:

a. Stop all research and development efforts on the drug Vyacon until after year-end. This change would delay the drug going to market by at least 6 months. It is possible that in the meantime a BrisCor competitor could make it to market with a similar drug.

b. Sell off rights to the drug Martek. The company had not planned on doing this because, under current market conditions, it would get less than fair value. It would, however, result in a one-time gain that could offset the budget shortfall. Of course, all future profits from Martek would be lost.

c. Capitalize some of the company's R&D expenditures, reducing R&D expense on the income statement. This transaction would not be in accordance with GAAP, but Jackson thought it was justifiable, since the Vyacon drug was going to market early next year. Jackson would argue that capitalizing R&D costs this year and expensing them next year would better match revenues and expenses.

Required

1. Referring to the "Standards of Ethical Behavior for Practitioners of Management Accounting and Financial Management," Exhibit 1-7 (page 17), which of the preceding items (**a–c**) are acceptable to use? Which are unacceptable?
2. What would you recommend Jackson do?

1-27 Professional ethics and end-of-year actions. Linda Butler is the new division controller of the snack-foods division of Daniel Foods. Daniel Foods has reported a minimum 15% growth in annual earnings for each of the past 5 years. The snack-foods division has reported annual earnings growth of more than 20% each year in this same period. During the current year, the economy went into a recession. The corporate controller estimates a 10% annual earnings growth rate for Daniel Foods this year. One month before the December 31 fiscal year-end of the current year, Butler estimates the snack-foods division will report an annual earnings growth of only 8%. Rex Ray, the snack-foods division president, is not happy, but he notes that the "end-of-year actions" still need to be taken.

Butler makes some inquiries and is able to compile the following list of end-of-year actions that were more or less accepted by the previous division controller:

a. Deferring December's routine monthly maintenance on packaging equipment by an independent contractor until January of next year.

b. Extending the close of the current fiscal year beyond December 31 so that some sales of next year are included in the current year.

c. Altering dates of shipping documents of next January's sales to record them as sales in December of the current year.

d. Giving salespeople a double bonus to exceed December sales targets.

e. Deferring the current period's advertising by reducing the number of television spots run in December and running more than planned in January of next year.

f. Deferring the current period's reported advertising costs by having Daniel Foods' outside advertising agency delay billing December advertisements until January of next year or by having the agency alter invoices to conceal the December date.

g. Persuading carriers to accept merchandise for shipment in December of the current year even though they normally would not have done so.

Required

1. Why might the snack-foods division president want to take these end-of-year actions?
2. Butler is deeply troubled and reads the "Standards of Ethical Behavior for Practitioners of Management Accounting and Financial Management" in Exhibit 1-7 (page 17). Classify each of the end-of-year actions (**a–g**) as acceptable or unacceptable according to that document.
3. What should Butler do if Ray suggests that these end-of-year actions are taken in every division of Daniel Foods and that she will greatly harm the snack-foods division if she does not cooperate and paint the rosiest picture possible of the division's results?

1-28 Professional ethics and end-of-year actions. Macon Publishing House produces consumer magazines. The house and home division, which sells home-improvement and home-decorating magazines, has seen a 20% reduction in operating income over the past 9 months, primarily due to an economic recession and a depressed consumer housing market. The division's controller, Rhett Gable, has felt pressure from the CFO to improve his division's operating results by the end of the year. Gable is considering the following options for improving the division's performance by year-end:

a. Cancelling two of the division's least profitable magazines, resulting in the layoff of 25 employees.
b. Selling the new printing equipment that was purchased in January and replacing it with discarded equipment from one of the company's other divisions. The previously discarded equipment no longer meets current safety standards.
c. Recognizing unearned subscription revenue (cash received in advance for magazines that will be delivered in the future) as revenue when cash is received in the current month (just before fiscal year-end) instead of showing it as a liability.
d. Reducing the division's Allowance for Bad Debt Expense. This transaction alone would increase operating income by 5%.
e. Recognizing advertising revenues that relate to January in December.
f. Switching from declining balance to straight line depreciation to reduce depreciation expense in the current year.

Required

1. What are the motivations for Gable to improve the division's year-end operating earnings?
2. From the point of view of the "Standards of Ethical Behavior for Practitioners of Management Accounting and Financial Management," Exhibit 1-7 (page 17), which of the preceding items (**a–f**) are acceptable? Which are unacceptable?
3. What should Gable do about the pressure to improve performance?

1-29 Ethical challenges, global company. Andahl Logistics, a U.S. shipping company, has just begun distributing goods across the Atlantic to Norway. The company began operations in 2011, transporting goods to South America. The company's earnings are currently trailing behind its competitors and Andahl's investors are becoming anxious. Some of the company's largest investors are even talking of selling their interest in the shipping newcomer. Andahl's CEO, Max Chang, calls an emergency meeting with his executive team. Chang needs a plan before his upcoming conference call with uneasy investors. Andahl's executive staff make the following suggestions for salvaging the company's short-term operating results:

a. Stop all transatlantic shipping efforts. The startup costs for the new operations are hurting current profit margins.
b. Make deep cuts in pricing through the end of the year to generate additional revenue.
c. Pressure current customers to take early delivery of goods before the end of the year so that more revenue can be reported in this year's financial statements.
d. Sell off distribution equipment prior to year-end. The sale would result in one-time gains that could offset the company's lagging profits. The owned equipment could be replaced with leased equipment at a lower cost in the current year.
e. Record executive year-end bonus compensation for the current year in the next year when it is paid after the December fiscal year-end.
f. Recognize sales revenues on orders received, but not shipped as of the end of the year.
g. Establish corporate headquarters in Ireland before the end of the year, lowering the company's corporate tax rate from 28% to 12.5%.

Required

1. As the management accountant for Andahl, evaluate each of the preceding items (**a–g**) in the context of the "Standards of Ethical Behavior for Practitioners of Management Accounting and Financial Management," Exhibit 1-7 (page 17). Which of the items are in violation of these ethics standards and which are acceptable?
2. What should the management accountant do with regard to those items that are in violation of the ethical standards for management accountants?

Case

British Motor Company: Organization of Accounting Department

The following quotation is from an address made by an officer of the British Motor Company:

> We can all, I think, take pride in the way cost accounting has kept pace with business development in this country. Tremendous strides have been made during the last quarter of a century, and I'm sure that much more progress will be made in the future. In fact, progress will ***have*** to be made if we are to keep the science of management accounting abreast of the times. The whole of industry is now operating on a different level than we have known before—a higher plateau, on which management accounting appears in a new light and becomes more and more significant as a factor in business management.
>
> It is my experience that the function of cost determination is basic to every other function of a modern business. Cost factors thread their way through every phase of a business and, to a large extent, influence the makeup of the entire enterprise—its products, its markets, and its methods of operation.
>
> We must, of necessity, have rather complex and extensive costing organizations, but the principle according to which they work is the same—finding out what each of the operations costs before it is too late to avoid doing the wrong thing.
>
> I am sure you would be interested in knowing that regional controllers now report to the regional managers not to the corporate controller . . . as local organizations prepare to assume the responsibilities involved . . . accounting offices are being placed under the direct jurisdiction of the managers of the operations they serve. . . .
>
> Each region, division, and activity has its own complete accounting service. . . . Each separate activity, such as each assembly plant, has been provided with an accounting office to compile its own internal operating reports for its own use, and to forward the financial statements required by the central office.

Required

1. What do you think is meant by the statement that "the whole of industry is now operating on a different level than we have known before—a higher plateau . . . "?
2. (a) What are the advantages of each region, division, and activity having its own accounting functions? Does this pose any ethical challenges? (b) Are there any areas of responsibility of the CFO described in Chapter 1 that you would not transfer to the local accounting organization?
3. Draw three boxes on an organizational chart, one each for the corporate controller, the plant controller, and the plant manager. Draw appropriate lines between the boxes that would accord with the system described in the quotation. Use a dashed line to denote "staff management" relationship and a solid line to denote "line management" relationship. Describe some major advantages and complications of the new organization arrangements.
4. The plant controller must frequently fulfill two roles simultaneously, as a helper of the plant manager and as a spy for the corporate controller. How can accountants' duties be organized to cope with these conflicting roles?

Source: From IMA Statement of Ethical Professional Practice, Institute of Management Accountants, www.imanet.org. Reprinted with permission.

2 An Introduction to Cost Terms and Purposes

Learning Objectives

1. Define and illustrate a cost object
2. Distinguish between direct costs and indirect costs
3. Explain variable costs and fixed costs
4. Interpret unit costs cautiously
5. Distinguish inventoriable costs from period costs
6. Illustrate the flow of inventoriable and period costs
7. Explain why product costs are computed in different ways for different purposes
8. Describe a framework for cost accounting and cost management

What does the word *cost* mean to you? Is it the price you pay for something of value, like a cell phone? A cash outflow, like monthly rent? Something that affects profitability, like salaries? Organizations, like individuals, deal with different types of costs. At different times organizations put more or less emphasis on these costs. When times are good, companies often focus on selling as much as they can, with costs taking a backseat. But when times get tough, companies shift their emphasis from selling to cutting costs. Unfortunately, when times are really bad, companies may find that they are unable to cut costs fast enough, leading to Chapter 11 bankruptcy. That has been the recent experience of companies as diverse as General Motors, AMR Corporation (the parent company of American Airlines), and Ritz Camera Centers.

As these examples illustrate, managers must pay close attention to understanding and managing their costs. Organizations as varied as the United Way, the Mayo Clinic, and Sony generate reports containing a variety of cost concepts and terms that managers need to understand to effectively use the reports to run their businesses. This chapter discusses cost concepts and terms that are the basis of accounting information used for internal and external reporting. The Chapter at a Glance, below, provides a summary.

Chapter at a Glance

- To determine the cost of an object, such as a component, organizations first *accumulate* or gather costs by categories and then *assign costs* to the object of interest.
- It is easiest to assign costs that can be traced to an object. When costs cannot be traced, or it is too expensive to do so, costs have to be allocated instead using proxies.
- For a given time period and activity, variable costs are those that vary in total in proportion to changes in activity, whereas fixed costs are unaffected by the level of activity.
- Inventoriable costs are all costs of a product that are placed on the balance sheet when incurred and are expensed as cost of goods sold only when the product is sold; all costs in the income statement other than inventoriable costs are period costs.
- For a manufacturing firm, all categories of manufacturing costs—direct materials, direct manufacturing labor, and manufacturing overhead—are inventoriable costs.
- Inventoriable costs in a manufacturing firm pass through three inventory accounts—direct materials, work-in-process, and finished goods—before flowing into cost of goods sold to be matched against revenues.
- All costs other than cost of goods sold, for example, marketing and distribution costs, are period costs. These costs are matched against revenues in the period in which they occur.

- The cost of products or services can be computed in different ways, depending on why the organization is making the calculation.
- Cost information is useful to managers for strategic decisions about pricing, product mix, and cost management, as well as for planning, control, and performance measurement.

Costs and Cost Terminology

Learning Objective 1

Define and illustrate a cost object

. . . examples of cost objects are products, services, activities, processes, and customers

Organizations define **cost** as a resource sacrificed or forgone to achieve a specific objective. A cost (such as direct materials or advertising) is usually measured as the monetary amount that must be paid to acquire goods or services. An **actual cost** is the cost incurred (a historical or past cost), as distinguished from a **budgeted cost,** which is a predicted or forecasted cost (a future cost).

When you think of cost, you invariably think of it in the context of finding the cost of a particular thing. We call this "thing" a **cost object,** which is anything for which a measurement of costs is desired. Suppose that you were a manager at the BMW plant in Spartanburg, South Carolina, where the company makes cars and sport activity vehicles. Can you identify some cost objects? Now look at Exhibit 2-1.

You will see that BMW managers not only want to know the cost of various products, such as the BMW X6 sports activity coupe, but they also want to know the costs of projects, services, customers, activities, and departments. Managers use their knowledge of these costs to guide decisions about, for example, product innovation, quality, and customer service.

Now think about whether a manager at BMW might want to know the *budgeted cost* or the *actual cost* of a cost object. Managers almost always need to know both types of costs when making decisions. For example, comparing budgeted costs to actual costs helps managers evaluate how well they did controlling costs and learn about how they can do better in the future.

How does a cost system determine the costs of various cost objects? Typically in two basic stages: accumulation followed by assignment. **Cost accumulation** is the collection of cost data in some organized way by means of an accounting system. For example, at its Spartanburg plant, BMW collects (accumulates) costs in various categories such as different types of materials, different classifications of labor, and costs incurred for supervision. The accumulated costs are then *assigned* to designated cost objects, such as the different models of cars that BMW manufactures at the plant. BMW managers use this cost information in two main ways: (1) when *making* decisions, for instance, on how to price different models of cars or how much to invest in R&D and marketing and (2) for *implementing* decisions, by influencing and motivating employees to act and learn, for example, by providing bonuses to employees for reducing costs.

Now that we know why it is useful for managers to assign costs, we turn our attention to some concepts that will help us do it. Again, think of the different types of costs that we just discussed—materials, labor, and supervision. You are probably thinking that some costs, such as costs of materials, are easier to assign to a cost object than others, such as costs of supervision. As you will see, this is indeed the case.

Keys to Success

The cost of an object is determined in two stages: costs are first accumulated, or collected, in various categories, and the accumulated costs are then assigned to designated objects.

Exhibit 2-1

Examples of Cost Objects at BMW

Cost Object	Illustration
Product	A BMW X6 sports activity coupe
Service	Telephone hotline providing information and assistance to BMW dealers
Project	R&D project on enhancing the DVD system in BMW cars
Customer	Herb Chambers Motors, the BMW dealer that purchases a broad range of BMW vehicles
Activity	Setting up machines for production or maintaining production equipment
Department	Environmental, health, and safety department

Learning Objective 2

Distinguish between direct costs

. . . costs that are traced to the cost object

and indirect costs

. . . costs that are allocated to the cost object

Direct Costs and Indirect Costs

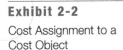

We now describe how costs are classified as direct and indirect costs and the methods used to assign these costs to cost objects.

- **Direct costs of a cost object** are related to the particular cost object and can be traced to it in an economically feasible (cost-effective) way. For example, the cost of steel or tires is a direct cost of BMW X6s. The cost of the steel or tires can be easily traced to or identified with the BMW X6. The workers on the BMW X6 line request materials from the warehouse and the material requisition document identifies the cost of the materials supplied to the X6. Similarly, individual workers record the time spent working on the X6 on time sheets. The cost of this labor can easily be traced to the X6 and is another example of a direct cost. The term **cost tracing** is used to describe the assignment of direct costs to a particular cost object.
- **Indirect costs of a cost object** are related to the particular cost object but cannot be traced to it in an economically feasible (cost-effective) way. For example, the salaries of plant administrators (including the plant manager) who oversee production of the many different types of cars produced at the Spartanburg plant are an indirect cost of the X6s. Plant administration costs are related to the cost object (X6s) because plant administration is necessary for managing the production of X6s. Plant administration costs are indirect costs because plant administrators also oversee the production of other products, such as the Z4 Roadster. Unlike the cost of steel or tires, there is no requisition of plant administration services, and it is virtually impossible to trace plant administration costs to the X6 line. The term **cost allocation** is used to describe the assignment of indirect costs to a particular cost object. **Cost assignment** is a general term that encompasses both (1) tracing direct costs to a cost object and (2) allocating indirect costs to a cost object. Exhibit 2-2 depicts direct costs and indirect costs and both forms of cost assignment—cost tracing and cost allocation—using the example of the BMW X6.

Challenges in Cost Allocation

Managers want to assign costs accurately to cost objects because inaccurate product costs will mislead managers about the profitability of different products and could cause managers to unknowingly promote unprofitable products while deemphasizing profitable products. Generally, managers are more confident about the accuracy of direct costs of cost objects, such as the cost of steel and tires of the X6.

Consider the cost to lease the Spartanburg plant. This cost is an indirect cost of the X6—there is no separate lease agreement for the area of the plant where the X6 is made. But BMW *allocates* to the X6 a part of the lease cost of the building—for example, on the basis of an estimate of the percentage of the building's floor space occupied for the production of the X6 relative to the total floor space used to produce all models of cars. This approach measures the building resources used by each car model reasonably and accurately. The more floor space that a car model occupies, the greater the lease costs assigned to it. Accurately allocating other indirect costs, such as plant administration, to the X6, however, is more difficult. For example, should these costs be allocated on the basis of the number of workers working on each car model or the number of cars produced of each model? How to measure the share of plant administration used by each car model is not clear-cut.

Exhibit 2-2
Cost Assignment to a Cost Object

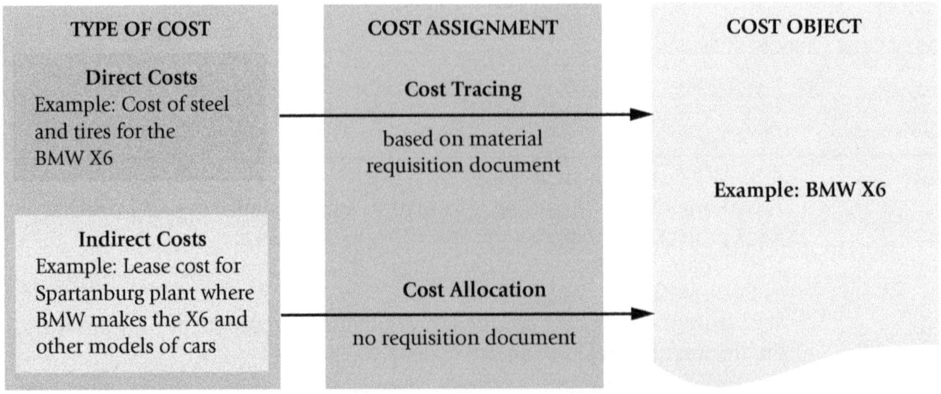

Factors Affecting Direct/Indirect Cost Classifications

Several factors affect the classification of a cost as direct or indirect:

- **The materiality of the cost in question.** The smaller the amount of a cost—that is, the more immaterial the cost is—the less likely that it is economically feasible to trace that cost to a particular cost object. Consider a mail-order catalog company such as Lands' End. It would be economically feasible to trace the courier charge for delivering a package to an individual customer as a direct cost. In contrast, the cost of the invoice paper included in the package would be classified as an indirect cost. Why? Although the cost of the paper can be traced to each customer, it is not cost-effective to do so. The benefits of knowing that, say, exactly 0.5¢ worth of paper is included in each package do not exceed the data processing and administrative costs of tracing the cost to each package. The time of the sales administrator, who earns a salary of $45,000 a year, is better spent organizing customer information to assist in focused marketing efforts than on tracking the cost of paper.
- **Available information-gathering technology.** Improvements in information-gathering technology make it possible to consider more and more costs as direct costs. Bar codes, for example, allow manufacturing plants to treat certain low-cost materials such as clips and screws, which were previously classified as indirect costs, as direct costs of products. At Dell, component parts such as the computer chip and the DVD drive display a bar code that can be scanned at every point in the production process. Bar codes can be read into a manufacturing cost file by waving a "wand" in the same quick and efficient way supermarket checkout clerks enter the cost of each item purchased by a customer.
- **Design of operations.** Classifying a cost as direct is easier if a company's facility (or some part of it) is used exclusively for a specific cost object, such as a specific product or a particular customer. For example, the cost of the General Chemicals facility dedicated to manufacturing soda ash (sodium carbonate) is a direct cost of soda ash.

Be aware that a specific cost may be both a direct cost of one cost object and an indirect cost of another cost object. *That is, the direct/indirect classification depends on the choice of the cost object.* For example, the salary of an assembly department supervisor at BMW is a direct cost if the cost object is the assembly department, but it is an indirect cost if the cost object is a product such as the BMW X6 sport activity coupe, because the assembly department assembles many different models. A useful rule to remember is that the broader the definition of the cost object—the assembly department rather than the X6—the higher the proportion of total costs that are direct costs and the more confidence a manager has in the accuracy of the resulting cost amounts.

Keys to Success

Direct costs are those costs that a manager can trace directly to a cost object in an economically feasible manner. Managers can allocate indirect costs, but it is more challenging to assign them in an accurate manner. As information technology improves and becomes less expensive, more costs can be categorized as direct, thereby allowing managers to avoid the more imprecise allocation of indirect costs.

Cost-Behavior Patterns: Variable Costs and Fixed Costs

Learning Objective 3

Explain variable costs and fixed costs

. . . the two basic ways in which costs behave

Costing systems record the cost of resources acquired, such as materials, labor, and equipment, and track how those resources are used to produce and sell products or services. Recording the costs of resources acquired and used allows managers to see how costs behave. Consider two basic types of cost-behavior patterns found in many accounting systems. A **variable cost** changes *in total* in proportion to changes in the related level of total activity or volume. A **fixed cost** remains unchanged *in total* for a given time period, despite wide changes in the related level of total activity or volume. Costs are defined as variable or fixed for *a specific activity* and for *a given time period.* Identifying a cost as variable or fixed provides valuable information for making many management decisions and is an important input when evaluating performance. To illustrate these two basic types of costs, again consider costs at the Spartanburg, South Carolina, plant of BMW.

1. **Variable costs.** If BMW buys a steering wheel at $600 for each of its BMW X6 vehicles, then the total cost of steering wheels is $600 times the number of vehicles produced, as the following table illustrates.

Number of X6s Produced (1)	Variable Cost per Steering Wheel (2)	Total Variable Cost of Steering Wheels (3) = (1) × (2)
1	$600	$ 600
1,000	600	600,000
3,000	600	1,800,000

The steering wheel cost is an example of a variable cost because *total cost* changes in proportion to changes in the number of vehicles produced. The cost per unit of a variable cost is constant. It is precisely because the variable cost per steering wheel in column 2 is the same for each steering wheel that the total variable cost of steering wheels in column 3 changes proportionately with the number of X6s produced in column 1. When considering how variable costs behave, always focus on *total* costs.

Exhibit 2-3, Panel A, is a graph that illustrates the total variable cost of steering wheels. The cost is represented by a straight line that climbs from left to right. The phrases "strictly variable" and "proportionately variable" are sometimes used to describe the variable cost in Panel A.

Consider an example of a variable cost for a different activity—the $20 hourly wage paid to each worker to set up machines at the Spartanburg plant. Setup labor cost is a variable cost for setup hours because setup cost changes in total in proportion to the number of setup hours used.

2. **Fixed costs.** Suppose BMW incurs a total cost of $2,000,000 per year for supervisors who work exclusively on the X6 line. These costs are unchanged in total over a designated range of the number of vehicles produced during a given time span (see Exhibit 2-3, Panel B). Fixed costs become smaller and smaller on a per-unit basis as the number of vehicles assembled increases, as the following table shows.

Annual Total Fixed Supervision Costs for BMW X6 Assembly Line (1)	Number of X6s Produced (2)	Fixed Supervision Cost per X6 (3) = (1) ÷ (2)
$2,000,000	10,000	$200
$2,000,000	25,000	80
$2,000,000	50,000	40

It is precisely because *total* line supervision costs are fixed at $2,000,000 that fixed supervision cost per X6 decreases as the number of X6s produced increases; the same fixed cost is spread over a larger number of X6s. Do not be misled by the change in fixed cost per unit. Just as in the case of

Exhibit 2-3

Graphs of Variable and Fixed Costs

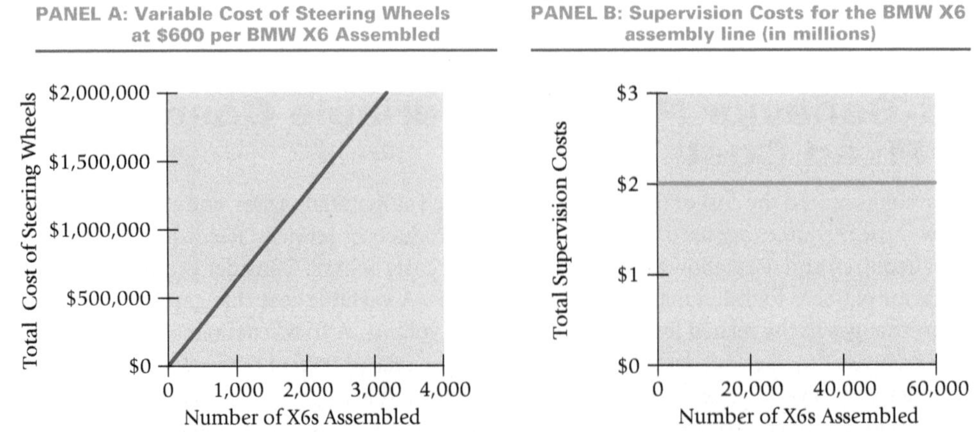

variable costs, when considering fixed costs, always focus on *total costs.* Costs are fixed when total costs remain unchanged despite significant changes in the level of total activity or volume.

Why are some costs variable and other costs fixed? Recall that a cost is usually measured as the amount of money that must be paid to acquire goods and services. Total cost of steering wheels is a variable cost because BMW buys the steering wheels only when they are needed. As more X6s are produced, proportionately more steering wheels are acquired and proportionately more costs are incurred.

Contrast the description of variable costs with the $2,000,000 of fixed costs per year incurred by BMW for supervision of the X6 assembly line. This level of supervision is acquired and put in place well before BMW uses it to produce X6s and before BMW even knows how many X6s it will produce. Suppose that BMW puts in place supervisors capable of supervising the production of 60,000 X6s each year. If the demand is for only 55,000 X6s, there will be idle capacity. Supervisors on the X6 line could have supervised the production of 60,000 X6s but will supervise only 55,000 X6s because of the lower demand. However, BMW must pay for the unused line supervision capacity because the cost of supervision cannot be reduced in the short run. If demand is even lower—say only 50,000 X6s—line supervision costs will still be the same $2,000,000, and idle capacity will increase.

Unlike variable costs, fixed costs of resources (such as for line supervision) cannot be quickly and easily changed to match the resources needed or used. Over time, however, managers can take actions to reduce fixed costs. For example, if the X6 line needs to be run for fewer hours because of low demand for X6s, BMW may lay off supervisors or move them to another production line. Unlike variable costs that go away automatically if the resources are not used, reducing fixed costs requires active intervention on the part of managers.

Do not assume that individual cost items are inherently variable or fixed. Consider labor costs. Labor costs can be purely variable for units produced when workers are paid on a piece-unit (piece-rate) basis. For example, some garment workers are paid on a per-shirt-sewed basis. In contrast, labor costs at a plant in the coming year are sometimes appropriately classified as fixed. For instance, a labor union agreement might set annual salaries and conditions, contain a no-layoff clause, and severely restrict a company's flexibility to assign workers to any other plant that has demand for labor. Japanese companies have for a long time had a policy of lifetime employment for their workers. Although such a policy entails higher fixed labor costs, the benefits are increased loyalty and dedication to the company and higher productivity. Such a policy increases the risk of losses during economic downturns as revenues decrease, while fixed costs remain unchanged. The recent global economic crisis has made companies very reluctant of locking in fixed costs. Concepts in Action: Zipcar Helps Twitter Reduce Fixed Costs describes how a car-sharing service offers companies the opportunity to convert the fixed costs of owning corporate cars into variable costs by renting cars on an as-needed basis.

A particular cost item could be variable for one level of activity and fixed for another. Consider annual registration and license costs for a fleet of planes owned by an airline company. Registration and license costs would be a variable cost as a function of the number of planes owned. But registration and license costs for a particular plane are fixed for the miles flown by that plane during a year.

To focus on key concepts, we have classified the behavior of costs as variable or fixed. Some costs have both fixed and variable elements and are called *mixed* or *semivariable* costs. For example, a company's telephone costs may have a fixed monthly payment and a charge per phone-minute used. We discuss mixed costs and techniques to separate out their fixed and variable components in Chapter 8.

Cost Drivers

A **cost driver** is a variable, such as the level of activity or volume that causally affects costs over a given time span. An *activity* is an event, task, or unit of work with a specified purpose—for example, designing products, setting up machines, or testing products. The level of activity or volume is a cost driver if there is a cause-and-effect relationship between a change in the level of activity or volume and a change in the level of total costs. For example, if product-design costs change with the number of parts in a product, the number of parts is a cost driver of product-design costs. Similarly, miles driven is often a cost driver of distribution costs.

The cost driver of a variable cost is the level of activity or volume whose change causes proportionate changes in the variable cost. For example, the number of vehicles assembled is the cost driver of the total cost of steering wheels. If setup workers are paid an hourly wage, the number of setup hours is the cost driver of total (variable) setup costs.

Costs that are fixed in the short run have no cost driver in the short run but may have a cost driver in the long run. Consider the costs of testing, say, 0.1% of the color printers produced at a

Hewlett-Packard plant. These costs consist of equipment and staff costs of the testing department that are difficult to change and, so, are fixed in the short run for changes in the volume of production. In this case, volume of production is not a cost driver of testing costs in the short run. In the long run, however, Hewlett-Packard will increase or decrease the testing department's equipment and staff to the levels needed to support future production volumes. In the long run, volume of production is a cost driver of testing costs. Costing systems that identify the cost of each activity such as testing, design, or setup are called *activity-based costing systems.*

Relevant Range

Relevant range is the band or range of normal activity level or volume in which there is a specific relationship between the level of activity or volume and the cost in question. For example, a fixed cost is fixed only in relation to a given wide range of total activity or volume (at which the company is expected to operate) and only for a given time span (usually a particular budget period). Suppose that BMW contracts with Thomas Transport Company (TTC) to transport X6s to BMW dealerships. TTC rents two trucks, and each truck has annual fixed rental costs of $40,000. The maximum annual usage of each truck is 120,000 miles. In the current year (2012), the predicted combined total hauling of the two trucks is 170,000 miles.

Exhibit 2-4 shows how annual fixed costs behave at different levels of miles of hauling. Up to 120,000 miles, TTC can operate with one truck; from 120,001 to 240,000 miles, it operates with two trucks; and from 240,001 to 360,000 miles, it operates with three trucks. This pattern will continue as TTC adds trucks to its fleet to provide more miles of hauling. Given the predicted 170,000-mile usage for 2012, the range from 120,001 to 240,000 miles hauled is the range in which TTC expects to operate, resulting in fixed rental costs of $80,000. Within this relevant range, changes in miles hauled will not affect the annual fixed costs.

Concepts in Action: Zipcar Helps Twitter Reduce Fixed Costs

In some cities, Zipcar has emerged as a way for corporations to reduce the spending on gas, insurance, and parking of corporate cars. Zipcar—which provides an "on-demand" option for urban individuals and businesses to rent a car by the week, the day, or even the hour—has rates beginning around $8 per hour and $78 per day (including gas, insurance, and around 180 miles per day).

Source: Jeremy Breningstall/ZUMA Press/Newscom

Let's think about what Zipcar means for companies. Many small businesses own a company car or two for getting to meetings, making deliveries, and running errands. Similarly, many large companies own a fleet of cars to shuttle visiting executives and clients back and forth from appointments, business lunches, and the airport. Traditionally, owning these cars has involved very high fixed costs, including buying the asset (car), maintenance costs, and insurance for multiple drivers.

Now, however, companies like Twitter can use Zipcar for on-demand mobility while reducing their transportation and overhead costs. Based in downtown San Francisco, Twitter managers use Zipcar to meet venture capitalists and partners in Silicon Valley. "We would get in a Zipcar to drive down to San Jose to pitch investors or go across the city," says Jack Dorsey, the micro-blogging service's co-founder. From a business perspective, Zipcar allows Twitter and other companies to convert the fixed costs of owning a company car to variable costs. If business slows, or a car isn't required to visit a client, Twitter is not saddled with the fixed costs of car ownership. Of course, when business is good, causing Twitter managers to use Zipcar more often, they can end up paying more overall than they would have paid if they purchased and maintained the car themselves.

Sources: Based on Paul Keegan, "Zipcar–the best new idea in business." *Fortune* (August 27, 2009); Elizabeth Olsen, "Car sharing reinvents the company wheels." *New York Times* (May 7, 2009); Zipcar, Inc., "Zipcar for business case studies"; Zipcar, Inc., "Zipcar rates and plans."

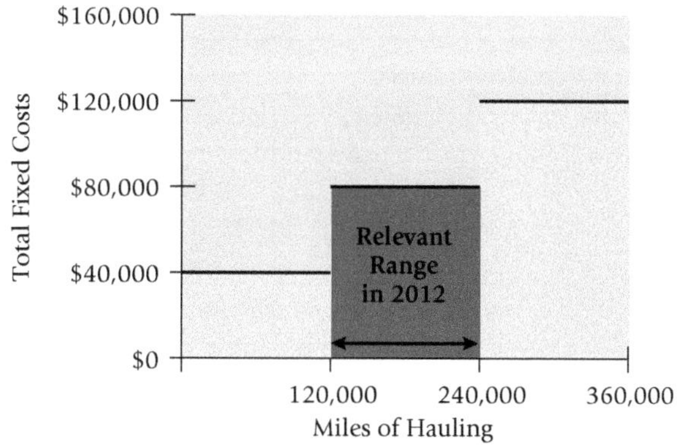

Exhibit 2-4
Fixed-Cost Behavior at Thomas Transport Company

Fixed costs may change from one year to the next. For example, if the total rental fee of the two trucks is increased by $2,000 for 2013, the total level of fixed costs will increase to $82,000 (all else remaining the same). If that increase occurs, total rental costs will be fixed at this new level of $82,000 for 2013 for miles hauled in the 120,001 to 240,000 range.

The basic assumption of the relevant range also applies to variable costs. That is, outside the relevant range, variable costs, such as direct materials, may not change proportionately with changes in production volume. For example, above a certain volume, direct material costs may increase at a lower rate because of price discounts on purchases greater than a certain quantity.

Relationships of Types of Costs

We have introduced two major classifications of costs: direct/indirect and variable/fixed. Costs may simultaneously be as follows:

- Direct and variable
- Direct and fixed
- Indirect and variable
- Indirect and fixed

Exhibit 2-5 shows examples of costs in each of these four cost classifications for the BMW X6.

Keys to Success

Variable costs change *in total* in proportion to changes in the related level of total activity. Fixed costs remain unchanged *in total* for a given time period, despite changes in the related level of total activity. The relevant range is the region of activity in which a particular relationship holds between a driver and a cost.

Total Costs and Unit Costs

Learning Objective 4

Interpret unit costs cautiously

. . . for many decisions, managers should use total costs, not unit costs

The preceding section concentrated on the behavior patterns of total costs in relation to activity or volume levels. We now consider unit costs.

Unit Costs

Generally, the decision maker should think in terms of total costs rather than unit costs. In many decision contexts, however, calculating a unit cost is essential. Consider the booking agent who has to make the decision to book Lady Gaga to play at the new Yankee Stadium. She estimates the cost of the event to be $3,000,000. This knowledge is helpful for the decision, but it is not enough.

Before reaching a decision, the booking agent also must predict the number of people who will attend. Without knowledge of both total cost and number of attendees, she cannot make an informed decision on a possible admission price to recover the cost of the event or even on whether to have the event at all. So she computes the unit cost of the event by dividing the total

Exhibit 2-5

Examples of Costs in Combinations of the Direct/Indirect and Variable/Fixed Cost Classifications for a Car Manufacturer

Cost-Behavior Pattern	Assignment of Costs to Cost Object: Direct Costs	Assignment of Costs to Cost Object: Indirect Costs
Variable Costs	• Cost object: BMW X6s produced Example: Tires used in assembly of automobile	• Cost object: BMW X6s produced Example: Power costs at Spartanburg plant. Power usage is metered only to the plant, where multiple products are assembled.
Fixed Costs	• Cost object: BMW X6s produced Example: Salary of supervisor on BMW X6 assembly line	• Cost object: BMW X6s produced Example: Annual lease costs at Spartanburg plant. Lease is for whole plant, where multiple products are produced.

cost ($3,000,000) by the expected number of people who will attend. If 60,000 people attend, the unit cost is $50 ($3,000,000 ÷ 60,000) per person; if 30,000 attend, the unit cost increases to $100 ($3,000,000 ÷ 30,000).

Unless the total cost is "unitized" (that is, averaged by the level of activity or volume), the $3,000,000 cost is difficult to interpret. The unit cost combines the total cost and the number of people in a simple and understandable way.

Accounting systems typically report both total-cost amounts and average-cost-per-unit amounts. A **unit cost,** also called an **average cost,** is calculated by dividing total cost by the related number of units. The units might be expressed in various ways. Examples are automobiles assembled, packages delivered, or hours worked. Consider Tennessee Products, a manufacturer of speaker systems with a plant in Memphis. Suppose that, in 2012, its first year of operations, the company incurs $40,000,000 of manufacturing costs to produce 500,000 speaker systems. Then the unit cost is $80:

$$\frac{\text{Total manufacturing costs}}{\text{Number of units manufactured}} = \frac{\$40{,}000{,}000}{500{,}000 \text{ units}} = \$80 \text{ per unit}$$

If 480,000 units are sold and 20,000 units remain in ending inventory, the unit-cost concept helps managers determine total costs in the income statement and balance sheet and, therefore, the financial results Tennessee Products reports to shareholders, banks, and the government.

Cost of goods sold in the income statement, 480,000 units × $80 per unit	$38,400,000
Ending inventory in the balance sheet, 20,000 units × $80 per unit	1,600,000
Total manufacturing costs of 500,000 units	$40,000,000

Unit costs are found in all areas of the value chain—for example, unit cost of product design, of sales visits, and of customer-service calls. By summing unit costs throughout the value chain, managers calculate the unit cost of the different products or services they deliver and determine the profitability of each product or service. Managers use this information, for example, to decide the products in which they should invest more resources, such as R&D and marketing, and the prices they should charge.

Use Unit Costs Cautiously

Although unit costs are regularly used in financial reports and for making product mix and pricing decisions, *managers should think in terms of total costs rather than unit costs for many decisions.* Consider the manager of the Memphis plant of Tennessee Products. Assume the $40,000,000 in costs in 2012 consist of $10,000,000 of fixed costs and $30,000,000 of variable costs (at $60 variable cost per speaker system produced). Suppose the total fixed cost and the variable cost per speaker system in 2013 are expected to be unchanged from 2012. The budgeted costs for 2013 at different production levels, calculated on the basis of total variable costs, total fixed costs, and total costs, are:

Units Produced (1)	Variable Cost per Unit (2)	Total Variable Costs (3) = (1) × (2)	Total Fixed Costs (4)	Total Costs (5) = (3) + (4)	Unit Cost (6) = (5) ÷ (1)
100,000	$60	$ 6,000,000	$10,000,000	$16,000,000	$160.00
200,000	$60	$12,000,000	$10,000,000	$22,000,000	$110.00
500,000	$60	$30,000,000	$10,000,000	$40,000,000	$ 80.00
800,000	$60	$48,000,000	$10,000,000	$58,000,000	$ 72.50
1,000,000	$60	$60,000,000	$10,000,000	$70,000,000	$ 70.00

A plant manager who uses the 2012 unit cost of $80 per unit will underestimate actual total costs if 2013 output is below the 2012 level of 500,000 units. If actual volume is 200,000 units due to, say, the presence of a new competitor, actual costs would be $22,000,000. The unit cost of $80 times 200,000 units equals $16,000,000, which underestimates the actual total costs by $6,000,000 ($22,000,000 − $16,000,000). *The unit cost of $80 applies only when the company produces 500,000 units.*

An overreliance on unit cost in this situation could lead to insufficient cash being available to pay costs if volume declines to 200,000 units. As the table indicates, for making this decision, managers should think in terms of total variable costs, total fixed costs, and total costs rather than unit cost. As a general rule, first calculate total costs, then compute a unit cost, if it is needed for a particular decision.

Keys to Success

Unit cost or average cost is the ratio of total costs to the number of units produced. In general, managers should focus on total costs rather than unit costs when making decisions.

Business Sectors, Types of Inventory, Inventoriable Costs, and Period Costs

Learning Objective 5

Distinguish inventoriable costs

. . . assets when incurred, then cost of goods sold

from period costs

. . . expenses of the period when incurred

In this section, we describe the different sectors of the economy, the different types of inventory that companies hold, and some commonly used classifications of manufacturing costs.

Manufacturing-, Merchandising-, and Service-Sector Companies

We define three sectors of the economy and provide examples of companies in each sector.

1. **Manufacturing-sector companies** purchase materials and components and convert them into various finished goods. Examples are automotive companies such as Jaguar, cellular phone producers such as Nokia, food-processing companies such as Heinz, and computer companies such as Toshiba.
2. **Merchandising-sector companies** purchase and then sell tangible products without changing their basic form. This sector includes companies engaged in retailing (for example, bookstores such as Barnes and Noble and department stores such as Target), distribution (for example, a supplier of hospital products, such as Owens and Minor), or wholesaling (for example, a supplier of electronic components such as Arrow Electronics).
3. **Service-sector companies** provide services (intangible products)—for example, legal advice or audits—to their customers. Examples are law firms such as Wachtell, Lipton, Rosen & Katz; accounting firms such as Ernst and Young; banks such as Barclays; mutual fund companies such as Fidelity; insurance companies such as Aetna; transportation companies such as Singapore Airlines; advertising agencies such as Saatchi & Saatchi; television stations such as Turner Broadcasting; Internet service providers such as Comcast; travel agencies such as American Express; and brokerage firms such as Merrill Lynch.

Types of Inventory

Manufacturing-sector companies purchase materials and components and convert them into various finished goods. These companies typically have one or more of the following three types of inventory:

1. **Direct materials inventory.** Direct materials in stock and awaiting use in the manufacturing process (for example, computer chips and components needed to manufacture cellular phones).
2. **Work-in-process inventory.** Goods partially worked on but not yet completed (for example, cellular phones at various stages of completion in the manufacturing process). This is also called **work in progress.**
3. **Finished goods inventory.** Goods (for example, cellular phones) completed but not yet sold.

Merchandising-sector companies purchase tangible products and then sell them without changing their basic form. These companies hold only one type of inventory, which is products in their original purchased form, called *merchandise inventory.* Service-sector companies provide only services or intangible products and so do not hold inventories of tangible products.

Commonly Used Classifications of Manufacturing Costs

Three terms commonly used when describing manufacturing costs are direct material costs, direct manufacturing labor costs, and indirect manufacturing costs. These terms build on the direct versus indirect cost distinction we described earlier, in the context of manufacturing costs.

1. **Direct material costs** are the acquisition costs of all materials that eventually become part of the cost object (work in process and then finished goods) and can be traced to the cost object in an economically feasible way. Acquisition costs of direct materials include freight-in (inward delivery) charges, sales taxes, and customs duties. Examples of direct material costs are the steel and tires used to make the BMW X6 and the computer chips used to make cellular phones.
2. **Direct manufacturing labor costs** include the compensation of all manufacturing labor that can be traced to the cost object (work in process and then finished goods) in an economically feasible way. Examples include wages and fringe benefits paid to machine operators and assembly-line workers who convert direct materials purchased to finished goods.
3. **Indirect manufacturing costs** are all manufacturing costs that are related to the cost object (work in process and then finished goods) but cannot be traced to that cost object in an economically feasible way. Examples include supplies, indirect materials such as lubricants, indirect manufacturing labor such as plant maintenance and cleaning labor, plant rent, plant insurance, property taxes on the plant, plant depreciation, and the compensation of plant managers. This cost category is also referred to as **manufacturing overhead costs** or **factory overhead costs.** We use *indirect manufacturing costs* and *manufacturing overhead costs* interchangeably in this book.

We now describe the distinction between inventoriable costs and period costs.

Inventoriable Costs

Inventoriable costs are all costs of a product that are considered as assets in the balance sheet when they are incurred and that become cost of goods sold only when the product is sold. For manufacturing-sector companies, all manufacturing costs are inventoriable costs. Consider Cellular Products, a manufacturer of cellular phones. Costs of direct materials, such as computer chips, issued to production (from direct material inventory), direct manufacturing labor costs, and manufacturing overhead costs create new assets, starting as work in process and becoming finished goods (the cellular phones). So, manufacturing costs are included in work-in-process inventory and in finished goods inventory (they are "inventoried") to accumulate the costs of creating these assets.

When the cellular phones are sold, the cost of manufacturing them is matched against **revenues,** which are inflows of assets (usually cash or accounts receivable) received for products or services customers purchase. The cost of goods sold includes all manufacturing costs (direct materials, direct manufacturing labor, and manufacturing overhead costs) incurred to produce them. The cellular phones may be sold during a different accounting period than the period in which they were manufactured. Thus, inventorying manufacturing costs in the balance sheet during the accounting period when goods are manufactured and expensing the manufacturing costs in a later income statement when the goods are sold matches revenues and expenses.

For merchandising-sector companies such as Walmart, inventoriable costs are the costs of purchasing the goods that are resold in their same form. These costs comprise the costs of the goods themselves plus any incoming freight, insurance, and handling costs for those goods. Service-sector companies provide only services or intangible products. The absence of inventories of tangible products for sale means there are no inventoriable costs.

Period Costs

Period costs are all costs in the income statement other than cost of goods sold. Period costs, such as marketing, distribution, and customer service costs, are treated as expenses of the accounting period in which they are incurred because managers expect those costs to benefit revenues in only that period and not in future periods. Some costs such as R&D costs are treated as period costs because, although these costs may benefit revenues in a future period if the R&D efforts are successful, it is highly uncertain if and when these benefits will occur. Expensing period costs as they are incurred best matches expenses to revenues.

For manufacturing-sector companies, period costs in the income statement are all nonmanufacturing costs (for example, design costs and costs of shipping products to customers). For merchandising-sector companies, period costs in the income statement are all costs not related to the cost of goods purchased for resale. Examples of these period costs are labor costs of sales floor personnel and advertising costs. Because there are no inventoriable costs for service-sector companies, all costs in the income statement are period costs.

Exhibit 2-5 showed examples of inventoriable costs in direct/indirect and variable/fixed cost classifications for a car manufacturer. Exhibit 2-6 shows examples of period costs in direct/indirect and variable/fixed cost classifications at a bank.

Keys to Success

Inventoriable costs are placed on the balance sheet and expensed when products are sold. Period costs are expensed in the income statement in the period they are incurred.

Learning Objective 6

Illustrate the flow of inventoriable and period costs

. . . period costs are always expensed as incurred; in manufacturing settings, inventoriable costs flow through work-in-process and finished goods accounts, and are expensed when goods are sold

Illustrating the Flow of Inventoriable Costs and Period Costs

We illustrate the flow of inventoriable costs and period costs through the income statement of a manufacturing company, where the distinction between inventoriable costs and period costs is most detailed.

Exhibit 2-6

Examples of Period Costs in Combinations of the Direct/Indirect and Variable/Fixed Cost Classifications at a Bank

		Assignment of Costs to Cost Object	
		Direct Costs	**Indirect Costs**
Cost-Behavior Pattern	**Variable Costs**	• Cost object: Number of mortgage loans Example: Fees paid to property appraisal company for each mortgage loan	• Cost object: Number of mortgage loans Example: Postage paid to deliver mortgage-loan documents to lawyers/homeowners
	Fixed Costs	• Cost object: Number of mortgage loans Example: Salary paid to executives in mortgage loan department to develop new mortgage-loan products	• Cost object: Number of mortgage loans Example: Cost to the bank of sponsoring annual golf tournament

Manufacturing-Sector Example

Follow the flow of costs for Cellular Products in Exhibit 2-7 and Exhibit 2-8. Exhibit 2-7 visually highlights the differences in the flow of inventoriable and period costs for a manufacturing-sector company. Note how, as described in the previous section, inventoriable costs go through the balance sheet accounts of work-in-process inventory and finished goods inventory before entering cost of goods sold in the income statement. Period costs are expensed directly in the income statement. Exhibit 2-8 takes the visual presentation in Exhibit 2-7 and shows how inventoriable costs and period expenses would appear in the income statement and schedule of cost of goods manufactured of a manufacturing company.

We start by tracking the flow of direct materials shown on the left in Exhibit 2-7 and in Panel B in Exhibit 2-8. For ease of exposition, all numbers are expressed in thousands, except for the per unit amounts.

Step 1: Cost of Direct Materials Used in 2012. Note how the arrows in Exhibit 2-7 for beginning inventory, $12,000, and direct material purchases, $73,000, "fill up" the direct material inventory box and how direct material used, $77,000, "empties out" direct material inventory, leaving an ending inventory of direct materials of $8,000 that becomes the beginning inventory for the next year.

The cost of direct materials used is calculated in Exhibit 2-8, Panel B (light blue shaded area), as follows:

Beginning inventory of direct materials, January 1, 2012	$12,000
+ Purchases of direct materials in 2012	73,000
− Ending inventory of direct materials, December 31, 2012	8,000
= Direct materials used in 2012	$77,000

Step 2: Total Manufacturing Costs Incurred in 2012. Total manufacturing costs refers to all direct manufacturing costs and manufacturing overhead costs incurred during 2012 for all goods worked on during the year. Cellular Products classifies its manufacturing costs into the three categories described earlier.

Exhibit 2-7

Flow of Revenue and Costs for a Manufacturing-Sector Company, Cellular Products (in thousands)

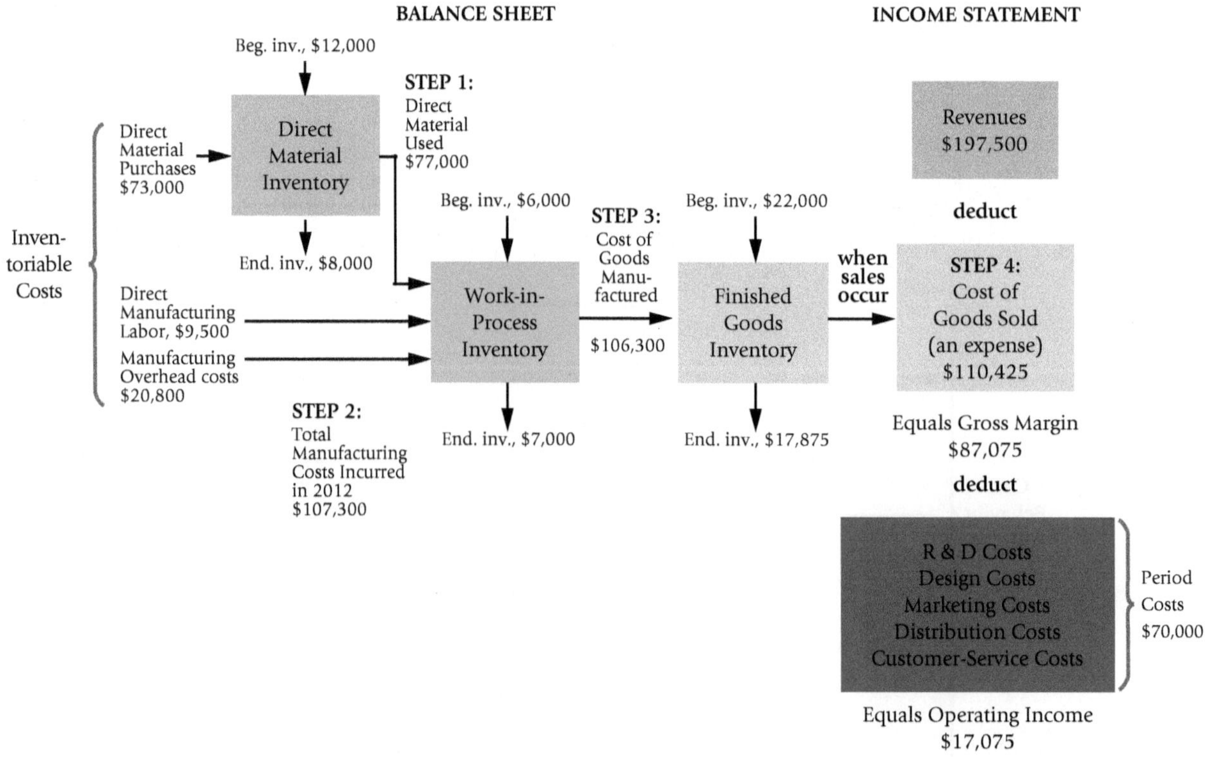

Exhibit 2-8

Income Statement and Schedule of Cost of Goods Manufactured of a Manufacturing-Sector Company, Cellular Products

Home Insert Page Layout Formulas Data Review View

Step		A	B	C	D
	1	**PANEL A: INCOME STATEMENT**			
	2	**Cellular Products**			
	3	**Income Statement**			
	4	**For the Year Ended December 31, 2012 (in thousands)**			
	5	Revenues		$197,500	
STEP 4	6	Cost of goods sold			
STEP 4	7	Beginning finished goods inventory, January 1, 2012	$ 22,000		
STEP 4	8	Cost of goods manufactured (see Panel B)	106,300	←	
STEP 4	9	Cost of goods available for sale	128,300		
STEP 4	10	Ending finished goods inventory, December 31, 2012	17,875		
STEP 4	11	Cost of goods sold		110,425	
	12	Gross margin (or gross profit)		87,075	
	13	Operating costs			
	14	R&D, design, marketing, distribution, and customer-service cost	70,000		
	15	Total operating costs		70,000	
	16	Operating income		$17,075	
	17				
	18	**PANEL B: COST OF GOODS MANUFACTURED**			
	19	**Cellular Products**			
	20	**Schedule of Cost of Goods Manufactured[a]**			
	21	**For the Year Ended December 31, 2012 (in thousands)**			
STEP 1	22	Direct materials			
STEP 1	23	Beginning inverntory, January 1, 2012	$12,000		
STEP 1	24	Purchases of direct materials	73,000		
STEP 1	25	Cost of direct materials available for use	85,000		
STEP 1	26	Ending inventory, December 31, 2012	8,000		
STEP 1 / STEP 2	27	Direct materials used		$ 77,000	
STEP 2	28	Direct manufacturing labor		9,500	
STEP 2	29	Manufacturing overhead costs			
STEP 2	30	Supplies	1,900		
STEP 2	31	Indirect labor	2,500		
STEP 2	32	Utilities	3,400		
STEP 2	33	Lease rent—plant building	5,000		
STEP 2	34	Plant equipment lease cost	7,000		
STEP 2	35	Miscellaneous	1,000		
STEP 2	36	Total manufacturing overhead costs		20,800	
STEP 2 / STEP 3	37	Manufacturing costs incurred during 2012		107,300	
STEP 3	38	Beginning work-in-process inventory, January 1, 2012		6,000	
STEP 3	39	Total manufacturing costs to account for		113,300	
STEP 3	40	Ending work-in-process inventory, December 31, 2012		7,000	
STEP 3	41	Cost of goods manufactured (to income statement)		$106,300	
	42	[a]Note that this schedule can become a schedule of cost of goods manufactured and sold simply by including the beginning and ending finished goods inventory figures in the supporting schedule rather than in the body of the income statement.			

(i) Direct materials used in 2012 (shaded light blue in Exhibit 2-8, Panel B)	$ 77,000
(ii) Direct manufacturing labor in 2012 (shaded blue in Exhibit 2-8, Panel B)	9,500
(iii) Manufacturing overhead costs in 2012 (shaded dark blue in Exhibit 2-8, Panel B)	20,800
Total manufacturing costs incurred in 2012	$107,300

Note how in Exhibit 2-7 these costs increase work-in-process inventory.

Step 3: Cost of Goods Manufactured in 2012. Cost of goods manufactured refers to the cost of goods brought to completion, whether they were started before or during the current accounting period.

Note how the work-in-process inventory box in Exhibit 2-7 has a very similar structure to the direct material inventory box described in Step 1. Beginning work-in-process inventory of $6,000 and total manufacturing costs incurred in 2012 of $107,300 "fill up" the work-in-process inventory box. Some of the manufacturing costs incurred during 2012 are held back as the cost of the ending work-in-process inventory. The ending work-in-process inventory of $7,000 becomes the beginning inventory for the next year, and the cost of goods manufactured during 2012 of $106,300 "empties out" the work-in-process inventory while "filling up" the finished goods inventory box.

The cost of goods manufactured in 2012 (shaded green) is calculated in Exhibit 2-8, Panel B, as follows:

Beginning work-in-process inventory, January 1, 2012	$ 6,000
+ Total manufacturing costs incurred in 2012	107,300
= Total manufacturing costs to account for	113,300
− Ending work-in-process inventory, December 31, 2012	7,000
= Cost of goods manufactured in 2012	$106,300

Step 4: Cost of Goods Sold in 2012. The cost of goods sold is the cost of finished goods inventory sold to customers during the current accounting period. Looking at the finished goods inventory box in Exhibit 2-7, we see that the beginning inventory of finished goods of $22,000 and cost of goods manufactured in 2012 of $106,300 "fill up" the finished goods inventory box. The ending inventory of finished goods of $17,875 becomes the beginning inventory for the next year, and the cost of goods sold during 2012 of $110,425 "empties out" the finished goods inventory.

This cost of goods sold is an expense that is matched against revenues. The cost of goods sold for Cellular Products (shaded brown) is computed in Exhibit 2-8, Panel A, as follows:

Beginning inventory of finished goods, January 1, 2012	$ 22,000
+ Cost of goods manufactured in 2012	106,300
− Ending inventory of finished goods, December 31, 2012	17,875
= Cost of goods sold in 2012	$110,425

Exhibit 2-9 shows related general ledger T-accounts for Cellular Products' manufacturing cost flow. Note how the cost of goods manufactured ($106,300) is the cost of all goods completed during the accounting period. These costs are all inventoriable costs. Goods completed during the period are transferred to finished goods inventory. These costs become cost of goods sold in the accounting period when the goods are sold. Also note that the direct materials, direct manufacturing labor, and manufacturing overhead costs of the units in work-in-process inventory ($7,000) and finished goods inventory ($17,875) as of December 31, 2012, will appear as an asset in the balance sheet. These costs will become expenses next year when these units are sold.

We can now prepare Cellular Products' income statement for 2012. The income statement of Cellular Products is shown on the right side in Exhibit 2-7 and in Exhibit 2-8, Panel A. Cellular Products sold 1,975,000 units in 2012 at $100 apiece for total revenues of $197,500 (as indicated earlier, all numbers in this example are expressed in thousands except for per unit amounts). Inventoriable costs expensed during 2012 equal cost of goods sold of $110,425.

Gross margin = Revenues − Cost of goods sold = $197,500 − $110,425 = $87,075

The $70,000 of operating costs comprising R&D, design, marketing, distribution, and customer-service costs are period costs of Cellular Products. These period costs include, for example, salaries of salespersons, depreciation on computers and other equipment used in marketing, and the cost of leasing warehouse space for distribution. **Operating income** equals total revenues from operations minus cost of goods sold and operating (period) costs (excluding interest expense and income

Exhibit 2-9

General Ledger T-Accounts for Cellular Products' Manufacturing Cost Flow (in thousands)

Work-in-Process Inventory

Bal. Jan. 1, 2012	6,000	Cost of goods manufactured	106,300
Direct materials used	77,000		
Direct manuf. labor	9,500		
Indirect manuf. costs	20,800		
Bal. Dec. 31, 2012	7,000		

Finished Goods Inventory

Bal. Jan. 1, 2012	22,000	Cost of goods sold	110,425
	106,300		
Bal. Dec. 31, 2012	17,875		

Cost of Goods Sold

110,425	

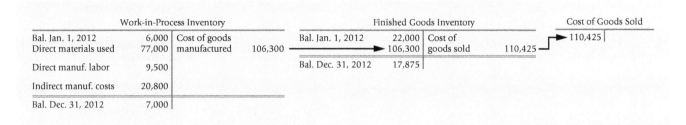

taxes) or equivalently, gross margin minus period costs. The operating income of Cellular Products is \$17,075 (gross margin, \$87,075 − period costs, \$70,000). If you are familiar with financial accounting, recall that period costs are typically called selling, general, and administrative expenses in the income statement.

Newcomers to cost accounting frequently assume that indirect costs such as rent, telephone, and depreciation are always costs of the period in which they are incurred and are not associated with inventories. When these costs are incurred in marketing or in corporate headquarters, they are period costs. However, when these costs are incurred in manufacturing, they are manufacturing overhead costs and are inventoriable.

Note that since costs that are inventoried are not expensed till units are sold, a manager can produce more units than are expected to be sold in a period without reducing a firm's net income. In fact, building up inventory in this way helps to defer the expensing of current period fixed manufacturing costs till units are sold in a subsequent period, thereby actually *increasing* the firm's gross margin and operating income. This important effect is illustrated in detail in the chapter appendix, where we also describe ways in which firms may attempt to dissuade managers from engaging in such potentially risky practices.

Recap of Inventoriable Costs and Period Costs

Exhibit 2-7 highlights the differences between inventoriable costs and period costs for a manufacturing company. The manufacturing costs of finished goods include direct materials, other direct manufacturing costs such as direct manufacturing labor, and manufacturing overhead costs such as supervision, production control, and machine maintenance. All these costs are inventoriable: They are assigned to work-in-process inventory until the goods are completed and then to finished goods inventory until the goods are sold. All nonmanufacturing costs, such as R&D, design, and distribution costs, are period costs.

Inventoriable costs and period costs flow through the income statement at a merchandising company similar to the way costs flow at a manufacturing company. At a merchandising company, however, the flow of costs is much simpler to understand and track. Exhibit 2-10 shows the inventoriable costs and period costs for a retailer or wholesaler who buys goods for resale. The only inventoriable cost is the cost of merchandise. (This corresponds to the cost of finished goods manufactured for a manufacturing company.) Purchased goods are held as merchandise inventory, the cost of which is shown as an asset in the balance sheet. As the goods are sold, their costs are shown in the income statement as cost of goods sold. A retailer or wholesaler also has a variety of marketing, distribution, and customer-service costs, which are period costs. In the income statement, period costs are deducted from revenues without ever having been included as part of inventory. Concepts in Action: Cost Structure at Nordstrom Spurs Growth shows the importance of having the right cost structure for period expenses for a retailer.

Prime Costs and Conversion Costs

Two terms used to describe cost classifications in manufacturing costing systems are prime costs and conversion costs. **Prime costs** are all direct manufacturing costs. For Cellular Products,

Prime costs = Direct material costs + Direct manufacuturing labor costs = \$77,000 + \$9,500 = \$86,500

As we have already discussed, the greater the proportion of prime costs in a company's cost structure, the more confident managers can be about the accuracy of the costs of products. As information-gathering technology improves, companies can add more and more direct-cost categories. For

Exhibit 2-10

Flow of Revenues and Costs for a Merchandising Company (Retailer or Wholesaler)

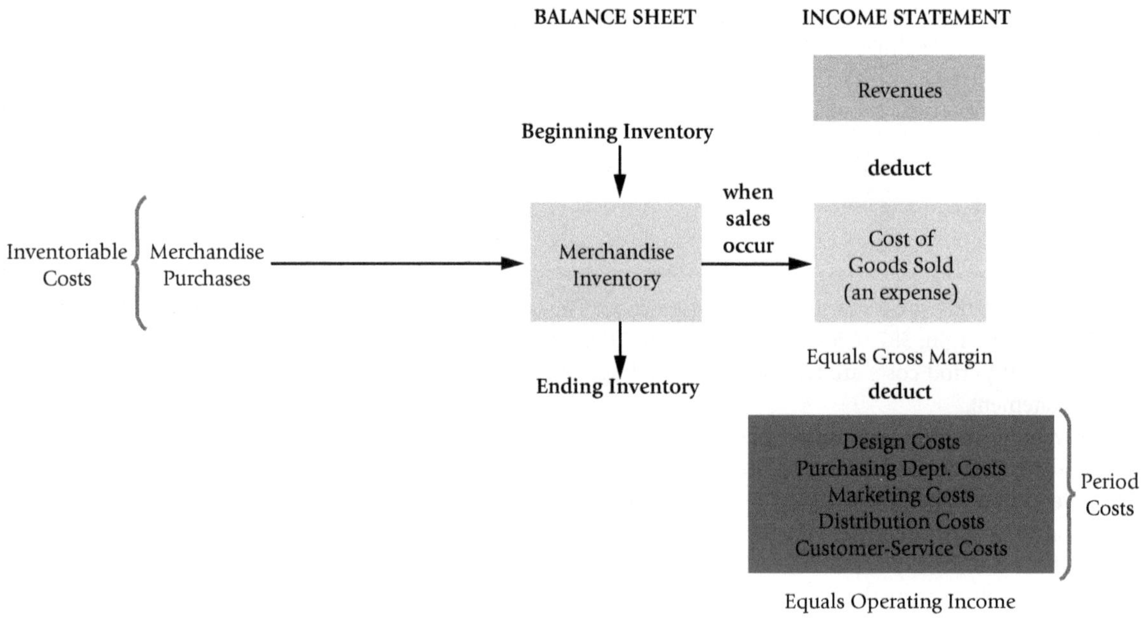

Concepts in Action: Cost Structure at Nordstrom Spurs Growth

During the recent global recession, the retail industry was hit hard due to declining economic conditions and changing consumer shopping habits. Since 2009, many long-standing retailers including Circuit City, Blockbuster, and Borders went out of business as their revenues failed to keep pace with the high fixed costs of the retail business, which include high rents and payroll. While some retailers closed their doors, however, other retailers became stronger and were prepared to grow as consumer spending recovered.

Source: Emily Harris/Bloomberg/Getty Images

While many failed retailers had high fixed costs, Nordstrom, an upscale department store chain, has a more variable cost structure. At Nordstrom, the company's operations are mainly based on a variable cost business model with about 40–45% of its selling, general, and administrative (SGA) costs being variable. These costs include compensation (most salespeople earn a commission), benefits, advertising, and shipping and handling. As consumer spending dropped during the recession, the company reduced costs to mitigate the impact of sluggish sales trends on margins. Similarly, its cost structure enabled Nordstrom to quickly capitalize on the emerging opportunities when market conditions improved.

For example, in 2009 Nordstrom's SGA expenses were 25.5% of its $8.2 billion in revenue. In 2011, its SGA expenses increased to 26.7%, but revenues were $10.5 billion. The company's variable cost flexibility allowed the company to first cut costs and then to aggressively pursue growth while incurring slightly higher SGA costs.

Sources: Based on Nordstrom, Inc., 2012. 2011 Annual Report. Seattle, WA: Nordstrom, Inc.; Zacks Equity Research, "Nordstrom Pinned to Neutral," May 22, 2012.

example, power costs might be metered in specific areas of a plant and identified as a direct cost of specific products. Furthermore, if a production line were dedicated to the manufacture of a specific product, the depreciation on the production equipment would be a direct manufacturing cost and would be included in prime costs. Computer software companies often have a "purchased technology" direct manufacturing cost item. This item, which represents payments to suppliers who develop software algorithms for a product, is also included in prime costs. **Conversion costs** are all manufacturing costs other than direct material costs. Conversion costs represent all manufacturing costs incurred to convert direct materials into finished goods. For Cellular Products,

$$\text{Conversion costs} = \frac{\text{Direct manufacturing}}{\text{labor costs}} + \frac{\text{Manufacturing}}{\text{overhead costs}} = \$9{,}500 + \$20{,}800 = \$30{,}300$$

Note that direct manufacturing labor costs are a part of both prime costs and conversion costs.

Some manufacturing operations, such as computer-integrated manufacturing (CIM) plants, have very few workers. The workers' roles are to monitor the manufacturing process and to maintain the equipment that produces multiple products. Costing systems in CIM plants do not have a direct manufacturing labor cost category because direct manufacturing labor cost is relatively small and because it is difficult to trace this cost to products. In CIM plants, the only prime cost is direct material costs, and conversion costs consist only of manufacturing overhead costs.

Keys to Success

For manufacturing companies, manufacturing costs (direct material, direct labor, and manufacturing overhead) are inventoriable costs; nonmanufacturing costs are expensed as period costs. For merchandising companies, the only inventoriable cost is the cost of merchandise.

Measuring Costs Requires Judgment

Learning Objective 7

Explain why product costs are computed in different ways for different purposes

. . . examples are pricing and product-mix decisions, government contracts, and financial statements

Measuring costs requires judgment. That's because there are alternative ways for managers to define and classify costs. Different companies or sometimes even different subunits within the same company may define and classify costs differently. Be careful to define and understand the ways costs are measured in a company or situation. We first illustrate this point using labor cost measurement.

Measuring Labor Costs

Consider labor costs for software programming at companies such as Apple where programmers work on different software applications for products like the iMac, the iPad, and the iPhone. Although labor cost classifications vary among companies, many companies use multiple labor cost categories:

- Direct programming labor costs that can be traced to individual products
- Overhead (examples of prominent labor components of overhead follow):
  - Indirect labor compensation for
    - Office staff
    - Office security
    - Rework labor (time spent by direct laborers correcting software errors)
    - Overtime premium paid to software programmers (explained next)
    - Idle time (explained next)
  - Salaries for managers, department heads, and supervisors
  - Payroll fringe costs, for example, health care premiums and pension costs (explained later)

Note how *indirect labor costs* are commonly divided into many subclassifications, for example, office staff and idle time, to retain information on different categories of indirect labor. Note also that managers' salaries usually are not classified as indirect labor costs. Instead, the compensation of supervisors, department heads, and all others who are regarded as management is placed in a separate classification of labor-related overhead.

Overtime Premium and Idle Time

The purpose of classifying costs in detail is to associate an individual cost with a specific cause or reason for why it was incurred. Managers need to pay special attention to two classes of indirect labor—overtime premium and idle time. **Overtime premium** is the wage rate paid to workers (for both direct labor and indirect labor) in *excess* of their straight-time wage rates. Overtime premium is usually considered to be a part of indirect costs or overhead. Consider the example of George Flexner, a junior software programmer who writes software for multiple products. He is paid $20 per hour for straight-time and $30 per hour (time and a half) for overtime. His overtime premium is $10 per overtime hour. If he works 44 hours, including 4 overtime hours, in one week, his gross compensation would be classified as follows:

Direct programming labor: 44 hours × $20 per hour	$880
Overtime premium: 4 hours × $10 per hour	40
Total compensation for 44 hours	$920

In this example, why is the overtime premium of direct programming labor usually considered an overhead cost rather than a direct cost? After all, the premium can be traced to specific products that George worked on while working overtime. Overtime premium is generally not considered a direct cost because the particular job that George worked on during the overtime hours is a matter of chance. For example, assume that George worked on two products for 5 hours each on a specific workday of 10 hours, including 2 overtime hours. Should the product George worked on during hours 9 and 10 be assigned the overtime premium? Or should the premium be prorated over both products? Prorating the overtime premium does not "penalize"—add to the cost of—a particular product solely because it happened to be worked on during the overtime hours. *Instead, the overtime premium is considered to be attributable to the heavy overall volume of work. Its cost is regarded as part of overhead, which is borne by both products.*

Sometimes overtime is not random. For example, a launch deadline for a particular product may clearly be the sole source of overtime. In such instances, the overtime premium is regarded as a direct cost of that product.

Another subclassification of indirect labor is the idle time of both direct and indirect labor. **Idle time** is wages paid for unproductive time caused by lack of orders, machine or computer breakdowns, work delays, poor scheduling, and the like. For example, if George had no work for 3 hours during that week while waiting to receive code from another colleague, George's earnings would be classified as follows:

Direct programming labor: 41 hours × $20/hour	$820
Idle time (overhead): 3 hours × $20/hour	60
Overtime premium (overhead): 4 hours × $10/hour	40
Total earnings for 44 hours	$920

Clearly, the idle time is not related to a particular product, nor, as we have already discussed, is the overtime premium. Both overtime premium and idle time are considered overhead costs.

Benefits of Defining Accounting Terms

Managers, accountants, suppliers, and others will avoid many problems if they thoroughly understand and agree on the classifications and meanings of the cost terms introduced in this chapter and later in this book.

Consider the classification of programming labor *payroll fringe costs,* which include employer payments for employee benefits such as Social Security, life insurance, health insurance, and pensions. Consider, for example, a software programmer who is paid a wage of $20 an hour with fringe benefits totaling, say, $5 per hour. Some companies classify the $20 as a direct programming labor cost of the product for which the software is being written and the $5 as overhead cost. Other companies classify the entire $25 as direct programming labor cost. The latter approach is preferable because the stated wage and the fringe benefit costs together are a fundamental part of acquiring direct software programming labor services.

Caution: In every situation, it is important for managers to pinpoint clearly what direct labor includes and what direct labor excludes. Achieving clarity may prevent disputes regarding cost-reimbursement contracts, income tax payments, and labor union matters, which often take up a substantial amount of management time. Consider that some countries, such as Costa Rica and Mauritius, offer substantial income tax savings to foreign companies that generate employment within their borders. In some cases, to qualify for the tax benefits, the direct labor costs must at least equal a specified percentage of the total costs.

When managers do not precisely define direct labor costs, disputes have arisen about whether payroll fringe costs should be included as part of direct labor costs when calculating the direct labor percentage for qualifying for such tax benefits. Companies have sought to classify payroll fringe costs as part of direct labor costs to make direct labor costs a higher percentage of total costs. Tax authorities have argued that payroll fringe costs are part of overhead. In addition to fringe benefits, other debated items are compensation for training time, idle time, vacations, sick leave, and overtime premium. To prevent disputes, contracts and laws should be as specific as possible regarding definitions and measurements.

Different Meanings of Product Costs

Many cost terms used by organizations have ambiguous meanings. Consider the term *product cost.* A **product cost** is the sum of the costs assigned to a product for a specific purpose. Different purposes can result in different measures of product cost, as the brackets on the value chain in Exhibit 2-11 illustrate:

- **Pricing and product-mix decisions.** For the purposes of making decisions about pricing and which products provide the most profits, the manager is interested in the overall (total) profitability of different products and, consequently, assigns costs incurred in all business functions of the value chain to the different products.
- **Reimbursement under government contracts.** Government contracts often reimburse contractors on the basis of the "cost of a product" plus a prespecified margin of profit. Such cost-plus arrangements are typically used for services and development contracts where it is not easy to predict the amount of money required to design, fabricate, and test items. Because these contracts transfer the risk of cost overruns to the government, agencies such as the Department of Defense and Department of Energy provide detailed guidelines on the cost items they will allow (and disallow) when calculating the cost of a product. For example, some government agencies explicitly exclude marketing, distribution, and customer-service costs from the product costs that qualify for reimbursement, and they may only partially reimburse R&D costs. These agencies want to reimburse contractors for only those costs most closely related to delivering products under the contract. The second bracket in Exhibit 2-11 shows how the product-cost calculations for a specific contract may allow for all design and production costs but only part of R&D costs.
- **Preparing financial statements for external reporting under Generally Accepted Accounting Principles (GAAP).** Under GAAP, only manufacturing costs can be assigned to inventories in the financial statements. For purposes of calculating inventory costs, product costs include only inventoriable (manufacturing) costs.

As Exhibit 2-11 illustrates, product-cost measures range from a narrow set of costs for financial statements—a set that includes only inventoriable costs—to a broader set of costs for

Exhibit 2-11
Different Product Costs for Different Purposes

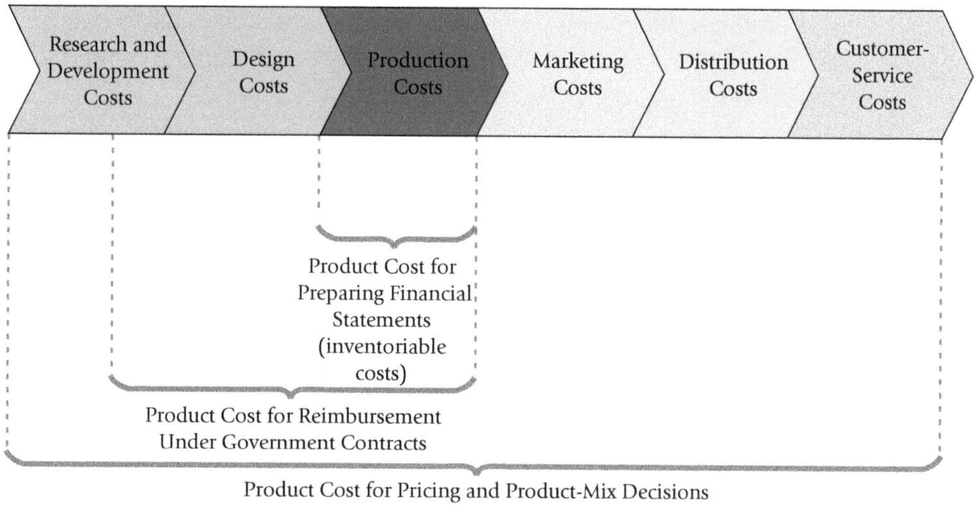

Exhibit 2-12

Alternative Classifications of Costs

1. Business function
   a. Research and development
   b. Design of products and processes
   c. Production
   d. Marketing
   e. Distribution
   f. Customer service
2. Assignment to a cost object
   a. Direct cost
   b. Indirect cost
3. Behavior pattern in relation to the level of activity or volume
   a. Variable cost
   b. Fixed cost
4. Aggregate or average
   a. Total cost
   b. Unit cost
5. Assets or expenses
   a. Inventoriable cost
   b Period cost

reimbursement under a government contract to a still broader set of costs for pricing and product-mix decisions.

This section focused on how different purposes result in the inclusion of different cost items of the value chain of business functions when product costs are calculated. Managers need to be clear and precise about cost concepts and their measurement for every cost classification introduced in this chapter. Exhibit 2-12 summarizes the key cost classifications.

Using the five-step process described in Chapter 1, think about how these different classifications of costs help managers make decisions and evaluate performance.

1. *Identify the problem and uncertainties.* Consider a decision about how much to price a product. This decision often depends on how much it costs to make the product.
2. *Obtain information.* Managers identify direct and indirect costs of a product in each business function. Managers also gather other information about customers, competitors, and prices of substitute products.
3. *Make predictions about the future.* Managers estimate what it will cost to make the product in the future. This requires predictions about the quantity of product that managers expect to sell and an understanding of fixed and variable costs.
4. *Make decisions by choosing among alternatives.* Managers choose a price to charge based on a thorough understanding of costs and other information.
5. *Implement the decision, evaluate performance, and learn.* Managers control costs and learn by comparing actual total and unit costs against predicted amounts.

The next section describes how the basic concepts introduced in this chapter lead to a framework for understanding cost accounting and cost management that can then be applied to the study of many topics, such as strategy evaluation, quality, and investment decisions.

Keys to Success

Managers can assign different costs to the same cost object (such as a product) depending on the purpose for which the cost is being calculated. It is important therefore to understand and agree on the classification and meaning of cost terms.

Learning Objective 8

Describe a framework for cost accounting and cost management

. . . three features that help managers make decisions

A Framework for Cost Accounting and Cost Management

Three features of cost accounting and cost management across a wide range of applications are as follows:

1. Calculating the cost of products, services, and other cost objects
2. Analyzing the relevant information for making decisions
3. Obtaining information for planning and control and performance evaluation

We develop these ideas in different sections of the book.

Calculating the Cost of Products, Services, and Other Cost Objects

We have already seen the different purposes and measures of product costs. Whatever the purpose, the costing system traces direct costs and allocates indirect costs to products. Chapters 4, 5, 6, and 7 describe systems such as job costing, process costing, and activity-based costing to calculate total costs and unit costs of products and services. The chapters also discuss how managers use this information to formulate strategy and make pricing, product-mix, and cost-management decisions.

Analyzing the Relevant Information for Making Decisions

When making decisions about strategy design and strategy implementation, managers must understand which revenues and costs to consider and which ones to ignore. Management accountants help managers identify what information is relevant and what information is irrelevant. Consider a decision about whether to buy a product from an outside vendor or to make it in-house. The costing system indicates that it costs $25 per unit to make the product in-house. A vendor offers the product for $22 per unit. At first glance, it seems it will cost less for the company to buy the product rather than make it. Suppose, however, that of the $25 to make the product in-house, $5 consists of plant lease costs that the company has already paid under the lease contract. Furthermore, if the product is bought, the plant will remain idle. That is, there is no opportunity to profit by putting the plant to some alternative use. Under these conditions, it will cost less to make the product than to buy it. That's because making the product costs only an *additional* $20 per unit ($25 – $5), compared with an *additional* $22 per unit if it is bought. The $5 per unit of lease cost is irrelevant to the decision because it is a *past* (or *sunk*) cost that has already been incurred regardless of whether the product is made or bought. Analyzing relevant information is a key aspect of making decisions.

When making strategic decisions about which products and how much to produce, managers must know how revenues and costs vary with changes in output levels. For this purpose, managers need to distinguish fixed costs from variable costs. Chapter 3 analyzes how operating income changes with changes in units sold and how managers use this information to make decisions such as how much to spend on advertising. Chapter 8 describes methods to estimate the fixed and variable components of costs. Chapter 9 applies the concept of relevance to decision making in many different situations and describes methods managers use to maximize income given the resource constraints they face. Chapter 10 introduces the relevant revenues and costs of quality, inventory, and time. Chapter 11 identifies relevant revenues and costs for capital investment decisions.

Obtaining Information for Planning and Control and Performance Evaluation

Budgeting is the most commonly used tool for planning and control. A budget forces managers to look ahead, to translate strategy into plans, to coordinate and communicate within the organization, and to provide a benchmark for evaluating performance. Budgeting often plays a major role in affecting behavior and decisions because managers strive to meet budget targets. Chapter 12 describes budgeting systems.

At the end of a reporting period, managers compare actual results to planned performance. The manager's tasks are to understand why differences (called variances) between actual and planned performances arose and to use the information provided by these variances as feedback to promote learning and future improvement. Managers also use variances as well as nonfinancial measures, such as defect rates and customer satisfaction ratings, to control and evaluate the performance of various departments, divisions, and managers. Chapter 13 discusses variance analysis. Chapter 14 introduces the balanced scorecard as a tool for implementing strategy. Chapter 15 describes the benefits and costs of decentralization and the use of transfer prices to coordinate the actions of different managers. Chapter 16 presents various measures for evaluating performance designed to align the interests of managers and owners. Chapters 12 through 16 collectively focus on the techniques managers use to execute strategy.

Problem for Self-Study

Foxwood Company is a metal- and woodcutting manufacturer, selling products to the home construction market. Consider the following data for 2012:

Sandpaper	$ 2,000
Materials-handling costs	70,000
Lubricants and coolants	5,000
Miscellaneous indirect manufacturing labor	40,000
Direct manufacturing labor	300,000
Direct materials inventory, Jan. 1, 2012	40,000
Direct materials inventory, Dec. 31, 2012	50,000
Finished goods inventory, Jan. 1, 2012	100,000
Finished goods inventory, Dec. 31, 2012	150,000
Work-in-process inventory, Jan. 1, 2012	10,000
Work-in-process inventory, Dec. 31, 2012	14,000
Plant-leasing costs	54,000
Depreciation—plant equipment	36,000
Property taxes on plant equipment	4,000
Fire insurance on plant equipment	3,000
Direct materials purchased	460,000
Revenues	1,360,000
Marketing promotions	60,000
Marketing salaries	100,000
Distribution costs	70,000
Customer-service costs	100,000

Required

1. Prepare an income statement with a separate supporting schedule of cost of goods manufactured. For all manufacturing items, classify costs as direct costs or indirect costs and indicate by V or F whether each is basically a variable cost or a fixed cost (when the cost object is a product unit). If in doubt, decide on the basis of whether the total cost will change substantially over a wide range of units produced.
2. Suppose that both the direct material costs and the plant-leasing costs are for the production of 900,000 units. What is the direct material cost of each unit produced? What is the plant-leasing cost per unit? Assume that the plant-leasing cost is a fixed cost.
3. Suppose Foxwood Company manufactures 1,000,000 units next year. Repeat the computation in requirement 2 for direct materials and plant-leasing costs. Assume the implied cost-behavior patterns persist.
4. As a management consultant, explain concisely to the company president why the unit cost for direct materials did not change in requirements 2 and 3 but the unit cost for plant-leasing costs did change.

Solution

1.

Foxwood Company
Income Statement
For the Year Ended December 31, 2012

Revenues		$1,360,000
Cost of goods sold		
Beginning finished goods inventory, January 1, 2012	$ 100,000	
Cost of goods manufactured (see the following schedule)	960,000	
Cost of goods available for sale	1,060,000	
Deduct ending finished goods inventory, December 31, 2012	150,000	910,000
Gross margin (or gross profit)		450,000
Operating costs		
Marketing promotions	60,000	
Marketing salaries	100,000	
Distribution costs	70,000	
Customer-service costs	100,000	330,000
Operating income		$ 120,000

Foxwood Company
Schedule of Cost of Goods Manufactured
For the Year Ended December 31, 2012

Direct materials		
Beginning inventory, January 1, 2012		$ 40,000
Purchases of direct materials		460,000
Cost of direct materials available for use		500,000
Ending inventory, December 31, 2012		50,000
Direct materials used		450,000 (V)
Direct manufacturing labor		300,000 (V)
Indirect manufacturing costs		
Sandpaper	$ 2,000 (V)	
Materials-handling costs	70,000 (V)	
Lubricants and coolants	5,000 (V)	
Miscellaneous indirect manufacturing labor	40,000 (V)	
Plant-leasing costs	54,000 (F)	
Depreciation—plant equipment	36,000 (F)	
Property taxes on plant equipment	4,000 (F)	
Fire insurance on plant equipment	3,000 (F)	214,000
Manufacturing costs incurred during 2012		964,000
Beginning work-in-process inventory, January 1, 2012		10,000
Total manufacturing costs to account for		974,000
Ending work-in-process inventory, December 31, 2012		14,000
Cost of goods manufactured (to income statement)		$960,000

2. Direct material unit cost = Direct materials used ÷ Units produced

= \$450,000 ÷ 900,000 units = \$0.50 per unit

Plant-leasing unit cost = Plant-leasing costs ÷ Units produced

= \$54,000 ÷ 900,000 units = \$0.06 per unit

3. The direct material costs are variable, so they would increase in total from \$450,000 to \$500,000 (1,000,000 units × \$0.50 per unit). However, their unit cost would be unaffected: \$500,000 ÷ 1,000,000 units = \$0.50 per unit.

In contrast, the plant-leasing costs of \$54,000 are fixed, so they would not increase in total. However, the plant-leasing cost per unit would decline from \$0.060 to \$0.054: \$54,000 ÷ 1,000,000 units = \$0.054 per unit.

4. The explanation would begin with the answer to requirement 3. As a consultant, you should stress that the unitizing (averaging) of costs that have different behavior patterns can be misleading. A common error is to assume that a total unit cost, which is often a sum of variable unit cost and fixed unit cost, is an indicator that total costs change in proportion to changes in production levels. The next chapter demonstrates the necessity for distinguishing between cost-behavior patterns. You must be wary, especially about average fixed cost per unit. Too often, unit fixed cost is erroneously regarded as being indistinguishable from unit variable cost.

Decision Points

The following question-and-answer format summarizes the chapter's learning objectives. Each decision presents a key question related to a learning objective. The guidelines are the answer to that question.

Decision	Guidelines
1. What is a cost object?	A cost object is anything for which a manager needs a separate measurement of cost. Examples include a product, a service, a project, a customer, a brand category, an activity, and a department.

Decision	Guidelines
2. How do managers decide whether a cost is a direct or an indirect cost?	A direct cost is any cost that is related to a particular cost object and can be traced to that cost object in an economically feasible way. Indirect costs are related to the particular cost object but cannot be traced to it in an economically feasible way. The same cost can be direct for one cost object and indirect for another cost object. This book uses *cost tracing* to describe the assignment of direct costs to a cost object and *cost allocation* to describe the assignment of indirect costs to a cost object.
3. How do managers decide whether a cost is a variable or a fixed cost?	A variable cost changes *in total* in proportion to changes in the related level of total activity or volume. A fixed cost remains unchanged *in total* for a given time period despite wide changes in the related level of total activity or volume.
4. How should managers estimate and interpret cost information?	In general, focus on total costs, not unit costs. When making total cost estimates, think of variable costs as an amount per unit and fixed costs as a total amount. Interpret the unit cost of a cost object cautiously when it includes a fixed-cost component.
5. What are the differences in the accounting for inventoriable versus period costs?	Inventoriable costs are all costs of a product that a firm regards as an asset in the accounting period when they are incurred and become cost of goods sold in the accounting period when the product is sold. Period costs are expensed in the accounting period in which they are incurred and are all of the costs in an income statement other than cost of goods sold.
6. What is the flow of inventoriable and period costs in manufacturing and merchandising settings?	In manufacturing settings, inventoriable costs flow through work-in-process and finished goods accounts, and are expensed as cost of goods sold. Period costs are expensed as incurred. In merchandising settings, only the cost of merchandise is treated as inventoriable.
7. Why do managers assign different costs to the same cost objects?	Managers can assign different costs to the same cost object depending on the purpose. For example, for the external reporting purpose in a manufacturing company, the inventoriable cost of a product includes only manufacturing costs. In contrast, costs from all business functions of the value chain often are assigned to a product for pricing and product-mix decisions.
8. What are the three key features of cost accounting and cost management?	Three features of cost accounting and cost management are (1) calculating the cost of products, services, and other cost objects; (2) analyzing relevant information for making decisions and (3) obtaining information for planning and control and performance evaluation.

Appendix

Variable Costing and Absorption Costing

Managers in companies with high fixed costs, such as those in semiconductor, automobile, or steel industries, must manage capacity levels and make decisions about the use of available capacity. Managers must also decide on a production and inventory policy. These decisions and the accounting choices managers make affect the operating incomes of manufacturing companies.

In this appendix, we focus on alternative inventory-costing choices for manufacturing costs. Recall that manufacturing costs are inventoriable costs that are recorded as assets when they are incurred and expensed as cost of goods sold when the product is sold. **Absorption costing** is a method of inventory costing in which *all* manufacturing costs are included as inventoriable costs. Absorption costing measures the cost of all manufacturing resources, whether variable or fixed, necessary to produce inventory. The Cellular Products example is an illustration of an absorption costing system. Absorption costing is the required inventory method for external reporting in most countries.

Undesirable Buildup of Inventories

One problem with absorption costing is that it enables a manager to increase operating income in a specific period by increasing production—even if there is no customer demand for the additional production! By producing more ending inventory, the firm's margins and operating income can be made higher. To align the interests of managers and shareholders, managers are frequently evaluated and rewarded on the basis of reported operating income. Producing for inventory makes the manager's performance look better.

To illustrate this effect, we return to the Cellular Products example. We provide the following additional information, consistent with the cost information in the example. All numbers are in thousands except per unit amounts.

- The cost driver for all variable manufacturing costs is units produced.
- The beginning finished goods inventory of $22,000 consists of 400 units at $55 each.
- Direct materials cost per unit is $40, and direct manufacturing labor cost per unit is $5.
- The only item of variable manufacturing overhead is supplies at a cost of $1 per unit.
- Fixed manufacturing overhead costs total $18,900. Cellular Products incurs these fixed manufacturing overhead costs to support the production of 2,100 units so that the fixed manufacturing overhead cost per unit is $9 ($18,900 ÷ 2,100 units). Consequently each unit in finished goods inventory has a fixed manufacturing overhead cost of $9. This is the case regardless of the units produced in 2012. For example, if Cellular Products produces 100 units during the year and all these units are in inventory, each unit will have a fixed manufacturing overhead cost of $9 per unit (for a total of $900) and not a fixed manufacturing overhead cost of $189 per unit ($18,900 ÷ 100). The fixed manufacturing overhead cost associated with unused production capacity of 2,000 units (2,100 units − 100 units) is expensed ($9 × 2,000 units = $18,000).
- The manufacturing cost per unit under absorption costing is $55 per unit (direct materials, $40 per unit; direct manufacturing labor, $5 per unit; variable manufacturing overhead, $1 per unit; and fixed manufacturing overhead, $9 per unit). As a result, each unit in finished goods inventory is valued at $55 per unit.
- The operating (period) costs of $70,000 are fixed.
- The beginning and ending work-in-process inventory consists of direct materials that have just begun to be processed. This information simplifies the exposition by allowing us to focus only on finished goods inventory. Companies can also report higher operating income by increasing almost-completed ending work in process inventory.

Exhibit 2-13 shows how Cellular Products' absorption costing income for 2012 changes as the production level changes. The first two columns depict the cost of goods manufactured and income statement from Exhibit 2-8 where physical units in beginning inventory is 400 units, production is 1,900 units, sales are 1,975 units, and ending inventory is 325 units. In this case, Cellular Products has a cost of goods sold of $110,425 and an operating income of $17,075. Note from Exhibit 2-13, Panel B, that for the 1,900 units produced and other work done in 2012, total manufacturing costs equal $107,300, which is composed of:

Direct materials manufacturing costs = $40 per unit × 1,900 units = $76,000 + $1,000 of additional direct materials in work-in-process inventory = $77,000

Direct manufacturing labor = $5 per unit × 1,900 units = $9,500

Variable manufacturing overhead costs = $1 × 1,900 units = $1,900

Total fixed manufacturing overhead costs = $18,900 (indirect labor, $2,500; utilities, $3,400; lease rent—plant building, $5,000; plant equipment lease cost, $7,000; miscellaneous, $1,000)

The third and fourth columns illustrate the effect of *producing for inventory* where physical units in beginning inventory is 400 units, production is 2,100 units instead of 1,900 units (200 units more), sales are the same 1,975 units, and ending inventory is 525 units instead of 325 units. In this case, Cellular Products has a cost of goods sold of $108,625 and an operating income of $18,875. Note from Exhibit 2-13, Panel B, that for the 2,100 units produced and other work done in 2012, total manufacturing costs equal $116,500. This is the sum of:

Direct materials manufacturing costs = $40 per unit × 2,100 units = $84,000 + $1,000 of additional direct materials in work-in-process inventory = $85,000

Direct manufacturing labor = $5 per unit × 2,100 units = $10,500

Variable manufacturing overhead costs = $1 × 2,100 units = $2,100

Exhibit 2-13

Effect on Absorption-Costing Income of Different Production Levels for Cellular Products Company: Income Statement for 2012 at Production of 2,100 Units Instead of 1,900 Units for the same level of Sales of 1,975 units (all numbers in thousands except per unit amounts).

	A	B	C	D	E
1	**PANEL A: UNIT DATA AND INCOME STATEMENT**				
2	**Cellular Products**				
3	**For the Year Ended December 31, 2012 (in thousands)**				
4		Production of 1,900 units during 2012 (as in Exhibit 2-8)		Production of 2,100 units during 2012	
5	**Units Data**				
6	Beginning inventory		400		400
7	Production		1,900		2,100
8	Units available for sale		2,300		2,500
9	Sales		1,975		1,975
10	Ending inventory		325		525
11	**Income Statement**				
12	Revenues ($100 per unit × 1,975 units; $100 per unit × 1,975 units)		$197,500		$197,500
13	Cost of goods sold				
14	Begining finished goods inventory, January 1, 2012 ($55 per unit × 400 units; $55 per unit × 400 units)	$ 22,000		$ 22,000	
15	Cost of goods manufactured (see Panel B) (1,900 units; 2,100 units)	106,300		115,500	
16	Cost of goods available for sale (2,300 units; 2,500 units)	128,300		137,500	
17	Ending finished goods inventory, December 31, 2012 ($55 per unit × 325 units; 525 units)	17,875		28,875	
18	Cost of goods sold (1,975 units; 1,975 units)		110,425		108,625
19	Gross margin		87,075		88,875
20	Operating costs				
21	R&D, design, marketing, distribution, and customer-service costs	70,000		70,000	
22	Total operating costs		70,000		70,000
23	Operating income		$ 17,075		$ 18,875

Total fixed manufacturing overhead costs (the same as in Columns 1 and 2) = $18,900 (indirect labor, $2,500; utilities, $3,400; lease rent—plant building, $5,000; plant equipment lease cost, $7,000; miscellaneous, $1,000)

By making 2,100 phones instead of 1,900 phones, Cellular Products increases its operating income by $1,800, or 10.5% ($1,800 ÷ $17,075). The reason is that under absorption costing, producing an additional 200 units for inventory moves $1,800 of the fixed manufacturing overhead costs ($9 per unit × 200 units) to finished goods inventory, so those costs are not expensed in 2012. The 200 units of additional finished goods inventory absorbs $11,000 of costs ($55 × 200 = $11,000). To produce those 200 units, however, Cellular Products incurs only an additional $9,200 of variable manufacturing costs ($46 × 200 units). Despite not resulting in any additional fixed manufacturing costs, the 200 units in ending finished goods inventory absorbs $1,800 of fixed manufacturing costs that would otherwise have been expensed, thereby increasing the operating income of Cellular Products from $17,075 to $18,875.

Exhibit 2-13 (cont'd.)

Effect on Absorption-Costing Income of Different Production Levels for Cellular Products Company: Income Statement for 2012 at Production of 2,100 Units Instead of 1,900 Units for the same level of Sales of 1,975 units (all numbers in thousands except per unit amounts).

	A	B	C	D	E
1	**PANEL B: COST OF GOODS MANUFACTURED**				
2	**Cellular Products**				
	Schedule of Cost of Goods Manufactured				
3	**For the Year Ended December 31, 2012**				
4		Production of 1,900 units during 2012 (as in Exhibit 2-8)		Production of 2,100 units during 2012	
5	Direct Materials				
6	Beginning inventory, January 1, 2012	$12,000		$12,000	
7	Purchases of direct materials	73,000		73,000	
8	Cost of direct materials available for use	85,000		85,000	
9	Ending inventory, December 31, 2012	8,000		0	
10	Direct materials used		$ 77,000		$ 85,000
11	Direct manufacturing labor		9,500		10,500
12	Manufacturing Overhead Costs:				
13	Supplies	1,900		2,100	
14	Indirect labor	2,500		2,500	
15	Utilities	3,400		3,400	
16	Lease rent---plant building	5,000		5,000	
17	Plant equipment lease cost	7,000		7,000	
18	Miscellaneous	1,000		1,000	
19	Total manufacturing overhead costs		20,800		21,000
20	Manufacturing costs incurred during 2012		107,300		116,500
21	Beginning work-in-process inventory, January 1, 2012		6,000		6,000
22	Total manufacturing costs to account for		113,300		122,500
23	Ending work-in-process inventory, December 31, 2012		7,000		7,000
24	Cost of goods manufactured (to income statement)		$106,300		$115,500

Why might Cellular Products' managers engage in this behavior? One possibility is that the firm's managers anticipate rapid growth in demand and want to make and store additional units to deal with possible production shortages in the next year. This is a risky strategy, however, especially in industries with volatile demand or high risk of product obsolescence. Another motivation may be that managers are tempted to build inventory in order to get higher bonuses based on absorption-costing operating income. Generally, higher operating income also results in higher taxes. Many would argue that it is unethical for managers to take actions that are not in the best interests of the company with the sole purpose of increasing their compensation.

Can top management implement checks and balances that limit managers from producing for inventory under absorption costing? While the answer is yes, as we will see in the next section, producing for inventory cannot completely be prevented. There are many subtle ways a manager can produce for inventory that, if done to a limited extent, may not be easy to detect. For example:

- A plant manager may switch to manufacturing products that absorb the highest amount of fixed manufacturing overhead costs, regardless of the customer demand for these products (called "cherry picking" the production line), resulting in failure to meet promised customer delivery dates (which, over time, can result in unhappy customers).

- To increase production, a manager may defer maintenance beyond the current period. Although operating income in this period may increase as a result, future operating income could decrease by a larger amount if repair costs increase and equipment becomes less efficient.

The example in Exhibit 2-13 focuses on only 1 year (2012). A manager who built up ending inventories of phones to 525 units in 2012 would have to further increase ending inventories in 2013 to increase that year's operating income by producing for inventory. There are limits to how much inventory levels can be increased over time (because of physical constraints on storage space and management supervision and controls). Such limits reduce the likelihood of continuously implementing some of the undesirable effects of absorption costing, such as excess inventory. Nevertheless, a manager could produce for inventory in a period when a company's performance is weak to increase operating income and reduce inventory with a corresponding decrease in operating income in periods when the company's performance is good.

Proposals for Revising Performance Evaluation

Top management can take several steps to reduce the undesirable effects of absorption costing.

- Focus on careful planning and budgeting of inventory amounts to reduce managers' freedom to build up excess inventory. If actual inventories exceed these dollar amounts, top management can investigate the inventory buildups.
- Incorporate a carrying charge for inventory in the internal accounting system to create a disincentive for managers to build up inventory. For example, the company could assess an inventory carrying charge of 1% per month on the investment tied up in inventory and for spoilage and obsolescence when it evaluates a manager's performance. An increasing number of companies are beginning to adopt this inventory carrying charge.
- Place greater weight on rewarding performance over longer periods, say 3–5 years, reducing a manager's temptation to produce for inventory at the end of each year.
- Include nonfinancial as well as financial variables in the measures used to evaluate performance. Examples of nonfinancial measures that can be used to monitor the performance of Cellular Products' managers are as follows (using the second scenario in Exhibit 2-13):

$$\textbf{(a)}\ \frac{\text{Beginning inventory in units in 2013}}{\text{Ending inventory in units in 2013}} = \frac{400}{525} = 0.76$$

$$\textbf{(b)}\ \frac{\text{Units produced in 2013}}{\text{Units sold in 2013}} = \frac{2{,}100}{1{,}975} = 1.02$$

  Top management would want to see the first ratio get bigger and the second ratio smaller.
- Use an alternative method of inventory costing for internal purposes that does not create incentives for managers to produce for inventory. We examine one such method next.

Besides the formal performance measurement systems, companies develop codes of conduct to discourage behavior that benefits managers but not the company, and build values and cultures that focus on doing the right things. We discuss these topics in more detail later in Chapter 16.

Variable Costing

Variable costing is a method of inventory costing in which fixed manufacturing costs are excluded from inventoriable costs and are treated instead as costs of the period in which they are incurred. As in absorption costing, all variable manufacturing costs (direct and indirect) are included as inventoriable costs, and variable nonmanufacturing costs are treated as period costs and are expensed.

Comparing Income Statements

What will Cellular Products' operating income be if the company uses variable costing instead of absorption costing? The differences between these methods are apparent from Exhibit 2-14, which shows the income statement under variable costing for the two scenarios analyzed under absorption costing in Exhibit 2-13. The variable-costing income statement uses a *contribution-margin* format. (**Contribution margin** refers to the difference between total revenues and total variable costs. We discuss this concept at length in Chapter 3.) Why these differences in format? The distinction

Exhibit 2-14

Effect on Variable-Costing Income of Different Production Levels for Cellular Products Company: Income Statement for 2012 at Production of 1,900 Units and 2,100 Units for the same level of Sales of 1,975 units (all numbers in thousands except per unit amounts).

	A	B	C	D	E
1	Unit Data and Income Statement				
2	Cellular Products				
3	For the Year Ended December 31, 2012 (in thousands)				
4		Production of 1,900 units during 2012		Production of 2,100 units during 2012	
5	**Units Data**				
6	Beginning inventory		400		400
7	Production		1,900		2,100
8	Units available for sale		2,300		2,500
9	Sales		1,975		1,975
10	Ending inventory		325		525
11	**Income Statement**				
12	Revenues ($100 per unit × 1975 units; $100 per unit × 1975)		$197,500		$197,500
13	Cost of goods sold				
14	Begining finished goods inventory, January 1, 2012 ($46 per unit × 400 units; $46 per unit × 400 units)	$ 18,400		$ 18,400	
15	Variable cost of goods manufactured ($46 per unit × 1,900 units; 2,100 units)	87,400*		96,600**	
16	Cost of goods available for sale (2,300 units; 2,500 units)	105,800		115,000	
17	Ending finished goods inventory, December 31, 2012 ($46 per unit × 325 units; 525 units)	14,950		24,150	
18	Variable cost of goods sold (1,975 units; 1,975 units)		90,850		90,850
19	Contribution margin		106,650		106,650
20	Fixed manufacturing overhead costs		18,900*		18,900**
21	Operating costs				
22	R&D, design, marketing, distribution, customer-service costs	70,000		70,000	
23	Total operating costs		70,000		70,000
24	Operating income		$ 17,750		$ 17,750

*The total cost of goods manufactured, $106,300 in Exhibit 2-13 equals variable cost of goods manufactured, $87,400 plus fixed manufacturing overhead costs, $18,900 in Exhibit 2-14.

**The total cost of goods manufactured, $115,500 in Exhibit 2-13 equals variable cost of goods manufactured, $96,600 plus fixed manufacturing overhead costs, $18,900 in Exhibit 2-14.

between manufacturing and nonmanufacturing costs is central to absorption costing, and it is highlighted by the gross-margin format. Similarly, the distinction between variable costs and fixed costs is central to variable costing, and it is highlighted by the contribution-margin format.

Notice how the fixed manufacturing overhead costs of $18,900 are accounted for under variable costing and absorption costing. The income statement under variable costing deducts all the $18,900 of fixed manufacturing overhead costs as an expense in 2012. In contrast, under absorption costing, the $18,900 is initially treated as an inventoriable cost. Of this $18,900, only a portion subsequently becomes a part of cost of goods sold in 2012, depending on the level of sales relative to the units produced. The remaining amount remains an asset—part of ending finished goods inventory on December 31, 2012.

Whether Cellular Products produces 1,900 or 2,100 units, the variable-costing operating income is the same, \$17,750. The variable-costing operating income of \$17,750 is less than the absorption-costing operating income of \$18,875, a difference of \$1,125 if Cellular Products produces more units (2,100) than it sells (1,975). The reason is that \$9 × 2,100 units = \$18,900 of fixed manufacturing overhead costs are inventoried and \$9 × 1,975 = \$17,775 of fixed manufacturing overhead costs are expensed under absorption costing, a difference of \$1,125, whereas none of the fixed manufacturing overhead costs are inventoried under variable costing. Note that the variable manufacturing cost of \$46 per unit is accounted for the same way in both income statements in Exhibits 2-13 and 2-14. The variable-costing operating income of \$17,750 is more than the absorption-costing operating income of \$17,075 by \$675 if Cellular Products produces fewer units (1,900) than it sells (1,975). The reason is that \$9 × 1,900 = \$17,100 of fixed manufacturing overhead costs are inventoried and \$9 × 1,975 units = \$17,775 of fixed manufacturing overhead costs are expensed under absorption costing, a difference of \$675, whereas none of the fixed manufacturing overhead costs are inventoried under variable costing.

Exhibit 2-14 points out another important aspect of variable costing. The operating income depends only on the level of sales and in particular is invariant to the quantity produced. Regardless of whether Cellular Products makes 1,900 or 2,100 phones, the eventual operating income from selling 1,975 phones is the same—\$17,750. Under variable costing, Cellular Products' managers cannot increase operating income by "producing for inventory." Why not? Because, as you can see from the preceding computations, when using variable costing, only the quantity of units sold drives operating income.

Comparing Absorption Costing and Variable Costing

Why do variable costing and absorption costing usually report different operating income numbers? In general, if production exceeds sales in a period, that is, inventory increases, greater operating income will be reported under absorption costing than variable costing. Conversely, if inventory decreases, more operating income will be reported under variable costing than absorption costing. The difference in reported operating income is due solely to (1) moving fixed manufacturing costs into inventories as inventories increase and (2) moving fixed manufacturing costs out of inventories as inventories decrease.

We can compute the difference between operating income under absorption costing and variable costing by using the following formula, which focuses on fixed manufacturing overhead costs in beginning inventory and ending inventory:

	Absorption costing operating income	−	Variable costing operating income	=	Fixed manufacturing overhead costs in ending inventory under absorption costing	−	Fixed manufacturing overhead costs in beginning inventory under absorption costing
Production (1,900 units) less than sales (1,975 units) or ending finished goods inventory (325 units) less than beginning finished goods inventory (400 units)	\$17,075	−	\$17,750	=	325 × \$9 per unit	−	400 × \$9 per unit
			\$(675) \$(675)	= =	\$2,925 \$(675)	−	\$3,600
Production (2,100 units) greater than sales (1,975 units) or ending finished goods inventory (525 units) greater than beginning finished goods inventory (400 units)	\$18,875	−	\$17,750	=	525 × \$9 per unit	−	400 × \$9 per unit
			\$1,125 \$1,125	= =	\$4,725 \$1,125	−	\$3,600

Fixed manufacturing overhead costs in ending inventory are deferred to a future period under absorption costing. For example, when 2,100 units are produced and 1,975 units are sold, $4,725 of fixed manufacturing overhead is deferred to 2013 as part of ending finished goods inventory at December 31, 2012, while $3,600 of fixed costs from beginning finished goods inventory enters cost of goods sold. Under variable costing, none of the fixed manufacturing overhead costs are included in inventory. Thus operating income under absorption costing is greater by $1,125 ($4,725 – $3,600).

Managers face increasing pressure to reduce inventory levels. Some companies are achieving steep reductions in inventory levels using policies such as just-in-time production—a production system under which products are manufactured only when needed. The formula illustrates that, as Cellular Products reduces its inventory levels, operating income differences between absorption costing and variable costing become immaterial. Consider, for example, the formula for 2012. If instead of 325 units in ending inventory and 400 units in beginning inventory, Cellular Products had only 20 units in ending inventory and 15 units in beginning inventory, the difference between absorption-costing operating income and variable-costing operating income would drop from $(675) to just $45 (20 × $9 per unit − 15 × $9 per unit).

To summarize, the main difference between variable costing and absorption costing is the accounting for fixed manufacturing costs:

- Under variable costing, fixed manufacturing costs are not inventoried; they are treated as an expense of the period.
- Under absorption costing, fixed manufacturing costs are inventoriable costs and are absorbed into finished goods inventory.

The use of variable costing for internal reporting removes the undesirable incentives to build up inventories that absorption costing can create. Variable costing also focuses attention on distinguishing variable manufacturing costs from fixed manufacturing costs. This distinction is important for short-run decision making (as in cost–volume–profit analysis in Chapter 3 and in planning and control in Chapters 12 and 13).

Companies that use both methods for internal reporting—variable costing for short-run decisions and performance evaluation and absorption costing for long-run decisions—benefit from the different advantages of both. Surveys sponsored by Chartered Institute of Management Accountants (United Kingdom), the world's largest professional body of management accountants, have shown that while most organizations employ absorption costing systems, over 75% indicate the use of variable costing information as either the most important or second most important measure for decision-making purposes.

Terms to Learn

This chapter contains more basic terms than any other in this book. The chapter and the Glossary at the end of the book contain definitions of the following important terms:

absorption costing (p. 52)
actual cost (p. 29)
average cost (p. 36)
budgeted cost (p. 29)
contribution margin (p. 56)
conversion costs (p. 45)
cost (p. 29)
cost accumulation (p. 29)
cost allocation (p. 30)
cost assignment (p. 30)
cost driver (p. 33)
cost object (p. 29)
cost of goods manufactured (p. 42)
cost tracing (p. 30)
direct costs of a cost object (p. 30)
direct manufacturing labor costs (p. 38)
direct material costs (p. 38)
direct materials inventory (p. 38)
factory overhead costs (p. 38)
finished goods inventory (p. 38)
fixed cost (p. 31)
idle time (p. 46)
indirect costs of a cost object (p. 30)
indirect manufacturing costs (p. 38)
inventoriable costs (p. 38)
manufacturing overhead costs (p. 38)
manufacturing-sector companies (p. 37)
merchandising-sector companies (p. 37)
operating income (p. 42)
overtime premium (p. 46)
period costs (p. 39)
prime costs (p. 43)
product cost (p. 47)
relevant range (p. 34)
revenues (p. 38)
service-sector companies (p. 37)
unit cost (p. 36)
variable cost (p. 31)
variable costing (p. 56)
work-in-process inventory (p. 38)
work in progress (p. 38)

Assignment Material

Questions

2-1 Define cost object and give three examples.

2-2 Why do managers consider direct costs to be more accurate than indirect costs?

2-3 Name three factors that will affect the classification of a cost as direct or indirect.

2-4 Define variable cost and fixed cost. Give an example of each.

2-5 What is a cost driver? Give one example.

2-6 What is the relevant range? What role does the relevant-range concept play in explaining how costs behave?

2-7 Explain why unit costs must often be interpreted with caution.

2-8 Distinguish between inventoriable costs and period costs.

2-9 Define product cost. Describe three different purposes for computing product costs.

2-10 Explain the main conceptual issue under variable costing and absorption costing regarding the timing for the release of fixed manufacturing overhead as expense.

Exercises

2-11 Computing and interpreting manufacturing unit costs. Massachusetts Office Products (MOP) produces three different paper products at its Vaasa lumber plant: Supreme, Deluxe, and Regular. Each product has its own dedicated production line at the plant. MOP currently uses the following three-part classification for its manufacturing costs: direct materials, direct manufacturing labor, and manufacturing overhead costs. Total manufacturing overhead costs of the plant in July 2013 are $190 million ($25 million of which are fixed). This total amount is allocated to each product line on the basis of the direct manufacturing labor costs of each line. Summary data (in millions) for July 2013 are:

	Supreme	Deluxe	Regular
Direct material costs	$88	$ 53	$64
Direct manufacturing labor costs	$11	$ 20	$19
Manufacturing overhead costs	$41	$ 88	$61
Units produced	50	100	80

Required

1. Compute the manufacturing cost per unit for each product produced in July 2013.
2. Suppose that in August 2013, production was 90 million units of Supreme, 140 million units of Deluxe, and 160 million units of Regular. Why might the July 2013 information on manufacturing cost per unit be misleading when predicting total manufacturing costs in August 2013?

2-12 Direct, indirect, fixed, and variable costs. Best Breads manufactures two types of bread, which it sells as wholesale products to various specialty retail bakeries. Each loaf of bread requires a three-step process. The first step is mixing. The mixing department combines all of the necessary ingredients to create the dough and processes it through high-speed mixers. The dough is then left to rise before baking. The second step is baking, which is an entirely automated process. The baking department molds the dough into its final shape and bakes each loaf of bread in a high-temperature oven. The final step is finishing, which is an entirely manual process. The finishing department coats each loaf of bread with a special glaze, allows the bread to cool, and then carefully packages each loaf in a specialty carton for sale in retail bakeries.

Required

1. Costs involved in the process are listed next. For each cost, indicate whether it is a direct variable, direct fixed, indirect variable, or indirect fixed cost, assuming "units of production of each kind of bread" is the cost object.

Costs:

Yeast	Mixing department manager
Flour	Materials handlers in each department
Packaging materials	Custodian in factory
Depreciation on ovens	Night guard in factory
Depreciation on mixing machines	Machinist (running the mixing machine)
Rent on factory building	Machine maintenance personnel in each department
Fire insurance on factory building	Maintenance supplies for factory
Factory utilities	Cleaning supplies for factory
Finishing department hourly laborers	

2. If the cost object were the "mixing department" rather than units of production of each kind of bread, which preceding costs would now be direct instead of indirect costs?

2-13 Classification of costs, service sector. Clear Focus is a marketing research firm that organizes focus groups for consumer-product companies. Each focus group has eight individuals who are paid $60 per session to provide comments on new products. These focus groups meet in hotels and are led by a trained, independent marketing specialist hired by Clear Focus. Each specialist is paid a fixed retainer to conduct a minimum number of sessions and a per session fee of $2,200. A Clear Focus staff member attends each session to ensure that all the logistical aspects run smoothly.

Required

Classify each cost item **(A–H)** as follows:

a. Direct or indirect (D or I) costs of each individual focus group.

b. Variable or fixed (V or F) costs of how the total costs of Clear Focus change as the number of focus groups conducted changes. (If in doubt, select on the basis of whether the total costs will change substantially if there is a large change in the number of groups conducted.)

You will have two answers (D or I; V or F) for each of the following items:

Cost Item	D or I	V or F
A. Payment to individuals in each focus group to provide comments on new products		
B. Annual subscription of Clear Focus to *Consumer Reports* magazine		
C. Phone calls made by Clear Focus staff member to confirm individuals will attend a focus group session (Records of individual calls are not kept.)		
D. Retainer paid to focus group leader to conduct 18 focus groups per year on new medical products		
E. Meals provided to participants in each focus group		
F. Lease payment by Clear Focus for corporate office		
G. Cost of tapes used to record comments made by individuals in a focus group session (These tapes are sent to the company whose products are being tested.)		
H. Gasoline costs of Clear Focus staff for company-owned vehicles (Staff members submit monthly bills with no mileage breakdowns.)		

2-14 Classification of costs, merchandising sector. Big Box Entertainment (BBE) operates a large store in Denver, Colorado. The store has both a movie (DVD) section and a music (CD) section. BBE reports revenues for the movie section separately from the music section.

Required

Classify each cost item **(A–H)** as follows:

a. Direct or indirect (D or I) costs of the total number of DVDs sold.

b. Variable or fixed (V or F) costs of how the total costs of the movie section change as the total number of DVDs sold changes. (If in doubt, select on the basis of whether the total costs will change substantially if there is a large change in the total number of DVDs sold.)

You will have two answers (D or I; V or F) for each of the following items:

Cost Item	D or I	V or F
A. Annual retainer paid to a DVD distributor		
B. Electricity costs of the BBE store (single bill covers entire store)		
C. Costs of DVDs purchased for sale to customers		
D. Subscription to *DVD Trends* magazine		
E. Leasing of computer software used for financial budgeting at the BBE store		

Cost Item	D or I	V or F
F. Cost of popcorn provided free to all customers of the BBE store		
G. Earthquake insurance policy for the BBE store		
H. Freight-in costs of DVDs purchased by BBE		

2-15 Classification of costs, manufacturing sector. The Kitakyushu, Japan, plant of Nissan Motor Corporation assembles two types of cars (Teanas and Muranos). Separate assembly lines are used for each type of car.

Required Classify each cost item **(A–H)** as follows:

a. Direct or indirect (D or I) costs for the total number of cars of each type assembled (Teana or Murano).

b. Variable or fixed (V or F) costs depending on how the total costs of the plant change as the total number of cars of each type assembled changes. (If in doubt, select on the basis of whether the total costs will change substantially if there is a large change in the total number of cars of each type assembled.)

You will have two answers (D or I; V or F) for each of the following items:

Cost Item	D or I	V or F
A. Cost of tires used on Muranos		
B. Salary of public relations manager for Kitakyushu plant		
C. Annual awards dinner for Teana suppliers		
D. Salary of engineer who monitors design changes on Murano		
E. Freight costs of Teana engines shipped from Yokohama to Kitakyushu		
F. Electricity costs for Kitakyushu plant (single bill covers entire plant)		
G. Wages paid to temporary assembly-line workers hired in periods of high production (paid on hourly basis)		
H. Annual fire-insurance policy cost for Kitakyushu plant		

2-16 Variable costs, fixed costs, total costs. Bridget Jackson is getting ready to open a small restaurant. She is on a tight budget and must choose between the following long-distance phone plans:

Plan A: Pay 8 cents per minute of long-distance calling.
Plan B: Pay a fixed monthly fee of $17 for up to 320 long-distance minutes, and 6 cents per minute thereafter (if she uses fewer than 320 minutes in any month, she still pays $17 for the month).
Plan C: Pay a fixed monthly fee of $21 for up to 500 long-distance minutes and 4 cents per minute thereafter (if she uses fewer than 500 minutes, she still pays $21 for the month).

Required

1. Draw a graph of the total monthly costs of the three plans for different levels of monthly long-distance calling. Your graph should resemble some combination of those in Panels A and B in Exhibit 2-3.
2. Which plan should Jackson choose if she expects to make 100 minutes of long-distance calls? 320 minutes? 520 minutes?

2-17 Variable costs and fixed costs. Combined Minerals (CM) owns the rights to extract minerals from beach sands on Fraser Island. CM has costs in three areas:

a. Payment to a mining subcontractor who charges $90 per ton of beach sand mined and returned to the beach (after being processed on the mainland to extract three minerals: ilmenite, rutile, and zircon).

b. Payment of a government mining and environmental tax of $30 per ton of beach sand mined.

c. Payment to a barge operator. This operator charges $140,000 per month to transport up to 100 tons of beach sand per day to the mainland and then return to Fraser Island (i.e., 0–100 tons per day = $140,000 per month; 101–200 tons per day = $280,000 per month; etc.).

Each barge operates 25 days per month. The $140,000 monthly charge must be paid even if fewer than 100 tons are transported on any day and even if CM requires fewer than 25 days of barge transportation in that month.

Required CM is currently mining 180 tons of beach sand per day for 25 days per month.

1. What is the variable cost per ton of beach sand mined? What is the fixed cost to CM per month?
2. Plot a graph of the variable costs and another graph of the fixed costs of CM. Your graphs should be similar to Exhibit 2-3, Panel A (page 32), and Exhibit 2-4 (page 35). Is the concept of relevant range applicable to your graphs? Explain.
3. What is the unit cost per ton of beach sand mined (a) if 180 tons are mined each day and (b) if 210 tons are mined each day? Explain the difference in the unit-cost figures.

2-18 Variable costs, fixed costs, relevant range. Gumball Candies manufactures jaw-breaker candies in a fully automated process. The company recently purchased a machine that can produce 4,500 candies per month. The machine costs $8,000 and is depreciated using straight-line depreciation over 10 years assuming zero residual value. Rent for the factory space and warehouse and other fixed manufacturing overhead costs total $700 per month.

Gumball currently makes and sells 3,100 jaw-breakers per month. Gumball buys just enough materials each month to make the jaw-breakers it needs to sell. Materials cost 40 cents per jawbreaker.

Next year Gumball expects demand to increase by 100%. At this volume of materials purchased, it will get a 10% discount on price. Rent and other fixed manufacturing overhead costs will remain the same.

Required

1. What is Gumball's current annual relevant range of output?
2. What is Gumball's current annual fixed manufacturing cost within the relevant range? What is the annual variable manufacturing cost?
3. What will Gumball's relevant range of output be next year? How, if at all, will total annual fixed and variable manufacturing costs change next year? Assume that Gumball could buy an identical machine at the same cost as the one it already has.

2-19 Cost drivers and value chain. Rubin Mobility Company (RMC) is developing a new touch-screen smartphone to compete in the cellular phone industry. The company will sell the phones at wholesale prices to cell phone companies, which will in turn sell them in retail stores to the final customer. RMC has undertaken the following activities in its value chain to bring its product to market:

Identify customer needs (What do smartphone users want?)
Perform market research on competing brands
Design a prototype of the RMC smartphone
Market the new design to cell phone companies
Manufacture the RMC smartphone
Process orders from cell phone companies
Package the RMC smartphones
Deliver the RMC smartphones to the cell phone companies
Provide online assistance to cell phone users for use of the RMC smartphone
Make design changes to the smartphone based on customer feedback

During the process of product development, production, marketing, distribution, and customer service, RMC has kept track of the following cost drivers:

Number of smartphones shipped by RMC
Number of design changes
Number of deliveries made to cell phone companies
Engineering hours spent on initial product design
Hours spent researching competing market brands
Customer-service hours
Number of smartphone orders processed
Number of cell phone companies purchasing the RMC smartphone
Machine hours required to run the production equipment
Number of surveys returned and processed from competing smartphone users

Required

1. Identify each value chain activity listed at the beginning of the exercise with one of the following value-chain categories:
   a. Design of products and processes
   b. Production
   c. Marketing
   d. Distribution
   e. Customer service
2. Use the list of preceding cost drivers to find one or more reasonable cost drivers for each of the activities in RMC's value chain.

2-20 Cost drivers and functions. The list of representative cost drivers in the right column of this table are randomized so they do not match the list of functions in the left column.

Function	Representative Cost Driver
1. Accounting	**A.** Number of invoices sent
2. Human resources	**B.** Number of purchase orders
3. Data processing	**C.** Number of research scientists
4. Research and development	**D.** Hours of computer processing unit (CPU)
5. Purchasing	**E.** Number of employees
6. Distribution	**F.** Number of transactions processed
7. Billing	**G.** Number of deliveries made

Required

1. Match each function with its representative cost driver.
2. Give a second example of a cost driver for each function.

2-21 Total costs and unit costs. A student association has hired a band and a caterer for a graduation party. The band will charge a fixed fee of $2,000 for an evening of music, and the caterer will charge a fixed fee of $1,200 for the party setup and an additional $18 per person who attends. The caterer will provide snacks and soft drinks for the duration of the party. Students attending the party will pay $10 each at the door to help reduce the student association's cost of holding the event.

Required

1. Draw a graph depicting the fixed cost, the variable cost, and the total cost to the student association for different attendance levels.
2. Suppose 100 people attend the party. What is the total cost to the student association? What is the cost per person?
3. Suppose 500 people attend the party. What is the total cost to the student association and the cost per attendee?
4. Draw a graph depicting the cost per attendee for different attendance levels. As president of the student association, you want to request a grant to cover some of the party costs. Will you use the per attendee cost numbers to make your case? Why or why not?

2-22 Total and unit cost, decision making. Geoffrey's Glassworks makes glass flanges for scientific use. Materials cost $3 per flange, and the glass blowers are paid a wage rate of $25 per hour. A glass blower blows 10 flanges per hour. Fixed manufacturing costs for flanges are $23,000 per period. Period (nonmanufacturing) costs of flanges are $17,000 per period, and are fixed.

Required

1. Graph the fixed, variable, and total manufacturing cost for flanges, using units (number of flanges) on the *x*-axis (the horizontal axis).
2. Assume Geoffrey's Glassworks manufactures and sells 4,000 flanges this period. Its competitor, Flora's Flasks, sells flanges for $10.50 each. Can Geoffrey sell below Flora's price and still make a profit on the flanges?
3. How would your answer to requirement 2 differ if Geoffrey's Glassworks made and sold 10,000 flanges this period? Why? What does this indicate about the use of unit cost in decision making?

2-23 Inventoriable costs versus period costs. Each of the following cost items pertains to one of these companies: Whole Foods (a merchandising-sector company), Whirlpool (a manufacturing-sector company), and Google (a service-sector company):

a. Evian mineral water purchased by Whole Foods for sale to its customers
b. Electricity used to provide lighting for assembly-line workers at a Whirlpool refrigerator-assembly plant
c. Depreciation on Google's computer equipment used to update directories of Web sites
d. Electricity used to provide lighting for Whole Foods' store aisles
e. Depreciation on Whirlpool's computer equipment used for quality testing of refrigerator components during the assembly process
f. Salaries of Whole Foods' marketing personnel planning local-newspaper advertising campaigns
g. Perrier mineral water purchased by Google for consumption by its software engineers
h. Salaries of Google's marketing personnel selling banner advertising

Required

1. Distinguish between manufacturing-, merchandising-, and service-sector companies.
2. Distinguish between inventoriable costs and period costs.
3. Classify each of the cost items (**a–h**) as an inventoriable cost or a period cost. Explain your answers.

Problems

2-24 Computing cost of goods purchased and cost of goods sold. The following data are for Maurice Department Store. The account balances (in thousands) are for 2013.

Marketing, distribution, and customer-service costs	$ 30,000
Merchandise inventory, January 1, 2013	25,000
Utilities	10,000
General and administrative costs	42,000
Merchandise inventory, December 31, 2013	38,000
Purchases	156,000
Miscellaneous costs	6,000
Transportation-in	8,000
Purchase returns and allowances	5,000
Purchase discounts	9,000
Revenues	295,000

Required

1. Compute **(a)** the cost of goods purchased and **(b)** the cost of goods sold.
2. Prepare the income statement for 2013.

2-25 Cost of goods purchased, cost of goods sold, and income statement. The following data are for Carolina Retail Outlet Stores. The account balances (in thousands) are for 2013.

Marketing and advertising costs	$ 14,000
Merchandise inventory, January 1, 2013	33,750
Shipping of merchandise to customers	1,500
Building depreciation	3,150
Purchases	195,000
General and administrative costs	24,000
Merchandise inventory, December 31, 2013	39,000
Merchandise freight-in	7,500
Purchase returns and allowances	8,250
Purchase discounts	6,750
Revenues	240,000

Required

1. Compute **(a)** the cost of goods purchased and **(b)** the cost of goods sold.
2. Prepare the income statement for 2013.

2-26 Flow of Inventoriable Costs. Salamone Heaters' selected data for October 2013 are presented here (in millions):

Direct materials inventory, 10/1/2013	$ 75
Direct materials purchased	335
Direct materials used	380
Total manufacturing overhead costs	495
Variable manufacturing overhead costs	260
Total manufacturing costs incurred during October 2013	1,580
Work-in-process inventory, 10/1/2013	215
Cost of goods manufactured	1,650
Finished goods inventory, 10/1/2013	165
Cost of goods sold	1,760

Required

Calculate the following costs:

1. Direct materials inventory, 10/31/2013
2. Fixed manufacturing overhead costs for October 2013
3. Direct manufacturing labor costs for October 2013
4. Work-in-process inventory, 10/31/2013
5. Cost of finished goods available for sale in October 2013
6. Finished goods inventory, 10/31/2013

2-27 Cost of finished goods manufactured, income statement, manufacturing company. Consider the following account balances (in thousands) for the Rouse Company:

	Beginning of 2013	End of 2013
Direct materials inventory	$27,000	$ 28,000
Work-in-process inventory	29,000	22,000
Finished goods inventory	16,000	25,000
Purchases of direct materials		73,000
Direct manufacturing labor		24,000
Indirect manufacturing labor		18,000
Plant insurance		6,000
Depreciation—plant, building, and equipment		17,000
Repairs and maintenance—plant		2,000
Marketing, distribution, and customer-service costs		111,000
General and administrative costs		36,000

Required

1. Prepare a schedule for the cost of goods manufactured for 2013.
2. Revenues for 2013 were $265 million. Prepare the income statement for 2013.

2-28 Income statement and schedule of cost of goods manufactured. The Alderman Corporation has the following account balances (in millions):

For Specific Date		For Year 2013	
Direct materials inventory, Jan. 1, 2013	$19	Purchases of direct materials	$305
Work-in-process inventory, Jan. 1, 2013	10	Direct manufacturing labor	115
Finished goods inventory, Jan. 1, 2013	70	Depreciation—plant and equipment	60
Direct materials inventory, Dec. 31, 2013	24	Plant supervisory salaries	6
Work-in-process inventory, Dec. 31, 2013	6	Miscellaneous plant overhead	30
Finished goods inventory, Dec. 31, 2013	54	Revenues	925
		Marketing, distribution, and customer-service costs	235
		Plant supplies used	10
		Plant utilities	34
		Indirect manufacturing labor	68

Required

Prepare an income statement and a supporting schedule of cost of goods manufactured for the year ended December 31, 2013. (For additional questions regarding these facts, see the next problem.)

2-29 Interpretation of statements (continuation of 2-28).

Required

1. How would you change the answer to Problem 2-28 if you were asked for a schedule of cost of goods manufactured and sold instead of a schedule of cost of goods manufactured? Be specific.
2. Would the sales manager's salary (included in marketing, distribution, and customer-service costs) be accounted for any differently if the Alderman Corporation were a merchandising-sector company instead of a manufacturing-sector company? Using the flow of manufacturing costs outlined in Exhibit 2-9 (page 43), describe how the wages of an assembler in the plant would be accounted for in this manufacturing company.
3. Plant supervisory salaries are usually regarded as manufacturing overhead costs. When might some of these costs be regarded as direct manufacturing costs? Give an example.
4. Suppose that both the direct materials used and the plant and equipment depreciation are related to the manufacture of 1 million units of product. What is the unit cost for the direct materials assigned to those units? What is the unit cost for plant and equipment depreciation? Assume that yearly plant and equipment depreciation is computed on a straight-line basis.

5. Assume that the implied cost-behavior patterns in requirement 4 persist. That is, direct material costs behave as a variable cost, and plant and equipment depreciation behaves as a fixed cost. Repeat the computations in requirement 4, assuming that the costs are being predicted for the manufacture of 1.2 million units of product. How would the total costs be affected?
6. As a manager, explain concisely to the president why the unit costs differed in requirements 4 and 5.

2-30 Income statement and schedule of cost of goods manufactured. The following items (in millions) pertain to Chester Corporation:

Chester's manufacturing costing system uses a three-part classification of direct materials, direct manufacturing labor, and manufacturing overhead costs.

For Specific Date		For Year 2013	
Work-in-process inventory, Jan. 1, 2013	$12	Plant utilities	$ 6
Direct materials inventory, Dec. 31, 2013	7	Indirect manufacturing labor	26
Finished goods inventory, Dec. 31, 2013	19	Depreciation—plant and equipment	8
Accounts payable, Dec. 31, 2013	21	Revenues	354
Accounts receivable, Jan. 1, 2013	54	Miscellaneous manufacturing overhead	17
Work-in-process inventory, Dec. 31, 2013	5	Marketing, distribution, and customer-service costs	97
Finished goods inventory, Jan 1, 2013	43	Direct materials purchased	88
Accounts receivable, Dec. 31, 2013	33	Direct manufacturing labor	40
Accounts payable, Jan. 1, 2013	45	Plant supplies used	9
Direct materials inventory, Jan. 1, 2013	30	Property taxes on plant	3

Required

Prepare an income statement and a supporting schedule of cost of goods manufactured. (For additional questions regarding these facts, see the next problem.)

2-31 Terminology, interpretation of statements (continuation of 2-30).

Required

1. Calculate total prime costs and total conversion costs.
2. Calculate total inventoriable costs and period costs.
3. Design costs and R&D costs are not considered product costs for financial statement purposes. When might managers regard some of these costs as product costs? Give an example.
4. Suppose that both the direct materials used and the depreciation on plant and equipment are related to the manufacture of 1 million units of product. Determine the unit cost for the direct materials assigned to those units and the unit cost for depreciation on plant and equipment. Assume that yearly depreciation is computed on a straight-line basis.
5. Assume that the implied cost-behavior patterns in requirement 4 persist. That is, direct material costs behave as a variable cost and depreciation on plant and equipment behaves as a fixed cost. Repeat the computations in requirement 4, assuming that the costs are being predicted for the manufacture of 2 million units of product. Determine the effect on total costs.
6. Assume that depreciation on the equipment (but not the plant) is computed based on the number of units produced because the equipment deteriorates with units produced. The depreciation rate on equipment is $2 per unit. Calculate the depreciation on equipment assuming (a) 1 million units of product are produced and (b) 2 million units of product are produced.

2-32 Labor cost, overtime, and idle time. Jerome Anderson works in the production department of Midcity Steelworks as a machine operator. Jerome, a long-time employee of Midcity, is paid on an hourly basis at a rate of $40 per hour. Jerome works five 8-hour shifts per week Monday–Friday (40 hours). Any time Jerome works over and above these 40 hours is considered overtime for which he is paid at a rate of time and a half ($60 per hour). If the overtime falls on weekends, Jerome is paid at a rate of double time ($80 per hour). Jerome is also paid double time for any holidays worked, even if it is part of his regular 40 hours.

Jerome is paid his regular wages even if the machines are down (not operating) due to regular machine maintenance, slow order periods, or unexpected mechanical problems. These hours are considered "idle time."

During December, Jerome worked the following hours:

	Hours Worked Including Machine Downtime	Machine Downtime
Week 1	48	3.9
Week 2	46	6.6
Week 3	54	6.1
Week 4	51	2.8

Included in the total hours worked above are two company holidays (Christmas Eve and Christmas Day) during Week 4. All overtime worked by Jerome was Monday–Friday, except for the hours worked in Week 3. All of the Week 3 overtime hours were worked on a Saturday.

Required

1. Calculate (a) direct manufacturing labor, (b) idle time, (c) overtime and holiday premium, and (d) total earnings for Jerome in December.
2. Is idle time and overtime premium a direct or indirect cost of the products that Jerome worked on in December? Explain.

2-33 Missing records, computing inventory costs. Ron Williams recently took over as the controller of Mission Manufacturing. Last month, the previous controller left the company with little notice and left the accounting records in disarray. Ron needs the ending inventory balances to report first-quarter numbers.

For the previous month (March 2013) Ron was able to piece together the following information:

Direct materials purchased	$120,000
Work-in-process inventory, 3/1/2013	$ 35,000
Direct materials inventory, 3/1/2013	$ 12,500
Finished goods inventory, 3/1/2013	$160,000
Conversion costs	$330,000
Total manufacturing costs added during the period	$420,000
Cost of goods manufactured	4 times direct materials used
Gross margin as a percentage of revenues	20%
Revenues	$518,750

Required

Calculate the cost of:

1. Finished goods inventory, 3/31/2013
2. Work-in-process inventory, 3/31/2013
3. Direct materials inventory, 3/31/2013

2-34 Comprehensive problem on unit costs, product costs. Tampa Office Equipment manufactures and sells metal shelving. It began operations on January 1, 2013. Costs incurred for 2013 are as follows (V stands for variable; F stands for fixed):

Direct materials used	$144,500 V
Direct manufacturing labor costs	23,500 V
Plant energy costs	5,000 V
Indirect manufacturing labor costs	18,000 V
Indirect manufacturing labor costs	16,000 F
Other indirect manufacturing costs	8,000 V
Other indirect manufacturing costs	23,000 F
Marketing, distribution, and customer-service costs	126,000 V
Marketing, distribution, and customer-service costs	40,000 F
Administrative costs	54,000 F

Variable manufacturing costs are variable to units produced. Variable marketing, distribution, and customer-service costs are variable to units sold.

Inventory data are as follows:

	Beginning: January 1, 2013	Ending: December 31, 2013
Direct materials	0 lb	1,900 lbs
Work in process	0 units	0 units
Finished goods	0 units	? units

Production in 2013 was 106,250 units. Two pounds of direct materials are used to make one unit of finished product.

Revenues in 2013 were $481,250. The selling price per unit and the purchase price per pound of direct materials were stable throughout the year. The company's ending inventory of finished goods is carried at the average unit manufacturing cost for 2013. Finished-goods inventory at December 31, 2013, was $22,400.

Required

1. Calculate direct materials inventory, total cost, December 31, 2013.
2. Calculate finished-goods inventory, total units, December 31, 2013.
3. Calculate selling price in 2013.
4. Calculate operating income for 2013.

2-35 Absorption versus variable costing. Griswold Company began operations in 2013. The company manufacturers a professional-grade vacuum cleaner and can make up to 18,000 units each year. Actual data for 2013 are given as follows:

	A	B
1	Units produced	18,000
2	Units sold	17,500
3	Selling price	$ 425
4	Variable costs:	
5	Manufacturing cost per unit produced	
6	Direct materials	30
7	Direct manufacturing labor	25
8	Manufacturing overhead	60
9	Marketing cost per unit sold	45
10	Fixed costs:	
11	Manufacturing cost	1,080,000
12	Administrative cost	965,450
13	Marketing	1,366,400

Required

1. Prepare a 2013 income statement for Griswold Company using variable costing.
2. Prepare a 2013 income statement for Griswold Company using absorption costing.
3. Explain the differences in operating incomes obtained in requirement 1 and requirement 2.
4. Griswold's management is considering implementing a bonus for the supervisors based on gross margin under absorption costing. What incentives will this create for the supervisors? What modifications could Griswold management make to improve such a plan? Explain briefly.

2-36 Comparison of costing methods. The Roberts Company sells its razors at $3 per unit. The company incurs fixed manufacturing overhead costs of $700,000 each year to support production of 1,400,000 units so that the fixed manufacturing overhead cost per unit equals $0.50 ($700,000 ÷ 1,400,000 units). The following data are related to its first 2 years of operation, all numbers are in thousands:

	2012	2013
Sales	1,000 units	1,200 units
Production	1,400 units	1,000 units
Costs		
Variable manufacturing	$ 700	$ 500
Fixed manufacturing	700	700
Variable operating (marketing)	1,000	1,200
Fixed operating (marketing)	400	400

Required

1. Prepare income statements based on variable costing for each of the 2 years.
2. Prepare income statements based on absorption costing for each of the 2 years.

3. Prepare a numerical reconciliation and explanation of the difference between operating income for each year under absorption costing and variable costing.
4. Critics have claimed that a widely used accounting system has led to undesirable buildups of inventory levels. (a) Is variable costing or absorption costing more likely to lead to such buildups? Why? (b) What can be done to counteract undesirable inventory buildups?

2-37 Cost classification: ethics. Scott Higgins, the new plant manager of Old State Manufacturing Plant Number 7, has just reviewed a draft of his year-end financial statements. Higgins receives a year-end bonus of 11.5% of the plant's operating income before tax. The year-end income statement provided by the plant's controller was disappointing to say the least. After reviewing the numbers, Higgins demanded that his controller go back and "work the numbers" again. Higgins insisted that if he didn't see a better operating income number the next time around he would be forced to look for a new controller.

Old State Manufacturing classifies all costs directly related to the manufacturing of its product as product costs. These costs are inventoried and later expensed as costs of goods sold when the product is sold. All other expenses, including finished goods warehousing costs of $3,630,000, are classified as period expenses. Higgins had suggested that warehousing costs be included as product costs because they are "definitely related to our product." The company produced 220,000 units during the period and sold 190,000 units.

As the controller reworked the numbers, she discovered that if she included warehousing costs as product costs, she could improve operating income by $495,000. She was also sure these new numbers would make Higgins happy.

Required

1. Show numerically how operating income would improve by $495,000 just by classifying the preceding costs as product costs instead of period expenses.
2. Is Higgins correct in his justification that these costs "are definitely related to our product."
3. By how much will Higgins profit personally if the controller makes the adjustments in requirement 1?
4. What should the plant controller do?

Case

Justin Anson Distillery, Inc.

In early August 2012, Craig Anson, president and chief operating officer (COO) of Justin Anson Distillery, Inc., of Oakwoods, Tennessee, sat in his office pondering the results of the previous day's meeting of the board of directors and wondering whether he should submit the 2012 financial statements (Justin Anson Distillery Exhibits 1 and 2) to the Valley National Bank of Nashville, Tennessee in support of a recent loan request for $3.3 million, or whether he should wait until after next month's board meeting to clarify some of the preceding day's discussion. A great deal of controversy had arisen over the 2012 reported loss of $895,000 and how this result should be reported to the bank. The controversy revolved principally around the accounting treatment of various expenses reported in the "other costs" section of the operating statement. Mr. Anson knew that a decision had to be reached on these matters quickly, because the company had reached a point where additional working capital was needed immediately if it was to remain solvent.

Company History

Justin Anson began distilling whiskey in 1935. Justin had come to Oakwoods, Tennessee from Scotland the preceding year and had decided to carry on in the family tradition of beverage manufacture. He purchased a tract of land on a high knoll adjacent to a small stream fed by a limestone spring and began to distill bourbon whiskey in an old barn behind his home. His business grew from a trickling in 1935 to a million-dollar firm by 1960. He attributed this growth to the high-quality, distinctive bourbon whiskey that he produced. The quality of "Old Trailridge," Anson's only brand of whiskey, was claimed to be the result of the unusual iron-free spring water used in the distillation process and the specially prepared fire-charred white oak barrels used in the aging process.

In 1997, Craig Anson, great-grandson of Justin, took over as COO of the company and nearly doubled sales revenue during the next 10 years. In 2011, the company produced just over 2% of the whiskey distilled in the United States. Since the mid-2000s, the company's production had been stable; the financial statements for 2011 (Justin Anson Distillery Exhibits 1 and 2) were typical of the results of the preceding several years. After a surge in demand in the 1990s, no special effort had been made to gain a larger share of the market, but at a board meeting in December 2010, a decision had been made to expand production to try to capture a larger than proportionate share of the increase in whiskey consumption that Mr. Anson had forecasted, based on an industry research report. This report showed that the consumption of straight bourbon whiskey was increasing as the members of Generation Y matured. Based on this report and other industry forecasts, Mr. Anson had forecasted a doubling of straight whiskey consumption from 2011 to 2019. In view of this assumption, and because bourbon whiskey had to be aged for at least four years, the board had decided to increase the production of whiskey in 2012 by 50% of the 2011 volume (see Justin Anson Distillery Exhibit 2) in order to meet the anticipated increase in consumer demand for straight bourbon whiskey from 2014 through 2019.

The Manufacturing and Maturing Process

Old Trailridge was a straight bourbon whiskey and thus, by law, had to be made from a mixture of grains containing at least 51% corn and be aged in new (not reused) charred white oak barrels. Once the ground corn was put through the "mashing" and fermentation processes, the distilled

---

Source: Reprinted by permission of Harvard Business School

Harvard Business School case 9-189-065
The case was prepared by W. Bruns as the basis for class discussion rather than to illustrate either effective or ineffective handling of an administrative situation.

liquor that emerged was mixed with limestone spring water to obtain the desired proof (percent of alcohol by volume where one degree of proof equals 0.5% alcohol).

At this point the whiskey was a clear liquid with a sharp, biting taste and had to be mellowed before consumption. For this process, it was pumped into 50-gallon barrels and moved to an aging warehouse. The cost accumulated in the product prior to its entry into barrels, including all direct and indirect materials and labor consumed in the production process, was approximately $1.15 per gallon (see Justin Anson Distillery Exhibit 2). The volume of production had been the same for each of the years 1984 to 2011, and all costs during this period had been substantially the same as the 2011 costs shown in Justin Anson Distillery Exhibit 2.

In order to mellow the whiskey, improve its taste, and give it a rich amber color, the new bourbon whiskey had to be matured or aged for a period of time of not less than four years under controlled temperature and humidity conditions. The new whiskey reacted with the charred oak and assimilated some of the flavor and color of the fire-charred oak during the period of aging.

Since the quality of the aging barrel was an important factor in determining the ultimate taste and character of the final product, Anson had his 50-gallon barrels manufactured under a unique patented process at a cost of $69.30 per barrel. The barrels could not be reused for aging future batches of bourbon whiskey and were disposed of at negligible value at the end of the aging period.

The filled barrels were next placed in open "ricks" in an aging warehouse rented by Anson or in that half of the factory building converted into warehousing space. The increased production in 2012 necessitated the leasing of an additional warehouse at an annual rental cost of $330,000. The temperature and humidity of the warehouse space had to be controlled, since the quality of the whiskey could be ruined by its aging too fast or too slowly, a process determined by temperature and humidity conditions.

Every six months, the barrels had to be rotated from a high rick to a lower rick or vice versa and sampled. If the quality or character of the whisky was not up to standard, certain measures were taken, such as adjusting the aging process, to bring it up to standard. At this time, each barrel was also checked for leaks or seepage, and the required repairs were made.

At the end of the four-year aging period, the barrels were removed from the ricks and dumped into regauging tanks where the charred oak residue was filtered out and volume was measured. On average, the volume of liquid in a barrel declined by 30% during the aging period because of evaporation and leakage. Thus, a barrel originally filled with 50 gallons of new bourbon would produce only 35 gallons of aged bourbon. The regauging operation was supervised by a government liquor tax agent, since it was at this point that federal excise tax of $23.10 per gallon was levied on the whiskey removed from the warehouse. Once the bourbon had been removed from the aging warehouse, it was bottled and shipped to wholesalers with the greatest speed possible because of the large amount of cash tied up in taxes on the finished product. During both 2011 and 2012, the company sold 30,100 regauged barrels of whiskey, equivalent to 43,000 barrels of original production.

Excerpts from Board of Directors' Meeting—August 3, 2012

Craig Anson: I'm quite concerned over the prospect of obtaining the $3.3 million loan we need in light of our 2012 loss of $895,000. We have shown annual profits since 1998, and our net sales of $46.2 million this year are the same as last year, and yet we incurred a net loss for the year. I'm afraid that the loan officers at the Valley National Bank will hesitate in granting us a loan. It appears that we are becoming less efficient in our production operation.

Carlos Sanchez (Production Manager): That's not quite so Craig. You know as well as I do that we increased production by 50% this year, and with this increased production our costs are bound to increase. You can't produce something for nothing.

Anita Tyler (Controller): Well, that's not quite so, Carlos. Granted that our production costs must rise when production increases, but our inventory account takes care of the increased costs of deferring these product costs until a future period when the product is actually sold. As you can see by looking at our 2012 profit and loss (P&L) statement, our cost of goods sold did not increase in 2012, since the volume of sales was the same in 2012 as in 2011. The largest share of the increase in production costs has been deferred until future periods, as you can see by looking at the increase in our inventory account of more than $1.1 million. I believe that the real reason for our loss this year was the large increase in other costs, composed chiefly of warehousing costs. The "Occupancy Costs" category in our P&L is really the summation of a group of expense accounts, including building depreciation or rent, heat, light, power, building maintenance, labor and supplies, real estate taxes, and insurance. In addition, warehouse labor cost also rose substantially in 2012. Even administrative and general expenses went up, due primarily to higher interest expense on the additional money needed to finance our increase in inventory.

Craig Anson: Well, what's our explanation for the large increase in warehousing costs, Carlos?

Carlos Sanchez: As I said before, Craig, we increased production, and this also means an increase in warehousing costs, since the increased production has to be aged for several years. You just can't age 50% more whiskey for the same amount of money.

Craig Anson: But I thought Anita said that increased production costs were taken care of in the inventory account. Isn't that so, Anita?

Anita Tyler: Well, yes and no, Craig. The inventory account can only be charged with those costs associated with the production of whiskey, and our warehousing costs are handling or carrying costs, certainly not production costs.

Carlos Sanchez: Now just a minute, Anita, I think that some of those costs are just as valid production costs as are direct labor and materials going into the distillation of the new bourbon. The manufacturing process doesn't stop with the newly produced bourbon; why it isn't even marketable in that form. Aging is an absolutely essential part of the manufacturing process, and I think the cost of barrels and part of the warehouse labor should be treated as inventoriable costs.

Craig Anson: Great, Carlos! I agree with you that warehousing and aging costs are an absolutely essential ingredient of our final product. We certainly couldn't market the bourbon before it had been aged. I think that all the costs associated with aging the product should be charged to the inventory account. I think that most of the "other costs" should be considered an inventoriable cost. Don't you agree, Anita?

Anita Tyler: Sure, Craig! Let's capitalize depreciation, interest expenses, your salary, the shareholders' dividends, our advertising costs, your secretary's salary—why, let's capitalize all our costs! That way we can show a huge inventory balance and small expenses!

Craig Anson: I think you're being facetious, Anita. I'm afraid I really don't see why we couldn't charge all of those costs you mentioned to the inventory account, since it seems to me that they are all necessary ingredients in producing our final product. What distinction do you draw between these so-called "inventoriable" costs you mentioned and the aging costs?

Anita Tyler: By inventoriable costs, I mean those costs that are necessary to convert raw materials into the whiskey that goes into the aging barrels. This is our cost of approximately $1.15 per gallon and includes the cost of raw materials going into the product such as grain, yeast, and malt; the direct labor necessary to convert these materials into whiskey; and the cost of any other overhead items that are needed to permit the workers to convert grain into whiskey. I don't see how aging costs can be included under the generally accepted accounting definition of the inventory cost of the product.

Craig Anson: I think we'd better defer further discussion of this entire subject until our meeting next month. In the meantime, I am going to try to get this thing squared away in my own mind.

Required

1. Assuming Anson decided to charge barrel costs (but not warehousing and aging costs) to inventory, what 2012 income statement and balance sheet items would change, and what would the new amounts be? (Assume no change in work-in-process inventory.)
2. If Anson's suggestion of including all warehousing and aging costs in inventory were accepted, how would the 2012 financial statements be affected? (Assume no change in work-in-process inventory.)
3. In your opinion, what costs should be included in Anson's inventory when preparing financial statements to be submitted to Valley National Bank?

Justin Anson Distillery Exhibit 1

Justin Anson Distillery, Inc., Balance Sheet as of June 30, 2011 and 2012 ($ thousands)

	2011	2012
Current Assets		
Cash	$ 2,892	$ 792
Accounts receivable—trade	3,139	4,028
Inventories:		
Bulk whiskey in barrels at average production cost (no excise tax included)	9,914	11,067
Bottled and cased whiskey, 175,000 gallons in each year at an average cost of $24.75 per gallon (including excise tax)	4,331	4,331
Inventory in process	222	222
Raw materials and supplies	880	519
Prepaid expenses	970	854
Total current assets	22,348	21,813

Fixed Assets	Cost		Accumulated Depreciation		Net	
	2011	2012	2011	2012	2011	2012
Land	$ 66	$ 66			$ 66	$ 66
Building[a]	4,202	4,642	$1,760	$1,877	2,442	2,765
Factory equipment	158	158	57	83	101	75
Warehouse equipment	77	141	53	75	24	66

	2011	2012
(Fixed assets, net)	2,633	2,972
Total assets	$24,981	$24,785
Current Liabilities		
Short-term notes payable to banks	$ 2,420	$ 3,300
Current maturities of long-term debt	506	1,062
Accounts payable	2,330	1,175
Federal excise taxes payable	902	-
Total current liabilities	6,158	5,537
Noncurrent Liabilities		
Notes payable (9 1/2%) secured by deed of trust on warehouse property	7,700	9,020
Stockholders' Equity		
Common stock held principally by members of the Anson family	3,960	3,960
Earnings retained in the business	7,163	6,268
Total liabilities and capital	$24,981	$24,785

[a]In June 2012, payment was made for work that had been performed during the year in adding to and improving the warehousing space in the building owned by Justin Anson Distillery.

Justin Anson Distillery Exhibit 2

Justin Anson Distillery, Inc., Statement of Income for the Years Ended June 30, 2011 and 2012 ($ thousands)

		2011		2012
Net sales:				
Sale of whiskey to wholesalers		$46,200		$46,200
Cost of goods sold:				
Federal excise taxes—on barrels sold		34,766		34,766
Cost of product charged to sales:				
Bulk whiskey inventory July 1, of each year—172,000 barrels	$ 9,914		$ 9,914	
Plus: Cost of whiskey produced to inventory (43,000 barrels in 2011 and 63,000 barrels in 2012 at an average cost of $57.63 per 50-gallon barrel in both years)	2,478		3,631	
	12,392		13,545	
Less: Bulk whiskey inventory June 30 of respective year (172,000 and 192,000 barrels, at average production cost)	9,914	2,478	11,067	2,478
Cased goods and in process July 1, of respective year	4,554		4,554	
Cased goods and in process June 30, of respective year	4,554	-	4,554	-
		37,244		37,244
Other costs charged to Cost of Goods Sold:				
Cost of barrels used during year at $69.30 per barrel	2,980		4,366	
Occupancy costs: factory building	291		327	
rented building	299		629	
Warehouse labor and warehouse supervisor	207		367	
Labor and supplies expense of chemical laboratory	150		183	
Depreciation: factory equipment	26		26	
warehouse equipment	13		22	
Cost of government supervision and bonding facilities	7		15	
Cost of bottling liquor (labor, glass, and miscellaneous supplies)	504	4,477	504	6,439
Total cost of goods sold		41,721		43,683
Gross profit from operations		4,479		2,517
Less: Selling and advertising expenses	1,725		2,061	
Administrative and general expense	1,100	2,825	1,351	3,412
Net profit (loss)		$ 1,654		$ (895)

3 Cost–Volume–Profit Analysis

Learning Objectives

1. Explain the features of cost–volume–profit (CVP) analysis
2. Determine the breakeven point and output level needed to achieve a target operating income
3. Understand how income taxes affect CVP analysis
4. Explain how managers use CVP analysis in decision making
5. Explain how sensitivity analysis helps managers cope with uncertainty
6. Use CVP analysis to plan variable and fixed costs
7. Apply CVP analysis to a company producing multiple products
8. Apply CVP analysis in service and not-for-profit organizations
9. Distinguish contribution margin from gross margin

All managers want to know how profits will change as the units sold of a product or service change. Home Depot managers, for example, might wonder how many units of a new power drill must be sold to break even or make a certain amount of profit. Procter & Gamble managers might ask themselves how expanding their business in Nigeria would affect costs, selling price, and profits. These questions have a common "what-if" theme: What if we sold more power drills? or What if we start selling in Nigeria? Examining the results of these what-if possibilities and alternatives helps managers make better decisions.

Businesses that have high fixed costs have to pay particular attention to the "what-ifs" because making the wrong choices could be disastrous. Examples of well-known companies with high fixed costs included Swiss and United Airlines in the airline industry and Global Crossing and WorldCom in the telecommunications industry. High fixed costs means that these companies needed significant revenues just to break even. For example, the profits that most airlines make come from the last two to five passengers that board each flight! When revenues declined at Swiss and United Airlines during 2001 and 2002 and fixed costs remained high, these companies declared bankruptcy. In this chapter, we see how cost–volume–profit (CVP) analysis helps managers minimize such risks.

The Chapter at a Glance previews the techniques managers use to make these decisions and to manage risks.

Chapter at a Glance

- Cost–volume–profit (CVP) analysis distinguishes fixed costs from variable costs and examines how total revenues, total costs, and operating income change with changes in units sold, selling price, variable cost per unit, or fixed costs.
- CVP analysis helps managers determine the breakeven point (how much revenue must the company earn to avoid making a loss); how much revenue is needed to achieve a certain target income; how much money should be spent on advertising; and whether the selling price should be changed.
- Recognizing uncertainty, managers test the sensitivity of how CVP relationships and outcomes will change as a result of changes in underlying assumptions.
- The level of fixed and variable costs in a company's cost structure affects the risk of loss and the amount of operating income as the number of units sold changes. Managers choose alternative cost structures taking into account these risk–return tradeoffs.
- CVP analysis can be adapted to multiproduct and multicost driver situations and to service and nonprofit organizations.

Essentials of CVP Analysis

Learning Objective 1

Explain the features of cost–volume–profit (CVP) analysis

. . . how operating income changes with changes in output level, selling prices, variable costs, or fixed costs

In Chapter 2, we discussed total revenues, total costs, and income. **Cost-volume-profit (CVP) analysis** studies the behavior and relationship among these elements as changes occur in the number of units sold, the selling price, the variable cost per unit, or the fixed costs of a product. Let's consider an example to illustrate CVP analysis.

> Emma Jones is a young entrepreneur who recently used *GMAT Success*, a test prep book and software package for the business school admission test. She loved the program and received a high score on the GMAT. After graduation, she contracted with the book's publisher to sell the book. She recently sold the book at a college fair in Boston and is now thinking of selling the book at a college fair in Chicago. Emma knows she can purchase this package from a wholesaler at $120 per package, with the privilege of returning all unsold packages and receiving a full $120 refund per package. She also knows that she must pay $2,000 to the organizers for the booth rental at the fair. She will incur no other costs. She must decide whether she should rent a booth.

Emma, like most managers who face such a situation, will need to work through a series of steps in order to make the most profitable decisions.

1. **Identify the problem and uncertainties.** Every managerial decision involves selecting a course of action. The decision to rent the booth hinges on how Emma resolves two important uncertainties: the price she can charge and the number of packages she can sell at that price. Emma must decide knowing that the outcome of the chosen action is uncertain and will only be known in the future. The more confident Emma is about selling a large number of packages at a good price, the more willing she will be to rent the booth.
2. **Obtain information.** When faced with uncertainty, managers obtain information that might help them understand the uncertainties more clearly. For example, Emma gathers information about the type of individuals likely to attend the fair and other test-prep packages that might be sold at the fair. She also gathers data on her past experiences selling *GMAT Success* at fairs very much like the Chicago fair.
3. **Make predictions about the future.** Managers make predictions using all the information available to them. Emma predicts that she can charge $200 for *GMAT Success*. At that price, she is reasonably confident that she will be able to sell at least 30 packages and possibly as many as 60. In making these predictions, Emma must be realistic and exercise careful judgment. If her predictions are too optimistic, Emma will rent the booth when she should not. If her predictions are too pessimistic, Emma will not rent the booth when she should.

   Emma's predictions rest on the belief that her experience at the Chicago fair will be similar to her experience at a comparable Boston fair 4 months earlier. Yet, Emma is uncertain about several aspects of her prediction. Is the comparison between Boston and Chicago appropriate? Have conditions and circumstances changed over the last 4 months? Are there any biases creeping into her thinking? She is keen on selling at the Chicago fair because sales in the last couple of months have been lower than expected. Is this experience making her predictions overly optimistic? Has she ignored some of the competitive risks? Will the other test prep vendors at the fair reduce their prices?

   Emma reviews her thinking. She retests her assumptions. She obtains data about student attendance and purchases in past years from the organizers of the fair. In the end, she feels quite confident that her predictions are reasonable, accurate, and carefully thought through.
4. **Make decisions by choosing among alternatives.** Emma uses the CVP analysis that follows, and decides to rent the booth at the Chicago fair.
5. **Implement the decision, evaluate performance, and learn.** Thoughtful managers never stop learning. They compare their actual performance to predicted performance to understand why things worked out the way they did and what they might learn. At the end of the Chicago fair, for example, Emma would want to evaluate whether her predictions about price and the number of packages she could sell were correct. Such feedback would be very helpful to Emma as she makes decisions about renting booths at subsequent fairs.

How does Emma use CVP analysis in Step 4 to make her decision? Emma begins by identifying which costs are fixed and which costs are variable and then calculates *contribution margin.*

Contribution Margin

The booth-rental cost of $2,000 is a fixed cost because it will not change no matter how many packages Emma sells. The cost of the package itself is a variable cost because it increases in proportion to the number of packages sold. Emma will incur a cost of $120 for each package that she sells. To get an idea of how operating income will change as a result of selling different quantities of packages, Emma calculates operating income if sales are 5 packages and if sales are 40 packages.

	5 packages sold	40 packages sold
Revenues	$ 1,000 ($200 per package × 5 packages)	$8,000 ($200 per package × 40 packages)
Variable purchase costs	600 ($120 per package × 5 packages)	4,800 ($120 per package × 40 packages)
Fixed costs	2,000	2,000
Operating income	$(1,600)	$1,200

The only numbers that change from selling different quantities of packages are *total revenues* and *total variable costs*. The difference between total revenues and total variable costs is called **contribution margin**. That is,

$$\text{Contribution margin} = \text{Total revenues} - \text{Total variable costs}$$

Contribution margin indicates why operating income changes as the number of units sold changes. The contribution margin when Emma sells 5 packages is $400 ($1,000 in total revenues minus $600 in total variable costs); the contribution margin when Emma sells 40 packages is $3,200 ($8,000 in total revenues minus $4,800 in total variable costs). When calculating the contribution margin, be sure to subtract all variable costs. For example, if Emma had variable selling costs because she paid a commission to salespeople for each package they sold at the fair, variable costs would include the cost of each package plus the sales commission.

Contribution margin per unit is a useful tool for calculating contribution margin and operating income. It is defined as:

$$\text{Contribution margin per unit} = \text{Selling price} - \text{Variable cost per unit}$$

In the *GMAT Success* example, contribution margin per package, or per unit, is $200 − $120 = $80. Contribution margin per unit recognizes the tight coupling of selling price and variable cost per unit. Unlike fixed costs, Emma will only incur the variable cost per unit of $120 when she sells a unit of *GMAT Success* for $200.

Contribution margin per unit provides a second way to calculate contribution margin:

$$\text{Contribution margin} = \text{Contribution margin per unit} \times \text{Quantity of units sold}$$

For example, when Emma sells 40 packages, contribution margin = $80 per unit × 40 units = $3,200.

Even before she gets to the fair, Emma incurs $2,000 in fixed costs. Because the contribution margin per unit is $80, Emma will recover $80 for each package that she sells at the fair. Emma hopes to sell enough packages to fully recover the $2,000 she spent for renting the booth and to then start making a profit.

Exhibit 3-1 presents contribution margins for different quantities of packages sold. The income statement in Exhibit 3-1 is called a **contribution income statement** because it groups costs into variable costs and fixed costs to highlight contribution margin.

$$\text{Operating income} = \text{Contribution margin} - \text{Fixed costs}$$

Each additional package sold from 0 to 1 to 5 increases contribution margin by $80 per package, recovering more of the fixed costs and reducing the operating loss. If Emma sells 25 packages, contribution margin equals $2,000 ($80 per package × 25 packages), exactly recovering fixed costs and resulting in $0 operating income. If Emma sells 40 packages, contribution margin increases by another $1,200 ($3,200 − $2,000), all of which becomes operating income. As you look across

	A	B	C	D	E	F	G	H
1				Number of Packages Sold				
2				0	1	5	25	40
3	Revenues	$ 200	per package	$ 0	$ 200	$ 1,000	$5,000	$8,000
4	Variable costs	$ 120	per package	0	120	600	3,000	4,800
5	Contribution margin	$ 80	per package	0	80	400	2,000	3,200
6	Fixed costs	$2,000		2,000	2,000	2,000	2,000	2,000
7	Operating income			$(2,000)	$(1,920)	$(1,600)	$ 0	$1,200

Exhibit 3-1

Contribution Income Statement for Different Quantities of *GMAT Success* Packages Sold

Exhibit 3-1 from left to right, you see that the increase in contribution margin exactly equals the increase in operating income (or the decrease in operating loss).

When companies, such as American Apparel and Prada, have many products, calculating contribution margin per unit is cumbersome. Instead of expressing contribution margin in dollars per unit, these companies express it as a percentage called **contribution margin percentage** (or **contribution margin ratio**):

$$\text{Contribution margin percentage (or contribution margin ratio)} = \frac{\text{Contribution margin}}{\text{Revenues}}$$

Consider any sales level, for example, sales of 40 units (see Exhibit 3-1),

$$\text{Contribution margin percentage} = \frac{\$3{,}200}{\$8{,}000} = 0.40, \text{ or } 40\%$$

Contribution margin percentage is the contribution margin per dollar of revenue. Emma earns 40% of each dollar of revenue (equal to 40 cents). Contribution margin percentage is a handy way to calculate contribution margin for different dollar amounts of revenue. Rearranging terms in the equation defining contribution margin percentage, we get:

$$\text{Contribution margin} = \text{Contribution margin percentage} \times \text{Revenues (in dollars)}$$

To derive the relationship between operating income and contribution margin percentage, recall that

$$\text{Operating income} = \text{Contribution margin} - \text{Fixed costs}$$

Substituting for contribution margin in the above equation:

$$\text{Operating income} = \text{Contribution margin percentage} \times \text{Revenues} - \text{Fixed costs}$$

For example, in Exhibit 3-1, if Emma sells 40 packages:

Revenues	$8,000
Contribution margin percentage	40%
Contribution margin, 40% × $8,000	$3,200
Fixed costs	2,000
Operating income	$1,200

When there is only one product, as in our example, we can divide both the numerator and denominator by the quantity of units sold and calculate contribution margin percentage as follows:

$$\text{Contribution margin percentage} = \frac{\text{Contribution margin/Quantity of units sold}}{\text{Revenues/Quantity of units sold}}$$

$$= \frac{\text{Contribution margin per unit}}{\text{Selling price}}$$

In our example,

$$\text{Contribution margin percentage} = \frac{\$80}{\$200} = 0.40, \text{ or } 40\%$$

Contribution margin percentage is a useful tool to calculate the effect of a change in revenues on contribution margin. Observe in Exhibit 3-1 that as revenues increase by $3,000 from $5,000 to $8,000, contribution margin increases by $1,200 from $2,000 to $3,200.

Contribution margin at revenue of \$8,000, 0.40 × \$8,000	\$3,200
Contribution margin at revenue of \$5,000, 0.40 × \$5,000	2,000
Change in contribution margin when revenue increases by \$3,000, 0.40 × \$3,000	\$1,200

Change in contribution margin = Contribution margin percentage × Change in revenues

Contribution margin analysis is a widely used technique. For example, managers at Home Depot use contribution margin analysis to evaluate how fluctuations in sales—for example, during a recession—impact profitability.

Keys to Success

Managers use contribution margin analysis as a quick and handy way to evaluate the effect of changes in revenues on operating income.

Expressing CVP Relationships

How was the Excel spreadsheet in Exhibit 3-1 constructed? Underlying the exhibit are some equations that express the CVP relationships. To make good decisions using CVP analysis, we must understand these relationships and the structure of the contribution income statement in Exhibit 3-1. There are three related ways (we will call them "methods") to think more deeply about and model CVP relationships:

1. The equation method
2. The contribution margin method
3. The graph method

The equation method and the contribution margin method are most useful when managers want to determine operating income at few specific levels of sales (for example, 5, 15, 25, and 40 units sold). The graph method helps managers visualize the relationship between units sold and operating income over a wide range of quantities of units sold. As we shall see later in the chapter, different methods are useful for different decisions.

Equation Method. Each column in Exhibit 3-1 is expressed as an equation.

$$\text{Revenues} - \text{Variable costs} - \text{Fixed costs} = \text{Operating income}$$

How are revenues in each column calculated?

$$\text{Revenues} = \text{Selling price } (SP) \times \text{Quantity of units sold } (Q)$$

How are variable costs in each column calculated?

$$\text{Variable costs} = \text{Variable cost per unit } (VCU) \times \text{Quantity of units sold } (Q)$$

So,

$$\left[\left(\begin{matrix}\text{Selling}\\\text{price}\end{matrix} \times \begin{matrix}\text{Quantity of}\\\text{units sold}\end{matrix}\right) - \left(\begin{matrix}\text{Variable cost}\\\text{per unit}\end{matrix} \times \begin{matrix}\text{Quantity of}\\\text{units sold}\end{matrix}\right)\right] - \begin{matrix}\text{Fixed}\\\text{costs}\end{matrix} = \begin{matrix}\text{Operating}\\\text{income}\end{matrix} \qquad \textbf{(Equation 1)}$$

Equation 1 becomes the basis for calculating operating income for different quantities of units sold. For example, if you go to cell F7 in Exhibit 3-1, the calculation of operating income when Emma sells 5 packages is

$$(\$200 \times 5) - (\$120 \times 5) - \$2{,}000 = \$1{,}000 - \$600 - \$2{,}000 = -\$1{,}600$$

Contribution Margin Method. Rearranging equation 1,

$$\left[\left(\begin{matrix}\text{Selling}\\\text{price}\end{matrix} - \begin{matrix}\text{Variable cost}\\\text{per unit}\end{matrix}\right) \times \left(\begin{matrix}\text{Quantity of}\\\text{units sold}\end{matrix}\right)\right] - \begin{matrix}\text{Fixed}\\\text{costs}\end{matrix} = \begin{matrix}\text{Operating}\\\text{income}\end{matrix}$$

$$\left(\begin{matrix}\text{Contribution margin}\\\text{per unit}\end{matrix} \times \begin{matrix}\text{Quantity of}\\\text{units sold}\end{matrix}\right) - \begin{matrix}\text{Fixed}\\\text{costs}\end{matrix} = \begin{matrix}\text{Operating}\\\text{income}\end{matrix} \qquad \textbf{(Equation 2)}$$

In our *GMAT Success* example, contribution margin per unit is \$80 (\$200 − \$120), so when Emma sells 5 packages,

$$\text{Operating income} = (\$80 \times 5) - \$2{,}000 = -\$1{,}600$$

Equation 2 expresses the basic idea we described earlier; each unit sold helps Emma recover $80 (in contribution margin) of the $2,000 in fixed costs.

Graph Method. The graph method helps managers visualize the relationships between total revenues and total costs. In the graph method, each relationship is shown as a line on a graph. Exhibit 3-2 illustrates the graph method for selling *GMAT Success*. Because we have assumed that total costs and total revenues behave in a linear fashion, we need only two points to plot the line representing each of them.

1. **Total costs line.** The total costs line is the sum of fixed costs and variable costs. Fixed costs are $2,000 for all quantities of units sold within the relevant range. To plot the total costs line, use as one point the $2,000 fixed costs at zero units sold (point A) because variable costs are $0 when no units are sold. Select a second point by choosing any other output level (say, 40 units sold) and determine the corresponding total costs. Total variable costs at this output level are $4,800 (40 units × $120 per unit). Remember, fixed costs are $2,000 at all quantities of units sold within the relevant range, so total costs at 40 units sold equal $6,800 ($2,000 + $4,800), which is point B in Exhibit 3-2. The total costs line is the straight line from point A to point B.
2. **Total revenues line.** One convenient starting point is $0 revenues at 0 units sold, which is point C in Exhibit 3-2. Select a second point by choosing any other convenient output level and determining the corresponding total revenues. At 40 units sold, total revenues are $8,000 ($200 per unit × 40 units), which is point D in Exhibit 3-2. The total revenues line is the straight line from point C to point D.

   Profit or loss at any sales level can be determined by the vertical distance between the two lines at that level in Exhibit 3-2. For quantities fewer than 25 units sold, total costs exceed total revenues, and the purple area indicates operating losses. For quantities greater than 25 units sold, total revenues exceed total costs, and the blue-green area indicates operating incomes. At 25 units sold, total revenues equal total costs. Emma will break even by selling 25 packages.

Many companies, particularly small- and medium-sized companies, use the graph method to picture how their revenues and costs will change as the quantity of units sold changes. The graph helps them understand the regions of profitability and the risks they face of making a loss.

Cost–Volume–Profit Assumptions

Now that you have seen how CVP analysis works, think about the following assumptions we made during the analysis:

Exhibit 3-2

Cost–Volume Graph for *GMAT Success*

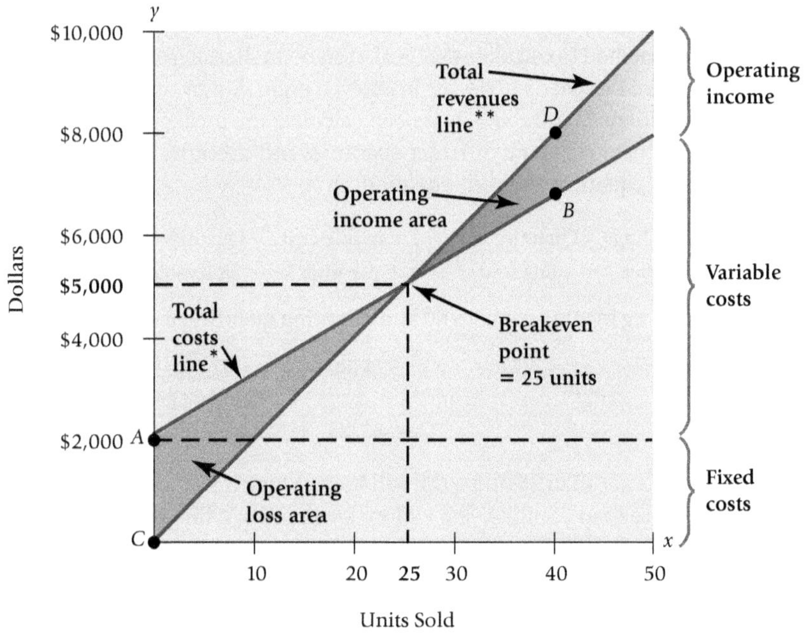

*Slope of the total costs line is the variable cost per unit = $120

**Slope of the total revenues line is the selling price = $200

1. Changes in the levels of revenues and costs arise only because of changes in the number of product (or service) units sold. The number of units sold is the only revenue driver and the only cost driver. Just as a cost driver is any factor that affects costs, a **revenue driver** is a variable, such as volume, that causally affects revenues.
2. Total costs can be separated into two components: a fixed component that does not vary with units sold (such as Emma's booth fee of $2,000) and a variable component that changes based on units sold (such as the $120 cost per package of purchasing *GMAT Success*).
3. When represented graphically, the behaviors of total revenues and total costs are linear (meaning they can be represented as a straight line) in relation to units sold within a relevant range (and time period).
4. Selling price, variable cost per unit, and total fixed costs (within a relevant range and time period) are known and constant.

As the CVP assumptions make clear, an important feature of CVP analysis is distinguishing fixed from variable costs. Always keep in mind, however, that whether a cost is variable or fixed depends on the time period for a decision.

The shorter the time horizon, the higher the percentage of total costs considered fixed. For example, suppose an American Airlines plane will depart from its gate in the next hour and currently has 20 seats unsold. A potential passenger arrives with a transferable ticket from a competing airline. The variable costs (such as one more drink) to American of placing one more passenger in an otherwise empty seat is negligible. At the time of this decision, with only an hour to go before the flight departs, virtually all costs (such as crew costs and baggage-handling costs) are fixed.

Alternatively, suppose American Airlines must decide whether to keep this flight on its flight schedule. This decision will have a 1-year planning horizon. If American Airlines decides to cancel this flight because very few passengers during the last year have taken it, many more costs, including crew costs, baggage-handling costs, and airport fees, would be considered variable: Over this longer 1-year time period, American Airlines would not have to incur these costs if the flight were no longer operating. Always consider the relevant range, the length of the time horizon, and the specific decision situation when classifying costs as variable or fixed.

Learning Objective 2

Determine the breakeven point and output level needed to achieve a target operating income

. . . compare contribution margin and fixed costs

Breakeven Point and Target Operating Income

Managers and entrepreneurs like Emma always want to know how much they must sell to earn a given amount of income. Equally important, they want to know how much they must sell to avoid a loss.

Breakeven Point

The **breakeven point (BEP)** is that quantity of output sold at which total revenues equal total costs—that is, the quantity of output sold that results in $0 of operating income. We have already seen how to use the graph method to calculate the breakeven point. Recall from Exhibit 3-1 that operating income was $0 when Emma sold 25 units, the breakeven point. But by understanding the equations underlying the calculations in Exhibit 3-1, we can calculate the breakeven point directly for selling *GMAT Success* rather than trying out different quantities and checking when operating income equals $0.

Recall the equation method (equation 1):

$$\left[\left(\begin{matrix}\text{Selling}\\\text{price}\end{matrix} \times \begin{matrix}\text{Quantity of}\\\text{units sold}\end{matrix}\right) - \left(\begin{matrix}\text{Variable cost}\\\text{per unit}\end{matrix} \times \begin{matrix}\text{Quantity of}\\\text{units sold}\end{matrix}\right)\right] - \begin{matrix}\text{Fixed}\\\text{costs}\end{matrix} = \begin{matrix}\text{Operating}\\\text{income}\end{matrix}$$

Setting operating income equal to $0 and denoting quantity of output units that must be sold by Q,

$$(\$200 \times Q) - (\$120 \times Q) - \$2{,}000 = \$0$$
$$\$80 \times Q = \$2{,}000$$
$$Q = \$2{,}000 \div \$80 \text{ per unit} = 25 \text{ units}$$

If Emma sells fewer than 25 units, she will incur a loss; if she sells 25 units, she will break even; and if she sells more than 25 units, she will make a profit. While this breakeven point is expressed in units, it can also be expressed in revenues: 25 units $\times$ $200 selling price $=$ $5,000.

Recall the contribution margin method (equation 2):

$$\left(\begin{matrix}\text{Contribution}\\\text{margin per unit}\end{matrix} \times \begin{matrix}\text{Quantity of}\\\text{units sold}\end{matrix}\right) - \text{Fixed costs} = \text{Operating income}$$

At the breakeven point, operating income is by definition $0 and so,

$$\text{Contribution margin per unit} \times \text{Breakeven quantity of units} = \text{Fixed cost} \qquad \textbf{(Equation 3)}$$

Rearranging equation 3 and entering the data,

$$\frac{\text{Breakeven}}{\text{quantity of units}} = \frac{\text{Fixed costs}}{\text{Contribution margin per unit}} = \frac{\$2{,}000}{\$80 \text{ per unit}} = 25 \text{ units}$$

$$\text{Breakeven revenues} = \text{Breakeven quantity of units} \times \text{Selling price}$$
$$= 25 \text{ units} \times \$200 \text{ per unit} = \$5{,}000$$

In practice (because they have multiple products), management accountants usually calculate the breakeven point directly in terms of revenues using contribution margin percentages. Recall that in the *GMAT Success* example,

$$\frac{\text{Contribution margin}}{\text{percentage}} = \frac{\text{Contribution margin per unit}}{\text{Selling price}} = \frac{\$80}{\$200} = 0.40, \text{ or } 40\%$$

That is, 40% of each dollar of revenue, or 40 cents, is contribution margin. To break even, contribution margin must equal fixed costs of $2,000. To earn $2,000 of contribution margin, when $1 of revenue earns $0.40 of contribution margin, revenues must equal $2,000 ÷ 0.40 = $5,000.

$$\frac{\text{Breakeven}}{\text{revenues}} = \frac{\text{Fixed costs}}{\text{Contribution margin \%}} = \frac{\$2{,}000}{0.40} = \$5{,}000$$

While the breakeven point tells managers how much they must sell to avoid a loss, managers are equally interested in how they will achieve the operating income targets underlying their strategies and plans. In our example, selling 25 units at a price of $200 (equal to revenue of $5,000) assures Emma that she will not lose money if she rents the booth. While this news is comforting, how does Emma determine how much she needs to sell to achieve a targeted amount of operating income?

Keys to Success

Breakeven point helps managers distinguish when their operations will be profitable and when they might make a loss.

Target Operating Income

We illustrate target operating income calculations by asking the following question: How many units must Emma sell to earn an operating income of $1,200? One approach is to keep plugging in different quantities into Exhibit 3-1 and check when operating income equals $1,200. Exhibit 3-1 shows that operating income is $1,200 when 40 packages are sold. A more convenient approach is to use equation 1 from page 80.

$$\left[\left(\begin{matrix}\text{Selling}\\\text{price}\end{matrix} \times \begin{matrix}\text{Quantity of}\\\text{units sold}\end{matrix}\right) - \left(\begin{matrix}\text{Variable cost}\\\text{per unit}\end{matrix} \times \begin{matrix}\text{Quantity of}\\\text{units sold}\end{matrix}\right)\right] - \begin{matrix}\text{Fixed}\\\text{costs}\end{matrix} = \begin{matrix}\text{Operating}\\\text{income}\end{matrix} \qquad \textbf{(Equation 1)}$$

We denote by Q the unknown quantity of units Emma must sell to earn an operating income of $1,200. Selling price is $200, variable cost per package is $120, fixed costs are $2,000, and target operating income is $1,200. Substituting these values into equation 1, we have

$$(\$200 \times Q) - (\$120 \times Q) - \$2{,}000 = \$1{,}200$$
$$\$80 \times Q = \$2{,}000 + \$1{,}200 = \$3{,}200$$
$$Q = \$3{,}200 \div \$80 \text{ per unit} = 40 \text{ units}$$

Alternatively, we could use equation 2,

$$\left(\begin{matrix}\text{Contribution margin}\\\text{per unit}\end{matrix} \times \begin{matrix}\text{Quantity of}\\\text{units sold}\end{matrix}\right) - \begin{matrix}\text{Fixed}\\\text{costs}\end{matrix} = \begin{matrix}\text{Operating}\\\text{income}\end{matrix} \qquad \textbf{(Equation 2)}$$

Given a target operating income ($1,200 in this case), we can rearrange terms to get equation 4.

$$\frac{\text{Quantity of units}}{\text{required to be sold}} = \frac{\text{Fixed costs} + \text{Target operating income}}{\text{Contribution margin per unit}} \quad \textbf{(Equation 4)}$$

$$\frac{\text{Quantity of units}}{\text{required to be sold}} = \frac{\$2{,}000 + \$1{,}200}{\$80 \text{ per unit}} = 40 \text{ units}$$

Proof:

Revenues, $200 per unit × 40 units	$8,000
Variable costs, $120 per unit × 40 units	4,800
Contribution margin, $80 per unit × 40 units	3,200
Fixed costs	2,000
Operating income	$1,200

The revenues needed to earn an operating income of $1,200 can also be calculated directly by recognizing (1) that $3,200 of contribution margin must be earned (fixed costs of $2,000 plus operating income of $1,200) and (2) that $1 of revenue earns $0.40 (40 cents) of contribution margin. To earn $3,200 of contribution margin, revenues must equal $3,200 ÷ 0.40 = $8,000.

$$\text{Revenues needed to earn operating income of } \$1{,}200 = \frac{\$2{,}000 + \$1{,}200}{0.40} = \frac{\$3{,}200}{0.40} = \$8{,}000$$

Could we use the graph method and the graph in Exhibit 3-2 to answer the question, How many units must Emma sell to earn an operating income of $1,200? Yes, but it is not as easy to determine the precise point at which the difference between the total revenues line and the total costs line equals $1,200. Recasting Exhibit 3-2 in the form of a profit–volume (PV) graph, however, makes it easier to answer this question.

A **PV graph** shows how changes in the quantity of units sold affect operating income. Exhibit 3-3 is the PV graph for *GMAT Success* (fixed costs, $2,000; selling price, $200; and variable cost per unit, $120). The PV line can be drawn using two points. One convenient point (M) is the operating loss at 0 units sold, which is equal to the fixed costs of $2,000, shown at –$2,000 on the vertical axis. A second convenient point (N) is the breakeven point, which is 25 units in our example (see page 82). The PV line is the straight line from point M through point N. To find the number of units Emma must sell to earn an operating income of $1,200, draw a horizontal line parallel to the *x*-axis corresponding to $1,200 on the vertical axis (that's the *y*-axis). At the point where this line intersects the PV line, draw a vertical line down to the horizontal axis (that's the *x*-axis). The vertical line intersects the *x*-axis at 40 units, indicating that by selling 40 units Emma will earn an operating income of $1,200.

Exhibit 3-3

Profit–Volume Graph for *GMAT Success*

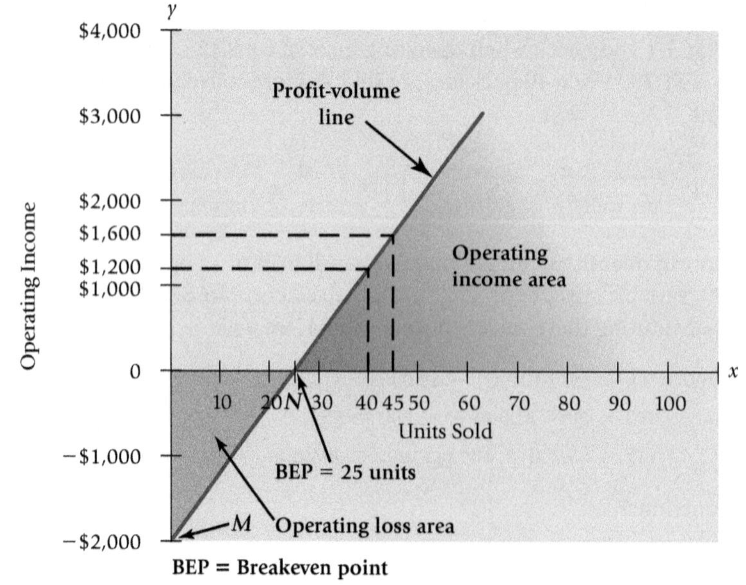

Just like Emma, managers at larger companies such as California Pizza Kitchen use profit-volume analysis to understand how profits change with sales volume. They use this understanding to target the sales levels they need to achieve to meet their profit plans.

> **Keys to Success**
> A PV graph is a visual way for managers to understand the relationship between quantity of units sold and operating income.

Target Net Income and Income Taxes

Learning Objective 3

Understand how income taxes affect CVP analysis

. . . focus on net income

Net income is operating income plus nonoperating revenues (such as interest revenue) minus nonoperating costs (such as interest cost) minus income taxes. For simplicity, throughout this chapter we assume nonoperating revenues and nonoperating costs are zero. Thus,

$$\text{Net income} = \text{Operating income} - \text{Income taxes}$$

Until now, we have ignored the effect of income taxes in our CVP analysis. In many companies, the income targets for managers in their strategic plans are expressed in terms of net income, because top management wants subordinate managers to take into account the effects their decisions have on operating income after income taxes. Some decisions may not result in large operating incomes, but they may have favorable tax consequences, making them attractive on a net income basis—the measure that drives shareholders' dividends and returns.

To make net income evaluations, CVP calculations for target income must be stated in terms of target net income instead of target operating income. For example, Emma may be interested in knowing the quantity of units of *GMAT Success* she must sell to earn a net income of \$960, assuming an income tax rate of 40%.

$$\text{Target net income} = \left(\begin{array}{c}\text{Target}\\\text{operating income}\end{array}\right) - \left(\begin{array}{c}\text{Target}\\\text{operating inome}\end{array} \times \text{Tax rate}\right)$$

$$\text{Target net income} = (\text{Target operating income}) \times (1 - \text{Tax rate})$$

$$\text{Target operating income} = \frac{\text{Target net income}}{1 - \text{Tax rate}} = \frac{\$960}{1 - 0.40} = \$1{,}600$$

In other words, to earn a target net income of \$960, Emma's target operating income is \$1,600.

Proof:

Target operating income	\$1,600
Tax at 40% (0.40 × \$1,600)	640
Target net income	\$ 960

The key step is to take the target net income number and convert it into the corresponding target operating income number. We can then use equation 1 for target operating income and substitute numbers from our *GMAT Success* example.

$$\left[\left(\begin{array}{c}\text{Selling}\\\text{price}\end{array} \times \begin{array}{c}\text{Quantity of}\\\text{units sold}\end{array}\right) - \left(\begin{array}{c}\text{Variable cost}\\\text{per unit}\end{array} \times \begin{array}{c}\text{Quantity of}\\\text{unit sold}\end{array}\right)\right] - \begin{array}{c}\text{Fixed}\\\text{costs}\end{array} = \begin{array}{c}\text{Operating}\\\text{income}\end{array} \quad \textbf{(Equation 1)}$$

$$(\$200 \times Q) - (\$120 \times Q) - \$2{,}000 = \$1{,}600$$

$$\$80 \times Q = \$3{,}600$$

$$Q = \$3{,}600 \div \$80 \text{ per unit} = 45 \text{ units}$$

Alternatively, we can calculate the number of units Emma must sell by using the contribution margin method and equation 4:

$$\begin{array}{c}\text{Quantity of units}\\\text{required to be sold}\end{array} = \frac{\text{Fixed costs} + \text{Target operating income}}{\text{Contribution margin per unit}} \quad \textbf{(Equation 4)}$$

$$= \frac{\$2{,}000 + \$1{,}600}{\$80 \text{ per unit}} = 45 \text{ units}$$

Proof:

Revenues, \$200 per unit × 45 units	\$9,000
Variable costs, \$120 per unit × 45 units	5,400
Contribution margin	3,600
Fixed costs	2,000
Operating income	1,600
Income taxes, \$1,600 × 0.40	640
Net income	\$ 960

Emma can also use the PV graph in Exhibit 3-3. To earn target operating income of \$1,600, Emma needs to sell 45 units.

Focusing the analysis on target net income instead of target operating income will not change the breakeven point, because, by definition, operating income at the breakeven point is \$0, and no income taxes are paid when there is no operating income.

Learning Objective 4

Explain how managers use CVP analysis in decision making.

. . . choose the alternative that maximizes operating income

Using CVP Analysis for Decision Making

We have seen how CVP analysis is useful for calculating the units that need to be sold to break even, or to achieve a target operating income or target net income. Managers also use CVP analysis to guide other decisions, many of them strategic decisions. Consider a decision about choosing additional features for an existing product such as the engine size, transmission system, or steering system for a new car model. Different choices can affect selling prices, variable cost per unit, fixed costs, units sold, and operating income. CVP analysis helps managers make product decisions by estimating the expected profitability of these choices. We return to our *GMAT Success* example to illustrate how to use CVP analysis for strategic decisions about advertising and selling price.

Decision to Advertise

Suppose Emma anticipates selling 40 units of *GMAT Success* at the fair. Exhibit 3-3 indicates that Emma's operating income will be \$1,200. Emma is considering placing an advertisement describing the product and its features in the fair brochure. The advertisement will be a fixed cost of \$500. Emma thinks that advertising will increase sales by 10% to 44 packages. Should Emma advertise? The following table presents the CVP analysis.

	40 Packages Sold with No Advertising (1)	44 Packages Sold with Advertising (2)	Difference (3) = (2) − (1)
Revenues (\$200 × 40; \$200 × 44)	\$8,000	\$8,800	\$ 800
Variable costs (\$120 × 40; \$120 × 44)	4,800	5,280	480
Contribution margin (\$80 × 40; \$80 × 44)	3,200	3,520	320
Fixed costs	2,000	2,500	500
Operating income	\$1,200	\$1,020	\$(180)

Operating income will decrease from \$1,200 to \$1,020, so Emma should not advertise. Note that Emma could focus only on the difference column and come to the same conclusion: If Emma advertises, contribution margin will increase by \$320 (revenues, \$800 − variable costs, \$480), and fixed costs will increase by \$500, resulting in a \$180 decrease in operating income.

As you become more familiar with CVP analysis, try evaluating decisions based on differences rather than mechanically working through the contribution income statement. What if advertising costs were \$400 or \$600 instead of \$500? Analyzing differences allows managers to get to the heart of CVP analysis and sharpens intuition by focusing only on the revenues and costs that will change as a result of a decision.

Decision to Reduce Selling Price

Having decided not to advertise, Emma is contemplating whether to reduce the selling price to \$175. At this price, she thinks she will sell 50 units. At this quantity, the test-prep package wholesaler who supplies *GMAT Success* will sell the packages to Emma for \$115 per unit instead of \$120. Should Emma reduce the selling price?

Contribution margin from lowering price to \$175: (\$175 − \$115) per unit × 50 units	\$3,000
Contribution margin from maintaining price at \$200: (\$200 − \$120) per unit × 40 units	3,200
Change in contribution margin from lowering price	\$ (200)

Decreasing the price will reduce contribution margin by \$200 and, because the fixed costs of \$2,000 will not change, it will also reduce operating income by \$200. Emma should not reduce the selling price.

Determining Target Prices

Emma could also ask, "At what price can I sell 50 units (purchased at \$115 per unit) and continue to earn an operating income of \$1,200?" The answer is \$179, as the following calculations show.

Target operating income	\$1,200
Add fixed costs	2,000
Target contribution margin	\$3,200
Divided by number of units sold	÷ 50 units
Target contribution margin per unit	\$ 64
Add variable cost per unit	115
Target selling price	\$ 179

Proof:

Revenues, \$179 per unit × 50 units	\$8,950
Variable costs, \$115 per unit × 50 units	5,750
Contribution margin	3,200
Fixed costs	2,000
Operating income	\$1,200

Emma should also examine the effects of other decisions, such as simultaneously increasing advertising costs and increasing or lowering prices. In each case, Emma will estimate the effects these actions are likely to have on the demand for *GMAT Success*. She will then compare the changes in contribution margin (through the effects on selling prices, variable costs, and quantities of units sold) to the changes in fixed costs, and choose the alternative that provides the highest operating income. Concepts in Action: Irish Rock Band U2 Turned a Big Profit—Despite High Fixed Costs describes how the band U2 used CVP analysis to make decisions on fixed costs and ticket prices on its recent world music tour.

Strategic decisions invariably entail risk. Managers can use CVP analysis to evaluate how operating income will be affected if the original predicted data are not achieved—say, if sales are 10% lower than estimated. Evaluating this risk affects other strategic decisions a manager might make. For example, if the probability of a decline in sales seems high, a manager may take actions to change the cost structure to have more variable costs and fewer fixed costs.

> **Keys to Success**
> Comparing changes in contribution margin to changes in fixed costs is a convenient way for managers to evaluate decision alternatives.

Sensitivity Analysis and Margin of Safety

Learning Objective 5

Explain how sensitivity analysis helps managers cope with uncertainty

. . . determine the effect on operating income of different assumptions

Before deciding on a course of action, managers frequently analyze the sensitivity of their decisions to changes in underlying assumptions. Companies such as Boeing and Airbus Industries use CVP analysis to evaluate how many airplanes they need to sell in order to recover the multibillion-dollar cost of designing and developing a new airplane. They test the sensitivity of their conclusions to different assumptions about market size, market share, and selling prices.

Sensitivity analysis is a "what-if" technique that managers use to examine how an outcome will change if the original predicted data are not achieved or if an underlying assumption changes. In the context of CVP analysis, sensitivity analysis answers questions such as "What will operating income be if the quantity of units sold decreases by 5% from the original prediction?" and "What will operating income be if variable cost per unit increases by 10%?" Sensitivity analysis broadens managers' perspectives to possible outcomes that might occur *before* the company commits to funding the project.

Electronic spreadsheets, such as Excel, enable managers to systematically and efficiently conduct CVP-based sensitivity analyses and to examine the effect and interaction of changes in selling price, variable cost per unit, and fixed costs on target operating income. Exhibit 3-4 displays a spreadsheet for the *GMAT Success* example.

Concepts in Action: Irish Rock Band U2 Turned a Big Profit—Despite High Fixed Costs

When U2 embarked on its recent world tour, *Rolling Stone* magazine called it "the biggest rock show ever." Visiting large stadiums around the world, the Irish band performed on an imposing 164-foot high stage that resembled a spaceship, complete with a massive video screen and footbridges leading to ringed catwalks. With an ambitious itinerary, U2 actually had three separate stages leapfrogging its global itinerary—each one costing nearly $40 million. As a result, the tour's success was dependent not only on each night's concert, but also recouping its tremendous fixed costs—costs that did not change with the number of fans in the audience.

Source: Ettore Ferrari/EPA/Newscom

To cover its high fixed costs and make a profit, U2 needed to sell a lot of tickets. To maximize revenue, the tour employed a unique in-the-round stage configuration, which boosted stadium capacity by roughly 20%, and sold tickets for as little as $30, far less than most large outdoor concerts. The band's plan worked—despite a broader music industry slump and global recession, U2 shattered attendance records in most of the venues it played. By the end of the tour in 2011, the band played to over 7 million fans and racked up more than $700 million in ticket and merchandise sales, making it the biggest music tour ever.

Sources: Based on Edna Gundersen, "U2 Turns 360 Stadium Tour Into Attendance-Shattering Sellouts," *USA Today* (October 4, 2009); and Ray Waddell, "U2's '360' Tour Gross: $734,137,344!" *Billboard* (July 29, 2011).

Exhibit 3-4

Spreadsheet Analysis of CVP Relationships for *GMAT Success*

Home | Insert | Page Layout | Formulas | Data | Review | View

D5 ▼ *fx* =($A5+D$3)/(F1-$B5)

	A	B	C	D	E	F
1			**Number of units required to be sold at $200**			
2			**Selling Price to Earn Target Operating Income of**			
3		**Variable Costs**	**$0**	**$1,200**	**$1,600**	**$2,000**
4	**Fixed Costs**	**per Unit**	**(Breakeven point)**			
5	$2,000	$100	20	32[a]	36	40
6	$2,000	$120	25	40	45	50
7	$2,000	$150	40	64	72	80
8	$2,400	$100	24	36	40	44
9	$2,400	$120	30	45	50	55
10	$2,400	$150	48	72	80	88
11	$2,800	$100	28	40	44	48
12	$2,800	$120	35	50	55	60
13	$2,800	$150	56	80	88	96
14						
15–16	[a]Number of units required to be sold	=	$\frac{\text{Fixed costs + Target operating income}}{\text{Contribution margin per unit}}$	=	$\frac{\$2{,}000 + \$1{,}200}{\$200 - \$100}$	= 32

Using the spreadsheet, Emma can immediately see how many units she needs to sell to achieve particular operating-income levels, given alternative levels of fixed costs and variable cost per unit that she may face. For example, she must sell 32 units to earn an operating income of \$1,200 if fixed costs are \$2,000 and variable cost per unit is \$100. Emma can also use Exhibit 3-4 to determine that she needs to sell 56 units to break even if fixed cost of the booth rental at the Chicago fair is raised to \$2,800 and if the variable cost per unit charged by the test-prep package supplier increases to \$150. Emma can use information about costs and sensitivity analysis, together with realistic predictions about how much she can sell, to decide if she should rent a booth at the fair.

Keys to Success

Sensitivity analysis is a "what-if" technique that managers use to recognize uncertainty by examining how an outcome will change if the original predicted data or assumptions change.

Another aspect of sensitivity analysis is **margin of safety**:

$$\text{Margin of safety} = \text{Budgeted (or actual) revenues} - \text{Breakeven revenues}$$
$$\text{Margin of safety (in units)} = \text{Budgeted (or actual) sales quantity} - \text{Breakeven quantity}$$

The margin of safety answers the "what-if" question: If budgeted revenues are above breakeven and drop, how far can they fall below budget before the breakeven point is reached? Sales might decrease as a result of factors such as a competitor introducing a better product or a poorly executed marketing program. Assume that Emma has fixed costs of \$2,000, a selling price of \$200, and variable cost per unit of \$120. From Exhibit 3-1, if Emma sells 40 units, budgeted revenues are \$8,000 and budgeted operating income is \$1,200. The breakeven point is 25 units or \$5,000 in total revenues.

$$\text{Margin of safety} = \begin{array}{c}\text{Budgeted}\\ \text{revenues}\end{array} - \begin{array}{c}\text{Breakeven}\\ \text{revenues}\end{array} = \$8{,}000 - \$5{,}000 = \$3{,}000$$

$$\begin{array}{c}\text{Margin of}\\ \text{safety (in units)}\end{array} = \begin{array}{c}\text{Budgeted}\\ \text{sales (units)}\end{array} - \begin{array}{c}\text{Breakeven}\\ \text{sales (units)}\end{array} = 40 - 25 = 15 \text{ units}$$

Sometimes margin of safety is expressed as a percentage:

$$\text{Margin of safety percentage} = \frac{\text{Margin of safety in dollars}}{\text{Budgeted (or actual) revenues}}$$

In our example, margin of safety percentage $= \dfrac{\$3{,}000}{\$8{,}000} = 37.5\%$

This result means that revenues would have to decrease substantially, by 37.5%, to reach breakeven revenues. The high margin of safety gives Emma confidence that she is unlikely to suffer a loss.

If, however, Emma expects to sell only 30 units, budgeted revenues would be \$6,000 (\$200 per unit × 30 units) and the margin of safety would equal:

$$\text{Budgeted revenues} - \text{Breakeven revenues} = \$6{,}000 - \$5{,}000 = \$1{,}000$$

$$\begin{array}{c}\text{Margin of}\\ \text{safety percentage}\end{array} = \frac{\text{Margin of safety in dollars}}{\text{Budgeted (or actual) revenues}} = \frac{\$1{,}000}{\$6{,}000} = 16.67\%$$

The analysis implies that if revenues decrease by more than 16.67%, Emma would suffer a loss. A low margin of safety increases the risk of a loss, which means that Emma would need to look for ways to lower the breakeven point by reducing fixed costs or increasing contribution margin. For example, she would need to evaluate if her product is attractive enough to customers to allow her to charge a higher price without reducing demand; or if she could purchase the software at a lower cost from the wholesaler. If Emma can neither reduce fixed costs nor increase contribution margin and if Emma does not have the tolerance for this level of risk, she will prefer not to rent a booth at the fair.

Sensitivity analysis is a simple approach to recognizing **uncertainty**, which is the possibility that an actual amount will deviate from an expected amount. Sensitivity analysis gives managers a good feel for the risks involved in a decision. A more comprehensive approach to recognizing uncertainty is to compute expected values using probability distributions. This approach is illustrated in the appendix to this chapter.

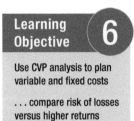

Learning Objective 6

Use CVP analysis to plan variable and fixed costs

. . . compare risk of losses versus higher returns

Cost Planning and CVP

Managers have the ability to choose the levels of fixed and variable costs in their cost structures. This is a strategic decision. In this section, we describe various factors that managers and management accountants consider as they make this decision.

Alternative Fixed-Cost/Variable-Cost Structures

CVP-based sensitivity analysis highlights the risks and returns as fixed costs are substituted for variable costs in a company's cost structure. In Exhibit 3-4, compare line 6 and line 11.

			Number of units required to be sold at $200 selling price to earn target operating income of	
	Fixed Cost	Variable Cost	$0 (Breakeven point)	$2,000
Line 6	$2,000	$120	25	50
Line 11	$2,800	$100	28	48

Compared to line 6, line 11, with higher fixed costs and lower variable costs, has more risk of loss (has a higher breakeven point) but requires fewer units to be sold (48 vs. 50) to earn operating income of $2,000. CVP analysis can help managers evaluate various fixed-cost/variable-cost structures. We next consider the effects of these choices in more detail. Suppose the Chicago college fair organizers offer Emma three rental alternatives:

Option 1: $2,000 fixed fee

Option 2: $800 fixed fee plus 15% of *GMAT Success* revenues

Option 3: 25% of *GMAT Success* revenues with no fixed fee

Emma's variable cost per unit is $120. Emma is interested in how her choice of a rental agreement will affect the income she earns and the risks she faces. Exhibit 3-5 graphically depicts the profit–volume relationship for each option.

Exhibit 3-5

Profit–Volume Graph for Alternative Rental Options for *GMAT Success*

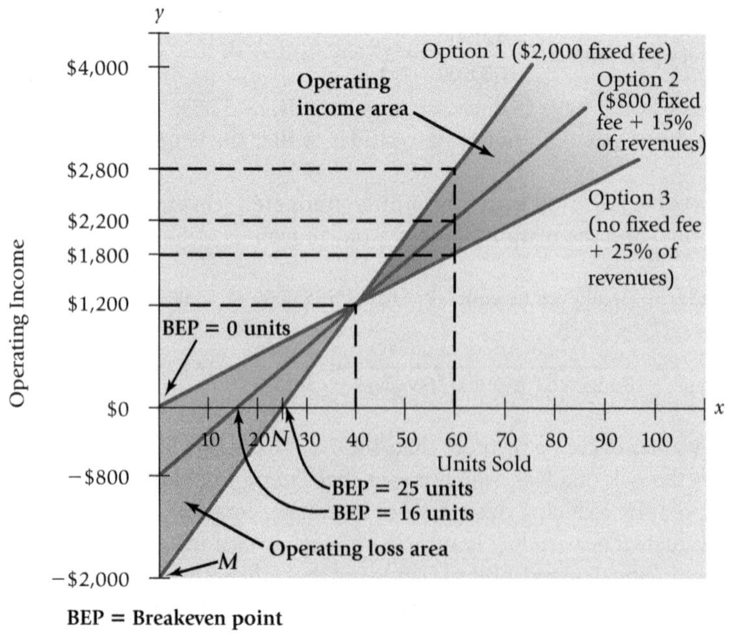

- The line representing the relationship between units sold and operating income for Option 1 is the same as the line in the PV graph shown in Exhibit 3-3 (fixed costs of $2,000 and contribution margin per unit of $80).
- The line representing Option 2 shows fixed costs of $800 and a contribution margin per unit of $50 [selling price, $200, minus variable cost per unit, $120, minus variable rental fees per unit, $30 (0.15 × $200)].
- The line representing Option 3 has fixed costs of $0 and a contribution margin per unit of $30 [$200 − $120 − $50 (0.25 × $200)].

Option 3 has the lowest breakeven point (0 units), and Option 1 has the highest breakeven point (25 units). Option 1 has the highest risk of loss if sales are low, but it also has the highest contribution margin per unit ($80) and so the highest operating income when sales are high (greater than 40 units).

The choice among Options 1, 2, and 3 is a strategic decision. As in most strategic decisions, what Emma decides now will significantly affect her operating income (or loss), depending on the demand for *GMAT Success*. Faced with this uncertainty, Emma's choice will be influenced by her confidence in the level of demand for *GMAT Success* and her willingness to risk losses if demand is low. For example, if Emma's tolerance for risk is high, she will choose Option 1 with its high potential rewards. If, however, Emma is averse to taking risk, she will prefer Option 3, where the rewards are smaller if sales are high but where she never suffers a loss if sales are low.

Operating Leverage

The risk–return tradeoff across alternative cost structures can be measured as *operating leverage*. **Operating leverage** describes the effects that fixed costs have on changes in operating income as changes occur in units sold and contribution margin. Organizations with a high proportion of fixed costs in their cost structures, as is the case under Option 1, have high operating leverage. The line representing Option 1 in Exhibit 3-5 is the steepest of the three lines. Small increases in sales lead to large increases in operating income. Small decreases in sales result in relatively large decreases in operating income, leading to a greater risk of operating losses. *At any given level of sales,*

$$\text{Degree of operating leverage} = \frac{\text{Contribution margin}}{\text{Operating income}}$$

The following table shows the **degree of operating leverage** at sales of 40 units for the three rental options.

	Option 1	Option 2	Option 3
1. Contribution margin per unit (see above)	$ 80	$ 50	$ 30
2. Contribution margin (row 1 × 40 units)	$3,200	$2,000	$1,200
3. Operating income (from Exhibit 3-5)	$1,200	$1,200	$1,200
4. Degree of operating leverage (row 2 ÷ row 3)	$\frac{\$3,200}{\$1,200} = 2.67$	$\frac{\$2,000}{\$1,200} = 1.67$	$\frac{\$1,200}{\$1,200} = 1.00$

These results indicate that, when sales are 40 units, a percentage change in sales and contribution margin will result in 2.67 times that percentage change in operating income for Option 1, but the same percentage change (1.00) in operating income for Option 3. Consider, for example, a sales increase of 50% from 40 to 60 units. Contribution margin will increase by 50% under each option. Operating income, however, will increase by 2.67 × 50% = 133% from $1,200 to $2,800 in Option 1, but it will increase by only 1.00 × 50% = 50% from $1,200 to $1,800 in Option 3 (see Exhibit 3-5). The degree of operating leverage at a given level of sales helps managers calculate the effect of sales fluctuations on operating income.

Keep in mind that, in the presence of fixed costs, the degree of operating leverage is different at different levels of sales. For example, at sales of 60 units, the degree of operating leverage under each of the three options is as follows:

	Option 1	Option 2	Option 3
1. Contribution margin per unit (p. 91)	$ 80	$ 50	$ 30
2. Contribution margin (row 1 × 60 units)	$4,800	$3,000	$1,800
3. Operating income (from Exhibit 3-5)	$2,800	$2,200	$1,800
4. Degree of operating leverage (row 2 ÷ row 3)	$\frac{\$4,800}{\$2,800} = 1.71$	$\frac{\$3,000}{\$2,200} = 1.36$	$\frac{\$1,800}{\$1,800} = 1.00$

The degree of operating leverage decreases from 2.67 (at sales of 40 units) to 1.71 (at sales of 60 units) under Option 1 and from 1.67 to 1.36 under Option 2. In general, whenever there are fixed costs, the degree of operating leverage decreases as the level of sales increases beyond the breakeven point. If fixed costs are $0 as in Option 3, contribution margin equals operating income, and the degree of operating leverage equals 1.00 at all sales levels.

But why must managers monitor operating leverage carefully? Again, consider companies such as General Motors and United Airlines. Their high operating leverage was a major reason for their financial problems. Anticipating high demand for their services, these companies borrowed money to acquire assets, resulting in high fixed costs. As sales declined, these companies suffered losses and could not generate sufficient cash to service their interest and debt, causing them to seek bankruptcy protection. Managers and management accountants should distinguish fixed from variable costs and then evaluate how the level of fixed costs and variable costs they choose will affect the risk–return tradeoff. In several contexts, as in the examples discussed in this chapter, discerning fixed from variable costs is fairly straightforward. In other contexts, classifying costs as fixed or variable can be more challenging because costs do not vary only with the number of units sold but with the number of different types of products or services offered, the number of batches in which products are produced, or the complexity of operations. Chapter 8 describes techniques managers can use to separate fixed costs from variable costs. Often, though, differentiating fixed from variable costs requires careful judgment.

What actions are managers taking to reduce their fixed costs? Nike, the shoe and apparel company, does no manufacturing and incurs no fixed costs of operating and maintaining manufacturing plants. Instead, it buys its products from various suppliers. As a result, all the costs of producing products are variable costs. Nike reduces its risk of loss by increasing variable costs and reducing fixed costs. Concepts in Action: Cost–Volume–Profit Analysis Makes Megabus a Mega-Success describes how Megabus, an intercity bus operator, developed an innovative business model to reduce fixed costs.

To reduce both fixed costs and variable costs, many companies are moving their manufacturing facilities from the United States to lower-cost countries, such as Mexico and China. Other companies, such as General Electric and Hewlett-Packard have shifted service functions, such as after-sales customer service, to their customer call centers in countries such as India. These decisions by companies are often controversial. Some economists argue that outsourcing helps to keep costs, and therefore prices, low and enables U.S. companies to remain globally competitive. Others argue that outsourcing reduces job opportunities in the United States and hurts working-class families.

Keys to Success

Managers choose the variable-cost/fixed-cost structure strategically to balance the risk of losses if revenues are low and higher profits if revenues are high.

Learning Objective 7

Apply CVP analysis to a company producing multiple products

. . . assume sales mix of products remains constant as total units sold changes

Effects of Sales Mix on Income

Sales mix is the quantities (or proportion) of various products (or services) that constitute total unit sales of a company. Suppose Emma is now budgeting for a subsequent college fair in New York. She plans to sell two different test-prep packages—*GMAT Success* and *GRE Guarantee*—and budgets the following:

	GMAT Success	*GRE Guarantee*	Total
Expected sales	60	40	100
Revenues, $200 and $100 per unit	$12,000	$4,000	$16,000
Variable costs, $120 and $70 per unit	7,200	2,800	10,000
Contribution margin, $80 and $30 per unit	$ 4,800	$1,200	6,000
Fixed costs			4,500
Operating income			$ 1,500

What is the breakeven point? In contrast to the single-product (or service) situation, the total number of units that must be sold to break even in a multiproduct company depends on the sales mix—the combination of the number of units of *GMAT Success* sold and the number of units of *GRE Guarantee* sold. We assume that the budgeted sales mix (60 units of *GMAT Success* sold for every 40 units of *GRE Guarantee* sold, that is, a ratio of 3:2) will not change at different levels of total unit sales. That is, we think of Emma selling a bundle of 3 units of *GMAT Success* and 2 units of *GRE Guarantee*. (Note that this does not mean that Emma physically bundles the two products together into one big package.)

Each bundle yields a contribution margin of $300, calculated as follows:

	Number of Units of *GMAT Success* and *GRE Guarantee* in Each Bundle	Contribution Margin per Unit for *GMAT Success* and *GRE Guarantee*	Contribution Margin of the Bundle
GMAT Success	3	$80	$240
GRE Guarantee	2	30	60
Total			$300

Concepts in Action: Cost–Volume–Profit Analysis Makes Megabus a Mega-Success

Many travelers are shunning airlines and leaving their cars at home to take the low-fare Megabus between major U.S. cities. Megabus, one of a growing number of express bus services, has a simple business model. Most tickets are sold online and are paperless. The first passengers to reserve seats on each bus get the cheapest prices, often starting at $1, and fares vary based on demand. Buses outfitted with free Wi-Fi connections and other perks link city centers such as Boston, New York, and Philadelphia. The buses make few if any stops, so travel times are often the same as driving and only slightly longer than taking the train, at a fraction of the price.

Source: Seth Wenig/AP Images

To offer rock-bottom prices and good service, Megabus is fanatical about keeping costs down. Aside from buses and a barebones back-office staff, Megabus has virtually no fixed costs. Riders are picked up at the curb—no fees for gate space at a terminal—and customers pay extra to order tickets from an agent. The bus fleet is also in constant use. As chief executive Dale Moser stated, "You cut all that overhead out of your business, you find you can pass that savings on to customers, thus driving volume." Without high fixed costs, Megabus can also easily add and subtract departures profitably. During Thanksgiving and Christmas 2010, Megabus sold as many tickets as were requested on its Web site, adding buses as needed.

Since hitting the road in 2006, Megabus has changed the way many Americans—especially those aged 18 to 34—travel. In 2010, Megabus did $100 million in business from 4 million passengers traveling on 135 of its buses.

Sources: Based on Ben Austen, "The Megabus Effect," *Bloomberg Businessweek* (April 7, 2011); Ken Belson, "Thinking Outside Rails and Runways, and Taking the Bus," *The New York Times* (May 5, 2010); and Dave Demerjian, "Low-Fare Buses Doing Big Business," Wired.com 'Autopia' blog (September 30, 2008).

To compute the breakeven point, we calculate the number of bundles Emma needs to sell.

$$\text{Breakeven point in bundles} = \frac{\text{Fixed costs}}{\text{Contribution margin per bundle}} = \frac{\$4{,}500}{\$300 \text{ per bundle}} = 15 \text{ bundles}$$

Breakeven point in units of *GMAT Success* and *GRE Guarantee* is as follows:

GMAT Success: 15 bundles × 3 units per bundle	45 units
GRE Guarantee: 15 bundles × 2 units per bundle	30 units
Total number of units to break even	75 units

Breakeven point in dollars for *GMAT Success* and *GRE Guarantee* is as follows:

GMAT Success: 45 units × $200 per unit	$ 9,000
GRE Guarantee: 30 units × $100 per unit	3,000
Breakeven revenues	$12,000

When there are multiple products, it is often convenient to use contribution margin percentage. Under this approach, Emma also calculates the revenues from selling a bundle of 3 units of *GMAT Success* and 2 units of *GRE Guarantee*:

	Number of Units of *GMAT Success* and *GRE Guarantee* in Each Bundle	Selling Price for *GMAT Success* and *GRE Guarantee*	Revenue of the Bundle
GMAT Success	3	$200	$600
GRE Guarantee	2	100	200
Total			$800

$$\text{Contribution margin percentage for the bundle} = \frac{\text{Contribution margin of the bundle}}{\text{Revenue of the bundle}} = \frac{\$300}{\$800} = 0.375, \text{ or } 37.5\%$$

$$\text{Breakeven revenues} = \frac{\text{Fixed costs}}{\text{Contribution margin \% for the bundle}} = \frac{\$4{,}500}{0.375} = \$12{,}000$$

$$\text{Number of bundles required to be sold to break even} = \frac{\text{Breakeven revenues}}{\text{Revenue per bundle}} = \frac{\$12{,}000}{\$800 \text{ per bundle}} = 15 \text{ bundles}$$

The breakeven point in units and dollars for *GMAT Success* and *GRE Guarantee* are as follows:

GMAT Success: 15 bundles × 3 units per bundle = 45 units × $200 per unit = $9,000
GRE Guarantee: 15 bundles × 2 units per bundle = 30 units × $100 per unit = $3,000

Recall that in all our calculations we have assumed that the budgeted sales mix (3 units of *GMAT Success* for every 2 units of *GRE Guarantee*) will not change at different levels of total unit sales.

Of course, there are many different sales mixes (in units) that result in a contribution margin of $4,500 and cause Emma to break even, as the following table shows:

Sales Mix (Units)		Contribution Margin from		
GMAT Success (1)	*GRE Guarantee* (2)	*GMAT Success* (3) = $80 × (1)	*GRE Guarantee* (4) = $30 × (2)	Total Contribution Margin (5) = (3) + (4)
48	22	$3,840	$ 660	$4,500
36	54	2,880	1,620	4,500
30	70	2,400	2,100	4,500

If for example, the sales mix changes to 3 units of *GMAT Success* for every 7 units of *GRE Guarantee*, the breakeven point increases from 75 units to 100 units, comprising 30 units of *GMAT Success* and 70 units of *GRE Guarantee*. The breakeven quantity increases because the sales mix has shifted toward the lower-contribution-margin product, *GRE Guarantee* ($30 per unit compared to *GMAT Success*'s $80 per unit). In general, for any given total quantity of units sold, as the sales mix shifts toward units with lower contribution margins (more units of *GRE Guarantee* compared to *GMAT Success*), operating income will be lower.

How do companies choose their sales mix? They adjust their mix to respond to demand changes. For example, as gasoline prices increase and customers want smaller cars, auto companies, such as Ford, Volkswagen, and Toyota, shift their production mix to produce smaller cars. This shift to smaller cars might result in an increase in the breakeven point because the sales mix has shifted toward lower contribution margin products. Despite this increase in the breakeven point, shifting the sales mix to smaller cars is the correct decision because the demand for larger cars has decreased. At no point should a manager focus on changing the sales mix to lower the breakeven point without taking into account customer preferences and demand. Of course, the shift in sales mix to smaller cars prompts managers at Ford, Volkswagen, and Toyota to take other actions such as reducing fixed costs and increasing contribution margins on smaller cars by charging higher prices for features that customers are willing to pay or lowering variable costs.

Emma's multiproduct case has two cost drivers, *GMAT Success* and *GRE Guarantee*. The multiproduct case shows how CVP and breakeven analysis can be adapted to the case of multiple cost drivers. The key point is that many different combinations of cost drivers can result in a given contribution margin.

Keys to Success

Managers adapt CVP analysis to the case of multiple products because the sales mix of products sold often remains unchanged as the total quantity of units sold changes.

CVP Analysis in Service and Not-for-Profit Organizations

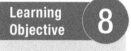

Learning Objective 8

Apply CVP analysis in service and not-for-profit organizations

. . . define appropriate output measures

So far, our CVP analysis has focused on a merchandising company. Managers can also apply CVP to decisions at manufacturing companies such as BMW, service companies such as Bank of America, and not-for-profit organizations such as the United Way. To apply CVP analysis in service and not-for-profit organizations, we need to focus on measuring their output, which is different from the tangible units sold by manufacturing and merchandising companies. Examples of output measures in various service and nonprofit industries are as follows:

Industry	Measure of Output
Airlines	Passenger miles
Hotels/motels	Room-nights occupied
Hospitals	Patient days
Universities	Student credit-hours

Consider an agency of the Oregon Department of Social Services, which has a $900,000 budget appropriation (its revenues) for 2013. This not-for-profit agency assists handicapped people seeking employment. On average, the agency supplements each person's income by $5,000 annually. The agency's only other costs are fixed costs of rent and administrative salaries equal to $270,000. The agency manager wants to know how many people could be assisted in 2013. We can use CVP analysis here by setting operating income to $0. Let Q be the number of handicapped people to be assisted:

$$\begin{aligned}
&\text{Revenues} - \text{Variable costs} - \text{Fixed costs} && = 0\\
&\$900{,}000 - \$5{,}000\,Q - \$270{,}000 && = 0\\
&\$5{,}000\,Q = \$900{,}000 - \$270{,}000 && = \$630{,}000\\
&Q = \$630{,}000 \div \$5{,}000 \text{ per person} && = 126 \text{ people}
\end{aligned}$$

Suppose the manager is concerned that the total budget appropriation for 2013 will be reduced by 15% to $900,000 × (1 − 0.15) = $765,000. The manager wants to know how many handicapped people could be assisted with this reduced budget. Assume the same amount of monetary assistance per person and the same fixed costs:

$$\$765{,}000 - \$5{,}000\,Q - \$270{,}000 = 0$$
$$\$5{,}000\,Q = \$765{,}000 - \$270{,}000 = \$495{,}000$$
$$Q = \$495{,}000 \div \$5{,}000 \text{ per person} = 99 \text{ people}$$

Note the following two characteristics of the CVP relationships in this nonprofit situation:

1. The percentage drop in the number of people assisted, (126 − 99) ÷ 126, or 21.4%, is greater than the 15% reduction in the budget appropriation. It is greater because the $270,000 in fixed costs still must be paid, leaving a proportionately lower budget to assist people. The percentage drop in service exceeds the percentage drop in budget appropriation.
2. Given the reduced budget appropriation (revenues) of $765,000, the manager can adjust operations to stay within this appropriation in one or more of three basic ways: (a) reduce the number of people assisted from the current 126, (b) reduce the variable cost (the extent of assistance per person) from the current $5,000 per person, or (c) reduce the total fixed costs from the current $270,000.

The description cost–volume–*profit* (CVP) analysis might suggest that CVP principles only apply to for-profit organizations. This section shows that CVP analysis can be adapted to service and not-for-profit organizations. The more general point is to always think about how the lessons learned in one industry and context can apply to another.

Learning Objective 9

Distinguish contribution margin

. . . revenues minus all variable costs

from gross margin

. . . revenues minus cost of goods sold

Contribution Margin Versus Gross Margin

So far, we have developed two important concepts relating to profit margin—contribution margin in this chapter and gross margin in Chapter 2. Is there a relationship between these two concepts? In the following equations, we clearly distinguish contribution margin, which provides information for CVP analysis, from gross margin, a measure of competitiveness, as defined in Chapter 2.

$$\text{Gross margin} = \text{Revenues} - \text{Cost of goods sold}$$
$$\text{Contribution margin} = \text{Revenues} - \text{All variable costs}$$

Gross margin measures how much a company can charge for its products over and above the cost of acquiring or producing them. Companies, such as branded pharmaceutical producers, have high gross margins because their products provide unique and distinctive benefits to consumers. Products such as televisions that operate in competitive markets have low gross margins. Contribution margin indicates how much of a company's revenues are available to cover fixed costs. It helps in assessing risk of loss. For example, the risk of loss is low if contribution margin exceeds fixed costs even when sales are low. Gross margin and contribution margin are related but give different insights. For example, a company operating in a competitive market with a low gross margin will have a low risk of loss if its fixed costs are small.

Consider the distinction between gross margin and contribution margin in the context of manufacturing companies. In the manufacturing sector, contribution margin and gross margin differ in two ways: fixed manufacturing costs and variable nonmanufacturing costs. The following example (figures assumed) illustrates this difference:

Contribution Income Statement Emphasizing Contribution Margin (in 000s)			Financial Accounting Income Statement Emphasizing Gross Margin (in 000s)	
Revenues		$1,000	Revenues	$1,000
Variable manufacturing costs	$250		Cost of goods sold (variable manufacturing costs, $250 + fixed manufacturing costs, $160)	410
Variable nonmanufacturing costs	270	520		
Contribution margin		480	Gross margin	590
Fixed manufacturing costs	160		Nonmanufacturing costs (variable, $270 + fixed, $138)	408
Fixed nonmanufacturing costs	138	298		
Operating income		$ 182	Operating income	$ 182

Fixed manufacturing costs of $160,000 are not deducted from revenues when computing contribution margin but are deducted when computing gross margin. Cost of goods sold in a manufacturing company includes all variable manufacturing costs and all fixed manufacturing costs ($250,000 + $160,000). Variable nonmanufacturing costs (such as commissions paid to salespersons) of $270,000 are deducted from revenues when computing contribution margin but are not deducted when computing gross margin.

Like contribution margin, gross margin can be expressed as a total, as an amount per unit, or as a percentage. For example, the **gross margin percentage** is the gross margin divided by revenues—59% ($590 ÷ $1,000) in our manufacturing-sector example.

One reason why managers may confuse gross margin and contribution margin with each other is that the two are often identical in the case of merchandising companies because cost of goods sold equals the variable cost of goods purchased (and subsequently sold).

Problem for Self-Study

Wembley Travel Agency specializes in flights between Los Angeles and London. It books passengers on United Airlines at $900 per round-trip ticket. Until last month, United paid Wembley a commission of 10% of the ticket price paid by each passenger. This commission was Wembley's only source of revenues. Wembley's fixed costs are $14,000 per month (for salaries, rent, etc.), and its variable costs, such as sales commissions and bonuses, are $20 per ticket purchased for a passenger.

United Airlines has just announced a revised payment schedule for all travel agents. It will now pay travel agents a 10% commission per ticket up to a maximum of $50. Any ticket costing more than $500 generates only a $50 commission, regardless of the ticket price. Wembley's managers are concerned about how United's new payment schedule will affect its breakeven point and profitability.

Required

1. Under the old 10% commission structure, how many round-trip tickets must Wembley sell each month (a) to break even and (b) to earn an operating income of $7,000?
2. How does United's revised payment schedule affect your answers to (a) and (b) in requirement 1?

Solution

1. Wembley receives a 10% commission on each ticket: 10% × $900 = $90. Thus,

Selling price = $90 per ticket
Variable cost per unit = $20 per ticket
Contribution margin per unit = $90 − $20 = $70 per ticket
Fixed costs = $14,000 per month

a. $$\text{Breakeven number of tickets} = \frac{\text{Fixed costs}}{\text{Contribution margin per unit}} = \frac{\$14{,}000}{\$70 \text{ per ticket}} = 200 \text{ tickets}$$

b. When target operating income = $7,000 per month,

$$\text{Quantity of tickets required to be sold} = \frac{\text{Fixed costs} + \text{Target operating income}}{\text{Contribution margin per unit}}$$

$$= \frac{\$14{,}000 + \$7{,}000}{\$70 \text{ per ticket}} = \frac{\$21{,}000}{\$70 \text{ per ticket}} = 300 \text{ tickets}$$

2. Under the new system, Wembley would receive only $50 on the $900 ticket. Thus,

Selling price = $50 per ticket
Variable cost per unit = $20 per ticket
Contribution margin per unit = $50 − $20 = $30 per ticket
Fixed costs = $14,000 per month

a. $\text{Breakeven number of tickets} = \dfrac{\$14{,}000}{\$30 \text{ per ticket}} = 467 \text{ tickets (rounded up)}$

b. $\text{Quantity of tickets required to be sold} = \dfrac{\$21{,}000}{\$30 \text{ per ticket}} = 700 \text{ tickets}$

The $50 cap on the commission paid per ticket causes the breakeven point to more than double (from 200 to 467 tickets) and the tickets required to be sold to earn $7,000 per month to also more than double (from 300 to 700 tickets). As would be expected, managers at Wembley reacted very negatively to the United Airlines announcement to change commission payments. Unfortunately for Wembley, other airlines also changed their commission structure in similar ways.

Decision Points

The following question-and-answer format summarizes the chapter's learning objectives. Each decision presents a key question related to a learning objective. The guidelines are the answer to that question.

Decision	Guidelines
1. How can CVP analysis assist managers?	CVP analysis assists managers in understanding the behavior of a product's or service's total costs, total revenues, and operating income as changes occur in the output level, selling price, variable costs, or fixed costs.
2. How can managers determine the breakeven point or the output needed to achieve a target operating income?	The breakeven point is the quantity of output at which total revenues equal total costs. The three methods for computing the breakeven point and the quantity of output to achieve target operating income are the equation method, the contribution margin method, and the graph method. Each method is merely a restatement of the others. Managers often select the method they find easiest to use in the specific decision situation.
3. How can managers incorporate income taxes into CVP analysis?	Income taxes can be incorporated into CVP analysis by using target net income to calculate the corresponding target operating income. The breakeven point is unaffected by income taxes because no income taxes are paid when operating income equals zero.
4. How do managers use CVP analysis to make decisions?	Managers compare how revenues, costs, and contribution margins change across various alternatives. They then choose the alternative that maximizes operating income.
5. What can managers do to cope with uncertainty or changes in underlying assumptions?	Sensitivity analysis, a "what-if" technique, examines how an outcome will change if the original predicted data are not achieved or if an underlying assumption changes. When making decisions, managers use CVP analysis to compare contribution margins and fixed costs under different assumptions. Managers also calculate the margin of safety equal to budgeted revenues minus breakeven revenues.
6. How should managers choose between different variable-cost/fixed-cost structures?	Choosing the variable-cost/fixed-cost structure is a strategic decision for companies. CVP analysis helps managers compare the risk of losses when revenues are low and the upside profits when revenues are high for different proportions of variable and fixed costs in a company's cost structure.
7. How can managers apply CVP analysis to a company producing multiple products?	Managers apply CVP analysis in a company producing multiple products by assuming the sales mix of products sold remains constant as the total quantity of units sold changes.

Decision	Guidelines
8. How do managers apply CVP analysis in service and non-profit organizations?	Managers define output measures such as passenger-miles in the case of airlines or patient-days in the context of hospitals and identify costs that are fixed and those that vary with these measures of output.
9. What is the difference between contribution margin and gross margin?	Contribution margin is revenues minus all variable costs whereas gross margin is revenues minus cost of goods sold. Contribution margin measures the risk of loss while gross margin measures the competitiveness of a product.

Appendix

Decision Models and Uncertainty[1]

This appendix explores the characteristics of uncertainty, describes an approach managers can use to make decisions in a world of uncertainty, and illustrates the insights gained when uncertainty is recognized in CVP analysis. In the face of uncertainty, managers rely on decision models to help them make the right choices.

Role of a Decision Model

Uncertainty is the possibility that an actual amount will deviate from an expected amount. In the *GMAT Success* example, Emma might forecast sales at 42 units, but actual sales might turn out to be 30 units or 60 units. A decision model helps managers deal with such uncertainty. It is a formal method for making a choice, commonly involving both quantitative and qualitative analyses. The quantitative analysis usually includes the following steps:

Step 1: Identify a choice criterion. A **choice criterion** is an objective that can be quantified, such as maximize income or minimize costs. Managers use the choice criterion to choose the best alternative action. Emma's choice criterion is to maximize expected operating income at the Chicago college fair.

Step 2: Identify the set of alternative actions that can be taken. We use the letter *a* with subscripts $_{1, 2,}$ and $_3$ to distinguish each of Emma's three possible actions:

a_1 = Pay \$2,000 fixed fee

a_2 = Pay \$800 fixed fee plus 15% of *GMAT Success* revenues

a_3 = Pay 25% of *GMAT Success* revenues with no fixed fee

Step 3: Identify the set of events that can occur. An **event** is a possible relevant occurrence, such as the actual number of *GMAT Success* packages Emma might sell at the fair. The set of events should be mutually exclusive and collectively exhaustive. Events are mutually exclusive if they cannot occur at the same time. Events are collectively exhaustive if, taken together, they make up the entire set of possible relevant occurrences (no other event can occur). Examples of mutually exclusive and collectively exhaustive events are growth, decline, or no change in industry demand, and increase, decrease, or no change in interest rates. Only one event out of the entire set of mutually exclusive and collectively exhaustive events will actually occur.

Suppose Emma's only uncertainty is the number of units of *GMAT Success* that she can sell. For simplicity, suppose Emma estimates that sales will be either 30 or 60 units. This set of events is mutually exclusive because clearly sales of 30 units and 60 units cannot both occur at the same time. It is collectively exhaustive because under our assumptions, sales cannot be anything other than 30 or 60 units. We use the letter *x* with subscripts $_1$ and $_2$ to distinguish the set of mutually exclusive and collectively exhaustive events:

x_1 = 30 units

x_2 = 60 units

[1] The presentation here draws (in part) from teaching notes prepared by R. Williamson.

Step 4: Assign a probability to each event that can occur. A **probability** is the likelihood or chance that an event will occur. The decision model approach to coping with uncertainty assigns probabilities to events. A **probability distribution** describes the likelihood, or the probability, that each of the mutually exclusive and collectively exhaustive set of events will occur. In some cases, there will be much evidence to guide the assignment of probabilities. For example, the probability of obtaining heads in the toss of a coin is 1/2 and that of drawing a particular playing card from a standard, well-shuffled deck is 1/52. In business, the probability of having a specified percentage of defective units may be assigned with great confidence on the basis of production experience with thousands of units. In other cases, there will be little evidence supporting estimated probabilities—for example, expected sales of a new pharmaceutical product next year.

Suppose that Emma, on the basis of past experience, assesses a 60% chance, or a 6/10 probability, that she will sell 30 units and a 40% chance, or a 4/10 probability, that she will sell 60 units. Using P(*x*) as the notation for the probability of an event, the probabilities are as follows:

$$P(x_1) = 6/10 = 0.60$$

$$P(x_2) = 4/10 = 0.40$$

The sum of these probabilities must equal 1.00 because these events are mutually exclusive and collectively exhaustive.

Step 5: Identify the set of possible outcomes. Outcomes specify, in terms of the choice criterion, the predicted economic results of the various possible combinations of actions and events. In the *GMAT Success* example, the outcomes are the six possible operating incomes displayed in the decision table in Exhibit 3-6. A **decision table** is a summary of the alternative actions, events, outcomes, and probabilities of events.

Distinguish among actions, events, and outcomes. Actions are decision choices available to managers—for example, the particular rental alternatives that Emma can choose. Events are the set of all relevant occurrences that can happen—for example, the different quantities of *GMAT Success* packages that may be sold at the fair. The outcome is operating income, which depends both on the action the manager selects (rental alternative chosen) and the event that occurs (the quantity of packages sold).

Exhibit 3-7 presents an overview of relationships among a decision model, the implementation of a chosen action, its outcome, and subsequent performance evaluation. Thoughtful managers step back and evaluate what happened and learn from their experiences. This learning serves as feedback for adapting the decision model for future actions.

Exhibit 3-6

Decision Table for *GMAT Success*

Home | Insert | Page Layout | Formulas | Data | Review | View

	A	B	C	D	E	F	G	H	I
1	Selling price =	$200			Outcomes: Operating Income				
2	Package cost =	$120			Under Each Possible Event				
3			Percentage						
4		Fixed	of Fair	Event x_1: Units Sold =	30		Event x_2: Units Sold =	60	
5	Actions	Fee	Revenues	Probability(x_1) =	0.60		Probability(x_2) =	0.40	
6	a_1: Pay $2,000 fixed fee	$2,000	0%	$400[l]			$2,800[m]		
7	a_2: Pay $800 fixed fee plus 15% of revenues	$ 800	15%	$700[n]			$2,200[p]		
8	a_3: Pay 25% of revenues with no fixed fee	$ 0	25%	$900[q]			$1,800[r]		
9									
10	[l]Operating income = ($200 – $120)(30) – $2,000	=	$ 400						
11	[m]Operating income = ($200 – $120)(60) – $2,000	=	$2,800						
12	[n]Operating income = ($200 – $120 – 15% × $200)(30) – $800	=	$ 700						
13	[p]Operating income = ($200 – $120 – 15% × $200)(60) – $800	=	$2,200						
14	[q]Operating income = ($200 – $120 – 25% × $200)(30)	=	$ 900						
15	[r]Operating income = ($200 – $120 – 25% × $200)(60)	=	$1,800						

Exhibit 3-7

A Decision Model and Its Link to Performance Evaluation

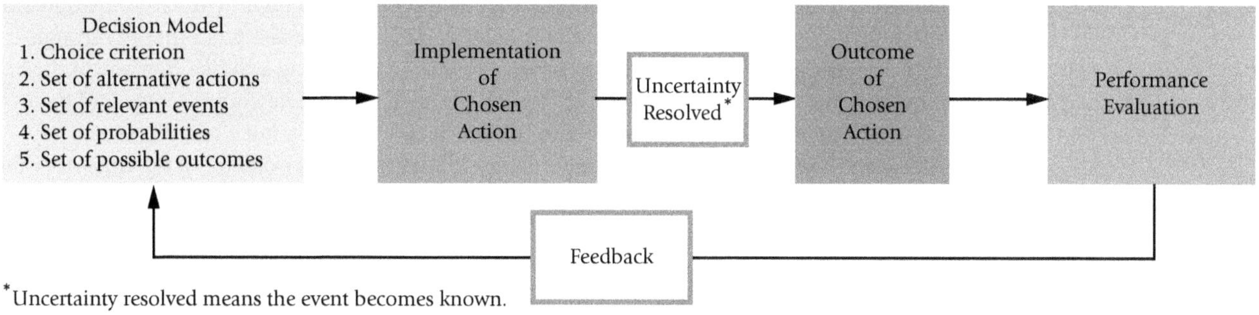

*Uncertainty resolved means the event becomes known.

Expected Value

An **expected value** is the weighted average of the outcomes, with the probability of each outcome serving as the weight. When the outcomes are measured in monetary terms, expected value is often called **expected monetary value.** Using information in Exhibit 3-6, the expected monetary value of each booth-rental alternative denoted by $E(a_1)$, $E(a_2)$, and $E(a_3)$ is as follows:

Pay $2,000 fixed fee:	$E(a_1) = (0.60 \times \$400) + (0.40 \times \$2{,}800) = \$1{,}360$
Pay $800 fixed fee plus 15% of revenues:	$E(a_2) = (0.60 \times \$700) + (0.40 \times \$2{,}200) = \$1{,}300$
Pay 25% of revenues with no fixed fee:	$E(a_3) = (0.60 \times \$900) + (0.40 \times \$1{,}800) = \$1{,}260$

To maximize expected operating income, Emma should select action a_1—pay the fair organizers a $2,000 fixed fee.

To interpret the expected value of selecting action a_1, imagine that Emma attends many fairs, each with the probability distribution of operating incomes given in Exhibit 3-6. For a specific fair, Emma will earn operating income of either $400, if she sells 30 units, or $2,800, if she sells 60 units. But if Emma attends 100 fairs, she will expect to earn $400 operating income 60% of the time (at 60 fairs), and $2,800 operating income 40% of the time (at 40 fairs), for a total operating income of $136,000 ($\$400 \times 60 + \$2{,}800 \times 40$). The expected value of $1,360 is the operating income per fair that Emma will earn when averaged across all fairs ($\$136{,}000 \div 100$). Of course, in many real-world situations, managers must make one-time decisions under uncertainty. Even in these cases, expected value is a useful tool for choosing among alternatives.

Consider the effect of uncertainty on the preferred action choice. If Emma were certain she would sell only 30 units (that is, $P(x_1) = 1$), she would prefer alternative a_3—pay 25% of revenues with no fixed fee. To follow this reasoning, examine Exhibit 3-6. When 30 units are sold, alternative a_3 yields the maximum operating income of $900. Because fixed costs are $0, booth-rental costs are lower, equal to $1,500 (25% of revenues $= 0.25 \times \$200$ per unit $\times$ 30 units), when sales are low.

However, if Emma were certain she would sell 60 packages (that is, $P(x_2) = 1$), she would prefer alternative a_1—pay a $2,000 fixed fee. Exhibit 3-6 indicates that when 60 units are sold, alternative a_1 yields the maximum operating income of $2,800. That's because, when 60 units are sold, rental payments under a_2 ($\$800 + 0.15 \times \$200$ per unit $\times$ 60 units $= \$2{,}600$) and a_3 ($0.25 \times \$200$ per unit $\times$ 60 units $= \$3{,}000$) are more than the fixed $2,000 fee under a_1.

Despite the high probability of selling only 30 units, Emma still prefers to take action a_1, which is to pay a fixed fee of $2,000. That's because the high risk of low operating income (the 60% probability of selling only 30 units) is more than offset by the high return from selling 60 units, which has a 40% probability. If Emma were more averse to risk (measured in our example by the difference between operating incomes when 30 vs. 60 units are sold), she might have preferred action a_2 or a_3. For example, action a_2 ensures an operating income of at least $700, greater than the operating income of $400 that she would earn under action a_1 if only 30 units were sold. Of course, choosing a_2 limits the upside potential to $2,200 relative to $2,800 under a_1, if 60 units are sold. If Emma is very concerned about downside risk, however, she may be willing to forgo some upside benefits to protect against a $400 outcome by choosing a_2.[2]

[2] For more formal approaches, refer to Moore, J., and L. Weatherford, *Decision modeling with Microsoft Excel*, 6th ed. (Upper Saddle River, NJ: Prentice Hall, 2001).

Good Decisions and Good Outcomes

Always distinguish between a good decision and a good outcome. One can exist without the other. Suppose you are offered a one-time-only gamble tossing a coin. You will win $20 if the outcome is heads, but you will lose $1 if the outcome is tails. As a decision maker, you proceed through the logical phases: gathering information, assessing outcomes, and making a choice. You accept the bet. Why? Because the expected value is $9.50 [0.5($20) + 0.5(−$1)]. The coin is tossed and the outcome is tails. You lose. From your viewpoint, this was a good decision but a bad outcome.

A decision can be made only on the basis of information that is available at the time of evaluating and making the decision. By definition, uncertainty rules out guaranteeing that the best outcome will always be obtained. As in our example, it is possible that bad luck will produce bad outcomes even when good decisions have been made. A bad outcome does not mean a bad decision was made. The best protection against a bad outcome is a good decision.

Terms to Learn

This chapter and the Glossary at the end of the book contain definitions of the following important terms:

breakeven point (BEP) (p. 82)
choice criterion (p. 99)
contribution income statement (p. 78)
contribution margin (p. 78)
contribution margin per unit (p. 78)
contribution margin percentage (p. 79)
contribution margin ratio (p. 79)
cost–volume–profit (CVP) analysis (p. 77)
decision table (p. 100)
degree of operating leverage (p. 91)
event (p. 99)
expected monetary value (p. 101)
expected value (p. 101)
gross margin percentage (p. 97)
margin of safety (p. 89)
net income (p. 85)
operating leverage (p. 91)
outcomes (p. 100)
probability (p. 100)
probability distribution (p. 100)
PV graph (p. 84)
revenue driver (p. 82)
sales mix (p. 92)
sensitivity analysis (p. 87)
uncertainty (p. 90)

Assignment Material

Note: To underscore the basic CVP relationships, the assignment material ignores income taxes unless stated otherwise.

Questions

3-1 Describe the assumptions underlying CVP analysis.

3-2 Describe three methods that managers can use to express CVP relationships.

3-3 Why is it more accurate to describe the subject matter of this chapter as CVP analysis rather than as breakeven analysis?

3-4 "CVP analysis is both simple and simplistic. If you want realistic analysis to underpin your decisions, look beyond CVP analysis." Do you agree? Explain.

3-5 Describe sensitivity analysis. How has the advent of the electronic spreadsheet affected the use of sensitivity analysis?

3-6 Give an example of how a manager can decrease variable costs while increasing fixed costs.

3-7 Give an example of how a manager can increase variable costs while decreasing fixed costs.

3-8 What is operating leverage? How is knowing the degree of operating leverage helpful to managers?

3-9 "There is no such thing as a fixed cost. All costs can be 'unfixed' given sufficient time." Do you agree? What is the implication of your answer for CVP analysis?

3-10 "In CVP analysis, gross margin is a less-useful concept than contribution margin." Do you agree? Explain briefly.

Exercises

3-11 CVP computations. Fill in the blanks for each of the following independent cases.

Case	Revenues	Variable Costs	Fixed Costs	Total Costs	Operating Income	Contribution Margin Percentage
a.		$800		$1,000	$1,500	
b.	$2,000		$200		$ 300	
c.	$ 500	$300		$ 500		
d.	$1,600		$200			75%

3-12 CVP exercises. The Delightful Donut owns and operates six doughnut outlets in and around Kansas City. You are given the following corporate budget data for next year:

Revenues	$10,500,000
Fixed costs	$ 1,400,000
Variable costs	$ 7,700,000

Variable costs change based on the number of doughnuts sold.

Required

Compute the budgeted operating income for each of the following deviations from the original budget data. (Consider each case independently.)

1. A 9% increase in contribution margin, holding revenues constant.
2. A 9% decrease in contribution margin, holding revenues constant.
3. A 3% increase in fixed costs.
4. A 3% decrease in fixed costs.
5. A 7% increase in units sold.
6. A 7% decrease in units sold.
7. A 9% increase in fixed costs and a 9% increase in units sold.
8. A 3% increase in fixed costs and a 3% decrease in variable costs.

Which of these alternatives yields the highest budgeted operating income? Explain why this is the case.

3-13 CVP exercises. The Brewer Company manufactures and sells pens. Currently, 5,400,000 units are sold per year at $0.60 per unit. Fixed costs are $860,000 per year. Variable costs are $0.40 per unit. Consider each case separately:

Required

1a. What is the current annual operating income?

1b. What is the present breakeven point in revenues?

Compute the new operating income for each of the following changes:

2. A $0.06 per unit increase in variable costs.
3. A 20% increase in fixed costs and a 20% increase in units sold.
4. A 40% decrease in fixed costs, a 40% decrease in selling price, a 30% decrease in variable cost per unit, and a 35% increase in units sold.

Compute the new breakeven point in units for each of the following changes:

5. A 20% increase in fixed costs
6. A 20% increase in selling price and a $20,000 increase in fixed costs

3-14 CVP analysis, income taxes. Diego Motors is a small car dealership. On average, it sells a car for $30,000, which it purchases from the manufacturer for $26,000. Each month, Diego Motors pays $55,000 in rent and utilities and $75,000 for salespeople's salaries. In addition to their salaries, salespeople are paid a commission of $800 for each car they sell. Diego Motors also spends $14,000 each month for local advertisements. Its tax rate is 40%.

Required

1. How many cars must Diego Motors sell each month to break even?
2. Diego Motors has a target monthly net income of $59,520. What is its target monthly operating income? How many cars must the company sell each month to reach the target monthly net income of $59,520?

3-15 CVP analysis, sensitivity analysis. Tomas King is a new author for SingleDay Publishing. SingleDay Publishing is negotiating to publish Tomas's new book, which promises to be an instant best-seller. The fixed costs of producing and marketing the book will be $575,000. The variable costs of producing and marketing will be $4.50 per copy sold. These costs are before any payments to Tomas. Tomas negotiates an up-front payment of $2.5 million, plus a 10% royalty rate on the net sales price of each book. The net sales price is the listed bookstore price of $35, minus the margin paid to the bookstore to sell the book. The normal bookstore margin of 30% of the listed bookstore price is expected to apply.

Required

1. Prepare a PV graph for SingleDay Publishing.
2. How many copies must SingleDay Publishing sell to (a) break even and (b) earn a target operating income of $850,000?
3. Examine the sensitivity of the breakeven point to the following changes:
   a. Increasing the royalty rate to 12% of the net sales price of each book.
   b. Increasing the listed bookstore price to $40 while keeping the royalty rate at 10%.
   c. Comment on the results and indicate which option you would prefer and why, indicating clearly any assumptions that you have made.

3-16 CVP analysis, margin of safety. Suppose McKnight Corp.'s breakeven point is revenues of $1,500,000. Fixed costs are $720,000.

Required

1. Compute the contribution margin percentage.
2. Compute the selling price if variable costs are $13 per unit.
3. Suppose 85,000 units are sold. Compute the margin of safety in units and dollars.
4. What does this tell you about the risk of McKnight making a loss? What are the most likely reasons for this risk to increase?

3-17 Operating leverage. Curt Rugs is holding a two-week carpet sale at Josh's Club, a local warehouse store. Curt Rugs plans to sell carpets for $850 each. The company will purchase the carpets from a local distributor for $340 each, with the privilege of returning any unsold units for a full refund. Josh's Club has offered Curt Rugs two payment alternatives for the use of space.

- Option 1: A fixed payment of $18,870 for the sale period
- Option 2: 20% of total revenues earned during the sale period

Assume Curt Rugs will incur no other costs.

Required

1. Calculate the breakeven point in units for (a) option 1 and (b) option 2.
2. At what level of revenues will Curt Rugs earn the same operating income under either option?
   a. For what range of unit sales will Curt Rugs prefer Option 1?
   b. For what range of unit sales will Curt Rugs prefer Option 2?
3. Calculate the degree of operating leverage at sales of 185 units for the two rental options.
4. Briefly explain and interpret your answer to requirement 3.

3-18 Sales mix, new and upgrade customers. Record 1-2-3 is a top-selling electronic spreadsheet product. Record is about to release version 5.0. It divides its customers into two groups: new customers and upgrade customers (those who previously purchased Record 1-2-3, 4.0 or earlier versions). Although the same physical product is provided to each customer group, sizable differences exist in selling prices and variable marketing costs:

	New Customers		Upgrade Customers	
Selling price		$195		$115
Variable costs				
Manufacturing	$15		$15	
Marketing	50	65	20	35
Contribution margin		$130		$ 80

The fixed costs of Record 1-2-3, 5.0 are $16,500,000. The planned sales mix in units is 60% new customers and 40% upgrade customers.

Required

1. What is the Record 1-2-3, 5.0 breakeven point in units, assuming that the planned 60%:40% sales mix is attained?
2. If the sales mix is attained, what is the operating income when 220,000 total units are sold?
3. Show how the breakeven point in units changes with the following customer mixes:
   a. New 40% and Upgrade 60%
   b. New 80% and Upgrade 20%
   c. Comment on the results.

3-19 Sales mix, three products. The Janowski Company has three product lines of belts—A, B, and C—with contribution margins of $5, $4, and $3, respectively. The president foresees sales of 168,000 units in the coming period, consisting of 24,000 units of A, 96,000 units of B, and 48,000 units of C. The company's fixed costs for the period are $405,000.

Required

1. What is the company's breakeven point in units, assuming that the given sales mix is maintained?
2. If the sales mix is maintained, what is the total contribution margin when 168,000 units are sold? What is the operating income?
3. What would operating income be if the company sold 24,000 units of A, 48,000 units of B, and 96,000 units of C? What is the new breakeven point in units if these relationships persist in the next period?
4. Comparing the breakeven points in requirements 1 and 3, is it always better for a company to choose the sales mix that yields the lower breakeven point? Explain.

3-20 CVP, Not-for-profit. Madison Classical Music Society is a not-for-profit organization that brings guest artists to the community's greater metropolitan area. The Music Society just bought a small concert hall in the center of town to house its performances. The lease payments on the concert hall are expected to be $4,000 per month. The organization pays its guest performers $1,500 per concert and anticipates corresponding ticket sales to be $4,500 per event. The Music Society also incurs costs of approximately $1,600 per concert for marketing and advertising. The organization pays its artistic director $30,000 per year and expects to receive $29,000 per year in donations in addition to its ticket sales.

Required

1. If the Madison Classical Music Society just breaks even, how many concerts does it hold each year?
2. In addition to the organization's artistic director, the Music Society would like to hire a marketing director for $28,000 per year. What is the breakeven point? The Music Society anticipates that the addition of a marketing director would allow the organization to increase the number of concerts to 53 per year. What is the Music Society's operating income/(loss) if it hires the new marketing director?
3. The Music Society expects to receive a grant that would provide the organization with an additional $14,000 toward the payment of the marketing director's salary. What is the breakeven point if the Music Society hires the marketing director and receives the grant?

3-21 Contribution margin, decision making. Wharton Men's Clothing's revenues and cost data for 2012 are as follows:

Revenues		$500,000
Cost of goods sold		200,000
Gross margin		300,000
Operating costs:		
Salaries fixed	$190,000	
Sales commissions (11% of sales)	55,000	
Depreciation of equipment and fixtures	14,000	
Store rent ($5,000 per month)	60,000	
Other operating costs	35,000	354,000
Operating income (loss)		$ (54,000)

Mr. Wharton, the owner of the store, is unhappy with the operating results. An analysis of other operating costs reveals that it includes $25,000 variable costs, which vary with sales volume, and $10,000 fixed costs.

Required

1. Compute the contribution margin of Wharton Men's Clothing.
2. Compute the contribution margin percentage.
3. Mr. Wharton estimates that he can increase revenues by 25% by incurring additional advertising costs of $15,000. Calculate the impact of the additional advertising costs on operating income.
4. What other actions can Mr. Wharton take to improve operating income?

3-22 Contribution margin, gross margin, and margin of safety. Sweet Aroma manufactures and sells scented oils to small specialty stores in the greater Dallas area. It presents the monthly operating income statement shown here to Hal Shaw, a potential investor in the business. Help Mr. Shaw understand Sweet Aroma's cost structure.

Sweet Aroma		
Operating Income Statement, November 2012		
Units sold		8,000
Revenues		$64,000
Cost of goods sold		
Variable manufacturing costs	$43,200	
Fixed manufacturing costs	12,000	
Total		55,200
Gross margin		8,800
Operating costs		
Variable marketing costs	$ 1,600	
Fixed marketing and administration costs	3,000	
Total operating costs		4,600
Operating income		$ 4,200

Required

1. Recast the income statement to emphasize contribution margin.
2. Calculate the contribution margin percentage and breakeven point in units and revenues for November 2012.
3. What is the margin of safety (in units) for November 2012?
4. If sales in November were only 7,500 units and Sweet Aroma's tax rate is 30%, calculate its net income.

3-23 Uncertainty and expected costs. (Appendix) Dawmart Corp., an international retail giant, is considering implementing a new business-to-business (B2B) information system for processing purchase orders. The current system costs Dawmart $1,000,000 per month and $45 per order. Dawmart has two options, a partially automated B2B and a fully automated B2B system. The partially automated B2B system will have a fixed cost of $11,000,000 per month and a variable cost of $25 per order. The fully automated B2B system has a fixed cost of $19,000,000 per month and $10 per order.

Based on data from the last 2 years, Dawmart has determined the following distribution on monthly orders:

Monthly Number of Orders	Probability
400,000	0.10
500,000	0.25
600,000	0.45
700,000	0.15
800,000	0.05

Required

1. Prepare a table showing the cost of each plan for each quantity of monthly orders.
2. What is the expected cost of each plan? Which plan would you recommend? Explain.
3. In addition to the information system costs, what other factors should Dawmart consider before deciding to implement a new B2B system?

Problems

3-24 CVP analysis, service firm. Outback Escapes generates revenue of $7,500 per person on its five-day package tours to wildlife parks in Kenya. The variable costs per person are as follows:

Airfare	$1,600
Hotel accommodations	3,100
Meals	600
Ground transportation	300
Park tickets and other costs	700
Total	$6,300

Annual fixed costs total $570,000.

Required

1. Calculate the number of package tours that must be sold to break even.
2. Calculate the revenue needed to earn a target operating income of $102,000.
3. If fixed costs increase by $19,000, what decrease in variable cost per person must be achieved to maintain the breakeven point calculated in requirement 1?
4. The general manager at Outback Escapes proposes to increase the price of the package tour to $8,200 to decrease the breakeven point. Using information in the original problem, calculate the new breakeven point. What factors should the general manager consider before deciding to increase the price of the package tour?

3-25 CVP analysis, margin of safety. (CMA, adapted) Creative Solutions sells office-organizing units for small businesses. The current selling price per unit is $320. Operating income for 2012 is $400,000 based on a sales volume of 12,000 units. Variable costs of producing the units are $100 per unit sold plus an additional cost of $20 per unit for shipping and handling. Creative Solutions' annual fixed costs are $2,000,000.

Required

1. Calculate Creative Solutions' breakeven point and margin of safety in units in 2012.
2. In 2013, management expects that the variable production cost per unit of the office-organizing units will increase by 20%, but the shipping and handling costs per unit will decrease by 10%. Calculate the Creative Solutions operating income in 2013 if the selling price remains unchanged, assuming all other data as in the original problem.
3. Under the assumptions made in requirement 2, calculate the margin of safety in units. As a manager, would you be concerned? What actions, if any, might you consider taking in response and why?
4. Under the assumptions made in requirement 2, how many units must Creative Solutions sell to earn the same operating income as in 2012?

3-26 CVP analysis, income taxes. (CMA, adapted) J.T. Lu and Company, a manufacturer of quality handmade walnut bowls, has had a steady growth in sales for the past 5 years. However, increased competition has led Mr. Lu, the president, to believe that an aggressive marketing campaign will be necessary next year to maintain the company's present growth. To prepare for next year's marketing campaign, the company's controller has prepared and presented Mr. Lu with the following data for the current year, 2012:

Variable cost (per bowl)	
Direct materials	$ 3.75
Direct manufacturing labor	8.50
Variable overhead (manufacturing, marketing, distribution, and customer service)	1.25
Total variable cost per bowl	$ 13.50
Fixed costs	
Manufacturing	$ 14,000
Marketing, distribution, and customer service	133,000
Total fixed costs	$147,000
Selling price	24.00
Expected sales, 20,000 units	$480,000
Income tax rate	40%

Required

1. What is the projected net income for 2012?
2. What is the breakeven point in units for 2012?
3. Mr. Lu has set the revenue target for 2013 at a level of $540,000 (or 22,500 bowls). He believes an additional marketing cost of $10,500 for advertising in 2013, with all other costs remaining constant, will be

necessary to attain the revenue target. What is the net income for 2013 if the additional $10,500 is spent and the revenue target is met?

4. What is the breakeven point in revenues for 2013 if the additional $10,500 is spent for advertising?
5. If the additional $10,500 is spent, what are the required 2013 revenues for 2013 net income to equal 2012 net income?
6. At a sales level of 22,500 units, what maximum amount can be spent on advertising if a 2013 net income of $47,100 is desired?

3-27 CVP, sensitivity analysis. The Derby Shoe Company produces its famous shoe, the Divine Loafer, which sells for $70 per pair. Operating income for 2012 is as follows:

Sales revenue ($70 per pair)	$280,000
Variable cost ($30 per pair)	120,000
Contribution margin	160,000
Fixed cost	80,000
Operating income	$ 80,000

Derby Shoe Company would like to increase its profitability over the next year by at least 25%. To do so, the company is considering the following options:

1. Replace a portion of its variable labor with an automated machining process. This would result in a 15% decrease in variable cost per unit, but a 10% increase in fixed costs. Sales would remain the same.
2. Spend $20,000 on a new advertising campaign, which would increase sales by 40%.
3. Increase both selling price by $10 per unit and variable costs by $8 per unit by using a higher quality leather material in the production of its shoes. The higher priced shoe would cause demand to drop by 15%.
4. Add a second manufacturing facility, which would double Derby's fixed costs but would increase sales by 60%.

Required Evaluate each of the alternatives considered by Derby Shoes. Do any of the options meet or exceed Derby's targeted increase in income of 25%? What should Derby do?

3-28 CVP analysis, clothing stores. The Dress4Less Company operates a chain of men's clothing stores that sells 10 different styles of inexpensive men's suits with identical unit costs and selling prices. A unit is defined as one suit. Each store has a manager who is paid a fixed salary. Individual salespeople receive a fixed salary and a sales commission. Dress4Less is considering opening another store that is expected to have the revenue and cost relationships shown here:

Unit Variable Data (per suit)		Annual Fixed Costs	
Selling price	$160.00	Rent	$ 45,000
Cost of suits	$120.00	Salaries	200,000
Sales commission	8.00	Advertising	50,000
Variable cost per unit	$128.00	Other fixed costs	25,000
		Total fixed costs	$320,000

Consider each question independently:

Required

1. What is the annual breakeven point in (a) units sold and (b) revenues?
2. If 8,000 units are sold, what will be the store's operating income (loss)?
3. If sales commissions are discontinued and fixed salaries are raised by a total of $90,000, what would be the annual breakeven point in (a) units sold and (b) revenues?
4. Refer to the original data. If, in addition to his fixed salary, the store manager is paid a commission of $0.75 per unit sold, what would be the annual breakeven point in (a) units sold and (b) revenues?
5. Refer to the original data. If, in addition to his fixed salary, the store manager is paid a commission of $0.75 *per unit in excess of the breakeven point*, what would be the store's operating income if 15,000 units were sold?

3-29 CVP analysis, shoe stores (continuation of 3-28). Refer to requirement 3 of Problem 3-28. In this problem, assume the role of the owner of Dress4Less.

Required

1. Calculate the number of units sold at which the owner of Dress4Less would be indifferent between the original salary-plus-commissions plan for salespeople and the higher fixed-salaries-only plan.
2. As owner, which sales compensation plan would you choose if forecasted annual sales of the new store were at least 12,000 units? What do you think of the motivational effect on sales of your chosen compensation plan?
3. Suppose the target operating income is $180,000. How many units must be sold to reach the target operating income under (a) the original salary-plus-commissions plan and (b) the higher-fixed-salaries-only plan? Which method would you prefer? Explain briefly.
4. You open the new store on January 1, 2013, with the original salary-plus-commission compensation plan in place. Because you expect the cost of the suits to rise due to inflation, you place a firm bulk order for 20,000 suits and lock in the $120.00 price per unit. But, toward the end of the year, only 18,000 suits are sold, and you authorize a markdown of the remaining inventory to $100 per unit. Finally, all units are sold. Salespeople, as usual, get paid a commission of 5% of revenues. What is the annual operating income for the store?

3-30 Alternate cost structures, uncertainty, and sensitivity analysis. Integral Printing Company currently leases its only copy machine for $1,200 a month. The company is considering replacing this leasing agreement with a new contract that is entirely commission based. Under the new agreement, Integral would pay a commission for its printing at a rate of $20 for every 500 pages printed. The company currently charges $0.15 per page to its customers. The paper used in printing costs the company $0.04 per page and other variable costs, including hourly labor, amount to $0.05 per page.

Required

1. What is the company's breakeven point under the current leasing agreement? What is it under the new commission-based agreement?
2. For what range of sales levels will Integral prefer, (a) the fixed lease agreement or (b) the commission agreement?
3. Do this question only if you have covered the chapter appendix in your class. Integral estimates that the company is equally likely to sell 20,000; 30,000; 40,000; 50,000; 60,000 pages of print. Using information from the original problem, prepare a table that shows the expected profit at each sales level under the fixed leasing agreement and under the commission-based agreement. What is the expected value of each agreement? Which agreement should Integral choose?

3-31 CVP, alternative cost structures. Crabapple Phones has just opened its doors. The new retail store sells refurbished phones at a significant discount from market prices. The phones cost Crabapple $55 to purchase and require additional variable costs of $45, which includes labor for refurbishing of $35 and wages for sales personnel of $10. The newly refurbished phones are resold to customers for $150. Rent on the retail store costs the company $5,000 per month.

Required

1. How many phones does Crabapple have to sell each month to break even?
2. If Crabapple wants to earn $4,000 per month after all expenses, how many phones does the company need to sell?
3. Crabapple can purchase already refurbished phones for $77.50. This would mean that all labor required to refurbish the phones could be eliminated. What would Crabapple's new breakeven point be if it decided to purchase the phones already refurbished?
4. Instead of paying the monthly rental fee for the retail space, Crabapple has the option of paying its landlord a 20% commission on sales. Assuming the original facts in the problem, at what sales level would Crabapple be indifferent between paying a fixed amount of monthly rent and paying a 20% commission on sales?
5. What factors would you consider in deciding whether Crabapple should pay the monthly rental fee or the commission on sales?

3-32 CVP analysis, income taxes, sensitivity. (CMA, adapted) Skudder Inc. sells blades that attach to garden tractors. For its 2013 budget, Skudder estimates the following:

Selling price	$ 750
Variable cost per engine	$ 350
Annual fixed costs	$750,000
Net income	$150,000
Income tax rate	25%

The first-quarter income statement, as of March 31, reported that sales were not meeting expectations. During the first quarter, only 500 units had been sold at the current price of $750. The income statement showed that variable and fixed costs were as planned, which meant that the 2013 annual net income projection would not be met unless management took action. A management committee was formed and presented the following mutually exclusive alternatives to the president:

a. Reduce the selling price by 20%. The sales organization forecasts that at this significantly reduced price, 2,800 units can be sold during the remainder of the year. Total fixed costs and variable cost per unit will stay as budgeted.

b. Lower variable cost per unit by $15 through the use of less-expensive direct materials. The selling price will also be reduced by $100, and sales of 2,300 units are expected for the remainder of the year.

c. Reduce fixed costs by 20% and lower the selling price by 10%. Variable cost per unit will be unchanged. Sales of 2,100 units are expected for the remainder of the year.

Required

1. If no changes are made to the selling price or cost structure, determine the number of units that Skudder must sell (a) to break even and (b) to achieve its net income objective.
2. Determine which alternative Skudder should select to achieve its net income objective. Show your calculations.

3-33 Choosing between compensation plans, operating leverage. (CMA, adapted) Diem Corporation manufactures fertilizer products that are sold through a network of external sales agents. The agents are paid a commission of 20% of revenues. Diem is considering replacing the sales agents with its own salespeople, who would be paid a commission of 15% of revenues and total salaries of $1,750,000. The income statement for the year ending December 31, 2012, under the two scenarios is shown here.

Diem Corporation Income Statement				
For the Year Ended December 31, 2012				
	Using Sales Agents		Using Own Sales Force	
Revenues		$35,000,000		$35,000,000
Cost of goods sold				
Variable	$19,250,000		$19,250,000	
Fixed	4,750,000	24,000,000	4,750,000	24,000,000
Gross margin		11,000,000		11,000,000
Marketing costs				
Commissions	7,000,000		5,250,000	
Fixed	1,450,000	8,450,000	3,200,000	8,450,000
Operating income		$ 2,550,000		$ 2,550,000

Required

1. Calculate Diem's 2012 contribution margin percentage, breakeven revenues, and degree of operating leverage under the two scenarios.
2. Describe the advantages and disadvantages of each type of sales alternative.
3. In 2013, Diem uses its own salespeople, who demand an 18% commission. If all other cost behavior patterns are unchanged, how much revenue must the salespeople generate in order to earn the same operating income as in 2012?

3-34 Multiproduct CVP and decision making. JumpUP Inc. produces two types of trampolines. One is smaller and is primarily used in gyms for exercise classes. The other is a larger model designed for recreational use.

The smaller trampoline sells for $200 and has variable costs of $120.

The larger trampoline sells for $600 and has variable costs of $420.

JumpUP sells four smaller models for every one larger model sold. Fixed costs equal $1,250,000.

Required

1. What is the breakeven point in unit sales and dollars for each type of trampoline at the current sales mix?

2. JumpUP is considering buying new production equipment. The new equipment will increase fixed cost by $202,000 per year and will decrease the variable cost of the small and large trampolines by $15 and $45, respectively. Assuming the same sales mix, how many of each type of trampoline does JumpUP need to sell to break even?
3. Assuming the same sales mix, at what total sales level would JumpUP be indifferent between using the old equipment and buying the new production equipment? If total sales are expected to be 13,000 units, should JumpUP buy the new production equipment?

3-35 Sales mix, two products. The Wharton Company retails two products: a standard and a deluxe version of a luggage carrier. The budgeted income statement for next period is as follows:

	Standard Carrier	Deluxe Carrier	Total
Units sold	180,000	60,000	240,000
Revenues at $30 and $38 per unit	$5,400,000	$2,280,000	$7,680,000
Variable costs at $24 and $28 per unit	4,320,000	1,680,000	6,000,000
Contribution margins at $6 and $10 per unit	$1,080,000	$ 600,000	1,680,000
Fixed costs			1,050,000
Operating income			$ 630,000

Required

1. Compute the breakeven point in units, assuming that the company achieves its planned sales mix.
2. Compute the breakeven point in units (a) if only standard carriers are sold and (b) if only deluxe carriers are sold.
3. Suppose 240,000 units are sold but only 40,000 of them are deluxe. Compute the operating income. Compute the breakeven point in units. Compare your answer with the answer to requirement 1. What is the major lesson of this problem?

3-36 Ethics, CVP analysis. Freddie Corporation produces a molded plastic casing, LX201, for desktop computers. Summary data from its 2012 income statement are as follows:

Revenues	$3,000,000
Variable costs	2,100,000
Fixed costs	1,050,000
Operating income	$ (150,000)

Terra Foreman, Freddie's president, is very concerned about Freddie Corporation's poor profitability. She asks Julian Vang, production manager, and Seth Madden, controller, to see if there are ways to reduce costs.

After 2 weeks, Julian returns with a proposal to reduce variable costs to 58% of revenues by reducing the costs Freddie currently incurs for safe disposal of wasted plastic. Seth is concerned that this would expose the company to potential environmental liabilities. He tells Julian, "We would need to estimate some of these potential environmental costs and include them in our analysis." "You can't do that," Julian replies. "We are not violating any laws. There is some possibility that we may have to incur environmental costs in the future, but if we bring it up now, this proposal will not go through because our senior management always assumes these costs to be larger than they turn out to be. The market is very tough, and we are in danger of shutting down the company, costing all of us our jobs. The only reason our competitors are making money is because they are doing exactly what I am proposing."

Required

1. Calculate Freddie Corporation's breakeven revenues for 2012.
2. Calculate Freddie Corporation's breakeven revenues if variable costs are 58% of revenues.
3. Calculate Freddie Corporation's operating income for 2012 if variable costs had been 58% of revenues.
4. Given Julian Vang's comments, what should Seth Madden do?

3-37 Deciding where to produce. (CMA, adapted) Portal Corporation produces the same laser printer in two Utah plants, a new plant in Ogden and an older plant in Sandy. The following data are available for the two plants:

	Ogden		Sandy	
Selling price		$ 320.00		$ 320.00
Variable manufacturing cost per unit	$95.00		$110.00	
Fixed manufacturing cost per unit	48.00		24.00	
Variable marketing and distribution cost per unit	15.00		15.00	
Fixed marketing and distribution cost per unit	22.00		15.00	
Total cost per unit		180.00		164.00
Operating income per unit		$ 140.00		$ 156.00
Production rate per day	250 units		200 units	
Normal annual capacity usage	240 days		240 days	
Maximum annual capacity	300 days		300 days	

All fixed costs per unit are calculated based on a normal capacity usage consisting of 240 working days. When the number of working days exceeds 240, overtime charges raise the variable manufacturing costs of additional units by $5.00 per unit in Ogden and $10.00 per unit in Sandy.

Portal Corporation is expected to produce and sell 120,000 laser printers during the coming year. Wanting to take advantage of the higher operating income per unit at Sandy, the company's production manager has decided to manufacture 60,000 units at each plant, resulting in a plan in which Sandy operates at maximum capacity (200 units per day × 300 days) and Ogden operates at its normal volume (250 units per day × 240 days).

Required

1. Calculate the breakeven point in units for the Ogden plant and for the Sandy plant.
2. Calculate the operating income that would result from the production manager's plan to produce 60,000 units at each plant.
3. Determine how the production of 120,000 units should be allocated between the Ogden and Sandy plants to maximize operating income for Portal Corporation. Show your calculations.

Case

ON-THE-GO: Cost–Volume–Profit Analysis

Peter Kankel, the CFO of On-the-Go convenience stores, had only a couple of hours to decide what he would recommend. Decisions to add products are often challenging. Kankel knows that modern convenience stores have to do more than just remain open late into the evening and offer a diverse product assortment; they have to change with the times or face extinction. Over the years, On-the-Go has stocked new products and services, such as gasoline, lottery tickets, and even Internet shopping and delivery services. A walk through any of its stores is likely to reveal in excess of 2,000 different products and services, often available 24 hours a day, seven days a week. There are close to 150,000 convenience stores scattered across the United States. The industry generated $350 billion in sales for 2011.

On-the-Go Stores, based in Newport, Rhode Island, operates 82 stores in its chain of convenience stores. Locations are primarily in the New England and Mid-Atlantic regions of the United States, where there are about 20,000 convenience stores—approximately 13% of the country's total. The average sale is $3.00, with a gross margin of 30%.

Recently, On-the-Go has faced some challenging decisions. For example, company managers recently evaluated the effect on income of the store's sales mix and performed sensitivity analysis to see the effect on operating income of changing the selling price of milk. Kankel was currently evaluating two major decisions.

The first decision related to the sale of money orders at its stores. This was a new product area for the company—a "financial service," much like what a bank would offer. By offering this new service, On-the-Go hoped to boost its customer count. Previous studies had shown that customers were likely to buy more than just the items they originally intended to purchase. So, On-the-Go wanted to boost sales revenue by giving customers another reason to come into the store—and buy more than intended.

Kankel had obtained the following information. The cost of renting the machine for each store to prepare money orders is $30 per month. The lease rent for the store is $5,000. For each money order processed, On-the-Go would pay a processing fee of 6 cents. After conducting an informal survey of banks and other local businesses that offered money order services, On-the-Go found that most charged 99 cents for each money order transaction. On-the-Go planned to set its money order fee at 79 cents to undercut local competition. Kankel estimated that a money order transaction would take one counter clerk 90 seconds to complete, versus only 30 seconds for ringing up a product sale. The average hourly wage for a store clerk is $12.00 per hour. On-the-Go does not plan to hire any new clerks or ask existing clerks to work longer hours if it decides to sell money orders.

Kankel then turned to the second major decision he faced: Should On-the-Go sell in-store deli sandwiches to lunchtime customers? If it chose to sell deli sandwiches, On-the-Go could either prepare these sandwiches in-store or purchase prepackaged deli sandwiches from an outside vendor. It would cost $3.50 to purchase the sandwiches. If it made the sandwiches, the cost of the ingredients would be $2.50 per sandwich. One of On-the-Go's senior employees, who is paid $15 per hour, would prepare the sandwiches during the lunch hour. On-the-Go would then have to hire a temporary worker for the 2-hour lunchtime period to manage other activities in the store. The temporary worker would be paid $10 per hour. The average selling price of a deli sandwich is $4.50. On-the-Go anticipates selling 12 sandwiches per hour. All other costs would be unchanged whether On-the-Go buys the sandwiches, makes the sandwiches, or chooses not to sell sandwiches at all.

John Lefarge, the marketing manager is very keen to add more products: "The name of the game is to add more and more products to drive traffic through the store regardless of whether we make money on each one. On the bundle of products that the customer buys, we are bound to make money."

Susan Polk, the operations manager, has a different view: "We know that convenience store customers don't like to wait in line for service. They want to be in and out fast. The more products we add and the more complexity we create, the longer it takes for customers to find what they want and to check out of the store. Also, different tasks require different skills. For example, if we make deli sandwiches, we need one of our more senior workers to prepare the sandwiches so it costs more to do that activity than to stock the shelves. I hope our accounting systems correctly reflect these higher costs."

Kankel wondered how he should consider these arguments. He knew he could not put numbers on what Lefarge and Polk were saying, but they seemed like important points for him to consider as he made recommendations to the CEO, Patrick Newhouse.

Required

1. (a) Calculate the contribution margin per unit for money orders. (b) Calculate how many money orders each On-the-Go location would need to sell each month to break even on the service. (c) Calculate how many money orders each On-the-Go location would need to sell each month to earn an operating income of $140 per month.
2. On the basis of financial considerations alone, should On-the-Go sell deli sandwiches? If so, should the store purchase prepackaged sandwiches or make them in the store? What other factors, if any, regarding the sandwiches should Peter Kankel consider?
3. Suppose On-the-Go can sell 300 money orders each month and 24 deli sandwiches during lunchtime each day. What should Peter Kankel recommend to Patrick Newhouse about selling money orders and deli sandwiches? How should Kankel consider the issues that Lefarge and Polk raised in reaching his recommendation?

Job Costing 4

Learning Objectives

1. Describe the building-block concepts of costing systems
2. Distinguish job costing from process costing
3. Describe the approaches to evaluating and implementing job-costing systems
4. Outline the seven-step approach to normal costing
5. Distinguish actual costing from normal costing
6. Track the flow of costs in a job-costing system
7. Dispose of under- or overallocated manufacturing overhead costs at the end of the fiscal year using alternative methods
8. Apply variations from normal costing

It's fair to say that no one likes to lose money. Whether a company is a new startup venture providing marketing consulting services or an established manufacturer of custom-built motorcycles, knowing how to job cost—or knowing how much it costs to produce an individual product—is critical if a company wants to generate a profit.

For example, managers at Nissan want to know how much it costs to manufacture its new Leaf electric car, and managers at Ernst & Young want to know what it costs to audit Whole Foods, the organic grocer. Knowing the costs and profitability of jobs helps managers pursue their business strategies, develop pricing plans, and meet external reporting requirements. Of course, when making decisions, managers combine cost information with noncost information, such as personal observations of operations, and nonfinancial performance measures, like quality and customer satisfaction.

The Chapter at a Glance provides a roadmap for the major elements of this chapter: (1) the different types of costing systems, (2) how managers assign costs to individual jobs as the job is being completed, (3) how entries are made in the accounting system at the end of each month, and (4) the adjustments that need to be made at the end of each year.

Chapter at a Glance

- Managers use two basic kinds of costing systems to assign costs to products and services: job costing and process costing. The costing systems of most companies combine elements of both systems.
- Companies use job-costing systems to determine the cost of direct materials, direct labor, and overhead costs required to complete individual jobs.
- The actual costs of direct materials and direct labor are available as the job is being done but actual overhead costs allocated to a job can only be calculated at the end of the year.
- To provide more timely information about job costs, companies use normal-costing systems that use actual direct material and labor costs but use a predetermined overhead cost rate to estimate overhead costs as the job is being done.
- At the end of each month, entries are made in the general ledger to account for the costs and revenues of all jobs worked during that month.
- The use of estimates to allocate overhead costs to jobs results in different amounts of total overhead costs incurred and total overhead costs allocated at the end of the year. Accounting systems determine the difference between overhead costs incurred and overhead costs allocated and make end-of-year adjustments to account for the difference.

Learning Objective 1

Describe the building-block concepts of costing systems

. . . the building blocks are cost object, direct costs, indirect costs, cost pools, and cost-allocation bases

Building-Block Concepts of Costing Systems

Before we begin our discussion of costing systems, let's review cost-related terms from Chapter 2 and introduce the new terms that we will need for our primary discussion.

1. A *cost object* is anything for which a measurement of costs is desired—for example, a product, such as an iMac computer, or a service, such as the cost of repairing an iMac computer.
2. The *direct costs of a cost object* are costs related to a particular cost object that can be traced to that cost object in an economically feasible (cost-effective) way—for example, the cost of purchasing the main computer board or the cost of parts used to make an iMac computer.
3. The *indirect costs of a cost object* are costs related to a particular cost object that cannot be traced to that cost object in an economically feasible (cost-effective) way—for example, the salaries of supervisors who oversee multiple products, only one of which is the iMac, or the rent paid for the repair facility that repairs many different Apple computer products besides the iMac. Indirect costs are allocated to the cost object using a cost-allocation method.

Recall that *cost assignment* is a general term for assigning costs, whether direct or indirect, to a cost object. *Cost tracing* is a specific term for assigning direct costs; *cost allocation* refers to assigning indirect costs. The relationship among these three concepts can be graphically represented as

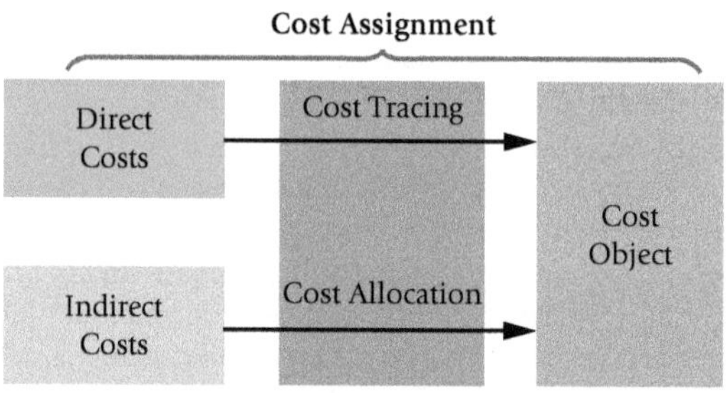

Throughout this chapter, the costs assigned to a cost object, such as a BMW Mini Cooper car, or a service, such as an audit of the MTV network, include both variable costs and costs that are fixed in the short run. Managers cost products and services to guide long-run strategic decisions (for example, the mix of products and services to produce and sell or the prices to charge for various products). In the long run, managers want revenues to exceed total (variable plus fixed) costs.

We also need to introduce and explain two more terms before discussing costing systems:

4. **Cost pool.** A **cost pool** is a grouping of individual indirect cost items. Cost pools can range from broad, such as all manufacturing-plant costs, to narrow, such as the costs of operating metal-cutting machines. Cost pools are often organized in conjunction with cost-allocation bases.
5. **Cost-allocation base.** How should a company allocate costs to operate metal-cutting machines among different products? One way to allocate costs is based on the number of machine-hours used to produce different products. The **cost-allocation base** (number of machine-hours) is a systematic way to link an indirect cost or group of indirect costs (operating costs of all metal-cutting machines) to cost objects (different products). For example, if indirect costs of operating metal-cutting machines is \$500,000 based on running these machines for 10,000 hours, the cost allocation rate is \$500,000 ÷ 10,000 hours = \$50 per machine-hour. If a product uses 800 machine-hours, it will be allocated \$40,000, \$50 per machine-hour × 800 machine-hours. The ideal cost-allocation base is the cost driver of the indirect costs, because there is a cause-and-effect relationship between the cost allocation base and the indirect costs. A cost-allocation base can be either financial (such as direct labor costs) or nonfinancial (such as the number of machine-hours). When the cost object is a job, product, or customer, the cost-allocation base is also called a **cost-application base.**

   Sometimes a cost may need to be allocated where the cause-and-effect relationship is not clear-cut. Consider a corporatewide advertising program that promotes the general image of the corporation and its operating businesses, rather than the image of an individual product. Many companies, such as Pepsico, allocate the costs of this program to individual businesses on the basis of revenues—the higher the revenue, the higher the business's allocated cost of the advertising program. Allocating costs on this basis follows the criterion of *benefits received* rather than cause-and-effect. Businesses with higher revenues benefit from the advertising more than divisions with lower revenues and, therefore, ought to be allocated more of the advertising costs.

Another criterion for allocating some costs is the cost object's *ability to bear* costs allocated to it. The city government of Houston, Texas, for example, distributes the costs of the city manager's office to other city departments—including the police department, fire department, library system, and others—based on the size of their budget, under the rationale that larger departments should absorb a larger share of the costs. Organizations generally use the cause-and-effect criterion to allocate costs, followed by benefits received, and finally, and more rarely, by ability to bear.

The concepts represented by these five terms constitute the building blocks that we will use to design the costing systems described in this chapter.

> **Keys to Success**
> **Measuring direct costs and using cost pools and cost-allocation bases to allocate indirect costs help managers understand the costs of a cost object and to make decisions based on those costs.**

Job-Costing and Process-Costing Systems

Learning Objective 2

Distinguish job costing

. . . job costing is used to cost a distinct product

from process costing

. . . process costing is used to cost masses of identical or similar units

Management accountants use two basic types of costing systems to assign costs to products or services:

1. **Job-costing system.** In a job-costing system, the cost object is a unit or multiple units of a distinct product or service called a **job.** Each job generally uses different amounts of resources. The product or service is often a single unit, such as a specialized machine made at Hitachi, a construction project managed by Bechtel Corporation, a repair job done at an Audi Service Center, or an advertising campaign produced by Saatchi & Saatchi. Each special machine made by Hitachi is unique and distinct from the other machines made at the plant. An advertising campaign for one client at Saatchi and Saatchi is unique and distinct from advertising campaigns for other clients. Job costing is also used by companies such as Ethan Allen to cost multiple identical units of distinct furniture products. Because the products and services are distinct, job-costing systems accumulate costs separately for each product or service.
2. **Process-costing system.** In a process-costing system, the cost object is masses of identical or similar units of a product or service. For example, Citibank provides the same service to all its customers when processing customer deposits. Intel provides the same product (say, a Pentium 6 chip) to each of its customers. All Minute Maid consumers receive the same frozen orange juice product. In each period, process-costing systems divide the total costs of producing an identical or similar product or service by the total number of units produced to obtain a per-unit cost. This per-unit cost is the average unit cost that applies to each of the identical or similar units produced in that period.

Exhibit 4-1 presents examples of job costing and process costing in the service, merchandising, and manufacturing sectors. These two types of costing systems lie at opposite ends of a continuum; in between, one type of system can blur into the other to some degree.

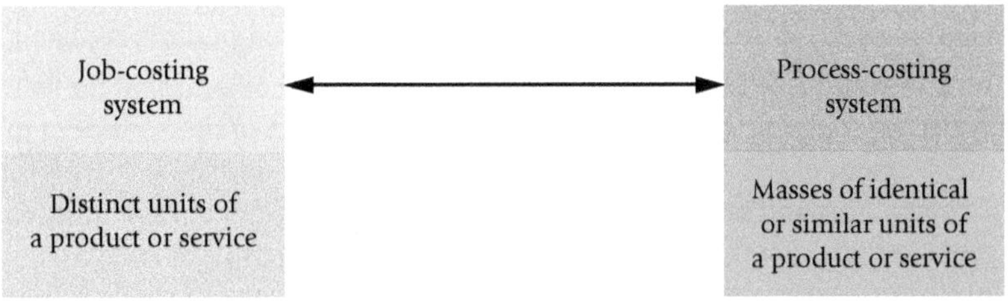

Exhibit 4-1

Examples of Job Costing and Process Costing in the Service, Merchandising, and Manufacturing Sectors

	Service Sector	Merchandising Sector	Manufacturing Sector
Job Costing Used	• Audit engagements done by Price Waterhouse Coopers • Consulting engagements done by McKinsey & Co. • Advertising-agency campaigns run by Ogilvy & Mather • Individual legal cases argued by Hale & Dorr • Computer-repair jobs done by CompUSA • Movies produced by Universal Studios	• L. L. Bean sending individual items by mail order • Special promotion of new products by Walmart	• Assembly of individual aircrafts at Boeing • Construction of ships at Litton Industries
Process Costing Used	• Bank-check clearing at Bank of America • Postal delivery (standard items) by U.S. Postal Service	• Grain dealing by Arthur Daniel Midlands • Lumber dealing by Weyerhauser	• Oil refining by Shell Oil • Beverage production by PepsiCo

Many companies have costing systems that are neither pure job costing nor pure process costing but have elements of both job- and process-costing systems tailored to the underlying operations. For example, Kellogg Corporation uses job costing to calculate the total cost to manufacture each of its different and distinct types of products—such as Corn Flakes, Crispix, and Froot Loops—and process costing to calculate the per-unit cost of producing each identical box of Corn Flakes. In this chapter, we focus on job-costing systems. Chapter 5 discusses process-costing systems.

Keys to Success

Managers choose costing systems based on the product or service—job-costing systems if the product or service is distinct and process-costing systems if the product or service is identical or similar.

Learning Objective 3

Describe the approaches to evaluating and implementing job-costing systems

. . . to determine costs of jobs in a timely manner

Job Costing: Evaluation and Implementation

We illustrate job costing using the example of Robinson Company, which manufactures and installs specialized machinery for the paper-making industry. In early 2012, Robinson receives a request to bid for the manufacturing and installation of a new paper-making machine for the Western Pulp and Paper Company (WPP). Robinson had never made a machine quite like this one, and its managers wonder what to bid for the job. In order to make decisions about the job, Robinson's management team works through the five-step decision-making process.

1. **Identify the problems and uncertainties.** The decision of whether and how much to bid for the WPP job depends on how management resolves two critical uncertainties: (1) what it will cost to complete the job and (2) the prices that Robinson's competitors are likely to bid.
2. **Obtain information.** Robinson's managers first evaluate whether doing the WPP job is consistent with the company's strategy. Do they want to do more of these kinds of jobs? Is this an attractive segment of the market? Will Robinson be able to develop a competitive advantage over its competitors and satisfy customers? After completing the requisite research, Robinson's managers conclude that the WPP job fits well with the company's strategy.

   Robinson's managers study the drawings and engineering specifications provided by WPP and decide on technical details of the machine. They compare the specifications of this machine to similar machines they have made in the past, identify competitors who might bid on the job, and gather information on what these bids might be.

3. **Make predictions about the future.** Robinson's managers estimate the cost of direct materials, direct manufacturing labor, and overhead for the WPP job. They also consider qualitative factors and risk factors and evaluate any biases they might have. For example, do engineers and employees working on the WPP job have the necessary skills and technical competence? Would they find the experience valuable and challenging? How accurate are the cost estimates, and what is the likelihood of cost overruns? What biases do Robinson's managers have to be careful about? Remember, Robinson has not made a machine quite like this one. Robinson's managers need to avoid drawing inappropriate analogies and to seek the most relevant information when making their judgments.
4. **Make decisions by choosing among alternatives.** Robinson's managers consider several alternatives. Should they bid on the WPP job? If they do, which of several alternative prices should they bid taking into account likely bids by competitors, technical and business risks, and qualitative factors? They decide to bid $15,000 for the WPP job. The manufacturing cost estimate is $10,000, which yields a markup of 50% over manufacturing cost.
5. **Implement the decision, evaluate performance, and learn.** Robinson wins the bid for the WPP job. As Robinson works on the WPP job, managers keep careful track of all the costs incurred (which are detailed later in this chapter). Ultimately, Robinson's managers will compare the predicted amounts against actual costs to evaluate how well they did on the WPP job.

In its job-costing system, Robinson accumulates costs incurred on a job in different parts of the value chain, such as manufacturing, marketing, and customer service. We focus here on Robinson's manufacturing function (which also includes product installation). To make a machine, Robinson purchases some components from outside suppliers and makes others itself. Each of Robinson's jobs also has a service element: installing a machine at a customer's site, integrating it with the customer's other machines and processes, and ensuring the machine meets customer expectations.

One form of a job-costing system that Robinson can use is **actual costing,** which is a costing system that traces direct costs to a cost object based on the actual direct-cost rates times the actual quantities of the direct-cost inputs. It allocates indirect costs based on the actual indirect-cost rates times the actual quantities of the cost-allocation bases. The *actual indirect-cost rate* is calculated by dividing actual annual indirect costs by the actual annual quantity of the cost-allocation base.

$$\text{Actual indirect cost rate} = \frac{\text{Actual annual indirect costs}}{\text{Actual annual quantity of the cost-allocation base}}$$

As its name suggests, actual-costing systems calculate the actual costs of jobs. Yet, actual-costing systems are not commonly found in practice because actual costs cannot be computed in a *timely* manner.[1] The problem is not with computing direct-cost rates for direct materials and direct manufacturing labor. For example, Robinson records the actual prices paid for materials. As it uses these materials, the prices paid serve as actual direct-cost rates for charging material costs to jobs. As we discuss next, calculating actual indirect-cost rates on a timely basis each week or each month is, however, a problem. Robinson can only calculate actual indirect-cost rates at the end of the fiscal year and Robinson's managers are unwilling to wait that long to learn the costs of various jobs because they need cost information to monitor and manage the cost of jobs while the jobs are still being worked on. Ongoing cost information about jobs also helps managers bid on new jobs that come up for bids while the old jobs are in process.

Time Period Used to Compute Indirect-Cost Rates

There are two reasons for using longer periods, such as a year, to calculate indirect-cost rates.

1. **The numerator reason (indirect-cost pool).** The shorter the period, the greater the influence of seasonal patterns on the amount of costs. For example, if indirect-cost rates were calculated each month, costs of heating (included in the numerator) would be charged to production only during the winter months. An annual period incorporates the effects of all four seasons into a single, annual indirect-cost rate.

   Levels of total indirect costs are also affected by nonseasonal erratic costs. Nonseasonal erratic costs are the costs incurred in a particular month that benefit operations during future

[1] Actual costing is presented in more detail on pages 127–129.

months, such as costs of equipment repairs and maintenance and costs of vacation and holiday pay for employees. If monthly indirect-cost rates were calculated, jobs done in a month with high, nonseasonal erratic costs would be charged with these costs. Pooling all indirect costs together over the course of a full year and calculating a single annual indirect-cost rate helps smooth some of the erratic bumps in costs associated with shorter periods.

2. **The denominator reason (quantity of the cost-allocation base).** Another reason for longer periods is to avoid spreading monthly fixed indirect costs over fluctuating levels of monthly output and fluctuating quantities of the cost-allocation base. Consider the following example.

Reardon and Pane is a firm of tax accountants whose work follows a highly seasonal pattern with very busy months during tax season, January–April, and less busy months at other times of the year. Reardon and Pane has both variable indirect costs and fixed indirect costs. Variable indirect costs (such as supplies, food, power, and indirect support labor) vary with the quantity of the cost-allocation base (direct professional labor hours). Fixed indirect costs (depreciation and general administrative support) do not vary with short-run fluctuations in the quantity of the cost-allocation base:

	Indirect Costs			Direct Professional Labor-Hours	Variable Indirect Cost Rate per Direct Professional Labor-Hour	Fixed Indirect Cost Rate per Direct Professional Labor-Hour	Total Allocation Rate per Direct Professional Labor-Hour
	Variable (1)	Fixed (2)	Total (3)	(4)	(5) = (1) ÷ (4)	(6) = (2) ÷ (4)	(7) = (3) ÷ (4)
High-output month	$40,000	$60,000	$100,000	3,200	$12.50	$18.75	$31.25
Low-output month	10,000	60,000	70,000	800	$12.50	$75.00	87.50

Variable indirect costs change in proportion to changes in direct professional labor-hours. Therefore, the variable indirect-cost rate is the same in both the high-output months and the low-output months. Sometimes overtime payments can cause the variable indirect-cost rate to be higher in high-output months. In such cases, variable indirect costs will be allocated at a higher rate to production in high-output months relative to production in low-output months.

Consider now the fixed costs of $60,000. The fixed costs cause monthly total indirect-cost rates to vary considerably—from $31.25 per hour to $87.50 per hour. Few managers believe that identical jobs done in different months should be allocated such significantly different indirect-cost charges per hour ($87.50 ÷ $31.25 = 2.80, or 280%) because of fixed costs. Furthermore, if fees for preparing tax returns are based on costs, fees would be high in low-output months leading to lost business, when in fact management wants to accept more bids to use idle capacity.

Reardon and Pane chose a specific level of capacity based on a time horizon far beyond a mere month. An average, annualized rate based on the relationship of total annual indirect costs to the total annual level of output smoothes the effect of monthly variations in output levels and is more representative of the total costs and total output that management considered when choosing the level of capacity and, therefore, fixed costs. Another denominator reason for using annual overhead rates is that the number of Monday-to-Friday workdays in a month affects the calculation of monthly indirect-cost rates. The number of workdays per month varies from 20 to 23 during a year. If separate rates are computed each month, jobs in February would bear a greater share of indirect costs (such as depreciation and property taxes) than jobs in other months, because February has the fewest workdays (and consequently labor-hours) in a month. Many managers believe such differences in allocation of indirect costs to be an unrepresentative and unreasonable way to determine indirect costs of otherwise identical jobs that happen to be done in different months. An annual period reduces the effect that the number of working days per month has on unit costs.

Keys to Success

Managers use annual periods to calculate indirect-cost rates to avoid effects of seasonal, erratic costs and fluctuating quantities of the cost-allocation base.

Normal Costing

The difficulty of calculating actual indirect-cost rates on a weekly or monthly basis means managers cannot calculate the actual costs of jobs as they are completed. However, managers, including those at Robinson, want a close approximation of the costs of various jobs regularly during the year, not just at the end of the fiscal year. Managers want to know manufacturing costs (and other costs, such as marketing costs) for ongoing uses, including pricing jobs, monitoring and managing costs, evaluating the success of the job, learning about what did and did not work, bidding on new jobs, and preparing interim financial statements. Because of the need for immediate access to job costs, few companies wait to allocate overhead costs until the end of the accounting year when the actual manufacturing overhead is finally known. Instead, a *predetermined* or *budgeted* indirect-cost rate is calculated for each cost pool at the beginning of a fiscal year, and overhead costs are allocated to jobs as work progresses. For the numerator and denominator reasons already described, the **budgeted indirect-cost rate** for each cost pool is computed as follows:

$$\text{Budgeted indirect cost rate} = \frac{\text{Budgeted annual indirect cost}}{\text{Budgeted annual quantity of the cost-allocation base}}$$

Using budgeted indirect-cost rates gives rise to normal costing.

Normal costing is a costing system that (1) traces direct costs to a cost object by using the actual direct-cost rates times the actual quantities of the direct-cost inputs and (2) allocates indirect costs based on the *budgeted* indirect-cost rates times the actual quantities of the cost-allocation bases.

Keys to Success

Under normal costing, managers use a predetermined or budgeted indirect-cost rate rather than an actual indirect-cost rate to cost jobs on a timely basis.

General Approach to Job Costing Using Normal Costing

Learning Objective 4

Outline the seven-step approach to normal costing

. . . the seven-step approach is used to compute direct and indirect costs of a job

We illustrate normal costing for the Robinson Company example using the following seven steps to assign costs to an individual job. This approach is commonly used by companies in the manufacturing, merchandising, and service sectors.

Step 1: Identify the Job That Is the Chosen Cost Object. The cost object in the Robinson Company example is Job WPP 298, manufacturing a paper-making machine for Western Pulp and Paper (WPP) in 2012. Robinson's managers and management accountants gather information to cost jobs through source documents. A **source document** is an original record (such as a labor time card on which an employee's work hours are recorded) that supports journal entries in an accounting system. The main source document for Job WPP 298 is a job-cost record. A **job-cost record,** also called a **job-cost sheet,** records and accumulates all the costs assigned to a specific job, starting when work begins. Exhibit 4-2 shows the job-cost record for the paper-making machine ordered by WPP. Follow the various steps in costing Job WPP 298 on the job-cost record in Exhibit 4-2.

Step 2: Identify the Direct Costs of the Job. Robinson identifies two direct-manufacturing cost categories: direct materials and direct manufacturing labor.

- **Direct materials:** On the basis of the engineering specifications and drawings provided by WPP, a manufacturing engineer orders materials from the storeroom with a basic source document called a **materials-requisition record,** which contains information about the cost of direct materials used on a specific job and in a specific department. Exhibit 4-3, Panel A, shows a materials-requisition record for the Robinson Company. See how the record specifies the job for which the material is requested (WPP 298), the description of the material (Part Number MB 468-A, metal brackets), the actual quantity (8), the actual unit cost ($14), and the actual total cost ($112). The $112 actual total cost also appears on the job-cost record in Exhibit 4-2. If we add the cost of all material requisitions, the total actual direct material cost is $4,606, which is shown in the Direct Materials panel of the job-cost record in Exhibit 4-2.
- **Direct manufacturing labor:** The accounting for direct manufacturing labor is similar to the accounting described for direct materials. The source document for direct manufacturing labor

Exhibit 4-2

Source Documents at Robinson Company: Job-Cost Record

	A	B	C	D	E	
1			**JOB-COST RECORD**			
2	JOB NO:	WPP 298		CUSTOMER:	Western Pulp and Paper	
3	Date Started:	Feb. 6, 2012		Date Completed	Feb. 29, 2012	
4						
5						
6	**DIRECT MATERIALS**					
7	Date	Materials		Quantity	Unit	Total
8	Received	Requisition No.	Part No.	Used	Cost	Costs
9	Feb. 6, 2012	2012: 198	MB 468-A	8	$14	$ 112
10	Feb. 6, 2012	2012: 199	TB 267-F	12	63	756
11						•
12						•
13	Total					$ 4,606
14						
15	**DIRECT MANUFACTURING LABOR**					
16	Period	Labor Time	Employee	Hours	Hourly	Total
17	Covered	Record No.	No.	Used	Rate	Costs
18	Feb. 6-12, 2012	LT 232	551-87-3076	25	$18	$ 450
19	Feb. 6-12, 2012	LT 247	287-31-4671	5	19	95
20				•		•
21				•		•
22	Total			88		$ 1,579
23						
24	**MANUFACTURING OVERHEAD***					
25		Cost Pool		Allocation Base	Allocation-	Total
26	Date	Category	Allocation Base	Quantity Used	Base Rate	Costs
27	Feb. 29, 2012	Manufacturing	Direct Manufacturing	88 hours	$40	$ 3,520
28			Labor-Hours			
29						
30	Total					$ 3,520
31	**TOTAL MANUFACTURING COST OF JOB**					$ 9,705
32						
33						
34	*The Robinson Company uses a single manufacturing-overhead cost pool. The use of multiple overhead cost pools					
35	would mean multiple entries in the "Manufacturing Overhead" section of the job-cost record.					
36						

is a **labor-time sheet,** which contains information about the amount of labor time used for a specific job in a specific department. Exhibit 4-3, Panel B, shows a typical weekly labor-time sheet for a particular employee (G. L. Cook). Each day Cook records the time spent on individual jobs (in this case WPP 298 and JL 256), as well as the time spent on other tasks, such as maintenance of machines or cleaning, that are not related to a specific job.

The 25 hours that Cook spent on Job WPP 298 appears on the job-cost record in Exhibit 4-2 at a cost of $450 (25 hours × $18 per hour). Similarly, the job-cost record for Job JL 256 will carry a cost of $216 (12 hours × $18 per hour). The three hours of time spent on maintenance and cleaning at $18 per hour equals $54. This cost is part of indirect manufacturing costs because it is not traceable to any particular job. This indirect cost is included as part of the manufacturing-overhead cost pool allocated to jobs. The total direct manufacturing labor costs of $1,579 for the paper-making machine that appears in the Direct Manufacturing

Exhibit 4-3

Source Documents at Robinson Company: Materials-Requisition Record and Labor-Time Sheet

PANEL A:

MATERIALS-REQUISITION RECORD

Materials-Requisition Record No. 2012: 198

Job No. WPP 298 Date: FEB. 6, 2012

Part No.	Part Description	Quantity	Unit Cost	Total Cost
MB 468-A	Metal Brackets	8	$14	$112

Issued By: B. Clyde Date: Feb. 6, 2012

Received By: L. Daley Date: Feb. 6, 2012

PANEL B:

LABOR-TIME SHEET

Labor-Time Record No: LT 232

Employee Name: G. L. Cook Employee No: 551-87-3076

Employee Classification Code: Grade 3 Machinist

Hourly Rate: $18

Week Start: Feb. 6, 2012 Week End: Feb. 12, 2012

Job. No.	M	T	W	Th	F	S	Su	Total
WPP 298	4	8	3	6	4	0	0	25
JL 256	3	0	4	2	3	0	0	12
Maintenance	1	0	1	0	1	0	0	3
Total	8	8	8	8	8	0	0	40

Supervisor: R. Stuart Date: Feb. 12, 2012

Labor panel of the job-cost record in Exhibit 4-2 is the sum of all the direct manufacturing labor costs charged to Job WPP 298 by different employees.

All costs other than direct materials and direct manufacturing labor are classified as indirect costs.

Step 3: Select the Cost-Allocation Bases to Use for Allocating Indirect Costs to the Job. Indirect manufacturing costs are costs that are necessary to do a job but that cannot be traced to a specific job. It would be impossible to complete a job without incurring indirect costs such as supervision, manufacturing engineering, utilities, and repairs. Managers must allocate these costs to jobs in a systematic way because these costs cannot be traced to a specific job and different jobs require different quantities of indirect resources.

Companies often use multiple cost-allocation bases to allocate indirect costs because different indirect costs have different cost drivers. For example, some indirect costs such as depreciation and repairs of machines are more closely related to machine-hours. Other indirect costs such as supervision and production support are more closely related to direct manufacturing labor-hours. Robinson, however, chooses direct manufacturing labor-hours as the sole allocation base for linking all indirect manufacturing costs to jobs because, in its labor-intensive environment, Robinson believes that the number of direct manufacturing labor-hours drives the manufacturing overhead resources required by individual jobs. (We will see in the appendix to this chapter and in Chapter 6 that managers in many manufacturing environments often need to broaden the set of cost drivers.) In 2012, Robinson budgets 28,000 direct manufacturing labor-hours.

Step 4: Identify the Indirect Costs Associated with Each Cost-Allocation Base. Because Robinson believes that a single cost-allocation base—direct manufacturing labor-hours—can be used to allocate indirect manufacturing costs to jobs, Robinson creates a single cost pool called manufacturing overhead costs. This pool represents all indirect costs of the Manufacturing Department that are difficult to trace directly to individual jobs. In 2012, budgeted manufacturing overhead costs total $1,120,000.

As we saw in Steps 3 and 4, managers first identify cost-allocation bases and then identify the costs related to each cost-allocation base, not the other way around. They choose this order because managers must first understand the cost driver, the reasons why costs are being incurred (such as for setting up machines, moving materials, or designing jobs), before they can determine the costs associated with each cost driver. Otherwise, there is nothing to guide the creation of cost pools. Of course, Steps 3 and 4 are often done almost simultaneously.

Step 5: Compute the Rate per Unit of Each Cost-Allocation Base Used to Allocate Indirect Costs to the Job. For each cost pool, the budgeted indirect-cost rate is calculated by dividing budgeted total indirect costs in the pool (determined in Step 4) by the budgeted total quantity of the cost-allocation base (determined in Step 3). Robinson calculates the allocation rate for its single manufacturing overhead cost pool as follows:

$$\text{Budgeted manufacturing overhead rate} = \frac{\text{Budgeted manufacturing overhead costs}}{\text{Budgeted total quantity of cost-allocation base}}$$

$$= \frac{\$1{,}120{,}000}{28{,}000 \text{ direct manufacturing labor-hours}}$$

$$= \$40 \text{ per direct manufacturing labor-hour}$$

Step 6: Compute the Indirect Costs Allocated to the Job. The indirect costs of a job are calculated by multiplying the *actual* quantity of each different allocation base (one allocation base for each cost pool) associated with the job by the *budgeted* indirect cost rate of each allocation base (computed in Step 5). Recall that Robinson's managers selected direct manufacturing labor-hours as the only cost-allocation base. Robinson uses 88 direct manufacturing labor-hours on the WPP 298 job. Manufacturing overhead costs allocated to WPP 298 equal $3,520 ($40 per direct manufacturing labor-hour × 88 hours) and appear in the Manufacturing Overhead panel of the WPP 298 job-cost record in Exhibit 4-2.

Keys to Success

To calculate the indirect costs of a job, managers determine cost-allocation bases and their related costs, calculate cost-allocation rates, and multiply them with the quantity of cost-allocation bases associated with the job.

Step 7: Compute the Total Cost of the Job by Adding All Direct and Indirect Costs Assigned to the Job. Exhibit 4-2 shows that the total manufacturing costs of the WPP job are $9,705.

Direct manufacturing costs		
Direct materials	$4,606	
Direct manufacturing labor	1,579	$6,185
Manufacturing overhead costs		
($40 per direct manufacturing labor-hour × 88 hours)		3,520
Total manufacturing costs of job WPP 298		$9,705

Recall that Robinson bid a price of $15,000 for the job. At that revenue, the normal-costing system shows a gross margin of $5,295 ($15,000 − $9,705) and a gross-margin percentage of 35.3% ($5,295 ÷ $15,000 = 0.353).

Robinson's manufacturing managers and sales managers can use the gross margin and gross-margin percentage calculations to compare the profitability of different jobs to try to understand the reasons why some jobs show low profitability. Have direct materials been wasted? Was direct manufacturing labor too high? Were there ways to improve the efficiency of these jobs? Were these jobs simply underpriced? Job-cost analysis provides the information needed for judging the performance of manufacturing and sales managers and for making future improvements (see Concepts in Action: The Job Costing "Game Plan" at the New Cowboys Stadium).

Exhibit 4-4 is an overview of Robinson Company's job-costing system. This exhibit represents the concepts comprising the five building blocks—(1) cost object, (2) direct costs of a cost object, (3) indirect (overhead) costs of a cost object, (4) indirect-cost pool, and (5) cost-allocation base—of job-costing systems that were first introduced at the beginning of this chapter. Costing-system overviews such as Exhibit 4-4 are important learning tools. We urge you to sketch one when you need to understand a costing system in manufacturing, merchandising, or service companies. (The symbols in Exhibit 4-4 are used consistently in the costing-system overviews presented in this book. A triangle always identifies a direct cost, a rectangle represents the indirect-cost pool, and an octagon describes the cost-allocation base.) Note the parallel between the overview diagram and the cost of the WPP 298 job described in Step 7. Exhibit 4-4 shows two direct-cost categories (direct materials and direct manufacturing labor) and one indirect-cost category (manufacturing overhead) used to allocate indirect costs. The costs in Step 7 also have three dollar amounts, each corresponding respectively to the two direct-cost and one indirect-cost categories.

Concepts in Action: The Job Costing "Game Plan" at the New Cowboys Stadium

Source: ZUMA Press/Newscom

Although the Dallas Cowboys have won five Super Bowls, many football fans recognize the team for its futuristic new home, Cowboys Stadium in Arlington, Texas. The 73,000-seat stadium, built in three years, features two arches spanning a quarter-mile in length over the dome, a retractable roof, the largest retractable glass doors in the world (in each end zone), canted glass exterior walls, and a 600-ton JumboTron. For Manhattan Construction, the company that managed the $1.2 billion Cowboys Stadium project, understanding the costs of these features was critical for making successful pricing decisions and ensuring that the project was profitable.

The Cowboys Stadium project had five stages: (1) conceptualization, (2) design and planning, (3) preconstruction, (4) construction, and (5) finalization and delivery. During this process, Manhattan Construction hired architects and subcontractors, created blueprints, purchased and cleared land, constructed the stadium, built out and finished interiors, and completed last-minute changes before the stadium's 2009 opening. To ensure proper allocation and accounting of resources, project managers used a job-costing system. The system first calculated the budgeted cost of more than 500 line items of direct materials and labor costs. It then allocated estimated overhead costs (supervisor salaries, rent, materials handling, etc.) to the job using direct material costs and direct labor-hours as allocation bases. Manhattan Construction was able to estimate the project's profitability based on the percentage of work completed and revenue earned, while providing the Dallas Cowboys with clear, concise, and transparent costing data.

Just like quarterback Tony Romo navigating opposing defenses, Manhattan Construction was able to leverage its job-costing system to ensure the successful construction of a stadium as iconic as the blue star on the Cowboys' helmets.

Sources: Based on David Dillon, "New Cowboys Stadium Has Grand Design, but Discipline Isn't Compromised," *The Dallas Morning News* (June 3, 2009); and Brooke Knudson, "Profile: Dallas Cowboys Stadium," *Construction Today* (December 22, 2008).

The Role of Technology

To improve the efficiency of their operations, managers use costing information about products and jobs to control materials, labor, and overhead costs. Modern information technology provides managers with quick and accurate information, making it easier to manage and control jobs. For example, in many costing systems, source documents exist only in the form of computer records. Bar coding and other forms of online information recording reduce human intervention and improve the accuracy of materials and labor time records for individual jobs.

Consider, for example, direct materials charged to jobs for product-costing purposes. Managers control these costs as materials are purchased and used. Using Electronic Data Interchange (EDI) technology, companies like Robinson order materials from their suppliers by clicking a few keys on a computer keyboard. EDI, an electronic computer link between a company and its suppliers, ensures that the order is transmitted quickly and accurately with minimal paperwork and costs. A bar code scanner records the receipt of incoming materials. The computer matches the receipt with the order, prints out a check to the supplier, and records the material received. When an operator on the production floor transmits a request for materials via a computer terminal, the computer prepares a materials-requisition record, instantly recording the issue of materials in the materials and job-cost records. Each day, the computer sums the materials-requisition records charged to a particular job or manufacturing department. A performance report is then prepared monitoring actual costs of direct materials. Direct material usage can be reported hourly—if the benefits exceed the cost of such frequent reporting. The Concepts in Action: Home Depot Undergoes an Inventory Management "Fix It" describes Home Depot's use of technology to manage its inventory.

Exhibit 4-4

Job-Costing Overview for Determining Manufacturing Costs of Jobs at Robinson Company

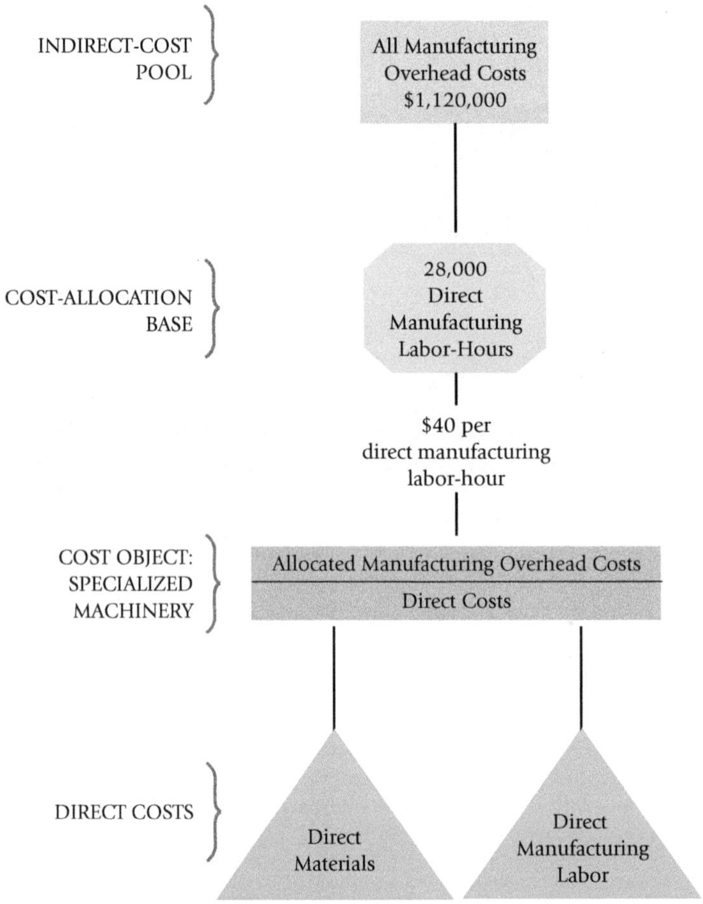

Concepts in Action: Home Depot Undergoes an Inventory Management "Fix-It"

Source: Chris Rank/Bloomberg/Getty Images

At the end of 2010, Home Depot had $10.6 billion worth of inventory. For many years, however, the world's largest home-improvement retailer struggled to know where that entire inventory was at any given time due to dated technology. As a result, Home Depot performed its own renovation to transform its inventory management using state-of-the-art technology across more than 2,200 stores in the United States and abroad.

Today, Home Depot uses advanced databases and hand-held devices that help workers locate and manage inventory on the spot. When merchandise is scanned at the checkout, computer systems are automatically alerted when additional inventory is needed on store shelves. While Home Depot previously sent half-empty trucks to individual stores, new "rapid deployment" distribution centers now combine shipments to area stores, which trims costs and cuts truck trips by 50 percent. The company also deployed mobile computers, with bar-code scanners and cameras, to sales staff that allows them to check inventory (including online), provide product information, print labels, communicate with other employees, even check out customers with debit or credit cards from anywhere in the store.

Home Depot's inventory management fix-it efforts have yielded significant benefits for the company. The new technology has helped more effectively manage inventory volume, reduce stockouts, reduce the need to sell overstocked items at clearance prices, and churn through inventory at a faster pace.

Sources: Based on Miguel Bustillo, "Home Depot Undergoes Renovation," *The Wall Street Journal* (February 24, 2010); Meridith Levinson Sun, "Home Improvement," *CIO* (August 2004); Rachel Tobin Ramos, "Home Depot Getting Better Handle on Products," *The Atlanta Journal-Constitution* (March 29, 2010); Jayne O'Donnell and Laura Petrecca, "Customers May Shop Online While in Store," *USA Today* (November 24, 2011); and The Home Depot, Inc., 2011 Form 10-K (March 24, 2011).

Similarly, information about direct manufacturing labor is obtained as employees log into computer terminals and key in the job numbers, their employee numbers, and start and end times of their work on different jobs. The computer automatically prints the labor time record and, using hourly rates stored for each employee, calculates the direct manufacturing labor costs of individual jobs. Information technology also provides managers with instantaneous feedback to help control manufacturing overhead costs, jobs in process, jobs completed, and jobs shipped and installed at customer sites.

As Concepts in Action: Lockheed Martin Settles with the U.S. Government for Overbilling indicates, the technology and systems for job costing need to be very accurate when companies do contract work for the U.S. government. Many contracts for the Department of Defense are cost-plus contracts. Errors in accounting for costs can then lead to overcharging the government and penalties and fines for the companies.

Actual Costing

Learning Objective 5

Distinguish actual costing

. . . actual costing uses actual indirect-cost rates

from normal costing

. . . normal costing uses budgeted indirect-cost rates

How would the cost of Job WPP 298 change if Robinson had used actual costing rather than normal costing? Both actual costing and normal costing trace direct costs to jobs in the same way because source documents identify the actual quantities and actual rates of direct materials and direct manufacturing labor for a job as the work is being done. The only difference between costing a job with normal costing and actual costing is that normal costing uses *budgeted* indirect-cost rates, whereas actual costing uses *actual* indirect-cost rates calculated annually at the end of the year. Exhibit 4-5 distinguishes actual costing from normal costing.

The following actual data for 2012 are for Robinson's manufacturing operations:

	Actual
Total manufacturing overhead costs	$1,215,000
Total direct manufacturing labor-hours	27,000

Steps 1 and 2 are the same in both normal and actual costing: Step 1 identifies WPP 298 as the cost object; Step 2 calculates actual direct material costs of $4,606, and actual direct manufacturing labor costs of $1,579. Recall from Step 3 that Robinson uses a single cost-allocation base, direct manufacturing labor-hours, to allocate all manufacturing overhead costs to jobs. The actual quantity of direct manufacturing labor-hours for 2012 is 27,000 hours. In Step 4, Robinson groups all actual indirect manufacturing costs of $1,215,000 into a single manufacturing overhead cost pool. In Step 5, the **actual indirect-cost rate** is calculated by dividing actual total indirect costs in the pool (determined in Step 4) by the actual total quantity of the cost-allocation base (determined in Step 3). Robinson calculates the actual manufacturing overhead rate in 2012 for its single manufacturing overhead cost pool as follows:

$$\begin{aligned}\text{Actual manufacturing overhead rate} &= \frac{\text{Actual annual manufacturing overhead costs}}{\text{Actual annual quantity of the cost-allocation base}}\\ &= \frac{\$1{,}215{,}000}{27{,}000 \text{ direct manufacturing labor-hours}}\\ &= \$45 \text{ per direct manufacturing labor-hour}\end{aligned}$$

In Step 6, under an actual-costing system,

$$\begin{aligned}\text{Manufacturing overhead costs allocated to WPP 298} &= \text{Actual manufacturing overhead rate} \times \text{Actual quantity of direct manufacturing labor-hours}\\ &= \$45 \text{ per direct manuf. labor-hour} \times 88 \text{ direct manufacturing labor-hours}\\ &= \$3{,}960\end{aligned}$$

Exhibit 4-5

Actual-Costing and Normal-Costing Methods

	Actual Costing	Normal Costing
Direct Costs	*Actual direct-cost rates* × actual quantities of direct-cost inputs	*Actual direct-cost rates* × actual quantities of direct-cost inputs
Indirect Costs	*Actual indirect-cost rates* × actual quantities of cost-allocation bases	*Budgeted indirect-cost rates* × actual quantities of cost-allocation bases

In Step 7, the cost of the job under actual costing is $10,145, calculated as follows:

Direct manufacturing costs		
Direct materials	$4,606	
Direct manufacturing labor	1,579	$ 6,185
Manufacturing overhead costs		
($45 per direct manufacturing labor-hour × 88 actual direct manufacturing labor-hours)		3,960
Total manufacturing costs of job		$10,145

The manufacturing cost of the WPP 298 job is higher by $440 under actual costing ($10,145) than it is under normal costing ($9,705) because the actual indirect-cost rate is $45 per hour, whereas the budgeted indirect-cost rate is $40 per hour. That is, ($45 − $40) × 88 actual direct manufacturing labor-hours = $440.

As we discussed previously, manufacturing costs of a job are available much earlier in a normal-costing system. Consequently, Robinson's manufacturing and sales managers can evaluate the profitability of different jobs, the efficiency with which the jobs are done, and the pricing of different jobs as soon as the jobs are completed, while the experience is still fresh in everyone's mind. Another advantage of normal costing is that managers can take corrective actions, such as improving labor efficiency or reducing overhead costs, much sooner. At the end of the year, though, costs allocated using normal costing will not, in general, equal actual costs incurred. If the differences are significant, adjustments will need to be made so that the cost of jobs and the costs in various inventory accounts are based on actual rather than normal costing. We describe these adjustments later in the chapter.

Concepts in Action: Lockheed Martin Settles with the U.S. Government for Overbilling

The U.S. government spent $553 billion on defense in 2011, excluding the cost of the wars in Afghanistan and Iraq. As in prior years, a portion of this money is allocated to private companies to carry out specific contracted services for the U.S. Department of Defense. In recent years, the U.S. government has pursued cases against defense contractors for overcharging it.

In 2010, Lockheed Martin reached a $10.2 million settlement with the U.S. Department of Justice to resolve a case involving allegations that the defense contractor "inflated the overhead rates that it used to price and bill government contracts performed for the U.S. Air Force and U.S. Navy." According to the government, Lockheed Martin improperly billed the Air Force and Navy for costs associated with a private venture with an Italian aerospace company. There have been other instances of Lockheed Martin overbilling or making accounting errors that led to settlements with the government. In 2000, the company paid the government $5 million to settle claims that it overcharged the Navy for anti-submarine devices. Three years later, Lockheed Martin paid $37.9 million to settle charges that it inflated costs on four Air Force contracts, intending to use the extra money to offset cost overruns on other Air Force projects.

To protect taxpayers from future overbilling, the U.S. Department of Defense is imposing a new contract provision that calls for withholding as much as 10 percent of payments to defense contractors when it finds "significant" shortcomings in systems used to track the performance and cost of weapons programs or services.

Source: M.L. Gray/MCT/Newscom

Sources: Based on Rob Hotakainen and Adam Ashton, "Angst at Lewis-McChord Over Defense Cuts," *The Seattle Times* (September 25, 2011); "Lockheed Settles Marietta Mischarge Claims," *Atlanta Business Chronicle* (December 17, 2010); and Rhonda Cook, "Lockheed Agrees to Pay Feds $10M for Marietta Overcharges to Air Force and Navy," *The Atlanta Journal-Constitution* (December 17, 2010).

> **Keys to Success**
> Managers are interested in actual costing because it uses actual indirect-cost rates rather than predetermined or budgeted indirect-cost rates and actual direct costs to calculate actual costs of jobs.

The next section explains how a normal job-costing system aggregates the costs and revenues for all jobs worked during a particular month. *Instructors and students who do not wish to explore these details can go directly to page 134 to the section "Budgeted Indirect Costs and End-of-Accounting-Year Adjustments" without any loss of continuity.*

A Normal Job-Costing System in Manufacturing

Learning Objective 6

Track the flow of costs in a job-costing system

. . . from purchase of materials to sale of finished goods

Continuing with the Robinson Company example, the following illustration considers events that occurred in February 2012. Before getting into the details of normal costing, study Exhibit 4-6, which provides a broad framework for understanding the flow of costs in job costing.

The upper part of Exhibit 4-6 shows the flow of inventoriable costs from the purchase of materials and other manufacturing inputs, to their conversion into work-in-process and finished goods, to the sale of finished goods.

Direct materials used and direct manufacturing labor can be easily traced to jobs. They become part of work-in-process inventory on the balance sheet because direct manufacturing labor transforms direct materials into another asset, work-in-process inventory. Robinson also incurs manufacturing overhead costs (including indirect materials and indirect manufacturing labor) to convert direct materials into work-in-process inventory. The overhead (indirect) costs, however, cannot be easily traced to individual jobs. Manufacturing overhead costs, therefore, are first accumulated in a manufacturing overhead account and then allocated to individual jobs. As manufacturing overhead costs are allocated, they become part of work-in-process inventory.

As individual jobs are completed, work-in-process inventory becomes another balance sheet asset, finished goods inventory. Only when finished goods are sold is the expense of cost of goods sold recognized in the income statement and matched against revenues earned.

The lower part of Exhibit 4-6 shows the period costs—marketing and customer-service costs. These costs do not create any assets on the balance sheet because they are not incurred to transform materials into a finished product. Instead, they are expensed in the income statement, as they are incurred, to best match revenues.

We next describe the entries made in the general ledger.

Exhibit 4-6

Flow of Costs in Job Costing

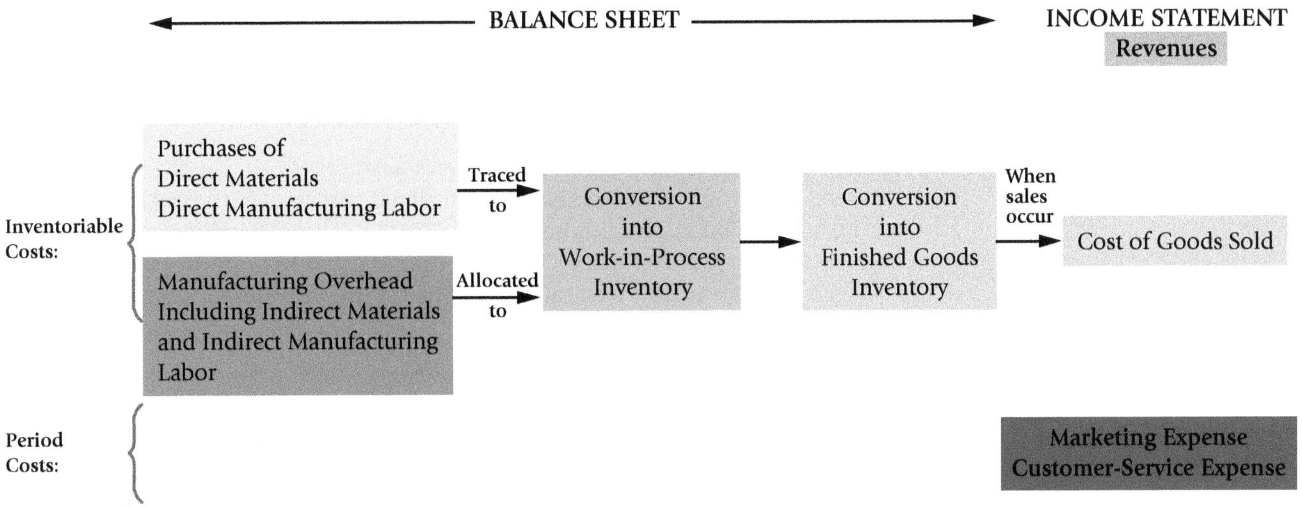

General Ledger

You know by this point that a job-costing system has a separate job-cost record for each job. A summary of the job-cost record is typically found in a subsidiary ledger. The general ledger account Work-in-Process Control presents the total of these separate job-cost records pertaining to all unfinished jobs. The job-cost records and Work-in-Process Control account track job costs from when jobs start until they are complete. When jobs are completed or sold, they are recorded in the finished goods inventory records of jobs in the subsidiary ledger. The general ledger account Finished Goods Control records the total of these separate job-cost records for all finished jobs completed and for all jobs sold.

Exhibit 4-7 shows T-account relationships for Robinson Company's general ledger. The general ledger gives a "bird's-eye view" of the costing system. The amounts shown in Exhibit 4-7 are based on the monthly transactions that follow. As you go through each transaction, use Exhibit 4-7 to see how the various entries being made come together. General ledger accounts with "Control" in the titles (for example, Materials Control and Accounts Payable Control) have underlying subsidiary ledgers that contain additional details, such as each type of material in inventory and individual suppliers that Robinson must pay.

Explanations of Transactions

We next look at a summary of Robinson Company's transactions for February 2012 and the corresponding entries for those transactions in the general ledger T-accounts.

1. Purchases of materials (direct and indirect) on credit, $89,000, which results in a debit to Materials Control and a credit to Accounts Payable Control. Recall that debit entries are made on the left side and credit entries on the right side of T-accounts and that assets (in this case Materials) are recorded on the left side and liabilities (in this case Accounts Payable) and owners' equity are recorded on the right side of T-accounts.

Materials Control				Accounts Payable Control			
1.	89,000					1.	89,000

2. Across all job-cost records for February 2012, the cost of direct materials used is $81,000 and the cost of indirect materials used is $4,000. The use of direct materials results in a debit to Work-in-Process Control of $81,000 and the use of indirect materials to a debit to Manufacturing Overhead Control of $4,000 to represent the creation of new assets. The corresponding credit is to Materials Control of $85,000, representing a decrease in the materials asset. The T-accounts show the buildup of each of the accounts affected by transaction 2. Note that the cost of indirect materials used cannot be traced to individual jobs and so it is not debited to Work-in-Process Control. Instead, like all other indirect manufacturing costs, indirect materials are accumulated in Manufacturing Overhead Control. Indirect manufacturing costs are allocated to individual job records and to Work-in-Process Control in step 5 to follow.

Materials Control				Work-in-Process Control				Manufacturing Overhead Control			
1.	89,000	2.	85,000	2.	81,000			2.	4,000		

3. The sum of total wages paid in cash to all employees for February 2012 is $54,000. Of these, total direct manufacturing labor costs recorded in all job-cost records (the subsidiary ledger for Work-in-Process Control) for February 2012 is $39,000. The total indirect manufacturing labor costs for February 2012 are $15,000. This results in debits to Work-in-Process Control of $39,000 and Manufacturing Overhead Control of $15,000 to represent a buildup in these assets and a credit to Cash Control of $54,000 to represent a decrease in this asset.

Work-in-Process Control				Manufacturing Overhead Control				Cash Control			
2.	81,000			2.	4,000					3.	54,000
3.	39,000			3.	15,000						

Exhibit 4-7

Manufacturing Job-Costing System Using Normal Costing: Diagram of General Ledger Relationships for February 2012

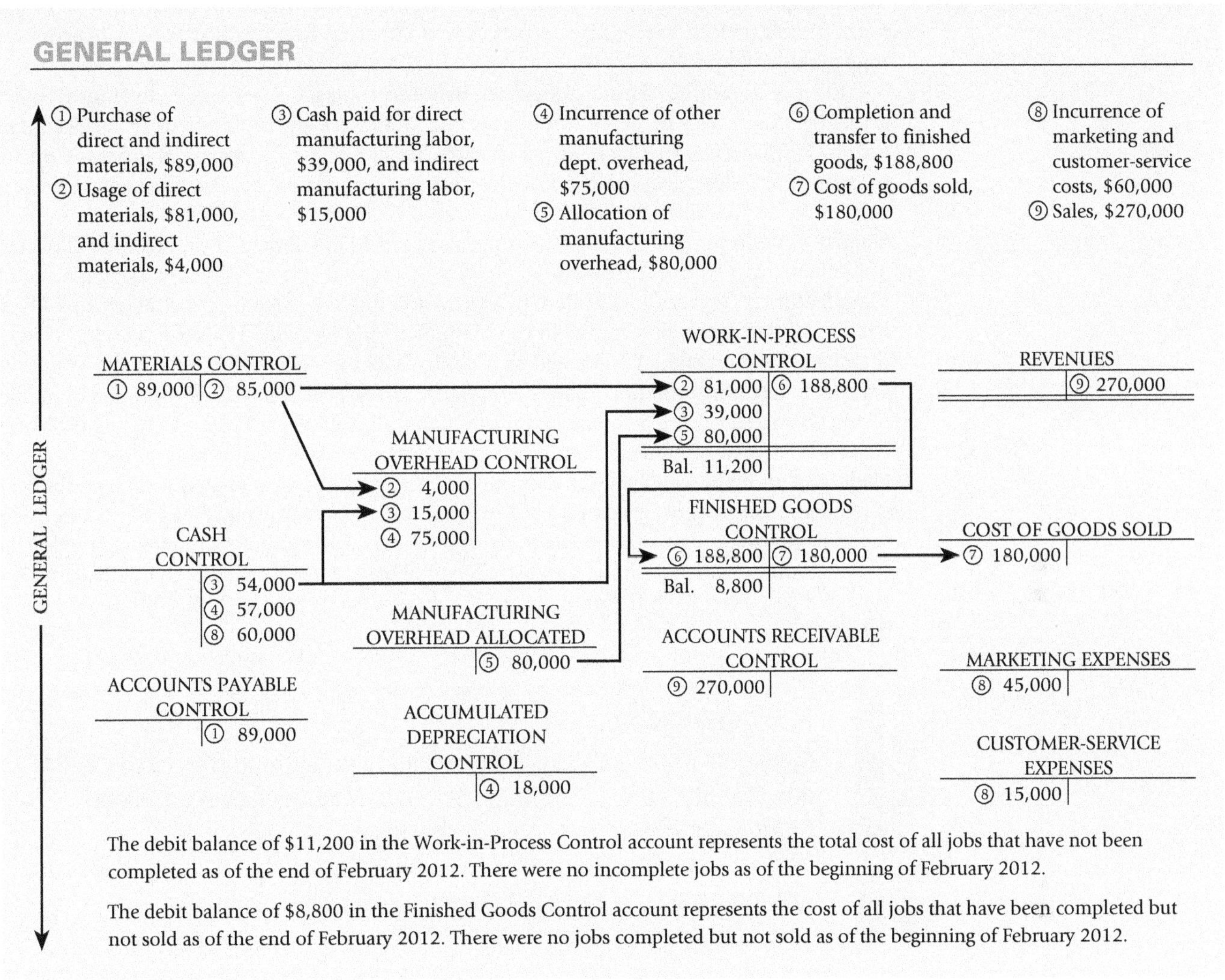
GENERAL LEDGER
① Purchase of direct and indirect materials, $89,000
② Usage of direct materials, $81,000, and indirect materials, $4,000
③ Cash paid for direct manufacturing labor, $39,000, and indirect manufacturing labor, $15,000
④ Incurrence of other manufacturing dept. overhead, $75,000
⑤ Allocation of manufacturing overhead, $80,000
⑥ Completion and transfer to finished goods, $188,800
⑦ Cost of goods sold, $180,000
⑧ Incurrence of marketing and customer-service costs, $60,000
⑨ Sales, $270,000
GENERAL LEDGER
MATERIALS CONTROL
① 89,000 ② 85,000
MANUFACTURING OVERHEAD CONTROL
② 4,000
③ 15,000
④ 75,000
CASH CONTROL
③ 54,000
④ 57,000
⑧ 60,000
MANUFACTURING OVERHEAD ALLOCATED
⑤ 80,000
ACCOUNTS PAYABLE CONTROL
① 89,000
ACCUMULATED DEPRECIATION CONTROL
④ 18,000
WORK-IN-PROCESS CONTROL
② 81,000 ⑥ 188,800
③ 39,000
⑤ 80,000
Bal. 11,200
FINISHED GOODS CONTROL
⑥ 188,800 ⑦ 180,000
Bal. 8,800
ACCOUNTS RECEIVABLE CONTROL
⑨ 270,000
REVENUES
⑨ 270,000
COST OF GOODS SOLD
⑦ 180,000
MARKETING EXPENSES
⑧ 45,000
CUSTOMER-SERVICE EXPENSES
⑧ 15,000
The debit balance of $11,200 in the Work-in-Process Control account represents the total cost of all jobs that have not been completed as of the end of February 2012. There were no incomplete jobs as of the beginning of February 2012.
The debit balance of $8,800 in the Finished Goods Control account represents the cost of all jobs that have been completed but not sold as of the end of February 2012. There were no jobs completed but not sold as of the beginning of February 2012.

4. Other manufacturing overhead costs incurred during February, $75,000, consisting of
   - supervision and engineering salaries, $44,000 (paid in cash);
   - plant utilities, repairs, and insurance, $13,000 (paid in cash); and
   - plant depreciation, $18,000.

   These transactions result in a debit to Manufacturing Overhead Control of $75,000 (increase in asset) and credits to Cash Control of $57,000 and Accumulated Depreciation Control of $18,000 to represent decreases in these assets.

Manufacturing Overhead Control			Cash Control			Accumulated Depreciation Control		
2.	4,000			3.	54,000		4.	18,000
3.	15,000			4	57,000			
4.	75,000							

5. The 2,000 actual direct manufacturing labor-hours that were used for all jobs in February 2012 results in a total manufacturing overhead allocation of $40 per labor-hour × 2,000 direct manufacturing labor-hours equal to $80,000. This transaction results in a debit to Work-in-Process Control and a credit to Manufacturing Overhead Allocated.

Work-in-Process Control			Manufacturing Overhead Allocated		
2.	81,000			5.	80,000
3.	39,000				
5.	80,000				

Under normal costing, **manufacturing overhead allocated**—or **manufacturing overhead applied**—is the amount of manufacturing overhead costs allocated to individual jobs based on the budgeted rate multiplied by actual quantity used of the allocation base. Manufacturing overhead allocated contains all manufacturing overhead costs, which are assigned to jobs using a cost-allocation base because these costs cannot be traced specifically to jobs in an economically feasible way.

Keep in mind the distinct difference between transactions 4 and 5. In transaction 4, actual overhead costs incurred throughout the month are added (debited) to the Manufacturing Overhead Control account. These costs are not debited to Work-in-Process Control, because unlike direct costs, they cannot be traced to individual jobs. Manufacturing overhead costs are added (debited) to individual jobs and to Work-in-Process Control *only when* manufacturing overhead costs are allocated in transaction 5. At the time these costs are allocated, Manufacturing Overhead Control is, *in effect,* decreased (credited) via its contra account, Manufacturing Overhead Allocated. By contra account, we mean that Manufacturing Overhead Allocated represents credits in the Manufacturing Overhead Control account. Having Manufacturing Overhead Allocated as a contra account allows the job-costing system to separately retain information about the manufacturing overheads incurred in the Manufacturing Overhead Control account and the amounts allocated in the Manufacturing Overhead Allocated account rather than combine these important pieces of information in one account. Under the normal-costing system described in our Robinson Company transaction, the budgeted manufacturing overhead rate of $40 per direct manufacturing labor-hour is calculated at the beginning of the year on the basis of predictions of annual manufacturing overhead costs and the annual quantity of the cost-allocation base. Almost certainly, the actual amounts allocated will differ from the predictions. We discuss what to do with this difference later in the chapter.

Keys to Success

Managers must distinguish between Manufacturing Overhead Control and Manufacturing Overhead Allocated. Manufacturing Overhead Control accumulates manufacturing overhead costs as they are incurred. Manufacturing Overhead Allocated allocates manufacturing overhead costs to individual jobs (Work-in-Process Control).

6. The sum of all individual jobs completed and transferred to finished goods in February 2012 is $188,800. This results in a debit to Finished Goods Control (increase in finished goods assets) and a credit to Work-in-Process Control (decrease in work-in-process assets).

Work-in-Process Control				Finished Goods Control			
1.	81,000	6.	188,800	6.	188,800		
3.	39,000						
5.	80,000						

7. Total cost of goods sold of all individual jobs completed and transferred in February 2012 is $180,000. This results in a debit to Cost of Goods Sold (an expense or decrease in owners' equity) and a credit to Finished Goods Control (decrease in finished goods assets).

Finished Goods Control				Cost of Goods Sold			
6.	188,800	7.	180,000	7.	180,000		

8. Marketing costs for February 2012, $45,000, and customer-service costs for February 2012, $15,000, paid in cash. This results in debits to Marketing Expenses of $45,000 and Customer-Service Expenses of $15,000 (decrease in owners' equity) and a credit to Cash Control of $60,000 (decrease in assets).

Marketing Expenses		Customer-Service Expenses		Cash Control	
8. 45,000		8. 15,000			3. 54,000
					4. 57,000
					8. 60,000

9. Sales revenues from all jobs sold and delivered in February 2012, all on credit, $270,000. This results in a debit to Accounts Receivable Control (increase in assets) and a credit to Revenues (increase in owners' equity).

Accounts Receivable Control		Revenues	
9. 270,000			9. 270,000

At this point, pause and review the nine entries in this illustration. Exhibit 4-7 is a handy summary of all nine general-ledger entries presented in T-account form. Be sure to trace each transaction, step-by-step, to T-accounts in the general ledger presented in Exhibit 4-7. Robinson's managers will use this information to evaluate how Robinson has performed on the WPP job.

Exhibit 4-8 provides Robinson's income statement for February 2012 using information from entries 7, 8, and 9. Managers could further subdivide the cost of goods sold calculations and present them in the format of Exhibit 2-8 (page 41). The benefit of using the subdivided format is that it allows managers to discern detailed trends in performance that helps them increase efficiency on future jobs.

Nonmanufacturing Costs and Job Costing. Chapter 2 (pages 47–48) pointed out that companies use product costs for different purposes. The product costs reported as inventoriable costs to shareholders may differ from product costs reported to managers for guiding pricing and product-mix decisions. Managers must keep in mind that even though marketing and customer-service costs are expensed when incurred for financial accounting purposes, companies often trace or allocate these costs to individual jobs for pricing, product-mix, and cost-management decisions.

To identify marketing and customer-service costs of individual jobs, Robinson can use the same approach to job costing described earlier in a manufacturing context. Robinson can trace the direct marketing costs and customer-service costs to jobs. Assume marketing and customer-service costs have the same cost-allocation base, revenues, and are included in a single cost pool. Robinson can then calculate a budgeted indirect-cost rate by dividing budgeted indirect marketing costs plus budgeted indirect customer-service costs by budgeted revenues. Robinson can use this rate to allocate these indirect costs to jobs. For example, if this rate were 22% of revenues, Robinson would allocate $3,300 to Job WPP 298 (0.22 × $15,000, the revenue from the job). By assigning both manufacturing costs and nonmanufacturing costs to jobs, Robinson can compare all costs against the revenues that different jobs generate.

Exhibit 4-8

Robinson Company Income Statement for the Month Ending February 2012

Revenues		$270,000
Cost of goods sold ($180,000 + $14,000[1])		194,000
Gross margin		76,000
Operating costs		
Marketing costs	$45,000	
Customer-service costs	15,000	
Total operating costs		60,000
Operating income		$ 16,000

[1]Cost of goods sold has been increased by $14,000, the difference between the Manufacturing overhead control account ($94,000) and the Manufacturing overhead allocated ($80,000). In a later section of this chapter, we discuss this adjustment, which represents the amount by which actual manufacturing overhead cost exceeds the manufacturing overhead allocated to jobs during February 2012.

Keys to Success

It is important for managers to recognize that inventoriable costs flow from purchase of materials and other manufacturing inputs into work-in-process, then to finished goods, and finally to cost of goods sold to be matched against revenues when the job is sold. Marketing and customer-service costs are noninventoriable or period costs and are expensed immediately to be matched against revenues when the job is sold.

Learning Objective 7

Dispose of under- or overallocated manufacturing overhead costs at the end of the fiscal year using alternative methods

. . . for example, writing off this amount to the Cost of Goods Sold account

Budgeted Indirect Costs and End-of-Accounting-Year Adjustments

Managers use budgeted indirect-cost rates and normal costing instead of actual costing because indirect costs can be assigned to individual jobs on an ongoing and timely basis, rather than only at the end of the fiscal year when actual costs are known. Recall that for the numerator and denominator reasons discussed earlier (pp. 119–121), we do *not* expect actual overhead costs incurred each month to equal overhead costs allocated each month. Even at the end of the year, budgeted rates are unlikely to equal actual rates because they are based on estimates made up to 12 months before actual costs are incurred. We now describe adjustments that managers need to make when, at the end of the fiscal year, indirect costs allocated differ from actual indirect costs incurred. These adjustments affect the reported income numbers used to evaluate managerial performance.

Underallocated and Overallocated Indirect Costs

Underallocated indirect costs occur when the allocated amount of indirect costs in an accounting period is less than the actual (incurred) amount. **Overallocated indirect costs** occur when the allocated amount of indirect costs in an accounting period is greater than the actual (incurred) amount.

Underallocated (overallocated) indirect costs = Actual indirect costs incurred − Indirect costs allocated

Underallocated (overallocated) indirect costs are also called **underapplied (overapplied) indirect costs** and **underabsorbed (overabsorbed) indirect costs.**

Consider the manufacturing overhead cost pool at Robinson Company. There are two indirect-cost accounts in the general ledger that have to do with manufacturing overhead:

1. Manufacturing Overhead Control, the record of the actual costs in all the individual overhead categories (such as indirect materials, indirect manufacturing labor, supervision, engineering, utilities, and plant depreciation)
2. Manufacturing Overhead Allocated, the record of the manufacturing overhead allocated to individual jobs on the basis of the budgeted rate multiplied by actual direct manufacturing labor-hours

At the end of the year, the overhead accounts show the following amounts.

Manufacturing Overhead Control			Manufacturing Overhead Allocated	
Bal. Dec. 31, 2012	1,215,000		Bal. Dec. 31, 2012	1,080,000

The $1,080,000 credit balance in Manufacturing Overhead Allocated results from multiplying the 27,000 actual direct manufacturing labor-hours worked on all jobs in 2012 by the budgeted rate of $40 per direct manufacturing labor-hour.

The $135,000 ($1,215,000 − $1,080,000) difference (a net debit) is an underallocated amount because actual manufacturing overhead costs are greater than the allocated amount. This difference arises from two reasons related to the computation of the $40 budgeted hourly rate:

1. **Numerator reason (indirect-cost pool).** Actual manufacturing overhead costs of $1,215,000 are greater than the budgeted amount of $1,120,000.

2. **Denominator reason (quantity of allocation base).** Actual direct manufacturing labor-hours of 27,000 are fewer than the budgeted 28,000 hours.

There are three main approaches to accounting for the $135,000 underallocated manufacturing overhead caused by Robinson underestimating manufacturing overhead costs and overestimating the quantity of the cost-allocation base: (1) adjusted allocation-rate approach, (2) proration approach, and (3) writeoff to cost of goods sold approach.

Adjusted Allocation-Rate Approach

The **adjusted allocation-rate approach** restates all overhead entries in the general ledger and job-cost records to represent actual cost rates rather than budgeted cost rates. The result is that at year-end, every job-cost record and finished goods record—as well as the ending Work-in-Process Control, Finished Goods Control, and Cost of Goods Sold accounts—represent actual manufacturing overhead costs incurred.

The widespread adoption of computerized accounting systems has greatly reduced the cost of using the adjusted allocation-rate approach. In our Robinson example, the actual manufacturing overhead ($1,215,000) exceeds the manufacturing overhead allocated ($1,080,000) by 12.5% [($1,215,000 − $1,080,000) ÷ $1,080,000]. At year-end, Robinson could increase the manufacturing overhead allocated to each job in 2012 by 12.5% using a single software command. The command would adjust both the job-cost records and the general ledger.

Consider the Western Pulp and Paper machine job, WPP 298. Under normal costing, the manufacturing overhead allocated to the job is $3,520 (the budgeted rate of $40 per direct manufacturing labor-hour × 88 hours). Increasing the manufacturing overhead allocated by 12.5%, or $440 ($3,520 × 0.125), means the adjusted amount of manufacturing overhead allocated to Job WPP 298 equals $3,960 ($3,520 + $440). Note from page 127 that using actual costing, manufacturing overhead allocated to this job is $3,960 (the actual rate of $45 per direct manufacturing labor-hour × 88 hours). Making this adjustment under normal costing for each job-cost record ensures that actual manufacturing overhead costs of $1,215,000 are allocated to jobs.

The adjusted allocation-rate approach yields the benefits of both the *timeliness and convenience of normal costing during the year and the allocation of actual manufacturing overhead costs at year-end.* Each individual job-cost record and the end-of-year account balances for inventories and cost of goods sold are adjusted to actual costs. These adjustments, in turn, affect reported income. After-the-fact analysis of actual profitability of individual jobs provides managers with accurate and useful insights for future decisions about job pricing, which jobs to emphasize, and ways to manage job costs.

Proration Approach

Proration spreads underallocated overhead or overallocated overhead among ending work-in-process inventory, finished goods inventory, and cost of goods sold. Materials inventory is not included in this proration because no manufacturing overhead costs have been allocated to it. We illustrate end-of-year proration in the Robinson Company example. Assume the following actual results for Robinson Company in 2012:

	A	B	C
1	Account	Account Balance (Before Proration)	Allocated Manufacturing Overhead Included in Each Account Balance (Before Proration)
2	Work-in-process control	$ 50,000	$ 16,200
3	Finished goods control	75,000	31,320
4	Cost of goods sold	2,375,000	1,032,480
5		$2,500,000	$1,080,000

How should Robinson prorate the underallocated $135,000 of manufacturing overhead at the end of 2012?

Robinson prorates underallocated or overallocated amounts on the basis of the total amount of manufacturing overhead allocated in 2012 (before proration) in the ending balances of Work-in-Process Control, Finished Goods Control, and Cost of Goods Sold. The $135,000 underallocated overhead is prorated over the three affected accounts in proportion to the total amount of manufacturing overhead allocated (before proration) in column 2 of the following table, resulting in the ending balances (after proration) in column 5 at actual costs.

	A	B	C	D	E	F	G
10		Account Balance (Before Proration)	Allocated Manufacturing Overhead Included in Each Account Balance (Before Proration)	Allocated Manufacturing Overhead Included in Each Account Balance as a Percent of Total	Proration of $135,000 of Underallocated Manufacturing Overhead		Account Balance (After Proration)
11	Account	(1)	(2)	(3) = (2) / $1,080,000	(4) = (3) x $135,000		(5) = (1) + (4)
12	Work-in-process control	$ 50,000	$ 16,200	1.5%	0.015 x $135,000 =	$ 2,025	$ 52,025
13	Finished goods control	75,000	31,320	2.9%	0.029 x 135,000 =	3,915	78,915
14	Cost of goods sold	2,375,000	1,032,480	95.6%	0.956 x 135,000 =	129,060	2,504,060
15	Total	$2,500,000	$1,080,000	100.0%		$135,000	$2,635,000

Prorating on the basis of the manufacturing overhead allocated (before proration) results in allocating manufacturing overhead based on actual manufacturing overhead costs. Recall that the actual manufacturing overhead ($1,215,000) in 2012 exceeds the manufacturing overhead allocated ($1,080,000) in 2012 by 12.5%. The proration amounts in column 4 can also be derived by multiplying the balances in column 2 by 0.125. For example, the $3,915 proration to Finished Goods is 0.125 × $31,320. Adding these amounts effectively means allocating manufacturing overhead at 112.5% of what had been allocated before. In the general ledger, Work-in-Process Control is debited by $2,025, Finished Goods Control is debited by $3,915, Cost of Goods Sold is debited by $129,060, Manufacturing Overhead Allocated is debited by $1,080,000 (to close out or make the account zero), and Manufacturing Overhead Control is credited by $1,215,000 (to close out or make the account zero).[2] The net effect is to restate the 2012 ending balances for Work-in-Process Control, Finished Goods Control, and Cost of Goods Sold to what they would have been if actual manufacturing overhead rates had been used rather than budgeted manufacturing overhead rates. This method reports the same 2012 ending balances in the general ledger as the adjusted allocation-rate approach. However, unlike the adjusted allocation-rate approach, no adjustments from budgeted to actual manufacturing overhead rates are made in the individual job-cost records. The objective of the proration approach is to only adjust the general ledger to actual manufacturing overhead rates for purposes of financial reporting. The increase in cost of goods sold expense by $129,060 as a result of the proration causes reported operating income to decrease by the same amount.

Writeoff to Cost of Goods Sold Approach

Under the writeoff approach, the total under- or overallocated manufacturing overhead is included in this year's Cost of Goods Sold. In the general ledger, Cost of Goods Sold is debited by $135,000, Manufacturing Overhead Allocated is debited by $1,080,000 (to make the account zero, also called closing out), and Manufacturing Overhead Control is credited by $1,215,000 (to close out or make

[2] The effect of proration in the T-accounts is as follows:

Work-in-Process Control		Finished Goods Control		Cost of Goods Sold		Manufacturing Overhead Allocated		Manufacturing Overhead Control	
2,025		3,915		129,060		1,080,000			1,215,000

the account zero).[3] The Cost of Goods Sold account after the writeoff equals $2,510,000, the balance before the writeoff of $2,375,000 *plus the underallocated* manufacturing overhead amount of $135,000, resulting in operating income decreasing by $135,000.

Choice Among Approaches

Which of these three approaches of dealing with underallocated overhead and overallocated overhead is the best one to use? In making this decision, managers are guided by the amount of underallocation or overallocation and the purpose of the adjustment, as the following table indicates.

If the purpose of the adjustment is to . . .	and the amount of underallocation or overallocation is . . .	then managers prefer to use the . . .
state balance sheet and income statements based on actual rather than budgeted manufacturing overhead rates	big, relative to total operating income or some other measure of materiality and inventory levels are high	proration method because it is the most accurate method of allocating actual manufacturing overhead costs to the general ledger accounts.
state balance sheet and income statements based on actual rather than budgeted manufacturing overhead rates	small, relative to total operating income or some other measure of materiality or inventory levels are low	writeoff to cost of goods sold expense method because it is a good approximation to the more accurate proration method.
provide an accurate record of actual individual job costs for profitability analysis and learning for managing costs and bidding on future jobs		adjusted-allocation rate method because it makes adjustments in individual job records in addition to the general ledger accounts.

Many management accountants and managers argue that to the extent that the underallocated or overallocated overhead cost measures inefficiency during the period, it should be written off to Cost of Goods Sold instead of being prorated to the Work-in-Process or Finished Goods inventory accounts. This line of reasoning favors applying a combination of the writeoff and proration methods. For example, the portion of the underallocated overhead cost that is due to inefficiency (say, because of excessive spending or idle capacity) and that could have been avoided should be written off to Cost of Goods Sold, whereas the portion that is unavoidable should be prorated. Unlike full proration, this approach avoids carrying the costs of inefficiency as part of inventory assets.

As our discussion suggests, choosing which method to use and determining the amount to be written off is often a matter of judgment. The method that managers choose affects the operating income a company reports. In the case of underallocated overhead, writing off to cost of goods sold results in lower operating income compared to proration. In the case of overallocated overhead, proration results in lower operating income compared to writing off to cost of goods sold. Reporting lower operating income lowers tax payments, saving the company cash and increasing the company's value. On the other hand, reporting a higher operating income may increase a manager's compensation even though it results in higher tax payments. Top managers design compensation plans to encourage managers to take actions that increase a company's value. For example, the compensation plan might reward after-tax cash flow metrics, in addition to operating income metrics, to align decision making and performance evaluation. Occasionally, in times of financial difficulty, managers may prefer to report higher operating income to avoid showing losses that could result in loans and borrowings coming due. Despite these incentives, managers should choose the method that increases the company's value and best represents its performance. At no time should managers make choices that are illegal or violate corporate ethics. We discuss these issues in more detail in Chapter 16.

Robinson's managers believed that a single manufacturing overhead cost pool with direct manufacturing labor dollars as the cost-allocation base was appropriate for allocating all manufacturing overhead costs to jobs. Had Robinson's managers felt that different departments used overhead resources differently, they would have assigned overhead costs to each department and calculated a separate overhead allocation rate for each department (see the appendix). The general ledger would contain Manufacturing Overhead Control and Manufacturing Overhead Allocated for each department, resulting in end-of-year adjustments for underallocated or overallocated overhead costs for each department.

[3] The effect on the T-accounts is as follows:

Cost of Goods Sold		Manufacturing Overhead Allocated		Manufacturing Overhead Control	
135,000		1,080,000			1,215,000

Keys to Success

Managers use the Adjusted Allocation-Rate Approach, the Proration Approach, and the Writeoff to Cost of Goods Sold approach to make adjustments at the end of the year to account for any overhead costs that are either underallocated or overallocated so that overhead costs allocated equal the overhead costs incurred. The approach managers use depends on the amount of underallocation or overallocation, the purpose of the adjustment, and other incentives.

Learning Objective 8

Apply variations from normal costing

. . . variations from normal costing use budgeted direct-cost rates

Variations from Normal Costing: A Service-Sector Example

Job costing is also very useful in service organizations such as accounting and consulting firms, advertising agencies, auto repair shops, and hospitals. In an accounting firm, each audit is a job. The costs of each audit are accumulated in a job-cost record, much like the document used by Robinson Company, based on the seven-step approach described earlier. On the basis of labor-time sheets, direct labor costs of the professional staff—audit partners, audit managers, and audit staff—are traced to individual jobs. Other direct costs, such as travel, out-of-town meals and lodging, phone, fax, and copying, are also traced to jobs. The costs of secretarial support, office staff, rent, and depreciation of furniture and equipment are indirect costs because these costs cannot be traced to jobs in an economically feasible way. Indirect costs are allocated to jobs, for example, using a cost-allocation base such as number of professional labor-hours.

In some service organizations, a variation from normal costing is helpful because actual direct-labor costs, the largest component of total costs, can be difficult to trace to jobs as they are completed. For example, the actual direct-labor costs of an audit may include bonuses that become known only at the end of the year (a numerator reason). Also, the hours worked each period might vary significantly depending on the number of working days each month and the demand for services (a denominator reason). In situations like these, a company needing timely information during the progress of an audit will use budgeted rates for some direct costs and budgeted rates for indirect costs. All budgeted rates are calculated at the start of the fiscal year. In contrast, normal costing uses actual cost rates for all direct costs and budgeted cost rates only for indirect costs.

The mechanics of using budgeted rates for direct costs are similar to the methods employed when using budgeted rates for indirect costs in normal costing. We illustrate this for Donahue and Associates, a public accounting firm. For 2012, Donahue budgets total direct-labor costs of \$14,400,000, total indirect costs of \$12,960,000, and total direct (professional) labor-hours of 288,000. In this case,

$$\text{Budgeted direct-labor cost rate} = \frac{\text{Budgeted total direct-labor costs}}{\text{Budgeted total direct-labor hours}}$$

$$= \frac{\$14{,}400{,}000}{288{,}000 \text{ direct labor-hours}} = \$50 \text{ per direct labor-hour}$$

Assuming only one indirect-cost pool and total direct-labor costs as the cost-allocation base,

$$\text{Budgeted indirect cost rate} = \frac{\text{Budgeted total costs in indirect cost pool}}{\text{Budgeted total quantity of cost-allocation base (direct-labor costs)}}$$

$$= \frac{\$12{,}960{,}000}{\$14{,}400{,}000} = 0.90, \text{ or } 90\% \text{ of direct-labor costs}$$

Suppose that in March 2012, an audit of Hanley Transport, a client of Donahue, uses 800 direct labor-hours. Donahue calculates the direct-labor costs of the Hanley Transport audit by multiplying the budgeted direct-labor cost rate, \$50 per direct labor-hour, by 800, the actual quantity of direct labor-hours. The indirect costs allocated to the Hanley Transport audit are determined by multiplying the budgeted indirect-cost rate (90%) by the direct-labor costs assigned to the job

($40,000). Assuming no other direct costs for travel and the like, the cost of the Hanley Transport audit is as follows:

Direct-labor costs, $50 × 800	$40,000
Indirect costs allocated, 90% × $40,000	36,000
Total	$76,000

At the end of the fiscal year, the direct costs traced to jobs using budgeted rates will generally not equal actual direct costs because the actual rate and the budgeted rate are developed at different times using different information. End-of-year adjustments for under- or overallocated direct costs would need to be made in the same way that adjustments are made for under- or overallocated indirect costs.

The Donahue and Associates example illustrates that all costing systems do not exactly match either the actual-costing system or the normal-costing system described earlier in the chapter. As another example, engineering consulting firms, such as Tata Consulting Engineers in India and Terracon Consulting Engineers in the United States, often have some actual direct costs (cost of making blueprints or fees paid to outside experts), other direct costs (professional-labor costs) assigned to jobs using a budgeted rate, and indirect costs (engineering and office-support costs) allocated to jobs using a budgeted rate. Therefore, users of costing systems should be aware of the different systems that they may encounter.

Keys to Success

Managers use a variation of normal costing by using budgeted rates to assign direct costs when actual direct costs are difficult to trace to jobs as they are being completed.

Problem for Self-Study

Your manager asks you to bring the following incomplete accounts of Endeavor Printing, Inc., up-to-date through January 31, 2013. Consider the data that appear in the T-accounts as well as the following information in items (a) through (j).

Endeavor's normal-costing system has two direct-cost categories (direct material costs and direct manufacturing labor costs) and one indirect-cost pool (manufacturing overhead costs, which are allocated using direct manufacturing labor costs).

Materials Control			
12-31-2012 Bal.	15,000		

Wages Payable Control			
		1-31-2013 Bal.	3,000

Work-in-Process Control			

Manufacturing Overhead Control			
1-31-2013 Bal.	57,000		

Finished Goods Control			
12-31-2012 Bal.	20,000		

Costs of Goods Sold			

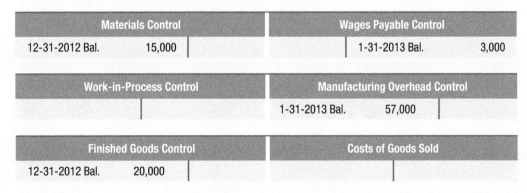

Additional information follows:

a. Manufacturing overhead is allocated using a budgeted rate that is set every December. You forecast next year's manufacturing overhead costs and next year's direct manufacturing labor costs. The budget for 2013 is $600,000 for manufacturing overhead costs and $400,000 for direct manufacturing labor costs.

b. The only job unfinished on January 31, 2013, is No. 419, on which direct manufacturing labor costs are $2,000 (125 direct manufacturing labor-hours) and direct material costs are $8,000.

- **c.** Total direct materials issued to production during January 2013 are $90,000.
- **d.** Cost of goods completed during January is $180,000.
- **e.** Materials inventory as of January 31, 2013, is $20,000.
- **f.** Finished goods inventory as of January 31, 2013, is $15,000.
- **g.** All plant workers earn the same wage rate. Direct manufacturing labor-hours used for January total 2,500 hours. Other labor costs total $10,000.
- **h.** The gross plant payroll paid in January equals $52,000. Ignore withholdings.
- **i.** All "actual" manufacturing overhead cost incurred during January has already been posted.
- **j.** All materials are direct materials.

Required

Calculate the following:

1. Materials purchased during January
2. Cost of Goods Sold during January
3. Direct manufacturing labor costs incurred during January
4. Manufacturing Overhead Allocated during January
5. Balance, Wages Payable Control, December 31, 2012
6. Balance, Work-in-Process Control, January 31, 2013
7. Balance, Work-in-Process Control, December 31, 2012
8. Manufacturing Overhead Underallocated or Overallocated for January 2013

Solution

Amounts from the T-accounts are labeled "(T)."

1. From Materials Control T-account, Materials purchased: $90,000 (c) + $20,000 (e) − $15,000 (T) = $95,000
2. From Finished Goods Control T-account, Cost of Goods Sold: $20,000 (T) + $180,000 (d) − $15,000 (f) = $185,000
3. Direct manufacturing wage rate: $2,000 (b) ÷ 125 direct manufacturing labor-hours (b) = $16 per direct manufacturing labor-hour
   Direct manufacturing labor costs: 2,500 direct manufacturing labor-hours (g) × $16 per hour = $40,000
4. Manufacturing overhead rate: $600,000 (a) ÷ $400,000 (a) = 150%
   Manufacturing Overhead Allocated: 150% of $40,000 = 1.50 × $40,000 (see 3) = $60,000
5. From Wages Payable Control T-account, Wages Payable Control, December 31, 2012: $52,000 (h) + $3,000 (T) − $40,000 (see 3) − $10,000 (g) = $5,000
6. Work-in-Process Control, January 31, 2013: $8,000 (b) + $2,000 (b) + 150% of $2,000 (b) = $13,000 (This answer is used in item 7.)
7. From Work-in-Process Control T-account, Work-in-Process Control, December 31, 2012: $180,000 (d) + $13,000 (see 6) − $90,000 (c) − $40,000 (see 3) − $60,000 (see 4) = $3,000
8. Manufacturing overhead overallocated: $60,000 (see 4) −$57,000 (T) = $3,000.
   Letters alongside entries in T-accounts correspond to letters in the preceding additional information. Numbers alongside entries in T-accounts correspond to numbers in the preceding requirements.

Materials Control				
December 31, 2012, Bal.	(given)	15,000		
	(1)	95,000*	(c)	90,000
January 31, 2013, Bal.	(e)	20,000		

* Can be computed only after all other postings in the account have been made.

Work-in-Process Control				
December 31, 2012	(7)	3,000	(d)	180,000
Direct materials	(c)	90,000		
Direct manufacturing labor	(b) (g) (3)	40,000		
Manufacturing overhead allocated	(3) (a) (4)	60,000		
January 31, 2013, Bal.	(b) (6)	13,000		

Finished Goods Control					
December 31, 2012, Bal.	(given)	20,000		(2)	185,000
	(d)	180,000			
January 31, 2013, Bal.	(f)	15,000			

Wages Payable Control					
	(h)	52,000	December 31, 2012, Bal.	(5)	5,000
				(g) (3)	40,000
				(g)	10,000
			January 31, 2013	(given)	3,000

Manufacturing Overhead Control					
Total January charges	(given)	57,000			

Manufacturing Overhead Allocated					
				(3) (a) (4)	60,000

Cost of Goods Sold					
	(d) (f) (2)	185,000			

Decision Points

The following question-and-answer format summarizes the chapter's learning objectives. Each decision presents a key question related to a learning objective. The guidelines are the answer to that question.

Decision	Guidelines
1. What are the building-block concepts of a costing system?	The building-block concepts of a costing system are cost object, direct costs of a cost object, indirect costs of a cost object, cost pool, and cost-allocation base. Costing-system overview diagrams represent these concepts in a systematic way. Costing systems aim to report cost numbers that reflect the way chosen cost objects (such as products or services) use the resources of an organization.
2. How do you distinguish job costing from process costing?	Job-costing systems assign costs to distinct units of a product or service. Process-costing systems assign costs to masses of identical or similar units and compute unit costs on an average basis. These two costing systems represent opposite ends of a continuum. The costing systems of many companies combine some elements of both job costing and process costing.
3. What is the main challenge of implementing job-costing systems?	The main challenge of implementing job-costing systems is estimating actual costs of jobs in a timely manner.
4. How do you implement a normal-costing system?	A general seven-step approach to normal costing requires identifying (1) the job, (2) the actual direct costs, (3) the budgeted cost-allocation bases, (4) the budgeted indirect-cost pools, (5) the budgeted cost-allocation rates, (6) the allocated indirect costs (budgeted rate times actual quantity), and (7) the total direct and indirect costs of a job.

Decision	Guidelines
5. How do you distinguish actual costing from normal costing?	Actual costing and normal costing differ in the type of indirect-cost rates used: (see table below) Both systems use actual quantities of inputs for tracing direct costs and actual quantities of the allocation bases for allocating indirect costs.
6. How are transactions recorded in a manufacturing job-costing system?	A job-costing system in manufacturing records the flow of inventoriable costs for (a) acquisition of materials and other manufacturing inputs, (b) their conversion into work in process, (c) their conversion into finished goods, and (d) the sale of finished goods. The job-costing system expenses period costs, such as marketing costs, as they are incurred.
7. How should managers dispose of under- or overallocated manufacturing overhead costs at the end of the accounting year?	The two standard approaches to disposing of under- or overallocated manufacturing overhead costs at the end of the accounting year for stating balance sheet and income statement amounts at actual costs are (1) to adjust the allocation rate and (2) to prorate on the basis of the total amount of the allocated manufacturing overhead cost in the ending balances of Work-in-Process Control, Finished Goods Control, and Cost of Goods Sold. Many companies, however, simply write off amounts of under- or overallocated manufacturing overhead to Cost of Goods Sold when amounts are immaterial.
8. What are some variations from normal costing?	In some variations from normal costing, organizations use budgeted rates to assign direct costs, as well as indirect costs, to jobs.

	Actual Costing	Normal Costing
Direct-cost rates	Actual rates	Actual rates
Indirect-cost rates	Actual rates	Budgeted rates

Appendix

Allocating Costs with Multiple Overhead Cost Pools

The Robinson company example assumed that a single manufacturing overhead cost pool with direct manufacturing labor-hours as the cost-allocation base is a good measure for allocating all manufacturing overhead costs to jobs. Robinson would have used multiple cost-allocation bases, say, direct manufacturing labor-hours and machine-hours, to allocate manufacturing overhead costs to jobs if its managers believed that the benefits of the information generated by adding one or more pools (such as more-accurate costing and pricing of jobs or a better ability to manage costs) exceeds the additional costs of the costing system.

In this appendix, we describe a normal-costing system with two overhead cost pools. We follow the seven-step approach to assigning costs to an individual job described on pages 121–124 of the chapter. Steps 1 and 2 are exactly as before:

Step 1 identifies WPP 298 as the cost object.

Step 2 calculates actual direct material costs of $4,606, and actual direct manufacturing labor costs of $1,579.

Step 3 requires the management accountant to "select the cost-allocation bases to use for allocating indirect costs to jobs."

Robinson has two manufacturing departments—the Machining Department and the Assembly Department. Each department has a different overhead cost driver—machine-hours in the

Machining Department and assembly labor-hours in the Assembly Department. Different jobs need different amounts of machining and assembly resources. Robinson's managers decide to allocate Machining Department overhead costs using machine-hours and Assembly Department overhead costs using labor-hours.

Step 4 "identifies the indirect costs associated with each cost-allocation base" (page 123). Exhibit 4-9, column 6, provides details of Robinson's total budgeted manufacturing overhead costs of $1,120,000 for 2012, for example, supervision salaries, $200,000; depreciation and maintenance, $193,000; indirect labor, $195,000; and rent, utilities, and insurance, $160,000. In Step 4, Robinson allocates the $1,120,000 of total budgeted manufacturing overhead costs to the Machining and Assembly Departments.

Columns (1) through (5) in Exhibit 4-9 show the various manufacturing departments to which each category of cost is either traced or allocated (Plant Administration, Engineering and Production Control, Materials Management, Machining, and Assembly). Note that the Machining and Assembly Departments are labeled as operating departments. An **operating department,** also called a **production department,** directly adds value to a product or service. The other departments, Plant Administration, Engineering and Production Control, and Materials Management, are support departments. A **support department,** which is also called a **service department,** provides the services that assist other internal departments (operating departments and other support departments) in the company.

Let's look more closely at Robinson's three support departments, all of which, like the operating departments, are expected to operate at capacity. The Plant Adminstration Department is responsible for managing all activities in the plant. That is, its costs are incurred to support, and can be thought of, as part of the supervision costs of all the other departments.

The Engineering and Production Control Department supports all the engineering activity in the other departments. In other words, its costs are incurred to support the engineering costs of the other departments.

The Materials Management Department is responsible for managing and moving materials and components required for different jobs. Each job at Robinson is different and requires small quantities of unique components to be machined and assembled. Materials Management Department costs vary with the number of material-handling labor-hours incurred in each department. Material-handling labor costs are included as part of the indirect labor costs of each department. They are a substantial component of indirect labor costs of the Assembly Department but a much smaller component of the indirect labor costs of the other departments.

In Step 4, Robinson allocates all support department costs to the Machining and Assembly Departments using the following steps.

Step A: Trace or allocate each cost to various support and operating departments. Exhibit 4-9 shows calculations for this step. For example, supervision salaries are traced to the departments in which the supervisors work. As described on page 123, supervision costs are an indirect cost of individual jobs because supervisory costs cannot be traced to individual jobs. They are a direct cost of the different departments, however, because they can be identified with each department in an economically feasible way. Rent, utilities, and insurance costs cannot be traced to each department because these costs are incurred for all of Robinson's manufacturing facility. They are therefore allocated to different departments on the basis of the square feet area—the cost driver for rent, utilities, and insurance costs.

Step B: Allocate plant administration costs to other support departments and operating departments. Plant administration supports supervisors in each department, so plant administration costs are allocated to departments on the basis of supervision costs.

Some companies prefer not to allocate plant administration costs to products because these costs are fixed and independent of the level of activity in the plant. However, most companies, like Robinson, allocate plant administration costs to departments and products because allocating all costs allows companies to calculate the full manufacturing costs of products.

$$\frac{\text{Plant administration}}{\text{cost-allocation rate}} = \frac{\text{Total plant administration costs}}{\text{Total supervision salaries}} = \frac{\$100{,}000}{\$200{,}000} = 0.50$$

The bottom part of Exhibit 4-9 shows how Robinson uses the 0.50 cost-allocation rate and supervision salaries to allocate plant adminstration costs to the other support and operating departments.

Exhibit 4-9

Details of Budgeted Manufacturing Overhead at Robinson Company for 2012

	Support Departments			Operating Departments		
Step A	Plant Administration Department (1)	Engineering and Production Control Department (2)	Materials Management Department (3)	Machining Department (4)	Assembly Department (5)	Total (6)
Plant manager's salary	$ 92,000					$ 92,000
Supervision salaries (traced to each department)		$ 48,000	$40,000	$52,000	$ 60,000	200,000
Engineering salaries (traced to each department)		110,000	36,000	60,000	24,000	230,000
Depreciation and maintenance (traced to each department)		39,000	55,000	79,000	20,000	193,000
Indirect materials (traced to each department)		20,000	12,000	11,000	7,000	50,000
Indirect labor (traced to each department)		43,000	63,000	44,000	45,000	195,000
Rent, utilities, and insurance (allocated to each department based on square feet area; $8[1] × 1,000; 2,000; 3,000; 8,000; 6,000 sq.ft.)	8,000	16,000	24,000	64,000	48,000	160,000
Total	$100,000	$276,000	$230,000	$310,000	$204,000	$1,120,000
Step B						
Allocation of plant administration costs 0.50[2] × $48,000; $40,000; $52,000; $60,000	$(100,000)	24,000	20,000	26,000	30,000	0
Total	$ 0	$300,000	$250,000	$336,000	$234,000	$1,120,000

[1] $160,000 ÷ 20,000 square feet total area = $8 per square foot

[2] $$\text{Plant administration cost-allocation rate} = \frac{\text{Total plant administration costs}}{\text{Total supervision salaries}} = \frac{\$100{,}000}{\$200{,}000} = 0.50$$

Step C: Allocate Engineering and Production Control and Materials Management Costs to the Machining and Assembly Operating Departments. Note that the two support departments whose costs are being allocated—Engineering and Production Control and Materials Management—provide reciprocal support to each other as well as support to the operating departments. That is, the Engineering and Production Control Department provides services to the Material Handling Department (for example, engineering services for material-handling equipment), while the Materials Management Department provides services to the Engineering and Production Control Department (for example, delivering materials). Exhibit 4-10 displays the data.

To understand the percentages in this exhibit, consider the Engineering and Production Control Department. This department supports the engineering activity in the other departments and so the costs of this department are allocated based on engineering salaries in each of the other departments. From Exhibit 4-9, budgeted engineering salaries are $36,000 in the Materials Management Department, $60,000 in the Machining Department, and $24,000 in the Assembly Department for a total of $120,000 ($36,000 + $60,000 + $24,000). Thus, the Engineering and Production Control Department provides support of 30% ($36,000 ÷ $120,000 = 0.30) to the Materials Management Department, 50% ($60,000 ÷ $120,000 = 0.50) to the Machining Department, and 20% ($24,000 ÷ $120,000 = 0.20) to the Assembly Department. Similarly, the Materials Management Department supports 4,000 material handling labor-hours in the other

Exhibit 4-10

Data for Allocating Budgeted Support Department Costs at Robinson Company for 2012

	A	B	C	D	E	F	G
1		**SUPPORT DEPARTMENTS**			**OPERATING DEPARTMENTS**		
2		**Engineering and Production Control**	**Materials Management**		**Machining**	**Assembly**	**Total**
3	Budgeted overhead costs						
4	before any interdepartment cost allocations	$ 300,000	$ 250,000		$336,000	$234,000	$1,120,000
5	Support work furnished:						
6	By Engineering and Production Control						
7	Budgeted Engineering salaries	—	$ 36,000		$60,000	$24,000	$120,000
8	Percentage	—	30%		50%	20%	100%
9	By Materials Management						
10	Budgeted material-handling labor-hours	400	—		800	2,800	4,000
11	Percentage	10%	—		20%	70%	100%

departments: 10% (400 ÷ 4,000 = 0.10) for the Engineering and Production Control Department, 20% (800 ÷ 4,000 = 0.20) for the Machining Department, and 70% (2,800 ÷ 4,000 = 0.70) for the Assembly Department.

We describe three methods of allocating budgeted overhead costs from the support departments to the Machining Department and the Assembly Department: *direct, step-down,* and *reciprocal.*

Direct Method

The **direct method** allocates each support department's costs to operating departments only. The direct method does not allocate support department costs to other support departments. Exhibit 4-11 illustrates this method using the data in Exhibit 4-10. The base used to allocate Engineering and Production Control costs to the operating departments is the budgeted engineering salaries in the operating departments: $60,000 + $24,000 = $84,000. This amount excludes the $36,000 of budgeted engineering salaries in the Materials Management Department, even though the Engineering and Production Control Department supports engineering services in the Materials Management Department. Similarly, the base used for allocation of Materials Management costs to the operating departments is 800 + 2,800 = 3,600 budgeted material-handling labor-hours, which excludes the 400 hours of budgeted material-handling labor-hours in the Engineering and Production Control Department, even though the Materials Management Department supports material-handling labor in the Engineering and Production Control Department.

An equivalent approach to implementing the direct method involves calculating a budgeted rate for each support department's costs. For example, the rate for the Engineering and Production Control Department costs is $300,000 ÷ $84,000, or 357.143%. The Machining Department is then allocated $214,286 (357.143% × $60,000), while the Assembly Department is allocated $85,714 (357.143% × $24,000). For ease of explanation throughout this section, we use the fraction of the support department services used by other departments, rather than calculate budgeted rates, to allocate support department costs.

Most managers adopt the direct method because it is easy to use. The benefit of the direct method is simplicity. There is no need to predict the usage of support department services by other support departments. A disadvantage of the direct method is that it ignores information about reciprocal services provided among support departments and can therefore lead to inaccurate estimates of the cost of operating departments. We now examine a second approach, which partially recognizes the services provided among support departments.

Exhibit 4-11

Direct Method of Allocating Budgeted Support-Department Costs at Robinson Company for 2012

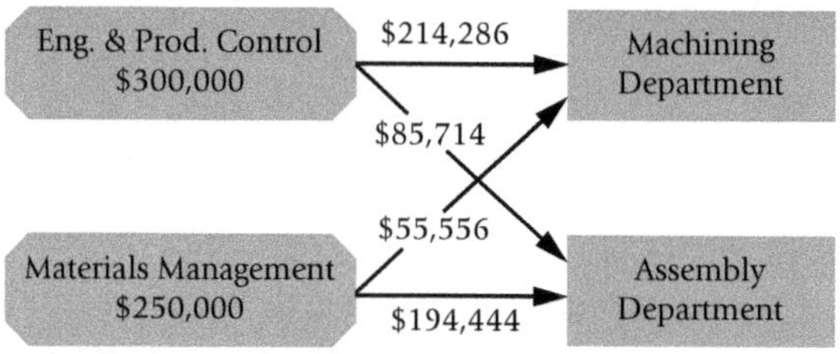

	A	B	C	D	E	F	G
1		SUPPORT DEPARTMENTS			OPERATING DEPARTMENTS		
2		Engineering and Production Control	Materials Management		Machining	Assembly	Total
3	Budgeted overhead costs						
4	before any interdepartment cost allocations	$300,000	$250,000		$336,000	$234,000	$1,120,000
5	Allocation of Eng. and Prod. Control (5/7, 2/7)[a]	(300,000)			214,286	85,714	
6	Allocation of Materials Management (2/9, 7/9)[b]		(250,000)		55,556	194,444	
7							
8	Total budgeted overhead of operating departments	$ 0	$ 0		$605,842	$514,158	$1,120,000
9							
10	[a]Base is ($60,000 + $24,000), or $84,000; $60,000 ÷ $84,000 = 5/7; $24,000 ÷ $84,000 = 2/7.						
11	[b]Base is (800 + 2,800), or 3,600 hours; 800 ÷ 3,600 = 2/9; 2,800 ÷ 3,600 = 7/9.						

Step-Down Method

Some organizations use the **step-down method**—also called the **sequential allocation method**—which allocates support-department costs to other support departments and to operating departments in a sequential manner that partially recognizes the mutual services provided among all support departments.

Exhibit 4-12 shows the step-down method. The Engineering and Production Control costs of $300,000 are allocated first. Exhibit 4-10 shows that Engineering and Production Control provides 30% of its services to Materials Management, 50% to Machining, and 20% to Assembly. Therefore, $90,000 is allocated to Materials Management (30% of $300,000), $150,000 to Machining (50% of $300,000), and $60,000 to Assembly (20% of $300,000). The Materials Management Department costs now total $340,000: budgeted costs of the Materials Management Department before any interdepartmental cost allocations, $250,000, plus $90,000 from the allocation of Engineering and Production Control costs to the Materials Management Department. The $340,000 is then only allocated between the two operating departments based on the proportion of the Materials Management Department services provided to Machining and Assembly. From Exhibit 4-10, the Materials Management Department provides 20% of its services to Machining and 70% to Assembly, so $75,556 (2/9 × $340,000) is allocated to Machining and $264,444 (7/9 × $340,000) is allocated to Assembly.

Note that this method requires managers to rank (sequence) the support departments in the order that the step-down allocation is to proceed. In our example, the costs of the Engineering and Production Control Department were allocated first to all other departments, including the Materials Management Department. The costs of the Materials Management support department were allocated second, but only to the two operating departments and not to the Engineering and Production Control Department even though the Materials Management Department delivers materials to the Engineering and Production Control Department. Different sequences will result in different allocations of support-department costs to operating departments—for example, if the Materials

Exhibit 4-12

Step-Down Method of Allocating Budgeted Support-Department Costs at Robinson Company for 2012

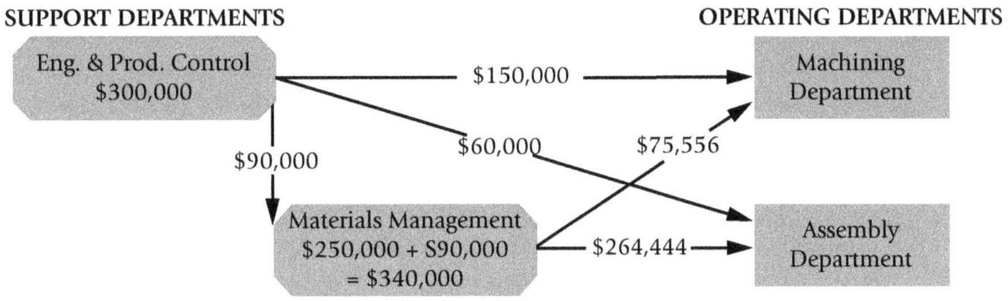

	A	B	C	D	E	F	G
1		SUPPORT DEPARTMENTS			OPERATING DEPARTMENTS		
2		Engineering and Production Control	Materials Management		Machining	Assembly	Total
3	Budgeted overhead cost before any						
4	interdepartment cost allocations	$ 300,000	$ 250,000		$336,000	$234,000	$1,120,000
5	Allocation of Eng. and Prod. Control (3/10, 5/10, 2/10)[a]	(300,000)	90,000		150,000	60,000	
6			340,000				
7	Allocation of Material Management (2/9, 7/9)[b]		(340,000)		75,556	264,444	
8							
9	Total budgeted overhead of operating departments	$ 0	$ 0		$561,556	$558,444	$1,120,000
10							
11	[a]Base is ($36,000 + $60,000 + $24,000), or $120,000; $36,000 ÷ $120,000 = 3/10; $60,000 ÷ $120,000 = 5/10; $24,000 ÷ $120,000 = 2/10.						
12	[b]Base is (800 + 2,800), or 3,600 hours; 800 ÷ 3,600 = 2/9; 2,800 ÷ 3,600 = 7/9.						

Management Department costs had been allocated first and the Engineering and Production Control Department costs second. A popular step-down sequence begins with the support department that renders the highest percentage of its total services to *other support departments.* The sequence continues with the department that renders the next-highest percentage, and so on, ending with the support department that renders the lowest percentage.[4] In our example, costs of the Engineering and Production Control Department were allocated first because it provides 30% of its services to the Materials Management Department, whereas the Materials Management Department provides only 10% of its services to the Engineering and Production Control Department (see Exhibit 4-10).

Under the step-down method, once a support department's costs have been allocated, no subsequent support-department costs are allocated back to it. Once the Engineering and Production Control Department costs are allocated, it receives no further allocation from other (lower-ranked) support departments. The result is that the step-down method does not recognize the total services that support departments provide to each other. The reciprocal method fully recognizes all such services, as you will see next.

Reciprocal Method

The **reciprocal method** allocates support-department costs to operating departments by fully recognizing the mutual services provided among all support departments. For example, the Engineering and Production Control Department provides engineering services to the Materials Management Department. Similarly, Materials Management handles materials for Engineering and

[4] An alternative approach to selecting the sequence of allocations is to begin with the support department that renders the highest dollar amount of services to other support departments. The sequence ends with the allocation of the costs of the department that renders the lowest dollar amount of services to other support departments.

Production Control. The reciprocal method fully incorporates interdepartmental relationships into the support-department cost allocations.

Exhibit 4-13 presents one way to understand the reciprocal method. First, Engineering and Production Control costs are allocated to all other departments, including the Materials Management support department (Materials Management, 30%; Machining, 50%; Assembly, 20%). The costs in the Materials Management Department then total \$340,000 (\$250,000 + \$90,000 from the first-round allocation), as in Exhibit 4-12. The \$340,000 is then allocated to all other departments that the Materials Management Department supports, including the Engineering and Production Control support department—Engineering and Production Control, 10%; Machining, 20%; and Assembly, 70% (see Exhibit 4-10). The Engineering and Production Control costs that had been brought down to \$0 now have \$34,000 from the Materials Management Department allocation. These costs are again reallocated to all other departments, including Materials Management, in the same ratio that the Engineering and Production Control costs were previously assigned. Now the Materials Management Department costs that had been brought down to \$0 have \$10,200 from the Engineering and Production Control Department allocations. These costs are again allocated in the same ratio that the Materials Management Department costs were previously assigned. Successive rounds result in smaller and smaller amounts being allocated to and reallocated from the support departments until eventually all support department costs are allocated to the operating departments.

An alternative way to implement the reciprocal method is to formulate and solve linear equations. This process requires three steps.

Exhibit 4-13

Reciprocal Method of Allocating Budgeted Support-Department Costs Using Repeated Iterations at Robinson Company for 2012

	A	B	C	D	E	F	G
1		SUPPORT DEPARTMENTS			OPERATING DEPARTMENTS		
2		Engineering and Production Control	Materials Management		Machining	Assembly	Total
3	Budgeted overhead costs before any						
4	interdepartment cost allocations	\$300,000	\$250,000		\$336,000	\$234,000	\$1,120,000
5	1st Allocation of Eng. & Prod. Control (3/10, 5/10, 2/10)[a]	(300,000)	90,000		150,000	60,000	
6			340,000				
7	1st Allocation of Material Management (1/10, 2/10, 7/10)[b]	34,000	(340,000)		68,000	238,000	
8	2nd Allocation of Eng. & Prod. Control (3/10, 5/10, 2/10)[a]	(34,000)	10,200		17,000	6,800	
9	2nd Allocation of Material Management (1/10, 2/10, 7/10)[b]	1,020	(10,200)		2,040	7,140	
10	3rd Allocation of Eng. & Prod Control (3/10, 5/10, 2/10)[a]	(1,020)	306		510	204	
11	3rd Allocation of Material Management (1/10, 2/10, 7/10)[b]	31	(306)		61	214	
12	4th Allocation of Eng. & Prod Control (3/10, 5/10, 2/10)[a]	(31)	9		15	7	
13	4th Allocation of Material Management (1/10, 2/10, 7/10)[b]	1	(9)		2	6	
14	5th Allocation of Eng. & Prod. Control (3/10, 5/10, 2/10)[a]	(1)	0		1	0	
15							
16	Total budgeted overhead of operating departments	\$ 0	\$ 0		\$573,629	\$546,371	\$1,120,000
17							
18	Total support department amounts allocated and reallocated (the numbers in parentheses in the first two columns):						
19	Eng. & Prod. Control: \$300,000 + \$34,000 + \$1,020 + \$31 + \$1 = \$335,052						
20	Materials Management: \$340,000 + \$10,200 + \$306 + \$9 = \$350,515						
21							
22	[a]Base is (\$36,000 + \$60,000 + \$24,000), or \$120,000; \$36,000 ÷ \$120,000 = 3/10; \$60,000 ÷ \$120,000 = 5/10; \$24,000 ÷ \$120,000 = 2/10.						
23	[b]Base is (400 + 800 + 2,800), or 4,000 hours; 400 ÷ 4,000 = 1/10; 800 ÷ 4,000 = 2/10; 2,800 ÷ 4,000 = 7/10.						

Step 1: Express Support Department Costs and Reciprocal Relationships in the Form of Linear Equations. Let *EPC* be the *complete reciprocated costs* of Engineering and Production Control and *MM* be the *complete reciprocated costs* of Materials Management. By **complete reciprocated costs,** we mean the support department's own costs plus any interdepartmental cost allocations. We then express the data in Exhibit 4-10 as follows:

$$EPC = \$300{,}000 + 0.1MM \qquad \textbf{(Equation 1)}$$
$$MM = \$250{,}000 + 0.3EPC \qquad \textbf{(Equation 2)}$$

The $0.1MM$ term in equation (1) is the percentage of the Materials Management services *used by* Engineering and Production Control. The $0.3EPC$ term in equation (2) is the percentage of Engineering and Production Control services *used by* Materials Management. The complete reciprocated costs in equations (1) and (2) are sometimes called the **artificial costs** of the support departments.

Step 2: Solve the Set of Linear Equations to Obtain the Complete Reciprocated Costs of Each Support Department. Substituting equation (1) into (2):

$$MM = \$250{,}000 + [0.3(\$300{,}000 + 0.1\ MM)]$$
$$MM = \$250{,}000 + \$90{,}000 + 0.03\ MM$$
$$0.97MM = \$340{,}000$$
$$MM = \$350{,}515$$

Substituting this into equation (1):

$$EPC = \$300{,}000 + 0.1(\$350{,}515)$$
$$EPC = \$300{,}000 + \$35{,}052 = \$335{,}052$$

When there are more than two support departments with reciprocal relationships, managers can use software such as Excel to calculate the complete reciprocated costs of each support department. The complete-reciprocated-cost figures also appear at the bottom of Exhibit 4-13 as the total amounts allocated and reallocated (subject to minor rounding differences).

Step 3: Allocate the Complete Reciprocated Costs of Each Support Department to All Other Departments (Both Support Departments and Operating Departments) on the Basis of the Usage Percentages (Based on Total Units of Service Provided to All Departments). Consider, for example, the Materials Management Department. The complete reciprocated costs of $350,515 are allocated as follows:

To Engineering and Production Control (1/10) × $350,515	= $ 35,052
To Machining (2/10) × $350,515	= 70,103
To Assembly (7/10) × $350,515	= 245,360
Total	$350,515

Exhibit 4-14 presents summary data based on the reciprocal method.

Robinson's $685,567 complete reciprocated costs of the support departments exceeds the budgeted amount of $550,000:

Support Department	Complete Reciprocated Costs	Budgeted Costs	Difference
Engineering and Production Control	$335,052	$300,000	$ 35,052
Materials Management	350,515	250,000	100,515
Total	$685,567	$550,000	$135,567

Each support department's complete reciprocated cost is greater than the budgeted amount to take into account that the allocation of support costs will be made to all departments using its services and not just to operating departments. This step ensures that the reciprocal method fully recognizes all interrelationships among support departments, as well as relationships between support and operating departments. The difference between complete reciprocated costs and budgeted costs for each support department reflects the costs allocated among support departments. The total cost allocated to the operating departments in Exhibit 4-14 under the reciprocal method equals the total cost of the support departments, $550,000 ($167,526 + $67,011 + $70,103 + $245,360).

Exhibit 4-14

Reciprocal Method of Allocating Budgeted Support-Department Costs Using Linear Equations at Robinson Company for 2012

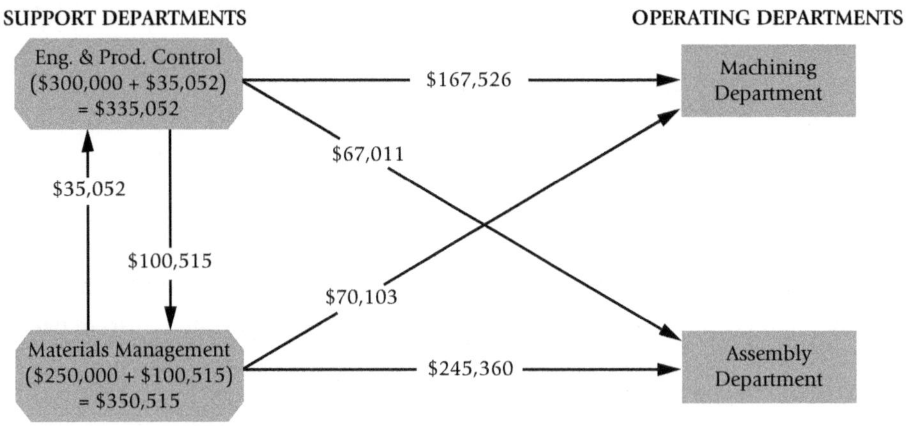

Home Insert Page Layout Formulas Data Review View

	A	B	C	D	E	F	G
1		SUPPORT DEPARTMENTS			OPERATING DEPARTMENTS		
2		Engineering and Production Control	Materials Management		Machining	Assembly	Total
3	Budgeted overhead costs before any						
4	interdepartment cost allocations	$300,000	$250,000		$336,000	$234,000	$1,120,000
5	Allocation of Eng. & Prod. Control (3/10, 5/10, 2/10)[a]	(335,052)	100,515		167,526	67,011	
6	Allocation of Material Management (1/10, 2/10, 7/10)[b]	35,052	(350,515)		70,103	245,360	
7							
8	Total budgeted overhead of operating departments	$ 0	$ 0		$573,629	$546,371	$1,120,000
9							
10	[a]Base is ($36,000 + $60,000 + $24,000), or $120,000; $36,000 ÷ $120,000 = 3/10; $60,000 ÷ $120,000 = 5/10; $24,000 ÷ $120,000 = 2/10.						
11	[b]Base is (400 + 800 + 2,800), or 4,000 hours; 400 ÷ 4,000 = 1/10; 800 ÷ 4,000 = 2/10; 2,800 ÷ 4,000 = 7/10.						

Overview of Methods

The amount of manufacturing overhead costs allocated to the Machining and Assembly Departments will differ depending on the method used to allocate support-department costs. Differences among the three methods' allocations increase (1) as the magnitude of the reciprocal allocations increases and (2) as the differences across operating departments' usage of each support department's services increase. The method of allocation becomes particularly important in the case of cost-reimbursement contracts that require allocation of support-department costs. To avoid disputes, managers should always clarify the method to be used for allocation. For example, Medicare reimbursements and federal contracts with universities that pay for the recovery of indirect costs typically mandate use of the step-down method, with explicit requirements about the costs that can be included in the indirect-cost pools.

The reciprocal method is conceptually the most precise method because it considers the mutual services provided among all support departments. The advantage of the direct and step-down methods is that they are simple to compute and understand relative to the reciprocal method. If the costs allocated to the operating departments using the direct or step-down methods closely approximate the costs allocated using the reciprocal method, the simpler direct or step-down methods should be used. However, as computing power to perform repeated iterations (as in Exhibit 4-13) or to solve sets of simultaneous equations (as on page 149) increases, more companies find the reciprocal method easier to implement.

Another advantage of the reciprocal method is that it highlights the complete reciprocated costs of support departments and how these costs differ from budgeted or actual costs of the departments. Knowing the complete reciprocated costs of a support department is a key input for decisions about whether to outsource all the services that the support department provides.

Suppose all of Robinson's support-department costs are variable over the period of a possible outsourcing contract. Consider a third party's bid to provide, say, all services currently provided by the Materials Management Department. Do not compare the bid to the $250,000 costs reported for the Materials Management Department. The complete reciprocated costs of the Materials Management Department, which include the services the Engineering and Production Control Department provides the Materials Management Department, are $350,515 to deliver 4,000 hours of material-handling labor to other departments at Robinson. The complete reciprocated costs for material-handling labor are $87.63 per hour ($350,515 ÷ 4,000 hours). Other things being equal, a third party's bid to provide the same materials management services as Robinson's internal department at less than $350,515, or $87.63 per hour (even if much greater than $250,000), would improve Robinson's operating income.

To see this point, note that the relevant savings from shutting down the Materials Management Department are $250,000 of Materials Management Department costs *plus* $100,515 of Engineering and Production Control Department costs. By closing down the Materials Management Department, Robinson will no longer incur the 30% of reciprocated Engineering and Production Control Department costs (equal to $100,515) that were incurred to support the Materials Management Department. Therefore, the total cost savings are $350,515 ($250,000 + $100,515).[5] Neither the direct nor the step-down methods can provide this relevant information for outsourcing decisions.

Calculating the Cost of Job WPP 298

Step 5 of a job-costing system "computes the rate per unit of each cost-allocation base used to allocate the indirect costs to the job." Robinson budgets 20,000 direct labor-hours for the Assembly Department (of the 28,000 total direct manufacturing labor-hours) and 10,000 machine-hours for the Machining Department.

The budgeted overhead allocation rates for each operating department by allocation method are:

	Total Budgeted Overhead Costs After Allocation of All Support-Department Costs		Budgeted Overhead Rate per Hour for Product-Costing Purposes	
Support Department Cost-Allocation Method	Machining	Assembly	Machining (10,000 machine-hours)	Assembly (20,000 labor-hours)
Direct	$605,842	$514,158	$60.58	$25.71
Step-down	561,556	558,444	56.16	27.92
Reciprocal	573,629	546,371	57.36	27.32

Note that while the final allocations under the reciprocal method are in between those under the direct and step-down methods in our example, this is not true in general.

Step 6 "computes the indirect costs allocated to the job." Robinson uses 42 labor-hours in the Assembly Department (out of 88 direct manufacturing labor-hours) and 46 machine-hours in the Machining Department (each worker works on one machine) for the WPP 298 job. The overhead costs allocated to the WPP 298 job under the three methods would be

Direct: $3,866 (46 × $60.58 + 42 × $25.71)

Step-down: $3,756 (46 × $56.16 + 42 × $27.92)

Reciprocal: $3,786 (46 × $57.36 + 42 × $27.32)

The manufacturing overhead costs allocated to WPP 298 differs only a little under the three methods because the WPP 298 job requires roughly equal amounts of machine-hours and assembly labor-hours. These differences would be larger if a job required many more machine-hours than assembly hours or vice versa.

[5] Technical issues when using the reciprocal method in outsourcing decisions are discussed in R. S. Kaplan and A. A. Atkinson, *Advanced Management Accounting*, 3rd ed. (Upper Saddle River, NJ: Prentice Hall, 1998, pp. 73–81).

Using normal costing and multiple cost-allocation bases also results in higher indirect manufacturing costs allocated to Job WPP 298, \$3,798 (under the reciprocal method) compared to \$3,520 allocated using direct manufacturing labor-hours as the sole allocation base (page 124). Two cost-allocation bases—machine-hours and assembly labor-hours—are better able to model the drivers of manufacturing overhead costs.

Step 7 "computes the total cost of the job by adding all direct and indirect costs assigned to the job." Under the reciprocal method, the total manufacturing costs of the WPP 298 job are as follows:

Direct manufacturing costs		
Direct materials	\$4,606	
Direct manufacturing labor	1,579	\$6,185
Manufacturing overhead costs		
Machining Department		
(\$57.36 per machine-hour × 46 machine-hours)	2,639	
Assembly Department		
(\$27.32 per labor-hour × 42 labor-hours)	1,147	3,786
Total manufacturing costs of Job WPP 298		\$9,971

Note that the costs in Step 7 have four dollar amounts, each corresponding respectively to the two direct-cost and two indirect-cost categories in the costing system.

At the end of the year, actual manufacturing overhead costs of the Machining Department and the Assembly Department would be compared to the manufacturing overhead allocated for each department. Management accountants would then make end-of-year adjustments (pages 134–138) separately for each cost pool for under- or overallocated overhead costs.

Terms to Learn

This chapter and the Glossary at the end of the book contain definitions of the following important terms:

actual costing (p. 119)
actual indirect-cost rate (p. 127)
adjusted allocation-rate approach (p. 135)
artificial costs (p. 149)
budgeted indirect-cost rate (p. 121)
complete reciprocated costs (p. 149)
cost-allocation base (p. 116)
cost-application base (p. 116)
cost pool (p. 116)
direct method (p. 145)
job (p. 117)
job-cost record (p. 121)
job-cost sheet (p. 121)
job-costing system (p. 117)
labor-time sheet (p. 122)
manufacturing overhead allocated (p. 132)
manufacturing overhead applied (p. 132)
materials-requisition record (p. 121)
normal costing (p. 121)
operating department (p. 143)
overabsorbed indirect costs (p. 134)
overallocated indirect costs (p. 134)
overapplied indirect costs (p. 134)
process-costing system (p. 117)
production department (p. 143)
proration (p. 135)
reciprocal method (p. 147)
sequential allocation method (p. 146)
service department (p. 143)
source document (p. 121)
step-down method (p. 146)
support department (p. 143)
underabsorbed indirect costs (p. 134)
underallocated indirect costs (p. 134)
underapplied indirect costs (p. 134)

Assignment Material

Questions

4-1 How does a job-costing system differ from a process-costing system?

4-2 Why might an advertising agency use job costing for an advertising campaign by Pepsi, whereas a bank might use process costing to determine the cost of checking account deposits?

4-3 Give two reasons why most organizations use an annual period rather than a weekly or monthly period to compute budgeted indirect-cost rates.

4-4 Distinguish between actual costing and normal costing.

4-5 Describe two ways in which a house construction company may use job-cost information.

4-6 Comment on the following statement: "In a normal-costing system, the amounts in the Manufacturing Overhead Control account will always equal the amounts in the Manufacturing Overhead Allocated account."

4-7 Describe three different debit entries to the Work-in-Process Control T-account under normal costing.

4-8 Describe three alternative ways to dispose of under- or overallocated overhead costs.

4-9 When might a company use budgeted costs rather than actual costs to compute direct-labor rates?

4-10 Distinguish among the three methods of allocating the costs of support departments to operating departments.

Exercises

4-11 Job costing, process costing. In each of the following situations, determine whether job costing or process costing would be more appropriate.

a. A CPA firm
b. An oil refinery
c. A custom furniture manufacturer
d. A tire manufacturer
e. A textbook publisher
f. A pharmaceutical company
g. An advertising agency
h. An apparel manufacturing plant
i. A flour mill
j. A paint manufacturer
k. A medical care facility
l. A landscaping company
m. A cola-drink-concentrate producer
n. A movie studio
o. A law firm
p. A commercial aircraft manufacturer
q. A management consulting firm
r. A breakfast-cereal company
s. A catering service
t. A paper mill
u. An auto repair shop

4-12 Actual costing, normal costing, accounting for manufacturing overhead. Desert Products uses a job-costing system with two direct-cost categories (direct materials and direct manufacturing labor) and one manufacturing overhead cost pool. Desert allocates manufacturing overhead costs using direct manufacturing labor costs. Desert provides the following information:

	Budget for 2012	Actual Results for 2012
Direct material costs	$2,250,000	$2,100,000
Direct manufacturing labor costs	1,700,000	1,650,000
Manufacturing overhead costs	2,975,000	2,970,000

Required

1. Compute the actual and budgeted manufacturing overhead rates for 2012.
2. During March, the job-cost record for Job 626 contained the following information:

Direct materials used	$55,000
Direct manufacturing labor costs	$40,000

   Compute the cost of Job 626 using (a) actual costing and (b) normal costing.
3. At the end of 2012, compute the under- or overallocated manufacturing overhead under normal costing. Why is there no under- or overallocated overhead under actual costing?
4. Why might managers at Desert Products prefer to use normal costing?

4-13 Job costing, normal and actual costing. Acre Construction assembles residential houses. It uses a job-costing system with two direct-cost categories (direct materials and direct labor) and one indirect-cost pool (assembly support). Direct labor-hours is the allocation base for assembly support costs. In December 2011, Acre budgets 2012 assembly-support costs to be $8,700,000 and 2012 direct labor-hours to be 145,000.

At the end of 2012, Acre is comparing the costs of several jobs that were started and completed in 2012.

	Laguna Model	Mission Model
Construction period	Feb–June 2012	May–Oct 2012
Direct material costs	$106,440	$127,625
Direct labor costs	$ 36,325	$ 41,750
Direct labor-hours	980	1,000

Direct materials and direct labor are paid for on a contract basis. The costs of each are known when direct materials are used or when direct labor-hours are worked. The 2012 actual assembly-support costs were $7,470,000, and the actual direct labor-hours were 166,000.

Required

1. Compute the (a) budgeted indirect-cost rate and (b) actual indirect-cost rate. Why do they differ?
2. What are the job costs of the Laguna Model and the Mission Model using (a) normal costing and (b) actual costing?
3. Why might Acre Construction prefer normal costing over actual costing?

4-14 Budgeted manufacturing overhead rate, allocated manufacturing overhead. Rovet Company uses normal costing. It allocates manufacturing overhead costs using a budgeted rate per machine-hour. The following data are available for 2012:

Budgeted manufacturing overhead costs	$4,250,000
Budgeted machine-hours	250,000
Actual manufacturing overhead costs	$4,120,000
Actual machine-hours	245,000

Required

1. Calculate the budgeted manufacturing overhead rate.
2. Calculate the manufacturing overhead allocated during 2012.
3. Why do Rovet's managers want to calculate a budgeted manufacturing overhead rate?
4. Calculate the amount of under- or overallocated manufacturing overhead. Why do Rovet's managers need to calculate this amount?

4-15 Job costing, consulting firm. Taylor & Associates, a consulting firm, has the following condensed budget for 2012:

Revenues		$20,000,000
Total costs:		
Direct costs		
Professional labor	$ 5,000,000	
Indirect costs		
Client support	13,000,000	18,000,000
Operating income		$ 2,000,000

Taylor has a single direct-cost category (professional labor) and a single indirect-cost pool (client support). Indirect costs are allocated to jobs on the basis of professional labor costs.

Required

1. Prepare an overview diagram of the job-costing system. Calculate the 2012 budgeted indirect-cost rate for Taylor & Associates.
2. The markup rate for pricing jobs is intended to produce operating income equal to 10% of revenues. Calculate the markup rate as a percentage of professional labor costs.
3. Taylor is bidding on a consulting job for Tasty Chicken, a fast-food chain specializing in poultry meats. The budgeted breakdown of professional labor on the job is as follows:

Professional Labor Category	Budgeted Rate per Hour	Budgeted Hours
Director	$200	3
Partner	100	16
Associate	50	40
Assistant	30	160

Calculate the budgeted cost of the Tasty Chicken job. How much will Taylor bid for the job if it is to earn its target operating income of 10% of revenues?

4-16 Time period used to compute indirect-cost rates. Splunge Manufacturing produces outdoor wading and slide pools. The company uses a normal-costing system and allocates manufacturing overhead on the basis of direct manufacturing labor-hours. Most of the company's production and sales occur in the first and second quarters of the year. The company is in danger of losing one of its larger customers, Solar Wholesale, due to large fluctuations in price. The owner of Splunge has requested an analysis of the manufacturing cost per unit in the second and third quarters. You have been provided the following budgeted information for the coming year:

	Quarter			
	1	2	3	4
Pools manufactured and sold	965	750	375	310

It takes 1 direct manufacturing labor-hour to make each pool. The actual direct material cost is $15 per pool. The actual direct manufacturing labor rate is $29 per hour. The budgeted variable manufacturing overhead rate is $22 per direct manufacturing labor-hour. Budgeted fixed manufacturing overhead costs are $15,000 each quarter.

Required

1. Calculate the total manufacturing cost per unit for the second and third quarter assuming the company allocates manufacturing overhead costs based on the budgeted manufacturing overhead rate determined for each quarter.
2. Calculate the total manufacturing cost per unit for the second and third quarter assuming the company allocates manufacturing overhead costs based on an annual budgeted manufacturing overhead rate.
3. Splunge Manufacturing prices its pools at manufacturing cost plus 30%. Why might Solar Wholesale be seeing large fluctuations in the prices of pools? Which of the methods described in requirements 1 and 2 would you recommend Splunge use? Explain.

4-17 Accounting for manufacturing overhead. Consider the following selected cost data for the All-In Company for 2012.

Budgeted manufacturing overhead costs	$4,520,000
Budgeted labor-hours	226,000
Actual manufacturing overhead costs	$4,388,000
Actual labor-hours	217,000

The company uses normal costing. Its job-costing system has a single manufacturing overhead cost pool. Costs are allocated to jobs using a budgeted labor-hour rate. Any amount of under- or overallocation is written off to Cost of Goods Sold.

Required

1. Compute the budgeted manufacturing overhead rate.
2. Prepare T-accounts to record the allocation of manufacturing overhead.
3. Compute the amount of under- or overallocation of manufacturing overhead. Is the amount large enough to require the manager to prorate overhead costs between cost of goods sold, work-in-process inventory, and finished goods inventory? Explain. Record entries in T-accounts to dispose of this amount.

4-18 Job costing, T-accounts. The University of Chicago Press is wholly owned by the university. It performs the bulk of its work for other university departments, which pay as though the press were an outside business enterprise. The press also publishes and maintains a stock of books for general sale. The press uses normal costing to cost each job. Its job-costing system has two direct-cost categories (direct materials and direct manufacturing labor) and one indirect-cost pool (manufacturing overhead, allocated on the basis of direct manufacturing labor costs).

The following data (in thousands) pertain to 2012:

Direct materials and supplies purchased on credit	$ 820
Direct materials used	750
Indirect materials issued to various production departments	120
Direct manufacturing labor	1,360
Indirect manufacturing labor incurred by various production departments	930
Depreciation on building and manufacturing equipment	440

Miscellaneous manufacturing overhead* incurred by various production departments (ordinarily would be detailed as repairs, photocopying, utilities, etc.)	540
Manufacturing overhead allocated at 150% of direct manufacturing labor costs	?
Cost of goods manufactured	4,100
Revenues	8,200
Cost of goods sold (before adjustment for under- or overallocated manufacturing overhead)	4,030
Inventories, December 31, 2011 (not 2012):	
Materials Control	150
Work-in-Process Control	80
Finished Goods Control	540

*The term *manufacturing overhead* is not used uniformly. Other terms that are often encountered in printing companies include *job overhead* and *shop overhead.*

Required

1. Prepare an overview diagram of the job-costing system at the University of Chicago Press.
2. Prepare T-accounts to record the 2012 transactions for inventories, revenues, and costs. As your final entry, dispose of the year-end under- or overallocated manufacturing overhead as a writeoff to Cost of Goods Sold. Number your entries.
3. How did the University of Chicago Press perform in 2012?

4-19 Job costing, T-accounts. Construction Company produces gadgets for the coveted small appliance market. The following data shows activity for the year 2012:

Costs incurred:	
Purchases of direct materials (net) on credit	$126,000
Direct manufacturing labor cost	85,000
Indirect labor	54,300
Depreciation, factory equipment	37,000
Depreciation, office equipment	7,700
Maintenance, factory equipment	24,000
Miscellaneous factory overhead	9,800
Rent, factory building	79,000
Advertising expense	94,000
Sales commissions	36,000
Inventories:	

	January 1, 2012	December 31, 2012
Direct materials	$ 9,900	$11,000
Work in process	6,100	28,000
Finished goods	61,000	32,000

Construction Co. uses a normal-costing system and allocates overhead to work in process at a rate of $2.90 per direct manufacturing labor dollar. Indirect materials are insignificant, so there is no inventory account for indirect materials.

Required

Prepare T-accounts for inventories and costs to record the transactions for 2012 including an entry to close out over- or underallocated overhead to cost of goods sold.

4-20 Job costing, T-accounts. Docks Transport assembles prestige manufactured homes. Its job-costing system has two direct-cost categories (direct materials and direct manufacturing labor) and one indirect-cost pool (manufacturing overhead allocated at a budgeted $25 per machine-hour in 2012). The following data (in millions) show operation costs for 2012:

Materials Control, beginning balance, January 1, 2012	$15
Work-in-Process Control, beginning balance, January 1, 2012	8
Finished Goods Control, beginning balance, January 1, 2012	8
Materials and supplies purchased on credit	158
Direct materials used	151
Indirect materials (supplies) issued to various production departments	15
Direct manufacturing labor	91
Indirect manufacturing labor incurred by various production departments	39
Depreciation on plant and manufacturing equipment	29

Miscellaneous manufacturing overhead incurred (ordinarily would be detailed as repairs, utilities, etc., with a corresponding credit to various liability accounts)	14
Manufacturing overhead allocated, 2,400,000 actual machine-hours	?
Cost of goods manufactured	298
Revenues	402
Cost of goods sold	298

Required

1. Prepare an overview diagram of Docks Transport's job-costing system.
2. Prepare T-accounts. What is the ending balance of Work-in-Process Control?
3. Dispose of under- or overallocated manufacturing overhead directly as a year-end writeoff to Cost of Goods Sold.
4. How did Docks Transport perform in 2012?

4-21 Job costing, unit cost, ending work in process. Ronald Company produces pipes for concert-quality organs. Each job is unique. In April 2012, it completed all outstanding orders, and then, in May 2012, it worked on only two jobs, M1 and M2:

	A	B	C
1	**Ronald Company, May 2012**	**Job M1**	**Job M2**
2	Direct materials	$ 76,000	$ 58,000
3	Direct manufacturing labor	277,000	205,000

Direct manufacturing labor is paid at the rate of $25 per hour. Manufacturing overhead costs are allocated at a budgeted rate of $16 per direct manufacturing labor-hour. Only Job M1 was completed in May.

Required

1. Calculate the total cost for Job M1.
2. 1,600 pipes were produced for Job M1. Calculate the cost per pipe.
3. What is the ending balance in the Work-in-Process Control account?

4-22 Job costing; actual, normal, and variation from normal costing. Kirac & Partners, a Quebec-based public accounting partnership, specializes in audit services. Its job-costing system has a single direct-cost category (professional labor) and a single indirect-cost pool (audit support, which contains all costs of the Audit Support Department). Audit support costs are allocated to individual jobs using actual professional labor-hours. Kirac & Partners employs 10 professionals to perform audit services.

Budgeted and actual amounts for 2012 are as follows:

	A	B	C
1	**Kirac & Partners**		
2	**Budget for 2012**		
3	Professional labor compensation	$1,120,000	
4	Audit support department costs	$ 688,000	
5	Professional labor-hours billed to clients	16,000	hours
6			
7	**Actual results for 2012**		
8	Audit support department costs	$ 738,000	
9	Professional labor-hours billed to clients	16,400	
10	Actual professional labor cost rate	$ 55	per hour

Required

1. Compute the direct-cost rate and the indirect-cost rate per professional labor-hour for 2012 under (a) actual costing, (b) normal costing, and (c) the variation from normal costing that uses budgeted rates for direct costs.
2. Which job-costing system would you recommend Kirac & Partners use? Explain.
3. Kirac's 2012 audit of Pierre & Co. was budgeted to take 170 hours of professional labor time. The actual professional labor time spent on the audit was 190 hours. Compute the cost of the Pierre & Co. audit using

(a) actual costing, (b) normal costing, and (c) the variation from normal costing that uses budgeted rates for direct costs. Explain any differences in the job cost.

4-23 Job costing; actual, normal, and variation from normal costing. Braun Brothers, Inc., is an architecture firm specializing in high-rise buildings. Its job-costing system has a single direct-cost category (architectural labor) and a single indirect-cost pool, which contains all costs of supporting the office. Office support costs are allocated to individual jobs using architect labor-hours. Braun Brothers employs 15 architects.

Budgeted and actual amounts for 2012 are as follows:

Braun Brothers, Inc.

Budget for 2012	
Architect labor cost	$3,613,500
Office support costs	$2,226,500
Architect labor-hours billed to clients	36,500 hours
Actual results for 2012	
Office support costs	$2,340,000
Architect labor-hours billed to clients	39,000 hours
Actual architect labor cost rate	$ 103 per hour

Required

1. Compute the direct-cost rate and the indirect-cost rate per architectural labor-hour for 2012 under (a) actual costing, (b) normal costing, and (c) the variation from normal costing that uses budgeted rates for direct costs.
2. Which job-costing system would you recommend Braun Brothers use? Explain.
3. Braun Brothers' architectural sketches for Champ Tower in Houston was budgeted to take 380 hours of architectural labor time. The actual architectural labor time spent on the job was 340 hours. Compute the cost of the Champ Tower sketches using (a) actual costing, (b) normal costing, and (c) the variation from normal costing that uses budgeted rates for direct costs.

4-24 Proration of overhead. The Ride-On-Wonder Company (ROW) produces a line of non-motorized boats. ROW uses a normal-costing system and allocates manufacturing overhead using direct manufacturing labor cost. The following data are for 2012:

Budgeted manufacturing overhead cost	$127,050
Budgeted direct manufacturing labor cost	$231,000
Actual manufacturing overhead cost	$123,000
Actual direct manufacturing labor cost	$220,000

Inventory balances on December 31, 2012, were as follows:

Account	Ending balance	2012 direct manufacturing labor cost in ending balance
Work in process	$ 51,000	$ 19,800
Finished goods	238,000	59,400
Cost of goods sold	561,000	140,800

Required

1. Calculate the budgeted manufacturing overhead allocation rate.
2. Compute the amount of under- or overallocated manufacturing overhead.
3. Calculate the ending balances in work in process, finished goods, and cost of goods sold if under- and overallocated manufacturing overhead is as follows:
   a. Written off to cost of goods sold
   b. Prorated based on the overhead allocated in 2012 in the ending balances (before proration) in each of the three accounts
4. Which method makes the most sense? Justify your answer.

Problems

4-25 Job costing, accounting for manufacturing overhead, budgeted rates. The Carlson Company uses a job-costing system at its Dover, Delaware, plant. The plant has a machining department and a finishing department. Carlson uses normal costing with two direct-cost categories (direct materials and direct manufacturing labor) and two manufacturing overhead cost pools (the machining department with machine-hours as the allocation base, and the finishing department with direct manufacturing labor costs as the allocation base). The 2012 budget for the plant is as follows:

	Machining Department	Finishing Department
Manufacturing overhead costs	$9,870,000	$7,644,000
Direct manufacturing labor costs	$980,000	$3,900,000
Direct manufacturing labor-hours	32,000	170,000
Machine-hours	210,000	33,000

Required

1. Prepare an overview diagram of Carlson's job-costing system.
2. What is the budgeted manufacturing overhead rate in the machining department? In the finishing department?
3. During the month of January, the job-cost record for Job 431 shows the following:

	Machining Department	Finishing Department
Direct materials used	$13,000	$3,500
Direct manufacturing labor costs	$700	$1,450
Direct manufacturing labor-hours	20	60
Machine-hours	110	15

Compute the total manufacturing overhead cost allocated to Job 431.

4. Assuming that Job 431 consisted of 100 units of product, what is the cost per unit?
5. Actual amounts at the end of 2012 are as follows:

	Machining Department	Finishing Department
Manufacturing overhead incurred	$11,380,000	$8,628,000
Direct manufacturing labor costs	$1,030,000	$4,300,000
Machine-hours	240,000	30,000

Compute the under- or overallocated manufacturing overhead for each department and for the Dover plant as a whole.

6. Why might Carlson use two different manufacturing overhead cost pools in its job-costing system?

4-26 Service industry, job costing, law firm. Kahn & Associates is a law firm specializing in labor relations and employee-related work. It employs 30 professionals (10 partners and 20 associates) who work directly with its clients. The average budgeted total compensation per professional for 2012 is $105,000. Each professional is budgeted to have 1,500 billable hours to clients in 2012. All professionals work for clients to their maximum 1,500 billable hours available. All professional labor costs are included in a single direct-cost category and are traced to jobs on a per-hour basis. All costs of Kahn & Associates other than professional labor costs are included in a single indirect-cost pool (legal support) and are allocated to jobs using professional labor-hours as the allocation base. The budgeted level of indirect costs in 2012 is $2,835,000.

Required

1. Prepare an overview diagram of Kahn's job-costing system.
2. Compute the 2012 budgeted direct-cost rate per hour of professional labor.
3. Compute the 2012 budgeted indirect-cost rate per hour of professional labor.
4. Kahn & Associates is considering bidding on two jobs:

   a. Litigation work for Richardson, Inc., which requires 120 budgeted hours of professional labor

   b. Labor contract work for Punch, Inc., which requires 145 budgeted hours of professional labor

   Prepare a cost estimate for each job.

4-27 Service industry, job costing, two direct- and two indirect-cost categories, law firm (continuation of 4-26). Kahn has just completed a review of its job-costing system. This review included a detailed analysis of how past jobs used the firm's resources and interviews with personnel about what factors drive the level of indirect costs. Management concluded that a system with two direct-cost categories (professional partner labor and professional associate labor) and two indirect-cost categories (general support and secretarial support) would yield more accurate job costs. Budgeted information for 2012 related to the two direct-cost categories is as follows:

	Professional Partner Labor	Professional Associate Labor
Number of professionals	10	20
Hours of billable time per professional	1,500 per year	1,500 per year
Total compensation (average per professional)	$195,000	$60,000

Budgeted information for 2012 relating to the two indirect-cost categories is as follows:

	General Support	Secretarial Support
Total costs	$2,250,000	$585,000
Cost-allocation base	Professional labor-hours	Partner labor-hours

Required

1. Compute the 2012 budgeted direct-cost rates for (a) professional partners and (b) professional associates.
2. Compute the 2012 budgeted indirect-cost rates for (a) general support and (b) secretarial support.
3. Compute the budgeted costs for the Richardson and Punch jobs, given the following information:

	Richardson, Inc.	Punch, Inc.
Professional partners	48 hours	29 hours
Professional associates	72 hours	116 hours

4. Comment on the results in requirement 3. Why are the job costs different from those computed in Problem 4-26?
5. Would you recommend Kahn & Associates use the job-costing system in Problem 4-26 or the job-costing system in this problem? Explain.

4-28 Proration of overhead. (Z. Iqbal, adapted) The Solar Radiator Company uses a normal-costing system with a single manufacturing overhead cost pool and machine-hours as the cost-allocation base. The following data are for 2012:

Budgeted manufacturing overhead costs	$4,875,000
Overhead allocation base	Machine-hours
Budgeted machine-hours	75,000
Manufacturing overhead costs incurred	$5,125,000
Actual machine-hours	80,000

Machine-hours data and the ending balances (before proration of under- or overallocated overhead) are as follows:

	Actual Machine-Hours	2012 End-of-Year Balance
Cost of Goods Sold	60,000	$8,500,000
Finished Goods Control	12,000	1,000,000
Work-in-Process Control	8,000	500,000

Required

1. Compute the budgeted manufacturing overhead rate for 2012.
2. Compute the under- or overallocated manufacturing overhead of Solar Radiator in 2012. Dispose of this amount using the following:
   a. Writeoff to Cost of Goods Sold
   b. Proration based on the overhead allocated in 2012 (before proration) in the ending balances of Work-in-Process Control, Finished Goods Control, and Cost of Goods Sold
3. Which method do you prefer in requirement 2? Explain.

4-29 Normal costing, overhead allocation, working backward. Garven Manufacturing uses normal costing for its job-costing system, which has two direct-cost categories (direct materials and direct manufacturing labor) and one indirect-cost category (manufacturing overhead). The following information is obtained for 2012:

- Total manufacturing costs, $8,350,000
- Manufacturing overhead allocated, $3,900,000 (allocated at a rate of 250% of direct manufacturing labor costs)
- Work-in-process inventory on January 1, 2012, $390,000
- Cost of finished goods manufactured, $8,040,000

Required

1. Use information in the first two bullet points to calculate (a) direct manufacturing labor costs in 2012 and (b) cost of direct materials used in 2012.
2. Calculate the ending work-in-process inventory on December 31, 2012.

4-30 General ledger relationships, under- and overallocation. (S. Sridhar, adapted) Southwick Company uses normal costing in its job-costing system. Partially completed T-accounts and additional information for Southwick for 2012 are as follows:

Direct Materials Control		
1-1-2012	25,000	234,000
	240,000	

Work-in-Process Control		
1-1-2012	44,000	
Dir. manuf. labor	348,000	

Finished Goods Control		
1-1-2012	10,000	880,000
	925,000	

Manufacturing Overhead Control	
514,000	

Manufacturing Overhead Allocated	

Cost of Goods Sold	

Additional information follows:

a. Direct manufacturing labor wage rate was $12 per hour.
b. Manufacturing overhead was allocated at $16 per direct manufacturing labor-hour.
c. During the year, sales revenues were $1,050,000, and marketing and distribution costs were $125,000.

Required

1. What was the amount of direct materials issued to production during 2012?
2. What was the amount of manufacturing overhead allocated to jobs during 2012?
3. What was the total cost of jobs completed during 2012?
4. What was the balance of work-in-process inventory on December 31, 2012?
5. What was the cost of goods sold before proration of under- or overallocated overhead?
6. What was the under- or overallocated manufacturing overhead in 2012?
7. Dispose of the under- or overallocated manufacturing overhead by writing off to Cost of Goods Sold.
8. Calculate Southwick's operating income for 2012.
9. What alternative method could Southwick have used to dispose of the under- or overallocated manufacturing overhead? Without doing any further calculations, explain how this alternative method would have affected Southwick's operating income. Which method would you recommend Southwick use? Explain your answer briefly.

4-31 Allocation and proration of overhead. InStep Company prints custom training material for corporations. The business was started January 1, 2012. The company uses a normal-costing system. It has two direct cost pools, materials and labor, and one indirect cost pool, overhead. Overhead is charged to printing jobs on the basis of direct labor cost. The following information is available for 2012.

Budgeted direct labor costs	$225,000
Budgeted overhead costs	$315,000
Costs of actual material used	$148,500
Actual direct labor costs	$213,500
Actual overhead costs	$302,100

There were two jobs in process on December 31, 2012: Job 11 and Job 12. Costs added to each job as of December 31 are as follows:

	Direct materials	Direct labor
Job 11	$4,870	$5,100
Job 12	$5,910	$6,800

InStep Company has no finished goods inventories because all printing jobs are transferred to cost of goods sold when completed.

Required

1. Compute the overhead allocation rate.
2. Calculate the balance in ending work in process and cost of goods sold before any adjustments for under- or overallocated overhead.
3. Calculate under- or overallocated overhead.
4. Calculate the ending balances in work in process and cost of goods sold if the under- or overallocated overhead amount is as follows:
   a. Written off to cost of goods sold
   b. Prorated using the overhead allocated in 2012 (before proration) in the ending balances of cost of goods sold and work-in-process control accounts
5. Which of the methods in requirement 4 would you choose? Explain.

4-32 Support-department cost allocation; direct, step-down, and reciprocal methods. Phoenix Partners provides management consulting services to government and corporate clients. Phoenix has two support departments—administrative services (AS) and information systems (IS)—and two operating departments—government consulting (GOVT) and corporate consulting (CORP). For the first quarter of 2012, Phoenix's cost records indicate the following:

Home Insert Page Layout Formulas Data Review View

	A	B	C	D	E	F	G
1		SUPPORT			OPERATING		
2		AS	IS		GOVT	CORP	Total
3	Budgeted overhead costs before any						
4	interdepartment cost allocations	$660,000	$3,300,000		$8,850,000	$12,470,000	$25,280,000
5	Support work supplied by AS (budgeted head count)	—	20%		48%	32%	100%
6	Support work supplied by IS (budgeted computer time)	10%	—		27%	63%	100%

Required

1. Allocate the two support departments' costs to the two operating departments using the following methods:
   a. Direct method
   b. Step-down method (allocate AS first)
   c. Step-down method (allocate IS first)
2. Compare and explain differences in the support-department costs allocated to each operating department.
3. What approaches might a manager use to decide the sequence in which to allocate support departments when using the step-down method?

4. Allocate the two support departments' costs to the two operating departments using the reciprocal method. Use (a) linear equations and (b) repeated iterations.
5. Which of the methods described in requirements 1 and 4 do you prefer? Explain briefly.

4-33 Support-department cost allocations; single-department cost pools; direct, step-down, and reciprocal methods. The Arrow Company has two products. Product 1 is manufactured entirely in department X. Product 2 is manufactured entirely in department Y. To produce these two products, the Arrow Company has two support departments: A (a materials-handling department) and B (a power-generating department).

An analysis of the work done by departments A and B in a typical period follows:

	Used by			
Supplied by	A	B	X	Y
A	—	200	500	300
B	750	—	125	375

The work done in department A is measured by the direct labor-hours of materials-handling time. The work done in department B is measured by the kilowatt-hours of power. The budgeted costs of the support departments for the coming year are as follows:

	Department A (Materials Handling)	Department B (Power Generation)
Variable indirect labor and indirect materials cost	$150,000	$15,000
Supervision	45,000	25,000
Depreciation	15,000	50,000
	$210,000	$90,000

The budgeted costs of the operating departments for the coming year are $1,250,000 for department X and $950,000 for department Y.

Supervision costs are salary costs. Depreciation in department B is the straight-line depreciation of power-generation equipment in its 19th year of an estimated 25-year useful life. The equipment is old but well maintained.

1. What are the allocations of costs of support departments A and B to operating departments X and Y using (a) the direct method, (b) the step-down method (allocate department A first), (c) the step-down method (allocate department B first), and (d) the reciprocal method?
2. An outside company has offered to supply all the power needed by the Arrow Company and to provide all the services of the present power department. The cost of this service will be $80 per kilowatt-hour of power. Should Arrow accept? Explain.

4-34 Support-department cost allocations; single-department cost pools; direct, step-down, and reciprocal methods. Mountain Extreme manufactures mountain biking clothes and shoes. The company has two product lines (clothing and shoes), which are produced in separate manufacturing facilities; however, both manufacturing facilities share the same support services for information technology and human resources. The following shows the total costs for each manufacturing facility and for each support department (in thousands):

	Variable Costs	Fixed Costs	Total Costs by Department
Information technology (IT)	$ 600	$ 2,000	$ 2,600
Human resources (HR)	$ 400	$ 1,000	$ 1,400
Clothing	$2,500	$ 8,000	$10,500
Shoes	$3,000	$ 4,500	$ 7,500
Total costs	$6,500	$15,500	$22,000

The total costs of the support departments (IT and HR) are allocated to the production departments (clothing and shoes) using a single rate based on the following:

Information technology:	Number of IT labor-hours worked by department
Human resources:	Number of employees supported by department

Data on the bases, by department, are given as follows:

Department	IT Hours Used	Number of Employees
Clothing	5,040	220
Shoes	3,960	88
Information technology	—	92
Human resources	3,000	—

1. What are the total costs of the production departments (clothing and shoes) *after* the support department costs of IT and HR have been allocated using (a) the direct method, (b) the step-down method (allocate IT first), (c) the step-down method (allocate HR first), and (d) the reciprocal method.
2. Assume that all of the work of the IT department could be outsourced to an independent company for $97.50 per hour. If Mountain Extreme no longer operated its own IT department, 30% of the fixed costs of the IT department could be eliminated. Should Mountain Extreme outsource its IT services? What other factors besides cost should managers consider in this decision?

4-35 Job costing, contracting, ethics. Rand Company manufactures modular homes. The company has two main products that it sells commercially: a 1,000-square-foot, one-bedroom model and a 1,500-square-foot, two-bedroom model. The company recently began providing emergency housing (huts) to FEMA, the Federal Emergency Management Agency. The emergency housing is similar to the 1,000-square-foot model.

FEMA has requested Rand to create a bid for 150 emergency huts to be sent for wildfire victims in the west. Your manager has asked that you prepare this bid. In preparing the bid, you find a recent invoice to FEMA for 200 huts provided during the most recent hurricane season in the south. You also have a standard cost sheet for the 1,000-square-foot model sold commercially. Both are provided as follows:

Standard cost sheet: 1,000-sq.-ft. one-bedroom model

Direct materials		$ 9,500
Direct manufacturing labor	32 hours	704
Manufacturing overhead*	$3.50 per direct labor dollar	2,464
Total cost		$ 12,668
Retail markup on total cost		25%
Retail price		$ 15,835

INVOICE:	
DATE: September 15, 2012	
BILL TO: FEMA	
FOR: 200 Emergency Huts	
SHIP TO: Sarasota, Florida	
Direct materials	$2,090,000
Direct manufacturing labor**	164,400
Manufacturing overhead	575,400
Total cost	2,829,800
Government contract markup on total cost	20%
Total due	$3,395,760

*Overhead cost pool includes inspection labor ($15 per hour), setup labor ($12 per hour), and other indirect costs associated with production.

**Direct manufacturing labor includes 30 production hours per unit, 4 inspection hours per unit, and 6 setup hours per unit.

Required

1. Calculate the total bid if you base your calculations on the standard cost sheet assuming a cost plus 20% government contract.
2. Calculate the total bid if you base your calculations on the September 15, 2012, invoice assuming a cost plus 20% government contract.
3. What are the main discrepancies between the bids you calculated in requirements 1 and 2?
4. What bid should you present to your manager? What principles from the IMA *Standards of Ethical Conduct for Practitioners of Management Accounting and Financial Management*, as described in Chapter 1, should guide your decision? As the manager, what would you do?

4-36 Job costing—service industry. Jordan Brady schedules gigs for local bands and creates CDs and t-shirts to sell at each gig. Brady uses a normal-costing system with two direct-cost pools, labor and materials, and one indirect-cost pool, general overhead. General overhead is allocated to each gig based on 120% of labor cost. Actual overhead equaled allocated overhead in March 2012. Actual overhead in April was $1,980. All costs incurred during the planning stage for a gig and during the gig are gathered in a balance sheet account called "Gigs in Progress (GIP)." When a gig is completed, the costs are transferred to an income statement account called "Cost of Completed Gigs (CCG)." Following is cost information for April 2012:

	From Beginning GIP		Incurred in April	
Band	Materials	Labor	Materials	Labor
Irok	$570	$750	$110	$200
Freke Out	700	550	140	100
Bottom Rung	250	475	310	250
Dish Towel	—	—	540	450
Rail Ride	—	—	225	250

As of April 1, there were three gigs in progress: *Irok, Freke Out, and Bottom Rung.* The gigs for *Dish Towel* and *Rail Ride* were started during April. The gigs for *Freke Out* and *Dish Towel* were completed during April.

Required

1. Calculate GIP at the end of April.
2. Calculate CCG for April.
3. Calculate under/overallocated overhead at the end of April.
4. Calculate the ending balances in GIP and CCG if the under/overallocated overhead amount is as follows:
   a. Written off to CCG
   b. Prorated based on the overhead allocated in April in the ending balances of GIP and CCG (before proration)
5. Which method would you choose? Explain. Would your choice depend on whether overhead cost is underallocated or overallocated? Explain.

Case

Colorscope, Inc. (Abridged)

Introduction

Andrew Cha, the founder of Colorscope, Inc., a small, vibrant firm in the graphic arts industry, had seen his business change dramatically over the years. The rapid development of such technologies as desktop publishing and the World Wide Web as well as the consolidation of several major players within the industry had radically altered his company's relative positioning on the competitive landscape. Preparing to celebrate the company's 35th anniversary on March 2013, Cha pondered the issues involved in moving Colorscope ahead.

Company History

Born in Anhui, China, in 1938, Andrew Cha immigrated to the United States in 1967 to seek a better life. Cha worked as a cook and busboy in a downtown Chinese restaurant in Los Angeles, but he eventually found jobs that took advantage of his artistic skills in draftsmanship and photography. A succession of promotions in one graphic arts company convinced him that he had the skills to start his own business. On March 1, 1976, Cha founded Colorscope, Inc. as a special-effects photography laboratory serving local advertising agencies in southern California.

As Cha's reputation grew, so did the business. Sales increased steadily over the years. The company served agency giants such as Saatchi & Saatchi, Grey Advertising, and J. Walter Thompson and large retailing and entertainment companies such as The Walt Disney Company and R. H. Macy & Co. To improve service to these customers, Cha invested in expensive proprietary computer equipment to continue providing ever more complicated print special effects.

While serving his existing base of high-margin clients, Cha ignored certain trends in the business, particularly the price pressures brought on by cheaper PC- and Mac-based microcomputers. These computers were equipped with increasingly sophisticated page layout and color correction software, so small ad agencies and print shops began to take pieces of business away from larger graphic art companies like Colorscope. Cha, however, had felt protected from the trend by the strong personal relationships he had built with key clients over his career.

Market pressures, however, forced Cha to reduce his own basic prices. This, however, proved to be insufficient. His largest account, representing about 80% of his business, announced that it was purchasing its own graphic design and production equipment, replacing Colorscope with an internal group. To rebuild the business, Cha had to reevaluate the industry, his company's position in the prepress segment, its pricing policy, and its operations.

The Prepress Production Process

Although technology dramatically changed the means by which production was conducted as well as the corresponding values to each phase, the basic process for print material, known in the industry as prepress or color separations, remained essentially the same. A content provider, such as a magazine or direct mail cataloger, designed and laid out a "book" or "project" for distribution (1 week). Once the book's layout was approved, a photographer captured and developed the images, received approvals from the client, and sent them to the prepress house or "color separator," in this case Colorscope (1 week). Once in production, images were processed or digitized via laser scanner and compiled with text and other graphics to form a master file for the printer (2 weeks).

Source: Reprinted by permission of Harvard Business School

Harvard Business School case 9-113-025
The case was prepared by VG Narayanan as the basis for class discussion rather than to illustrate either effective or ineffective handling of an administrative situation.

During this process, the magazine or direct-mail client saw iterations, or proofs, of their "book" with digital and conventional proofing devices. At these intervals, the clients could ask for changes, ranging from simple price and copy adjustments to sophisticated special effects, adjusting colors, or clearing blemishes in products and people. A very important qualitative component of the separator's task was to understand the product's desired "look and feel" and translate the direction the client desired into the actual images on each page. Typically, the prepress house charged a base rate for digitizing, assembling, and proofing each page, with an additional fee for the special effects. When the "books" were ultimately produced on paper, the images were filed and stored in the separator's database for future use.

After the client approved the project, Colorscope sent the "master book," or file, to the printer electronically. At this point, the separator had converted all of the client's information, digital text, graphics, and photographs (described in a postscript or dpi format) into a printer-acceptable (line screen) format. Printing took about 1 week.

Industry Dynamics

For the individual prepress firm the market had drastically changed. Thus Colorscope's previous position as a high-quality, high-service player appeared unsustainable in a marketplace full of service providers that claimed the same quality at lower prices. While in the past prosperous relationships could last several years, with customers consistently able and willing to pay for top quality separations, current technology blurred the clear distinctions in quality of the actual output. As more prepress houses bought desktop equipment and lowered their prices, customers in the catalog arena defected to even lower-cost providers. Given that the basic scanning and proofing functions of a prepress house could be easily replicated on a smaller scale with minimal investment,[1] and given the significant overcapacity in the industry, Cha knew that the downward pressure on prices was likely to continue.

Direct Competition

Although the number of larger direct-mail clients had remained flat for several years, the competition for them was intense. Cha's competitors came in three main types. First were larger, more technically savvy printing companies, such as R. R. Donnelley & Sons Co. and Quad Graphics, with professional salespeople pushing bundled pricing, integrating prepress services with printing in a single package. Another significant rival type was represented by the horizontally integrated national prepress houses or "trade shops" such as American Color and Wace/Techtron—highly entrenched, multimillion-dollar prepress service providers backed by national sales networks of service professionals and multiple physical plant locations across the United States. These companies competed in several different submarkets beyond catalogs, for example, inserts, comic syndications, and coupons. A third rival type comprised other standalone firms that competed with loose affiliations to other printers or advertising agencies, or that literally set up shop next door to their largest accounts to fend off potential competitors. Cha currently lacked a sales infrastructure similar to that of these competitor types.

Work Flow Organization at Colorscope

A "job" at Colorscope began when the customer placed an order. Customer service representatives interacted with the customer on the phone and recorded the job specification details. Each order was "owned" by a particular representative, who, based on the specifications, did a "job preparation." A separate "job bag" was opened for each set of four pages for the order. The template of the job was created by physically cutting and pasting text, graphics, and photographs; extensive markings on the template specified the changes in font, color, shading, and layout. The next step in the production process was scanning, whereby the pictures were digitized and output as a computer file. Colorscope had three laser scanners.

The following step was assembly, performed on nine high-end Macintosh computers, each with oversized computer terminals. The computers were networked and hooked up to the scanners,

[1] Local service bureaus could scan color film, layout pages, and output printer-specified film with a minimal capital investment of less than $100,000.

output devices, and a powerful file server that contained archives of optical images. Operators worked on the computers composing the "job" with scanned images and text input from the keyboard. At this stage the operators changed colors and shades of the scanned picture to the exact specifications the customer demanded. Once a job was fully assembled, it was output on one of two high-end output devices. The output was a large sheet of four-color film that was then developed.

The "job" then flowed to Quality Control (QC) for proofing, where an employee compared the hardcopy output with customer specifications. Reworks were initiated at this stage. QC might, for instance, require the job to be rescanned if it determined that the original scanning was flawed. The rescanned image would then have to be reassembled, re-output, and pass QC all over again. Once a job passed QC, it was shipped to the customer's printer either on a computer disk or, more usually, on film.

Colorscope's operators were cross-trained and could work at any stage of the production process. Work flow and production procedures were standardized but not documented. Colorscope relied instead on the institutional knowledge of its employees and frequent supervision by Andy Cha to maintain and improve operational efficiency.

The Future

Cha realized that Colorscope had to capitalize on its biggest assets, its employees, who were all well trained and worked effectively as a team to meet deadlines. The short-term strategy was to increase marketing efforts to drum up new business for the lean months that preceded the huge rush of orders to do prepress for catalogs in the fall season before holiday shopping started. Colorscope Exhibit 1 gives details of jobs completed in June 2012 and revenue generated from each customer. Revenue per page, however, was unlikely to improve due to competitive pressures. Cost containment and improving operational efficiency were therefore critical, particularly in reducing the amount of rework. This effort required the cooperation of its workers, and Cha was considering sharing the gains of such improvement with its employees. With this objective in mind, Colorscope began tracking hours spent on rework, which was broken down into hours spent on rework initiated by customer due to change in specifications and rework caused by errors in-house. Colorscope compensated its line workers on an hourly wage basis. To keep track of hours worked, employees logged the hours spent on various jobs into a centralized computer from remote terminals. (Colorscope Exhibit 2 gives the hours spent at different workstations by different jobs in June 2012.)

Colorscope Exhibit 1

Jobs Completed in June 2012*

Job	Pages	Revenue
601	32	$ 19,200
602	32	23,000
603	32	23,000
604	112	76,000
605	128	50,000
606	48	26,600
607	32	16,000
608	16	11,000
609	16	11,000
610	32	20,000
611	8	3,400
612	32	18,000
613	8	6,000
614	17	12,000
Total	545	$315,200

* All figures are disguised.

Tracking rework hours was fairly straightforward; employees recorded both types of rework hours separately for each job. (Colorscope Exhibit 3 gives the rework hours recorded during June 2012.)

Another area for improvement was product pricing. At present, Colorscope quoted more or less the same per-page price for different customers, plus additional charges for special effects. Yet different customers placed different demands on organizational resources, and this was not appropriately reflected in the price charged. However, Colorscope could not afford expensive accounting systems or to hire consultants to design a state-of-the-art activity-based cost system. Colorscope Exhibit 4 gives selected financial information and Colorscope Exhibit 5 gives materials expense, broken down by jobs, for the month of June 2012.

Colorscope Exhibit 2

Hours Clocked at Different Workstations in June 2012*

Job #	Job Preparation	Scanning	Assembly	Output	Quality Control	Total
601	7	56	80	16	15	174
602	7	40	75	16	8	146
603	8	32	58	8	8	114
604	23	112	212	28	25	400
605	15	130	250	32	30	457
606	13	56	104	12	13	198
607	8	39	66	12	10	135
608	4	21	39	4	4	72
609	4	20	40	8	7	79
610	7	26	60	8	9	110
611	4	10	21	3	2	40
612	8	40	80	8	8	144
613	3	10	23	3	2	41
614	6	20	44	5	6	81
Idle Time	43	28	128	37	13	249
Capacity	160	640	1,280	200	160	2,440

Hours clocked in different workstations include rework hours given in Exhibit 3.

* All figures are disguised.

Colorscope Exhibit 3

Rework Hours*

Rework due to change in specifications by customer

Job #	Job Preparation	Scanning	Assembly	Output	Quality Control	Total
601	0	24	16	8	5	53
605	2	5	10	2	2	21
609	1	4	8	1	0	14
613	1	2	7	1	0	11
Total	4	35	41	12	7	99

* All figures are disguised.

Quality Control initiated rework of house errors

Job #	Job Preparation	Scanning	Assembly	Output	Quality Control	Total
605	1	3	4	1	1	10
607	0	19	30	4	3	56
611	1	3	3	1	0	8
Total	2	25	37	6	4	74

In all four jobs that were subsequently reworked because Quality Control initiated rework, the original defects were introduced in the scanning stage of the operation. However, when a job is rescanned, assembly, output, and quality control all have to be redone.

Colorscope Exhibit 4

Selected Financial Information for June 2012*

Description	Job Preparation	Scanning	Assembly	Output	Quality Control	Idle	Total
Wages	$8,000	$32,000	$64,000	$10,000	$11,000		$125,000
Depreciation	$500	$25,000	$10,000	$14,000	$500		50,000
Rent							30,000
Others							20,000
Total overhead							$225,000
Floor space in sq. ft.	1000	1000	4000	2000	500	6,500	15,000

Colorscope Exhibit 5

Materials Expense in June 2012*

Job #	Total Materials Expense[2]	Customer-Initiated Rework	Correction of House Error
601	$ 8,900	$3,800	
602	4,500		
603	3,300		
604	13,400		
605	13,000	1,000	$1,000
606	5,900		
607	7,000		2,000
608	2,200		
609	3,600	1,500	
610	3,300		
611	1,600		500
612	4,600		
613	3,300	2,000	
614	2,400		
Total	$75,000	$8,300	$3,500

[2] Includes materials for rework.

* All figures are disguised.

Required

1. Set up a two-stage cost system to calculate the profitability of different jobs. You will have to choose resource drivers to allocate the cost of resources to cost pools. Then choose cost drivers to allocate the costs in various cost pools to jobs. Compute the cost driver rates. Calculate profitability of all jobs by allocating costs to jobs using the cost-driver rates that you estimated. It might be useful to diagram this system before you start calculating the cost pools and cost-driver rates.
2. Assignment question 1 is a full-cost analysis. Is full cost the right metric for job profitability, or should we only allocate direct costs of jobs? What assumptions are we making about the variability of overhead costs when we do a "full-cost" analysis?
3. What is the financial consequence of rework? What should Colorscope do about rework? How?
4. Should Colorscope change its incentive system?
5. How can Colorscope improve its operations and profitability?

Process Costing and Cost Allocation

5

Learning Objectives

1. Identify the situations in which process-costing systems are appropriate
2. Understand the basic concepts of process costing and compute average unit costs
3. Describe the five steps in process costing and calculate equivalent units
4. Use the weighted-average method and first-in, first-out (FIFO) method of process costing
5. Understand the need for hybrid-costing systems such as operation costing
6. Understand why and how managers allocate joint and common costs

Many companies use mass-production techniques to produce identical or similar units of a product or service: Apple (cell phones), Coca-Cola (soft drinks), ExxonMobil (gasoline), JP MorganChase (processing of checks), Kellogg (cereals), and Novartis (pharmaceuticals). Managerial accountants at companies like these use process costing because it helps them (1) determine how many units of the product the firm has on hand at the end of an accounting reporting period, (2) evaluate the units' stages of completion, and (3) assign costs to units produced and in inventory. There are different methods for process costing based on different assumptions about flow of product costs (for example, the FIFO or weighted-average method). As you studied in your financial accounting class, the choice of method results in different operating income, affects the taxes a company pays, and the performance evaluation of the manager.

Chapter at a Glance

- Managers use process-costing systems to determine the cost of a product or service when masses of identical or similar units are produced.
- Average unit costs are computed by dividing total costs in a given accounting period by total units produced in that period. The key step is to convert partially completed output units into equivalent units of completed output units. The key challenge is estimating the degree of completion of partially completed units.
- Two commonly used methods of process costing are the weighted-average method (based on all costs incurred to date) and the first-in, first-out (FIFO) method (based on costs incurred during the current period). Managers choose the method of process costing after considering various factors such as the effect on taxes, operating income, performance evaluation, and debt covenants.
- Many production systems have aspects of both custom-order production and mass production. In these circumstances, managers use hybrid-costing systems that blend characteristics from both job-costing and process-costing systems.
- The simultaneous production of products leads to joint costs. Managers allocate joint costs on the basis of the sales values of the products produced.
- The sharing of an activity or facility among multiple users leads to common costs. Managers use various methods to determine the "fair" share of the cost to be borne by each user.

Learning Objective 1

Identify the situations in which process-costing systems are appropriate

. . . when masses of identical or similar units are produced

Illustrating Process Costing

Before examining process costing in more detail, let's briefly review the distinction between job costing and process costing that we explained in Chapter 4. Job-costing and process-costing systems are best viewed as ends of a continuum:

Job-costing system	**Process-costing system**
Distinct, identifiable units of a product or service (for example, custom-made machines and houses, consulting engagements)	Masses of identical or similar units of a product or service (for example, food or chemical processing, postal delivery)

In a *process-costing system,* the unit cost of a product or service is obtained by assigning total costs to many identical or similar units of output. In other words, unit costs are calculated by dividing total costs incurred by the number of units of output from the production process. In a manufacturing process-costing setting, each unit receives the same or similar amounts of direct material costs, direct manufacturing labor costs, and indirect manufacturing costs (manufacturing overhead).

The main difference between process costing and job costing is the *extent of averaging* used to compute unit costs of products or services. In a job-costing system, individual jobs use different quantities of production resources, so it would be incorrect to cost each job at the same average production cost. In contrast, when identical or similar units of products or services are mass-produced, not processed as individual jobs, process costing is used to calculate an average production cost for all units produced. Some processes, such as clothes manufacturing, have aspects of both process costing (cost per unit of each operation, such as cutting or sewing, is identical) and job costing (different materials are used in different batches of clothing, say, wool versus cotton). A later section in this chapter describes "hybrid" costing systems that combine elements of both job and process costing.

Consider the following example of process costing: Suppose that Pacific Electronics manufactures a variety of cell phone models. These models are assembled in the assembly department. Upon completion, units are transferred to the testing department. We focus on the assembly department process for one cell phone model, SG-40. All units of SG-40 are identical and must meet a set of demanding performance specifications for clear reception. The process-costing system for SG-40 in the assembly department has a single direct-cost category—direct materials—and a single indirect-cost category—conversion costs. Conversion costs are all manufacturing costs other than direct material costs, including manufacturing labor, energy, plant depreciation, and so on. Direct materials, such as circuit board, antenna, and microphone are added at the beginning of the assembly process. Conversion costs are added evenly during assembly.

The following illustrates the process-costing system:

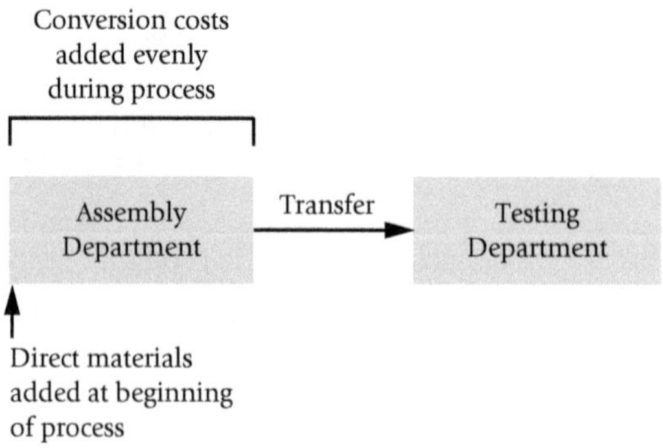

Process-costing systems separate costs into cost categories according to *when costs are introduced into the process.* Often, as in our Pacific Electronics example, managers need only two cost classifications—direct materials and conversion costs—to assign costs to products. Why only two? Because *all* direct materials are added to the process at one time, and all conversion costs generally are added to the process evenly during manufacturing of the product. Sometimes the situation is different.

1. If two different direct materials—such as the circuit board and microphone—are added to the process at different times, two different direct-materials categories would be needed to assign these costs to products.
2. If manufacturing labor costs are added to the process at a different time compared to other conversion costs, an additional cost category—direct manufacturing labor costs—would be needed to assign these costs to products.

We illustrate process costing using three cases of increasing complexity:

- **Case 1**—Process costing with zero beginning and zero ending work-in-process inventory of SG-40. (That is, all units are started and fully completed within the accounting period.) *This case presents the most basic concepts of process costing and illustrates the feature of averaging of costs.*
- **Case 2**—Process costing with zero beginning work-in-process inventory and some ending work-in-process inventory of SG-40. (That is, some units of SG-40 started during the accounting period are incomplete at the end of the period.) *This case introduces the five steps of process costing and the concept of equivalent units.*
- **Case 3**—Process costing with both some beginning and some ending work-in-process inventory of SG-40. *This case adds more complexity and illustrates the effect of weighted-average and first-in, first-out (FIFO) cost flow assumptions on cost of units completed and cost of work-in-process inventory.*

Keys to Success

Managers use process costing systems to determine the cost of a product or service when masses of identical or similar units are produced.

Case 1: Process Costing with No Beginning or Ending Work-in-Process Inventory

Learning Objective 2

Understand the basic concepts of process costing and compute average unit costs

. . . divide total costs by total units in a given accounting period

On January 1, 2013, there was no beginning inventory of SG-40 units in the assembly department. During the month of January, Pacific Electronics started, completely assembled, and transferred 400 units to the testing department.

Data for the assembly department for January 2013 are as follows:

Physical Units for January 2013

Work in process, beginning inventory (January 1)	0 units
Started during January	400 units
Completed and transferred out during January	400 units
Work in process, ending inventory (January 31)	0 units

Physical units refer to the number of output units, whether complete or incomplete. In January 2013, all 400 physical units started were completed.

Total Costs for January 2013

Direct material costs added during January	$32,000
Conversion costs added during January	24,000
Total assembly department costs added during January	$56,000

Pacific Electronics records direct material costs and conversion costs in the assembly department as these costs are incurred. By averaging, the assembly cost of SG-40 is itemized as follows:

Direct material cost per unit ($32,000 ÷ 400 units)	$80
Conversion cost per unit ($24,000 ÷ 400 units)	60
Assembly department cost per unit	$140

In Case 1, average unit costs are calculated by dividing total costs in a given accounting period by total units produced in that period. Because each unit is identical, managers assume all units receive the same amount of direct material costs and conversion costs. Case 1 applies whenever a company produces a homogeneous product or service but has no incomplete units when each accounting period ends, which is a common situation in service-sector organizations. For example, a bank can adopt this process-costing approach to compute the unit cost of processing 100,000 customer deposits made in a month because each deposit is processed in the same way regardless of the amount of the deposit.

Learning Objective 3

Describe the five steps in process costing

. . . to assign total costs to units completed and to units in work in process

and calculate equivalent units

. . . output units adjusted for incomplete units

Case 2: Process Costing with Zero Beginning and Some Ending Work-in-Process Inventory

In February 2013, Pacific Electronics' managers place another 400 units of SG-40 into production. Because all units placed into production in January were completely assembled, there is no beginning inventory of partially completed units in the assembly department on February 1. Some customers order late, so not all units started in February are completed by the end of the month. Only 175 units are completed and transferred to the testing department.

Data for the assembly department for February 2013 are as follows:

	A	B	C	D	E
1		Physical Units (SG-40s) (1)	Direct Materials (2)	Conversion Costs (3)	Total Costs (4) = (2) + (3)
2	Work in process, beginning inventory (February 1)	0			
3	Started during February	400			
4	Completed and transferred out during February	175			
5	Work in process, ending inventory (February 28)	225			
6	Degree of completion of ending work in process		100%	60%	
7	Total costs added during February		$32,000	$18,600	$50,600

The 225 partially assembled units as of February 28, 2013 are fully processed for direct materials, because all direct materials in the assembly department are added at the beginning of the assembly process. Conversion costs, however, are added evenly during assembly. An assembly department supervisor evaluates the work completed relative to the total work required to complete the SG-40 units still in process at the end of February and estimates that the partially assembled units are, on average, 60% complete for conversion costs.

The accuracy of the completion estimate of conversion costs depends on the care, skill, and experience of the estimator and the nature of the conversion process. Estimating the degree of completion is usually easier for direct material costs than for conversion costs, because the quantity of direct materials needed for a completed unit and the quantity of direct materials in a partially completed unit can be measured more accurately. In contrast, the conversion sequence usually consists of a number of operations, each for a specified period of time, at various steps in the production process. The degree of completion for conversion costs depends on the proportion of the total conversion costs needed to complete one unit (or a batch of production) that has already been incurred on the units still in process.

Department supervisors and line managers are most familiar with the conversion process, so they most often estimate conversion costs. Still, in some industries, such as semiconductor manufacturing, no exact estimate is possible because manufacturing occurs inside sealed equipment that is only opened after the process is complete. In other settings, such as the textile industry, vast quantities of unfinished products such as shirts and pants make the task of estimation too costly. In these cases, it is necessary for managers to assume that all work in process in a department is complete to some preset degree for conversion costs (for example, one-third, one-half, or two-thirds).

The point to understand here is that a partially assembled unit is not the same as a fully assembled unit. Faced with some fully assembled units and some partially assembled units, managers use a common metric called *equivalent units* to compare the work done in each category and, more importantly, obtain a total measure of work done. We explain this concept in greater detail next as we explore the five steps managers at Pacific Electronics need to take to calculate (1) the cost of fully assembled units in February 2013 and (2) the cost of partially assembled units still in process at the end of that month. The five steps of process costing are as follows:

Step 1: Summarize the flow of physical units of output.

Step 2: Compute output in terms of equivalent units.

Step 3: Summarize total costs to account for.

Step 4: Compute cost per equivalent unit.

Step 5: Assign total costs to units completed and to units in ending work in process.

Physical Units and Equivalent Units (Steps 1 and 2)

In **Step 1,** managers track physical units of output. Recall that physical units are the number of output units, whether complete or incomplete. Managers ask, Where did physical units come from? Where did they go? The physical-units column in Exhibit 5-1 tracks the 400 physical units started, the 175 units completed and transferred out, and the 225 units in ending inventory. Remember, when there is no beginning inventory, units started must equal the sum of units transferred out and ending inventory.

Because not all 400 physical units are fully completed, managers compute output in **Step 2** in *equivalent units,* not in *physical units.* To see what is meant by equivalent units, suppose that during a month, 50 physical units were started but not completed. Managers estimate that these 50 units in ending inventory are 70% complete for conversion costs. Consider those units from the perspective of the conversion costs already incurred to get the units to be 70% complete. Suppose all the conversion costs represented in the 70% were used to make fully completed units. How many units could have been 100% complete by the end of the month? The answer is 35 units. Why? Because 70% of conversion costs incurred on 50 incomplete units could have been incurred to make 35 (0.70 × 50) complete units by the end of the month. That is, if all the conversion-cost input in the 50 units in inventory had been used to make completed output units, the company would have produced 35 completed units (also called *equivalent units*) of output.

Equivalent units is a derived amount of output units that (1) combines the quantity of each input (factor of production) in units completed and in incomplete units of work in process and (2) converts the quantity of input into the amount of completed output units that could be produced with that quantity of input. Note that equivalent units are calculated separately for each

Exhibit 5-1

Steps 1 and 2: Summarize Output in Physical Units and Compute Output in Equivalent Units for Assembly Department of Pacific Electronics for February 2013

Home Insert Page Layout Formulas Data Review View

	A	B	C	D
1		(Step 1)	(Step 2)	
2			Equivalent Units	
3	Flow of Production	Physical Units	Direct Materials	Conversion Costs
4	Work in process, beginning	0		
5	Started during current period	400		
6	To account for	400		
7	Completed and transferred out during current period	175	175	175
8	Work in process, ending[a]	225		
9	(225 × 100%; 225 × 60%)		225	135
10	Accounted for	400		
11	Equivalent units of work done in current period		400	310
12				
13	[a]Degree of completion in this department; direct materials, 100%; conversion costs, 60%.			

input (such as direct materials and conversion costs). Moreover, every completed unit, by definition, is composed of one equivalent unit of each input required to make it. This chapter focuses on equivalent-unit calculations in manufacturing settings. Managers in nonmanufacturing companies also use equivalent units. For example, universities convert their part-time student enrollments into "full-time student equivalents" to get a better measure, for example, of faculty–student ratios over time. Without this adjustment, an increase in part-time students would erroneously suggest a deterioration in the faculty–student ratio and in the quality of instruction, when in fact, part-time students take considerably fewer academic courses and so do not need the same number of faculty per student compared to full-time students.

When calculating equivalent units in Step 2, focus on quantities. Disregard dollar amounts until after equivalent units are computed. In the Pacific Electronics example, all 400 physical units—the 175 fully assembled units and the 225 partially assembled units—are 100% complete for direct materials because all direct materials are added in the assembly department at the start of the process. Therefore, Exhibit 5-1 shows output as 400 *equivalent units* for direct materials: 175 equivalent units for the 175 physical units assembled and transferred out and 225 equivalent units for the 225 physical units in ending work-in-process inventory.

The 175 fully assembled units are also completely processed for conversion costs. The partially assembled units in ending work in process are 60% complete (on average). Therefore, conversion costs in the 225 partially assembled units are *equivalent* to conversion costs in 135 (60% of 225) fully assembled units. Exhibit 5-1 shows output as 310 *equivalent units* for conversion costs: 175 equivalent units for the 175 physical units assembled and transferred out and 135 equivalent units for the 225 physical units in ending work-in-process inventory.

Calculation of Product Costs (Steps 3, 4, and 5)

Exhibit 5-2 shows Steps 3, 4, and 5. Together, they are called the *production cost worksheet.*

In **Step 3,** managers summarize total costs to account for. Because the beginning balance of work-in-process inventory is zero on February 1, total costs to account for (that is, the total charges or debits to the Work in Process—Assembly account) consist only of costs added during February: direct materials of $32,000 and conversion costs of $18,600, for a total of $50,600.

In **Step 4,** managers calculate cost per equivalent unit separately for direct materials and for conversion costs by dividing direct material costs and conversion costs added during February by the related quantity of equivalent units of work done in February (as calculated in Exhibit 5-1).

To see why it is important for managers to understand equivalent units in unit-cost calculations, compare conversion costs for January and February 2013. Total conversion costs of $18,600 for the 400 units worked on during February are lower than the conversion costs of $24,000 for the 400 units worked on in January. However, in this example, the conversion costs to fully assemble a unit are $60 in both January and February. Total conversion costs are lower in February because fewer equivalent units of conversion-costs work were completed in February (310) than in January (400). Using physical units instead of equivalent units in the per-unit calculation would have led managers to the erroneous conclusion that conversion costs per unit declined from $60 in January to $46.50 ($18,600 ÷ 400 units) in February. This incorrect costing might have prompted Pacific Electronics' managers to presume that the assembly department had achieved greater efficiencies in processing than was the case and to lower the price of SG-40, for example, when in fact costs had not declined.

In **Step 5,** managers assign these costs to units completed and transferred out and to units still in process at the end of February 2013. The idea is to attach dollar amounts to the equivalent output units for direct materials and conversion costs of (a) units completed and (b) ending work in process, calculated in Exhibit 5-1, Step 2. *Equivalent output units for each input are multiplied by cost per equivalent unit, as calculated in Step 4 in Exhibit 5-2.* For example, costs assigned to the 225 physical units in ending work-in-process inventory are as follows:

Direct material costs of 225 equivalent units (Exhibit 5-1, Step 2) × $80 cost per equivalent unit of direct materials calculated in Step 4	$18,000
Conversion costs of 135 equivalent units (Exhibit 5-1, Step 2) × $60 cost per equivalent unit of conversion costs calculated in Step 4	8,100
Total cost of ending work-in-process inventory	$26,100

Note that total costs to account for in Step 3 ($50,600) equal total costs accounted for in Step 5.

Exhibit 5-2

Steps 3, 4, and 5: Summarize Total Costs to Account For, Compute Cost per Equivalent Unit, and Assign Total Costs to Units Completed and to Units in Ending Work in Process for Assembly Department of Pacific Electronics for February 2013

	A	B	C	D	E
1			Total Production Costs	Direct Materials	Conversion Costs
2	(Step 3)	Costs added during February	$50,600	$32,000	$18,600
3		Total costs to account for	$50,600	$32,000	$18,600
4					
5	(Step 4)	Costs added in current period	$50,600	$32,000	$18,600
6		Divide by equivalent units of work done in current period (Exhibit 5-1)		÷ 400	÷ 310
7		Cost per equivalent unit		$ 80	$ 60
8					
9	(Step 5)	Assignment of costs:			
10		Completed and transferred out (175 units)	$24,500	(175[a] × $80) +	(175[a] × $60)
11		Work in process, ending (225 units):	26,100	(225[b] × $80) +	(135[b] × $60)
12		Total costs accounted for	$50,600	$32,000 +	$18,600
13					
14	[a]Equivalent units completed and transferred out from Exhibit 5-1, step 2.				
15	[b]Equivalent units in ending work in process from Exhibit 5-1, step 2.				

T-Account Entries

The T-account entries in process-costing systems are similar to the T-account entries made in job-costing systems for direct materials and conversion costs. The main difference is that, in process costing, there is one Work in Process account for each process. In our example, there are accounts for Work in Process—Assembly and Work in Process—Testing. Pacific Electronics purchases direct materials as needed. These materials are delivered directly to the assembly department.

Using amounts from Exhibit 5-2, Exhibit 5-3 shows the entries recorded in February in various T-accounts and a general framework for the flow of costs through these accounts for the transactions summarized in the following table:

Entry Recorded in T-Accounts for . . .	In the Amount of . . .	Results in a Debit to . . .	And Results in a Credit to . . .
Purchase of direct materials used in production	$32,000	Work in Process—Assembly	Accounts Payable Control
Conversion costs incurred (for example, manufacturing labor, plant depreciation, energy, manufacturing supplies)	$18,600	Work in Process—Assembly	various accounts such as Wages Payable Control and Accumulated Depreciation
Physical transfer of completed goods from the Assembly Department to the Testing Department	$24,500	Work in Process—Testing	Work in Process—Assembly

The T-account Work in Process—Assembly shows February 2013's ending balance of $26,100, which is the beginning balance of Work in Process—Assembly in March 2013. Follow the arrows in Exhibit 5-3 from Work in Process—Testing to Finished Goods as finished goods are completed and from Finished Goods to Cost of Goods Sold when finished goods are sold. Now think about what happens if managers overestimate the degree of completion of partially completed units in ending work in process.

Exhibit 5-3

Flow of Costs in a Process-Costing System for Assembly Department of Pacific Electronics for February 2013

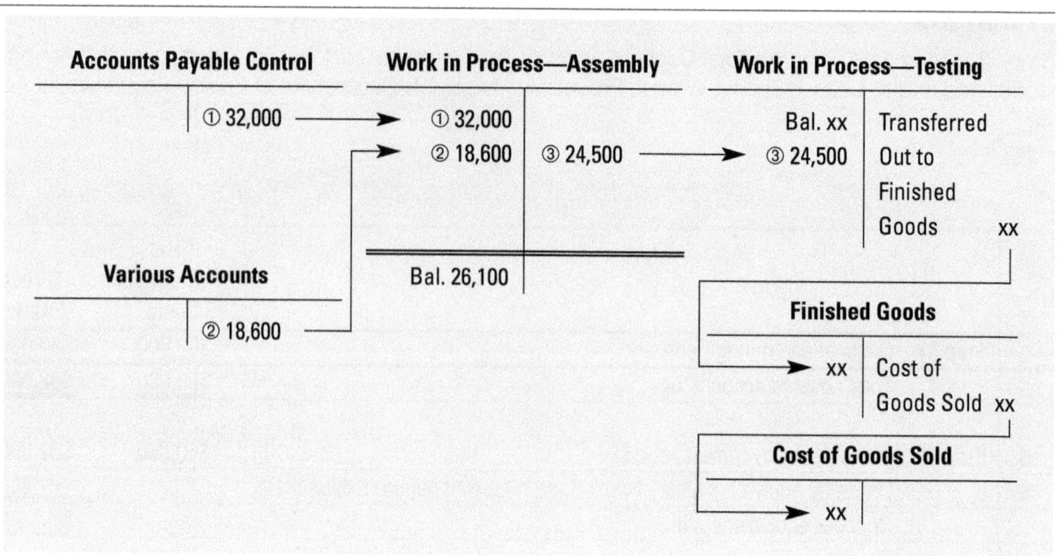

Suppose, for example, that Pacific Electronics' managers overestimate the degree of completion for conversion costs at 80% instead of 60%. The computations would change as follows:

- Exhibit 5-1, Step 2

  Equivalent units of conversion costs in ending Work in Process—Assembly = 80% × 225 = 180

  Equivalent units of conversion costs for work done in the current period = 175 + 180 = 355
- Exhibit 5-2, Step 4

  Cost per equivalent unit of conversion costs = \$18,600 ÷ 355 = \$52.39

  Cost per equivalent unit of direct materials is the same, \$80
- Exhibit 5-2, Step 5

  Cost of 175 units of goods completed and transferred out = 175 × \$80 + 175 × \$52.39 = \$23,168.25

This amount is lower than the \$24,500 of costs assigned to goods completed and transferred out calculated in Exhibit 5-2. Overestimating the degree of completion decreases the costs assigned to goods transferred out and eventually to cost of goods sold and increases operating income.

Managers must ensure that department supervisors avoid introducing personal biases into estimates of degrees of completion. To show better performance, for example, a department supervisor might report a higher degree of completion resulting in overstated operating income. If performance for the period is very good, the department supervisor may be tempted to report a lower degree of completion, reducing income in the current period. This has the effect of reducing the costs carried in ending inventory and the costs carried to the following year in beginning inventory. In other words, estimates of degree of completion can help to smooth earnings from one period to the next.

To guard against the possibility of bias, managers should ask supervisors specific questions about the process they followed to prepare estimates. Top management should always emphasize obtaining the correct answer, regardless of how it affects reported performance. This emphasis drives ethical actions throughout the organization.

Keys to Success

Average unit costs are computed by dividing total costs in a given accounting period by total units produced in that period. The key step is to convert partially completed output units into equivalent units of completed output units. The key challenge for managers is accurately estimating the degree of completion of partially completed units.

Case 3: Process Costing with Some Beginning and Some Ending Work-in-Process Inventory

At the beginning of March 2013, Pacific Electronics had 225 partially assembled SG-40 units in the Assembly Department. It started production of another 275 units in March. Data for the Assembly Department for March are as follows:

Home Insert Page Layout Formulas Data Review View

	A	B	C	D	E
1		Physical Units (SG-40s) (1)	Direct Materials (2)	Conversion Costs (3)	Total Costs (4) = (2) + (3)
2	Work in process, beginning inventory (March 1)	225	$18,000[a]	$8,100[a]	$26,100
3	Degree of completion of beginning work in process		100%	60%	
4	Started during March	275			
5	Completed and transferred out during March	400			
6	Work in process, ending inventory (March 31)	100			
7	Degree of completion of ending work in process		100%	50%	
8	Total costs added during March		$19,800	$16,380	$36,180
9					
10					
11	[a]Work in process, beginning inventory (equals work in process, ending inventory for February)				
12	Direct materials: 225 physical units × 100% completed × $80 per unit = $18,000				
13	Conversion costs: 225 physical units × 60% completed × $60 per unit = $8,100				

Learning Objective 4

Use the weighted-average method of process costing

. . . assigns costs based on total costs and equivalent units completed to date

and the first-in, first-out (FIFO) method of process costing

. . . assigns costs based on costs and equivalent units of work done in the current period

Pacific Electronics now has incomplete units in both beginning work-in-process inventory and ending work-in-process inventory for March 2013. We can still use the five steps described earlier to calculate (1) cost of units completed and transferred out and (2) cost of ending work in process. To assign costs to each of these categories, however, we first need to select an inventory-valuation method. Which method should managers at Pacific Electronics choose? To answer this question, we first need to understand two of the most commonly used methods—the *weighted-average method* and the *first-in, first-out method.* These different valuation methods produce different amounts for cost of units completed and for ending work in process when the unit cost of inputs changes from one period to the next.

Weighted-Average Method

The **weighted-average process-costing method** calculates cost per equivalent unit of all *work done to date* (regardless of the accounting period in which it was done) and assigns this cost to equivalent units completed and transferred out of the process and to equivalent units in ending work-in-process inventory. The weighted-average cost is the total of all costs entering the Work in Process account (whether the costs are from beginning work in process or from work started during the current period) divided by total equivalent units of work done to date. We now describe the weighted-average method using the five-step procedure introduced on page 175.

Step 1: Summarize the Flow of Physical Units of Output. The physical-units column in Exhibit 5-4 shows where the units came from—225 units from beginning inventory and 275 units started during the current period—and where the units went—400 units completed and transferred out and 100 units in ending inventory.

Step 2: Compute Output in Terms of Equivalent Units. We use the relationship shown in the following equation:

$$\begin{matrix}\text{Equivalent units} & & \text{Equivalent units} & & \text{Equivalent units} & & \text{Equivalent units} \\ \text{in beginning work} & + & \text{of work done in} & = & \text{completed and transferred} & + & \text{in ending work} \\ \text{in process} & & \text{current period} & & \text{out in current period} & & \text{in process}\end{matrix}$$

Although we are interested in calculating the left side of the preceding equation, it is easier to calculate this sum using the equation's right side: (1) equivalent units completed and transferred out in the current period plus (2) equivalent units in ending work in process. *Note that the stage of completion of the current-period beginning work in process is not used in this computation.*

The equivalent-units columns in Exhibit 5-4 show equivalent units of work done to date: 500 equivalent units of direct materials and 450 equivalent units of conversion costs. All completed and transferred-out units are 100% complete in both direct materials and conversion costs. Partially completed units in ending work in process are 100% complete as to direct materials because direct materials are introduced at the beginning of the process, and 50% complete as to conversion costs, based on estimates from the assembly department manager.

Step 3: Summarize Total Costs to Account For. Exhibit 5-5 presents Step 3. Total costs to account for in March 2013 are described in the example data on page 179:

Beginning work in process (direct materials, \$18,000 + conversion costs, \$8,100)	\$26,100
Costs added during March (direct materials, \$19,800 + conversion costs, \$16,380)	36,180
Total costs to account for in March	\$62,280

Step 4: Compute Cost per Equivalent Unit. Exhibit 5-5, Step 4, shows the computation of weighted-average cost per equivalent unit for direct materials and conversion costs. Weighted-average cost per equivalent unit is obtained by dividing the sum of costs for beginning work in process plus costs for work done in the current period by total equivalent units of work done to date. We calculate weighted-average conversion cost per equivalent unit in Exhibit 5-5, for example, as follows:

Total conversion costs (beginning work in process, \$8,100 + work done in current period, \$16,380)	\$24,480
Divide by total equivalent units of work done to date (equivalent units of conversion costs in beginning work in process and in work done in current period)	÷ 450
Weighted-average cost per equivalent unit	\$54.40

Step 5: Assign Total Costs to Units Completed and to Units in Ending Work in Process. Step 5 in Exhibit 5-5 takes the equivalent units completed and transferred out and equivalent units in ending work in process calculated in Exhibit 5-4, Step 2, and assigns dollar amounts to the units using the weighted-average cost per equivalent unit for direct materials and conversion costs calculated in Step 4. For example, total costs of the 100 physical units in ending work in process are as follows:

Direct materials:	
100 equivalent units × weighted-average cost per equivalent unit of \$75.60	\$ 7,560
Conversion costs:	
50 equivalent units × weighted-average cost per equivalent unit of \$54.40	2,720
Total costs of ending work in process	\$10,280

The following table summarizes total costs to account for (\$62,280) and how they are accounted for in Exhibit 5-5. The arrows indicate that the costs of units completed and transferred out and units in ending work in process are calculated using weighted-average total costs obtained after merging costs of beginning work in process and costs added in the current period.

Costs to Account for			Costs Accounted for Calculated Using the Weighted-Average Method	
Beginning work in process	\$26,100	→	Completed and transferred out	\$52,000
Costs added in current period	36,180	→	Ending work in process	10,280
Total costs to account for	\$62,280		Total costs accounted for	\$62,280

Before proceeding, review Exhibits 5-4 and 5-5 to check your understanding of the weighted-average method. Note: Exhibit 5-4 deals with only physical and equivalent units, not costs. Exhibit 5-5 shows the cost amounts.

Exhibit 5-4

Steps 1 and 2: Summarize Output in Physical Units and Compute Output in Equivalent Units Using Weighted-Average Method of Process Costing for Assembly Department of Pacific Electronics for March 2013

	A	B	C	D
1		(Step 1)	(Step 2)	
2			Equivalent Units	
3	Flow of Production	Physical Units	Direct Materials	Conversion Costs
4	Work in process, beginning (given, p. 179)	225		
5	Started during current period (given, p. 179)	275		
6	To account for	500		
7	Completed and transferred out during current period	400	400	400
8	Work in process, ending[a] (given, p. 179)	100		
9	(100 × 100%; 100 × 50%)		100	50
10	Accounted for	500		
11	Equivalent units of work done to date		500	450
12				
13	[a]Degree of completion in this department; direct materials, 100%; conversion costs, 50%.			

Using amounts from Exhibit 5-5, Steps 3 and 5, the T-account Work in Process—Assembly, under the weighted-average method, is as follows:

Work in Process—Assembly			
Beginning inventory, March 1	26,100	③ Completed and transferred out to Work in Process—Testing	52,000
① Direct materials	19,800		
② Conversion costs	16,380		
Ending inventory, March 31	10,280		

Exhibit 5-5

Steps 3, 4, and 5: Summarize Total Costs to Account For, Compute Cost per Equivalent Unit, and Assign Total Costs to Units Completed and to Units in Ending Work in Process Using Weighted-Average Method of Process Costing for Assembly Department of Pacific Electronics for March 2013

	A	B	C	D		E
1			Total Production Costs	Direct Materials		Conversion Costs
2	(Step 3)	Work in process, beginning (given, p. 179)	$26,100	$18,000		$ 8,100
3		Costs added in current period (given, p. 179)	36,180	19,800		16,380
4		Total costs to account for	$62,280	$37,800		$24,480
5						
6	(Step 4)	Costs incurred to date		$37,800		$24,480
7		Divide by equivalent units of work done to date (Exhibit 5-4)		÷ 500		÷ 450
8		Cost per equivalent unit of work done to date		$ 75.60		$ 54.40
9						
10	(Step 5)	Assignment of costs:				
11		Completed and transferred out (400 units)	$52,000	(400[a] × $75.60)	+	(400[a] × $54.40)
12		Work in process, ending (100 units):	10,280	(100[b] × $75.60)	+	(50[b] × $54.40)
13		Total costs accounted for	$62,280	$37,800	+	$24,480
14						
15	[a]Equivalent units completed and transferred out from Exhibit 5-4, Step 2.					
16	[b]Equivalent units in ending work in process from Exhibit 5-4, Step 2.					

First-In, First-Out Method

The **first-in, first-out (FIFO) process-costing method** (1) assigns the cost of the previous accounting period's equivalent units in beginning work-in-process inventory to the first units completed and transferred out of the process, and (2) assigns the cost of equivalent units worked on during the *current* period first to complete beginning inventory, next to start and complete new units, and finally to units in ending work-in-process inventory. The FIFO method assumes that the earliest equivalent units in work in process are completed first.

A distinctive feature of the FIFO process-costing method is that it keeps separate work done on beginning inventory before the current period from work done in the current period. Costs incurred and units produced in the current period are used to calculate cost per equivalent unit of work done in the current period. In contrast, equivalent-unit and cost-per-equivalent-unit calculations under the weighted-average method *merge* units and costs in beginning inventory with units and costs of work done in the current period.

We now describe the FIFO method using the five-step procedure introduced on page 175.

Step 1: Summarize the Flow of Physical Units of Output. Exhibit 5-6, Step 1, traces the flow of physical units of production and explains the calculation of physical units using the FIFO method.

- The first physical units assumed to be completed and transferred out during the period are 225 units from beginning work-in-process inventory.
- The March data on page 179 indicate that 400 physical units were completed during March. The FIFO method assumes that of these 400 units, 175 units (400 units − 225 units from beginning work-in-process inventory) must have been started and completed during March.
- Ending work-in-process inventory consists of 100 physical units—the 275 physical units started minus the 175 units that were started and completed.
- The physical units "to account for" equal the physical units "accounted for" (500 units).

Step 2: Compute Output in Terms of Equivalent Units. Exhibit 5-6 also presents the computations for Step 2 under the FIFO method. *The equivalent-unit calculations for each cost category focus on equivalent units of work done in the current period (March) only.*

Under the FIFO method, equivalent units of work done in March on the beginning work-in-process inventory equal 225 physical units times *the percentage of work remaining to be done in March to complete these units:* 0% for direct materials, because beginning work in process is 100% complete for direct materials, and 40% for conversion costs, because beginning work in process is 60% complete for conversion costs. The results are 0 (0% × 225) equivalent units of work for direct materials and 90 (40% × 225) equivalent units of work for conversion costs.

The equivalent units of work done on the 175 physical units started and completed equals 175 units times 100% for both direct materials and conversion costs because all work on these units is done in the current period.

The equivalent units of work done on the 100 units of ending work in process equal 100 physical units times 100% for direct materials (because all direct materials for these units are added in the current period) and 50% for conversion costs (because 50% of the conversion-costs work on these units is done in the current period).

Step 3: Summarize Total Costs to Account For. Exhibit 5-7 presents Step 3 and summarizes total costs to account for in March 2013 (beginning work in process, $26,100 and costs added in the current period, $36,180) of $62,280, as described in the example data (page 179).

Step 4: Compute Cost per Equivalent Unit. Exhibit 5-7 shows the Step 4 computation of cost per equivalent unit for *work done in the current period only* for direct materials and conversion costs. For example, conversion cost per equivalent unit of $52 is obtained by dividing current-period conversion costs of $16,380 by current-period conversion-costs equivalent units of 315.

Step 5: Assign Total Costs to Units Completed and to Units in Ending Work in Process. Exhibit 5-7 shows the assignment of costs under the FIFO method. Costs of work done in the current period are assigned (1) first to the additional work done to complete the beginning work in process, then (2) to work done on units started and completed during the current period, and finally (3) to ending work in process. *Step 5 takes each quantity of equivalent units calculated in Exhibit 5-6, Step 2, and assigns dollar amounts to them (using the cost-per-equivalent-unit calculations in Step 4).* The goal is to use the cost of work done in the current period to determine total costs of all units

Exhibit 5-6

Steps 1 and 2: Summarize Output in Physical Units and Compute Output in Equivalent Units Using FIFO Method of Process Costing for Assembly Department of Pacific Electronics for March 2013

1		**(Step 1)**	**(Step 2)**	
2			**Equivalent Units**	
3	**Flow of Production**	**Physical Units**	**Direct Materials**	**Conversion Costs**
4	Work in process, beginning (given, p. 179)	225	(work done before current period)	
5	Started during current period (given, p. 179)	275		
6	To account for	500		
7	Completed and transferred out during current period:			
8	From beginning work in process[a]	225		
9	[225 × (100% – 100%); 225 × (100% – 60%)]		0	90
10	Started and completed	175[b]		
11	(175 × 100%; 175 × 100%)		175	175
12	Work in process, ending[c] (given, p. 179)	100		
13	(100 × 100%; 100 × 50%)		100	50
14	Accounted for	500		
15	Equivalent units of work done in current period		275	315
16				
17	[a]Degree of completion in this department; direct materials, 100%; conversion costs, 60%.			
18	[b]400 physical units completed and transferred out minus 225 physical units completed and			
19	transferred out from beginning work-in-process inventory.			
20	[c]Degree of completion in this department: direct materials, 100%; conversion costs, 50%.			

completed from beginning inventory and from work started and completed in the current period, and costs of ending work in process.

Of the 400 completed units, 225 units are from beginning inventory and 175 units are started and completed during March. The FIFO method starts by assigning the costs of beginning work-in-process inventory of $26,100 to the first units completed and transferred out. As we saw in Step 2, an additional 90 equivalent units of conversion costs are needed to complete these units in the current period. Current-period conversion cost per equivalent unit is $52, so $4,680 (90 equivalent units × $52 per equivalent unit) of additional costs are incurred to complete beginning inventory. Total production costs for units in beginning inventory are $26,100 + $4,680 = $30,780. The 175 units started and completed in the current period consist of 175 equivalent units of direct materials and 175 equivalent units of conversion costs. These units are costed at the cost per equivalent unit in the current period (direct materials, $72, and conversion costs, $52) for a total production cost of $21,700 [175 × ($72 + $52)].

Under FIFO, ending work-in-process inventory comes from units that were started but not fully completed during the current period. Total costs of the 100 partially assembled physical units in ending work in process are as follows:

Direct materials:	
100 equivalent units × $72 cost per equivalent unit in March	$7,200
Conversion costs:	
50 equivalent units × $52 cost per equivalent unit in March	2,600
Total cost of work in process on March 31	$9,800

The following table summarizes total costs to account for and costs accounted for of $62,280 in Exhibit 5-7. Notice how the FIFO method keeps separate the layers of beginning work in process and costs added in the current period. The arrows indicate where the costs in each layer go—that is, to units completed and transferred out or to ending work in process. Be sure to include costs of beginning work in process ($26,100) when calculating costs of units completed from beginning inventory.

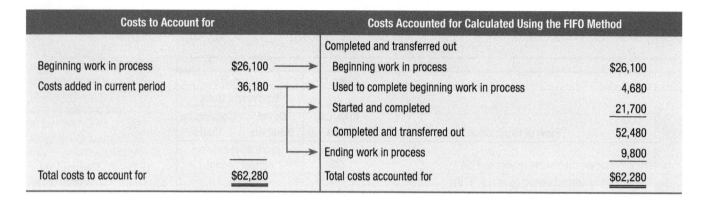

Costs to Account for		Costs Accounted for Calculated Using the FIFO Method	
		Completed and transferred out	
Beginning work in process	$26,100	Beginning work in process	$26,100
Costs added in current period	36,180	Used to complete beginning work in process	4,680
		Started and completed	21,700
		Completed and transferred out	52,480
		Ending work in process	9,800
Total costs to account for	$62,280	Total costs accounted for	$62,280

Before proceeding, review Exhibits 5-6 and 5-7 to check your understanding of the FIFO method. Note: Exhibit 5-6 deals with only physical and equivalent units, not costs. Exhibit 5-7 shows the cost amounts.

The T-account entries under the FIFO method are identical to the T-account entries under the weighted-average method except for one difference. The entry to record the cost of goods completed and transferred out would be $52,480 under the FIFO method instead of $52,000 under the weighted-average method.

Exhibit 5-7

Steps 3, 4, and 5: Summarize Total Costs to Account For, Compute Cost per Equivalent Unit, and Assign Total Costs to Units Completed and to Units in Ending Work in Process Using FIFO Method of Process Costing for Assembly Department of Pacific Electronics for March 2013

Home Insert Page Layout Formulas Data Review View

	A	B	C	D	E
1			**Total Production Costs**	**Direct Material**	**Conversion Costs**
2	**(Step 3)**	Work in process, beginning (given, p. 184)	$26,100	$18,000	$ 8,100
3		Costs added in current period (given, p. 184)	36,180	19,800	16,380
4		Total costs to account for	$62,280	$37,800	$24,480
5					
6	**(Step 4)**	Costs added in current period		$19,800	$16,380
7		Divide by equivalent units of work done in current period (Exhibit 5-6)		÷ 275	÷ 315
8		Cost per equivalent unit of work done in current period		$ 72	$ 52
9					
10	**(Step 5)**	Assignment of costs:			
11		Completed and transferred out (400 units):			
12		Work in process, beginning (225 units)	$26,100	$18,000 +	$8,100
13		Costs added to beginning work in process in current period	4,680	(0^a × $72) +	(90^a × $52)
14		Total from beginning inventory	30,780		
15		Started and completed (175 units)	21,700	(175^b × $72) +	(175^b × $52)
16		Total costs of units completed and transferred out	52,480		
17		Work in process, ending (100 units):	9,800	(100^c × $72) +	(50^c × $52)
18		Total costs accounted for	$62,280	$37,800 +	$24,480
19					
20	[a]Equivalent units used to complete beginning work in process from Exhibit 5-6, Step 2.				
21	[b]Equivalent units started and completed from Exhibit 5-6, Step 2.				
22	[c]Equivalent units in ending work in process from Exhibit 5-6, Step 2.				

Comparison of Weighted-Average and FIFO Methods

Consider the summary of the costs assigned to units completed and to units still in process under the weighted-average and FIFO process-costing methods in our example for March 2013:

	Weighted Average (from Exhibit 5-5) (1)	FIFO (from Exhibit 5-7) (2)	Difference (3) = (2) − (1)
Cost of units completed and transferred out	$52,000	$52,480	+$480
Work in process, ending	10,280	9,800	−$480
Total costs accounted for	$62,280	$62,280	

The weighted-average ending inventory is higher than the FIFO ending inventory by $480, or 4.9% ($480 ÷ $9,800 = 0.049, or 4.9%). This would be a significant difference when aggregated over the many thousands of products that Pacific Electronics makes. When completed units are sold, the weighted-average method in our example leads to a lower cost of goods sold than the FIFO method. To see why, recall the data on page 179. Direct material cost per equivalent unit in beginning work-in-process inventory is $80, and conversion cost per equivalent unit in beginning work-in-process inventory is $60. These costs are greater, respectively, than the $72 direct materials cost and the $52 conversion cost per equivalent unit of work done during the current period. The current-period costs are lower partly because of a decline in the prices of direct materials and conversion-cost inputs, and partly as a result of Pacific Electronics becoming more efficient in its processes by using smaller quantities of inputs per unit of output.

FIFO assumes that (1) all the higher-cost units from the previous period in beginning work in process are the first to be completed and transferred out of the process and (2) ending work in process consists of only the lower-cost current-period units. The weighted-average method, however, smooths out cost per equivalent unit by assuming that (1) more of the lower-cost units are completed and transferred out and (2) some of the higher-cost units are placed in ending work in process. Cost of units completed differ materially between the weighted-average and FIFO methods when (1) direct material or conversion cost per equivalent unit varies significantly from period to period and (2) physical-inventory levels of work in process are large in relation to the total number of units transferred out of the process. As differences in unit costs and inventory levels from period to period decrease, the difference in cost of units completed under the weighted-average and FIFO methods also decrease.[1]

When the cost of units completed under the weighted-average and FIFO methods differ substantially, which method should a manager choose? In a period of falling prices, as in the Pacific Electronics case, the higher cost of goods sold under the FIFO method will lead to lower operating income and lower tax payments, saving the company cash and increasing the company's value. FIFO is the preferred choice, but managers may not make this choice. If the manager's compensation, for instance, is based on operating income, the manager may prefer the weighted-average method, which increases operating income even though it results in higher tax payments. Top managers must carefully design compensation plans to encourage managers to take actions that increase a company's value. For example, the compensation plan might reward after-tax cash flow metrics, in addition to operating income metrics, to align decision making and performance evaluation.

Occasionally, choosing a process-costing method can be more difficult. Suppose, for example, that by using FIFO a company would violate its debt covenants (agreements between a company and its creditors that the company will maintain certain financial ratios) resulting in its loans coming due. In this case, a manager may prefer the weighted-average method even though it results in higher taxes because the company does not have the liquidity to repay its loans.

[1] For example, suppose beginning work-in-process inventory for March were 125 physical units (instead of 225), and suppose costs per equivalent unit of work done in the current period (March) were direct materials, $75, and conversion costs, $55. Assume that all other data for March are the same as in our example. In this case, the cost of units completed and transferred out would be $52,833 under the weighted-average method and $53,000 under the FIFO method. The work-in-process ending inventory would be $10,417 under the weighted-average method and $10,250 under the FIFO method (calculations not shown). These differences are much smaller than in the chapter example. The weighted-average ending inventory is higher than the FIFO ending inventory by only $167 ($10,417 − $10,250), or 1.6% ($167 ÷ $10,250 = 0.016, or 1.6%), compared with 4.9% higher in the chapter example.

In a period of rising prices, the weighted-average method will decrease taxes because cost of goods sold will be higher and operating income lower. Once again, though, for the reasons described earlier, managers may not make this preferred choice. Concepts in Action: Why Does ExxonMobil Use LIFO? describes how Exxon uses the last-in, first-out (LIFO) method (not presented in this chapter) to save taxes.[2]

From an information and control standpoint, FIFO has the advantage that it identifies changes in costs from one period to the next. For example, the $72 direct material cost and $52 conversion cost in March is valuable information for making pricing and product-mix decisions and also for evaluating how well Pacific Electronics managed costs in 2013 compared to the budget.

Keys to Success

Companies typically use two methods of process costing: the weighted-average method and the first-in, first-out (FIFO) method. The weighted-average method computes unit cost by dividing total costs incurred to date by the total equivalent units completed to date and assigns this cost to units completed and to units in ending work-in-process inventory. The FIFO method computes unit costs based only on costs incurred during the current period and equivalent units of work done during the current period. Managers choose the method of process costing after considering various factors such as the effect on taxes, operating income, and debt covenants.

Concepts in Action: Why Does ExxonMobil Use LIFO?

In 2012, ExxonMobil led the *Fortune* 500 annual ranking of the largest U.S. companies with 2011 revenue of $452 billion and more than $41 billion in profits. Believe it or not, however, by one measure ExxonMobil's profits are understated. ExxonMobil uses last-in, first-out (LIFO) accounting for financial reporting and tax purposes. Under this treatment, ExxonMobil records its cost of goods sold at the latest price paid for oil in the open market, even though it is often selling oil produced at a much lower cost. This increases the company's cost of goods sold, which in turn reduces profits and tax payments.

Source: Jason Reed/Reuters

Assigning costs to inventory is a critical part of process costing, and a company's choice of method can result in substantially different profits. For instance, ExxonMobil's 2011 net income would have been $3.5 billion higher under FIFO. Moreover, if ExxonMobil had used FIFO accounting in prior years, its operating income in those years would have been higher by $25.6 billion, resulting in an incremental tax burden of almost $9 billion assuming a marginal tax rate of approximately 35%.

Sources: Based on Exxon Mobil Corporation, 2012. *2011 Annual Report*, Irving, TX: Exxon Mobil Corporation; Izabella Kaminska, "Shell, BP, and the increasing cost of inventory," *Financial Times*, "FT Alphaville" blog (April 29, 2010); and David Reilly, "Big oil's accounting methods fuel criticism," *The Wall Street Journal* (August 8, 2006).

[2] In reading the box, students not familiar with the LIFO method need only note that in a period of rising prices, the LIFO method reduces operating income and taxes even more than the weighted-average method.

Using Budgeted Rates

Recall that managers use process-costing systems when the output consists of masses of identical or similar units. The production of similar units means that it is fairly easy to budget for the quantities of inputs needed to produce a unit of output. The budgeted cost per input unit (called a standard input cost) can then be multiplied by the budgeted quantity of inputs per unit of output (standard-inputs) to develop a budgeted cost per output unit (standard cost of output).

The weighted-average and FIFO methods become very complicated when used in process industries, such as textiles, ceramics, paints, and packaged food, that produce a wide variety of similar products. For example, a steel-rolling mill uses various steel alloys and produces sheets of various sizes and finishes. The different types of direct materials used and the operations performed are few, but used in various combinations, they yield a wide variety of products. In these cases, if managers use the broad averaging procedure of *actual* process costing, the result would be inaccurate costs for each product. Therefore, managers in these industries typically use the standard-costing method of process costing.

Under the standard-costing method, teams of design and process engineers, operations personnel, and management accountants work together to determine *separate* standard costs per equivalent unit on the basis of different technical processing specifications for each product. Identifying standard costs for each product overcomes the disadvantage of costing all products at a single average amount, as under actual costing.

The application of the standard-costing method is identical to the FIFO method discussed earlier. The only difference is that a standard cost of direct materials and conversion costs for each output unit is predetermined at the start of the year. Suppose Pacific Electronics determines the standard direct material cost per equivalent unit to be $74 and the standard conversion cost per equivalent unit to be $54 in 2013. All costs would then be assigned to completed units and to units in work in process at these standard amounts. At the end of the year, variances between the standard amounts assigned to products and the actual costs incurred would be identified and analyzed using methods described in Chapter 13.

Hybrid-Costing Systems

Learning Objective 5

Understand the need for hybrid costing systems such as operation costing

. . . when product costing does not fall into job-costing or process-costing categories

Product-costing systems do not always fall neatly into either job-costing or process-costing categories. Consider Ford Motor Company. Automobiles may be manufactured in a continuous flow (suited to process costing), but individual units may be customized with a special combination of engine size, transmission, music system, and so on (which requires job costing). A **hybrid-costing system** blends characteristics from both job-costing and process-costing systems. Many production systems are a hybrid: They have some features of custom-order manufacturing and other features of mass-production manufacturing. Managers must design product-costing systems to fit the particular characteristics of different production systems.

Manufacturers of a relatively wide variety of closely related standardized products (for example, televisions, dishwashers, washing machines, and shoes) tend to use hybrid-costing systems, process costing to account for conversion costs and job costing for the material and customizable components. Consider Nike, which has a message for shoppers looking for the hottest new shoe design: Just do it . . . yourself! While athletic apparel manufacturers have long individually crafted shoes for professional athletes, Nike has taken the idea a step further by allowing customers to design their own shoes and clothing. With NikeID, customers use the Internet and mobile applications to personalize Nike apparel, such as Jordan-brand sneakers, with their own colors and patterns. (Concepts in Action: Hybrid Costing for Mi Adidas Customized Sneakers describes a hybrid-costing system at Adidas.) The next section explains *operation costing*, a common type of hybrid-costing system.

Overview of Operation-Costing Systems

An **operation** is a standardized method or technique that is performed repetitively, often on different materials, resulting in different finished goods. Multiple operations are usually conducted within a department. For instance, a suit maker may have a cutting operation and a hemming operation within a single department. The term *operation*, however, is often used loosely. It may be a synonym for a department or process. For example, some companies may call their finishing department a finishing process or a finishing operation.

An **operation-costing system** is a hybrid-costing system applied to batches of similar, but not identical, products. Each batch of products is often a variation of a single design, and it proceeds through a sequence of operations. Within each operation, all product units are treated exactly alike, using identical amounts of the operation's resources. A key point in the operation system is that each batch does not necessarily move through the same operations as other batches. Batches are also called production runs.

In a company that makes suits, management may select a single basic design for every suit to be made, but depending on specifications, each batch of suits varies somewhat from other batches. Batches may vary depending on the material used or the type of stitching. Semiconductors, textiles, and shoes are also manufactured in batches and may have similar variations from batch to batch.

An operation-costing system uses work orders that specify the needed direct materials and step-by-step operations. Product costs are compiled for each work order. Direct materials that are unique to different work orders are specifically identified with the appropriate work order, as in job costing. However, each unit is assumed to use an identical amount of conversion costs for a given operation, as in process costing. A single average conversion cost per unit is calculated for each operation by dividing total conversion costs for that operation by the number of units that pass through it. This average cost is then assigned to each unit passing through the operation. Units that do not pass through an operation are not allocated any costs of that operation. Our examples assume only two cost categories—direct materials and conversion costs—but operation costing can have more than two cost categories. Costs in each category are identified with specific work orders using job-costing or process-costing methods as appropriate.

Managers find operation costing useful in cost management because operation costing focuses on control of physical processes, or operations, of a given production system. For example, in clothing manufacturing, managers are concerned with fabric waste, how many fabric layers that can be cut at one time, and so on. Operation costing measures, in financial terms, how well managers have controlled physical processes.

Concepts in Action: Hybrid Costing for Mi Adidas Customized Sneakers

The mi adidas customization offering is available online at adidas.com/miadidas and in 25 stores globally. Consumers can choose from over 25 styles across 7 sports and lifestyle categories. mi adidas offers the opportunity to create individual, custom shoes for performance, fit and design. Once the designs are created and purchased, the design and product data are transferred to manufacturing plants where the product is then built to order and shipped directly to the consumer.

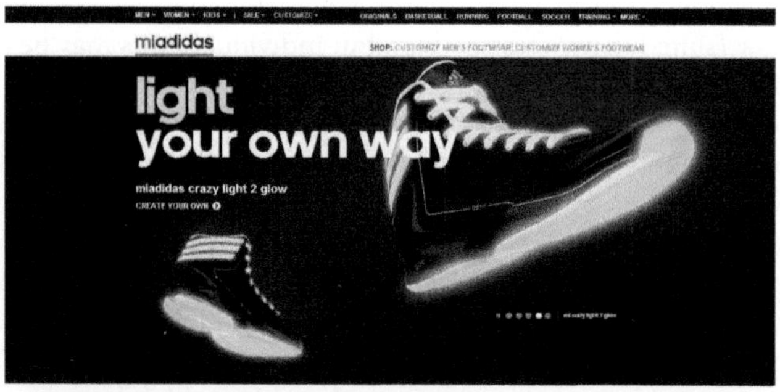

Source: The adidas Group. Used by permission.

Adidas uses a hybrid-costing system. Accounting for individual customization requires job costing but the similar process used to make sneakers lends itself to process costing. The cost of making each pair of shoes is calculated by accumulating all production costs and dividing by the number of shoes made. In other words, even though each pair of shoes is different, the conversion cost is roughly the same.

The combination of customization with certain features of mass production is called mass customization. It is the consequence of being able to digitize information that individual customers indicate is important to them. Various products that companies can customize within a mass-production setting (personal computers, blue jeans, and bicycles) still require job costing of materials and considerable human intervention. However, as manufacturing systems become flexible, companies are also using process costing to account for the standardized conversion costs.

Sources: Based on "Jordan Spik'ize on NikeID," Nike, Inc. press release. Beaverton, OR, April 24, 2012; Marina Kamenev, "Adidas' high tech footwear," *Businessweek* (November 3, 2006); "Nike designs can get personal," *Los Angeles Times* (May 30, 2005); and Ralf Seifert, "The 'mi adidas' mass customization initiative," IMD No. 159. Lausanne, Switzerland: International Institute for Management Development, 2003.

Illustration of an Operation-Costing System

The Baltimore Clothing Company produces two lines of blazers for department stores: those made of wool and those made of polyester. Wool blazers use better-quality materials and undergo more operations than polyester blazers. Operations information on Work Order 423 for 50 wool blazers and Work Order 424 for 100 polyester blazers is as follows:

	Work Order 423	Work Order 424
Direct materials	Wool	Polyester
	Satin full lining	Rayon partial lining
	Bone buttons	Plastic buttons
Operations		
1. Cutting cloth	Use	Use
2. Checking edges	Use	Do not use
3. Sewing body	Use	Use
4. Checking seams	Use	Do not use
5. Machine sewing of collars and lapels	Do not use	Use
6. Hand sewing of collars and lapels	Use	Do not use

Cost data for these work orders, started and completed in March 2013, are as follows:

	Work Order 423	Work Order 424
Number of blazers	50	100
Direct material costs	$ 6,000	$3,000
Conversion costs allocated:		
Operation 1	580	1,160
Operation 2	400	—
Operation 3	1,900	3,800
Operation 4	500	—
Operation 5	—	875
Operation 6	700	—
Total manufacturing costs	$10,080	$8,835

As in process costing, all product units in any work order are assumed to consume identical amounts of conversion costs of a particular operation. Baltimore's operation-costing system uses a budgeted rate to calculate the conversion costs of each operation. The budgeted rate for Operation 1 (amounts assumed) is as follows:

$$\begin{aligned}\text{Operation 1 budgeted conversion-cost rate for 2013} &= \frac{\text{Operation 1 budgeted conversion costs for 2013}}{\text{Operation 1 budgeted product units for 2013}}\\ &= \frac{\$232{,}000}{20{,}000 \text{ units}}\\ &= \$11.60 \text{ per unit}\end{aligned}$$

Budgeted conversion costs of Operation 1 include labor, power, repairs, supplies, depreciation, and other overhead of this operation. If some units have not been completed (so all units in Operation 1 have not received the same amounts of conversion costs), the conversion-cost rate is computed by dividing budgeted conversion costs by *equivalent units* of conversion costs, as in process costing.

As the company manufactures blazers, managers allocate conversion costs to the work orders processed in Operation 1 by multiplying the $11.60 conversion cost per unit by the number of units processed. Conversion costs of Operation 1 for 50 wool blazers (Work Order 423) are $11.60 per blazer × 50 blazers = $580, and for 100 polyester blazers (Work Order 424) are $11.60 per blazer × 100 blazers = $1,160. When equivalent units are used to calculate the conversion-cost rate, costs are allocated to work orders by multiplying conversion cost per equivalent unit by number of equivalent units in the work order. Direct material costs of $6,000 for the 50 wool blazers (Work Order 423) and $3,000 for the 100 polyester blazers (Work Order 424) are specifically identified with each order, as in job costing. Remember the basic point in operation costing: Managers assume operation unit costs are the same regardless of the work order, but direct material costs vary across orders when the materials used for each work order vary.

T-Account Entries

Suppose that of the $3,000 of direct materials for Work Order 424, $2,975 are used in Operation 1, and the remaining $25 of materials are used in another operation. T-account entries for assigning costs to polyester blazers (Work Order 424) at Operation 1 follow. Entries for wool blazers would be similar. The entries record the $2,975 of direct materials used at Operation 1, the conversion costs of $1,160 incurred on polyester blazers at Operation 1, and the transfer of the 100 polyester blazers (at a cost of $2,975 + $1,160) from Operation 1 to Operation 3 (polyester blazers do not go through Operation 2).

Work in Process, Operation 1			
① Direct materials	2,975	③ Transferred to Operation 3	4,135
② Conversion costs allocated	1,160		
Ending inventory, March 31	0		

Costs of the blazers are transferred through the operations in which blazers are worked on and then to finished goods in the usual manner. Costs are added throughout the fiscal year in the Conversion Costs Control account and the Conversion Costs Allocated account. Any overallocation or underallocation of conversion costs is disposed of in the same way as overallocated or underallocated manufacturing overhead in a job-costing system (see pages 134–138).

Keys to Success

Many production systems have aspects of both custom-order production and mass production. In these circumstances, managers use hybrid-costing systems that blend characteristics from both job-costing and process-costing systems. Managers always choose costing systems to match production systems.

Learning Objective 6

Understand why and how managers allocate joint costs

. . . to calculate cost of goods sold and inventory values for individual products usually based on sales value at splitoff

and common costs

. . . to determine the "fair" share of cost to be borne by each user using stand-alone, incremental, and Shapley value cost-allocation methods

Cost Allocation for Joint Costs and Common Costs

Our process-costing example focused on a single product, the SG-40 cell phone. Process-costing computations determine the costs assigned to completed goods and to ending work-in-process inventory. In other words, process costing focuses on the assignment of costs between the current period (costs of completed goods) and the next period (cost of ending work-in-process inventory). Some processes, however, yield more than one product. Other processes involve sharing of costs across two or more users. These situations result in joint cost allocations and common cost allocations.

Allocating Joint Costs

Consider petroleum production that yields crude oil and natural gas or the distillation of coal, which yields coke, natural gas, and other products. These contexts give rise to **joint costs,** which are the costs of a production process that yields multiple products simultaneously. The costs of distillation are joint costs. The **splitoff point** is the juncture in a joint production process when two or more products become separately identifiable, for example, the point at which coal becomes coke, natural gas, and other products. **Separable costs** are all costs—manufacturing, marketing, distribution, and so on—incurred beyond the splitoff point that are assignable to each of the specific products identified at the splitoff point.

The question is how to allocate joint costs to two or more products when all products appear together—no individual product can be produced without the accompanying products appearing. In this section, we describe the basic issues managers face. The accounting details are beyond the scope of this book.

Managers are interested in joint-cost allocation mainly for calculating cost of goods sold and inventory values for the individual products. But joint-cost allocation is arbitrary because there is no obvious way to allocate costs that are fundamentally joint to individual products. What method should the manager choose? The most common method is to allocate costs on the basis of the sales value of the products at the splitoff point, a measure of the benefits each product received as a result of joint processing. If the sales value at the splitoff point is not available, managers frequently approximate the sales value at splitoff by determining the value of the product sold after further processing minus the separable costs. Joint-cost allocation is arbitrary and managers generally have a lot less discretion in choosing a method, unlike the choice of the weighted-average or FIFO method in process costing.

Allocating Common Costs

Managers sometimes must evaluate *common costs*. A **common cost** is a cost of operating a facility, department, activity, or similar cost object that two or more users share. Common costs exist because each user obtains a lower cost by sharing than the separate cost that would result by operating independently. Consider two companies, Delpin Corporation and Cambry Inc., responsible for the environmental cleanup of some land. It will cost Delpin Corporation \$120 million and Cambry Inc. \$80 million to remediate its own share of the environmental waste. If the two companies remediated together the total cost would be \$150 million because there are common activities such as digging the ground which they would share and save costs. The \$150 million is a common cost that benefits both companies because it is less than the \$200 million (\$120 million + \$80 million) that the two companies would incur if they each operated independently.

What is a reasonable way to allocate the common costs of \$150 million? There are two methods of allocating this common cost between the two companies: the stand-alone method and the incremental method.

Stand-Alone Cost-Allocation Method

The **stand-alone cost-allocation method** determines the weights for cost allocation by considering each user of the cost as a separate entity. The stand-alone costs of \$120 million and \$80 million are used to allocate the common cost of \$150 million:

$$\text{Delpin Corporation: } \frac{\$120}{\$120 + \$80} \times \$150 = 0.60 \times \$150 = \$90 \text{ million}$$

$$\text{Cambry Inc.: } \frac{\$80}{\$80 + \$120} \times \$150 = 0.40 \times \$150 = \$60 \text{ million}$$

Advocates of this method often emphasize its fairness or equity. The method is viewed as reasonable because each company bears a proportionate share of total costs in relation to the individual stand-alone costs.

Incremental Cost-Allocation Method

The **incremental cost-allocation method** ranks the individual users of a cost object in the order of users most responsible for the common cost and then uses this ranking to allocate cost among those users. The first-ranked user of the cost object is the *primary user* (also called the *primary party*) and is allocated costs up to the costs of the primary user as a stand-alone user. The second-ranked user is the *first-incremental user* (*first-incremental party*) and is allocated the additional cost that arises from two users instead of only the primary user. The third-ranked user is the *second-incremental user* (*second-incremental party*) and is allocated the additional cost that arises from three users instead of two users, and so on.

To see how this method works in our example, assume Delpin Corp. is viewed as the primary party because it has greater responsibility for the cleanup. The cost allocations would be as follows:

Party	Costs Allocated (in millions)	Cumulative Costs Allocated (in millions)
Delpin (primary)	$120	$120
Cambry (incremental)	30 ($150 − $120)	$150
Total	$150	

Delpin is allocated its full cost. The unallocated part of the total cost is then allocated to Cambry. If Cambry had been chosen as the primary party, the cost allocations would have been Cambry $80 million (its stand-alone cost) and Delpin $70 ($150 − $80) million. When there are more than two parties, this method requires them to be ranked from first to last (such as by the extent of their responsibility for the environmental damage).

Under the incremental method, the primary party typically receives the highest allocation of the common costs. The difficulty with the method is that every user would prefer to be viewed as the incremental party!

One approach managers can use to sidestep disputes in such situations is to use the stand-alone cost-allocation method. Another approach is to use the *Shapley value,* which considers each party as first the primary party and then the incremental party. From the calculations shown earlier, Delpin is allocated $120 million as the primary party and $70 million as the incremental party, for an average of $95 [($120 + $70) ÷ 2] million. Cambry is allocated $80 million as the primary party and $30 million as the incremental party, for an average of $55 [($80 + 30) ÷ 2] million. The Shapley value method allocates, to each company, the average of the costs allocated as the primary party and as the incremental party: $95 million to Delpin and $55 million to Cambry.[3]

As our discussion suggests, allocating common costs is not clear-cut and can generate disputes. Whenever feasible, managers should specify the rules for such allocations in advance. If this is not done, then, rather than blindly follow one method or another, managers should exercise judgment when allocating common costs by thinking carefully about allocation methods that appear fair to each party.

[3] For further discussion of the Shapley value, see J. Demski, "Cost Allocation Games," in *Joint Cost Allocations,* ed. S. Moriarity, (University of Oklahoma Center for Economic and Management Research, 1981); L. Kruz and P. Bronisz, "Cooperative Game Solution Concepts to a Cost Allocation Problem," *European Journal of Operations Research* 122 (2000): 258–271.

Problem for Self-Study

Allied Chemicals operates a thermo-assembly process as the first of three processes at its plastics plant. Direct materials in thermo-assembly are added at the end of the process. Conversion costs are added evenly during the process. The following data pertain to the thermo-assembly department for June 2013:

	A	B	C	D
1		Physical Units	Direct Materials	Conversion Costs
2	Work in process, beginning inventory	50,000		
3	Degree of completion of beginning work in process		0%	80%
4	Started during June	200,000		
5	Completed and transferred out during June	210,000		
6	Work in process, ending inventory	?		
7	Degree of completion of ending work in process		0%	40%

Required

1. Compute equivalent units under (1) the weighted-average method and (2) the FIFO method.
2. What issues should the manager of the thermo-assembly department focus on when computing equivalent units?

Solution

1. The weighted-average method uses equivalent units of work done to date to compute cost per equivalent unit. The calculations of equivalent units follow:

	A	B	C	D
1		**(Step 1)**	**(Step 2)**	
2			**Equivalent Units**	
3	**Flow of Production**	**Physical Units**	**Direct Materials**	**Conversion Costs**
4	Work in process, beginning (given)	50,000		
5	Started during current period (given)	200,000		
6	To account for	250,000		
7	Completed and transferred out during current period	210,000	210,000	210,000
8	Work in process, ending[a]	40,000[b]		
9	(40,000 × 0%; 40,000 × 40%)		0	16,000
10	Accounted for	250,000		
11	Equivalent units of work done to date		210,000	226,000
12				
13	[a]Degree of completion in this department: direct materials, 0%; conversion costs, 40%.			
14	[b]250,000 physical units to account for minus 210,000 physical units completed and transferred out.			

2. The FIFO method uses equivalent units of work done in the current period only to compute cost per equivalent unit. The calculations of equivalent units follow:

	A	B	C	D
1		**(Step 1)**	**(Step 2)**	
2			**Equivalent Units**	
3	**Flow of Production**	**Physical Units**	**Direct Materials**	**Conversion Costs**
4	Work in process, beginning (given)	50,000		
5	Started during current period (given)	200,000		
6	To account for	250,000		
7	Completed and transferred out during current period:			
8	From beginning work in process[a]	50,000		
9	[50,000 × (100% – 0%); 50,000 × (100% – 80%)]		50,000	10,000
10	Started and completed	160,000[b]		
11	(160,000 × 100%; 160,000 × 100%)		160,000	160,000
12	Work in process, ending[c]	40,000[d]		
13	(40,000 × 0%; 40,000 × 40%)		0	16,000
14	Accounted for	250,000		
15	Equivalent units of work done in current period		210,000	186,000
16				
17	[a]Degree of completion in this department: direct materials, 0%; conversion costs, 80%.			
18	[b]210,000 physical units completed and transferred out minus 50,000 physical units completed and transferred out from beginning work-in-process inventory.			
19	[c]Degree of completion in this department: direct materials, 0%; conversion costs, 40%.			
20	[d]250,000 physical units to account for minus 210,000 physical units completed and transferred out.			

3. The manager of the thermo-assembly department must be careful that estimates of degrees of completion are meticulously done. The process of estimation is subject to measurement error and judgment, the precise circumstances when biases inevitably creep in. To show better performance, for example, a department supervisor might report a higher degree of completion resulting in overstated operating income. If performance for the period is very good, the department supervisor may be tempted to report a lower degree of completion, reducing income in the current period. This has the effect of reducing the costs carried in ending inventory, and therefore the costs carried to the following year in beginning inventory. In other words, estimates of degree of completion can help to smooth earnings from one period to the next.

   The manager of the thermo-assembly department should guard against this possibility by asking department managers specific and detailed questions to ensure that they followed good and consistent processes of estimation. Managers should always emphasize the importance of obtaining the correct answer, regardless of its effect on reported performance.

Decision Points

The following question-and-answer format summarizes the chapter's learning objectives. Each decision presents a key question related to a learning objective. The guidelines are the answer to that question.

Decision	Guidelines
1. Under what conditions is a process-costing system used?	A process-costing system is used to determine cost of a product or service when masses of identical or similar units are produced. Industries using process-costing systems include food, textiles, and oil refining.
2. How are average unit costs computed when no inventories are present?	Average unit costs are computed by dividing total costs in a given accounting period by total units produced in that period.
3. What are the five steps in a process-costing system and how are equivalent units calculated?	The five steps in a process-costing system are (1) summarize the flow of physical units of output, (2) compute output in terms of equivalent units, (3) summarize total costs to account for, (4) compute cost per equivalent unit, and (5) assign total costs to units completed and to units in ending work in process. Equivalent units is a derived amount of output units that (a) takes the quantity of each input (factor of production) in units completed or in incomplete units in work in process and (b) converts the quantity of input into the amount of completed output units that could be made with that quantity of input.
4. What are the weighted-average and first-in, first-out methods of process costing? Under what conditions will they yield different levels of operating income?	The weighted-average method computes unit costs by dividing total costs in the Work in Process account by total equivalent units completed to date, and assigns this average cost to units completed and to units in ending work-in-process inventory. The first-in, first-out (FIFO) method computes unit costs based on costs incurred during the current period and equivalent units of work done in the current period. Operating income can differ materially between the two methods when (1) direct material or conversion cost per equivalent unit varies significantly from period to period and (2) physical-inventory levels of work in process are large in relation to the total number of units transferred out of the process.
5. What is an operation-costing system, and when is it a better approach to product-costing?	Operation costing is a hybrid-costing system that blends characteristics from both job-costing (for direct materials) and process-costing systems (for conversion costs). It is a better approach to product costing when production systems share some features of custom-order manufacturing and other features of mass-production manufacturing.

Decision	Guidelines
6. Why and how do managers allocate joint and common costs?	Managers allocate joint costs (costs that yield multiple products simultaneously) to calculate cost of goods sold and inventory values for individual products usually on the basis of the sales values of the products at the splitoff point (the benefits received). Managers allocate common costs (costs of operating a shared activity) to determine the "fair" share of the cost to be borne by each user using the stand-alone, incremental, or Shapley value-based cost-allocation method.

Terms to Learn

This chapter and the Glossary at the end of the book contain definitions of the following important terms:

common cost (p. 191)
equivalent units (p. 175)
first-in, first-out (FIFO) process-costing method (p. 182)
hybrid-costing system (p. 187)
incremental cost-allocation method (p. 191)
joint costs (p. 190)
operation (p. 187)
operation-costing system (p. 188)
separable costs (p. 191)
splitoff point (p. 191)
stand-alone cost-allocation method (p. 191)
weighted-average process-costing method (p. 179)

Assignment Material

Questions

5-1 In process costing, why are costs often divided into two main classifications?

5-2 Explain equivalent units. Why are equivalent-unit calculations necessary in process costing?

5-3 What are the key managerial issues in computing equivalent units?

5-4 Describe the distinctive characteristic of weighted-average computations in assigning costs to units completed and to units in ending work in process and distinguish it from the distinctive characteristic of FIFO computations in assigning costs to units completed and to units in ending work in process.

5-5 What factors should managers consider when choosing a process-costing method.

5-6 "Using budgeted rates is particularly applicable to process-costing situations." Do you agree? Explain briefly.

5-7 Describe hybrid-costing systems.

5-8 "Many companies need to use both job costing and process costing." Do you agree? Explain briefly.

5-9 "There's no reason for me to get excited about the choice between the weighted-average and FIFO methods in my process-costing system. I have long-term contracts with my materials suppliers at fixed prices." Do you agree with this statement made by a plant controller? Explain.

5-10 "Managers must carefully choose the best method to allocate joint costs." Do you agree? Explain briefly.

Exercises

5-11 Equivalent units, zero beginning inventory. Candid, Inc., is a manufacturer of digital cameras. The company has two departments: assembly and testing. In January 2013, the company incurred $825,000 on direct materials and $820,000 on conversion costs, for a total manufacturing cost of $1,645,000.

Required

1. Assume there was no beginning inventory of any kind on January 1, 2013. During January, 20,000 cameras were placed into production and all 20,000 were fully completed at the end of the month. What is the unit cost of an assembled camera in January?

2. Assume that during February 20,000 cameras are placed into production. Further assume the same total assembly costs for January are also incurred in February, but only 15,000 cameras are fully completed at the end of the month. All direct materials have been added to the remaining 5,000 cameras. However, on average, these remaining 5,000 cameras are only 60% complete as to conversion costs. (a) What are the equivalent units for direct materials and conversion costs and their respective costs per equivalent unit for February? (b) What is the unit cost of an assembled camera in February 2013?
3. Explain the difference in your answers to requirements 1 and 2.

5-12 T-account entries (continuation of 5-11). Refer to requirement 2 in Exercise 5-11.

Required Prepare summary T-account entries for the use of direct materials and incurrence of conversion costs and to transfer out the cost of goods completed.

5-13 Zero beginning inventory, materials introduced in middle of process. Felding Chemicals has a mixing department and a refining department. Its process-costing system in the mixing department has two direct material cost categories (chemical P and chemical Q) and one conversion costs pool. The following data pertain to the mixing department for July 2013:

Units	
Work in process, July 1	0
Units started	53,500
Completed and transferred to refining department	39,000
Costs	
Chemical P	$374,500
Chemical Q	117,000
Conversion costs	249,375

Chemical P is introduced at the start of operations in the mixing department, and chemical Q is added when the product is 85% completed in the mixing department. Conversion costs are added evenly during the process. The ending work in process in the mixing department is 75% complete.

Required

1. Compute the equivalent units in the mixing department for July 2013 for each cost category.
2. What issues should the manager focus on when reviewing the equivalent units calculation?
3. Compute (a) the cost of goods completed and transferred to the refining department during July and (b) the cost of work in process as of July 31, 2013.

5-14 Weighted-average method, equivalent units. Consider the following data for the assembly division of Cranberry Watches, Inc.,

The assembly division uses the weighted-average method of process costing.

	Physical Units (Watches)	Direct Materials	Conversion Costs
Beginning work in process (May 1)[a]	100	$ 547,100	$ 141,600
Started in May 2013	510		
Completed during May 2013	450		
Ending work in process (May 31)[b]	160		
Total costs added during May 2013		$3,585,600	$1,748,460

[a]Degree of completion: direct materials, 80%; conversion costs, 35%.
[b]Degree of completion: direct materials, 80%; conversion costs, 80%.

Required

1. Compute equivalent units for direct materials and conversion costs. Show physical units in the first column of your schedule.
2. What issues should the manager focus on when reviewing the equivalent units calculation?

5-15 Weighted-average method, assigning costs (continuation of 5-14).

Required For the data in Exercise 5-14, summarize total costs to account for, calculate cost per equivalent unit for direct materials and conversion costs, and assign total costs to units completed (and transferred out) and to units in ending work in process.

5-16 FIFO method, equivalent units. Refer to the information in Exercise 5-14. Suppose the assembly division at Cranberry Watches, Inc., uses the FIFO method of process costing instead of the weighted-average method.

Required

1. Compute equivalent units for direct materials and conversion costs. Show physical units in the first column of your schedule.
2. What issues should the manager focus on when reviewing the equivalent units calculation?

5-17 FIFO method, assigning costs (continuation of 5-16).

Required

1. For the data in Exercise 5-14, use the FIFO method to summarize total costs to account for, calculate cost per equivalent unit for direct materials and conversion costs, and assign total costs to units completed (and transferred out) and to units in ending work in process.
2. If you did Exercise 5-15, should Cranberry's managers choose the weighted-average method or the FIFO method? Explain briefly.

5-18 Operation Costing. Nature's Bounty Bakery needs to determine the cost of two work orders for the month of June. Work Order 215 is for 1,500 packages of dinner rolls and Work Order 216 is for 1,100 loaves of multigrain bread. Dinner rolls are mixed and cut into individual rolls before being baked and then packaged. Multigrain loaves are mixed and shaped before being baked, sliced, and packaged. The following information applies to Work Order 215 and Work Order 216:

	Work Order 215	Work Order 216
Quantity (packages)	1,500	1,100
Operations		
1. Mix	Use	Use
2. Shape loaves	Do not use	Use
3. Cut rolls	Use	Do not use
4. Bake	Use	Use
5. Slice loaves	Do not use	Use
6. Package	Use	Use

Selected budget information for June follows:

	Dinner Rolls	Multigrain Loaves	Total
Packages	4,500	8,000	12,500
Direct material costs	$2,250	$4,800	$ 7,050

Budgeted conversion costs for each operation for June follow:

Mixing	$ 9,375
Shaping	1,760
Cutting	810
Baking	7,500
Slicing	640
Packaging	11,250

Required

1. Use budgeted number of packages as the denominator to calculate the budgeted conversion-cost rates for each operation.
2. Use the information in requirement 1 to calculate the budgeted cost of goods manufactured for the two June work orders.
3. Calculate the cost per package of dinner rolls and multigrain loaves for Work Order 215 and 216.

5-19 Weighted-average method, assigning costs. Fielding Corporation is a biotech company that makes a cancer-treatment drug in a single processing department. Direct materials are added at the start of the process. Conversion costs are added evenly during the process. Fielding uses the weighted-average method of process costing. The following information for July 2013 is available.

		Equivalent Units	
	Physical Units	Direct Materials	Conversion Costs
Work in process, July 1	8,700[a]	8,700	1,305
Started during July	34,500		
Completed and transferred out during July	32,000	32,000	32,000
Work in process, July 31	11,200[b]	11,200	7,840

[a]Degree of completion: direct materials, 100%; conversion costs, 15%.
[b]Degree of completion: direct materials, 100%; conversion costs, 70%.

Total Costs for July 2013		
Work in process, beginning		
Direct materials	$61,500	
Conversion costs	43,200	$104,700
Direct materials added during July		301,380
Conversion costs added during July		498,624
Total costs to account for		$904,704

Required

1. Calculate equivalent units for direct materials and conversion costs.
2. Summarize total costs to account for, and assign total costs to units completed (and transferred out) and to units in ending work in process.

5-20 FIFO method, assigning costs.

Required

1. Do Exercise 5-19 using the FIFO method. Note that you first need to calculate the equivalent units of work done in the current period (for direct materials and conversion costs) to complete beginning work in process, to start and complete new units, and to produce ending work in process.
2. If you did Exercise 5-19, should Fielding's managers choose the weighted-average method or the FIFO method? Explain briefly.

5-21 Process costing, weighted-average method. Alpaca Knitwear, Inc., is a manufacturer of fine alpaca sweaters. It has a knitting department and a finishing department. This exercise focuses on the knitting department. Direct materials are added at the beginning of the process. Conversion costs are added evenly during the process. Alpaca uses the weighted-average method of process costing. The following information for June 2013 is available.

	Physical Units	Direct Materials	Conversion Costs
Beginning work in process (June 1)[a]	750	$ 23,000	$ 5,500
Started in June 2013	3,200		
Completed during June 2013	3,300		
Ending work in process (June 30)[b]	650		
Total costs added during June 2013		$87,600	$78,380

[a]Degree of completion: direct materials, 100%; conversion costs, 40%.
[b]Degree of completion: direct materials, 100%; conversion costs, 30%.

Required

1. Calculate equivalent units of direct materials and conversion costs.
2. What issues should the manager focus on when reviewing the equivalent units calculation?

3. Summarize total costs to account for, and calculate the cost per equivalent unit for direct materials and conversion costs.
4. Assign total costs to units completed (and transferred out) and to units in ending work in process.

5-22 Process costing, FIFO method. Refer to the information in Exercise 5-21. Suppose that Alpaca uses the FIFO method instead of the weighted-average method in all of its departments.

Required

1. Calculate equivalent units of direct materials and conversion costs.
2. What issues should the manager focus on when reviewing the equivalent units calculation?
3. Summarize total costs to account for, and calculate the cost per equivalent unit for direct materials and conversion costs.
4. Assign total costs to units completed (and transferred out) and to units in ending work in process.
5. If you did Exercise 5-21, should Alpaca's managers choose the weighted-average method or the FIFO method? Explain briefly.

5-23 Operation Costing. Sunrise Vitamin Company manufactures three different types of vitamins: vitamin A, vitamin B, and a multivitamin. The company uses four operations to manufacture the vitamins: mixing, tableting, encapsulating, and bottling. Vitamins A and B are produced in tablet form (in the tableting department) and the multivitamin is produced in capsule form (in the encapsulating department). Each bottle contains 200 vitamins, regardless of the product.

Conversion costs are applied based on the number of bottles in the tableting and encapsulating departments. Conversion costs are applied based on labor-hours in the mixing department. It takes 1½ minutes to mix the ingredients for a 200-unit bottle for each product. Conversion costs are applied based on machine-hours in the bottling department. It takes 0.3 minutes of machine time to fill a 200-unit bottle, regardless of the product.

The budgeted number of bottles and expected direct material cost for each type of vitamin is as follows:

	Vitamin A	Vitamin B	Multivitamin
Number of 200 unit bottles	11,000	8,000	21,000
Direct material cost	$21,450	$20,000	$52,500

The budgeted conversion costs for each department for July are as follows:

Department	Budgeted Conversion Cost
Mixing	$ 8,000
Tableting	22,800
Encapsulating	30,450
Bottling	1,000

Required

1. Calculate the conversion cost rates for each department.
2. Calculate the budgeted cost of goods manufactured for vitamin A, vitamin B, and the multivitamin for the month of July.
3. Calculate the cost per 200-unit bottle for each type of vitamin for the month of July.

5-24 Common costs. Wright Inc. and Brown Inc. are two small clothing companies that are considering leasing a dyeing machine together. The companies estimated that in order to meet production, Wright needs the machine for 800 hours and Brown needs it for 200 hours. If each company rents the machine on its own, the fee will be $50 per hour of usage. If they rent the machine together, the fee will decrease to $42 per hour of usage.

Required

1. Calculate Wright's and Brown's respective share of fees under the stand-alone cost-allocation method.
2. Calculate Wright's and Brown's respective share of fees using the incremental cost-allocation method. Assume Wright to be the primary party.
3. Calculate Wright's and Brown's respective share of fees using the Shapley value method.
4. Which method would you recommend Wright and Brown use to share the fees?

Problems

5-25 Weighted-average method. Hoffman Company manufactures car seats in its Miami plant. Each car seat passes through the assembly department and the testing department. This problem focuses on the assembly department. The process-costing system at Hoffman Company has a single direct-cost category (direct materials) and a single indirect-cost category (conversion costs). Direct materials are added at the beginning of the process. Conversion costs are added evenly during the process. When the assembly department finishes work on each car seat, it is immediately transferred to testing.

Hoffman Company uses the weighted-average method of process costing. Data for the assembly department for October 2013 are as follows:

	Physical Units (Car Seats)	Direct Materials	Conversion Costs
Work in process, October 1[a]	4,000	$1,248,000	$ 241,650
Started during October 2013	22,500		
Completed during October 2013	26,000		
Work in process, October 31[b]	500		
Total costs added during October 2013		$4,635,000	$2,575,125

[a]Degree of completion: direct materials, ?%; conversion costs, 45%.
[b]Degree of completion: direct materials, ?%; conversion costs, 65%.

Required

1. For each cost category, compute equivalent units in the assembly department. Show physical units in the first column of your schedule.
2. What issues should the manager focus on when reviewing the equivalent units calculation?
3. For each cost category, summarize total assembly department costs for October 2013 and calculate the cost per equivalent unit.
4. Assign total costs to units completed and transferred out and to units in ending work in process.

5-26 T-account entries (continuation of 5-25).

Required Prepare summary T-account entries for the use of direct materials and incurrence of conversion costs and to transfer out the cost of goods completed.

5-27 FIFO method (continuation of 5-25).

Required

1. Do Problem 5-25 using the FIFO method of process costing. Explain any difference between the cost per equivalent unit in the assembly department under the weighted-average method and the FIFO method.
2. Should Hoffman's managers choose the weighted-average method or the FIFO method? Explain briefly.

5-28 Weighted-average method. Jackson Company is a manufacturer of rocking chairs. Each chair passes through the assembly department and finishing department. This problem focuses on the assembly department. Direct materials are added at the beginning of the process. Conversion costs are added evenly during the assembly department's process. As work in assembly is completed, each unit is immediately transferred to finishing.

Jackson Company uses the weighted-average method of process costing. Data for the assembly department for October 2012 are as follows:

	Physical Units (Rocking Chairs)	Direct Materials	Conversion Costs
Work in process, October 1[a]	15,000	$ 480,000	$ 544,240
Started during October 2012	?		
Completed during October 2012	46,600		
Work in process, October 31[b]	9,700		
Total costs added during October 2012		$1,321,600	$1,919,500

[a]Degree of completion: direct materials, ?%; conversion costs, 80%.
[b]Degree of completion: direct materials, ?%; conversion costs, 60%.

Required

1. What is the percentage of completion for (a) direct materials in beginning work-in-process inventory, and (b) direct materials in ending work-in-process inventory?
2. What issues should the manager focus on when reviewing the equivalent-units calculation?
3. For each cost category, compute equivalent units in the assembly department. Show physical units in the first column of your schedule.
4. For each cost category, summarize total assembly department costs for October 2012, calculate the cost per equivalent unit, and assign total costs to units completed (and transferred out) and to units in ending work in process.

5-29 FIFO method (continuation of 5-28). Refer to the information in Problem 5-28. Suppose that Jackson Company uses the FIFO method instead of the weighted-average method in all of its departments.

Required

1. Using the FIFO process-costing method, complete Problem 5-28.
2. If you did Exercise 5-28, should Jackson Company's managers choose the weighted-average method or the FIFO method? Explain briefly.

5-30 Weighted-average method. Porter Handcraft is a manufacturer of picture frames for large retailers. Every picture frame passes through two departments: the assembly department and the finishing department. This problem focuses on the assembly department. The process-costing system at Porter has a single direct-cost category (direct materials) and a single indirect-cost category (conversion costs). Direct materials are added when the assembly department process is 5% complete. Conversion costs are added evenly during the assembly department's process.

Porter uses the weighted-average method of process costing. Consider the following data for the assembly department in April 2013:

	Physical Unit (Frames)	Direct Materials	Conversion Costs
Work in process, April 1[a]	120	$ 2,140	$2,916
Started during April 2013	485		
Completed during April 2013	445		
Work in process, April 30[b]	160		
Total costs added during April 2013		$18,430	$9,315

[a]Degree of completion: direct materials, 100%; conversion costs, 40%.
[b]Degree of completion: direct materials, 100%; conversion costs, 5%.

Required

1. Summarize total assembly department costs for April 2013, and assign total costs to units completed (and transferred out) and to units in ending work in process.
2. What issues should the manager focus on in regard to the equivalent-units calculation?

5-31 T-Account entries (continuation of 5-30). Refer to requirement 1 in Problem 5-30.

Required

Prepare summary T-account entries for the use of direct materials and incurrence of conversion costs and to transfer out the cost of goods completed.

5-32 FIFO method (continuation of 5-30).

Required

1. Do Problem 5-30 using the FIFO method of process costing. If you did Problem 5-30, explain any difference between the cost of work completed and transferred out and the cost of ending work in process in the assembly department under the weighted-average method and the FIFO method.
2. Should Porter's managers choose the weighted-average method or the FIFO method? Explain briefly.

5-33 Weighted-average method. Charleston Biscuit Company (CBC) makes cheese crackers that it packs in decorative one-pound tins and sells to specialty stores throughout the southeast United States. The crackers pass through three departments: the mixing department, the baking department, and the packaging department. This problem focuses on the mixing department. The process-costing system at CBC has a single direct-cost category (direct materials) and a single indirect-cost category (conversion costs). Direct materials are added when the mixing department process is 10% complete. Conversion costs are added evenly during the mixing department's process.

CBC uses the weighted-average method of process costing. Consider the following data for the mixing department in September 2012:

	Physical Unit (Pounds)	Direct Materials	Conversion Costs
Work in process, September 1[a]	2,000	$ 4,460	$ 4,175
Started during September 2012	13,400		
Completed during September 2012	14,150		
Work in process, September 30[b]	1,250		
Total costs added during September 2012		$37,120	$39,400

[a]Degree of completion: direct materials, 100%; conversion costs, 60%.
[b]Degree of completion: direct materials, 100%; conversion costs, 30%.

Required

1. Summarize total mixing department costs for September 2012, and assign total costs to units completed (and transferred out) and to units in ending work in process.
2. What issues should the manager focus on when reviewing the equivalent units calculation?

5-34 FIFO method (continuation of 5-33).

Required

1. Complete Problem 5-33 using the FIFO method of process costing.
2. If you did Problem 5-33, explain any difference between the cost of work completed and transferred out and the cost of ending work in process in the mixing department under the weighted-average method and the FIFO method. Should CBC's managers choose the weighted-average method or the FIFO method? Explain briefly.

5-35 Allocation of common costs. Dave Dandy Auto Sales uses television, radio, newspapers, and other types of media to advertise its products. At the end of 2012, the company president, Dave Dickens, decided that all advertising costs would be incurred by corporate headquarters and allocated to each of the company's four sales locations based on number of vehicles sold. Dave was confident that his corporate purchasing manager could negotiate better advertising contracts on a corporatewide basis than each of the sales managers could on his or her own. Dickens budgeted total advertising cost for 2013 to be $1.9 million. He introduced the new plan to his sales managers just before the New Year.

The manager of the east sales location, Tom Stevens, was not happy. He complained that the new allocation method was unfair and would increase his advertising costs significantly over the prior year. The east location sold high volumes of low-priced used cars and most of the corporate advertising budget was related to new car sales.

Following Tom's complaint, Dave decided to take another hard look at what each of the divisions were paying for advertising before the new allocation plan. The results were as follows:

Sales Location	Actual Number of Cars Sold in 2012	Actual Advertising Cost Incurred in 2012
East	3,900	$ 282,750
West	1,040	435,000
North	2,730	652,500
South	5,330	804,750
	13,000	$2,175,000

Required

1. Using 2012 data as the cost bases, show the amount of the 2013 advertising cost ($1,900,000) that would be allocated to each of the divisions under the following criteria:
   a. Dickens's allocation method based on number of cars sold
   b. The stand-alone method
   c. The incremental-allocation method, with divisions ranked on the basis of dollars spent on advertising in 2012
2. Which method do you think is most equitable to the divisional sales managers? What other options might President Dave Dickens have for allocating the advertising costs?

5-36 Joint-cost allocation, insurance settlement. Organic Chicken grows and processes chickens. Each chicken is disassembled into five main parts. Information pertaining to production in July 2013 is as follows:

Parts	Pounds of Product	Wholesale Selling Price per Pound When Production Is Complete
Breasts	90	$0.50
Wings	25	0.25
Thighs	35	0.45
Bones	45	0.15
Feathers	5	0.10

Joint cost of production in July 2013 was $40.

A fire destroys a special shipment of 75 pounds of breasts and 20 pounds of wings. Organic Chicken's insurance policy provides reimbursement for the cost of the items destroyed. The insurance company permits Organic Chicken to use a joint-cost-allocation method. The splitoff point is assumed to be at the end of the production process.

Required

Compute the cost of the special shipment destroyed using the sales value at splitoff method.

5-37 Weighted-average and FIFO methods. McKee Foods, Inc., manufactures snack cakes under the brand name Little Debbie. Production of Swiss cake rolls occurs in four departments: mixing, baking, icing, and drying and packaging. Consider the mixing department, where direct materials are added at the beginning of the process. Conversion costs are added evenly during the process. The accounting records of a McKee Foods plant provide the following information for Swiss cake rolls in its mixing department during a weekly period (week 31):

	Physical Units (Cases)	Direct Materials	Conversion Costs
Beginning work in process[a]	10,500	$ 32,160	$ 36,888
Completed during week 31	45,000		
Ending work in process, week 31[b]	12,400		
Total costs added during week 31		$159,000	$177,940

[a]Degree of completion: direct materials, ?%; conversion costs, 20%.
[b]Degree of completion: direct materials, ?%; conversion costs, 40%.

Required

1. Using the weighted-average method, summarize the total mixing department costs for week 31, and assign total costs to units completed (and transferred out) and to units in ending work in process.
2. Assume that the FIFO method is used for the mixing department. Summarize the total mixing department costs for week 31, and assign total costs to units completed and transferred out and to units in ending work in process using the FIFO method.
3. McKee management seeks to have a more consistent cost per equivalent unit. Which method of process costing should the company choose and why?

Case

Shamrock Inc.

You drive on it, walk on it, wear it, and even brush your teeth with it. What is it? Limestone. It's a versatile natural resource found in asphalt highways, concrete sidewalks, cosmetics and toothpaste, to name a few things. Shamrock Inc. has been a primary supplier of quality limestone products since the mid-1950s. Over the years, the company has seen many changes as its business and the local economy have matured.

Considered a commodity, limestone rock is extracted from underground mines located 350 feet below the surface. Limestone used to be mined on the surface, but the supply of quality surface rock has been exhausted. Engineers estimate that millions of tons of quality limestone rock still remain to be mined underground.

To mine limestone, the rock is first blasted with dynamite charges to loosen it. The large pieces of limestone rocks are loaded into 35-ton capacity trucks for transport to rock-crushing plants. Shamrock operates 20 rock-crushing plants. Shamrock buys the large limestone pieces from several mines (quarries), and workers dump them into a crusher that breaks the rocks into smaller pieces. All rocks are processed in a relatively homogeneous way. These pieces are then loaded onto trucks for customers or moved to a storage pile away from the crushing plant.

Pricing is very competitive, so Shamrock's managers keep a close eye on costs to ensure that the operations remain profitable. Major costs for the business include the cost of the large limestone rocks, depreciation on the equipment, labor, repairs, maintenance, and safety and environmental protection.

Eugene Johnson is the corporate controller of Shamrock. Each plant uses a process-costing system. At the end of each year, each plant manager submits a production report and a production-cost report. The cost data have been particularly useful for identifying how well different plants have been managing their costs in the very competitive environment in which they operate.

The production report includes the plant manager's estimates of the percentage of completion of (1) the ending work-in-process as to direct materials and conversion costs and (2) the limestone inventory in the storage pile. Johnson uses these estimates to compare costs across plants by computing the equivalent units of work done in each plant and the cost per equivalent unit of work done for both direct materials and conversion costs in each year. Plants are ranked from 1 to 20 based on (a) cost per equivalent unit of direct materials and (b) cost per equivalent unit of conversion costs. Shamrock rewards the three top-ranked plants in each category with a bonus and writes about their achievement in the company newsletter.

Johnson has been pleased with the success of his benchmarking program. However, he has just received some unsigned letters stating that two plant managers have been manipulating their estimates of percentage of completion and limestone inventory in an attempt to obtain best-in-class status.

Required

1. Do you agree with Shamrock Inc.'s use of a process-costing system? Why? Explain.
2. Why do you think Johnson was benchmarking one plant against another?
3. Why and how might plant managers manipulate their estimates of percentage of completion and limestone inventory?
4. Johnson's first reaction is to contact each plant controller and discuss the problem raised by the unsigned letters. Is that a good idea?

5. Assume that the plant controller's primary reporting responsibility is to the plant manager and that each plant controller receives the phone call from Johnson mentioned in requirement 4. What is the ethical responsibility of each plant controller to (a) Eugene Johnson and (b) to Shamrock Inc. when reporting the equivalent-unit information and limestone inventory each plant provides?
6. How might Johnson learn whether the equivalent unit and limestone inventory figures provided by particular plants are being manipulated?
7. What should Johnson do?

6 Activity-Based Costing and Activity-Based Management

Learning Objectives

1. Explain how broad averaging undercosts and overcosts products or services
2. Present three guidelines for refining a costing system
3. Distinguish between simple and activity-based costing systems
4. Describe a four-part cost hierarchy
5. Cost products or services using activity-based costing
6. Evaluate the costs and benefits of implementing activity-based costing systems
7. Explain how managers use activity-based costing systems in activity-based management

A good mystery never fails to capture the imagination.

Money is stolen or lost, property disappears, or someone meets with foul play. On the surface, what appears unremarkable to the untrained eye can turn out to be quite a revelation once the facts and details are uncovered. Getting to the bottom of the case, understanding what happened and why, and taking action can make the difference between a solved case and an unsolved one. Business and organizations face similar situations. Their costing systems are often mysteries with unresolved questions: Why are we bleeding red ink? Are we pricing our products accurately? Activity-based costing can help unravel the mystery and result in improved operations.

Most companies, such as Dell, Oracle, JP Morgan Chase, and Honda, offer more than one product (or service). Dell Computer, for example, produces desktops, laptops, and servers. Manufacturing these products entails three basic activities: (1) designing computers, (2) ordering component parts, and (3) assembly. Different products require different quantities of the three activities. A server, for example, has a more complex design, many more parts, and a more complex assembly than a desktop.

Dell separately tracks activity costs by product in its activity-based costing (ABC) system. In this chapter, we describe these types of systems and how they help companies make better decisions about pricing and product mix. We show how ABC systems help managers make cost management decisions by improving product designs, processes, and efficiency.

Chapter at a Glance

- Simple costing systems that broadly average overhead costs give managers incorrect information about the resources organizations use to produce products and the profitability of different products.
- Companies refine their costing systems by classifying more costs as direct costs, expanding the number of indirect cost pools, and identifying cost drivers for those cost pools.
- Activity-based costing (ABC) systems refine costing systems by identifying individual activities, tasks, or units of work. Managers then use the cost of those activities to calculate product and customer profitability.
- A cost hierarchy categorizes costs into different types of cost drivers based on if a cost is (1) related to each individual unit of product or service (energy), (2) a batch of products or services (setup costs), (3) a product or service (design costs), or (4) the organization as a whole (general administration).

- ABC systems are likely to yield the most decision-making benefits when indirect costs are a high percentage of total costs or when different products and services demand very different amounts of indirect resources. In these cases, managers find ABC systems useful for decisions such as pricing, product and process redesign, cost reduction, and process improvement.
- The main challenge implementing ABC systems are the measurements needed to implement and maintain the system.

Broad Averaging and Its Consequences

Learning Objective 1

Explain how broad averaging undercosts and overcosts products or services

. . . it does not measure the different resources consumed by different products and services

Historically, companies (such as television and automobile manufacturers) produced a limited variety of products. These companies used few overhead resources to support these simple operations, so indirect (or overhead) costs were a relatively small percentage of total costs. Managers used simple costing systems to allocate overhead costs broadly in an easy, inexpensive, and reasonably accurate way. But as product diversity and indirect costs increased, broad averaging led to inaccurate product costs. That's because simple *peanut-butter costing* (yes, that's what it's called) broadly averages or spreads the cost of resources uniformly to cost objects (such as products or services) when, in fact, the individual products or services use those resources in nonuniform ways.

Undercosting and Overcosting

The following example illustrates how averaging can result in inaccurate and misleading cost data. Consider the cost of a restaurant bill for four colleagues who meet monthly to discuss business developments. Each diner orders separate entrees, desserts, and drinks. The restaurant bill for the most recent meeting is as follows.

	Emma	James	Jessica	Matthew	Total	Average
Entree	$11	$20	$15	$14	$ 60	$15
Dessert	0	8	4	4	16	4
Drinks	4	14	8	6	32	8
Total	$15	$42	$27	$24	$108	$27

If the $108 total restaurant bill is divided evenly, $27 is the average cost per diner. This cost-averaging approach treats each diner the same. When costs are averaged across all four diners, both Emma and Matthew are overcosted, James is undercosted, and Jessica is (by coincidence) accurately costed. Emma, especially, may object to paying the average bill of $27, because her individual bill is only $15.

Broad averaging often leads to undercosting or overcosting of products or services:

- **Product undercosting**—a product consumes a high level of resources per unit but is reported to have a low cost per unit (James's dinner).
- **Product overcosting**—a product consumes a low level of resources per unit but is reported to have a high cost per unit (Emma's dinner).

What are the strategic consequences of product undercosting and overcosting? Suppose a manager uses cost information about products to guide pricing decisions. Undercosted products will be underpriced and may even lead to sales that actually result in losses, since the sales may bring in less revenue than the cost of resources they use. Overcosted products will lead to overpricing, causing those products to lose market share to competitors producing similar products. But what if prices are determined by the market based on competition among companies? In this case, product undercosting and overcosting causes managers to focus on the wrong products, drawing attention to overcosted products that show low profits when costs may in fact be perfectly reasonable and ignoring undercosted products that show high profits but which in fact consume large amounts of resources.

Product-Cost Cross-Subsidization

Product-cost cross-subsidization means that if a company undercosts one of its products, it will overcost at least one of its other products. Similarly, if a company overcosts one of its products, it will undercost at least one of its other products. Product-cost cross-subsidization is very common when a cost is uniformly spread—meaning it is broadly averaged—across multiple products without managers recognizing the amount of resources consumed by each product.

In the restaurant-bill example, the amount of cost cross-subsidization of each diner can be readily computed *because all cost items can be traced as direct costs to each diner.* If all diners pay $27, Emma is paying $12 more than her actual cost of $15. She is cross-subsidizing James who is paying $15 less than his actual cost of $42. Calculating the amount of cost cross-subsidization takes more work when there are indirect costs to be considered. Why? Because when two or more diners use the resources represented by indirect costs, we need to find a way to allocate costs to each diner. Consider, for example, a $40 bottle of wine whose cost is shared equally. Each diner would pay $10 ($40 ÷ 4). Suppose Matthew drinks two glasses of wine, while Emma, James, and Jessica drink one glass each for a total of five glasses. Allocating the cost of the bottle of wine on the basis of the glasses of wine that each diner drinks would result in Matthew paying $16 ($40 × 2/5) and each of the others $8 ($40 × 1/5). In this case, by sharing the cost equally, Emma, James, and Jessica are each paying $2 ($10 − $8) more and are cross-subsidizing Matthew who is paying $6 ($16 − $10) less for his wine for the night.

To see the effects of broad averaging on direct and indirect costs, we next consider Plastim Corporation's costing system.

Keys to Success

Managers must always be aware of product undercosting (overcosting) that occurs when a product or service consumes a high (low) level of resources but is reported to have a low (high) cost. It arises when costs are assigned uniformly to products while the products use resources in a nonuniform way.

Simple Costing System at Plastim Corporation

Plastim Corporation manufactures lenses for the rear taillights of automobiles. A lens, made from black, red, orange, or white plastic, is the part of the lamp visible on the automobile's exterior. Lenses are made by injecting molten plastic into a mold to give the lamp its desired shape. The mold is cooled to allow the molten plastic to solidify, and the lens is removed.

Under its contract with Giovanni Motors, a major automobile manufacturer, Plastim makes two types of lenses: a complex lens, CL5, and a simple lens, S3. The complex lens is a large lens with special features, such as multicolor molding (when more than one color is injected into the mold) and a complex shape that wraps around the corner of the car. Manufacturing CL5 lenses is complicated because various parts in the mold must align and fit precisely. The S3 lens is simpler to make because it has a single color and few special features.

Design, Manufacturing, and Distribution Processes

The sequence of steps to design, produce, and distribute lenses, whether simple or complex, is:

- **Design products and processes.** Each year Giovanni Motors specifies details of the simple and complex lenses it needs for its new models of cars. Plastim's design department designs the new molds and specifies the manufacturing process to make the lenses.
- **Manufacture lenses.** The lenses are molded, finished, cleaned, and inspected.
- **Distribute lenses.** Finished lenses are packed and sent to Giovanni Motors. Plastim is operating at capacity and incurs very low marketing costs. Because of its high-quality products, Plastim has minimal customer-service costs. Plastim competes with several other companies who also manufacture simple lenses. At a recent meeting, Giovanni's purchasing manager informed Plastim's sales manager that Bandix, which makes only simple lenses, is offering to supply the S3 lens to Giovanni at a price of $53, well below the $63 price that Plastim is currently projecting and budgeting for 2013. Unless Plastim can lower its selling price, it will lose the Giovanni business for the simple lens for the upcoming model year. Fortunately, the same competitive pressures do not exist for the complex lens, which Plastim currently sells to Giovanni at $137 per lens.

Plastim's managers have two primary options:

- Give up the Giovanni business in simple lenses if selling them is unprofitable. Bandix makes only simple lenses and perhaps, therefore, uses simpler technology and processes than Plastim. The simpler operations may give Bandix a cost advantage that Plastim cannot match. If so, it is better for Plastim to not supply the S3 lens to Giovanni.
- Reduce the price of the simple lens and either accept a lower margin or aggressively seek to reduce costs.

To make these long-run strategic decisions, managers first need to understand the costs to design, make, and distribute the S3 and CL5 lenses.

Bandix makes only simple lenses and can fairly accurately calculate the cost of a lens by dividing total costs by the number of simple lenses produced. Plastim's costing environment is more challenging because the manufacturing overhead costs support the production of both simple and complex lenses. Plastim's managers and management accountants need to find a way to allocate overhead costs to each type of lens.

In computing costs, Plastim assigns both variable costs and costs that are fixed in the short run to the S3 and CL5 lenses. Managers cost products and services to guide long-run strategic decisions (for example, what mix of products and services to produce and sell and what prices to charge for them). In the long run, managers have the ability to influence all costs. The firm will only survive in the long run if revenues exceed total costs, whether variable or fixed in the short run.

To guide pricing and cost-management decisions, Plastim's managers assign both manufacturing and nonmanufacturing costs to the S3 and CL5 lenses. If managers had wanted to calculate the cost of inventory, Plastim's management accountants would have assigned only manufacturing costs to the lenses, as required by Generally Accepted Accounting Principles. Surveys of company practice across the globe indicate that the vast majority of companies use costing systems not just for inventory costing but also for strategic purposes, such as pricing and product-mix decisions and decisions about cost reduction, process improvement, design, and planning and budgeting. Managers of these companies assign all costs to products and services. Even merchandising-sector companies (for whom inventory costing is straightforward) and service-sector companies (who have no inventory) expend considerable resources in designing and operating their costing systems.

Simple Costing System Using a Single Indirect-Cost Pool

Plastim currently has a simple costing system that allocates indirect costs using a single indirect-cost rate, the type of system described in Chapter 4. The only difference between these two chapters is that Chapter 4 focuses on jobs and here the cost objects are products. Exhibit 6-1 shows an overview of Plastim's simple costing system. Use this exhibit as a guide as you study the following steps, each of which is marked in Exhibit 6-1.

Step 1: Identify the Products That Are the Chosen Cost Objects. The cost objects are the 60,000 simple S3 lenses and the 15,000 complex CL5 lenses that Plastim will produce in 2013. Plastim's management accountants first calculate the total costs and then the unit cost of designing, manufacturing, and distributing lenses.

Step 2: Identify the Direct Costs of the Products. The direct costs are direct materials and direct manufacturing labor. Exhibit 6-2 shows the direct and indirect costs for the S3 and the CL5 lenses using the simple costing system. The direct cost calculations appear on lines 5, 6, and 7 in Exhibit 6-2. Plastim's simple costing system classifies all costs other than direct materials and direct manufacturing labor as indirect costs.

Step 3: Select the Cost-Allocation Bases to Use for Allocating Indirect (or Overhead) Costs to the Products. A majority of the indirect costs consist of salaries paid to supervisors, engineers, manufacturing support, and maintenance staff that support direct manufacturing labor. Plastim's managers use direct manufacturing labor-hours as the only allocation base to allocate all manufacturing and nonmanufacturing indirect costs to S3 and CL5. In 2013, Plastim's managers budget 39,750 direct manufacturing labor-hours.

Step 4: Identify the Indirect Costs Associated with Each Cost-Allocation Base. Because Plastim uses only a single cost-allocation base, Plastim's management accountants group all budgeted indirect costs of $2,385,000 for 2013 into a single overhead cost pool.

Step 5: Compute the Rate per Unit of Each Cost-Allocation Base.

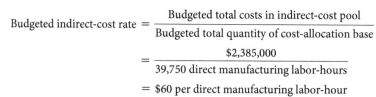

$$\text{Budgeted indirect-cost rate} = \frac{\text{Budgeted total costs in indirect-cost pool}}{\text{Budgeted total quantity of cost-allocation base}}$$

$$= \frac{\$2{,}385{,}000}{39{,}750 \text{ direct manufacturing labor-hours}}$$

$$= \$60 \text{ per direct manufacturing labor-hour}$$

Exhibit 6-1

Overview of Plastim's Simple Costing System

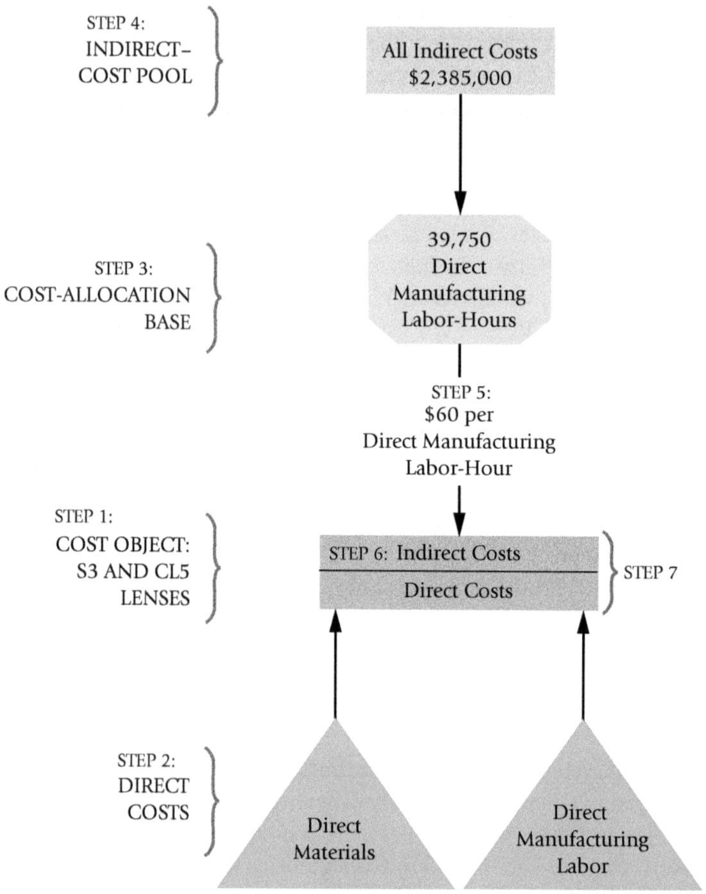

Exhibit 6-2

Plastim's Product Costs Using the Simple Costing System

	A	B	C	D	E	F	G
1		60,000			15,000		
2		Simple Lenses (S3)			Complex Lenses (CL5)		
3		Total	per Unit		Total	per Unit	Total
4		(1)	(2) = (1) ÷ 60,000		(3)	(4) = (3) ÷ 15,000	(5) = (1) + (3)
5	Direct materials	$1,125,000	$18.75		$ 675,000	$45.00	$1,800,000
6	Direct manufacturing labor	600,000	10.00		195,000	13.00	795,000
7	Total direct costs (Step 2)	1,725,000	28.75		870,000	58.00	2,595,000
8	Indirect costs allocated (Step 6)	1,800,000	30.00		585,000	39.00	2,385,000
9	Total costs (Step 7)	$3,525,000	$58.75		$1,455,000	$97.00	$4,980,000
10							

Step 6: Compute the Indirect Costs Allocated to the Products. Plastim's managers budget 30,000 total direct manufacturing labor-hours to make the 60,000 S3 lenses and 9,750 total direct manufacturing labor-hours to make the 15,000 CL5 lenses. Exhibit 6-2 shows indirect costs of \$1,800,000 (\$60 per direct manufacturing labor-hour × 30,000 direct manufacturing labor-hours) allocated to the simple lens and \$585,000 (\$60 per direct manufacturing labor-hour × 9,750 direct manufacturing labor-hours) allocated to the complex lens.

Step 7: Compute the Total Cost of the Products by Adding All Direct and Indirect Costs Assigned to the Products. Exhibit 6-2 presents the product costs for the simple and complex lenses. The direct costs are calculated in Step 2 and the indirect costs in Step 6. Be sure you see the parallel between the simple costing system overview diagram (Exhibit 6-1) and the costs calculated in Step 7. Exhibit 6-1 shows two direct-cost categories and one indirect-cost category. Therefore, the budgeted cost of each type of lens in Step 7 (Exhibit 6-2) has three line items: two for direct costs and one for allocated indirect costs. It is very helpful to draw overview diagrams to see the big picture of costing systems before getting into the detailed costing of products and services. The budgeted cost per S3 lens is \$58.75, well above the \$53 selling price quoted by Bandix. The budgeted cost per CL5 lens is \$97.

Applying the Five-Step Decision-Making Process at Plastim

To decide how it should respond to the threat that Bandix poses to its S3 lens business, Plastim's managers work through the five-step decision-making process introduced in Chapter 1.

Step 1: Identify the Problem and Uncertainties. The problem is clear: If Plastim wants to retain the Giovanni business for S3 lenses and make a profit, it must find a way to reduce the price and costs of the S3 lens. The two major uncertainties Plastim faces are (1) whether Plastim's technology and processes for the S3 lens are competitive with Bandix's and (2) whether the S3 lens is overcosted by the simple costing system.

Step 2: Obtain Information. Senior management asks a team of its design and process engineers to analyze and evaluate the design, manufacturing, and distribution operations for the S3 lens. The team is very confident that the technology and processes for the S3 lens are not inferior to those of Bandix and other competitors because Plastim has many years of experience in manufacturing and distributing the S3 lens with a history and culture of continuous process improvements. If anything, the team is less certain about Plastim's capabilities in manufacturing and distributing complex lenses because it only recently started making this type of lens. Given these doubts, senior management is happy that Giovanni Motors considers the price of the CL5 lens to be competitive. It is somewhat of a puzzle, though, how at the currently budgeted prices, Plastim is expected to earn a very large profit margin percentage (operating income ÷ revenues) on the CL5 lenses and a small profit margin on the S3 lenses:

	60,000 Simple Lenses (S3)		15,000 Complex Lenses (CL5)		
	Total (1)	per Unit (2) = (1) ÷ 60,000	Total (3)	per Unit (4) = (3) ÷ 15,000	Total (5) = (1) + (3)
Revenues	\$3,780,000	\$63.00	\$2,055,000	\$137.00	\$5,835,000
Total costs	3,525,000	58.75	1,455,000	97.00	4,980,000
Operating income	\$ 255,000	\$ 4.25	\$ 600,000	\$ 40.00	\$ 855,000
Profit margin percentage		6.75%		29.20%	

As they continue to gather information, Plastim's managers begin to ponder why the profit margins (and process) are under so much pressure for the S3 lens, where the company has strong capabilities, but are high on the newer, less-established CL5 lens. Plastim is not deliberately charging a low price for S3, so managers begin to focus their attention on the costing system. Plastim's simple costing system may be overcosting the simple S3 lens (assigning too much cost to it) and undercosting the complex CL5 lens (assigning too little cost to it).

Step 3: Make Predictions About the Future. Plastim's key challenge is to get a better estimate of what it will cost to design, make, and distribute the S3 and CL5 lenses. Managers are fairly confident about the direct material and direct manufacturing labor cost of each lens because these costs are easily traced to the lenses. But managers are quite concerned about how accurately the simple costing system measures the indirect resources used by each type of lens. They believe the costing system can be substantially improved.

Even as they come to this conclusion, managers want to ensure that no biases enter their thinking. In particular, they want to be careful that the desire to be competitive on the S3 lens does not lead to assumptions that bias them in favor of lowering costs of the S3 lens.

Step 4: Make Decisions by Choosing Among Alternatives. On the basis of predicted costs, and taking into account how Bandix might respond, Plastim's managers must decide whether they should bid for Giovanni Motors' S3 lens business and, if they do bid, what price they should offer.

Step 5: Implement the Decision, Evaluate Performance, and Learn. If Plastim bids and wins Giovanni's S3 lens business, it must compare actual costs, as it makes and ships S3 lenses, to predicted costs and learn why actual costs deviate from predicted costs. Such evaluation and learning form the basis for future improvements.

The next few sections focus on Steps 3, 4, and 5: (3) how Plastim improves the allocation of indirect costs to the S3 and CL5 lenses, (4) how it uses these predictions to bid for the S3 lens business, and (5) how it evaluates performance, makes product design and process improvements, and learns using the new system.

Learning Objective 2

Present three guidelines for refining a costing system

... classify more costs as direct costs, expand the number of indirect-cost pools, and identify cost drivers

Refining a Costing System

A **refined costing system** reduces the use of broad averages for assigning the cost of resources to cost objects (such as jobs, products, and services) and provides better measurement of the costs of indirect resources used by different cost objects, no matter how differently various cost objects use indirect resources.

Reasons for Refining a Costing System

Three principal reasons have accelerated the demand for refinements.

1. **Increase in product diversity.** The growing demand for customized products has led managers to increase the variety of products and services their companies offer. Kanthal, a Swedish manufacturer of heating elements, for example, produces more than 10,000 different types of electrical heating wires and thermostats. Banks, such as the Cooperative Bank in the United Kingdom, offer many different types of accounts and services: special passbook accounts, ATMs, credit cards, and electronic banking. These products differ in the demands they place on the resources needed to produce them because of differences in volume, process, and complexity. The use of broad averages fails to capture these differences in demand and leads to distorted and inaccurate cost information.
2. **Increase in indirect costs.** The use of product and process technology such as computer-integrated manufacturing (CIM) and flexible manufacturing systems (FMS) has led to an increase in indirect costs and a decrease in direct costs, particularly direct manufacturing labor costs. In CIM and FMS, computers on the manufacturing floor give instructions to set up and run equipment quickly and automatically. The computers accurately measure hundreds of production parameters and directly control the manufacturing processes to achieve high-quality output. Managing complex technology and producing diverse products also requires additional support function resources for activities such as production scheduling, product and process design, and engineering. Because direct manufacturing labor is not a cost driver of these costs, allocating indirect costs on the basis of direct manufacturing labor (as in Plastim's simple costing system) does not accurately measure how resources are being used by different products.
3. **Competition in product markets.** As markets have become more competitive, managers have felt the need to obtain more accurate cost information to help them make important strategic decisions, such as how to price products and which products to sell. Making correct pricing and product mix decisions is critical in competitive markets because competitors quickly capitalize on a manager's mistakes.

Whereas the preceding factors identify reasons for the increase in *demand* for refined cost systems, *advances in information technology* facilitate its implementation. Costing system refinements require more data gathering and more analysis, and improvements in information technology have drastically reduced the costs to gather, validate, store, and analyze vast quantities of data.

Guidelines for Refining a Costing System

There are three main guidelines for refining a costing system:

1. **Direct-cost tracing.** Identify as many direct costs as is economically feasible. This guideline aims to reduce the amount of costs classified as indirect, thereby minimizing the extent to which costs have to be allocated, rather than traced.
2. **Indirect-cost pools.** Expand the number of indirect-cost pools until each pool is more homogeneous. All costs in a *homogeneous cost pool* have the same or a similar cause-and-effect (or benefits-received) relationship with a single cost driver that is used as the cost-allocation base. Consider, for example, a single indirect-cost pool containing both indirect machining costs and indirect distribution costs that are allocated to products using machine-hours. This pool is not homogeneous because machine-hours are a cost driver of machining costs but not of distribution costs, which has a different cost driver, number of shipments. If, instead, machining costs and distribution costs are separated into two indirect-cost pools (with machine-hours as the cost-allocation base for the machining cost pool and number of shipments as the cost-allocation base for the distribution cost pool), each indirect-cost pool would become homogeneous.
3. **Cost-allocation bases.** As we describe later in the chapter, whenever possible, managers should use the cost driver (the cause of indirect costs) as the cost-allocation base for each homogeneous indirect-cost pool (the effect).

> **Keys to Success**
>
> **Managers refine a costing system by tracing more direct costs to products or services, creating more homogeneous indirect cost pools, and identifying cost drivers, all with the goal of better measuring the way different cost objects use resources.**

Activity-Based Costing Systems

Learning Objective 3

Distinguish between simple and activity-based costing systems

. . . unlike simple systems, ABC systems calculate costs of individual activities to cost products

One of the best tools for refining a costing system is *activity-based costing.* **Activity-based costing (ABC)** refines a costing system by identifying individual activities as the fundamental cost objects. An **activity** is an event, task, or unit of work with a specified purpose—for example, designing products, setting up machines, operating machines, and distributing products. More informally, activities are verbs; they are things that a firm does. To help make strategic decisions, ABC systems identify activities in all functions of the value chain, calculate costs of individual activities, and assign costs to cost objects such as products and services on the basis of the mix of activities needed to produce each product or service.[1]

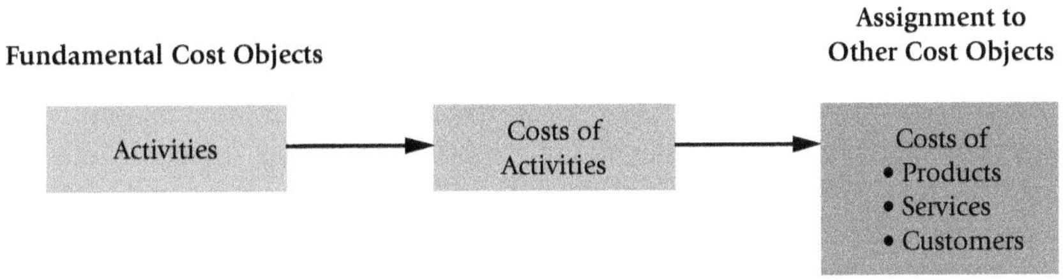

[1] For more details on ABC systems, see R. Cooper and R. S. Kaplan, *The Design of Cost Management Systems* (Upper Saddle River, NJ: Prentice Hall, 1999); G. Cokins, *Activity-Based Cost Management: An Executive's Guide* (Hoboken, NJ: Wiley, 2001); and R. S. Kaplan and S. Anderson, *Time-Driven Activity-Based Costing: A Simpler and More Powerful Path to Higher Profits* (Boston: Harvard Business School Press, 2007).

Plastim's ABC System

After reviewing its simple costing system and the potential miscosting of product costs, Plastim's managers decide to implement an ABC system. Direct material costs and direct manufacturing labor costs can be traced to products easily, so the ABC system focuses on refining the assignment of indirect costs to departments, processes, products, or other cost objects. To identify activities, Plastim organizes a team of managers from design, manufacturing, distribution, accounting, and administration. Plastim's ABC system then uses these activities to break down its current single indirect cost pool into finer pools of costs related to the various activities.

Defining activities is difficult. The team evaluates hundreds of tasks performed at Plastim. It must decide which tasks should be classified as separate activities and which should be combined. For example, should maintenance of molding machines, operations of molding machines, and process control be regarded as separate activities or combined into a single activity? An activity-based costing system with many activities becomes overly detailed and unwieldy to operate. An activity-based costing system with too few activities may not be refined enough to measure cause-and-effect relationships between cost drivers and various indirect costs. To achieve an effective balance, Plastim's team focuses on activities that account for a sizable fraction of indirect costs and combines activities that have the same cost driver into a single activity. For example, the team decides to combine maintenance of molding machines, operations of molding machines, and process control into a single activity—molding machine operations—because all these activities have the same cost driver: molding machine-hours.

The team identifies the following seven activities by developing a flowchart of all the steps and processes needed to design, manufacture, and distribute S3 and CL5 lenses.

a. Design products and processes
b. Set up molding machines to ensure that the molds are properly held in place and parts are properly aligned before manufacturing starts
c. Operate molding machines to manufacture lenses
d. Clean and maintain the molds after lenses are manufactured
e. Prepare batches of finished lenses for shipment
f. Distribute lenses to customers
g. Administer and manage all processes at Plastim

These activity descriptions (or *activity list* or *activity dictionary*) form the basis of the activity-based costing system. Compiling the list of tasks, however, is only the first step in implementing activity-based costing systems. Plastim must also identify the cost of each activity and the related cost driver. To do so, Plastim uses the three guidelines for refining a costing system described on page 213.

1. **Direct-cost tracing.** Plastim's ABC system subdivides the single indirect cost pool into seven smaller cost pools related to the different activities. The costs in the cleaning and maintenance activity cost pool (item d) consist of salaries and wages paid to workers who clean the mold. These costs are direct costs, because they can be economically traced to a specific mold and lens.

2. **Indirect-cost pools.** The remaining six activity cost pools are indirect cost pools. Unlike the single indirect cost pool of Plastim's simple costing system, each of the activity-related cost pools is homogeneous. That is, each activity cost pool includes only those narrow and focused sets of costs that have the same cost driver. For example, the distribution cost pool includes only those costs (such as wages of truck drivers) that, over time, increase as the cost driver of distribution costs, cubic feet of packages delivered, increases. In the simple costing system, all indirect costs were lumped together and the cost-allocation base, direct manufacturing labor-hours, was not a cost driver of the indirect costs and managers were unable to measure how different cost objects used resources.

   Determining costs of activity pools requires assigning costs accumulated in various account classifications (salaries, wages, maintenance, power, etc.) to each of the activity cost pools, commonly referred to as *first-stage allocation.* For example, as we will see later in the chapter, of the \$2,385,000 in the total indirect-cost pool, Plastim identifies setup costs of \$300,000. Setup costs include depreciation and maintenance costs of setup equipment, wages of setup workers, and allocated salaries of design engineers, process engineers, and supervisors. We next focus on the *second-stage allocation,* the allocation of costs of activity cost pools to products.

3. **Cost-allocation bases.** For each activity cost pool, Plastim uses the cost driver (whenever possible) as the cost-allocation base. To identify cost drivers, Plastim's managers consider various alternatives and use their knowledge of operations to choose among them. For example, Plastim's managers choose setup-hours rather than the number of setups as the cost driver of setup costs because Plastim's managers believe that more complex setups take more time and are more costly. Over time, Plastim's managers can use data to test their beliefs. (Chapter 8 discusses several methods to estimate the relationship between a cost driver and costs.)

The logic of ABC systems is twofold. First, when managers structure activity cost pools more finely with cost drivers for each activity cost pool as the cost-allocation base, it leads to more accurate costing of activities. Second, allocating these costs to products by measuring the cost-allocation bases of different activities used by different products leads to more accurate product costs. We illustrate this logic by focusing on the setup activity at Plastim.

Setting up molding machines frequently entails trial runs, fine-tuning, and adjustments. Improper setups cause quality problems such as scratches on the surface of the lens. The resources needed for each setup depend on the complexity of the manufacturing operation. Complex lenses require more setup resources (setup-hours) per setup than simple lenses. Furthermore, complex lenses can be produced only in small batches because the molds for complex lenses need to be cleaned more often than molds for simple lenses. Thus, relative to simple lenses, complex lenses not only use more setup-hours per setup, but they also require more frequent setups.

Setup data for the simple S3 lens and the complex CL5 lens are as follows.

		Simple S3 Lens	Complex CL5 Lens	Total
1	Quantity of lenses produced	60,000	15,000	
2	Number of lenses produced per batch	240	50	
3 = (1) ÷ (2)	Number of batches	250	300	
4	Setup time per batch	2 hours	5 hours	
5 = (3) × (4)	Total setup-hours	500 hours	1,500 hours	2,000 hours

Recall that in its simple costing system, Plastim uses direct manufacturing labor-hours to allocate all \$2,385,000 of indirect costs (which includes \$300,000 of indirect setup costs) to products. The following table compares how setup costs allocated to simple and complex lenses will be different if Plastim allocates setup costs to lenses based on setup-hours rather than direct manufacturing labor-hours. Of the \$60 total rate per direct manufacturing labor-hour (page 210), the setup cost per direct manufacturing labor-hour amounts to \$7.54717 (\$300,000 ÷ 39,750 total direct manufacturing labor-hours). The setup cost per setup-hour equals \$150 (\$300,000 ÷ 2,000 total setup-hours).

	Simple S3 Lens	Complex CL5 Lens	Total
Setup cost allocated using direct manufacturing labor-hours: \$7.54717 × 30,000; \$7.54717 × 9,750	\$226,415	\$ 73,585	\$300,000
Setup cost allocated using setup-hours: \$150 × 500; \$150 × 1,500	\$ 75,000	\$225,000	\$300,000

ABC systems that use available time (setup hours in our example) to calculate the cost of a resource and to allocate costs to cost objects are sometimes called *time-driven activity-based costing (TDABC) systems.* As we have already discussed when presenting guidelines 2 and 3, setup-hours, not direct manufacturing labor-hours, are the cost driver of setup costs. The CL5 lens uses substantially more setup-hours than the S3 lens (1,500 hours ÷ 2,000 hours = 75% of the total setup-hours) because the CL5 requires a greater number of setups (batches) and each setup is more challenging and requires more setup-hours.

The ABC system therefore allocates significantly more setup costs to CL5 than to S3. When direct manufacturing labor-hours rather than setup-hours are used to allocate setup costs in the simple costing system, it is the S3 lens that is allocated a very large share of the setup costs because the

S3 lens uses a larger proportion of direct manufacturing labor-hours (30,000 ÷ 39,750 = 75.47%). As a result, the simple costing system overcosts the S3 lens with regard to setup costs. As we will see later in the chapter, ABC systems provide valuable information to managers beyond more accurate product costs. For example, identifying setup hours as the cost driver correctly orients managers' cost reduction efforts on reducing setup hours and cost per setup hour. Note that setup-hours are related to batches (or groups) of lenses made, not the number of individual lenses. Activity-based costing attempts to identify the most relevant cause-and-effect relationship for each activity pool, without restricting the cost driver to only units of output or variables related to units of output (such as direct manufacturing labor-hours). As our discussion of setups illustrates, limiting cost-allocation bases to only units of output weakens the cause-and-effect relationship between the cost-allocation base and the costs in a cost pool.

Keys to Success

Managers use activity-based costing (ABC) systems to track indirect resources by identifying homogeneous indirect-cost pools for different activities and by using cost drivers as allocation bases. Without ABC systems, managers will be unable to understand the drivers of overhead costs and the demands different products place on overhead resources.

Learning Objective 4

Describe a four-part cost hierarchy

. . . a four-part cost hierarchy is used to categorize costs based on different types of cost drivers—for example, costs that vary with each unit of a product versus costs that vary with each batch of products

Cost Hierarchies

A **cost hierarchy** categorizes various activity cost pools on the basis of the different types of cost drivers, cost-allocation bases, or different degrees of difficulty in determining cause-and-effect (or benefits-received) relationships. ABC systems commonly use a cost hierarchy with four levels—(1) *output unit-level costs,* (2) *batch-level costs,* (2) *product-sustaining costs,* and (4) *facility-sustaining costs*—to identify cost-allocation bases that are cost drivers of the activity cost pools.

Output unit-level costs are the costs of activities performed on each individual unit of a product or service. Machine operations costs (such as the cost of energy, machine depreciation, and repair) related to the activity of running the automated molding machines are output unit-level costs because, over time, the cost of this activity increases with additional units of output produced (or machine-hours used). Plastim's ABC system uses molding machine-hours, an output unit-level cost-allocation base, to allocate machine operations costs to products.

Batch-level costs are the costs of activities related to a group of units of a product or service rather than each individual unit of product or service. In the Plastim example, setup costs are batch-level costs because, over time, the cost of this setup activity increases with setup-hours needed to produce batches (groups) of lenses. As described in the table on page 215, the S3 lens requires 500 setup-hours (2 setup-hours per batch × 250 batches). The CL5 lens requires 1,500 setup-hours (5 setup-hours per batch × 300 batches). The total setup costs allocated to S3 and CL5 depend on the total setup-hours required by each type of lens, not on the number of units of S3 and CL5 produced. (Setup costs being a batch-level cost cannot be avoided by producing one less unit of S3 or CL5.) Plastim's ABC system uses setup-hours, a batch-level cost-allocation base, to allocate setup costs to products. Other examples of batch-level costs are material-handling and quality-inspection costs associated with batches (not the quantities) of products produced, and costs of placing purchase orders, receiving materials, and paying invoices related to the number of purchase orders placed rather than the quantity or value of materials purchased.

Product-sustaining costs (service-sustaining costs) are the costs of activities undertaken to support individual products or services regardless of the number of units or batches in which the units are produced. In the Plastim example, design costs are product-sustaining costs. Over time, design costs depend largely on the time designers spend on designing and modifying the product, the mold, and the process. These design costs are a function of the complexity of the mold, measured by the number of parts in the mold multiplied by the area (in square feet) over which the molten plastic must flow (12 parts × 2.5 square feet, or 30 parts-square feet for the S3 lens, and 14 parts × 5 square feet, or 70 parts-square feet for the CL5 lens). As a result, the total design costs allocated to S3 and CL5 depend on the complexity of the mold, regardless of the number of units or batches of production. Plastim can't avoid design costs by producing fewer units or running fewer batches. Plastim's ABC system uses parts-square feet, a product-sustaining cost-allocation base, to allocate design costs to products. Other examples of product-sustaining costs at companies such as Volvo, Samsung, and General Electric are product research and development costs, costs of making engineering changes, and marketing costs to launch new products.

Facility-sustaining costs are the costs of activities that cannot be traced to individual products or services but that support the organization as a whole. In the Plastim example, and at companies such as Volvo, Samsung, and General Electric, the general administration costs (including top management compensation, rent, and building security) are facility-sustaining costs. It is usually difficult to find a good cause-and-effect relationship between these costs and the cost-allocation base, so some companies deduct facility-sustaining costs as a separate lump-sum amount from operating income rather than allocate them to products. If they follow this approach, managers need to keep in mind that when making decisions based on costs (such as pricing), some lump-sum costs have not been allocated. They may only be willing to sell products at prices that are much greater than the allocated costs to recover some of the unallocated facility-sustaining costs. Other companies, such as Plastim, allocate facility-sustaining costs to products on some basis—for example, direct manufacturing labor-hours—because management believes all costs should be allocated to products even though these costs are allocated to products in a somewhat arbitrary way. Allocating all costs to products or services ensures that managers have taken into account all costs when making decisions based on costs (such as pricing). So long as managers are aware of the nature of facility-sustaining costs and the pros and cons of allocating them, which method a manager chooses is a matter of personal preference.

Keys to Success

A cost hierarchy is helpful to managers because it categorizes costs into different cost pools on the basis of different types of cost drivers depending on whether a cost is related to each individual unit of product or service (machine depreciation), a batch of products or services (setup costs), a product or service (design costs), or the organization as a whole (general administration).

Implementing Activity-Based Costing

Learning Objective 5

Cost products or services using activity-based costing

. . . use cost rates for different activities to compute indirect costs of a product

Now that you understand the basic concepts of ABC, let's see how Plastim's managers refine the simple costing system, evaluate the two systems, and identify the factors to consider when deciding whether or not to develop the ABC system.

Implementing ABC at Plastim

To implement ABC, Plastim's managers follow the seven-step approach to costing and the three guidelines for refining costing systems (increase direct-cost tracing, create homogeneous indirect-cost pools, and identify cost-allocation bases that have cause-and-effect relationships with costs in the cost pool). Exhibit 6-3 shows an overview of Plastim's ABC system. Use this exhibit as a guide as you study the following steps, each of which is marked in Exhibit 6-3.

Step 1: Identify the Products That Are the Chosen Cost Objects. The cost objects are the 60,000 S3 and the 15,000 CL5 lenses that Plastim will produce in 2013. Plastim's managers want to determine the total costs and then the per-unit cost of designing, manufacturing, and distributing these lenses.

Step 2: Identify the Direct Costs of the Products. The managers identify the following direct costs of the lenses because these costs can be economically traced to a specific mold and lens: direct material costs, direct manufacturing labor costs, and mold cleaning and maintenance costs.

Exhibit 6-5 shows the direct and indirect costs for the S3 and CL5 lenses using the ABC system. The direct costs calculations appear on lines 6, 7, 8, and 9 in Exhibit 6-5. Plastim's managers classify all other costs as indirect costs, as we will see in Exhibit 6-4.

Step 3: Select the Activities and Cost-Allocation Bases to Use for Allocating Indirect Costs to the Products. Following guidelines 2 and 3 for refining a costing system (page 213), Plastim's managers identify six activities for allocating indirect costs to products: (a) design, (b) molding

Exhibit 6-3

Overview of Plastim's Activity-Based Costing System

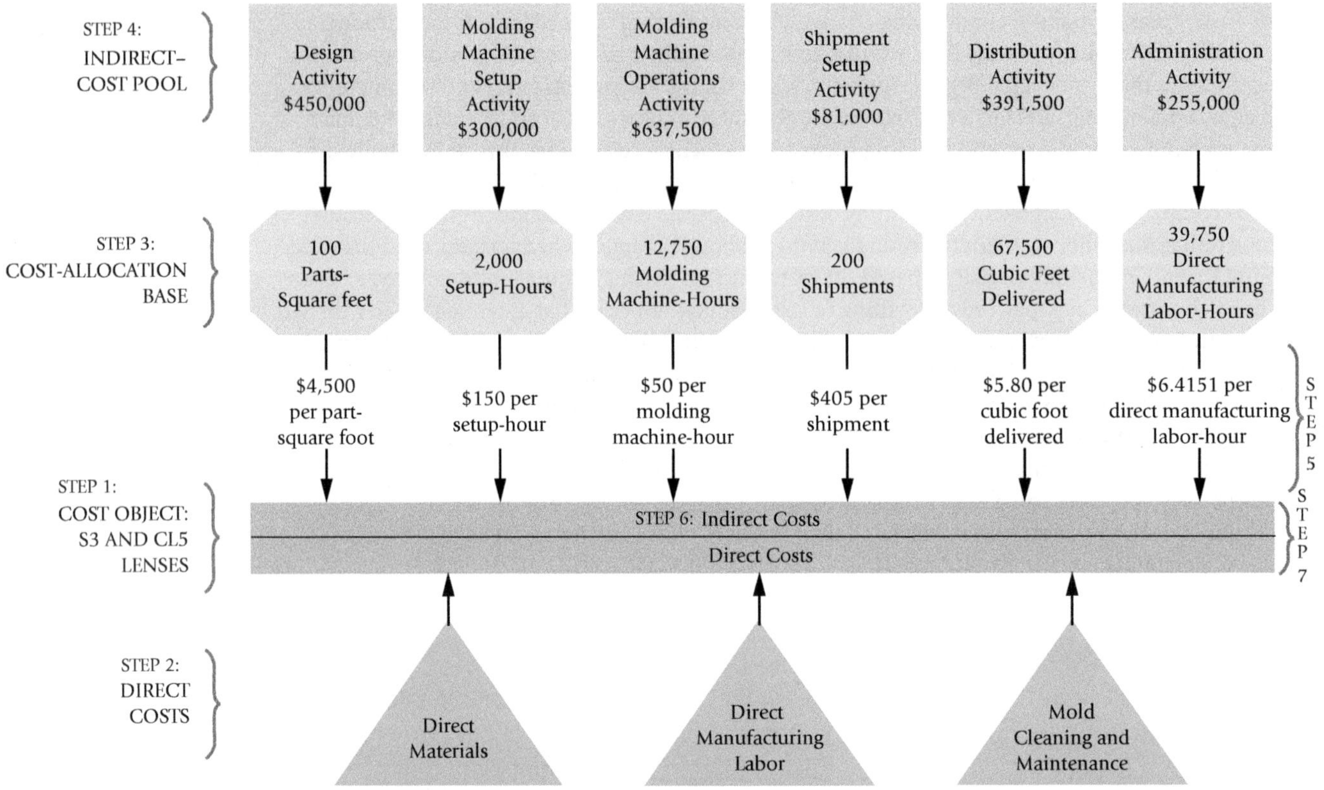

Exhibit 6-4

Activity-Cost Rates for Indirect-Cost Pools

Home Insert Page Layout Formulas Data Review View

	A	B	C	D	E	F	G	H
1			(Step 4)	(Step 3)		(Step 5)		
2	Activity	Cost Hierarchy Category	Total Budgeted Indirect Costs	Budgeted Quantity of Cost-Allocation Base		Budgeted Indirect Cost Rate		Cause-and-Effect Relationship Between Allocation Base and Activity Cost
3	(1)	(2)	(3)	(4)		(5) = (3) ÷ (4)		(6)
4	Design	Product-sustaining	$450,000	100	parts-square feet	$ 4,500	per part-square foot	Design Department indirect costs increase with more complex molds (more parts, larger surface area).
5	Setup molding machines	Batch-level	$300,000	2,000	setup-hours	$ 150	per setup-hour	Indirect setup costs increase with setup-hours.
6	Machine operations	Output unit–level	$637,500	12,750	molding machine-hours	$ 50	per molding machine-hour	Indirect costs of operating molding machines increases with molding machine-hours.
7	Shipment setup	Batch-level	$ 81,000	200	shipments	$ 405	per shipment	Shipping costs incurred to prepare batches for shipment increase with the number of shipments.
8	Distribution	Output unit–level	$391,500	67,500	cubic feet delivered	$ 5.80	per cubic foot delivered	Distribution costs increase with cubic feet of packages delivered.
9	Administration	Facility sustaining	$255,000	39,750	direct manuf. labor-hours	$6.4151	per direct manuf. labor-hour	The demand for administrative resources increases with direct manufacturing labor-hours.

Exhibit 6-5

Plastim's Product Costs Using Activity-Based Costing System

	A	B	C	D	E	F	G
1		60,000			15,000		
2		Simple Lenses (S3)			Complex Lenses (CL5)		
3		Total	per Unit		Total	per Unit	Total
4	**Cost Description**	(1)	(2) = (1) ÷ 60,000		(3)	(4) = (3) ÷ 15,000	(5) = (1) + (3)
5	Direct Costs						
6	Direct materials	$1,125,000	$18.75		$ 675,000	$ 45.00	$1,800,000
7	Direct manufacturing labor	600,000	10.00		195,000	13.00	795,000
8	Direct mold cleaning and maintenance costs	120,000	2.00		150,000	10.00	270,000
9	Total direct costs (Step 2)	1,845,000	30.75		1,020,000	68.00	2,865,000
10	Indirect Costs of Activities						
11	Design						
12	S3: 30 parts-sq.ft. × $4,500	135,000	2.25				} 450,000
13	CL5: 70 parts-sq.ft. × $4,500				315,000	21.00	
14	Setup of molding machines						
15	S3: 500 setup-hours × $150	75,000	1.25				} 300,000
16	CL5: 1,500 setup-hours × $150				225,000	15.00	
17	Machine operations						
18	S3: 9,000 molding machine-hours × $50	450,000	7.50				} 637,500
19	CL5: 3,750 molding machine-hours × $50				187,500	12.50	
20	Shipment setup						
21	S3: 100 shipments × $405	40,500	0.67				} 81,000
22	CL5: 100 shipments × $405				40,500	2.70	
23	Distribution						
24	S3: 45,000 cubic feet delivered × $5.80	261,000	4.35				} 391,500
25	CL5: 22,500 cubic feet delivered × $5.80				130,500	8.70	
26	Administration						
27	S3: 30,000 dir. manuf. labor-hours × $6.4151	192,453	3.21				} 255,000
28	CL5: 9,750 dir. manuf. labor-hours × $6.4151				62,547	4.17	
29	Total indirect costs allocated (Step 6)	1,153,953	19.23		961,047	64.07	2,115,000
30	Total Costs (Step 7)	$2,998,953	$49.98		$1,981,047	$132.07	$4,980,000
31							

machine setups, (c) machine operations, (d) shipment setup, (e) distribution, and (f) administration. Exhibit 6-4, column 2, shows the cost hierarchy category, and column 4 shows the cost-allocation base and the budgeted quantity of the cost-allocation base for each activity described in column 1.

Identifying the cost-allocation bases defines the number of activity pools into which costs must be grouped in an ABC system. For example, rather than define the design activities of product design, process design, and prototyping as separate activities, Plastim's managers define these three activities together as a combined "design" activity and form a homogeneous design cost pool. Why? Because the same cost driver, the complexity of the mold, drives the costs of each design activity. A second consideration for choosing a cost-allocation base is the availability of reliable data and measures. For example, in its ABC system, Plastim's managers measure mold complexity in terms of the number of parts in the mold and the surface area of the mold (parts-square feet). If these data are difficult to obtain or measure, Plastim's managers may be forced to use some other measure of complexity, such as the amount of material flowing through the mold that may only be weakly related to the cost of the design activity.

Step 4: Identify the Indirect Costs Associated with Each Cost-Allocation Base. In this step, Plastim's managers assign budgeted indirect costs for 2013 to activities (see Exhibit 6-4, column 3), to the extent possible, on the basis of a cause-and-effect relationship between the cost-allocation base for an activity and the cost. For example, all costs that have a cause-and-effect relationship to cubic feet of packages moved are assigned to the distribution cost pool. Of course, the strength of the cause-and-effect relationship between the cost-allocation base and the cost of an activity varies across cost pools. For example, the cause-and-effect relationship between direct manufacturing labor-hours and administration activity costs, which as we discussed earlier is somewhat arbitrary, is not as strong as the relationship between setup-hours and setup activity costs, where setup hours is the cost driver of setup costs.

Some costs can be directly identified with a particular activity. For example, salaries paid to design engineers and depreciation of equipment used in the design department are directly identified with the design activity. Other costs need to be allocated across activities. For example, on the basis of interviews or time records, manufacturing engineers and supervisors estimate the time they will spend on design, molding machine setup, and molding machine operations. For example, if a manufacturing engineer spends 15% of her time on design, 45% of her time managing molding machine setups, and 40% of her time on molding operations, the manufacturing engineer's salary would be allocated to each of these activities in proportion to the time spent. Still other costs are allocated to activity-cost pools using allocation bases that measure how these costs support different activities. For example, rent costs are allocated to activity cost pools on the basis of square-feet area used by different activities.

The point here is that all costs do not fit neatly into activity categories. Often, costs may first need to be allocated to activities (Stage 1 of the two-stage cost-allocation model) before the costs of the activities can be allocated to products (Stage 2).

The following table shows the assignment of costs to the seven activities identified earlier. Recall that Plastim's management accountants reclassify mold cleaning costs as a direct cost because these costs can be easily traced to a specific mold and lens.

	Design	Molding Machine Setups	Molding Operations	Mold Cleaning	Shipment Setup	Distribution	Administration	Total
Salaries (supervisors, design engineers, process engineers)	$320,000	$105,000	$137,500	$ 0	$21,000	$ 61,500	$165,000	$ 810,000
Wages of support staff	65,000	115,000	70,000	234,000	34,000	125,000	40,000	683,000
Depreciation	24,000	30,000	290,000	18,000	11,000	140,000	15,000	528,000
Maintenance	13,000	16,000	45,000	12,000	6,000	25,000	5,000	122,000
Power and fuel	18,000	20,000	35,000	6,000	5,000	30,000	10,000	124,000
Rent	10,000	14,000	60,000	0	4,000	10,000	20,000	118,000
Total	$450,000	$300,000	$637,500	$270,000	$81,000	$391,500	$255,000	$2,385,000

Step 5: Compute the Rate per Unit of Each Cost-Allocation Base. Exhibit 6-4, column 5, summarizes the calculation of the budgeted indirect-cost rates using the budgeted quantity of the cost-allocation base from Step 3 and the total budgeted indirect costs of each activity from Step 4.

Step 6: Compute the Indirect Costs Allocated to the Products. Exhibit 6-5 shows total budgeted indirect costs of $1,153,953 allocated to the simple lens and $961,047 allocated to the complex lens. Follow the budgeted indirect cost calculations for each lens in Exhibit 6-5. For each activity, Plastim's operations personnel indicate the total quantity of the cost-allocation base that will be used by each type of lens (recall that Plastim operates at capacity). For example, lines 15 and 16 in Exhibit 6-5 show that of the 2,000 total setup-hours, the S3 lens is budgeted to use 500 hours and the CL5 lens 1,500 hours. The budgeted indirect cost rate is $150 per setup-hour (Exhibit 6-4, column 5, line 5). Therefore, the total budgeted cost of the setup activity allocated to the S3 lens is $75,000 (500 setup-hours × $150 per setup-hour) and to the CL5 lens is $225,000 (1,500 setup-hours × $150 per setup-hour). Budgeted setup cost per unit equals $1.25 ($75,000 ÷ 60,000 units) for the S3 lens and $15 ($225,000 ÷ 15,000 units) for the CL5 lens.

Step 7: Compute the Total Cost of the Products by Adding All Direct and Indirect Costs Assigned to the Products. Exhibit 6-5 presents the product costs for the simple and complex lenses. The direct costs are calculated in Step 2, and the indirect costs are calculated in Step 6. The ABC system overview in Exhibit 6-3 shows three direct-cost categories and six indirect-cost categories. The budgeted cost of each lens type in Exhibit 6-5 has nine line items, three for direct costs and six for indirect costs. The differences between the ABC product costs of S3 and CL5 calculated in Exhibit 6-5 highlight how each of these products uses different amounts of direct and indirect costs in each activity area.

We emphasize two features of ABC systems. First, these systems identify all costs used by products, whether the costs are variable or fixed in the short run. When making long-run strategic decisions using ABC information, managers want revenues to exceed total costs. Otherwise, they will continue to make losses and will be unable to continue in business. Second, recognizing the hierarchy of costs is critical when allocating costs to products. Management accountants use the cost hierarchy to first calculate the total costs of each product. They then derive per-unit costs by dividing total costs by the number of units produced.

Comparing Alternative Costing Systems

Exhibit 6-6 compares the simple costing system using a single indirect-cost pool (Exhibit 6-1 and Exhibit 6-2) that Plastim had been using and the ABC system (Exhibit 6-3 and Exhibit 6-5). Note three points in Exhibit 6-6, consistent with the guidelines for refining a costing system: (1) ABC systems trace more costs as direct costs; (2) ABC systems create homogeneous cost pools linked to different activities; and (3) for each activity-cost pool, ABC systems seek a cost-allocation base that has a cause-and-effect relationship with costs in the cost pool.

The homogeneous cost pools and the choice of cost-allocation bases, tied to the cost hierarchy, give Plastim's managers greater confidence in the activity and product cost numbers from the ABC system. The bottom part of Exhibit 6-6 shows that allocating costs to lenses using only an output unit-level allocation base—direct manufacturing labor-hours, as in the single indirect-cost pool system used prior to ABC—overcosts the simple S3 lens by \$8.77 per unit and undercosts the complex CL5 lens by \$35.07 per unit. The CL5 lens uses a disproportionately larger amount of output

Exhibit 6-6
Comparing Alternative Costing Systems

	Simple Costing System Using a Single Indirect-Cost Pool (1)	ABC System (2)	Difference (3) = (2) − (1)
Direct-cost categories	2 Direct materials Direct manufacturing labor	3 Direct materials Direct manufacturing labor Direct mold cleaning and maintenance labor	1
Total direct costs	\$2,595,000	\$2,865,000	\$270,000
Indirect-cost pools	1 Single indirect-cost pool allocated using direct manufacturing labor-hours	6 Design (parts-square feet)[1] Molding machine setup (setup-hours) Machine operations (molding machine-hours) Shipment setup (number of shipments) Distribution (cubic feet delivered) Administration (direct manufacturing labor-hours)	5
Total indirect costs	\$2,385,000	\$2,115,000	(\$270,000)
Total costs assigned to simple (S3) lens	\$3,525,000	\$2,998,953	(\$526,047)
Cost per unit of simple (S3) lens	\$58.75	\$49.98	(\$8.77)
Total costs assigned to complex (CL5) lens	\$1,455,000	\$1,981,047	\$526,047
Cost per unit of complex (CL5) lens	\$97.00	\$132.07	\$35.07

[1]Cost drivers for the various indirect-cost pools are shown in parentheses.

unit-level, batch-level, and product-sustaining costs than is represented by the direct manufacturing labor-hour cost-allocation base. The S3 lens uses a disproportionately smaller amount of these costs.

The benefit of an ABC system is that it provides information to make better decisions. But managers must weigh this benefit against the measurement and implementation costs of an ABC system.

Learning Objective 6

Evaluate the costs and benefits of implementing activity-based costing systems

. . . measurement difficulties versus more accurate costs that aid in decision making

Considerations in Implementing Activity-Based Costing Systems

Managers choose the level of detail to use in a costing system by evaluating the expected costs of the system against the expected benefits that result from better decisions.

Benefits and Costs of Activity-Based Costing Systems

There are telltale signs of when an ABC system is likely to provide the most benefits. Here are some of these signs:

- Significant amounts of indirect costs are allocated using only one or two cost pools.
- All or most indirect costs are identified as output unit-level costs (few indirect costs are described as batch-level costs, product-sustaining costs, or facility-sustaining costs).
- Products make diverse demands on resources because of differences in volume, process steps, batch size, or complexity.
- Products that a company is well suited to make and sell show small profits, whereas products that a company is less suited to produce and sell show large profits.
- Operations staff has substantial disagreement with the reported costs of manufacturing and marketing products and services.

When managers decide to implement ABC, they must make important choices about the level of detail to use. Should they choose many finely specified activities, cost drivers, and cost pools, or would a few suffice? For example, Plastim's managers could identify a different molding machine-hour rate for each different type of molding machine. In making such choices, managers weigh the benefits against the costs and limitations of implementing a more detailed costing system.

The main costs and limitations of an ABC system are the measurements necessary to implement it. ABC systems require managers to estimate costs of activity pools and to identify and measure cost drivers for these pools to serve as cost-allocation bases. Even basic ABC systems require many calculations to determine costs of products and services. These measurements are costly. Activity-cost rates also need to be updated regularly.

As ABC systems get very detailed and more cost pools are created, more allocations are necessary to calculate activity costs for each cost pool, which increases the chances of misidentifying the costs of different activity cost pools. For example, supervisors are more prone to incorrectly identify the time they spend on different activities if they have to allocate their time over five activities rather than only two activities.

Occasionally, managers are also forced to use allocation bases for which data are readily available rather than allocation bases they would have liked to use. For example, a manager might be forced to use the number of loads moved, instead of the degree of difficulty and distance of different loads moved, as the allocation base for material-handling costs because data on degree of difficulty and distance of moves are difficult to obtain. When incorrect cost-allocation bases are used, activity-cost information can be misleading. For example, if the cost per load moved decreases, a company may conclude that it has become more efficient in its materials-handling operations. In fact, the lower cost per load moved may have resulted solely from moving many lighter loads over shorter distances.

Many companies, such as Kanthal, a Swedish heating elements manufacturer, have found the strategic and operational benefits of a less-detailed ABC system to be good enough to not warrant incurring the costs and challenges of operating a more detailed system. Other organizations, such as Hewlett-Packard, have implemented ABC in certain divisions (such as the Roseville Networks Division, which manufactures printed circuit boards) or functions (such as procurement and production). As improvements in information technology and accompanying declines in measurement costs continue, more detailed ABC systems have become a practical alternative in many companies. As these advancements become more widespread, more detailed ABC systems will be better able to pass the cost–benefit test.

Global surveys of company practice suggest that ABC implementation varies among companies. Nevertheless, its framework and ideas provide a standard for judging whether any simple costing system is good enough for a particular management's purposes. Any contemplated changes in a simple costing system will inevitably be improved by ABC thinking.

Behavioral Issues in Implementing Activity-Based Costing Systems

Successfully implementing ABC systems requires more than an understanding of the technical details. ABC implementation often represents a significant change in the costing system and, as the chapter indicates, requires a manager to choose how to define activities and the level of detail. What then are some of the behavioral issues that managers must be sensitive to?

1. **Gaining support of top management and creating a sense of urgency for the ABC effort.** This requires managers to clearly communicate the strategic benefits (for example, the resulting improvements in product and process design) of the ABC project. For example, at USAA Federal Savings Bank, managers demonstrated how the information gained from ABC would provide insights into the efficiency of bank operations, which was previously unavailable.
2. **Creating a guiding coalition of managers throughout the value chain for the ABC effort.** ABC systems measure how the resources of an organization are used. Managers responsible for these resources have the best knowledge about activities and cost drivers. Getting managers to cooperate and take the initiative for implementing ABC is essential for gaining the required expertise, the proper credibility, greater commitment, valuable coordination, and the necessary leadership.
3. **Educating and training employees in ABC as a basis for employee empowerment.** Disseminating information about ABC throughout an organization allows workers in all areas of a business to use their knowledge of ABC to make improvements. For example, WS Industries, an Indian manufacturer of insulators, not only shared ABC information with its workers but also established an incentive plan that gave employees a percentage of the cost savings. The results were dramatic because employees were empowered and motivated to implement numerous cost-saving projects.
4. **Seeking small short-run successes as proof that the ABC implementation is yielding results.** Too often, managers seek big results and major changes far too quickly. In many situations, achieving a significant change overnight is difficult. However, showing how ABC information has helped improve a process and save costs, even if only in small ways, motivates the team to stay on course and build momentum. The credibility gained from small victories leads to additional and bigger improvements involving larger numbers of people and different parts of the organization. Eventually ABC and ABM become rooted in the culture of the organization. Sharing short-term successes also helps motivate employees to be innovative. At USAA Federal Savings Bank, managers created a "process improvement" mailbox in Microsoft Outlook to facilitate the sharing of process improvement ideas.
5. **Recognizing that ABC information is not perfect because it balances the need for better information against the costs of creating a complex system that few managers and employees can understand.** Managers must recognize both the value and the limitations of ABC and not oversell it. Open and honest communication about ABC ensures that managers use ABC thoughtfully to make good decisions. Critical judgments can then be made without being adversarial, and tough questions can be asked to help drive better decisions about the system.

Keys to Success

ABC systems are likely to yield the most decision-making benefits when indirect costs are a high percentage of total costs or when products and services make diverse demands on indirect resources. The main costs of ABC systems are the difficulties of the measurements necessary to implement and update the systems. When implementing ABC systems, managers should be sensitive to the behavioral challenges of making changes.

Learning Objective 7

Explain how managers use activity-based costing systems in activity-based management

. . . such as pricing decisions, product-mix decisions, and cost reduction

Activity-Based Management

The emphasis of this chapter so far has been on the role of ABC systems in obtaining better product costs. However, Plastim's managers must now use this information to make decisions (Step 4 of the five-step decision process, page 212) and to implement the decision, evaluate performance, and learn (Step 5, page 212). **Activity-based management (ABM)** is a method of management decision making that uses activity-based costing information to improve customer satisfaction and profitability. We define ABM broadly to include decisions about pricing and product mix, cost reduction, process improvement, and product and process design.

Pricing and Product-Mix Decisions

An ABC system gives managers information about the costs of making and selling diverse products. With this information, managers can make pricing and product-mix decisions. For example, the ABC system indicates that Plastim can match its competitor's price of $53 for the S3 lens and still make a profit because the ABC cost of S3 is $49.98 (see Exhibit 6-5).

Plastim's managers offer Giovanni Motors a price of $52 for the S3 lens. Plastim's managers are confident that they can use the deeper understanding of costs that the ABC system provides to improve efficiency and further reduce the cost of the S3 lens. Without information from the ABC system, Plastim managers might have erroneously concluded that they would incur an operating loss on the S3 lens at a price of $53. This incorrect conclusion would have probably caused Plastim to reduce or exit its business in simple lenses and focus instead on complex lenses, where its single indirect-cost-pool system indicated it is very profitable.

Focusing on complex lenses would have been a mistake. The ABC system indicates that the cost of making the complex lens is much higher—$132.07 versus $97 indicated by the direct manufacturing labor-hour-based costing system Plastim had been using. As Plastim's operations staff had thought all along, Plastim has no competitive advantage in making CL5 lenses. At a price of $137 per lens for CL5, the profit margin is very small ($137.00 − $132.07 = $4.93). As Plastim reduces its prices on simple lenses, it would need to negotiate a higher price for complex lenses with Giovanni Motors.

Cost Reduction and Process Improvement Decisions

Manufacturing and distribution personnel use ABC systems to focus on how and where to reduce costs. Managers set cost reduction targets in terms of reducing the cost per unit of the cost-allocation base in different activity areas. For example, the supervisor of the distribution activity area at Plastim could have a performance target of decreasing distribution cost per cubic foot of products delivered from $5.80 to $5.40 by reducing distribution labor and warehouse rental costs. The goal is to reduce these costs by improving the way work is done without compromising customer service or the actual or perceived value (usefulness) customers obtain from the product or service. That is, the supervisor will attempt to take out only those costs that are *nonvalue added.* Controlling physical cost drivers, such as setup-hours or cubic feet delivered, is another fundamental way that operating personnel manage costs. For example, the distribution department can decrease distribution costs by packing the lenses in a way that reduces the bulkiness of the packages delivered.

The following table shows the reduction in distribution costs of the S3 and CL5 lenses as a result of actions that lower cost per cubic foot delivered (from $5.80 to $5.40) and total cubic feet of deliveries (from 45,000 to 40,000 for S3 and 22,500 to 20,000 for CL5).

	60,000 (S3) Lenses		15,000 (CL5) Lenses	
	Total (1)	per Unit (2) = (1) ÷ 60,000	Total (3)	per Unit (4) = (3) ÷ 15,000
Distribution costs (from Exhibit 6-5)				
S3: 45,000 cubic feet × $5.80/cubic foot	$261,000	$4.35		
CL5: 22,500 cubic feet × $5.80/cubic foot			$130,500	$8.70
Distribution costs as a result of process improvements				
S3: 40,000 cubic feet × $5.40/cubic foot	216,000	3.60		
CL5: 20,000 cubic feet × $5.40/cubic foot			108,000	7.20
Savings in distribution costs from process improvements	$ 45,000	$0.75	$ 22,500	$1.50

In the long run, total distribution costs will decrease from \$391,500 (\$261,000 + \$130,500) to \$324,000 (\$216,000 + \$108,000). In the short run, however, distribution costs may be fixed and may not decrease. Suppose all \$391,500 of distribution costs are fixed costs in the short run. The efficiency improvements (using less distribution labor and space) mean that the same \$391,500 of distribution costs can now be used to distribute 72,500 $\left(= \dfrac{\$391{,}500}{\$5.40 \text{ per cubic feet}} \right)$ cubic feet of lenses. In this case, how should costs be allocated to the S3 and CL5 lenses?

ABC systems distinguish costs incurred from resources used to design, manufacture, and deliver products and services. For the distribution activity, after process improvements,

$$\text{Costs incurred} = \$391{,}500$$
$$\text{Resources used} = \$216{,}000 \text{ (for S3 lens)} + \$108{,}000 \text{ (for CL5 lens)} = \$324{,}000$$

On the basis of the resources used by each product, Plastim's ABC system allocates \$216,000 to S3 and \$108,000 to CL5 for a total of \$324,000. The difference of \$67,500 (\$391,500 − \$324,000) is shown as costs of unused but available distribution capacity. Plastim's ABC system does not allocate the costs of unused capacity to products so as not to burden the product costs of S3 and CL5 with the cost of resources not used by these products. Instead, the system highlights the amount of unused capacity as a separate line item to signal to managers the need to reduce these costs, such as by redeploying labor to other uses or laying off workers. Concepts in Action: Activity-Based Costing at LG Electronics describes how LG Electronics used ABC to improve its purchasing practices.

Design Decisions

ABC systems help managers to evaluate the effect of current product and process designs on activities and costs and to identify new designs to reduce costs. For example, design decisions that decrease complexity of the mold reduce costs of design, materials, labor, machine setups, machine operations, and mold cleaning and maintenance. Plastim's customers may be willing to give up

Concepts in Action: Activity-Based Costing at LG Electronics

Source: Achmad Ibrahim/AP Photo

LG Electronics is one of the world's largest manufacturers of flat-screen televisions and mobile phones. To make its many electronic devices, the Seoul, South Korea–based company spends nearly \$40 billion annually on the procurement of semiconductors, metals, connectors, and other materials.

Until recently, however, LG Electronics did not have a centralized procurement system to leverage its scale and control rising supply costs. When LG Electronics hired its first chief procurement officer, he turned to activity-based costing (ABC) to identify opportunities for improvement. ABC analysis of the company's procurement system revealed that most company resources were applied to administrative and not strategic tasks. Furthermore, the administrative tasks were done manually and at a very high cost.

The ABC analysis led LG Electronics to change many of its procurement practices and processes, improve efficiency, and focus on the highest-value tasks such as managing costs of commodity products and negotiating with suppliers. Furthermore, the company developed a global procurement strategy for its televisions, mobile phones, computers, and home theater systems by implementing competitive bidding among suppliers, standardizing parts across product lines, and developing the capability to purchase more goods in China.

Sources: Based on J. Carbone, "LG Electronics centralizes purchasing to save," *Purchasing* (April 2009); K. Yoou-chul, "CPO expects to save \$1 billion in procurement," *The Korea Times* (April 1, 2009); "Linton's goals" (May 12, 2009); and M. Ihlwan, "Innovation Close-up: LG Electronics," *Bloomberg Businessweek* (April 15, 2010).

some features of the lens in exchange for a lower price. Note that Plastim's previous costing system, which used direct manufacturing labor-hours as the cost-allocation base for all indirect costs, would have mistakenly signaled that Plastim choose those designs that most reduce direct manufacturing labor-hours when, in fact, there is a weak cause-and-effect relationship between direct manufacturing labor-hours and indirect costs.

Planning and Managing Activities

Most managers implementing ABC systems for the first time start by analyzing actual costs to identify activity-cost pools and activity-cost rates. Managers then calculate a budgeted rate (as in the Plastim example) that they use for planning, making decisions, and managing activities. At year-end, managers compare budgeted costs and actual costs to evaluate how well activities were managed and make adjustments for underallocated or overallocated indirect costs for each activity using methods described in Chapter 4. As activities and processes change, managers calculate new activity-cost rates.

We return to activity-based management in later chapters. Management decisions that use activity-based costing information are described in Chapter 7, where we evaluate alternative design choices to improve efficiency and reduce non-value-added costs; in Chapter 9, where we discuss outsourcing and adding or dropping business segments; in Chapter 10, where we explain quality improvements and how to evaluate suppliers; in Chapter 12, where we discuss activity-based budgeting; and in Chapter 14, where we present reengineering and downsizing.

Keys to Success

Managers distinguish costs incurred from resources used and find ABC systems useful for decisions such as pricing, product and process redesign, cost reduction, and process improvement.

ABC in Service and Merchandising Companies

Although many early examples of ABC originated in manufacturing, managers also use ABC in service and merchandising companies. For instance, the Plastim example includes the application of ABC to a service activity—design—and to a merchandising activity—distribution. Companies such as the Cooperative Bank, Braintree Hospital, BCTel in the telecommunications industry, and Union Pacific in the railroad industry have implemented some form of ABC systems to identify profitable product mixes, improve efficiency, and satisfy customers. Similarly, many retail and wholesale companies—for example, Supervalu, a retailer and distributor of grocery store products, and Owens and Minor, a medical supplies distributor—have used ABC systems.

The widespread use of ABC systems in service and merchandising companies reinforces the idea that ABC systems are used by managers for strategic decisions rather than for inventory valuation. (Inventory valuation is fairly straightforward in merchandising companies and not needed in service companies.) Service companies, in particular, find great value from ABC because a vast majority of their cost structure comprises indirect costs. After all, there are few direct costs when a bank makes a loan or when a representative answers a phone call at a call center. As we have seen, a major benefit of ABC is its ability to assign indirect costs to cost objects by identifying activities and cost drivers. As a result, ABC systems provide greater insight than traditional systems into the management of these indirect costs. The general approach to ABC in service and merchandising companies is similar to the ABC approach in manufacturing.

The Cooperative Bank followed the approach described in this chapter when it implemented ABC in its retail banking operations. Managers calculated the cost rates of various activities, such as performing ATM transactions, opening and closing accounts, administering mortgages, and processing Visa transactions by dividing the cost of these activities by the time available to do them. They used these time-based rates to cost individual products, such as checking accounts, mortgages, and Visa cards, and the costs of supporting different types of customers. Information from this time-driven activity-based costing system helped the Cooperative Bank to improve its processes and to identify profitable products and customer segments. Concepts in Action: Hospitals Use Time-Driven Activity-Based Costing to Reduce Costs and Improve Care describes how hospitals, such as the M.D. Anderson Cancer Research Center in Houston and Children's Hospital in Boston, have similarly benefited from using ABC analysis.

Activity-based costing raises some interesting issues when it is applied to a public service institution, such as the U.S. Postal Service. The costs of delivering mail to remote locations are far greater than the costs of delivering mail within urban areas. However, for fairness and community-building reasons, the Postal Service cannot charge higher prices to customers in remote areas. In this case, activity-based costing is valuable for understanding, managing, and reducing costs but not for pricing decisions.

Concepts in Action: Hospitals Use Time-Driven Activity-Based Costing to Reduce Costs and Improve Care

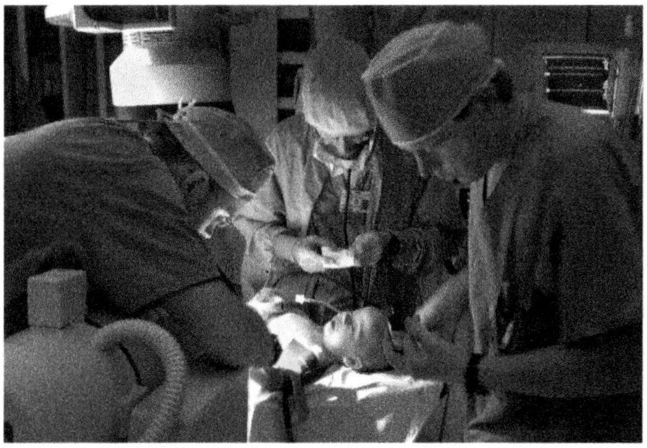
Source: Susan Stocker KRT/Newscom

In the United States, health care costs in 2012 exceeded 17% of gross domestic product and continue to rise. Several medical centers, such as the M.D. Anderson Cancer Center in Houston and Children's Hospital in Boston, are using time-driven activity-based costing (TDABC) to help bring accurate cost and value measurement practices into the health-care delivery system.

TDABC assigns all of the organization's resource costs to cost objects using a framework that requires two sets of estimates. TDABC first calculates the cost of supplying resource capacity, such as a doctor's time. The total cost of resources—including personnel, supervision, insurance, space occupancy, technology, and supplies—is divided by the available capacity—the time available for doctors to do their work—to obtain the capacity cost rate. Next, TDABC uses the capacity cost rate to drive resource costs to cost objects, such as the number of patients seen, by estimating the demand for resource capacity (time) that the cost object requires.

Medical centers implementing TDABC have succeeded in "bending the health care cost curve." For head and neck procedures at the M.D. Anderson Cancer Center, the TDABC-modified process resulted in a 16% reduction in process time, a 12% decrease in costs for technical staff, and a 67% reduction in costs for professional staff (physicians and other providers). As a result, total costs fell 36% per patient. Prior to implementing TDABC, managers did not have the necessary information to make decisions to reduce costs.

More broadly, health-care providers implementing TDABC have found that better outcomes for patients often go hand in hand with lower total costs. For example, spending more on early detection and better diagnosis of disease spares patients suffering and often leads to less-complex and less-expensive care. With the insights from TDABC, health-care providers can utilize medical staff, equipment, facilities, and administrative resources far more efficiently; streamline the path of patients through the system; and select treatment approaches that improve outcomes while eliminating services that do not.

Sources: Based on R. S. Kaplan and S. R. Anderson, "The Innovation of Time-Driven Activity-Based Costing," *Cost Management* (March-April 2007); R. S. Kaplan and S. R. Anderson, "Time-Drive Activity-Based Costing" (Boston, MA: Harvard Business School Press, 2007); and R. S. Kaplan and M. E. Porter, "How to Solve the Cost Crisis in Health Care," *Harvard Business Review* (September 2011).

Problem for Self-Study

Family Supermarkets (FS) has decided to increase the size of its Memphis store. It wants information about the profitability of individual product lines: soft drinks, fresh produce, and packaged food. FS provides the following data for 2013 for each product line:

	Soft Drinks	Fresh Produce	Packaged Food
Revenues	$317,400	$840,240	$483,960
Cost of goods sold	$240,000	$600,000	$360,000
Cost of bottles returned	$4,800	$0	$0
Number of purchase orders placed	144	336	144
Number of deliveries received	120	876	264
Hours of shelf-stocking time	216	2,160	1,080
Items sold	50,400	441,600	122,400

FS also provides the following information for 2013:

Activity (1)	Description of Activity (2)	Total Support Costs (3)	Cost-Allocation Base (4)
1. Bottle returns	Returning of empty bottles to store	$ 4,800	Direct tracing to soft-drink line
2. Ordering	Placing of orders for purchases	$ 62,400	624 purchase orders
3. Delivery	Physical delivery and receipt of merchandise	$100,800	1,260 deliveries
4. Shelf-stocking	Stocking of merchandise on store shelves and ongoing restocking	$ 69,120	3,456 hours of shelf-stocking time
5. Customer support	Assistance provided to customers, including checkout and bagging	$122,880	614,400 items sold
Total		$360,000	

Required

1. Family Supermarkets currently allocates store support costs (all costs other than cost of goods sold) to product lines on the basis of cost of goods sold of each product line. Calculate the operating income and operating income as a percentage of revenues for each product line.
2. If Family Supermarkets allocates store support costs (all costs other than cost of goods sold) to product lines using an ABC system, calculate the operating income and operating income as a percentage of revenues for each product line.
3. Comment on your answers in requirements 1 and 2.

Solution

1. The following table shows the operating income and operating income as a percentage of revenues for each product line. All store support costs (all costs other than cost of goods sold) are allocated to product lines using cost of goods sold of each product line as the cost-allocation base. Total store support costs equal $360,000 (cost of bottles returned, $4,800 + cost of purchase orders, $62,400 + cost of deliveries, $100,800 + cost of shelf-stocking, $69,120 + cost of customer support, $122,880). The allocation rate for store support costs = $360,000 ÷ $1,200,000 (soft drinks, $240,000 + fresh produce, $600,000 + packaged food, $360,000) = 30% of cost of goods sold. To allocate support costs to each product line, FS multiplies the cost of goods sold of each product line by 0.30.

	Soft Drinks	Fresh Produce	Packaged Food	Total
Revenues	$317,400	$840,240	$483,960	$1,641,600
Cost of goods sold	240,000	600,000	360,000	1,200,000
Store support cost				
($240,000; $600,000; $360,000) × 0.30	72,000	180,000	108,000	360,000
Total costs	312,000	780,000	468,000	1,560,000
Operating income	$ 5,400	$ 60,240	$ 15,960	$ 81,600
Operating income ÷ Revenues	1.70%	7.17%	3.30%	4.97%

2. The ABC system identifies bottle-return costs as a direct cost because these costs can be traced to the soft drink product line. FS then calculates cost-allocation rates for each activity area (as in Step 5 of the seven-step costing system, described earlier on page 220). The activity rates are as follows.

Activity (1)	Cost Hierarchy (2)	Total Costs (3)	Quantity of Cost-Allocation Base (4)	Overhead Allocation Rate (5) = (3) ÷ (4)
Ordering	Batch-level	$62,400	624 purchase orders	$100 per purchase order
Delivery	Batch-level	$100,800	1,260 deliveries	$80 per delivery
Shelf-stocking	Output unit–level	$69,120	3,456 shelf-stocking hours	$20 per stocking-hour
Customer support	Output unit–level	$122,880	614,400 items sold	$0.20 per item sold

Store support costs for each product line by activity are obtained by multiplying the total quantity of the cost-allocation base for each product line by the activity cost rate. Operating income and operating income as a percentage of revenues for each product line are as follows.

	Soft Drinks	Fresh Produce	Packaged Food	Total
Revenues	$317,400	$840,240	$483,960	$1,641,600
Cost of goods sold	240,000	600,000	360,000	1,200,000
Bottle-return costs	4,800	0	0	4,800
Ordering costs				
(144; 336; 144) purchase orders × $100	14,400	33,600	14,400	62,400
Delivery costs				
(120; 876; 264) deliveries × $80	9,600	70,080	21,120	100,800
Shelf-stocking costs				
(216; 2,160; 1,080) stocking-hours × $20	4,320	43,200	21,600	69,120
Customer-support costs				
(50,400; 441,600; 122,400) items sold × $0.20	10,080	88,320	24,480	122,880
Total costs	283,200	835,200	441,600	1,560,000
Operating income	$ 34,200	$ 5,040	$ 42,360	$ 81,600
Operating income ÷ Revenues	10.78%	0.60%	8.75%	4.97%

3. Managers believe the ABC system is more credible than the simple costing system. The ABC system distinguishes the different types of activities at FS more precisely. It also tracks more accurately how individual product lines use resources. Rankings of relative profitability—operating

income as a percentage of revenues—of the three product lines under the simple costing system and under the ABC system are as follows.

Simple Costing System		ABC System	
1. Fresh produce	7.17%	1. Soft drinks	10.78%
2. Packaged food	3.30%	2. Packaged food	8.75%
3. Soft drinks	1.70%	3. Fresh produce	0.60%

The percentage of revenues, cost of goods sold, and activity costs for each product line are as follows.

	Soft Drinks	Fresh Produce	Packaged Food
Revenues	19.34%	51.18%	29.48%
Cost of goods sold	20.00	50.00	30.00
Bottle returns	100.00	0	0
Activity areas:			
Ordering	23.08	53.84	23.08
Delivery	9.53	69.52	20.95
Shelf-stocking	6.25	62.50	31.25
Customer Support	8.20	71.88	19.92

Soft drinks have fewer deliveries and require less shelf-stocking time and customer support than either fresh produce or packaged food. Most major soft-drink suppliers deliver merchandise to the store shelves and stock the shelves themselves. In contrast, the fresh produce area has the most deliveries and consumes a large percentage of shelf-stocking time. It also has the highest number of individual sales items and so requires the most customer support. The simple costing system assumed that each product line used the resources in each activity area in the same ratio as their respective individual cost of goods sold to total cost of goods sold. Clearly, this assumption is incorrect. Relative to cost of goods sold, soft drinks and packaged food use fewer resources while fresh produce uses more resources. As a result, the ABC system reduces the costs assigned to soft drinks and packaged food and increases the costs assigned to fresh produce. The simple costing system is an example of averaging that is too broad.

FS managers can use the ABC information to guide decisions such as how to allocate a planned increase in floor space. An increase in the percentage of space allocated to soft drinks is warranted. Note, however, that ABC information is only one input into decisions about shelf-space allocation. In many situations, companies cannot make product decisions in isolation but must consider the effect that dropping or deemphasizing a product might have on customer demand for other products. For example, FS will have a minimum limit on the shelf space allocated to fresh produce because reducing the choice of fresh produce will lead to customers not shopping at FS, resulting in loss of sales of other, more profitable products.

Pricing decisions can also be made in a more informed way with ABC information. For example, suppose a competitor announces a 5% reduction in soft-drink prices. Given the 10.78% margin FS currently earns on its soft-drink product line, it has flexibility to reduce prices and still make a profit on this product line. In contrast, the simple costing system erroneously implied that soft drinks only had a 1.70% margin, leaving little room to counter a competitor's pricing initiatives.

Decision Points

The following question-and-answer format summarizes the chapter's learning objectives. Each decision presents a key question related to a learning objective. The guidelines are the answer to that question.

Decision	Guidelines
1. When does product undercosting or overcosting occur?	Product undercosting (overcosting) occurs when a product or service consumes a high (low) level of resources but is reported to have a low (high) cost. Broad averaging, or peanut-butter costing, a common cause of undercosting or overcosting, is the result of using broad averages that uniformly assign, or spread, the cost of resources to products when the individual products use those resources in a nonuniform way. Product-cost cross-subsidization exists when one undercosted (overcosted) product results in at least one other product being overcosted (undercosted).
2. How do managers refine a costing system?	Refining a costing system means making changes that result in cost numbers that better measure the way different cost objects, such as products, use different amounts of resources of the company. These changes can require additional direct-cost tracing, the choice of more homogeneous indirect cost pools, or the use of cost drivers as cost-allocation bases.
3. What is the difference between the design of a simple costing system and an activity-based costing (ABC) system?	The ABC system differs from the simple system by its fundamental focus on activities. The ABC system typically has more homogeneous indirect-cost pools than the simple system, and more cost drivers are used as cost-allocation bases.
4. What is a cost hierarchy?	A cost hierarchy categorizes costs into different cost pools on the basis of the different types of cost-allocation bases or different degrees of difficulty in determining cause-and-effect (or benefits-received) relationships. A four-part hierarchy to cost products consists of output unit-level costs, batch-level costs, product-sustaining or service-sustaining costs, and facility-sustaining costs.
5. How do managers cost products or services using ABC systems?	In ABC, managers calculate costs of activities and use activity-cost rates to assign costs to other cost objects such as products or services based on the activities the products or services consume.
6. What should managers consider when deciding to implement ABC systems?	ABC systems are likely to yield the most decision-making benefits when indirect costs are a high percentage of total costs or when products and services make diverse demands on indirect resources. The main costs of ABC systems are the difficulties of the measurements necessary to implement and update the systems.
7. How can ABC systems be used to manage better?	Activity-based management (ABM) is a management method of decision making that uses ABC information to satisfy customers and improve profits. Managers use ABC systems to make decisions such as pricing, product mix, cost reduction, process improvement, product and process redesign, and planning and managing activities.

Terms to Learn

This chapter and the Glossary at the end of this book contain definitions of the following important terms:

activity (p. 213)
activity-based costing (ABC) (p. 213)
activity-based management (ABM) (p. 224)
batch-level costs (p. 216)
cost hierarchy (p. 216)
facility-sustaining costs (p. 217)
output unit-level costs (p. 216)
product-cost cross-subsidization (p. 207)
product overcosting (p. 207)
product-sustaining costs (p. 216)
product undercosting (p. 207)
refined costing system (p. 212)
service-sustaining costs (p. 216)

Assignment Material

Questions

6-1 What is broad averaging and what consequences can it have on costs?

6-2 Why is it important to classify costs into a cost hierarchy?

6-3 What are the key reasons for product-cost differences between simple costing systems and ABC systems?

6-4 What is the benefit of distinguishing costs incurred from resources used?

6-5 Describe four signs that help indicate when ABC systems are likely to provide the most benefits.

6-6 Describe four decisions for which ABC information is useful. What are the main costs and limitations of implementing ABC systems?

6-7 "ABC systems only apply to manufacturing companies." Do you agree? Explain.

6-8 "Activity-based costing is the wave of the present and the future. All companies should adopt it." Do you agree? Explain.

6-9 "Increasing the number of indirect-cost pools is guaranteed to sizably increase the accuracy of product or service costs." Do you agree? Why?

6-10 The controller of a retail company has just had a $50,000 request to implement an ABC system quickly turned down. A senior vice president, in rejecting the request, noted, "Given a choice, I will always prefer a $50,000 investment in improving things a customer sees or experiences, such as our shelves or our store layout. How does a customer benefit by our spending $50,000 on a supposedly better accounting system?" How should the controller respond?

Exercises

6-11 Cost hierarchy. Harrison, Inc., manufactures karaoke machines for several well-known companies. The machines differ significantly in their complexity and their manufacturing batch sizes. The following costs were incurred in 2013:

a. Indirect manufacturing labor costs such as supervision that supports direct manufacturing labor, $725,000

b. Procurement costs of placing purchase orders, receiving materials, and paying suppliers related to the number of purchase orders placed, $425,000

c. Cost of indirect materials, $137,500

d. Costs incurred to set up machines each time a different product needs to be manufactured, $315,000

e. Designing processes, drawing process charts, making engineering process changes for products, $387,500

f. Machine-related overhead costs such as depreciation, maintenance, and production engineering, $750,000 (These resources relate to the activity of running the machines.)

g. Plant management, plant rent, and plant insurance, $462,500

Required

1. Classify each of the preceding costs as output unit-level, batch-level, product-sustaining, or facility-sustaining. Explain each answer.

2. Consider two types of karaoke machines made by Harrison, Inc. One machine, designed for professional use, is complex to make and is produced in many batches. The other machine, designed for home use, is simple to make and is produced in few batches. Suppose that Harrison needs the same number of machine-hours to make each type of karaoke machine and that Harrison allocates all overhead costs using machine-hours as the only allocation base. How, if at all, would the machines be miscosted? Briefly explain why.
3. How is the cost hierarchy helpful to Harrison in managing its business?

6-12 ABC, cost hierarchy, service. (CMA, adapted) Ayer Test Laboratories does heat testing (HT) and stress testing (ST) on materials and operates at capacity. Under its current simple costing system, Ayer aggregates all operating costs of $1,330,000 into a single overhead cost pool. Ayer calculates a rate per test-hour of $14 ($1,330,000 ÷ 95,000 total test-hours). HT uses 55,000 test-hours, and ST uses 40,000 test-hours. Gary Daley, Ayer's controller, believes that there is enough variation in test procedures and cost structures to establish separate costing and billing rates for HT and ST. The market for test services is becoming competitive. Without this information, any miscosting and mispricing of its services could cause Ayer to lose business. Daley divides Ayer's costs into four activity-cost categories.

a. Direct-labor costs, $222,000. These costs can be directly traced to HT, $155,000, and ST, $67,000.
b. Equipment-related costs (rent, maintenance, energy, and so on), $475,000. These costs are allocated to HT and ST on the basis of test-hours.
c. Setup costs, $385,000. These costs are allocated to HT and ST on the basis of the number of setup-hours required. HT requires 13,000 setup-hours, and ST requires 4,500 setup-hours.
d. Costs of designing tests, $248,000. These costs are allocated to HT and ST on the basis of the time required for designing the tests. HT requires 3,000 hours, and ST requires 1,000 hours.

Required

1. Classify each activity cost as output unit-level, batch-level, product- or service-sustaining, or facility-sustaining. Explain each answer.
2. Calculate the cost per test-hour for HT and ST using ABC. Explain briefly the reasons why these numbers differ from the $14 per test-hour that Ayer calculated using its simple costing system.
3. Explain the accuracy of the product costs calculated using the simple costing system and the ABC system. How might Ayer's management use the cost hierarchy and ABC information to better manage its business?

6-13 Alternative allocation bases for a professional services firm. The Wilmer Group (WG) provides tax advice to multinational firms. WG charges clients for (a) direct professional time (at an hourly rate) and (b) support services (at 30% of the direct professional costs billed). The three professionals in WG and their rates per professional hour are as follows.

Professional	Billing Rate per Hour
Mark Wilmer	$500
Ashley Bennet	170
John Amesbury	70

WG has just prepared the May 2013 bills for two clients. The hours of professional time spent on each client are as follows.

	Hours per Client	
Professional	San Antonio Dominion	Amsterdam Enterprises
Wilmer	21	3
Bennet	4	11
Amesbury	30	41
Total	55	55

Required

1. What amounts did WG bill to San Antonio Dominion and Amsterdam Enterprises for May 2013?
2. Suppose support services were billed at $55 per professional labor-hour (instead of 30% of professional labor costs). How would this change affect the amounts WG billed to the two clients for May 2013? Comment on the differences between the amounts billed in requirements 1 and 2.

3. How would you determine whether professional labor costs or professional labor-hours is the more appropriate allocation base for WG's support services?

6-14 Plantwide and ABC indirect cost rates. Driven Products (DP) designs and produces automotive parts. In 2013, actual manufacturing overhead is $617,200. DP's simple costing system allocates manufacturing overhead to its three customers based on machine-hours and prices its contracts based on full costs. One of its customers has regularly complained of being charged noncompetitive prices, so DP's controller Mike Jones realizes that it is time to examine the consumption of overhead resources more closely by adopting an activity-based costing (ABC) system. He knows that there are three main activities that consume overhead resources: design, production, and engineering. Interviews with operating personnel and examination of time records yield the following detailed information:

			Usage of Cost Drivers by Customer Contract		
Activity	Cost Driver	Manufacturing Overhead in 2013	Bates Motors	Hathaway Motors	Landon Auto
Design	CAD-design-hours	$ 78,000	110	200	80
Production	Engineering-hours	59,200	70	60	240
Engineering	Machine-hours	480,000	120	2,800	1,080
Total		$617,200			

Required

1. Compute the manufacturing overhead allocated to each customer in 2013 using the simple costing system that uses machine-hours as the allocation base.
2. Compute the manufacturing overhead allocated to each customer in 2013 using activity-based manufacturing overhead rates.
3. Comment on your answers in requirements 1 and 2. Which customer do you think was complaining about being overcharged in the simple system? If the new activity-based rates are used to price contracts, which customer(s) will be unhappy? How would you respond to these concerns?
4. How else might DP use the information available from its activity-based costing analysis of manufacturing overhead costs?
5. DP's managers are wondering if they should further refine the ABC system by identifying more activities. Under what conditions would it not be worthwhile to further refine the ABC system?

6-15 Department and activity-cost rates. Triumph Trophies makes trophies and plaques and operates at capacity. Triumph does large custom orders, such as the participant trophies for the Minnetonka Little League. The controller has asked you to compare Triumph's current costing system that allocates total overhead costs of each department to products and an activity-based costing system.

Triumph Trophies Budgeted Information for the Year Ended November 30, 2013

Forming Department	Trophies	Plaques	Total
Direct materials	$26,000	$22,500	$48,500
Direct manufacturing labor	31,200	18,000	49,200
Overhead costs			
Setup			24,000
Supervision			20,772
Assembly Department	**Trophies**	**Plaques**	**Total**
Direct materials	$ 5,200	$18,750	$23,950
Direct manufacturing labor	15,600	21,000	36,600
Overhead costs			
Setup			46,000
Supervision			21,920

Other information follows.

Setup costs in each department vary with the number of batches processed in each department. The budgeted number of batches for each product line in each department is as follows.

	Trophies	Plaques
Forming department	40	116
Assembly department	43	103

Supervision costs in each department vary with direct manufacturing labor costs in each department.

Required

1. Calculate the budgeted cost of trophies and plaques based on departmental overhead rates, where forming department overhead costs are allocated based on direct manufacturing labor costs of the forming department, and assembly department overhead costs are allocated based on total direct costs of the assembly department.
2. Calculate the budgeted cost of trophies and plaques if Triumph allocates overhead costs in each department using activity-based costing.
3. Explain how the disaggregation of information could improve or reduce decision quality.

6-16 ABC, process costing. Potvin Company produces mathematical and financial calculators and operates at capacity. Data related to the two products are presented here:

	Mathematical	Financial
Annual production in units	25,000	50,000
Direct material costs	$62,500	$125,000
Direct manufacturing labor costs	$25,000	$ 50,000
Direct manufacturing labor-hours	1,250	2,500
Machine-hours	20,000	50,000
Number of production runs	50	50
Inspection hours	800	400

Total manufacturing overhead costs are as follows.

	Total
Machining costs	$350,000
Setup costs	117,000
Inspection costs	96,000

Required

1. Choose a cost driver for each overhead cost pool and calculate the manufacturing overhead cost per unit for each product.
2. Compute the manufacturing cost per unit for each product.
3. How might Potvin use the new cost information from its activity-based costing system to better manage its business?

6-17 Activity-based costing, service company. Speediprint Corporation owns a small printing press that prints leaflets, brochures, and advertising materials. Speediprint classifies its various printing jobs as standard jobs or special jobs. Speediprint's simple job-costing system has two direct-cost categories (direct materials and direct labor) and a single indirect-cost pool. Speediprint operates at capacity and allocates all indirect costs using printing machine-hours as the allocation base.

Speediprint is concerned about the accuracy of the costs assigned to standard and special jobs and therefore is planning to implement an activity-based costing system. Speediprint's ABC system would have the same direct-cost categories as its simple costing system. However, instead of a single indirect-cost pool there would now be six categories for assigning indirect costs: design, purchasing, setup, printing machine operations, marketing, and administration. To see how activity-based costing would affect the costs of standard and special jobs, Speediprint collects the following information for the fiscal year 2013 that just ended.

	Standard Job	Special Job	Total	Cause-and-Effect Relationship Between Allocation Base and Activity Cost
Number of printing jobs	400	200		
Price per job	$ 600	$ 750		
Cost of supplies per job	$ 100	$ 125		
Direct labor cost per job	$ 90	$ 100		
Printing machine-hours per job	10	10		
Cost of printing machine operations			$75,000	Indirect costs of operating printing machines increase with printing machine hours
Setup-hours per job	4	7		
Setup costs			$45,000	Indirect setup costs increase with setup-hours
Total number of purchase orders	400	500		
Purchase order costs			$18,000	Indirect purchase order costs increase with the number of purchase orders
Design costs	$4,000	$16,000	$20,000	Design costs are allocated to standard and special jobs based on a special study of the design department
Marketing costs as a percentage of revenues	5%	5%	$19,500	
Administration costs			$24,000	Demand for administrative resources increases with direct labor costs

Required

1. Calculate the cost of a standard job and a special job under the simple costing system.
2. Calculate the cost of a standard job and a special job under the activity-based costing system.
3. Compare the costs of a standard job and a special job in requirements 1 and 2. Why do the simple and activity-based costing systems differ in the cost of a standard job and a special job?
4. How might Speediprint use the new cost information from its activity-based costing system to better manage its business?

6-18 Activity-based costing, manufacturing. Decorative Doors, Inc., produces two types of doors, interior and exterior. The company's simple costing system has two direct cost categories (materials and labor) and one indirect cost pool. The simple costing system allocates indirect costs on the basis of machine-hours. Recently, the owners of Decorative Doors have been concerned about a decline in the market share for their interior doors, usually their biggest seller. Information related to Decorative Doors production for the most recent year follows.

	Interior	Exterior
Units sold	3,200	1,800
Selling price	$ 125	$ 200
Direct material cost per unit	$ 30	$ 45
Direct manufacturing labor cost per hour	$ 16	$ 16
Direct manufacturing labor-hours per unit	1.50	2.25
Production runs	40	85
Material moves	72	168
Machine setups	45	155
Machine-hours	5,500	4,500
Number of inspections	250	150

The owners have heard of other companies in the industry that are now using an activity-based costing system and are curious how an ABC system would affect their product costing decisions. After analyzing the indirect cost pool for Decorative Doors, six activities were identified as generating indirect costs: production scheduling, material handling, machine setup, assembly, inspection, and marketing. Decorative Doors collected the following data related to the indirect cost activities:

Activity	Activity Cost	Activity Cost Driver
Production scheduling	$95,000	Production runs
Material handling	$45,000	Material moves
Machine setup	$25,000	Machine setups
Assembly	$60,000	Machine-hours
Inspection	$ 8,000	Number of inspections

Marketing costs were determined to be 3% of the sales revenue for each type of door.

Required

1. Calculate the cost of an interior door and an exterior door under the existing simple costing system.
2. Calculate the cost of an interior door and an exterior door under an activity-based costing system.
3. Compare the costs of the doors in requirements 1 and 2. Why do the simple and activity-based costing systems differ in the cost of an interior and exterior door?
4. How might Decorative Doors, Inc., use the new cost information from its activity-based costing system to address the declining market share for interior doors?

6-19 ABC, retail product-line profitability. Granger Supermarkets (GS) operates at capacity and decides to apply ABC analysis to three product lines: baked goods, milk and fruit juice, and frozen foods. It identifies four activities and their activity cost rates:

Ordering	$98 per purchase order
Delivery and receipt of merchandise	$81 per delivery
Shelf-stocking	$22 per hour
Customer support and assistance	$0.18 per item sold

The revenues, cost of goods sold, store support costs, the activities that account for the store support costs, and activity-area usage of the three product lines are as follows.

	Baked Goods	Milk and Fruit Juice	Frozen Products
Financial data			
Revenues	$58,000	$64,000	$52,500
Cost of goods sold	$37,000	$45,000	$36,000
Store support	$11,100	$13,500	$10,800
Activity-area usage (cost-allocation base)			
Ordering (purchase orders)	35	30	20
Delivery (deliveries)	85	45	30
Shelf-stocking (hours)	175	155	25
Customer support (items sold)	12,000	16,000	7,000

Under its simple costing system, GS allocated support costs to products at the rate of 30% of cost of goods sold.

Required

1. Use the simple costing system to prepare a product-line profitability report for GS.
2. Use the ABC system to prepare a product-line profitability report for GS.
3. What new insights does the ABC system in requirement 2 provide to GS's managers?

6-20 ABC, wholesale, customer profitability. Ruiz Wholesalers operates at capacity and sells furniture items to four department-store chains (customers). Mr. Ruiz commented, "We apply ABC to determine product-line profitability. The same ideas apply to customer profitability, and we should find out our customer profitability as well." Ruiz Wholesalers sends catalogs to corporate purchasing departments on a monthly basis. The customers are entitled to return unsold merchandise within a 6-month period from the purchase date and receive a full purchase price refund. The following data were collected from last year's operations:

	Chain			
	1	2	3	4
Gross sales	$75,000	$45,000	$95,000	$85,000
Sales returns:				
Number of items	101	28	68	35
Amount	$15,000	$ 6,500	$ 6,650	$ 8,000
Number of orders:				
Regular	65	165	57	90
Rush	18	56	9	40

Ruiz has calculated the following activity rates:

Activity	Cost-Driver Rate
Regular order processing	$32 per regular order
Rush order processing	$160 per rush order
Returned items processing	$20 per item
Catalogs and customer support	$1,000 per customer

Customers pay the transportation costs. The cost of goods sold averages 80% of sales.

Required Determine the contribution to profit from each chain last year. Comment on your solution.

6-21 ABC, activity area cost-driver rates, product cross-subsidization. Ionia Potatoes (IP) operates at capacity and processes potatoes into potato cuts at its highly automated Pocatello plant. It sells potatoes to the retail consumer market and to the institutional market, which includes hospitals, cafeterias, and university dormitories.

IP's simple costing system, which does not distinguish between potato cuts processed for retail and institutional markets, has a single direct-cost category (direct materials; that is, raw potatoes) and a single indirect-cost pool (production support). Support costs, which include packaging materials, are allocated on the basis of pounds of potato cuts processed. The company uses 1,800,000 pounds of raw potatoes to process 1,600,000 pounds of potato cuts. At the end of 2013, IP unsuccessfully bid for a large institutional contract. Its bid was reported to be 30% above the winning bid. This feedback came as a shock because IP included only a minimum profit margin on its bid, and the Pocatello plant was acknowledged as the most efficient in the industry.

As a result of its review process of the lost contract bid, IP decided to explore ways to refine its costing system. The company determined that 90% of the direct materials (raw potatoes) related to the retail market and 10% to the institutional market. In addition, the company identified that packaging materials could be directly traced to individual jobs ($190,000 for retail and $9,000 for institutional). Also, the company used ABC to identify three main activity areas that generated support costs: cleaning, cutting, and packaging.

- **Cleaning Activity Area**—The cost-allocation base is pounds of raw potatoes cleaned.
- **Cutting Activity Area**—The production line produces (a) 150 pounds of retail potato cuts per cutting-hour and (b) 200 pounds of institutional potato cuts per cutting-hour. The cost-allocation base is cutting-hours on the production line.
- **Packaging Activity Area**—The packaging line packages (a) 25 pounds of retail potato cuts per packaging-hour and (b) 80 pounds of institutional potato cuts per packaging-hour. The cost-allocation base is packaging-hours on the production line.

The following table summarizes the actual costs for 2013 before and after the preceding cost analysis.

	Before the Cost Analysis	After the Cost Analysis			
		Production Support	Retail	Institutional	Total
Direct materials used					
Potatoes	$ 231,000		$207,900	$23,100	$ 231,000
Packaging			190,000	9,000	199,000
Production support	1,689,000				
Cleaning		$ 270,000			270,000
Cutting		624,000			624,000
Packaging		596,000			596,000
Total	$1,920,000	$1,490,000	$397,900	$32,100	$1,920,000

Required

1. Using the simple costing system, what is the cost per pound of potato cuts produced by IP?
2. Calculate the cost rate per unit of the cost driver in the (a) cleaning, (b) cutting, and (c) packaging activity areas.
3. Suppose IP uses information from its activity cost rates to calculate costs incurred on retail potato cuts and institutional potato cuts. Using the ABC system, what is the cost per pound of (a) retail potato cuts and (b) institutional potato cuts?
4. Comment on the cost differences between the two costing systems in requirements 1 and 3. How might IP use the information in requirement 3 to make better decisions?

6-22 Activity-based costing. The job costing system at Sheri's Custom Framing has five indirect cost pools (purchasing, material handling, machine maintenance, product inspection, and packaging). The company is in the process of bidding on two jobs; Job 215, an order of 15 intricate personalized frames, and Job 325, an order of 6 standard personalized frames. The controller wants you to compare overhead allocated under the current simple job-costing system and a newly designed activity-based job-costing system. Total budgeted costs in each indirect cost pool and the budgeted quantity of activity driver are as follows.

	Budgeted Overhead	Activity Driver	Budgeted Quantity of Activity Driver
Purchasing	$ 35,000	Purchase orders processed	2,000
Material handling	43,750	Material moves	5,000
Machine maintenance	118,650	Machine-hours	10,500
Product inspection	9,450	Inspections	1,200
Packaging	19,950	Units produced	3,800
	$226,800		

Information related to Job 215 and Job 325 follows. Job 215 incurs more batch-level costs because it uses more types of materials that need to be purchased, moved, and inspected relative to Job 325.

	Job 215	Job 325
Number of purchase orders	25	8
Number of material moves	10	4
Machine-hours	40	60
Number of inspections	9	3
Units produced	15	6

Required

1. Compute the total overhead allocated to each job under a simple costing system, where overhead is allocated based on machine-hours.

2. Compute the total overhead allocated to each job under an activity-based costing system using the appropriate activity drivers.
3. Explain why Sheri's Custom Framing might favor the ABC job-costing system over the simple job-costing system, especially in its bidding process.

6-23 ABC, product costing at banks, cross-subsidization. United International Bank (UIB) is examining the profitability of its Premier Account, a combined savings and checking account. Depositors receive a 7% annual interest rate on their average deposit. UIB earns an interest rate spread of 3% (the difference between the rate at which it lends money and the rate it pays depositors) by lending money for home loan purposes at 10%. Thus, UIB would gain $60 on the interest spread if a depositor had an average Premier Account balance of $2,000 in 2013 ($\$2,000 \times 3\% = \$60$).

The Premier Account allows depositors unlimited use of services such as deposits, withdrawals, checking accounts, and foreign currency drafts. Depositors with Premier Account balances of $1,000 or more receive unlimited free use of services. Depositors with minimum balances of less than $1,000 pay a $20-a-month service fee for their Premier Account.

UIB recently conducted an activity-based costing study of its services. It assessed the following costs for six individual services. The use of these services in 2013 by three customers is as follows.

	Activity-Based Cost per "Transaction"	Account Usage		
		Harvin	Slaton	Flynn
Deposit/withdrawal with teller	$ 2.40	41	54	6
Deposit/withdrawal with automatic teller machine (ATM)	0.80	12	18	13
Deposit/withdrawal on prearranged monthly basis	0.60	0	10	64
Bank checks written	7.90	8	2	4
Foreign currency drafts	12.00	5	3	7
Inquiries about account balance	1.70	10	18	6
Average Premier Account balance for 2013		$1,325	$850	$25,400

Assume Harvin and Flynn always maintain a balance above $1,000, whereas Slaton always has a balance below $1,000.

Required

1. Compute the 2013 profitability of the Harvin, Slaton, and Flynn Premier Accounts at UIB.
2. Why might UIB worry about the profitability of individual customers if the Premier Account product offering is profitable as a whole?
3. What changes would you recommend for UIB's Premier Account?

Problems

6-24 Job costing with single direct-cost category, single indirect-cost pool, law firm. Timlin Associates is a recently formed law partnership. Ellery Hanley, the managing partner of Timlin Associates, has just finished a tense phone call with Martin Offiah, president of Widnes Coal. Offiah strongly complained about the price Timlin charged for some legal work done for Widnes Coal.

Hanley also received a phone call from its only other client, St. Helen's Glass, which was very pleased with both the quality of the work and the price charged on its most recent job.

Timlin Associates operates at capacity and uses a cost-based approach to pricing (billing) each job. Currently, it uses a simple costing system with a single direct-cost category (professional labor-hours) and a single indirect-cost pool (general support). Indirect costs are allocated to cases on the basis of professional labor-hours per case. The job files show the following:

	Widnes Coal	St. Helen's Glass
Professional labor	115 hours	95 hours

Professional labor costs at Timlin Associates are $83 an hour. Indirect costs are allocated to cases at $120 an hour. Total indirect costs in the most recent period were $25,200.

Required

1. Why is it important for Timlin Associates to understand the costs associated with individual jobs?
2. Compute the costs of the Widnes Coal and St. Helen's Glass jobs using Timlin's simple costing system.

6-25 Job costing with multiple direct-cost categories, single indirect-cost pool, law firm (continuation of 6-24). Hanley asks his assistant to collect details on those costs included in the $25,200 indirect-cost pool that can be traced to each individual job. After analysis, Timlin is able to reclassify $18,900 of the $25,200 as direct costs:

Other Direct Costs	Widnes Coal	St. Helen's Glass
Research support labor	$1,900	$ 6,850
Computer time	750	1,600
Travel and allowances	700	4,500
Telephones/faxes	300	1,300
Photocopying	250	750
Total	$3,900	$15,000

Hanley decides to calculate the costs of each job as if Timlin had used six direct cost-pools and a single indirect-cost pool. The single indirect-cost pool would have $6,300 of costs and would be allocated to each case using the professional labor-hours base.

Required

1. What is the revised indirect-cost allocation rate per professional labor-hour for Timlin Associates when total indirect costs are $6,300?
2. Compute the costs of the Widnes and St. Helen's jobs if Timlin Associates had used its refined costing system with multiple direct-cost categories and one indirect-cost pool.
3. Compare the costs of the Widnes and St. Helen's jobs in requirement 2 with those in requirement 2 in Problem 6-24. Comment on the results.

6-26 Job costing with multiple direct-cost categories, multiple indirect-cost pools, law firm (continuation of 6-24 and 6-25). Timlin has two classifications of professional staff: partners and associates. Hanley asks his assistant to examine the relative use of partners and associates on the recent Widnes Coal and St. Helen's jobs. The Widnes job used 30 partner-hours and 85 associate-hours. The St. Helen's job used 60 partner-hours and 35 associate-hours. Therefore, totals of the two jobs together were 90 partner-hours and 120 associate-hours. Hanley decides to examine how using separate direct-cost rates for partners and associates and using separate indirect-cost pools for partners and associates would have affected the costs of the Widnes and St. Helen's jobs. Indirect costs in each indirect-cost pool would be allocated on the basis of total hours of that category of professional labor. From the total indirect cost-pool of $6,300, $3,600 is attributable to the activities of partners, and $2,700 is attributable to the activities of associates.

The rates per category of professional labor are as follows.

Category of Professional Labor	Direct Cost per Hour	Indirect Cost per Hour
Partner	$115.00	$3,600 ÷ 90 hours = $40.00
Associate	59.00	$2,700 ÷ 120 hours = $22.50

Required

1. Compute the costs of the Widnes and St. Helen's cases using Timlin's further refined system, with multiple direct-cost categories and multiple indirect-cost pools.
2. For what decisions might Timlin Associates find it more useful to use this job-costing approach rather than the approaches in Problem 6-24 or 6-25?

6-27 First stage allocation, activity-based costing, manufacturing sector. Marshall Precision Devices uses activity-based costing to allocate overhead to customer orders for pricing purposes. Many customer orders are won through competitive bidding. Direct material and direct manufacturing labor costs are traced directly to each order. Marshall's direct manufacturing labor rate is $18 per hour. The company reports the following yearly overhead costs:

Wages and salaries	$400,000
Depreciation	50,000
Rent	100,000
Other overhead	200,000
Total overhead costs	$750,000

Marshall has established four activity cost pools:

Activity Cost Pool	Activity Measure	Total Activity for the Year
Direct manufacturing labor support	Number of direct manufacturing labor-hours	30,000 direct manufacturing labor-hours
Order processing	Number of customer orders	500 orders
Design support	Number of custom designs	100 custom designs
Other	Facility-sustaining costs that are not allocated to orders	Not applicable

Only about 20% of Marshall's yearly orders require custom designs.

Jen Chandler, Marshall's controller, has prepared the following estimates regarding distribution of the overhead costs across the four activity cost pools:

	Direct Manufacturing Labor Support	Order Processing	Design Support	Other	Total
Wages and salaries	50%	25%	20%	5%	100%
Depreciation	25%	10%	15%	50%	100%
Rent	30%	5%	10%	55%	100%
Other overhead	40%	20%	15%	25%	100%

Order 448200 required $10,550 of direct materials, 120 direct manufacturing labor-hours, and one custom design.

Required

1. Allocate the overhead costs to each activity cost pool. Calculate the activity rate for each pool.
2. Determine the cost of Order 448200.
3. How does activity-based costing enhance Marshall's ability to price its orders? If Marshall used a traditional costing system allocating all overhead to orders on the basis of direct manufacturing labor-hours, how might this have impacted Marshall's profitability?

6-28 Department and activity-cost rates, service sector. Raynham's Radiology Center (RRC) performs X-rays, ultrasounds, computer tomography (CT) scans, and magnetic resonance imaging (MRI). RRC has developed a reputation as a top Radiology Center in the state. RRC has achieved this status because it constantly reexamines its processes and procedures. RRC has been using a single, facilitywide overhead allocation rate. The vice president of finance believes that RRC can make better process improvements if it uses more disaggregated cost information. She says, "We have state-of-the-art medical imaging technology. Can't we have state-of-the-art accounting technology?"

Raynham's Radiology Center Budgeted Information for the Year Ended May 30, 2013

	X-Rays	Ultrasounds	CT scans	MRIs	Total
Technician labor	$ 62,000	$101,000	$155,000	$ 103,000	$ 421,000
Depreciation	42,240	256,000	424,960	876,800	1,600,000
Materials	22,600	16,400	23,600	31,500	94,100
Administration					20,000
Maintenance					250,000

	X-Rays	Ultrasounds	CT scans	MRIs	Total
Sanitation					252,500
Utilities					151,100
	$126,840	$373,400	$603,560	$1,011,300	$2,788,700
Number of procedures	3,842	4,352	2,924	2,482	
Minutes to clean after each procedure	5	5	15	35	
Minutes for each procedure	5	15	25	40	

RRC operates at capacity. The proposed allocation bases for overhead are:

Administration	Number of procedures
Maintenance (including parts)	Capital cost of the equipment (use Depreciation)
Sanitation	Total cleaning minutes
Utilities	Total procedure minutes

Required

1. Calculate the budgeted cost per service for X-rays, ultrasounds, CT scans, and MRI using direct technician labor costs as the allocation basis.
2. Calculate the budgeted cost per service of X-rays, ultrasounds, CT scans, and MRI if RRC allocated overhead costs using activity-based costing.
3. Explain how the disaggregation of information could be helpful to RRC's intention to continuously improve its services.

6-29 First-stage allocation, activity-based costing, service sector. Green Thumb, Inc., provides lawn care and landscaping services to commercial clients. Green Thumb uses activity-based costing to bid on jobs and to evaluate their profitability. Green Thumb reports the following annual costs:

Wages and salaries	$300,000
Depreciation	60,000
Supplies	100,000
Other overhead	240,000
Total overhead costs	$700,000

John Gibson, controller of Green Thumb, has established four activity cost pools:

Activity Cost Pool	Activity Measure	Total Activity for the Year
Estimating jobs	Number of job estimates	250 estimates
Lawn care	Number of direct labor-hours	10,000 direct labor-hours
Landscape design	Number of design hours	500 design hours
Other	Facility-sustaining costs that are not allocated to jobs	Not applicable

He estimates that Green Thumb's costs are distributed to the activity-cost pools as follows.

	Estimating Jobs	Lawn Care	Landscape Design	Other	Total
Wages and salaries	5%	70%	15%	10%	100%
Depreciation	10%	65%	10%	15%	100%
Supplies	0%	100%	0%	0%	100%
Other overhead	15%	50%	20%	15%	100%

Vista Office Park, a new development in a nearby community, has contacted Green Thumb to provide an estimate on landscape design and annual lawn maintenance. The job is estimated to require a single landscape design requiring 40 design hours in total and 250 direct labor-hours annually. Green Thumb has a policy of pricing estimates at 150% of allocated cost.

Required

1. Allocate Green Thumb's costs to the activity-cost pools and determine the activity rate for each pool.
2. Estimate total cost for the Vista Office Park job.

3. How much should Green Thumb bid to perform the job?
4. Vista Office Park asks Green Thumb to give an estimate for providing its services for a 2-year period. What are the advantages and disadvantages for Green Thumb to provide a 2-year estimate? ?

6-30 Activity-based costing, merchandising. Medtech, Inc., a distributor of special pharmaceutical products, operates at capacity and has three main market segments:

a. General supermarket chains
b. Drugstore chains
c. Mom-and-pop single-store pharmacies

Evan Kennedy, the new controller of Medtech, reported the following data for 2013:

	General Supermarket Chains	Drugstore Chains	Mom-and-Pop Single Store	Medtech
Revenues	$3,708,000	$3,150,000	$1,980,000	$8,838,000
Cost of goods sold	3,600,000	3,000,000	1,800,000	8,400,000
Gross margin	$ 108,000	$ 150,000	$ 180,000	438,000
Other operating costs				301,080
Operating income				$ 136,920

For many years, Medtech has used gross margin percentage [(Revenue − Cost of goods sold) ÷ Revenue] to evaluate the relative profitability of its market segments. However, Kennedy recently attended a seminar on activity-based costing and is considering using it at Medtech to analyze and allocate "other operating costs." He meets with all the key managers and several of his operations and sales staff and they agree that there are five key activities that drive other operating costs at Medtech:

Activity Area	Cost Driver
Order processing	Number of customer purchase orders
Line-item processing	Number of line items ordered by customers
Delivering to stores	Number of store deliveries
Cartons shipped to store	Number of cartons shipped
Stocking of customer store shelves	Hours of shelf-stocking

Each customer order consists of one or more line items. A line item represents a single product (such as Extra-Strength Tylenol tablets). Each product line item is delivered in one or more separate cartons. Each store delivery entails the delivery of one or more cartons of products to a customer. Medtech's staff stacks cartons directly onto display shelves in customers' stores. Currently, there is no additional charge to the customer for shelf-stocking and not all customers use Medtech for this activity. The level of each activity in the three market segments and the total cost incurred for each activity in 2013 is as follows.

	A	B	C	D	E
13					
14	**Activity-Based Cost Data**		**Activity Level**		
15	**Medtech, Inc., 2013**	**General**			**Total Cost**
16		**Supermarket**	**Drugstore**	**Mom-and-Pop**	**of Activity**
17	**Activity**	**Chains**	**Chains**	**Single Stores**	**in 2013**
18	Orders processed (number)	140	360	1,500	$ 80,000
19	Line-items ordered (number)	1,960	4,320	15,000	63,840
20	Store deliveries made (number)	120	360	1,000	71,000
21	Cartons shipped to stores (number)	36,000	24,000	16,000	76,000
22	Shelf stocking (hours)	360	180	100	10,240
23					$301,080

Required

1. Compute the 2013 gross-margin percentage for each of Medtech's three market segments.
2. Compute the cost driver rates for each of the five activity areas.
3. Use the activity-based costing information to allocate the $301,080 of "other operating costs" to each of the market segments. Compute the operating income for each market segment.
4. Comment on the results. What new insights are available with the activity-based costing information?

6-31 Choosing cost drivers, activity-based costing, activity-based management. Pink Bags (PB) is a designer of high-quality backpacks and purses. Each design is made in small batches. Each spring, PB comes out with new designs for the backpack and for the purse. The company uses these designs for a year, and then moves on to the next trend. The bags are all made on the same fabrication equipment, which is expected to operate at capacity. The equipment must be switched over to a new design and set up to prepare for the production of each new batch of products. When completed, each batch of products is immediately shipped to a wholesaler. Shipping costs vary with the number of shipments. Budgeted information for the year is as follows.

Pink Bags Budget for Costs and Activities for the Year Ended February 28, 2013

Direct materials—purses	$ 283,575
Direct materials—backpacks	496,625
Direct manufacturing labor—purses	95,000
Direct manufacturing labor—backpacks	119,000
Setup	65,000
Shipping	72,400
Design	162,500
Plant utilities and administration	253,500
Total	$1,547,600

Other budget information follows.

	Backpacks	Purses	Total
Number of bags	6,250	3,100	9,350
Hours of production	1,600	2,625	4,225
Number of batches	125	75	200
Number of designs	2	3	5

Required

1. Identify the cost hierarchy level for each cost category.
2. Identify the most appropriate cost driver for each cost category. Explain briefly your choice of cost driver.
3. Calculate the budgeted cost per unit of cost driver for each cost category.
4. Calculate the budgeted total costs and cost per unit for each product line.
5. Explain how you could use the information in requirement 4 to reduce costs.

6-32 ABC, health care. Crossroads Health Center runs two programs: drug addict rehabilitation and aftercare (counseling and support of patients after release from a mental hospital). The center's budget for 2013 follows.

Professional salaries:		
4 physicians × $165,000	$660,000	
12 psychologists × $82,500	990,000	
16 nurses × $33,000	528,000	$2,178,000
Medical supplies		242,000
Rent and clinic maintenance		138,600
Administrative costs to manage patient charts, food, laundry		484,000
Laboratory services		92,400
Total		$3,135,000

Kim Yu, the director of the center, is keen on determining the cost of each program. Yu compiled the following data describing employee allocations to individual programs:

	Drug	Aftercare	Total Employees
Physicians	4		4
Psychologists	4	8	12
Nurses	6	10	16

Yu has recently become aware of activity-based costing as a method to refine costing systems. She asks her accountant, Gus Gates, how she should apply this technique. Gates obtains the following budgeted information for 2013:

	Drug	Aftercare	Total
Square feet of space occupied by each program	9,000	12,000	21,000
Patient-years of service	50	60	110
Number of laboratory tests	1,400	700	2,100

Required

1. a. Selecting cost-allocation bases that you believe are the most appropriate for allocating indirect costs to programs, calculate the budgeted indirect cost rates for medical supplies; rent and clinic maintenance; administrative costs for patient charts, food, and laundry; and laboratory services.
   b. Using an activity-based costing approach to cost analysis, calculate the budgeted cost of each program and the budgeted cost per patient-year of the drug program.
   c. What benefits can Crossroads Health Center obtain by implementing the ABC system?
2. What factors, other than cost, do you think Crossroads Health Center should consider in allocating resources to its programs?

6-33 Unused capacity, activity-based costing, activity-based management. Wybock's Netballs is a manufacturer of high-quality basketballs and volleyballs. Setup costs are driven by the number of batches. Equipment and maintenance costs increase with the number of machine-hours, and lease rent is paid per square foot. Capacity of the facility is 17,000 square feet and Wybock is using only 80% of this capacity. Wybock records the cost of unused capacity as a separate line item, and not as a product cost. The following is the budgeted information for Wybock.

Wybock's Netballs Budgeted Costs and Activities for the Year Ended August 31, 2013

Direct materials—basketballs	$ 169,180
Direct materials—volleyballs	343,400
Direct manufacturing labor—basketballs	99,620
Direct manufacturing labor—volleyballs	110,250
Setup	127,500
Equipment and maintenance costs	110,250
Lease rent	272,000
Total	$1,232,200

Other budget information follows.

	Basketballs	Volleyballs
Number of balls	58,000	110,000
Machine-hours	10,000	14,500
Number of batches	500	350
Square footage of production space used	3,250	10,350

Required

1. Calculate the budgeted cost per unit of cost driver for each indirect cost pool.
2. What is the budgeted cost of unused capacity?

3. What is the budgeted total cost and the cost per unit of resources used to produce (a) basketballs and (b) volleyballs?
4. What factors should Wybock consider if it has the opportunity to manufacture a new line of footballs?

6-34 Unused capacity, activity-based costing, activity-based management. Whitewater Adventures manufactures two models of kayaks, Basic and Deluxe, using a combination of machining and hand finishing. Machine setup costs are driven by the number of setups. Indirect manufacturing labor costs increase with direct manufacturing labor costs. Equipment and maintenance costs increase with the number of machine-hours, and facility rent is paid per square foot. Capacity of the facility is 6,250 square feet and Whitewater is using only 80% of this capacity. Whitewater records the cost of unused capacity as a separate line item, and not as a product cost. For the current year, Whitewater has budgeted the following.

Whitewater Adventures Budgeted Costs and Activities for the Year Ended December 31, 2013

Direct materials—Basic kayaks	$ 325,000
Direct materials—Deluxe kayaks	240,000
Direct manufacturing labor—Basic kayaks	110,000
Direct manufacturing labor—Deluxe kayaks	130,000
Indirect manufacturing labor costs	72,000
Machine setup costs	40,500
Equipment and maintenance costs	235,000
Facility rent	200,000
Total	$1,352,500

Other budget information follows.

	Basic	Deluxe
Number of kayaks	5,000	3,000
Machine-hours	11,000	12,500
Number of batches	300	200
Square footage of production space used	2,860	2,140

Required

1. Calculate the cost per unit of each cost-allocation base.
2. What is the budgeted cost of unused capacity?
3. Calculate the budgeted total cost and the cost per unit for each model.
4. Why might excess capacity be beneficial for Whitewater? What are some of the issues Whitewater should consider before increasing production to use the space?

6-35 Activity-based job costing, unit-cost comparisons. The Taylor Corporation has a machining facility specializing in jobs for the aircraft-components market. Taylor's previous simple job-costing system had two direct-cost categories (direct materials and direct manufacturing labor) and a single indirect-cost pool (manufacturing overhead, allocated using direct manufacturing labor-hours). The indirect cost-allocation rate of the simple system for 2013 would have been $113 per direct manufacturing labor-hour.

Recently a team with members from product design, manufacturing, and accounting used an ABC approach to refine its job-costing system. The two direct-cost categories were retained. The team decided to replace the single indirect-cost pool with five indirect-cost pools. The cost pools represent five activity areas at the plant, each with its own supervisor and budget responsibility. Pertinent data are as follows.

Activity Area	Cost-Allocation Base	Cost-Allocation Rate
Materials handling	Parts	$ 0.40
Lathe work	Lathe turns	0.35
Milling	Machine-hours	14.00
Grinding	Parts	0.50
Testing	Units tested	13.00

Information-gathering technology has advanced to the point at which the data necessary for budgeting in these five activity areas are collected automatically.

Two representative jobs processed under the ABC system at the plant in the most recent period had the following characteristics:

	Job 410	Job 411
Direct material cost per job	$19,512	$55,204
Direct manufacturing labor cost per job	$ 475	$ 6,950
Number of direct manufacturing labor-hours per job	19	278
Parts per job	550	2,300
Lathe turns per job	14,323	15,383
Machine-hours per job	190	825
Units per job (all units are tested)	15	170

Required

1. Compute the manufacturing cost per unit for each job under the previous simple job-costing system.
2. Compute the manufacturing cost per unit for each job under the activity-based costing system.
3. Compare the per-unit cost figures for Jobs 410 and 411 computed in requirements 1 and 2. Why do the simple and the activity-based costing systems differ in the manufacturing cost per unit for each job? Why might these differences be important to Taylor Corporation?
4. How might Taylor Corporation use information from its ABC system to better manage its business?

6-36 ABC, implementation, ethics. (CMA, adapted) Plum Electronics, a division of Berry Corporation, manufactures two large-screen television models: the Mammoth, which has been produced since 2009 and sells for $990, and the Maximum, a newer model introduced in early 2011 that sells for $1,254. Based on the following income statement for the year ended November 30, 2013, senior management at Berry have decided to concentrate Plum's marketing resources on the Maximum model and to begin to phase out the Mammoth model because Maximum generates a much bigger operating income per unit.

Plum Electronics Income Statement for the Fiscal Year Ended November 30, 2013

	Mammoth	Maximum	Total
Revenues	$21,780,000	$5,016,000	$26,796,000
Cost of goods sold	13,794,000	3,511,200	17,305,200
Gross margin	7,986,000	1,504,800	9,490,800
Selling and administrative expense	6,413,000	1,075,800	7,488,800
Operating income	$ 1,573,000	$ 429,000	$ 2,002,000
Units produced and sold	22,000	4,000	
Operating income per unit sold	$71.50	$107.25	

Details for cost of goods sold for Mammoth and Maximum are as follows.

	Mammoth		Maximum	
	Total	Per Unit	Total	Per Unit
Direct materials	$ 5,033,600	$228.80	$2,569,600	$642.40
Direct manufacturing labor[a]	435,600	19.80	184,800	46.20
Machine costs[b]	3,484,800	158.40	316,800	79.20
Total direct costs	$ 8,954,000	$407.00	$3,071,200	$767.80
Manufacturing overhead costs[c]	$ 4,840,000	$220.00	$ 440,000	$110.00
Total cost of goods sold	$13,794,000	$627.00	$3,511,200	$877.80

[a]Mammoth requires 1.5 hours per unit and Maximum requires 3.5 hours per unit. The direct manufacturing labor cost is $13.20 per hour.

[b]Machine costs include lease costs of the machine, repairs, and maintenance. Mammoth requires 8 machine-hours per unit and Maximum requires 4 machine-hours per unit. The machine hour rate is $19.80 per hour.

[c]Manufacturing overhead costs are allocated to products based on machine-hours at the rate of $27.50 per hour.

Plum's controller, Steve Jacobs, is advocating the use of activity-based costing and activity-based management and has gathered the following information about the company's manufacturing overhead costs for the year ended November 30, 2013.

		Units of the Cost-Allocation Base		
Activity Center (Cost-Allocation Base)	Total Activity Costs	Mammoth	Maximum	Total
Soldering (number of solder points)	$1,036,200	1,185,000	385,000	1,570,000
Shipments (number of shipments)	946,000	16,200	3,800	20,000
Quality control (number of inspections)	1,364,000	56,200	21,300	77,500
Purchase orders (number of orders)	1,045,440	80,100	109,980	190,080
Machine power (machine-hours)	63,360	176,000	16,000	192,000
Machine setups (number of setups)	825,000	16,000	14,000	30,000
Total manufacturing overhead	$5,280,000			

After completing his analysis, Jacobs shows the results to Charles Clark, the Plum division president. Clark does not like what he sees. "If you show headquarters this analysis, they are going to ask us to phase out the Maximum line, which we have just introduced. This whole costing stuff has been a major problem for us. First Mammoth was not profitable and now Maximum."

"Looking at the ABC analysis, I see two problems. First, we do many more activities than the ones you have listed. If you had included all activities, maybe your conclusions would be different. Second, you used number of setups and number of inspections as allocation bases. The numbers would be different had you used setup-hours and inspection-hours instead. I know that measurement problems precluded you from using these other cost-allocation bases, but I believe you ought to make some adjustments to our current numbers to compensate for these issues. I know you can do better. We can't afford to phase out either product."

Jacobs knows that his numbers are fairly accurate. As a quick check, he calculates the profitability of Maximum and Mammoth using more and different allocation bases. The set of activities and activity rates had used results in numbers that closely approximate those based on more detailed analyses. He is confident that headquarters, knowing that Maximum was introduced only recently, will not ask Plum to phase it out. He is also aware that a sizable portion of Clark's bonus is based on division revenues. Phasing out either product would adversely affect his bonus. Still, he feels some pressure from Clark to do something.

Required

1. Using activity-based costing, calculate the gross margin per unit of the Maximum and Mammoth models.
2. Explain briefly why these numbers differ from the gross margin per unit of the Maximum and Mammoth models calculated using Plum's existing simple costing system.
3. Comment on Clark's concerns about the accuracy and limitations of ABC.
4. How might Plum find the ABC information helpful in managing its business?
5. What should Steve Jacobs do in response to Clark's comments?

6-37 Activity-based costing, activity-based management, merchandising. Super Bookstore (SB) is a large city bookstore that sells books and music CDs and has a café. SB operates at capacity and allocates selling, general, and administration (S, G & A) costs to each product line using the cost of merchandise of each product line. SB wants to optimize the pricing and cost management of each product line. SB is wondering if its accounting system is providing it with the best information for making such decisions.

Super Bookstore Product Line Information for the Year Ended December 31, 2012

	Books	CDs	Café
Revenues	$3,720,480	$2,315,360	$736,216
Cost of merchandise	$2,656,727	$1,722,311	$556,685
Cost of café cleaning	—	—	$ 18,250
Number of purchase orders placed	2,800	2,500	2,000
Number of deliveries received	1,400	1,700	1,600
Hours of shelf-stocking time	15,000	14,000	10,000
Items sold	124,016	115,768	368,108

Super Bookstore incurs the following selling, general, and administration costs.

Super Bookstore S, G & A Costs for the Year Ended December 31, 2012

Purchasing department expenses	$ 474,500
Receiving department expenses	432,400
Shelf-stocking labor expense	487,500
Customer support expense (cashiers and floor employees)	91,184
	$1,485,584

Required

1. Suppose Super Bookstore uses cost of merchandise to allocate all S, G & A costs. Prepare product line and total company income statements.
2. Identify an improved method for allocating costs to the three product lines. Explain. Use the method for allocating S, G & A costs that you propose to prepare new product line and total company income statements. Compare your results to the results in requirement 1.
3. Write a memo to Super Bookstore's management describing how the improved system might be useful for managing Super Bookstore.

Case

Wilkerson Company

Robert S. Kaplan

Robert Parker, president of the Wilkerson Company, was discussing operating results in the latest month with Peggy Knight, his controller, and John Scott, his manufacturing manager. The meeting among the three was taking place in an atmosphere tinged with apprehension because competitors had been reducing prices on pumps, Wilkerson's major product line. Since pumps were a commodity product, Parker had seen no alternative but to match the reduced prices to maintain volume. But the price cuts had led to declining company profits, especially in the pump line (summary operating results for the previous month, March 2000, are shown in Wilkerson Exhibits 1 and 2).

Wilkerson supplied products to manufacturers of water purification equipment. The company had started with a unique design for valves that it could produce to tolerances that were better than any in the industry. Parker quickly established a loyal customer base because of the high quality of its manufactured valves. He and Scott realized that Wilkerson's existing labor skills and machining equipment could also be used to produce pumps and flow controllers, products that were also purchased by its customers. They soon established a major presence in the high-volume pump product line and the more customized flow controller line.

Wilkerson's production process started with the purchase of semi-finished components from several suppliers. It machined these parts to the required tolerances and assembled them in the company's modern manufacturing facility. The same equipment and labor were used for all three product lines, and production runs were scheduled to match customer shipping requirements.

Wilkerson Exhibit 1

Wilkerson Company: Operating Results (March 2000)

Sales		$2,152,500	100%
Direct Labor Expense		271,250	
Direct Materials Expense		458,000	
Manufacturing overhead			
Machine-related expenses	$336,000		
Setup labor	40,000		
Receiving and production control	180,000		
Engineering	100,000		
Packaging and shipping	150,000		
Total Manufacturing Overhead		806,000	
Gross Margin		$617,250	29%
General, Selling & Admin. Expense		559,650	
Operating Income (pre-tax)		$ 57,600	3%

The case was prepared by Robert Kaplan as the basis for class discussion rather than to illustrate either effective or ineffective handling of an administrative situation.

Wilkerson Exhibit 2

Product Profitability Analysis (March 2000)

	Valves	Pumps	Flow Controllers
Direct labor cost	$10.00	$ 12.50	$ 10.00
Direct material cost	16.00	20.00	22.00
Manufacturing overhead (@300%)	30.00	37.50	30.00
Standard unit costs	$56.00	$ 70.00	$ 62.00
Target selling price	$86.15	$107.69	$ 95.38
Planned gross margin (%)	35%	35%	35%
Actual selling price	$86.00	$ 87.00	$105.00
Actual gross margin (%)	34.9%	19.5%	41.0%

Suppliers and customers had agreed to just-in-time deliveries, and products were packed and shipped as completed.

Valves were produced by assembling four different machined components. Scott had designed machines that held components in fixtures so that they could be machined automatically. The valves were standard products and could be produced and shipped in large lots. Although Scott felt several competitors could now match Parker's quality in valves, none had tried to gain market share by cutting price, and gross margins had been maintained at a standard 35%.

The manufacturing process for pumps was practically identical to that for valves. Five components were machined and then assembled into the final product. The pumps were shipped to industrial product distributors after assembly. Recently, it seemed as if each month brought new reports of reduced prices for pumps. Wilkerson had matched the lower prices so that it would not give up its place as a major pump supplier. Gross margins on pump sales in the latest month had fallen below 20%, well below the company's planned gross margin of 35%.

Flow controllers were devices that controlled the rate and direction of flow of chemicals. They required more components and more labor, than pumps or valves, for each finished unit. Also, there was much more variety in the types of flow controllers used in industry, so many more production runs and shipments were performed for this product line than for valves. Wilkerson had recently raised flow controller prices by more than 10% with no apparent effect on demand.

Wilkerson had always used a simple cost accounting system. Each unit of product was charged for direct material and labor cost. Material cost was based on the prices paid for components under annual purchasing agreements. Labor rates, including fringe benefits, were $25 per hour, and were charged to products based on the standard run times for each product (see Wilkerson Exhibit 3). The company had only one producing department, in which components were both machined and assembled into finished products. The overhead costs in this department were allocated to products as a percentage of production-run direct labor cost. Currently, the rate was 300%. Since direct labor cost had to be recorded anyway to prepare factory payroll, this was an inexpensive way to allocate overhead costs to products.

Knight noted that some companies didn't allocate any overhead costs to products, treating them as period, not product, expenses. For these companies, product profitability was measured at the contribution margin level—price less all variable costs. Wilkerson's variable costs were only its direct material and direct labor costs. On that basis, all products, including pumps, would be generating substantial contribution to overhead and profits. She thought that perhaps some of Wilkerson's competitors were following this procedure and pricing to cover variable costs.

Knight had recently led a small task force to study Wilkerson's overhead costs since they had now become much larger than the direct labor expenses. The study had revealed the following information:

1. Workers often operated several of the machines simultaneously once they were set up. For other operations, however, workers could operate only one machine. Thus machine-related

Wilkerson Exhibit 3
Product Data

Product Lines	Valves	Pumps	Flow Controllers
Materials per unit	4 components	5 components	10 components
	2 @ $2 = $4	3 @ $2 = $6	4 @ $1 = $4
	2 @ 6 = 12	2 @ 7 = 14	5 @ 2 = 10
			1 @ 8 = 8
Materials cost per unit	$16	$20	$22
Direct labor per unit	.40 DL hours	.50 DL hours	.40 DL hours
Direct labor $/unit @ $25/DL hour (including employee benefits)	$10	$12.50	$10.00
Machine hours per unit	0.5	0.5	0.3

expenses might relate more to the machine hours of a product than to its production-run labor hours.

2. A set-up had to be performed each time a batch of components had to be machined in a production run. Each component in a product required a separate production run to machine the raw materials or purchased part to the specifications for the product.
3. People in the receiving and production control departments ordered, processed, inspected, and moved each batch of components for a production run. This work required about the same amount of time whether the components were for a long or a short production run, or whether the components were expensive or inexpensive.
4. The work in the packaging and shipping area had increased during the past couple of years as Wilkerson increased the number of customers it served. Each time products were packaged and shipped, about the same amount of work was required, regardless of the number of items in the shipment.

Knight's team had collected the data shown in Wilkerson Exhibit 4 based on operations in March 2000. The team felt that this month was typical of ongoing operations. Some people recalled, however, that when demand was really heavy last year, the machines had worked 12,000 hours in a month and the factory handled up to 180 production runs and 400 shipments without experiencing any production delays or use of overtime.

Required

1. Develop and diagram an activity-based costing system using information in the case. Calculate the profitability of Wilkerson's three product lines. Are these profitabilities different from the profitabilities Wilkerson reports based on its current costing system.
2. Based on your analysis, what actions should Wilkerson's management take to improve profitability.

Wilkerson Exhibit 4
Monthly Production and Operating Statistics (March 2000)

	Valves	Pumps	Flow Controllers	Total
Production (units)	7,500	12,500	4,000	24,000
Machine hours	3,750	6,250	1,200	11,200
Production runs	10	50	100	160
Number of shipments	10	70	220	300
Hours of engineering work	250	375	625	1,250

7 Pricing Decisions, Customer Profitability, and Cost Management

Learning Objectives

1. Discuss the three major factors that affect pricing decisions
2. Understand how companies make long-run pricing decisions
3. Price products using the target-costing approach
4. Apply the concepts of cost incurrence and locked-in costs
5. Price products using the cost-plus approach
6. Discuss why a company's revenues and costs differ across customers and the actions managers can take based on this information
7. Use life-cycle budgeting and costing when making pricing decisions
8. Describe two pricing practices in which noncost factors are important when setting prices and the effects of antitrust laws on pricing

Most companies carefully analyze their input costs and the prices of their products. They know if the price is too high, customers will go to competitors; if the price is too low, the company won't be able to cover the cost of making the product. Many successful companies, such as Samsung and Tata Motors, however, understand that it is possible to charge a low price to stimulate demand and meet customer needs while relentlessly managing costs to earn a profit.

Managers at many innovative companies, such as IKEA, Unilever, and Walmart, are strategic in their pricing decisions. The Chapter at a Glance describes how managers evaluate demand at different prices and manage customers and costs across the value chain and over a product's life cycle to achieve profitability.

Chapter at a Glance

- The demand for a product and the supply of that product determines its price. Customers, competitors, and costs influence demand and supply.
- The most common market-based approach to pricing decisions is target pricing, where managers estimate a price that customers are willing to pay for a product. Managers use this price to determine a target cost. Using value engineering methods, managers make cost improvements to meet the target cost.
- Many costs are locked in, for example, at the time the products are designed and before costs are actually incurred. Once costs are locked in, they are hard to influence so managers make decisions to control costs before costs are locked in.
- Cost-plus pricing starts with some measure of cost and adds a margin (the plus) to arrive at a price that earns a targeted profit. Often, managers modify the margin in response to competitive pressures.
- Companies make more profit from some customers than others, depending on the quantity of goods purchased, price discounts, and costs needed to provide customer service. Managers treat customers differently based on the profits the company makes from them.
- Factors other than costs affect the prices managers charge for their products. For example, managers charge some customers a higher price than other customers and also charge higher prices when demand for a product approaches the capacity available to produce it. Managers must always comply with antitrust laws against predatory and collusive pricing.

Major Factors that Affect Pricing Decisions

Learning Objective 1

Discuss the three major factors that affect pricing decisions

. . . customers, competitors, and costs

Consider for a moment how managers at Adidas might price their newest line of sneakers, or how decision makers at Comcast would determine how much to charge for a monthly subscription of Comcast. How managers price a product or a service ultimately depends on the demand and supply for it. Three influences on demand and supply are customers, competitors, and costs.

Customers

Customers influence price through their effect on the demand for a product or service, based on factors such as the features of a product and its quality. Managers at companies such as Adidas, Toyota, and Fidelity Investments always examine pricing decisions through the eyes of their customers and then manage costs to earn a profit.

Competitors

No business operates in a vacuum. Managers must always be aware of the actions of their competitors. At one extreme, for companies such as Home Depot or Texas Instruments, alternative or substitute products of competitors hurt demand and cause them to lower prices. At the other extreme, companies such as Apple and Porsche have distinctive products and limited competition and are free to set higher prices. When there are competitors, managers try to learn about competitors' technologies, plant capacities, and operating strategies to estimate competitors' costs—valuable information when setting prices.

Because competition spans international borders, fluctuations in exchange rates between different countries' currencies affect costs and pricing decisions. For example, if the yuan weakens against the U.S. dollar, Chinese producers receive more yuan for each dollar of sales. These producers can lower prices and still make a profit; Chinese products become cheaper for American consumers and, consequently, more competitive in U.S. markets.

Costs

Costs influence prices because they affect supply. The lower the cost of producing a product, such as a Toyota Prius or a Nokia cell phone, the greater the quantity of product the company is willing to supply. That's because as companies increase supply, the cost of producing an additional unit initially declines but eventually increases; companies supply products as long as the revenue from selling additional units exceeds the cost of producing them. Managers who understand the cost of producing products set prices that make the products attractive to customers while maximizing operating income.

Weighing Customers, Competitors, and Costs

Surveys indicate that managers weigh customers, competitors, and costs differently when making pricing decisions. At one extreme, companies operating in a perfectly competitive market sell very similar commodity products, such as wheat, rice, steel, and aluminum. The managers at these companies have no control over setting prices and must accept the price determined by a market consisting of many participants. Cost information is only helpful to them in deciding the quantity of output to produce to maximize operating income.

In less-competitive markets, such as those for cameras, televisions, and cellular phones, products are differentiated, and all three factors affect prices: The value customers place on a product and the prices charged for competing products affect demand, and the costs of producing and delivering the product affect supply.

As competition lessens even more, such as in microprocessors and operating software, the key factor affecting pricing decisions is the customer's willingness to pay based on the value that customers place on the product or service, not costs or competitors. In the extreme, there are monopolies. A monopolist has no competitors and has much more leeway to set high prices. Nevertheless, there are limits. The higher the price a monopolist sets, the lower the demand for the monopolist's product as customers seek substitute products or forgo buying the product.

Learning Objective 2

Understand how companies make long-run pricing decisions

... consider all future variable and fixed costs and earn a target return on investment

Costing and Pricing for the Long Run

Long-run pricing is a strategic decision designed to build long-run relationships with customers based on stable and predictable prices. Managers prefer a stable price because it reduces the need for continuous monitoring of prices, improves planning, and builds long-run buyer–seller relationships. But to charge a stable price and earn the target long-run return, managers must know and manage long-run costs of supplying products to customers, which includes *all* future fixed and variable costs. McDonald's does this with its Dollar Menu of fast-food items, as does Apple, which always prices its new entry-level iPad at $499.

Calculating Product Costs for Long-Run Pricing Decisions

Consider Astel Computers. Astel manufactures two brands of personal computers (PCs): Deskpoint, Astel's top-of-the-line product, and Provalue, a less-powerful Pentium chip–based machine. Astel's managers must decide the price to charge for Provalue.

Astel's managers start by reviewing data for the year just ended, 2012. Astel has no beginning or ending inventory of Provalue and manufactures and sells 150,000 units during the year. Astel uses activity-based costing (ABC) to calculate the manufacturing cost of Provalue. Astel's ABC system has:

- Three direct manufacturing costs: direct materials, direct manufacturing labor, and direct machining costs.
- Three manufacturing overhead cost pools: ordering and receiving components, testing and inspection of final products, and rework (correcting and fixing errors and defects).

Astel considers machining costs as a direct cost of Provalue because these machines are dedicated to manufacturing Provalue.[1]

Astel uses a long-run time horizon to price Provalue. Over this horizon, Astel's managers observe the following:

- Direct material costs vary with the number of units of Provalue produced.
- Direct manufacturing labor costs vary with the number of direct manufacturing labor-hours used.
- Direct machining costs are fixed costs of leasing 300,000 machine-hours of capacity each year for multiple years. These costs do not vary with the number of machine-hours used each year. Each unit of Provalue requires 2 machine-hours. In 2012, Astel uses the entire machining capacity to manufacture Provalue (2 machine-hours per unit × 150,000 units = 300,000 machine-hours).
- Ordering and receiving, testing and inspection, and rework costs vary with the quantity of their respective cost drivers. For example, ordering and receiving costs vary with the number of orders. In the long run, staff members responsible for placing orders can be reassigned or laid off if fewer orders need to be placed, or increased if more orders need to be processed.

The following Excel spreadsheet summarizes manufacturing cost information to produce 150,000 units of Provalue in 2012. Astel's managers derive the indirect cost per unit of the cost driver in column (6) by dividing the total costs in each cost pool by the quantity of cost driver calculated in column (5). (Calculations not shown.)

[1] Recall that Astel makes two types of PCs: Deskpoint and Provalue. If Deskpoint and Provalue had shared the same machines, Astel would have allocated machining costs on the basis of the budgeted machine-hours used to manufacture the two products and would have treated these costs as fixed overhead costs.

Home Insert Page Layout Formulas Data Review View

	A	B	C	D	E	F	G	H
1		Manufacturing Cost Information						
2		to Produce 150,000 Units of Provalue						
3	Cost Category	Cost Driver	Details of Cost Driver Quantities				Total Quantity of Cost Driver	Cost per Unit of Cost Driver
4	(1)	(2)	(3)		(4)		(5) = (3) × (4)	(6)
5	**Direct Manufacturing Costs**							
6	Direct materials	No. of kits	1	kit per unit	150,000	units	150,000	$460
7	Direct manufacturing labor (DML)	DML hours	3.2	DML hours per unit	150,000	units	480,000	$ 20
8	Direct machining (fixed)	Machine-hours					300,000	$ 38
9	**Manufacturing Overhead Costs**							
10	Ordering and receiving	No. of orders	50	orders per component	450	components	22,500	$ 80
11	Testing and inspection	Testing-hours	30	testing-hours per unit	150,000	units	4,500,000	$ 2
12	Rework				8%	defect rate		
13		Rework-hours	2.5	rework-hours per defective unit	12,000[a]	defective units	30,000	$ 40
14								
15	[a]8% defect rate × 150,000 units = 12,000 defective units							

Exhibit 7-1 shows the total cost of manufacturing Provalue in 2012 of $102 million subdivided into the various categories of direct costs and indirect costs. The manufacturing cost per unit in Exhibit 7-1 is $680. Manufacturing, however, is just one business function in the value chain. To set long-run prices, Astel's managers must calculate the *full cost* of producing and selling Provalue.

For each nonmanufacturing business function, Astel's managers trace direct costs to products and allocate indirect costs using cost pools and cost drivers that measure cause-and-effect relationships (supporting calculations not shown). Exhibit 7-2 summarizes Provalue's 2012 operating income and shows that Astel earned $15 million from Provalue, or $100 per unit sold in 2012.

Alternative Long-Run Pricing Approaches

How should managers at Astel use product cost information to price Provalue in 2013? Two different approaches for pricing decisions are (1) market-based and (2) cost-based, which is also called cost-plus.

The market-based approach to pricing starts by asking, "Given what our customers want and how our competitors will react to what we do, what price should we charge?" Based on this price, managers control costs to earn a target return on investment. The cost-based approach to pricing starts by asking, "Given what it costs us to make this product, what price should we charge that will recoup our costs and achieve a target return on investment?"

Companies operating in *competitive* markets (for example, commodities such as steel, oil, and natural gas) use the market-based approach. The products produced or services provided by one company are very similar to products produced or services provided by others. Companies in these markets must accept the prices set by the market.

Exhibit 7-1

Manufacturing Costs of Provalue for 2012 Using Activity-Based Costing

	A	B	C
1		Total Manufacturing	
2		Costs for	Manufacturing
3		150,000 Units	Cost per Unit
4		(1)	(2) = (1) ÷ 150,000
5	Direct manufacturing costs		
6	Direct material costs		
7	(150,000 kits × $460 per kit)	$ 69,000,000	$460
8	Direct manufacturing labor costs		
9	(480,000 DML-hours × $20 per hour)	9,600,000	64
10	Direct machining costs		
11	(300,000 machine-hours × $38 per machine-hour)	11,400,000	76
12	Direct manufacturing costs	90,000,000	600
13			
14	Manufacturing overhead costs		
15	Ordering and receiving costs		
16	(22,500 orders × $80 per order)	1,800,000	12
17	Testing and inspection costs		
18	(4,500,000 testing-hours × $2 per hour)	9,000,000	60
19	Rework costs		
20	(30,000 rework-hours × $40 per hour)	1,200,000	8
21	Manufacturing overhead cost	12,000,000	80
22	Total manufacturing costs	$102,000,000	$680

Exhibit 7-2

Product Profitability of Provalue for 2012 Using Value-Chain Activity-Based Costing

	A	B	C
1		Total Amounts	
2		for 150,000 Units	Per Unit
3		(1)	(2) = (1) ÷ 150,000
4	Revenues	$150,000,000	$1,000
5	Costs of goods sold[a] (from Exhibit 7-1)	102,000,000	680
6	Operating costs[b]		
7	R&D costs	2,400,000	16
8	Design cost of product and process	3,000,000	20
9	Marketing and administration costs	15,000,000	100
10	Distribution costs	9,000,000	60
11	Customer-service costs	3,600,000	24
12	Operating costs	33,000,000	220
13	Full cost of the product	135,000,000	900
14	Operating income	$ 15,000,000	$ 100
15			
16	[a]Cost of goods sold = Total manufacturing costs because there is no beginning or ending inventory		
17	of Provalue in 2012		
18	[b]Numbers for operating cost line-items are assumed without supporting calculations		

Companies operating in *less competitive* markets offer products or services that differ from each other (for example, automobiles, computers, management consulting, and legal services) and can use either the market-based or cost-based approach as the starting point for pricing decisions. Some companies use the cost-based approach: They first look at costs because cost information is more easily available and then consider customers and competitors. Other companies use the market-based approach: They first look at customers and competitors and then look at costs. Both approaches consider customers, competitors, and costs. Only their starting points differ. Managers must always keep in mind market forces, regardless of which pricing approach they use. For example, building contractors often bid on a cost-plus basis but then reduce their prices during negotiations to respond to other lower-cost bids.

Companies operating in markets that are *not competitive* favor cost-based approaches. That's because these companies do not need to respond or react to competitors' prices. The margin they add to costs to determine price depends on the ability and willingness of customers to pay for the product or service.

We consider first the market-based approach.

Target Costing for Target Pricing

Learning Objective 3

Price products using the target-costing approach

. . . target costing identifies an estimated price customers are willing to pay and then computes a target cost to earn the desired profit

Market-based pricing starts with a **target price,** which is the estimated price for a product or service that potential customers are willing to pay. Managers base this estimate on an understanding of customers' perceived value for a product or service and how competitors will price competing products or services. Managers need to understand customers and competitors for three reasons:

1. Lower-cost competitors continually restrain prices.
2. Products have shorter lives, which leaves companies less time and opportunity to recover from pricing mistakes, loss of market share, and loss of profitability.
3. Customers are more knowledgeable because they have easy access to price and other information online and demand high-quality products at low prices.

Understanding Customers' Perceived Value

A company's sales and marketing organization, through close contact and interaction with customers, identifies customer needs and perceptions of product value. Companies such as Toshiba and Dell also conduct market research on what customers want and the prices they are willing to pay.

Doing Competitor Analysis

To gauge how competitors might react to a prospective price, a manager must understand competitors' technologies, products or services, costs, and financial conditions. In general, the more distinctive a product or service, the higher the price a company can charge. Where do companies like Ford Motors or PPG Industries obtain information about their competitors? Usually from former customers, suppliers, and employees of competitors. Some companies *reverse-engineer*—disassemble and analyze competitors' products to determine product designs and materials and to understand the technologies competitors use. At no time should a manager resort to illegal or unethical means to obtain information about competitors. For example, a manager should never pay off current employees or pose as a supplier or customer in order to obtain competitor information.

Implementing Target Pricing and Target Costing

We use the Provalue example to illustrate the five steps in developing target prices and target costs.

Step 1: Develop a Product That Satisfies the Needs of Potential Customers. Astel's managers use the customer insights they have gained and information about competitors' products to finalize product features and design modifications for Provalue in 2013. Their market research indicates that customers do not value Provalue's extra features, such as special audio elements and designs that accommodate upgrades to make the PC run faster. Instead, customers want Astel to redesign Provalue into a no-frills but reliable PC and to sell it at a much lower price.

Step 2: Choose a Target Price. Astel's managers expect competitors to lower the prices to distributors of PCs that compete with Provalue to $850. They want to respond aggressively, reducing the price Astel charges for Provalue by 20%, from $1,000 to $800 per unit. At this lower price, Astel's marketing manager forecasts an increase in annual sales from 150,000 to 200,000 units.

Step 3: Derive a Target Cost per Unit by Subtracting Target Operating Income per Unit from the Target Price. Target operating income per unit is the operating income that a company aims to earn per unit of a product or service sold. **Target cost per unit** is the estimated long-run cost per unit of a product or service that enables the company to achieve its target operating income per unit when selling at the target price.[2] *Target cost per unit* is the target price minus *target operating income per unit* and is often lower than the existing *full cost of the product.* Target cost per unit is really just that—a target—something the company must commit to achieve.

To earn the target return on capital, Astel needs to earn 10% target operating income per unit on the 200,000 units of Provalue it plans to sell.

Target price	= \$800 per unit
Target operating income per unit	= 10% × \$800 = \$80
Target cost per unit	= Target price − Target operating income per unit
	= \$800 per unit − \$80 per unit = \$720 per unit
Current full cost per unit of Provalue	= \$900 (from Exhibit 7-2, column 2)

Provalue's \$720 target cost per unit is \$180 below its existing \$900 unit cost. Astel's managers must reduce costs in all parts of the value chain—from R&D to customer service, for example, by reducing prices of materials and components while maintaining quality.

Target costs include *all* future costs, variable costs, and costs that are fixed in the short run because in the long run a company's prices and revenues must recover all its costs if it is to remain in business. In contrast, for short-run pricing or one-time-only special order decisions, managers consider only those costs that change in the short run, mostly but not exclusively variable costs.

Step 4: Perform Cost Analysis. Astel's managers analyze specific aspects of the product to target for cost reduction:

- The functions performed by different component parts, such as the motherboard, disk drives, and graphics and video cards.
- The importance customers place on different functional features. For example, Provalue's customers value reliability more than video quality.
- The relationship and tradeoffs between functional features and component parts. For example, a simpler motherboard enhances reliability but cannot support a top-of-the-line video card.

Step 5: Perform Value Engineering to Achieve Target Cost. Value engineering is a systematic evaluation of all aspects of the value chain, with the objective of reducing costs and achieving a quality level that satisfies customers. Value engineering entails improvements in product designs, changes in materials specifications, and modifications in process methods. (Concepts in Action: Extreme Target Pricing and Cost Management at IKEA describes IKEA's approach to target pricing and target costing.)

Learning Objective 4

Apply the concepts of cost incurrence

. . . when resources are consumed

and locked-in costs

. . . when resources are committed to be incurred in the future

Value Engineering, Cost Incurrence, and Locked-In Costs

To implement value engineering, managers distinguish value-added activities and costs from non-value-added activities and costs. A **value-added cost** is a cost that, if eliminated, would reduce the actual or perceived value or utility (usefulness) customers experience from using the product or service. In the Provalue example, value-added costs are specific product features and attributes desired by customers, such as reliability, adequate memory, preloaded software, clear images, and prompt customer service.

A **non-value-added cost** is a cost that, if eliminated, would not reduce the actual or perceived value or utility (usefulness) customers gain from using the product or service. Examples of non-value-added costs are the costs of defective products and machine breakdowns. Companies seek to minimize non-value-added costs because they do not provide benefits to customers.

[2] For a more detailed discussion of target costing, see S. Ansari, J. Bell, and the CAM-I Target Cost Core Group, *Target Costing: The Next Frontier in Strategic Cost Management* (Martinsville, IN: Mountain Valley Publishing, 2009). For implementation information, see S. Ansari, D. Swenson, and J. Bell, "A Template for Implementing Target Costing," *Cost Management* (September–October 2006): 20–27.

Activities and costs do not always fall neatly into value-added or non-value-added categories, so managers often have to apply judgment to classify costs. Several costs, such as supervision and production control, have both value-added and non-value-added components. When in doubt, some managers prefer to classify costs as non-value-added to focus organizational attention on cost reduction. The risk with this approach is that an organization may cut some costs that are value-adding, leading to poor customer experiences. Managers must exercise careful judgment when classifying costs as value-added or non-value-added.

Despite these difficult gray areas, managers find it useful to distinguish value-added from non-value-added costs for value engineering. In the Provalue example, direct materials, direct manufacturing labor, and direct machining costs are value-added costs; ordering, receiving, testing, and inspection costs have both value-added and non-value-added components; and rework costs are non-value-added costs.

Astel's managers next distinguish cost incurrence from locked-in costs. **Cost incurrence** describes when a resource is consumed (or benefit forgone) to meet a specific objective. Costing systems measure cost incurrence. For example, Astel recognizes direct material costs of Provalue only when Provalue is assembled and sold. But Provalue's direct material cost per unit is *locked in*, or *designed in*, much earlier, when product designers choose the specific components in Provalue. **Locked-in costs,** or **designed-in costs,** are costs that have not yet been incurred but will be incurred in the future based on decisions that have already been made.

Concepts in Action: Extreme Target Pricing and Cost Management at IKEA

IKEA is a global furniture retailing industry phenomenon. Known for products named after Swedish towns, modern design, flat packaging, and do-it-yourself instructions, IKEA has grown into the world's largest furniture retailer with 287 stores in 26 countries. How did this happen? Through aggressive target pricing, coupled with relentless cost management. IKEA's prices typically run 30–50% below its competitors' prices. Moreover, while the prices of other companies' products have increased over time, IKEA's prices have dropped 2–3% each year since 2000.

Source: JFP/Alamy

When IKEA decides to create new items, product developers survey competitors to determine how much they charge for similar items, if offered, and then select a target price that is 30–50% less than competitors' prices. With a product and price established, IKEA then determines what materials will be used and selects one of its 1,800 suppliers to manufacture the item through a competitive-bidding process. This value-engineering process promotes volume-based cost efficiencies throughout design and production. Aggressive cost management does not stop there. All IKEA products are designed to be shipped unassembled in flat packages, as the company estimates that shipping costs would be at least six times greater if all products were assembled before shipping.

What about products that have already been developed? IKEA applies the same cost management techniques to those products, too. For example, one of IKEA's best-selling products is the Lack bedside table, which has retailed for the same low price since 1981. Since hitting store shelves, more than 100 technical development projects have been performed on the Lack table. Despite the steady increase in the cost of raw materials and wages, IKEA has aggressively sought to reduce product and distribution costs to maintain the Lack table's initial retail price without jeopardizing the company's profit on the product. As founder Ingvar Kamprad once summarized, "Waste of resources is a mortal sin at IKEA. Expensive solutions are a sign of mediocrity, and an idea without a price tag is never acceptable."

Sources: Based on Enrico Baraldi and Torkel Strömsten, "Managing product development the IKEA way. Using target costing in interorganizational networks," Working Paper, December 2009; Lisa Margonelli, "How IKEA designs its sexy price tags," Business 2.0, October 2002; Daniel Terdiman, "Anatomy of an IKEA product," CNET News.com, April 19, 2008; and Deniz Caglar, Marco Kesteloo, and Art Kleiner, "How IKEA Reassembled Its Growth Strategy," *Strategy + Business*, May 7, 2012.

The best opportunity to manage costs is before costs are locked in, so Astel's managers model the effect of different product design choices on costs such as scrap and rework that will only be incurred later during manufacturing. They then control these costs by making wise design choices. Similarly, managers in the software industry reduce costly and difficult-to-fix errors that appear during coding and testing through better software design and analysis.

Exhibit 7-3 illustrates the locked-in cost curve and the cost-incurrence curve for Provalue. The bottom curve uses information from Exhibit 7-2 to plot the cumulative cost per unit incurred in different business functions of the value chain. The top curve plots cumulative locked-in costs. (The specific numbers underlying this curve are not presented.) Total cumulative cost per unit for both curves is $900 but there is *wide divergence between locked-in costs and costs incurred.* For example, product design decisions lock in more than 86% ($780 ÷ $900) of the unit cost of Provalue (including costs of direct materials, ordering, testing, rework, distribution, and customer service), when Astel incurs only about 4% ($36 ÷ $900) of the unit cost!

Value-Chain Analysis and Cross-Functional Teams

A cross-functional value-engineering team consisting of marketing managers, product designers, manufacturing engineers, purchasing managers, suppliers, dealers, and management accountants redesign Provalue (called Provalue II) to reduce costs while retaining features that customers value. Some of the team's ideas are:

- Use a simpler, more reliable motherboard without complex features to reduce manufacturing and repair costs.
- Snap-fit rather than solder parts together to decrease direct manufacturing labor-hours and related costs.
- Use fewer components to decrease ordering, receiving, testing, and inspection costs.
- Make Provalue lighter and smaller to reduce distribution and packaging costs.

Management accountants use their understanding of the value chain to estimate cost savings.

The team focuses on design decisions to reduce costs before costs get locked in. However, not all costs are locked in at the design stage. Managers use *kaizen,* or *continuous improvement* techniques, to reduce the time it takes to do a task, eliminate waste, and improve operating efficiency and productivity. To summarize, the key steps in value-engineering are:

1. Understanding customer requirements, value-added, and non-value-added costs.
2. Anticipating how costs are locked in before they are incurred.
3. Using cross-functional teams to redesign products and processes to reduce costs while meeting customer needs.

Exhibit 7-3

Pattern of Cost Incurrence and Locked-In Costs for Provalue

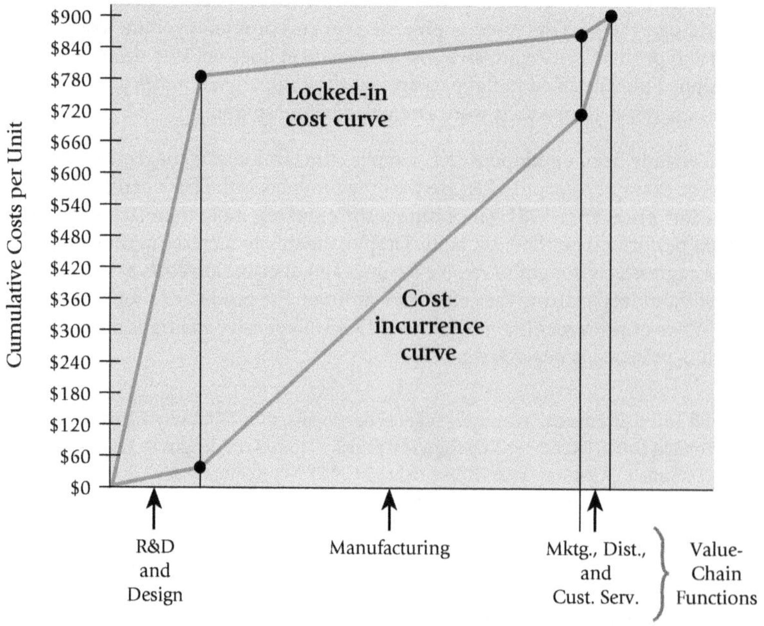

Achieving the Target Cost per Unit for Provalue

Exhibit 7-4 uses an activity-based approach to compare cost-driver quantities and rates for the 150,000 units of Provalue manufactured and sold in 2012 and the 200,000 units of Provalue II budgeted for 2013. Value engineering decreases both value-added costs (by designing Provalue II to reduce direct materials and component costs, direct manufacturing labor-hours, and testing-hours) and non-value-added costs (by simplifying Provalue II's design to reduce rework). Value engineering also reduces the machine-hours required to make Provalue II to 1.5 hours per unit. Astel can now use the 300,000 machine-hours of capacity to make 200,000 units of Provalue II (vs. 150,000 units for Provalue), reducing machining cost per unit. For simplicity, we assume that value engineering will not reduce the $20 cost per direct manufacturing labor-hour, the $80 cost per order, the $2 cost per testing-hour, or the $40 cost per rework-hour. (The Problem for Self-Study, page 281, explores how value engineering can also reduce these cost-driver rates.)

Exhibit 7-5 presents the target manufacturing costs of Provalue II, using cost driver and cost-driver rate data from Exhibit 7-4. For comparison, Exhibit 7-5 also shows the actual 2012

Exhibit 7-4

Cost-Driver Quantities and Rates for Provalue in 2012 and Provalue II for 2013 Using Activity-Based Costing

	A	B	C	D	E	F	G	H	I	J	K	L	M	N
1–2				Manufacturing Cost Information for 150,000 Units of Provalue in 2012					Manufacturing Cost Information for 200,000 Units of Provalue II for 2013					
3	Cost Category	Cost Driver	Details of Actual Cost Driver Quantities				Actual Total Quantity of Cost Driver	Actual Cost per Unit of Cost Driver (p.257)	Details of Budgeted Cost Driver Quantities				Budgeted Total Quantity of Cost Driver	Budgeted Cost per Unit of Cost Driver (Given)
4	(1)	(2)	(3)		(4)		(5)=(3)×(4)	(6)	(7)		(8)		(9)=(7)×(8)	(10)
5	Direct Manufacturing Costs													
6	Direct materials	No. of kits	1	kit per unit	150,000	units	150,000	$460	1	kit per unit	200,000	units	200,000	$385
7	Direct manuf. labor (DML)	DML hours	3.2	DML hours per unit	150,000	units	480,000	$ 20	2.65	DML hours per unit	200,000	units	530,000	$ 20
8	Direct machining (fixed)	Machine-hours					300,000	$ 38					300,000	$ 38
9	Manufacturing Overhead Costs													
10	Ordering and receiving	No. of orders	50	orders per component	450	compo-nents	22,500	$ 80	50	orders per compo-nent	425	compo-nents	21,250	$ 80
11	Testing and inspection	Testing-hours	30	testing-hours per unit	150,000	units	4,500,000	$ 2	15	testing hours per unit	200,000	units	3,000,000	$ 2
12	Rework				8%	defect rate					6.5%	defect rate		
13		Rework-hours	2.5	rework-hours per defective unit	12,000[a]	defective units	30,000	$ 40	2.5	rework-hours per defective unit	13,000[b]	defective units	32,500	$ 40
14														
15	[a]8% defect rate × 150,000 units = 12,000 defective units													
16	[b]6.5% defect rate × 200,000 units = 13,000 defective units													

Exhibit 7-5

Target Manufacturing Costs of Provalue II for 2013

	A	B	C	D	E	F
1		PROVALUE II				PROVALUE
2		Budgeted		Budgeted		Actual Manufacturing
3		Manufacturing Costs		Manufacturing		Cost per Unit
4		for 200,000 Units		Cost per Unit		(Exhibit 7-1)
5		(1)		(2) = (1) ÷ 200,000		(3)
6	Direct manufacturing costs					
7	Direct material costs					
8	(200,000 kits × $385 per kit)	$ 77,000,000		$385.00		$460.00
9	Direct manufacturing labor costs					
10	(530,000 DML-hours × $20 per hour)	10,600,000		53.00		64.00
11	Direct machining costs					
12	(300,000 machine-hours × $38 per machine-hour)	11,400,000		57.00		76.00
13	Direct manufacturing costs	99,000,000		495.00		600.00
14	Manufacturing overhead costs					
15	Ordering and receiving costs					
16	(21,250 orders × $80 per order)	1,700,000		8.50		12.00
17	Testing and inspection costs					
18	(3,000,000 testing-hours × $2 per hour)	6,000,000		30.00		60.00
19	Rework costs					
20	(32,500 rework-hours × $40 per hour)	1,300,000		6.50		8.00
21	Manufacturing overhead costs	9,000,000		45.00		80.00
22	Total manufaturing costs	$108,000,000		$540.00		$680.00

manufacturing cost per unit of Provalue from Exhibit 7-1. Astel's managers expect the new design to reduce total manufacturing cost per unit by $140 (from $680 to $540) and cost per unit in other business functions from $220 (Exhibit 7-2) to $180 (calculations not shown) at the budgeted sales quantity of 200,000 units. The budgeted full unit cost of Provalue II is $720 ($540 + $180), the target cost per unit. At the end of 2013, Astel's managers will compare actual costs and target costs to gain insight about improvements they can make in subsequent target-costing efforts.

Unless managed properly, value engineering and target costing can have undesirable effects:

- Employees may feel frustrated if they fail to attain target costs.
- The cross-functional team may add too many features just to accommodate the different wishes of team members.
- A product may be in development for a long time as the team repeatedly evaluates alternative designs.
- Organizational conflicts may develop as the burden of cutting costs falls unequally on different business functions in the company's value chain, for example, more on manufacturing than on marketing.

To avoid these pitfalls, target-costing efforts should always (1) encourage employee participation and celebrate small improvements toward achieving the target cost, (2) focus on the customer, (3) pay attention to schedules, and (4) set cost-cutting targets for all value-chain functions to encourage a culture of teamwork and cooperation.

Keys to Success

In the market-based approach to pricing, managers (1) determine a target price that potential customers are willing to pay for a product; (2) derive a target cost per unit to achieve a desired level of profitability; and (3) apply value engineering methods to make cost improvements before costs are locked in to achieve the target cost.

Cost-Plus Pricing

Learning Objective 5

Price products using the cost-plus approach

. . . cost-plus pricing is based on some measure of cost plus a markup

Instead of using the market-based approach for long-run pricing decisions, managers sometimes use a cost-based approach. The general formula for setting a cost-based selling price adds a markup component to the cost base. Because a markup is added, cost-based pricing is often called cost-plus pricing, where the plus refers to the markup component. Costco uses cost-plus pricing when deciding how much to charge for products in its warehouse stores. Managers use the cost-plus pricing formula as a starting point. The markup component is usually flexible, depending on the behavior of customers and competitors. In other words, market conditions ultimately determine the markup component.[3]

Cost-Plus Target Rate of Return on Investment

Suppose Astel uses a 12% markup on the full unit cost of Provalue II to compute the selling price. The cost-plus price is:

Cost base (full unit cost of Provalue II)	$720.00
Markup component of 12% (0.12 × $720)	86.40
Prospective selling price	$806.40

How do managers determine the markup percentage of 12%? One way is to choose a markup to earn a **target rate of return on investment,** which is the target annual operating income divided by invested capital. Invested capital can be defined in many ways. In this chapter, we define it as total assets—that is, long-term assets plus current assets. Suppose Astel's (pretax) target rate of return on investment is 18%, and Provalue II's capital investment is $96 million. The target annual operating income for Provalue II is:

Invested capital	$96,000,000
Target rate of return on investment	18%
Target annual operating income (0.18 × $96,000,000)	$17,280,000
Target operating income per unit of Provalue II ($17,280,000 ÷ 200,000 units)	$ 86.40

This calculation indicates that Astel needs to earn a target operating income of $86.40 on each unit of Provalue II. The markup ($86.40) expressed as a percentage of the full unit cost of the product ($720) equals 12% ($86.40 ÷ $720).

Do not confuse the 18% target rate of return on investment with the 12% markup percentage.

- The 18% target rate of return on investment expresses Astel's expected annual operating income as a percentage of investment.
- The 12% markup expresses operating income per unit as a percentage of the full product cost per unit.

Astel uses the target rate of return on investment to calculate the markup percentage.

Alternative Cost-Plus Methods

Computing the specific amount of capital invested in a product is challenging because it requires difficult and arbitrary allocations of investments in equipment and buildings to individual products. The following table uses alternative cost bases (without supporting calculations) and assumed markup percentages to set prospective selling prices for Provalue II without explicitly calculating invested capital to set prices.

The different cost bases and markup percentages give four prospective selling prices that are close to each other. In practice, a company chooses a reliable cost base and markup percentage to recover its costs and earn a target return on investment. For example, consulting companies often choose the full cost of a client engagement as their cost base because it is difficult to distinguish variable costs from fixed costs.

[3] Exceptions are pricing of electricity and natural gas in many countries, where prices are set by the government on the basis of costs plus a return on invested capital. In these situations, products are not subject to competitive forces and cost accounting techniques substitute for markets as the basis for setting prices.

Cost Base	Estimated Cost per Unit (1)	Markup Percentage (2)	Markup Component (3) = (1) × (2)	Prospective Selling Price (4) = (1) + (3)
Variable manufacturing cost	$475.00	65%	$308.75	$783.75
Variable cost of the product	547.00	45	246.15	793.15
Manufacturing cost	540.00	50	270.00	810.00
Full cost of the product	720.00	12	86.40	806.40

The markup percentages in the preceding table vary a great deal, from a high of 65% on variable manufacturing cost to a low of 12% on full cost of the product. Why the wide variation? When determining a prospective selling price, a cost base such as variable manufacturing cost that includes fewer costs requires a higher markup percentage because the price needs to be set to earn a profit margin *and* to recover costs (fixed manufacturing costs and all nonmanufacturing costs) that have been excluded from the base.

Surveys indicate that most managers use the full cost of the product for cost-based pricing decisions—that is, they include variable costs and costs that are fixed in the short run when calculating the cost per unit. Managers include fixed cost per unit in the cost base for several reasons:

1. **Full recovery of all costs of the product.** In the long run, the price of a product must exceed the full cost of the product if a company is to remain in business. Using just the variable cost as a base may tempt managers to cut prices as long as prices are above variable cost and generate a positive contribution margin. As the experience in the airline industry has shown, variable cost pricing may cause companies to lose money because revenues are too low to recover the full cost of the product. Using the full cost of the product as a basis for pricing reduces the temptation to cut prices below full costs.
2. **Price stability.** Limiting the ability and temptation of salespersons to cut prices by using the full cost of a product as the basis for pricing decisions also promotes price stability. Stable prices facilitate more accurate forecasting and planning for both sellers and buyers.
3. **Simplicity.** A full-cost formula for pricing does not require the management accountant to perform a detailed analysis of cost-behavior patterns to separate product costs into fixed and variable components. Variable and fixed cost components are difficult to identify for many costs such as testing, inspection, and setups.

Including fixed cost per unit in the cost base for pricing can cause problems. Allocating fixed costs to products can be arbitrary. Also, calculating fixed cost per unit requires a denominator level that is based on an estimate of capacity or expected units of future sales. Errors in these estimates will cause actual full cost per unit of the product to differ from the estimated amount.

Cost-Plus Pricing and Target Pricing

The selling prices computed under cost-plus pricing are *prospective* prices. Suppose Astel's initial product design results in a $750 full cost for Provalue II. Assuming a 12% markup, Astel sets a prospective price of $840 [$750 + (0.12 × $750)]. In the competitive personal computer market, customer and competitor reactions to this price may force Astel to reduce the markup percentage and lower the price to, say, $800. Astel may then want to redesign Provalue II to reduce the full cost to $720 per unit, as in our example, and achieve a markup close to 12% while keeping the price at $800. The eventual design and cost-plus price must balance cost, markup, and customer reactions.

The target-pricing approach reduces the need to go back and forth among prospective cost-plus prices, customer reactions, and design modifications. In contrast to cost-plus pricing, target pricing first determines product characteristics and target price on the basis of customer preferences and expected competitor responses, and then computes a target cost.

Suppliers who provide unique products and services, such as accountants and management consultants, usually use cost-plus pricing. Professional service firms set prices based on hourly cost-plus billing rates of partners, managers, and associates. These prices are, however, lowered in competitive situations. Professional service firms also take a multiple-year client perspective when deciding prices because clients prefer to work with a firm over multiple periods. Certified public accountants, for example, sometimes charge a client a low price initially to get the account and recover the lower profits or losses in the intial years by charging higher prices in later years.

Service companies such as home repair services, automobile repair services, and architectural firms use a cost-plus pricing method called the *time-and-materials method.* Individual jobs are priced based on materials and labor time. The price charged for materials equals the cost of materials plus a markup. The price charged for labor represents the cost of labor plus a markup. That is, the price charged for each direct cost item includes its own markup. Companies choose the markups to recover overhead costs and to earn a profit.

We have so far focused on the overall pricing decision for Provalue. But Astel does not sell Provalue at the same price to all customers. For example, Astel sells Provalue through different distribution channels: wholesalers who distribute Provalue to different electronic retail stores and direct sales to business customers. Astel's pricing arrangements differ across these channels and even for customers within each channel. At the same time, the resources Astel uses to support different customers varies across customers. As we discuss in the next section, these differences result in individual customers delivering varying amounts of profitability.

Keys to Success

In the cost-plus approach to pricing, managers determine price by adding a markup component to a cost base to achieve a desired level of profit. They decide the size of the "plus" component after taking into account customer reactions and competitor responses.

Learning Objective 6

Discuss why a company's revenues and costs differ across customers

. . . revenues differ because of differences in quantities purchased and price discounts while costs differ because of different demands placed on a company's resources

and the actions managers can take based on this information

. . . expand relationships with profitable customers and change behavior patterns of unprofitable customers

Customer-Profitability Analysis

Customer-profitability analysis is the reporting and assessment of revenues earned from customers and the costs incurred to earn those revenues. An analysis of customer differences in revenues and costs reveals why differences exist in the operating income earned from different customers. Managers use this information to ensure that customers making large contributions to the operating income of a company receive a high level of attention from the company and that loss-making customers do not use more resources than the revenues they provide. At Best Buy, managers use customer-profitability analysis to segment customers into "angels," the profitable customers the company is seeking, and "devils," or unprofitable customers that should be avoided.

Consider again Astel Computers' data for the year just-ended in 2012 (Exhibit 7-2). Astel sells the same Provalue computer to wholesalers and to business customers, so the full manufacturing cost of Provalue, $680, is the same regardless of where it is sold. Provalue's listed selling price in 2012 was $1,100 but price discounts reduced the average selling price to $1,000. We focus on customer-profitability in Astel's wholesale distribution channel.

Customer-Revenue Analysis

Consider revenues from 4 of Astel's 10 wholesale customers in 2012:

Home Insert Page Layout Formulas Data Review View

	A	B	C	D	E
1			CUSTOMER		
2		A	B	G	J
3	Units of Provalue sold	30,000	25,000	5,000	4,000
4	List selling price	$ 1,100	$ 1,100	$ 1,100	$ 1,100
5	Price discount	$ 100	$ 50	$ 150	—
6	Invoice price	$ 1,000	$ 1,050	$ 950	$ 1,100
7	Revenues (Row 3 x Row 6)	$30,000,000	$26,250,000	$4,750,000	$4,400,000

Two variables explain revenue differences across these four wholesale customers: (1) the number of computers they purchased and (2) the magnitude of price discounting. A **price discount** is the reduction in selling price below list selling price to encourage customers to purchase more quantities. Companies that record only the final invoice price in their information system cannot readily track the magnitude of their price discounting.[4]

Price discounts are a function of multiple factors, including the volume of product purchased (higher-volume customers receive higher discounts) and the desire to sell to a customer who might help promote sales to other customers. In some cases, discounts result from poor negotiating by a salesperson or the unwanted effect of a company's incentive plan based only on revenues. At no time, however, should price discounts stem from illegal activities such as price discrimination, predatory pricing, or collusive pricing (pages 278–280).

Tracking price discounts by customer and by salesperson helps improve customer profitability. For example, Astel's managers may decide to strictly enforce its volume-based price discounting policy. The company may also require its salespeople to obtain approval for giving large discounts to customers who do not normally qualify for such discounts. In addition, the company could track future sales to customers who have received sizable price discounts on the basis of their "high growth potential." For example, Astel should track future sales to customer G to see if the $150-per-computer discount translates into higher future sales.

Customer revenues are one element of customer profitability. The other, equally important element is the cost of acquiring, serving, and retaining customers.

Customer-Cost Analysis

We apply to customers the cost hierarchy discussed in Chapter 6 (pages 216–217). A **customer-cost hierarchy** categorizes costs related to customers into different cost pools on the basis of different types of cost drivers, or cost-allocation bases, or different degrees of difficulty in determining cause-and-effect or benefits-received relationships. Astel's customer costs comprise (1) marketing and administration costs, $15,000,000; (2) distribution costs, $9,000,000; and (3) customer-service costs, $3,600,000 (see Exhibit 7-2). Astel identifies five categories of indirect costs in its customer-cost hierarchy:

1. **Customer output unit–level costs**—costs of activities to sell each unit (computer) to a customer. An example is product-handling costs of each computer sold.
2. **Customer batch-level costs**—costs of activities related to a group of units (computers) sold to a customer. Examples are costs incurred to process orders or to make deliveries.
3. **Customer-sustaining costs**—costs of activities to support individual customers, regardless of the number of units or batches of product delivered to the customer. Examples are costs of visits to customers or costs of displays at customer sites.
4. **Distribution-channel costs**—costs of activities related to a particular distribution channel rather than to each unit of product, each batch of product, or specific customers. An example is the salary of the manager of Astel's wholesale distribution channel.
5. **Corporate (division)-sustaining costs**—costs of activities that cannot be traced to individual customers or distribution channels. Examples are general-administration costs such as the salary of the Provalue division manager.

Note from these descriptions that four of the five levels of Astel's cost hierarchy closely parallel the cost hierarchy described in Chapter 6, except that Astel focuses on *customers* whereas the cost hierarchy in Chapter 6 focused on *products*. Astel has one additional cost hierarchy category, distribution-channel costs, for the costs it incurs to support its wholesale and business-sales channels.

Customer-Level Costs

Exhibit 7-6 summarizes details of the costs incurred in marketing and administration, distribution, and customer service by activity. It also identifies the cost driver (where appropriate), the total costs incurred for the activity, the total quantity of the cost driver, the cost per unit of the cost driver, and the customer cost-hierarchy category for each activity.

For example, here is how Astel spends $15,000,000 on marketing and administration:

- $6,750,000 on the sales order activity, which includes negotiating, finalizing, issuing, and collecting on 6,000 sales orders at a cost of $1,125 ($6,750,000 ÷ 6,000) per sales order. Recall that sales-order costs are customer batch-level costs because these costs vary with the number of sales orders issued and not with the number of Provalue computers in a sales order.

[4] Further analysis of customer revenues could distinguish gross revenues from net revenues. This approach highlights differences across customers in sales returns. Additional discussion of ways to analyze revenue differences across customers is in R. S. Kaplan and R. Cooper, *Cost and Effect* (Boston: Harvard Business School Press, 1998), Chapter 10; and G. Cokins, *Activity-Based Cost Management: An Executive's Guide* (New York: Wiley, 2001), Chapter 3.

Exhibit 7-6

Marketing, Distribution, and Customer Service Activities, Costs, and Cost Driver Information

	A	B	C	D	E	F	G	H
1	Marketing, Distribution, and Customer Service Costs for 150,000 units of Provalue in 2012							
2								
3	Activity Area	Cost Driver	Total Cost of Activity	Total Quantity of Cost Driver		Rate per Unit of Cost Driver		Cost Hierarchy Category
4	(1)	(2)	(3)	(4)		(5) = (3) ÷ (4)		(6)
5	**Marketting**							
6	Sales order	Number of sales orders	$ 6,750,000	6,000	sales orders	$1,125	per sales order	Customer batch-level costs
7	Customer visits	Number of customer visits	4,200,000	750	customer visits	$5,600	per customer visit	Customer-sustaining costs
8	Wholesale channel marketing		800,000					Distribution-channel costs
9	Business-sales channel marketing		1,350,000					Distribution-channel costs
10	Provalue division administration		1,900,000					Corporate (division)-sustaining costs
11	Total marketing costs		$15,000,000					
12								
13	**Distribution**							
14	Product handling	Number of cubic feet moved	$ 4,500,000	300,000	cubic feet	$ 15	per cubic foot	Customer output unit-level costs
15	Regular shipments	Number of regular shipments	3,750,000	3,000	regular shipments	$1,250	per regular shipment	Customer batch-level costs
16	Rush shipments	Number of rush shipments	750,000	150	rush shipments	$5,000	per rush shipment	Customer batch-level costs
17	Total distribution costs		$ 9,000,000					
18								
19	**Customer Service**							
20	Customer service	Number of units shipped	$ 3,600,000	150,000	units shipped	$ 24	per unit shipped	Customer output unit-level costs

- $4,200,000 for customer visits, which are customer-sustaining costs. The amount per customer varies with the number of visits rather than the number of units or batches of Provalue delivered to a customer.
- $800,000 on managing the wholesale channel, which are distribution-channel costs.
- $1,350,000 on managing the business-sales channel, which are distribution-channel costs.
- $1,900,000 on marketing the Provalue brand and on general administration of the Provalue division, which are corporate (division)-sustaining costs.

As we discussed in an earlier chapter (Chapter 6), it is difficult to find a cost driver for distribution-channel and corporate (division)-sustaining costs. As a result, Astel chooses not to allocate distribution-channel and corporate (division)-sustaining costs to individual customers. Instead, as we will see in the next section, Astel deducts these costs as separate lump-sum amounts when calculating operating income.

Astel's managers have particular interest in analyzing *customer-level indirect costs*—costs incurred in the first three categories of the customer-cost hierarchy: customer output unit–level costs, customer batch-level costs, and customer-sustaining costs. They want to work with customers to reduce these costs. They believe customer actions will have less impact on distribution-channel and corporate (division)-sustaining costs. Information on the quantity of cost drivers used by each of four representative wholesale customers follows:

	A	B	C	D	E	F
1			CUSTOMER			
2	Activity	Quantity of Cost Driver	A	B	G	J
3	**Marketing**					
4	Sales orders	Number of sales orders	1,200	1,000	600	300
5	Customer visits	Number of customer visits	150	100	50	25
6	**Distribution**					
7	Product handling	Number of cubic feet moved	60,000	50,000	10,000	8,000
8	Regular shipments	Number of regular shipments	600	400	300	120
9	Rush shipments	Number of rush shipments	25	5	20	3
10	**Customer Service**					
11	Customer service	Number of unit shipped	30,000	25,000	5,000	4,000

Exhibit 7-7

Customer-Profitability Analysis for Four Wholesale Channel Customers of Astel Computers for 2012

Home Insert Page Layout Formulas Data Review View

	A	B	C	D	E
1		**A**	**B**	**G**	**J**
2	Revenues at list price	$33,000,000	$27,500,000	$5,500,000	$4,400,000
3	Price discount	3,000,000	1,250,000	750,000	-
4	Revenues	30,000,000	26,250,000	4,750,000	4,400,000
5					
6	Cost of goods sold[a]	20,400,000	17,000,000	3,400,000	2,720,000
7					
8	Gross margin	9,600,000	9,250,000	1,350,000	1,680,000
9					
10	**Customer-level operating costs**				
11	**Marketing Costs**				
12	Sales orders[b]	1,350,000	1,125,000	675,000	337,500
13	Customer visits[c]	840,000	560,000	280,000	140,000
14	**Distribution Costs**				
15	Product handling[d]	900,000	750,000	150,000	120,000
16	Regular shipments[e]	750,000	500,000	375,000	150,000
17	Rush shipments[f]	125,000	25,000	100,000	15,000
18	**Customer Service Costs**				
19	Customer service[g]	720,000	600,000	120,000	96,000
20					
21	Total customer-level operating costs	4,685,000	3,560,000	1,700,000	858,500
22					
23	Customer-level operating income	$ 4,915,000	$ 5,690,000	$ (350,000)	$ 821,500
24	[a]$680 x 30,000; 25,000; 5,000; 4,000 [b]$1,125 x 1,200; 1,000; 600; 300 [c]$5,600 x 150; 100; 50; 25 [d]$15 x 60,000; 50,000; 10,000;				
25	8,000 [e]$1,250 x 600; 400; 300; 120 [f]$5,000 x 25; 5; 20; 3 [g]$24 x 30,000; 25,000; 5,000; 4,000				

Exhibit 7-7 shows customer-level operating income for the four wholesale customers using information on customer revenues previously presented (page 267) and customer-level indirect costs obtained, by multiplying the rate per unit of cost driver (from Exhibit 7-6) by the quantities of the cost driver used by each customer (page 269). Exhibit 7-7 shows that Astel is losing money on Customer G (the cost of resources used by Customer G exceeds revenues) while it makes money on Customer J on smaller revenues. Astel sells fewer computers to Customer B compared to Customer A but has higher operating income from Customer B than Customer A.

Astel's managers can use the information in Exhibit 7-7 to work with customers to reduce the quantity of activities needed to support them. Consider, for example, a comparison of Customer G and Customer J. Customer G purchases 25% more computers than customer J purchases (5,000 vs. 4,000) but the company offers Customer G significant price discounts to achieve these sales. Compared with Customer J, Customer G places twice as many sales orders, requires twice as many customer visits, and generates two-and-a-half times as many regular shipments and seven times as many rush shipments. Selling smaller quantities of units is profitable, provided Astel's salespeople limit the amount of price discounting and customers do not use large amounts of Astel's resources. For example, by implementing an additional charge for customers who use large amounts of marketing and distribution services, Astel's managers might be able to induce customer G to place fewer but larger sales orders, and require fewer customer visits, regular shipments, and rush shipments while looking to increase sales in the future. Astel's managers would perform a similar analysis to understand the reasons for the lower profitability of Customer A relative to Customer B.

Owens and Minor, a distributor of medical supplies to hospitals, follows this approach. Owens and Minor strategically prices each of its services separately. For example, if a hospital wants a rush delivery or special packaging, Owens and Minor charges the hospital an additional price for each particular service. How have Owens and Minor's customers reacted? Hospitals that value these services continue to demand and pay for them, while hospitals that do not value these services stop asking for them, saving Owens and Minor some costs. Owens and Minor's pricing strategy influences customer behavior in a way that increases its revenues or decreases its costs.

The ABC system also highlights a second opportunity for cost reduction. Astel's managers can reduce the costs of each activity by applying the same value-engineering process described earlier in the chapter to nonmanufacturing costs. For example, improving the efficiency of the ordering process (such as by having customers order electronically) reduces sales order costs even if customers place the same number of orders. Simplifying the design and reducing the weight of the newly designed Provalue II for 2013 reduces the cost per cubic foot of handling Provalue and total product-handling costs. By influencing customer behavior and improving marketing, distribution, and customer service operations, Astel's managers aim to reduce the nonmanufacturing cost of Provalue to $180 per computer and achieve the target cost of $720 for Provalue II.

Customer Profitability Profiles

Customer-profitability profiles provide a useful tool for managers. Exhibit 7-8 ranks Astel's 10 wholesale customers based on customer-level operating income. (We analyzed four of these customers in Exhibit 7-7.)

Column 4, computed by adding the individual amounts in column 1, shows the cumulative customer-level operating income. For example, Customer C has a cumulative income of $13,260,000 in column 4. This $13,260,000 is the sum of $5,690,000 for Customer B, $4,915,000 for Customer A, and $2,655,000 for Customer C.

Column 5 shows what percentage the $13,260,000 *cumulative* total for customers B, A, and C is of the total customer-level operating income of $15,027,500 earned in the wholesale distribution channel from all 10 customers. The three most profitable customers contribute 88% of

Exhibit 7-8

Customer-Profitability Analysis for Wholesale Channel Customers: Astel Computers 2012

	A	B	C	D	E	F
1	Retail Customer Code	Customer-Level Operating Income	Customer Revenue	Customer-Level Operating Income Divided by Revenue	Cumulative Customer-Level Operating Income	Cumulative Customer-Level Operating Income as a % of Total Customer-Level Operating Income
2		(1)	(2)	(3) = (1) ÷ (2)	(4)	(5) = (4) ÷ $15,027,500
3	B	$ 5,690,000	$26,250,000	21.7%	$ 5,690,000	38%
4	A	4,915,000	30,000,000	16.4%	10,605,000	71%
5	C	2,655,000	13,000,000	20.4%	13,260,000	88%
6	D	1,445,000	7,250,000	19.9%	14,705,000	98%
7	F	986,000	5,100,000	19.3%	15,691,000	104%
8	J	821,500	4,400,000	18.7%	16,512,500	110%
9	E	100,000	1,800,000	5.6%	16,612,500	111%
10	G	(350,000)	4,750,000	−7.4%	16,262,500	108%
11	H	(535,000)	2,400,000	−22.3%	15,727,500	105%
12	I	(700,000)	2,600,000	−26.9%	15,027,500	100%
13	Total	$15,027,500	$97,550,000			

total customer-level operating income. These customers deserve the highest service and priority. Companies try to keep their best customers happy in a number of ways: special phone numbers and upgrade privileges for elite-level frequent flyers, free usage of luxury hotel suites and big credit limits for high-rollers at casinos, and so on. In many companies, it is common for a small number of customers to contribute a high percentage of operating income. Microsoft uses the phrase "not all revenue dollars are endowed equally in profitability" to stress this point.

Column 3 shows the profitability per dollar of revenue by customer. This measure of customer profitability indicates that, although Customer A contributes the second-highest operating income, the profitability per dollar of revenue is lowest among the top six customers because of high price discounts and higher customer-level costs. Astel's managers would like to increase profit margins for Customer A by decreasing price discounts or saving customer-level costs while maintaining or increasing sales. Customers D, F, and J have high profit margins but low total sales. The challenge for Astel's managers with these customers is to maintain margins while increasing sales. With Customers E, G, H, and I, Astel's managers have the dual challenge of boosting profits and sales.

Presenting Profitability Analysis

Exhibit 7-9 illustrates two common ways of displaying the results of customer-profitability analysis. Managers often find the bar chart presentation in Exhibit 7-9, Panel A, to be an intuitive way to visualize customer profitability because (1) the highly profitable customers clearly stand out and (2) the number of "unprofitable" customers and the magnitude of their losses are apparent. Exhibit 7-9, Panel B is a popular alternative way to express customer profitability. It plots the contents of column 5 in Exhibit 7-8. This chart is called the **whale curve** because it is backward-bending at the point where customers start to become unprofitable, and thus resembles a humpback whale.[5]

Astel's managers must explore ways to make unprofitable customers profitable. Exhibits 7-6 to 7-9 emphasize annual customer profitability. Managers should also consider other factors when allocating resources among customers, including:

- **Likelihood of customer retention.** The more likely a customer will continue to do business with a company, the more valuable the customer, for example, wholesalers who have sold Provalue each year over the last several years. Customers differ in their loyalty and their willingness to frequently "shop their business."
- **Potential for sales growth.** The higher the likely growth of the customer's sales, the more valuable the customer. Moreover, customers to whom a company can cross-sell other products are more desirable, for example, wholesalers willing to distribute both Astel's Provalue and Deskpoint brands.
- **Long-run customer profitability.** This factor is influenced by the first two factors and the cost of customer-support staff and special services required to support the customer.
- **Increase in overall demand from having well-known customers.** Customers with established reputations help generate sales from other customers through product endorsements.
- **Ability to learn from customers.** Customers who provide ideas about new products or ways to improve existing products are especially valuable, for example, wholesalers who give Astel feedback about key features such as size of memory or video displays.

Managers should be cautious when deciding to discontinue customers. In Exhibit 7-8, the current unprofitability of Customer G, for example, may provide misleading signals about G's profitability in the long run. Moreover, as in any ABC-based system, the costs assigned to Customer G are not all variable. In the short run, it may well be efficient for Astel's managers to use spare capacity to serve G on a contribution-margin basis. Discontinuing Customer G will not eliminate all costs assigned to Customer G, and may result in losing more revenues than costs saved.

---

[5] In practice, the curve of the chart can be quite steep. The whale curve for cumulative profitability usually reveals that the most profitable 20% of customers generate between 150% and 300% of total profits, the middle 70% of customers break even, and the least profitable 10% of customers lose from 50% to 200% of total profits (see Robert Kaplan and V. G. Narayanan, Measuring and Managing Customer Profitability, *Journal of Cost Management* (September/October 2001): 1–11.

Exhibit 7-9

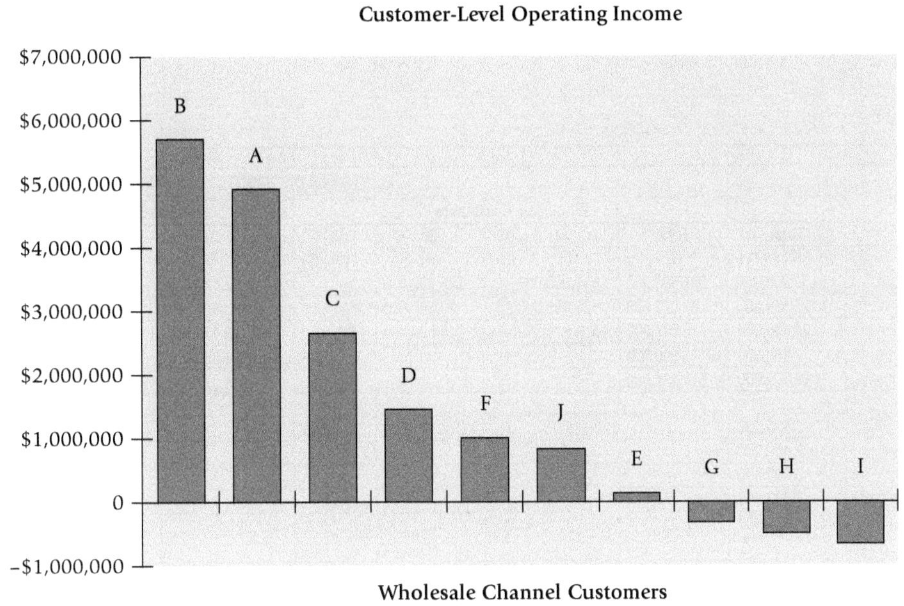

Panel A: Bar Chart of Customer-Level Operating Income for Astel Computer's Wholesale Channel Customers in 2012

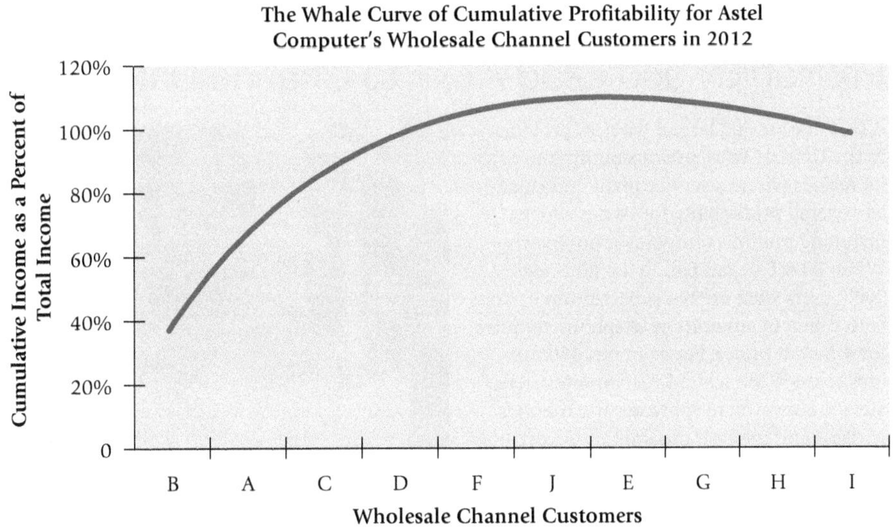

Panel B: The Whole Curve of Cumulative Profitability for Astel Computer's Wholesale Channel Customers in 2012

Of course, particular customers might be chronically unprofitable and hold limited future prospects. Or they might fall outside a company's target market or require unsustainably high levels of service relative to the company's strategies and capabilities. In such cases, organizations are becoming increasingly aggressive in severing customer relationships. For example, ING Direct, the largest direct lender and fastest-growing financial services organization in the United States, asks 10,000 "high-maintenance" customers (for example, customers who maintain low balances and make frequent deposits and withdrawals) to close their accounts each month.[6] Concepts in Action: iPhone "Apps" Challenge Profitability and Lead AT&T to Change Data Pricing describes how AT&T has had to struggle with managing its resources and profitability without affecting the satisfaction of its customers.

Cost Hierarchy-Based Operating Income Statement

Exhibit 7-10 shows an operating income statement for Astel Computers for 2012. The customer-level operating income of Customers A and B in Exhibit 7-7 is shown in columns 3 and 4 in Exhibit 7-10. The format of Exhibit 7-10 is based on Astel's cost hierarchy. As described in Exhibit 7-6, some

[6] See, for example, "The New Math of Customer Relationships" at http://hbswk.hbs.edu/item/5884.html.

Exhibit 7-10

Income Statement of Astel Computers for 2012 Using the Cost Hierarchy

	A	B	C	D	E	F	G	H	I	J	K	L	M	N	O
1				CUSTOMER DISTRIBUTION CHANNELS											
2				Wholesale Customers							Business-Sales Customers				
3		Total	Total	A*		B*		A3			Total	A	B	C	
4		1 = (2) + (7)	(2)	(3)		(4)		(5)	(6)		(7)	(8)	(9)	(10)	(11)
5	Revenues (at actual prices)	$150,000,000	$97,550,000	$30,000,000		$26,250,000		-	-		$52,450,000	$7,000,000	$6,250,000	-	-
6	Customer-level costs	125,550,000	82,522,500	25,085,000	a	20,560,000	a	-	-		43,027,500	5,385,000	4,760,000	-	-
7	Customer-level operating income	24,450,000	15,027,500	$ 4,915,000		$ 5,690,000		-	-		9,422,500	$1,615,000	$1,490,000	-	-
8	Distribution-channel costs	2,150,000	800,000								1,350,500				
9	Distribution-channel-level operating income	22,300,000	$14,227,500								$ 8,072,500				
10	Corporate (division)-sustaining costs														
11	Marketing and administration costs	1,900,000													
12	R&D Costs	2,400,000													
13	Design Costs	3,000,000													
14	Total corporate (division)-sustaining costs	7,300,000													
15	Operating income	$ 15,000,000													
16															
17	*Full details are presented in Exhibit 7-7														
18	[a]Cost of Goods sold + total customer-level operating costs from Exhibit 7-7														

Concepts in Action: iPhone "Apps" Challenge Profitability and Lead AT&T to Change Data Pricing

Source: ZUMA Press/Newscom

AT&T, the second largest wireless provider in the United States, uses accounting to price its various wireless service plans and calculate overall profitability for its customers, including millions of Apple's iPhone owners. When AT&T began selling the iPhone in 2007, users were offered subscription options with different amounts of telephone minutes for different prices. For example, 450 minutes cost $59.99, while 1,350 minutes were $99.99. However, to showcase the iPhone's wireless and Internet capabilities, AT&T only offered one data package, an unlimited plan.

While the unlimited data package proved initially lucrative, technology developments added significant costs to AT&T. When Apple introduced the iPhone 3G in 2008, the new data capabilities encouraged software developers to build new programs for the iPhone platform. By 2012, more than 500,000 applications were available, ranging from Pandora's music player to the Words With Friends game, draining AT&T's bandwidth.

Recall that AT&T did not charge iPhone subscribers for marginal bandwidth use. As a result, subscribers who downloaded and used many iPhone applications became unprofitable for the company. Moreover, with wireless data volume on its network doubling annually, AT&T had to invest more than $95 billion to make improvements to its data network from 2007 to 2011. As a result, the company stopped offering its unlimited data plan in 2010 and began pricing data based on how much people used their phones to access videos, music, and data. While many iPhone owners were unhappy, the move proved profitable for AT&T. In 2011 alone, the company booked $22 billion in wireless data revenue, with growth projected well into the future.

Sources: Based on AT&T Inc. and Apple Inc., "AT&T and Apple announce simple, affordable service plans for iPhone," AT&T Inc. and Apple Inc. Press Release, June 26, 2007; Roben Fazard, "AT&T's iPhone mess," *Businessweek*, February 3, 2010; AT&T Inc. 2011 Annual Report. Dallas, Texas: AT&T Inc., 2012; Chris Velazco, "AT&T's Wireless Data Traffic Doubles Every Year, But Throttling Is Not The Solution," TechCrunch.com blog February 14, 2012; and David Lieberman, "New AT&T smartphone users won't get one-price Net," *USA Today*, June 4, 2010.

costs of serving customers, such as the salary of the wholesale distribution-channel manager, are not customer-level costs and are therefore not allocated to customers in Exhibit 7-10. Managers identify these costs as distribution-channel costs because changes in customer behavior will have no effect on these costs. Only decisions pertaining to the channel, such as a decision to discontinue wholesale distribution, will influence these costs. Astel's managers also believe that salespersons responsible for managing individual customer accounts would lose motivation if sales bonuses were adversely affected as a result of Astel allocating to customers distribution-channel costs over which they had minimal influence.

Next, consider division-sustaining costs such as general-administration costs of the Provalue division- and corporate-sustaining costs such as R&D and Design. Astel's managers believe there is no cause-and-effect or benefits-received relationship between any cost-allocation base and division or corporate-sustaining costs. Consequently, allocation of corporate sustaining or division-sustaining costs serves no useful purpose in decision making, performance evaluation, or motivation. Suppose, for example, that Astel allocates the $7,300,000 of division and corporate-sustaining costs to its distribution channels and that in some subsequent period this allocation results in the business-sales channel showing a loss. Should Astel shut down the business-sales distribution channel?

No, because (as we will discuss in more detail in Chapter 9), if business-sales distribution was discontinued, division and corporate-sustaining costs would be unaffected. Allocating division and corporate-sustaining costs to distribution channels gives the misleading impression that potential cost savings from discontinuing a distribution channel are greater than the likely amount.

Some managers and management accountants advocate fully allocating all costs to customers and distribution channels so that (1) the sum of operating incomes of all customers in a distribution channel (segment) equals the operating income of the distribution channel and (2) the sum of the distribution-channel operating incomes equals companywide operating income. These managers and management accountants argue that customers and products must eventually be profitable on a full-cost basis. As we discussed earlier in this chapter, for some decisions such as pricing, allocating all costs ensures that long-run prices are set at a level to cover the cost of all resources used to produce and sell products. Nevertheless, the value of the hierarchical format in Exhibit 7-10 is to distinguish among various degrees of objectivity when allocating costs so that it dovetails with the different levels at which managers make decisions and evaluate performance. The issue of when and what costs to allocate is another example of the "different costs for different purposes" theme emphasized throughout this book.

Using the Five-Step Decision-Making Process to Manage Customer Profitability

The different types of customer analyses provide companies with key information to guide the allocation of resources across customers. Use the five-step decision-making process (introduced in Chapter 1), to think about how managers use these analyses to make customer-management decisions.

1. *Identify the problem and uncertainties.* The problem is how to manage and allocate resources across customers.
2. *Obtain information.* Managers identify past revenues generated by each customer and customer-level costs incurred in the past to support each customer.
3. *Make predictions about the future.* Managers estimate the revenues they expect from each customer and the customer-level costs they will incur in the future. In making these predictions, managers consider the effects that future price discounts will have on revenues, the effect that pricing for different services (such as rush deliveries) will have on the demand for these services by customers, and ways to reduce the cost of providing services. For example, Deluxe Corporation, a leading check printer, initiated process modifications to rein in its cost to serve customers by opening an electronic channel to shift customers from paper to automated ordering.
4. *Make decisions by choosing among alternatives.* Managers use the customer-profitability profiles to identify the small set of customers who deserve the highest service and priority. They also identify ways to make less-profitable customers (such as Astel's Customer G) more profitable. Banks, for example, often impose minimum balance requirements on customers. Distribution firms may require minimum order quantities or levy a surcharge for smaller or customized orders. In making resource-allocation decisions, managers also consider long-term effects,

such as the potential for future sales growth and the opportunity to leverage a particular customer account, to make sales to other customers.

5. *Implement the decision, evaluate performance, and learn.* After the decision is implemented, managers compare actual results to predicted outcomes to evaluate the decision they made, its implementation, and ways in which they might improve profitability.

Keys to Success

Customer profitability differs across customers because of differences in the quantity purchased, price discounts given, and demands that different customers make on a company's resources. Managers should devote resources to maintain and expand relationships with the most profitable customers and should limit the use of resources by unprofitable customers.

Learning Objective 7

Use life-cycle budgeting and costing when making pricing decisions

. . . accumulate all costs of a product from initial R&D to final customer service for each year of the product's life

Life-Cycle Product Budgeting and Costing

Managers sometimes need to consider target prices and target costs over a multiple-year product life cycle. The **product life cycle** spans the time from initial R&D on a product to when customer service and support is no longer offered for that product. For automobile companies such as DaimlerChrysler, Ford, and Nissan, the product life cycle is 12–15 years to design, introduce, sell, and service different car models. For pharmaceutical products, the life cycle at companies such as Pfizer, Merck, and GlaxoSmithKline may be 15–20 years. For banks such as Wells Fargo and Chase, a product such as a newly designed savings account with specific privileges can have a life cycle of 10–20 years. Personal computers have a shorter life cycle of 3–5 years because rapid innovations in the computing power and speed of microprocessors that run the computers make older models obsolete.

In **life-cycle budgeting,** managers estimate the revenues and business function costs across the entire value chain from a product's initial R&D to its final customer service and support. **Life-cycle costing** tracks and accumulates business function costs across the entire value chain from a product's initial R&D to its final customer service and support. Life-cycle budgeting and life-cycle costing span several years.

Life-Cycle Budgeting and Pricing Decisions

Budgeted life-cycle costs provide useful information for strategically evaluating pricing decisions. Consider Insight, Inc., a computer software company, which is developing a new accounting package, "General Ledger." Assume the following budgeted amounts for General Ledger over a 6-year product life cycle:

Years 1 and 2	Total Fixed Costs
R&D costs	$240,000
Design costs	160,000

Years 3–6	Total Fixed Costs	Variable Cost per Package
Production costs	$100,000	$25
Marketing costs	70,000	24
Distribution costs	50,000	16
Customer-service costs	80,000	30

Exhibit 7-11 presents the 6-year life-cycle budget for General Ledger for three alternative selling-price/sales-quantity combinations.

Several features make life-cycle budgeting particularly important:

1. **The development period for R&D and design is long and costly.** When a high percentage of total life-cycle costs are incurred before any production begins and any revenues are received, as in the General Ledger example, managers need to evaluate revenues and costs over the life cycle of the product in order to decide whether to begin the costly R&D and design activities.
2. **Many costs are locked in at R&D and design stages, even if R&D and design costs themselves are small.** In our General Ledger example, a poorly designed accounting software package, which is difficult to install and use, would result in higher marketing, distribution, and customer-service costs in several subsequent years. These costs would be even higher if the product failed to meet promised quality-performance levels. A life-cycle revenue-and-cost budget prevents Insight's managers from overlooking these multiple-year relationships among business-function costs. Life-cycle budgeting highlights costs throughout the product's life cycle and, in doing so, facilitates target pricing, target costing, and value engineering at the design stage before costs are locked in. The amounts presented in Exhibit 7-11 are the outcome of value engineering.

Insight's managers decide to sell the General Ledger package for $480 per package because this price maximizes life-cycle operating income. They then compare actual costs to life-cycle budgets to obtain feedback and to learn about how to estimate costs better for subsequent products. Exhibit 7-11 assumes that the selling price per package is the same over the entire life cycle. For strategic reasons, however, Insight's managers may decide to skim the market by charging higher prices to eager customers when General Ledger is first introduced and then lowering prices later as the product matures. In these later stages, managers may even add new features to differentiate the product to maintain prices and sales. The life-cycle budget must then incorporate the revenues and costs of these strategies.

Exhibit 7-11

Budgeting Life-Cycle Revenues and Costs for "General Ledger" Software Package of Insight, Inc.[a]

	Alternative Selling-Price/ Sales-Quantity Combinations		
	A	B	C
Selling price per package	$400	$480	$600
Sales quantity in units	5,000	4,000	2,500
Life-cycle revenues			
($400 × 5,000; $480 × 4,000; $600 × 2,500)	$2,000,000	$1,920,000	$1,500,000
Life-cycle costs			
R&D costs	240,000	240,000	240,000
Design costs of product/process	160,000	160,000	160,000
Production costs			
$100,000 + ($25 × 5,000); $100,000 + ($25 × 4,000); $100,000 + ($25 × 2,500)	225,000	200,000	162,500
Marketing costs			
$70,000 + ($24 × 5,000); $70,000 + ($24 × 4,000); $70,000 + ($24 × 2,500)	190,000	166,000	130,000
Distribution costs			
$50,000 + ($16 × 5,000); $50,000 + ($16 × 4,000); $50,000 + ($16 × 2,500)	130,000	114,000	90,000
Customer-service costs			
$80,000 + ($30 × 5,000); $80,000 + ($30 × 4,000); $80,000 + ($30 × 2,500)	230,000	200,000	155,000
Total life-cycle costs	1,175,000	1,080,000	937,500
Life-cycle operating income	$ 825,000	$ 840,000	$ 562,500

[a]This exhibit does not take into consideration the time value of money when computing life-cycle revenues or life-cycle costs. Chapter 11 outlines how this important factor can be incorporated into such calculations.

Management of environmental costs provides another example of life-cycle costing and value engineering. Environmental laws like the U.S. Clean Air Act and the U.S. Superfund Amendment and Reauthorization Act have introduced tougher environmental standards, imposed stringent cleanup requirements, and introduced severe penalties for polluting the air and contaminating subsurface soil and groundwater. Environmental costs that are incurred over several years of the product's life cycle are often locked in at the product- and process-design stage. To avoid environmental liabilities, managers in industries such as oil refining, chemical processing, and automobile manufacturing practice value engineering; they design products and processes to prevent and reduce pollution over the product's life cycle. For example, laptop computer manufacturers like Hewlett-Packard and Apple have introduced costly recycling programs to ensure that chemicals from nickel-cadmium batteries do not leak hazardous chemicals into the soil.

Customer Life-Cycle Costing

A different notion of life-cycle costs is *customer life-cycle costs.* **Customer life-cycle costs** focus on the total costs incurred by a customer to acquire, use, maintain, and dispose of a product or service. Customer life-cycle costs influence the prices a company can charge for its products. For example, Ford can charge a higher price and/or gain market share if its cars require minimal maintenance for 100,000 miles. Similarly, Maytag charges higher prices for appliances that save electricity and have low maintenance costs. Boeing Corporation justifies a higher price for the Boeing 777 because the plane's design allows mechanics easier access to different areas of the plane to perform routine maintenance, reduces the time and cost of maintenance, and significantly decreases the life-cycle cost of owning the plane.

Learning Objective 8

Describe two pricing practices in which noncost factors are important when setting prices

... price discrimination—charging different customers different prices for the same product—and peak-load pricing—charging higher prices when demand approaches capacity limits

and the effects of antitrust laws on pricing

... antitrust laws attempt to counteract pricing below costs to drive out competitors or fixing prices artificially high to harm consumers

Additional Considerations for Pricing Decisions

In some cases, cost is *not* a major factor in setting prices. We explore some of the ways that market structures, ability to pay, capacity limits, and laws and regulations influence price-setting outside of cost.

Price Discrimination

Consider the prices airlines charge for a round-trip flight from Boston to San Francisco. A coach-class ticket for a flight with a 7-day advance purchase is $450 if the passenger stays in San Francisco over a Saturday night. It is $1,000 if the passenger returns without staying over a Saturday night. Can this price difference be explained by the difference in the cost to the airline of these round-trip flights? No, because it costs the same amount to transport the passenger from Boston to San Francisco and back, regardless of whether the passenger stays in San Francisco over a Saturday night. This difference in price is due to *price discrimination.*

Price discrimination is the practice of charging different customers different prices for the same product or service. How does price discrimination work in the airline example? The demand for airline tickets comes from two main sources: business travelers and pleasure travelers. Business travelers must travel to conduct business for their organizations, so their demand for air travel is relatively insensitive to price. Airlines can earn higher operating incomes by charging business travelers higher prices. Insensitivity of demand to price changes is called *demand inelasticity.* Also, business travelers generally go to their destinations, complete their work, and return home without staying over a Saturday night. Pleasure travelers, in contrast, usually don't need to return home during the week, and prefer to spend weekends at their destinations. Because they pay for their tickets themselves, pleasure travelers' demand is price-elastic; lower prices stimulate demand while higher prices restrict demand. Airlines can earn higher operating incomes by charging pleasure travelers lower prices.

How can airlines keep fares high for business travelers while keeping fares low for pleasure travelers? Requiring a Saturday night stay discriminates between the two customer segments. The airlines price-discriminate by taking advantage of different sensitivities to prices exhibited by business travelers and pleasure travelers. Prices differ even though there is no difference in cost in serving the two customer segments.

What if economic conditions weaken such that business travelers become more sensitive to price? The airlines may then need to lower the prices they charge to business travelers. Following the terrorist attacks on the Unites States on September 11, 2001, airlines started offering discounted fares on certain routes without requiring a Saturday night stay to stimulate business travel. Business travel picked up and airlines started filling more seats than they otherwise would have. Unfortunately, travel did not pick up enough, and the airline industry as a whole suffered severe losses over the next few years.

Peak-Load Pricing

In addition to price discrimination, other noncost factors such as capacity constraints affect pricing decisions. **Peak-load pricing** is the practice of charging a higher price for the same product or service when demand approaches the physical limit of the capacity to produce that product or service. When demand is high and production capacity and therefore supply is limited, customers are willing to pay more to get the product or service. In contrast, slack or excess capacity leads companies to lower prices in order to stimulate demand and utilize capacity. Peak-load pricing occurs in the telephone, telecommunications, hotel, car rental, and electric-utility industries. During the 2012 Summer Olympics in London, for example, hotels charged very high rates and required multiple-night stays. Airlines charged high fares for flights into and out of many cities in the region for roughly a month around the time of the Games. Demand far exceeded capacity and the hospitality industry and airlines employed peak-load pricing to increase their profits.

International Pricing

Another example of factors other than costs affecting prices occurs when the same product is sold in different countries. Consider software, books, and medicines produced in one country and sold globally. The prices charged in each country vary much more than the costs of delivering the product to each country. These price differences arise because of differences in the purchasing power of consumers in different countries (a form of price discrimination) and government restrictions that may limit the prices that companies can charge.

Antitrust Laws

Legal considerations also affect pricing decisions. Companies are not always free to charge whatever price they like. For example, under the U.S. Robinson-Patman Act of 1936, a manufacturer cannot price-discriminate between two customers if the intent is to lessen or prevent competition for customers. Two key features of price-discrimination laws are:

1. Price discrimination is permissible if differences in prices can be justified by differences in costs.
2. Price discrimination is illegal only if the intent is to lessen or prevent competition.

The price discrimination by airline companies described earlier is legal because their practices do not hinder competition.

Predatory Pricing. To comply with U.S. antitrust laws, such as the Sherman Act, the Clayton Act, the Federal Trade Commission Act, and the Robinson-Patman Act, pricing must not be predatory.[7] A company engages in **predatory pricing** when it deliberately prices below its costs in an effort to drive competitors out of the market and restrict supply, and then raises prices rather than enlarge demand.[8]

The U.S. Supreme Court established the following conditions to prove that predatory pricing has occurred:

- The predator company charges a price below an appropriate measure of its costs.
- The predator company has a reasonable prospect of recovering in the future, through larger market share or higher prices, the money it lost by pricing below cost.

The Supreme Court has not specified the "appropriate measure of costs."[9]

---

[7] Discussion of the Sherman Act and the Clayton Act is in A. Barkman and J. Jolley, "Cost Defenses for Antitrust Cases," *Management Accounting* 67, no. 10 (1986): 37–40.

[8] For more details, see W. Viscusi, J. Harrington, and J. Vernon, *Economics of Regulation and Antitrust*, 4th ed. (Cambridge, MA: MIT Press, 2006); and J. L. Goldstein, "Single Firm Predatory Pricing in Antitrust Law: The Rose Acre Recoupment Test and the Search for an Appropriate Judicial Standard," *Columbia Law Review* 91 (1991): 1557–1592.

[9] *Brooke Group* v. *Brown & Williamson Tobacco*, 113 S. Ct. (1993); T. J. Trujillo, "Predatory Pricing Standards Under Recent Supreme Court Decisions and Their Failure to Recognize Strategic Behavior as a Barrier to Entry," *Iowa Journal of Corporation Law* (Summer 1994): 809–831.

Most courts in the United States have defined the "appropriate measure of costs" as the short-run marginal or average variable costs.[10] In *Adjustor's Replace-a-Car* v. *Agency Rent-a-Car,* Adjustor's (the plaintiff) claimed that it was forced to withdraw from the Austin and San Antonio, Texas, markets because Agency had engaged in predatory pricing.[11] To prove predatory pricing, Adjustor pointed to "the net loss from operations" in Agency's income statement, calculated after allocating Agency's headquarters overhead. The judge, however, ruled that Agency had not engaged in predatory pricing because the price it charged for a rental car never dropped below its average variable costs.

The Supreme Court decision in *Brooke Group* v. *Brown & Williamson Tobacco* (*BWT*) increased the difficulty of proving predatory pricing. The Court ruled that pricing below average variable costs is not predatory if the company does not have a reasonable chance of later increasing prices or market share to recover its losses.[12] The defendant, BWT, a cigarette manufacturer, sold brand-name cigarettes and had 12% of the cigarette market. The introduction of generic cigarettes threatened BWT's market share. BWT responded by introducing its own version of generics priced below average variable cost, thereby making it difficult for generic manufacturers to continue in business. The Supreme Court ruled that BWT's action was a competitive response and not predatory pricing. That's because, given BWT's small 12% market share and the existing competition within the industry, it would be unable to later charge a monopoly price to recoup its losses.

Dumping. Closely related to predatory pricing is dumping. Under U.S. laws, **dumping** occurs when a non-U.S. company sells a product in the United States at a price below the market value in the country where it is produced, and this lower price materially injures or threatens to materially injure an industry in the United States. If dumping is proven, an antidumping duty can be imposed under U.S. tariff laws equal to the amount by which the foreign price exceeds the U.S. price. Cases related to dumping have occurred in the cement, computer, lumber, paper, semiconductor, steel, sweater, and tire industries. In September 2009, the U.S. Commerce Department announced it would place import duties of 25–35% on imports of automobile and light-truck tires from China.[13] China challenged the decision to the dispute settlement panel of the World Trade Organization (WTO), an international institution created with the goal of promoting and regulating trade practices among countries. The WTO upheld US's claim.

Collusive Pricing. Another violation of antitrust laws is **collusive pricing,** which occurs when companies in an industry conspire in their pricing and production decisions to achieve a price above the competitive price and so restrain trade. In 2008, for example, LG of South Korea agreed to pay $400 million and Sharp of Japan agreed to pay $120 million for colluding to fix prices of LCD picture tubes in the United States.

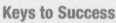

Keys to Success

To maximize profits, managers price-discriminate by charging some customers a higher price for a given product. They also charge higher prices when demand approaches peak loads. At no time should a manager violate antitrust laws or engage in predatory pricing, collusive pricing, or dumping.

[10] An exception is *McGahee* v. *Northern Propane Gas Co.* [858 F, 2d 1487 (1988)], in which the Eleventh Circuit Court held that prices below average total cost constitute evidence of predatory intent. For more discussion, see P. Areeda and D. Turner, "Predatory Pricing and Related Practices under Section 2 of Sherman Act," *Harvard Law Review* 88 (1975): 697–733. For an overview of case law, see W. Viscusi, J. Harrington, and J. Vernon, *Economics of Regulation and Antitrust,* 4th ed. (Cambridge, MA: MIT Press, 2006). See also the "Legal Developments" section of the *Journal of Marketing* for summaries of court cases.

[11] *Adjustor's Replace-a-Car, Inc.* v. *Agency Rent-a-Car,* 735 2d 884 (1984).

[12] *Brooke Group* v. *Brown & Williamson Tobacco,* 113 S. Ct. (1993).

[13] Edmund Andrews, "U.S. Adds Tariffs on Chinese Tires," *New York Times* (September 11, 2009).

Problem for Self-Study

Reconsider the Astel Computer example (pages 256–257). Astel's marketing manager realizes that a further reduction in price is necessary to sell 200,000 units of Provalue II. To maintain a target profitability of $16 million, or $80 per unit, Astel will need to reduce costs of Provalue II by $6 million, or $30 per unit. Astel targets a reduction of $4 million, or $20 per unit, in manufacturing costs, and $2 million, or $10 per unit, in marketing, distribution, and customer-service costs. The cross-functional team assigned to this task proposes the following changes to manufacture a different version of Provalue, called Provalue III:

1. Reduce direct materials and ordering costs by purchasing subassembled components rather than individual components.
2. Reengineer ordering and receiving to reduce ordering and receiving costs per order.
3. Reduce testing time and the labor and power required per hour of testing.
4. Develop new rework procedures to reduce rework costs per hour.

No changes are proposed in direct manufacturing labor cost per unit and in total machining costs.

The following table summarizes the cost-driver quantities and the cost per unit of each cost driver for Provalue III compared with Provalue II.

	A	B	C	D	E	F	G	H	I	J	K	L	M	N
1			Manufacturing Cost Information						Manufacturing Cost Information					
2			for 200,000 Units of Provalue II for 2013						for 200,000 Units of Provalue III for 2013					
3	Cost Category	Cost Driver	Details of Budgeted Cost Driver Quantities				Budgeted Total Quantity of Cost Driver	Budgeted Cost per Unit of Cost Driver	Details of Budgeted Cost Driver Quantities				Budgeted Total Quantity of Cost Driver	Budgeted Cost per Unit of Cost Driver
4	(1)	(2)		(3)		(4)	(5)=(3)×(4)	(6)		(7)		(8)	(9)=(7)×(8)	(10)
5	Direct materials	No. of kits	1	kit per unit	200,000	units	200,000	$385	1	kit per unit	200,000	units	200,000	$375
6	Direct manuf. labor (DML)	DML hours	2.65	DML hours per unit	200,000	units	530,000	$ 20	2.65	DML hours per unit	200,000	units	530,000	$ 20
7	Direct machining (fixed)	Machine-hours					300,000	$ 38					300,000	$ 38
8	Ordering and receiving	No. of orders	50	orders per component	425	components	21,250	$ 80	50	orders per component	400	components	20,000	$ 60
9	Test and inspection	Testing-hours	15	testing-hours per unit	200,000	units	3,000,000	$ 2	14	testing-hours per unit	200,000	units	2,800,000	$ 1.70
10	Rework				6.5%	defect rate					6.5%	defect rate		
11		Rework-hours	2.5	rework-hours per defective unit	13,000[a]	defective units	32,500	$ 40	2.5	rework-hours per defective unit	13,000[a]	defective units	32,500	$ 32
12														
13	[a]6.5% defect rate × 200,000 units = 13,000 defective units													

Required

Will the proposed changes achieve Astel's targeted reduction of $4 million, or $20 per unit, in manufacturing costs for Provalue III? Show your computations.

Solution

Exhibit 7-12 presents the manufacturing costs for Provalue III based on the proposed changes. Manufacturing costs will decline from $108 million, or $540 per unit (Exhibit 7-5), to $104 million, or $520 per unit (Exhibit 7-12), and will achieve the target reduction of $4 million, or $20 per unit.

Exhibit 7-12

Target Manufacturing Costs of Provalue III for 2013 Based on Proposed Changes

	A	B	C	D
1		Budgeted		Budgeted
2		Manufacturing Costs		Manufacturing
3		for 200,000 Units		Cost per Unit
4		(1)		(2) = (1) ÷ 200,000
5	Direct manufacturing costs			
6	Direct material costs			
7	(200,000 kits × $375 per kit)	$ 75,000,000		$375.00
8	Direct manufacturing labor costs			
9	(530,000 DML-hours × $20 per hour)	10,600,000		53.00
10	Direct machining costs			
11	(300,000 machine-hours × $38 per machine-hour)	11,400,000		57.00
12	Direct manufacturing costs	97,000,000		485.00
13				
14	Manufacturing overhead costs			
15	Ordering and receiving costs			
16	(20,000 orders × $60 per order)	1,200,000		6.00
17	Testing and inspection costs			
18	(2,800,000 testing-hours × $1.70 per hour)	4,760,000		23.80
19	Rework costs			
20	(32,500 rework-hours × $32 per hour)	1,040,000		5.20
21	Manufacturing overhead costs	7,000,000		35.00
22	Total manufacturing costs	$104,000,000		$520.00

Decision Points

The following question-and-answer format summarizes the chapter's learning objectives. Each decision presents a key question related to a learning objective. The guidelines are the answers to that question.

Decision	Guidelines
1. What are the three major factors affecting pricing decisions?	Customers, competitors, and costs influence prices through their effects on demand and supply; customers and competitors affect demand, and costs affect supply.
2. How do companies make long-run pricing decisions?	Companies consider all future costs (whether variable or fixed in the short run) and use a market-based or a cost-based pricing approach to earn a target return on investment.
3. How do companies determine target costs?	One approach to long-run pricing is to use a target price. Target price is the estimated price that potential customers are willing to pay for a product or service. Target cost per unit equals target price minus target operating income per unit. Target cost per unit is the estimated long-run cost of a product or service that when sold enables the company to achieve target operating income per unit. Value-engineering methods help a company make the cost improvements necessary to achieve target cost.

Decision	Guidelines
4. Why is it important for managers to distinguish cost incurrence from locked-in costs?	Cost incurrence describes when a resource is sacrificed. Locked-in costs are costs that have not yet been incurred but, based on decisions that have already been made, will be incurred in the future. To reduce costs, techniques such as value engineering are most effective *before* costs are locked in.
5. How do companies price products using the cost-plus approach?	The cost-plus approach to pricing adds a markup component to a cost base as the starting point for pricing decisions. Many different costs, such as full cost of the product or manufacturing cost, can serve as the cost base in applying the cost-plus formula. Prices are then modified on the basis of customers' reactions and competitors' responses. Therefore, the size of the "plus" is determined by the marketplace.
6. How can a company's revenues and costs differ across customers, and what actions do these differences prompt managers to take?	Revenues differ because of differences in the quantity purchased and price discounts. Costs differ because different customers place different demands on a company's resources in terms of processing sales orders, making deliveries, and customer support. Managers should devote sufficient resources to support and expand relationships with profitable customers and design incentives to change behavior patterns of unprofitable customers.
7. Describe life-cycle budgeting and life-cycle costing and when companies should use these techniques.	Life-cycle budgeting estimates and life-cycle costing tracks and accumulates the costs (and revenues) attributable to a product from its initial R&D to its final customer service and support. These life-cycle techniques are particularly important when (a) a high percentage of total life-cycle costs are incurred before production begins and revenues are earned over several years, and (b) a high fraction of the life-cycle costs are locked in at the R&D and design stages.
8. Describe price discrimination and peak-load pricing and how antitrust laws affect pricing.	Price discrimination is charging some customers a higher price for a given product or service than other customers. Peak-load pricing is charging a higher price for the same product or service when demand approaches physical-capacity limits. Under price discrimination and peak-load pricing, prices differ among market segments and across time periods even though the cost of providing the product or service is approximately the same. To comply with antitrust laws, a company must not engage in predatory pricing, dumping, or collusive pricing, which lessens competition, puts another company at an unfair competitive disadvantage, or harms consumers.

Terms to Learn

The chapter and the Glossary at the end of the book contain definitions of the following important terms:

collusive pricing (p. 280)
cost incurrence (p. 261)
customer-cost hierarchy (p. 268)
customer life-cycle costs (p. 278)
customer-profitability analysis (p. 267)
designed-in costs (p. 261)
dumping (p. 280)
life-cycle budgeting (p. 276)
life-cycle costing (p. 276)
locked-in costs (p. 261)
non-value-added cost (p. 260)
peak-load pricing (p. 279)
predatory pricing (p. 279)
price discount (p. 267)
price discrimination (p. 278)
product life cycle (p. 276)
target cost per unit (p. 260)
target operating income per unit (p. 260)
target price (p. 259)
target rate of return on investment (p. 265)
value-added cost (p. 260)
value engineering (p. 260)
whale curve (p. 272)

Assignment Material

Questions

7-1 How is activity-based costing useful for pricing decisions?

7-2 What is a target cost per unit?

7-3 Describe value engineering and its role in target costing.

7-4 "It's not important for a company to distinguish between cost incurrence and locked-in costs." Do you agree? Explain.

7-5 Describe three alternative cost-plus pricing methods.

7-6 "A customer-profitability profile highlights those customers a company should drop to improve profitability." Do you agree? Explain.

7-7 Give examples of three different levels of costs in a customer-cost hierarchy.

7-8 Give two examples in which the difference in the costs of two products or services is much smaller than the difference in their prices.

7-9 What is life-cycle budgeting?

7-10 Define predatory pricing, dumping, and collusive pricing.

Exercises

7-11 Value-added, non-value-added costs. The McGowan Repair Shop repairs and services machine tools. A summary of its costs (by activity) for 2012 is as follows:

a. Materials and labor for servicing machine tools	$500,000
b. Rework costs	150,000
c. Expediting costs caused by work delays	75,000
d. Materials-handling costs	50,000
e. Materials-procurement and inspection costs	60,000
f. Preventive maintenance of equipment	40,000
g. Breakdown maintenance of equipment	75,000

Required

1. Classify each cost as value-added, non-value-added, or in the gray area between.
2. For any cost classified in the gray area, assume 65% is value-added and 35% is non-value-added. How much of the total of all seven costs is value-added and how much is non-value-added?
3. McGowan is considering the following changes: (a) introducing quality-improvement programs whose net effect will be to reduce rework and expediting costs by 60% and materials and labor costs for servicing machine tools by 5%; (b) working with suppliers to reduce materials-procurement and inspection costs by 20% and materials-handling costs by 25%; and (c) increasing preventive-maintenance costs by 40% to reduce breakdown-maintenance costs by 50%. Calculate the effect of programs (a), (b), and (c) on value-added costs, non-value-added costs, and total costs. Comment briefly.

7-12 Target operating income, value-added costs, service company. Charlton Associates prepares architectural drawings to conform to local structural-safety codes. Its income statement for 2013 is as follows:

Revenues	$731,850
Salaries of professional staff (8,200 hours × $47 per hour)	385,400
Travel	21,000
Administrative and support costs	154,160
Total costs	560,560
Operating income	$171,290

Following is the percentage of time spent by professional staff on various activities:

Making calculations and preparing drawings for clients	75%
Checking calculations and drawings	4
Correcting errors found in drawings (not billed to clients)	7
Making changes in response to client requests (billed to clients)	6
Correcting own errors regarding building codes (not billed to clients)	8
Total	100%

Assume administrative and support costs vary with professional-labor costs. Consider each requirement independently.

Required

1. How much of the total costs in 2013 are value-added, non-value-added, or in the gray area between? Explain your answers briefly. What actions can Charlton take to reduce its costs?
2. What are the consequences of misclassifying a non-value-added cost as a value-added cost? When in doubt, would you classify a cost as a value-added or non-value-added cost? Explain briefly.
3. Suppose Charlton could eliminate all errors so that it did not need to spend any time making corrections and, as a result, could proportionately reduce professional-labor costs. Calculate Charlton's operating income for 2013.
4. Now suppose Charlton could take on as much business as it could complete, but it could not add more professional staff. Assume Charlton could eliminate all errors so that it does not need to spend any time correcting errors. Assume Charlton could use the time saved to increase revenues proportionately. Assume travel costs will remain at $21,000. Calculate Charlton's operating income for 2013.

7-13 Target prices, target costs, activity-based costing. Bright Tiles is a small distributor of marble tiles. Bright identifies its three major activities and cost pools as ordering, receiving and storage, and shipping, and it reports the following details for 2012:

Activity	Cost Driver	Quantity of Cost Driver	Cost per Unit of Cost Driver
1. Placing and paying for orders of marble tiles	Number of orders	800	$70 per order
2. Receiving and storage	Loads moved	5,000	$40 per load
3. Shipping of marble tiles to retailers	Number of shipments	2,200	$50 per shipment

For 2012, Bright buys 300,000 marble tiles at an average cost of $4 per tile and sells them to retailers at an average price of $7 per tile. Assume Bright has no fixed costs and no inventories.

Required

1. Calculate Bright's operating income for 2012.
2. For 2013, retailers are demanding a 5% discount off the 2012 price. Bright's suppliers are only willing to give a 4% discount. Bright expects to sell the same quantity of marble tiles in 2013 as in 2012. If all other costs and cost-driver information remain the same, calculate Bright's operating income for 2013.
3. Suppose further that Bright decides to make changes in its ordering and receiving-and-storing practices. By placing long-run orders with its key suppliers, Bright expects to reduce the number of orders to 500 and the cost to $35 per order. By redesigning the layout of the warehouse and reconfiguring the crates in which the marble tiles are moved, Bright expects to reduce the number of loads moved to 4,125 and the cost per load moved to $38. Will Bright achieve its target operating income of $1.92 per tile in 2013? Show your calculations.

7-14 Target costs, effect of product-design changes on product costs. Patient Care Instruments uses a manufacturing costing system with one direct-cost category (direct materials) and three indirect-cost categories:

a. Setup, production order, and materials-handling costs that vary with the number of batches
b. Manufacturing-operations costs that vary with machine-hours
c. Costs of engineering changes that vary with the number of engineering changes made

In response to competitive pressures at the end of 2011, Patient Care Instruments used value-engineering techniques to reduce manufacturing costs. Actual information for 2011 and 2012 is as follows:

	2011	2012
Setup, production-order, and materials-handling costs per batch	$ 8,900	$8,000
Total manufacturing-operations cost per machine-hour	$ 64	$ 48
Cost per engineering change	$16,000	$8,000

The management of Patient Care Instruments wants to evaluate whether value engineering has succeeded in reducing the target manufacturing cost per unit of one of its products, HJ6, by 5%.

Actual results for 2011 and 2012 for HJ6 are:

	Actual Results for 2011	Actual Results for 2012
Units of HJ6 produced	2,700	4,600
Direct material cost per unit of HJ6	$ 1,400	$ 1,300
Total number of batches required to produce HJ6	60	70
Total machine-hours required to produce HJ6	20,000	30,000
Number of engineering changes made	24	7

Required

1. Calculate the manufacturing cost per unit of HJ6 in 2011.
2. Calculate the manufacturing cost per unit of HJ6 in 2012.
3. Did Patient Care Instruments achieve the target manufacturing cost per unit for HJ6 in 2012? Explain.
4. Explain how Patient Care Instruments reduced the manufacturing cost per unit of HJ6 in 2012.
5. What challenges might managers at Patient Care Instruments encounter in achieving the target cost and how might they overcome these challenges?

7-15 Target costs, effect of process-design changes on service costs. Sun Systems provides energy audits in residential areas of southern Ohio. The energy audits provide information to homeowners on the benefits of solar energy. A consultant from Sun Systems educates the homeowner about federal and state rebates and tax credits available for purchases and installations of solar heating systems. A successful energy audit results in the homeowner purchasing a solar heating system. Sun Systems does not install the solar heating system, but arranges for the installation with a local company. Sun Systems completes all necessary paperwork related to the rebates, tax credits, and financing. Sun Systems has identified three major activities that drive the cost of energy audits: identifying new contacts (that varies with the number of new contacts), travelling to and between appointments (that varies with the number of miles driven), and preparing and filing rebates and tax forms (that varies with the number of clerical hours). Actual costs for each of these activities in 2011 and 2012 are:

	2011	2012
Consultant labor cost per hour	$35.00	$35.00
Average cost per new contact	9.00	7.00
Travel cost per mile	0.55	0.65
Preparing and filing cost per clerical hour	9.10	9.50

In 2012, Sun Systems used value engineering to reduce the cost of the energy audits. The management of Sun Systems wants to evaluate whether value engineering has succeeded in reducing the target cost per audit by 5%.

Actual results for 2011 and 2012 for Sun Systems are:

	Actual Results for 2011	Actual Results for 2012
Successful audits performed	150	178
Number of new contacts	215	275
Miles driven	1,756	1,327
Total clerical hours	1,218	1,367
Consultant labor hours per audit	2.2	2

Required

1. Calculate the cost per audit in 2011.
2. Calculate the cost per audit in 2012.
3. Did Sun Systems achieve the target cost per audit in 2012? Explain.
4. What challenges might managers at Sun Systems encounter in achieving the target cost and how might they overcome these challenges?

7-16 Cost-plus target return on investment pricing. John Branch is the managing partner of a business that has just finished building a 60-room motel. Branch anticipates that he will rent these rooms for 16,000 nights next year (or 16,000 room-nights). All rooms are similar and will rent for the same price. Branch estimates the following operating costs for next year:

Variable operating costs	$4 per room-night
Fixed costs	
Salaries and wages	$170,000
Maintenance of building and pool	48,000
Other operating and administration costs	122,000
Total fixed costs	$340,000

The capital invested in the motel is $1,000,000. The partnership's target return on investment is 20%. Branch expects demand for rooms to be uniform throughout the year. He plans to price the rooms at full cost plus a markup on full cost to earn the target return on investment.

Required

1. What price should Branch charge for a room-night? What is the markup as a percentage of the full cost of a room-night?
2. Branch's market research indicates that if the price of a room-night determined in requirement 1 is reduced by 10%, the expected number of room-nights Branch could rent would increase by 10%. Should Branch reduce prices by 10%? Show your calculations.

7-17 Cost-plus, target pricing, working backward. TinRoof, Inc., manufactures and sells a do-it-yourself storage shed kit. In 2012, it reported the following:

Units produced and sold	3,200
Investment	$2,400,000
Markup percentage on full cost	8%
Rate of return on investment	12%
Variable cost per unit	$500

Required

1. What was TinRoof's operating income in 2012? What was the full cost per unit? What was the selling price? What was the percentage markup on variable cost?
2. TinRoof is considering increasing the annual spending on advertising by $175,000. The managers believe that the investment will translate into a 10% increase in unit sales. Should the company make the investment? Show your calculations.
3. Refer back to the original data. In 2013, TinRoof believes that it will only be able to sell 2,900 units at the price calculated in requirement 1. Management has identified $125,000 in fixed cost that can be eliminated. If TinRoof wants to maintain an 8% markup on full cost, what is the target variable cost per unit?

7-18 Customer profitability, customer-cost hierarchy. Enviro-Tech has only two retail and two wholesale customers. Information relating to each customer for 2012 follows (in thousands):

	Wholesale Customers		Retail Customers	
	North America Wholesaler	South America Wholesaler	Green Energy	Global Power
Revenues at list prices	$375,000	$590,000	$175,000	$130,000
Discounts from list prices	25,800	47,200	8,400	590
Cost of goods sold	285,000	510,000	144,000	95,000
Delivery costs	4,550	6,710	2,230	2,145
Order processing costs	3,820	5,980	2,180	1,130
Cost of sales visit	6,300	2,620	2,620	1,575

Enviro-Tech's annual distribution-channel costs are $33 million for wholesale customers and $12 million for retail customers. The company's annual corporate-sustaining costs, such as salary for top management and general-administration costs, are $48 million. There is no cause-and-effect or benefits-received relationship between any cost-allocation base and corporate-sustaining costs. That is, Enviro-Tech could save corporate-sustaining costs only if the company completely shuts down.

Required

1. Calculate customer-level operating income using the format in Exhibit 7-7.
2. Prepare a customer-cost hierarchy report, using the format in Exhibit 7-10.
3. Enviro-Tech's management decides to allocate all corporate-sustaining costs to distribution channels: $38 million to the wholesale channel and $10 million to the retail channel. As a result, distribution channel costs are now $71 million ($33 million + $38 million) for the wholesale channel and $22 million ($12 million + $10 million) for the retail channel. Calculate the distribution channel–level operating income. On the basis of these calculations, what actions, if any, should Enviro-Tech's managers take? Explain.
4. How might Enviro-Tech use the new cost information from its activity-based costing system to better manage its business?

7-19 Customer profitability, service company. Secure Data provides onsite data storage and server management services for five multisite companies in a tristate area. Secure Data's costs consist of the cost of technicians and equipment that are directly traceable to the customer site and a pool of office overhead. Until recently, Secure Data estimated customer profitability by allocating the office overhead to each customer based on revenues. For 2012, Secure Data reported the following results:

	Manning	Decker	Thomas	Bailey	Willis	Total
Revenues	$ 320,000	$185,000	$338,000	$115,000	$221,000	$1,179,000
Technician and equipment cost	224,000	161,800	236,180	100,500	185,500	$ 907,980
Office Overhead allocated	38,677	22,360	40,852	13,899	26,711	$ 142,500
Operating income	$ 57,323	$ 840	$ 60,567	$ 601	8,789	$ 128,520

Todd Burns, Secure Data's new controller, notes that office overhead is more than 10% of total costs, so he spends a couple of weeks analyzing the consumption of office overhead resources by customers. He collects the following information:

	Manning	Decker	Thomas	Bailey	Willis
Number of service calls	140	240	45	135	190
Number of Web-based parts orders	160	190	70	140	140
Number of bills (or reminders)	25	85	85	75	130

Activity Area	Cost Driver Rate
Service call handling	$82 per service call
Parts ordering	$90 per Web-based parts ordered
Billing and collection	$45 per bill

Required

1. Compute customer-level operating income using the new information that Todd has gathered.
2. Prepare exhibits for Secure Data similar to Exhibits 7-8 and 7-9. Comment on the results.
3. What options should Secure Data consider for individual customers in light of the new data and analysis of office overhead?

7-20 Life-cycle product costing. Brooks, Inc., develops and manufactures kitchen gadgets that it then sells through infomercials. Currently, the company is designing a cookie press that it intends to begin manufacturing and marketing next year. Because of the rapidly changing nature of the kitchen gadget industry, Brooks management projects that the company will produce and sell the cookie press for only 3 years. At the end of the product's life cycle, Brooks plans to sell the rights to the cookie press to an overseas company for $125,000. Cost information concerning the cookie press follows:

		Total Fixed Costs over Four Years	Variable Cost per Unit
Year 1	Design costs	$450,000	—
Years 2–4	Production costs	$120,000	$10 per unit
Years 2–4	Marketing and distribution costs	$ 70,000	$2 per unit

For simplicity, ignore the time value of money.

Required

1. Suppose the managers at Brooks price the cookie press at $20 per unit. How many units do they need to sell to break even?
2. The managers at Brooks are thinking of two alternative pricing strategies.
   a. Sell the press at $20 each from the outset. At this price, the managers expect to sell 175,000 units over its life cycle.
   b. Increase the selling price of the cookie press in year 2 when it first comes out to $25 per unit. At this price, the managers expect to sell 72,000 units in year 2. In years 3 and 4, drop the price to $15 per unit. The managers expect to sell 100,000 units each year in years 3 and 4. Which pricing strategy would you recommend? Explain.

7-21 Considerations other than cost in pricing decisions. Fun Stay Express operates a 100-room hotel near a busy amusement park. During June, a 30-day month, Fun Stay Express experienced a 65% occupancy rate from Monday evening through Thursday evening (weeknights). On Friday through Sunday evenings (weekend nights), however, occupancy increases to 90%. (There were 18 weeknights and 12 weekend nights in June.) Fun Stay Express charges $85 per night for a suite. Fun Stay Express recently hired Gina Johnson to manage the hotel to increase the hotel's profitability. The following information relates to Fun Stay Express' costs:

	Fixed Cost	Variable Cost
Depreciation	$25,000 per month	
Administrative costs	$38,000 per month	
Housekeeping and supplies	$16,000 per month	$30 per room-night
Breakfast	$12,000 per month	$6 per breakfast served

Fun Stay Express offers free breakfast to guests. In June, there were an average of 2 breakfasts served per room night on weeknights and 4 breakfasts served per room night on weekend nights.

Required

1. Calculate the average cost per room-night for June. What was Fun Stay Express' operating income or loss for the month?
2. Gina Johnson estimates that if Fun Stay Express decreases the nightly rates to $75, weeknight occupancy will increase to 75%. She also estimates that if the hotel increases the nightly rate on weekend nights to $105, occupancy on those nights will remain at 90%. Would this be a good move for Fun Stay Express? Show your calculations.
3. Why would the guests tolerate a $30 price difference between weeknights and weekend nights?
4. A discount travel clearinghouse has approached Fun Stay Express with a proposal to offer last-minute deals on empty rooms on both weeknights and weekend nights. Assuming that there will be an average of three breakfasts served per night per room, what is the minimum price that Fun Stay Express could accept on the last-minute rooms?

Problems

7-22 Cost-plus, target pricing, working backward. The new CEO of Ruiz Manufacturing has asked for a variety of information about the operations of the firm from last year. The CEO is given the following information, but with some data missing:

Total sales revenue	?
Number of units produced and sold	500,000 units
Selling price	?
Operating income	$230,000
Total investment in assets	$2,500,000
Variable cost per unit	$3.50
Fixed costs for the year	$2,850,000

Required

1. Find (a) total sales revenue, (b) selling price, (c) rate of return on investment, and (d) markup percentage on full cost for this product.
2. The new CEO has a plan to reduce fixed costs by $250,000 and variable costs by $0.50 per unit while continuing to produce and sell 500,000 units. Using the same markup percentage as in requirement 1, calculate the new selling price.
3. Assume the CEO institutes the changes in requirement 2 including the new selling price. However, the reduction in variable cost has reduced product quality, resulting in 5% fewer units being sold compared to before the change. Calculate operating income (loss).
4. What concerns, if any, other than the quality problem described in requirement 3, do you see in implementing the CEO's plan? Explain briefly.

7-23 Target prices, target costs, value engineering, cost incurrence, locked-in costs, activity-based costing. Bell Electronics makes an MP3 player, CE100, which has 80 components. Bell sells 7,000 units each month for $70 each. The costs of manufacturing CE100 are $45 per unit, or $315,000 per month. Monthly manufacturing costs are:

Direct material costs	$182,000
Direct manufacturing labor costs	28,000
Machining costs (fixed)	31,500
Testing costs	35,000
Rework costs	14,000
Ordering costs	3,360
Engineering costs (fixed)	21,140
Total manufacturing costs	$315,000

Bell's management identifies the activity cost pools, the cost driver for each activity, and the cost per unit of the cost driver for each overhead cost pool as:

Manufacturing Activity	Description of Activity	Cost Driver	Cost per Unit of Cost Driver
1. Machining costs	Machining components	Machine-hour capacity	$4.50 per machine-hour
2. Testing costs	Testing components and final product (each unit of CE100 is tested individually)	Testing-hours	$2 per testing-hour
3. Rework costs	Correcting and fixing errors and defects	Units of CE100 reworked	$20 per unit
4. Ordering costs	Ordering of components	Number of orders	$21 per order
5. Engineering costs	Designing and managing of products and processes	Engineering-hour capacity	$35 per engineering-hour

Bell's management views direct material costs and direct manufacturing labor costs as variable for the units of CE100 manufactured. Over a long-run horizon, each of the overhead costs described in the preceding table varies, as described, with the chosen cost drivers.

The following additional information describes the existing design:

a. Testing time per unit is 2.5 hours.

b. Ten percent of the CE100s manufactured are reworked.

c. Bell places two orders with each component supplier each month. A different supplier supplies each component.
d. It currently takes 1 hour to manufacture each unit of CE100.

In response to competitive pressures, Bell must reduce its price to $62 per unit and its costs by $8 per unit. No additional sales are anticipated at this lower price. However, Bell stands to lose significant sales if it does not reduce its price. Managers ask manufacturing to reduce its costs by $6 per unit. Improvements in manufacturing efficiency are expected to yield a net savings of $1.50 per MP3 player, but that is not enough. The chief engineer has proposed a new modular design that reduces the number of components to 50 and also simplifies testing. The newly designed MP3 player, called "New CE100" will replace CE100.

The expected effects of the new design are:

a. Direct material cost for the New CE100 is expected to be lower by $2.20 per unit.
b. Direct manufacturing labor cost for the New CE100 is expected to be lower by $0.50 per unit.
c. Machining time required to manufacture the New CE100 is expected to be 20% less, but machine-hour capacity will not be reduced.
d. Time required for testing the New CE100 is expected to be lower by 20%.
e. Rework is expected to decline to 4% of New CE100s manufactured.
f. Engineering-hours capacity will remain the same.

Assume that the cost per unit of each cost driver for CE100 continues to apply to New CE100.

Required

1. Calculate Bell's manufacturing cost per unit of New CE100.
2. Will the new design achieve the per-unit cost-reduction targets that have been set for the manufacturing costs of New CE100? Show your calculations.
3. The problem describes two strategies to reduce costs: (a) improving manufacturing efficiency and (b) modifying product design. Which strategy has more impact on Bell's costs? Why? Explain briefly.
4. What challenges might managers at Bell Electronics encounter in achieving the target cost and how might they overcome these challenges?

7-24 Target service costs, value engineering, activity-based costing. Lagoon is an amusement park that offers family-friendly entertainment and attractions. The park boasts over 25 acres of fun. The admission price to enter the park, which includes access to all attractions, is $35. At this entrance price, Lagoon's target profit is 35% of revenues. Lagoon's managers have identified the major activities that drive the cost of operating the park. The activity cost pools, the cost driver for each activity, and the cost per unit of the cost driver for each pool are:

Activity	Description of Activity	Cost Driver	Cost per Unit of Cost Driver
1. Ticket sales	Selling tickets on-site for entry into the park	Number of tickets sold	$2 per ticket sold
2. Ticket verification	Verifying tickets purchased at park and online ticket purchases	Number of patrons	$1.50 per patron
3. Operating attractions	Loading, monitoring, off-loading patrons on attraction	Number of runs	$90 per run
4. Litter patrol	Roaming the park and cleaning up waste as necessary	Number of litter patrol hours	$20 per hour

The following additional information describes the existing operations:

a. The park operating hours are 10:00 a.m.–8:00 p.m., 7 days a week. The average number of patrons per week is 55,000.
b. Lagoon maintains an online website for advance ticket purchases. This site is maintained by an outside company, which charges $1 per ticket sold. Only 15% of the tickets are purchased online.
c. Once the ticket is purchased, another park employee checks the ticket and stamps the patron for potential exit and reentry.
d. The park has 27 attractions. A run is the complete cycle of loading, monitoring, and off-loading of patrons. On average, the attractions can make six runs an hour. The cost of operating the attractions includes wages of operator, maintenance, and depreciation of equipment
e. The cleaning crew are assigned to 1-acre areas. One person can cover approximately 1 acre per hour. Each acre is covered continuously. The cost of litter patrol includes the wages of the employee and cleaning supplies.

In response to competitive pressures and to continue to attract 55,000 patrons per week, Lagoon has decided to lower ticket prices to $33 per patron. To maintain the same level of profits as before, Lagoon is looking to make the following improvements to reduce operating costs:

a. Spend $1,000 per week on advertising to promote awareness of the available online ticket purchase. Lagoon's managers expect that this will increase online purchases to 40% of total ticket sales. At this volume the cost per online ticket sold will decrease to $0.75.
b. Reduce the operating hours for eight of the attractions that are not very popular from 10 hours per day to 7 hours per day.
c. Increase the number of refuse containers in the park at an additional cost of $250 per week. Litter patrol employees will be able to cover 1.25 acres per hour.

The cost per unit of cost driver for all other activities will remain the same.

Required

1. Does Lagoon currently achieve its target profit of 35% of sales?
2. Will the new changes and improvements allow Lagoon to achieve the same target profit in dollars? Show your calculations.
3. What challenges might managers at Lagoon encounter in achieving the target cost and how might they overcome these challenges?

7-25 Cost-plus, target return on investment pricing. Gold-o-licious makes candy bars for vending machines and sells them to vendors in cases of 30 bars. Although Gold-o-licious makes a variety of candy, the cost differences are insignificant, and the cases all sell for the same price.

Gold-o-licious has a total capital investment of $20,000,000. It expects to produce and sell 650,000 cases of candy next year. Gold-o-licious requires a 10% target return on investment.

Expected costs for next year are:

Variable production costs	$4.00 per case
Variable marketing and distribution costs	$1.00 per case
Fixed production costs	$1,050,000
Fixed marketing and distribution costs	$650,000
Other fixed costs	$200,000

Gold-o-licious prices the cases of candy at full cost plus markup to generate profits equal to the target return on capital.

Required

1. What is the target operating income?
2. What is the selling price Gold-o-licious needs to charge to earn the target operating income? Calculate the markup percentage on full cost.
3. Gold-o-licious's closest competitor has just increased its candy case price to $13, although it sells 36 candy bars per case. Gold-o-licious is considering increasing its selling price to $12 per case. Assuming production and sales decrease by 5%, calculate Gold-o-licious' return on investment. Is increasing the selling price a good idea?

7-26 Cost-plus, time and materials, ethics. T&W Mechanical sells and services plumbing, heating, and air conditioning systems. T&W's cost accounting system tracks two cost categories: direct labor and direct materials. T&W uses a time-and-materials pricing system, with direct labor marked up 100% and direct materials marked up 50% to recover indirect costs of support staff, support materials, and shared equipment and tools, and to earn a profit.

During a hot summer day, the T&W central air conditioning in Michelle Lowry's home stops working. T&W technician Tony Dickerson arrives at Lowry's home and inspects the air conditioner. He considers two options: replace the compressor or repair it. The cost information available to Dickerson follows:

	Labor	Materials
Repair option	6 hrs.	$170
Replace option	3 hrs.	$260
Labor rate	$45 per hour	

Required

1. If Dickerson presents Lowry with the replace or repair options, what price would he quote for each?
2. If the two options were equally effective for the 3 years that Lowry intends to live in the home, which option would she choose?
3. If Dickerson's objective is to maximize profits, which option would he recommend to Lowry? What would be the ethical course of action?

7-27 Cost-plus and market-based pricing. Nevada Temps, a large labor contractor, supplies contract labor to building-construction companies. For 2013, Nevada Temps has budgeted to supply 84,000 hours of contract labor. Its variable costs are $13 per hour, and its fixed costs are $168,000. Roger Mason, the general manager, has proposed a cost-plus approach for pricing labor at full cost plus 20%.

Required

1. Calculate the price per hour that Nevada Temps should charge based on Mason's proposal.
2. The marketing manager supplies the following information on demand levels at different prices:

Price per Hour	Demand (Hours)
$16	124,000
17	104,000
18	84,000
19	74,000
20	61,000

Nevada Temps can meet any of these demand levels. Fixed costs will remain unchanged for all the demand levels. On the basis of this additional information, calculate the price per hour that Nevada Temps should charge to maximize operating income.

3. Comment on your answers to requirements 1 and 2. Why are the answers the same or different?

7-28 Cost-plus and market-based pricing. (CMA, adapted) Quick Test Laboratories evaluates the reaction of materials to extreme increases in temperature. Much of the company's early growth was attributable to government contracts, but recent growth has come from expansion into commercial markets. Two types of testing at Quick Test are Heat Testing (HTT) and Arctic-Condition Testing (ACT). Currently, all of the budgeted operating costs are collected in a single overhead pool. All of the estimated testing-hours are also collected in a single pool. One rate per test-hour is used for both types of testing. This hourly rate is marked up by 30% to recover administrative costs and taxes, and to earn a profit.

George Barton, Quick Test's controller, believes that there is enough variation in the test procedures and cost structure to establish separate costing rates and billing rates at a 30% markup. He also believes that the inflexible rate structure the company is currently using is inadequate in today's competitive environment. After analyzing the company data, he has divided operating costs into the following three cost pools:

Labor and supervision	$ 470,800
Setup and facility costs	456,475
Utilities	389,400
Total budgeted costs for the period	$1,316,675

George Barton budgets 107,000 total test-hours for the coming period. Test-hours is also the cost driver for labor and supervision. The budgeted quantity of cost driver for setup and facility costs is 950 setup hours. The budgeted quantity of cost driver for utilities is 11,000 machine-hours.

George has estimated that HTT uses 70% of the testing hours, 30% of the setup hours, and half the machine-hours.

Required

1. Find the single rate for operating costs based on test-hours and the hourly billing rate for HTT and ACT.
2. Find the three activity-based rates for operating costs.
3. What will the billing rate for HTT and ACT be based on the activity-based costing structure? State the rates in terms of testing hours. Referring to both requirements 1 and 2, which rates make more sense for Quick Test?
4. If Quick Test's competition all charge $24 per hour for arctic testing, what can Quick Test do to stay competitive?

7-29 Customer profitability, distribution. Green Paper Delivery has decided to analyze the profitability of five new customers. It buys recycled paper at $20 per case and sells to retail customers at a list price of $26 per case. Data pertaining to the five customers are:

	Customer				
	1	2	3	4	5
Cases sold	1,830	6,780	44,500	31,200	1,950
List selling price	$26	$26	$26	$26	$26
Actual selling price	$26	$25.20	$24.30	$25.80	$23.90
Number of purchase orders	10	18	35	16	35
Number of customer visits	3	5	12	4	12
Number of deliveries	12	28	65	25	35
Miles traveled per delivery	14	4	8	6	45
Number of expedited deliveries	0	0	0	0	3

Green Paper Delivery's five activities and their cost drivers are:

Activity	Cost Driver Rate
Order taking	$90 per purchase order
Customer visits	$75 per customer visit
Deliveries	$3 per delivery mile traveled
Product handling	$1.20 per case sold
Expedited deliveries	$250 per expedited delivery

Required

1. Compute the customer-level operating income of each of the five retail customers now being examined (1, 2, 3, 4, and 5). Comment on the results.
2. What insights do managers gain by reporting both the list selling price and the actual selling price for each customer?
3. What factors should managers consider in deciding whether to drop one or more of the five customers?

7-30 Customer profitability in a manufacturing firm. Antelope Manufacturing makes a component called A1030. This component is manufactured only when ordered by a customer, so Antelope keeps no inventory of A1030. The list price is $115 per unit, but customers who place "large" orders receive a 12% discount on price. The customers are manufacturing firms. Currently, the salespeople decide whether an order is large enough to qualify for the discount. When the product is finished, it is packed in cases of 10. If the component needs to be exchanged or repaired, customers can come back within 10 days for free exchange or repair.

The full cost of manufacturing a unit of A1030 is $95. In addition, Antelope incurs customer-level costs. Customer-level cost-driver rates are:

Order taking	$360 per order
Product handling	$15 per case
Rush order processing	$560 per rush order
Exchange and repair costs	$50 per unit

Information about Antelope's five biggest customers follows:

	A	B	C	D	E
Number of units purchased	5,400	1,800	1,200	4,400	8,100
Discounts given	12%	12%	0	12%	12% on half the units
Number of orders	8	16	52	20	16
Number of cases	540	180	120	440	810
Number of rush orders	1	6	1	0	5
Number of units exchanged/repaired	14	72	16	40	180

All customers except E ordered units in the same order size. Customer E's order quantity varied, so E got a discount part of the time but not all the time.

Required

1. Calculate the customer-level operating income for these five customers. Use the format in Exhibit 7-7. Prepare a customer-profitability analysis by ranking the customers from most to least profitable, as in Exhibit 7-8.
2. Discuss the results of your customer-profitability analysis. Does Antelope have unprofitable customers? Is there anything Antelope should do differently with its five customers?

7-31 Life-cycle costing. Maximum Metal Recycling and Salvage receives the opportunity to salvage scrap metal and other materials from an old industrial site. The current owners of the site will sign over the site to Maximum at no cost. Maximum intends to extract scrap metal at the site for 24 months, and then will clean up the site, return the land to useable condition, and sell it to a developer. Projected costs associated with the project follow:

		Fixed	Variable
Months 1–24	Metal extraction and processing	$5,000 per month	$110 per ton
Months 1–27	Rent on temporary buildings	$4,000 per month	—
	Administration	$9,000 per month	—
Months 25–27	Cleanup	$27,000 per month	—
	Land restoration	$938,000 total	—
	Cost of selling land	$110,000 total	—

Ignore time value of money.

Required

1. Assuming that Maximum expects to salvage 40,000 tons of metal from the site, what is the total project life-cycle cost?
2. Suppose Maximum can sell the metal for $190 per ton and wants to earn a profit (before taxes) of $60 per ton. At what price must Maximum sell the land at the end of the project to achieve its target profit per ton?
3. Now suppose Maximum can only sell the metal for $180 per ton and the land at $132,000 less than what you calculated in requirement 2. If Maximum wanted to maintain the same markup percentage on total project life-cycle cost as in requirement 2, by how much would the company have to reduce its total project life-cycle cost?

7-32 Airline pricing, considerations other than cost in pricing. Northern Airways is about to introduce a daily round-trip flight from New York to Los Angeles and is determining how to price its round-trip tickets.

The market research group at Northern Airways segments the market into business and pleasure travelers. It provides the following information on the effects of two different prices on the number of seats expected to be sold and the variable cost per ticket, including the commission paid to travel agents:

		Number of Seats Expected to Be Sold	
Price Charged	Variable Cost per Ticket	Business	Pleasure
$ 800	$ 85	300	150
1,800	195	285	30

Pleasure travelers start their travel during one week, spend at least one weekend at their destination, and return the following week or thereafter. Business travelers usually start and complete their travel within the same work week. They do not stay over weekends.

Assume that round-trip fuel costs are fixed costs of $24,700 and that fixed costs allocated to the round-trip flight for airplane-lease costs, ground services, and flight-crew salaries total $183,000.

Required

1. If you could charge different prices to business travelers and pleasure travelers, would you? Show your computations.
2. Explain the key factor (or factors) for your answer in requirement 1.
3. How might Northern Airways implement price discrimination? That is, what plan could the airline formulate so that business travelers and pleasure travelers each pay the price the airline desires?

7-33 Ethics and pricing. Instyle Interior Designs has been requested to prepare a bid to decorate 4 model homes for a new development. Winning the bid would be a big boost for sales representative Jim Doogan, who works entirely on commission. Sara Groom, the cost accountant for Instyle, prepares the bid based on the following cost information:

Direct costs		
Design costs		$ 20,000
Furniture and artwork		70,000
Direct labor		10,000
Delivery and installation		20,000
Overhead costs		
Design software	5,200	
Furniture handling	4,800	
General and administration	8,000	
Total overhead costs		18,000
Full product costs		$138,000

Based on the company policy of pricing at 120% of full cost, Groom gives Doogan a figure of $165,600 to submit for the job. Doogan is very concerned. He tells Groom that at that price, Instyle has no chance of winning the job. He confides in her that he spent $600 of company funds to take the developer to a basketball playoff game where the developer disclosed that a bid of $156,000 would win the job. He hadn't planned to tell Groom because he was confident that the bid she developed would be below that amount. Doogan reasons that the $600 he spent will be wasted if Instyle doesn't capitalize on this valuable information. In any case, the company will still make money if it wins the bid at $156,000 because it is higher than the full cost of $138,000.

Required

1. Groom suggests that if Doogan is willing to use cheaper furniture and artwork, he can achieve a bid of $156,000. The designs have already been reviewed and accepted and cannot be changed without additional cost, so the entire amount of reduction in cost will need to come from furniture and artwork. What is the target cost of furniture and artwork that will allow Doogan to submit a bid of $156,000 assuming a target markup of 20% of full cost?
2. Evaluate whether Groom's suggestion to Doogan to use the developer's tip is unethical. Would it be unethical for Doogan to redo the project's design to arrive at a lower bid? What steps should Doogan and Groom take to resolve this situation?

7-34 Customer profitability and ethics. KC Corporation manufactures an air-freshening device called GoodAir, which it sells to six merchandising firms. The list price of a GoodAir is $30, and the full manufacturing costs are $18. Salespeople receive a commission on sales, but the commission is based on number of orders taken, not on sales revenue generated or number of units sold. Salespeople receive a commission of $10 per order (in addition to regular salary).

KC Corporation makes products based on anticipated demand. KC carries an inventory of GoodAir, so rush orders do not result in any extra manufacturing costs over and above the $18 per unit. KC ships finished product to the customer at no additional charge for either regular or expedited delivery. KC incurs significantly higher costs for expedited deliveries than for regular deliveries. Customers occasionally return shipments to KC, and the company subtracts these returns from gross revenue. The customers are not charged a restocking fee for returns.

Budgeted (expected) customer-level cost driver rates are:

Order taking (excluding sales commission)	$15 per order
Product handling	$1 per unit
Delivery	$1.20 per mile driven
Expedited (rush) delivery	$175 per shipment
Restocking	$50 per returned shipment
Visits to customers	$125 per customer

Because salespeople are paid $10 per order, they often break up large orders into multiple smaller orders. This practice reduces the actual order-taking cost by $7 per smaller order (from $15 per order to $8 per order) because the smaller orders are all written at the same time. This lower cost rate is not included in budgeted rates because salespeople create smaller orders without telling management or the accounting department. All other actual costs are the same as budgeted costs.

Information about KC's clients follows:

	AC	DC	MC	JC	RC	BC
Total number of units purchased	225	520	295	110	390	1,050
Number of actual orders	5	20	4	6	9	18
Number of written orders	10	20*	9	12	24	36
Total number of miles driven to deliver all products	360	580	350	220	790	850
Total number of units returned	15	40	0	0	35	40
Number of returned shipments	3	2	0	0	1	5
Number of expedited deliveries	0	8	0	0	3	4

*Because DC places 20 separate orders, its order costs are $15 per order. All other orders are multiple smaller orders and so have actual order costs of $8 each.

Required

1. Classify each of the customer-level operating costs as a customer output unit–level, customer batch-level, or customer-sustaining cost.
2. Using the preceding information, calculate the expected customer-level operating income for the six customers of KC Corporation. Use the number of written orders at $15 each to calculate expected order costs.
3. Recalculate the customer-level operating income using the number of written orders but at their actual $8 cost per order instead of $15 (except for DC, whose actual cost is $15 per order). How will KC Corporation evaluate customer-level operating cost performance this period?
4. Recalculate the customer-level operating income if salespeople had not broken up actual orders into multiple smaller orders. Don't forget to also adjust sales commissions.
5. How is the behavior of the salespeople affecting the profit of KC Corporation? Is their behavior ethical? What could KC Corporation do to change the behavior of the salespeople?

7-35 Value engineering, target pricing, and locked-in costs. Wood Creations designs, manufactures, and sells modern wood sculptures. Sally Jensen is an artist for Wood Creations. Jensen has spent much of the past month working on the design of an intricate abstract piece. Jim Smoot, product development manager, likes the design. However, he wants to make sure that the sculpture can be priced competitively. Alexis Nampa, Wood's cost accountant, presents Smoot with the following cost data for the expected production of 75 sculptures:

Design cost	$ 8,000
Direct materials	32,000
Direct manufacturing labor	38,000
Variable manufacturing overhead	32,000
Fixed manufacturing overhead	26,000
Marketing	14,000

Required

1. Smoot thinks that Wood Creations can successfully market each piece for $2,500. The company's target operating income is 25% of revenue. Calculate the target full cost of producing the 75 sculptures. Does the cost estimate developed by Nampa meet Wood's requirements? Is value engineering needed?
2. Smoot discovers that Jensen has designed the sculpture using the highest grade wood available, rather than the standard grade of wood that Wood Creations normally uses. Replacing the grade of wood will lower the cost of direct materials by 60%. However, the redesign will require an additional $1,100 of design cost, and the sculpture will be sold for $2,400 each. Will this design change allow the sculpture to meet its target cost? Are the costs of wood a locked-in cost?
3. Jensen insists that the higher grade wood is a necessity in terms of the sculpture's design. She believes that spending an additional $3,000 on better marketing will allow Wood Creations to sell each sculpture for $2,700. If this is the case, will the sculptures' target cost be achieved without any value engineering?
4. Compare the total operating income on the 75 sculptures for requirements 2 and 3. What do you recommend Wood Creations do, based solely on your calculations? Explain briefly.
5. What challenges might managers at Wood Creations encounter in achieving the target cost and how might they overcome these challenges?

Case

Dakota Office Products

Robert S. Kaplan

John Malone, General Manager of Dakota Office Products (DOP) was concerned about the financial results for calendar year 2000. Despite a sales increase from the prior year, the company had just suffered the first loss in its history (see summary income statement in Dakota Office Products Exhibit 1).

Dakota Office Products was a regional distributor of office supplies to institutions and commercial businesses. It offered a comprehensive product line ranging from simple writing implements (such as pens, pencils, and markers) and fasteners to specialty paper for modern high-speed copiers and printers. DOP had an excellent reputation for customer service and responsiveness.

DOP operated several distribution centers in which personnel unloaded truckload shipments of products from manufacturers, and moved the cartons into designated storage locations until customers requested the items. Each day, after customer orders had been received, DOP personnel drove forklift trucks around the warehouse to accumulate the cartons of items and prepared them for shipment.

Typically, DOP shipped products to its customers using commercial truckers. Recently, DOP had attracted new business by offering a "desktop" option by delivering the packages of supplies directly to individual locations at the customer's site. Dakota operated a small fleet of trucks and assigned warehouse personnel as drivers to make the desktop deliveries. Dakota charged a small price premium (up to an additional 2% markup) for the convenience and savings such direct delivery orders provided to customers. The company believed that the added price for this service could improve margins in its highly competitive office supplies distribution business.

DOP ordered supplies from many different manufacturers. It priced products to its end-use customers by first marking up the purchased product cost by about 15% to cover the cost of

Dakota Office Products Exhibit 1

Dakota Office Products: Income Statement CY2000

Sales	$42,500,000	121.4%
Cost of Items Purchased	35,000,000	100.0%
Gross margin	7,500,000	21.4%
Warehouse Personnel Expense	2,400,000	6.9%
Warehouse Expenses (excluding personnel)	2,000,000	5.7%
Freight	450,000	1.3%
Delivery Truck Expenses	200,000	0.6%
Order entry expenses	800,000	2.3%
General and selling expenses	2,000,000	5.7%
Interest expense	120,000	0.3%
Net Income Before Taxes	$ (470,000)	−1.3%

warehousing, distribution, and freight. Then it added another markup to cover the approximate cost for general and selling expenses, plus an allowance for profit. The markups were determined at the start of each year, based on actual expenses in prior years and general industry and competitive trends. Actual prices to customers were adjusted based on long-term relationships and competitive situations, but were generally independent of the specific level of service provided to that customer, except for desktop deliveries.

Dakota had introduced electronic data interchange (EDI) in 1999, and a new Internet site in 2000, which allowed customer orders to arrive automatically so that clerks would not have to enter customer and order data manually. Several customers had switched to this electronic service because of the convenience to them. Yet Dakota's costs continued to rise. Malone was concerned that even after introducing innovations such as desktop delivery and electronic order entry, the company could not earn a profit. He wondered about what actions he should take to regain profitability.

Distribution Center: Activity Analysis

Malone turned to his controller, Melissa Dunhill, and director of operations, Tim Cunningham, for help. Tim suggested:

> If we can figure out, without going overboard of course, what exactly goes on in the distribution centers, maybe we can get a clearer picture about what it costs to serve our various customers.

Melissa and Tim went into the field to get more specific information. They visited one of Dakota's distribution facilities. Site manager Wilbur Smith confirmed, "All we do is store the cartons, process the orders, and ship them to customers." With Wilbur's help, Melissa and Tim identified four primary activities done at the distribution center—process cartons in and out of the facility, the new desktop delivery service, order handling, and data entry.

Wilbur described some details of these activities:

> The amount of warehouse space we need and the people to move cartons in and out of storage and get them ready for shipment just depends on the number of cartons. All items have about the same inventory turnover so space and handling costs are proportional to the number of cartons that go through the facility.
>
> We use commercial freight for normal shipments, and the cost is based more on volume than on anything else. Each carton we ship costs about the same, regardless of the weight or distance. Of course, any carton that we deliver ourselves, through our new desktop delivery service, avoids the commercial shipping charges.

The team confirmed the information with the warehouse supervisor who noted:

> This desktop delivery is a real pain for my people. Sure, we offer the service, and it's attracted increased business. But I have had to add people since existing personnel already had more than enough to do.

Melissa and Tim next checked on the expenses of entering and validating customer order data. The order entry expenses included the data processing system and the data entry operators. They spoke with Hazel Nutley, a data entry operator at Dakota for 17 years.

> All I do is key in the orders, line by line by line. I start by entering the customer ID and validating our customer information. Beyond that, the only thing that really matters is how many lines I have to enter. Each line item on the order has to be entered separately. Of course, any order that comes in through our new EDI system or Internet page sets up automatically without any intervention from me. I just do quick check to make sure the customer hasn't made an obvious error, and that everything looks correct. This validity check takes about the same time for all electronic orders; it doesn't depend on the number of items ordered.

Melissa and Tim collected information from company data bases and learned the following:

- The distribution centers processed 80,000 cartons in year 2000. Of these, 75,000 cartons were shipped by commercial freight. The remaining 5,000 cartons were shipped under the desktop delivery option. DOP made 2,000 desktop deliveries during the year.
- People felt this total amount of handling, processing, and shipping was about the capacity that could be handled with existing resources.
- The data entry operators processed 16,000 manual orders, and validated 8,000 EDI orders. The 16,000 manual orders had an average of nearly 10 items per order, or 150,000 order lines in total. As with the carton handling, shipping, and delivery personnel, supervisors felt that the data entry operators were operating at capacity rates with the existing business.

They then formed two small project teams, one made up of distribution center personnel and the other of data entry operators, to estimate the amount of time people spent on the various activities they had identified. The teams conducted interviews, asked some people to keep track of their time for several days, and observed other people as they went about their daily jobs.

The distribution center team reported that 90% of the workers processed cartons in and out of the facility. The remaining 10% of workers were assigned to the desktop delivery service. All of the other warehouse expenses (rent, building and equipment depreciation, utilities, insurance, and property taxes) were associated with the receipt, storage, and handling of cartons. The delivery trucks were used only for desktop delivery orders. These estimates were reviewed by supervisors and felt to be representative of operations not just in the current year, but in the past year (2000) as well.

The data entry team, from monitoring computer records, learned that operators worked 10,000 hours during year 2000. Further analysis of the records revealed the following distribution of time for each of the activities performed by data entry operators.

Activity	Data Entry Operators Time
Set up a manual customer order	2,000 hours
Enter individual order lines in an order	7,500 hours
Validate an EDI/Internet order	500 hours
Total	10,000 hours

Understanding Customer Profitability

Melissa looked through the customer accounts and found two typical accounts of similar size and activity volumes. Customers A and B had each generated sales in year 2000 slightly above $100,000. The costs of the products ordered were also identical at $85,000. The overall markups (21.2% for Customer A, and 22.4% for B) were in the range of markups targeted by Dakota Office Products. The markup for Customer B was slightly higher because of the premium charges for desktop delivery. Both customers had ordered 200 cartons during the year. The existing customer profitability system (see Dakota Office Products Exhibit 2) indicated that both customers generated a contribution margin sufficient to cover normal general and selling expenses and return a profit for the company.

Dakota Office Products Exhibit 2

Customer Profitability Report (Current Method)

	Customer A		Customer B	
Sales	$103,000	121.2%	$104,000	122.4%
Cost of Items Purchased	85,000	100.0%	85,000	100.0%
Gross margin	18,000	21.2%	19,000	22.4%
Warehousing, Distribution, and Order Entry	12,750	15.0%	12,750	15.0%
Contribution to general and selling expenses, and profit	$ 5,250	6.2%	$ 6,250	7.4%

Dakota Office Products Exhibit 3

Services Provided in Year 2000 to Customers A and B

	Customer A	Customer B
Number of cartons ordered	200	200
Number of cartons shipped commercial freight	200	150
Number of desktop deliveries	–	25
Number of orders, manual	6	100
Number of line items, manual	60	180
Number of EDI orders	6	–
Average accounts receivable	$9,000	$30,000

Melissa noticed, however, that the two accounts differed on the service demands made on Dakota. Customer A placed a few large orders, and had started to use EDI to place its orders (half its orders, in year 2000, arrived electronically). Customer B, in contrast, placed many more orders, so its average size of order was much smaller than for Customer A. Also, all of Customer B's orders were either paper or phone orders, requiring manual data entry; and 25% of B's orders requested the desktop delivery option.

Melissa, concerned about increases in Dakota's borrowings from the bank, also noticed that Customer A generally paid its bills within 30 days, while Customer B often took 90 or more days to pay its bills. A quick study revealed that the average accounts receivable balance during the year for A was $9,000, while it was $30,000 for B. With Dakota paying interest of 10% per year on its working capital line of credit, Melissa thought this difference might be significant.

Dakota Office Products Exhibit 3 shows Melissa's summary of the actual ordering, delivery and payment statistics for the two customers. She believed she was now ready to assess the actual profitability of customers, and make recommendations about how to reverse Dakota's recent profit slide.

Required

1. Why was Dakota Office Products' existing pricing system inadequate for its current operating environment?
2. Develop an activity-based costing system for Dakota Office Products (DOP) based on year 2000 data. Calculate the activity cost-driver rate for each DOP activity in 2000.
3. Using your answer in requirement 2, calculate the profitability of Customer A and Customer B. What explains any difference in profitability between the two customers?
4. What are the limitations, if any, to the estimates of the profitability of the two customers?
5. Is there any additional information you would like to have to explain the relative profitability of the two customers?
6. Assume Dakota Office Products applies the analysis done in requirement 3 to its entire customer base. How could such information help the Dakota Office Products' managers increase company profits?
7. Suppose a major customer switched from placing all its orders manually to placing all its orders over the internet site. How would this affect the activity cost driver rates calculated in requirement 2? How would the switch affect Dakota Office Products profitability?

8 Determining How Costs Behave

Learning Objectives

1. Describe linear cost functions and three common ways in which they behave
2. Explain nonlinear cost functions
3. Explain the importance of causality in estimating cost functions
4. Understand various methods of cost function estimation
5. Outline six steps in estimating a cost function using quantitative analysis
6. Describe three criteria managers use to evaluate and choose cost drivers
7. Understand the data problems managers encounter in estimating cost functions

What is the value of looking at the past? Perhaps it is to recall fond memories of family and friends or help you understand historical events. Maybe your return to the past helps you to better understand and predict the future. An organization looks at the past to analyze its performance and determine the best decisions for improving performance in the future. This activity requires managers to gather information about costs and how they behave so that managers can predict what they will be "down the road." Gaining a deeper understanding of cost behavior can also motivate an organization to reorganize its operations in innovative ways and tackle important challenges past results have revealed.

Understanding how costs behave is a valuable technical skill. When making decisions, managers find it helpful to identify cost drivers, estimate cost relationships, and determine the fixed and variable components of costs. Boeing's managers use their understanding of how costs behave to make strategic and operating decisions. For example, when Boeing overran by $600 million its budget on the contract to build the U.S. shield against intercontinental ballistic missiles, its managers and management accountants used cost estimation and analysis to identify testing delays as the reason for the cost overruns. As the Chapter at a Glance describes, this chapter focuses on how managers determine cost drivers and cost-behavior patterns and how these patterns help them make future decisions.

Chapter at a Glance

- Managers use past cost and activity data to estimate a relationship between the cost and the level of activity and use this estimated cost function to predict future costs.
- Cost functions are not always linear. Nonlinear cost functions can arise because of quantity discounts, costs increasing in steps, and the effects of learning.
- The most important step in estimating a cost function is determining whether an economically plausible cause-and-effect relationship exists (for example, based on knowledge of operations) between the cost and the level of activity.
- Some methods of estimating cost functions (for example, the conference or account analysis method) are qualitative and rely on judgment. Other methods (such as regression analysis) are quantitative and objectively determine a line or curve that best "fits" the data.
- One advantage of quantitative (objective) methods is that managers can use these techniques to evaluate different activities (cost drivers) using not only the criteria of economic plausibility but also which cost driver best "fits" the data.
- A difficult task in cost estimation is collecting high-quality, reliably measured data on the costs and the level of the activity. Common problems include missing data, extreme values of observations, and changes in technology that change the relationship between the level of the activity and the costs.

Basic Assumptions of Linear Cost Functions

Managers are able to understand cost behavior through cost functions, which are the basic building blocks for estimating costs. A **cost function** is a mathematical description of how a cost changes with changes in the level of an activity relating to that cost. Cost functions can be plotted on a graph by measuring the level of an activity, such as number of batches produced or number of machine-hours used, on the horizontal axis (called the *x*-axis) and the amount of total costs corresponding to—or, preferably, dependent on—the levels of that activity on the vertical axis (called the *y*-axis).

Learning Objective 1

Describe linear cost functions

. . . graph of cost function is a straight line

and three common ways in which they behave

. . . variable, fixed, and mixed

Basic Assumptions

Managers often estimate cost functions based on two assumptions:

1. Variations in the level of a single activity (the cost driver) explain variations in the related total costs.
2. Cost behavior is approximated by a linear cost function within the relevant range. Recall from Chapter 2 that a *relevant range* is the range of the activity in which there is a relationship between total cost and the level of activity. For a **linear cost function** represented graphically, total cost versus the level of a single activity related to that cost is a straight line within the relevant range.

We use these two assumptions throughout most, but not all, of this chapter. Not all cost functions are linear and can be explained by a single activity. Later sections in this chapter discuss cost functions that do not rely on these assumptions.

Linear Cost Functions

To understand three basic types of linear cost functions and to see the role of cost functions in business decisions, consider the negotiations between Cannon Services and World Wide Communications (WWC) for exclusive use of a videoconferencing line between New York and Paris.

- **Alternative 1:** $5 per minute used. Total cost to Cannon changes in proportion to the number of minutes used. The number of minutes used is the only factor whose change causes a change in total cost.

  Panel A in Exhibit 8-1 presents this *variable cost* for Cannon Services. Under alternative 1, there is no fixed cost. We write the cost function in Panel A of Exhibit 8-1 as

$$y = \$5X$$

  where X measures the number of minutes used (on the *x*-axis) and y measures the total cost of the minutes used (on the *y*-axis), calculated using the cost function. Panel A illustrates the

Exhibit 8-1

Examples of Linear Cost Functions

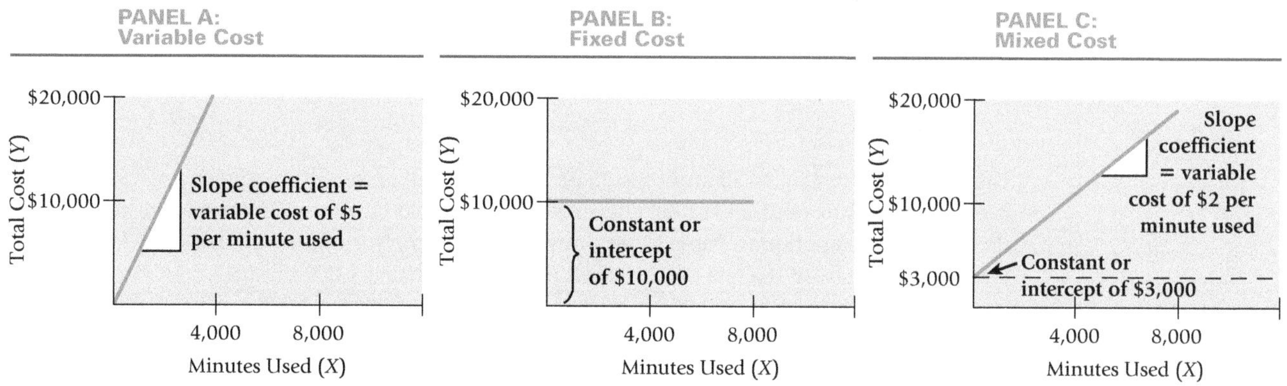

$5 **slope coefficient,** the amount by which total cost changes when a one-unit change occurs in the level of activity (1 minute of usage in the Cannon example). *Throughout the chapter, uppercase letters, such as X, refer to the actual observations, and lowercase letters, such as y, represent estimates or calculations made using a cost function.*

- **Alternative 2:** Total cost will be fixed at $10,000 per month, regardless of the number of minutes used. (We use the same activity measure, number of minutes used, to compare cost-behavior patterns under the three alternatives.)

  Panel B in Exhibit 8-1 presents this *fixed cost* for Cannon Services. We write the cost function in Panel B as

$$y = \$10{,}000$$

  The fixed cost of $10,000 is called a **constant;** it is the component of total cost that does not vary with changes in the level of the activity. Under alternative 2, the constant accounts for all the cost because there is no variable cost. Graphically, the slope coefficient of the cost function is zero; this cost function intersects the *y*-axis at the constant value, and therefore the *constant* is also called the **intercept.**

- **Alternative 3:** $3,000 per month plus $2 per minute used. This is an example of a **mixed cost**—also called a **semivariable cost**—because it has both fixed and variable elements.

Panel C in Exhibit 8-1 presents this *mixed cost* for Cannon Services. We write the cost function in Panel C of Exhibit 8-1 as

$$y = \$3{,}000 + \$2X$$

Unlike the graphs for alternatives 1 and 2, Panel C has both a constant, or intercept, value of $3,000 and a slope coefficient of $2. In the case of a mixed cost, total cost in the relevant range increases as the number of minutes used increases. Note that total cost does not vary strictly in proportion to the number of minutes used within the relevant range. For example, with 4,000 minutes of usage, the total cost equals $11,000 [$3,000 + ($2 per minute × 4,000 minutes)], but when 8,000 minutes are used, total cost equals $19,000 [$3,000 + ($2 per minute × 8,000 minutes)]. Although the usage in terms of minutes has doubled, total cost has increased by only about 73% [($19,000 − $11,000) ÷ $11,000].

Cannon's managers must understand the cost-behavior patterns in the three alternatives to choose the best deal with WWC. Suppose Cannon expects to do at least 4,000 minutes of videoconferencing per month. Its cost for 4,000 minutes under the three alternatives would be as follows.

- **Alternative 1:** $20,000 ($5 per minute × 4,000 minutes)
- **Alternative 2:** $10,000
- **Alternative 3:** $11,000 [$3,000 + ($2 per minute × 4,000 minutes)]

Alternative 2 is the least costly. Moreover, if Cannon were to use more than 4,000 minutes, as is likely to be the case, alternatives 1 and 3 would be even more costly. Cannon's managers, therefore, should choose alternative 2.

Note that the graphs in Exhibit 8-1 are linear. That is, they appear as straight lines. We simply need to know the constant, or intercept, amount (commonly designated *a*) and the slope coefficient (commonly designated *b*). For any linear cost function based on a single activity (recall our two assumptions discussed at the start of this section), knowing *a* and *b* is sufficient to describe and graphically plot all the values within the relevant range of number of minutes used. We write a general form of this linear cost function as

$$y = a + bX$$

Under alternative 1, $a = \$0$ and $b = \$5$ per minute used; under alternative 2, $a = \$10{,}000$ and $b = \$0$ per minute used; and under alternative 3, $a = \$3{,}000$ and $b = \$2$ per minute used. To plot the mixed-cost function in Panel C, we draw a line starting from the point marked $3,000 on the *y*-axis and increasing at a rate of $2 per minute used, so that at 1,000 minutes, total costs increase by $2,000 ($2 per minute × 1,000 minutes) to $5,000 ($3,000 + $2,000) and at 2,000 minutes, total costs increase by $4,000 ($2 per minute × 2,000 minutes) to $7,000 ($3,000 + $4,000) and so on.

Nonlinear Cost Functions and Cost Classifications

Learning Objective 2

Explain nonlinear cost functions

. . . graph of cost function is not a straight line, for example, because of quantity discounts, costs changing in steps, or learning effects

In practice, cost functions are not always linear. In a **nonlinear cost function,** the graph of total costs (based on the level of a single activity) is not a straight line within the relevant range. To see what a nonlinear cost function looks like, consider Exhibit 8-2. Exhibit 8-2 plots the relationship (over several years) between total direct manufacturing labor costs and the number of snowboards produced each year by Winter Sports Authority at its Vermont plant. If the relevant range is set for the region from 0 to 80,000 snowboards produced, it is evident that the cost function over this range is graphically represented by a line that is not straight. The nonlinearities outside the range of 20,000–65,000 snowboards occur because of labor and other inefficiencies (first because workers are learning to produce snowboards and later because capacity limits are being stretched). If, however, the relevant range is set at 20,000–65,000 snowboards (as indicated in the darkened portion of Exhibit 8-2), the cost function is linear. Knowing the relevant range is essential to properly classify costs.

Consider another example. Economies of scale in advertising enable an advertising agency to produce double the number of advertisements for less than double the costs. Even direct material costs are not always linear variable costs because of quantity discounts on direct material purchases. As shown in Exhibit 8-3, Panel A, total direct material costs rise as the units of direct materials purchased increase. But, because of quantity discounts, these costs rise more slowly (as indicated by the slope coefficient) as the units of direct materials purchased increase. This cost function has $b = \$25$ per unit for 1–1,000 units purchased, $b = \$15$ per unit for 1,001–2,000 units purchased, and $b = \$10$ per unit for 2,001–3,000 units purchased. The direct material cost per unit falls at each price break; the cost per unit decreases with larger purchase orders. If managers are interested in understanding cost behavior over the relevant range from 1 to 3,000 units, the cost function is nonlinear—not a straight line. If, however, managers are only interested in understanding cost behavior over a more narrow relevant range (for example, from 1 to 1,000 units), the cost function is linear.

Step cost functions are also examples of nonlinear cost functions. A **step cost function** is a cost function in which the cost remains the same over various ranges of the level of activity, but the cost increases by discrete amounts—that is, increases in steps—as the level of activity increases from one range to the next. Panel B in Exhibit 8-3 shows a *step variable-cost function,* a step cost function in which cost remains the same over *narrow* ranges of the level of activity in each relevant range. Panel B presents the relationship between units of production and setup costs. The pattern is a step cost function because, as we described in Chapter 6 on activity-based costing, setup costs are related to each production batch started. If the relevant range is considered to be from 0 to 6,000 production units, the cost function is nonlinear. However, as shown by the blue line in Panel B, managers often approximate step variable costs with a continuously variable cost function. This type of step cost pattern also occurs when production inputs such as materials-handling labor, supervision, and process-engineering labor are acquired in discrete quantities but used in fractional quantities.

Panel C in Exhibit 8-3 shows a *step fixed-cost function* for Crofton Steel, a company that operates large heat-treatment furnaces to harden steel parts. Looking at Panel C and Panel B, you can see that the main difference between a step variable-cost function and a step fixed-cost function is that the cost in a step fixed-cost function remains the same over *wide* ranges of the activity in each relevant range. The ranges indicate the number of furnaces being used (operating costs of each

Exhibit 8-2

Linearity within Relevant Range for Winter Sports Authority, Inc.

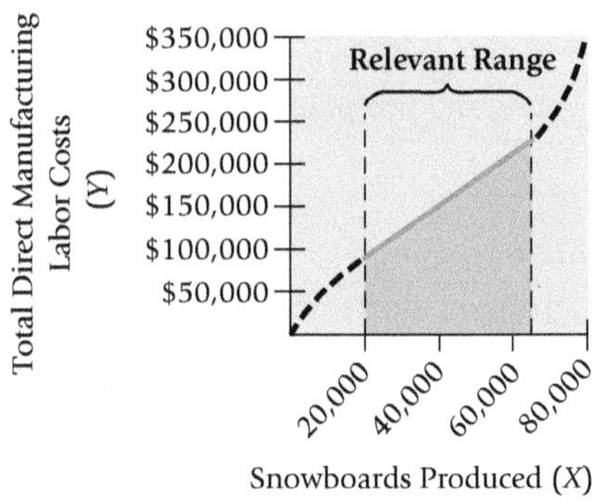

Exhibit 8-3

Examples of Nonlinear Cost Functions

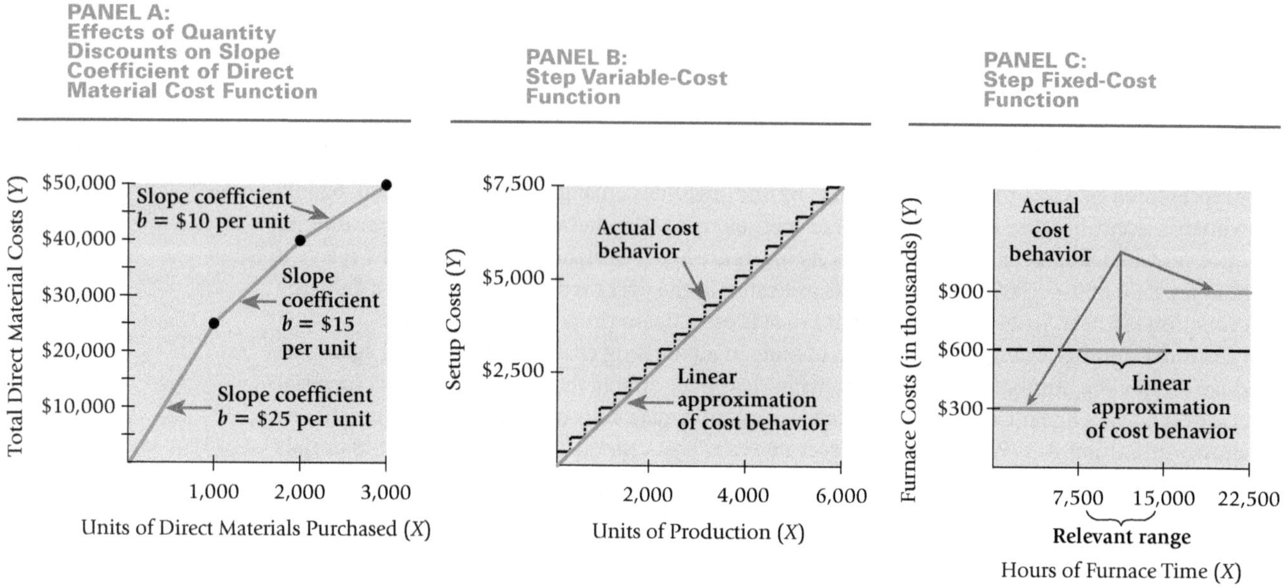

furnace are $300,000). The cost increases from one range to the next higher range when the hours of furnace time needed require the use of another furnace. The relevant range of 7,500–15,000 hours of furnace time indicates that the company expects to operate with two furnaces at a cost of $600,000. Management considers the cost of operating furnaces as a fixed cost within this relevant range of operation. However, if the relevant range is considered to be from 0 to 22,500 hours, the cost function is nonlinear: The graph in Panel C is not a single straight line; it is three broken lines.

Learning Curves

Nonlinear cost functions also result from learning curves. A **learning curve** is a function that measures how labor-hours per unit decline as units of production increase because workers are learning and becoming better at their jobs. Managers use learning curves to predict how labor-hours, or labor costs, will increase as more units are produced.

The aircraft-assembly industry first documented the effect that learning has on efficiency. In general, as workers become more familiar with their tasks, their efficiency improves. Managers learn how to improve the scheduling of work shifts and how to operate the plant more efficiently. As a result of improved efficiency, unit costs decrease as productivity increases, and the unit-cost function behaves nonlinearly. These nonlinearities must be considered when estimating and predicting unit costs.

Managers have extended the learning-curve notion beyond labor-hours to all business functions in the value chain. The term *experience curve* describes this broader application of the learning curve. An **experience curve** is a function that measures the decline in cost per unit in various business functions of the value chain, such as marketing, distribution, and customer service, as the amount of these activities increases. For companies such as Dell Computer, Walmart, and McDonald's, learning curves and experience curves are key elements of their profit-maximization strategies. These companies use learning curves and experience curves to reduce costs and increase customer satisfaction, market share, and profitability.

Keys to Success

Managers should never assume that a cost function is linear and should always plot the function on a graph to see if it is a straight line within a relevant range. If they ignore this step, they may mistakenly believe a cost function is linear when it is not, misestimate how costs actually behave, and make incorrect decisions.

Review of Cost Classification

Before we discuss issues related to the estimation of cost functions, let's briefly review the three criteria laid out in Chapter 2 for classifying a cost. If we can classify costs into fixed and variable costs, we can estimate simple linear cost functions to estimate cost-behavior relationships. If we cannot classify costs into only fixed and variable costs, we need to estimate nonlinear cost functions, which are beyond the scope of this book.

Choice of Cost Object. A particular cost item could be variable for one cost object and fixed for another cost object. Consider Super Shuttle, an airport transportation company. If the fleet of vans it owns is the cost object, then the annual van registration and license costs would be variable costs for the number of vans owned. But if a particular van is the cost object, then the registration and license costs for that van are fixed costs for the miles driven during a year.

Time Horizon. Whether a cost is variable or fixed for a particular activity depends on the time horizon managers are considering when making decisions. The longer the time horizon, all other things being equal, the more likely that the cost will be variable. For example, inspection costs at Boeing Company are typically fixed in the short run for inspection-hours used because inspectors earn a fixed salary in a given year regardless of the number of inspection-hours of work done. But, in the long run, Boeing's total inspection costs will vary with the inspection-hours required: More inspectors will be hired if more inspection-hours are needed, and some inspectors will be reassigned to other tasks or laid off if fewer inspection-hours are needed. As shown in Exhibit 8-3, Panel B, inspection costs are step-variable costs that can be approximated as variable costs.

Relevant Range. Managers should never forget that variable and fixed cost-behavior patterns are valid for linear cost functions only within a given relevant range. Outside the relevant range, variable and fixed cost-behavior patterns may change, causing costs to become nonlinear.

Identifying Cost Drivers

Learning Objective 3

Explain the importance of causality in estimating cost functions

. . . only a cause-and-effect relationship establishes an economically plausible relationship between an activity and its costs

In the Cannon Services/WWC example, we discussed variable-, fixed-, and mixed-cost functions using information about *future* cost structures proposed to Cannon by WWC. Often, however, cost functions are estimated from *past* cost data. Managers use **cost estimation** to measure a relationship based on data from past costs and the related level of an activity. For example, managers at Sony use cost estimation to evaluate the costs of alternative design choices, and combine this information with customer insights about what customers are willing to pay, to choose design features for its new television models. Similarly, marketing managers at Volkswagen use cost estimation to understand what causes their customer-service costs to change from year to year (for example, the number of new car models introduced or the total number of cars sold) and the fixed and variable components of these costs. Managers at Volkswagen are interested in estimating past cost-behavior functions primarily because these estimates can help them make more accurate **cost predictions,** or forecasts, of future costs. Better cost predictions help managers make informed planning and control decisions, such as preparing next year's customer-service budget. But better management decisions, cost predictions, and estimation of cost functions can be achieved only if managers correctly identify the factors that affect costs.

The Cause-and-Effect Criterion

The most important issue in estimating a cost function is determining whether a cause-and-effect relationship exists between the level of an activity and the costs related to that level of activity. Without a cause-and-effect relationship, managers will be less confident about their ability to estimate or predict costs. Recall from Chapter 2 that when a cause-and-effect relationship exists between a change in the level of an activity and a change in the level of total costs, we refer to the activity measure as a *cost driver.* We use the terms *level of activity* and *level of cost driver* interchangeably when estimating cost functions. Understanding the drivers of costs is critical for managing costs. The cause-and-effect relationship might arise as a result of the following.

- **A physical relationship between the level of activity and costs.** An example of a physical relationship is when units of production are used as the activity that affects direct material costs. For example, producing more snowboards requires more plastic, which results in higher total direct material costs.

- **A contractual arrangement.** We saw a contractual agreement in the Cannon Services example described earlier. The contract specifies the number of minutes used as the level of activity that affects the telephone-line costs.
- **Knowledge of operations.** An example of knowledge of operations is when the number of parts is used as the activity measure of ordering costs. A Lenovo computer with many parts will incur higher ordering costs than will a newer model that has fewer parts.

Managers must be careful not to interpret a high correlation, or connection, in the relationship between two variables to mean that either variable causes the other. Consider total direct material costs and labor costs at Winston Furniture, which makes two types of identical tables, one with a granite surface (granite table) and the other with a wooden surface (wooden table). Granite tables have higher direct material costs compared to wooden tables because granite is much more costly than wood, but it is purchased in precut blocks and so requires less direct manufacturing labor costs than wooden tables. Winston currently sells 10,000 granite tables and 30,000 wooden tables.

If Winston sells 20% more tables consisting of 20% more granite tables (10,000 + 0.20 × 10,000 = 12,000) and 20% more wooden tables (30,000 + 0.20 × 30,000 = 36,000), total direct material cost and total direct manufacturing labor cost will each increase by 20%. Total direct material cost and total direct manufacturing labor cost are highly correlated, but neither causes the other. Using direct manufacturing labor costs to predict direct material costs is problematic. To see why, suppose Winston sells 20% more tables (40,000 + 0.20 × 40,000 = 48,000) but now comprising 4,000 granite tables and 44,000 wooden tables. That is, Salem sells 6,000 fewer granite tables (10,000 - 4,000) and 14,000 more wooden tables (44,000 - 30,000). Direct manufacturing labor costs are higher for wooden tables compared to granite tables and so total direct manufacturing labor cost will increase more than 20%. Direct material costs are much lower for wooden tables compared to granite tables and so total direct material cost will decrease. Total direct manufacturing labor cost is a poor predictor of total direct material cost. By contrast, factors that drive total direct material cost, such as the number of granite tables and wooden tables produced, would have more accurately predicted the changes in total direct material cost.

Only a cause-and-effect relationship—not merely correlation—establishes an economically plausible relationship between the level of an activity and its costs. Economic plausibility is critical because it gives analysts and managers confidence that the estimated relationship will appear again and again in other sets of data from the same situation. Identifying cost drivers also gives managers insights into ways to reduce costs and the confidence that reducing the quantity of the cost drivers will lead to a decrease in costs.

To identify cost drivers on the basis of data gathered over time, managers should always use a long time horizon. Why? Because costs may be fixed in the short run (during which time they have no cost driver), but they are usually variable and have a cost driver in the long run. Focusing on the short run may inadvertently cause a manager to believe that a cost has no cost driver.

Keys to Success

Before estimating a cost function, managers must first determine whether an economically plausible cause-and-effect relationship exists between the level of the activity and the costs and then estimate this relationship over a long time horizon.

Cost Drivers and the Decision-Making Process

Consider Elegant Rugs, which uses state-of-the-art automated weaving machines to produce carpets for homes and offices. Management has changed manufacturing processes and wants to introduce new styles of carpets. Elegant Rugs' managers follow the five-step decision-making process outlined in Chapter 1 to evaluate how these changes have affected costs and what styles of carpets they should introduce.

Step 1: Identify the Problem and Uncertainties. Managers had specifically targeted changes to the manufacturing process to reduce indirect manufacturing labor costs, and they now want to know whether costs such as supervision, maintenance, and quality control did, in fact, decrease. One option is to simply compare indirect manufacturing labor costs before and after the process change. The problem with this approach, however, is that the volume of activity and the style of carpet produced before and after the process change are very different, so costs need to be compared after taking into account these changes.

Elegant Rugs' managers are fairly confident about the direct material and direct manufacturing labor costs of the new styles of carpets. They are less certain about the impact that the choice of different styles will have on indirect manufacturing costs.

Step 2: Obtain Information. Managers gather information about potential cost drivers—factors such as machine-hours or direct manufacturing labor-hours that cause indirect manufacturing labor costs to be incurred. They also begin to consider different techniques (discussed in the next section) for estimating the magnitude of the effect of the cost driver on indirect manufacturing labor costs. Their goal is to identify the best possible single cost driver.

Step 3: Make Predictions About the Future. Managers use past data to estimate the relationship between cost drivers and costs and use this relationship to predict future costs.

Step 4: Make Decisions by Choosing Among Alternatives. As we will describe later (pages 317–319), managers choose machine-hours as the cost driver of indirect manufacturing labor costs. Using the regression analysis estimate of indirect manufacturing labor cost per machine-hour, managers estimate the costs of alternative styles of carpets and introduce the most profitable styles.

Step 5: Implement the Decision, Evaluate Performance, and Learn. A year after the managers at Elegant Rugs introduced the new carpet styles, they focused on evaluating the results of their decision. Comparing predicted to actual costs helped managers determine how accurate the estimates were, set targets for continuous improvement, and seek ways to improve efficiency and effectiveness.

Cost Estimation Methods

Learning Objective 4

Understand various methods of cost function estimation

. . . for example, the regression analysis method determines the line that best fits past data

Four methods of cost estimation are (1) the industrial engineering method, (2) the conference method, (3) the account analysis method, and (4) the quantitative analysis method (which takes different forms). These methods differ based on how expensive they are to implement, the assumptions they make, and the information they provide about the accuracy of the estimated cost function. The methods are not mutually exclusive, so many organizations use a combination of methods.

Industrial Engineering Method

Description of method. The **industrial engineering method,** also called the **work-measurement method,** estimates cost functions by analyzing the relationship between inputs and outputs in physical terms. Consider Elegant Rugs. It uses inputs of cotton, wool, dyes, direct manufacturing labor, machine time, and power. Production output is square yards of carpet. Time-and-motion studies analyze the time required to perform the various operations to produce a carpet. For example, a time-and-motion study may conclude that to produce 10 square yards of carpet requires one hour of direct manufacturing labor. Standards and budgets transform these physical input measures into costs. The result is an estimated cost function relating direct manufacturing labor costs to the cost driver, square yards of carpet produced.

Advantages and challenges. The industrial engineering method is a very thorough and detailed way to estimate a cost function when there is a physical relationship between inputs and outputs. While it can be very time consuming, some government contracts mandate its use. Many organizations, such as Bose and Nokia, use it to estimate direct manufacturing costs but find it too costly or impractical for analyzing their entire cost structure. For example, physical relationships between inputs and outputs are difficult to specify for some items, such as indirect manufacturing costs, R&D costs, and advertising costs.

Conference Method

Description of method. The **conference method** estimates cost functions on the basis of analysis and opinions about costs and their drivers gathered from various departments of a company (purchasing, process engineering, manufacturing, employee relations, etc.). The Cooperative Bank in the United Kingdom has a cost-estimating department that develops cost functions for its retail banking products (checking accounts, Visa cards, mortgages, etc.) based on the consensus of estimates from personnel of the particular departments. Elegant Rugs gathers opinions from supervisors and production engineers about how indirect manufacturing labor costs vary with machine-hours and direct manufacturing labor-hours.

Advantages and challenges. The conference method encourages interdepartmental cooperation. The pooling of expert knowledge from different business functions of the value chain gives the conference method credibility. Because the conference method does not require detailed analysis of data, cost functions and cost estimates can be developed quickly. However, the emphasis on opinions rather than systematic estimation means that the accuracy of the cost estimates depends largely on the care and skill of the people providing the inputs.

Account Analysis Method

Description of method. The **account analysis method** estimates cost functions by classifying various cost accounts as variable, fixed, or mixed in regard to the identified level of activity. Typically, managers use qualitative rather than quantitative analysis when making these cost-classification decisions.

Consider indirect manufacturing labor costs for a small production area (or cell) at Elegant Rugs. Indirect manufacturing labor costs include wages paid for supervision, maintenance, quality control, and setups. During the most recent 12-week period, Elegant Rugs ran the machines in the cell for a total of 862 hours and incurred total indirect manufacturing labor costs of $12,501. Using qualitative analysis, the manager and the management accountant determine that over this 12-week period indirect manufacturing labor costs are mixed costs with only one cost driver—machine-hours. As machine-hours vary, one component of the cost (such as supervision cost) is fixed, whereas another component (such as maintenance cost) is variable. The goal is to use account analysis to estimate a linear cost function for indirect manufacturing labor costs with number of machine-hours as the cost driver. The manufacturing manager and the management accountant use experience and judgment to separate total indirect manufacturing labor costs ($12,501) into costs that are fixed ($2,157, based on 950 hours of machine capacity for the cell over a 12-week period) and costs that are variable ($10,344) in regard to the number of machine-hours used. Variable cost per machine-hour is $10,344 ÷ 862 machine-hours = $12 per machine-hour. The linear cost equation, $y = a + bX$, in this example is:

$$\text{Indirect manufacturing labor costs} = \$2{,}157 + (\$12 \text{ per machine-hour} \times \text{Number of machine-hours})$$

Management at Elegant Rugs can use the cost function to estimate the indirect manufacturing labor costs of using, say, 950 machine-hours to produce carpet in the next 12-week period. Estimated costs equal $2,157 + (950 machine-hours × $12 per machine-hour) = $13,557. The indirect manufacturing labor cost per machine-hour is currently $12,501 ÷ 862 machine-hours = $14.50 per machine-hour. The indirect manufacturing labor cost per machine-hour decreases to $13,557 ÷ 950 machine-hours = $14.27 per machine-hour, as fixed costs of $2,157 are spread over a greater number of machine-hours.

Advantages and challenges. The account analysis approach is widely used because it is reasonably accurate, cost-effective, and easy to use. To obtain reliable estimates of the fixed and variable components of cost, organizations must take care to ensure that individuals with thorough knowledge of the operations make the cost-classification decisions. Supplementing the account analysis method with the conference method improves credibility. The accuracy of the account analysis method depends on the accuracy of the qualitative judgments that managers and management accountants make about which costs are fixed and which costs are variable.

Quantitative Analysis Method

Description of method. Quantitative analysis uses a formal mathematical method to fit cost functions to past data observations. Excel is a useful tool for performing quantitative analysis. Columns B and C of Exhibit 8-4 show the breakdown of Elegant Rugs' total machine-hours (862) and total indirect manufacturing labor costs ($12,501) into weekly data for the most recent 12-week period. Note that the data are paired; for each week, there is data for the number of machine-hours and corresponding indirect manufacturing labor costs. For example, week 12 shows 48 machine-hours and indirect manufacturing labor costs of $963. The next section uses the data in Exhibit 8-4 to illustrate how to estimate a cost function using quantitative analysis. We examine two techniques:

Exhibit 8-4
Weekly Indirect Manufacturing Labor Costs and Machine-Hours for Elegant Rugs

	A	B	C
1	Week	Cost Driver: Machine-Hours	Indirect Manufacturing Labor Costs
2		(X)	(Y)
3	1	68	$ 1,190
4	2	88	1,211
5	3	62	1,004
6	4	72	917
7	5	60	770
8	6	96	1,456
9	7	78	1,180
10	8	46	710
11	9	82	1,316
12	10	94	1,032
13	11	68	752
14	12	48	963
15	Total	862	$12,501
16			

the relatively simple high–low method as well as the more common quantitative tool used to examine and understand data, regression analysis.

Advantages and challenges. Quantitative analysis is the most rigorous approach to estimate costs. Increases in computing power have made quantitative analysis and, in particular, regression analysis, much easier to use. But regression analysis requires more detailed information about costs, cost drivers, and cost functions, and is therefore more time consuming to implement.

Steps in Estimating a Cost Function Using Quantitative Analysis

Learning Objective 5

Outline six steps in estimating a cost function using quantitative analysis

. . . the end result (Step 6) is to evaluate the cost driver of the estimated cost function

There are six steps in estimating a cost function using quantitative analysis of a past cost relationship. We illustrate the steps as follows using the Elegant Rugs example.

Step 1: Choose the Dependent Variable. Which **dependent variable** (the cost to be predicted and managed) managers choose will depend on the specific cost function being estimated. In the Elegant Rugs example, the dependent variable is indirect manufacturing labor costs.

Step 2: Identify the Independent Variable, or Cost Driver. The **independent variable** (level of activity or cost driver) is the factor used to predict the dependent variable (costs). When the cost is an indirect cost, as it is with Elegant Rugs, the independent variable is also called a cost-allocation base. Although these terms are sometimes used interchangeably, we use the term *cost driver* to describe the independent variable. Frequently, the management accountant, working with the management team, will cycle through the six steps several times, trying alternative economically plausible cost drivers to identify which one best fits the data.

Recall that a cost driver should be measurable and have an *economically plausible* relationship with the dependent variable. Economic plausibility means that the relationship (describing how changes in the cost driver lead to changes in the costs being considered) is based on a physical relationship, a contract, or knowledge of operations and makes economic sense to the operating manager and the management accountant. As we saw in Chapter 6, all the individual items of costs included in the dependent variable should have the same cost driver, that is, the cost pool should be homogeneous. When all items of costs in the dependent variable do not have the same cost driver, the management accountant should investigate the possibility of creating homogeneous cost pools and estimating more than one cost function, one for each cost item/cost driver pair.

As an example, consider several types of fringe benefits paid to employees and the cost drivers of the benefits:

Fringe Benefit	Cost Driver
Health benefits	Number of employees
Cafeteria meals	Number of employees
Pension benefits	Salaries of employees
Life insurance	Salaries of employees

The costs of health benefits and cafeteria meals can be combined into one homogeneous cost pool because they have the same cost driver—the number of employees. Pension benefits and life insurance costs have a different cost driver—the salaries of employees—and, therefore, should not be combined with health benefits and cafeteria meals. Instead, pension benefits and life insurance costs should be combined into a separate homogeneous cost pool. The cost pool comprising pension benefits and life insurance costs can be estimated using salaries of employees receiving these benefits as the cost driver.

Keys to Success

Managers should estimate the cost function only after they verify that cost pools are homogeneous.

Step 3: Collect Data on the Dependent Variable and the Cost Driver. Data collection is usually the most difficult step in cost analysis. Management accountants obtain data from company documents, from interviews with managers, and through special studies. These data may be time-series data or cross-sectional data.

Time-series data pertain to the same entity (such as an organization, plant, or activity) over successive past periods. Weekly observations of indirect manufacturing labor costs and number of machine-hours at Elegant Rugs are examples of time-series data. The ideal time-series database would contain numerous observations for a company whose operations have not been affected by economic or technological change. A stable economy and technology ensure that data collected during the estimation period represent the same underlying relationship between the cost driver and the dependent variable. Moreover, the periods used to measure the dependent variable and the cost driver should be consistent throughout the observations.

Cross-sectional data pertain to different entities during the same period. For example, studies of loans processed and the related personnel costs at 50 individual, yet similar, branches of a bank during March 2013 would produce cross-sectional data for that month. The cross-sectional data should be drawn from entities that, within each entity, have a similar relationship between the cost driver and costs. Later in this chapter, we describe the problems that arise in data collection.

Step 4: Plot the Data. Managers can easily see the general relationship between the cost driver and costs in a graphical representation of the data, which is commonly called a plot of the data. The plot provides insight into the relevant range of the cost function, and reveals whether the relationship between the driver and costs is approximately linear. Moreover, the plot highlights extreme observations (observations outside the general pattern) that analysts should check. Was there an error in recording the data or an unusual event, such as a work stoppage, that makes these observations unrepresentative of the normal relationship between the cost driver and the costs?

Exhibit 8-5 is a plot of the weekly data from columns B and C of the Excel spreadsheet in Exhibit 8-4 (with the week number indicated alongside each point). This graph provides strong visual evidence of a positive linear relationship between number of machine-hours and indirect manufacturing labor costs (i.e., when machine-hours go up, so do indirect manufacturing labor costs). There do not appear to be any extreme observations in Exhibit 8-5. The relevant range is from 46 to 96 machine-hours per week (weeks 8 and 6, respectively).

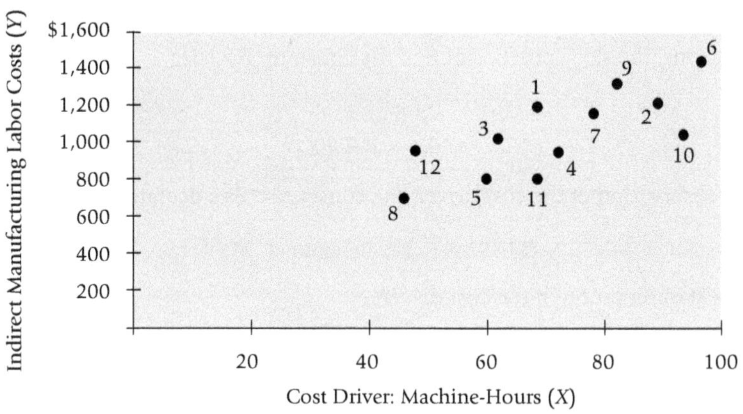

Exhibit 8-5

Plot of Weekly Indirect Manufacturing Labor Costs and Machine-Hours for Elegant Rugs

Keys to Success

Plotting time-series data or cross-sectional data helps managers to observe the general relationship between the cost driver and costs and to identify extreme observations that need to be checked.

Step 5: Estimate the Cost Function. The two most common forms of quantitative analysis managers and accountants use to estimate a cost function are the high–low method and regression analysis. The widespread availability of computer packages such as Excel makes regression analysis much easier to use. Still, we describe the simpler high–low method to provide some basic intuition for the idea of drawing a line to "fit" a number of data points. We present these methods after Step 6.

Step 6: Evaluate the Cost Driver of the Estimated Cost Function. In this step, we describe criteria for evaluating the cost driver of the estimated cost function, but to do so we need to understand the high–low method and regression analysis. Identifying cost drivers is a critical aspect of managing costs and improving profitability and therefore a vital component in a manager's toolkit.

High–Low Method

The simplest form of quantitative analysis to "fit" a line to data points is the **high–low method.** It uses only the highest and lowest observed values of the cost driver within the relevant range and their respective costs to estimate the slope coefficient and the constant of the cost function. The method provides a first cut at understanding the relationship between a cost driver and costs. We illustrate the high–low method using data from Exhibit 8-4.

	Cost Driver: Machine-Hours (*X*)	Indirect Manufacturing Labor Costs (*Y*)
Highest observation of cost driver (week 6)	96	$1,456
Lowest observation of cost driver (week 8)	46	710
Difference	50	$ 746

The slope coefficient, *b*, is calculated as:

$$\text{Slope coefficient} = \frac{\text{Difference between costs associated with highest and lowest observations of the cost driver}}{\text{Difference between highest and lowest observations of the cost driver}}$$

$$= \$746 \div 50 \text{ machine-hours} = \$14.92 \text{ per machine-hour}$$

To compute the constant, we can use either the highest or the lowest observation of the cost driver. Both calculations yield the same answer because the solution technique solves two linear equations with two unknowns, the slope coefficient and the constant. Because

$$y = a + bX$$
$$a = y - bX$$

At the highest observation of the cost driver, the constant, *a*, is calculated as:

$$\text{Constant} = \$1{,}456 - (\$14.92 \text{ per machine-hour} \times 96 \text{ machine-hours}) = \$23.68$$

And at the lowest observation of the cost driver,

$$\text{Constant} = \$710 - (\$14.92 \text{ per machine-hour} \times 46 \text{ machine-hours}) = \$23.68$$

Thus, the high–low estimate of the cost function is:

$$y = a + bX$$
$$y = \$23.68 + (\$14.92 \text{ per machine-hour} \times \text{Number of machine-hours})$$

The purple line in Exhibit 8-6 shows the estimated cost function using the high–low method (based on the data in Exhibit 8-4). The estimated cost function is a straight line joining the observations with the highest and lowest values of the cost driver (number of machine-hours). Note how this simple high–low line falls "in between" the data points with three observations on the line, four above it, and five below it. The intercept ($a = \$23.68$), the point where the dashed extension of the purple line meets the *y*-axis, is the constant component of the equation that provides the best linear approximation of how a cost behaves *within the relevant range* of 46–96 machine-hours. Managers should *not* interpret the intercept as an estimate of the fixed costs of Elegant Rugs if no machines were run because running no machines and shutting down the plant—that is, using zero machine-hours—is *outside the relevant range.*

Suppose indirect manufacturing labor costs in week 6 were \$1,280, instead of \$1,456, while 96 machine-hours were used. In this case, the highest observation of the cost driver (96 machine-hours in week 6) will not coincide with the newer highest observation of the costs (\$1,316 in week 9). How would this change affect our high–low calculation? Given that the cause-and-effect relationship runs *from* the cost driver *to* the costs in a cost function, we choose the highest and lowest observations of the cost driver (the factor that causes the costs to change). The high–low method would still estimate the new cost function using data from weeks 6 (high) and 8 (low).

It is dangerous for managers to rely on only two observations to estimate a cost function. Suppose that because a labor contract guarantees certain minimum payments in week 8, indirect manufacturing labor costs in week 8 were \$1,000 instead of \$710, when only 46 machine-hours were used. The blue line in Exhibit 8-6 shows the cost function that would be estimated by the high–low method using this revised cost. Other than the two points used to draw the line, all other data lie on or below the line. In this case, choosing the highest and lowest observations for machine-hours would result in an estimated cost function that poorly describes the underlying linear cost relationship between number of machine-hours and indirect manufacturing labor costs. In such situations,

Exhibit 8-6

High–Low Method for Weekly Indirect Manufacturing Labor Costs and Machine-Hours for Elegant Rugs

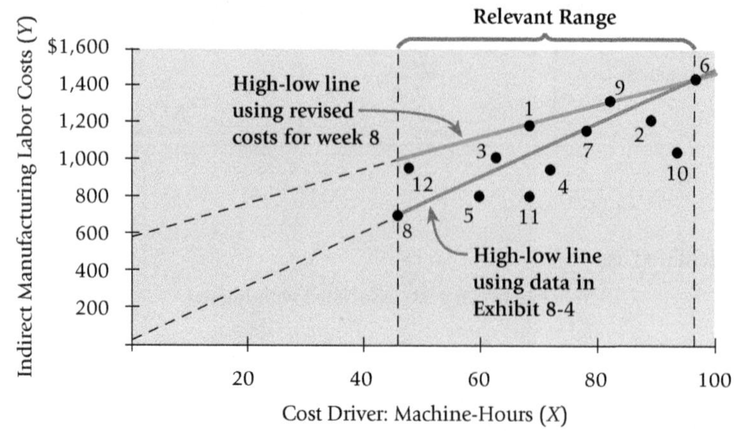

managers can modify the high–low method so that the two observations chosen to estimate the cost function are a *representative high* and a *representative low.* By using this adjustment, managers can avoid having extreme observations, which arise from abnormal events, influence the estimate of the cost function. The modification allows managers to estimate a cost function that is representative of the relationship between the cost driver and costs and, therefore, is more useful for making decisions (such as pricing and performance evaluation).

The advantage of the high–low method is that it is simple to compute and easy to understand; it gives a quick, initial insight into how the cost driver—number of machine-hours—affects indirect manufacturing labor costs. The disadvantage is that the method ignores information from all but two observations when estimating the cost function. We next describe the regression analysis method of quantitative analysis that uses all available data to estimate the cost function.

Keys to Success

The high–low method of quantitative analysis is a rough and easy way to estimate a cost function that fits the data.

Regression Analysis Method

Regression analysis is widely used because it helps managers "get behind the numbers" to understand why costs behave the way they do, the factors that drive costs, and what managers can do to influence them. Managers at Analog Devices, for example, use regression analysis to evaluate how and why quality and defect rates change over time. Managers who understand these relationships gain greater insights into their businesses, make more judicious decisions, and manage more effectively.

Regression analysis is a statistical method that measures the average amount of change in the dependent variable associated with a unit change in one or more independent variables. In the Elegant Rugs example, the dependent variable is total indirect manufacturing labor costs. The independent variable, or cost driver, is number of machine-hours. **Simple regression** analysis estimates the relationship between the dependent variable and *one* independent variable. **Multiple regression** analysis estimates the relationship between the dependent variable and *two or more* independent variables. Multiple regression analysis for Elegant Rugs might use as the independent variables, or cost drivers, number of machine-hours and number of batches.

The following discussion emphasizes how managers interpret and use the output from regression analysis programs such as Excel to make critical strategic and operating decisions. The actual techniques are typically covered in statistics courses. Exhibit 8-7 shows the line developed using regression analysis that best fits the data in columns B and C of Exhibit 8-4. Excel estimates the cost function to be

$$y = \$300.98 + \$10.31X$$

The regression line in Exhibit 8-7 is derived using the least-squares technique. The least-squares technique determines the regression line by minimizing the sum of the squared vertical

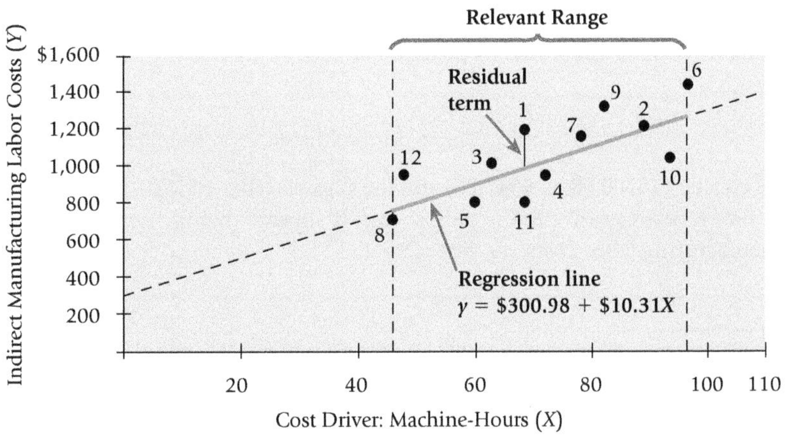

Exhibit 8-7

Regression Model for Weekly Indirect Manufacturing Labor Costs and Machine-Hours for Elegant Rugs

differences from the data points (the various points in the graph) to the regression line. The vertical difference, called the **residual term,** measures the distance between actual cost and estimated cost for each observation of the cost driver. Exhibit 8-7 shows the residual term for the week 1 data. The line from the observation to the regression line is drawn perpendicular to the horizontal axis, or *x*-axis. The smaller the residual terms, the better the fit between actual cost observations and estimated costs. *Goodness of fit* indicates the strength of the relationship between the cost driver and costs[1]. The regression line in Exhibit 8-7 rises from left to right. The positive slope of this line and small residual terms indicate that, on average, indirect manufacturing labor costs increase as the number of machine-hours increases. The vertical dashed lines in Exhibit 8-7 indicate the relevant range, the range within which the cost function applies.

Keys to Success

Regression analysis is a sophisticated quantitative technique that managers use to estimate a cost function. The technique uses all data points to fit a line that minimizes the sum of the squared vertical differences from the data points to the regression line.

The estimate of the slope coefficient, *b*, indicates that indirect manufacturing labor costs vary at the average amount of $10.31 for every machine-hour used within the relevant range. Management can use the regression equation when budgeting for future indirect manufacturing labor costs. For instance, if 90 machine-hours are budgeted for the upcoming week, the predicted indirect manufacturing labor costs would be

$$y = \$300.98 + (\$10.31 \text{ per machine-hour} \times 90 \text{ machine-hours}) = \$1{,}228.88$$

As we have already mentioned, the regression method is more accurate than the high–low method because the regression equation estimates costs using information from all observations, whereas the high–low equation uses information from only two observations. The inaccuracies of the high–low method can mislead managers. Consider the high–low method equation in the preceding section, $y = \$23.68 + \$14.92$ per machine-hour × Number of machine-hours. For 90 machine-hours, the predicted weekly cost based on the high–low method equation is $23.68 + ($14.92 per machine-hour × 90 machine-hours) = $1,366.48. Suppose that for 7 weeks over the next 12-week period, Elegant Rugs runs its machines for 90 hours each week. Assume average indirect manufacturing labor costs for those 7 weeks are $1,300. Based on the high–low method prediction of $1,366.48, Elegant Rugs would conclude it has performed well because actual costs are less than predicted costs. But comparing the $1,300 performance with the more accurate $1,228.88 prediction of the regression model tells a much different story and would probably prompt Elegant Rugs to search for ways to improve its cost performance.

Accurate cost estimation helps managers predict future costs and evaluate the success of cost-reduction initiatives. Suppose the manager at Elegant Rugs is interested in evaluating whether recent strategic decisions that led to changes in the production process and resulted in the data in Exhibit 8-4 have reduced indirect manufacturing labor costs, such as supervision, maintenance, and quality control. Using data on number of machine-hours used and indirect manufacturing labor costs of the previous process (not shown here), the manager estimates the regression equation,

$$y = \$546.26 + (\$15.86 \text{ per machine-hour} \times \text{Number of machine-hours})$$

The constant ($300.98 vs. $545.26) and the slope coefficient ($10.31 vs. $15.86) are both smaller for the new process relative to the old process. It appears that the new process has decreased indirect manufacturing labor costs.

[1] The regression analysis method computes a measure of goodness of fit called the coefficient of determination (denoted by r^2), which measures the percentage of variation in *Y* (costs) explained by *X* (cost driver). The value of r^2 increases as the predicted values, *y*, more closely approximate the actual observations, *Y*. The range of r^2 is from 0 (implying no explanatory power) to 1 (implying perfect explanatory power). Generally, an r^2 of 0.30 passes the goodness-of-fit test.

Evaluating Cost Drivers of the Estimated Cost Function

Learning Objective 6

Describe three criteria managers use to evaluate and choose cost drivers

. . . economically plausible relationships, goodness of fit, and significant effect of the cost driver on costs

How does a company determine the best cost driver when estimating a cost function? In many cases, managers need to understand both operations and cost accounting.

To see why managers need to understand operations, consider the costs to maintain and repair metal-cutting machines at Helix Corporation, a manufacturer of treadmills. Helix schedules repairs and maintenance at a time when production is at a low level to avoid having to take machines out of service when they are needed most. An analysis of the monthly data will then show high repair costs in months of low production and low repair costs in months of high production. Someone unfamiliar with operations might conclude that there is an inverse relationship between production and repair costs. The engineering link between units produced and repair costs, however, is usually clear-cut. Over time, there is a cause-and-effect relationship: the higher the level of production, the higher the repair costs. To estimate the relationship correctly, operating managers and analysts will recognize that repair costs will tend to lag behind periods of high production, and so they will use production of prior periods as the cost driver.

In other cases, choosing a cost driver is more subtle and difficult. Consider again indirect manufacturing labor costs at Elegant Rugs. Management believes that both the number of machine-hours and the number of direct manufacturing labor-hours are plausible cost drivers of indirect manufacturing labor costs. However, management is not sure which is the better cost driver. Exhibit 8-8 presents weekly data (in Excel) on indirect manufacturing labor costs and number of machine-hours for the most recent 12-week period from Exhibit 8-4, together with data on the number of direct manufacturing labor-hours for the same period.

Choosing Among Cost Drivers

What guidance do the different cost-estimation methods provide for choosing among cost drivers? The industrial engineering method relies on analyzing physical relationships between cost drivers and costs, relationships that are difficult to specify in this case. The conference method and the account analysis method use subjective assessments to choose a cost driver and to estimate the fixed and variable components of the cost function. In these cases, managers must rely on their best

Exhibit 8-8

Weekly Indirect Manufacturing Labor Costs, Machine-Hours, and Direct Manufacturing Labor-Hours for Elegant Rugs

Home | Insert | Page Layout | Formulas | Data | Review

	A	B	C	D
1	Week	Original Cost Driver: Machine-Hours	Alternate Cost Driver: Direct Manufacturing Labor-Hours (X)	Indirect Manufacturing Labor Costs (Y)
2	1	68	30	$ 1,190
3	2	88	35	1,211
4	3	62	36	1,004
5	4	72	20	917
6	5	60	47	770
7	6	96	45	1,456
8	7	78	44	1,180
9	8	46	38	710
10	9	82	70	1,316
11	10	94	30	1,032
12	11	68	29	752
13	12	48	38	963
14	Total	862	462	$12,501
15				

judgment. Managers cannot use these methods to test and try alternative cost drivers. The major advantages of quantitative methods are that they are objective—a given data set and estimation method result in a unique estimated cost function—and managers can use them to evaluate different cost drivers. We use the regression analysis approach to illustrate how to evaluate different cost drivers.

First, the management accountant at Elegant Rugs enters data in columns C and D in Exhibit 8-8 in Excel and estimates the following regression equation of indirect manufacturing labor costs based on number of direct manufacturing labor-hours:

$$y = \$744.67 + \$7.72X$$

Exhibit 8-9 shows the plot of the data points for number of direct manufacturing labor-hours and indirect manufacturing labor costs, and the regression line that best fits the data. Recall that Exhibit 8-7 shows the corresponding graph when number of machine-hours is the cost driver. To decide which of the two cost drivers Elegant Rugs should choose, the analyst compares the machine-hour regression equation and the direct manufacturing labor-hour regression equation. There are three criteria used to make this evaluation:

1. **Economic plausibility.** Both cost drivers are economically plausible. However, in the state-of-the-art, highly automated production environment at Elegant Rugs, managers familiar with the operations believe that costs such as machine maintenance are likely to be more closely related to number of machine-hours used than to number of direct manufacturing labor-hours used.
2. **Goodness of fit.** Compare Exhibits 8-7 and 8-9. The vertical differences between actual costs and predicted costs are much smaller for the machine-hours regression than for the direct manufacturing labor-hours regression. Number of machine-hours used, therefore, has a stronger relationship—or goodness of fit—with indirect manufacturing labor costs.[2]
3. **Significance of independent variable.** Again compare Exhibits 8-7 and 8-9 (both of which have been drawn to roughly the same scale). The machine-hours regression line has a steep slope relative to the slope of the direct manufacturing labor-hours regression line. *For the same (or more) scatter of observations about the line (goodness of fit)*, a flat, or slightly sloped, regression line indicates a weak relationship between the cost driver and costs. In our example, changes in direct manufacturing labor-hours appear to have a small influence or effect on indirect manufacturing labor costs.

Based on this evaluation, managers at Elegant Rugs select number of machine-hours as the cost driver and use the cost function $y = \$300.98 + (\$10.31 \text{ per machine-hour} \times \text{Number of machine-hours})$ to predict future indirect manufacturing labor costs.

Exhibit 8-9

Regression Model for Weekly Indirect Manufacturing Labor Costs and Direct Manufacturing Labor-Hours for Elegant Rugs

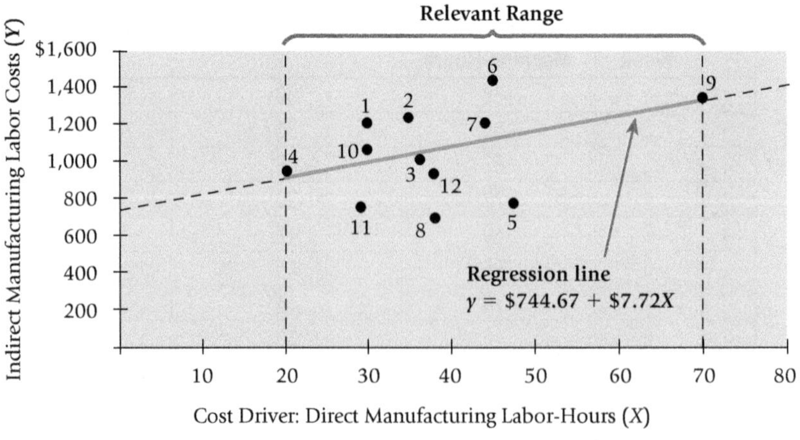

[2] The value of r^2 for the machine-hours regression is 0.52, while the value of r^2 for the direct manufacturing labor-hours regression is 0.17.

Why is choosing the correct cost driver to estimate indirect manufacturing labor costs important? Because identifying the wrong drivers or misestimating cost functions can lead management to incorrect (and costly) decisions along a variety of dimensions. Consider the following strategic decision that management at Elegant Rugs must make. The company is thinking of introducing a new style of carpet that, from a manufacturing standpoint, is similar to the carpets it has manufactured in the past. Prices are set by the market, and sales of 650 square yards of this carpet are expected each week. Management estimates the company needs 72 machine-hours and 21 direct manufacturing labor-hours per week to produce the 650 square yards of carpet needed. Using the machine-hour regression equation, Elegant Rugs would predict indirect manufacturing labor costs of $y = \$300.98 + (\$10.31 \text{ per machine-hour} \times 72 \text{ machine-hours}) = \$1{,}043.30$. If the company used direct manufacturing labor-hours as the cost driver, it would incorrectly predict costs of $\$744.67 + (\$7.72 \text{ per labor-hour} \times 21 \text{ labor-hours}) = \$906.79$. If Elegant Rugs chose similarly incorrect cost drivers for other indirect costs as well and systematically underestimated costs, it would conclude that the costs of manufacturing the new style of carpet would be low and basically fixed (fixed because the regression line is nearly flat). But the actual costs driven by number of machine-hours used and other correct cost drivers would be higher. By failing to identify the proper cost drivers, managers would be misled into believing the new style of carpet would be more profitable than it actually is. Managers might decide to introduce the new style of carpet, whereas if they identify the correct cost driver they would realize it is not as profitable and may decide not to introduce the new carpet.

Incorrectly estimating the cost function would also have repercussions for cost management and cost control. Suppose number of direct manufacturing labor-hours were used as the cost driver, and actual indirect manufacturing labor costs for the new carpet were $970. Actual costs would then be higher than the predicted costs of $906.79. Management would feel compelled to find ways to cut costs. In fact, on the basis of the preferred machine-hour cost driver, the plant would have actual costs lower than the $1,043.30 predicted costs—a performance that management should seek to replicate, not change!

Cost Drivers and the Environment

Understanding how costs behave is a critical input for managers as they make strategic and operating decisions to improve profitability and positively impact the environment. After estimating the fuel consumption of its old planes, managers at FedEx decided to replace these planes with new Boeing 757s that reduced fuel consumption by 36%, while increasing capacity by 20%. At Clorox, managers used past costs and market research to estimate the costs and revenues of new nonsynthetic cleaning products that were better for the environment. They created a new category of "green" cleaning products worth about $200 million annually. Concepts in Action: Cisco Understands Its Costs While Helping the Environment describes how Cisco used its understanding of costs to improve profitability and its environmental impact.

> **Keys to Success**
> **When estimating costs, managers should choose drivers that are economically plausible, fit the data points, and significantly affect costs. Identifying the correct cost drivers helps managers make better strategic decisions and manage costs more effectively.**

Cost Drivers and Activity-Based Costing

Activity-based costing (ABC) systems focus on individual activities, such as product design, machine setup, materials handling, distribution, or customer service, as the fundamental cost objects. To implement ABC systems, managers must identify a cost driver for each activity. Consider, for example, a manager at Westronics, a manufacturer of electronic products. Using methods described in this chapter, the manager must decide whether the number of loads moved or the weight of loads moved is the cost driver of materials-handling costs.

Concepts in Action: Cisco Understands Its Costs While Helping the Environment

Can understanding how costs behave contribute to environmental sustainability? At Cisco Systems, an in-depth understanding of the company's costs and operations led to reduced costs, while also helping the environment. Cisco, makers of computer networking equipment including routers and wireless switches, traditionally regarded the used equipment it received back from its business customers as scrap and recycled it at a cost of about $8 million a year. In 2005, Cisco began trying to find uses for the equipment, mainly because 80% of the returns were in working condition.

Source: Caro/Alamy

A value recovery team at Cisco identified groups within the company that could use the returned equipment. These included its customer service group, which supports warranty claims and service contracts, and the labs that provide technical support, training, and product demonstrations. Based on the initial success of the value recovery team, Cisco designated its recycling group as a company business unit, set clear objectives for it, and assigned the group its own income statement. As a result, the reuse of equipment rose from 5% in 2004 to 45% in 2008, and Cisco's recycling costs fell by 40%. By 2010, the company reused or recycled all returned electronic equipment. The unit has become a profit center that contributed $203 million to Cisco's bottom line in 2010.

Sources: Based on R. Nidumolu, C. Prahalad, and M. Rangaswami. 2009. "Why Sustainability is Now the Key Driver of Innovation," *Harvard Business Review* (September 2009); Cisco Systems, Inc., 2010 Corporate Social Responsibility Report. San Jose, CA: Cisco Systems, Inc., 2011.

To choose the cost driver and use it to estimate the cost function in this materials-handling example, the manager collects data on materials-handling costs and the quantities of the two competing cost drivers over a reasonably long period. Why a long period? Because in the short run, materials-handling costs may be fixed and, therefore, will not vary with changes in the level of the cost driver. In the long run, however, there is a clear cause-and-effect relationship between materials-handling costs and the cost driver. Suppose number of loads moved is the cost driver of materials-handling costs. Increases in the number of loads moved will require more materials-handling labor and equipment; decreases will result in equipment being sold and labor being reassigned to other tasks.

ABC systems have a great number and variety of cost drivers and cost pools. That means ABC systems require managers to estimate many cost relationships. In estimating the cost function for each cost pool, the manager must pay careful attention to the cost hierarchy. For example, if a cost is a batch-level cost such as setup cost, the manager must only consider batch-level cost drivers like number of setup-hours. In some cases, the costs in a cost pool may have more than one cost driver from different levels of the cost hierarchy. In the Elegant Rugs example, the cost drivers for indirect manufacturing labor costs could be machine-hours and number of production batches of carpet manufactured. Furthermore, it may be difficult to subdivide the indirect manufacturing labor costs into two cost pools and to measure the costs associated with each cost driver. In these cases, companies use multiple regression to estimate costs based on more than one independent variable, but these techniques are beyond the scope of this book.

As Concepts in Action: Activity-Based Costing: Identifying Cost Drivers illustrates, managers implementing ABC systems use a variety of methods—industrial engineering, conference, and regression analysis—to estimate slope coefficients. In making these choices, managers trade off level of detail, accuracy, feasibility, and costs of estimating cost functions. For example, to estimate the cost of an activity such as opening a bank account or making a transfer payment, Bankinter in Spain uses work measurement methods, while the Co-operative Bank in the United Kingdom uses the conference method.

Data Collection and Adjustment Issues

Learning Objective 7

Understand the data problems managers encounter in estimating cost functions

... for example, unreliable data and poor record keeping, extreme observations, treating fixed costs as if they are variable, and a changing relationship between a cost driver and cost

The ideal database for estimating cost functions quantitatively has two characteristics:

1. **The database should contain numerous reliably measured observations of the cost driver (the independent variable) and the related costs (the dependent variable).** Errors in measuring the costs and the cost driver are serious. They result in inaccurate estimates of the effect of the cost driver on costs.
2. **The database should consider many values spanning a wide range for the cost driver.** Using only a few values of the cost driver that are grouped closely together causes managers to consider too small a segment of the relevant range and reduces the confidence in the estimates obtained.

Unfortunately, management accountants typically do not have the advantage of working with a database having both characteristics. This section outlines some frequently encountered data problems and steps the management accountant can take to overcome these problems. Managers should ask about these problems and how they have been resolved before they rely on cost estimates.

1. **The time period for measuring the dependent variable does not properly match the period for measuring the cost driver.** This problem often arises when a company does not keep accounting records on the accrual basis. Consider a cost function for a transport company with engine-lubricant costs as the dependent variable and number of truck-hours as the cost driver. Assume that the lubricant is purchased sporadically and stored for later use. Records maintained on the basis of lubricants purchased will indicate little lubricant costs in many months and large lubricant costs in other months. These records present an obviously inaccurate picture of what is actually taking place. The management accountant should use accrual accounting to measure cost of lubricants consumed to better match costs with the truck-hours cost driver in this example.
2. **Fixed costs are allocated as if they are variable.** For example, costs such as depreciation, insurance, or rent may be allocated to products to calculate cost per unit of output. *The danger for managers is to regard these costs as variable rather than as fixed. They seem to be variable because of the allocation methods used.* To avoid this problem, managers and accountants should carefully distinguish fixed costs from variable costs and not treat allocated fixed cost per unit as a variable cost.
3. **Data are either not available for all observations or are not uniformly reliable.** Missing cost observations often arise from a failure to record a cost or from classifying a cost incorrectly. For example, marketing costs may be understated because costs of sales visits to customers may be incorrectly recorded as customer-service costs. Recording data manually rather than electronically tends to result in a higher percentage of missing observations and erroneously entered observations. Errors also arise when data on cost drivers originate outside the internal accounting system. For example, the accounting department may obtain data on testing-hours for medical instruments from the company's manufacturing department and data on number of items shipped to customers from the distribution department. One or both of these departments might not keep accurate records. To minimize these problems, managers should ensure that management accountants design data collection reports that regularly and routinely obtain the required data and should follow up immediately whenever data are missing.
4. **Extreme values of observations occur.** These values arise from (a) errors in recording costs (for example, a misplaced decimal point), (b) from nonrepresentative periods (for example, from a period in which a major machine breakdown occurred or from a period in which a delay in delivery of materials from an international supplier curtailed production), or (c) from observations outside the relevant range. Analysts should adjust or eliminate unusual observations before estimating a cost relationship.
5. **There is no homogeneous relationship between the cost driver and the individual cost items in the dependent variable-cost pool.** A homogeneous relationship exists when each activity whose costs are included in the dependent variable has the same cost driver. In this case, a single cost function can be estimated. As discussed in Step 2 for estimating a cost function using quantitative analysis (page 311), when the cost driver for each activity is different,

separate cost functions (each with its own cost driver) should be estimated for each activity. Alternatively, managers should ask the management accountant to estimate the cost function with more than one independent variable using multiple regression.

6. **The relationship between the cost driver and the cost is not stationary.** This occurs when the underlying process that generated the observations has not remained stable over time. For example, the relationship between number of machine-hours and manufacturing overhead costs is unlikely to be stationary when the data cover a period in which new technology was introduced. One way to see if the relationship is stationary is to split the sample into two parts and estimate separate cost relationships—one for the period before the technology was introduced and one for the period after the technology was introduced. Then, if the estimated coefficients for the two periods are similar, the analyst can pool the data to estimate a single cost relationship. When feasible, pooling data provides a larger data set for the estimation, which increases confidence in the cost predictions being made.
7. **Inflation has affected costs, the cost driver, or both.** For example, inflation may cause costs to change even when there is no change in the level of the cost driver. To study the underlying cause-and-effect relationship between the level of the cost driver and costs, the analyst should remove purely inflationary price effects from the data by dividing each cost by the price index on the date the cost was incurred.

In many cases, a management accountant must expend considerable effort to reduce the effect of these problems before estimating a cost function on the basis of past data. Before making any decisions, a manager should carefully review any data that seems suspect and work closely with the company's management accountants to obtain and process the correct and relevant information.

Concepts in Action: Activity-Based Costing: Identifying Cost Drivers

Many cost estimation methods presented in this chapter are essential when implementing activity-based costing across the globe. In the United Kingdom, the City of London police force uses input–output relationships (the industrial engineering method) to identify cost drivers and the cost of an activity. Using a surveying methodology, officials can determine the total costs associated with responding to house robberies, dealing with burglaries, and filling out police reports. The industrial engineering method is also used by U.S. government agencies such as the U.S. Postal Service to determine the cost of each post office transaction and the U.S. Patent and Trademark Office to identify the costs of each patent examination.

Source: Brian Southam/Alamy

Managers also use regression analysis to determine the cost drivers of activities. Consider how fuel service retailers (that is, gas stations with convenience stores) identify the principal cost driver for labor within their operations. Two economically plausible cost drivers are gasoline sales and convenience store sales. Gasoline sales are batch-level activities because payment transactions occur only once for each purchase, regardless of the volume of gasoline purchased, whereas convenience store sales are output unit-level activities that vary based on the amount of food, drink, and other products sold. Fuel service retailers generally use convenience store sales as the basis for assigning labor costs because regression analyses confirm that convenience store sales, not gasoline sales, are the major cost driver of labor for fuel service retailers.

Sources: Based on T. Carter, A. Sedaghat, and T. Williams, "How ABC Changed the Post Office," *Management Accounting* (February 1998); J. Peckenpaugh, "Teaching the ABCs," *Government Executive* (April 1, 2002); B. Leapman, "Police Spend £ 500m Filling in Forms." *Daily Telegraph* (January 22, 2006); United Kingdom Home Office. *The Police Service National ABC Model: Manual of Guidance* (London: Her Majesty's Stationary Office, 2007).

Problem for Self-Study

Goldstein Corporation manufactures a children's bicycle, model CT8. Goldstein currently manufactures the bicycle frame. During 2012, Goldstein made 32,000 frames at a total cost of $1,056,000. Ryan Corporation has offered to supply as many frames as Goldstein wants at a cost of $32.50 per frame. Goldstein anticipates needing 35,000 frames each year for the next few years.

Required

1. **a.** What is the average cost of manufacturing a bicycle frame in 2012? How does it compare to Ryan's offer?
   b. Can Goldstein use the answer in requirement 1a to determine the cost of manufacturing 35,000 bicycle frames? Explain.
2. Goldstein's management accountant uses annual data from past years to estimate the following regression equation with total manufacturing costs of the bicycle frame as the dependent variable and bicycle frames produced as the independent variable:

$$y = \$435{,}000 + \$19X$$

   During the years used to estimate the regression equation, the production of bicycle frames varied from 31,000 to 35,000. Using this equation, estimate how much it would cost Goldstein to manufacture 35,000 bicycle frames. How much more or less costly is it to manufacture the frames rather than to acquire them from Ryan?
3. What other information would Goldstein's managers need to be confident that the equation in requirement 2 accurately predicts the cost of manufacturing bicycle frames?

Solution

1. **a.**

$$\text{Average cost of manufacturing a bicycle frame} = \frac{\text{Total manufacturing costs}}{\text{Number of bicycle frames}}$$

$$= \frac{\$1{,}056{,}000}{32{,}000} = \$33 \text{ per frame}$$

   This cost is higher than the $32.50 per frame that Ryan has quoted.

   b. Goldstein cannot take the average manufacturing cost in 2012 of $33 per frame and multiply it by 35,000 bicycle frames to determine the total cost of manufacturing 35,000 bicycle frames. The reason is that some of the $1,056,000 (or equivalently the $33 cost per frame) are fixed costs and some are variable costs. Without distinguishing fixed from variable costs, Goldstein cannot determine the cost of manufacturing 35,000 frames. For example, if all costs are fixed, the manufacturing costs of 35,000 frames will continue to be $1,056,000. If, however, all costs are variable, the cost of manufacturing 35,000 frames would be $\$33 \times 35{,}000 = \$1{,}155{,}000$. If some costs are fixed and some are variable, the cost of manufacturing 35,000 frames will be somewhere between $1,056,000 and $1,155,000.

   Another reason for not being able to determine the cost of manufacturing 35,000 bicycle frames is that not all costs are output unit–level costs. If some costs are, for example, batch-level costs, managers would need more information on the number of batches in which the 35,000 bicycle frames would be produced in order to determine the cost of manufacturing 35,000 bicycle frames.

2.

$$\text{Expected cost to make 35,000 bicycle frames} = \$435{,}000 + \$19 \times 35{,}000$$

$$= \$435{,}000 + \$665{,}000 = \$1{,}100{,}000$$

   Purchasing bicycle frames from Ryan will cost $\$32.50 \times 35{,}000 = \$1{,}137{,}500$. So, it will cost Goldstein $\$1{,}137{,}500 - \$1{,}100{,}000 = \$37{,}500$ more to purchase the frames from Ryan rather than manufacture them in-house.

3. Goldstein's managers would need to consider several factors before being confident that the equation in requirement 2 accurately predicts the cost of manufacturing bicycle frames.
   a. Is the relationship between total manufacturing costs and quantity of bicycle frames economically plausible? For example, is the quantity of bicycles made the only cost driver or are there other cost drivers (for example batch-level costs of setups, production orders, or materials handling) that affect manufacturing costs?
   b. How good is the goodness of fit? That is, how well does the estimated line fit the data?
   c. Is the relationship between the number of bicycle frames produced and total manufacturing costs linear?
   d. Does the slope of the regression line indicate that a strong relationship exists between manufacturing costs and the number of bicycle frames produced?
   e. Are there any data problems such as, for example, errors in measuring costs, trends in prices of materials, labor or overheads that might affect variable or fixed costs over time, extreme values of observations, or a nonstationary relationship over time between total manufacturing costs and the quantity of bicycles produced?

Decision Points

The following question-and-answer format summarizes the chapter's learning objectives. Each decision presents a key question related to a learning objective. The guidelines are the answer to that question.

Decision	Guidelines
1. What is a linear cost function and what types of cost behavior can it represent?	A linear cost function is a cost function in which, within the relevant range, the graph of total costs based on the level of a single activity is a straight line. Linear cost functions can be described by a constant, *a*, which represents the estimate of the total cost component that, within the relevant range, does not vary with changes in the level of the activity; and a slope coefficient, *b*, which represents the estimate of the amount by which total costs change for each unit change in the level of the activity within the relevant range. Three types of linear cost functions are variable, fixed, and mixed (or semivariable).
2. What is a nonlinear cost function and how does it arise?	A nonlinear cost function is a cost function in which the graph of total costs based on the level of a single activity is not a straight line within the relevant range. Nonlinear costs can arise because of quantity discounts, step cost functions, and learning-curve effects.
3. What is the most important issue in estimating a cost function?	The most important issue in estimating a cost function is determining whether a cause-and-effect relationship exists between the level of an activity and the costs related to that level of activity. Only a cause-and-effect relationship—not merely correlation—establishes an economically plausible relationship between the level of an activity and its costs.
4. What are the different methods that managers can use to estimate a cost function?	Four methods for estimating cost functions are the industrial engineering method, the conference method, the account analysis method, and the quantitative analysis method (which includes the high–low method and the regression analysis method). If possible, the manager should apply more than one method. Each method is a check on the others.
5. What are the steps to estimate a cost function using quantitative analysis?	There are six steps to estimate a cost function using quantitative analysis: (a) choose the dependent variable; (b) identify the cost driver; (c) collect data on the dependent variable and the cost driver; (d) plot the data; (e) estimate the cost function; and (f) evaluate the cost driver of the estimated cost function. In most situations, working closely with operations managers, the management accountant will cycle through these steps several times before identifying an acceptable cost function.

Decision	Guidelines
6. How should a company evaluate and choose cost drivers?	Three criteria for evaluating and choosing cost drivers are (a) economic plausibility, (b) goodness of fit, and (c) significance of the independent variable.
7. What are the common data problems a company must watch for when estimating cost functions?	The most difficult task in cost estimation is collecting high-quality, reliably measured data on the costs and the cost driver. Common problems include missing data, extreme values of observations, changes in technology, and distortions resulting from inflation.

Terms to Learn

This chapter and the Glossary at the end of this book contain definitions of the following important terms:

account analysis method (p. 310)
conference method (p. 309)
constant (p. 304)
cost estimation (p. 307)
cost function (p. 303)
cost predictions (p. 307)
dependent variable (p. 311)
experience curve (p. 306)
high–low method (p. 313)
independent variable (p. 311)
industrial engineering method (p. 309)
intercept (p. 304)
learning curve (p. 306)
linear cost function (p. 303)
mixed cost (p. 304)
multiple regression (p. 315)
nonlinear cost function (p. 305)
regression analysis (p. 315)
residual term (p. 316)
semivariable cost (p. 304)
simple regression (p. 315)
slope coefficient (p. 304)
step cost function (p. 305)
work-measurement method (p. 309)

Assignment Material

Questions

8-1 What is the difference between a linear and a nonlinear cost function? Give an example of each type of cost function.

8-2 "A cost can be variable or fixed depending on the time horizon." Do you agree? Explain.

8-3 "High correlation between two variables means that one is the cause and the other is the effect." Do you agree? Explain.

8-4 Describe the conference method for estimating a cost function. What are two advantages of this method?

8-5 Describe the account analysis method for estimating a cost function.

8-6 When using the high–low method, should you base the high and low observations on the dependent variable or on the cost driver?

8-7 Describe three criteria for evaluating cost functions and choosing cost drivers.

8-8 Why might a manager prefer the regression analysis method over the high–low method?

8-9 Discuss four frequently encountered problems when collecting cost data on variables included in a cost function.

8-10 "All the independent variables in a cost function estimated with regression analysis are cost drivers." Do you agree? Explain.

Exercises

8-11 Estimating a cost function. The controller of the Dorsey Company wants you to estimate a cost function from the following two observations in a general ledger account called Maintenance:

Month	Machine-Hours	Maintenance Costs Incurred
January	8,000	$4,200
February	12,000	5,600

Required

1. Estimate the cost function for maintenance.
2. Can the constant in the cost function be used as an estimate of fixed maintenance cost per month? Explain.
3. How might a manager use the cost function above?

8-12 Identifying variable-, fixed-, and mixed-cost functions. The Rolling Hills Corporation operates car rental agencies at more than 20 airports. Customers can choose from one of three contracts for car rentals of one day or less:

- Contract 1: $50 for the day
- Contract 2: $30 for the day plus $0.20 per mile traveled
- Contract 3: $1 per mile traveled

Required

1. Plot separate graphs for each of the three contracts, with costs on the vertical axis and miles traveled on the horizontal axis.
2. Express each contract as a linear cost function of the form $y = a + bX$.
3. Identify each contract as a variable-, fixed-, or mixed-cost function.

8-13 Various cost-behavior patterns. (CPA, adapted) Select the graph that matches the numbered manufacturing cost data (requirements 1–9). Indicate by letter which graph best fits the situation or item described.

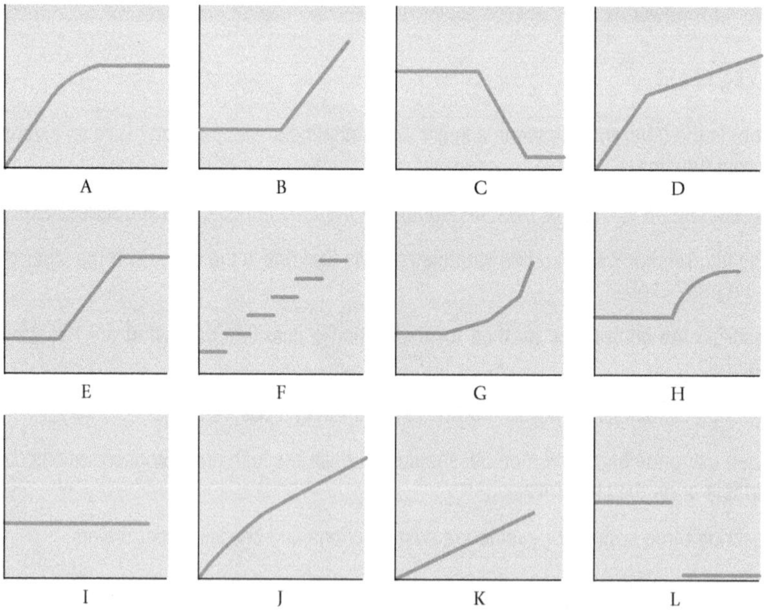

The vertical axes of the graphs represent total cost, and the horizontal axes represent units produced during a calendar year. In each case, the zero point of dollars and production is at the intersection of the two axes. The graphs may be used more than once.

1. Annual depreciation of equipment, where the amount of depreciation charged is computed by the machine-hours method.
2. Electricity bill—a flat fixed charge, plus a variable cost after a certain number of kilowatt-hours are used, in which the quantity of kilowatt-hours used varies proportionately with quantity of units produced.

3. City water bill, which is computed as:

First 1,000,000 gallons or less	$1,000 flat fee
Next 10,000 gallons	$0.003 per gallon used
Next 10,000 gallons	$0.006 per gallon used
Next 10,000 gallons	$0.009 per gallon used
and so on	and so on

The gallons of water used vary proportionately with the quantity of production output.

4. Cost of direct materials, where direct material cost per unit produced decreases with each pound of material used (e.g., if 1 pound is used, the cost is $10; if 2 pounds are used, the cost is $19.98; if 3 pounds are used, the cost is $29.94), with a minimum cost per unit of $9.20.
5. Annual depreciation of equipment, where the amount is computed by the straight-line method. When the depreciation schedule was prepared, it was anticipated that the obsolescence factor would be greater than the wear-and-tear factor.
6. Rent on a manufacturing plant donated by the city, where the agreement calls for a fixed-fee payment unless 200,000 labor-hours are worked, in which case no rent is paid.
7. Salaries of repair personnel, where one person is needed for every 1,000 machine-hours or less (for exmaple, 0–1,000 hours requires one person, 1,001–2,000 hours requires two people, etc.).
8. Cost of direct materials used (assume no quantity discounts).
9. Rent on a manufacturing plant donated by the county, where the agreement calls for rent of $100,000 to be reduced by $1 for each direct manufacturing labor-hour worked in excess of 200,000 hours, but a minimum rental fee of $20,000 must be paid.

8-14 Matching graphs with descriptions of cost and revenue behavior. (D. Green, adapted) Given here are a number of graphs.

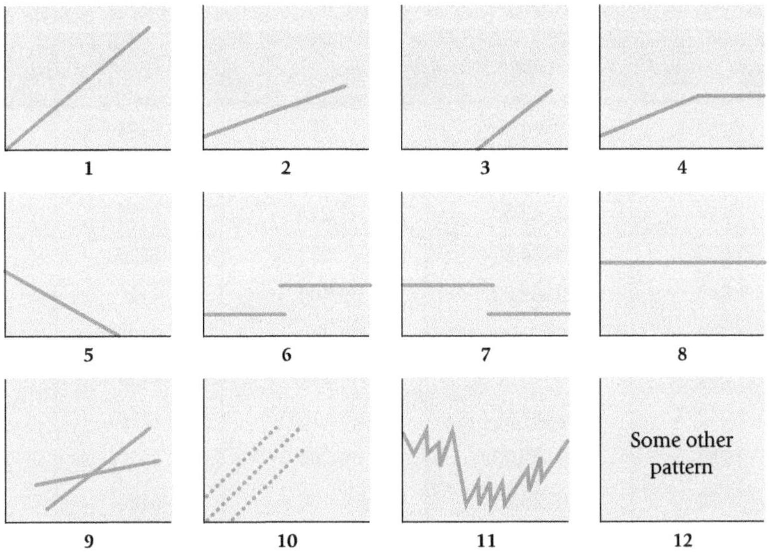

The horizontal axis represents the units produced over the year, and the vertical axis represents total cost or revenues. Indicate by number which graph best fits the situation or item described (a–h). Some graphs may be used more than once; some may not apply to any of the situations.

a. Direct material costs

b. Supervisors' salaries for one shift and two shifts

c. A cost–volume–profit graph

d. Mixed costs—for example, car rental fixed charge plus a rate per mile driven

e. Depreciation of plant, computed on a straight-line basis

f. Data supporting the use of a variable-cost rate, such as manufacturing labor cost of $14 per unit produced

g. Incentive bonus plan that pays managers $0.10 for every unit produced above some level of production

h. Interest expense on $2 million borrowed at a fixed rate of interest

8-15 Account analysis method. Henley operates a mobile car detailing service. Henley travels to a customer's home or place of business to wash and detail their car. Since many locations are remote, Henley's trucks carry water to the location where the car will be washed. Typically, only one car is washed and detailed per location. Henley serviced 60,000 cars in 2012. Henley reports the following costs for 2012:

Account Description	Costs
Car wash labor	$240,000
Soap, cloth, and supplies	39,000
Water	36,000
Fuel and other transportation costs	132,000
Depreciation	68,000
Salaries	52,000

Required

1. Classify each account as variable or fixed for the number of cars washed. Explain.
2. Suppose Henley washed 75,000 cars in 2012. Use the cost classification you developed in requirement 1 to estimate Henley's total costs in 2012. Depreciation is computed on a straight-line basis.
3. Why is it important to correctly classify costs as variable or fixed? That is, what would happen if Henley misclassified some of the costs? Explain.

8-16 Account analysis, high–low method. Highland Exports wants to find an equation to estimate monthly utility costs. Highland Exports has been in business for 1 year and has collected the following cost data for utilities:

Month	Electricity Bill	Kilowatt Hours Used	Telephone Bill	Telephone Minutes Used	Water Bill	Gallons of Water Used
January	$ 770	1,100	$122.00	1,100	$120	30,560
February	$ 910	1,300	$125.30	1,060	$120	26,800
March	$1,218	1,740	$142.50	1,240	$120	31,450
April	$ 714	1,020	$134.00	980	$120	29,965
May	$1,288	1,840	$152.00	1,400	$120	30,568
June	$1,365	1,950	$157.00	1,440	$120	25,540
July	$1,281	1,830	$140.00	1,170	$120	32,690
August	$1,407	2,010	$147.60	1,310	$120	31,222
September	$1,561	2,230	$141.00	1,280	$120	33,540
October	$1,484	2,120	$136.80	1,190	$120	31,970
November	$1,323	1,890	$124.00	1,050	$120	28,600
December	$1,470	2,100	$148.70	1,350	$120	34,100

Required

1. Which of the preceding costs is variable? Fixed? Mixed? Explain.
2. Using the high–low method, determine the cost function for each cost.
3. Combine the preceding information to get a monthly utility cost function for Highland Exports.
4. Next month, Highland Exports expects to use 2,200 kilowatt hours of electricity, make 1,500 minutes of telephone calls, and use 32,000 gallons of water. Estimate total cost of utilities for the month.
5. If you are the manager relying on the cost function determined in requirement 3 to accurately predict costs, what additional concerns would you have when using the high–low method of cost estimation?

8-17 Account analysis method. Gorham, Inc., a manufacturer of plastic products, reports the following manufacturing costs and account analysis classification for the year ended December 31, 2012.

Account	Classification	Amount
Direct materials	All variable	$290,000
Direct manufacturing labor	All variable	181,250
Power	All variable	36,250
Supervision labor	20% variable	43,500
Materials-handling labor	50% variable	72,500
Maintenance labor	50% variable	58,000
Depreciation	0% variable	100,000
Rent, property taxes, and administration	0% variable	110,000

Gorham, Inc., produced 72,500 units of product in 2012. Gorham's management is estimating costs for 2013 on the basis of 2012 numbers. The following additional information is available for 2013.

a. Direct materials prices in 2013 are expected to increase by 10% compared with 2012.

b. Under the terms of the labor contract, direct manufacturing labor wage rates are expected to increase by 5% in 2013 compared with 2012.

c. Power rates and wage rates for supervision, materials handling, and maintenance are not expected to change from 2012 to 2013.

d. Depreciation costs are expected to increase by 8%, and rent, property taxes, and administration costs are expected to increase by 7%.

e. Gorham expects to manufacture and sell 82,500 units in 2013.

Required

1. Prepare a schedule of variable, fixed, and total manufacturing costs for each account category in 2013. Estimate total manufacturing costs for 2013.
2. Calculate Gorham's total manufacturing cost per unit in 2012, and estimate total manufacturing cost per unit in 2013.
3. How can you obtain better estimates of fixed and variable costs? Why would these better estimates be useful to Gorham?

8-18 Estimating a cost function, high-low method. Rapp Travel offers helicopter service from suburban towns to John F. Kennedy International Airport in New York City. Each of its seven helicopters makes between 1,300 and 2,300 round-trips per year. The records indicate that a helicopter that has made 1,300 round-trips in the year incurs an average operating cost of $600 per round-trip, and one that has made 2,300 round-trips in the year incurs an average operating cost of $450 per round-trip.

Required

1. Using the high–low method, estimate the linear relationship $y = a + bX$, where y is the total annual operating cost of a helicopter and X is the number of round-trips it makes to JFK Airport during the year.
2. Give examples of costs that would be included in a and in b.
3. If Rapp Travel expects each helicopter to make, on average, 1,700 round-trips in the coming year, what should its estimated operating budget for the helicopter fleet be?
4. What factors might influence the accuracy of the cost prediction in requirement 3?

8-19 Estimating a cost function, high-low method. Sue North is examining customer-service costs in the southern region of Capitol Products. Capitol Products has more than 200 separate electrical products that it sells with a 6-month guarantee of full repair or replacement with a new product. When a customer returns a product, a service report is prepared. This service report includes details of the problem and the time and cost of resolving the problem. Weekly data for the most recent 8-week period are:

Week	Customer-Service Department Costs	Number of Service Reports
1	$13,700	190
2	20,900	275
3	13,000	115
4	18,800	395
5	14,000	265
6	21,500	455
7	16,900	340
8	21,000	305

Required

1. Plot the relationship between customer-service costs and number of service reports. Is the relationship economically plausible?
2. Use the high–low method to compute the cost function, relating customer-service costs to the number of service reports.
3. What other variables, besides number of service reports, might be cost drivers of weekly customer-service costs of Capitol Products? How might Sue North go about determining which cost driver best explains customer-service department costs?

8-20 Linear cost approximation. Bill Hide, managing partner of the law firm Hide & Associates, is examining how secretarial support costs behave with changes in monthly professional labor-hours billed to clients. Assume the following historical data:

Total Secretarial Support Costs	Professional Labor-Hours Billed to Clients
$35,000	2,000
38,000	3,000
39,500	4,000
49,000	5,000
52,000	6,500
58,000	7,500

Required

1. Compute the linear cost function, relating total secretarial support costs to professional labor-hours, using the representative observations of 3,000 and 6,500 hours. Plot the linear cost function. Does the constant component of the cost function represent the fixed secretarial support costs of Hide & Associates? Why?
2. What would be the predicted total overhead costs for (a) 4,000 hours and (b) 7,500 hours using the cost function estimated in requirement 1? Plot the predicted costs and actual costs for 4,000 and 7,500 hours.
3. Hide had a chance to accept a special job that would have boosted professional labor-hours from 3,000 to 4,000 hours. Suppose Hide, guided by the linear cost function, rejected this job because it would have brought a total increase in contribution margin (sales minus all variable costs) of $3,200, before deducting the predicted increase in total overhead cost, $4,000. What is the actual effect of this decision on overall firm income?

8-21 Cost–volume–profit and regression analysis. Husker Corporation manufactures a garden tractor for residential use. Husker currently manufactures the wheel assembly for the tractors. During 2012, Husker made 2,500 wheel assemblies at a total cost of $325,000. Axel Corporation has offered to supply as many wheel assemblies as Husker wants at a cost of $125 per assembly. Husker anticipates needing 3,000 wheel assemblies each year for the next few years.

Required

1 a. What is the average cost of manufacturing a wheel assembly in 2012? How does it compare to Axel's offer?

b. Can Husker use the answer in requirement 1a to determine the cost of manufacturing 3,000 wheel assemblies? Explain.

2. Husker's management accountant uses annual data from past years to estimate the following regression equation with total manufacturing costs of the wheel assembly as the dependent variable and wheel assemblies produced as the independent variable:

$$y = \$165{,}000 + \$65X$$

During the years used to estimate the regression equation, the production of wheel assemblies varied from 1,800 to 3,500. Using this equation, estimate how much it would cost Husker to manufacture 3,000 wheel assemblies. How much more or less costly is it to manufacture the wheel assemblies rather than to acquire them from Axel?

3. What other information would you need to be confident that the equation in requirement 2 accurately predicts the cost of manufacturing wheel assemblies?

8-22 Regression analysis, service company. (CMA, adapted) Sara Nye owns a party-planning company that provides planning as well as food and beverages. For a standard party, the cost on a per-person basis is as follows.

Food and beverages	$20.00
Labor (0.5 hour × $15 per hour)	7.50
Overhead (0.5 hour × $12.50 per hour)	6.25
Total cost per person	$33.75

Sara is quite certain about her estimates of the food, beverage, and labor costs but is not as comfortable with the overhead estimate. The overhead estimate was based on the actual data for the past 12 months, which are presented here. These data indicate that overhead costs vary with the direct labor-hours used. The $12.50 estimate was determined by dividing total overhead costs for the 12 months by total labor-hours.

Month	Labor-Hours	Overhead Costs
January	2,100	$ 48,000
February	2,400	54,500
March	3,800	52,500
April	4,900	62,500
May	7,500	78,500
June	9,300	83,000
July	8,900	84,000
August	5,800	71,500
September	5,200	63,000
October	4,700	63,000
November	3,240	58,000
December	5,200	69,500
Total	63,040	$788,000

Sara has recently become aware of regression analysis. She estimated the following regression equation with overhead costs as the dependent variable and labor-hours as the independent variable:

$$y = \$39{,}826 + \$4.92X$$

Required

1. Plot the relationship between overhead costs and labor-hours. Draw the regression line and evaluate it using the criteria of economic plausibility, goodness of fit, and slope of the regression line.
2. Using data from the regression analysis, what is the variable cost per person for a standard party?
3. Sara Nye has been asked to prepare a bid for a 200-person standard party to be given next month. Determine the minimum bid price that Sara would be willing to submit to recoup variable costs.
4. What other factors should Sara Nye consider when preparing her bid?

8-23 High-low, regression. Thom Betow is the new manager of the materials storeroom for Manning Industries. Thom has been asked to estimate future monthly purchase costs for part#18, used in two of Manning's products. Thom has purchase cost and quantity data for the past 9 months as follows.

Month	Cost of Purchase	Quantity Purchased
January	$13,950	3,490 parts
February	11,600	2,480
March	15,200	3,600
April	13,100	3,250
May	11,800	2,390
June	12,750	2,780
July	12,350	2,970
August	10,100	1,900
September	13,400	3,050

Estimated monthly purchases for this part based on expected demand of the two products for the rest of the year are as follows.

Month	Purchase Quantity Expected
October	2,750 parts
November	3,260
December	2,610

Required

1. The computer in Thom's office is down and Thom has been asked to immediately provide an equation to estimate the future purchase cost for part#18. Thom grabs a calculator and uses the high–low method to estimate a cost equation. What equation does he get?
2. Using the equation from requirement 1, calculate the future expected purchase costs for each of the last 3 months of the year.
3. After a few hours Thom's computer is fixed. Thom uses the first 9 months of data and regression analysis to estimate the relationship between the quantity purchased and purchase costs of part#18. The regression line Thom obtains is:

$$y = \$5{,}337.90 + 2.56X$$

   Evaluate the regression line using the criteria of economic plausibility, goodness of fit, and significance of the independent variable. Compare the regression equation to the equation based on the high–low method. Which is a better fit? Why?
4. Use the regression results to calculate the expected purchase costs for October, November, and December. Compare the expected purchase costs to the expected purchase costs calculated using the high–low method in requirement 2. Comment on your results.

8-24 Cost estimation, pricing decisions. GottaRun is a local company that custom-prints tech running shirts for organized racing events. The company has been in business for 2 years. Normal demand for the tech running shirts is approximately 600 shirts per event. On average, there are two events per month. The company has the following direct costs per shirt:

Direct material (tech shirts)	$5.00
Direct labor (printing)	$1.00
Direct labor (design)	$2.50
Total direct costs	$8.50

The company has historically estimated selling price based on the direct cost of providing the tech shirts. Prices reflected a 40% desired profit margin above direct costs. Recently, GottaRun has experienced lower-than-normal profits and suspects that the prices it is charging are not covering all costs (direct and indirect) of providing the tech shirts. Indirect costs of the company include depreciation on the printing machines and utilities. The following data from the most recent year relate to these indirect costs:

Month	Depreciation	Tech Shirts	Utilities
January	$400	650	$1,990
February	$400	780	$1,870
March	$400	980	$1,890
April	$400	1,450	$2,640
May	$400	1,210	$2,340
June	$400	1,400	$3,390
July	$400	1,580	$3,480
August	$400	1,610	$3,560
September	$400	1,320	$2,780
October	$400	1,220	$2,750
November	$400	860	$2,280
December	$400	790	$2,150

The management accountant estimates the following regression equation with utilities as the dependent variable and the number of tech shirts as the independent variable:

$$y = \$689 + \$1.65X$$

Required

1. If monthly sales are 1,200 tech shirts, what is the full cost per tech shirt?
2. Why has GottaRun been experiencing lower-than-normal profits?
3. What price must GottaRun charge to recover all costs and earn a 25% margin on all sales?
4. What implications will a potential price increase have on GottaRun and/or its customers? How might the owners address any negative reactions from customers?

8-25 Equipment replacement and regression analysis. Brightlite Company uses a special machine to manufacture streetlights. It currently produces 500 streetlights per month at a total cost of $68,000. Ergo, Inc., has been pressuring Brightlite Company to purchase as many streetlights as it needs from Ergo at a cost of $130 per light.

Required

1. What is the average total cost of manufacturing a streetlight? How does it compare to the cost of purchasing the lights from Ergo? Can Brightlite use the average cost of manufacturing to determine the cost of manufacturing 600 streetlights? Explain.
2. Brightlite's management accountant uses annual data from past years when production varied from 500 to 800 streetlights to estimate the following equation with total manufacturing costs of the streetlights as the dependent variable and streetlights produced as the independent variable:

   $$y = \$23{,}000 + \$90X$$

   Using this equation, estimate how much it would cost Brightlite to manufacture 600 streetlights. How much more or less costly would it be to manufacture the lights rather than purchase the streetlights from Ergo?
3. What other information would Brightlite need to be confident that the equation in requirement 2 accurately predicts the cost of manufacturing streetlights?

Problems

8-26 High-low method. Ken Howard, financial analyst at QTY Corporation, is examining the behavior of quarterly maintenance costs for budgeting purposes. Howard collects the following data on machine-hours worked and maintenance costs for the past 12 quarters.

Quarter	Machine-Hours	Maintenance Costs
1	75,000	$195,000
2	95,000	230,000
3	85,000	210,000
4	105,000	250,000
5	70,000	180,000
6	90,000	225,000
7	80,000	205,000
8	100,000	245,000
9	80,000	200,000
10	100,000	235,000
11	90,000	190,000
12	130,000	285,000

Required

1. Estimate the cost function for the quarterly data using the high–low method.
2. Plot and comment on the estimated cost function.
3. Howard anticipates that QTY will operate machines for 75,000 hours in quarter 13. Calculate the predicted maintenance costs in quarter 13 using the cost function estimated in requirement 1.
4. Would there be much value to estimating the cost function using the regression method instead of the high–low method used in requirement 1? Explain.

8-27 High-low method and regression analysis. True Orchard, a cooperative of organic family-owned farms outside of Portland, Oregon, has recently started a fresh produce club to provide support to the group's member farms and to promote the benefits of eating organic, locally produced food to the nearby suburban community. Families pay a seasonal membership fee of $50, and place their orders a week in advance for a price of $41 per week. In turn, True Harvest delivers fresh-picked seasonal local produce to several neighborhood distribution points. Eight hundred families joined the club for the first season, but the number of orders varied from week to week.

Sam Young has run the produce club for the first 10-week season. Before becoming a farmer, Sam had been a business major in college, and he remembers a few things about cost analysis. In planning for next year, he wants to know how many orders will be needed each week for the club to break even, but first he must estimate the club's fixed and variable costs. He has collected the following data over the club's first 10 weeks of operation:

Week	Number of Orders per Week	Weekly Total Costs
1	344	$17,580
2	380	20,560
3	420	21,980
4	445	22,350
5	415	22,350
6	490	24,550
7	460	23,780
8	457	22,690
9	532	25,400
10	515	24,900

Required

1. Plot the relationship between number of orders per week and weekly total costs.
2. Estimate the cost equation using the high–low method, and draw this line on your graph.
3. Sam uses his computer to calculate the following regression formula:

   Total weekly costs = $5,631 + ($38.10 × Number of weekly orders)

   Draw the regression line on your graph. Use your graph to evaluate the regression line using the criteria of economic plausibility, goodness of fit, and significance of the independent variable. Is the cost function estimated using the high–low method a close approximation of the cost function estimated using the regression method? Explain briefly.
4. Did True Orchard break even this season? Remember that each of the families paid a seasonal membership fee of $50.
5. Assume that 900 families join the club next year, and that prices and costs do not change. Using the regression equation, how many orders, on average, must True Orchard receive each week to break even?
6. For the number of orders calculated in requirement 5, calculate True Orchard's estimated profit using the high–low method. Comment on your results.

8-28 High-low method; regression analysis. (CIMA, adapted) Tina Reese, financial manager at the local Players Theater, is checking to see if there is any relationship between newspaper advertising and sales revenues at the theater. She obtains the following data for the past 10 months:

Month	Revenues	Advertising Costs
March	$28,000	$2,000
April	73,000	3,000
May	58,000	1,500
June	65,000	3,500
July	55,000	1,000

Month	Revenues	Advertising Costs
August	65,000	2,000
September	45,000	1,500
October	85,000	4,000
November	55,000	2,300
December	60,000	2,500

She estimates the following regression equation:

Monthly revenues = \$33,818 + (\$10.765 × Advertising costs)

Required

1. Plot the relationship between advertising costs and revenues.
2. Draw the regression line and evaluate it using the criteria of economic plausibility, goodness of fit, and slope of the regression line.
3. Use the high–low method to compute the function, relating advertising costs and revenues.
4. Using (a) the regression equation and (b) the high–low equation, what is the increase in revenues for each \$1,000 spent on advertising within the relevant range? Which method should Tina use to predict the effect of advertising costs on revenues? Explain briefly.
5. What other factors should Tina consider before using the method you chose in requirement 4?

8-29 Regression, activity-based costing, choosing cost drivers. Bayland Manufacturing has been using activity-based costing to determine the cost of product B-190. One of the activities, "Inspection," occurs just before the product is finished. Bayland inspects every 10th unit and has been using "number of units inspected" as the cost driver for inspection costs. A significant component of inspection costs is the cost of the test kit used in each inspection.

Meena Ley, the line manager, is wondering if inspection labor-hours might be a better cost driver for inspection costs. Meena gathers information for weekly inspection costs, units inspected, and inspection labor-hours as follows.

Week	Units Inspected	Inspection Labor-Hours	Inspection Costs
1	1,700	190	\$4,000
2	700	80	2,100
3	2,100	230	4,900
4	2,700	240	6,300
5	2,300	210	5,700
6	1,000	70	3,100
7	1,200	130	3,200

Meena runs regressions on each of the possible cost drivers and estimates these cost functions:

Inspection costs = \$772 + (\$2.04 × Number of units inspected)
Inspection costs = \$988 + (\$19.47 × Inspection labor-hours)

Required

1. Explain why number of units inspected and inspection labor-hours are plausible cost drivers of inspection costs.
2. Plot the data and regression line for units inspected and inspection costs. Plot the data and regression line for inspection labor-hours and inspection costs. Which cost driver of inspection costs would you choose? Explain.
3. Meena expects inspectors to work 120 hours next period and to inspect 1,500 units. Using the cost driver you chose in requirement 2, what amount of inspection costs should Meena budget?
4. What, if any, are the implications of Meena choosing the cost driver you did not choose in requirement 2 to budget inspection costs?

8-30 Interpreting regression results, matching time periods. Bender, Inc., produces industrial blenders for smoothie and health food shops. It has four peak periods, each lasting 2 months, for manufacturing the merchandise suited for spring, summer, fall, and winter. In the off-peak periods, Bender schedules equipment maintenance. Bender's controller, Gina Hood, wants to understand the drivers of equipment maintenance costs.

The data collected is as follows.

Month	Machine-Hours	Maintenance Costs
January	5,150	$ 1,250
February	4,600	2,150
March	1,120	13,100
April	5,360	1,650
May	5,650	2,680
June	1,750	15,100
July	7,250	1,900
August	6,050	2,690
September	1,950	15,400
October	6,200	1,750
November	5,800	2,850
December	1,450	14,900

A regression analysis of 1 year of monthly data yields the following relationships:

$$\text{Maintenance costs} = \$17{,}983 - (\$2.683 \times \text{Number of machine-hours})$$

Upon examining the results, Hood comments, "So, all I have to do to reduce maintenance costs is run my machines longer? This is hard to believe, but numbers don't lie! I would have guessed just the opposite."

Required

1. Explain why Hood made this comment. What is wrong with her analysis?
2. Upon further reflection, Hood reanalyzes the data, this time comparing quarterly machine-hours with quarterly maintenance expenditures. This time, the results are very different. The regression yields the following formula:

$$\text{Maintenance costs} = \$8{,}580.20 + (\$0.785 \times \text{Number of machine-hours})$$

What caused the formula to change, in light of the fact that the data was the same?

8-31 Regression, activity-based costing, customer costs. Soaring, Inc., makes paragliders, most of which are custom-designed for the customer. Customer costs, the costs incurred to support customers, are a major component of the company's income statement. The owners of Soaring would like to have a more accurate picture of what is driving customer costs and have collected the following data related to paraglider sales:

Month	Customer Costs	Number of Customer Orders	Number of Design-Hours
1	$4,500	50	190
2	2,600	20	80
3	5,300	75	230
4	6,550	60	240
5	5,850	55	210
6	3,370	10	70
7	3,480	45	130

The management accountant runs regressions on each of the possible cost drivers and estimates these cost functions:

$$\text{Customer costs} = \$1{,}391 + (\$19.057 \times \text{Number of design-hours})$$

$$\text{Customer costs} = \$2{,}267 + (\$50.097 \times \text{Number of customer orders})$$

Required

1. Plot the data and draw the regression line for customer costs and number of customer orders. Plot the data and draw the regression line for customer costs and number of design-hours. Which driver would you choose to predict customer costs?

2. Soaring received a call from a customer who would like to order a paraglider that could hold two passengers. The design of this type of glider would require 10 design hours. What are the expected customer costs for this customer if design hours is used to predict customer costs? The company may get additional orders from other customers for a similar design. Should Soaring charge the customer for all the customer costs related to this order?
3. The owners of Soaring anticipate many return customers in the following months. Return customers require fewer custom designs since existing designs for these customers provide a significant reduction in design time. How does this information affect your choice of the driver for customer costs?

8-32 Regression, choosing best cost driver. Heywood Game Systems produces a variety of video game consoles. The company has been using activity-based costing to determine the cost of the "Ultimate" game block. Heywood incurs setup costs for each batch of consoles it produces. Currently the company is using the number of setups as the cost driver for setup costs. Jerry Crofton has been hired recently to assist in the production department. He frequently boasts about the managerial accounting classes he has taken as a student. He thinks that setup hours may be a better driver for setup costs. Heywood has collected the following data related to setting up the machines for production of the game consoles:

Month	Number of Setups	Number of Setup Hours	Setup Costs
1	18	36	$520
2	20	45	620
3	22	40	530
4	25	42	535
5	17	35	500
6	15	26	415
7	14	30	460
8	13	28	464

Jerry runs regressions on each of the possible cost drivers and estimates these cost functions:

$$\text{Setup costs} = \$327.25 + (\$9.83 \times \text{Number of setups})$$
$$\text{Setup costs} = \$212.89 + (\$8.26 \times \text{Setup hours})$$

Required

1. Explain why number of setups and setup-hours are plausible cost drivers of setup costs.
2. Plot the data and regression line for number of setups and setup costs. Plot the data and regression line for setup hours and setup costs. Which cost driver of setup costs would you choose? Explain.
3. What, if any, are the implications of Heywood choosing the cost driver you did not choose in requirement 2 when evaluating the production process?

8-33 Interpreting regression results, data shifts. FunSkis Company manufactures snow and water skis. Snow skis are the primary product for the company. However, to keep part of the facility operating during the offseason for snow skiing, the company manufactures water skis during the offseason months. The company produces snow skis from July through January and water skis from February through June. During the months of February through June, the company significantly reduces the labor force and approximately two-thirds of the production equipment sits idle. FunSkis would like to better predict overhead cost and has chosen machine-hours as the cost driver for overhead cost. The following data has been gathered for the most recent year:

Month	Number of Machine-Hours	Overhead Costs
January	390	$ 4,520
February	289	1,110
March	268	1,100
April	215	950
May	190	820
June	245	990

continued

Month	Number of Machine-Hours	Overhead Costs
July	385	4,490
August	442	4,760
September	480	4,780
October	510	4,870
November	458	4,790
December	418	4,600

A regression analysis of 1 year of monthly data yields the following relationships:

$$\text{Overhead costs} = (\$16.347 \times \text{Number of machine-hours}) - \$2{,}695.80$$

Required

1. How should FunSkis interpret the negative intercept term based on the most recent 12-month period?
2. Plot the relationship between overhead costs and machine hours. What issue(s) do you recognize with the data?
3. Upon further reflection, FunSkis reanalyzes the data. The company realizes that it has two distinct operating "seasons": July through January and February through June.

   Regression line for July through January:
   $\text{Overhead costs} = \$3.087 \times \text{Number of machine-hours} + \$3{,}327.40$

   Regression line for February through June:
   $\text{Overhead costs} = \$2.914 \times \text{Number of machine-hours} + \$290.55$

   a. Plot the data and the regression line for overhead costs and number of machine-hours for the period of July through January.

   b. Plot the data and the regression line for overhead costs and number of machine-hours for the period of February through June.
4. What, if any, are the implications of FunSkis using the regression line with all 12 months of data to budget for overhead costs, without adjusting for seasonality?

8-34 Interpreting regression results, matching time periods, ethics. Jayne Barbour is working as a summer intern at Mode, a trendy store specializing in clothing for twenty-somethings. Jayne has been working closely with her cousin, Gail Hubbard, who plans promotions for Mode. The store has only been in business for 10 months, and Valerie Parker, the store's owner, has been unsure of the effectiveness of the store's advertising. Wanting to impress Valerie with the regression analysis skills she acquired in a cost accounting course the previous semester, Jayne decides to prepare an analysis of the effect of advertising on revenues. Jayne performs a regression analysis, comparing each month's advertising expense with that month's revenue, and obtains the following formula:

$$\text{Revenue} = \$47{,}801 - (1.92 \times \text{Advertising expense})$$
$$r^2 = 0.43;$$

Required

1. Plot the preceding data on a graph and draw the regression line. What does the cost formula indicate about the relationship between monthly advertising expense and monthly revenues? Is the relationship economically plausible?
2. Jayne worries that if she makes her presentation to the owner as planned, it will reflect poorly on her cousin Gail's performance. Is she ethically obligated to make the presentation?
3. Jayne thinks further about her analysis, and discovers a significant flaw in her approach. She realizes that advertising done in a given month should be expected to influence the following month's sales, not necessarily the current month's. She modifies her analysis by comparing, for example, October advertising expense with November sales revenue. The modified regression yields:

$$\text{Revenue} = \$23{,}538 + (5.92 \times \text{Previous month's advertising expense})$$
$$r^2 = 0.71;$$

   What does the revised cost formula indicate? Plot the revised data on a graph. Is this relationship economically plausible?
4. Can Jayne conclude that there is a cause-and-effect relationship between advertising expense and sales revenue? Why or why not?

Case

United Packaging

Janice Kerry is the management accountant at the can manufacturing plant of United Packaging. She looked a little puzzled as she stared at the regression equation for estimating the relationship between total engineering support costs reported in the plant records and machine-hours. As she looked up from the computer she mumbled to herself, "I have to dive deeper to understand this. Why do engineering support costs decrease when we run our machines harder?"

United Packaging has been facing pressure from customers to reduce prices. To respond to this challenge, Terrence Jimenez, the general manager of the plant, has put in place a cost reduction program to increase United's competitiveness. To implement this program, he has asked Kerry to gain a better understanding of the spending in various categories of overhead costs. In his speeches to employees, Jimenez would often emphasize the importance of managing based on data and repeat his favorite mantra, "You cannot manage that which you cannot measure."

United Packaging has been in business for over 30 years. When the company started operations, its major customer was General Mills Corporation. Over the years, United's business grew several-fold matching the growth in its customers' businesses. The company took advantage of scale economies and lower costs to add more customers and further grow the business. The company had a reputation for excellent quality and very good customer service. This further strengthened its customer relationships. In the most recent year, the plant had annual sales of $300 million and a gross margin percentage of 30%.

Jimenez had a good sense of direct costs such as direct materials. He knew how much direct material was needed for each can and how much material was being wasted. Manufacturing teams were already working on plans to cut down waste and reduce direct material costs by 7%. Overhead costs were a different matter. Jimenez and his team were just not sure about the drivers of overhead costs and therefore what they needed to do to manage these costs.

Kerry chose engineering support costs as the first overhead cost category to analyze because she was fairly confident about the cost driver of those costs. Engineering support costs are costs incurred on maintenance and fine-tuning of machines to ensure the production of high-quality products. Kerry believed that the more United ran its machines, the greater would be the need for engineering support.

Engineering support costs have two components: (1) labor, which is paid monthly, and (2) materials and parts, which are purchased from an outside vendor every three months. By consolidating purchases each quarter, United was able to get a discounted price on the larger purchase quantities. The accounting system recorded the monthly labor payments and the quarterly materials and parts purchases. Kerry took this accounting data, described in columns 1, 2, and 4 of United Packaging Exhibit 1, and ran a regression analysis of engineering support reported costs and machine hours to obtain the estimates obtained in regression 1 as follows:

Regression 1: Engineering support reported costs = $1,393.20 − ($14.23 × Machine-hours)

This is the regression equation that Kerry was having trouble understanding. Increasing machine-hours appeared to decrease engineering support costs, when in fact she had reasoned that it should have increased these costs. She decided to call the operating manager, Roger Liston. Here is their dialogue:

Kerry: "Roger, I've collected accounting data on engineering support costs and machine hours. My results are showing that as machine-hours increase, engineering support costs decrease. Can you explain why this might be the case?"

Liston: "Janice, I don't know what data you've collected but let me think out aloud about what happens in the plant. The more I run the machines, the greater the materials and parts I order from the store because the greater the number of parts that I need to replace. Why might you find a negative relationship in a particular month? Because sometimes we schedule the maintenance of the machines during periods when the machines are used less. In this case, it could be that engineering support costs are high in periods when machine-hours are low. I am pretty sure this was not the case last year, but it is something you may want to check. In any event, I think you need to take a good look at the numbers you are using."

Kerry: "Your comments suddenly triggered a thought in my mind. I think I know exactly what I need to do. Thank you very much for your help."

As soon as Kerry put down the phone, she began gathering some additional data. These data are shown in Column 3 of United Packaging Exhibit 1. Notice that the total of the cost numbers used in Column 3 do not equal the total of the cost numbers reported in Column 2. Kerry then ran a regression analysis of engineering support restated costs and machine hours to obtain the estimates obtained in regression 2 as follows:

Regression 2: Engineering support restated costs = \$176.38 + (\$11.44 × Machine-hours)

Required

1. What data do you think Kerry collected to obtain the numbers in column 3? That is, what do the numbers in column 3 represent?
2. Plot the cost functions for (i) the *reported costs* for total engineering support and machine-hours and (ii) the *restated costs* for total engineering support and machine-hours. Contrast and evaluate the cost function estimated with regression analysis using restated data for materials and parts with the cost function estimated with regression analysis using the data reported in the plant records. Which cost function would you choose to best represent the relationship between engineering support costs and machine-hours? Explain briefly.
3. Is it important for Kerry to choose the correct cost function? That is, what potential problems could Kerry encounter by choosing a cost function other than the one you chose in requirement 2. Explain briefly.
4. What problems might Kerry encounter when restating the materials and parts costs recorded in column 3 of United Packaging Exhibit 1?
5. Do you think Kerry should estimate any other cost function? Why? Explain briefly.

United Packaging Exhibit 1

(All numbers in thousands)

Month	Labor: Reported Costs (1)	Materials and Parts: Reported Costs (2)	Materials and Parts: Restated Costs (3)	Total Engineering Support: Reported Costs (4) = (1) + (2)	Total Engineering Support: Restated Costs (5) = (1) + (3)	Machine-Hours (6)
March	\$347	\$847	\$182	\$1,194	\$529	30
April	521	0	411	521	932	63
May	398	0	268	398	666	49
June	355	961	228	1,316	583	38
July	473	0	348	473	821	57
August	617	0	349	617	966	73
September	245	821	125	1,066	370	19
October	487	0	364	487	851	53
November	431	0	290	431	721	42

Decision Making and Relevant Information

9

Learning Objectives

1. Use the five-step decision-making process to make decisions
2. Distinguish relevant from irrelevant information in decision situations
3. Explain the concept of opportunity cost and why managers consider it when making decisions
4. Know how to choose which products to produce when there are capacity constraints
5. Explain how to manage bottlenecks
6. Discuss factors managers must consider when adding or dropping customers or segments
7. Explain why book value of equipment is irrelevant to managers making equipment-replacement decisions
8. Explain how conflicts can arise between the decision model a manager uses and the performance-evaluation model companies use to evaluate managers
9. Explain why joint costs are irrelevant in a sell-or-process-further decision

How many decisions have you made today?

Maybe you made a big decision today, such as accepting a job offer. Or maybe your decision was as simple as settling on your plans for the weekend or choosing a restaurant for dinner. Regardless of whether decisions are significant or routine, most people follow a simple, logical process when making them. This process involves gathering information, making predictions, making a choice, acting on the choice, and evaluating results. The process also includes deciding what costs and benefits each choice offers. For decisions that involve costs, some costs are irrelevant. For example, once you purchase a coffee maker, its cost is irrelevant when calculating how much money you save each time you brew coffee at home versus buy it at Starbucks. You incurred the cost of the coffee maker in the past, and you can't recoup that money. The Chapter at a Glance explains which costs and benefits are relevant and which are not—and how you should think of them when choosing among alternatives.

Chapter at a Glance

- When making decisions, two criteria help managers decide whether a revenue or cost is relevant: (1) whether it is an expected future revenue or expected future cost and (2) whether it differs among alternative courses of action. Managers also consider nonfinancial and qualitative factors.
- The relevant cost of any decision is (1) the incremental cost of the decision plus (2) the opportunity cost of the profit forgone from making that decision rather than using a limited resource in its next-best alternative use. Allocated costs are irrelevant.
- When resources are constrained, managers select the product that yields the highest contribution margin per unit of the constraining or bottleneck resource (factor). To increase profits, managers increase bottleneck utilization, efficiency, and capacity.
- The book value of existing equipment is a past cost (also called a historical or sunk cost) and, therefore, irrelevant to managers deciding whether to replace equipment.
- Top management must ensure that the performance-evaluation model of lower-level managers is consistent with the decision model.
- Joint costs arise when a production process yields multiple products simultaneously. Joint costs are irrelevant in the decision to sell or further process these products because joint costs are the same regardless of whether further processing occurs.

Managers in corporations around the world use a decision process. Managers at JPMorgan Chase gather information about financial markets, consumer preferences, and economic trends before determining whether to offer new services to customers. Managers at Macy's examine all the relevant information related to domestic and international clothing manufacturing before selecting vendors. Managers at Porsche gather cost information to decide whether to manufacture a component part or purchase it from a supplier. The decision process may not always be easy, but as Peter Drucker said, "Wherever you see a successful business, someone once made a courageous decision."

Learning Objective 1

Use the five-step decision-making process to make decisions

. . . the five steps are identify the problem and uncertainties; obtain information; make predictions about the future; make decisions by choosing among alternatives; and implement the decision, evaluate performance, and learn

Information and the Decision Process

Managers usually follow a *decision model* for choosing among different courses of action. A **decision model** is a formal method of making a choice that often involves both quantitative and qualitative analyses. Management accountants analyze and present relevant data to guide managers' decisions.

Consider a strategic decision facing managers at Precision Sporting Goods, a manufacturer of golf clubs: Should it reorganize its manufacturing operations to reduce manufacturing labor costs? Precision Sporting Goods has only two alternatives: do not reorganize or reorganize.

Reorganization will eliminate all manual handling of materials. Current manufacturing labor consists of 20 workers: 15 workers operate machines and 5 workers handle materials. The 5 materials-handling workers have been hired on contracts that permit layoffs without additional payments. Each worker works 2,000 hours annually. Reorganization is predicted to cost \$90,000 each year (mostly for new equipment leases). The reorganization will not affect the production output of 25,000 units, the selling price of \$250, the direct material cost per unit of \$50, manufacturing overhead of \$750,000, or marketing costs of \$2,000,000.

Managers use the five-step decision-making process presented in Exhibit 9-1 and first introduced in Chapter 1 to make this decision. Study the sequence of steps in this exhibit and note how Step 5 evaluates performance to provide feedback about actions taken in the previous steps. This feedback might affect future predictions, the prediction methods used, the way choices are made, or the implementation of the decision.

Learning Objective 2

Distinguish relevant from irrelevant information in decision situations

. . . only costs and revenues that are expected to occur in the future and differ among alternative courses of action are relevant

The Concept of Relevance

Much of this chapter focuses on Step 4 in Exhibit 9-1 and on the concepts of relevant costs and relevant revenues when choosing among alternatives.

Relevant Costs and Relevant Revenues

Relevant costs are *expected future costs* and **relevant revenues** are *expected future revenues* that differ among the alternative courses of action being considered. Revenues and costs that are *not relevant* are said to be *irrelevant.* It is important to recognize that to be relevant costs and relevant revenues they *must:*

- **Occur in the future**—every decision deals with a manager selecting a course of action based on its expected future results.
- **Differ among the alternative courses of action**—costs and revenues that do not differ will not matter and, therefore, will have no bearing on the decision being made.

The question is always, "What difference will a particular action make?"

Exhibit 9-2 presents the financial data underlying the choice between the do-not-reorganize and reorganize alternatives for Precision Sporting Goods. Managers can analyze the data in two ways: by considering "all revenues and costs" or considering only "relevant revenues and costs."

The first two columns describe the first way and present *all data.* The last two columns describe the second way and present *only relevant costs:* the \$640,000 and \$480,000 expected future manufacturing labor costs and the \$90,000 expected future reorganization costs that differ between the two alternatives. Managers can ignore the revenues, direct materials, manufacturing overhead, and marketing items because these costs will remain the same whether or not Precision Sporting Goods reorganizes. These costs do not differ between the alternatives and, therefore, are irrelevant.

Note, the past (historical) manufacturing hourly wage rate of \$14 and total past (historical) manufacturing labor costs of \$560,000 (20 workers × 2,000 hours per worker per year × \$14 per hour) do not appear in Exhibit 9-2. *Although they may be a useful basis for making informed predictions of*

Exhibit 9-1

Five-Step Decision-Making Process for Precision Sporting Goods

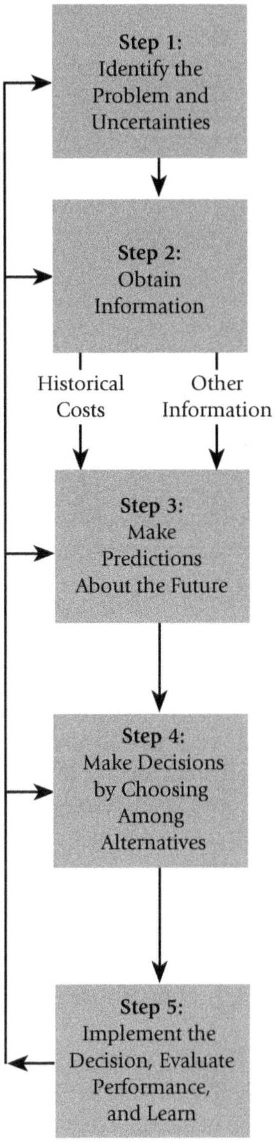

Should Precision Sporting Goods reorganize its manufacturing operations to reduce manufacturing labor costs? An important uncertainty is how the reorganization will affect employee morale.

Historical hourly wage rates are $14 per hour. However, a recently negotiated increase in employee benefits of $2 per hour will increase wages to $16 per hour. The reorganization of manufacturing operations is expected to reduce the number of workers from 20 to 15 by eliminating all 5 workers who handle materials. The reorganization is likely to have negative effects on employee morale.

Managers use information from Step 2 as a basis for predicting future manufacturing labor costs. Under the existing do-not-reorganize alternative, costs are predicted to be $640,000 (20 workers × 2,000 hours per worker per year × $16 per hour), and under the reorganize alternative, costs are predicted to be $480,000 (15 workers × 2,000 hours per worker per year ×$16 per hour). Recall, the reorganization is predicted to cost $90,000 per year.

Managers compare the predicted benefits calculated in Step 3 ($640,000 − $480,000 = $160,000—that is, savings from eliminating materials-handling labor costs, 5 workers × 2,000 hours per worker per year × $16 per hour = $160,000) against the cost of the reorganization ($90,000) along with other considerations (such as likely negative effects on employee morale). Management chooses the reorganize alternative because the financial benefits are significant and the effects on employee morale are expected to be temporary and relatively small.

Evaluating performance after the decision is implemented provides critical feedback for managers, and the five-step sequence is then repeated in whole or in part. Managers learn from actual results that the new manufacturing labor costs are $540,000, rather than the predicted $480,000, because of lower-than-expected manufacturing labor productivity. This (now) historical information can help managers make better subsequent predictions that allow for more learning time. Alternatively, managers may improve implementation via employee training and better supervision.

the expected future manufacturing labor costs of $640,000 and $480,000, historical costs themselves are past costs that, therefore, are irrelevant to decision making. Past costs are also called **sunk costs** because they are unavoidable and cannot be changed no matter what action is taken.

The analysis in Exhibit 9-2 indicates that reorganizing the manufacturing operations will increase predicted operating income by $70,000 each year. Note that the managers at Precision Sporting Goods reach the same conclusion whether they use all data or include only relevant data in the analysis. By confining the analysis to only relevant data, managers can clear away the clutter of potentially confusing irrelevant data. Focusing on relevant data is especially helpful when all the information needed to prepare a detailed income statement is unavailable. Understanding which costs are relevant and which are irrelevant helps the decision maker concentrate on obtaining only the pertinent data.

Qualitative and Quantitative Relevant Information

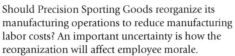

Managers divide the outcomes of decisions into two broad categories: *quantitative* and *qualitative.* **Quantitative factors** are outcomes that are measured in numerical terms. Some quantitative factors are financial; they can be expressed in monetary terms. Examples include the cost of direct

Exhibit 9-2

Determining Relevant Revenues and Relevant Costs for Precision Sporting Goods

	All Revenues and Costs		Relevant Revenues and Costs	
	Alternative 1: Do Not Reorganize	Alternative 2: Reorganize	Alternative 1: Do Not Reorganize	Alternative 2: Reorganize
Revenues[a]	$6,250,000	$6,250,000	—	—
Costs:				
Direct materials[b]	1,250,000	1,250,000	—	—
Manufacturing labor	640,000[c]	480,000[d]	$ 640,000[c]	$ 480,000[d]
Manufacturing overhead	750,000	750,000	—	—
Marketing	2,000,000	2,000,000	—	—
Reorganization costs	—	90,000	—	90,000
Total costs	4,640,000	4,570,000	640,000	570,000
Operating income	$1,610,000	$1,680,000	$(640,000)	$(570,000)
	$70,000 Difference		$70,000 Difference	

[a]25,000 units × $250 per unit = $6,250,000
[b]25,000 units × $50 per unit = $1,250,000
[c]20 workers × 2,000 hours per worker × $16 per hour = $640,000
[d]15 workers × 2,000 hours per worker × $16 per hour = $480,000

materials, direct manufacturing labor, and marketing. Other quantitative factors are nonfinancial; they can be measured numerically, but they are not expressed in monetary terms. Examples include reduction in new product-development time for companies such as Microsoft and the percentage of on-time flight arrivals for companies such as Jet Blue. **Qualitative factors** are outcomes that are difficult to measure accurately in numerical terms. Employee morale is an example.

Relevant-cost analysis generally emphasizes quantitative factors that can be expressed in financial terms. *Although qualitative factors and quantitative nonfinancial factors cannot be measured easily in financial terms, they are important for managers to consider.* In the Precision Sporting Goods example, managers carefully considered the negative effect on employee morale of laying off materials-handling workers, a qualitative factor, before choosing the reorganize alternative. It is often challenging for managers to compare and trade off nonfinancial and financial considerations.

Exhibit 9-3 summarizes the key features of relevant information. The concept of relevance applies to all decision situations. We present some of these decision situations in this chapter. Later chapters describe other decision situations that require application of the relevance concept, such as quality, timeliness, inventory management, and supplier evaluation (Chapter 10); capital investment (Chapter 11); and transfer pricing (Chapter 15). We start our discussion on relevance by considering managerial decisions that affect output levels, such as whether to introduce a new product or to try to sell more units of an existing product.

One-Time-Only Special Orders

One type of decision that affects output levels involves accepting or rejecting special orders when there is idle production capacity and the special orders have no long-run implications. We use the term **one-time-only special order** to describe these conditions.

Exhibit 9-3

Key Features of Relevant Information

- Past (historical) costs may be helpful as a basis for making *predictions*. However, past costs themselves are always irrelevant when making *decisions*.
- Different alternatives can be compared by examining differences in expected total future revenues and expected total future costs.
- Not all expected future revenues and expected future costs are relevant. Expected future revenues and expected future costs that do not differ among alternatives are irrelevant and, hence, can be eliminated from the analysis. The key question is always, "What difference will an action make?"
- Appropriate weight must be given to qualitative factors and quantitative nonfinancial factors.

Example 1: Surf Gear manufactures quality beach towels at its highly automated Burlington, North Carolina, plant. The plant has a production capacity of 45,000 towels each month. Current monthly production is 30,000 towels. Retail department stores account for all existing sales. Exhibit 9-4 shows the expected results for the coming month (August). (These amounts are predictions based on past costs.) We assume that in the short run, all costs can be classified as either fixed or variable for a single cost driver (units of output).

As a result of a worker strike at its existing towel supplier, Azelia, a luxury hotel chain, has offered to buy 5,000 towels from Surf Gear in August at $11 per towel. Based on the following facts, should Surf Gear's managers accept Azelia's offer?

- No subsequent sales to Azelia are anticipated.
- Fixed manufacturing costs are based on the 45,000-towel production capacity. That is, fixed manufacturing costs relate to the production capacity available and not the actual capacity used. If Surf Gear accepts the special order, it will use existing idle capacity to produce the 5,000 towels and fixed manufacturing costs will not change.
- No marketing costs will be necessary for the 5,000-unit one-time-only special order.
- Accepting this special order is not expected to affect the selling price or the quantity of towels sold to regular customers.

The management accountant prepares the data shown in Exhibit 9-4 on an absorption-costing basis (both variable and fixed manufacturing costs are included in inventoriable costs and cost of goods sold). In this exhibit, the manufacturing cost of $12 per unit and the marketing cost of $7 per unit include both variable and fixed costs. The sum of all costs (variable and fixed) in a particular business function of the value chain, such as manufacturing costs or marketing costs, are called **business function costs. Full costs of the product,** in this case $19 per unit, are the sum of all variable and fixed costs in all business functions of the value chain (R&D, design, production, marketing, distribution, and customer service). For Surf Gear, full costs of the product consist of costs in manufacturing and marketing because these are the only business functions. Because no marketing costs are necessary for the special order, the manager of Surf Gear will focus only on manufacturing costs. Based on the manufacturing cost per unit of $12, which is greater than the $11-per-unit price Azelia offered, the manager might decide to reject the offer.

Exhibit 9-4

Budgeted Income Statement for August, Absorption-Costing Format for Surf Gear[a]

	A	B	C	D
1		**Total**	**Per Unit**	
2	Units sold	30,000		
3				
4	Revenues	$600,000	$20.00	
5	Cost of goods sold (manufacturing costs)			
6	Variable manufacturing costs	225,000	7.50[b]	
7	Fixed manufacturing costs	135,000	4.50[c]	
8	Total cost of goods sold	360,000	12.00	
9	Marketing costs			
10	Variable marketing costs	150,000	5.00	
11	Fixed marketing costs	60,000	2.00	
12	Total marketing costs	210,000	7.00	
13	Full costs of the product	570,000	19.00	
14	Operating income	$ 30,000	$ 1.00	
15				
16	[a]Surf Gear incurs no R&D, product-design, distribution, or customer-service costs			
17	[b]Variable manufacturing = Direct material + Variable direct manufacturing + Variable manufacturing			
18	cost per unit cost per unit labor cost per unit overhead cost per unit			
19	= $6.00 + $0.50 + $1.00 = $7.50			
20	[c]Fixed manufacturing = Fixed direct manufacturing + Fixed manufacturing			
21	cost per unit labor cost per unit overhead cost per unit			
22	= $1.50 + $3.00 = $4.50			

In Exhibit 9-5, the management accountant separates manufacturing and marketing costs into their variable- and fixed-cost components and presents data in the format of a contribution income statement. The relevant revenues and costs are the expected future revenues and costs that differ as a result of Surf Gear accepting the special offer: revenues of $55,000 ($11 per unit × 5,000 units) and variable manufacturing costs of $37,500 ($7.50 per unit × 5,000 units). The fixed manufacturing costs and all marketing costs (*including variable marketing costs*) are irrelevant in this case because these costs will not change in total whether the special order is accepted or rejected. Surf Gear would gain an additional $17,500 (relevant revenues, $55,000 − relevant costs, $37,500) in operating income by accepting the special order. In this example, by comparing total amounts for 30,000 units versus 35,000 units or focusing only on the relevant amounts in the difference column in Exhibit 9-5, the manager avoids a misleading implication: to reject the special order because the $11-per-unit selling price is lower than the manufacturing cost per unit of $12 (Exhibit 9-4), which includes both variable and fixed manufacturing costs.

The assumption of no long-run or strategic implications is crucial to a manager's analysis of the one-time-only special-order decision. Suppose the manager concludes that the retail department stores (Surf Gear's regular customers) will demand a lower price if Surf Gear sells towels at $11 apiece to Azelia. In this case, revenues from regular customers will be relevant. Why? Because the future revenues from regular customers will differ depending on whether Surf Gear accepts the special order. The Surf Gear manager would need to modify the relevant-revenue and relevant-cost analysis of the Azelia order to consider both the short-run benefits from accepting the order and the long-run consequences on profitability if Surf Gear lowered prices to all regular customers.

Exhibit 9-5

One-Time-Only Special-Order Decision for Surf Gear: Comparative Contribution Income Statements

Home | Insert | Page Layout | Formulas | Data | Review | View

	A	B	C	D	E	F	G	H
1		Without the Special Order				With the Special Order		Difference: Relevant Amounts
2		30,000				35,000		for the
3		Units to be Sold				Units to be Sold		5,000
4		Per Unit		Total		Total		Units Special Order
5		(1)		(2) = (1) × 30,000		(3)		(4) = (3) − (2)
6	Revenues	$20.00		$600,000		$655,000		$55,000[a]
7	Variable costs:							
8	Manufacturing	7.50		225,000		262,500		37,500[b]
9	Marketing	5.00		150,000		150,000		0[c]
10	Total variable costs	12.50		375,000		412,500		37,500
11	Contribution margin	7.50		225,000		242,500		17,500
12	Fixed costs:							
13	Manufacturing	4.50		135,000		135,000		0[d]
14	Marketing	2.00		60,000		60,000		0[d]
15	Total fixed costs	6.50		195,000		195,000		0
16	Operating income	$ 1.00		$ 30,000		$ 47,500		$17,500
17								
18	[a]5,000 units × $11.00 per unit = $55,000.							
19	[b]5,000 units × $7.50 per unit = $37,500.							
20	[c]No variable marketing costs would be incurred for the 5,000-unit one-time-only special order.							
21	[d]Fixed manufacturing costs and fixed marketing costs would be unaffected by the special order.							

Potential Problems in Relevant-Cost Analysis

Managers should avoid two potential problems in relevant-cost analysis. First, they must watch for incorrect general assumptions, such as all variable costs are relevant and all fixed costs are irrelevant. In the Surf Gear example, the variable marketing cost of $5 per unit is irrelevant because Surf Gear will incur no extra marketing costs by accepting the special order. But fixed manufacturing costs could be relevant. The extra production of 5,000 towels per month from 30,000 towels to 35,000 towels does not affect fixed manufacturing costs because we assumed that the existing level of fixed manufacturing cost can support any level of production in the relevant range from 30,000 to 45,000 towels per month. In some cases, however, producing the extra 5,000 towels might increase fixed manufacturing costs (and also increase variable manufacturing cost per unit). Suppose Surf Gear would need to run three shifts of 15,000 towels per shift to achieve full capacity of 45,000 towels per month. Increasing monthly production from 30,000 to 35,000 would require a partial third shift (or overtime) because two shifts could produce only 30,000 towels. The partial shift would increase fixed manufacturing costs, thereby making these additional fixed manufacturing costs relevant for this decision.

Second, unit-fixed-cost data can potentially mislead managers in two ways:

1. **When irrelevant costs are included.** Consider the $4.50 of fixed manufacturing cost per unit (direct manufacturing labor, $1.50 per unit + manufacturing overhead, $3.00 per unit) included in the $12-per-unit manufacturing cost in the one-time-only special-order decision (see Exhibits 9-4 and 9-5). This $4.50-per-unit cost is irrelevant because these costs will not change if the one-time-only special order is accepted, and so should be excluded.
2. **When the same unit fixed costs are used at different output levels.** Generally, managers use total fixed costs rather than unit fixed costs because total fixed costs are easier to work with and reduce the chance for erroneous conclusions. Then, if desired, the total fixed costs can be unitized. In the Surf Gear example, total fixed manufacturing costs remain at $135,000 even if the company accepts the special order and produces 35,000 towels. Including the fixed manufacturing cost per unit of $4.50 as a cost of thve special order would lead managers to the erroneous conclusion that total fixed manufacturing costs would increase to $157,500 ($4.50 per towel × 35,000 towels).

The best way for managers to avoid these two potential problems is to keep focusing on (1) total fixed costs (rather than unit fixed cost) and (2) the relevance concept. Managers should always require all items included in an analysis to be expected total future revenues and expected total future costs that differ among the alternatives.

Short-Run Pricing Decisions

In the one-time-only special-order decision in the previous section, Surf Gear's managers had to decide whether to accept or reject Azelia's offer to supply towels at $11 each. Sometimes managers must decide how much to bid on a one-time-only special order. This is an example of a short-run pricing decision—decisions that have a time horizon of only a few months.

Consider a short-run pricing decision facing managers at Surf Gear. Cranston Corporation has asked Surf Gear to bid on supplying 5,000 towels in September after Surf Gear has fulfilled its obligation to Azelia in August. Cranston is unlikely to place any future orders with Surf Gear. Cranston will sell Surf Gear's towels under its own brand name in regions and markets where Surf Gear does not sell its towels. Whether Surf Gear accepts or rejects this order will not affect Surf Gear's revenues—neither the units sold nor the selling price—from existing sales channels.

Relevant Costs for Short-Run Pricing Decisions. As before, Surf Gear's managers estimate how much it will cost to supply the 5,000 towels. There are no incremental marketing costs, so the relevant costs are the variable manufacturing costs of $7.50 calculated in the previous section. As before, the extra production of 5,000 towels in September from 30,000 to 35,000 towels does not affect fixed manufacturing costs because the relevant range is from 30,000 to 45,000 towels per month. Any selling price above $7.50 will improve Surf Gear's profitability in the short run. What price should Surf Gear's managers bid for the 5,000-towel order?

Strategic and Other Factors in Short-Run Pricing. Based on market intelligence, Surf Gear's managers believe that competing bids will be between $10 and $11 per towel, so they decide to bid $10 per towel. If Surf Gear wins this bid, operating income will increase by $12,500 (relevant *revenues*, $10 × 5,000 = $50,000 − relevant costs, $7.50 × 5,000 = $37,500). In light of the extra capacity and strong competition, management's strategy is to bid as high above $7.50 as possible while remaining lower than competitors' bids. Note how Surf Gear chooses the price after looking at the problem through the eyes of its competitors, not based on just its own costs.

What if Surf Gear was the only supplier and Cranston could undercut Surf Gear's selling price in Surf Gear's current markets? The relevant cost of the bidding decision would then include the contribution margin lost on sales to existing customers. What if there were many parties eager to bid and win the Cranston contract? In this case, the contribution margin lost on sales to existing customers would be irrelevant to the decision because the existing business would be undercut by Cranston regardless of whether Surf Gear wins the contract.

In contrast to the Surf Gear case, in some short-run situations, a company may experience strong demand for its products or have limited capacity. In these circumstances, managers will strategically increase prices in the short run to as much as the market will bear. We observe high short-run prices in the case of new products or new models of older products, such as microprocessors, computer chips, cellular telephones, and software.

Keys to Success

Managers use two criteria to decide whether a revenue or cost is relevant for a decision: (1) It must be an expected future revenue or expected future cost and (2) it must differ among alternative courses of action. When making decisions, managers also consider nonfinancial factors and qualitative factors.

Learning Objective 3

Explain the concept of opportunity-cost and why managers consider it when making decisions

. . . in all decisions, it is important to consider the contribution to income forgone by choosing a particular alternative and rejecting others

Insourcing-Versus-Outsourcing and Make-or-Buy Decisions

We now apply the concept of relevance to another strategic decision: whether a company should make a component part or buy it from a supplier. We again assume idle capacity.

Outsourcing and Idle Facilities

Outsourcing is purchasing goods and services from outside vendors rather than **insourcing,** producing the same goods or providing the same services within an organization. For example, Kodak prefers to manufacture its own film (insourcing) but has IBM do its data processing (outsourcing). Honda relies on outside vendors to supply some component parts (outsourcing) but chooses to manufacture other parts internally (insourcing).

Decisions about whether a producer of goods or services will insource or outsource are called **make-or-buy decisions.** Surveys of companies indicate that managers consider quality, dependability of suppliers, and costs as the most important factors in the make-or-buy decision. Sometimes, however, qualitative factors dominate management's make-or-buy decision. For example, Dell Computer buys the Pentium chip for its personal computers from Intel because Dell does not have the know-how and technology to make the chip itself. In contrast, to maintain the secrecy of its formula, Coca-Cola does not outsource the manufacture of its concentrate.

Example 2: The Soho Company manufactures a two-in-one video system consisting of a DVD player and a digital media receiver (that downloads movies and video from Internet sites such as Netflix). Columns 1 and 2 of the following table show the expected total and per-unit costs for manufacturing the DVD player of the video system. Soho plans to manufacture the 250,000 units in 2,000 batches of 125 units each. Variable batch-level costs of $625 per batch vary with the number of batches, not the total number of units produced.

Broadfield, Inc., a manufacturer of DVD players, offers to sell Soho 250,000 DVD players next year for $64 per unit on Soho's preferred delivery schedule. Assume that financial factors will be the basis of this make-or-buy decision. Should Soho's managers make or buy the DVD player?

	Expected Total Costs of Producing 250,000 Units in 2,000 Batches Next Year (1)	Expected Cost per Unit (2) = (1) ÷ 250,000
Direct materials ($36 per unit × 250,000 units)	$ 9,000,000	$36.00
Direct manufacturing labor ($10 per unit × 250,000 units)	2,500,000	10.00
Variable manufacturing overhead costs of power and utilities ($6 per unit × 250,000 units)	1,500,000	6.00
Mixed (variable and fixed) batch-level manufacturing overhead costs of materials handling and setup [$750,000 + ($625 per batch × 2,000 batches)]	2,000,000	8.00
Fixed manufacturing overhead costs of plant lease, insurance, and administration	3,000,000	12.00
Total manufacturing cost	$18,000,000	$72.00

Columns 1 and 2 of the preceding table indicate the expected total costs and expected cost per unit of producing 250,000 DVD players next year. The expected manufacturing cost per unit for next year is $72. At first glance, it appears that Soho's managers should buy DVD players because the expected $72-per-unit cost of making the DVD player is more than the $64 per unit to buy it. But a make-or-buy decision is rarely obvious. To make a decision, managers need to answer the question, "What is the difference in relevant costs between the alternatives?"

For the moment, suppose (1) the capacity now used to make the DVD players will become idle next year if the DVD players are purchased, (2) the $3,000,000 of fixed manufacturing overhead will continue to be incurred next year regardless of the decision made and (3) the $750,000 in fixed salaries to support materials handling and setup will not be incurred if the manufacture of DVD players is completely shut down.

Exhibit 9-6 presents the relevant-cost computations, which shows that Soho will *save* $1,000,000 by making the DVD players rather than buying them from Broadfield. Based on this analysis, Soho's managers decide to make the DVD players.

Note how the key concepts of relevance presented in Exhibit 9-3 apply here:

- Exhibit 9-6 compares differences in expected total future revenues and expected total future costs. Past costs are always irrelevant when making decisions.

Exhibit 9-6

Relevant (Incremental) Items for Make-or-Buy Decision for DVD Players at Soho Company

	Total Relevant Costs		Relevant Cost Per Unit	
Relevant Items	**Make**	**Buy**	**Make**	**Buy**
Outside purchase of parts ($64 × 250,000 units)		$16,000,000		$64
Direct materials	$ 9,000,000		$36	
Direct manufacturing labor	2,500,000		10	
Variable manufacturing overhead	1,500,000		6	
Mixed (variable and fixed) materials-handling and setup overhead	2,000,000		8	
Total relevant costs[a]	$15,000,000	$16,000,000	$60	$64
Difference in favor of making DVD players	$1,000,000		$4	

[a]The $3,000,000 of plant lease, insurance, and administration costs could be included under both alternatives. Conceptually, they do not belong in a listing of relevant costs because these costs are irrelevant to the decision. Practically, some managers may want to include them in order to list all costs that will be incurred under each alternative.

- Exhibit 9-6 shows $2,000,000 of future materials-handling and setup costs under the make alternative but not under the buy alternative. Why? Because buying DVD players and not manufacturing them will save $2,000,000 in future variable costs per batch and avoidable fixed costs. The $2,000,000 represents future costs that differ between the alternatives and so is relevant to the make-or-buy decision.
- Exhibit 9-6 excludes the $3,000,000 of plant-lease, insurance, and administration costs under both alternatives. Why? Because these future costs will not differ between the alternatives, so they are irrelevant.

A common term in decision making is *incremental cost*. An **incremental cost** is the additional total cost incurred for an activity. In Exhibit 9-6, the incremental cost of making DVD players is the additional total cost of $15,000,000 that Soho will incur if it decides to make DVD players. The $3,000,000 of fixed manufacturing overhead is not an incremental cost because Soho will incur these costs whether or not it makes DVD players. Similarly, the incremental cost of buying DVD players from Broadfield is the additional total cost of $16,000,000 that Soho will incur if it decides to buy DVD players. A **differential cost** is the difference in total cost between two alternatives. In Exhibit 9-6, the differential cost between the make-DVD-players and buy-DVD-players alternatives is $1,000,000 ($16,000,000 − $15,000,000). Note that *incremental cost* and *differential cost* are sometimes used interchangeably in practice. When faced with these terms, always be sure to clarify what they mean.

We define *incremental revenue* and *differential revenue* similarly to incremental cost and differential cost. **Incremental revenue** is the additional total revenue from an activity. **Differential revenue** is the difference in total revenue between two alternatives.

Strategic and Qualitative Factors

Strategic and qualitative factors affect outsourcing decisions. For example, Soho's managers may prefer to manufacture DVD players in-house to retain control over design, quality, reliability, and delivery schedules. Conversely, despite the cost advantages documented in Exhibit 9-6, Soho's managers may prefer to outsource, become a leaner organization, and focus on areas of its core competencies, the manufacture and sale of video systems. For example, advertising companies, such as J. Walter Thompson, only focus on the creative and planning aspects of advertising (their core competencies), and outsource production activities, such as film, photographs, and illustrations.

Outsourcing is risky. As a company's dependence on its suppliers increases, suppliers could increase prices and let quality and delivery performance slip. To minimize these risks, managers generally enter into long-run contracts specifying costs, quality, and delivery schedules with their suppliers. Wise managers go so far as to build close partnerships or alliances with a few key suppliers. For example, Toyota sends its own engineers to improve suppliers' processes. Suppliers of companies such as Ford, Hyundai, Panasonic, and Sony have researched and developed innovative products, met demands for increased quantities, maintained quality and on-time delivery, and lowered costs—actions that the companies themselves would not have had the competencies to achieve.

Outsourcing decisions invariably have a long-run horizon in which the financial costs and benefits of outsourcing become more uncertain. Almost always, strategic and qualitative factors become important determinants of the outsourcing decision. Weighing all these factors requires the exercise of considerable management judgment and care.

International Outsourcing

What additional factors would Soho's managers have to consider if the DVD-player supplier was based in Mexico? One important factor would be exchange-rate risk. Suppose the Mexican supplier offers to sell Soho 250,000 DVD players for 192,000,000 pesos. Should Soho make or buy? The answer depends on the exchange rate that Soho's managers expect next year. If they forecast an exchange rate of 12 pesos per $1, Soho's expected purchase cost equals $16,000,000 (192,000,000 pesos ÷ 12 pesos per $), greater than the $15,000,000 relevant costs for making the DVD players in Exhibit 9-6, so Soho's managers would prefer to make DVD players rather than buy them. If, however, Soho's managers anticipate an exchange rate of 13.50 pesos per $1, Soho's expected purchase cost equals $14,222,222 (192,000,000 pesos ÷ 13.50 pesos per $), which

Concepts in Action: The LEGO Group

For decades, Denmark-based LEGO Group has delighted children of all ages with its sets of construction toys. The fifth-largest toymaker in the world produces billions of its small building bricks annually, but a decision to outsource a major chunk of its production nearly jeopardized the company's global supply chain and operations. In response to near bankruptcy in 2004, the company outsourced 80% of its internal Western European production to three lower-cost countries: the Czech Republic, Hungary, and Mexico. While LEGO Group sought to reduce costs and gain economies of scale, it failed to account for managing the complexity of an outsourced global production network.

Source: Nathan Denette/AP Images

LEGO Group had several major challenges with its new offshoring arrangement: controlling its multicontinent production facilities, transferring production knowledge to its outsourcing partners, and allowing for seasonal fluctuations in demand (60% of LEGO production occurs in the second half of the year to accommodate Christmas holiday demand). These problems led to unanticipated production delays and costs. As a result, the company cancelled its outsourcing contracts and brought all production back in-house by 2009.

LEGO Group's experience demonstrates the costs of outsourcing and offshoring, the outsourcing of business processes and jobs to other countries. While offshoring often yields significant cost savings, there are significant costs associated with international taxation, global supply chain coordination, and shuttering existing facilities. For LEGO Group, these challenges proved insurmountable, and the company evolved its outsourcing journey to better deliver its Star Wars, Harry Potter, and Pirates of the Caribbean–themed toys to children across the globe.

Sources: Based on LEGO Group, Annual Report 2011. Billund, Denmark: LEGO Group, 2012; Marcus Moller Larsen, Torben Pedersen, and Dmitrij Slepniov, "Lego Group: An Outsourcing Journey." Richard Ivey School of Business No. 910M94. London, Ontario: Richard Ivey School of Business Foundation, 2010.

is less than the $15,000,000 relevant costs for making the DVD players, so Soho's managers would prefer to buy rather than make the DVD players.

Soho's managers have yet another option. Soho could enter into a forward contract to purchase 192,000,000 pesos. A forward contract allows Soho to contract today to purchase pesos next year at a predetermined, fixed cost, thereby protecting itself against exchange rate risk. If Soho's managers choose this route, they would make (buy) DVD players if the cost of the contract is greater (less) than $15,000,000.

International outsourcing requires managers to evaluate manufacturing and transportation costs, exchange rate risks, and the other strategic and qualitative factors discussed earlier such as quality, reliability, and efficiency of the supply chain. Concepts in Action: The LEGO Group describes how LEGO struggled with outsourcing production to lower-cost European countries and eventually brought back all production to Denmark.

The Total Alternatives Approach

In the simple make-or-buy decision in Exhibit 9-6, we assumed that the capacity currently used to make DVD players will remain idle if Soho purchases DVDs from Broadfield. Often, however, the released capacity can be used for other, profitable purposes. In this case, Soho's managers must choose whether to make or buy based on how best to use available production capacity.

Example 3: If Soho decides to buy DVD players for its video systems from Broadfield, then Soho's best use of the capacity that becomes available is to produce 100,000 Digiteks, a portable, stand-alone DVD player. From a manufacturing standpoint, Digiteks are similar to DVD players made for the video system. With help from operating managers, Soho's management accountant estimates the following future revenues and costs if Soho decides to manufacture and sell Digiteks:

Incremental future revenues		$8,000,000
Incremental future costs		
Direct materials	$3,400,000	
Direct manufacturing labor	1,000,000	
Variable overhead (such as power, utilities)	600,000	
Materials-handling and setup overheads	500,000	
Total incremental future costs		5,500,000
Incremental future operating income		$2,500,000

Because of capacity constraints, Soho can make either DVD players for its video-system unit or Digiteks, but not both. Which of the two alternatives should Soho's managers choose: (1) make video-system DVD players and do not make Digiteks or (2) buy video-system DVD players and make Digiteks?

Exhibit 9-7, Panel A, summarizes the "total-alternatives" approach, the future costs and revenues for *all* products. Soho's managers will choose Alternative 2, buying video-system DVD players and using the available capacity to make and sell Digiteks. The future incremental costs of buying video-system DVD players from an outside supplier ($16,000,000) exceed the future incremental costs of making video-system DVD players in-house ($15,000,000). But Soho can use the capacity freed up by buying video-system DVD players to gain $2,500,000 in operating income (incremental future revenues of $8,000,000 minus total incremental future costs of $5,500,000) by making and selling Digiteks. The *net relevant* costs of buying video-system DVD players and making and selling Digiteks are $16,000,000 − $2,500,000 = $13,500,000.

The Opportunity-Cost Approach

Deciding to use a resource one way means a manager must forgo the opportunity to use the resource in any other way. This lost opportunity is a cost that the manager must consider when making a

Exhibit 9-7

Total-Alternatives Approach and Opportunity-Cost Approach to Make-or-Buy Decisions for Soho Company

	Alternatives for Soho	
Relevant Items	**1. Make Video-System DVD Players and Do Not Make Digitek**	**2. Buy Video-System DVD Players and Make Digitek**
PANEL A Total-Alternatives Approach to Make-or-Buy Decisions		
Total incremental future costs of making/buying video-system DVD players (from Exhibit 9-6)	$15,000,000	$16,000,000
Deduct excess of future revenues over future costs from Digitek	0	(2,500,000)
Total relevant costs under total-alternatives approach	$15,000,000	$13,500,000
	1. Make Video-System DVD Players	**2. Buy Video-System DVD Players**
PANEL B Opportunity-Cost Approach to Make-or-Buy Decisions		
Total incremental future costs of making/buying video-system DVD players (from Exhibit 9-6)	$15,000,000	$16,000,000
Opportunity cost: Profit contribution forgone because capacity will not be used to make Digitek, the next-best alternative	2,500,000	0
Total relevant costs under opportunity-cost approach	$17,500,000	$16,000,000

Note that the differences in costs across the columns in Panels A and B are the same: The cost of alternative 2 is $1,500,000 less than the cost of alternative 1.

decision. **Opportunity cost** is the contribution to operating income that is forgone by not using a limited resource in its next-best alternative use. For example, the (relevant) cost of going to school for an MBA degree is not only the cost of tuition, books, lodging, and food, but also the income sacrificed (opportunity cost) by not working. Presumably, however, the estimated future benefits of obtaining an MBA (such as a higher-paying career) will exceed these costs.

Exhibit 9-7, Panel B, displays the opportunity-cost approach for analyzing the alternatives Soho faces. *Note that the alternatives are defined differently under the two approaches:*

In the total alternatives approach:	In the opportunity cost approach:
1. Make video-system DVD players and do not make Digitek	1. Make video-system DVD players
2. Buy video-system DVD players and make Digitek	2. Buy video-system DVD players

The opportunity cost approach does not reference Digiteks. Under the opportunity-cost approach, the cost of each alternative includes (1) the incremental costs and (2) the opportunity cost, the profit forgone from not making Digiteks. This opportunity cost arises because Digitek is excluded from formal consideration in the alternatives.

Consider alternative 1, making video-system DVD players. What are all the costs of making video-system DVD players? Certainly Soho will incur $15,000,000 of incremental costs to make video-system DVD players, but is this the entire cost? No, because by deciding to use limited manufacturing resources to make video-system DVD players, Soho will give up the opportunity to earn $2,500,000 by not using these resources to make Digiteks. Therefore, the relevant costs of making video-system DVD players are the incremental costs of $15,000,000 plus the opportunity cost of $2,500,000.

Next, consider alternative 2, buy video-system DVD players. The incremental cost of buying video-system DVD players is $16,000,000. The opportunity cost is zero. Why? Because by choosing this alternative, Soho will not forgo the profit it can earn from making and selling Digiteks.

Panel B leads managers to the same conclusion as Panel A: buying video-system DVD players and making Digiteks is the preferred alternative.

Panels A and B in Exhibit 9-7 describe two consistent approaches to decision making with capacity constraints. The total-alternatives approach in Panel A includes all future incremental costs and revenues. For example, under alternative 2, the additional future operating income from *using capacity to make and sell Digiteks* ($2,500,000) is subtracted from the future incremental cost of buying video-system DVD players ($16,000,000). The opportunity-cost analysis in Panel B takes the opposite approach. It focuses only on video-system DVD players. Whenever capacity is not going to be used to make and sell Digiteks, the future forgone operating income is added as an opportunity cost of making video-system DVD players, as in alternative 1. (Note that when Digiteks are made, as in alternative 2, there is no "opportunity cost of not making Digiteks.") Therefore, whereas Panel A *subtracts* $2,500,000 under alternative 2, Panel B *adds* $2,500,000 under alternative 1. *Panel B highlights the idea that when capacity is constrained, the relevant revenues and costs of any alternative equal (1) the incremental future revenues and costs plus (2) the opportunity cost.* However, when managers are considering more than two alternatives simultaneously, it is generally easier for them to use the total-alternatives approach.

Opportunity costs are not recorded in financial accounting systems. Why? Because historical record keeping is limited to transactions involving alternatives that managers *actually selected* rather than alternatives that they rejected. Rejected alternatives do not produce transactions and are not recorded. If Soho makes video-system DVD players, it will not make Digiteks, and it will not record any accounting entries for Digiteks. Yet the opportunity cost of making video-system DVD players, which equals the operating income that Soho forgoes by not making Digiteks, is a crucial input into the make-or-buy decision. Consider again Exhibit 9-7, Panel B. On the basis of only the incremental costs that are systematically recorded in accounting systems, it is less costly for Soho to make rather than buy video-system DVD players. Recognizing the opportunity cost of $2,500,000 leads to a different conclusion: buying video-system DVD players is preferable to making them.

Suppose Soho has sufficient capacity to make Digiteks even if it makes video-system DVD players. In this case, the opportunity cost of making video-system DVD players is $0 because Soho does not give up the $2,500,000 operating income from making Digiteks even if it chooses to make video-system DVD players. The relevant costs are $15,000,000 (incremental costs of $15,000,000 plus opportunity cost of $0). Under these conditions, Soho's managers would prefer to make video-system DVD players, rather than buy them, and also make Digiteks. Concepts in Action: Relevant Costs, JetBlue, and Twitter describes how JetBlue prices tickets based on whether a plane is operating at capacity or below it.

Concepts in Action: Relevant Costs, JetBlue, and Twitter

What does it cost JetBlue to fly one customer round trip from New York City to Nantucket? The incremental cost is only around $5 for beverages. The other costs, such as the fuel for the plane and salaries of the pilots, ticket agents, and baggage handlers, are fixed costs. Because most costs are fixed, would it be worthwhile for JetBlue to fill one seat provided it earns at least $5 for that seat? The answer depends on whether the flight is full.

Source: Adam Rountree/Bloomberg/Getty Images

Suppose JetBlue normally charges $330 for this round-trip ticket. If the flight is full, JetBlue would not sell the ticket for less than $330 because there are customers willing to pay this fare and the opportunity cost of the ticket is high. What if there are empty seats? Selling a ticket for more than $5 is better for JetBlue than leaving the seat empty and earning nothing.

If a customer uses the Internet to purchase the ticket a month in advance, JetBlue will likely quote $330 because it expects the flight to be full. On the Monday before the scheduled Friday departure, if JetBlue finds that the plane will not be full, the airline may be willing to lower its prices dramatically in hopes of attracting more customers and earning a profit on the unfilled seats.

Enter Twitter. Like the e-mails that Jet Blue has sent out to customers for years, the widespread messaging service allows JetBlue to quickly connect with customers and fill seats on flights that might otherwise take off less than full. The flights fill up quickly once JetBlue begins promoting last-minute fare sales on Twitter and recipients learn that $330 round-trip tickets from New York City to Nantucket are available for just $18. JetBlue's Twitter fare sales usually last only eight hours, or until all available seats are sold. To use such a pricing strategy requires a deep understanding of costs in different decision situations.

Source: Based on Charisse Jones, "JetBlue and United give Twitter a try to sell airline seats fast." *USA Today*, August 2, 2009.

Besides quantitative considerations, managers also consider strategic and qualitative factors in make-or-buy decisions. In deciding to buy video-system DVD players from an outside supplier, Soho's managers consider factors such as the supplier's reputation for quality and timely delivery. They also consider the strategic consequences of selling Digiteks. For example, will selling Digiteks take Soho's focus away from its video-system business?

Carrying Costs of Inventory

To see another example of an opportunity cost, consider the following data for Soho's DVD player purchasing decision:

Annual estimated video-system DVD player requirements for next year	250,000 units
Cost per unit when each purchase is equal to 2,500 units	$64.00
Cost per unit when each purchase is equal to or greater than 30,000 units ($64 − 0.5% discount)	$63.68
Cost of a purchase order	$150
Soho's managers are evaluating the following alternatives:	
A. Make 100 purchases (twice a week) of 2,500 units each during next year	
B. Make 8 purchases (twice a quarter) of 31,250 units during the year	
Average investment in inventory:	
A. (2,500 units × $64.00 per unit) ÷ 2[a]	$80,000
B. (31,250 units × $63.68 per unit) ÷ 2[a]	$995,000
Annual rate of return if cash is invested elsewhere (for example, bonds or stocks) at the same level of risk as investment in inventory	12%

[a] The example assumes that video-system-DVD-player purchases will be used uniformly throughout the year. The average investment in inventory during the year is the cost of the inventory when a purchase is received plus the cost of inventory just before the next purchase is delivered (in our example, zero) divided by 2.

Soho will pay cash for the video-system DVD players it buys. Which purchasing alternative is more economical for Soho?

The management accountant presents the following analysis to her managers using the total alternatives approach, recognizing that Soho has, on average, $995,000 of cash available to invest. If Soho invests only $80,000 in inventory as in alternative A, it will have $915,000 ($995,000 − $80,000) of cash available to invest elsewhere, which at a 12% rate of return will yield a total return of $109,800. This income is subtracted from the ordering and purchasing costs incurred under alternative A. If Soho invests all $995,000 in inventory as in alternative B, it will have $0 ($995,000 − $995,000) available to invest elsewhere and will earn no return on the cash.

	Alternative A: Make 100 Purchases of 2,500 Units Each During the Year and Invest Any Excess Cash (1)	Alternative B: Make 8 Purchases of 31,250 Units Each During the Year and Invest Any Excess Cash (2)	Difference (3) = (1) − (2)
Annual purchase-order costs (100 purchase orders × $150/purchase order; 8 purchase orders × $150/purchase order)	$ 15,000	$ 1,200	$ 13,800
Annual purchase costs (250,000 units × $64.00/unit; 250,000 units × $63.68/unit)	16,000,000	15,920,000	80,000
Deduct annual rate of return earned by investing cash not tied up in inventory elsewhere at the same level of risk [0.12 × ($995,000 − $80,000); 0.12 × ($995,000 − $995,000)]	(109,800)	0	(109,800)
Relevant costs	$15,905,200	$15,921,200	$ (16,000)

Consistent with the trends toward holding smaller inventories, it is more economical for Soho's managers to purchase smaller quantities of 2,500 units 100 times a year than to purchase 31,250 units 8 times a year by $16,000.

The following table presents the management accountant's analysis of the two alternatives using the opportunity cost approach. Each alternative is defined only in terms of the two purchasing choices with no explicit reference to investing the excess cash.

	Alternative A: Make 100 Purchases of 2,500 Units Each During the Year (1)	Alternative B: Make 8 Purchases of 31,250 Units Each During the Year (2)	Difference (3) = (1) − (2)
Annual purchase-order costs (100 purchase orders × $150/purchase order; 8 purchase orders × $150/purchase order)	$ 15,000	$ 1,200	$ 13,800
Annual purchase costs (250,000 units × $64.00/unit; 250,000 units × $63.68/unit)	16,000,000	15,920,000	80,000
Opportunity cost: Annual rate of return that could be earned if investment in inventory were invested elsewhere at the same level of risk (0.12 × $80,000; 0.12 × $995,000)	9,600	119,400	(109,800)
Relevant costs	$16,024,600	$16,040,600	$ (16,000)

Recall that under the opportunity-cost approach, the relevant cost of any alternative is (1) the incremental cost of the alternative plus (2) the opportunity cost of the profit forgone from choosing that alternative. The opportunity cost of holding inventory is the income forgone by tying up money in inventory and not investing it elsewhere. The opportunity cost would not be recorded in the accounting system because, once the money is invested in inventory, there is no money available to invest elsewhere, and so no return related to this investment to record. On the basis of the costs recorded in the accounting system (purchase-order costs and purchase costs), Soho's managers would erroneously conclude that making eight purchases of 31,250 units each is the less costly alternative. Column 3, however, indicates that, as in the total-alternatives approach, purchasing smaller quantities of 2,500 units 100 times a year is more economical than purchasing 31,250 units eight times during the year by $16,000. Why? Because the lower opportunity cost of holding smaller inventory exceeds the higher purchase and ordering costs. If the opportunity cost of money tied up in inventory were greater than 12% per year, or if other incremental benefits of holding lower inventory were considered, such as lower insurance, materials-handling, storage, obsolescence, and breakage cost, making 100 purchases would be even more economical.

Keys to Success

Managers determine the relevant cost of any decision as (1) the incremental cost of the decision plus (2) the opportunity cost of the profit forgone from making that decision rather than using a limited resource in its next-best alternative use.

Learning Objective 4

Know how to choose which products to produce when there are capacity constraints

. . . select the product with the highest contribution margin per unit of the limiting resource

Product-Mix Decisions with Capacity Constraints

We now examine how the concept of relevance applies to **product-mix decisions,** the decisions managers make about which products to sell and in what quantities. These decisions usually have only a short-run focus because they typically arise in the context of capacity constraints that can be relaxed in the long run. In the short run, for example, BMW, the German car manufacturer, continually adapts the mix of its different models of cars (for example, 325i, 525i, and 740i) to fluctuations in selling prices and demand.

To determine product mix, managers maximize operating income, subject to constraints such as capacity and demand. Throughout this section, we assume that as short-run changes in product mix occur, the only costs that change are costs that are variable with the number of units produced (and sold). Under this assumption, the analysis of individual product contribution margins provides insight into the product mix that maximizes operating income.

Example 4: Power Recreation assembles two engines, a snowmobile engine and a boat engine, at its Lexington, Kentucky, plant.

	Snowmobile Engine	Boat Engine
Selling price	$800	$1,000
Variable cost per unit	560	625
Contribution margin per unit	$240	$ 375
Contribution margin percentage ($240 ÷ $800; $375 ÷ $1,000)	30%	37.5%

Only 600 machine-hours are available daily for assembling engines. Additional capacity cannot be obtained in the short run. Power Recreation can sell as many engines as it produces. The constraining resource, then, is machine-hours. It takes two machine-hours to produce one snowmobile engine and five machine-hours to produce one boat engine. What product mix should Power Recreation's managers choose to maximize operating income?

In terms of contribution margin per unit and contribution margin percentage, boat engines are more profitable than snowmobile engines. The product that Power Recreation should produce and sell, however, is not necessarily the product with the higher individual contribution margin per unit or contribution margin percentage. Managers should choose the product with *the highest contribution margin per unit of the constraining resource (factor).* That's the resource that restricts or limits the production or sale of products.

	Snowmobile Engine	Boat Engine
Contribution margin per unit	$240	$375
Machine-hours required to produce one unit	2 machine-hours	5 machine-hours
Contribution margin per machine-hour		
$240 per unit ÷ 2 machine-hours/unit	$120/machine-hour	
$375 per unit ÷ 5 machine-hours/unit		$75/machine-hour
Total contribution margin for 600 machine-hours		
$120/machine-hour × 600 machine-hours	$72,000	
$75/machine-hour × 600 machine-hours		$45,000

The number of machine-hours is the constraining resource in this example and snowmobile engines earn more contribution margin per machine-hour ($120/machine-hour) compared to boat engines ($75/machine-hour). Therefore, choosing to produce and sell snowmobile engines maximizes *total* contribution margin ($72,000 vs. $45,000 from producing and selling boat engines) and operating income. Other constraints in manufacturing settings can be the availability of direct materials, components, or skilled labor, as well as financial and sales factors. In a retail department store, the constraining resource may be linear feet of display space. Regardless of the specific constraining resource, managers should always focus on maximizing *total* contribution margin by choosing products that give the highest contribution margin per unit of the constraining resource.

In many cases, a manufacturer or retailer has the challenge of trying to maximize total operating income for a variety of products, each with more than one constraining resource. Some constraints may require a manufacturer or retailer to stock minimum quantities of products even if these products are not very profitable. For example, supermarkets must stock less-profitable products, such as paper towels and toilet paper, because customers will be willing to shop at a supermarket only if it carries a wide range of products. To determine the most profitable production schedule and the most profitable product mix, the manufacturer or retailer needs to determine the maximum total contribution margin in the face of many constraints. Optimization techniques, such as linear programming discussed in the appendix to this chapter, help solve these more complex problems.

We next turn to the question of managing the bottleneck constraint to increase output and, therefore, contribution margin when some operations are bottlenecks and others are not.

Theory of Constraints and Throughput-Margin Analysis

Learning Objective 5

Explain how to manage bottlenecks . . .

. . . keep bottlenecks busy and increase their efficiency and capacity by increasing throughput (contribution) margin

Suppose the snowmobile engine must go through a forging operation before it goes to the assembly operation. Power Recreation has 1,200 hours of daily forging capacity dedicated to the manufacture of snowmobile engines. The company takes 3 hours to forge each snowmobile engine, so Power Recreation can forge 400 snowmobile engines per day (1,200 hours ÷ 3 hours per snowmobile engine). It can assemble only 300 snowmobile engines per day (600 machine-hours ÷ 2 machine-hours per snowmobile engine). The production of snowmobile engines is constrained by the assembly operation, not the forging operation.

The **theory of constraints (TOC)** describes methods to maximize operating income when faced with some bottleneck and some nonbottleneck operations.[1] The TOC defines these three measures:

1. **Throughput margin** equals revenues minus the direct material costs of the goods sold.
2. *Investments* equal the sum of material costs in direct materials, work-in-process, and finished goods inventories; R&D costs; and capital costs of equipment and buildings.
3. *Operating costs* equal all costs of operations (other than direct materials) incurred to earn throughput margin. Operating costs include salaries and wages, rent, utilities, depreciation, and the like.

[1] See E. Goldratt and J. Cox, *The Goal* (New York: North River Press, 1986); E. Goldratt, *The Theory of Constraints* (New York: North River Press, 1990); E. Noreen, D. Smith, and J. Mackey, *The Theory of Constraints and Its Implications for Management Accounting* (New York: North River Press, 1995); and M. Woeppel, *Manufacturers' Guide to Implementing the Theory of Constraints* (Boca Raton, FL: Lewis Publishing, 2000).

The objective of the TOC is to increase throughput margin while decreasing investments and operating costs. *The TOC considers a short-run time horizon of a few months and assumes operating costs are fixed and direct material costs are the only variable costs. In a situation where some of the operating costs are also variable in the short run, throughput margin is replaced by contribution margin.* In the Power Recreation example, each snowmobile engine sells for $800. We assume that the variable costs of $560 consist only of direct material costs (incurred in the forging department) so throughput margin equals contribution margin. For ease of exposition and consistency with the previous section, we use the term "contribution margin" instead of "throughput margin" throughout this section.

TOC focuses on managing bottleneck operations, as explained in the following steps:

Step 1: Recognize that the bottleneck operation determines contribution margin of the entire system. In the Power Recreation example, output in the assembly operation determines the output of snowmobile engines.

Step 2: Identify the bottleneck operation by identifying operations with large quantities of inventory waiting to be worked on. As snowmobile engines are produced at the forging operation, inventories will build up at the assembly operation because daily assembly capacity of 300 snowmobile engines is less than the daily forging capacity of 400 snowmobile engines.

Step 3: Keep the bottleneck operation busy and subordinate all nonbottleneck operations to the bottleneck operation. That is, the needs of the bottleneck operation determine the production schedule of the nonbottleneck operations.

To maximize operating income, the manager must maximize contribution margin of the constrained or bottleneck resource. The bottleneck assembly operation must always be kept running; it should not be waiting for work. To achieve this objective, Power Recreation's managers maintain a small buffer inventory of snowmobile engines that have gone through the forging operation and are waiting to be assembled. The bottleneck assembly operation sets the pace for the nonbottleneck forging operations. Operating managers maximize contribution margin by ensuring the assembly operation is operating at capacity by developing a detailed production schedule at the forging operation to ensure that the assembly operation is not waiting for work. At the same time, forging more snowmobile engines that cannot be assembled does not increase output or contribution margin; it only creates excess inventory of unassembled snowmobile engines.

Step 4: Take actions to increase the efficiency and capacity of the bottleneck operation as long as the incremental contribution margin exceeds the incremental costs of increasing efficiency and capacity.

We illustrate Step 4 using data from the forging and assembly operations of Power Recreation.

	Forging	Assembly
Capacity per day	400 units	300 units
Daily production and sales	300 units	300 units
Other fixed operating costs per day (excluding direct materials)	$24,000	$18,000
Other fixed operating costs per unit produced ($24,000 ÷ 300 units; $18,000 ÷ 300 units)	$80 per unit	$60 per unit

Power Recreation's output is constrained by the capacity of 300 units in the assembly operation. What can Power Recreation's managers do to relieve the bottleneck constraint of the assembly operation?

Desirable actions include the following:

1. **Eliminate idle time at the bottleneck operation (time when the assembly machine is neither being set up to assemble nor actually assembling snowmobile engines).** Power Recreation's manager is evaluating permanently positioning two workers at the assembly operation to unload snowmobile engines as soon as they are assembled and to set up the machine to begin assembling the next batch of snowmobile engines. This action will cost $320 per day and bottleneck output will increase by 3 snowmobile engines per day. Should Power Recreation's managers incur the additional costs? Yes, because Power Recreation's contribution margin will increase by $720 per day ($240 per snowmobile engine × 3 snowmobile engines), which is greater than the incremental cost of $320 per day. All other costs are irrelevant.

2. **Shift products that do not have to be made on the bottleneck machine to nonbottleneck machines or to outside processing facilities.** Suppose Spartan Corporation, an outside contractor, offers to assemble 5 snowmobile engines each day at \$75 per snowmobile engine from engines that have gone through the forging operation at Power Recreation. Spartan's quoted price is greater than Power Recreation's own operating costs in the assembly department of \$60 per snowmobile engine. Should Power Recreation's managers accept the offer? Yes, because assembly is the bottleneck operation. Getting additional snowmobile engines assembled by Spartan will increase contribution margin by \$1,200 per day (\$240 per snowmobile engine × 5 snowmobile engines), while the relevant cost of increasing capacity will be \$375 per day (\$75 per snowmobile engine × 5 snowmobile engines). The fact that Power Recreation's unit cost is less than Spartan's quoted price is irrelevant.

   Suppose Gemini Industries, another outside contractor, offers to do the forging operation for 8 snowmobile engines per day for \$65 per snowmobile engine from direct materials supplied by Power Recreation. Gemini's price is lower than Power Recreation's operating cost of \$80 per snowmobile engine in the forging department. Should Power Recreation's managers accept the offer? No, because other operating costs are fixed costs. Power Recreation will not save any costs by subcontracting the forging operations. Instead, its costs will increase by \$520 per day (\$65 per snowmobile engine × 8 snowmobile engines) with no increase in contribution margin, which is constrained by assembly capacity.

3. **Reduce setup time and processing time at bottleneck operations (for example, by simplifying the design or reducing the number of parts in the product).** Suppose Power Recreation can assemble 10 more snowmobile engines each day at a cost of \$1,000 per day by reducing setup time at the assembly operation. Should Power Recreation's managers incur this cost? Yes, because contribution margin will increase by \$2,400 per day (\$240 per snowmobile engine × 10 snowmobile engines), which is greater than the incremental costs of \$1,000 per day. Will Power Recreation's managers find it worthwhile to incur costs to reduce machining time at the nonbottleneck forging operation? No. Other operating costs will increase, while contribution margin will remain unchanged because bottleneck capacity of the assembly operation will not increase.

4. **Improve the quality of parts or products manufactured at the bottleneck operation.** Poor quality is more costly at a bottleneck operation than at a nonbottleneck operation. The cost of poor quality at a nonbottleneck operation is the cost of materials wasted. If Power Recreation produces 5 defective snowmobile engines at the forging operation, the cost of poor quality is \$2,800 (direct material cost per snowmobile engine, \$560 × 5 snowmobile engines). No contribution margin is forgone because forging has unused capacity. Despite the defective production, forging can produce and transfer 300 good-quality snowmobile engines to the assembly operation. At a bottleneck operation, the cost of poor quality is the cost of materials wasted *plus* the opportunity cost of lost contribution margin. Bottleneck capacity not wasted in producing defective snowmobile engines could be used to generate additional contribution margin. If Power Recreation produces 5 defective units at the assembly operation, the cost of poor quality is the lost revenue of \$4,000 (\$800 per snowmobile engine × 5 snowmobile engines) or, alternatively stated, direct material costs of \$2,800 (direct material cost per snowmobile engine, \$560 × 5 snowmobile engines) plus forgone contribution margin of \$1,200 (\$240 per snowmobile engine × 5 snowmobile engines).

   The high cost of poor quality at the bottleneck operation means that bottleneck time should not be wasted processing units that are defective. That is, engines should be inspected before the bottleneck operation to ensure that only good-quality parts are processed at the bottleneck operation. Furthermore, quality-improvement programs should place special emphasis on minimizing defects at bottleneck machines.

If successful, the actions in Step 4 will increase the capacity of the assembly operation until it eventually exceeds the capacity of the forging operation. The bottleneck will then shift to the forging operation. Power Recreation would then focus continuous-improvement actions on increasing forging operation efficiency and capacity. For example, the contract with Gemini Industries to forge 8 snowmobile engines per day at \$65 per snowmobile engine from direct material supplied by Power Recreation will become attractive because contribution margin will increase by \$1,920 per day (\$240 per snowmobile engine × 8 snowmobile engines), which is greater than the incremental costs of \$520 (\$65 per snowmobile engine × 8 snowmobile engines).

The theory of constraints emphasizes management of bottleneck operations as the key to improving performance of production operations as a whole. It focuses on short-run maximization of contribution margin. Because TOC regards operating costs as difficult to change in the short run, it does not identify individual activities and drivers of costs. TOC is, therefore, less useful for the long-run management of costs. In contrast, activity-based costing (ABC) systems take a long-run perspective and focus on improving processes by eliminating non-value-added activities and reducing the costs of performing value-added activities. ABC systems, therefore, are more useful for long-run pricing, cost control, and capacity management. The short-run TOC emphasis on maximizing contribution margin by managing bottlenecks complements the long-run strategic-cost-management focus of ABC.[2]

Keys to Success

When resources are constrained, managers should select the product that yields the highest contribution margin per unit of the constraining or bottleneck resource (factor). To increase profits, managers should increase bottleneck utilization, efficiency, and capacity.

Learning Objective 6

Discuss factors managers must consider when adding or dropping customers or segments

. . . managers should focus on how total costs differ among alternatives and ignore allocated overhead costs

Customer Profitability, Activity-Based Costing, and Relevant Costs

Not only must managers make choices about which products and how much of each product to produce, they must often make decisions about adding or dropping a product line or a business segment. Similarly, if the cost object is a customer, managers must decide about adding or dropping customers (analogous to a product line) or a branch office (analogous to a business segment). We illustrate relevant-revenue and relevant-cost analysis for these kinds of decisions using customers rather than products as the cost object.

Example 5: Allied West, the West Coast sales office of Allied Furniture, a wholesaler of specialized furniture, supplies furniture to three local retailers: Vogel, Brenner, and Wisk. Exhibit 9-8 presents expected revenues and costs of Allied West by customer for the upcoming year using its ABC system. Allied West's management accountant assigns costs to customers based on the activities needed to support each customer. Information on Allied West's costs for different activities at various levels of the cost hierarchy are:

- Furniture-handling labor costs vary with the number of units of furniture shipped to customers.
- Allied West reserves different areas of the warehouse to stock furniture for different customers. For simplicity, we assume that furniture-handling equipment in an area and depreciation costs on the equipment that Allied West has already acquired are identified with individual customers (customer-level costs). Any unused equipment remains idle. The equipment has a 1-year useful life and zero disposal value.
- Allied West allocates its fixed rent costs to each customer on the basis of the amount of warehouse space reserved for that customer.
- Marketing costs vary with the number of sales visits made to customers.
- Sales-order costs are batch-level costs that vary with the number of sales orders received from customers; delivery-processing costs are batch-level costs that vary with the number of shipments made.
- Allied West allocates fixed general-administration costs (facility-level costs) to customers on the basis of customer revenues.
- Allied Furniture allocates its fixed corporate-office costs to sales offices on the basis of the budgeted costs of each sales office. Allied West then allocates these costs to customers on the basis of customer revenues.

[2] For an excellent evaluation of TOC, operations management, cost accounting, and the relationship between TOC and activity-based costing, see A. Atkinson, "Cost Accounting, the Theory of Constraints, and Costing" (Issue Paper, CMA Canada, December 2000).

Exhibit 9-8
Customer Profitability Analysis for Allied West

	Customer			
	Vogel	Brenner	Wisk	Total
Revenues	$500,000	$300,000	$400,000	$1,200,000
Cost of goods sold	370,000	220,000	330,000	920,000
Furniture-handling labor	41,000	18,000	33,000	92,000
Furniture-handling equipment cost written off as depreciation	12,000	4,000	9,000	25,000
Rent	14,000	8,000	14,000	36,000
Marketing support	11,000	9,000	10,000	30,000
Sales-order and delivery processing	13,000	7,000	12,000	32,000
General administration	20,000	12,000	16,000	48,000
Allocated corporate-office costs	10,000	6,000	8,000	24,000
Total costs	491,000	284,000	432,000	1,207,000
Operating income	$ 9,000	$ 16,000	$ (32,000)	$ (7,000)

In the following sections, we consider several decisions that Allied West's managers face: Should Allied West drop the Wisk account? Should it add a fourth customer, Loral? Should Allied Furniture close down Allied West? Should it open another sales office, Allied South, whose revenues and costs are identical to those of Allied West?

Relevant-Revenue and Relevant-Cost Analysis of Dropping a Customer

Exhibit 9-8 indicates a loss of $32,000 on the Wisk account. Allied West's managers believe the reason for the loss is that Wisk places low-margin orders with Allied, and has relatively high sales-order, delivery-processing, furniture-handling, and marketing costs. Allied West's managers are considering several possible actions for the Wisk account: reducing the costs of supporting Wisk by becoming more efficient, cutting back on some of the services Allied West offers Wisk; asking Wisk to place larger, less frequent orders; charging Wisk higher prices; or dropping the Wisk account. The following analysis focuses on the operating-income effect of dropping the Wisk account for the year.

Allied West's managers and management accountants first identify the relevant revenues and relevant costs. Dropping the Wisk account will:

- Save cost of goods sold, furniture-handling labor, marketing support, sales-order, and delivery-processing costs incurred on the account.
- Leave idle the warehouse space and furniture-handling equipment currently used to supply products to Wisk.
- Not affect the fixed rent costs, general-administration costs, or corporate-office costs.

Exhibit 9-9, column 1, presents the relevant-revenue and relevant-cost analysis using data from the Wisk column in Exhibit 9-8. Allied West's operating income will be $15,000 lower if it drops the Wisk account—the cost savings from dropping the Wisk account, $385,000, will not be enough to offset the $400,000 loss in revenues—so Allied West's managers decide to keep the Wisk account. They will, of course, continue to find ways to become more efficient, change Wisk's ordering patterns, or charge higher prices.

Depreciation on equipment that Allied West has already acquired is a past cost and therefore irrelevant. Rent, general-administration, and corporate-office costs are future costs that will not change if Allied West drops the Wisk account, and are also irrelevant.

Overhead costs allocated to the sales office and individual customers are always irrelevant. The only question is, will expected total corporate-office costs decrease as a result of dropping the Wisk account? In our example, they will not, so these costs are irrelevant. *If expected total corporate-office costs* were to decrease by dropping the Wisk account, those savings would be relevant even if *the amount allocated to Wisk did not change.*

Note that there is no opportunity cost of using warehouse space and equipment for Wisk because there is no alternative use of the space and equipment. That is, the space and equipment

Exhibit 9-9

Relevant-Revenue and Relevant-Cost Analysis for Dropping the Wisk Account and Adding the Loral Account

	(Relevant Loss in Revenues) and Relevant Savings in Costs from Dropping Wisk Account (1)	Relevant Revenues and (Relevant Costs) from Adding Loral Account (2)
Revenues	$(400,000)	$400,000
Cost of goods sold	330,000	(330,000)
Furniture-handling labor	33,000	(33,000)
Furniture-handling equipment cost written off as depreciation	0	(9,000)
Rent	0	0
Marketing support	10,000	(10,000)
Sales-order and delivery processing	12,000	(12,000)
General administration	0	0
Corporate-office costs	0	0
Total costs	385,000	(394,000)
Effect on operating income (loss)	$ (15,000)	$ 6,000

will remain idle if managers drop the Wisk account. But suppose Allied West could lease the available extra space and equipment to Sanchez Corporation for $20,000 per year. Then $20,000 would be Allied West's opportunity cost of continuing to use the warehouse to service Wisk. Allied West would gain $5,000 by dropping the Wisk account ($20,000 from lease revenue minus lost operating income of $15,000). Under the total alternatives approach, the revenue loss from dropping the Wisk account would be $380,000 ($400,000 − $20,000) versus the savings in costs of $385,000 (Exhibit 9-9, Column 1). Before reaching a decision, Allied West's managers must examine whether Wisk can be made more profitable so that supplying products to Wisk earns more than the $20,000 from leasing to Sanchez. The managers must also consider strategic factors such as the effect of dropping the Wisk account on Allied West's reputation for developing stable, long-run business relationships with its customers.

Relevant-Revenue and Relevant-Cost Analysis of Adding a Customer

Suppose that Allied West's managers are evaluating the profitability of adding another customer, Loral, to its existing customer base of Vogel, Brenner, and Wisk. There is no other alternative use of the Allied West facility. Loral has a customer profile much like Wisk's. Suppose Allied West's managers predict revenues and costs of doing business with Loral to be the same as the revenues and costs described under the Wisk column in Exhibit 9-8. In particular, Allied West would have to acquire furniture-handling equipment for the Loral account costing $9,000, with a 1-year useful life and zero disposal value. If Loral is added as a customer, warehouse rent costs ($36,000), general-administration costs ($48,000), and *actual total* corporate-office costs will not change. Should Allied West's managers add Loral as a customer?

Exhibit 9-9, column 2, shows relevant revenues exceed relevant costs by $6,000. The opportunity cost of adding Loral is $0 because there is no alternative use of the Allied West facility. On the basis of this analysis, Allied West's managers would recommend adding Loral as a customer. Rent, general-administration, and corporate-office costs are irrelevant because these costs will not change if Loral is added as a customer. However, the cost of new equipment to support the Loral order (written off as depreciation of $9,000 in Exhibit 9-9, column 2), is relevant. That's because this cost can be avoided if Allied West decides not to add Loral as a customer. Note the critical distinction here: *Depreciation cost is irrelevant in deciding whether to drop Wisk as a customer because depreciation on equipment that has already been purchased is a past cost, but the cost of purchasing new equipment in the future that will then be written off as depreciation is relevant in deciding whether to add Loral as a customer.*

Exhibit 9-10
Relevant-Revenue and Relevant-Cost Analysis for Closing Allied West and Opening Allied South

	(Relevant Loss in Revenues) and Relevant Savings in Costs from Closing Allied West (1)	Relevant Revenues and (Relevant Costs) from Opening Allied South (2)
Revenues	$(1,200,000)	$1,200,000
Cost of goods sold	920,000	(920,000)
Furniture-handling labor	92,000	(92,000)
Furniture-handling equipment cost written off as depreciation	0	(25,000)
Rent	36,000	(36,000)
Marketing support	30,000	(30,000)
Sales-order and delivery processing	32,000	(32,000)
General administration	48,000	(48,000)
Corporate-office costs	0	0
Total costs	1,158,000	(1,183,000)
Effect on operating income (loss)	$ (42,000)	$ 17,000

Relevant-Revenue and Relevant-Cost Analysis of Closing or Adding Branch Offices or Segments

Companies periodically confront decisions about closing or adding branch offices or business segments. For example, given Allied West's expected loss of $7,000 (see Exhibit 9-8), should Allied Furniture's managers close Allied West for the year? Closing Allied West will save all costs currently incurred at Allied West. Recall that there is no disposal value for the equipment that Allied West has already acquired. Closing Allied West will have no effect on total corporate-office costs.

Exhibit 9-10, column 1, presents the relevant-revenue and relevant-cost analysis using data from the "Total" column in Exhibit 9-8. The revenue losses of $1,200,000 will exceed the cost savings of $1,158,000, leading to a decrease in operating income of $42,000. Allied West should not be closed. The key reasons are that closing Allied West will not save depreciation cost or actual total corporate-office costs. Depreciation cost is past or sunk because it represents the cost of equipment that Allied West has already purchased. Corporate-office costs allocated to various sales offices will change *but the total amount of these costs will not decline.* The $24,000 no longer allocated to Allied West will be allocated to other sales offices. Therefore, the $24,000 of allocated corporate-office costs is irrelevant because it does not represent expected cost savings from closing Allied West.

Now suppose Allied Furniture has the opportunity to open another sales office, Allied South, whose revenues and costs are identical to Allied West's costs, including a cost of $25,000 to acquire furniture-handling equipment with a 1-year useful life and zero disposal value. Opening this office will have no effect on total corporate-office costs. Should Allied Furniture's managers open Allied South? Exhibit 9-10, column 2, indicates that they should because opening Allied South will increase operating income by $17,000. As before, the cost of new equipment to be purchased in the future (and written off as depreciation) is relevant and *allocated* corporate-office costs are irrelevant because total corporate-office costs will not change if Allied South is opened.

Keys to Success

When making decisions about adding or dropping customers or adding or discontinuing branch offices and segments, managers should focus only on incremental costs and opportunity costs. Managers should ignore allocated overhead costs.

Learning Objective 7

Explain why book value of equipment is irrelevant to managers making equipment-replacement decisions

. . . it is a past cost

Irrelevance of Past Costs and Equipment-Replacement Decisions

At several points in this chapter, when discussing the concept of relevance, we reasoned that past (historical or sunk) costs are irrelevant to decision making. That's because a decision cannot change something that has already happened. We now apply this concept to decisions about replacing equipment. We stress the idea that **book value**—original cost minus accumulated depreciation—of existing equipment is a past cost that is irrelevant.

Example 6: Toledo Company, a manufacturer of aircraft components, is considering replacing a metal-cutting machine with a newer model. The new machine is more efficient than the old machine, but it has a shorter life. Revenues from aircraft parts ($1.1 million per year) will be unaffected by the replacement decision. Here are the data the management accountant prepares for the existing (old) machine and the replacement (new) machine:

	Old Machine	New Machine
Original cost	$1,000,000	$600,000
Useful life	5 years	2 years
Current age	3 years	0 years
Remaining useful life	2 years	2 years
Accumulated depreciation	$600,000	Not acquired yet
Book value	$400,000	Not acquired yet
Current disposal value (in cash)	$40,000	Not acquired yet
Terminal disposal value (in cash 2 years from now)	$0	$0
Annual operating costs (maintenance, energy, repairs, coolants, etc.)	$800,000	$460,000

Toledo Corporation uses straight-line depreciation. To focus on relevance, we ignore the time value of money and income taxes.[3] Should Toledo's managers replace its old machine?

Exhibit 9-11 presents a cost comparison of the two machines. Consider why each of the following four items in Toledo's equipment-replacement decision are relevant or irrelevant:

Exhibit 9-11

Operating Income Comparison: Replacement of Machine, Relevant, and Irrelevant Items for Toledo Company

	Two Years Together		
	Keep (1)	Replace (2)	Difference (3) = (1) − (2)
Revenues	$2,200,000	$2,200,000	—
Operating costs			
Cash operating costs ($800,000/yr. × 2 years; $460,000/yr. × 2 years)	1,600,000	920,000	$ 680,000
Book value of old machine			
Periodic write-off as depreciation or	400,000	—	—
Lump-sum write-off	—	400,000[a]	
Current disposal value of old machine	—	(40,000)[a]	40,000
New machine cost, written off periodically as depreciation	—	600,000	(600,000)
Total operating costs	2,000,000	1,880,000	120,000
Operating income	$ 200,000	$ 320,000	$(120,000)

[a]In a formal income statement, these two items would be combined as "loss on disposal of machine" of $360,000.

[3] See Chapter 11 for a discussion of time-value-of-money and income-tax considerations in capital investment decisions.

Exhibit 9-12
Cost Comparison: Replacement of Machine, Relevant Items Only, for Toledo Company

	Two Years Together		
	Keep (1)	**Replace (2)**	**Difference (3) = (1) − (2)**
Cash operating costs	$1,600,000	$ 920,000	$680,000
Current disposal value of old machine	—	(40,000)	40,000
New machine cost, written off periodically as depreciation	—	600,000	(600,000)
Total relevant costs	$1,600,000	$1,480,000	$120,000

1. **Book value of old machine, $400,000.** Irrelevant, because it is a past or sunk cost. All past costs are "down the drain." Nothing can change what the company has already spent or what has already happened.
2. **Current disposal value of old machine, $40,000.** Relevant, because it is an expected future benefit that will only occur if the company replaces the machine.
3. **Loss on disposal, $360,000.** This is the difference between amounts in items 1 and 2. It is a meaningless combination blurring the distinction between the irrelevant book value and the relevant disposal value. Managers should consider each value separately, as was done in items 1 and 2.
4. **Cost of new machine, $600,000.** Relevant, because it is an expected future cost that will only occur if the company purchases the machine.

Exhibit 9-11 should clarify these four assertions. Column 3 in Exhibit 9-11 shows that the book value of the old machine does not differ between the alternatives and could be ignored for decision-making purposes. No matter what the timing of the writeoff—whether a lump-sum charge in the current year or depreciation charges over the next 2 years—the total amount is still $400,000 because it is a past (historical) cost. In contrast, the $600,000 cost of the new machine and the current disposal value of $40,000 for the old machine are relevant because they would not arise if Toledo's managers decided not to replace the machine. Considering the cost of replacing the machine and savings in cash operating costs, Toledo's managers should replace the machine because the operating income from replacing it is $120,000 higher for the 2 years together.

Exhibit 9-12 concentrates only on relevant items and leads to the same answer—replacing the machine leads to lower costs and higher operating income of $120,000—even though book value is omitted from the calculations. The only relevant items are the cash operating costs, the disposal value of the old machine, and the cost of the new machine, which is represented as depreciation in Exhibit 9-12.

Learning Objective 8

Explain how conflicts can arise between the decision model a manager uses and the performance-evaluation model companies use to evaluate the managers

. . . tell managers to take a multiple-year view in decision making but judge their performance only on the basis of the current year's operating income

> **Keys to Success**
> **Book value of existing equipment is a past (historical or sunk) cost and, therefore, irrelevant in equipment-replacement decisions.**

Decisions and Performance Evaluation

Consider our equipment-replacement example in light of the five-step sequence in Exhibit 9-1 (page 343).

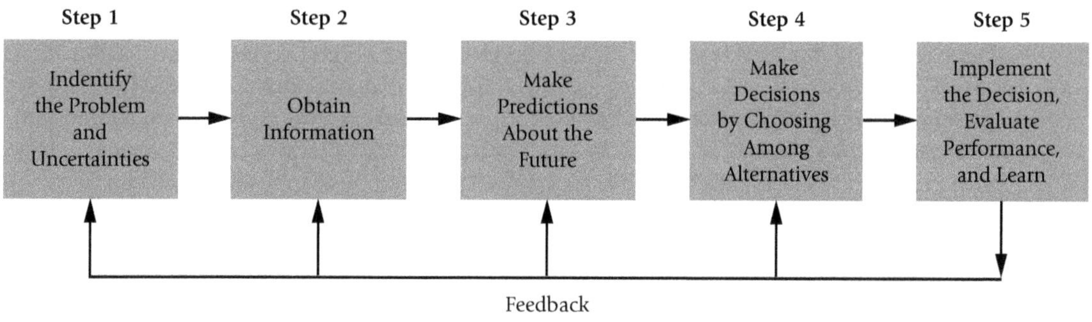

The decision model analysis (Step 4), which is presented in Exhibits 9-11 and 9-12, dictates replacing the machine rather than keeping it. In the real world, however, would the manager replace it? An important factor in replacement decisions is the manager's perception of whether the decision model is consistent with how the manager's performance will be judged after the decision is implemented (the performance-evaluation model in Step 5).

From the perspective of their own careers, it is no surprise that managers tend to favor the alternative that makes their performance look better. In our examples throughout this chapter, the decision model and the performance-evaluation model were consistent. If, however, the performance-evaluation model conflicts with the decision model, the performance-evaluation model often prevails in influencing managers' decisions. The following table shows Toledo's accrual accounting income for the first year and the second year if it keeps or replaces the machine.

	Accrual Accounting First-Year Results		Accrual Accounting Second-Year Results	
	Keep	Replace	Keep	Replace
Revenues	$1,100,000	$1,100,000	$1,100000	$1,100,000
Operating costs				
Cash-operating costs	800,000	$ 460,000	800,000	460,000
Depreciation	200,000	300,000	200,000	300,000
Loss on disposal	—	360,000		
Total operating costs	1,000,000	1,120,000	1,000,000	760,000
Operating income (loss)	$ 100,000	$ (20,000)	$ 100,000	$ 340,000

Total accrual accounting income for the 2 years together is $120,000 higher if the machine is replaced, as in Exhibit 9-11. But if the promotion or bonus of the manager at Toledo hinges on his or her first year's operating income performance under accrual accounting, the manager's temptation not to replace would be very strong. Why? Because the accrual accounting model for measuring performance will show a first-year operating income of $100,000 if the old machine is kept versus an operating loss of $20,000 if the machine is replaced. Even though top management's goals encompass the 2-year period (consistent with the decision model), the manager will focus on first-year results if his or her evaluation is based on short-run measures such as the first-year's operating income.

Resolving the conflict between the decision model and the performance-evaluation model is frequently a baffling problem in practice. In theory, resolving the difficulty seems obvious: Design models that are consistent. Consider our replacement example. Year-by-year effects on operating income of replacement can be budgeted for the 2-year planning horizon. The manager then would be evaluated on the expectation that the first year would be poor and the next year would be much better. Doing this for every decision, however, makes the performance-evaluation model very cumbersome. As a result of these practical difficulties, accounting systems rarely track each decision separately. Performance evaluation focuses on responsibility centers for a specific period, not on projects or individual items of equipment over their useful lives. Thus, the effects of many different decisions are combined in a single performance report and evaluation measure, say operating income. Lower-level managers make decisions to maximize operating income, and top management—through the reporting system—is rarely aware of particular desirable alternatives that were *not* chosen by lower-level managers because of conflicts between the decision and performance-evaluation models.

Consider another conflict between the decision model and the performance-evaluation model. Suppose a manager buys a particular machine only to discover shortly afterward that a better machine could have been purchased instead. The decision model may suggest replacing the machine that was just bought with the better machine, but will the manager do so? Probably not. Why? Because replacing the machine so soon after its purchase will reflect badly on the manager's capabilities and performance. If the manager's bosses have no knowledge of the better machine, the manager may prefer to keep the recently purchased machine rather than alert them to the better machine.

Many managers consider it unethical to take actions that make their own performance look good when these actions are not in the best interests of the firm. They believe that it was precisely these kinds of behaviors that contributed to the recent global financial crisis. To discourage such behaviors, managers develop codes of conduct, emphasize values, and build cultures that focus on doing the right things. Chapter 16 discusses performance-evaluation models, ethics, and ways to reduce conflict between the decision model and the performance-evaluation model in more detail.

In the next section, we consider relevant and irrelevant costs in the context of joint costs (Chapter 5).

Keys to Success

Top management faces a persistent challenge: making sure that the performance-evaluation model of lower-level managers is consistent with the decision model. A common inconsistency is to tell managers to take a multiple-year view in their decision making but to then judge their performance only on the basis of the current year's operating income.

Irrelevance of Joint Costs for Decision Making

Learning Objective 9

Explain why joint costs are irrelevant in a sell-or-process-further decision . . .

because joint costs are the same whether or not further processing occurs

Joint costs arise when a production process yields multiple products simultaneously, such as when coal is distilled to yield coke, natural gas, and other products. The costs of this distillation are joint costs. The *splitoff point* is the juncture in a joint production process when two or more products become separately identifiable. An example is the point at which coal becomes coke, natural gas, and other products. *Separable costs* are all costs, such as manufacturing, marketing, or distribution, incurred beyond the splitoff point that are assignable to each of the specific products identified at the splitoff point.

Consider this example. Farmers' Dairy purchases raw milk from individual farms and processes it until the splitoff point, when two products—cream and liquid skim—emerge. The following data is available for May 2013:

- Farmers' Dairy processes 110,000 gallons of raw milk at a cost of $400,000.
- During processing, 10,000 gallons are lost due to evaporation and spillage, yielding 25,000 gallons of cream and 75,000 gallons of liquid skim.
- Cream can be sold for $8 per gallon and liquid skim for $4 per gallon.
- The 25,000 gallons of cream can be processed further to yield 20,000 gallons of buttercream at additional processing costs of $280,000. Buttercream can be sold for $25 per gallon.
- The 75,000 gallons of liquid skim can be processed further to yield 50,000 gallons of condensed milk at additional processing costs of $520,000. Condensed milk can be sold for $22 per gallon.

Should managers at Farmers' Dairy sell the joint products, cream and liquid skim, at the splitoff point or further process them into buttercream and condensed milk?

Exhibit 9-13, Panel A depicts (1) how raw milk is converted into cream and liquid skim in the joint production process and (2) how cream is separately processed into buttercream and liquid skim is separately processed into condensed milk. Exhibit 9-13, Panel B presents additional information about inventories, production, sales, and selling prices.

The decision to incur additional costs for further processing should be based on the incremental operating income attainable beyond the splitoff point for each product separately. The relevant cost analysis for the decision to process further versus selling joint products at the splitoff point is:

Further Processing Cream into Buttercream

Incremental revenues	
($25 per gallon × 20,000 gallons) − ($8 per gallon × 25,000 gallons)	$300,000
Deduct incremental processing costs	280,000
Increase in operating income from buttercream	$ 20,000

Further Processing Liquid Skim into Condensed Milk

Incremental revenues	
($22 per gallon × 50,000 gallons) − ($4 per gallon × 75,000 gallons)	$800,000
Deduct incremental processing costs	520,000
Increase in operating income from condensed milk	$280,000

Exhibit 9-13

Graphical Presentation of the Joint Production Process for Raw Milk

PANEL A: Graphical Presentation of Process for Example

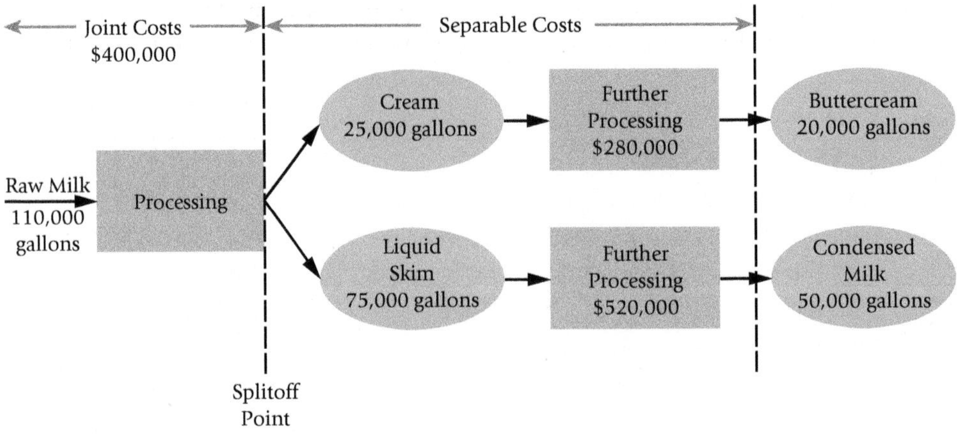

PANEL B: Data for Example

	A	B	C	D	E
1		Joint Costs		Buttercream	Condensed Milk
2	Joint costs (costs of 110,000 gallons raw milk and processing to splitoff point)	$400,000			
3	Separable cost of processing 25,000 gallons cream into 20,000 gallons buttercream			$280,000	
4	Separable cost of processing 75,000 gallons liquid skim into 50,000 gallons condensed milk				$520,000
5					
6		Cream	Liquid Skim	Buttercream	Condensed Milk
7	Beginning inventory (gallons)	0	0	0	0
8	Production (gallons)	25,000	75,000	20,000	50,000
9	Transfer for further processing (gallons)	25,000	75,000		
10	Sales (gallons)			12,000	45,000
11	Ending inventory (gallons)	0	0	8,000	5,000
12	Selling price per gallon	$ 8	$ 4	$ 25	$ 22

In this example, processing beyond the splitoff point increases operating income for each product. Therefore, the manager decides to process cream into buttercream and liquid skim into condensed milk. *The $400,000 joint costs incurred before the splitoff point are irrelevant in deciding whether to process further.* Why? Because the joint costs of $400,000 are the same whether the products are sold at the splitoff point or processed further.

Recall that incremental costs are the additional costs incurred for an activity, such as further processing. *Do not assume all separable costs are always incremental costs.* Some separable costs may be fixed costs, such as lease costs on buildings where the further processing is done; some separable costs may be sunk costs, such as depreciation on the equipment that converts cream into buttercream; and some separable costs may be allocated costs, such as corporate costs allocated to the condensed milk operations. None of these costs will differ between the alternatives of selling products at the splitoff point or processing further; therefore, they are irrelevant.

Joint-Cost Allocation and Performance Evaluation

The potential conflict between cost concepts used for decision making and cost concepts used for evaluating the performance of managers could also arise in sell-or-process-further decisions. To see how, let us continue with our Farmers' Dairy example. Suppose *allocated* fixed corporate and administrative costs of further processing cream into buttercream equal $30,000 and that these costs will be allocated only to buttercream and to the manager's product-line income statement if buttercream is produced. How might this policy affect the manager's decision to process further?

As we have seen, on the basis of incremental revenues and incremental costs, Farmers' operating income will increase by $20,000 if it processes cream into buttercream. However, producing the buttercream also results in an additional charge for allocated fixed costs of $30,000. If the manager is evaluated on a full-cost basis (that is, after allocating all costs), processing cream into buttercream will lower the manager's performance-evaluation measure by $10,000 (incremental operating income, $20,000 − allocated fixed costs, $30,000). Therefore, the manager may be tempted to sell cream at splitoff and not process it into buttercream. Reducing this inconsistency between the decision model and the performance evaluation model is an important organizational goal.

Keys to Success

Managers should only consider incremental revenues and incremental separable costs in a sell-or-process-further decision. Joint costs are irrelevant in the sell-or-process further decision because joint costs are the same regardless of whether further processing occurs.

Problem for Self-Study

Wally Lewis is manager of the engineering development division of Goldcoast Products. Lewis has just received a proposal signed by all 15 of his engineers to replace the workstations with networked personal computers (networked PCs). Lewis is not enthusiastic about the proposal.

Data on workstations and networked PCs are:

	Workstations	Networked PCs
Original cost	$300,000	$135,000
Useful life	5 years	3 years
Current age	2 years	0 years
Remaining useful life	3 years	3 years
Accumulated depreciation	$120,000	Not acquired yet
Current book value	$180,000	Not acquired yet
Current disposal value (in cash)	$95,000	Not acquired yet
Terminal disposal value (in cash 3 years from now)	$0	$0
Annual computer-related cash operating costs	$40,000	$10,000
Annual revenues	$1,000,000	$1,000,000
Annual non-computer-related operating costs	$880,000	$880,000

Lewis's annual bonus includes a component based on division operating income. He has a promotion possibility next year that would make him a group vice president of Goldcoast Products.

Required

1. Compare the costs of workstations and networked PCs. Consider the cumulative results for the 3 years together, ignoring the time value of money and income taxes.
2. Why might Lewis be reluctant to purchase the networked PCs?

Solution

1. The following table considers all cost items when comparing future costs of workstations and networked PCs:

All Items	Three Years Together Workstations (1)	Networked PCs (2)	Difference (3) = (1) − (2)
Revenues	$3,000,000	$3,000,000	—
Operating costs			
Non-computer-related operating costs ($880,000 per year × 3 years)	2,640,000	2,640,000	—
Computer-related cash operating costs ($40,000 per year; $10,000 per year × 3 years)	120,000	30,000	$ 90,000
Workstations' book value			
Periodic writeoff as depreciation or	180,000	—	—
Lump-sum writeoff	—	180,000	
Current disposal value of workstations	—	(95,000)	95,000
Networked PCs, written off periodically as depreciation	—	135,000	(135,000)
Total operating costs	2,940,000	2,890,000	50,000
Operating income	$ 60,000	$ 110,000	$ (50,000)

Alternatively, the analysis could focus on only those items in the preceding table that differ between the alternatives.

Relevant Items	Three Years Together Workstations	Networked PCs	Difference
Computer-related cash operating costs ($40,000 per year × 3 years: $10,000 per year × 3 years)	$120,000	$ 30,000	$ 90,000
Current disposal value of workstations	—	(95,000)	95,000
Networked PCs, written off periodically as depreciation	—	135,000	(135,000)
Total relevant costs	$120,000	$ 70,000	$ 50,000

The analysis suggests that it is cost-effective to replace the workstations with the networked PCs.

2. The accrual-accounting operating incomes *for the first year* under the alternatives of "keep workstations" versus the "buy networked PCs" are:

	Keep Workstations		Buy Networked PCs	
Revenues		$1,000,000		$1,000,000
Operating costs				
Non-computer-related operating costs	$880,000		$880,000	
Computer-related cash operating costs	40,000		10,000	
Depreciation	60,000		45,000	
Loss on disposal of workstations	—		85,000[a]	
Total operating costs		980,000		1,020,000
Operating income (loss)		$ 20,000		$ (20,000)

[a] $85,000 = Book value of workstations, $180,000 − Current disposal value, $95,000.

Lewis would be less happy with the expected operating loss of $20,000 if the networked PCs are purchased than he would be with the expected operating income of $20,000 if the workstations are kept. Buying the networked PCs would eliminate the component of his bonus based on operating income. He might also perceive the $20,000 operating loss as reducing his chances of being promoted to group vice president.

Decision Points

The following question-and-answer format summarizes the chapter's learning objectives. Each decision presents a key question related to a learning objective. The guidelines are the answer to that question.

Decision	Guidelines
1. What is the five-step process that managers can use to make decisions?	The five-step decision-making process is (a) identify the problem and uncertainties, (b) obtain information, (c) make predictions about the future, (d) make decisions by choosing among alternatives, and (e) implement the decision, evaluate performance, and learn.
2. When is a revenue or cost item relevant for a particular decision and what potential problems should managers avoid in relevant-cost analysis?	To be relevant for a particular decision, a revenue or cost item must meet two criteria: (a) It must be an expected future revenue or expected future cost and (b) it must differ among alternative courses of action. Quantitative outcomes are measured in numerical terms. Relevant revenue and relevant cost analysis only consider quantitative outcomes that can be expressed in financial terms. The outcomes of alternative actions can also have nonfinancial quantitative and qualitative effects. Qualitative factors, such as employee morale, are difficult to measure accurately in numerical terms. But managers must consider qualitative factors and nonfinancial quantitative factors when making decisions. Two potential problems to avoid in relevant-cost analysis are (a) making incorrect general assumptions—such as all variable costs are relevant and all fixed costs are irrelevant—and (b) losing sight of total fixed costs and focusing instead on unit fixed costs.
3. What is an opportunity cost and why should managers consider it when making decisions?	Opportunity cost is the contribution to income that is forgone by not using a limited resource in its next-best alternative use. Opportunity cost is included in decision making because the relevant cost of any decision is (a) the incremental cost of the decision plus (b) the opportunity cost of the profit forgone from making that decision.
4. When a resource is constrained, how should managers choose which of multiple products to produce and sell?	When a resource is constrained, managers should select the product that yields the highest contribution margin per unit of the constraining or limiting resource (factor). In this way, total contribution margin will be maximized.
5. What steps can managers take to manage bottlenecks?	Managers can take four steps to manage bottlenecks: (a) recognize that the bottleneck operation determines throughput (contribution) margin, (b) identify the bottleneck, (c) keep the bottleneck busy and subordinate all nonbottleneck operations to the bottleneck operation, and (d) increase bottleneck efficiency and capacity.
6. In deciding to add or drop customers or to add or discontinue branch offices or segments, what should managers focus on and how should they take into account allocated overhead costs?	When making decisions about adding or dropping customers or adding or discontinuing branch offices and segments, managers should focus on only those costs that will change and any opportunity costs. Managers should ignore allocated overhead costs.
7. Is book value of existing equipment relevant in equipment-replacement decisions?	Book value of existing equipment is a past (historical or sunk) cost and, therefore, is irrelevant in equipment-replacement decisions.

Decision	Guidelines
8. How can conflicts arise between the decision model a manager uses and the performance-evaluation model the company uses to evaluate that manager?	Top management faces a persistent challenge: making sure that the performance-evaluation model of lower-level managers is consistent with the decision model. A common inconsistency is to tell these managers to take a multiple-year view in their decision making but then to judge their performance only on the basis of the current year's operating income.
9. What revenues and costs should managers consider in a sell-or-process-further decision?	Managers should only consider incremental revenues and incremental separable costs in a sell-or-process-further decision. Joint costs are irrelevant in the sell-or-process-further decision because joint costs are the same regardless of whether further processing occurs.

Appendix

Linear Programming

In this chapter's Power Recreation example (pages 356–357), suppose both the snowmobile and boat engines must be tested on a very expensive machine before they are shipped to customers. The available machine-hours for testing are limited. Production data are:

		Use of Capacity in Hours per Unit of Product		Daily Maximum Production in Units	
Department	Available Daily Capacity in Hours	Snowmobile Engine	Boat Engine	Snowmobile Engine	Boat Engine
Assembly	600 machine-hours	2.0 machine-hours	5.0 machine-hours	300[a] snowmobile engines	120 boat engines
Testing	120 testing-hours	1.0 testing-hour	0.5 testing-hour	120 snowmobile engines	240 boat engines

[a] For example, 600 machine-hours ÷ 2.0 machine-hours per snowmobile engine = 300, the maximum number of snowmobile engines that the assembly department can make if it works exclusively on snowmobile engines.

Exhibit 9-14 summarizes these and other relevant data. In addition, as a result of material shortages for boat engines, Power Recreation cannot produce more than 110 boat engines per day. How many engines of each type should Power Recreation's managers produce and sell daily to maximize operating income?

Because there are multiple constraints, managers can use a technique called *linear programming (LP)* to determine the number of each type of engine Power Recreation should produce. LP models typically assume that all costs are either variable or fixed for a single cost driver (units of output). As we shall see, LP models also require certain other linear assumptions to hold. When these assumptions fail, managers should consider other decision models.[4]

Steps in Solving an LP Problem

We use the data in Exhibit 9-14 to illustrate the three steps in solving an LP problem. Throughout this discussion, *S* equals the number of units of snowmobile engines produced and sold, and *B* equals the number of units of boat engines produced and sold.

Step 1: Determine the Objective Function. The **objective function** of a linear program expresses the objective or goal to be maximized (say, operating income) or minimized (say, operating costs). In our example, the objective is to find the combination of snowmobile engines and boat engines

[4] Other decision models are described in J. Moore and L. Weatherford, *Decision Modeling with Microsoft Excel*, 6th ed. (Upper Saddle River, NJ: Prentice Hall, 2001); and S. Nahmias, *Production and Operations Analysis*, 6th ed. (New York: McGraw-Hill/Irwin, 2008).

Exhibit 9-14
Operating Data for Power Recreation

	Department Capacity (per Day) In Product Units				
	Assembly	Testing	Selling Price	Variable Cost per Unit	Contribution Margin per Unit
Only snowmobile engines	300	120	\$ 800	\$560	\$240
Only boat engines	120	240	\$1,000	\$625	\$375

that maximizes total contribution margin. Fixed costs remain the same regardless of the product-mix decision and are irrelevant. The linear function expressing the objective for the total contribution margin (*TCM*) is:

$$TCM = \$240S + \$375B$$

Step 2: Specify the Constraints. A **constraint** is a mathematical inequality or equality that must be satisfied by the variables in a mathematical model. The following linear inequalities express the relationships in our example:

Assembly department constraint	$2S + 5B \leq 600$
Testing department constraint	$1S + 0.5B \leq 120$
Materials-shortage constraint for boat engines	$B \leq 110$
Negative production is impossible	$S \geq 0$ and $B \geq 0$

The three solid lines on the graph in Exhibit 9-15 show the existing constraints for assembly and testing and the materials-shortage constraint.[5] The feasible or technically possible alternatives are those combinations of quantities of snowmobile engines and boat engines that satisfy all the constraining resources or factors. The shaded "area of feasible solutions" in Exhibit 9-15 shows the boundaries of those product combinations that are feasible.

Step 3: Compute the Optimal Solution. Linear programming (LP) is an optimization technique used to maximize the *objective function* when there are multiple *constraints*. We present two approaches for finding the optimal solution using LP: trial-and-error approach and graphic

Exhibit 9-15
Linear Programming: Graphic Solution for Power Recreation

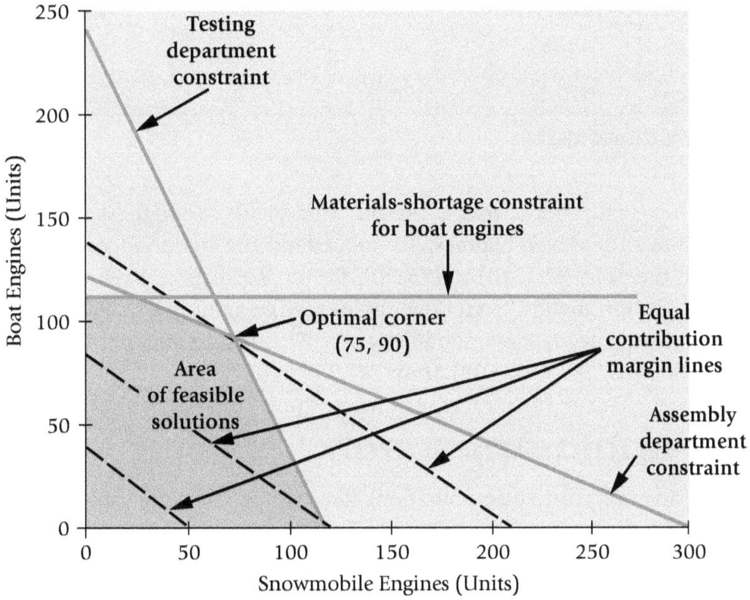

[5] As an example of how the lines are plotted in Exhibit 9-15, use equal signs instead of inequality signs and assume for the assembly department that $B = 0$; then $S = 300$ (600 machine-hours ÷ 2 machine-hours per snowmobile engine). Assume that $S = 0$; then $B = 120$ (600 machine-hours ÷ 5 machine-hours per boat engine). Connect those two points with a straight line.

approach. These approaches are easy to use in our example because there are only two variables in the objective function and a small number of constraints. Understanding these approaches provides insight into LP. In most real-world LP applications, managers use computer software packages to calculate the optimal solution.[6]

Trial-and-Error Approach

Managers can find the optimal solution by trial and error, by working with coordinates of the corners of the area of feasible solutions.

First, select any set of corner points and compute the total contribution margin. Five corner points appear in Exhibit 9-15. It is helpful to use simultaneous equations to obtain the exact coordinates in the graph. To illustrate, the corner point ($S = 75, B = 90$) can be derived by solving the two pertinent constraint inequalities as simultaneous equations:

$$2S + 5B = 600 \quad (1)$$

$$1S + 0.5B = 120 \quad (2)$$

Multiplying (2) by 2: $$2S + B = 240 \quad (3)$$

Subtracting (3) from (1): $$4B = 360$$

Therefore, $$B = 360 \div 4 = 90$$

Substituting for B in (2): $$1S + 0.5(90) = 120$$

$$S = 120 - 45 = 75$$

Given $S = 75$ snowmobile engines and $B = 90$ boat engines, TCM = (\$240 per snowmobile engine × 75 snowmobile engines) + (\$375 per boat engine × 90 boat engines) = \$51,750.

Second, move from corner point to corner point and compute the total contribution margin at each corner point.

Trial	Corner Point (S, B)	Snowmobile Engines (S)	Boat Engines (B)	Total Contribution Margin
1	(0, 0)	0	0	\$240(0) +\$375(0) = \$0
2	(0, 110)	0	110	\$240(0) +\$375(110) = \$41,250
3	(25,110)	25	110	\$240(25) +\$375(110) = \$47,250
4	(75, 90)	75	90	\$240(75) +\$375(90) = \$51,750[a]
5	(120, 0)	120	0	\$240(120) +\$375(0) = \$28,800

[a] The optimal solution.

The optimal product mix is the mix that yields the highest total contribution: 75 snowmobile engines and 90 boat engines. To understand the solution, consider what happens when moving from the point (25,110) to (75, 90). Power Recreation gives up \$7,500 [\$375 × (110 − 90)] in contribution margin from boat engines while gaining \$12,000 [\$240 × (75 − 25)] in contribution margin from snowmobile engines. This results in a net increase in contribution margin of \$4,500 (\$12,000 − \$7,500), from \$47,250 to \$51,750.

Graphic Approach

Consider all possible combinations that will produce the same total contribution margin of, say, \$12,000. That is,

$$\$240S + \$375B = \$12,000$$

[6] Standard computer software packages rely on the simplex method. The *simplex method* is an iterative step-by-step procedure for determining the optimal solution to an LP problem. The procedure starts with a specific feasible solution and then tests it by substitution to see whether the result can be improved. These substitutions continue until no further improvement is possible and the optimal solution is obtained.

This set of \$12,000 contribution margins is a straight dashed line through [$S = 50$ (\$12,000 ÷ \$240); $B = 0$)] and [$S = 0$, $B = 32$ (\$12,000 ÷ \$375)] in Exhibit 9-15. Other equal total contribution margins can be represented by lines parallel to this one. In Exhibit 9-15, we show three dashed lines. Lines drawn farther from the origin represent more sales of both products and higher amounts of equal contribution margins.

The optimal line is the one farthest from the origin but still passing through a point in the area of feasible solutions. This line represents the highest total contribution margin. The optimal solution—the number of snowmobile engines and boat engines that will maximize the objective function, total contribution margin—is the corner point ($S = 75$, $B = 90$). This solution will become apparent if you put a straight-edge ruler on the graph and move it outward from the origin and parallel with the \$12,000 contribution margin line. Move the ruler as far away from the origin as possible—that is, increase the total contribution margin—without leaving the area of feasible solutions. In general, the optimal solution in a maximization problem lies at the corner where the dashed line intersects an extreme point of the area of feasible solutions. Moving the ruler out any farther puts it outside the area of feasible solutions.

Sensitivity Analysis

What are the implications of uncertainty about the accounting or technical coefficients used in the objective function (such as the contribution margin per unit of snowmobile engines or boat engines) or the constraints (such as the number of machine-hours it takes to make a snowmobile engine or a boat engine)? Consider how a change in the contribution margin of snowmobile engines from \$240 to \$300 per unit would affect the optimal solution. Assume the contribution margin for boat engines remains unchanged at \$375 per unit. The revised objective function will be:

$$TCM = \$300S + \$375B$$

Using the trial-and-error approach to calculate the total contribution margin for each of the five corner points described in the previous table, the optimal solution is still ($S = 75$, $B = 90$). What if the contribution margin of snowmobile engines falls to \$160 per unit? The optimal solution remains the same ($S = 75$, $B = 90$). Thus, big changes in the contribution margin per unit of snowmobile engines have no effect on the optimal solution in this case. That's because, although the slopes of the equal contribution margin lines in Exhibit 9-15 change as the contribution margin of snowmobile engines changes from \$240 to \$300 to \$160 per unit, the farthest point at which the equal contribution margin lines intersect the area of feasible solutions is still ($S = 75$, $B = 90$).

Terms to Learn

This chapter and the Glossary at the end of the book contain definitions of the following important terms:

book value (p. 364)
business function costs (p. 345)
constraint (p. 373)
decision model (p. 342)
differential cost (p. 350)
differential revenue (p. 350)
full costs of the product (p. 345)
incremental cost (p. 350)
incremental revenue (p. 350)
insourcing (p. 348)
linear programming (LP) (p. 373)
make-or-buy decisions (p. 348)
objective function (p. 372)
one-time-only special order (p. 344)
opportunity cost (p. 353)
outsourcing (p. 348)
product-mix decisions (p. 356)
qualitative factors (p. 344)
quantitative factors (p. 343)
relevant costs (p. 342)
relevant revenues (p. 342)
sunk costs (p. 343)
theory of constraints (TOC) (p. 357)
throughput margin (p. 357)

Assignment Material

Questions

9-1 Outline the five-step sequence in a decision process.

9-2 "All future costs are relevant." Do you agree? Why?

9-3 "Variable costs are always relevant, and fixed costs are always irrelevant." Do you agree? Why?

9-4 "A component part should be purchased whenever the purchase price is less than its total manufacturing cost per unit." Do you agree? Why?

9-5 "Management should always maximize sales of the product with the highest contribution margin per unit." Do you agree? Why?

9-6 Describe the four key steps in managing bottleneck operations.

9-7 "A branch office or business segment that shows negative operating income should be shut down." Do you agree? Explain briefly.

9-8 "Cost written off as depreciation on equipment already purchased is always irrelevant." Do you agree? Why?

9-9 "Managers will always choose the alternative that maximizes operating income or minimizes costs in the decision model." Do you agree? Why?

9-10 Managers should consider only additional revenues and separable costs when making decisions about selling at splitoff or processing further." Do you agree? Explain.

Exercises

9-11 Multiple choice. (CPA) Choose the best answer.

1. The Fluffy Company manufactures slippers and sells them at $13 a pair. Variable manufacturing cost is $4.75 a pair, and allocated fixed manufacturing cost is $3.00 a pair. Fluffy has enough idle capacity available to accept a one-time-only special order of 25,000 pairs of slippers at $7.75 a pair. Fluffy will not incur any marketing costs as a result of the special order. What would the effect on operating income be if Fluffy could accept the special order without affecting normal sales: (a) $0, (b) $75,000 increase, (c) $118,750 increase, or (d) $193,750 increase? Show your calculations.
2. The Chicago Company manufactures Part No. 498 for use in its production line. The manufacturing cost per unit for 35,000 units of Part No. 498 is:

Direct materials	$ 8
Direct manufacturing labor	35
Variable manufacturing overhead	15
Fixed manufacturing overhead allocated	20
Total manufacturing cost per unit	$78

The Bench Company has offered to sell 35,000 units of Part No. 498 to Chicago for $74 per unit. Chicago will make the decision to buy the part from Bench if there is an overall savings of at least $30,000 for Chicago. If Chicago accepts Bench's offer, $5 per unit of the fixed overhead allocated would be eliminated. Furthermore, Chicago has determined that it could use the released facilities to save relevant costs in the manufacture of Part No. 575. For Chicago to achieve an overall savings of $30,000, the amount of relevant costs that would have to be saved by using the released facilities in the manufacture of Part No. 575 would be which of the following: (a) $140,000, (b) $415,000, (c) $65,000, or (d) $525,000? Show your calculations. What other factors might Chicago consider before outsourcing to Bench?

9-12 Special order, activity-based costing. (CMA, adapted) The Medal Plus Company manufactures medals for winners of athletic events and other contests. Its manufacturing plant has the capacity to produce 12,000 medals each month. Current production and sales are 10,000 medals per month. The company normally charges $300 per medal. Cost information for the current activity level is as follows:

Variable costs that vary with number of units produced	
Direct materials	$ 600,000
Direct manufacturing labor	450,000
Variable costs (for setups, materials handling, quality control, etc.) that vary with number of batches, 200 batches × $1,500 per batch	300,000
Fixed manufacturing costs	250,000
Fixed marketing costs	50,000
Total costs	$1,650,000

Medal Plus has just received a one-time-only special order for 2,000 medals at $250 per medal. Accepting the special order would not affect the company's regular business. Medal Plus makes medals for its existing customers in batch sizes of 50 medals (200 batches $\times$ 50 medals per batch $=$ 10,000 medals). The special order requires Medal Plus to make the medals in 40 batches of 50 each.

Required

1. Should Medal Plus accept this special order? Show your calculations.
2. Suppose plant capacity were only 11,000 medals instead of 12,000 medals each month. Medal Plus must accept or reject the special order in full. Should Medal Plus accept the special order? Show your calculations.
3. As in requirement 1, assume that monthly capacity is 12,000 medals. Medal Plus is concerned that if it accepts the special order, its existing customers will immediately demand a price discount of $20 in the month in which the special order is being filled. Existing customers would argue that Medal Plus' capacity costs are now being spread over more units and that they should get the benefit of these lower costs. Should Medal Plus accept the special order under these conditions? Show your calculations.

9-13 Make versus buy, activity-based costing. The Summer Corporation manufactures cellular modems. It manufactures its own cellular modem circuit boards (CMCB), an important part of the cellular modem. The company reports the following cost information about the costs of making CMCBs in 2012 and the expected costs in 2013:

	Current Costs in 2012	Expected Costs in 2013
Variable manufacturing costs		
Direct material cost per CMCB	$ 185	$ 165
Direct manufacturing labor cost per CMCB	60	44
Variable manufacturing cost per batch for setups, materials handling, and quality control	1,750	1,700
Fixed manufacturing cost		
Fixed manufacturing overhead costs that can be avoided if CMCBs are not made	590,000	595,000
Fixed manufacturing overhead costs of plant depreciation, insurance, and administration that cannot be avoided even if CMCBs are not made	1,030,000	1,020,000

Summer manufactured 16,200 CMCBs in 2012 in 80 batches of 190 each. In 2013, Summer anticipates needing 17,000 CMCBs. The CMCBs would be produced in 100 batches of 170 each.

The Manson Corporation has approached Summer about supplying CMCBs to Summer in 2013 at $280 per CMCB on whatever delivery schedule Summer wants.

Required

1. Calculate the total expected manufacturing cost per unit of making CMCBs in 2013.
2. Suppose the capacity currently used to make CMCBs will become idle if Summer purchases CMCBs from Manson. On the basis of financial considerations alone, should Summer make CMCBs or buy them from Manson? Show your calculations.
3. Now suppose that if Summer purchases CMCBs from Manson, its best alternative use of the capacity currently used for CMCBs is to make and sell special circuit boards (CB3s) to the Essex Corporation. Summer estimates the following incremental revenues and costs from CB3s:

Total expected incremental future revenues	$2,200,000
Total expected incremental future costs	$2,425,000

On the basis of financial considerations alone, should Summer make CMCBs or buy them from Manson? Show your calculations.

9-14 Inventory decision, opportunity costs. Lawnwolf, a manufacturer of lawn mowers, predicts that it will purchase 240,000 spark plugs next year. Lawnwolf estimates that 20,000 spark plugs will be required each month. A supplier quotes a price of $11 per spark plug. The supplier also offers a special discount option: If Lawnwolf purchases all 240,000 spark plugs at the start of the year, the supplier gives a discount of 4% off the $11 price. Lawnwolf can invest its cash at 10% per year. Lawnwolf spends $220 to place each purchase order.

Required

1. What is the opportunity cost for Lawnwolf of interest forgone from purchasing all 240,000 units at the start of the year instead of in 12 monthly purchases of 20,000 units per order?
2. Would managers record this opportunity cost in the accounting system? Why?
3. Should Lawnwolf purchase 240,000 units at the start of the year or 20,000 units each month? Show your calculations.
4. What other factors should Lawnwolf consider when making its decision?

9-15 Relevant costs, contribution margin, product emphasis. The Shell Hunter is a take-out food store at a popular beach resort. Susan Sexton, owner of the Shell Hunter, is deciding how much refrigerator space to devote to four different drinks. Pertinent data on these four drinks are:

	Cola	Lemonade	Punch	Natural Orange Juice
Selling price per case	$19.10	$19.75	$26.90	$38.80
Variable cost per case	$14.20	$15.60	$20.90	$30.25
Cases sold per foot of shelf space per day	5	10	25	12

Sexton has a maximum front shelf space of 12 feet to devote to the four drinks. She wants a minimum of 1 foot and a maximum of 6 feet of front shelf space for each drink.

Required

1. Calculate the contribution margin per case of each type of drink.
2. A coworker of Sexton's recommends that she maximize the shelf space devoted to those drinks with the highest contribution margin per case. Do you agree with this recommendation? Explain briefly.
3. What shelf-space allocation for the four drinks would you recommend for the Shell Hunter? Show your calculations.

9-16 Selection of most profitable product. Java Giant, Inc., produces two basic types of espresso makers, Model A and Model B. Pertinent data are:

	Per Unit	
	Model A	Model B
Selling price	$200.00	$140.00
Costs		
Direct material	56.00	26.00
Direct manufacturing labor	30.00	50.00
Variable manufacturing overhead*	50.00	25.00
Fixed manufacturing overhead*	20.00	10.00
Marketing (all variable)	28.00	20.00
Total cost	184.00	131.00
Operating income	$ 16.00	$ 9.00

*Allocated on the basis of machine-hours

The specialty coffee craze suggests that Java Giant can sell enough of either Model A or Model B to keep the plant operating at full capacity. Both products are processed through the same production departments.

Required

Which products should the company produce? Briefly explain your answer.

9-17 Theory of constraints, throughput margin, and relevant costs. Montana Industries manufactures electronic testing equipment. The company also installs the equipment at customers' sites and ensures that it functions smoothly. Additional information on the manufacturing and installation departments is as follows (capacities are expressed in terms of the number of units of electronic testing equipment):

	Equipment Manufactured	Equipment Installed
Annual capacity	500 units per year	450 units per year
Equipment manufactured and installed	450 units per year	450 units per year

Montana manufactures only 450 units per year because that is the maximum capacity of the installation department. The equipment sells for $30,000 per unit (installed) and has direct material costs of $10,000. All costs other than direct material costs are fixed. The following requirements refer only to the preceding data. There is no connection between the requirements.

Required

1. Montana's engineers have found a way to reduce equipment manufacturing time. The new method would cost an additional $30 per unit and would allow Montana to manufacture 22 additional units a year. Should Montana implement the new method? Show your calculations.
2. Montana's designers have proposed a change in direct materials that would increase direct material costs by $1,500 per unit. This change would enable Montana to install 475 units of equipment each year. If Montana makes the change, it will implement the new design on all equipment sold. Should Montana use the new design? Show your calculations.
3. Montana has developed a new installation technique that will enable its engineers to install 17 additional units of equipment a year. The new method will increase installation costs by $70,000 each year. Should Montana implement the new technique? Show your calculations.
4. Montana is considering how to motivate workers to improve their productivity (output per hour). One proposal is to evaluate and compensate workers in the manufacturing and installation departments on the basis of their productivities. Do you think the new proposal is a good idea? Explain briefly.

9-18 Closing and opening stores. GST Corporation runs two convenience stores, one in Minneapolis and one in St. Paul. Operating income for each store in 2013 is:

	Minneapolis Store	St. Paul Store
Revenues	$2,140,000	$1,720,000
Operating costs		
Cost of goods sold	1,500,000	1,320,000
Lease rent (renewable each year)	180,000	150,000
Labor costs (paid on an hourly basis)	84,000	84,000
Depreciation of equipment	50,000	44,000
Utilities (electricity, heat)	86,000	92,000
Allocated corporate overhead	100,000	80,000
Total operating costs	2,000,000	1,770,000
Operating income (loss)	$ 140,000	$ (50,000)

The equipment has a zero disposal value. In a senior management meeting, Sven Larsen, management accountant at GST Corporation, comments: "GST can increase its profitability by closing down the St. Paul store or by adding another store like it."

Required

1. By closing down the St. Paul store, GST can reduce overall corporate overhead costs by $88,000. Calculate GST's operating income if it closes the St. Paul store. Is Sven Larsen's statement about the effect of closing the St. Paul store correct? Explain.
2. Calculate GST's operating income if it keeps the St. Paul store open and opens another store with revenues and costs identical to the St. Paul store (including a cost of $44,000 to acquire equipment with a 1-year useful life and zero disposal value). Opening this store will increase corporate overhead costs by $8,000. Is Sven Larsen's statement about the effect of adding another store like the St. Paul store correct? Explain.

9-19 Choosing customers. Speedy Printers operates a printing press with a monthly capacity of 1,000 machine-hours. Speedy has two main customers: Ace Corporation and Jacks Corporation. Data on each customer for January are:

	Ace Corporation	Jacks Corporation	Total
Revenues	$60,000	$40,000	$100,000
Variable costs	21,000	24,000	45,000
Contribution margin	39,000	16,000	55,000
Fixed costs (allocated)	30,000	20,000	50,000
Operating income	$ 9,000	$ (4,000)	$ 5,000
Machine-hours required	750 hours	250 hours	1,000 hours

Jacks Corporation indicates that it wants Speedy to do an *additional* $40,000 worth of printing jobs during February. These jobs are identical to the existing business Speedy did for Jacks in January in terms of variable costs and machine-hours required. Speedy anticipates that the business from Ace Corporation in February will be the same as that in January. Speedy can choose to accept as much of the Ace and Jacks business for February as its capacity allows. Assume that total machine-hours and fixed costs for February will be the same as in January.

Required What action should Speedy take to maximize its operating income? Show your calculations.

9-20 Relevance of equipment costs. Shiny Car Wash has just today paid for and installed a special machine for polishing cars at one of its several outlets. It is the first day of the company's fiscal year. The machine costs $40,000, and its annual cash operating costs total $30,000. The machine will have a 4-year useful life and a zero terminal disposal value.

After the Shiny Car Wash uses the machine for only one day, a salesperson offers a different machine that promises to do the same job at annual cash operating costs of $18,000. The new machine will cost $48,000 cash, installed. The "old" machine is unique and can be sold outright for only $20,000, minus $4,000 removal cost. The new machine, like the old one, will have a 4-year useful life and zero terminal disposal value.

Revenues, all in cash, will be $300,000 annually, and other cash costs will be $220,000 annually, regardless of this decision.

For simplicity, ignore income taxes and the time value of money.

Required

1. a. Prepare a statement of cash receipts and disbursements for each of the 4 years under each alternative. What is the cumulative difference in cash flow for the 4 years taken together?
   b. Prepare income statements for each of the 4 years under each alternative. Assume straight-line depreciation. What is the cumulative difference in operating income for the 4 years taken together?
   c. What are the irrelevant items in your presentations in requirements a and b? Why are the items irrelevant?
2. Suppose the cost of the "old" machine was $1 million rather than $40,000. Nevertheless, the old machine can be sold outright for only $20,000, minus $4,000 removal cost. Would the net differences in requirements 1a and 1b change? Explain.
3. Is there any conflict between the decision model and the incentives of the manager who has just purchased the "old" machine and is considering replacing it a day later?

9-21 Equipment upgrade versus replacement. (A. Spero, adapted) The Furnitech Company produces and sells 7,500 modular computer desks per year at a selling price of $375 each. Its current production equipment, purchased for $900,000 and with a 5-year useful life, is only 2 years old. The equipment has a terminal disposal value of $0 and is depreciated on a straight-line basis. The equipment has a current disposal price of $225,000. However, the emergence of a new molding technology has led Furnitech to consider either upgrading or replacing the production equipment. The following table presents data for the two alternatives:

	Upgrade	Replace
One-time equipment costs	$1,500,000	$2,400,000
Variable manufacturing cost per desk	$ 75.00	$ 37.50
Remaining useful life of equipment (years)	3	3
Terminal disposal value of equipment	$ 0	$ 0

All equipment costs will continue to be depreciated on a straight-line basis. For simplicity, ignore income taxes and the time value of money.

Required

1. Should Furnitech upgrade its production line or replace it? Show your calculations.
2. Now suppose the one-time equipment cost to replace the production equipment is somewhat negotiable. All other data are as given previously. What is the maximum one-time equipment cost that Furnitech would be willing to pay to replace rather than upgrade the old equipment?
3. Assume that the capital expenditures to replace and upgrade the production equipment are as given in the original exercise, but that the production and sales quantity is not known. For what production and sales quantity would Furnitech (i) upgrade the equipment or (ii) replace the equipment?
4. Assume that all data are as given in the original exercise. Dan Douglas is Furnitech's manager, and his bonus is based on operating income. Because he is likely to relocate after about a year, his current bonus is his primary concern. Which alternative would Douglas choose? Explain.

9-22 Joint-costs, further-process decision. The Sinclair Spirits Division of the Pilgrim Company produces two products—turpentine and methanol (wood alcohol)—by a joint process. Joint costs amount to $116,000 per batch of output. Each batch totals 13,000 gallons: 25% methanol and 75% turpentine. Both products could be processed further without gain or loss in volume. Separable processing costs are $2 per gallon for methanol and $1 per gallon for turpentine. Methanol sells for $20 per gallon. Turpentine sells for $15 per gallon.

Required

1. The company has discovered an additional process by which it can turn the methanol (wood alcohol) into a pleasant-tasting alcoholic beverage. The selling price of this beverage would be $45 a gallon. Additional processing would increase separable costs $6 per gallon (in addition to the $2 per gallon separable cost required to yield methanol). The company would have to pay excise taxes of 20% on the selling price of the beverage. Should the company produce the alcoholic beverage? Show your computations.
2. Describe a situation where the decision model might conflict with the performance-evaluation model.

Problems

9-23 Special Order. Homerun Corporation produces baseball bats for kids that it sells for $37 each. At capacity, the company can produce 50,000 bats a year. The costs of producing and selling 50,000 bats are:

	Cost per Bat	Total Costs
Direct materials	$16	$ 800,000
Direct manufacturing labor	4	200,000
Variable manufacturing overhead	1	50,000
Fixed manufacturing overhead	3	150,000
Variable selling expenses	4	200,000
Fixed selling expenses	2	100,000
Total costs	$30	$1,500,000

Required

1. Suppose Homerun is currently producing and selling 40,000 bats. At this level of production and sales, its fixed costs are the same as given in the preceding table. Ryan Corporation wants to place a one-time special order for 10,000 bats at $23 each. Homerun will incur no variable selling costs for this special order. Should Homerun accept this one-time special order? Show your calculations.
2. Now suppose Homerun is currently producing and selling 50,000 bats. If Homerun accepts Ryan's offer, it will have to sell 10,000 fewer bats to its regular customers.
   a. On financial considerations alone, should Homerun accept this one-time special order? Show your calculations.
   b. On financial considerations alone, at what price would Homerun be indifferent between accepting the special order and continuing to sell to its regular customers at $37 per bat?
   c. What other factors should Homerun consider in deciding whether to accept the one-time special order?

9-24 Short-run pricing, capacity constraints. Ohio Acres Dairy, maker of specialty cheeses, produces a soft cheese from the milk of Holstein cows raised on a special corn-based diet. One kilogram of soft cheese, which has a contribution margin of $8, requires 4 liters of milk. A well-known gourmet restaurant has asked Ohio Acres to produce 2,000 kilograms of a hard cheese from the same milk of Holstein cows. Knowing that the dairy has sufficient unused capacity, Elise Princiotti, owner of Ohio Acres, calculates the costs of making one kilogram of the desired hard cheese:

Milk (10 liters × $1.50 per liter)	$15
Variable direct manufacturing labor	4
Variable manufacturing overhead	2
Fixed manufacturing cost allocated	5
Total manufacturing cost	$26

Required

1. Suppose Ohio Acres can acquire all the Holstein milk that it needs. What is the minimum price per kilogram the company should charge for the hard cheese?
2. Now suppose that the Holstein milk is in short supply. Every kilogram of hard cheese Ohio Acres produces will reduce the quantity of soft cheese that it can make and sell. What is the minimum price per kilogram the company should charge to produce the hard cheese?

9-25 International outsourcing. Cuddly Critters, Inc., manufactures plush toys in a facility in Cleveland, Ohio. Recently, the company designed a group of collectible resin figurines to go with the plush toy line. Management is trying to decide whether to manufacture the figurines themselves in existing space in the Cleveland facility or to accept an offer from a manufacturing company in Indonesia. Data concerning the decision are:

Expected annual sales of figurines (in units)	400,000
Average selling price of a figurine	$5
Price quoted by Indonesian company, in Indonesian rupiah (IDR), for each figurine	27,300 IDR
Current exchange rate	9,100 IDR = $1
Variable manufacturing costs	$2.85 per unit
Incremental annual fixed manufacturing costs associated with the new product line	$200,000
Variable selling and distribution costs[a]	$0.50 per unit
Annual fixed selling and distribution costs[a]	$285,000

[a] Selling and distribution costs are the same regardless of whether the figurines are manufactured in Cleveland or imported.

Required

1. Should Cuddly Critters manufacture the 400,000 figurines in the Cleveland facility or purchase them from the Indonesian supplier? Explain.
2. Cuddly Critters believes that the U.S. dollar may weaken in the coming months against the Indonesian rupiah and does not want to face any currency risk. Assume that Cuddly Critters can enter into a forward contract today to purchase 27,300 IDRs for $3.40. Should Cuddly Critters manufacture the 400,000 figurines in the Cleveland facility or purchase them from the Indonesian supplier? Explain.
3. What are some of the qualitative factors that Cuddly Critters should consider when deciding whether to outsource the figurine manufacturing to Indonesia?

9-26 Relevant costs, opportunity costs. Larry Miller, general manager of McCormick Software, must decide when to release the new version of McCormick's spreadsheet package, Easyspread 2.0. Development of Easyspread 2.0 is complete; however, the company has not yet produced the compact discs and user manuals. The software can be shipped starting July 1, 2013.

The major problem is that McCormick has overstocked the previous version of its spreadsheet package, Easyspread 1.0. Miller knows that once Easyspread 2.0 is introduced, McCormick will not be able to sell any more units of Easyspread 1.0. Rather than just throwing away the inventory of Easyspread 1.0, Miller is wondering if it might be better to continue to sell Easyspread 1.0 for the next 3 months and introduce Easyspread 2.0 on October 1, 2013, when the inventory of Easyspread 1.0 will be sold out.

The following information is available:

	Easyspread 1.0	Easyspread 2.0
Selling price	$170	$215
Variable cost per unit of compact discs and user manuals	24	34
Development cost per unit	60	100
Marketing and administrative cost per unit	29	39
Total cost per unit	113	173
Operating income per unit	$ 57	$ 42

Development cost per unit for each product equals the total costs of developing the software product divided by the anticipated unit sales over the life of the product. Marketing and administrative costs are fixed costs in 2013, incurred to support all marketing and administrative activities of McCormick Software. Marketing and administrative costs are allocated to products on the basis of the budgeted revenues of each product. The preceding unit costs assume Easyspread 2.0 will be introduced on October 1, 2013.

Required

1. On the basis of financial considerations alone, should Miller introduce Easyspread 2.0 on July 1, 2013, or wait until October 1, 2013? Show your calculations, clearly identifying relevant and irrelevant revenues and costs.
2. What other factors might Larry Miller consider in making a decision?

9-27 Opportunity costs. (H. Schaefer, adapted) The Wild Orchid Corporation is working at full production capacity producing 13,000 units of a unique product, Everlast. Manufacturing cost per unit for Everlast is:

Direct materials	$10
Direct manufacturing labor	2
Manufacturing overhead	14
Total manufacturing cost	$26

Manufacturing overhead cost per unit is based on variable cost per unit of $8 and fixed costs of $78,000 (at full capacity of 13,000 units). Marketing cost per unit, all variable, is $4, and the selling price is $52.

A customer, the Apex Company, has asked Wild Orchid to produce 3,500 units of Stronglast, a modification of Everlast. Stronglast would require the same manufacturing processes as Everlast. Apex has offered to pay Wild Orchid $40 for a unit of Stronglast and share half of the marketing cost per unit.

Required

1. What is the opportunity cost to Wild Orchid of producing the 3,500 units of Stronglast? (Assume that no overtime is worked.)
2. The Chesapeake Corporation has offered to produce 3,500 units of Everlast for Wild Orchid so that Wild Orchid may accept the Apex offer. That is, if Wild Orchid accepts the Chesapeake offer, Wild Orchid would manufacture 9,500 units of Everlast and 3,500 units of Stronglast and purchase 3,500 units of Everlast from Chesapeake. Chesapeake would charge Wild Orchid $36 per unit to manufacture Everlast. On the basis of financial considerations alone, should Wild Orchid accept the Chesapeake offer? Show your calculations.
3. Suppose Wild Orchid had been working at less than full capacity, producing 9,500 units of Everlast at the time the Apex offer was made. Calculate the minimum price Wild Orchid should accept for Stronglast under these conditions. (Ignore the previous $40 selling price.)

9-28 Product mix, special order. (N. Melumad, adapted) Gunther Precision Tools makes cutting tools for metalworking operations. It makes two types of tools: A6, a regular cutting tool, and EX4, a high-precision cutting tool. A6 is manufactured on a regular machine, but EX4 must be manufactured on both the regular machine and a high-precision machine. The following information is available:

	A6	EX4
Selling price	$ 200	$ 300
Variable manufacturing cost per unit	$ 120	$ 200
Variable marketing cost per unit	$ 30	$ 70
Budgeted total fixed overhead costs	$700,000	$1,100,000
Hours required to produce one unit on the regular machine	1.0	0.5

Additional information includes the following:

a. Gunther faces a capacity constraint on the regular machine of 50,000 hours per year.

b. The capacity of the high-precision machine is not a constraint.

c. Of the $1,100,000 budgeted fixed overhead costs of EX4, $600,000 are lease payments for the high-precision machine. This cost is charged entirely to EX4 because Gunther uses the machine exclusively to produce EX4. The company can cancel the lease agreement for the high-precision machine at any time without penalties.

d. All other overhead costs are fixed and cannot be changed.

Required

1. What product mix—that is, how many units of A6 and EX4—will maximize Gunther's operating income? Show your calculations.
2. Suppose Gunther can increase the annual capacity of its regular machines by 15,000 machine-hours at a cost of $300,000. Should Gunther increase the capacity of the regular machines by 15,000 machine-hours? By how much will Gunther's operating income increase or decrease? Show your calculations.
3. Suppose that the capacity of the regular machines has been increased to 65,000 hours. Gunther has been approached by Clark Corporation to supply 20,000 units of another cutting tool, V2, for $240 per unit. Gunther must either accept the order for all 20,000 units or reject it totally. V2 is exactly like A6 except that its variable manufacturing cost is $140 per unit. (It takes 1 hour to produce one unit of V2 on the regular machine, and variable marketing cost equals $30 per unit.) What product mix should Gunther choose to maximize operating income? Show your calculations.

9-29 Theory of constraints, throughput margin, quality, and relevant costs. Agnello Industries manufactures pharmaceutical products in two departments: mixing and tablet making. Additional information on the two departments follows. Each tablet contains 0.7 gram of direct materials.

	Mixing	Tablet Making
Capacity per hour	200 grams	120 tablets
Monthly capacity (2,500 hours available in each department)	500,000 grams	300,000 tablets
Monthly production	210,000 grams	294,000 tablets
Fixed operating costs (excluding direct materials)	$14,700	$35,280
Fixed operating cost per unit ($14,700 ÷ 210,000 grams; $35,280 ÷ 294,000 tablets)	$0.07 per gram	$0.12 per tablet

The mixing department makes 210,000 grams of direct materials mixture (enough to make 300,000 tablets) because the tablet-making department has only enough capacity to process 300,000 tablets. All direct material costs of $147,000 are incurred in the mixing department. The tablet-making department manufactures only 294,000 tablets from the 210,000 grams of mixture processed; 2% of the direct materials mixture is lost in the tablet-making process. Each tablet sells for $1.25. All costs other than direct material costs are fixed costs. The following requirements refer only to the preceding data. There is no connection between the requirements.

Required

1. An outside contractor makes the following offer: If Agnello will supply the contractor with 12,000 grams of mixture, the contractor will manufacture 16,800 tablets for Agnello (allowing for the normal 2% loss of the mixture during the tablet-making process) at $0.15 per tablet. Should Agnello accept the contractor's offer? Show your calculations.
2. Another company offers to prepare 21,000 grams of mixture a month from direct materials Agnello supplies. The company will charge $0.11 per gram of mixture. Should Agnello accept the company's offer? Show your calculations.
3. Agnello's engineers have devised a method that would improve quality in the tablet-making department. They estimate that the 6,000 tablets currently being lost would be saved. The modification would cost $6,000 a month. Should Agnello implement the new method? Show your calculations.
4. Suppose that Agnello also loses 6,000 grams of mixture in its mixing department. The company can reduce these losses to zero if it spends $10,000 per month in quality-improvement methods. Should Agnello adopt the quality-improvement method? Show your calculations.
5. What are the benefits of improving quality in the mixing department compared with improving quality in the tablet-making department?

9-30 Dropping a product line, selling more units. The Northern Division of Shea Corporation makes and sells tables and beds. The following estimated revenue and cost information from the division's ABC system is available for 2013.

	4,000 Tables	5,000 Beds	Total
Revenues ($110 × 4,500; $340 × 8,250)	$495,000	$2,805,000	$3,300,000
Variable direct materials and direct manufacturing labor costs ($65 × 4,500; $265 × 8,250)	292,500	2,186,250	2,478,750
Depreciation on equipment used exclusively by each product line	52,000	62,000	114,000
Marketing and distribution costs			
$34,000 (fixed) + ($790 per shipment × 45 shipments)	69,550		
$70,000 (fixed) + ($790 per shipment × 165 shipments)		200,350	269,900
Fixed general-administration costs of the division allocated to product lines on the basis of revenue	63,000	357,000	420,000
Corporate-office costs allocated to product lines on the basis of revenues	26,250	148,750	175,000
Total costs	503,300	2,954,350	3,457,650
Operating income (loss)	$ (8,300)	$ (149,350)	$ (157,650)

Additional information includes the following:

a. On January 1, 2013, the equipment has a book value of $114,000, a 1-year useful life, and zero disposal value. Any equipment not used will remain idle.

b. Fixed marketing and distribution costs of a product line can be avoided if the line is discontinued.

c. Fixed general-administration costs of the division and corporate-office costs will not change if the company increases or decreases sales of individual product lines or if it adds or drops product lines.

Required

1. On the basis of financial considerations alone, should the Northern Division discontinue the tables product line for the year, assuming the released facilities remain idle? Show your calculations.
2. If Northern Division sold 4,000 more tables, how would that affect its operating income? Assume that to sell more beds the division would have to acquire additional equipment costing $52,000 with a one-year useful life and zero terminal disposal value. Assume further that the fixed marketing and distribution costs would not change but that the number of shipments would double. Show your calculations.
3. Given the Northern Division's expected operating loss of $157,650, should Shea Corporation shut it down for the year? Assume that shutting down the Northern Division will have no effect on corporate-office costs but will lead to savings of all general-administration costs of the division. Show your calculations.
4. Suppose Shea Corporation has the opportunity to open another division, the Southern Division, whose revenues and costs are expected to be identical to the Northern Division's revenues and costs (including a cost of $114,000 to acquire equipment with a 1-year useful life and zero terminal disposal value). Opening the new division will have no effect on corporate-office costs. Should Shea open the Southern Division? Show your calculations.

9-31 Make or buy, unknown level of volume. (A. Atkinson, adapted) Denver Engineering manufactures small engines that it sells to manufacturers who install them in products such as lawn mowers. The company currently manufactures all the parts used in these engines but is considering a proposal from an external supplier who wishes to supply the starter assemblies used in these engines.

The starter assemblies are currently manufactured in Division 3 of Denver Engineering. The costs relating to the starter assemblies for the past 12 months were as follows:

Direct materials	$ 400,000
Direct manufacturing labor	300,000
Manufacturing overhead	800,000
Total	$1,500,000

Over the past year, Division 3 manufactured 150,000 starter assemblies. The average cost for each starter assembly is $10 ($1,500,000 ÷ 150,000).

Further analysis of manufacturing overhead revealed the following information. Of the total manufacturing overhead, only 25% is considered variable. Of the fixed portion, $300,000 is an allocation of general overhead that will remain unchanged for the company as a whole if production of the starter assemblies is discontinued. A further $200,000 of the fixed overhead is avoidable if production of the starter assemblies is discontinued. The balance of the current fixed overhead, $100,000, is the division manager's salary. If Denver Engineering discontinues production of the starter assemblies, the manager of Division 3 will be transferred to Division 2 at the same salary. This move will allow the company to save the $80,000 salary that would otherwise be paid to attract an outsider to this position.

Required

1. Tutwiler Electronics, a reliable supplier, has offered to supply starter-assembly units at $8 per unit. Because this price is less than the current average cost of $10 per unit, the vice president of manufacturing is eager to accept this offer. On the basis of financial considerations alone, should Denver Engineering accept the outside offer? Show your calculations. (*Hint:* Production output in the coming year may be different from production output in the past year.)
2. How, if at all, would your response to requirement 1 change if the company could use the vacated plant space for storage and, in so doing, avoid $100,000 of outside storage charges currently incurred? Why is this information relevant or irrelevant?

9-32 Make versus buy, activity-based costing, opportunity costs. The Weston Company produces gas grills. This year's expected production is 20,000 units. Currently, Weston makes the side burners for its grills. Each grill includes two side burners. Weston's management accountant reports the following costs for making 40,000 burners:

	Cost per Unit	Costs for 40,000 Units
Direct materials	$10.00	$400,000
Direct manufacturing labor	5.00	200,000
Variable manufacturing overhead	2.50	100,000
Inspection, setup, materials handling		8,000
Machine rent		16,000
Allocated fixed costs of plant administration, taxes, and insurance		100,000
Total costs		$824,000

Weston has received an offer from an outside vendor to supply any number of burners Weston requires at a price of $18.50 per burner. The following additional information is available:

a. Inspection, setup, and materials-handling costs vary with the number of batches in which the burners are produced. Weston produces burners in batch sizes of 1,000 units. Weston will produce the 40,000 units in 40 batches.

b. Weston rents the machine it uses to make the burners. If Weston buys all of its burners from the outside vendor, it does not need to pay rent on this machine.

Required

1. Assume that if Weston purchases the burners from the outside vendor, the facility where the burners are currently made will remain idle. On the basis of financial considerations alone, should Weston accept the outside vendor's offer at the anticipated volume of 40,000 burners? Show your calculations.
2. For this question, assume that if the burners are purchased outside, the facilities where the burners are currently made will be used to upgrade the grills by adding a rotisserie attachment. (*Note:* Each grill contains two burners and one rotisserie attachment.) As a consequence, the selling price of grills will be raised by $60. The variable cost per unit of the upgrade would be $48, and additional tooling costs of $200,000 per year would be incurred. On the basis of financial considerations alone, should Weston make or buy the burners, assuming that 20,000 grills are produced (and sold)? Show your calculations.

3. The sales manager at Weston is concerned that the estimate of 20,000 grills may be high and believes that only 16,000 grills will be sold. Production will be cut back, freeing up work space. This space can be used to add the rotisserie attachments whether Weston buys the burners or makes them in-house. At this lower output, Weston will produce the burners in 32 batches of 1,000 units each. On the basis of financial considerations alone, should Weston purchase the burners from the outside vendor? Show your calculations.

9-33 Product mix, constrained resource. Wechsler Company produces three products: A110, B382, and C657. All three products use the same direct material, Voxx. Unit data for the three products are:

	Product		
	A110	B382	C657
Selling price	$168	$112	140
Variable costs			
Direct materials	48	30	18
Labor and other costs	56	54	80
Quantity of Voxx per unit	8 lb.	5 lb.	3 lb.

The demand for the products far exceeds the direct materials available to produce the products. Voxx costs $6 per pound and a maximum of 5,000 pounds is available each month. Wechsler must produce a minimum of 200 units of each product.

Required

1. How many units of product A110, B382, and C657 should Wechsler produce?
2. What is the maximum amount Wechsler would be willing to pay for another 1,200 pounds of Voxx?

9-34 Joint costs, sell immediately, or process further. Utah Soy Products (USP) buys soybeans and processes them into other soy products. Each ton of soybeans that USP purchases for $400 can be converted for an additional $210 into 675 pounds of soy meal and 80 gallons of soy oil. A pound of soy meal can be sold at splitoff for $1.12 and soy oil can be sold in bulk for $4.50 per gallon.

USP can process the 675 pounds of soy meal into 825 pounds of soy cookies at an additional cost of $380. Each pound of soy cookies can be sold for $2.12 per pound. The 80 gallons of soy oil can be packaged at a cost of $260 and made into 320 quarts of Soyola. Each quart of Soyola can be sold for $1.15.

Required

1. Should USP process each of the products further?
2. Describe a situation where the decision model might conflict with the performance-evaluation model?

9-35 Optimal product mix. (CMA, adapted) Diane Simpson, Inc., sells two popular brands of cookies: Diane's Delight and Bessie's Bourbon. Diane's Delight goes through the mixing and baking departments, and Bessie's Bourbon, a filled cookie, goes through the mixing, filling, and baking departments.

Michael Shirra, vice president of sales, believes that at the current price, Diane Simpson can sell all of its daily production of Diane's Delight and Bessie's Bourbon. Both cookies are made in batches of 3,000. In each department, the time required per batch and the total time available each day are:

Home Insert Page Layout Formulas Data Review

	A	B	C	D
1		Department Minutes		
2		Mixing	Filling	Baking
3	Della's Delight	30	0	10
4	Bonny's Bourbon	15	15	15
5	Total available per day	660	270	300

Revenue and cost data for each type of cookie are:

	A	B	C
7		Diane's	Bessie's
8		Delight	Bourbon
9	Revenue per batch	$ 475	$ 375
10	Variable cost per batch	175	125
11	Contribution margin per batch	$ 300	$ 250
12	Monthly fixed costs		
13	(allocated to each product)	$18,650	$22,350

Required

1. Using *D* to represent the batches of Diane's Delight and *B* to represent the batches of Bessie's Bourbon made and sold each day, formulate Shirra's decision as an LP model.
2. Compute the optimal number of batches of each type of cookie that Diane Simpson, Inc., should make and sell each day to maximize operating income.

9-36 Dropping a customer, activity-based costing, ethics. Jason Ackerman is the management accountant for Central Restaurant Supply (CRS). Beth Donaldson, the VRS sales manager, and Jason are meeting to discuss the profitability of one of the customers, Mama Leone's Pizza. Jason hands Beth the following analysis of Mama Leone's activity during the last quarter, taken from Central's activity-based costing system:

Sales	$23,400
Cost of goods sold (all variable)	14,025
Order processing (25 orders processed at $300 per order)	7,500
Delivery (2,500 miles driven at $0.75 per mile)	1,875
Rush orders (3 rush orders at $165 per rush order)	495
Sales calls (3 sales calls at $150 per call)	450
Operating income	$ (945)

Beth looks at the report and remarks, "I'm glad to see all my hard work is paying off with Mama Leone's. Sales have gone up 10% over the previous quarter!"

Jason replies, "Increased sales are great, but I'm worried about Mama Leone's margin, Beth. We were showing a profit with Mama Leone's at the lower sales level, but now we're showing a loss. Gross margin percentage this quarter was 40%, down five percentage points from the prior quarter. I'm afraid that corporate will push hard to drop them as a customer if things don't turn around."

"That's crazy," Beth responds. "A lot of that overhead for things like order processing, deliveries, and sales calls would just be allocated to other customers if we dropped Mama Leone's. This report makes it look like we're losing money on Mama Leone's when we're not. In any case, I am sure you can do something to make its profitability look closer to what we think it is. No one doubts that Mama Leone's is a very good customer."

Required

1. Assume that Beth is partly correct in her assessment of the report. Upon further investigation, it is determined that 10% of the order processing costs and 20% of the delivery costs would not be avoidable if CRS were to drop Mama Leone's. Would CRS benefit from dropping Mama Leone's? Show your calculations.
2. Beth's bonus is based on meeting sales targets. Based on the preceding information regarding gross margin percentage, what might Beth have done last quarter to meet her target and receive her bonus? How might CRS revise its bonus system to address this?
3. Should Jason rework the numbers? How should he respond to Beth's comments about making Mama Leone's look more profitable?

9-37 Equipment replacement decisions and performance evaluation. Sean Fitzpatrick manages the Chicago plant of Shamrock Manufacturing. A representative of Darien Engineering approaches Fitzpatrick about replacing a large piece of manufacturing equipment that Shamrock uses in its process with a more efficient model. While the representative made some compelling arguments in favor of replacing the 3-year-old equipment, Fitzpatrick is hesitant. Fitzpatrick is hoping to be promoted next year to manager of the larger Houston plant, and he knows that the accrual-basis net operating income of the Chicago plant will be evaluated closely as part of the promotion decision. The following information is available concerning the equipment replacement decision:

- The historic cost of the old machine is $150,000. It has a current book value of $60,000, 2 remaining years of useful life, and a market value of $36,000. Annual depreciation expense is $30,000. It is expected to have a salvage value of $0 at the end of its useful life.
- The new equipment will cost $90,000. It will have a 2-year useful life and a $0 salvage value. Shamrock uses straight-line depreciation on all equipment.
- The new equipment will reduce electricity costs by $17,500 per year, and will reduce direct manufacturing labor costs by $15,000 per year.

For simplicity, ignore income taxes and the time value of money.

Required

1. Assume that Fitzpatrick's priority is to receive the promotion, and he makes the equipment replacement decision based on next year's accrual-based net operating income. Which alternative would he choose? Show your calculations.
2. What are the relevant factors in the decision? Which alternative is in the best interest of the company over the next 2 years? Show your calculations.
3. At what cost would Fitzpatrick be willing to purchase the new equipment? Explain.

Case

To Trim Or Not To Trim: That Is The Question

The issue had come up again and again in various management meetings and company seminars. Novartis had too many products and needed to reduce the product proliferation that had occurred. Thomas Ebeling, Chief Operating Officer, Novartis Pharmaceuticals, wondered what he should do.

The merger of Ciba-Geigy and Sandoz to form Novartis on December 20, 1996 had resulted in a significant increase in the pharmaceutical product portfolio of Novartis's Pharma Sector. Combining the pharmaceutical product lines of Ciba-Geigy and Sandoz had given Novartis a leadership position in several therapeutic areas, including immunology and inflammatory diseases, as well as strong positions in central nervous system disorders, cardiovascular diseases, oncology, dermatology, and asthma. Novartis now had approximately 250 product brands (such as Sandimmun, Voltaren, Lamisil, and Foradil). The sales volumes of each of the different brands, however, were very different. In 1999, the top 20 brands accounted for 79% of pharmaceutical revenues while the remaining brands yielded 21% of revenues.

Novartis Exhibit 1 presents sales, anticipated sales growth rates, cost and other data for the 50 smallest global base business brands that account for CHF 422 million in sales (or approximately 2.7% of pharmaceutical product sales) in 1998. In addition to the base business brands listed in Novartis Exhibit 1, 15 other product brands contributed an additional CHF 2.4 million in revenues. Although these products generated very small revenues, they satisfied some important medical needs. For example, Visken had sales of CHF 114,000 in South Africa but it was unique among betablockers regarding the effect on serotonin 1a receptors for the onset of antidepressant action.

Novartis Exhibit 1 subdivides costs into variable costs and fixed costs. A *variable cost* changes in total in proportion to changes in the related level of total activity or volume. An example of a variable cost is direct materials used to make the product. If sales are small, variable costs are small. As sales increase, variable costs increase proportionately as well.

A *fixed cost* remains unchanged in total for a given time period despite wide changes in the related level of total activity or volume. Examples of fixed costs are costs of operating the plant and costs of drug regulatory affairs to maintain registration of products. In the long run, however, fixed costs can sometimes be adjusted to match the levels needed to support future activity levels or production volumes. Commenting on the fixed costs reported in Novartis Exhibit 1, Andre Khairallah, Head of Controlling, commented:

> Dropping a few products out of the 50 products shown in Appendix 1 will not result in savings in fixed costs even in the long run. We already have idle capacity in our plants so dropping a few of these products will only result in even more idle capacity. If we drop all 50 products, some of the fixed costs in technical operations, production scheduling, drug registration, warehousing and inventory management, and distribution will be saved. If we dropped all 50 products, we can reduce the headcount and space used to support these products, something we cannot do if we drop only two or three products. I estimate that we can save 50% of the total fixed costs if we dropped all

Source: Reprinted by permission of Harvard Business School

Harvard Business School case 9-100-105.
The case was prepared by Srikant Datar as the basis for class discussion rather than to illustrate either effective or ineffective handling of an administrative situation.

Novartis Exhibit 1

Base Business Brands for Global Divestment (Basic Projection)

Brands	No. of Countries In which Brand is Sold	Sales 1999 Million CHF	Growth % from 98-99	Growth % p.a. proj. 99-09 for Novartis	Variable Costs in Million CHF	Fixed Costs in Million CHF
Spasmo-Cibalgin/+ Comp.	14	29	−3%	1%	4.8	0.7
Slow-K/KCL-Retard	18	26	−23	0	2.1	1.4
Pamelor (L:Lilly)	2	27	−15	−15	1.3	1
Insidon	9	22	−21	−3	5.2	3.6
Trasicor/+ Comb.	WW	22	−14	−10	5.9	0.4
Restoril (L:Wyeth/Am.Ho.Pr.)	3	18	−35	−10	9.1	2.9
Lentaron (L: A. Brodie)	20	14	−44	−20	2.4	0.2
Termalgin	2	24	8	−5	8	3.5
Sintrom	18	24	1	5	8.3	0.6
Cibacalcin	7	15	−23	−15	7.4	0.2
Tonopan	7	15	−13	−5	5.1	0.5
Locacorten/-Vioform	WW	14	−7	−5	3.9	1.2
Calcibronat−/+ Vit.B1	6	0	−10	0	0.1	0.1
Parsel	8	11	−23	0	4.7	1.1
Locasalen /Logamel	WW	10	−18	−2	2.9	1
Norprolac	19	11	−8	8	4.5	0.2
Teronac	8	12	−4	−12	3.6	0.2
Adelphan-Esidrex	7	13	32	0	6.6	0.2
Apresolin	17	8	−24	−7	1.8	0.5
Bellergal/+ Retard	8	6	−43	0	0.6	0.1
Nitroglycerin/Triniplas	3	13	51	5	4.5	0.7
Esidrex	9	9	5	2	1.7	1.4
Torecan	8	8	−8	−10	1.8	0.4
Entumin	8	8	1	−5	2.4	1.3
Aminocardol	3	5	−24	−5	1.6	0.4
Digoxin	9	8	−1	0	2.5	0.2
Noveril	7	5	−8	−7	2.7	0.8
Sicorten/-Plus	10	5	−14	3	1.4	0.3
Talotren	3	6	−13	−10	2.1	0.9
Navispare	2	4	−18	−15	0.9	0.6
Ser-Ap-Es	5	4	−15	−20	1	0.5
Muricalm/ Calmixene	3	3	−11	−2	0.4	0.5
Tremaril	3	2	−53	−20	0.7	0.3
Leptilan (L:Welding)	6	3	−8	−11	1.2	0.1
Nepresol	3	3	−12	−15	0.8	0
Estulic	6	2	−7	−12	1.2	0.4
Nadex/Pridana	2	2	−26	0	0	0.3
Cortison-Ciba	2	2	−14	−12	1	0.2

continued

Novartis Exhibit 1 (cont'd.)

Brands	No. of Countries In which Brand is Sold	Sales 1999 Million CHF	Growth % from 98-99	Growth % p.a. proj. 99-09 for Novartis	Variable Costs in Million CHF	Fixed Costs in Million CHF
Yermonil	2	1	−27%	−12%	0.4	0.2
Anturan	4	1	−6	−20	0.4	0.1
Ultracorten	2	1	−4	−10	0.4	0.2
Visergil	2	1	−23	−10	0.9	0.2
Neo-Intestopan	2	1	3	−9	0.3	0.2
Vioform/-Hydrocortison	3	2	−29	−15	0.4	0.2
Resoferon	4	1	−13	−1	0	0.1
Pertofran	5	1	−2	−15	5.9	0
Esiteren	2	1	−4	−11	0.2	0.1
Sulfacol AG	2	1	−23	−5	0.1	0.1
Millicorten	2	1	0	0	0.3	0.1
Nupercainal	2	1	−30	−4	0.3	0.1
50 Brands		**422**			**125.6**	**30.8**
− growth in % c.a.			−13	−3		
− % of sales		2.7%				

Source: Novartis

50 products. Of course, this will result in a one-time restructuring charge such as for severance costs and disposal of equipment of CHF 15 million (which is roughly equal to 1 year's savings in fixed cost).

Andrew Kay, Head of Global Marketing, reflected on the products in Novartis Exhibit 1.

Many of these products consist of products whose sales are declining mainly because Novartis is either unable to or does not find it worthwhile to put marketing resources behind them. Of course, these products constitute a significant percentage of total sales in some countries and an insignificant percentage in others.

Novartis Exhibit 2 shows that brands slated for possible divestment constituted 11.1% of the sales in Chile but only 1.8% of the sales in Australia. One alternative before Ebeling was to simply stop producing these products. Novartis would lose revenues on these products but it would also save costs. Dropping products would simplify manufacturing operations and focus the organization and sales and marketing on a few key products. A concern was the negative effects such discontinuation or withdrawal would have on Novartis's relationships with Health Maintenance Organizations (HMOs), doctors, and patients in the different countries, particularly in countries where these products were a significant percentage of sales.

Ebeling wondered whether there were other alternatives to divestment that he should consider. One possibility was to increase the marketing resources put behind these products. Currently, the direct marketing costs incurred to support these products were minimal. The products were already in the mature phases of their life cycles and with little or no investment in them, the projected growth rates were mostly negative. Of course, in the late stages of their life cycles, it was unclear whether devoting marketing resources to these products would have any effect.

Another possibility was to find a company willing to buy these products from Novartis. Typically, such a company would be a smaller company with a lower cost structure than Novartis. A company buying these products would then have the right to produce, market, promote and sell these products over several years.

Novartis Exhibit 2

Impact of Divestment on Country Sales Organizations (CSOs)

	Sales 1999 CHF Million	Total Divestment CHF Million	Total Divestment in % CSO
Pharma Total	15,617	422	2.7%
Venezuela	63	7	10.9
Ecuador	19	1	7.7
Chile	39	4	11.1
France Export	91	3	3.0
PHA Pakistan	53	3	6.2
Spain	460	42	9.1
Italy	680	33	4.8
Germany	1,077	72	6.7
Peru	22	2	7.8
Czechoslovakia	40	1	3.4
India	89	2	1.8
Uruguay	28	2	6.8
Portugal	165	2	1.5
Switzerland	180	9	5.1
Morocco	15	1	7.1
Turkey	201	10	5.1
South Africa	88	5	5.5
Amer. Central & Carib.	92	4	4.0
Austria	127	4	3.5
Egypt Pharma	111	5	4.8
Bangladesh	8	0	5.0
Indonesia	18	1	5.4
Colombia	53	2	4.6
Mexico	248	12	4.8
Thailand	29	1	3.3
Brazil	497	18	3.7
Novartis Pharma Services	378	21	5.5
Hungary	64	3	5.2
Taiwan	78	4	4.5
Poland	89	2	2.1
Philippines	49	1	2.9
Nov. Ent. India	14	3	21.0
United Kingdom	540	11	2.0
Singapore	12	0	2.0
France	952	23	2.4
Novartis Pharma Basel	81	0	0.5
Greece	161	4	2.6
Argentina	166	4	2.3
Canada	305	7	2.3
Netherlands	112	2	2.0

continued

Novartis Exhibit 2 (cont'd.)

	Sales 1999 CHF Million	Total Divestment CHF Million	Total Divestment in % CSO
Belgium	181	3	1.8%
Japan	1,801	27	1.5
Hong Kong	33	1	1.8
Australia	167	3	1.8
Malaysia	10	0	1.5
New Zealand	32	1	2.1
Ireland	33	0	1.0
USA	5,487	50	0.9
China	87	1	1.5
Norway	26	0	0.9
Finland	72	1	0.8
Sweden	78	1	1.0
Denmark	39	0	0.7
South Korea	66	0	0.4

Source: Novartis

A final issue was the management reporting and incentive system. Country sector heads and their sales organizations were evaluated on the basis of sales minus local country costs—the items on the income statements that the country managers could most directly influence. In their performance evaluation systems the countries were not charged by Novartis for the costs incurred to manufacture the goods that were sold because the country managers had no control over these manufacturing costs. The effect of pruning or divesting products is that overall country sales revenues could be adversely affected without a corresponding decrease in local country costs. This could have a negative impact on a country's performance measures and hence on managers' bonus payments.

Assignment Questions

1. Please refer to the data on Pertofran and Visergil in Novartis Exhibit 1. Would you recommend that Novartis drop these products because the total cost of these products exceeds the total revenues?
2. What strategic factors would you consider in deciding whether to drop all 50 products shown in Novartis Exhibit 1 and the 15 other product brands described in paragraph 3 of the case?
3. Would you recommend that Novartis drop all the 50 products shown in Novartis Exhibit 1? What is the net present value gained or lost from dropping all these 50 products? Assume a discount rate of 12%. What are the factors that go into determining this rate?
4. Suppose Novartis was able to find a buyer for all the 50 products shown in Novartis Exhibit 1. What price should Novartis charge the buyer?
5. Comment on the incentive issues described in the last paragraph of the case. What, if anything, would you do to address these issues?
6. What would you recommend Thomas Ebeling should do with respect to the 50 products shown in Novartis Exhibit 1 and the 15 product brands described in paragraph 3 of the case?

Quality, Inventory Management, and Time

10

Learning Objectives

1. Explain the four cost categories in a costs-of-quality program
2. Develop nonfinancial measures and methods to improve quality
3. Combine financial and nonfinancial measures to make decisions and evaluate quality performance
4. Balance ordering costs with carrying costs using the economic-order-quantity (EOQ) decision model
5. Describe why companies are using just-in-time (JIT) purchasing
6. Identify the features and benefits of a just-in-time production system
7. Describe customer-response time and explain why delays happen and their costs

To satisfy ever-increasing customer expectations, managers at companies such as Samsung, Sony, Texas Instruments, and Toyota find cost-effective ways to continuously improve the quality of their products and services, shorten response times, and reduce the quantities of inventories they hold. They balance the costs of achieving these improvements against the benefits from higher performance. Improving quality, reducing inventories, and decreasing response times is hard work but when companies do not make these improvements, the losses can be substantial.

This chapter covers three topics that give companies a competitive advantage. The first topic addresses quality as a competitive tool, looking at quality from multiple perspectives—financial, customer, and process—before discussing how managers evaluate quality performance. The second topic describes the components of inventory management, relevant costs for different inventory-related decisions, and planning and control systems such as just-in-time systems for reducing inventory. The third topic addresses time as a competitive tool and focuses on customer response time, on-time performance, time drivers, and the cost of time. The Chapter at a Glance presents a summary of the key ideas presented in this chapter.

Chapter at a Glance

- Costs-of-quality are the prevention costs to reduce poor quality; appraisal costs to detect poor quality; internal failure costs when defective products are produced; and external failure costs when defective products are shipped to customers.
- Managers also measure quality using nonfinancial measures, such as number of customer complaints, percentage of defective and reworked products, and percentage of employees trained in quality.
- Techniques such as control charts, Pareto diagrams that indicate how frequently each type of failure occurs, and cause-and-effect diagrams to identify quality problems help managers make quality improvements.
- Managers make purchasing decisions using the economic order quantity decision model balancing the costs of ordering and carrying inventory. As companies improve quality and streamline ordering, managers make purchases just-in-time to meet production (or sales) needs.
- Many companies have implemented just-in-time (JIT) production systems, a "demand-pull approach" in which a company manufactures goods only after receiving customer orders. Managers find that JIT production improves flow of information, quality, and delivery performance and reduces costs.
- Delivering a product or service quickly to customers is a source of competitive advantage. Managers identify and manage bottlenecks to reduce costly delays.

Learning Objective 1

Explain the four cost categories in a costs-of-quality program

. . . prevention, appraisal, internal failure, and external failure costs

Quality as a Competitive Tool

The American Society for Quality defines **quality** as the total features and characteristics of a product or a service made or performed according to specifications to satisfy customers at the time of purchase and during use. Many companies throughout the world—like Cisco Systems and Motorola in the United States and Canada, British Telecom in the United Kingdom, Fujitsu and Honda in Japan, Crysel in Mexico, and Samsung in South Korea—emphasize quality as an important strategic initiative. These companies have found that focusing on the quality of a product or service generally builds expertise in producing it, lowers the costs of providing it, creates higher satisfaction for customers using it, and generates higher future revenues for the company selling it. Several high-profile awards, such as the Malcolm Baldrige National Quality Award in the United States, the Deming Prize in Japan, and the Premio Nacional de Calidad in Mexico, are given to companies that have produced high-quality products and services.

International quality standards have also emerged. ISO 9000, developed by the International Organization for Standardization, is a set of five international standards for quality management adopted by more than 85 countries. ISO 9000 enables companies to effectively document and certify the elements of their production processes that lead to quality. To ensure that their suppliers deliver high-quality products at competitive costs, companies such as DuPont and General Electric require their suppliers to obtain ISO 9000 certification. Documenting evidence of quality through ISO 9000 has become a necessary condition for competing in the global marketplace.

As corporations' responsibilities toward the environment grow, managers are applying the quality management and measurement practices discussed in this chapter to find cost-effective ways to reduce the environmental and economic costs of air pollution, wastewater, oil spills, and hazardous waste disposal. An environmental management standard, ISO 14000, encourages organizations to pursue environmental goals vigorously by developing (1) environmental management systems to reduce environmental costs and (2) environmental auditing and performance-evaluation systems to review and provide feedback on environmental goals. Nowhere has the issue of quality and the environment come together in a bigger way than at the British Petroleum (BP) Deepwater Horizon oil rig in the Gulf of Mexico. An explosion on the oil-drilling platform in April 2010 resulted in the deaths of 11 workers and millions of gallons of oil spilling out in the Gulf over 3 months, causing environmental damage over thousands of square miles and resulting in billions of dollars of cleanup costs for BP.

We focus on two basic aspects of quality: design quality and conformance quality. **Design quality** refers to how closely the characteristics of a product or service meet the needs and wants of customers. **Conformance quality** is the performance of a product or service relative to its design and product specifications. Apple Inc. has built a reputation for design quality by developing many innovative products such as the iPod, iPhone, and iPad that have uniquely met customers' music, telephone, entertainment, and business needs. Apple's products have also had excellent conformance quality; the products did what they were supposed to do. In the case of the iPhone 4, however, many customers complained about very weak signal receptions on their phones. The enthusiastic customer response to the iPhone 4 when Apple launched it in the summer of 2010 indicates good design quality, as customers liked what the iPhone 4 had to offer. The problem with its antenna that caused signals not to be received is a problem of conformance quality because the phone did not do what Apple designed it to do. The following diagram illustrates that actual performance can fall short of customer satisfaction because of design-quality failure and because of conformance-quality failure.

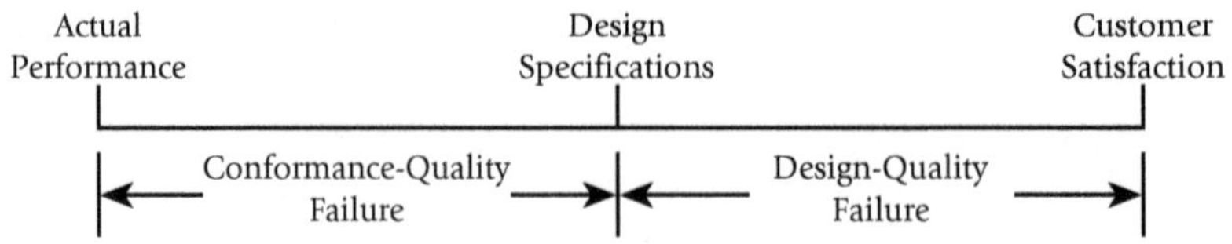

We illustrate the issues in managing quality—computing the costs of quality, identifying quality problems, and taking actions to improve quality—using Photon Corporation. While Photon makes many products, we focus only on Photon's photocopying machines, which earned an operating income of $24 million on revenues of $300 million (from sales of 20,000 copiers) in 2012.

The Financial Perspective: Costs of Quality

Financial measures include measures such as revenue and operating income growth that are impacted by quality. The most direct financial measure of quality, however, is *costs of quality*. **Costs of quality (COQ)** are the costs incurred to prevent the production of a low-quality product or the costs arising as a result of such products. Costs of quality are classified into the following four categories; examples for each category are listed in Exhibit 10-1.

1. **Prevention costs**—costs incurred to prevent the production of products that do not conform to specifications
2. **Appraisal costs**—costs incurred to detect which of the individual units of products do not conform to specifications
3. **Internal failure costs**—costs incurred on defective products *before* they are shipped to customers
4. **External failure costs**—costs incurred on defective products *after* they have been shipped to customers

The items in Exhibit 10-1 arise in all business functions of the value chain.

Photon determines the COQ of its photocopying machines by adapting the seven-step activity-based costing approach described in Chapter 6.

Step 1: Identify the Chosen Cost Object. The cost object is the quality of the photocopying machine that Photon made and sold in 2012. Photon's goal is to calculate the total costs of quality of these 20,000 machines.

Step 2: Identify the Direct Costs of Quality of the Product. The photocopying machines have no direct costs of quality because there are no resources such as inspection or repair workers dedicated to managing the quality of the photocopying machines.

Step 3: Select the Activities and Cost-Allocation Bases to Use for Allocating Indirect Costs of Quality to the Product. Column 1 in Exhibit 10-2, Panel A, classifies the activities that result in prevention, appraisal, and internal and external failure costs of quality at Photon Corporation and the business functions of the value chain in which these costs occur. For example, the quality-inspection activity results in appraisal costs and occurs in the manufacturing function. Photon identifies the total number of inspection-hours (across all products) as the cost-allocation base for the inspection activity. (To avoid details not needed to explain the concepts here, we do not show the total quantities of each cost-allocation base.)

Step 4: Identify the Indirect Costs of Quality Associated with Each Cost-Allocation Base. These are the total costs (variable and fixed) incurred for each of the costs-of-quality activities, such as inspections, across all of Photon's products. (To avoid details not needed to understand the points described here, we do not present these total costs.)

Step 5: Compute the Rate per Unit of Each Cost-Allocation Base. For each activity, total costs (identified in Step 4) are divided by total quantity of the cost-allocation base (calculated in Step 3) to compute the rate per unit of each cost-allocation base. Column 2 in Exhibit 10-2, Panel A, shows these rates (without supporting calculations).

Exhibit 10-1
Items Pertaining to Costs-of-Quality Reports

Prevention Costs	Appraisal Costs	Internal Failure Costs	External Failure Costs
Design engineering Process engineering Supplier evaluations Preventive equipment maintenance Quality training Testing of new materials	Inspection Online product manufacturing and process inspection Product testing	Spoilage Rework Scrap Machine repairs Manufacturing/process engineering on internal failures	Customer support Manufacturing/process engineering for external failures Warranty repair costs Liability claims

Exhibit 10-2

Analysis of Activity-Based Costs of Quality (COQ) for Photocopying Machines at Photon Corporation

Home Insert Page Layout Formulas Data Review View

	A	B	C	D	E	F	G
1	**PANEL A: ACCOUNTING COQ REPORT**						**Percentage of**
2		**Cost Allocation**		**Quantity of Cost**		**Total**	**Revenues**
3	**Cost of Quality and Value-Chain Category**	**Rate[a]**		**Allocation Base**		**Costs**	**(5) = (4) ÷**
4	**(1)**	**(2)**		**(3)**		**(4) = (2) x (3)**	**$300,000,000**
5	*Prevention costs*						
6	Design engineering (R&D/Design)	$ 80	per hour	40,000	hours	$ 3,200,000	1.1%
7	Process engineering (R&D/Design)	$ 60	per hour	45,000	hours	2,700,000	0.9%
8	Total prevention costs					5,900,000	2.0%
9	*Appraisal costs*						
10	Inspection (Manufacturing)	$ 40	per hour	240,000	hours	9,600,000	3.2%
11	Total appraisal costs					9,600,000	3.2%
12	*Internal failure costs*						
13	Rework (Manufacturing)	$100	per hour	100,000	hours	10,000,000	3.3%
14	Total internal failure costs					10,000,000	3.3%
15	*External failure costs*						
16	Customer support (Marketing)	$ 50	per hour	12,000	hours	600,000	0.2%
17	Transportation (Distribution)	$240	per load	3,000	loads	720,000	0.2%
18	Warranty repair (Customer service)	$110	per hour	120,000	hours	13,200,000	4.4%
19	Total external failure costs					14,520,000	4.8%
20	Total costs of quality					$40,020,000	13.3%
21							
22	[a]Calculations not shown.						
23							
24	**PANEL B: OPPORTUNITY COST ANALYSIS**						
25						**Total Estimated**	**Percentage**
26						**Contribution**	**of Revenues**
27	**Cost of Quality Category**					**Margin Lost**	**(3) = (2) ÷**
28	**(1)**					**(2)**	**$300,000,000**
29	*External failure costs*						
30	Estimated forgone contribution margin						
31	and income on lost sales					$12,000,000[b]	4.0%
32	Total external failure costs					$12,000,000	4.0%
33							
34	[b]Calculated as total revenues minus all variable costs (whether output-unit, batch, product-sustaining, or facility-sustaining) on						
35	lost sales in 2012. If poor quality causes Photon to lose sales in subsequent years as well, the opportunity costs will be						
36	even greater.						

Step 6: Compute the Indirect Costs of Quality Allocated to the Product. The indirect costs of quality of the photocopying machines, shown in Exhibit 10-2, Panel A, column 4, equal the cost-allocation rate from Step 5 (column 2) multiplied by the total quantity of the cost-allocation base used by the photocopying machines for each activity (column 3). For example, inspection costs for ensuring the quality of the photocopying machines are $9,600,000 ($40 per hour × 240,000 inspection-hours).

Step 7: Compute the Total Costs of Quality by Adding All Direct and Indirect Costs of Quality Assigned to the Product. Photon's total costs of quality in the COQ report for photocopying machines is $40.02 million (Exhibit 10-2, Panel A, column 4) or 13.3% of current revenues (column 5).

As we have seen in Chapter 9, opportunity costs are not recorded in financial accounting systems. Yet, a significant component of costs of quality is the opportunity cost of the contribution margin and income forgone from lost sales, lost production, and lower prices resulting from poor design and conformance quality. Photon's market research department estimates that design and conformance quality problems experienced by some customers resulted in lost sales of 2,000 photocopying machines in 2012 and forgone contribution margin and operating income of $12 million (Exhibit 10-2, Panel B). Total costs of quality, including opportunity costs, equal $52.02 million ($40.02 million recorded in the accounting system and shown in Panel A + $12 million of opportunity costs shown in Panel B), or 17.3% of current revenues. Opportunity costs account for 23.1% ($12 million ÷ $52.02 million) of Photon's total costs of quality.

We turn next to the leading indicators of external failure costs, the nonfinancial measures of customer satisfaction about the quality of Photon's photocopiers.

Keys to Success

Costs of quality help managers identify how much they are spending on prevention costs, appraisal costs, internal failure costs, and external failure costs. The objective is to reduce failure costs and total costs of quality.

Using Nonfinancial Measures to Evaluate and Improve Quality

Learning Objective 2

Develop nonfinancial measures

. . . customer satisfaction measures such as number of customer complaints, internal-business process measures such as percentage of defective and reworked products, and quality training measures such as employee empowerment and training

and methods to improve quality

. . . control charts, Pareto diagrams, and cause-and-effect diagrams

Companies such as Unilever, Federal Express, and TiVo use nonfinancial measures to manage quality. Almost always, the first step is to look at quality through the eyes of customers. Managers then turn their attention inward to build processes that help improve quality and cultures that help sustain it.

The Customer Perspective: Nonfinancial Measures of Customer Satisfaction

Photon's managers track the following measures of customer satisfaction:

- Market research information on customer preferences for and customer satisfaction with specific product features (to measure design quality)
- Market share
- Percentage of highly satisfied customers
- Number of defective units shipped to customers as a percentage of total units shipped
- Number of customer complaints (Companies estimate that for every customer who actually complains, there are 10–20 others who have had bad experiences with the product or service but did not complain.)
- Percentage of products that fail soon after delivery
- Average delivery delays (difference between the scheduled delivery date and the date requested by the customer)
- On-time delivery rate (percentage of shipments made on or before the scheduled delivery date)

Photon's managers monitor whether these numbers improve or deteriorate over time. Higher customer satisfaction should lead to lower external failure costs, lower costs of quality and higher future revenues from greater customer retention, loyalty, and positive word-of-mouth advertising. Lower customer satisfaction indicates that external failure costs and costs of quality will likely increase in the future. We next discuss internal business processes to identify and analyze quality problems that help to improve quality and increase customer satisfaction.

The Internal-Business-Process Perspective: Analyzing Quality Problems and Improving Quality

We present three techniques for identifying and analyzing quality problems: control charts, Pareto diagrams, and cause-and-effect diagrams.

Exhibit 10-3

Statistical Quality Control Charts: Daily Defect Rate for Photocopying Machines at Photon Corporation

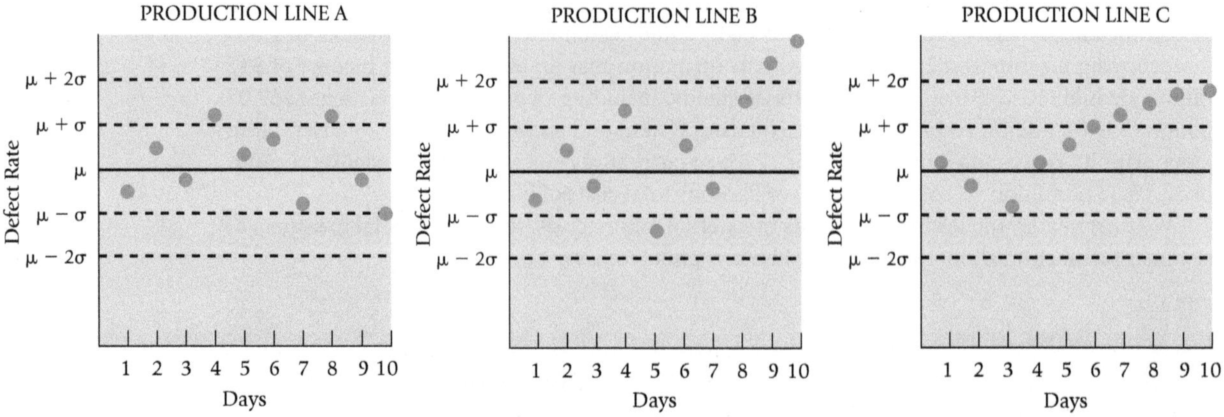

Control Charts. Statistical quality control (SQC), also called statistical process control (SPC), is a formal means of distinguishing between random and nonrandom variations in an operating process. Random variations occur, for example, when chance fluctuations in the speed of equipment cause defective products to be produced, such as copiers that produce fuzzy and unclear copies or copies that are too light or too dark. Nonrandom variations occur when defective products are produced as a result of a systematic problem such as an incorrect speed setting, a flawed part design, or mishandling of a component part. A **control chart,** an important tool in SQC, is a graph of a series of successive observations of a particular step, procedure, or operation taken at regular intervals of time. Each observation is plotted relative to specified ranges that represent the limits within which observations are expected to fall. Only those observations outside the control limits are ordinarily regarded as nonrandom and worth investigating.

Exhibit 10-3 presents control charts for the daily defect rates (defective copiers divided by the total number of copiers produced) observed at Photon's three photocopying-machine production lines. Defect rates in the prior 60 days for each production line were assumed to provide a good basis from which to calculate the distribution of daily defect rates. The arithmetic mean (μ, read as mu) and standard deviation (σ, read as sigma, how much an observation deviates from the mean) are the two parameters of the distribution that are used in the control charts in Exhibit 10-3. On the basis of experience, the company decides that managers should investigate any observation outside the $\mu \pm 2\sigma$ range.

For production line A, all observations are within the range of $\mu \pm 2\sigma$, so managers believe no investigation is necessary. For production line B, the last two observations signal that a much higher percentage of copiers are not performing as they should, indicating that the problem is probably because of a nonrandom, out-of-control occurrence such as an incorrect speed setting or mishandling of a component part. Given the $\pm 2\sigma$ rule, both observations would be investigated. Production line C illustrates a process that would not prompt an investigation under the $\pm 2\sigma$ rule but that may well be out of control because the last eight observations show a clear direction, and over the last 6 days, the percentage of defective copiers is increasing and getting further and further away from the mean. The pattern of observations moving away from the mean could be due, for example, to the tooling on a machine beginning to wear out, resulting in poorly machined parts. As the tooling deteriorates further, the trend in producing defective copiers is likely to persist until the production line is no longer in statistical control. Statistical procedures have been developed using the trend as well as the variation to evaluate whether a process is out of control.

Pareto Diagrams. Observations outside control limits serve as inputs for Pareto diagrams. A **Pareto diagram** is a chart that indicates how frequently each type of defect occurs, ordered from the most frequent to the least frequent. Exhibit 10-4 presents a Pareto diagram of quality problems for all observations outside the control limits at the final inspection point in 2012. Copiers that produce fuzzy and unclear copies are the most frequently recurring problem, and they result in high rework costs. Sometimes these problems are detected at customer sites and result in high warranty and repair costs and low customer satisfaction.

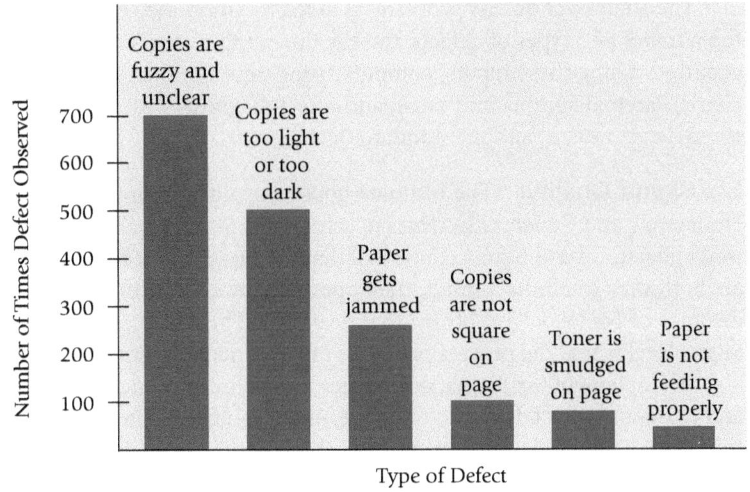

Exhibit 10-4
Pareto Diagram for Photocopying Machines at Photon Corporation

Cause-and-Effect Diagrams. The most frequently recurring and costly problems identified by the Pareto diagram are analyzed using cause-and-effect diagrams. A **cause-and-effect diagram** identifies potential causes of defects using a diagram that resembles the bone structure of a fish (so, cause-and-effect diagrams are also called *fishbone diagrams*).[1] Exhibit 10-5 presents the cause-and-effect diagram describing potential reasons for fuzzy and unclear copies. The "backbone" of the diagram represents the problem being examined. The large "bones" coming off the backbone represent the main categories of potential causes of failure. The exhibit identifies four of these: human factors, methods and design factors, machine-related factors, and materials and components factors. Photon's engineers identify the materials and components factor as an important reason for the fuzzy and unclear copies. Additional arrows or bones are added to provide more detailed reasons for each higher-level cause. For example, the engineers determine that two potential causes of material and component problems are variation in purchased components and incorrect component specifications. They quickly settle on variation in purchased components as the likely cause and focus on the use of multiple suppliers and mishandling of purchased parts as the root causes of variation in purchased components. Further analysis leads them to conclude that mishandling of the steel frame that holds in place various components of the copier such as drums, mirrors, and lenses results in the misalignment of these components, causing fuzzy and unclear copies.

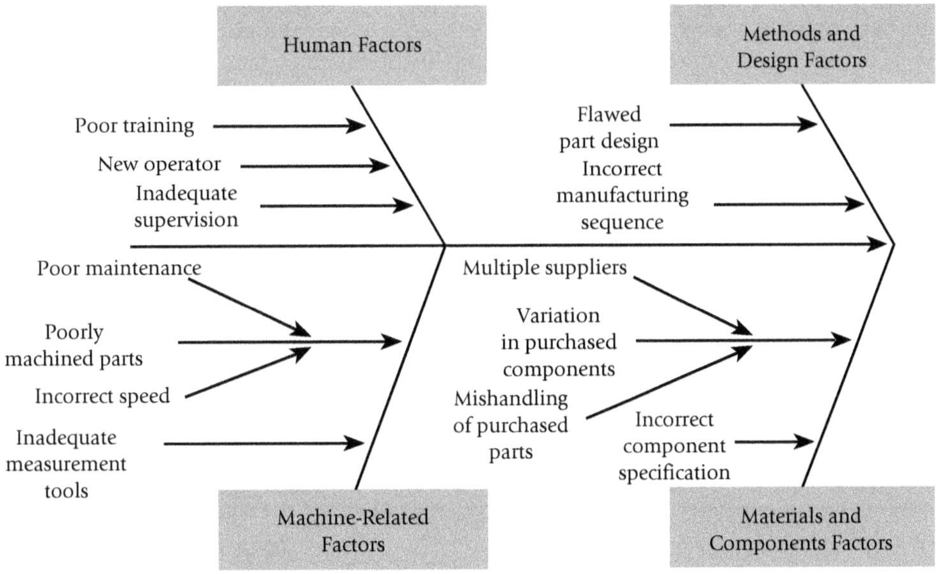

Exhibit 10-5
Cause-and-Effect Diagram for Fuzzy and Unclear Photocopies at Photon Corporation

[1] See P. Clark, "Getting the Most from Cause-and-Effect Diagrams," *Quality Progress* (June 2000).

The analysis of quality problems is aided by automated equipment and computers that record the number and types of defects and the operating conditions that existed at the time the defects occurred. Using these inputs, computer programs simultaneously and iteratively prepare control charts, Pareto diagrams, and cause-and-effect diagrams with the goal of continuously reducing the mean defect rate, μ, and the standard deviation, σ.

Six Sigma Quality. The ultimate goal of quality programs at companies such as Motorola, Honeywell, and General Electric is to achieve Six Sigma quality.[2] This means that the process is so well understood and tightly controlled that the mean defect rate, μ, and the standard deviation, σ, are both very small. As a result, the upper and lower control limits in Exhibit 10-3 can be set at a distance of 6σ (six sigma) from the mean (μ). The implication of controlling a process at a Six Sigma level is that the process produces only 3.4 defects per million products produced.

To implement Six Sigma, companies use techniques such as control charts, Pareto diagrams, and cause-and-effect diagrams to define, measure, analyze, improve, and control processes to minimize variability in manufacturing and achieve almost zero defects. Critics of Six Sigma argue that it emphasizes incremental rather than dramatic or disruptive innovation. Nevertheless, companies report substantial benefits from Six Sigma initiatives.

Nonfinancial Measures of Internal-Business-Process Quality

Companies routinely use nonfinancial measures to track the quality improvements they are making. Photon's managers use the following nonfinancial measures of internal-business-process quality:

- Percentage of defective products manufactured
- Percentage of reworked products
- Number of different types of defects analyzed using control charts, Pareto diagrams, and cause-and-effect diagrams
- Number of design and process changes made to improve design quality or reduce costs of quality

Photon's managers believe that improving these measures will lead to greater customer satisfaction, lower costs of quality, and better financial performance.

Quality Training and Quality Improvement Measures

What are the drivers of internal-business-process quality? Photon's managers believe that recruiting outstanding design engineers, providing more employee training, lowering employee turnover, and greater employee empowerment and satisfaction will reduce the number of defective products and increase customer satisfaction, leading to better financial performance. To create a quality culture, managers encourage employees to continuously strive to improve quality by identifying and eliminating root causes of defects. Photon measures the following factors:

- Experience and qualifications of design engineers
- Employee turnover (ratio of number of employees who leave the company to the average total number of employees)
- Employee empowerment (ratio of the number of processes in which employees have the right to make decisions without consulting supervisors to the total number of processes)
- Employee satisfaction (ratio of employees indicating high satisfaction ratings to the total number of employees surveyed)
- Employee training (percentage of employees trained in different quality-enhancing methods)

Concepts in Action: Toyota Plans Changes After Millions of Defective Cars Are Recalled describes quality initiatives at Toyota Motor Corporation and the challenges it faced as it focused on rapid growth.

[2] Six Sigma is a registered trademark of Motorola Inc.

Concepts in Action: Toyota Plans Changes After Millions of Defective Cars Are Recalled

Toyota Motor Corporation, the Japanese automaker, built its reputation on manufacturing reliable cars. The company trained workers in total quality management, statistical quality control, Six Sigma, Pareto diagrams, and fishbone diagrams. Toyota fostered a culture of continuous improvement and quality first by empowering workers to stop the production line if they observed defective products. In 2002, Toyota executives set an ambitious goal to grow sales by 50% to become the world's largest carmaker. The company succeeded but the focus on rapid growth appears to have come at a cost to its reputation for quality.

Source: EPA/Alamy

Between November 2009 and January 2010, Toyota was forced to recall 9 million vehicles worldwide because gas pedals began to stick and were causing unwanted acceleration on eight Toyota models. The company recalled 12 models and suspended the production and sales of eight new Toyota and Lexus models, including its popular Camry and Corolla sedans, resulting in a loss of revenue of as much as $500 million per week.

To restore its credibility and reputation for quality, Toyota (1) established a quality committee led by Akio Toyoda, the company's chief executive; (2) announced plans to add a brake override system to all new models; (3) added four new quality training facilities; and (4) promised faster decisions on future recall situations. "Listening to consumer voices is most important in regaining credibility from our customers," Mr. Toyoda said.

Sources: Based on Wendy Kaufman, "Can Toyota recover its reputation for quality?" *Morning Edition, National Public Radio* (February 9, 2010); Kate Linebaugh and Norihiko Shirouzu, "Toyota heir faces crisis at the wheel." *Wall Street Journal* (January 27, 2010); Micheline Maynard and Hiroko Tabuchi. "Rapid growth has its perils, Toyota learns." *New York Times* (January 27, 2010); Yuri Kageyama, "Toyota holds quality meeting to help repair reputation; promises quicker complaint response," *Associated Press* (March 29, 2010).

Keys to Success

Nonfinancial measures help managers understand quality from the customers' viewpoint. Managers use techniques such as control charts, Pareto diagrams, and cause-and-effect diagrams to improve quality.

Learning Objective 3

Combine financial and nonfinancial measures to make decisions and evaluate quality performance

. . . identify relevant incremental and opportunity costs to evaluate tradeoffs across costs of quality and nonfinancial measures to identify problem areas and to highlight leading indicators of future performance

Making Decisions and Evaluating Quality Performance

When making decisions and evaluating performance, managers combine financial and nonfinancial information. We use the Photon example to illustrate relevant revenues and relevant costs in the context of decisions to improve quality.

Relevant Costs and Benefits of Quality Improvement

Recall that the cause-and-effect diagram reveals that the steel frame (or chassis) of the copier is often mishandled as it travels from a supplier's warehouse to Photon's warehouse and then to the production line. The frame must meet very precise specifications or else copier components (such as drums, mirrors, and lenses) will not fit exactly on the frame. Mishandling frames during transport causes misalignment and results in fuzzy and unclear copies.

A team of engineers offers two solutions: (1) electronically inspect and test the frames before production starts or (2) redesign and strengthen the frames and their shipping containers to withstand mishandling during transportation. The cost structure for 2013 is expected to be the same as the cost structure for 2012 presented in Exhibit 10-2.

To evaluate each alternative versus the status quo, managers identify the relevant costs and benefits for each solution by focusing on *how total costs and total revenues will change under each alternative.* Relevant-cost and relevant-revenue analysis ignores allocated costs (see Chapter 9).

Photon uses only a 1-year time horizon (2013) for the analysis because it plans to introduce a completely new line of copiers at the end of 2013. The new line is so different that the choice of either the inspection or the redesign alternative will have no effect on the sales of copiers in future years. Exhibit 10-6 shows the relevant costs and benefits for each alternative.

1. **Estimated incremental costs:** $400,000 for the inspection alternative; $660,000 for the redesign alternative (process engineering, $300,000 + design engineering, $160,000 + additional cost of frames, $200,000).
2. **Cost savings from less rework, customer support, and repairs:** Exhibit 10-6, line 10, shows that reducing rework results in savings of $40 per rework-hour. Exhibit 10-2, Panel A, column 2, line 13, shows total rework cost per hour of $100. Why the difference? Because as it improves quality, Photon will only save the $40 variable cost per rework-hour, not the $60 fixed cost per rework-hour. Exhibit 10-6, line 10, shows total savings of $960,000 ($40 per rework-hour × 24,000 rework-hours saved) if it inspects the frames and $1,280,000 ($40 per rework-hour × 32,000 rework-hours saved) if it redesigns the frames. Photon's managers expect higher savings from focusing quality improvement efforts on eliminating root causes such as strengthening the frame rather than directing quality improvement efforts toward inspecting and detecting defective frames. Inspection has less impact on quality because suppliers are still shipping defective frames, some of which will escape detection. For this reason, companies such as Toyota always emphasize defect prevention ("front of the pipe solutions") over defect inspection ("back of the pipe solutions"). Exhibit 10-6 also shows expected variable-cost savings in customer support (line 11), transportation (line 12), and warranty repair (line 13) for the two alternatives.
3. **Increased contribution margin from higher sales as a result of building a reputation for quality and performance:** Exhibit 10-6, line 14 shows $1,500,000 in higher contribution margins from selling 250 more copiers under the inspection alternative and $1,800,000 from selling 300 more copiers under the redesign alternative. Management should always look for opportunities to generate higher revenues, not just cost reductions, from quality improvements.

Exhibit 10-6

Estimated Effects of Quality-Improvement Actions on Costs of Quality for Photocopying Machines at Photon Corporation

	A	B	C	D	E	F	G	H	I	J
1						Relevant Costs and Benefits of				
2				Further Inspecting Incoming Frames				Redesigning Frames		
3	Relevant Items	Relevant Benefit per Unit		Quantity		Total Benefits		Quantity		Total Benefits
4	(1)	(2)		(3)		(4)		(5)		(6)
5	Additional inspection and testing costs					$ (400,000)				
6	Additional process engineering costs									$ (300,000)
7	Additional design engineering costs									(160,000)
8	Additional cost of frames $10 per frame × 20,000 frames									(200,000)
9						(2) × (3)				(2) × (5)
10	Savings in rework costs	$ 40	per hour	24,000	hours	$ 960,000		32,000	hours	$1,280,000
11	Savings in customer-support costs	$ 20	per hour	2,000	hours	40,000		2,800	hours	56,000
12	Savings in transportation costs for repair parts	$ 180	per load	500	loads	90,000		700	loads	126,000
13	Savings in warranty repair costs	$ 45	per hour	20,000	hours	900,000		28,000	hours	1,260,000
14	Total contribution margin from additional sales	$6,000	per copier	250	copiers	1,500,000		300	copiers	1,800,000
15										
16	Net cost savings and additional contribution margin					$3,090,000				$3,862,000
17										
18	Difference in favor of redesigning frames **(J16) – (F16)**						772,000			

Exhibit 10-6 shows that both the inspection and the redesign alternatives yield net benefits relative to the status quo. However, consistent with value engineering, design for manufacturing, and kaizen or continuous improvement that emphasize eliminating the root causes of defects, Photon expects net benefits from the redesign alternative to be $772,000 greater.

Note how quality improvements affect the costs of quality. Redesigning the frame increases prevention costs (process engineering, design engineering, and additional cost of frames), but decreases internal failure costs (rework) and external failure costs (customer support, transportation costs, and warranty repairs). COQ reports provide more insight about quality improvements when managers compare trends over time. In successful quality programs, companies decrease costs of quality and, in particular, internal and external failure costs, as a percentage of revenues. Many companies, such as Hewlett-Packard, go further and believe they should eliminate all failure costs and have zero defects.

Photon's managers use both financial (COQ) and nonfinancial measures to evaluate quality performance because financial and nonfinancial measures of quality offer different benefits.

Advantages of COQ Measures

- Consistent with the attention-directing role of management accounting, COQ measures focus managers' attention on how poor quality affects operating income.
- Total COQ helps managers aggregate costs to evaluate tradeoffs among prevention costs, appraisal costs, internal failure costs, and external failure costs.
- COQ measures assist in problem solving by comparing costs and benefits of different quality-improvement programs and by setting priorities for cost reduction.

Advantages of Nonfinancial Measures of Quality

- Nonfinancial measures of quality are often easy to quantify and understand.
- Nonfinancial measures direct attention to physical processes that help managers identify the precise problem areas that need improvement.
- Nonfinancial measures, such as number of defects, provide immediate short-run feedback on whether quality-improvement efforts are succeeding.
- Nonfinancial measures such as measures of customer satisfaction and employee satisfaction are useful indicators of long-run performance.

COQ measures and nonfinancial measures complement each other. Without financial quality measures, companies could be spending more money on improving nonfinancial quality measures than it is worth. Without nonfinancial quality measures, quality problems might not be identified until it is too late. Most organizations use both types of measures to gauge quality performance. McDonald's, for example, evaluates employees and individual franchisees on multiple measures of quality and customer satisfaction. McDonald's hires an outside company who sends a "mystery shopper" to evaluate restaurant performance, scoring individual restaurants on quality, cleanliness, service, and value. McDonald's then evaluates the restaurant's performance across these dimensions over time and against other restaurants.

Keys to Success

When making decisions, managers estimate the relevant costs and relevant benefits of various alternatives and also consider non-financial factors such as customer satisfaction, process improvements, and employee satisfaction.

Learning Objective 4

Balance ordering costs with carrying costs using the economic-order-quantity (EOQ) decision model

. . . choose the inventory quantity per order to minimize these costs

Inventory Management

Many managers believe that holding units in inventory contributes to quality problems because of spoilage, shrinkage, mishandling while products are moved in and out of the warehouse, misclassification of items, and clerical errors in the recording and issuing of items in inventory. Photon's managers order large quantities of the steel frame in each order and store the frames in the warehouse before they are issued to production. To understand the inventory decisions that Photon's managers make, we first define some key terms.

1. **Purchasing costs** are the cost of goods acquired from suppliers, including incoming freight costs. These costs usually make up the largest cost category of goods in inventory. Discounts for various purchase-order sizes and supplier payment terms affect purchasing costs.
2. **Ordering costs** arise in preparing and issuing purchase orders, receiving and inspecting the items included in the orders, and matching invoices received, purchase orders, and delivery records to make payments. Ordering costs include the cost of obtaining purchase approvals, as well as other special processing costs.
3. **Carrying costs** arise while holding goods in inventory. Carrying costs include the opportunity cost of the investment tied up in inventory (see Chapter 9) and the costs associated with storage, such as space rental, insurance, obsolescence, and spoilage.
4. **Stockout costs** arise when a company runs out of a particular item for which there is customer demand, a *stockout.* The company must act quickly to replenish inventory to meet that demand or suffer the costs of not meeting it. A company may respond to a stockout by expediting an order from a supplier, which can be expensive because of additional ordering and manufacturing costs plus any associated transportation costs. Or the company may lose sales due to the stockout. In this case, the opportunity cost of the stockout includes lost contribution margin on the sale not made plus any contribution margin lost on future sales due to customer ill will.
5. **Costs of quality** are the costs incurred to prevent, or the costs arising as a result of, the production of a low-quality product. As discussed earlier in this chapter, there are four categories of quality costs: prevention costs, appraisal costs, internal failure costs, and external failure costs.
6. **Shrinkage costs** result from theft by outsiders, embezzlement by employees, misclassifications, and clerical errors. Shrinkage is measured by the difference between (a) the cost of inventory recorded on the books (after correcting errors) and (b) the cost of inventory when physically counted.

Note that not all inventory costs are available in financial accounting systems. For example, opportunity costs are not recorded in these systems and are a significant component in several of these cost categories.

Information-gathering technology increases the reliability and timeliness of inventory information and reduces costs in the six cost categories. For example, barcoding technology allows a scanner to record purchases and sales of individual units. As soon as a unit is scanned, an instantaneous record of inventory movements is created that helps in the management of purchasing, carrying, and stockout costs.

Economic-Order-Quantity Decision Model

Photon's managers make inventory purchase decisions using **economic order quantity (EOQ),** a decision model that, under a given set of assumptions, calculates the optimal quantity of inventory to order.

- The simplest version of the EOQ model assumes there are only ordering and carrying costs.
- The same quantity is ordered at each reorder point.
- Demand, ordering costs, and carrying costs are known with certainty. The **purchase-order lead time,** the time between placing an order and its delivery, is also known with certainty.
- Purchasing cost per unit is unaffected by the order quantity. This assumption makes purchasing costs irrelevant to determining EOQ because the purchase price is the same, whatever the order size.
- No stockouts occur. The basis for this assumption is that the costs of stockouts are so high that managers maintain adequate inventory to prevent them.
- In deciding on the size of a purchase order, managers consider costs of quality and shrinkage costs only to the extent that these costs affect ordering or carrying costs.

Given these assumptions, EOQ analysis ignores purchasing costs, stockout costs, costs of quality, and shrinkage costs. EOQ is the order quantity that minimizes the relevant ordering and carrying costs (that is, the ordering and carrying costs affected by the quantity of inventory ordered):

$$\text{Relevant total costs} = \text{Relevant ordering costs} + \text{Relevant carrying costs}$$

We use the following notations:

D = Demand in units for a specified period (1 year in this example)

Q = Size of each order (order quantity)

$$\text{Number of purchase orders per period (1 year)} = \frac{\text{Demand in units for a period (1 year)}}{\text{Size of each order (order quantity)}} = \frac{D}{Q}$$

Average inventory in units $= \frac{Q}{2}$, because each time the inventory goes down to 0, an order for Q units is received. The inventory varies from Q to 0 so the average inventory is $\frac{0 + Q}{2}$.

P = Relevant ordering cost per purchase order

C = Relevant carrying cost of one unit in stock for the time period used for D (1 year)

For any order quantity, Q,

$$\text{Annual relevant ordering costs} = \left(\begin{matrix}\text{Number of} \\ \text{purchase orders} \\ \text{per year}\end{matrix} \times \begin{matrix}\text{Relevant ordering} \\ \text{cost per} \\ \text{purchase order}\end{matrix}\right) = \left(\frac{D}{Q} \times P\right)$$

$$\text{Annual relevant carrying costs} = \left(\begin{matrix}\text{Average inventory} \\ \text{in units}\end{matrix} \times \begin{matrix}\text{Annual} \\ \text{relevant carrying} \\ \text{cost per unit}\end{matrix}\right) = \left(\frac{Q}{2} \times C\right)$$

$$\text{Annual relevant total costs} = \begin{matrix}\text{Annual} \\ \text{relevant ordering} \\ \text{costs}\end{matrix} + \begin{matrix}\text{Annual} \\ \text{relevant carrying} \\ \text{costs}\end{matrix} = \left(\frac{D}{Q} \times P\right) + \left(\frac{Q}{2} \times C\right)$$

The order quantity that minimizes annual relevant total costs is

$$EOQ = \sqrt{\frac{2DP}{C}}$$

The EOQ model is solved using calculus but the key intuition is that relevant total costs are minimized when relevant ordering costs equal relevant carrying costs. If carrying costs are less (greater) than ordering costs, total costs can be reduced by increasing (decreasing) the order quantity. To solve for EOQ, we set

$$\left(\frac{Q}{2} \times C\right) = \left(\frac{D}{Q} \times P\right)$$

Multiplying both sides by $\frac{2Q}{C}$, we get $Q^2 = \frac{2DP}{C}$

$$Q = \sqrt{\frac{2DP}{C}}$$

The formula indicates that EOQ increases with higher demand and/or higher ordering costs and decreases with higher carrying costs.

Let's see how EOQ analysis works in Photon's purchasing decision for frames. Photon needs one frame for each photocopying machine, so the annual demand for frames is 20,000 units. The cost of each frame is \$125. Photon requires a 12% annual rate of return on investment. Relevant ordering cost per purchase order is \$875.

Relevant carrying cost per frame per year is as follows:

Required annual return on investment, 0.12 × \$125	\$15.00
Relevant costs of insurance, materials handling, breakage, shrinkage, and so on, per year	20.00
Total	\$35.00

What is the EOQ for ordering frames?

Substituting D = 20,000 frames per year, P = \$875 per order, and C = \$35.00 per frame per year, in the EOQ formula, we get,

$$EOQ = \sqrt{\frac{2 \times 20{,}000 \times \$875}{\$35.00}} = \sqrt{1{,}000{,}000} = 1{,}000 \text{ frames}$$

Purchasing 1,000 frames per order minimizes total relevant ordering and carrying costs. Therefore, the number of deliveries each period (1 year in this example) is as follows:

$$\frac{D}{EOQ} = \frac{20{,}000}{1{,}000} = 20 \text{ deliveries}$$

Recall the annual relevant total costs (RTC) $= \left(\frac{D}{Q} \times P\right) + \left(\frac{Q}{2} \times C\right)$

For $Q = 1{,}000$ frames,

$$\begin{aligned} RTC &= \frac{20{,}000 \times \$875}{1{,}000} + \frac{1{,}000 \times \$35.00}{2} \\ &= \$17{,}500 + \$17{,}500 = \$35{,}000 \end{aligned}$$

Exhibit 10-7 graphs the annual relevant total costs of ordering (DP/Q) and carrying inventory ($QC/2$) under various order sizes (Q), and it illustrates the tradeoff between these two types of costs. The larger the order quantity, the lower the annual relevant ordering costs, but the higher the annual relevant carrying costs. *Annual relevant total costs are at a minimum at the EOQ at which the relevant ordering and carrying costs are equal.*

When to Order, Assuming Certainty

The second decision Photon's managers face is *when to order* the frames. The **reorder point** is the quantity level of inventory on hand that triggers a new purchase order. The reorder point is simplest to compute when both demand and purchase-order lead time are known with certainty:

$$\text{Reorder point} = \frac{\text{Number of units sold}}{\text{per time period}} \times \frac{\text{Purchase-order}}{\text{lead time}}$$

In our Photon example, suppose the purchase-order lead time is 2 weeks:

Economic order quantity	1,000 frames
Number of units sold per week	385 frames per week (20,000 frames ÷ 52 weeks)
Purchase-order lead time	2 weeks

$$\text{Reorder point} = 385 \text{ frames per week} \times 2 \text{ weeks} = 770 \text{ frames}$$

Exhibit 10-7

Graphic Analysis of Ordering Costs and Carrying Costs for `Frames at Photon Corporation

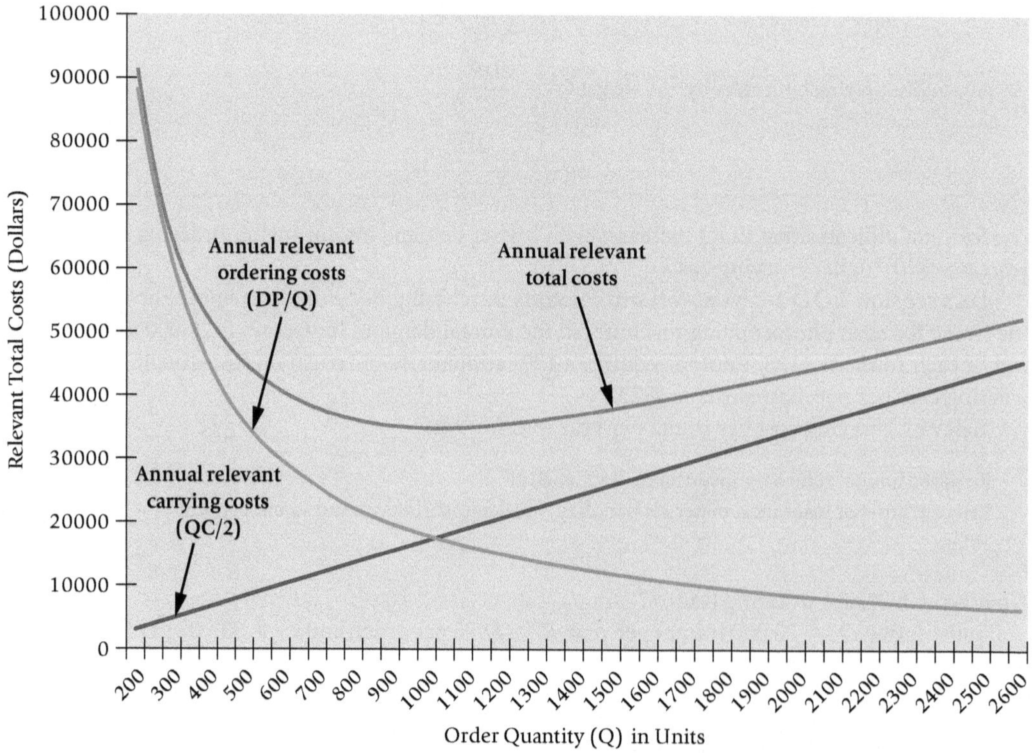

Exhibit 10-8

Inventory Level of Frames at Photon Corporation[a]

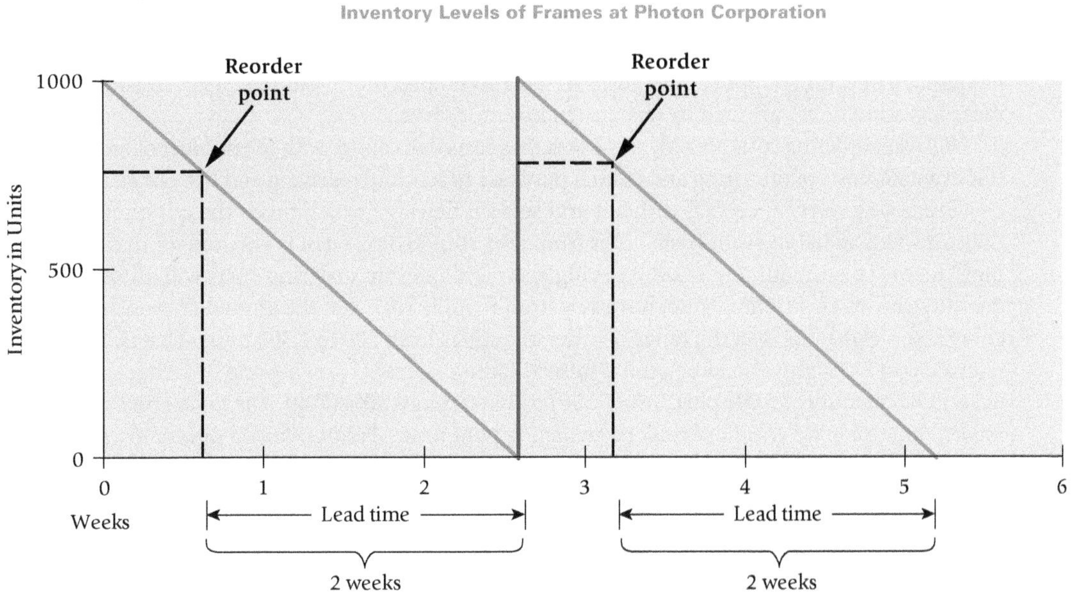

[a] This exhibit assumes that demand and purchase-order lead time are certain:
Demand = 385 frames per week
Purchase-order lead time = 2 weeks

Photon will order 1,000 frames each time inventory stock falls to 770 frames.[3] The graph in Exhibit 10-8 shows the behavior of the inventory level of frames, assuming demand occurs uniformly during each week. If purchase-order lead time is 2 weeks, a new order will be placed when the inventory level falls to 770 frames, so the 1,000 frames ordered will be received at the precise time that inventory reaches zero.

Safety Stock

Our preceding analysis assumed that Photon's managers know demand and purchase-order lead time with certainty. If managers at Photon are uncertain about demand, lead time, or the quantity that suppliers can provide, they will hold safety stock. **Safety stock** is inventory held at all times regardless of the quantity of inventory ordered using the EOQ model. Companies use safety stock as a buffer against unexpected increases in demand, uncertainty about lead time, and unavailability of stock from suppliers. The quantity of safety stock depends on the probabilities of different levels of demand and the relevant costs of stockouts. These safety stock computations are beyond the scope of this book.

Estimating Inventory-Related Relevant Costs and Their Effects

How do Photon's managers calculate the annual relevant carrying costs and ordering costs of inventory? Relevant inventory carrying costs consist of the *relevant incremental costs* plus the *relevant opportunity cost of capital.* What are the *relevant incremental costs* of carrying inventory? Only those costs, such as warehouse rent, warehouse workers' salaries, costs of obsolescence, costs of shrinkage, costs of breakage, and costs of insurance, that change with the quantity of inventory held. Salaries paid to clerks, stock keepers, and materials handlers are irrelevant if they are unaffected by changes in inventory levels. Suppose, however, that as inventories increase (decrease), total salary costs increase (decrease) as clerks, stock keepers, and materials handlers are added (transferred to other activities or laid off). In this case, salaries paid are relevant costs of carrying inventory. Similarly, costs of storage space owned that cannot be used for other profitable purposes when inventories decrease is irrelevant. But if the space has other profitable uses, or if total rental cost is tied to the amount of space occupied, storage costs are relevant costs of carrying inventory.

[3] This handy but special formula does not apply when receipt of the order fails to increase inventory to the reorder-point quantity (for example, when lead time is 3 weeks and the order is a 1-week supply). In these cases, orders will overlap.

What is the *relevant opportunity cost of capital?* It is the return forgone by investing capital in inventory rather than elsewhere. It is calculated as the required rate of return multiplied by the per-unit costs of acquiring inventory, such as the purchase price of units, incoming freight, and incoming inspection. Opportunity costs are also computed on investments (say, in equipment) if these investments are affected by changes in inventory levels.

Relevant ordering costs are only those ordering costs that change with the number of orders placed (for example, costs of preparing and issuing purchase orders and receiving and inspecting materials).

Predicting relevant costs is difficult and seldom flawless, which raises the question, "What is the cost when actual relevant costs differ from the estimated relevant costs used for decision making?" Errors in estimating relevant carrying costs and relevant ordering costs will affect the EOQ quantity chosen by Photon. Note, however, from Exhibit 10-7 that the annual relevant-total-costs curve is somewhat flat over the range of order quantities from 700 to 1,300 units. That is, the annual relevant cost is roughly the same even if misestimating relevant carrying and ordering costs results in an EOQ quantity of 1,000 plus 30% (1,300) or 1,000 minus 30% (700). *The square root in the EOQ model diminishes the effect of errors in predicting parameters because taking square roots results in the incorrect numbers becoming smaller.* However, if we consider other costs, such as costs of quality and shrinkage of holding large inventories or stock out costs of holding too little inventories, the effect of prediction errors are much bigger.

In the next section, we consider a planning-and-control and performance-evaluation issue that frequently arises when managing inventory.

Conflict Between the EOQ Decision Model and Managers' Performance Evaluation

What happens if the order quantity calculated based on the EOQ decision model differs from the order quantity that managers making inventory management decisions would choose to make their own performance look best? For example, because there are no opportunity costs recorded in financial accounting systems, conflicts may arise between the EOQ model's optimal order quantity and the order quantity that purchasing managers (who are evaluated on financial accounting numbers) will regard as optimal.

As a result of ignoring some carrying costs (the opportunity costs), managers will be inclined to purchase larger lot sizes of materials than the lot sizes calculated according to the EOQ model, particularly if larger lot sizes result in lower purchase prices. As we discussed in the previous section, the cost of these suboptimal choices is small if the quantities purchased are close to the EOQ. However, if the lot sizes become much greater, the cost to the company can be quite large. Moreover, if we consider other costs, such as costs of quality and shrinkage of holding large inventories, the cost to the company of purchasing in large lot sizes is even greater. To achieve congruence between the EOQ decision model and managers' performance evaluations, companies such as Walmart design performance-evaluation models that charge managers responsible for managing inventory levels with carrying costs that include a required return on investment.

Keys to Success

Managers use the economic-order-quantity (EOQ) decision model to balance ordering and carrying costs when calculating the optimal quantity of inventory to order. The EOQ model considers opportunity costs not recorded in the financial accounting system.

Learning Objective 5

Describe why companies are using just-in-time (JIT) purchasing

. . . high carrying costs, costs of quality, and shrinkage costs, low ordering costs, high-quality suppliers, and reliable supply chains

Just-in-Time Purchasing

Just-in-time (JIT) purchasing is the purchase of materials (or goods) so that they are delivered just as needed for production (or sales). Consider JIT purchasing for Hewlett-Packard's (HP's) manufacture of computer printers. HP has long-term agreements with suppliers for the major components of its printers. Each supplier is required to make frequent deliveries of small orders directly to the production floor, based on the production schedule that HP provides. Suppliers work hard to keep their commitments because failure to deliver components on time, or to meet agreed-upon quality standards, prevents the HP assembly plant from meeting its own scheduled deliveries for printers.

Exhibit 10-9

Sensitivity of EOQ to Variations in Relevant Ordering and Carrying Costs for Frames at Photon Corporation

Home Insert Page Layout Formulas Data Review View

	A	B	C	D	E	F	G
1				**Economic Order Quantity of Units**			
2				**At Different Ordering and Carrying Costs**			
3	Annual Demand (D) =	20,000	units				
4							
5	**Relevant Carrying Costs**			**Relevant Ordering Cost per Purchase Order (P)**			
6	**Per Package per Year (C)**			**$875.00**	**$625.00**	**$350.00**	**$100.00**
7	$35.00			1,000	845	632	338
8	$45.00			882	745	558	298
9	$55.00			798	674	505	270
10	$65.00			734	620	464	248

JIT Purchasing and EOQ Model Parameters

As Photon's managers examine the quality problems caused by defective frames held in inventory, they realize that carrying costs are actually much greater than estimated because costs of warehousing, handling, shrinkage, spoilage, and investment have not been fully identified. At the same time, the cost of placing a purchase order (parameter *P* in the EOQ model) has decreased because of the following:

- Photon is establishing long-term purchasing agreements that define price and quality terms over an extended period. Individual purchase orders covered by those agreements require no additional negotiation regarding price or quality.
- Photon is using electronic links to place purchase orders, tally delivery records, and make payments at a cost that is estimated to be a small fraction of the cost of placing orders by telephone or by mail.

Exhibit 10-9 tabulates the sensitivity of Photon's EOQ (page 407) to changes in carrying and ordering costs. Exhibit 10-9 supports moving toward JIT purchasing because, as relevant carrying costs increase and relevant ordering costs per purchase order decrease, EOQ decreases and ordering frequency increases.

Relevant Costs of JIT Purchasing

JIT purchasing is not guided solely by the EOQ model because that model only emphasizes the tradeoff between relevant carrying and ordering costs. Inventory management, however, also includes purchasing costs, stockout costs, costs of quality, and shrinkage costs. Photon's managers are concerned that ordering and storing large quantities of frames have contributed to quality and spoilage problems leading to fuzzy and unclear copies. Even as they strengthen the frame and the shipping containers to withstand mishandling during transportation, they are working on implementing JIT purchasing by asking the supplier to make more frequent deliveries of smaller sizes directly to the production floor. Photon has recently established an Internet business-to-business purchase-order link with its supplier, Sontek. Photon triggers a purchase order for frames by a single computer entry. Payments are made electronically for batches of deliveries, rather than for each individual delivery. These changes reduce ordering costs from $875 to only $100 per purchase order! Photon will use the Internet purchase-order link whether or not it shifts to JIT purchasing. We next evaluate the effect of JIT purchasing on quality and costs.

Description of Item	Current Purchasing Practice	JIT Purchasing Practice
Deliveries	1,000 frames 20 times per year	Sontek will deliver 160 frames 125 times per year (roughly 5 times every 2 weeks)
Purchasing costs	$125 per frame	$125.25 per frame because Photon will pay Sontek an extra $0.25 per frame (many companies do not pay a higher price) for more frequent deliveries.

continued

Description of Item	Current Purchasing Practice	JIT Purchasing Practice
Inspection of frames	Visual inspection of frames at the time of receipt and when issued to production at a cost of $0.50 per frame	Frames only need basic inspection at a cost of $0.20 per frame because Sontek must ensure that quality frames are delivered ready for use in production to support Photon's JIT purchasing.
Required rate of return on investment	12%	12%
Relevant carrying cost of insurance, materials handling, spoilage, etc.	$20 per frame per year	$20 per frame per year
Cost of repairing defective frames	3% of frames will require repair (3% × 20,000 = 600 frames at a cost of $25 per frame).	Fewer frames (1%) will require repair because of reduced handling of frames in and out of inventory and better quality management at both Sontek and Photon to support JIT systems (1% × 20,000 = 200 frames at a cost of $25 per frame).
Stockout costs	No stockout costs because demand and purchase-order lead times during each 2.6-week period (52 weeks ÷ 20 orders) are known with certainty.	Lower inventory levels from implementing JIT purchasing will lead to more stockouts because demand variations and delays in supplying frames are more likely in the short time intervals between orders under JIT purchasing. Photon expects to incur stockout costs on 225 frames per year under the JIT purchasing policy. When a stockout occurs, Photon must rush-order frames at an additional cost of $16 per frame.

Should Photon implement the JIT purchasing option of 125 deliveries per year? Exhibit 10-10 compares Photon's relevant total costs under the current purchasing policy and the JIT policy. It shows net cost savings of $11,598 per year by shifting to a JIT purchasing policy. The benefits of JIT purchasing arise from lower carrying costs, inspection costs, and repair costs as a result of better quality. JIT purchasing gives Photon's managers immediate feedback about defects and forces the company to improve quality by reducing the safety net afforded by large quantities of inventory. The benefits of JIT purchasing would be even greater if the analysis had included other costs of quality such as rework and warranty repair resulting from defects that are only discovered after the photocopiers have been manufactured or shipped to customers.

Supplier Evaluation and Relevant Costs of Quality and Timely Deliveries

Companies that implement JIT purchasing choose their suppliers carefully and develop long-term supplier relationships. Some suppliers are better positioned than others to support JIT purchasing. For example, Frito-Lay, a supplier of potato chips and other snack foods, has a corporate strategy

Exhibit 10-10

Annual Relevant Costs of Current Purchasing Policy and JIT Purchasing Policy for Frames at Photon Corporation

Home Insert Page Layout Formulas Data Review View

	A	B	C	D	E	F	G	H	I	J
1		Relevant Cost Under								
2		Current Purchasing Policy					JIT Purchasing Policy			
3	Relevant Items	Relevant Cost Per Unit		Quantity per Year	Total Costs		Relevant Cost Per Unit		Quantity Per Year	Total Costs
4	(1)	(2)		(3)	(4) = (2) x (3)		(5)		(6)	(7) = (5) x (6)
5	Purchasing costs	$ 125.00	per unit	20,000	$2,500,000		$ 125.25	per unit	20,000	$2,505,000
6	Ordering costs	$ 100.00	per order	20	2,000		$ 100.00	per order	125	12,500
7	Inspection costs	$ 0.50	per unit	20,000	10,000		$ 0.20	per unit	20,000	4,000
8	Opportunity carrying costs	$ 15.00[a]	per unit of average inventory per year	500[b]	7,500		$ 15.03[a]	per unit of average inventory per year	80[c]	1,202
9	Other carrying costs (insurance, materials handling, and so on)	$ 20.00	per unit of average inventory per year	500[b]	10,000		$ 20.00	per unit of average inventory per year	80[c]	1,600
10	Cost of repairing frames	$ 25.00	per unit repaired	600[d]	15,000		$ 25.00	per unit repaired	200[e]	5,000
11	Stockout costs	$ 16.00	per unit	0	-		$ 16.00	per unit	225	3,600
12	Total annual relevant costs				$2,544,500					$2,532,902
13	Annual difference in favor of JIT Purchasing					$ 11,598				
14										
15	(a) Purchasing cost per unit x 0.12 per year									
16	(b) Order quantity / 2 = 1000/2 = 500 units									
17	(c) Order quantity/2 = 160/2 = 80 units									
18	(d) 3% of units repaired x 20,000 units = 600 units									
19	(e) 1% of units repaired x 20,000 units = 200 units									

that emphasizes service, consistency, freshness, and quality of the delivered products. As a result, the company makes deliveries to retail outlets more frequently than many of its competitors.

What are the relevant total costs when choosing suppliers? Consider again the frames purchased by Photon Corporation. Denton Corporation, another supplier of frames, offers to supply all the frames that Photon needs. Photon requires the supplier to deliver 160 frames 125 times per year (roughly 5 times every 2 weeks). Photon will establish an Internet-based purchase-order link with whichever supplier it chooses, trigger a purchase order for frames by a single computer entry, and make payments electronically for batches of deliveries, rather than for each individual delivery. These changes will reduce ordering costs from $875 to only $100 per purchase order. The following table provides information about Denton and Sontek. Sontek charges a higher price than Denton but also supplies higher-quality frames. The information about Sontek is the same as that presented earlier. We only present it here to facilitate comparison with Denton.

Description of Item	Purchasing Terms from Denton	Purchasing Terms from Sontek
Purchasing costs	Denton offers a price of $124.75, which is better than Sontek's.	$125.25 per frame
Inspection of frames	Denton does not enjoy a sterling reputation for quality so Photon plans to do a more thorough inspection of frames at a cost of $0.60 per frame.	Photon has bought frames from Sontek in the past and knows that it will deliver quality frames on time. Photon does only the most basic inspection at a cost of $0.20 per frame.
Required rate of return on investment	12%	12%
Relevant carrying cost of insurance, materials handling, spoilage, etc.	$20 per frame per year	$20 per frame per year
Cost of repairing defective frames	2.75% of frames will require repair because Denton's frames are of poorer quality (2.75% × 20,000 = 550 frames at a cost of $25 per frame).	Fewer frames (1%) will require repair because of better quality management at Sontek (1% × 20,000 = 200 frames at a cost of $25 per frame).
Stockouts	Denton has less control over its processes, so Photon expects to incur stockout costs on 500 frames, each time initiating rush orders at a cost of $16 per frame.	Photon expects to incur stockout costs on 225 frames per year when it purchases from Sontek, each time resulting in a rush-order at a cost of $16 per frame.

Exhibit 10-11 shows the relevant total costs of purchasing from Sontek and Denton. Even though Denton is offering a lower price per frame, there is a net cost savings of $11,145 per year by purchasing frames from Sontek because of lower inspection, repair, and stockout costs. The benefit of purchasing from Sontek could be even greater if purchasing high-quality frames from Sontek enhances Photon's reputation and increases customer goodwill, leading to higher sales and profitability in the future.

Keys to Success

As ordering costs decrease, carrying costs increase, and quality improves, managers favor making purchases just-in-time from reliable suppliers to meet production (or sales) needs.

Learning Objective 6

Identify the features and benefits of a just-in-time production system

. . . for example, organizing work in manufacturing cells, improving quality, and reducing manufacturing lead time to reduce costs and earn higher margins

Inventory Management, MRP, and JIT Production

We now turn our attention from purchasing to managing production inventories in manufacturing companies. Two of the most widely used systems to plan and implement inventory activities within plants are materials requirements planning (MRP) and just-in-time (JIT) production.

Materials Requirements Planning

Companies such as Guidant, which manufactures medical devices and Philips, which makes consumer electronic products, use MRP systems. **Materials requirements planning (MRP)** is a "push-through" system that manufactures finished goods for inventory on the basis of demand

Exhibit 10-11

Annual Relevant Costs of Purchasing from Sontek and Denton

	A	B	C	D	E	F	G	H	I	J
1		Relevant Cost of Purchasing From								
2		Denton					Sontek			
3	Relevant Items	Relevant Cost Per Unit		Quantity per Year	Total Costs		Relevant Cost Per Unit		Quantity Per Year	Total Costs
4	(1)	(2)		(3)	(4) = (2) x (3)		(5)		(6)	(7) = (5) x (6)
5	Purchasing costs	$ 124.75	per unit	20,000	$2,495,000		$ 125.25	per unit	20,000	$2,505,000
6	Ordering costs	$ 100.00	per order	125	12,500		$ 100.00	per order	125	12,500
7	Inspection costs	$ 0.60	per unit	20,000	12,000		$ 0.20	per unit	20,000	4,000
8	Opportunity carrying costs	$ 14.97[a]	per unit of average inventory per year	80[b]	1,197		$ 15.03[a]	per unit of average inventory per year	80[b]	1,202
9	Other carrying costs (insurance, materials handling, and so on)	$ 20.00	per unit of average inventory per year	80[b]	1,600		$ 20.00	per unit of average inventory per year	80[b]	1,600
10	Cost of repairing frames	$ 25.00	per unit repaired	550[c]	13,750		$ 25.00	per unit repaired	200[d]	5,000
11	Stockout costs	$ 16.00	per unit	500	8,000		$ 16.00	per unit	225	3,600
12	Total annual relevant costs				$2,544,047					$2,532,902
13	Annual difference in favor of Sontek					$ 11,145				
14										
15	(a) Purchasing cost per unit x 0.12 per year									
16	(b) Order quantity / 2 = 160/2 = 80 units									
17	(c) 2.75% of units repaired x 20,000 units = 550 units									
18	(d) 1% of units repaired x 20,000 units = 200 units									

forecasts. To determine outputs at each stage of production, MRP uses (1) demand forecasts for final products; (2) a bill of materials detailing the materials, components, and subassemblies for each final product; and (3) available inventories of materials, components, and products. Taking into account the lead time required to purchase materials and to manufacture components and finished products, a master production schedule specifies the quantity and timing of each item to be produced. Once production starts as scheduled, the output of each department is pushed through the production line.

Just-in-Time (JIT) Production

In contrast, JIT production is a "demand-pull" approach, which is used by companies such as Toyota in the automobile industry, Dell in the computer industry, and Braun in the appliance industry. **Just-in-time (JIT) production,** which is also called **lean production,** is a "demand-pull" manufacturing system that manufactures each component in a production line as soon as, and only when, needed by the next step in the production line. Demand triggers each step of the production process, starting with customer demand for a finished product at the end of the process and working all the way back to the demand for direct materials at the beginning of the process. In this way, demand pulls an order through the production line. The demand-pull feature of JIT production systems achieves close coordination among workstations. It smooths the flow of goods, despite low quantities of inventory. JIT production systems aim to meet customer demand for high-quality products at the lowest possible total cost on a timely schedule.

Features of JIT Production Systems

A JIT production system has these features:

- Production is organized in **manufacturing cells,** groupings of all the different types of equipment used to make a given product. Materials move from one machine to another, and various operations are performed in sequence, minimizing materials-handling costs.
- Workers are hired and trained to be multiskilled and capable of performing a variety of operations and tasks, including minor repairs and routine equipment maintenance.
- Defects are aggressively eliminated. Because of the tight links between workstations in the production line and the minimal inventories at each workstation, defects arising at one workstation quickly affect other workstations in the line. JIT creates an urgency for solving problems immediately and eliminating the root causes of defects as quickly as possible. Low levels of

inventories allow workers to trace problems to and solve problems at earlier workstations in the production process, where the problems likely originated.

- *Setup time,* the time required to get equipment, tools, and materials ready to start the production of a component or product, and *manufacturing cycle time,* the time from when an order is received by manufacturing until it becomes a finished good, are reduced. Setup costs correspond to the ordering costs *P* in the EOQ model. Reducing setup time and costs makes production in smaller batches economical, which in turn reduces inventory levels. Reducing manufacturing cycle time enables a company to respond faster to customer demand (see also Concepts in Action: After the Encore: Just-in-Time Live Concert Recordings).
- Suppliers are selected on the basis of their ability to deliver quality materials in a timely manner. Most companies implementing *JIT production* also implement *JIT purchasing.* JIT plants expect JIT suppliers to make timely deliveries of high-quality goods directly to the production floor.

We next present a relevant-cost analysis for deciding whether to implement a JIT production system.

Financial Benefits of JIT and Relevant Costs

Early advocates saw the benefit of JIT production as lower carrying costs of inventory. But there are other benefits of lower inventories: heightened emphasis on improving quality by eliminating the specific causes of rework, scrap, and waste, and lower manufacturing cycle times. In computing the relevant benefits and costs of reducing inventories in JIT production systems, managers should take into account all benefits and all costs.

Consider again Photon Corporation. Photon is considering implementing a JIT production system for manufacturing the glide rails for its photocopying machines.

- To implement JIT production, Photon must incur $100,000 in annual tooling costs to reduce setup times.

Concepts in Action: After the Encore: Just-in-Time Live Concert Recordings

Each year, millions of music fans flock to concerts to see artists ranging from Pearl Jam to Phish. When fans stop by the merchandise stand to pick up a t-shirt or poster after the show ends, they increasingly have another option: buying a professional recording of the concert they just saw! Just-in-time production, enabled by advances in technology, now allows fans to relive the live concert experience just a few minutes after the final chord is played.

Source: Eddie Linssen/Alamy

Several companies, including Live Nation and Concert Live, employ microphones, recording and audio mixing hardware and software, and an army of high-speed computers to produce concert recordings during the show. As soon as each song is complete, engineers burn that track onto hundreds of CDs or USB drives. At the end of the show, they have to burn only one last song. Once completed, the CDs or USB drives are packaged and rushed to merchandise stands throughout the venue for instant sale.

Just-in-time production benefits the artists, fans, and producers: Artists get another revenue stream amidst declining album sales; fans enjoy immediate access to a high-quality recording of concerts; and producers such as Live Nation enjoy low finished-goods carrying costs. These recordings can also be downloaded through Apple's iTunes platform and artist Web sites, making live recordings more accessible than ever. With such opportunities, it's no wonder that bands like Pearl Jam and Phish augment their existing CD sales with just-in-time recordings.

Sources: Based on Jonathan Self, "Free (and Some Not Free) Live Music." *PC World* (November 24, 2009); Eliot Van Buskirk, "Apple unveils 'live music' in iTunes." *Wired,* "Epicenter" blog (November 24, 2009); Sabra Chartrand, "How to take the concert home." *New York Times* (May 3, 2004); Stephen Humphries, "Get your official 'bootleg' here." *Christian Science Monitor* (November 21, 2003); Mark Huffman, "Google Music Takes Aim at iTunes." *Consumer Affairs* (November 17, 2011).

- Photon expects JIT manufacturing to reduce (a) average inventory by $500,000 and (b) relevant costs of insurance, storage, materials handling, and setup by $30,000 per year.
- The required rate of return on inventory investments is 12% per year.

Should Photon implement a JIT production system?

On the basis of the information provided, we would be tempted to say "no" because annual relevant total cost savings amount to $90,000 [(12% of $500,000) + $30,000)], which is less than the additional annual tooling costs of $100,000.

Our analysis, however, is incomplete. We have not considered the other benefits of lower inventories in JIT production. Photon estimates that implementing JIT will (1) improve quality and reduce rework on 500 units each year, resulting in savings of $30 per unit and (2) reduce warranty repair costs on 200 units, yielding savings of $70 per unit.

The annual relevant benefits and costs from implementing JIT equal:

Incremental savings in insurance, storage, materials handling, and setup	$ 30,000
Incremental savings in inventory carrying costs (12% × $500,000)	60,000
Incremental savings from reduced rework costs ($30 per unit × 500 units)	15,000
Incremental savings from reduced warranty repair costs ($70 per unit × 200 units)	14,000
Incremental annual tooling costs	(100,000)
Net incremental benefit	$ 19,000

Therefore, Photon *should* implement the JIT production system. The relevant benefits of implementing JIT systems would be even greater if Photon considered the benefits of achieving higher sales and contribution margins as a result of better quality.

Enterprise Resource Planning (ERP) Systems[4]

The success of a JIT production system hinges on the speed of information flows from customers to manufacturers to suppliers. Information flows are a problem for large companies that have fragmented information systems spread over dozens of unlinked computer systems. An **enterprise resource planning (ERP) system** is an integrated set of software modules covering accounting, distribution, manufacturing, purchasing, human resources, and other functions. ERP uses a single database to collect and feed data into all software applications, allowing integrated, real-time information sharing, and providing visibility to the company's business processes as a whole. For example, using an ERP system, a salesperson can generate a contract for a customer in Germany, verify the customer's credit limits, and place a production order. The system then uses this same information to schedule manufacturing in, say, Brazil, requisition materials from inventory, order components from suppliers, and schedule shipments. At the same time, the system credits sales commissions to the salesperson and records all the costing and financial accounting information.

ERP systems give lower-level managers, workers, customers, and suppliers access to detailed and timely operating information. This benefit, coupled with tight coordination across business functions of the value chain, enables ERP systems to shift manufacturing and distribution plans rapidly in response to changes in supply and demand. Companies believe that an ERP system is essential to support JIT initiatives because of the effect it has on lead times. For example, using an ERP system, Autodesk, a maker of computer-aided design software, reduced order lead time from two weeks to one day; and Fujitsu, an information technology company, reduced lead time from 18 days to 1.5 days.

ERP systems are large and unwieldy. Because of its complexity, suppliers of ERP systems such as SAP and Oracle provide software packages that are standard but that can be customized, at significant cost. Without some customization, unique and distinctive features that confer strategic advantage will not be available. The challenge when implementing ERP systems is to strike the proper balance between the lower cost and reliability of standardized systems and the strategic benefits that accrue from customization.

[4] For an excellent discussion, see T. H. Davenport, "Putting the Enterprise into the Enterprise System," *Harvard Business Review* (July–August 1998); also see A. Cagilo, "Enterprise Resource Planning Systems and Accountants: Towards Hybridization?" *European Accounting Review* (May 2003).

Performance Measures and Control in JIT Production

In addition to personal observation, managers use financial and nonfinancial measures to evaluate and control JIT production. We now describe these measures and indicate the effect that JIT systems are expected to have on these measures.

1. Financial performance measures, such as inventory turnover ratio (Cost of goods sold ÷ Average inventory), which is expected to increase
2. Nonfinancial performance measures of inventory, quality, and time such as the following:
   - Number of days of inventory on hand, expected to decrease
   - Units produced per hour, expected to increase
   - $\frac{\text{Number of units scrapped or requiring rework}}{\text{Total number of units started and completed}}$, expected to decrease
   - Manufacturing time, expected to decrease
   - $\frac{\text{Total setup time for machines}}{\text{Total manufacturing time}}$, expected to decrease

Personal observation and nonfinancial performance measures provide the most timely, intuitive, and easy to understand measures of manufacturing performance. Rapid, meaningful feedback is critical because the lack of inventories in a demand-pull system makes it urgent for managers to detect and solve problems quickly.

Effect of JIT Systems on Product Costing

By reducing materials handling, warehousing, and inspection, JIT systems reduce overhead costs. JIT systems also aid in direct tracing of some costs usually classified as indirect. For example, the use of manufacturing cells makes it cost-effective to trace materials handling, machine operating, and inspection costs to specific products or product families made in these cells. These costs then become direct costs of those products. These changes have prompted some companies using JIT to adopt *lean accounting.*

Lean Accounting

Successful JIT production requires companies to focus on the entire value chain of business functions (from suppliers to manufacturing to customers) in order to reduce inventories, lead times, and waste. The emphasis on improvements throughout the value chain has led some JIT companies to develop organizational structures and costing systems that focus on **value streams,** which are all the value-added activities needed to design, manufacture, and deliver a given product or product line to customers. For example, a value stream can include the activities needed to develop and engineer products, advertise and market those products, process orders, purchase and receive materials, manufacture and ship orders, bill customers, and collect payments. The use of manufacturing cells in JIT systems that group together the operations needed to make a given product or product line helps the focus on value streams.

Lean accounting is a costing method that supports creating value for customers by costing value streams, as distinguished from individual products or departments, thereby eliminating waste in the accounting process.[5] If a company makes multiple, related products in a single value stream, it does not compute product costs for the individual products. Instead, it traces many actual costs directly to the value stream. Tracing more costs as direct costs to value streams is possible because companies using lean accounting often dedicate resources to individual value streams. We now illustrate lean accounting for Photon Corporation.

Photon Corporation manufactures toner cartridges and ink cartridges for use with its printers. It makes two models of toner cartridges in one manufacturing cell and two models of ink cartridges in another manufacturing cell. The following table lists, revenues, operating costs, operating income, and other information for the different products.

[5] See B. Baggaley, "Costing by Value Stream," *Journal of Cost Management* (May–June 2003).

	Toner Cartridges		Ink Cartridges	
	Model A	Model B	Model C	Model D
Revenues	$600,000	$700,000	$800,000	$550,000
Direct materials	340,000	400,000	410,000	270,000
Direct manufacturing labor	70,000	78,000	105,000	82,000
Manufacturing overhead costs (e.g., equipment lease, supervision, and unused facility costs)	112,000	130,000	128,000	103,000
Rework costs	15,000	17,000	14,000	10,000
Design costs	20,000	21,000	24,000	18,000
Marketing and sales costs	30,000	33,000	40,000	28,000
Total costs	587,000	679,000	721,000	511,000
Operating income	$ 13,000	$ 21,000	$ 79,000	$ 39,000
Direct materials purchased	$350,000	$420,000	$430,000	$285,000
Unused facility costs	$ 22,000	$ 38,000	$ 18,000	$ 15,000

Using lean accounting principles, Photon's managers calculate value-stream operating costs and operating income for toner cartridges and ink cartridges, not individual models, as follows:

	Toner Cartridges	Ink cartridges
Revenues		
($600,000 + $700,000; $800,000 + $550,000)	$1,300,000	$1,350,000
Direct material purchases		
($350,000 + $420,000; $430,000 + $285,000)	770,000	715,000
Direct manufacturing labor		
(70,000 + $78,000; $105,000 + $82,000)	148,000	187,000
Manufacturing overhead (after deducting unused facility costs)		
($112,000 − $22,000) + ($130,000 − $38,000); ($128,000 − $18,000) + ($103,000 − $15,000)	182,000	198,000
Design costs		
($20,000 + $21,000; $24,000 + $18,000)	41,000	42,000
Marketing and sales costs		
($30,000 + $33,000; $40,000 + $28,000)	63,000	68,000
Total value stream operating costs	1,204,000	1,210,000
Value stream operating income	$ 96,000	$ 140,000

Photon's lean accounting system, like many lean accounting systems, expenses the costs of all purchased materials in the period in which it buys direct materials to signal the need to reduce direct material and work-in-process inventory. In our example, the cost of direct material purchases under lean accounting exceeds the cost of direct materials used in the operating income statement.

Photon allocates facility costs (such as depreciation, property taxes, and leases) to value streams based on the square footage each value stream uses to encourage managers to use less space for holding and moving inventory. Note that Photon does not consider unused facility costs as manufacturing overhead costs of value streams. Instead, it treats these costs as plant or business unit expenses. Photon excludes unused facility costs because it only includes those costs that add value in value-stream costs. Increasing the visibility of unused capacity costs creates incentives to reduce these costs or to find alternative uses for capacity. Photon excludes rework costs when calculating value-stream costs and operating income because these costs are non-value-added costs. Companies also exclude from value stream costs common costs such as corporate or support department costs that cannot reasonably be assigned to value streams.

The analysis shows that while total cost for toner cartridges is $1,266,000 ($587,000 + $679,000), the value stream cost using lean accounting is $1,204,000 (95.1% of $1,266,000), indicating significant opportunities for improving profitability by reducing unused facility and rework costs, and by purchasing direct materials only as needed for production. Making improvements is particularly important because value stream operating income is only 7.4% ($96,000 ÷ $1,300,000) of revenues. Ink cartridges portray a different picture. Total cost for ink cartridges is $1,232,000 ($721,000 + $511,000) while the value-stream cost using lean accounting is $1,210,000 (98.2% of $1,232,000). The ink cartridges value stream has low unused facility and rework costs and is more efficient. Moreover, ink cartridges also have higher value stream operating income profitability of 10.4% ($140,000 ÷ $1,350,000).

Lean accounting is much simpler than traditional product costing. Why? Because calculating actual product costs by value streams require less overhead allocation. Consistent with JIT and lean production, lean accounting emphasizes improvements in the value chain from suppliers to customers. Lean accounting encourages practices—such as reducing direct material and work-in-process inventories, improving quality, using less space, and eliminating unused capacity—that reflect the goals of JIT production.

Lean accounting does not compute costs of individual products. Critics charge that this limits its usefulness for decision making. Proponents of lean accounting argue that the lack of individual product costs is not a problem because most decisions are made at the product line level rather than the individual product level, and that pricing decisions are based on the value created for the customer (market prices) and not product costs.

Another criticism is that lean accounting excludes certain support costs and unused capacity costs. As a result, the decisions based on only value stream costs will look profitable because they do not consider all costs. Proponents argue that lean accounting overcomes this problem by adding a larger markup on value stream costs to compensate for some of these excluded costs. Moreover, in a competitive market, prices will eventually settle at a level that represents a reasonable markup above value stream costs because customers will be unwilling to pay for non-value-added costs. The goal must therefore be to eliminate non-value-added costs.

A final criticism is that lean accounting does not correctly account for inventories under Generally Accepted Accounting Principles (GAAP). However, proponents are quick to point out that in lean accounting environments, work in process and finished goods inventories are immaterial from an accounting perspective.

JIT Systems and Supply-Chain Analysis in Retailing

JIT systems work well for retailers because the levels of inventories they hold are affected by (1) the demand patterns of their customers and (2) supply relationships with their distributors and manufacturers, the suppliers to their manufacturers, and so on. The *supply chain* describes the flow of goods, services, and information from the initial sources of materials and services to the delivery of products to consumers, regardless of whether those activities occur in the same company or in other companies. Retailers can purchase inventories on a JIT basis only if activities throughout the supply chain are properly planned, coordinated, and controlled.

Procter and Gamble's (P&G's) experience with its Pampers product illustrates the gains from supply-chain coordination. Retailers selling Pampers encountered variability in weekly demand because families purchased disposable diapers randomly. Anticipating even more demand variability and lacking information about available inventory with P&G, retailers' orders to P&G became more variable. This, in turn, increased variability of orders at P&G's suppliers, resulting in high levels of inventory at all stages in the supply chain.

How did P&G respond to these problems? By sharing information and planning and coordinating activities throughout the supply chain among retailers, P&G, and P&G's suppliers. Sharing sales information reduced the level of uncertainty that P&G and its suppliers had about retail demand for Pampers and led to (1) fewer stockouts at the retail level, (2) reduced manufacture of Pampers not immediately needed by retailers, (3) fewer manufacturing orders that had to be "rushed" or "expedited," and (4) lower inventories held by each company in the supply chain. The benefits of supply chain coordination at P&G have been so great that retailers such as Walmart have contracted with P&G to manage Walmart's retail inventories on a just-in-time basis. This practice is called *supplier- or vendor-managed inventory.* Supply-chain management, however, has challenges in sharing accurate, timely, and relevant information about sales, inventory, and sales forecasts caused by problems of communication, trust, incompatible information systems, and limited people and financial resources.

JIT in Service Industries

In addition to companies in the manufacturing and retail sectors, many service-sector companies use JIT purchasing and production methods. For example, a third of the costs in most hospitals are related to inventories and supplies, and the associated labor costs to manage them. By implementing a JIT purchasing and distribution system, Eisenhower Memorial Hospital in Palm Springs, California, reduced its inventories and supplies by 90% in 18 months. To achieve these savings, the hospital shared information electronically with distributors and trained employees to be materials service coordinators.

McDonald's has adapted JIT production practices to making hamburgers.[6] Before, McDonald's precooked a batch of hamburgers that were placed under heat lamps to stay warm until ordered. If the hamburgers didn't sell within a specified period of time, they were discarded, resulting in high inventory holding costs and spoilage costs. Moreover, the quality of hamburgers deteriorated the longer they sat under the heat lamps. Finally, customers placing a special order for a hamburger (such as a hamburger with no cheese) had to wait for the hamburger to be cooked. Today, the use of new technology (including an innovative bun toaster) and JIT production practices allow McDonald's to cook hamburgers only when they are ordered, significantly reducing inventory holding and spoilage costs. More importantly, JIT has improved customer satisfaction by increasing the quality of hamburgers and reducing the time needed for special orders.

As we have seen, JIT inventory systems help companies reduce inventory, improve quality, and streamline processes so that work gets done faster. To satisfy customer demand, companies must be able to produce and deliver products quickly. In the next section, we focus on various dimensions of time and how bottlenecks arise to cause delays.

Keys to Success

Just-in-time (JIT) production systems use a "demand-pull" approach to produce goods only after receiving a customer order. JIT production improves the flow of information, increases quality, lowers costs, speeds up delivery, and simplifies accounting.

Learning Objective 7

Describe customer-response time

. . . time between receipt of customer order and product delivery

and explain why delays happen and their costs

. . . uncertainty about the timing of customer orders and limited capacity lead to lower revenues and higher inventory carrying costs

Time as a Competitive Tool

Companies increasingly view time as a driver of strategy.[7] For example, CapitalOne has increased business on its Web site by promising home-loan approval decisions in 30 minutes or less. Companies such as AT&T, General Electric, and Walmart attribute not only higher revenues but also lower costs to doing things faster and on time. They cite, for example, the need to carry fewer inventories driven by their ability to respond rapidly to customer demands.

Managers need to measure time to manage it properly. In this section, we focus on two *operational measures of time: customer-response time,* which reveals how quickly companies respond to customers' demands for their products and services, and *on-time performance,* which indicates how reliably they meet scheduled delivery dates. We also show how managers measure the causes and costs of delays.

Customer-Response Time and On-Time Performance

Customer-response time is how long it takes from the time a customer places an order for a product or service to the time the product or service is delivered to the customer. Fast responses to customers are of strategic importance in industries such as construction, banking, car rental, and fast food. Some companies, such as Airbus, have to pay penalties to compensate their customers (airline companies) for lost revenues and profits (from being unable to operate flights) as a result of delays in delivering aircraft to them.

Exhibit 10-12 describes the components of customer-response time. *Receipt time* is how long it takes the marketing department to specify to the manufacturing department the exact requirements in the customer's order. **Manufacturing cycle time** (also called **manufacturing lead time**) is

[6] Charles Atkinson, "McDonald's, A Guide to the Benefits of JIT," *Inventory Management Review* (November 8, 2005).

[7] See K. Eisenhardt and S. Brown, "Time Pacing: Competing in Strategic Markets That Won't Stand Still," *Harvard Business Review* (March–April 1998); and T. Willis and A. Jurkus, "Product Development: An Essential Ingredient of Time-Based Competition," *Review of Business* (2001).

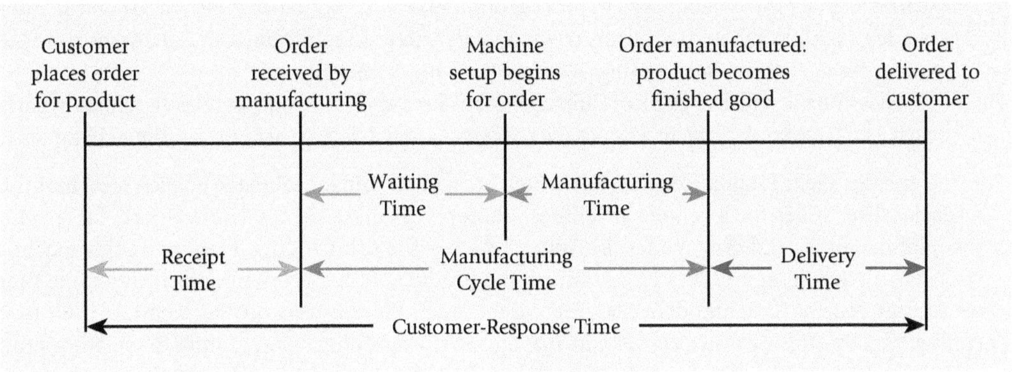

Exhibit 10-12
Components of Customer-Response Time

how long it takes from the time an order is received by manufacturing to the time a finished good is produced. Manufacturing cycle time is the sum of waiting time and manufacturing time for an order. For example, an aircraft order received by Airbus' manufacturing department may need to wait for components before the plane can be assembled. *Delivery time* is how long it takes to deliver a completed order to a customer.

Some companies evaluate their response time improvement efforts using a measure called **manufacturing cycle efficiency (MCE):**

$$\text{MCE} = (\text{Value-added manufacturing time} \div \text{Manufacturing cycle time})$$

Value-added manufacturing activities (see Chapter 7) are activities that customers perceive as adding value or utility to a product. The time spent efficiently assembling the product is value-added manufacturing time. The rest of manufacturing cycle time, such as the time the product spends waiting for parts, or for the next stage in the production process, or being repaired, represents non-value-added manufacturing time. Identifying and minimizing the sources of non-value-added manufacturing time increases customer responsiveness and reduces costs.

Similar measures apply to service-sector companies. Consider a 40-minute doctor's office visit, of which a patient spends 9 minutes on administrative tasks such as filling out forms, 20 minutes waiting in the reception area and examination room, and 11 minutes with a nurse or doctor. The service cycle efficiency for this visit equals 11 ÷ 40, or 0.275. In other words, only 27.5% of the time in the office added value to the patient/customer. Minimizing non-value-added service time in their medical delivery processes has allowed hospitals such as Alle-Kiski Medical Center in Pennsylvania to treat more patients in less time.

On-time performance is delivery of a product or service by the time it is scheduled to be delivered. Consider Federal Express, which specifies a price per package and a next-day delivery time of 10:30 A.M. for its overnight courier service. Federal Express measures on-time performance by how often it meets its stated delivery time of 10:30 A.M. On-time performance increases customer satisfaction. For example, commercial airlines gain loyal passengers as a result of consistent on-time service. But there is a tradeoff between a customer's desire for shorter customer-response time and better on-time performance. Scheduling longer customer-response times, such as airlines lengthening scheduled arrival times, displeases customers on the one hand but increases customer satisfaction on the other hand by improving on-time performance.

Bottlenecks and Time Drivers

Managing customer-response time and on-time performance requires managers to understand the causes and costs of delays that occur, for example, at a machine in a manufacturing plant or at a checkout counter in a store.

A **time driver** is any factor that causes a change in the speed of an activity when the factor changes. Two time drivers are:

1. **Uncertainty about when customers will order products or services.** For example, the more randomly Airbus receives orders for its airplanes, the more likely queues will form and delays will occur.
2. **Bottlenecks due to limited capacity.** A **bottleneck** occurs in an operation when the work to be performed approaches or exceeds the capacity available to do it. For example, a bottleneck results and causes delays when products that must be processed at a particular machine arrive

while the machine is being used to process other products. Bottlenecks also occur on the Internet, for example, when many users try to operate wireless mobile devices at the same time (see Concepts in Action: Overcoming Wireless Data Bottlenecks).

Many banks, such as Bank of China; grocery stores, such as Krogers; and entertainment parks, such as Disneyland, actively work to reduce queues and delays to better serve their customers.

Consider again Photon Corporation, which uses one turning machine to convert steel bars into a special fuser roller for its copier machines. Photon sells these rollers as spare parts for its photocopier machines and only makes this roller, which is the sole product it makes on this machine after its only wholesaler orders 1,000 units of the product. To focus on manufacturing cycle time, we assume receipt time and delivery time are minimal. Photon wants to differentiate itself from competitors by offering faster delivery. Its managers are examining opportunities to sell other products to increase profits without sacrificing the competitive advantage provided by short customer-response times. The managers examine these opportunities using the five-step decision-making process introduced in Chapter 1.

Step 1: Identify the Problem and Uncertainties. Photon's managers are considering introducing a second product, a fuser gear. The primary uncertainty is how the introduction of a second product will affect manufacturing cycle times for rollers.

Step 2: Obtain Information. Managers gather data on the number of orders for rollers Photon has received in the past, the time it takes to manufacture rollers, the available capacity, and the average manufacturing cycle time for rollers. Photon typically receives 30 orders for rollers each year, but it could receive 10, 30, or 50 orders. Each order is for 1,000 units and takes 100 hours of manufacturing time (8 hours of setup time to clean and prepare the machine, and 92 hours of processing time). Annual capacity of the machine is 4,000 hours. If Photon receives the 30 orders it expects, the total amount of manufacturing time required on the machine is 3,000 hours (100 hours per order × 30 orders), which is less than the available machine capacity of 4,000 hours. Even though capacity

Concepts in Action: Overcoming Wireless Data Bottlenecks

The wired world is quickly going wireless. In addition to the smartphone boom, emerging devices including e-book readers and machine-to-machine appliances (the so-called "Internet of things") will add to rapidly growing data traffic. Cisco recently forecast that data traffic will grow at a compound rate of 108% from 90,000 terabytes per month in 2009 to 3.6 million terabytes per month by 2014.

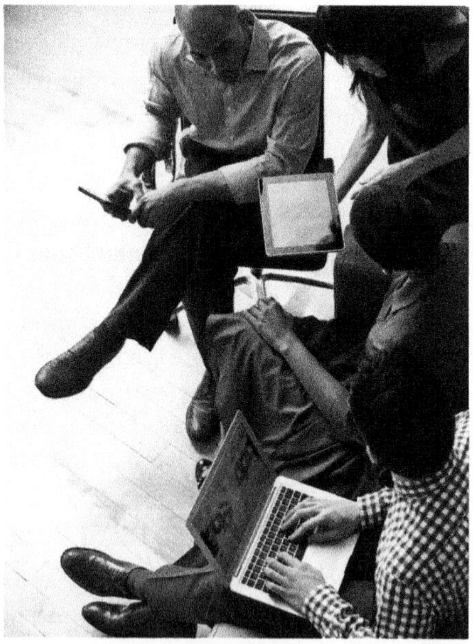

Source: Image Source/Alamy

This astronomical growth already causes many users to suffer from mobile bottlenecks caused by too many users trying to transfer mobile data at the same time in a given area. These bottlenecks are most harmful to companies, such as Amazon.com and e-Bay, buying and selling products and services over the mobile Internet. To relieve mobile bottlenecks, wireless providers and other high-tech companies are working on more efficient mobile broadband networks, such as LTE, that use complementary technologies to automatically choose the best available wireless network to increase capacity. Technology providers are also deploying Wi-Fi direct, which allows mobile users to freely transfer video, digital music, and photos between mobile devices without choking up valuable bandwidth. Companies and government agencies around the world are also trying to increase the wireless broadband spectrum. In the United States, for example, current holders of spectrum—such as radio stations—are being encouraged to sell their excess capacity to wireless providers in exchange for a share of the profits.

Sources: Based on Cliff Edwards, "Wi-fi direct seen as way to alleviate network congestion." *Businessweek* (January 7, 2010); John Morris, "CTIA: More spectrum, and other ways to break the wireless data bottleneck." *ZDNet*, "Laptops & Desktops" blog (March 24, 2010); George Pyle, "Wireless growth leading to bottlenecks." *Buffalo News* (May 9, 2010).

utilization is not strained, queues and delays still occur because uncertainty about when wholesalers place their orders causes an order to be received while the machine is processing an earlier order.

Average waiting time, the average amount of time that an order waits in line before the machine is set up and the order is processed equals,[8]

$$\frac{\text{Annual average number of orders for rollers} \times \left(\text{Manufacturing time per order for rollers}\right)^2}{2 \times \left[\text{Annual machine capacity} - \left(\text{Annual average number of orders for rollers} \times \text{Manufacturing time per order for rollers}\right)\right]}$$

$$= \frac{30 \times (100)^2}{2 \times [4{,}000 - (30 \times 100)]} = \frac{30 \times 10{,}000}{2 \times (4{,}000 - 3{,}000)} = \frac{300{,}000}{2 \times 1{,}000} = \frac{300{,}000}{2{,}000}$$

$$= 150 \text{ hours per order (for rollers)}$$

Therefore, the average manufacturing cycle time for an order is 250 hours (150 hours of average waiting time + 100 hours of manufacturing time). Note that manufacturing time per order is a squared term in the numerator. The squared term indicates the disproportionately large impact manufacturing time has on waiting time. As the manufacturing time lengthens, there is a much greater chance that the machine will be in use when an order arrives, leading to longer delays. The denominator in this formula is a measure of the unused capacity, or cushion. As the unused capacity becomes smaller, the chance that the machine is processing an earlier order becomes more likely, leading to greater delays.

The formula describes only the *average* waiting time. A particular order might arrive when the machine is free, in which case manufacturing will start immediately. In another situation, Photon may receive an order while two other orders are waiting to be processed, which means the delay will be longer than 150 hours.

Step 3: Make Predictions About the Future. The manager makes the following predictions about gears: Photon expects to receive 10 orders for gears, each order for 1,600 units, in the coming year. Each order will take 50 hours of manufacturing time, comprising 3 hours for setup and 47 hours of processing. Expected demand for rollers will be unaffected by whether Photon produces and sells gears.

Average waiting time *before* machine setup begins is expected to be as follows (the formula is an extension of the preceding formula for the single-product case):

$$\frac{\left[\text{Annual average number of orders for rollers} \times \left(\text{Manufacturing time per order for rollers}\right)^2\right] + \left[\text{Annual average number of orders for gears} \times \left(\text{Manufacturing time per order for gears}\right)^2\right]}{2 \times \left[\text{Annual machine capacity} - \left(\text{Annual average number of orders for rollers} \times \text{Manufacturing time per order for rollers}\right) - \left(\text{Annual average number of orders for gears} \times \text{Manufacturing time per order for gears}\right)\right]}$$

$$= \frac{[30 \times (100)^2] + [10 \times (50)^2]}{2 \times [4{,}000 - (30 \times 100) - (10 \times 50)]} = \frac{(30 \times 10{,}000) + (10 \times 2{,}500)}{2 \times (4{,}000 - 3{,}000 - 500)}$$

$$= \frac{300{,}000 + 25{,}000}{2 \times 500} = \frac{325{,}000}{1{,}000} = 325 \text{ hours per order (for rollers } \textit{and} \text{ gears)}$$

Introducing gears will cause average waiting time for an order to more than double, from 150 hours to 325 hours. Waiting time increases because introducing gears will cause unused capacity to shrink, increasing the probability that new orders will arrive while current orders are being manufactured or waiting to be manufactured. Average waiting time is very sensitive to the shrinking of unused capacity.

If the manager decides to make gears, average manufacturing cycle time will be 425 hours for a roller order (325 hours of average waiting time + 100 hours of manufacturing time), and 375 hours for a gear order (325 hours of average waiting time + 50 hours of manufacturing time). A roller

[8] The technical assumptions are (1) that customer orders for the product follow a Poisson distribution with a mean equal to the expected number of orders (30 in our example) and (2) that orders are processed on a first-in, first-out (FIFO) basis. The Poisson arrival pattern for customer orders has been found to be reasonable in many real-world settings. The FIFO assumption can be modified. Under the modified assumptions, the basic queuing and delay effects will still occur, but the precise formulas will be different.

order will spend 76.5% (325 hours ÷ 425 hours) of its manufacturing cycle time just waiting for manufacturing to start!

Step 4: Make decisions by choosing among alternatives. Given the anticipated effects on manufacturing cycle time of adding gears, should Photon's managers introduce gears? To help managers make a decision, the management accountant identifies and analyzes the relevant revenues and relevant costs of adding the gear product and, in particular, the cost of delays on all products. The rest of this section focuses on Step 4. While we do not cover Step 5 in this example, we discuss later in the chapter how to evaluate and learn about time-based performance.

Relevant Revenues and Relevant Costs of Time

To determine the relevant revenues and costs of adding gears under Step 4, the management accountant prepares the following additional information:

		Average Selling Price per Order If Average Manufacturing Cycle Time per Order Is			
Product	Annual Average Number of Orders	Less Than 300 Hours	More Than 300 Hours	Direct Material Cost per Order	Inventory Carrying Cost per Order per Hour
Rollers	30	$22,000	$21,500	$16,000	$1.00
Gears	10	10,000	9,600	8,000	0.50

Manufacturing cycle times affect both revenues and costs. Revenues are affected because customers are willing to pay a higher price for faster delivery. On the cost side, direct material costs and inventory carrying costs are the only relevant costs of introducing gears (all other costs are unaffected and therefore irrelevant). Inventory carrying costs equal the opportunity costs of investment tied up in inventory (see Chapter 9, pages 354–356) and the relevant costs of storage, such as space rental, spoilage, deterioration, and materials handling. Usually, companies calculate inventory carrying costs on a per-unit, per-year basis. To simplify calculations, the management accountant calculates inventory carrying costs on a per-order, per-hour basis. Also, Photon acquires direct materials at the time the order is received by manufacturing and, therefore, calculates inventory carrying costs for the duration of the manufacturing cycle time.

Exhibit 10-13 presents relevant revenues and relevant costs for the "introduce gears" and "do not introduce gears" alternatives. Based on the analysis, Photon's managers decide not to introduce gears, even though gears have a positive contribution margin of $1,600 ($9,600 − $8,000) per order and Photon has the capacity to process gears. If it produces gears, Photon will, on average, use only 3,500 (Rollers: 100 hours per order × 30 orders + Gears: 50 hours per order × 10 orders) of the available 4,000 machine-hours. So why is Photon better off not introducing gears? *Because of the negative effects that producing gears will have on the existing product, rollers.* The following table presents the *costs of time,* the expected loss in revenues and expected increase in carrying costs as a result of delays caused by using machine capacity to manufacture gears.

	Effect of Increasing Average Manufacturing Cycle Time		
Product	Expected Loss in Revenues for Rollers (1)	Expected Increase in Carrying Costs for All Products (2)	Expected Loss in Revenues Plus Expected Increase in Carrying Costs of Introducing Gears (3) = (1) + (2)
Rollers	$15,000[a]	$5,250[b]	$20,250
Gears	—	1,875[c]	1,875
Total	$15,000	$7,125	$22,125

[a] ($22,000 − $21,500) per order × 30 expected orders = $15,000.
[b] (425 − 250) hours per order × $1.00 per hour × 30 expected orders = $5,250.
[c] (375 − 0) hours per order × $0.50 per hour × 10 expected orders = $1,875.

Exhibit 10-13
Determining Expected Relevant Revenues and Relevant Costs for Photon's Decision to Introduce Gears

Relevant Items	Alternative 1: Introduce Gears (1)	Alternative 2: Do Not Introduce Gears (2)	Difference (3) = (1) − (2)
Expected revenues	$741,000[a]	$660,000[b]	$ 81,000
Expected variable costs	560,000[c]	480,000[d]	(80,000)
Expected inventory carrying costs	14,625[e]	7,500[f]	(7,125)
Expected total costs	574,625	487,500	(87,125)
Expected revenues minus expected costs	$166,375	$172,500	$ (6,125)

[a]($21,500 × 30) + ($9,600 × 10) = $741,000; average manufacturing cycle time will be more than 300 hours.

[b]($22,000 × 30) = $660,000; average manufacturing cycle time will be less than 300 hours.

[c]($16,000 × 30) + ($8,000 × 10) = $560,000.

[d]$16,000 × 30 = $480,000.

[e](Average manufacturing cycle time for rollers × Unit carrying cost per order for rollers × Expected number of orders for rollers) + (Average manufacturing cycle time for gears × Unit carrying cost per order for gears × Expected number of orders for gears) = (425 × $1.00 × 30) + (375 × $0.50 × 10) = $12,750 + $1,875 = $14,625.

[f]Average manufacturing cycle time for rollers × Unit carrying cost per order for rollers × Expected number of orders for rollers = 250 × $1.00 × 30 = $7,500.

Introducing gears causes the average manufacturing cycle time of rollers to increase from 250 hours to 425 hours. Longer manufacturing cycle times increase inventory carrying costs of rollers and decrease roller revenues (average manufacturing cycle time for rollers exceeds 300 hours so the average selling price per order decreases from $22,000 to $21,500). Together with the inventory carrying cost of gears, the expected cost of introducing gears, $22,125, exceeds the expected contribution margin of $16,000 ($1,600 per order × 10 expected orders) from selling gears by $6,125 (the difference calculated in Exhibit 10-13).

This example illustrates that when demand uncertainty is high, some unused capacity is desirable.[9] Increasing the capacity of a bottleneck resource reduces manufacturing cycle times and delays. One way to increase capacity is to reduce the time required for setups and processing via more efficient setups and processing. Another way to increase capacity is to invest in new equipment, such as flexible manufacturing systems that can be programmed to switch quickly from producing one product to producing another. Delays can also be reduced through careful scheduling of orders on machines, such as by batching similar jobs together for processing.

Time-Related Measures

In this section, we focus on the final step of the five-step decision-making process by tracking changes in time-based measures, evaluating and learning whether these changes affect financial performance, and modifying decisions and plans to achieve the company's goals. Examples of financial and nonfinancial measures are:

Financial measures

Revenue losses or price discounts attributable to delays

Carrying cost of inventories

Customer measures

Customer-response time (the time it takes to fulfill a customer order)

On-time performance (delivering a product or service by the scheduled time)

Internal-business-process measures

Average manufacturing time for key products

Manufacturing cycle efficiency for key processes

Average reduction in setup time and processing time at bottleneck operations

[9] Other complexities, such as analyzing a network of machines, priority scheduling, and allowing for uncertainty in processing times, are beyond the scope of this book. In these cases, the basic queuing and delay effects persist, but the precise formulas are more complex.

Training measures

Number of employees trained in managing bottleneck operations

To see the cause-and-effect linkages across these measures, consider the example of the Bell Group, a designer and manufacturer of equipment for the jewelry industry. A key financial measure was higher profit margin on a specific product line. To achieve this goal, the company set a 2-day turnaround time on all orders for the product based on operating a bottleneck machine 22 hours per day, 6 days a week. It trained new employees to carry out nonbottleneck operations to free experienced employees to operate the bottleneck machine. The Bell Group's emphasis on time-related measures allowed the company to substantially increase manufacturing throughput and slash response times, leading to higher revenues and increased profits.[10]

Keys to Success

Delays in serving customers occur because of uncertainty about when customers will order products and limited processing capacity. Delays result in lower revenues and higher costs. To avoid delays, managers need to maintain some slack capacity.

[10] Management Roundtable, "The Bell Group Uses the Balanced Scorecard with the Theory of Constraints to Keep Strategic Focus," FastTrack.roundtable.com, fasttrack.roundtable.com/app/content/knowledgesource/item/197 (accessed May 15, 2007).

Problem for Self-Study

The Sloan Moving Corporation transports household goods from one city to another within the continental United States. It measures quality of service in terms of (1) time required to transport goods, (2) on-time delivery (within 2 days of agreed-upon delivery date), and (3) number of lost or damaged items. Sloan is considering investing in a new scheduling-and-tracking system costing $160,000 per year, which should help it improve performance for items (2) and (3). The following information describes Sloan's current performance and the expected performance if the new system is implemented:

	Current Performance	Expected Future Performance
On-time delivery performance	85%	95%
Variable cost per carton lost or damaged	$60	$60
Fixed cost per carton lost or damaged	$40	$40
Number of cartons lost or damaged per year	3,000 cartons	1,000 cartons

Sloan expects each percentage point increase in on-time performance to increase revenue by $20,000 per year. Sloan's contribution margin percentage is 45%.

Required

1. Should Sloan acquire the new system? Show your calculations.
2. Sloan is very confident about the cost savings from fewer lost or damaged cartons as a result of introducing the new system but unsure about the increase in revenues. Calculate the minimum amount of increase in revenues needed to make it worthwhile for Sloan to invest in the new system.

Solution

1. Additional costs of the new scheduling-and-tracking system are $160,000 per year. Additional annual benefits of the new scheduling-and-tracking system are as follows:

Additional annual revenues from a 10% improvement in on-time performance, from 85% to 95%, $20,000 per 1% × 10 percentage points	$200,000
45% contribution margin from additional annual revenues (0.45 × $200,000)	$ 90,000
Decrease in costs per year from fewer cartons lost or damaged (only variable costs are relevant) [$60 per carton × (3,000 − 1,000) cartons]	120,000
Total additional benefits	$210,000

   Because the benefits of $210,000 exceed the costs of $160,000, Sloan should invest in the new system.

2. As long as Sloan earns a contribution margin of $40,000 (to cover incremental costs of $160,000 minus relevant variable-cost savings of $120,000) from additional annual revenues, investing in the new system is beneficial. This contribution margin corresponds to additional revenues of $40,000 ÷ 0.45 = $88,889.

Decision Points

The following question-and-answer format summarizes the chapter's learning objectives. Each decision presents a key question related to a learning objective. The guidelines are the answer to that question.

Decision	Guidelines
1. What are the four cost categories of a costs-of-quality program?	Four cost categories in a costs-of-quality program are prevention costs (costs incurred to prevent the production of products that do not conform to specifications), appraisal costs (costs incurred to detect which of the individual units of products do not conform to specifications), internal failure costs (costs incurred on defective products before they are shipped to customers), and external failure costs (costs incurred on defective products after they are shipped to customers).
2. What nonfinancial measures and methods can managers use to improve quality?	Nonfinancial quality measures managers can use include customer satisfaction measures such as number of customer complaints and percentage of defective units shipped to customers; internal-business process measures such as percentage of defective and reworked products; and training measures such as percentage of employees trained in and empowered to use quality principles. Three methods to identify quality problems and to improve quality are (a) control charts, to distinguish random from nonrandom variations in an operating process; (b) Pareto diagrams, to indicate how frequently each type of failure occurs; and (c) cause-and-effect diagrams, to identify and respond to potential causes of failure.
3. How do managers identify the relevant costs and benefits of quality improvement programs and use financial and nonfinancial measures to evaluate quality?	The relevant costs of quality improvement programs are the expected incremental costs to implement the program. The relevant benefits are the cost savings and the estimated increase in contribution margin from the higher revenues expected from quality improvements. Financial measures are helpful to evaluate tradeoffs among prevention costs, appraisal costs, and failure costs. Nonfinancial measures identify problem areas that need improvement and serve as indicators of future long-run performance.

Decision	Guidelines
4. What does the economic-order-quantity (EOQ) decision model help managers do and what is the effect on costs of errors in predicting parameters of the EOQ model?	The economic-order-quantity (EOQ) decision model helps managers to calculate the optimal quantity of inventory to order by balancing ordering costs and carrying costs. The larger the order quantity, the higher the annual carrying costs and the lower the annual ordering costs. The EOQ model includes costs recorded in the financial accounting system as well as opportunity costs not recorded in the financial accounting system. The cost of prediction errors when using the EOQ model is small.
5. Why are companies using just-in-time (JIT) purchasing?	Just-in-time (JIT) purchasing is making purchases in small order quantities just as needed for production (or sales). JIT purchasing is a response to high carrying costs, costs of quality, and shrinkage costs, and low ordering costs. JIT purchasing increases the focus of companies and suppliers on quality and timely deliveries.
6. What are the features and benefits of a just-in-time (JIT) production system?	Just-in-time (JIT) production systems use a "demand-pull" approach in which goods are manufactured only to satisfy customer orders. JIT production systems (a) organize production in manufacturing cells, (b) hire and train multiskilled workers, (c) emphasize total quality management, (d) reduce manufacturing lead time and setup time, and (e) build strong supplier relationships. The benefits of JIT production include lower costs and higher margins from better flow of information, higher quality, faster delivery, and simpler accounting systems.
7. What is customer-response time? What are the reasons for and the costs of delays?	Customer-response time is how long it takes from the time a customer places an order for a product or service to the time the product or service is delivered to the customer. Delays occur because of (a) uncertainty about when customers will order products or services and (b) bottlenecks due to limited capacity. Bottlenecks are operations at which the work to be performed approaches or exceeds available capacity. Costs of delays include lower revenues and higher inventory carrying costs.

Terms to Learn

This chapter and the Glossary at the end of the book contain definitions of the following important terms:

appraisal costs (p. 397)
average waiting time (p. 423)
bottleneck (p. 421)
carrying costs (p. 406)
cause-and-effect diagram (p. 401)
conformance quality (p. 396)
control chart (p. 400)
costs of quality (COQ) (p. 397)
customer-response time (p. 420)
design quality (p. 396)
economic order quantity (EOQ) (p. 406)
enterprise resource planning (ERP) system (p. 416)
external failure costs (p. 397)
internal failure costs (p. 397)
just-in-time (JIT) production (p. 414)
just-in-time (JIT) purchasing (p. 410)
lean accounting (p. 417)
lean production (p. 414)
manufacturing cells (p. 414)
manufacturing cycle efficiency (MCE) (p. 421)
manufacturing cycle time (p. 420)
manufacturing lead time (p. 420)
materials requirements planning (MRP) (p. 413)
on-time performance (p. 421)
ordering costs (p. 406)
Pareto diagram (p. 400)
prevention costs (p. 397)
purchase-order lead time (p. 406)
purchasing costs (p. 406)
quality (p. 396)
reorder point (p. 408)
safety stock (p. 409)
shrinkage costs (p. 406)
stockout costs (p. 406)
time driver (p. 421)
value streams (p. 417)

Assignment Material

Questions

10-1 How does conformance quality differ from design quality? Explain.

10-2 Describe three methods that companies use to identify quality problems.

10-3 "Companies should focus on financial measures of quality because these are the only measures of quality that can be linked to bottom-line performance." Do you agree? Explain.

10-4 Why might goal-congruence issues arise when managers use an EOQ model to guide decisions on how much to order?

10-5 "JIT purchasing has many benefits but also some risks." Do you agree? Explain briefly.

10-6 "You should always choose the supplier who offers the lowest price per unit." Do you agree? Explain.

10-7 What are the main features of JIT production and what are its benefits and costs?

10-8 Discuss the differences between lean accounting and traditional cost accounting.

10-9 "There is no tradeoff between customer-response time and on-time performance." Do you agree? Explain.

10-10 "Companies should always make and sell all products whose selling prices exceed variable costs." Assuming fixed costs are irrelevant, do you agree? Explain.

Exercises

10-11 Costs of quality. (CMA, adapted) Osborn, Inc., produces cell phone equipment. Amanda Westerly, Osborn's president, decided to devote more resources to the improvement of product quality after learning that her company had been ranked fourth in product quality in a 2010 survey of cell phone users. Osborn's quality-improvement program has now been in operation for 2 years, and the cost report shown here has recently been issued.

Semi-Annual COQ Report, Osborn, Inc. (in thousands)

	6/30/2011	12/31/2011	6/30/2012	12/31/2012
Prevention costs				
Machine maintenance	$ 480	$ 480	$ 440	$ 290
Supplier training	21	90	45	35
Design reviews	30	218	198	196
Total prevention costs	531	788	683	521
Appraisal costs				
Incoming inspections	109	124	89	55
Final testing	327	327	302	202
Total appraisal costs	436	451	391	257
Internal failure costs				
Rework	226	206	166	115
Scrap	127	124	68	65
Total internal failure costs	353	330	234	180
External failure costs				
Warranty repairs	182	89	70	67
Customer returns	594	510	263	186
Total external failure costs	776	599	333	253
Total quality costs	$2,096	$2,168	$1,641	$1,211
Total revenues	$8,220	$9,180	$9,260	$9,050

Required

1. For each period, calculate the ratio of each COQ category to revenues and to total quality costs.
2. Based on the results of requirement 1, would you conclude that Osborn's quality program has been successful? Prepare a short report to present your case.
3. Based on the 2010 survey, Amanda Westerly believed that Osborn had to improve product quality. In making her case to Osborn management, how might Westerly have estimated the opportunity cost of not implementing the quality-improvement program?

10-12 Costs of quality analysis. Safe Travel produces car seats for children from newborn to 2 years old. The company is worried because one of its competitors has recently come under public scrutiny because of product failure. Historically, Safe Travel's only problem with its car seats was stitching in the straps. The problem can usually be detected and repaired during an internal inspection. The cost of the inspection is \$6 per car seat, and the repair cost is \$1.25 per car seat. All 175,000 car seats were inspected last year and 5% were found to have problems with the stitching in the straps during the internal inspection. Another 1% of the 175,000 car seats had problems with the stitching, but the internal inspection did not discover them. Defective units that were sold and shipped to customers needed to be shipped back to Safe Travel and repaired. Shipping costs are \$9 per car seat, and repair costs are \$1.25 per car seat. However, the out-of-pocket costs (shipping and repair) are not the only costs of defects not discovered in the internal inspection. Negative publicity will result in a loss of contribution margin of \$168 for each external failure.

Required

1. Calculate appraisal cost.
2. Calculate internal failure cost.
3. Calculate out-of-pocket external failure cost.
4. Determine the opportunity cost associated with the external failures.
5. What are the total costs of quality?
6. Safe Travel is concerned with the high up-front cost of inspecting all 175,000 units. It is considering an alternative internal inspection plan that will cost only \$3.50 per car seat inspected. During the internal inspection, the alternative technique will detect only 2.5% of the 175,000 car seats that have stitching problems. The other 3.5% will be detected after the car seats are sold and shipped. What are the total costs of quality for the alternative technique?
7. What factors other than cost should Safe Travel consider before changing inspection techniques?

10-13 Costs of quality, ethical considerations. Refer to information in Exercise 10-12 in answering this question. Safe Travel has discovered a more serious problem with the plastic core of its car seats. An accident can cause the plastic in some of the seats to crack and break, resulting in serious injuries to the occupant. It is estimated that this problem will affect about 250 car seats in the next year. This problem could be corrected by using a higher quality of plastic that would increase the cost of every car seat produced by \$25. If this problem is not corrected, Safe Travel estimates that out of the 250 accidents, customers will realize that the problem is due to a defect in the seats in only six cases. Safe Travel's legal team has estimated that each of these six accidents would result in a lawsuit that could be settled for about \$675,000. All lawsuits settled would include a confidentiality clause, so Safe Travel's reputation would not be affected.

Required

1. Assuming that Safe Travel expects to sell 175,000 car seats next year, what would be the cost of increasing the quality of all 175,000 car seats?
2. What will be the total cost of the lawsuits next year if the problem is not corrected?
3. Suppose Safe Travel has decided not to increase the quality of the plastic because the cost of increasing the quality exceeds the benefits (saving the cost of lawsuits). What do you think of this decision? (*Note:* Because of the confidentiality clause, the decision will have no effect on Safe Travel's reputation.)
4. Are there any other costs or benefits that Safe Travel should consider?

10-14 Quality improvement, relevant costs, relevant revenues. On Time Print manufactures and sells 23,000 high-technology printing presses each year. The variable and fixed costs of rework and repair are as follows:

	Variable Cost	Fixed Cost	Total Cost
Rework cost per hour	\$80	\$140	\$220
Repair costs			
Customer support cost per hour	42	50	92
Transportation cost per load	370	140	510
Warranty repair cost per hour	86	140	226

On Time Print's current presses have a quality problem that causes variations in the shade of some colors. Its engineers suggest changing a key component in each press. The new component will cost $35 more than the old one. In the next year, however, On Time Print expects that with the new component it will (1) save 12,875 hours of rework, (2) save 500 hours of customer support, (3) move 250 fewer loads, (4) save 6,800 hours of warranty repairs, and (5) sell an additional 175 printing presses, for a total contribution margin of $1,750,000. On Time Print believes that even as it improves quality, it will not be able to save any of the fixed costs of rework or repair. On Time Print uses a 1-year time horizon for this decision because it plans to introduce a new press at the end of the year.

Required

1. Should On Time Print change to the new component? Show your calculations.
2. Suppose the estimate of 175 additional printing presses sold is uncertain. What is the minimum number of additional printing presses that On Time Print needs to sell to justify adopting the new component?
3. What other factors should managers at On Time Print consider when making their decision about changing to a new component?

10-15 Quality improvement, relevant costs, relevant revenues. Keswick Conference Center and Catering is a conference center and restaurant facility that hosts over 300 national and international events each year attended by 50,000 professionals. Due to increased competition and soaring customer expectations, the company has been forced to revisit its quality standards. In the company's 25-year history, customer demand has never been greater for high-quality products and services. Keswick has the following budgeted fixed and variable costs for 2013:

	Total Conference Center Fixed Costs	Variable Cost per Conference Attendee
Building and facilities	$4,320,000	
Management salaries	$1,680,000	
Customer support and service personnel		$ 66
Food and drink		$120
Conference materials		$ 42
Incidental products and services		$ 18

The company's budgeted operating income is $4,200,000.

After conducting a survey of 3,000 conference attendees, the company has learned that its customers would most like to see the following changes in the quality of the company's products and services: (1) more menu options and faster service, (2) more incidental products and services (wireless access in all meeting rooms, computer stations for Internet use, free local calling, etc.), and (3) upscale and cleaner meeting facilities. To satisfy these customer demands, the company would be required to increase fixed costs by 50% per year and increase variable costs by $12 per attendee as follows:

Customer support and service personnel	$4
Food and drink	$5
Conference materials	$0
Incidental products and services	$3

Keswick believes that the preceding improvements in product and service quality would increase overall conference attendance by 40%.

Required

1. What is the budgeted revenue per conference attendee?
2. Assuming budgeted revenue per conference attendee is unchanged, should Keswick implement the proposed changes?
3. Assuming budgeted revenue per conference attendee is unchanged, what is the variable cost per conference attendee at which Keswick would be indifferent between implementing and not implementing the proposed changes?

10-16 Economic order quantity for retailer. Super Shirts (SS) operates a megastore featuring sports merchandise. It uses an EOQ decision model to make inventory decisions. SS is now considering inventory decisions for its Los Angeles Galaxy jackets product line. This is a highly popular item. Data for 2013 are:

Expected annual demand for Galaxy jackets	9,000
Ordering cost per purchase order	$250
Carrying cost per year	$8 per jersey

Each jersey costs Super Shirts $50 and sells for $100. The $8 carrying cost per jersey per year comprises the required return on investment of $5.00 (10% × $50 purchase price) plus $3.00 in relevant insurance, handling, and theft-related costs. The purchasing lead time is 6 days. SS is open 365 days a year.

Required

1. Calculate the EOQ.
2. Calculate the number of orders that will be placed each year.
3. Calculate the reorder point.

10-17 Economic order quantity, effect of parameter changes (continuation of 10-16). Winning Textiles (WT) manufactures the Galaxy jackets that Super Shirts sells. WT has recently installed computer software that enables its customers to conduct "one-stop" purchasing using state-of-the-art Web site technology. SS's ordering cost per purchase order will be $40 using this new technology.

Required

1. Calculate the EOQ for the Galaxy jackets using the revised ordering cost of $40 per purchase order. Assume all other data from Exercise 10-16 are the same. Comment on the result.
2. Suppose WT proposes to "assist" SS. WT will allow SS customers to order directly from the WT Web site. WT would ship directly to these customers. WT would pay $15 to SS for every Galaxy jersey purchased by one of SS's customers. Comment qualitatively on how this offer would affect inventory management at SS. What factors should SS consider in deciding whether to accept WT's proposal?

10-18 EOQ for manufacturer. Turfpro Company produces lawn mowers and purchases 4,500 units of a rotor blade part each year at a cost of $30 per unit. Turfpro requires a 15% annual rate of return on investment. In addition, the relevant carrying cost (for insurance, materials handling, breakage, etc.) is $3 per unit per year. The relevant ordering cost per purchase order is $75.

Required

1. Calculate Turfpro's EOQ for the rotor blade part.
2. Calculate Turfpro's annual relevant ordering costs for the EOQ calculated in requirement 1.
3. Calculate Turfpro's annual relevant carrying costs for the EOQ calculated in requirement 1.
4. Assume that demand is uniform throughout the year and known with certainty so that there is no need for safety stocks. The purchase-order lead time is half a month. Calculate Turfpro's reorder point for the rotor blade part.

10-19 Inventory management. To support its just-in-time production system, Jarvis Sport Cycles (JSC) measures the percentage of employees who are cross-trained to perform a wide variety of production tasks. The internal business process measures are inventory turns and on-time delivery. JSC also measures customer satisfaction. JSC estimates that if it can increase the percentage of cross-trained employees by 5%, the resulting increase in labor productivity will reduce inventory-related costs by $200,000 per year and shorten delivery times by 10%. The 10% reduction in delivery times, in turn, is expected to increase customer satisfaction by 5%, and each 1% increase in customer satisfaction is expected to increase revenues by 2% due to higher prices.

Required

1. Assume that budgeted revenues in the coming year are $10,000,000. Ignoring the costs of training, what is the expected increase in operating income in the coming year if the number of cross-trained employees is increased by 5%?
2. What amount is the most JSC would be willing to pay to increase the percentage of cross-trained employees if it is only interested in maximizing operating income in the coming year?
3. What factors other than short-term profits should JSC consider when assessing the benefits from employee cross-training?

10-20 JIT production, relevant benefits, relevant costs. The Colonial Hardware Company manufactures specialty brass door handles at its Lynchburg plant. Colonial is considering implementing a JIT production system. The following are the estimated costs and benefits of JIT production:

a. Annual additional tooling costs would be $200,000.
b. Average inventory would decline by 80% from the current level of $2,000,000.
c. Insurance, space, materials-handling, and setup costs, which currently total $600,000 annually, would decline by 25%.
d. The emphasis on quality inherent in JIT production would reduce rework costs by 30%. Colonial currently incurs $400,000 in annual rework costs.
e. Improved product quality under JIT production would enable Colonial to raise the price of its product by $8 per unit. Colonial sells 40,000 units each year.

Colonial's required rate of return on inventory investment is 15% per year.

Required

1. Calculate the net benefit or cost to Colonial if it adopts JIT production at the Lynchburg plant.
2. What nonfinancial and qualitative factors should Colonial consider when making the decision to adopt JIT production?
3. Suppose Colonial implements JIT production at its Lynchburg plant. Give examples of performance measures Colonial could use to evaluate and control JIT production. What would be the benefit of Colonial implementing an enterprise resource planning (ERP) system?

10-21 Waiting time, service industry. The registration advisors at a small southwestern university (SSU) help 4,200 students develop each of their class schedules and register for classes each semester. Each advisor works for 10 hours a day during the registration period. SSU currently has 10 advisors. While advising an individual student can take anywhere from 2 to 30 minutes, it takes an average of 12 minutes per student. During the registration period, the 10 advisors see an average of 300 students a day on a first-come, first-served basis.

Required

1. Using the formula on page 423, calculate how long the average student will have to wait in the advisor's office before being advised.
2. The head of the registration advisors would like to increase the number of students seen each day, because at 300 students a day it would take 14 working days to see all of the students. This is a problem because the registration period lasts for only 2 weeks (10 working days). If the advisors could advise 420 students a day, it would take only 2 weeks (10 days). However, the head advisor wants to make sure that the waiting time is not excessive. What would be the average waiting time if 420 students were seen each day?
3. SSU wants to know the effect of reducing the average advising time on the average wait time. If SSU can reduce the average advising time to 10 minutes, what would be the average waiting time if 420 students were seen each day?

10-22 Waiting time, cost considerations, customer satisfaction. Refer to the information presented in Exercise 10-21. The head of the registration advisors at SSU has decided that the advisors must finish their advising in two weeks and therefore must advise 420 students a day. However, the average waiting time given a 12-minute advising period will result in student complaints, as will reducing the average advising time to 10 minutes. SSU is considering two alternatives:

a. Hire two more advisors for the 2-week (10-working day) advising period. This will increase the available number of advisors to 12 and therefore lower the average waiting time.
b. Increase the number of days that the advisors will work during the 2-week registration period to 6 days a week. If SSU increases the number of days worked to six per week, then the 10 advisors need only see 350 students a day to advise all of the students in 2 weeks.

Required

1. What would the average wait time be under alternative A and under alternative B?
2. If advisors earn $100 per day, which alternative would be cheaper for SSU (assume that if advisors work 6 days in a given work week, they will be paid time and a half for the sixth day)?
3. From a student satisfaction point of view, which of the two alternatives would be preferred? Why?

10-23 Nonfinancial measures of quality, manufacturing cycle efficiency. (CMA, adapted) Prescott Manufacturing evaluates the performance of its production managers based on a variety of factors, including cost, quality, and cycle time. The following are nonfinancial measures for quality and time for 2011 and 2012 for its only product:

Nonfinancial Quality Measures	2011	2012
Number of returned goods	750	915
Number of defective units reworked	2,200	1,640
Annual hours spent on quality training per employee	38	44
Number of units delivered on time	24,820	29,935

Annual Totals	2011	2012
Units of finished goods shipped	28,480	33,668
Average total hours worked per employee	2,000	2,000

The following information relates to the average amount of time needed to complete an order:

Time to Complete an Order	2011	2012
Wait time		
From customer placing order to order being received by production	15	14
From order received by production to machine being set up for production	13	12
Inspection time	4	2
Process time	8	8
Move time	4	4

Required

1. Compute the manufacturing cycle efficiency for an order for 2011 and 2012.
2. For each year 2011 and 2012, calculate the following:
   a. Percentage of goods returned
   b. Defective units reworked as a percentage of units shipped
   c. Percentage of on-time deliveries
   d. Percentage of hours spent by each employee on quality training
3. Evaluate management's performance on quality and timeliness in 2011 and 2012.

Problems

10-24 Quality improvement, relevant costs, and relevant revenues.

The Carson Corporation sells 250,000 V262 valves to the automobile and truck industry. Carson has a capacity of 150,000 machine-hours and can produce 2 valves per machine-hour. V262's contribution margin per unit is $10. Carson sells only 250,000 valves because 50,000 valves (20% of the valves sold) need to be reworked. It takes one machine-hour to rework 2 valves, so 25,000 hours of capacity are used in the rework process. Carson's rework costs are $450,000. Rework costs consist of the following:

- Direct materials and direct rework labor (variable costs): $5 per unit
- Fixed costs of equipment, rent, and overhead allocation: $4 per unit

Carson's process designers have developed a modification that would maintain the speed of the process and ensure 100% quality and no rework. The new process would cost $736,000 per year. The following additional information is available:

- The demand for Carson's V262 valves is 320,000 per year.
- The Brady Corporation has asked Carson to supply 17,000 T971 valves (another product) if Carson implements the new design. The contribution margin per T971 valve is $15. Carson can make one T971 valve per machine-hour with 100% quality and no rework.

Required

1. Suppose Carson's designers implement the new design. Should Carson accept Brady's order for 17,000 T971 valves? Show your calculations.
2. Should Carson implement the new design? Show your calculations.
3. What nonfinancial and qualitative factors should Carson consider in deciding whether to implement the new design?

10-25 Quality improvement, relevant costs, and relevant revenues.

The Harvest Corporation uses multicolor molding to make plastic lamps. The molding operation has a capacity of 100,000 units per year. The demand for lamps is very strong. Harvest will be able to sell whatever output quantities it can produce at $50 per lamp.

Harvest can start only 100,000 units into production in the molding department because of capacity constraints on the molding machines. If a defective unit is produced at the molding operation, it must be scrapped at a net disposal value of zero. Of the 100,000 units started at the molding operation, 10,000 defective units (10%) are produced. The cost of a defective unit, based on total (fixed and variable) manufacturing costs incurred up to the molding operation, equals $24 per unit, as follows:

Direct materials (variable)	$12 per unit
Direct manufacturing labor, setup labor, and materials-handling labor (variable)	2 per unit
Equipment, rent, and other allocated overhead, including inspection and testing costs on scrapped parts (fixed)	10 per unit
Total	$24 per unit

Harvest's designers have determined that adding a different type of material to the existing direct materials would result in no defective units being produced, but it would increase the variable costs by $3 per lamp in the molding department.

Required

1. Should Harvest use the new material? Show your calculations.
2. What nonfinancial and qualitative factors should Harvest consider in making the decision?

10-26 Statistical quality control. Harvest Cereals produces a wide variety of breakfast products. The company's three best-selling breakfast cereals are Double Bran Bits, Honey Wheat Squares, and Sugar King Pops. Each box of a particular type of cereal is required to meet pre-determined weight specifications, so that no single box contains more or less cereal than another. The company measures the mean weight per production run to determine if there are variances over or under the company's specified upper- and lower-level control limits. A production run that falls outside of the specified control limit does not meet quality standards and is investigated further by management to determine the cause of the variance. The three Harvest breakfast cereals had the following weight standards and production run data for the month of March:

Quality Standard: Mean Weight per Production Run

Double Bran Bits	Honey Wheat Squares	Sugar King Pops
17.97 ounces	14 ounces	16.02 ounces

Actual Mean Weight per Production Run (Ounces)

Production Run	Double Bran Bits	Honey Wheat Squares	Sugar King Pops
1	18.23	14.11	15.83
2	18.14	14.13	16.11
3	18.22	13.98	16.24
4	18.30	13.89	15.69
5	18.10	13.91	15.95
6	18.05	14.01	15.50
7	17.84	13.94	15.86
8	17.66	13.99	16.23
9	17.60	14.03	16.15
10	17.52	13.97	16.60
Standard Deviation	**0.28**	**0.16**	**0.21**

Required

1. Using the $\pm 2\sigma$ rule, what variance investigation decisions would be made?
2. Present control charts for each of the three breakfast cereals for March. What inferences can you draw from the charts?
3. What are the costs of quality in this example? How could Harvest employ Six Sigma programs to improve quality?

10-27 EOQ and JIT. Tech Works Corp. produces J-Pods, music players that can download thousands of songs. Tech Works forecasts that demand in 2013 will be 48,000 J-Pods. The variable production cost of each J-Pod is $54. Due to the large $10,000 cost per setup, Tech Works plans to produce J-Pods once a month in batches of 4,000 each. The carrying cost of a unit in inventory is $17 per year.

Required

1. What is the annual cost of producing and carrying J-Pods in inventory? (Assume that, on average, half of the units produced in a month are in inventory.)
2. A new manager at Tech Works has suggested that the company use the EOQ model to determine the optimal batch size to produce. (To use the EOQ model, Tech Works needs to treat the setup cost in the same way it would treat ordering cost in a traditional EOQ model.) Determine the optimal batch size and number of batches. Round up the number of batches to the nearest whole number. What would be the annual cost of producing and carrying J-Pods in inventory if it uses the optimal batch size? Compare this cost to the cost calculated in requirement 1. Comment briefly.
3. Tech Works is also considering switching to a JIT system. This will result in producing J-Pods in batch sizes of 600 J-Pods and will reduce obsolescence, improve quality, and result in a higher selling price. The frequency of production batches will force Tech Works to reduce setup time and will result in a reduction in setup cost. The new setup cost will be $500 per setup. What is the annual cost of producing and carrying J-Pods in inventory under the JIT system?

4. Compare the models analyzed in the previous parts of the problem. What are the advantages and disadvantages of each?

10-28 Effect of management evaluation criteria on EOQ model. Computer Depot purchases one model of computer at a wholesale cost of $300 per unit and resells it to end consumers. The annual demand for the company's product is 600,000 units. Ordering costs are $1,200 per order and carrying costs are $75 per computer, including $30 in the opportunity cost of holding inventory.

Required

1. Compute the optimal order quantity using the EOQ model.
2. Compute (a) the number of orders per year and (b) the annual relevant total cost of ordering and carrying inventory.
3. Assume that when evaluating the manager, the company excludes the opportunity cost of carrying inventory. If the manager makes the EOQ decision excluding the opportunity cost of carrying inventory, the relevant carrying cost would be $45 not $75. How would this affect the EOQ amount and the actual annual relevant cost of ordering and carrying inventory?
4. What is the cost impact on the company of excluding the opportunity cost of carrying inventory when making EOQ decisions? Why do you think the company currently excludes the opportunity costs of carrying inventory when evaluating the manager's performance? What could the company do to encourage the manager to make decisions more congruent with the goal of reducing total inventory costs?

10-29 JIT purchasing, relevant benefits, relevant costs. (CMA, adapted) The Greene Corporation is an automotive supplier that uses automatic turning machines to manufacture precision parts from steel bars. Greene's inventory of raw steel averages $300,000. John Oates, president of Greene, and Helen Gorman, Greene's controller, are concerned about the costs of carrying inventory. The steel supplier is willing to supply steel in smaller lots at no additional charge. Gorman identifies the following effects of adopting a JIT inventory program to virtually eliminate steel inventory:

- Without scheduling any overtime, lost sales due to stockouts would increase by 35,000 units per year. However, by incurring overtime premiums of $20,000 per year, the increase in lost sales could be reduced to 20,000 units per year. This would be the maximum amount of overtime that would be feasible for Greene.
- Two warehouses currently used for steel bar storage would no longer be needed. Greene rents one warehouse from another company under a cancelable leasing arrangement at an annual cost of $45,000. The other warehouse is owned by Greene and contains 12,000 square feet. Three-fourths of the space in the owned warehouse could be rented for $1.25 per square foot per year. Insurance and property tax costs totaling $7,000 per year would be eliminated.

Greene's required rate of return on investment is 20% per year. Greene's budgeted income statement for the year ending December 31, 2013 (in thousands), is:

Revenues (900,000 units)		$5, 400
Cost of goods sold		
Variable costs	$2,025	
Fixed costs	725	
Total costs of goods sold		2,750
Gross margin		2,650
Marketing and distribution costs		
Variable costs	$ 450	
Fixed costs	750	
Total marketing and distribution costs		1,200
Operating income		$1,450

Required

1. Calculate the estimated dollar savings (loss) for the Greene Corporation that would result in 2013 from the adoption of JIT purchasing.
2. Identify and explain other factors that Greene should consider before deciding whether to adopt JIT purchasing.

10-30 Supply chain effects on total relevant inventory cost. Peach Computer Co. outsources the production of motherboards for its computers. It is currently deciding which of two suppliers to use: Alpha or Beta. Due to differences in the product failure rates in the two companies, 5% of motherboards purchased from Alpha will be inspected and 25% of motherboards purchased from Beta will be inspected. The following data refers to costs associated with Alpha and Beta:

	Alpha	Beta
Number of orders per year	50	50
Annual motherboards demanded	10,000	10,000
Price per motherboard	$108	$105
Ordering cost per order	$13	$10
Inspection cost per unit	$6	$6
Average inventory level	100 units	100 units
Expected number of stockouts	100	300
Stockout cost (cost of rush order) per stockout	$4	$6
Units returned by customers for replacing motherboards	50	500
Cost of replacing each motherboard	$30	$30
Required annual return on investment	10%	10%
Other carrying cost per unit per year	$3.50	$3.50

Required

1. What is the relevant cost of purchasing from Alpha and Beta?
2. What factors other than cost should Peach consider?

10-31 Lean accounting. Reliable Security Devices (RSD) has introduced a just-in-time production process and is considering the adoption of lean accounting principles to support its new production philosophy. The company has two product lines: Mechanical Devices and Electronic Devices. Two individual products are made in each line. Product-line manufacturing overhead costs are traced directly to product lines, and then allocated to the two individual products in each line. The company's traditional cost accounting system allocates all plant-level facility costs and some corporate overhead costs to individual products. The latest accounting report using traditional cost accounting methods included the following information (in thousands of dollars):

	Mechanical Devices		Electronic Devices	
	Product A	Product B	Product C	Product D
Sales	$1,400	$1,000	$1,800	$900
Direct material (based on quantity used)	400	200	500	150
Direct manufacturing labor	300	150	400	120
Manufacturing overhead (equipment lease, supervision, production control)	180	240	400	190
Allocated plant-level facility costs	100	80	160	60
Design and marketing costs	190	100	210	84
Allocated corporate overhead costs	30	20	40	16
Operating income	$ 200	$ 210	$ 90	$280

RSD has determined that each of the two product lines represents a distinct value stream. It has also determined that out of the $400,000 ($100,000 + $80,000 + $160,000 + $60,000) plant-level facility costs, product A occupies 22% of the plant's square footage, product B occupies 18%, product C occupies 36%, and product D occupies 14%. The remaining 10% of square footage is not being used. Finally, RSD has decided that direct material should be expensed in the period it is purchased, rather than when the material is used. According to purchasing records, direct material purchase costs during the period were as follows:

	Mechanical Devices		Electronic Devices	
	Product A	Product B	Product C	Product D
Direct material (purchases)	$420	$240	$500	$180

Required

1. What are the cost objects in RSD's lean accounting system?
2. Compute operating income for the cost objects identified in requirement 1 using lean accounting principles. Why does operating income differ from the operating income computed using traditional cost accounting methods? Comment on your results.

10-32 Quality improvement, Pareto diagram, cause-and-effect diagram. Pauli's Pizza has recently begun collecting data on the quality of its customer order processing and delivery. Pauli's made 1,800 deliveries during the first quarter of 2013. The following quality data pertains to first-quarter deliveries:

Type of Quality Failure	Quality Failure Incidents First Quarter 2013
Late delivery	50
Damaged or spoiled product delivered	5
Incorrect order delivered	12
Service complaints by customer of delivery personnel	8
Failure to deliver incidental items with order (drinks, side items, etc.)	18

Required

1. Draw a Pareto diagram of the quality failures experienced by Pauli's Pizza.
2. Give examples of prevention activities that could reduce the failures experienced by Pauli's.
3. Draw a cause-and-effect diagram of possible causes for late deliveries. How might such a diagram be helpful to the manager of Pauli's Pizza?

10-33 Quality improvement, relevant costs. The Winchester Corporation makes printed cloth in two departments: weaving and printing. Currently, all product first moves through the weaving department and then through the printing department before it is sold to retail distributors for $2,500 per roll. Winchester provides the following information:

	Weaving	Printing
Monthly capacity	10,000 rolls	15,000 rolls
Monthly production	9,500 rolls	8,550 rolls
Direct material cost per roll of cloth processed at each operation	$1,000	$200
Fixed operating costs	$5,700,000	$855,000

Winchester can start only 10,000 rolls of cloth in the weaving department because of capacity constraints of the weaving machines. Of the 10,000 rolls of cloth started in the weaving department, 500 (5%) defective rolls are scrapped at zero net disposal value. The good rolls from the weaving department (called gray cloth) are sent to the printing department. Of the 9,500 good rolls started at the printing operation, 950 (10%) defective rolls are scrapped at zero net disposal value. The Winchester Corporation's total monthly sales of printed cloth equal the printing department's output.

Required

1. The printing department is considering buying 5,000 additional rolls of gray cloth from an outside supplier at $1,800 per roll, which is much higher than Winchester's cost to manufacture the roll. The printing department expects that 10% of the rolls obtained from the outside supplier will result in defective products. Should the printing department buy the gray cloth from the outside supplier? Show your calculations.
2. Winchester's engineers have developed a method that would lower the printing department's rate of defective products to 6% at the printing operation. Implementing the new method would cost $700,000 per month. Should Winchester implement the change? Show your calculations.
3. The design engineering team has proposed a modification that would lower the weaving department's rate of defective products to 3%. The modification would cost the company $350,000 per month. Should Winchester implement the change? Show your calculations.

10-34 Compensation linked with profitability, waiting time, and quality measures. West Coast Healthcare operates two medical groups, one in Seattle and one in San Francisco. The semi-annual bonus plan for each medical group's president has three components:

a. Profitability performance. Add 0.75% of operating income.

b. Average patient waiting time. Add $20,000 if the average waiting time for a patient to see a doctor after the scheduled appointment time is less than 10 minutes. If average patient waiting time is more than 10 minutes, add nothing.

c. Patient satisfaction performance. Deduct $20,000 if patient satisfaction (measured using a survey asking patients about their satisfaction with their doctor and their overall satisfaction with West Coast Healthcare) falls below 65 on a scale from 0 (lowest) to 100 (highest). No additional bonus is awarded for satisfaction scores of 65 or more.

Semi-annual data for 2012 for the Seattle and San Francisco groups are as follows:

	January–June	July–December
Seattle		
Operating income	$5,575,000	$5,250,000
Average waiting time	12 minutes	13 minutes
Patient satisfaction	75	73
San Francisco		
Operating income	$4,750,000	$2,937,500
Average waiting time	13 minutes	9 minutes
Patient satisfaction	58	69

Required

1. Compute the bonuses paid in each half year of 2012 to the Seattle and San Francisco medical group presidents.
2. Discuss the validity of the components of the bonus plan as measures of profitability, waiting time performance, and patient satisfaction. Suggest one shortcoming of each measure and how it might be overcome (by redesign of the plan or by another measure).
3. Why do you think West Coast Healthcare includes measures of both operating income and waiting time in its bonus plan for group presidents? Give one example of what might happen if waiting time was dropped as a performance measure.

10-35 Waiting times, manufacturing cycle times. The Seawall Corporation uses an injection molding machine to make a plastic product, Z39, after receiving firm orders from its customers. Seawall estimates that it will receive 50 orders for Z39 during the coming year. Each order of Z39 will take 80 hours of machine time. The annual machine capacity is 5,000 hours.

Required

1. Calculate (a) the average amount of time that an order for Z39 will wait in line before it is processed and (b) the average manufacturing cycle time per order for Z39.
2. Seawall is considering introducing a new product, Y28. The company expects it will receive 25 orders of Y28 in the coming year. Each order of Y28 will take 20 hours of machine time. Assuming the demand for Z39 will not be affected by the introduction of Y28, calculate (a) the average waiting time for an order received and (b) the average manufacturing cycle time per order for each product if Seawall introduces Y28.
3. The following table provides information on selling prices, variable costs, and inventory carrying costs for Z39 and Y28:

		Selling Price per Order if Average Manufacturing Cycle Time per Order Is			
Product	Annual Average Number of Orders	Less than 320 Hours	More than 320 Hours	Variable Cost per Order	Inventory Carrying Cost per Order per Hour
Z39	50	$27,000	$26,500	$15,000	$0.75
Y28	25	8,400	8,000	5,000	0.25

Should Seawall manufacture and sell Y28? Show your calculations.

10-36 Manufacturing cycle times, relevant revenues, and relevant costs. The Brandt Corporation makes wire harnesses for the aircraft industry only upon receiving firm orders from its customers. Brandt has recently purchased a new machine to make two types of wire harnesses, one for Boeing airplanes (B7) and the other for Airbus Industries airplanes (A3). The annual capacity of the new machine is 6,000 hours. The following information is available for next year:

			Selling Price per Order if Average Manufacturing Cycle Time per Order Is			
Customer	Annual Average Number of Orders	Manufacturing Time Required	Less Than 200 Hours	More Than 200 Hours	Variable Cost per Order	Inventory Carrying Cost per Order per Hour
B7	125	40 hours	$15,000	$14,400	$10,000	$0.50
A3	10	50 hours	13,500	12,960	9,000	0.45

Required

1. Calculate the average manufacturing cycle times per order (a) if Brandt manufactures only B7 and (b) if Brandt manufactures both B7 and A3.
2. Even though A3 has a positive contribution margin, Brandt's managers are evaluating whether Brandt should (a) make and sell only B7 or (b) make and sell both B7 and A3. Which alternative will maximize Brandt's operating income? Show your calculations.
3. What other factors should Brandt consider in choosing between the alternatives in requirement 2?

10-37 Ethics and quality. Weston Corporation manufactures auto parts for two leading Japanese automakers. Nancy Evans is the management accountant for one of Weston's largest manufacturing plants. The plant's general manager, Chris Sheldon, has just returned from a meeting at corporate headquarters where quality expectations were outlined for 2013. Chris calls Nancy into his office to relay the corporate quality objective that total quality costs will not exceed 10% of total revenues by plant under any circumstances. Chris asks Nancy to provide him with a list of options for meeting corporate headquarters's quality objective. The plant's initial budgeted revenues and quality costs for 2013 are as follows:

Revenue	5,100,000
Quality costs	
Testing of purchased materials	48,000
Quality control training for production staff	7,500
Warranty repairs	123,000
Quality design engineering	72,000
Customer support	55,500
Materials scrap	18,000
Product inspection	153,000
Engineering redesign of failed parts	31,500
Rework of failed parts	27,000

Prior to receiving the new corporate quality objective, Nancy had collected information for all of the plant's possible options for improving both product quality and costs of quality. She was planning to introduce the idea of reengineering the manufacturing process at a one-time cost of $112,500, which would decrease product inspection costs by approximately 25% per year and was expected to reduce warranty repairs and customer support by an estimated 40% per year. After seeing the new corporate objective, Nancy is reconsidering the reengineering idea.

Nancy returns to her office and crunches the numbers again to look for other alternatives. She concludes that by increasing the cost of quality control training for production staff by $22,500 per year, the company would reduce inspection costs by 10% annually and reduce warranty repairs and customer support costs by 20% per year, as well. She is leaning toward only presenting this latter option to Chris because this is the only option that meets the new corporate quality objective.

Required

1. Calculate the ratio of each costs-of-quality category (prevention, appraisal, internal failure, and external failure) to revenues for 2013. Are the total costs of quality as a percentage of revenues currently less than 10%?
2. Which of the two quality options should Nancy propose to the general manager, Chris Sheldon? Show the 2-year outcome for each option: (a) reengineer the manufacturing process for $112,500 and (b) increase quality training expenditure by $22,500 per year.
3. Suppose Nancy decides not to present the reengineering option to Chris. Is Nancy's action unethical? Explain.

10-38 JIT production, relevant benefits, relevant costs, ethics. Perez Container Corporation is considering implementing a JIT production system. The new system would reduce current average inventory levels of $4,000,000 by 75%, but it would require a much greater dependency on the company's core suppliers for on-time deliveries and high-quality inputs. The company's operations manager, Jim Ingram, is opposed to the idea of a new JIT system because he is concerned that the new system (a) will be too costly to manage; (b) will result in too many stockouts; and (c) will lead to the layoff of his employees, several of whom are currently managing inventory. He believes that these layoffs will affect the morale of his entire production department. The management accountant, Sue Winston, is in favor of the new system because of its likely cost savings. Jim wants Sue to rework the numbers because he is concerned that top management will give more weight to financial factors and not give due consideration to nonfinancial factors such as employee morale. In addition to the reduction in inventory described previously, Sue has gathered the following information for the upcoming year regarding the JIT system:

- Annual insurance and warehousing costs for inventory would be reduced by 60% of current budgeted level of $700,000.
- Payroll expenses for current inventory management staff would be reduced by 15% of the budgeted total of $1,200,000.
- Additional annual costs for JIT system implementation and management, including personnel costs, would equal $440,000.
- The additional number of stockouts under the new JIT system is estimated to be 5% of the total number of shipments annually. Ten thousand shipments are budgeted for the upcoming year. Each stockout would result in an average additional cost of $500.
- Perez's required rate of return on inventory investment is 10% per year.

Required

1. From a financial perspective, should Perez adopt the new JIT system?
2. Should Sue Winston rework the numbers?
3. How should she manage Jim Ingram's concerns?

Case

Ritz-Carlton Hotel Company

Senior executives at the Ritz Carlton strive to balance efficiency and quality with the goal of maintaining the hotel's reputation for creating an aura and experience of old-world elegance and legendary grandeur in locations ranging from the United States to Bahrain to China. If executives were to focus on quality, what precisely would this mean and how might they measure it?

Ritz Carlton's strategy is to create an outstanding experience for its guests. One way to create this experience is to build hotels with stunning lobbies and spacious and elegant rooms and to hire and train a staff that provides excellent customer service. Project teams build each hotel with the usual "Ritz-Carlton" splendor, and maintenance teams ensure that the hotel preserves this décor and high level of service.

A second way to create outstanding customer experience is to improve the efficiency of operations such as room service, guest reservation and registration, message delivery, and breakfast service. Ritz Carlton could do statistical measurement of process work flows and cycle times for areas such as room service delivery, reservations, valet parking, and housekeeping. Managers could use the results to develop benchmarks against which they could measure future performance. With specific, quantifiable targets in place, they could focus on the continuous improvement and monitoring of quality and take actions to prevent problems from arising. Managers can review these performances at daily and weekly management meetings and communicate results back to their employees.

Senior managers debated whether the Ritz-Carlton should emphasize quality. Some managers felt that attention to quality and efficiency would only be relevant if the company's focus was on cutting costs to charge lower prices. They felt that, as a premium-priced hotel, the Ritz-Carlton should concentrate on spending money to create an aura of grandeur and comfort. They also argued that emphasizing quality could be confusing to employees. For example, these managers believed that it was more important for the Ritz-Carlton to focus on the tastiness of the food rather than room service delivery times. If room service delivery times became an important measure, employees might cut corners on food preparation to serve customers more quickly. As one of these managers commented, "No one is arguing that the wait times for guest reservations and registration or valet parking should be long. I am just not sure that we should be focusing on these activities because it will distract from what makes Ritz-Carlton special."

Other managers had a different view. They saw quality as a daily commitment to meeting customer expectations and making sure each hotel was free of any deficiency in fulfilling those expectations. They believed that guests do not purchase a product, they buy an experience. Creating the right combination of elements to make the guests' experience outstanding is the challenge and goal of every employee, from maintenance to management. A manager who supported the focus on quality argued, "I think creating a quality mind set in every employee is important because each employee has the potential to affect the customer experience. For example, when a customer is waiting to register, it does not matter how beautiful the lobby of the hotel is if the registration waiting times get long. Customers will get upset. The registration staff must be polite and courteous and this means registration may take longer, but the focus on quality means that we employ more people to staff the counter to reduce delays."

Another manager who supported the quality initiative added, "I would go so far as to organize employees into 'self-directed' work teams within each functional area of the hotel, such as guest services, valet services, food and beverages, housekeeping, and maintenance. Managers should not operate in command-and-control mode, in which orders are dictated and expected to be carried out. Instead, employee teams should determine employee work scheduling, what work needs to be done, and what to do about quality problems in their areas. Managers should become facilitators and resources for helping the teams achieve their quality goals. Employees should be given the opportunity to take additional training on how the hotel is run, so they can see the relationship of their specific area's efforts to the overall goals of the hotel. Training topics should range from budgets and purchasing to payroll and controllable costs. Employees then should be tested and compensated for successful completion of training. A more-educated and informed employee will be in a better position to make decisions that are in the best interest of guests and the organization as a whole."

Several managers, including some who supported the quality initiative, were more skeptical about the "self-directed" approach, however. One such manager stated, "You cannot have 'self-directed' work teams because then actions cannot be properly coordinated. It is the manager's job to do employee work scheduling. I am not saying that employees must not be empowered to make some decisions, but hotel operations run best when there are well-established processes that employees must follow."

Questions

1. Consider the time it takes to register guests. Give an example of a cost in each costs of quality category—prevention costs, appraisal costs, internal failure costs, and external failure costs.
2. For each of the following perspectives, describe two measures that the Ritz-Carlton managers could use when evaluating quality, (a) customer perspective (b) internal business-process perspective and (c) employee perspective? Explain why you think your choices of measures are important for Ritz-Carlton.
3. What actions can Ritz-Carlton's managers, staff, and employees take to improve quality?
4. What do you think about the idea of organizing employees into "self-directed" teams? Explain.
5. Would you advise the Ritz-Carlton to focus on quality? Why? Explain.

11 Capital Investments

Learning Objectives

1. Understand the five stages of capital budgeting for a project
2. Use and evaluate the two main discounted cash flow (DCF) methods: the net present value (NPV) method and the internal rate-of-return (IRR) method
3. Use and evaluate the payback and discounted payback methods
4. Use and evaluate the accrual accounting rate-of-return (AARR) method
5. Identify relevant cash inflows and outflows that managers use to make capital budgeting decisions
6. Understand the challenges of implementing capital budgeting decisions and evaluating managerial performance
7. Explain how managers can use capital budgeting to achieve strategic goals

A firm's managers must make important decisions about whether to commit to major expenditures, or investments, which will have a significant effect on the company's future. For example, should Honda open a new plant in China or India? Should Sony invest in developing the next generation of PlayStation consoles? Should the Gap discontinue its children's clothing line and expand its women's athletic clothing line? Top executives have to figure out how and when to best allocate the firm's financial resources among alternative opportunities to create future value for the company. Because it's hard to know what the future holds and how much projects will ultimately cost, this can be a challenging task, but it's one that managers must constantly confront. To meet this challenge, companies such as Target and Chevron have developed special groups to make project-related capital budgeting decisions. As the Chapter at a Glance describes, this chapter explains the different methods managers use to choose the projects that will contribute the most value to their organizations.

Chapter at a Glance

- Capital budgeting is the process by which firms evaluate long-term investments.
- A key step in capital budgeting requires managers to estimate the lifespan after-tax cash flows for each project, from initial investment through annual operation to its eventual termination.
- Discounted cash flow (DCF) methods evaluate projects based on the present value of all expected future *cash* inflows and outflows, thus accounting for the time value of money.
- In addition to discounted cash flow methods, managers also use undiscounted cash flows or accounting earnings to select capital projects.
- It is inconsistent for a company to use discounted cash flow methods to choose projects while using periodic accounting earnings to evaluate managers.
- It is useful for companies to conduct post-investment audits because they reveal difficulties in project implementation and help deter managers from making overly optimistic initial projections of cash flows.
- Capital investment decisions are often made in support of a firm's strategic goals.

Stages of Capital Budgeting

Learning Objective 1

Understand the five stages of capital budgeting for a project

. . . identify the project; obtain information; make predictions; choose among alternatives; and implement the decision

Capital budgeting is the process of making long-run planning decisions for investments in projects. In choosing investments, managers make a selection from among a group of multiple projects, each of which may span several periods. Capital budgeting analyzes each project by considering all the lifespan cash flows from its initial investment through its termination, and is analogous to life-cycle budgeting and costing (Chapter 7, pages 276–278). For example, when Honda managers consider a new line of automobiles, they begin by estimating all potential revenues from the new line as well as any costs that will be incurred along its life cycle, which may be as long as 10 years. Only after examining the potential costs and benefits across all of the business functions in the value chain, from research and development (R&D) to customer service, across the entire lifespan of the new-car project, do Honda managers decide whether the new model is a wise investment.

Managers use capital budgeting as a decision-making and a control tool. Like the five-step decision process that we have emphasized in many chapters of this book, there are five stages to the capital budgeting process:

Stage 1: Identify Projects. *Identify potential capital investments that agree with the organization's strategy.* For example, Nike, an industry leader in product differentiation, makes significant investments in product innovation, engineering, and design, hoping to develop the next generation of high-quality sportswear. Alternatively, managers could promote projects that improve productivity and efficiency as a strategy of cost leadership. In the case of a manufacturer of computer hardware such as Dell, a strategy of cost leadership includes outsourcing certain components to lower-cost contract manufacturing facilities located overseas. Identifying which types of capital projects to invest in is largely the responsibility of senior line managers.

Stage 2: Obtain Information. *Gather information from all parts of the value chain to evaluate alternative projects.* Returning to the new car example at Honda, in this stage, top managers ask marketing managers for potential revenue numbers, plant managers for assembly times, and suppliers for prices and the availability of key components. Honda's top managers will ask the lower-level managers to validate the data provided and to explain the assumptions underlying them. The goal is to encourage open and honest communication of accurate estimates, so that the eventual decisions taken by the firm are in the best interests of the shareholders. Managers may even reject some projects at this stage. For example, suppose Honda learns that the car simply cannot be built using existing plants. It may then opt to cancel the project altogether.

Stage 3: Make Predictions. *Forecast all potential cash flows attributable to the alternative projects.* Capital investment projects generally involve substantial initial outlays, which are recouped over time through annual cash inflows and the disposal values from the termination of the project. As a result, they require the firm to make forecasts of cash flows several years into the future. BMW, for example, estimates yearly cash flows and sets its investment budgets accordingly using a 12-year planning horizon. Because of the significant uncertainty associated with these predictions, firms typically analyze a wide range of alternate circumstances. In the case of BMW, the marketing group is asked to estimate a band of possible sales figures within a 90% confidence interval. Firms also attempt to ensure that estimates, especially for the later years of a project, are grounded in realistic scenarios. It is tempting for managers to introduce biases into these projections in order to drive the outcome of the capital budgeting process to their preferred choice. This effect is exacerbated by the fact that managers may not expect to be employed at the firm during those years and therefore cannot be held accountable for their estimates.

Stage 4: Make Decisions by Choosing Among Alternatives. *Determine which investment yields the greatest benefit and the least cost to the organization.* Using the quantitative information obtained in stage 3, the firm uses any one of several capital budgeting methodologies to determine which project best meets organizational goals. While capital budgeting calculations are typically limited to financial information, managers use their judgment and intuition to factor in qualitative information and strategic considerations as well. For example, even if a proposed new line of cars meets its financial targets on a stand-alone basis, Honda might decide not to pursue the line if it will lessen how consumers perceive the quality of the firm's products. Moreover, Honda's top managers will try to ensure that a new car project is aligned with the strategic imperatives of the company on matters such as fuel consumption, environmental sustainability, and brand positioning. Finally, managers spend a significant amount of time assessing the risks of a project, in terms of both the uncertainty of the estimated cash flows as well as the potential downside risk to the project (as well as to the firm as a whole) if the worst-case scenario were to occur.

Stage 5: Implement the Decision, Evaluate Performance, and Learn. Given the complexities of capital investment decisions and their long time horizons, this stage can be separated into two phases:

- **Obtain funding and make the investments selected in stage 4.** Sources of funding include internally generated cash flow as well as equity and debt securities sold in capital markets. Making capital investments is often an arduous task, laden with the purchase of many different goods and services. If Honda opts to build a new car, it must order steel, aluminum, paint, and so on. If some of the planned supplies are unavailable, managers must revisit and determine the economic feasibility of substituting the missing material with alternative inputs.
- **Track realized cash flows, compare against estimated numbers, and revise plans if necessary.** As the cash outflows and inflows begin to accumulate, managers can verify whether the predictions made in stage 3 agree with the actual flows of cash from the project. When the BMW group initially released the new Mini in 2001, its realized sales were substantially higher than the original demand estimates. BMW responded by manufacturing more cars to meet the higher demand. It also decided to expand the Mini line to include convertibles and the larger Clubman model. It is equally important for a company to abandon projects that are performing poorly relative to expectations. A natural bias for managers is to escalate commitment to a project they chose to implement, for fear of revealing that they made an incorrect capital budgeting decision. It is in the firm's and the managers' long-term interest, however, to acknowledge the mistake when it is clear that the project is not financially sustainable. For example, TransAlta, a Canadian electricity generator, recently halted a CA$1.4 billion project to capture carbon in Alberta. After spending CA$30 million on engineering and design studies, the firm realized that even though costs were in line with expectations, revenue from carbon sales and the price of emissions reductions were insufficient to make the project economically viable.

To illustrate capital budgeting, consider Top-Spin tennis racquets. Top-Spin was one of the first major tennis-racquet producers to introduce graphite in its racquets. This innovation allowed Top-Spin to produce some of the lightest and stiffest racquets in the market. However, new carbon-fiber impregnated racquets are even lighter and stiffer than their graphite counterparts. Top-Spin wants to continue to innovate, so in stage 1, managers identify the carbon-fiber racquet project. In the information-gathering stage (stage 2), the company learns that it could feasibly begin using carbon fiber in its racquets as early as 2012 if it replaces one of its graphite-forming machines with a carbon-fiber weaving machine. After collecting additional data, Top-Spin's managers begin to forecast future cash flows if the firm were to invest in the new machine (stage 3). Top-Spin estimates that it can purchase a carbon-fiber weaving machine with a useful life of 5 years for a net after-tax initial investment of $379,100, which is calculated as:

Cost of new machine	$390,000
Investment in working capital	9,000
Cash flow from disposing of existing machine (after-tax)	(19,900)
Net initial investment for new machine	$379,100

Working capital refers to the difference between current assets and current liabilities. New projects often necessitate additional investments in current assets such as inventories and receivables. In the case of Top-Spin, the purchase of the new machine is accompanied by an outlay of $9,000 for supplies and spare parts inventory. At the end of the project, the $9,000 in supplies and spare parts inventory is liquidated, resulting in a cash inflow. However, the machine itself is believed to have no terminal disposal value after 5 years.

Managers estimate that by introducing carbon-fiber impregnated racquets, operating cash inflows (cash revenues minus cash operating costs) will increase by $100,000 (after tax) in the first 4 years and $91,000 in year 5. To simplify the analysis, suppose that all cash flows occur at the end of each year. Note that cash flow at the end of the fifth year also increases by $100,000, $91,000 in operating cash inflows and $9,000 in working capital. Management next calculates the costs and benefits of the proposed project (stage 4). This chapter discusses four capital budgeting methods to analyze financial information: (1) net present value (NPV), (2) internal rate of return (IRR), (3) payback, and (4) accrual accounting rate of return (AARR). Both the net present value (NPV) and internal rate-of-return (IRR) methods use *discounted cash flows,* which we discuss in the next section.

Keys to Success

Analogous to the five-step decision process, there are five stages of capital budgeting managers must follow for a project: identification, information gathering, forecasting, decision making, and evaluation.

Discounted Cash Flow

Learning Objective 2

Use and evaluate the two main discounted cash flow (DCF) methods: the net present value (NPV) method and the internal rate-of-return (IRR) method

. . . to explicitly consider all project cash flows and the time value of money

Discounted cash flow (DCF) methods measure all expected future cash inflows and outflows of a project discounted back to the present point in time. The key feature of DCF methods is the **time value of money,** which means that a dollar (or any other monetary unit) received today is worth more than a dollar received at any future time. The reason is that \$1 received today can be invested at, say, 10% per year so that it grows to \$1.10 at the end of 1 year. The time value of money is the opportunity cost (the return of \$0.10 forgone per year) from not having the money today. In this example, \$1 received 1 year from now is worth \$1 ÷ 1.10 = \$0.9091 today. In this way, discounted cash flow methods explicitly weigh cash flows by the time value of money. Note that DCF focuses exclusively on cash inflows and outflows rather than on operating income as determined by accrual accounting.

The compound interest tables and formulas used in DCF analysis are in the Appendix, pages 702–708. If you are unfamiliar with compound interest, do not proceed until you have studied the Appendix because we will use the tables in the appendix frequently in this chapter.

The two DCF methods we describe are the net present value (NPV) method and the internal rate-of-return (IRR) method. Both DCF methods use the **required rate of return (RRR),** the minimum acceptable annual rate of return on an investment. The RRR is internally set, usually by upper management, and typically represents the return that an organization could expect to receive elsewhere for an investment of comparable risk. The RRR is also called the **discount rate, hurdle rate, cost of capital,** or **opportunity cost of capital.** Suppose the CFO at Top-Spin has set the required rate of return for the firm's investments at 8% per year.

Net Present Value Method

The **net present value (NPV) method** calculates the expected monetary gain or loss from a project by discounting all expected future cash inflows and outflows back to the present point in time using the required rate of return. To use the NPV method, apply the following three steps:

Step 1: Draw a Sketch of Relevant Cash Inflows and Outflows. The right side of Exhibit 11-1 shows arrows that depict the cash flows of the new carbon-fiber machine. The sketch helps the decision maker visualize and organize the data in a systematic way. *Note that parentheses denote relevant cash outflows throughout all exhibits in this chapter.* Exhibit 11-1 includes the outflow for the acquisition of the new machine at the start of year 1 (also referred to as end of year 0), and the inflows over the subsequent 5 years. The NPV method specifies cash flows regardless of the source of the cash flows, such as from operations, purchase or sale of equipment, or investment in or recovery of working capital. However, accrual-accounting concepts such as sales made on credit or noncash expenses are not included since the focus is on *cash* inflows and outflows.

Step 2: Discount the Cash Flows Using the Correct Compound Interest Table from the Appendix and Sum Them. In the Top-Spin example, we can discount each year's cash flow separately using Table 2, or we can compute the present value of an annuity, a series of equal cash flows at equal time intervals, using Table 4. (Both tables are in the Appendix.) If we use Table 2, we find the discount factors for periods 1–5 under the 8% column. Approach 1 in Exhibit 11-1 uses the five discount factors. To obtain the present value amount, multiply each discount factor by the corresponding amount represented by the arrow on the right in Exhibit 11-1 (−\$379,100 × 1.000; \$100,000 × 0.926; and so on to \$100,000 × 0.681). Because the investment in the new machine produces an annuity, we may also use Table 4. Under Approach 2, we find that the annuity factor for five periods under the 8% column is 3.993, which is the sum of the five discount factors used in Approach 1. We multiply the uniform annual cash inflow by this factor to obtain the present value of the inflows (\$399,300 = \$100,000 × 3.993). Subtracting the initial investment then reveals the NPV of the project as \$20,200 (\$20,200 = \$399,300 − \$379,100).

Exhibit 11-1

Net Present Value Method: Top-Spin's Carbon-Fiber Machine

Home Insert Page Layout Formulas Data Review View

	A	B	C	D	E	F	G	H	I
1			Net initial investment	$379,100					
2			Useful life	5 years					
3			Annual cash inflow	$100,000					
4			Required rate of return	8%					
5									
6		Present Value	Present Value of		Sketch of Relevant Cash Flows at End of Each Year				
7		of Cash Flow	$1 Discounted at 8%	0	1	2	3	4	5
8	Approach 1: Discounting Each Year's Cash Flow Separately[a]								
9	Net initial investment	$(379,100) ←	1.000 ←	$(379,100)					
10		92,600 ←	0.926 ←		$100,000				
11		85,700 ←	0.857 ←			$100,000			
12	Annual cash inflow	79,400 ←	0.794 ←				$100,000		
13		73,500 ←	0.735 ←					$100,000	
14		68,100 ←	0.681 ←						$100,000
15	NPV if new machine purchased	$ 20,200							
16									
17	Approach 2: Using Annuity Table[b]								
18	Net initial investment	$(379,100) ←	1.000 ←	$(379,100)					
19					$100,000	$100,000	$100,000	$100,000	$100,000
20									
21	Annual cash inflow	399,300 ←	3.993 ←						
22	NPV if new machine purchased	$ 20,200							
23									
24	*Note:* Parentheses denote relevant cash outflows throughout all exhibits in Chapter 11.								
25	[a] Present values from Table 2, in the Appendix at the end of the book. For example, $0.857 = 1 \div (1.08)^2$.								
26	[b] Annuity present value from Table 4, in the Appendix. The annuity value of 3.993 is the sum of the individual discount rates 0.926 + 0.857 + 0.794 + 0.735 + 0.681.								

Step 3: Make the Project Decision on the Basis of the Calculated NPV. If NPV is zero or positive, financial considerations suggest that the company should accept the project because the expected rate of return equals or exceeds the required rate of return. If NPV is negative, the company should reject the project because its expected rate of return is below the required rate of return.

Exhibit 11-1 calculates an NPV of $20,200 at the required rate of return of 8% per year. The project is acceptable based on financial information. The cash flows from the project are adequate (1) to recover the net initial investment in the project and (2) to earn a return greater than 8% per year on the investment tied up in the project over its useful life.

> **Keys to Success**
>
> **Discounted cash flow methods incorporate the time value of money so that managers can evaluate projects with cash flows over multiple years on a common basis. The NPV criterion specifies that a manager should choose a project if and only if the sum of its discounted cash flows is positive.**

Managers must also weigh nonfinancial factors such as the effect that purchasing the machine will have on Top-Spin's brand. This is a nonfinancial factor because the financial benefits that accrue from Top-Spin's brand are very difficult to estimate. Nevertheless, managers must consider brand effects before reaching a final decision. Suppose, for example, that the NPV of the carbon-fiber machine is negative. Management may still decide to buy the machine if it maintains Top-Spin's brand and technological image and helps sell other Top-Spin products.

Internal Rate-of-Return Method

The **internal rate-of-return (IRR) method** calculates the discount rate at which an investment's present value of all expected cash inflows equals the present value of its expected cash outflows. That is, the IRR is the discount rate that makes NPV = \$0. Exhibit 11-2 presents the cash flows and shows the calculation of NPV using a 10% annual discount rate for Top-Spin's carbon-fiber project. At a 10% discount rate, the NPV of the project is \$0. Therefore, IRR is 10% per year.

Managers solving capital budgeting problems typically use a calculator or computer program to provide the internal rate of return. The following trial-and-error approach can also provide the answer.

Step 1: Use a discount rate and calculate the project's NPV.

Step 2: If the calculated NPV is less than zero, use a lower discount rate. (A *lower* discount rate will *increase* NPV. Remember that we are trying to find a discount rate for which NPV = \$0.) If NPV is greater than zero, use a higher discount rate. Keep adjusting the discount rate until NPV = \$0. In the Top-Spin example, a discount rate of 8% yields an NPV of +\$20,200 (see Exhibit 11-1). A discount rate of 12% yields an NPV of −\$18,600 (3.605, the present value annuity factor from Table 4 × \$100,000 − \$379,100). Therefore, the discount rate that makes NPV = \$0 must lie between 8% and 12%. We use 10% and get NPV = \$0, so the IRR is 10% per year.

The step-by-step computations of internal rate of return are easier when the cash inflows are constant, as in our Top-Spin example. Information from Exhibit 11-2 can be expressed as:

$$\$379{,}100 = \text{Present value of annuity of } \$100{,}000 \text{ at } X\% \text{ per year for 5 years}$$

Exhibit 11-2

Internal Rate-of-Return Method: Top-Spin's Carbon-Fiber Machine[a]

	A	B	C	D	E	F	G	H	I
1			Net initial investment	\$379,100					
2			Useful life	5 years					
3			Annual cash inflow	\$100,000					
4			Annual discount rate	10%					
5									
6		Present Value	Present Value of		Sketch of Relevant Cash Flows at End of Each Year				
7		of Cash Flow	\$1 Discounted at 10%[b]	0	1	2	3	4	5
8	**Approach 1: Discounting Each Year's Cash Flow Separately**								
9	Net initial investment	\$(379,100)	1.000	\$(379,100)					
10		90,900	0.909		\$100,000				
11		82,600	0.826			\$100,000			
12	Annual cash inflow	75,100	0.751				\$100,000		
13		68,300	0.683					\$100,000	
14		62,100	0.621						\$100,000
15	NPV if new machine purchased[c]	\$ 0							
16	(the zero difference proves that								
17	the internal rate of return is 10%)								
18									
19	**Approach 2: Using Annuity Table**								
20	Net initial investment	\$(379,100)	1.000	\$(379,100)					
21					\$100,000	\$100,000	\$100,000	\$100,000	\$100,000
22									
23	Annual cash inflow	379,100	3.791[d]						
24	NPV if new machine purchased	\$ 0							
25									
26	*Note: Parentheses denote relevant cash outflows throughout all exhibits in Chapter 11.*								
27	[a]The internal rate of return is computed by methods explained on pp. 449–450.								
28	[b]Present values from Table 2, in the Appendix at the end of the book.								
29	[c]Sum is \$(100) due to rounding. We round to \$0.								
30	[d]Annuity present value from Table 4, in the Appendix. The annuity table value of 3.791 is the sum of the individual discount rates								
31	0.909 + 0.826 + 0.751 + 0.683 + 0.621, subject to rounding.								

Or, what factor F in Table 4 (in the Appendix) will satisfy this equation?

$$\$379{,}100 = \$100{,}000F$$
$$F = \$379{,}100 \div \$100{,}000 = 3.791$$

On the five-period line in Table 4, find the percentage column that is closest to 3.791. It is exactly 10%. If the factor (F) falls between the factors in two columns, straight-line interpolation is used to approximate IRR. This interpolation is illustrated in the Problem for Self-Study (pages 465–466).

Managers accept a project only if IRR equals or exceeds the RRR. In the Top-Spin example, the carbon-fiber machine has an IRR of 10%, which is greater than the RRR of 8%. On the basis of financial factors, Top-Spin should invest in the new machine. In general, the NPV and IRR decision rules result in consistent project acceptance or rejection decisions. If IRR exceeds RRR, then the project has a positive NPV (favoring acceptance). If IRR equals RRR, NPV = \$0, so the company is indifferent between project acceptance and rejection. If IRR is less than RRR, NPV is negative (favoring rejection). Obviously, managers prefer projects with higher IRRs to projects with lower IRRs, if all other things are equal. The IRR of 10% means the cash inflows from the project are adequate to (1) recover the net initial investment in the project and (2) earn a return of exactly 10% on the investment tied up in the project over its useful life.

Comparison of Net Present Value and Internal Rate-of-Return Methods

The NPV method is the preferred method for project selection decisions because use of the NPV criterion leads to shareholder value maximization. At an intuitive level, this occurs because the NPV measure for a project captures the value, in today's dollars, of the surplus the project generates for the firm's shareholders, over and above the required rate of return.[1] Next, we highlight some of the limitations of the IRR method relative to the NPV technique.

One advantage of the NPV method is that it expresses computations in dollars, not in percentages. Therefore, we can sum NPVs of individual projects to calculate an NPV of a combination or portfolio of projects. In contrast, IRRs of individual projects cannot be added or averaged to represent the IRR of a combination of projects.

A second advantage is that the NPV of a project can always be expressed as a unique number. From the sign and magnitude of this number, the firm can then make an accurate assessment of the financial consequences of accepting or rejecting the project. Under the IRR method, it is possible that more than one IRR may exist for a given project. In other words, there may be multiple discount rates that equate the NPV of a set of cash flows to zero. This is especially true when the signs of the cash flows switch over time; that is, when there are outflows, followed by inflows, followed by additional outflows, and so forth. In such cases, it is difficult to know which of the IRR estimates should be compared to the firm's required rate of return.

A third advantage of the NPV method is that it can be used when the RRR varies over the life of a project. Suppose Top-Spin's management sets an RRR of 9% per year in years 1 and 2 and 12% per year in years 3, 4, and 5. Total present value of the cash inflows can be calculated as \$378,100 (computations not shown). It is not possible to use the IRR method in this case. That's because different RRRs in different years mean there is no single RRR that the IRR (a single figure) can be compared against to decide if the project should be accepted or rejected.

Finally, there are settings in which the IRR method is prone to indicating erroneous decisions, such as when comparing mutually exclusive projects with unequal lives or unequal levels of initial investment. The reason is that the IRR method implicitly assumes that project cash flows can be reinvested at the *project's* rate of return. The NPV method, in contrast, accurately assumes that project cash flows can only be reinvested at the *company's* required rate of return.

Despite its limitations, surveys report widespread use of the IRR method.[2] Why? Probably because managers find the percentage return computed under the IRR method easy to understand and compare. Moreover, in most instances where a single project is being evaluated, their decisions would likely be unaffected by using IRR or NPV.

[1] More detailed explanations of the preeminence of the NPV criterion can be found in corporate finance texts.

[2] In a recent survey, John Graham and Campbell Harvey found that 75.7% of CFOs always or almost always used IRR for capital budgeting decisions, while a slightly smaller number, 74.9%, always or almost always used the NPV criterion.

Keys to Success

The internal rate of return (IRR) is the discount rate that sets the NPV of a sequence of cash flows to zero. The IRR method has conceptual limitations when compared to the NPV method and, at times, gives managers differing recommendations regarding project selection.

Sensitivity Analysis

To present the basics of the NPV and IRR methods, we have assumed that the expected values of cash flows will occur *for certain*. In reality, there is substantial uncertainty associated with the prediction of future cash flows. To examine how a result will change if the predicted financial outcomes are not achieved or if an underlying assumption changes, managers use *sensitivity analysis*, a "what-if" technique introduced in Chapter 3.

A common way to apply sensitivity analysis in capital budgeting decisions is to vary each of the inputs to the NPV calculation by a certain percentage and assess the effect of the change on the project's NPV. Sensitivity analysis can take on other forms as well. Suppose the manager at Top-Spin believes forecasted cash flows are difficult to predict. She asks, "What are the minimum annual cash inflows that make the investment in a new carbon-fiber machine acceptable—that is, what inflows lead to an NPV = \$0?" For the data in Exhibit 11-1, let A = Annual cash flow and let NPV = \$0. Net initial investment is \$379,100, and the present value factor at the 8% required annual rate of return for a 5-year annuity of \$1 is 3.993. Then,

$$\begin{aligned} NPV &= \$0 \\ 3.993A - \$379{,}100 &= \$0 \\ 3.993A &= \$379{,}100 \\ A &= \$94{,}941 \end{aligned}$$

At the discount rate of 8% per year, the annual (after-tax) cash inflows can decrease to \$94,941 (a decline of \$100,000 − \$94,941 = \$5,059) before the NPV falls to \$0. If the manager believes she can attain annual cash inflows of at least \$94,941, she can justify investing in the carbon-fiber machine on financial grounds.

Exhibit 11-3 shows that variations in the annual cash inflows or RRR significantly affect the NPV of the carbon-fiber machine project. NPVs can also vary with different useful lives of a project. Sensitivity analysis helps managers to focus on decisions that are most sensitive to different assumptions and to worry less about decisions that are not so sensitive. It is also an important risk-management tool because it provides information to managers about the downside risk from projects as well as their potential impact on the health of the overall firm. Concepts in Action: Target Corporation Invests in the Shopping Experience illustrates the use of discounted cash flow and sensitivity analyses at a major U.S. corporation.

Keys to Success

Sensitivity analysis helps managers carry out what-if scenarios to assess the robustness of the recommendations provided by discounted cash flow methods.

Exhibit 11-3

Net Present Value Calculations for Top-Spin's Carbon-Fiber Machine Under Different Assumptions of Annual Cash Flows and Required Rates of Return[a]

Home Insert Page Layout Formulas Data Review View

	A	B	C	D	E	F
1	**Required**			**Annual Cash Flows**		
2	**Rate of Return**	**\$ 80,000**	**\$ 90,000**	**\$100,000**	**\$110,000**	**\$120,000**
3	6%	\$(42,140)	\$ (20)	\$ 42,100	\$ 84,220	\$126,340
4	8%	\$(59,660)	\$(19,730)	\$ 20,200	\$ 60,130	\$100,060
5	10%	\$(75,820)	\$(37,910)	\$ 0	\$ 37,910	\$ 75,820
6						
7	[a]All calculated amounts assume the project's useful life is five years.					

Concepts in Action: Target Corporation Invests in the Shopping Experience

In 2010, retailer Target Corporation spent more than $3.3 billion on opening new stores, remodeling and expanding existing stores, and investing in information technology and distribution infrastructure. With intense competition from Walmart, which focuses on low prices, Target's strategy is to consider the shopping experience as a whole. This experience is created by emphasizing store décor that gives just the right shopping ambiance.

Source: Scott Gries/PictureGroup

As a result, investments in the shopping experience are critical to Target. To manage these complex capital investments, Target has a Capital Expenditure Committee (CEC), composed of a team of top executives that reviews and approves all capital project requests in excess of $100,000. Project proposals that CEC reviews vary widely and include remodeling, relocating, rebuilding, and closing an existing store to build a new store.

Target's CEC considers several factors in determining whether to accept or reject a project. Projects need to meet a variety of financial objectives, starting with providing a suitable return as measured by discounted cash flow metrics net present value (NPV) and internal rate of return (IRR). Other financial considerations include projected profit and earnings per share impacts, total investment size, impact on sales of other nearby Target stores, and sensitivity of the NPV and IRR to sales variations, like the recent global economic recession.

Sources: Based on David Ding and Saul Yeaton, "Target Corporation," University of Virginia Darden School of Business No. UV1057, (Charlottesville, VA: Darden Business Publishing, 2008); Target Corporation, 2011 annual report (Minneapolis, MN: Target Corporation, 2012).

Learning Objective 3

Use and evaluate the payback and discounted payback methods

. . . to calculate the time it takes to recoup the investment

Payback Method

We now consider the third method for analyzing the financial aspects of projects. The **payback method** measures the time it will take to recoup, in the form of expected future cash flows, the net initial investment in a project. As in NPV and IRR, payback does not distinguish among the sources of cash flows, such as from operations, purchase or sale of equipment, or investment or recovery of working capital. As we'll see in the next section, payback is simpler to calculate when a project has uniform cash flows, as opposed to nonuniform cash flows.

Uniform Cash Flows

In the Top-Spin example, the carbon-fiber machine costs $379,100, has a 5-year expected useful life, and generates $100,000 *uniform* cash flow each year. Calculation of the payback period is:

$$\text{Payback period} = \frac{\text{Net initial investment}}{\text{Uniform increase in annual future cash flows}}$$

$$= \frac{\$379{,}100}{\$100{,}000} = 3.8 \text{ years}^{3}$$

[3] Cash inflows from the new carbon-fiber machine occur uniformly *throughout* the year, but for simplicity in calculating NPV and IRR, we assume they occur at the *end* of each year. A literal interpretation of this assumption would imply a payback of 4 years because Top-Spin will only recover its investment when cash inflows occur at the end of year 4. The calculations shown in the chapter, however, better approximate Top-Spin's payback on the basis of uniform cash flows throughout the year.

The payback method highlights liquidity, a factor that often plays a role in capital budgeting decisions, particularly when the investments are large. Managers prefer projects with shorter payback periods (projects that are more liquid) to projects with longer payback periods, if all other things are equal. Projects with shorter payback periods give an organization more flexibility because funds for other projects become available sooner. Also, managers are less confident about cash flow predictions that stretch far into the future, again favoring shorter payback periods.

Unlike the NPV and IRR methods where management selects an RRR, under the payback method, management chooses a cutoff period for a project. Projects with a payback period that is less than the cutoff period are considered acceptable, and those with a payback period that is longer than the cutoff period are rejected. Japanese companies favor the payback method over other methods and use cutoff periods ranging from 3 to 5 years depending on the risks involved with the project.[4] In general, modern risk management calls for using shorter cutoff periods for riskier projects. If Top-Spin's cutoff period under the payback method is 3 years, it will reject the new machine.

The payback method is easy to understand. As in DCF methods, the payback method is not affected by accrual accounting conventions such as depreciation. Payback is a useful measure when (1) preliminary screening of many proposals is necessary, (2) interest rates are high, and (3) the expected cash flows in later years of a project are highly uncertain. Under these conditions, companies give much more weight to cash flows in early periods of a capital budgeting project and to recovering the investments they have made, thereby making the payback criterion especially relevant.

Two weaknesses of the payback method are that (1) it fails to explicitly incorporate the time value of money and (2) it does not consider a project's cash flows after the payback period. Consider an alternative to the \$379,100 carbon-fiber machine. Another carbon-fiber machine, with a 3-year useful life and no terminal disposal value, requires only a \$300,000 net initial investment and will also result in cash inflows of \$100,000 per year. First, compare the payback periods:

$$\text{Machine 1} = \frac{\$379{,}100}{\$100{,}000} = 3.8 \text{ years}$$

$$\text{Machine 2} = \frac{\$300{,}000}{\$100{,}000} = 3.0 \text{ years}$$

The payback criterion favors machine 2, with the shorter payback. If the cutoff period were 3 years, machine 1 would fail to meet the payback criterion.

Consider next the NPV of the two investment options using Top-Spin's 8% required rate of return for the carbon-fiber machine investment. At a discount rate of 8%, the NPV of machine 2 is −\$42,300 (2.577, the present value annuity factor for 3 years at 8% per year from Table 4, times \$100,000 = \$257,700 minus net initial investment of \$300,000). Machine 1, as we know, has a positive NPV of \$20,200 (from Exhibit 11-1). The NPV criterion suggests Top-Spin should acquire machine 1. Machine 2, with a negative NPV, would fail to meet the NPV criterion.

The payback method gives a different answer from the NPV method in this example because the payback method ignores cash flows after the payback period and ignores the time value of money. Another problem with the payback method is that choosing too short a cutoff period for project acceptance promotes the selection of projects with high short-run cash flows. An organization will tend to reject long-run, positive-NPV projects. Despite these differences, companies find it useful to look at both NPV and payback when making capital investment decisions.

Nonuniform Cash Flows

When cash flows are not uniform, the payback computation takes a cumulative form: The cash flows over successive years are accumulated until the amount of net initial investment is recovered. Assume that Venture Law Group is considering the purchase of videoconferencing equipment for \$150,000. The firm expects the equipment to provide a total cash savings of \$340,000 over the next 5 years, due to reduced travel costs and more effective use of associates' time. The cash savings occur uniformly throughout each year, but are not uniform across years.

[4] A 2010 survey of Japanese firms found that 50.2% of them often or always used the payback method to make capital budgeting decisions. The NPV method came in a distant second at 30.5% (see T. Shinoda, "Capital Budgeting Management Practices in Japan," *Economic Journal of Hokkaido University* 39 (2010): 39–50).

Year	Cash Savings	Cumulative Cash Savings	Net Initial Investment Unrecovered at End of Year
0	—	—	$150,000
1	$50,000	$ 50,000	100,000
2	55,000	105,000	45,000
3	60,000	165,000	—
4	85,000	250,000	—
5	90,000	340,000	—

The chart shows that payback occurs during the third year. Straight-line interpolation within the third year reveals that the final $45,000 needed to recover the $150,000 investment (that is, $150,000 − $105,000 recovered by the end of year 2) will be achieved three-quarters of the way through year 3 (in which $60,000 of cash savings occur):

$$\text{Payback period} = 2 \text{ years} + \left(\frac{\$45{,}000}{\$60{,}000} \times 1 \text{ year}\right) = 2.75 \text{ years}$$

It is relatively simple to adjust the payback method to incorporate the time value of money by using a similar cumulative approach. The **discounted payback method** calculates the amount of time required for the discounted expected future cash flows to recoup the net initial investment in a project. For the videoconferencing example, we can modify the preceding chart by discounting the cash flows at the 8% required rate of return.

Year (1)	Cash Savings (2)	Present Value of $1 Discounted at 8% (3)	Discounted Cash Savings (4) = (2) × (3)	Cumulative Discounted Cash Savings (5)	Net Initial Investment Unrecovered at End of Year (6)
0	—	1.000	—	—	$150,000
1	$50,000	0.926	$46,300	$ 46,300	103,700
2	55,000	0.857	47,135	93,435	56,565
3	60,000	0.794	47,640	141,075	8,925
4	85,000	0.735	62,475	203,550	—
5	90,000	0.681	61,290	264,840	—

The fourth column represents the present values of the future cash savings. The chart shows that discounted payback occurs between years 3 and 4. At the end of the third year, $8,925 of the initial investment is still unrecovered. Comparing this amount to the $62,475 in present value of savings achieved in the fourth year, straight-line interpolation then reveals that the discounted payback period is exactly one-seventh of the way into the fourth year:

$$\text{Discounted payback period} = 3 \text{ years} + \left(\frac{\$8{,}925}{\$62{,}475} \times 1 \text{ year}\right) = 3.14 \text{ years}$$

While discounted payback does incorporate the time value of money, it is still subject to the other criticism of the payback method—cash flows beyond the discounted payback period are ignored, resulting in a bias toward projects with high short-run cash flows. Companies such as Hewlett-Packard value the discounted payback method (HP refers to it as "breakeven time") because they view longer-term cash flows as inherently unpredictable in high-growth industries, such as technology.

Finally, the videoconferencing example has a single cash outflow of $150,000 in year 0. When a project has multiple cash outflows occurring at different points in time, these outflows are first aggregated to obtain a total cash-outflow figure for the project. For computing the payback period, the cash flows are simply added, with no adjustment for the time value of money. For calculating the discounted payback period, the present values of the outflows are added instead.

> **Keys to Success**
> **The payback method evaluates projects on the basis of the time period over which the undiscounted capital investments are recouped by the firm. The discounted payback method informs managers of the breakeven time at which discounted cash inflows equal the discounted cash outflows of the project.**

Accrual Accounting Rate-of-Return Method

Learning Objective 4

Use and evaluate the accrual accounting rate-of-return (AARR) method

. . . after-tax operating income divided by investment

We now consider a fourth method for analyzing the financial aspects of capital budgeting projects. The **accrual accounting rate-of-return (AARR) method** divides the average annual (accrual accounting) income of a project by a measure of the investment in it. We illustrate AARR for the Top-Spin example using the project's net initial investment as the amount in the denominator:

$$\text{Accrual accounting rate of return} = \frac{\text{Increase in expected average annual after-tax operating income}}{\text{Net initial investment}}$$

If Top-Spin purchases the new carbon-fiber machine, its net initial investment is \$379,100. The increase in expected average annual after-tax operating cash inflows is \$98,200. This amount is the expected after-tax total operating cash inflows of \$491,000 (\$100,000 for 4 years and \$91,000 in year 5), divided by the time horizon of 5 years. Suppose that the new machine results in additional depreciation deductions of \$70,000 per year (\$78,000 in annual depreciation for the new machine, relative to \$8,000 per year on the existing machine).[5] The increase in expected average annual after-tax income is therefore \$28,200 (the difference between the cash flow increase of \$98,200 and the depreciation increase of \$70,000). The AARR on net initial investment is computed as:

$$AARR = \frac{\$98{,}200 - \$70{,}000}{\$379{,}100} = \frac{\$28{,}200 \text{ per year}}{\$379{,}100} = 0.074, \text{ or } 7.4\% \text{ per year}$$

The 7.4% figure for AARR indicates the average rate at which a dollar of investment generates after-tax operating income. The new carbon-fiber machine has a low AARR for two reasons: (1) the use of net initial investment as the denominator and (2) the use of income as the numerator, which necessitates deducting depreciation charges from the annual operating cash flows. To mitigate the first issue, many companies calculate AARR using an average level of investment. This alternative procedure recognizes that the book value of the investment declines over time. In its simplest form, average investment for Top-Spin is calculated as the arithmetic mean of the net initial investment of \$379,100 and the net terminal cash flow of \$9,000 (terminal disposal value of machine of \$0, plus the terminal recovery of working capital of \$9,000):

$$\text{Average investment over five years} = \frac{\text{Net initial investment} + \text{Net terminal cash flow}}{2}$$

$$= \frac{\$379{,}100 + \$9{,}000}{2} = \$194{,}050$$

The AARR on average investment is then calculated as:

$$AARR = \frac{\$28{,}200}{\$194{,}050} = 0.145, \text{ or } 14.5\% \text{ per year}$$

Our point here is that companies vary in how they calculate AARR. There is no uniformly preferred approach. Be sure you understand how AARR is defined in each individual situation. Managers consider projects acceptable if the AARR exceeds a specified hurdle required rate of return (the higher the AARR, the better the project is considered to be).

The AARR method is similar to the IRR method in that both methods calculate a rate-of-return percentage. The AARR method calculates return using operating-income numbers after considering accruals and taxes, whereas the IRR method calculates return using after-tax cash flows and the time value of money. Because cash flows and time value of money are central to capital budgeting decisions, managers regard the IRR method as better than the AARR method.

---

[5] We provide further details on these numbers in the next section; see page 457.

AARR computations are easy to understand, and they use numbers reported in the financial statements. AARR gives managers an idea of how the accounting numbers they will report in the future will be affected if a project is accepted. Unlike the payback method, which ignores cash flows after the payback period, the AARR method considers income earned *throughout* a project's expected useful life. Unlike the NPV method, the AARR method uses accrual accounting income numbers and not cash flows, and it ignores the time value of money. Critics cite these arguments as drawbacks of the AARR method.

Overall, keep in mind that companies frequently use multiple methods for evaluating capital investment decisions. When different methods lead to different rankings of projects, finance theory suggests that managers give more weight to the NPV method because the assumptions made by the NPV method are most consistent with making decisions that maximize company value.

Keys to Success
The accrual accounting rate of return (AARR) captures the average rate at which each dollar invested in a project yields after-tax operating income. The metric demonstrates to managers the impact of their project choices on future accounting earnings.

Learning Objective 5

Identify relevant cash inflows and outflows that managers use to make capital budgeting decisions

. . . the differences in expected future cash flows resulting from the investment

Relevant Cash Flows in Discounted Cash Flow Analysis

So far, we have examined methods for evaluating long-term projects in settings where the expected future cash flows of interest were assumed to be known. One of the biggest challenges in capital budgeting, particularly DCF analysis, however, is determining which cash flows are relevant in making an investment selection. Relevant cash flows are the differences in expected future cash flows as a result of making the investment. In the Top-Spin example, the relevant cash flows are the differences in expected future cash flows between continuing to use the old technology and updating its technology with the purchase of a new machine. *When reading this section, focus on identifying expected future cash flows and the differences in expected future cash flows.*

To illustrate relevant cash flow analysis, consider a more complex version of the Top-Spin example with these additional assumptions:

- Top-Spin is a profitable company. The income tax rate is 40% of operating income each year.
- The before-tax additional operating cash inflows from the carbon-fiber machine are $120,000 in years 1–4 and $105,000 in year 5.
- For tax purposes, Top-Spin uses the straight-line depreciation method and assumes no terminal disposal value.
- Gains or losses on the sale of depreciable assets are taxed at the same rate as ordinary income.
- The tax effects of cash inflows and outflows occur at the same time that the cash inflows and outflows occur.
- Top-Spin uses an 8% required rate of return for discounting after-tax cash flows.

Summary data for the machines are:

	Old Graphite Machine	New Carbon-Fiber Machine
Purchase price	—	$390,000
Current book value	$40,000	—
Current disposal value	6,500	Not applicable
Terminal disposal value 5 years from now	0	0
Annual depreciation	8,000[a]	78,000[b]
Working capital required	6,000	15,000

[a] $40,000 ÷ 5 years = $8,000 annual depreciation
[b] $390,000 ÷ 5 years = $78,000 annual depreciation

Relevant After-Tax Flows

We use the concepts of differential cost and differential revenue introduced in Chapter 9. We compare (1) the after-tax cash outflows as a result of replacing the old machine with (2) the additional after-tax cash inflows generated from using the new machine rather than the old machine.

As Benjamin Franklin said, "Two things in life are certain: death and taxes." Income taxes are a fact of life for most corporations and individuals. It is important first to understand how income taxes affect cash flows in each year. Exhibit 11-4 shows how investing in the new machine will affect Top-Spin's cash flow from operations and its income taxes in year 1. Recall that Top-Spin will generate \$120,000 in before-tax additional operating cash inflows by investing in the new machine (page 456), but it will record additional depreciation of \$70,000 (\$78,000 − \$8,000) for tax purposes.

Panel A shows that the year 1 cash flow from operations, net of income taxes, equals \$100,000, using two methods based on the income statement. The first method focuses on cash items only, the \$120,000 operating cash inflows minus income taxes of \$20,000. The second method starts with the \$30,000 increase in net income (calculated after subtracting the \$70,000 additional depreciation deductions for income tax purposes) and adds back that \$70,000 because depreciation is an operating cost that reduces net income but is a noncash item itself.

Panel B in Exhibit 11-4 describes a third method that we will use frequently to compute cash flow from operations, net of income taxes. The easiest way to interpret the third method is to think of the government as a 40% (equal to the tax rate) partner in Top-Spin. Each time Top-Spin obtains operating cash inflows, *C*, its income is higher by *C*, so it will pay 40% of the operating cash inflows (0.40*C*) in taxes. This results in additional after-tax cash operating flows of *C* − 0.40*C*, which in this example is \$120,000 − (0.40 × \$120,000) = \$72,000, or \$120,000 × (1 − 0.40) = \$72,000.

To achieve the higher operating cash inflows, *C*, Top-Spin incurs higher depreciation charges, *D*, from investing in the new machine. Depreciation costs do not directly affect cash flows because depreciation is a noncash cost, but higher depreciation cost *lowers* Top-Spin's taxable income by *D*, saving income tax cash outflows of 0.40*D*, which in this example is 0.40 × \$70,000 = \$28,000.

Letting *t* = tax rate, cash flow from operations, net of income taxes, in this example equals the operating cash inflows, *C*, minus the tax payments on these inflows, *t* × *C*, plus the tax savings on depreciation deductions, *t* × *D*: \$120,000 − (0.40 × \$120,000) + (0.40 × \$70,000) = \$120,000 − \$48,000 + \$28,000 = \$100,000.

Exhibit 11-4

Effect on Cash Flow from Operations, Net of Income Taxes, in Year 1 for Top-Spin's Investment in the New Carbon-Fiber Machine

PANEL A: Two Methods Based on the Income Statement

C	Operating cash inflows from investment in machine	\$120,000
D	Additional depreciation deduction	70,000
OI	Increase in operating income	50,000
T	Income taxes (Income tax rate *t* × *OI*) = 40% × \$50,000	20,000
NI	Increase in net income	\$ 30,000
	Increase in cash flow from operations, net of income taxes	
	Method 1: *C* − *T* = \$120,000 − \$20,000 = \$100,000 or	
	Method 2: *NI* + *D* = \$30,000 + \$70,000 = \$100,000	

PANEL B: Item-by-Item Method

	Effect of cash operating flows	
C	Operating cash inflows from investment in machine	\$120,000
t × *C*	Deduct income tax cash outflow at 40%	48,000
C − (*t* × *C*) = (1 − *t*) × *C*	After-tax cash flow from operations (excluding the depreciation effect)	72,000
	Effect of depreciation	
D	Additional depreciation deduction, \$70,000	
t × *D*	Income tax cash savings from additional depreciation deduction at 40% × \$70,000	28,000
(1 − *t*) × *C* + (*t* × *D*) = *C* − (*t* × *C*) + (*t* × *D*)	Cash flow from operations, net of income taxes	\$100,000

By the same logic, each time Top-Spin has a gain on the sale of assets, G, it will show tax outflows, $t \times G$; and each time Top-Spin has a loss on the sale of assets, L, it will show tax benefits or savings of $t \times L$.

Categories of Cash Flows

A capital investment project typically has three categories of cash flows: (1) net initial investment in the project, which includes the acquisition of assets and any associated additions to working capital, minus the after-tax cash flow from the disposal of existing assets; (2) after-tax cash flow from operations (including income tax cash savings from annual depreciation deductions); and (3) after-tax cash flow from terminal disposal of an asset and recovery of working capital. We use the Top-Spin example to discuss these three categories.

As you work through the cash flows in each category, refer to Exhibit 11-5. This exhibit sketches the relevant cash flows for Top-Spin's decision to purchase the new machine as described in items 1–3 here. Note that the total relevant cash flows for each year equal the relevant cash flows used in Exhibits 11-1 and 11-2 to illustrate the NPV and IRR methods.

1. **Net initial investment.** Three components of net-initial-investment cash flows are (a) cash outflow to purchase the machine, (b) cash outflow for working capital, and (c) after-tax cash inflow from current disposal of the old machine.

   1a. *Initial machine investment.* These outflows, made for purchasing plant and equipment, occur at the beginning of the project's life and include cash outflows for transporting and installing the equipment. In the Top-Spin example, the $390,000 cost (including transportation and installation) of the carbon-fiber machine is an outflow in year 0. These cash flows are relevant to the capital budgeting decision because they will be incurred only if Top-Spin decides to purchase the new machine.

   1b. *Initial working-capital investment.* Initial investments in plant and equipment are usually accompanied by additional investments in working capital. These additional investments take the form of current assets, such as accounts receivable and inventories, minus current liabilities, such as accounts payable. Working-capital investments are similar to plant and equipment investments in that they require cash. The magnitude of the investment

Exhibit 11-5

Relevant Cash Inflows and Outflows for Top-Spin's Carbon-Fiber Machine

	A	B	C	D	E	F	G	H
1				Sketch of Relevant Cash Flows at End of Year				
2			0	1	2	3	4	5
3	1a.	Initial machine investment	$(390,000)					
4	1b.	Initial working-capital investment	(9,000)					
5	1c.	After-tax cash flow from current disposal						
6		of old machine	19,900					
7	Net initial investment		(379,100)					
8	2a.	Annual after-tax cash flow from operations						
9		(excluding the depreciation effect)		$ 72,000	$ 72,000	$ 72,000	$ 72,000	$ 63,000
10	2b.	Income tax cash savings from annual						
11		depreciation deductions		28,000	28,000	28,000	28,000	28,000
12	3a.	After-tax cash flow from terminal disposal						
13		of machine						0
14	3b.	After-tax cash flow from recovery of						
15		working capital						9,000
16	Total relevant cash flows,							
17		as shown in Exhibits 11-1 and 11-2	$(379,100)	$ 100,000	$100,000	$100,000	$100,000	$100,000
18								

generally increases as a function of the level of additional sales generated by the project. However, the exact relationship varies based on the nature of the project and the operating cycle of the industry. For a given dollar of sales, a maker of heavy equipment, for example, would require more working capital support than Top-Spin, which in turn has to invest more in working capital than a retail grocery store.

The Top-Spin example assumes a $9,000 additional investment in working capital (for supplies and spare-parts inventory) if the new machine is acquired. The additional working-capital investment is the difference between working capital required to operate the new machine ($15,000) and working capital required to operate the old machine ($6,000). The $9,000 additional investment in working capital is a cash outflow in year 0 and is returned, that is, becomes a cash inflow, at the end of year 5.

1c. *After-tax cash flow from current disposal of old machine.* Any cash received from disposal of the old machine is a relevant cash inflow (in year 0) because it is an expected future cash flow that differs between the alternatives of investing and not investing in the new machine. Top-Spin will dispose of the old machine for $6,500 only if it invests in the new carbon-fiber machine. Recall from Chapter 9 (page 364) that the book value (which is original cost minus accumulated depreciation) of the old equipment is generally irrelevant to the decision since it is a past, or sunk, cost. However, when tax considerations are included, book value does play a role because the book value determines the gain or loss on the sale of the machine and, therefore, the taxes paid (or saved) on the transaction.

Consider the tax consequences of disposing of the old machine. We first have to compute the gain or loss on disposal:

Current disposal value of old machine (given, page 456)	$ 6,500
Deduct current book value of old machine (given, page 456)	40,000
Loss on disposal of machine	$(33,500)

Any loss on the sale of assets lowers taxable income and results in tax savings. The after-tax cash flow from disposal of the old machine is:

Current disposal value of old machine	$ 6,500
Tax savings on loss (0.40 × $33,500)	13,400
After-tax cash inflow from current disposal of old machine	$19,900

The sum of items 1a, 1b, and 1c appears in Exhibit 11-5 as the year 0 net initial investment for the new carbon-fiber machine equal to $379,100 (initial machine investment, $390,000, plus additional working-capital investment, $9,000, minus after-tax cash inflow from current disposal of the old machine, $19,900).[6]

2. Cash flow from operations. This category includes the difference between each year's cash flow from operations under the two alternatives. Organizations make capital investments to generate future cash inflows. These inflows may result from savings in operating costs or, as for Top-Spin, from producing and selling additional goods. Annual cash flow from operations can be net outflows in some years. Chevron makes periodic upgrades to its oil extraction equipment, and in years of upgrades, cash flow from operations tends to be negative for the site being upgraded, although in the long run such upgrades are NPV positive. Always focus on cash flow from operations, not on revenues and expenses under accrual accounting.

Top-Spin's additional operating cash inflows—$120,000 in each of the first 4 years and $105,000 in the fifth year—are relevant because they are expected future cash flows that will differ between the alternatives of investing and not investing in the new machine. The after-tax effects of these cash flows follow.

2a. *Annual after-tax cash flow from operations (excluding the depreciation effect).* The 40% tax rate reduces the benefit of the $120,000 additional operating cash inflows for years 1–4 with the new carbon-fiber machine. After-tax cash flow (excluding the depreciation effect) is:

[6] To illustrate the case when there is a gain on disposal, suppose that the old machine could be sold now for $50,000 instead. Then, the firm would record a gain on disposal of $10,000 ($50,000 less the book value of $40,000), resulting in additional tax payments of $4,000 (0.40 tax rate × $10,000 gain). The after-tax cash inflow from current disposal would therefore equal $46,000 (the disposal value of $50,000, less the tax payment of $4,000).

Annual cash flow from operations with new machine	\$120,000
Deduct income tax payments (0.40 × \$120,000)	48,000
Annual after-tax cash flow from operations	\$ 72,000

For year 5, the after-tax cash flow (excluding the depreciation effect) is:

Annual cash flow from operations with new machine	\$105,000
Deduct income tax payments (0.40 × \$105,000)	42,000
Annual after-tax cash flow from operations	\$ 63,000

Exhibit 11-5, item 2a, shows the \$72,000 amounts for each of the years 1–4 and \$63,000 for year 5.

To reinforce the idea about focusing on cash flows, consider the following additional fact about the Top-Spin example. Suppose the total plant overhead costs will not change whether the company purchases a new machine or keeps the old machine. The production plant's overhead costs are allocated to individual machines—Top-Spin has several—on the basis of the labor costs for operating each machine. Because the new carbon-fiber machine would have lower labor costs, overhead costs allocated to it would be \$30,000 less than the amount allocated to the machine it would replace. How should Top-Spin incorporate the decrease in allocated overhead costs of \$30,000 in the relevant cash flow analysis?

To answer that question, we need to ask, "Do *total* overhead costs decrease at Top-Spin's production plant as a result of acquiring the new machine?" In our example, they do not. Total overhead costs of the production plant remain the same whether or not the new machine is acquired. *Only the overhead costs allocated to individual machines change.* The overhead costs allocated to the new machine are \$30,000 less than the amount allocated to the machine it would replace. This \$30,000 difference in overhead would be allocated to *other* machines in the department. That is, no cash flow savings in total overhead would occur. Therefore, the \$30,000 should not be included as part of annual cash savings from operations.

Next consider the effects of depreciation. *The depreciation line item is itself irrelevant in DCF analysis.* That's because it's a noncash allocation of costs, whereas DCF is based on inflows and outflows of *cash.* In DCF methods, the initial cost of equipment is regarded as a *lump-sum* outflow of cash in year 0. Deducting depreciation expenses from operating cash inflows would result in counting the lump-sum amount twice. *However, depreciation results in income tax cash savings. These tax savings are a relevant cash flow.*

2b. *Income tax cash savings from annual depreciation deductions.* Tax deductions for depreciation, in effect, partially offset the cost of acquiring the new carbon-fiber machine. By purchasing the new machine, Top-Spin is able to deduct \$78,000 in depreciation each year, relative to the \$8,000 depreciation on the old graphite machine. The additional annual depreciation deduction of \$70,000 results in incremental income tax cash savings of \$70,000 × 0.4, or \$28,000 annually. Exhibit 11-5, item 2b, shows these \$28,000 amounts for years 1–5.[7]

For economic-policy reasons, usually to encourage (or in some cases, discourage) investments, tax laws specify which depreciation methods and which depreciable lives are permitted. Suppose the government permitted companies to use accelerated depreciation, allowing for higher depreciation deductions in earlier years. If allowable, should Top-Spin use accelerated depreciation? Yes, because there is a general rule in tax planning for profitable companies such as Top-Spin: When there is a legal choice, take the depreciation (or any other deduction) sooner rather than later. Doing so causes the (cash) income tax savings to occur earlier, which increases the project's NPV.

Keys to Success

Depreciation is relevant for capital budgeting decisions only to the extent that it results in cash tax savings; as with any tax deduction, it is optimal for the firm to depreciate assets as quickly as is legally allowed.

[7] If Top-Spin were a nonprofit foundation not subject to income taxes, cash flow from operations would equal \$120,000 in years 1–4 and \$105,000 in year 5. The revenues would not be reduced by 40%, nor would there be income tax cash savings from the depreciation deduction.

3. **Terminal disposal of investment.** The disposal of the new investment generally increases cash inflow when the project terminates. Errors in forecasting terminal disposal value are seldom critical for long-duration projects because the present value of amounts to be received in the distant future is usually small. Two components of the terminal disposal value of an investment are (a) after-tax cash flow from terminal disposal of machines and (b) after-tax cash flow from recovery of working capital.

3a. *After-tax cash flow from terminal disposal of machines.* At the end of the useful life of the project, the machine's terminal disposal value may be $0 or an amount considerably less than the net initial investment. The relevant cash inflow is the difference in expected after-tax cash inflow from terminal disposal at the end of 5 years under the two alternatives of purchasing the new machine or keeping the old machine.

Although the old machine has a positive terminal disposal value today (year 0), in year 5, it will have a zero terminal value. As such, both the existing and the new machines have zero after-tax cash inflow from terminal disposal in year 5. So, the difference in after-tax cash inflow from terminal disposal is also $0.

In this example, there are no tax effects at the terminal point because both the existing and new machine have disposal values that equal their book values at the time of disposal (in each case, this value is $0). What if either the existing or the new machine had a terminal value that differed from its book value at the time of disposal? In that case, the approach for computing the terminal inflow is identical to that for calculating the after-tax cash flow from current disposal, illustrated earlier in part 1c.

3b. *After-tax cash flow from terminal recovery of working-capital investment.* The initial investment in working capital is usually fully recouped when the project is terminated. At that time, inventories and accounts receivable necessary to support the project are no longer needed. Top-Spin receives cash equal to the book value of its working capital. There is no gain or loss on working capital and, so, there are no tax consequences. The relevant cash inflow is the difference in the expected working capital recovered under the two alternatives. At the end of year 5, Top-Spin recovers $15,000 cash from working capital if it invests in the new carbon-fiber machine versus $6,000 if it continues to use the old machine. The relevant cash inflow at the end of year 5 if Top-Spin invests in the new machine is thus $9,000 ($15,000 − $6,000).

Some capital investment projects *reduce* working capital. Assume that a computer-integrated manufacturing (CIM) project with a 7-year life will reduce inventories and, therefore, working capital by $20 million from, say, $50 million to $30 million. This reduction will be represented as a $20 million cash *inflow* for the project in year 0. At the end of 7 years, the recovery of working capital will show a relevant incremental cash *outflow* of $20 million. That's because, at the end of year 7, the company recovers only $30 million of working capital under CIM, rather than the $50 million of working capital it would have recovered had it not implemented CIM.

Exhibit 11-5 shows items 3a and 3b in the "year 5" column. The relevant cash flows in Exhibit 11-5 serve as inputs for the four capital budgeting methods described earlier in the chapter.

Keys to Success

There are three primary categories of cash flows relevant for evaluating capital investment projects: the net initial investment in the project, the after-tax cash flow from operations, and the after-tax cash flow from terminal disposal.

Learning Objective 6

Understand the challenges of implementing capital budgeting decisions and evaluating managerial performance

. . . the importance of postinvestment audits and the correct choice of performance measures

Project Management and Performance Evaluation

We have so far looked at ways to identify relevant cash flows and appropriate techniques for analyzing them. The final stage (stage 5) of capital budgeting begins with implementing the decision, or managing the project.[8] This includes management control of the investment activity itself, as well as management control of the project as a whole.

[8] In this section, we do not consider the different options for financing a project (refer to a text on corporate finance for details).

Capital budgeting projects, such as purchasing a carbon-fiber machine or videoconferencing equipment, are easier to implement than projects involving building shopping malls or manufacturing plants. The building projects are more complex, so monitoring and controlling the investment schedules and budgets are critical to successfully completing the investment activity. This leads to the second dimension of stage 5 in the capital budgeting process: evaluate performance and learn.

Postinvestment Audits

A postinvestment audit provides management with feedback about the performance of a project, so management can compare actual results to the costs and benefits expected at the time the project was selected. Suppose actual outcomes (such as additional operating cash flows from the new carbon-fiber machine in the Top-Spin example) are much lower than expected. Management must then determine if this result occurred because the original estimates were overly optimistic or because of implementation problems. Either of these explanations is a concern.

Optimistic estimates may cause managers to accept a project that they should reject. To discourage optimistic estimates, companies such as DuPont maintain records comparing actual results to the estimates individual managers make when seeking approval for capital investments. Postinvestment audits uncover inaccurate estimates, and therefore discourage unrealistic forecasts. This prevents managers from overstating project cash inflows and accepting projects that they should reject. Implementation problems, such as weak project management, poor quality control, or inadequate marketing, are also a concern. Postinvestment audits help to alert senior management to these problems so that they can be quickly corrected.

Companies should perform postinvestment audits only after project outcomes have stabilized because performing audits too early may yield misleading feedback. Obtaining actual results to compare against estimates is often difficult. For example, additional revenues from the new carbon-fiber technology may not be comparable to the estimated revenues because in any particular season, the rise or decline of a tennis star such as Roger Federer or Serena Williams can greatly affect the popularity of the sport and the subsequent demand for racquets. A better evaluation would look at the average revenues across a couple of seasons.

Keys to Success

Postinvestment audits help uncover problems in project implementation and also serve to dissuade managers from providing overly optimistic initial projections of cash flows.

Performance Evaluation

As the preceding discussions show, ideally companies should evaluate managers on a project-by-project basis and look at how well managers achieve the amounts and timing of forecasted cash flows. In practice, however, companies often evaluate managers based on aggregate information, especially when multiple projects are underway at any point in time. It is important then for companies to ensure that the method of evaluation does not conflict with the use of the NPV method for making capital budgeting decisions. For example, suppose that Top-Spin uses the accrual accounting rate of return generated in each period to assess managerial performance. We know from the NPV method that the manager of the racquet production plant should purchase the carbon-fiber machine because it has a positive NPV of $20,200. Despite that, the manager may reject the project if the AARR of 7.4% on the net initial investment is lower than the minimum accounting rate of return the manager is required to achieve.

There is an inconsistency between using the NPV method as best for capital budgeting decisions and then using a different method to evaluate performance. This inconsistency means managers are tempted to make capital budgeting decisions on the basis of the method by which they are being evaluated. Such temptations become more pronounced if managers are frequently transferred (or promoted), or if their bonuses are affected by the level of year-to-year accrual income.

Other conflicts between decision making and performance evaluation persist even if a company uses similar measures for both purposes. If the AARR on the carbon-fiber machine exceeds the minimum required AARR but is below the current AARR of the production plant, the manager may still be tempted to reject purchase of the carbon-fiber machine because the lower AARR of the carbon-fiber machine will reduce the AARR of the entire plant and hurt the manager's reported performance. Or, consider an example where the cash inflows from the carbon-fiber machine occur mostly in the later years of the project. Then, even if the AARR on the project exceeds the current AARR of the plant (as well as the minimum required return), the manager may still reject the purchase since it will have a negative effect on the realized accrual accounting rate of return for the first few years. In Chapter 16, we study these conflicts in greater depth and describe how performance evaluation models such as economic value added (EVA®) help achieve greater congruency with decision-making models.

Strategic Considerations in Capital Budgeting

Learning Objective 7

Explain how managers can use capital budgeting to achieve strategic goals

. . . critical investments whose benefits are uncertain or difficult to estimate

Managers consider a company's strategic goals when making capital budgeting decisions. Strategic decisions by United Airlines, Westin Hotels, Federal Express, and Pizza Hut to expand in Europe and Asia required capital investments in several countries (also see Concepts in Action: Walt Disney Switches Budget Approval Process for DisneySea in Japan). The strategic decision by Barnes & Noble to support book sales over the Internet required capital investments creating barnesandnoble.com and an Internet infrastructure. News Corp.'s decision to enlarge its online presence resulted in a large investment to purchase MySpace and additional supporting investments to integrate MySpace with the firm's pre-existing assets. Pfizer's decision to develop its cholesterol-reducing drug Lipitor led to major investments in R&D and marketing. Toyota's decision to offer a line of hybrids across both its Toyota and Lexus platforms required startup investments to form a hybrid division and ongoing investments to fund the division's continuing research efforts.

Capital investment decisions that are strategic in nature require managers to consider a broad range of factors that may be difficult to estimate. Consider some of the difficulties of justifying investments made by companies such as Mitsubishi, Sony, and Audi in computer-integrated manufacturing

Concepts in Action: Walt Disney Switches Budget Approval Process for DisneySea in Japan

The Walt Disney Company, one of the world's leading entertainment producers, had $40.9 billion in 2011 revenue through movies, television networks, branded products, and theme parks and resorts. In its theme park business, Disney spends more than $2 billion annually in capital investments for new theme parks, rides and attractions, and other park improvements.

Source: Kyodo/Newscom

Years ago, Disney developed a robust capital budgeting approval process. Project approval relied heavily on projected returns on capital investment as measured by net present value and internal rate-of-return calculations. While this worked well for Disney's domestic investments, the company experienced challenges when it considered building the DisneySea theme park near Tokyo, Japan, as Japanese firms frequently use the average accounting return (AAR) method instead. AAR is analogous to an accrual accounting rate-of-return measure based on average investment. However, AAR focuses on the first few years of a project (5 years, in the case of DisneySea) and ignores terminal values.

When Disney managers evaluated the DisneySea project, they found a negative rather than positive AAR. To account for the differences in capital budgeting techniques, managers at Disney introduced a third calculation method called average cash flow return. This hybrid method measured the average cash flow over the first 5 years, with the asset assumed to be sold for book value at the end of that period as a fraction of the initial investment in the project. Managers found that the resulting ratio exceeded the return on Japanese government bonds and so yielded a positive return for DisneySea. As a result, the DisneySea theme park was built next to Tokyo Disneyland and has become a profitable addition to Disney's Japanese operations.

Sources: Based on Mitsuru Misawa, "Tokyo Disneyland and the DisneySea Park: Corporate governance and differences in capital budgeting concepts and methods between American and Japanese companies," University of Hong Kong No. HKU568 (Hong Kong: University of Hong Kong Asia Case Research Center, 2006); The Walt Disney Company. 2011 Annual Report (Burbank, CA: The Walt Disney Company, 2012).

(CIM) technology. In CIM, computers give instructions that quickly and automatically set up and run equipment to manufacture many different products. Quantifying these benefits requires some notion of how quickly consumer demand will change in the future. CIM technology also increases worker knowledge of, and experience with, automation; however, the benefit of this knowledge and experience is difficult to measure. Managers must develop judgment and intuition to make these decisions.

Investment in Research and Development

Companies such as GlaxoSmithKline, in the pharmaceutical industry, and Intel, in the semiconductor industry, regard R&D projects as important strategic investments. The distant payoffs from R&D investments, however, are more uncertain than other investments such as new equipment. On the positive side, R&D investments are often staged: As time unfolds, companies can increase or decrease the resources committed to a project based on how successful it has been up to that point. This option feature of R&D investments, called real options, is an important aspect of R&D investments and increases the NPV of these investments because a company can limit its losses when things are going badly and take advantage of new opportunities when things are going well. As an example, a pharmaceutical company can increase or decrease its investment in an R&D joint venture based on the progress of the clinical trials of new drugs that are being developed by the venture.

Customer Value and Capital Budgeting

Finally, note that managers can use the framework described in this chapter to both evaluate investment projects and to make strategic decisions regarding in which customers to invest. Consider Potato Supreme, which makes potato products for sale to retail outlets. It is currently analyzing two of its customers: Shine Stores and Always Open. Potato Supreme predicts the following cash flow from operations, net of income taxes (in thousands), from each customer account for the next 5 years:

	2012	2013	2014	2015	2016
Shine Stores	$1,450	$1,305	$1,175	$1,058	$ 950
Always Open	690	1,160	1,900	2,950	4,160

Which customer is more valuable to Potato Supreme? Looking at only the current period, 2012, Shine Stores provides more than double the cash flow compared to Always Open ($1,450 vs. $690). A different picture emerges, however, when looking over the entire 5-year horizon. Potato Supreme anticipates Always Open's orders to increase; meanwhile, it expects Shine Stores' orders to decline. Using Potato Supreme's 10% RRR, the NPV of the Always Open customer is $7,610, compared to $4,591 for Shine Stores (computations not shown). Note how NPV captures in its estimate of customer value the future growth of Always Open. Potato Supreme uses this information to allocate more resources and salespersons to service the Always Open account. Potato Supreme can also use NPV calculations to examine the effects of alternative ways of increasing customer loyalty and retention, such as introducing frequent-purchaser cards.

A comparison of year-to-year changes in customer NPV estimates highlights whether managers have been successful in maintaining long-run profitable relationships with their customers. Suppose the NPV of Potato Supreme's customer base declines 15% in 1 year. Management can then examine the reasons for the decline, such as aggressive pricing by competitors, and devise new-product development and marketing strategies for the future.

Capital One, a financial-services company, uses NPV to estimate the value of different credit-card customers. Cellular telephone companies such as Cellular One and Verizon Wireless attempt to sign up customers for multiple years of service. The objective is to prevent "customer churn," customers switching frequently from one company to another. The higher the probability of customer churn, the lower the NPV of the customer.

Keys to Success

The capital budgeting framework is useful to managers for evaluating the lifetime value of customers as well as the benefits from customer-focused strategies.

Problem for Self-Study

Part A

Returning to the Top-Spin carbon-fiber machine project, assume that Top-Spin is a *nonprofit organization* and that the expected additional operating cash inflows are \$130,000 in years 1–4 and \$121,000 in year 5. Using data from page 456, the net initial investment is \$392,500 (new machine, \$390,000 + additional working capital, \$9,000 − terminal disposal value of old machine, \$6,500). All other facts are unchanged: a 5-year useful life, no terminal disposal value, and an 8% RRR. Year 5 cash inflows are \$130,000, which includes a \$9,000 recovery of working capital.

Required

Calculate the following:

1. Net present value
2. Internal rate of return
3. Payback
4. Accrual accounting rate of return on net initial investment

Solution

1. $NPV = (\$130{,}000 \times 3.993) - \$392{,}500$

   $= \$519{,}090 - \$392{,}500 = \$126{,}590$

2. There are several approaches to computing IRR. One approach is to use a calculator with an IRR function. This approach gives an IRR of 19.6%. Another approach is to use Table 4 in the Appendix at the end of the book:

$$\$392{,}500 = \$130{,}000F$$

$$F = \frac{\$392{,}500}{\$130{,}000} = 3.019$$

On the five-period line in Table 4, the column closest to 3.019 is 20%. To obtain a more accurate number, use straight-line interpolation:

	Present Value Factors	
18%	3.127	3.127
IRR	—	3.019
20%	2.991	—
Difference	0.136	0.108

$$IRR = 18\% + \frac{0.108}{0.136}(2\%) = 19.6\% \text{ per year}$$

3. $$\text{Payback period} = \frac{\text{Net initial investment}}{\text{Uniform increase in annual future cash flows}}$$

   $= \$392{,}500 \div \$130{,}000 = 3.0 \text{ years}$

4. $$AARR = \frac{\text{Increase in expected average annual operating income}}{\text{Net initial investment}}$$

$$\text{Increase in expected average annual operating cash inflows} = [(\$130{,}000 \times 4) + \$121{,}000] \div 5 \text{ years}$$

$$= \$641{,}000 \div 5 = \$128{,}200$$

$$\text{Increase in annual depreciation} = \$70{,}000\ (\$78{,}000 - \$8{,}000)\ (\text{see page 456})$$

$$\text{Increase in expected average annual operating income} = \$128{,}200 - \$70{,}000 = \$58{,}200$$

$$AARR = \frac{\$58{,}200}{\$392{,}500} = 14.8\% \text{ per year}$$

Part B

Assume that Top-Spin is subject to income tax at a 40% rate. All other information from Part A is unchanged. Compute the NPV of the new carbon-fiber machine project.

Solution

To save space, Exhibit 11-6 shows the calculations using a format slightly different from the format used in this chapter. Item 2a is where the new $130,000 cash flow assumption affects the NPV analysis (compared to Exhibit 11-5). All other amounts in Exhibit 11-6 are identical to the corresponding amounts in Exhibit 11-5. For years 1–4, after-tax cash flow (excluding the depreciation effect) is:

Annual cash flow from operations with new machine	$130,000
Deduct income tax payments (0.40 × $130,000)	52,000
Annual after-tax cash flow from operations	$ 78,000

For year 5, after-tax cash flow (excluding the depreciation effect) is:

Annual cash flow from operations with new machine	$121,000
Deduct income tax payments (0.40 × $121,000)	48,400
Annual after-tax cash flow from operations	$ 72,600

NPV in Exhibit 11-6 is $46,610. As computed in Part A, NPV when there are no income taxes is $126,590. The difference in these two NPVs illustrates the impact of income taxes in capital budgeting analysis.

Exhibit 11-6

Net Present Value Method Incorporating Income Taxes: Top-Spin's Carbon-Fiber Machine with Revised Annual Cash Flow from Operations

Home Insert Page Layout Formulas Data Review View

	A	B	C	D	E	F	G	H	I	J
1			Present	Present Value of						
2			Value of	$1 Discounted at		Sketch of Relevant Cash Flows at End of Year				
3			Cash Flow	8%	0	1	2	3	4	5
4	1a.	Initial machine investment	$(390,000)	1.000	$(390,000)					
5										
6	1b.	Initial working-capital investment	(9,000)	1.000	$ (9,000)					
7	1c.	After-tax cash flow from current								
8		disposal of old machine	19,900	1.000	$ 19,900					
9	Net initial investment		(379,100)							
10	2a.	Annual after-tax cash flow from								
11		operations (excluding the depreciation effect)								
12		Year 1	72,228	0.926		$78,000				
13		Year 2	66,846	0.857			$78,000			
14		Year 3	61,932	0.794				$78,000		
15		Year 4	57,330	0.735					$78,000	
16		Year 5	49,441	0.681						$72,600
17	2b.	Income tax cash savings from annual								
18		depreciation deductions								
19		Year 1	25,928	0.926		$28,000				
20		Year 2	23,996	0.857			$28,000			
21		Year 3	22,232	0.794				$28,000		
22		Year 4	20,580	0.735					$28,000	
23		Year 5	19,068	0.681						$28,000
24	3.	After-tax cash flow from								
25		**a.** Terminal disposal of machine	0	0.681						$ 0
26		**b.** Recovery of working capital	6,129	0.681						$ 9,000
27	NPV if new machine purchased		$ 46,610							
28										

Decision Points

The following question-and-answer format summarizes the chapter's learning objectives. Each decision presents a key question related to a learning objective. The guidelines are the answer to that question.

Decision	Guidelines
1. What are the five stages of capital budgeting?	Capital budgeting is long-run planning for proposed investment projects. The five stages of capital budgeting are: (1) Identify projects: Identify potential capital investments that agree with the organization's strategy; (2) Obtain information: Gather information from all parts of the value chain to evaluate alternative projects; (3) Make predictions: Forecast all potential cash flows attributable to the alternative projects; (4) Choose among alternatives: Determine which investment yields the greatest benefit and the least cost to the organization; and (5) Implement the decision: Obtain funding and make the investments selected in stage 4; track realized cash flows, compare against estimated numbers, and revise plans if necessary.
2. What are the two primary discounted cash flow (DCF) methods for project evaluation?	The two main DCF methods are the net present value (NPV) method and the internal rate-of-return (IRR) method. The NPV method calculates the expected net monetary gain or loss from a project by discounting to the present all expected future cash inflows and outflows, using the required rate of return. A project is acceptable in financial terms if it has a positive NPV. The IRR method computes the rate of return (also called the discount rate) at which the present value of expected cash inflows from a project equals the present value of expected cash outflows from the project. A project is acceptable in financial terms if its IRR exceeds the required rate of return. DCF is the best approach to capital budgeting. It explicitly includes all project cash flows and recognizes the time value of money. The NPV method is the preferred DCF method.
3. What are the payback and discounted payback methods? What are their main weaknesses?	The payback method measures the time it will take to recoup, in the form of cash inflows, the total cash amount invested in a project. The payback method neglects the time value of money and ignores cash flows beyond the payback period. The discounted payback method measures the time taken for the present value of cash inflows to equal the present value of outflows. It adjusts for the time value of money but overlooks cash flows after the discounted payback period.
4. What are the strengths and weaknesses of the accrual accounting rate-of-return (AARR) method for evaluating long-term projects?	The AARR divides an accrual accounting measure of average annual income from a project by an accrual accounting measure of its investment. AARR gives managers an idea of the effect of accepting a project on their future reported accounting profitability. However, AARR uses accrual accounting income numbers, does not track cash flows, and ignores the time value of money.
5. What are the relevant cash inflows and outflows for capital budgeting decisions? How should managers consider accrual accounting concepts?	Relevant cash inflows and outflows in DCF analysis are the differences in expected future cash flows as a result of making the investment. Only cash inflows and outflows matter; accrual accounting concepts are irrelevant for DCF methods. For example, the income taxes saved as a result of depreciation deductions are relevant because they decrease cash outflows, but the depreciation itself is a noncash item.

Decision	Guidelines
6. What conflicts can arise between using DCF methods for capital budgeting decisions and accrual accounting for performance evaluation? How can managers reduce these conflicts?	Using accrual accounting to evaluate the performance of a manager may create conflicts with using DCF methods for capital budgeting. Frequently, the decision made using a DCF method will not report good "operating income" results in the project's early years under accrual accounting. For this reason, managers are tempted to not use DCF methods even though the decisions based on them would be in the best interests of the company as a whole over the long run. This conflict can be reduced by evaluating managers on a project-by-project basis and by looking at their ability to achieve the amounts and timing of forecasted cash flows.
7. What strategic considerations arise in the capital budgeting process?	A company's strategy is the source of its strategic capital budgeting decisions. Such decisions require managers to consider a broad range of factors that may be difficult to estimate. Managers must develop judgment and intuition to make these decisions. R&D projects, for example, are important strategic investments, with distant and usually highly uncertain payoffs.

Appendix

Capital Budgeting and Inflation

The Top-Spin example (Exhibits 11-1 to 11-5) does not include adjustments for inflation in the relevant revenues and costs. **Inflation** is the decline in the general purchasing power of the monetary unit, such as dollars. An inflation rate of 10% per year means that an item bought for \$100 at the beginning of the year will cost \$110 at the end of the year.

Why is it important to account for inflation in capital budgeting? Because declines in the general purchasing power of the monetary unit will inflate future cash flows above what they would have been in the absence of inflation. These inflated cash flows will cause the project to look better than it really is unless the analyst recognizes that the inflated cash flows are measured in dollars that have less purchasing power than the dollars that were initially invested. When analyzing inflation, distinguish real rate of return from nominal rate of return:

> **Real rate of return** is the rate of return demanded to cover investment risk if there is no inflation. The real rate is made up of two elements: (1) a risk-free element (the pure rate of return on risk-free long-term government bonds when there is no expected inflation) and (2) a business-risk element (the risk premium demanded for bearing risk).
>
> **Nominal rate of return** is the rate of return demanded to cover investment risk and the decline in general purchasing power of the monetary unit as a result of expected inflation. The nominal rate is made up of three elements: (1) a risk-free element when there is no expected inflation, (2) a business-risk element, and (3) an inflation element. Items (1) and (2) make up the real rate of return to cover investment risk. The inflation element is the premium above the real rate. The rates of return earned in the financial markets are nominal rates because investors want to be compensated both for the investment risks they take and for the expected decline in the general purchasing power, as a result of inflation, of the money they get back.

Assume that the real rate of return for investments in high-risk cellular data-transmission equipment at Network Communications is 20% per year and that the expected inflation rate is 10% per year. Nominal rate of return is as follows:

$$\begin{aligned}\text{Nominal rate} &= (1 + \text{Real rate})(1 + \text{Inflation rate}) - 1\\ &= (1 + 0.20)(1 + 0.10) - 1\\ &= (1.20 \times 1.10) - 1 = 1.32 - 1 = 0.32, \text{ or } 32\%\end{aligned}$$

Nominal rate of return is related to the real rate of return and the inflation rate:

Real rate of return	0.20
Inflation rate	0.10
Combination (0.20 × 0.10)	0.02
Nominal rate of return	0.32

Note the nominal rate, 0.32, is slightly higher than 0.30, the real rate (0.20) plus the inflation rate (0.10). That's because the nominal rate recognizes that inflation of 10% also decreases the purchasing power of the real rate of return of 20% earned during the year. The combination component represents the additional compensation investors seek for the decrease in the purchasing power of the real return earned during the year because of inflation.[9]

Net Present Value Method and Inflation

When incorporating inflation into the NPV method, the key is *internal consistency.* There are two internally consistent approaches:

1. **Nominal approach** —predicts cash inflows and outflows in nominal monetary units *and* uses a nominal rate as the required rate of return
2. **Real approach** —predicts cash inflows and outflows in real monetary units *and* uses a real rate as the required rate of return

We limit our discussion to the simpler nominal approach. Consider an investment that is expected to generate sales of 100 units and a net cash inflow of $1,000 ($10 per unit) each year for 2 years *absent inflation.* Assume cash flows occur at the end of each year. If inflation of 10% is expected each year, net cash inflows from the sale of each unit would be $11 ($10 × 1.10) in year 1 and $12.10 ($11 × 1.10, or $10 × $(1.10)^2$) in year 2, resulting in net cash inflows of $1,100 in year 1 and $1,210 in year 2. The net cash inflows of $1,100 and $1,210 are nominal cash inflows because they include the effects of inflation. *Nominal cash flows are the cash flows that are recorded in the accounting system.* The cash inflows of $1,000 each year are real cash flows. The accounting system does not record these cash flows. The nominal approach is easier to understand and apply because it uses nominal cash flows from accounting systems and nominal rates of return from financial markets.

Assume that Network Communications can purchase equipment to make and sell a cellular data-transmission product at a net initial investment of $750,000. It is expected to have a 4-year useful life and no terminal disposal value. An annual inflation rate of 10% is expected over this 4-year period. Network Communications requires an after-tax nominal rate of return of 32% (see page 468). The following table presents the predicted amounts of real (that's assuming no inflation) and nominal (that's after considering cumulative inflation) net cash inflows from the equipment over the next 4 years (excluding the $750,000 investment in the equipment and before any income tax payments):

Year (1)	Before-Tax Cash Inflows in Real Dollars (2)	Cumulative Inflation Rate Factor[a] (3)	Before-Tax Cash Inflows in Nominal Dollars (4) = (2) × (3)
1	$500,000	$(1.10)^1 = 1.1000$	$550,000
2	600,000	$(1.10)^2 = 1.2100$	726,000
3	600,000	$(1.10)^3 = 1.3310$	798,600
4	300,000	$(1.10)^4 = 1.4641$	439,230

[a]1.10 = 1.00 + 0.10 inflation rate

[9] The real rate of return can be expressed in terms of the nominal rate of return as:

$$\text{Real rate} = \frac{1 + \text{Nominal rate}}{1 + \text{Inflation rate}} - 1 = \frac{1 + 0.32}{1 + 0.10} - 1 = 0.20, \text{ or } 20\%$$

Exhibit 11-7

Net Present Value Method Using Nominal Approach to Inflation for Network Communication's New Equipment

	A	B	C	D	E	F	G	H	I	J	K	L
1						**Present**	**Present Value**					
2						**Value of**	**Discount Factor[a] at**	**Sketch of Relevant Cash Flows at End of Each Year**				
3						**Cash Flow**	**32%**	**0**	**1**	**2**	**3**	**4**
4	1.	Net initial investment										
5		**Year**	**Investment Outflows**									
6		0	$(750,000)			$(750,000)	← 1.000 ←	$(750,000)				
7	2a.	Annual after-tax cash flow from										
8		operations (excluding the depreciation effect)										
9			**Annual**		**Annual**							
10			**Before-Tax**	**Income**	**After-Tax**							
11			**Cash Flow**	**Tax**	**Cash Flow**							
12		**Year**	**from Operations**	**Outflows**	**from Operations**							
13		**(1)**	**(2)**	**(3) = 0.40 x (2)**	**(4) = (2) - (3)**							
14		1	$550,000	$220,000	$330,000	250,140	← 0.758 ←		$330,000			
15		2	726,000	290,400	435,600	250,034	← 0.574 ←			$435,600		
16		3	798,600	319,440	479,160	208,435	← 0.435 ←				$479,160	
17		4	439,230	175,692	263,538	86,704	← 0.329 ←					$263,538
18						795,313						
19	2b.	Income tax cash savings from annual										
20		depreciation deductions										
21		**Year**	**Depreciation**	**Tax Cash Savings**								
22		**(1)**	**(2)**	**(3) = 0.40 x (2)**								
23		1	$187,500[b]	$75,000		56,850	← 0.758 ←		$ 75,000			
24		2	187,500	75,000		43,050	← 0.574 ←			$ 75,000		
25		3	187,500	75,000		32,625	← 0.435 ←				$ 75,000	
26		4	187,500	75,000		24,675	← 0.329 ←					$ 75,000
27						157,200						
28	NPV if new equipment purchased					$ 202,513						
29												
30												
31	[a]The nominal discount rate of 32% is made up of the real rate of return of 20% and the inflation rate of 10% [(1 + 0.20) (1 + 1.10)] – 1 = 0.32.											
32	[b]$750,000 ÷ 4 = $187,500											

We continue to make the simplifying assumption that cash flows occur at the end of each year. The income tax rate is 40%. For tax purposes, the cost of the equipment will be depreciated using the straight-line method.

Exhibit 11-7 shows the calculation of NPV using cash flows in nominal dollars and using a nominal discount rate. The calculations in Exhibit 11-7 include the net initial machine investment, annual after-tax cash flows from operations (excluding the depreciation effect), and income tax cash savings from annual depreciation deductions. The NPV is $202,513 and, based on financial considerations alone, Network Communications should purchase the equipment.

Terms to Learn

This chapter and the Glossary at the end of the book contain definitions of the following important terms:

accrual accounting rate-of-return (AARR) method (p. 455)
capital budgeting (p. 445)
cost of capital (p. 447)
discount rate (p. 447)
discounted cash flow (DCF) methods (p. 447)
discounted payback method (p. 454)
hurdle rate (p. 447)
inflation (p. 468)
internal rate-of-return (IRR) method (p. 449)
net present value (NPV) method (p. 447)
nominal rate of return (p. 468)
opportunity cost of capital (p. 447)
payback method (p. 452)
real rate of return (p. 468)
required rate of return (RRR) (p. 447)
time value of money (p. 447)

Assignment Material

Questions

11-1 List and briefly describe each of the five stages in capital budgeting.

11-2 What is the essence of the discounted cash flow methods?

11-3 How can managers incorporate sensitivity analysis in DCF analysis?

11-4 What is the payback method? What are its main strengths and weaknesses?

11-5 Describe the accrual accounting rate-of-return method. What are its main strengths and weaknesses?

11-6 Bill Watts, president of Western Publications, accepts a capital budgeting project proposed by division X. This is the division in which the president spent his first 10 years with the company. On the same day, the president rejects a capital budgeting project proposal from division Y. The manager of division Y is incensed. She believes that the division Y project has an internal rate of return at least 10 percentage points higher than the division X project. She comments, "What is the point of all our detailed DCF analysis? If Watts is panting over a project, he can arrange to have the proponents of that project massage the numbers so that it looks like a winner." What advice would you give the manager of division Y?

11-7 Distinguish different categories of cash flows to be considered in an equipment-replacement decision by a tax-paying company.

11-8 Describe three ways income taxes can affect the cash inflows or outflows in a motor vehicle replacement decision by a tax-paying company.

11-9 How can capital budgeting tools assist in evaluating a manager who is responsible for retaining customers of a cellular telephone company?

11-10 Distinguish the nominal rate of return from the real rate of return.

Exercises

11-11 Exercises in compound interest, no income taxes. To be sure that you understand how to use the tables in the Appendix at the end of this book, solve the following exercises. Ignore income tax considerations. The correct answers, rounded to the nearest dollar, appear on pages 479–480.

Required

1. You have just won $5,000. How much money will you accumulate at the end of 10 years if you invest it at 6% compounded annually? At 14%?
2. Ten years from now, the unpaid principal of the mortgage on your house will be $89,550. How much do you need to invest today at 6% interest compounded annually to accumulate the $89,550 in 10 years?
3. If the unpaid mortgage on your house in 10 years will be $89,550, how much money do you need to invest at the end of each year at 6% to accumulate exactly this amount at the end of the 10th year?
4. You plan to save $5,000 of your earnings at the end of each year for the next 10 years. How much money will you accumulate at the end of the 10th year if you invest your savings compounded at 12% per year?
5. You have just turned 65 and an endowment insurance policy has paid you a lump sum of $200,000. If you invest the sum at 6%, how much money can you withdraw from your account in equal amounts at the end of each year so that at the end of 10 years (age 75) there will be nothing left?
6. You have estimated that for the first 10 years after you retire you will need a cash inflow of $50,000 at the end of each year. How much money do you need to invest at 6% at your retirement age to obtain this annual cash inflow? At 20%?
7. The following table shows two schedules of prospective operating cash inflows, each of which requires the same net initial investment of $10,000 now:

	Annual Cash Inflows	
Year	Plan A	Plan B
1	$ 1,000	$ 5,000
2	2,000	4,000
3	3,000	3,000
4	4,000	2,000
5	5,000	1,000
Total	$15,000	$15,000

The required rate of return is 6% compounded annually. All cash inflows occur at the end of each year. In terms of net present value, which plan is more desirable? Show your computations.

11-12 Capital budgeting methods, no income taxes. Valleyview Company runs hardware stores in a tri-state area. Valleyview's management estimates that if it invests $325,000 in a new computer system, it can save $72,000 in annual cash operating costs. The system has an expected useful life of 8 years and no terminal disposal value. The required rate of return is 8%. Ignore income tax issues in your answers. Assume all cash flows occur at year-end except for initial investment amounts.

Required

1. Calculate the following for the new computer system:
   a. Net present value
   b. Payback period
   c. Discounted payback period
   d. Internal rate of return (using the interpolation method)
   e. Accrual accounting rate of return based on the net initial investment (assume straight-line depreciation)
2. What other factors should Valleyview consider in deciding whether to purchase the new computer system?

11-13 Capital budgeting methods, no income taxes. Techno Labs, a nonprofit organization, estimates that it can save $25,000 a year in cash operating costs for the next 8 years if it buys a special-purpose eye-testing machine at a cost of $120,000. No terminal disposal value is expected. Techno Labs' required rate of return is 12%. Assume all cash flows occur at year-end except for initial investment amounts. Techno Labs uses straight-line depreciation.

Required

1. Calculate the following for the special-purpose eye-testing machine:
   a. Net present value
   b. Payback period
   c. Internal rate of return
   d. Accrual accounting rate of return based on net initial investment
   e. Accrual accounting rate of return based on average investment
2. What other factors should Techno Labs consider in deciding whether to purchase the special-purpose eye-testing machine?

11-14 Capital budgeting, income taxes. Assume the same facts as in Exercise 11-13 except that Techno Labs is a tax-paying entity. The income tax rate is 30% for all transactions that affect income taxes.

Required

1. Do requirement 1 in Exercise 11-13.
2. How would your computations in requirement 1 be affected if the special-purpose machine had a $12,000 terminal disposal value at the end of 8 years? Assume depreciation deductions are based on the $120,000 purchase cost and zero terminal disposal value using the straight-line method. Answer briefly in words without further calculations.

11-15 Capital budgeting with uneven cash flows, no income taxes. America Cola is considering the purchase of a special-purpose bottling machine for $28,000. It is expected to have a useful life of 4 years with no terminal disposal value. The plant manager estimates the following savings in cash operating costs:

Year	Amount
1	$12,000
2	10,000
3	9,000
4	8,000
Total	$39,000

America Cola uses a required rate of return of 20% in its capital budgeting decisions. Ignore income taxes in your analysis. Assume all cash flows occur at year-end except for initial investment amounts.

Required

Calculate the following for the special-purpose bottling machine:

1. Net present value
2. Payback period
3. Discounted payback period
4. Internal rate of return (using the interpolation method)
5. Accrual accounting rate of return based on net initial investment (Assume straight-line depreciation. Use the average annual savings in cash operating costs when computing the numerator of the accrual accounting rate of return.)

11-16 Comparison of projects, no income taxes. (CMA, adapted) New Olgy Corporation is a rapidly growing biotech company that has a required rate of return of 14%. It plans to build a new facility in Santa Clara County. The building will take 2 years to complete. The building contractor offered New Olgy a choice of three payment plans:

- **Plan I** Payment of $325,000 at the time of signing the contract and $4,650,000 upon completion of the building. The end of the second year is the completion date.
- **Plan II** Payment of $1,625,000 at the time of signing the contract and $1,625,000 at the end of each of the two succeeding years.
- **Plan III** Payment of $450,000 at the time of signing the contract and $1,600,000 at the end of each of the three succeeding years.

Required

1. Using the net present value method, calculate the comparative cost of each of the three payment plans being considered by New Olgy.
2. Which payment plan should New Olgy choose? Explain.
3. Discuss the financial factors, other than the cost of the plan, and the nonfinancial factors that should be considered in selecting an appropriate payment plan.

11-17 Payback and NPV methods, no income taxes. (CMA, adapted) Clarabelles Construction is analyzing its capital expenditure proposals for the purchase of equipment in the coming year. The capital budget is limited to $10,000,000 for the year. Laura Bobo, staff analyst at Clarabelles, is preparing an analysis of the three projects under consideration by Calvin Clarabelles, the company's owner.

	A	B	C	D
1		Project A	Project B	Project C
2	Projected cash outflow			
3	Net initial investment	$5,000,000	$5,000,000	$5,000,000
4				
5	Projected cash inflows			
6	Year 1	$2,450,000	$3,200,000	$3,200,000
7	Year 2	2,450,000	1,400,000	2,200,000
8	Year 3		1,200,000	125,000
9	Year 4	2,450,000		25,000
10				
11	Required rate of return	8%	8%	8%

Required

1. Because the company's cash is limited, Clarabelles thinks the payback method should be used to choose between the capital budgeting projects.
   a. What are the benefits and limitations of using the payback method to choose between projects?
   b. Calculate the payback period for each of the three projects. Ignore income taxes. Using the payback method, which project should Clarabelles choose?
2. Bobo thinks that projects should be selected based on their NPVs. Assume all cash flows occur at the end of the year except for initial investment amounts. Calculate the NPV for each project. Ignore income taxes.
3. Which projects, if any, would you recommend funding? Briefly explain why.

11-18 DCF, accrual accounting rate of return, working capital, evaluation of performance, no income taxes. Compo Research plans to purchase a new centrifuge machine for its New Mexico facility. The machine costs $382,000 and is expected to have a useful life of 10 years, with a terminal disposal value of $47,000. Savings in cash operating costs are expected to be $79,000 per year. However, Compo Research needs additional working capital to keep the machine running efficiently. The working capital must continually be replaced, so an investment of $22,000 needs to be maintained at all times, but this investment is fully recoverable (will be "cashed in") at the end of the useful life. Compo Research's required rate of return is 12%. Ignore income taxes in your analysis. Assume all cash flows occur at year-end except for initial investment amounts. Compo Research uses straight-line depreciation for its machines.

Required

1. Calculate net present value.
2. Calculate internal rate of return.
3. Calculate accrual accounting rate of return based on net initial investment.
4. Calculate accrual accounting rate of return based on average investment.
5. You have the authority to make the purchase decision. Why might you be reluctant to base your decision on the DCF methods?

11-19 New equipment purchase, income taxes. Amanda's Bakery plans to purchase a new oven for its store. The oven has an estimated useful life of 4 years. The estimated pretax cash flows for the oven are as shown in the table that follows, with no anticipated change in working capital. Amanda's Bakery has an 8% after-tax required rate of return and a 34% income tax rate. Assume depreciation is calculated on a straight-line basis for tax purposes using the initial oven investment and estimated terminal disposal value of the oven. Assume all cash flows occur at year-end except for initial investment amounts.

Home Insert Page Layout Formulas Data Review View

	A	B	C	D	E	F
1		**Relevant Cash Flows at End of Each Year**				
2		**0**	**1**	**2**	**3**	**4**
3	Initial machine investment	($70,000)				
4	Annual cash flow from operations (excluding the depreciation effect)		$24,000	$24,000	$24,000	$24,000
5	Cash flow from terminal disposal of machine					$ 7,000

Required

1. Calculate (a) net present value, (b) payback period, and (c) internal rate of return.
2. Calculate the project's accrual accounting rate of return based on net initial investment.

11-20 New equipment purchase, income taxes. New Frontiers, Inc., is considering the purchase of a new industrial electric motor to improve efficiency at its Chico plant. The motor has an estimated useful life of 5 years. The estimated pretax cash flows for the motor are shown in the table that follows, with no anticipated change in working capital. New Frontiers has an 8% after-tax required rate of return and a 30% income tax rate. Assume depreciation is calculated on a straight-line basis for tax purposes. Assume all cash flows occur at year-end except for initial investment amounts.

	A	B	C	D	E	F	G
1		Relevant Cash Flows at End of Each Year					
2		0	1	2	3	4	5
3	Initial machine investment	($90,000)					
4	Annual cash flow from operations (excluding the depreciation effect)		$26,000	$26,000	$26,000	$26,000	$26,000
5	Cash flow from terminal disposal of machine						$ 0

Required

1. Calculate (a) net present value, (b) payback period, (c) discounted payback period, and (d) internal rate of return.
2. Compare and contrast the capital budgeting methods in requirement 1.

11-21 Selling a plant, income taxes. (CMA, adapted) The Lucky Seven Company is an international clothing manufacturer. Its Santa Monica plant will become idle on December 31, 2013. Peter Laney, the corporate controller, has been asked to look at three options regarding the plant:

- **Option 1** The plant, which has been fully depreciated for tax purposes, can be sold immediately for $900,000.
- **Option 2** The plant can be leased to the Preston Corporation, one of Lucky Seven's suppliers, for 4 years. Under the lease terms, Preston would pay Lucky Seven $220,000 rent per year (payable at year-end) and would grant Lucky Seven a $40,000 annual discount off the normal price of fabric purchased by Lucky Seven. (Assume that the discount is received at year-end for each of the 4 years.) Preston would bear all of the plant's ownership costs. Lucky Seven expects to sell this plant for $150,000 at the end of the 4-year lease.
- **Option 3** The plant could be used for 4 years to make souvenir jackets for the Olympics. Fixed overhead costs (a cash outflow) before any equipment upgrades are estimated to be $20,000 annually for the 4-year period. The jackets are expected to sell for $55 each. Variable cost per unit is expected to be $43. The following production and sales of jackets are expected: 2014, 18,000 units; 2015, 26,000 units; 2016, 30,000 units; 2017, 10,000 units. In order to manufacture the jackets, some of the plant equipment would need to be upgraded at an immediate cost of $160,000. The equipment would be depreciated using the straight-line depreciation method and zero terminal disposal value over the 4 years it would be in use. Because of the equipment upgrades, Lucky Seven could sell the plant for $270,000 at the end of 4 years. No change in working capital would be required.

Lucky Seven treats all cash flows as if they occur at the end of the year, and it uses an after-tax required rate of return of 10%. Lucky Seven is subject to a 35% tax rate on all income, including capital gains.

Required

1. Calculate net present value of each of the options and determine which option Lucky Seven should select using the NPV criterion.
2. What nonfinancial factors should Lucky Seven consider before making its choice?

Problems

11-22 Equipment replacement, no income taxes. A-1 Chips is a manufacturer of prototype chips based in Dublin, Ireland. Next year, in 2014, A-1 Chips expects to deliver 605 prototype chips at an average price of $110,000. A-1 Chips' marketing vice president forecasts growth of 55 prototype chips per year through 2020. That is, demand will be 605 in 2014, 660 in 2015, 715 in 2016, and so on.

The plant cannot produce more than 575 prototype chips annually. To meet future demand, A-1 Chips must either modernize the plant or replace it. The old equipment is fully depreciated and can be sold for $4,500,000 if the plant is replaced. If the plant is modernized, the costs to modernize it are to be capitalized and depreciated over the useful life of the updated plant. The old equipment is retained as part of the modernize alternative. The following data on the two options are:

	Modernize	Replace
Initial investment in 2014	$37,100,000	$66,300,000
Terminal disposal value in 2020	$ 6,400,000	$15,500,000
Useful life	7 years	7 years
Total annual cash operating costs per prototype chip	$ 94,000	$ 85,000

A-1 Chips uses straight-line depreciation, assuming zero terminal disposal value. For simplicity, we assume no change in prices or costs in future years. The investment will be made at the beginning of 2014, and all transactions thereafter occur on the last day of the year. A-1 Chips' required rate of return is 18%.

There is no difference between the modernize and replace alternatives in terms of required working capital. A-1 Chips has a special waiver on income taxes until 2020.

Required

1. Sketch the cash inflows and outflows of the modernize and replace alternatives over the 2014–2020 period.
2. Calculate payback period for the modernize and replace alternatives.
3. Calculate net present value of the modernize and replace alternatives.
4. What factors should A-1 Chips consider in choosing between the alternatives?

11-23 Equipment replacement, income taxes (continuation of 11-22). Assume the same facts as in Problem 11-22, except that the plant is located in Austin, Texas. A-1 Chips has no special waiver on income taxes. It pays a 25% tax rate on all income. Proceeds from sales of equipment above book value are taxed at the same 25% rate.

Required

1. Sketch the after-tax cash inflows and outflows of the modernize and replace alternatives over the 2014–2020 period.
2. Calculate the net present value of the modernize and replace alternatives.
3. Suppose A-1 Chips is planning to build several more plants. It wants to have the most advantageous tax position possible. A-1 Chips has been approached by Spain, Malaysia, and Australia to construct plants in their countries. Use the data in Problem 11-22 and this problem to briefly describe in qualitative terms the income tax features that would be advantageous to A-1 Chips.

11-24 DCF, sensitivity analysis, no income taxes. (CMA, adapted) Grace Corporation is an international manufacturer of fragrances for women. Management at Grace is considering expanding the product line to men's fragrances. From the best estimates of the marketing and production managers, annual sales (all for cash) for this new line is 1,400,000 units at $40 per unit; cash variable cost is $15 per unit; and cash fixed costs are $15,000,000 per year. The investment project requires $40,000,000 of cash outflow and has a project life of 6 years.

At the end of the 6-year useful life, there will be no terminal disposal value. Assume all cash flows occur at year-end except for initial investment amounts.

Men's fragrance is a new market for Grace, and management is concerned about the reliability of the estimates. The controller has proposed applying sensitivity analysis to selected factors. Ignore income taxes in your computations. Grace's required rate of return on this project is 16%.

Required

1. Calculate the net present value of this investment proposal.
2. Calculate the effect on the net present value of the following two changes in assumptions. (Treat each item independently of the other.)
   a. 10% reduction in the selling price
   b. 10% increase in the variable cost per unit
3. Discuss how managers would use the data developed in requirements 1 and 2 when considering the proposed capital investment.

11-25 NPV, IRR, and sensitivity analysis. Yummy Candy Company is considering expanding by buying a new (additional) machine that costs $124,000, has zero terminal disposal value, and has an 11-year useful life. The company expects the annual increase in cash revenues from the expansion to be $56,000 per year. It expects additional annual cash costs to be $36,000 per year. Its cost of capital is 8%. Ignore taxes.

Required

1. Calculate the net present value and internal rate of return for this investment.
2. Assume the finance manager of Yummy Candy Company is not sure about the cash revenues and costs. The revenues could be anywhere from 10% higher to 10% lower than predicted. Assume cash costs are still $36,000 per year. What are NPV and IRR at the high and low points for revenue?
3. The finance manager thinks that costs will vary with revenues, and if the revenues are 10% higher, the costs will be 7% higher. If the revenues are 10% lower, the costs will be 10% lower. Recalculate the NPV and IRR at the high and low revenue points with this new cost information.

4. The finance manager has decided that the company should earn 2% more than the cost of capital on any project. Recalculate the original NPV in requirement 1 using the new discount rate and evaluate the investment opportunity.
5. Discuss how the changes in assumptions have affected the decision to expand.

11-26 Payback methods, even and uneven cash flows. You have the opportunity to expand your business by purchasing new equipment for $222,000. The equipment has a useful life of 9 years. You expect to incur cash fixed costs of $79,000 per year to use this new equipment, and you expect to incur cash variable costs in the amount of 5% of cash revenues. Your cost of capital is 10%.

Required

1. Calculate the payback period and the discounted payback period for this investment, assuming you will generate $200,000 in cash revenues every year.
2. Assume instead that you expect the following cash revenue stream for this investment:

Year 1	$ 115,000
Year 2	105,000
Year 3	115,000
Year 4	185,000
Year 5	195,000
Year 6	185,000
Year 7	125,000
Year 8	135,000
Year 9	155,000

Based on this estimated revenue stream, what are the payback and discounted payback periods for this investment?

11-27 Replacement of a machine, income taxes, sensitivity. (CMA, adapted) The Frooty Company is a family-owned business that produces fruit jam. The company has a grinding machine that has been in use for 3 years. On January 1, 2013, Frooty is considering the purchase of a new grinding machine. Frooty has two options: (1) continue using the old machine or (2) sell the old machine and purchase a new machine. The seller of the new machine isn't offering a trade-in. The following information has been obtained:

	A	B	C
1		**Old Machine**	**New Machine**
2	Initial purchase cost of machines	$150,000	$190,000
3	Useful life from acquisition date (years)	8	5
4	Terminal disposal valve at the end of useful life on Dec. 31, 2017, assumed for depreciation purposes	$20,000	$25,000
5	Expected annual cash operating costs:		
6	Variable cost per can of jam	$0.25	$0.19
7	Total fixed costs	$25,000	$24,000
8	Depreciation method for tax purposes	Straight line	Straight line
9	Estimated disposal value of machines:		
10	January 1, 2013	$68,000	$190,000
11	December 31, 2017	$12,000	$22,000
12	Expected cans of jam made and sold each year	475,000	475,000

Frooty is subject to a 34% income tax rate. Assume that any gain or loss on the sale of machines is treated as an ordinary tax item and will affect the taxes paid by Frooty in the year in which it occurs. Frooty's after-tax required rate of return is 12%. Assume all cash flows occur at year-end except for initial investment amounts.

Required

1. A manager at Frooty asks you whether it should buy the new machine. To help in your analysis, calculate the following:
   a. One-time after-tax cash effect of disposing of the old machine on January 1, 2013
   b. Annual recurring after-tax cash operating savings from using the new machine (variable and fixed)

c. Cash tax savings due to differences in annual depreciation of the old machine and the new machine

d. Difference in after-tax cash flow from terminal disposal of new machine and old machine

2. Use your calculations in requirement 1 and the net present value method to determine whether Frooty should use the old machine or acquire the new machine.
3. How much more or less would the recurring after-tax cash operating savings of the new machine need to be for Frooty to earn exactly the 12% after-tax required rate of return? Assume that all other data about the investment do not change.
4. What other factors should Frooty consider when making its decision?

11-28 NPV and AARR, goal-congruence issues. Eric Scanzillo, a manager of the Plate Division for the Ore City Manufacturing Company, has the opportunity to expand the division by investing in additional machinery costing $430,000. He would depreciate the equipment using the straight-line method, and expects it to have no residual value. It has a useful life of 8 years. The firm mandates a required after-tax rate of return of 12% on investments. Eric estimates annual net cash inflows for this investment of $110,000 before taxes, and an investment in working capital of $7,500. The tax rate is 30%.

Required

1. Calculate the net present value of this investment.
2. Calculate the accrual accounting rate of return on initial investment for this project.
3. Should Eric accept the project? Will Eric accept the project if his bonus depends on achieving an accrual accounting rate of return of 12%? How can this conflict be resolved?

11-29 Recognizing cash flows for capital investment projects. Jane Fando owns a fitness center and is thinking of replacing the old Ab-O-Matic machine with a brand new Flab-Blaster 5000. The old Ab-O-Matic has a historical cost of $25,200 and accumulated depreciation of $23,000, but has a trade-in value of $2,700. It currently costs $600 per month in utilities and another $5,000 a year in maintenance to run the Ab-O-Matic. Jane feels that the Ab-O-Matic can be used for another 11 years, after which it would have no salvage value.

The Flab-Blaster 5000 would reduce the utilities costs by 30% and cut the maintenance cost in half. The Flab-Blaster 5000 costs $49,000, has an 11-year life, and an expected disposal value of $5,000 at the end of its useful life.

Jane charges customers $5 per hour to use the fitness center. Replacing the fitness machine will not affect the price of service or the number of customers she can serve.

Required

1. Jane wants to evaluate the Flab-Blaster 5000 project using capital budgeting techniques, but does not know how to begin. To help her, read through the problem and separate the cash flows into four groups: (1) net initial investment cash flows, (2) cash flow savings from operations, (3) cash flows from terminal disposal of investment, and (4) cash flows not relevant to the capital budgeting problem.
2. Assuming a tax rate of 40%, a required rate of return of 8%, and straight-line depreciation over remaining useful life of machines, should Jane buy the Flab-Blaster 5000?

11-30 Recognizing cash flows for capital investment projects, NPV. City Manufacturing manufactures over 20,000 different products made from metal, including building materials, tools, and furniture parts. The manager of the furniture parts division has proposed that his division expand into bicycle parts as well. The furniture parts division currently generates cash revenues of $5,300,000 and incurs cash costs of $3,750,000, with an investment in assets of $12,270,000. One-fifth of the cash costs are direct labor.

The manager estimates that the expansion of the business will require an investment in working capital of $70,000. Because the company already has a facility, there would be no additional rent or purchase costs for a building, but the project would generate an additional $300,000 in annual cash overhead. Moreover, the manager expects annual materials cash costs for bicycle parts to be $1,650,000, and labor for the bicycle parts to be about the same as the labor cash costs for furniture parts.

The controller of City, working with various managers, estimates that the expansion would require the purchase of equipment with a $2,430,000 cost and an expected disposal value of $450,000 at the end of its 6-year useful life. Depreciation would occur on a straight-line basis.

The CFO of City determines the firm's cost of capital as 12%. The CFO's salary is $200,000 per year. Adding another division will not change that. The CEO asks for a report on expected revenues for the project, and is told by the marketing department that it might be able to achieve cash revenues of $3,480,000 annually from bicycle parts. City Manufacturing has a tax rate of 40%.

Required

1. Separate the cash flows into four groups: (1) net initial investment cash flows, (2) cash flows from operations, (3) cash flows from terminal disposal of investment, and (4) cash flows not relevant to the capital budgeting problem.
2. Calculate the NPV of the expansion project and comment on your analysis.

11-31 NPV, inflation and taxes. Cheap-O Foods is considering replacing all 10 of its old cash registers with new ones. The old registers are fully depreciated and have no disposal value. The new registers cost $899,640 (in total). Because the new registers are more efficient than the old registers, Cheap-O will have annual incremental cash savings from using the new registers in the amount of $192,000 per year. The registers have a 7-year useful life and no terminal disposal value, and are depreciated using the straight-line method. Cheap-O requires an 8% real rate of return.

Required

1. Given the preceding information, what is the net present value of the project? Ignore taxes.
2. Assume the $192,000 cost savings are in current real dollars, and the inflation rate is 5.5%. Recalculate the NPV of the project.
3. Based on your answers to requirements 1 and 2, should Cheap-O buy the new cash registers?
4. Now assume that the company's tax rate is 30%. Calculate the NPV of the project assuming no inflation.
5. Again assuming that the company faces a 30% tax rate, calculate the NPV of the project under an inflation rate of 5.5%.
6. Based on your answers to requirements 4 and 5, should Cheap-O buy the new cash registers?

11-32 Net present value, internal rate of return, sensitivity analysis. Sally wants to purchase a Burger Barn franchise. She can buy one for $750,000. Burger Barn headquarters provides the following information:

Estimated annual cash revenues	$420,000
Typical annual cash operating expenses	$248,000

Sally will also have to pay Burger Barn a franchise fee of 10% of her revenues each year. Sally wants to earn at least 10% on the investment because she has to borrow the $750,000 at a cost of 6%. Use an 11-year window and ignore taxes.

Required

1. Find the NPV and IRR of Sally's investment.
2. Sally is nervous about the revenue estimate provided by Burger Barn headquarters. Calculate the NPV and IRR under alternative annual revenue estimates of $390,000 and $360,000. Assume cash operating expenses of $248,000 each year and a franchise fee of 10% of revenues.
3. Sally estimates that if her revenues are lower, her costs will be lower as well. For each revised level of revenue used in requirement 2, recalculate NPV and IRR with a proportional decrease in annual operating expenses.
4. Suppose Sally also negotiates a lower franchise and has to pay Burger Barn only 8% of annual revenues. Redo the calculations in requirement 3.
5. Discuss how the sensitivity analysis will affect Sally's decision to buy the franchise.

Answers to Exercises in Compound Interest (Exercise 11-11)

The general approach to these exercises centers on a key question: Which of the four basic tables in the Appendix should you use? You need to answer this basic question before doing any computations.

1. **From Table I.** The $5,000 is the present value P of your winnings. Their future value S in 10 years will be as follows:

$$S = P(1 + r)^n$$

The conversion factor, $(1 + r)^n$ is on line 10 of Table I.

$$\text{Substituting at 6\%: } S = \$5{,}000(1.791) = \$8{,}955$$

$$\text{Substituting at 14\%: } S = \$5{,}000(3.707) = \$18{,}535$$

2. **From Table 2.** The $89,550 is a future value. You want the present value of that amount. $P = S \div (1 + r)^n$ The conversion factor, $1 \div (1 + r)^n$, is on line 10 in Table 2. Substituting,

$$P = \$89,550\ (.558) = \$49,969$$

3. **From Table 3.** The $89,550 is a future value. You are seeking the uniform amount (annuity) to set aside annually. Note that $1 invested each year for 10 years at 6% has a future value of $13.181 after 10 years, from line 10 in Table 3.

$$\$89,550/13.181 = \$6,794$$

4. **From Table 3.** You need to find the future value of an annuity of $5,000 per year. Note that $1 invested each year for 10 years at 12% has a future value of $17.549 after 10 years.

$$\$5,000\ (17.549) = \$87,745$$

5. **From Table 4.** When you reach age 65, you will get $200,000, a present value at that time. You need to find the annuity that will exactly exhaust the invested principal in 10 years. To pay yourself $1 each year for 10 years when the interest rate is 6% requires you to have $7.360 today, from line 10 in Table 4.

$$\$200,000/7.360 = \$27,174$$

6. **From Table 4.** You need to find the present value of an annuity for 10 years at 6% and at 20%:

$$6\%: \$50,000\ (7.360) = \$368,000$$

$$20\%: \$50,000\ (4.192) = \$209,600$$

7. **Plan B is preferable.** The NPV of plan B exceeds that of plan A by $980.

		Plan A		Plan B	
Year	PV Factor at 6%	Cash Inflows	PV of Cash Inflows	Cash Inflows	PV of Cash Inflows
0	1.000	$(10,000)	$(10,000)	$(10,000)	$(10,000)
1	0.943	1,000	943	5,000	4,715
2	0.890	2,000	1,780	4,000	3,560
3	0.840	3,000	2,520	3,000	2,520
4	0.792	4,000	3,168	2,000	1,584
5	0.747	5,000	3,735	1,000	747
			$ 2,146		$ 3,126

Even though plans A and B have the same total cash inflows over the 5 years, plan B is preferred because it has greater cash inflows occurring earlier.

Case

Liquid Chemical

Liquid Chemical, Ltd. sells a range of high-grade chemical products throughout the Pacific Northwest from its main plant in Vancouver, British Columbia. The company's products, because of their chemical properties, call for careful packaging. The company has always emphasized the special properties of the containers used. Liquid Chemical had a special patented lining made from a material known as GHL, and the company operated a department specially to maintain its containers in good condition and to make new ones to replace the ones that were past repair.

Tom Walsh, the general manager, had for some time suspected that the firm might save money and get equally good service by buying its containers outside. After careful inquiries, he approached a firm specializing in container production, Packages, Inc., and obtained a quotation on the special containers. At the same time he asked Amy Dyer, the controller, to let him have an up-to-date statement of the cost of operating the Container Department.

Within a few days, the quotation from Packages, Inc. came in. They were prepared to supply all the new containers required, running at the rate of 3,000 a year, for $600,000 annually. The contract would run for a term of five years, and thereafter would be renewable from year to year. If the number of containers required increased, the contract price would be increased proportionally. Additionally, if the above contract was agreed upon, Packages, Inc. proposed to carry out maintenance work on the containers for a sum of $175,000 annually on the same contract terms.

Tom Walsh compared these figures with the cost data prepared by Amy Dyer covering a year's operations of the Container Department. Dyer's analysis is as follows:

Direct material (GHL)		$ 75,000
Direct material (other)		125,000
Direct labor		350,000
Departmental overhead:		
Department manager's salary	$80,000	
Rent	17,000	
Depreciation of machinery	60,000	
Maintenance of machinery	13,500	
Other overhead	63,000	233,500
		$783,500
Allocation of general administrative overhead from entire factory		69,500
Total cost of Container Department for one year		$853,000

Walsh's conclusion was that no time should be lost in closing down the Container Department and entering into the contract offered by Packages, Inc. However, he felt bound to give the manager of the department, Jake Duffy, an opportunity to question this conclusion before he acted on it. Walsh called Duffy in and put the facts before him, at the same time making it clear that Duffy's own position was not in jeopardy. Even if Duffy's department were closed down, there was another managerial position shortly becoming vacant to which Duffy could be moved without loss of pay or prospects.

Jake Duffy looked thoughtful, and asked for time to think the matter over. The next morning Duffy asked to speak to Walsh again, and said he thought there were a number of considerations that ought to be borne in mind before his department was closed down. "For instance," Duffy said, "what will you do with the machinery? It cost $480,000 four years ago, but you'd be lucky if you got $80,000 for it now, even though it's good for another five years. Then there's the stock of GHL we bought a year ago. That cost us $300,000. At the rate we're using it now, it'll last us another three years. We used up about a quarter of it last year. But it'll be tricky stuff to handle if we don't use it up. We bought well, paying $1,500 a ton for it. You couldn't buy it today for less than $1,800 a ton. But you wouldn't have more than $1,200 a ton left if you sold it, after you'd covered all the handling expenses."

Tom Walsh thought that Amy Dyer ought to be present during this discussion. He asked her to come in and then reviewed Duffy's points. "I don't much like all this conjecture," Dyer said. "I think my figures are pretty conclusive. Besides, if we are going to have all this talk about 'what will happen if,' don't forget the problem of space we're faced with. We're paying $27,500 a year in rent for a warehouse a couple of miles away. If we closed Duffy's department, we'd have all the warehouse space we need without renting."

"That's a good point," said Walsh, "though I must say, I'm a bit worried about the employees if we close the Container Department. I don't think we can find room for any of them elsewhere in the firm. I could see whether Packages, Inc. can take any of them. But some of them are getting on in years. There's Walters and Hines, for example. They've been with us since they left school many years ago. Their severance pay would cost us $10,000 a year each, for five years."

Duffy showed some relief at Walsh's comment. "But I still don't like Amy's figures," he said. "What about this $69,500 for general administrative overhead? You surely don't expect to fire anyone in the general office if I'm closed down, do you?" "Probably not," said Dyer, "but someone has to pay for these costs. We can't ignore them when we look at an individual department, because if we do that with each department in turn, we'll wind up by convincing ourselves that general managers, accountants, secretaries, and the like, don't have to be paid. And they do, believe me."

"Well, I think we've thrashed this out pretty fully," said Walsh, "but I've been wondering about the possibility of perhaps keeping on the maintenance work ourselves. What are your views on that, Duffy?" "I don't know," said Duffy, "but it's worth looking into. We shouldn't need any machinery for that, and I could hand the management over to a department supervisor. You'd save about $20,000 a year there. You'd only need about one-fifth of the employees, but you could keep the oldest. You wouldn't save any space, so I suppose the rent would be the same. I shouldn't think the other overhead expenses would be more than $26,000 a year." "What about materials?" asked Walsh. "We use about 10 percent of both GHL and other materials on maintenance," Duffy replied.

"Well, I've told Packages, Inc. that I'd let them know my decision within a week," said Walsh. "I'll let you know what I decide to do before I contact them."

Notes

i. Liquid Chemical's tax rate is 40%, and its after-tax hurdle rate is 10%.
ii. The company uses straight-line depreciation for tax purposes. The depreciation expense in each of the next four years is $60,000. The equipment will be fully depreciated at the end of that period.
iii. Liquid Chemical's annual net revenue is $2,000,000.

Required

Prepare a net present value analysis of Liquid Chemical's three alternatives. Use a five-year time horizon. You don't have to make additional assumptions (regarding inflation rates, for example) beyond the information provided in the case.

Master Budget and Responsibility Accounting

12

Learning Objectives

1. Describe the master budget and explain its benefits
2. Describe the advantages of budgets
3. Prepare the operating budget and its supporting schedules
4. Use computer-based financial planning models for sensitivity analysis
5. Describe responsibility centers and responsibility accounting
6. Recognize the human aspects of budgeting
7. Appreciate the special challenges of budgeting in multinational companies

During the global recession of 2007–2009, both households and businesses faced economic hardships. One of the hottest innovations to emerge during this recession was Web sites that enable users to get a snapshot of their financial data, including checking accounts, investment statements, and loans, and to create budgets to manage their spending and saving. Mint.com, a pioneer in these Web sites, was launched in 2007. In 2009, Intuit, Inc., the developer of Quicken and TurboTax, recognized the growing popularity of these financial Web sites and acquired Mint.com for $170 million.

Businesses, like individuals, need budgets. Without budgets, it's difficult for managers and their employees to know whether they're on target for their growth and spending goals. Adhering to budgets is important for all types of companies: large financial institutions, such as Citigroup, that suffered big financial losses after the bursting of the housing bubble in the mid 2000s; large retailers, such as Walmart, whose profit margins are slim; profitable computer companies, such as Apple, that sell high dollar-value goods; and luxury hotels, such as the Ritz-Carlton, that sell high dollar-value services.

In many profitable companies, a strict budget is a key to their success and decision-making process. Southwest Airlines, for example, uses budgets to monitor and manage fluctuating fuel costs. Walmart depends on its budget to maintain razor-thin margins as it competes with Target. Gillette uses budgets to plan marketing campaigns for its razors and blades.

Many young managers are often frustrated by the budgeting process because they find it difficult to predict the future and dislike superiors challenging them to improve their performance. If the budgets are stretched, these young managers may dislike having their performance measured against them and begin to view budgeting as a game: "If I I lower performance expectations, my actual performance will look good." We discuss these issues and the ways thoughtful managers deal with them later in this chapter. For now, we highlight some of the benefits that managers get from budgeting.

Budgets help managers:

1. Communicate directions and goals to different departments of a company to help them coordinate the actions they must pursue to satisfy customers and succeed in the marketplace.
2. Judge performance by measuring financial results against planned objectives, activities, and timelines and to learn about potential problems.
3. Motivate employees to achieve their goals.

Interestingly, even when it comes to entrepreneurial activities, research shows that business planning increases a new venture's probability of survival, as well as its product development and venture-organizing activities.[1] As the old adage goes: "If you fail to plan, you plan to fail."

[1] For more details, see F. Delmar and S. Shane, "Does Business Planning Facilitate the Development of New Ventures?" *Strategic Management Journal* (December 2003).

In this chapter, you will see that a budget is based on an organization's strategy and expresses its operating and financial plans. Most importantly, you will see that budgeting is a human activity that requires judgment and wise interpretation. The Chapter at a Glance previews these topics.

Chapter at a Glance

- A budget is a quantitative expression of a company's strategy and action plans and what needs to be done to implement those plans.
- The master budget expresses management's operating and financial plans for a specified period, promotes coordination and communication among subunits, provides a framework for judging performance and facilitating learning, and motivates managers and employees to achieve a company's goals.
- The operating budget comprises the budgeted income statement and its supporting schedules. Managers base this budget on activities that need to be performed and opportunities for continuous improvement.
- Top management determines operating budgets by responsibility centers, subunits of the organization with managers accountable for a specified set of activities. Managers do not fully control all the revenues and costs that they are accountable for, so responsibility accounting focuses on obtaining information, not fixing blame.
- Budgeting is not a mechanical tool but a human activity that requires persuasion, judgment, and intelligent interpretation. When administered wisely, budgeting creates commitment, accountability, and honest communication. When managed badly, it leads to game-playing and employee frustration.

Learning Objective 1

Describe the master budget

. . . the master budget is the initial budget prepared before the start of a period

and explain its benefits

. . . benefits include planning, coordination, and control

Budgets and the Budgeting Cycle

A *budget* is the quantitative expression of a proposed plan of action by management for a specified period and helps managers coordinate the activities that need to be done to implement the plan. A budget generally includes both financial and nonfinancial aspects of a plan, and serves as a blueprint for the company to follow in an upcoming period. A financial budget quantifies management's expectations regarding income, cash flows, and financial position. Just as financial statements are prepared for past periods, financial statements can be prepared for future periods—for example, a budgeted income statement, a budgeted statement of cash flows, or a budgeted balance sheet. Managers derive financial budgets using supporting information from nonfinancial budgets for, say, units manufactured or sold, number of employees, and number of new products being introduced to the marketplace.

Strategic Plans and Operating Plans

Budgeting is most useful when it is integrated with a company's strategy. *Strategy* specifies how an organization matches its own capabilities with the opportunities in the marketplace to accomplish its objectives. In developing successful strategies, managers consider questions such as the following:

- What are our objectives?
- How do we create value for our customers while distinguishing ourselves from our competitors?
- Are the markets for our products local, regional, national, or global? What trends affect our markets? How do the economy, our industry, and our competitors affect us?
- What organizational and financial structures serve us best?
- What are the risks and opportunities of alternative strategies, and what are our contingency plans if our preferred plan fails?

A company, such as Home Depot, can have a strategy of providing quality products or services at a low price. Another company, such as Porsche or the Ritz-Carlton, can have a strategy of providing a unique product or service that is priced higher than the products or services of competitors. Exhibit 12-1 shows that strategic plans are expressed through long-run budgets, and operating plans are expressed through short-run budgets. But there is more to the story! The exhibit shows

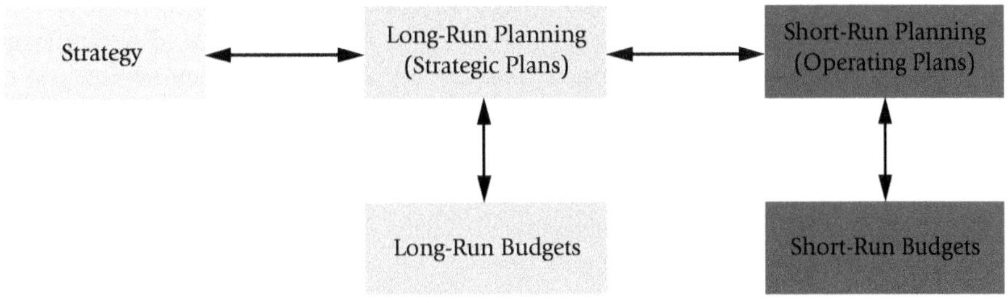

Exhibit 12-1
Strategy, Planning, and Budgets

arrows pointing backward as well as forward. The backward arrows show that budgets can lead to changes in plans and strategies. Budgets help managers assess strategic risks and opportunities by providing them with feedback about the likely effects of their strategies and plans. Sometimes the feedback prompts managers to revise their plans and possibly their strategies.

Boeing's experience with the 747-8 program illustrates how budgets can help managers rework their operating plans. Boeing believed that sharing design synergies with the ongoing 787 Dreamliner program was a relatively inexpensive way to reconfigure its 747 jumbo jet. However, continued cost overruns and delays undermined that strategy: In early 2012, the 747-8 program was already $2 billion over budget and a year behind schedule. Boeing revealed that it expects to earn no profit on virtually any of the 105 747-8 planes on its order books. With the budget revealing higher-than-expected costs in design, rework, and production, Boeing postponed plans to accelerate the jumbo's production to 2013. Some aerospace experts urged Boeing to consider more dramatic steps, including discontinuing the passenger aircraft version of the 747-8 program.

Budgeting Cycle and Master Budget

As you start your managerial career, budgeting will be a major part of your professional life. Well-managed companies usually cycle through the following steps during the course of the fiscal year:

1. Before the start of the fiscal year, managers at all levels take into account past performance, market feedback, and anticipated future changes to initiate plans for the next period. For example, an anticipated economic recovery from a recession may cause managers to plan for sales increases, higher production, and greater promotion expenses in the next period. Managers and management accountants work together to develop plans for the company as a whole and the performance of its subunits, such as departments or divisions.
2. At the beginning of the year, senior managers give subordinate managers a frame of reference, a set of specific financial or nonfinancial expectations against which they will compare actual results.
3. During the course of the year, management accountants help managers investigate variations from plans, such as an unexpected decline in sales. If necessary, corrective action follows, such as changes in product features, a reduction in price to boost sales, or cutting of costs to maintain profitability.

The preceding three steps describe the ongoing budget-related processes. The working document at the core of this process is called the *master budget.* The **master budget** expresses management's operating and financial plans for a specified period, usually a fiscal year, and it includes a set of budgeted financial statements. The master budget is the initial plan of what the company intends to accomplish in the budget period and evolves from both operating and financing decisions managers make along the way.

- Operating decisions deal with how to best use the limited resources of an organization.
- Financing decisions deal with how to obtain the funds to acquire those resources.

The terminology used to describe budgets varies among companies. For example, budgeted financial statements are sometimes called **pro forma statements.** Some companies, such as Hewlett-Packard, refer to budgeting as *targeting.* And many companies, such as Nissan Motor Company and Owens Corning, refer to the budget as a *profit plan.* Microsoft refers to goals as *commitments* and distributes firm-level goals across the company, connecting them to organizational, team, and ultimately individual commitments.

This book focuses on how management accounting helps managers make operating decisions, which is why operating budgets are emphasized here. Managers spend a significant part of their time preparing and analyzing budgets because budgeting yields many advantages

Learning Objective 2

Describe the advantages of budgets

. . . advantages include coordination, communication, performance evaluation, and managerial motivation

Advantages of Budgets

Budgets are an integral part of management control systems. When administered thoughtfully by managers, budgets do the following:

- Promote coordination and communication among subunits within the company
- Provide a framework for judging performance and facilitating learning
- Motivate managers and other employees

Coordination and Communication

Coordination is meshing and balancing all aspects of production or service and all departments in a company in the best way for the company to meet its goals. *Communication* is making sure all employees understand those goals.

Coordination forces executives to think of relationships among individual departments within the company, as well as between the company and its supply chain partners. Consider budgeting at Pace, a United Kingdom–based manufacturer of electronic products. A key product is Pace's digital set-top box for decoding satellite broadcasts. The production manager can achieve more timely production by coordinating and communicating with the company's marketing team to understand when set-top boxes need to ship to customers. In turn, the marketing team can make better predictions of future demand for set-top boxes by coordinating and communicating with Pace's customers.

Suppose BSkyB, one of Pace's largest customers, is planning to launch a new high-definition personal video recorder service. If Pace's marketing group is able to obtain information about the launch date for the service, it can share this information with Pace's manufacturing group. The manufacturing group must then coordinate and communicate with Pace's materials-procurement group, and so on. The point to understand is that Pace is more likely to have personal video recorders in the quantities that customers demand if Pace coordinates and communicates both within its business functions and with its customers and suppliers during the budgeting process as well as during the production process.

Framework for Judging Performance and Facilitating Learning

Budgets enable a company's managers to measure actual performance against predicted performance. Budgets can overcome two limitations of using past performance as a basis for judging actual results. One limitation is that past results often incorporate past miscues and substandard performance. Consider a cellular telephone company (Mobile Communications) examining the current-year (2013) performance of its sales force. Suppose the performance for 2012 incorporated the efforts of many salespeople who have since left Mobile because they did not have a good understanding of the marketplace. The president of Mobile said of those salespeople, "They could not sell ice cream in a heat wave." Using the sales record of those departed employees would set the performance bar for 2013 much too low.

The other limitation of using past performance is that future conditions can be expected to differ from the past. Consider again Mobile Communications. Suppose, in 2013, Mobile had a 20% revenue increase, compared with a 10% revenue increase in 2012. Does this increase indicate outstanding sales performance? Before you say yes, consider the following facts. In November 2012, an industry trade association correctly forecasts that the 2013 growth rate in industry revenues will be 40%. As a result, Mobile's 20% actual revenue gain in 2013 takes on a negative connotation, even though it exceeded the 2012 actual growth rate of 10%. Using the 40% budgeted sales growth rate provides a better measure of the 2013 sales performance than using the 2012 actual growth rate of 10%.

It is important to remember that the budget is not the only benchmark companies use to evaluate performance. Many companies also consider performance relative to peers. Using only the budget creates an incentive for subordinates to set targets that are relatively easy to achieve.[2] Of course, managers at all levels recognize this incentive, and therefore work to make the budget more challenging to achieve for the individuals who report to them. Still, the budget is the end product of negotiations among senior and subordinate managers. At the end of the year, senior managers gain information about the performance of competitors and external market conditions. This is valuable information that senior managers can use to judge the performance of subordinate managers.

One of the most valuable benefits of budgeting is that it helps managers gather information for improving future performance. When actual outcomes fall short of budgeted or planned results, it prompts thoughtful senior managers to ask questions about what happened and why, and how this knowledge can be used to ensure that such shortfalls do not occur again. This probing and learning is one of the most important reasons why budgeting helps improve performance.

Motivate Managers and Other Employees

Research shows employee performance improves when they receive a challenging budget because employees view falling short of budgeted numbers as a failure. Most employees are motivated to work more intensely to avoid failure than to achieve success. As employees get closer to a goal, they work harder to achieve it. Therefore, many executives like to set demanding but achievable goals for their subordinate managers and employees.[3] Creating a little anxiety improves performance, but overly ambitious and unachievable budgets increase anxiety without motivation because employees see little chance of avoiding failure. General Electric's former CEO, Jack Welch, describes challenging, yet achievable, budgets as energizing, motivating, and satisfying for managers and other employees, and capable of unleashing out-of-the-box and creative thinking.

Challenges in Administering Budgets

The budgeting process involves all levels of management. Top managers want lower-level managers to participate in the budgeting process because they have more specialized knowledge and firsthand experience with the day-to-day aspects of running the business. Participation also creates greater commitment and accountability toward the budget among lower-level managers. This is the bottom-up aspect of the budgeting process.

The budgeting process, however, is time-consuming. Estimates suggest that senior managers spend about 10–20% of their time on budgeting, and finance planning departments spend as much as 50% of their time on it.[4] For most organizations, the annual budget process is a months-long exercise that consumes a tremendous amount of resources.

The widespread use of budgets in companies ranging from major multinational corporations to small local businesses indicates that the advantages of budgeting systems outweigh the costs. To gain the benefits of budgeting, management at all levels of a company should understand and support the budget and all aspects of the management control system. This is critical for obtaining lower-level management's participation in the formulation of budgets and for successful administration of budgets. Lower-level managers who feel that top management does not "believe" in budgets are unlikely to be active participants in a budget process.

Budgets should not be administered rigidly. Attaining the budget is not an end in itself, especially when conditions change dramatically. A manager may commit to a budget, but if a situation arises in which some unplanned repairs or an unplanned advertising program would serve the long-run interests of the company, the manager should undertake the additional spending. On the flip side, the dramatic decline in consumer demand during the 2007–2009 recession led designers such as Gucci to slash their ad budgets and put on hold planned new boutiques. Macy's and other retailers, stuck with shelves of merchandise ordered before the financial crisis, had no recourse but to slash prices and cut their workforce. JCPenney eventually missed its sales projections for 2009 by $2 billion. However, its aggressive actions during the year enabled it to survive the recession and emerge with sophisticated new inventory management plans to profit from the next holiday season.

---

[2] For several examples, see J. Hope and R. Fraser, *Beyond Budgeting* (Boston: Harvard Business School Press, 2003). The authors also criticize the tendency for managers to administer budgets rigidly even when changing market conditions have rendered the budget obsolete.

[3] For a detailed discussion and several examples of the merits of setting specific hard goals, see G. Latham, "The Motivational Benefits of Goal-Setting," *Academy of Management Executive* 18, no. 4 (2004).

[4] See P. Horvath and R. Sauter, "Why Budgeting Fails: One Management System is Not Enough," *Balanced Scorecard Report* (September 2004).

Keys to Success

Managers use budgets to compel strategic analysis, promote coordination and communication across subunits of the company, provide a framework for judging performance and facilitating learning, and motivate fellow managers and other employees. To be useful, managers must support the budget and be flexible if economic conditions change.

Learning Objective 3

Prepare the operating budget

. . . the budgeted income statement

and its supporting schedules

. . . such as cost of goods sold and nonmanufacturing costs

Developing an Operating Budget

Budgets are typically developed for a set period, such as a month, quarter, or year, which can be then broken into subperiods. For example, a 12-month cash budget may be broken into 12 monthly periods so that cash inflows and outflows can be better coordinated.

Time Coverage of Budgets

The motive for creating a budget should guide a manager in choosing the period for the budget. For example, consider budgeting for a new Harley-Davidson 500-cc motorcycle. If the purpose is to budget for the total profitability of this new model, a 5-year period (or more) may be suitable and long enough to cover the product from design through to manufacture, sales, and after-sales support. In contrast, consider budgeting for a school play. If the purpose is to estimate all cash outlays, a 6-month period from the planning stage to the final performance should suffice.

The most frequently used budget period is 1 year, which is often subdivided into months and quarters. The budgeted data for a year are frequently revised as the year goes on. At the end of the second quarter, management may change the budget for the next two quarters in light of new information obtained during the first 6 months. For example, Amerigroup, a health insurance firm, had to make substantial revisions to its third-quarter and annual cost projections for 2009 because of higher-than-expected costs related to a flu epidemic caused by the H1N1 virus.

Businesses are increasingly using *rolling budgets.* A **rolling budget,** also called a **continuous budget** or **rolling forecast,** is a budget that is always available for a specified future period. It is created by continually adding a month, quarter, or year to the period that just ended. Consider Electrolux, a global appliance company, which has a 3- to 5-year strategic plan and a four-quarter rolling budget. A four-quarter rolling budget for the April 2012 to March 2013 period is superseded in the next quarter—that is in June 2012—by a four-quarter rolling budget for July 2012 to June 2013, and so on. There is always a 12-month budget (for the next year) in place. Rolling budgets constantly force Electrolux's management to think about the forthcoming 12 months, regardless of the quarter at hand. Some companies, such as Borealis, Europe's leading polyolefin plastics manufacturer; Millipore, a life sciences research and manufacturing firm headquartered in Massachusetts; and Nordea, the largest financial services group in the Nordic and Baltic Sea region, prepare rolling financial forecasts that look ahead five quarters. Other companies, such as EMC Corporation, the information infrastructure giant, employ a six-quarter rolling-forecast process so that budget allocations can be constantly adjusted to meet changing market conditions.

Steps in Preparing an Operating Budget

The best way to learn how to prepare an operating budget is by walking through the steps a company would take. Consider Stylistic Furniture, a company that makes two types of granite-top coffee tables: Casual and Deluxe. It is late 2012 and Stylistic's CEO, Rex Jordan, is very concerned about how to respond to the board of directors' mandate to increase profits by 10% in the coming year. Jordan goes through the five-step decision-making process introduced in Chapter 1.

1. **Identify the Problem and Uncertainties.** The problem is to identify a strategy and to build a budget to achieve a 10% profit growth. There are several uncertainties. Can Stylistic dramatically increase sales for its more profitable Deluxe tables? What price pressures is Stylistic likely to face? Will the cost of materials increase? Can Stylistic reduce costs through efficiency improvements?
2. **Obtain Information.** Stylistic's managers gather information about sales of tables in the current year. They are delighted to learn that sales of Deluxe tables have been stronger than expected. Moreover, one of the key competitors in Stylistic's Casual tables line has had quality

problems that are unlikely to be resolved until 2013. Unfortunately, Stylistic's managers also discover that the prices of direct materials have increased slightly during 2012.

3. **Make Predictions About the Future.** Stylistic's managers feel confident that with a little more marketing, they will be able to grow the Deluxe tables business and even increase prices slightly relative to 2012. They also do not expect significant price pressures on Casual tables during the year because of the quality problems faced by a key competitor.

   The purchasing manager anticipates that prices of direct materials will be about the same as in 2012. The manufacturing manager believes that efficiency improvements would allow costs of manufacturing tables to be maintained at 2012 costs despite an increase in the prices of other inputs. Achieving these efficiency improvements is important if Stylistic is to maintain its 12% operating margin (that is, operating income ÷ sales = 12%) and to grow sales and operating income.

4. **Make Decisions by Choosing Among Alternatives.** Jordan and his managers feel confident in their strategy of pushing sales of Deluxe tables. This decision has some risks but is the best option available for Stylistic to increase profits by 10%.

5. **Implement the Decision, Evaluate Performance, and Learn.** As we will discuss in Chapter 13, managers compare actual to predicted performance to learn why things turned out the way they did and how to do things better. Stylistic's managers would want to know whether their predictions about prices of Casual and Deluxe tables were correct. Did prices of direct materials increase more or less than anticipated? Did efficiency improvements occur? Such learning would be very helpful as Stylistic plans its budgets in subsequent years.

Stylistic's managers begin their work on the 2013 budget. Exhibit 12-2 shows the various parts of the master budget, which comprises the financial projections for the operating and financial budgets for Stylistic for 2013. The light, medium, and dark purple boxes in Exhibit 12-2 represent the budgeted income statement and its supporting budget schedules—together called the **operating budget.**

We show the revenues budget box in light purple to indicate that it is often the starting point of the operating budget. The supporting schedules—shown in medium purple—quantify the budgets for various business functions of the value chain, from research and development to distribution costs. These schedules build up to the budgeted income statement—the key summary statement in the operating budget—shown in dark purple.

The light and dark blue boxes in the exhibit are the **financial budget,** which is that part of the master budget made up of the capital expenditures budget, the cash budget, the budgeted balance sheet, and the budgeted statement of cash flows. A financial budget focuses on how operations and planned capital outlays affect cash—shown in light blue. Management accountants use the cash budget and the budgeted income statement to prepare two other summary financial statements—the budgeted balance sheet and the budgeted statement of cash flows—shown in dark blue.

Top management and managers responsible for various business functions in the value chain finalize the master budget after several rounds of discussions between them. We next present the steps in preparing an operating budget for Stylistic Furniture for 2013. Use Exhibit 12-2 as a guide for the steps that follow. The appendix to this chapter presents Stylistic's cash budget, which is another key component of the master budget.

Most companies have a budget manual that contains a company's particular instructions and information for preparing its budgets. Although the details differ among companies, the following basic steps are common for developing the operating budget for a manufacturing company. Beginning with the revenues budget, each of the other budgets follows step-by-step in logical fashion. As you go through the details for preparing a budget, think about two things: (1) the information needed to prepare each budget and (2) the actions that managers can plan to improve performance.

Step 1: Prepare the Revenues Budget. Stylistic currently sells two models of granite-top coffee tables: Casual and Deluxe. During 2012, Stylistic's managers had considered introducing a third coffee-table model but had decided against it. They must now budget for the quantities and prices of Casual and Deluxe tables in 2013.

A revenues budget is the usual starting point for the operating budget because the forecasted level of unit sales or revenues has a major impact on the production capacity and the inventory levels planned for 2013—and therefore manufacturing costs—as well as nonmanufacturing costs.

Many factors influence the sales forecast, including the sales volume in recent periods, general economic and industry conditions, market research studies, pricing policies, advertising and sales promotions, competition, and regulatory policies. Key to Stylistic achieving its goal of growing profits by 10% is growing sales of Deluxe tables from 8,000 tables in 2012 to 10,000 tables in 2013.

Exhibit 12-2

Overview of the Master Budget for Stylistic Furniture

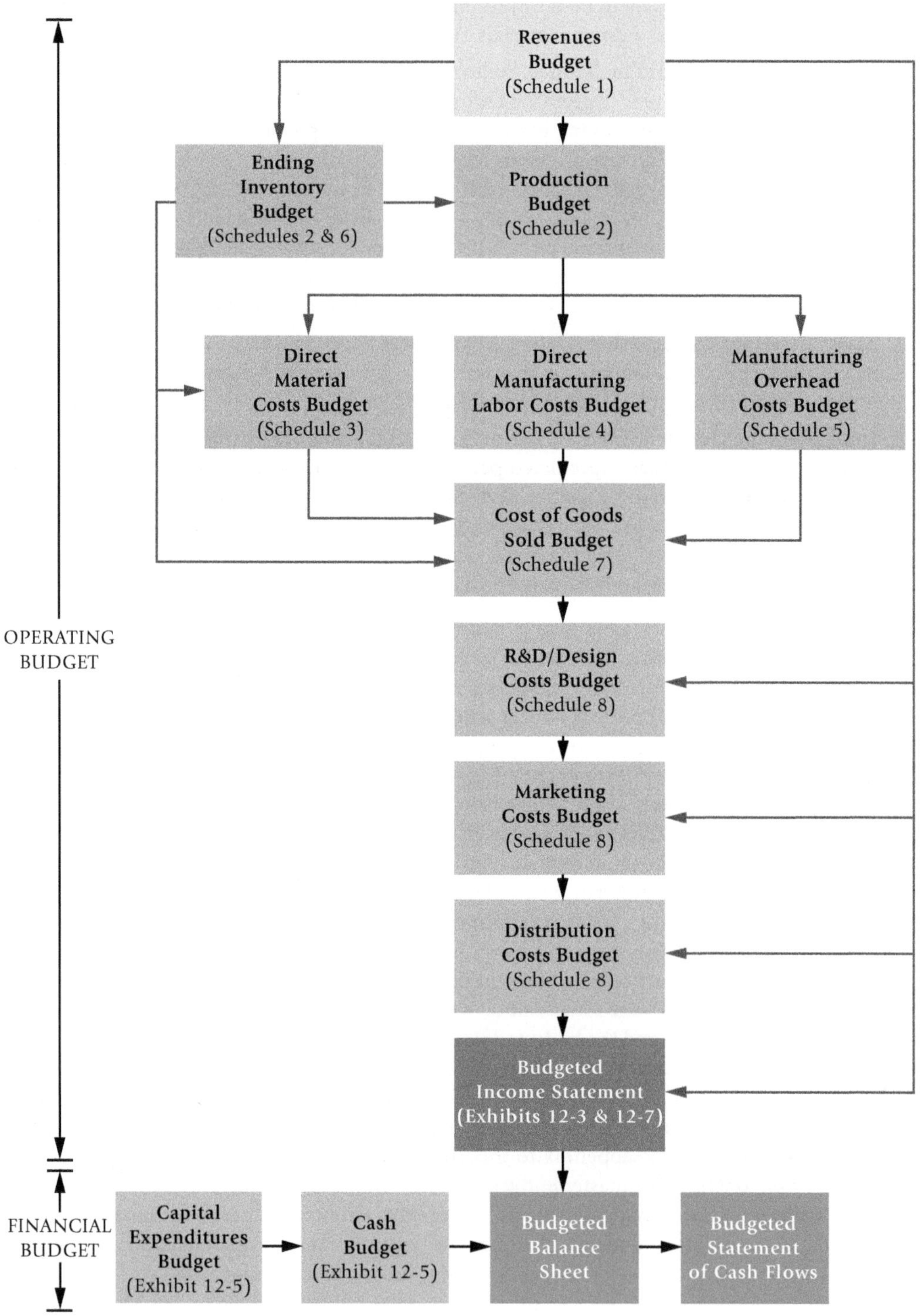

Sales managers and sales representatives build the revenues budget by gathering detailed information about customer needs, market potential, and competitors' products. They debate how best to position, price, and promote Casual and Deluxe tables relative to competitors' products. Together with top management, they consider various actions, such as adding product features, digital advertising, and changing sales incentives, to increase revenues. The cost of these actions are included in the various cost budgets.

Managers often gather this information through a customer response management (CRM) or sales management system. Statistical approaches such as regression and trend analysis also help in sales forecasting. These techniques use indicators of economic activity and past sales data to forecast future sales. Managers use statistical analysis only as one input to forecast sales. In the final analysis, the sales forecast represents the collective experience and judgment of managers.

After much discussion, top management decides on the budgeted sales quantities and prices presented in the revenues budget in Schedule 1. These are difficult or stretch targets designed to motivate the organization to achieve higher levels of performance.

Schedule 1: Revenues Budget for the Year Ending December 31, 2013			
	Units	Selling Price	Total Revenues
Casual	50,000	$600	$30,000,000
Deluxe	10,000	800	8,000,000
Total			$38,000,000

The $38,000,000 is the amount of revenues in the budgeted income statement.

Revenue budgets are usually based on expected demand because demand for a company's products is invariably the limiting factor for achieving profit goals. Occasionally, other factors, such as available production capacity (being less than demand) or a manufacturing input in short supply, limit budgeted revenues. In these cases, managers base the revenues budget on the maximum units that can be produced because sales will be limited by the amount produced.

Step 2: Prepare the Production Budget (in Units). After budgeting revenues, the logical next step is to plan the production of Casual and Deluxe tables so that the product is available when customers need it. The only new information managers need to prepare the production budget is the level of finished goods inventory Stylistic wants to maintain. As we discussed in Chapter 10, if inventory levels are high, it increases the cost of carrying inventory, the costs of quality, and shrinkage costs. Keeping inventory levels too low increases setup costs and lost sales from holding inadequate inventory. Over the course of the year, Stylistic's management decides to increase the inventory of Casual tables to avoid some of the supply shortages the company had encountered in the current year but to maintain the inventory level of Deluxe tables.

The manufacturing manager prepares the production budget, shown in Schedule 2. The total finished goods units to be produced depend on budgeted unit sales (calculated in Step 1), the target ending finished goods inventory, and the beginning finished goods inventory:

$$\text{Budget production (units)} = \text{Budget sales (units)} + \text{Target ending finished goods inventory (units)} - \text{Beginning finished goods inventory (units)}$$

Schedule 2: Production Budget (in Units) for the Year Ending December 31, 2013		
	Product	
	Casual	Deluxe
Budgeted unit sales (Schedule 1)	50,000	10,000
Add target ending finished goods inventory	11,000	500
Total required units	61,000	10,500
Deduct beginning finished goods inventory	1,000	500
Units of finished goods to be produced	60,000	10,000

The production budget then drives the various budgeted costs (for example, direct materials, direct manufacturing labor, and manufacturing overhead) that Stylistic plans to incur in 2013 to support its revenue budget, taking into account the efficiency improvements it expects to make in 2013. Recall from Step 3 in the decision-making process (page 489) that efficiency improvements are critical to offset anticipated increases in the cost of inputs and to maintain Stylistic's 12% operating margin. Some companies rely on past results and how these results might be improved when developing budgeted amounts; other companies rely on detailed engineering studies. Managers differ in how they compute their budgeted amounts, but they are always looking for opportunities to reduce costs, for example, by redesigning products, improving processes, streamlining manufacturing, and reducing the time it takes to complete various activities such as setting up machines or transporting materials. Making these changes improves a company's competitiveness but it also requires investment. The budgeting exercise is an ideal time for managers to evaluate their plans and request any financial resources that they might need. We start with the budget for direct materials.

Step 3: Prepare the Direct Material Usage Budget and Direct Material Purchases Budget. The number of units to be produced, calculated in Schedule 2, is the key to computing the usage of direct materials in quantities and in dollars. The direct material quantities used depend on the efficiency with which Stylistic's workers use materials to produce a table. In determining budgets, managers are constantly anticipating ways to make process improvements that increase quality and reduce waste, thereby reducing direct material usage and costs. Senior managers set budgets that push production managers to reduce direct material costs and keep negligible work-in-process inventory. We ignore work-in-process inventory when preparing Stylistic's budgets for 2013.

Like many companies, Stylistic has a *bill of materials* stored in its computer systems that it constantly updates for efficiency improvements. This document identifies how each product is manufactured, specifying all materials (and components), the sequence in which the materials are used, the quantity of materials in each finished unit, and the work centers where the operations are performed.

There are two types of direct materials: red oak (RO) and granite slabs (GS). Total direct material costs vary with units of output—coffee tables.

The bill of material indicates the following:

Content of Each Product Unit		
	Product	
	Casual Granite Table	Deluxe Granite Table
Red oak	12 board feet	12 board feet
Granite	6 square feet	8 square feet

Managers anticipate that the budgeted price of direct materials will remain the same throughout 2013 and not change from 2012:

Red oak	$ 7 per board foot (b.f.) (same as in 2012)
Granite	$10 per square foot (sq. ft.) (same as in 2012)

Direct materials inventory are costed using the first-in, first-out (FIFO) method. The management accountant uses this information to calculate the amounts in Schedule 3A.

Schedule 3A: Direct Material Usage Budget in Quantity and Dollars for the Year Ending December 31, 2013			
	Material		
	Red Oak	Granite	Total
Physical Units Budget			
Direct materials required for Casual tables (60,000 units × 12 b.f. and 6 sq. ft.)	720,000 b.f.	360,000 sq. ft.	
Direct materials required for Deluxe tables (10,000 units × 12 b.f. and 8 sq. ft.)	120,000 b.f.	80,000 sq. ft.	
Total quantity of direct materials to be used	840,000 b.f.	440,000 sq. ft.	
Cost Budget			
Available from beginning direct materials inventory (under a FIFO cost-flow assumption) (Given)			
Red oak: 70,000 b.f. × $7 per b.f.	$ 490,000		
Granite: 60,000 sq. ft. × $10 per sq. ft.		$ 600,000	
To be purchased this period			
Red oak: (840,000 − 70,000) b.f. × $7 per b.f.	5,390,000		
Granite: (440,000 − 60,000) sq. ft. × $10 per sq. ft.		3,800,000	
Direct materials to be used this period	$5,880,000	$4,400,000	$10,280,000

The only new information needed to prepare the purchasing budget is the level of direct materials inventory Stylistic wants to maintain. As we discussed in Chapter 10, if inventory levels are high, too much cash is tied up in inventory, increasing the cost of carrying inventory, the costs of quality, and shrinkage costs. Keeping inventory levels too low increases ordering costs and could result in lost production because there is inadequate inventory. Over the course of the year, Stylistic's management decides to increase the inventory of red oak but reduce the inventory of granite. The planned levels of beginning and ending inventory are:

	Direct Materials	
	Red Oak	Granite
Beginning inventory	70,000 b.f.	60,000 sq. ft.
Target ending inventory	80,000 b.f.	20,000 sq. ft.

The purchasing manager prepares the budget for direct material purchases, calculated in Schedule 3B:

$$\text{Purchases of direct materials} = \text{Direct materials used in production} + \text{Target ending inventory of direct materials} - \text{Beginning inventory of direct materials}$$

Schedule 3B: Direct Material Purchases Budget for the Year Ending December 31, 2013			
	Material		
	Red Oak	Granite	Total
Physical Units Budget			
To be used in production (from Schedule 3A)	840,000 b.f.	440,000 sq. ft.	
Add target ending inventory	80,000 b.f.	20,000 sq. ft.	
Total requirements	920,000 b.f.	460,000 sq. ft.	
Deduct beginning inventory	70,000 b.f.	60,000 sq. ft.	
Purchases to be made	850,000 b.f.	400,000 sq. ft.	
Cost Budget			
Red oak: 850,000 b.f. × $7 per b.f.	$5,950,000		
Granite: 400,000 sq. ft. × $10 per sq. ft.		$4,000,000	
Purchases	$5,950,000	$4,000,000	$9,950,000

Step 4: Prepare the Direct Manufacturing Labor Costs Budget. Having calculated the cost of direct materials, Stylistic's managers next budget for direct manufacturing labor costs. Manufacturing managers use *labor standards,* the time allowed per unit of output, to calculate the direct manufacturing labor costs budget in Schedule 4. To estimate these costs, Stylistic's managers estimate wage rates, production methods, process and efficiency improvements, and hiring plans. The company hires direct manufacturing labor workers on an hourly basis. These workers do not work overtime. The direct manufacturing labor rate is $20 per hour. Managers budget the following direct manufacturing labor-hours to make a Casual table and a Deluxe table:

	Casual Table	Deluxe Table
Direct manufacturing labor	4 hours	6 hours

Schedule 4 presents the direct manufacturing labor costs budget:

Schedule 4: Direct Manufacturing Labor Costs Budget for the Year Ending December 31, 2013					
	Output Units Produced (Schedule 2)	Direct Manufacturing Labor-Hours per Unit	Total Hours	Hourly Wage Rate	Total
Casual	60,000	4	240,000	$20	$4,800,000
Deluxe	10,000	6	60,000	20	1,200,000
Total			300,000		$6,000,000

Step 5: Prepare the Manufacturing Overhead Costs Budget. Stylistic's managers next budget for manufacturing overhead costs such as supervision, depreciation, maintenance, supplies, and power. Managing overhead costs is important but also challenging because it requires managers to understand the various activities needed to manufacture products and the cost drivers of those activities. Stylistic's managers identify two activities for manufacturing overhead costs in its activity-based costing system: manufacturing operations and machine setups. The following table presents the activities and their cost drivers.

Manufacturing Overhead Costs	Cost Driver of Variable Component of Overhead Costs	Cost Driver of Fixed Component of Overhead Costs	Manufacturing and Setup Capacity in 2013
Manufacturing Operations Overhead Costs	Direct manufacturing labor hours	Manufacturing capacity	300,000 direct manufacturing labor-hours
Machine Setup Overhead Costs	Setup labor hours	Setup capacity	15,000 setup labor-hours

The use of activity-based cost drivers gives rise to **activity-based budgeting (ABB),** a budgeting method that focuses on the budgeted cost of the activities necessary to produce and sell products and services.

In its activity-based costing system, Stylistic's manufacturing managers estimate various line items of overhead costs that constitute manufacturing operations overhead (that is, all costs for which direct manufacturing labor-hours is the cost driver). Managers identify opportunities for process and efficiency improvements, such as reducing defect rates and time to manufacture a table, and determine budgeted manufacturing operations overhead costs in the operating department. They also determine the resources that they will need from the two support departments—kilowatt hours of energy from the power department and hours of maintenance service from the maintenance department. The support department managers, in turn, plan the costs of personnel and supplies that they will need in order to provide the operating department with the support services it requires. The costs of the support departments are then allocated (first-stage cost allocation) as part of manufacturing operations overhead. The appendix to Chapter 4 describes the allocation of support department costs to operating departments when support departments provide services to each other and to operating departments. The first half of Schedule 5 (p. 495) shows the various line items of costs that constitute manufacturing operations overhead costs—that is, all variable and fixed overhead costs that are caused by the 300,000 direct manufacturing labor-hours (the cost driver).

Stylistic budgets costs differently for variable and fixed overhead costs. Consider variable overhead costs of supplies, Stylistic's managers use past historical data and their knowledge of operations to estimate the cost of supplies per direct manufacturing labor-hour = \$5. The total budgeted cost of supplies for 2013 is \$5 × 300,000 budgeted direct manufacturing labor-hours = \$1,500,000. The total variable manufacturing operations overhead cost equals \$21.60 per direct manufacturing labor-hour × 300,000 budgeted direct manufacturing labor-hours = \$6,480,000.

For fixed overhead costs, Stylistic's managers start the budgeting process by determining the total fixed manufacturing operations overhead costs of \$2,520,000 needed to support the 300,000 direct manufacturing labor-hours of capacity that Stylistic's managers have chosen to build. (Stylistic may not operate at full capacity each year but fixed manufacturing operations costs will still be \$2,520,000.) Fixed manufacturing overhead cost is \$2,520,000 ÷ 300,000 = \$8.40 per direct manufacturing labor-hour (regardless of the budgeted direct manufacturing labor-hours, which may be less than 300,000 in a particular year). That is, each direct manufacturing labor-hour will absorb \$21.60 of variable manufacturing operations overhead plus \$8.40 of fixed manufacturing operations overhead for a total of \$30 of manufacturing operations overhead per direct manufacturing labor-hour.

Stylistic's managers determine how setups should be done for the Casual and Deluxe line of tables, taking into account past experiences and potential improvements in setup efficiency.

For example, managers consider the following:

- Increasing the number of tables produced per batch so that fewer batches (and therefore fewer setups) are needed for the budgeted production of tables
- Decreasing the setup time per batch
- Reducing the supervisory time needed, for instance by increasing the skill base of workers

Stylistic's managers forecast the following setup information for the Casual and Deluxe tables:

	Casual Tables	Deluxe Tables	Total
1. Quantity of tables to be produced	60,000 tables	10,000 tables	
2. Number of tables to be produced per batch	50 tables/batch	40 tables/batch	
3. Number of batches (1) ÷ (2)	1,200 batches	250 batches	
4. Setup time per batch	10 hours/batch	12 hours/batch	
5. Total setup-hours (3) × (4)	12,000 hours	3,000 hours	15,000 hours
6. Setup-hours per table (5) ÷ (1)	0.2 hour	0.3 hour	

Using an approach similar to the one described for manufacturing operations overhead costs, Stylistic's managers estimate various line items of costs that comprise machine setup overhead costs—that is, all costs that are caused by the 15,000 setup labor-hours (the cost driver): (1) variable machine setup overhead costs per setup labor-hour = \$88 × the budgeted 15,000 setup labor-hours = \$1,320,000 and (2) fixed machine setup overhead costs of \$1,650,000 needed to support the 15,000 setup labor-hours of capacity that Stylistic's managers have chosen to build. (Stylistic may not operate at full capacity each year but fixed machine setup costs will still be \$1,680,000.) Fixed machine setup cost is \$1,680,000 ÷ 15,000 = \$112 per setup labor-hour (regardless of the budgeted setup labor-hours, which may be less than 15,000 in a particular year). That is, each setup labor-hour will absorb \$88 of variable machine setup overhead cost plus \$112 of fixed machine setup overhead cost for a total of \$200 of machine setup overhead cost per setup labor-hour.

Note how using activity-based cost drivers provide additional and detailed information that improves decision making compared with budgeting based solely on output-based cost drivers. Of course, managers must always evaluate whether the expected benefit of adding more cost drivers exceeds the expected cost.[5] The second half of Schedule 5 summarizes the variable and fixed machine setup overhead costs budget for 15,000 setup labor-hours.

Schedule 5: Manufacturing Overhead Costs Budget for the Year Ending December 31, 2013		
Manufacturing Operations Overhead Costs		
Variable costs (for 300,000 direct manufacturing labor-hours)		
Supplies (\$5 per direct manufacturing labor-hour)	\$1,500,000	
Indirect manufacturing labor (\$5.60 per direct manufacturing labor-hour)	1,680,000	
Power (support department costs) (\$7 per direct manufacturing labor-hour)	2,100,000	
Maintenance (support department costs) (\$4 per direct manufacturing labor-hour)	1,200,000	\$6,480,000
Fixed costs (to support capacity of 300,000 direct manufacturing labor-hours)		
Depreciation	1,020,000	
Supervision	390,000	
Power (support department costs)	630,000	
Maintenance (support department costs)	480,000	2,520,000
Total manufacturing operations overhead costs		\$9,000,000

[5] The Stylistic example illustrates ABB using manufacturing operations and setup costs included in Stylistic's manufacturing overhead costs budget. ABB implementations in practice include costs in many parts of the value chain. For an example, see S. Borjesson, "A Case Study on Activity-Based Budgeting," *Journal of Cost Management* 10, no. 4 (Winter 1997): 7–18.

Schedule 5: Manufacturing Overhead Costs Budget for the Year Ending December 31, 2013 (contd.)		
Machine Setup Overhead Costs		
Variable costs (for 15,000 setup labor-hours)		
Supplies ($26 per setup labor-hour)	$390,000	
Indirect manufacturing labor ($56 per setup labor-hour)	840,000	
Power (support department costs) ($6 per setup labor-hour)	90,000	$ 1,320,000
Fixed costs (to support capacity of 15,000 setup labor-hours)		
Depreciation	603,000	
Supervision	1,050,000	
Power (support department costs)	27,000	1,680,000
Total machine setup overhead costs		$ 3,000,000
Total manufacturing operations overhead costs		$12,000,000

Note that Stylistic is scheduled to operate at capacity. Therefore, the budgeted quantity of the cost allocation base/cost driver is the same for variable overhead costs and fixed overhead costs—300,000 direct manufacturing labor-hours for manufacturing operations overhead costs and 15,000 setup labor-hours for machine setup overhead costs. In this case, the budgeted rate for manufacturing operations overhead cost does not have to be calculated separately for variable costs and for fixed costs. It can be calculated directly by estimating total budgeted manufacturing operations overhead, $9,000,000 ÷ 300,000 direct manufacturing labor-hours = $30 per direct manufacturing labor-hour. Similarly the budgeted rate for machine setup overhead cost can be calculated as total budgeted machine setup overhead, $3,000,000 ÷ 15,000 budgeted setup hours = $200 per setup-hour.

Step 6: Prepare the Ending Inventories Budget. Steps 2–5 determine the total manufacturing costs Stylistic plans to incur in 2013. As we saw in Chapter 2, manufacturing costs are inventoriable costs: they are assigned to work-in-process inventory and then assigned to finished goods inventory until the goods are sold. These costs are only expensed as cost of goods sold when the finished goods are sold. To determine the budgeted cost of goods sold expense for 2013, Stylistic's management accountants calculate how much of the total manufacturing costs will be inventoried in finished goods at the end of 2013. Recall that work-in-process inventory is negligible and so ignored. In accordance with Generally Accepted Accounting Principles, Stylistic treats both variable and fixed manufacturing overhead as inventoriable (product) costs. Manufacturing operations overhead costs are allocated to finished goods inventory at the budgeted rate of $30 per direct manufacturing labor-hour. Machine setup overhead costs are allocated to finished goods inventory at the budgeted rate of $200 per setup-hour.

Schedule 6A shows the computation of the unit cost of coffee tables started and completed in 2013.

Schedule 6A: Unit Costs of Ending Finished Goods Inventory December 31, 2013					
		Product			
		Casual Tables		Deluxe Tables	
	Cost per Unit of Input	Input per Unit of Output	Total	Input per Unit of Output	Total
Red oak	$ 7	12 b.f.	$ 84	12 b.f.	$ 84
Granite	10	6 sq. ft.	60	8 sq. ft.	80
Direct manufacturing labor	20	4 hrs.	80	6 hrs.	120
Manufacturing operations overhead	30	4 hrs.	120	6 hrs.	180
Machine setup overhead	200	0.2 hrs.	40	0.3 hrs.	60
Total			$384		$524

Under the FIFO method, managers use this unit cost to calculate the cost of target ending inventories of finished goods in Schedule 6B.

Schedule 6B: Ending Inventories Budget December 31, 2013				
	Quantity	Cost per Unit		Total
Direct materials				
Red oak	80,000*	$ 7	$ 560,000	
Granite	20,000*	10	200,000	$ 760,000
Finished goods				
Casual	11,000**	$384***	$4,224,000	
Deluxe	500**	524***	262,000	4,486,000
Total ending inventory				$5,246,000

*Data are from page 493. **Data are from page 491. ***From Schedule 6A, this is based on 2013 costs of manufacturing finished goods because under the FIFO costing method, the units in finished goods ending inventory consists of units that are produced during 2013.

Step 7: Prepare the Cost of Goods Sold Budget. The manufacturing and purchase managers, together with the management accountant, use information from Schedules 3–6 to prepare Schedule 7—the cost of goods sold expense that will be matched against revenues to calculate Stylistic's budgeted gross margin for 2013.

Schedule 7: Cost of Goods Sold Budget for the Year Ending December 31, 2013			
	From Schedule		Total
Beginning finished goods inventory, January 1, 2013	Given*		$ 646,000
Direct materials used	3A	$10,280,000	
Direct manufacturing labor	4	6,000,000	
Manufacturing overhead	5	12,000,000	
Cost of goods manufactured			28,280,000
Cost of goods available for sale			28,926,000
Deduct ending finished goods inventory, December 31, 2013	6B		4,486,000
Cost of goods sold			$24,440,000

*Based on ending inventory values in 2012 for Casual tables, $384,000, and Deluxe tables, $262,000.

Step 8: Prepare the Nonmanufacturing Costs Budget. Schedules 2–7 represent budgets for Stylistic's manufacturing costs. Stylistic also incurs nonmanufacturing costs in other parts of the value chain—product design, marketing, and distribution. Just as in the case of manufacturing costs, the key to managing nonmanufacturing overhead costs is to understand the various activities needed to support the design, marketing, and distribution of Deluxe and Casual tables in 2013 and the cost drivers of those activities. Managers in these functions of the value chain build in process and efficiency improvements and prepare nonmanufacturing cost budgets on the basis of the quantities of cost drivers planned for 2013.

The number of design changes is the cost driver for product design costs. Product design costs of $1,024,000 are fixed costs for 2013, determined at the start of the year based on the number of design changes planned for 2013.

Total revenue is the cost driver for the variable portion of marketing (and sales) costs. The commission paid to sales people equals 6.5 cents per dollar (or 6.5%) of revenues. Managers budget the fixed component of marketing costs, $1,330,000, at the start of the year based on budgeted revenues for 2013.

Cubic feet of tables moved (Casual: 18 cubic feet × 50,000 tables + Deluxe: 24 cubic feet × 10,000 tables = 1,140,000 cubic feet) is the cost driver of the variable component of budgeted distribution costs. Variable distribution costs equal $2 per cubic foot. The fixed component of budgeted distribution costs equal to $1,596,000 varies with distribution capacity, which in 2013 is 1,140,000 cubic feet (to support the distribution of 50,000 Casual tables and 10,000 Deluxe tables). For brevity, Schedule 8 shows the product design, marketing, and distribution costs budget for 2013 in a single schedule.

Schedule 8: Nonmanufacturing Costs Budget for the Year Ending December 31, 2013

Business Function	Variable Costs	Fixed Costs	Total Costs
Product design	—	$1,024,000	$1,024,000
Marketing (Variable cost: $38,000,000 × 0.065)	$2,470,000	1,330,000	3,800,000
Distribution (Variable cost: $2 × 1,140,000 cu. ft.)	2,280,000	1,596,000	3,876,000
	$4,750,000	$3,950,000	$8,700,000

Step 9: Prepare the Budgeted Income Statement. The CEO and managers of various business functions, with help from the management accountant, use information in Schedules 1, 7, and 8 to finalize the budgeted income statement, shown in Exhibit 12-3. The style used in Exhibit 12-3 is typical, but managers and accountants could include more details in the income statement. As more details are put in the income statement, fewer supporting schedules are needed.

Budgeting is a cross-functional activity. Top management's strategies for achieving revenue and operating income goals influence the costs planned for the different business functions of the value chain. For example, the budgeted increase in sales at Stylistic based on spending more for marketing was matched with higher production costs to ensure that there is an adequate supply of tables and with higher distribution costs to ensure timely delivery of tables to customers. Concepts in Action: "Scrimping" at the Ritz: Master Budgets describes how Ritz-Carlton uses budgets to coordinate activities across different business functions and to improve performance.

Rex Jordan, the CEO of Stylistic Furniture, is very pleased with the 2013 budget. It calls for a 10% increase in operating income compared with 2012. The keys to achieving a higher operating income are a significant increase in sales of Deluxe tables and process improvements and efficiency gains throughout the value chain. As Rex studies the budget more carefully, however, he is struck

Exhibit 12-3

Budgeted Income Statement for Stylistic Furniture

	A	B	C	D
1	**Budgeted Income Statement for Stylistic Furniture**			
2	**For the Year Ending December 31, 2013**			
3	Revenues	Schedule 1		$38,000,000
4	Cost of goods sold	Schedule 7		24,440,000
5	Gross margin			13,560,000
6	Operating costs			
7	Product design costs	Schedule 8	$1,024,000	
8	Marketing costs	Schedule 8	3,800,000	
9	Distribution costs	Schedule 8	3,876,000	8,700,000
10	Operating income			$ 4,860,000

by two comments appended to the budget: First, to achieve the budgeted number of tables sold, Stylistic may need to reduce its selling prices by 3% to $582 for Casual tables and to $776 for Deluxe tables. Second, a supply shortage in direct materials may result in a 5% increase in the prices of direct materials (red oak and granite) above the material prices anticipated in the 2013 budget. Even if direct materials prices increase, selling prices are anticipated to remain the same. He asks Tina Larsen, a management accountant, to use Stylistic's financial planning model to evaluate how these outcomes will affect budgeted operating income.

Concepts in Action: "Scrimping" at the Ritz: Master Budgets

The motto of the luxury hotel chain the Ritz-Carlton is, "Ladies and gentlemen serving ladies and gentlemen." With locations ranging from South Beach (Miami) to South Korea, the Ritz is known for its indulgent luxury and sumptuous surroundings. However, the aura of the chain's elegance stands in contrast to its behind-the-scenes emphasis on cost control and budgets. It is this very emphasis, however, that makes it possible for the Ritz to offer the legendary grandeur its guests expect.

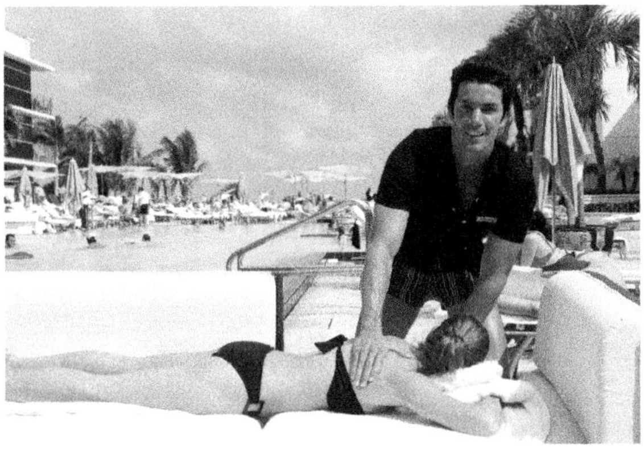

Source: Mark O'Flaherty/Alamy

Each Ritz hotel's performance is the responsibility of its general manager and controller or chief accounting officer. They prepare annual forecasts and budgets for the hotel, which serve as the basis of performance evaluations. The budget starts with the hotel's sales director, who is responsible for all revenues including hotel rooms, conventions, weddings, meeting facilities, merchandise, and food and beverage. The controller then seeks input about (1) standard costs, based on cost per occupied room, to build the budget for guest room stays; and (2) other standard costs, to build the budget for meeting rooms and food and beverages. After a series of meetings, corporate managers approve the final budget.

The managers of each hotel meet daily to review the hotel's performance to date relative to the plan and take corrective action such as adjusting room rates. Each month, the controller of each hotel receives a report from headquarters showing how the hotel performed against budget, as well as against the performance of other Ritz hotels. Ideas for boosting revenues and reducing costs are regularly shared among hotel managers. This thorough process allows the company to earn a profit and maintain its legendary service for guests around the world.

Keys to Success

Managers use operating income budgets to plan operations for the forthcoming year. After evaluating market opportunities, managers finalize a revenue budget and then identify cost drivers to determine the manufacturing and nonmanufacturing costs needed to deliver the revenues.

Learning Objective 4

Use computer-based financial planning models for sensitivity analysis

. . . for example, understand the effects of changes in selling prices and direct material prices on budgeted income

Financial Planning Models and Sensitivity Analysis

Financial planning models are mathematical representations of the relationships among operating activities, financing activities, and other factors that affect the master budget. Managers can use computer-based systems, such as enterprise resource planning (ERP) systems, to perform calculations for these planning models. Managers use budgeting tools within ERP systems to simplify budgeting, reduce the need to reinput data, and reduce the time required to prepare budgets. ERP systems store vast quantities of information about the materials, machines and equipment, labor, power, maintenance, and setups needed to manufacture different products. Once managers identify sales quantities for different products, the software can quickly compute the budgeted costs for manufacturing these products. ERP systems also help managers budget for nonmanufacturing costs.

As they prepare operating budgets, managers do not focus only on what they can achieve. They also identify the risks they face such as a potential decline in demand for the company's products, the entry of a new competitor, or an increase in the prices of different inputs. Sensitivity analysis is a useful tool that helps managers evaluate these risks. *Sensitivity analysis* is a "what-if" technique that examines how a result will change if the original predicted data are not achieved or if an underlying assumption changes. Software packages typically have a module on sensitivity analysis to assist managers in their planning and budgeting activities.

To see how sensitivity analysis works, we consider two scenarios identified as possibly affecting Stylistic Furniture's budget model for 2013.

Scenario 1: A 3% decrease in the selling price of the Casual table and a 3% decrease in the selling price of the Deluxe table.

Scenario 2: A 5% increase in the price per board foot of red oak and a 5% increase in the price per square foot of granite.

Exhibit 12-4 presents the budgeted operating income for the two scenarios.

Note that under Scenario 1, a change in the selling price per table affects revenues (Schedule 1) as well as variable marketing costs (sales commissions, Schedule 8). The Problem for Self-Study at the end of the chapter shows the revised schedules for Scenario 1. Similarly, a change in the price of direct materials affects the direct material usage budget (Schedule 3A), the unit cost of ending finished goods inventory (Schedule 6A), the ending finished goods inventories budget (in Schedule 6B), and the cost of goods sold budget (Schedule 7). Sensitivity analysis is especially useful in incorporating such interrelationships into budgeting decisions by managers.

Exhibit 12-4 shows a substantial decrease in operating income as a result of decreases in selling prices but a smaller decline in operating income if direct material prices increase by 5%. The sensitivity analysis prompts Stylistic's managers to put in place contingency plans. For example, should selling prices decline in 2013, Stylistic may choose to postpone some product development programs that it had included in its 2013 budget but that could be deferred to a later year. More generally, when the success or viability of a venture is highly dependent on attaining one or more targets, managers should frequently update their budgets as uncertainty is resolved. These updated budgets can help managers to adjust expenditure levels as circumstances change.

Earlier in this chapter we had described a rolling budget as a budget that is always available for a specified future period. The rolling budget is constantly updated to reflect the latest information and makes managers responsive to changing conditions and market needs. Concepts in Action: Rolling Budgets and LivingSocial's High-Growth Adventure describes how LivingSocial, a fast-growing online company offering daily deals much like Groupon, uses rolling budgets as a form of sensitivity analysis to flexibly allocate resources to capitalize on opportunities as they arise.

Exhibit 12-4

Effect of Changes in Budget Assumptions on Budgeted Operating Income for Stylistic Furniture

	A	B	C	D	E	F	G	H	I
1	Key Assumptions								
2		Units Sold		Selling Price		Direct Material Cost		Budgeted Operating Income	
3	What-If Scenario	Casual	Deluxe	Casual	Deluxe	Red Oak	Granite	Dollars	Change from Master Budget
4	Master budget	50,000	10,000	$600	$800	$7.00	$10.00	$4,860,000	
5	Scenario 1	50,000	10,000	582	776	$7.00	$10.00	3,794,100	22% decrease
6	Scenario 2	50,000	10,000	600	800	$7.35	$10.50	4,483,800	8% decrease

Concept in Action: Rolling Budgets and LivingSocial's High-Growth Adventure

Source: Web Pix/Alamy

LivingSocial is an online company that provides subscribers daily discount vouchers to local businesses. In the fast-growing daily deals business, LivingSocial has been on a high-growth adventure since its launch in 2007. The company has grown from 33 employees in its Washington, D.C., headquarters to 3,500 staffers in more than 20 countries. Facing competition from Groupon and others, LivingSocial has raised venture funding to add new sales employees, who persuade local merchants to offer online discounts on such products as meals, yoga classes, and weekend trips. With such a rapidly growing business, the company has adopted an innovative budgeting model where managers augment the traditional budgeting cycle and master budget with rolling budgets.

Rather than preset annual revenue and expense targets, LivingSocial reviews its enterprise and department projections monthly to allow for new income opportunities and cost reductions as needed. This framework allows managers to balance new business needs with the financial discipline required to achieve long-term profitability. Variable budgets are then tied to these rolling forecasts. For example, instead of allocating $500,000 to a sales manager for salaries each year, the company agrees to fund a set number of staff members per new market entered or per number of deals sold. Managers at LivingSocial use variable budgets to balance growth and spending targets in a high-growth environment. Using variable budgets enables the company to capitalize on opportunities as they arise. But rolling and variable budgets lack the long-term planning often needed to achieve coordination across different units of a company. For this reason, LivingSocial uses rolling and variable budgets to augment its master budget.

In recent years, economic events including the 2007–2009 global recession, spikes in oil prices, and currency exchange rates have capsized carefully prepared budgets. In response, companies ranging from Unilever, the consumer goods company, to Statoil, the Norwegian oil-and-gas producer, have adopted new tools that allow for flexibility in the budgeting and performance management process.

Sources: Banham, Russ, "Let It Roll," *CFO Magazine* (May 2011); O'Sullivan, Kate, "LivingSocial's High-Growth Adventure," *CFO Magazine* (October 2011); Adam Satariano, and Douglas MacMillan, "LivingSocial CEO Takes Unusual Low-Tech Path," *Bloomberg Businessweek* (May 17, 2011).

Keys to Success
Managers use financial planning models to conduct what-if (sensitivity) analysis to evaluate and respond to risks of failing to achieve the master budget as a result of changes in the original predicted data or underlying assumptions.

Learning Objective 5

Describe responsibility centers

. . . a part of an organization that a manager is accountable for

and responsibility accounting

. . . measurement of plans and actual results that a manager is accountable for

Instructors and students who, at this point, want to explore the cash budget for the Stylistic Furniture example can skip ahead to the Appendix on page 509.

Budgeting and Responsibility Accounting

To attain the goals described in the master budget, top management must coordinate the efforts of all its employees—from senior executives through middle levels of management to every supervised worker. To coordinate the company's efforts, top management assigns responsibility to managers and holds them accountable for their actions. How each company structures its own organization significantly shapes how the company coordinates its actions.

Organization Structure and Responsibility

Organization structure is an arrangement of lines of responsibility within an organization. A company such as ExxonMobil is organized by business function—exploration, refining, marketing, and so on—with the president of each business-line company having decision-making authority over his or her function. Other companies, such as Procter & Gamble, the household-products giant, are organized primarily by product line or brand. The managers of the individual divisions (toothpaste, soap, etc.) have decision-making authority concerning all the business functions (manufacturing, marketing, etc.) within that division.

Each manager, regardless of level, is in charge of a responsibility center. A **responsibility center** is a part, segment, or subunit of an organization whose manager is accountable for a specified set of activities. Higher-level managers have broader responsibility centers and a larger number of subordinates. **Responsibility accounting** is a system that measures the plans, budgets, actions, and actual results of each responsibility center. There are four types of responsibility centers:

1. **Cost center**—the manager is accountable for costs only.
2. **Revenue center**—the manager is accountable for revenues only.
3. **Profit center**—the manager is accountable for revenues and costs.
4. **Investment center**—the manager is accountable for investments, revenues, and costs.

The maintenance department of a Ritz-Carlton hotel is a cost center because the maintenance manager is responsible only for costs and the budget is based only on costs. The sales department is a revenue center because the sales manager is responsible primarily for revenues, and the budget is based only on revenues. The hotel manager is in charge of a profit center because the manager is accountable for both revenues and costs, and the budget is based on both revenues and costs. The regional manager responsible for determining the amount to be invested in new hotel projects and for revenues and costs generated from these investments is in charge of an investment center, and the budget is based on revenues, costs, and the investment base.

A responsibility center can be structured to promote better alignment of individual and company goals. For example, until recently, OPD, an office products distributor, operated its sales department as a revenue center. Each salesperson received a commission of 3% of the revenues per order, regardless of its size, the cost of processing it, or the cost of delivering the office products. Upon analyzing customer profitability, OPD found that many customers were unprofitable. The main reason was the high ordering and delivery costs of small orders. OPD's managers decided to make the sales department a profit center, accountable for revenues and costs, and to change the incentive system for salespeople to 15% of the monthly profits of their customers. The costs for each customer included the ordering and delivery costs. The effect of this change was immediate. The sales department began charging customers for ordering and delivery, and salespeople at OPD actively encouraged customers to consolidate their purchases into fewer orders. As a result, each order began producing larger revenues. Customer profitability increased because of a 40% reduction in ordering and delivery costs in 1 year.

Feedback

Budgets coupled with responsibility accounting provide feedback to top management about the performance relative to the budget of different responsibility center managers.

Differences between actual results and budgeted amounts—called *variances*—if properly used, can help managers implement and evaluate strategies in three ways:

1. **Early warning.** Variances alert managers early to events not easily or immediately evident. Managers can then take corrective actions or exploit the available opportunities. For example, after observing a small decline in sales this period, managers may want to investigate if this is an indication of an even steeper decline to follow later in the year.
2. **Performance evaluation.** Variances prompt managers to probe how well the company has performed in implementing its strategies. Were materials and labor used efficiently? Was R&D spending increased as planned? Did product warranty costs decrease as planned?
3. **Evaluating strategy.** Variances sometimes signal to managers that their strategies are ineffective. For example, a company seeking to compete by reducing costs and improving quality may find that it is achieving these goals but that it is having little effect on sales and profits. Top management may then want to reevaluate the strategy.

Responsibility and Controllability

Controllability is the degree of influence that a specific manager has over costs, revenues, or related items for which he or she is responsible. A **controllable cost** is any cost that is primarily subject to the influence of a given *responsibility center manager* for a given *period.* A responsibility accounting system could either exclude all uncontrollable costs from a manager's performance report or segregate such costs from the controllable costs. For example, a machining supervisor's performance report might be confined to direct materials, direct manufacturing labor, power, and machine maintenance costs and might exclude costs such as rent and taxes paid on the plant.

In practice, controllability is difficult to pinpoint for two main reasons:

1. Few costs are clearly under the sole influence of one manager. For example, prices of direct materials may be influenced by a purchasing manager, but these prices also depend on market conditions beyond the manager's control. Quantities used may be influenced by a production manager, but quantities used also depend on the quality of materials purchased. Moreover, managers often work in teams. Think about how difficult it is to evaluate individual responsibility in a team situation.
2. With a long enough time span, all costs will come under somebody's control. However, most performance reports focus on periods of a year or less. A current manager may benefit from a predecessor's accomplishments or may inherit a predecessor's problems and inefficiencies. For example, present managers may have to work with undesirable contracts with suppliers or labor unions that were negotiated by their predecessors. How can we separate what the current manager actually controls from the results of decisions other managers made? Exactly what is the current manager accountable for? Answers may not be clear-cut.

Executives differ in how they embrace the controllability notion when evaluating those reporting to them. Some CEOs regard the budget as a firm commitment that subordinates must meet and that "numbers always tell the story." Failure to meet the budget is viewed unfavorably. An executive once noted, "You can miss your plan once, but you wouldn't want to miss it twice." The behavioral effect of such an approach is that it forces managers to learn to perform under adverse circumstances and to deliver consistent results year after year. It removes the need to discuss which costs are controllable and which are noncontrollable because it does not matter whether poor performance was because of controllable or noncontrollable factors. The disadvantage of this approach is that it subjects the manager's compensation to greater risk. It also demotivates managers when uncontrollable factors result in a manager's performance being evaluated as poor when the manager has performed well on all factors that he or she could control.

Other CEOs believe that a focus on making the numbers in a budget puts excessive pressure on managers. These CEOs adjust for noncontrollable factors and evaluate managers only on factors that the managers can control, such as performance relative to competitors. Using relative performance measures takes out the effects of favorable or unfavorable business conditions that are outside the manager's control and affect all competing managers in the same way. The challenge is in finding the correct benchmarks. This measure, however, reduces the pressure on managers to perform when circumstances are difficult.

Managers should avoid thinking about controllability only in the context of performance evaluation. Responsibility accounting is more far-reaching. It focuses on gaining *information and knowledge,* not only on control. *Responsibility accounting helps managers to first focus on whom they should ask to obtain information and not on whom they should blame.* Comparing the shortfall of actual revenues to budgeted revenues is certainly relevant when evaluating the performance of the sales manager of a Ritz-Carlton hotel. But the more fundamental purpose of responsibility accounting is to gather information from the sales manager to enable future improvement. Holding the sales manager accountable for sales motivates the sales manager to learn about market conditions and dynamics that are outside his personal control but relevant when deciding the actions the hotel might take to increase future sales. Similarly, purchasing managers may be held accountable for total purchase costs, not because of their ability to control market prices, but because of their ability to predict and respond to uncontrollable prices and to explain uncontrollable price changes.

Performance reports for responsibility centers are sometimes designed to change managers' behavior in the direction top management desires even if it decreases controllability. Consider a manufacturing department. If the department is designated as a cost center, the manufacturing manager may emphasize efficiency and deemphasize the pleas of sales personnel for faster service and rush orders that reduce efficiency and increase costs. If evaluated as a profit center, the manufacturing manager will more likely consider activities such as rush orders that affect sales. She will weigh the impact of decisions on costs and revenues rather than on costs alone. Call centers provide another example. If designated as a cost center, the call-center manager will focus on controlling operating costs, for example, by decreasing the time customer representatives spend on each call. If designed as a profit center, the call-center manager will encourage customer-service representatives to balance efficiency with better customer service and efforts to upsell and cross-sell other products. Hewlett-Packard, Microsoft, Oracle, and others offer software platforms that seek to evolve the call center from cost center to profit center. The new adage is, "Every service call is a sales call."

Keys to Success

Top management uses responsibility accounting to measure the plans, budgets, actions, and actual results of each responsibility center manager. Performance reports of responsibility center managers often include costs, revenues, and investments that the managers cannot control. Responsibility accounting identifies financial items with managers on the basis of which manager has the most knowledge and information about specific items, regardless of the manager's ability to exercise full control.

Learning Objective 6

Recognize the human aspects of budgeting

. . . to engage subordinate managers in the budgeting process

Human Aspects of Budgeting

Why did we discuss the master budget and responsibility accounting in the same chapter? Primarily to emphasize that human factors are crucial in budgeting. Too often, budgeting is thought of as a mechanical tool because the budgeting techniques themselves are free of emotion. However, the administration of budgeting requires education, persuasion, and intelligent interpretation.

Budgetary Slack

As we discussed earlier in this chapter, budgeting is most effective when lower-level managers actively participate and meaningfully engage in the budgeting process. Participation adds credibility to the budgeting process and creates greater commitment and accountability toward the budget. But participation requires "honest" communication about the business from subordinates and lower-level managers to their bosses.

At times, subordinates may try to "play games" and build in *budgetary slack*. **Budgetary slack** is the practice of underestimating budgeted revenues, or overestimating budgeted costs, to make budgeted targets more easily to achieve. This practice frequently occurs when budget variances (the differences between actual results and budgeted amounts) are used to evaluate performance. Line managers are also unlikely to be fully honest in their budget communications if top management mechanically institutes across-the-board cost reductions (say, a 10% reduction in all areas) in the face of projected revenue reductions.

Budgetary slack provides managers with a hedge against unexpected adverse circumstances. But budgetary slack also misleads top management about the true profit potential of the company, which leads to inefficient resource planning and allocation and poor coordination of activities across different parts of the company.

To avoid problems of budgetary slack, some companies use budgets primarily for planning and to a lesser extent for performance evaluation. They evaluate managerial performance using multiple indicators that take into account various factors that become known during the course of the year, such as the prevailing business environment and performance relative to competitors. Evaluating performance in this way takes time and requires careful judgment.

One approach to dealing with budgetary slack is to obtain good benchmark data when setting the budget. Consider the plant manager of a beverage bottler. Suppose top management could purchase a consulting firm's study of productivity levels—such as the number of bottles filled per hour—at a number of comparable plants owned by other bottling companies. Top management could share this independent information with the plant manager and use it to set the budget. Using external benchmark performance measures reduces a manager's ability to set budget levels that are easy to achieve.

Rolling budgets is another approach to reducing budgetary slack. As we discussed earlier in the chapter, companies that use rolling budgets always have a budget for a defined period, say 12 months, by adding, at the end of each quarter, a budget for one more quarter to replace the quarter just ended. The continuous updating of budget information and the richer information it provides reduces the opportunity to create budgetary slack relative to when budgeting is done only annually.

Some companies, such as IBM and Kodak, have designed innovative performance evaluation measures that reward managers based on the subsequent accuracy of the forecasts used in preparing budgets. For example, the *higher and more accurate* the budgeted profit forecasts of division managers, the higher their incentive bonuses.[6]

Another approach to reducing budgetary slack is for managers to involve themselves regularly in understanding what their subordinates are doing. Such involvement should not result in managers dictating the decisions and actions of subordinates. Rather, a manager's involvement should take the form of providing support, challenging in a motivational way the assumptions subordinates make, and enhancing mutual learning about the operations. Regular interaction with subordinates allows managers to become knowledgeable about the operations and diminishes the ability of subordinates to create slack in their budgets. Subordinates and superiors have in-depth dialogues about performance. Managers evaluate performance using subjective (and objective) measures that naturally require a great deal of trust.

Part of top management's responsibility is to promote commitment among the employees to a set of core values and norms. These values and norms describe what constitutes acceptable and unacceptable behavior. For example, Johnson & Johnson (J&J) has a credo that describes its responsibilities to doctors, patients, employees, communities, and shareholders. Employees are trained in the credo to help them understand the behavior that is expected of them. Managers are often promoted from within and are therefore very familiar with the work of the employees reporting to them. Managers also have the responsibility to interact with and mentor their subordinates. These values and practices create a culture at J&J that discourages budgetary slack.

Stretch Targets

Many of the best performing companies, such as General Electric, Microsoft, and Novartis, set "stretch" targets. Stretch targets are challenging but achievable levels of expected performance, intended to create a little discomfort. Creating some performance anxiety motivates employees to exert extra effort and attain better performance, but setting targets that are very difficult or impossible to achieve hurts performance because employees give up on trying to achieve them. Organizations such as Goldman Sachs also use "horizontal" stretch goal initiatives. The aim is to enhance professional development of employees by asking them to take on significantly different responsibilities or roles outside their comfort zone.

A major rationale for stretch targets is its psychological motivation. Consider the following two compensation arrangements offered to a salesperson:

- In the first arrangement, the salesperson is paid $40,000 for achieving sales of $1,000,000 and 4 cents for every dollar of sales above $1,000,000 up to $1,100,000.
- In the second arrangement, the salesperson is paid $44,000 for achieving the sales target of $1,100,000 with a reduction in compensation of 4 cents for every dollar of sales less than $1,100,000 up to $1,000,000.

For simplicity we assume that sales will be between $1,000,000 and $1,100,000.

It should be clear that the salesperson receives the same level of compensation under the two arrangements for all levels of sales between $1,000,000 and $1,100,000. The question is whether the psychological motivation is the same in the two compensation arrangements. Many executives who favor stretch targets point to the asymmetric way in which salespeople psychologically perceive the two compensation arrangements. In the first arrangement, achieving sales of $1,000,000 is seen as good and everything above it as a bonus. In the second arrangement, not reaching $1,100,000 in sales is seen as a failure. If salespeople are loss averse, that is, they feel the pain of loss more than the joy of success, they will work harder under the second arrangement to achieve sales of $1,100,000 and not fail.

Ethics. At no point should the pressure for performance embedded in stretch targets push employees to engage in illegal or unethical practices. The more a company tries to push performance, the greater the emphasis it must place on training employees to follow its code of conduct to prohibit behavior that is out of bounds (for example, no bribery, side payments or dishonest dealings) and its norms and values (for example, putting customers first and not compromising on quality).

[6] For an excellent discussion of these issues, see Chapter 14 ("Formal Models in Budgeting and Incentive Contracts") in R. S. Kaplan and A. A. Atkinson, *Advanced Management Accounting*, 3rd ed. (Upper Saddle River, NJ: Prentice Hall, 1998).

Ethical questions are sometimes subtle and not clear-cut. Consider, for example, a division manager, faced with the choice of doing maintenance on a machine at the end of 2012 or early in 2013. It is preferable to do the maintenance in 2012 because delaying maintenance increases the probability of the machine breaking down. But doing so would mean that the manager will not reach his 2012 stretch target for operating income and lose some of his bonus. If the risks of a breakdown and loss are substantial, many observers would view delaying maintenance as unethical. If the risk is minimal, there may be more debate as to whether delaying maintenance is unethical.

Many managers regard budgets negatively. To them, the word budget is about as popular as, say, *downsizing, layoff,* or *strike.* Top managers must convince their subordinates that the budget is a tool designed to help them set and reach goals. As with all tools of management, it has its benefits and challenges. Budgets must be used thoughtfully and wisely, but whatever the manager's perspective on budgets—pro or con—they are not remedies for weak management talent, faulty organization, or a poor accounting system.

Kaizen Budgeting

Chapter 1 noted the importance of continuous improvement, or *kaizen* in Japanese. **Kaizen budgeting** explicitly incorporates continuous improvement anticipated during the budget period into the budget numbers. Many companies that have cost reduction as a strategic focus, including General Electric in the United States and Citizens Watch and Toyota in Japan, use kaizen budgeting to continuously reduce costs. Much of the cost reduction associated with kaizen budgeting arises from many small improvements rather than "quantum leaps." Many of these improvements come from employee suggestions as a result of managers creating a culture that values, recognizes, and rewards employee suggestions. Employees who actually do the job, whether in manufacturing, sales, or distribution, have the best information and knowledge of how the job can be done better.

As an example, throughout our nine budgeting steps for Stylistic Furniture, we assumed 4 hours of direct labor time to manufacture each Casual coffee table. A Kaizen budgeting approach would incorporate continuous improvement by prescribing 4.00 direct manufacturing labor-hours per table for the first quarter of 2013, 3.95 hours for the second quarter, 3.90 hours for the third quarter, and so on. The implications of these reductions would be lower direct manufacturing labor costs, as well as lower variable manufacturing overhead costs, because direct manufacturing labor is the driver of these costs. If Stylistic Furniture doesn't meet continuous improvement goals, its managers will explore the reasons behind it and either adjust the targets or seek inputs from employees to implement process changes to accelerate continuous improvement. Of course, top management should encourage managers at all levels to also seek larger, discontinuous reduction in costs by changing operating processes and supply-chain relationships.

Managers can also apply Kaizen budgeting to activities such as setups with the goal of reducing setup time and setup costs, or distribution with the goal of reducing the cost of moving each cubic foot of table. Kaizen budgeting for specific activities are key building blocks of the master budget for companies that use the Kaizen approach.

A growing number of cash-strapped states and agencies in the United States are using Kaizen techniques to bring together government workers, regulators, and end users of government processes to identify ways to reduce inefficiencies and eliminate bureaucratic procedures. Several state environmental agencies, for example, have conducted a kaizen session or are planning one.[7] As another example, the United States Postal Service has identified many different programs to reduce its costs. The success of these efforts will depend heavily on human factors such as the commitment and engagement of managers and other employees to make these changes.

Keys to Success

The administration of budgets requires education, participation, persuasion, and intelligent interpretation. By administering budgets wisely, managers create commitment, accountability, and honest communication. When badly managed, budgeting can lead to game-playing and budgetary slack.

[7] For details, see "State Governments, Including Ohio's, Embrace Kaizen to Seek Efficiency via Japanese Methods," www.cleveland.com (December 12, 2008).

Budgeting in Multinational Companies

Learning Objective 7

Appreciate the special challenges of budgeting in multinational companies

. . . exposure to currency fluctuations and to different legal, political, and economic environments

Multinational companies, such as Federal Express, Kraft, and Pfizer, have operations in many countries. An international presence has benefits—access to new markets and resources—and drawbacks—operating in less-familiar business environments and exposure to currency fluctuations. Multinational companies earn revenues and incur expenses in many different currencies and must translate their operating performance into a single currency (say, U.S. dollars) for reporting results to their shareholders each quarter. This translation is based on the average exchange rates that prevail during the quarter. As a result, managers in multinational companies budget in different currencies and also budget for foreign exchange rates. This requires management to anticipate potential changes in exchange rates that might occur during the year. To reduce the possible negative impact on performance caused by unfavorable exchange rate movements, finance managers frequently use sophisticated techniques such as forward, future, and option contracts to minimize exposure to foreign currency fluctuations (see Chapter 9). Besides currency issues, managers at multinational companies need to understand the political, legal, and, in particular, economic environments of the different countries in which they operate. For example, in countries such as Turkey, Zimbabwe, and Guinea, annual inflation rates are very high, resulting in sharp declines in the value of the local currency. Managers also need to consider differences in tax regimes, especially when the company transfers goods or services across the many countries in which it operates (see Chapter 15).

When there is considerable business and exchange rate uncertainty of operating in global environments and predicting outcomes, a natural question to ask is "Do managers of multinational companies find budgeting to be a helpful tool?" The answer is yes. However, the purpose of budgeting in such environments is not to evaluate performance relative to budgets, which is a meaningless comparison when conditions are so volatile, but to help managers throughout the organization to learn and to adapt their plans. As circumstances and conditions change, companies revise their budgets and use it as a tool to communicate and coordinate actions that need to be taken throughout the company. Senior managers evaluate performance more subjectively, based on how well subordinate managers have managed in constantly changing and volatile environments.

Keys to Success

Managers in multinational companies value budgeting despite the uncertainties of operating in multiple countries and the challenges of budgeting in different currencies and forecasting foreign exchange rates. Managers use budgets to help the organization to learn and adapt plans in response to changed circumstances rather than to evaluate performance.

Problem for Self-Study

Consider the Stylistic Furniture example described earlier. Suppose that to maintain its sales quantities, Stylistic needs to decrease selling prices to $582 per Casual table and $776 per Deluxe table, a 3% decrease in the selling prices used in the chapter illustration. All other data are unchanged.

Required

Prepare a budgeted income statement, including all necessary detailed supporting budget schedules that are different from the schedules presented in the chapter. Indicate those schedules that will remain unchanged.

Solution

Schedules 1 and 8 will change. Schedule 1 changes because a change in selling price affects revenues. Schedule 8 changes because revenues are a cost driver of marketing costs (sales commissions). The remaining schedules 2–7 will not change because a change in selling price has no effect on manufacturing costs. The revised schedules and the new budgeted income statement follow.

Schedule 1: Revenue Budget for the Year Ending December 31, 2013			
	Selling Price	Units	Total Revenues
Casual tables	$582	50,000	$29,100,000
Deluxe tables	776	10,000	7,760,000
Total			$36,860,000

Schedule 8: Nonmanufacturing Costs Budget for the Year Ending December 31, 2013			
Business Function	Variable Costs	Fixed Costs (as in Schedule 8, page 498)	Total Costs
Product design		$1,024,000	$1,024,000
Marketing (Variable cost: $36,860,000 × 0.065)	$2,395,900	1,330,000	3,725,900
Distribution (Variable cost: $2 × 1,140,000 cu. ft.)	2,280,000	1,596,000	3,876,000
	$4,675,900	$3,950,000	$8,625,900

Stylistic Furniture Budgeted Income Statement for the Year Ending December 31, 2013			
Revenues	Schedule 1		$36,860,000
Cost of goods sold	Schedule 7		24,440,000
Gross margin			12,420,000
Operating costs			
Product design	Schedule 8	$1,024,000	
Marketing costs	Schedule 8	3,725,900	
Distribution costs	Schedule 8	3,876,000	8,625,900
Operating income			$ 3,794,100

Decision Points

The following question-and-answer format summarizes the chapter's learning objectives. Each decision presents a key question related to a learning objective. The guidelines are the answer to that question.

Decision	Guidelines
1. What is the master budget and why is it useful?	The master budget summarizes the financial projections of all the company's budgets. It expresses management's operating and financing plans—the formalized outline of the company's financial objectives and how they will be attained. Budgets are tools that, by themselves, are neither good nor bad. Budgets are useful when administered skillfully.
2. When should a company prepare budgets? What are the advantages of preparing budgets?	Budgets should be prepared when their expected benefits exceed their expected costs. There are four key advantages of budgets: (a) they compel strategic analysis and planning, (b) they promote coordination and communication among subunits of the company, (c) they provide a framework for judging performance and facilitating learning, and (d) they motivate managers and other employees.

Decision	Guidelines
3. What is the operating budget and what are its components?	The operating budget is the budgeted income statement and its supporting budget schedules. The starting point for the operating budget is generally the revenues budget. The following supporting schedules are derived from the revenues budget and the activities needed to support the revenues budget: production budget, direct material usage budget, direct material purchases budget, direct manufacturing labor cost budget, manufacturing overhead costs budget, ending inventories budget, cost of goods sold budget, R&D/product design cost budget, marketing cost budget, distribution cost budget, and customer-service cost budget.
4. How can managers plan for changes in the assumptions underlying the budget and manage risk?	Managers can use financial planning models—mathematical statements of the relationships among operating activities, financing activities, and other factors that affect the budget. These models make it possible for managers to conduct what-if (sensitivity) analysis of the risks that changes in the original predicted data or changes in underlying assumptions would have on the master budget and to develop plans to respond to changed conditions.
5. How do companies use responsibility centers? Should performance reports of responsibility center managers include only costs the manager can control?	A responsibility center is a part, segment, or subunit of an organization whose manager is accountable for a specified set of activities. Four types of responsibility centers are cost centers, revenue centers, profit centers, and investment centers. Responsibility accounting systems are useful because they measure the plans, budgets, actions, and actual results of each responsibility center. Controllable costs are costs primarily subject to the influence of a given responsibility center manager for a given time period. Performance reports of responsibility center managers often include costs, revenues, and investments that the managers cannot control. Responsibility accounting associates financial items with managers on the basis of which manager has the most knowledge and information about the specific items, regardless of the manager's ability to exercise full control.
6. Why are human factors crucial in budgeting?	The administration of budgets requires education, participation, persuasion, and intelligent interpretation. When wisely administered, budgets create commitment, accountability, and honest communication among employees, and can be used as the basis for continuous improvement efforts. When badly managed, budgeting can lead to game-playing and budgetary slack—the practice of making budget targets more easily achievable.
7. What are the special challenges involved in budgeting at multinational companies?	Budgeting is a valuable tool for multinational companies but is challenging because of the uncertainties inherent in operating in multiple countries. In addition to budgeting in different currencies, managers in multinational companies also need to budget for foreign exchange rates and consider the political, legal, and economic environments of the different countries in which they operate. In times of high uncertainty, managers use budgets to help the organization to learn and adapt plans to changed circumstances rather than to evaluate performance.

Appendix

The Cash Budget

The chapter illustrated the operating budget, which is one part of the master budget. The other part is the financial budget, which comprises the capital expenditures budget, the cash budget, the budgeted balance sheet, and the budgeted statement of cash flows. This appendix focuses on the cash budget. We discussed capital budgeting in Chapter 11. The budgeted statement of cash flows and budgeted balance sheet are beyond the scope of this book, and are generally covered in financial accounting and corporate finance courses.

Why should Stylistic's managers want a cash budget in addition to the operating income budget presented in the chapter? Recall that Stylistic's management accountants prepared the operating budget on an accrual accounting basis consistent with how the company reports its actual operating income. But Stylistic's managers also need to plan cash flows to ensure that the company has adequate cash to pay vendors, meet payroll, and pay operating expenses as these payments come due. Stylistic could be very profitable, but the pattern of cash receipts from revenues might be delayed and result in insufficient cash being available to make scheduled payments. Stylistic's managers may then need to initiate a plan to borrow money to finance any shortfall. Building a profitable operating plan does not guarantee that adequate cash will be available, so Stylistic's managers need to prepare a cash budget in addition to an operating income budget.

Suppose Stylistic Furniture had a cash balance of $300,000 on December 31, 2012. The budgeted cash flows for 2013 are:

	Quarters			
	1	2	3	4
Collections from customers	$9,136,600	$10,122,000	$10,263,200	$8,561,200
Disbursements				
Direct materials	2,947,605	2,714,612	2,157,963	2,155,356
Payroll	3,604,512	2,671,742	2,320,946	2,562,800
Manufacturing overhead costs	2,109,018	1,530,964	1,313,568	1,463,450
Nonmanufacturing costs	1,847,750	1,979,000	1,968,250	1,705,000
Machinery purchase	—	—	758,000	—
Income taxes	725,000	400,000	400,000	400,000

The quarterly data are based on the budgeted cash effects of the operations formulated in Schedules 1–8 in the chapter, but the details of that formulation are not shown here to keep this illustration as brief and as focused as possible.

Stylistic wants to maintain a $350,000 minimum cash balance at the end of each quarter. The company can borrow or repay money at an interest rate of 12% per year. Management does not want to borrow any more short-term cash than is necessary. By special arrangement with the bank, Stylistic pays interest when repaying the principal. Assume, for simplicity, that borrowing takes place at the beginning and repayment at the end of the quarter under consideration (in multiples of $1,000). Interest is computed to the nearest dollar.

Suppose a management accountant at Stylistic receives the preceding data and the other data contained in the budgets in the chapter (pages 489–499). Her manager asks her to:

1. Prepare a cash budget for 2013 by quarter. That is, prepare a statement of cash receipts and disbursements by quarter, including details of borrowing, repayment, and interest.
2. Prepare a budgeted income statement for the year ending December 31, 2013. This statement should include interest expense and income taxes (at a rate of 40% of operating income).

Preparation of Budgets

1. The **cash budget** is a schedule of expected cash receipts and disbursements. It predicts the effects on the cash position at the given level of operations. Exhibit 12-5 presents the cash budget by quarters to show the impact of cash flow timing on bank loans and their repayment. In practice, monthly—and sometimes weekly or even daily—cash budgets are critical for cash planning and control. Cash budgets help avoid unnecessary idle cash and unexpected cash deficiencies. They thus keep cash balances in line with needs. Ordinarily, the cash budget has these main sections:

   a. **Cash available for needs (before any financing).** The beginning cash balance plus cash receipts equals the total cash available for needs before any financing. Cash receipts depend on collections of accounts receivable, cash sales, and miscellaneous recurring sources, such

Exhibit 12-5

Cash Budget for Stylistic Furniture for the Year Ending December 31, 2013

	A	B	C	D	E	F
1	**Stylistic Furniture**					
2	**Cash Budget**					
3	**For Year Ending December 31, 2013**					
4		**Quarters**				**Year as a**
5		**1**	**2**	**3**	**4**	**Whole**
6	Cash balance, beginning	$ 300,000	$ 350,715	$ 350,657	$ 350,070	$ 300,000
7	Add receipts					
8	Collections from customers	9,136,600	10,122,000	10,263,200	8,561,200	38,083,000
9	Total cash available for needs (x)	9,436,600	10,472,715	10,613,857	8,911,270	38,383,000
10	Deduct disbursements					
11	Direct materials	2,947,605	2,714,612	2,157,963	2,155,356	9,975,536
12	Payroll	3,604,512	2,671,742	2,320,946	2,562,800	11,160,000
13	Manufacturing overhead costs	2,109,018	1,530,964	1,313,568	1,463,450	6,417,000
14	Nonmanufacturing costs	1,847,750	1,979,000	1,968,250	1,705,000	7,500,000
15	Machinery purchase			758,000		758,000
16	Income taxes	725,000	400,000	400,000	400,000	1,925,000
17	Total disbursements (y)	11,233,885	9,296,318	8,918,727	8,286,606	37,735,536
18	Minimum cash balance desired	350,000	350,000	350,000	350,000	350,000
19	Total cash needed	11,583,885	9,646,318	9,268,727	8,636,606	38,085,536
20	Cash excess (deficiency)*	$(2,147,285)	$ 826,397	$ 1,345,130	$ 274,664	$ 297,464
21	Financing					
22	Borrowing (at beginning)	$ 2,148,000	$ 0	$ 0	$ 0	$ 2,148,000
23	Repayment (at end)	0	(779,000)	(1,234,000)	(135,000)	(2,148,000)
24	Interest (at 12% per year)**	0	(46,740)	(111,060)	(16,200)	(174,000)
25	Total effects of financing (z)	$ 2,148,000	$ (825,740)	$ (1,345,060)	$ (151,200)	$ (174,000)
26	Cash balance, ending***	$ 350,715	$ 350,657	$ 350,070	$ 473,464	$ 473,464
27	*Excess of total cash available for needs − Total cash needed before financing.					
28	**Note that the short-term interest payments pertain only to the amount of principal being repaid at the end of a quarter. The specific computations regarding interest are $779,000 × 0.12 × 0.5 = $46,740; $1,234,000 × 0.12 × 0.75 = $111,060; $135,000 × 0.12 = $16,200. Also note that *depreciation does not require a cash outlay.*					
29	***Ending cash balance = Total cash available for needs (x) − Total disbursements (y) + Total effects of financing (z)					

as rental or royalty receipts. Information on the expected collectibility of accounts receivable is needed for accurate predictions. Key factors include bad-debt (uncollectible accounts) experience (not an issue in the Stylistic case because Stylistic sells to only a few large wholesalers) and average time lag between sales and collections.

b. Cash disbursements Cash disbursements by Stylistic Furniture include:

i. *Direct material purchases.* Suppliers are paid in full in the month after the goods are delivered.

ii. *Direct labor and other wage and salary outlays.* All payroll-related costs are paid in the month in which the labor effort occurs.

iii. *Other costs.* These depend on timing and credit terms. (In the Stylistic case, all other costs are paid in the month in which the cost is incurred.) *Note, depreciation does not require a cash outlay.*

iv. *Other disbursements.* These include outlays for property, plant, equipment, and other long-term investments.

v. Income tax payments as shown each quarter.

Exhibit 12-6

Budgeted Income Statement for Stylistic Furniture for the Year Ending December 31, 2013

	A	B	C	D
1	**Stylistic Furniture**			
2	**Budgeted Income Statement**			
3	**For the Year Ending December 31, 2013**			
4	Revenues	Schedule 1		$38,000,000
5	Cost of goods sold	Schedule 7		24,440,000
6	Gross margin			13,560,000
7	Operating costs			
8	Product design costs	Schedule 8	$1,024,000	
9	Marketing costs	Schedule 8	3,800,000	
10	Distribution costs	Schedule 8	3,876,000	8,700,000
11	Operating income			4,860,000
12	Interest expense	Exhibit 12-5		174,000
13	Income before income taxes			4,686,000
14	Income taxes (at 40%)			1,874,400
15	Net income			$ 2,811,600

c. Financing effects. Short-term financing requirements depend on how the total cash available for needs [keyed as (x) in Exhibit 12-5] compares with the total cash disbursements [keyed as (y)], plus the minimum ending cash balance desired. The financing plans will depend on the relationship between total cash available for needs and total cash needed. If there is a deficiency of cash, Stylistic obtains loans. If there is excess cash, Stylistic repays any outstanding loans.

d. Ending cash balance. The cash budget in Exhibit 12-5 shows the pattern of short-term "self-liquidating" cash loans. In quarter 1, Stylistic budgets a $2,147,285 cash deficiency. The company therefore undertakes short-term borrowing of $2,148,000 that it pays off over the course of the year. Seasonal peaks of production or sales often result in heavy cash disbursements for purchases, payroll, and other operating outlays as the company produces and sells products. Cash receipts from customers typically lag behind sales. The loan is *self-liquidating* in the sense that the company uses the borrowed money to acquire resources that it uses to produce and sell finished goods, and uses the proceeds from sales to repay the loan. This self-liquidating cycle is the movement from cash to inventories to receivables and back to cash.

2. The budgeted income statement is presented in Exhibit 12-6. It is merely the budgeted operating income statement in Exhibit 12-3 (page 498) expanded to include interest expense and income taxes.

For simplicity, this example explicitly gave the cash receipts and disbursements. Usually, the receipts and disbursements are calculated based on the lags between the items reported on the accrual basis of accounting in an income statement and balance sheet and their related cash receipts and disbursements. Consider accounts receivable.

The budgeted sales for the year are broken down into sales budgets for each month and quarter. For example, Stylistic Furniture budgets sales by quarter of $9,282,000; $10,332,000; $10,246,000; and $8,140,000, which equal 2013 budgeted sales of $38,000,000.

	Quarter 1		Quarter 2		Quarter 3		Quarter 4	
	Casual	Deluxe	Casual	Deluxe	Casual	Deluxe	Casual	Deluxe
Budgeted sales in units	12,270	2,400	13,620	2,700	13,610	2,600	10,500	2,300
Selling price	$600	$800	$600	$800	$600	$800	$600	$800
Budgeted revenues	$7,362,000	$1,920,000	$8,172,000	$2,160,000	$8,166,000	$2,080,000	$6,300,000	$1,840,000
	$9,282,000		$10,332,000		$10,246,000		$8,140,000	

Notice that sales are expected to be higher in the second and third quarters relative to the first and fourth quarters when weather conditions limit the number of customers shopping for furniture.

Once Stylistic's managers determine the sales budget, a management accountant prepares a schedule of cash collections that serves as an input for the preparation of the cash budget. The receipts and disbursements are calculated based on the lags between the items reported on the accrual basis of accounting in the income statement and balance sheet and their related cash receipts and disbursements. In the first three quarters, Stylistic estimates that 80% of all sales made in a quarter are collected in the same quarter and 20% are collected in the following quarter. Estimated collections from customers each quarter are calculated in the following table.

Schedule of Cash Collections	Quarters			
	1	2	3	4
Accounts receivable balance on 1-1-2013 (Fourth-quarter sales from prior year collected in first quarter of 2013)	$1,711,000			
From first-quarter 2013 sales ($9,282,000 × 0.80; $9,282,000 × 0.20)	7,425,600	$ 1,856,400		
From second-quarter 2013 sales ($10,332,000 × 0.80; $10,332,000 × 0.20)		8,265,600	$ 2,066,400	
From third-quarter 2013 sales ($10,246,000 × 0.80; $10,246,000 × 0.20)			8,196,800	$2,049,200
From fourth-quarter 2013 sales ($8,140,000 × 0.80)				6,512,000
Total collections	$9,136,600	$10,122,000	$10,263,200	$8,561,200

Uncollected fourth-quarter 2013 sales of $1,628,000 ($8,140,000 × 0.20) appear as accounts receivable on the balance sheet of December 31, 2013.

Note that the quarterly cash collections from customers calculated in this schedule equal the cash collections by quarter shown on page 510.

Sensitivity Analysis and Cash Flows

Exhibit 12-4 (page 500) shows how differing assumptions about selling prices of coffee tables and direct material prices led to differing amounts for budgeted operating income for Stylistic Furniture. A key use of sensitivity analysis is to budget cash flow. Exhibit 12-7 outlines the short-term borrowing implications of the two combinations examined in Exhibit 12-4. Scenario 1, with the lower selling prices per table ($582 for the Casual table and $776 for the Deluxe table), requires $2,352,000 of short-term borrowing in quarter 1 that cannot be fully repaid as of December 31, 2013. Scenario 2, with the 5% higher direct material costs, requires $2,250,000 borrowing by Stylistic Furniture that also cannot be repaid by December 31, 2013. Sensitivity analysis helps managers anticipate such outcomes and take steps to minimize the effects of expected reductions in cash flows from operations.

Exhibit 12-7

Sensitivity Analysis: Effects of Key Budget Assumptions in Exhibit 12-4 on 2013 Short-Term Borrowing for Stylistic Furniture

Home Insert Page Layout Formulas Data Review View

	A	B	C	D	E	F	G	H	I	J
1				Direct Material			Short-Term Borrowing and Repayment by Quarter			
2		Selling Price		Purchase Costs		Budgeted	Quarters			
3	Scenario	Casual	Deluxe	Red Oak	Granite	Operating Income	1	2	3	4
4	1	$582	$776	$7.00	$10.00	$3,794,100	$2,352,000	($511,000)	($ 969,000)	($ 30,000)
5	2	$600	$800	7.35	10.50	4,483,800	2,250,000	(651,000)	(1,134,000)	(149,000)

Terms to Learn

The chapter and the Glossary at the end of the book contain definitions of the following important terms:

activity-based budgeting (ABB) (p. 494)
budgetary slack (p. 504)
cash budget (p. 510)
continuous budget (p. 488)
controllability (p. 503)
controllable cost (p. 503)
cost center (p. 502)
financial budget (p. 489)
financial planning models (p. 499)
investment center (p. 502)
Kaizen budgeting (p. 506)
master budget (p. 485)
operating budget (p. 489)
organization structure (p. 502)
pro forma statements (p. 485)
profit center (p. 502)
responsibility accounting (p. 502)
responsibility center (p. 502)
revenue center (p. 502)
rolling budget (p. 488)
rolling forecast (p. 488)

Assignment Material

Questions

12-1 "Strategy, plans, and budgets are unrelated to one another." Do you agree? Explain.

12-2 "Budgeted performance is a better criterion than past performance for judging managers." Do you agree? Explain.

12-3 "Production managers and marketing managers are like oil and water. They just don't mix." How can a budget assist in reducing battles between these two departments?

12-4 "Budgets meet the cost–benefit test. They force managers to act differently." Do you agree? Explain.

12-5 "The sales forecast is the cornerstone for budgeting." Why?

12-6 How can managers use sensitivity analysis to increase the benefits of budgeting?

12-7 What are the benefits of kaizen budgeting?

12-8 Describe how managers can incorporate non-output-based cost drivers into budgeting.

12-9 Explain how the manager's choice of the type of responsibility center (cost, revenue, profit, or investment) affects the behavior of other employees.

12-10 "Managers must prepare cash budgets before the operating income budget." Do you agree? Explain.

Exercises

12-11 Sales budget, service setting. In 2012, Canseco & Sons, a small environmental-testing firm, performed 12,400 radon tests for $310 each and 16,600 lead tests for $210 each. Because new homes are being built with lead-free pipes, lead-testing volume is expected to decrease by 13% next year. However, awareness of radon-related health hazards is expected to result in a 4% increase in radon-test volume each year in the near future. Jim Canseco feels that if he lowers his price for lead testing to $190 per test, he will have to face only a 6% decline in lead-test sales in 2013.

Required

1. Prepare a 2013 sales budget for Canseco & Sons assuming that Canseco holds prices at 2012 levels.
2. Prepare a 2013 sales budget for Canseco & Sons assuming that Canseco lowers the price of a lead test to $190. Should Canseco lower the price of a lead test in 2013 if its goal is to maximize sales revenue?
3. How might Jim Canseco use the budget developed in requirement 2 to better manage the company?

12-12 Production and material purchases budgets. The Howell Company has prepared a sales budget of 46,000 finished units for a 3-month period. The company has an inventory of 10,000 units of finished goods on hand at December 31 and has a target finished goods inventory of 13,000 units at the end of the succeeding quarter.

It takes 2 gallons of direct materials to make one unit of finished product. The company has an inventory of 62,000 gallons of direct materials at December 31 and has a target ending inventory of 52,000 gallons at the end of the succeeding quarter.

Required

1. How many gallons of direct materials should Howell Company purchase during the 3 months ending March 31?
2. What questions might the CEO ask of the operating manager when reviewing the budget?

12-13 Revenues, production, and purchases budgets. The Yoshida Co. in Japan has a division that manufactures two-wheel motorcycles. Its budgeted sales for Model G in 2013 is 895,000 units. Yoshida's target ending inventory is 90,000 units, and its beginning inventory is 120,000 units. The company's budgeted selling price to its distributors and dealers is 405,000 yen (¥) per motorcycle.

Yoshida buys all its wheels from an outside supplier. No defective wheels are accepted. (Yoshida's needs for extra wheels for replacement parts are ordered by a separate division of the company.) The company's target ending inventory is 74,000 wheels, and its beginning inventory is 56,000 wheels. The budgeted purchase price is 12,000 yen (¥) per wheel.

Required

1. Compute the budgeted revenues in yen.
2. Compute the number of motorcycles that Yoshida should produce.
3. Compute the budgeted purchases of wheels in units and in yen.
4. What actions can Yoshida's managers take to reduce budgeted purchasing costs of wheels assuming the same budgeted sales for Model G?

12-14 Revenues and production budget. Posh, Inc., bottles and distributes mineral water from the company's natural springs in northern Oregon. Posh markets two products: 12-ounce disposable plastic bottles and 1-gallon reusable plastic containers.

Required

1. For 2013, Posh marketing managers project monthly sales of 420,000 12-ounce bottles and 170,000 1-gallon containers. Average selling prices are estimated at $0.20 per 12-ounce bottle and $1.50 per 1-gallon container. Prepare a revenues budget for Posh, Inc., for the year ending December 31, 2013. What questions might the CEO ask of the marketing manager when reviewing the budget?
2. Posh begins 2013 with 890,000 12-ounce bottles in inventory. The vice president of operations requests that 12-ounce bottles ending inventory on December 31, 2013, be no less than 680,000 bottles. Based on sales projections as budgeted previously, what is the minimum number of 12-ounce bottles Posh must produce during 2013? What questions might the CEO ask of the operating manager when reviewing the budget?
3. The VP of operations requests that ending inventory of 1-gallon containers on December 31, 2013, be 240,000 units. If the production budget calls for Posh to produce 1,900,000 1-gallon containers during 2013, what is the beginning inventory of 1-gallon containers on January 1, 2013?

12-15 Budgeting, direct material usage, manufacturing cost, and gross margin. Xander Manufacturing Company manufactures blue rugs, using wool and dye as direct materials. One rug is budgeted to use 36 skeins of wool at a cost of $2 per skein and 0.8 gallons of dye at a cost of $6 per gallon. All other materials are indirect. At the beginning of the year Xander has an inventory of 458,000 skeins of wool at a cost of $961,800 and 4,000 gallons of dye at a cost of $23,680. Target ending inventory of wool and dye is zero. Xander uses the FIFO inventory cost flow method.

Xander blue rugs are very popular and demand is high, but because of capacity constraints the firm will produce only 200,000 blue rugs per year. The budgeted selling price is $2,000 each. There are no rugs in beginning inventory. Target ending inventory of rugs is also zero.

Xander makes rugs by hand, but uses a machine to dye the wool. Thus, overhead costs are accumulated in two cost pools—one for weaving and the other for dyeing. Weaving overhead is allocated to products based on direct manufacturing labor-hours (DMLH). Dyeing overhead is allocated to products based on machine-hours (MH).

There is no direct manufacturing labor cost for dyeing. Xander budgets 62 direct manufacturing labor-hours to weave a rug at a budgeted rate of $13 per hour. It budgets 0.2 machine-hours to dye each skein in the dyeing process.

The following table presents the budgeted overhead costs for the dyeing and weaving cost pools:

	Dyeing (based on 1,440,000 MH)	Weaving (based on 12,400,000 DMLH)
Variable costs		
Indirect materials	$ 0	$15,400,000
Maintenance	6,560,000	5,540,000
Utilities	7,550,000	2,890,000
Fixed costs		
Indirect labor	347,000	1,700,000
Depreciation	2,100,000	274,000
Other	723,000	5,816,000
Total budgeted costs	$17,280,000	$31,620,000

Required

1. Prepare a direct material usage budget in both units and dollars.
2. Calculate the budgeted overhead allocation rates for weaving and dyeing.
3. Calculate the budgeted unit cost of a blue rug for the year.
4. Prepare a revenue budget for blue rugs for the year, assuming Xander sells (a) 200,000 or (b) 185,000 blue rugs (that is, at two different sales levels).
5. Calculate the budgeted cost of goods sold for blue rugs under each sales assumption.
6. Find the budgeted gross margin for blue rugs under each sales assumption.
7. What actions might you take as a manager to improve profitability if sales drop to 185,000 blue rugs?
8. How might top management at Xander use the budget developed in requirements 1–6 to better manage the company?

12-16 Budgeting, service company. Sunshine Window Washers (SWW) provides window-washing services to commercial clients. The company has enjoyed considerable growth in recent years due to a successful marketing campaign and favorable reviews on service rating Web sites. Sunshine owner Sam Davis makes sales calls himself, and quotes on jobs based on square footage of window surface. Sunshine hires college students to drive the company vans to jobs and wash the windows. A part-time bookkeeper takes care of billing customers and other office tasks. Overhead is accumulated in two cost pools, one for travel to jobs, allocated based on miles driven, and one for window washing, allocated based on direct labor-hours (DLH).

Sam Davis estimates that his window washers will work a total of 2,000 jobs during the year Each job averages 2,000 square feet of window surface, and requires 5 direct labor-hours and 12.5 miles of travel. Davis pays his window washers $12 per hour. Taxes and benefits equal 20% of wages. Wages, taxes, and benefits are considered direct labor costs. The following table presents the budgeted overhead costs for the Travel and Window Washing cost pools:

	Travel (based on 25,000 miles driven)	Window Washing (based on 10,000 DLH)
Variable costs		
Supplies ($4.40 per DLH)	$ 0	$ 44,000
Fuel ($0.60 per mile)	15,000	0
Fixed costs (to support capacity of 30,000 miles driven and 12,000 direct labor-hours)		
Indirect labor	0	20,000
Depreciation	40,000	35,000
Other	5,000	23,000
Total budgeted costs	$60,000	$122,000

Required

1. Prepare a direct labor budget in both hours and dollars. Calculate the direct labor rate.
2. Calculate the budgeted overhead allocation rates for travel and window washing.
3. Calculate the budgeted total cost of all jobs for the year and the budgeted cost of an average 2,000-square-foot window-washing job.
4. Prepare a revenue budget for the year, assuming that Sunshine charges customers $0.10 per square foot.
5. Calculate the budgeted operating income.
6. Davis believes that spending $15,000 in additional advertising will lead to a 20% increase in the number of jobs. Recalculate the budgeted revenue and operating income assuming this change is made. Calculate expenses by multiplying the existing budgeted cost per job calculated in requirement 3 by the number of jobs and adding the $15,000 advertising cost. Based on the change in budgeted operating income, would you recommend the investment?
7. Do you see any flaw in this analysis? How could the analysis be improved? Should SWW spend $15,000 in additional advertising?
8. What is SWW's profitability if sales should decline to 1,800 jobs annually? What actions can Davis take to improve profitability?

12-17 Budgets for production and direct manufacturing labor. (CMA, adapted) Peterson Company makes and sells artistic picture frames for special events such as weddings and graduations. Bob Anderson, the controller, is responsible for preparing Peterson's master budget and has accumulated the following information for 2013:

	2013				
	January	February	March	April	May
Estimated sales in units	14,000	15,000	9,000	10,000	10,000
Selling price	$55.00	$52.50	$52.50	$52.50	$52.50
Direct manufacturing labor-hours per unit	2.5	2.5	1.0	1.0	1.0
Wage per direct manufacturing labor-hour	$12.00	$12.00	$12.00	$14.00	$14.00

In addition to wages, direct manufacturing labor-related costs include pension contributions of $0.40 per hour, worker's compensation insurance of $0.10 per hour, employee medical insurance of $0.30 per hour, and Social Security taxes. Assume that as of January 1, 2013, the Social Security tax rates are 7.5% for employers and 7.5% for employees. The cost of employee benefits paid by Peterson on its employees is treated as a direct manufacturing labor cost.

Peterson has a labor contract that calls for a wage increase to $14 per hour on April 1, 2013. The company will install new labor-saving machinery by March 1, 2013. Peterson expects to have 19,500 frames on hand at December 31, 2012, and it has a policy of carrying an end-of-month inventory of 100% of the following month's sales plus 50% of the second following month's sales.

Required

1. Prepare a production budget and a direct manufacturing labor budget for Peterson Company by month and for the first quarter of 2013. You may combine both budgets in one schedule. The direct manufacturing labor budget should include labor-hours and show the details for each labor cost category.
2. What actions has the budget process prompted Peterson's management to take?
3. How might Peterson's managers use the budget developed in requirement 1 to better manage the company?

12-18 Activity-based budgeting. The Georgetown store of Jiffy Mart, a chain of small neighborhood convenience stores, is preparing its activity-based budget for January 2013. Jiffy Mart has three product categories: soft drinks (35% of cost of goods sold [COGS]), fresh snacks (25% of COGS) , and packaged food (40% of COGS). The following table shows the four activities that consume indirect resources at the Georgetown store, the cost drivers and their rates, and the cost-driver amount budgeted to be consumed by each activity in January 2013.

		January 2013 Budgeted Cost-Driver Rate	January 2013 Budgeted Amount of Cost Driver Used		
Activity	Cost Driver		Soft Drinks	Fresh Snacks	Packaged Food
Ordering	Number of purchase orders	$ 45	14	24	14
Delivery	Number of deliveries	$ 41	12	62	19
Shelf stocking	Hours of stocking time	$10.50	16	172	94
Customer support	Number of items sold	$ 0.09	4,600	34,200	10,750

Required

1. What is the total budgeted indirect cost at the Georgetown store in January 2013? What is the total budgeted cost of each activity at the Georgetown store for January 2013? What is the budgeted indirect cost of each product category for January 2013?
2. Which product category has the largest fraction of total budgeted indirect costs?
3. Given your answer in requirement 2, what advantage does Jiffy Mart gain by using an activity-based approach to budgeting over, say, allocating indirect costs to products based on cost of goods sold?

12-19 Kaizen approach to activity-based budgeting (continuation of 12-18). Jiffy Mart has a kaizen (continuous improvement) approach to budgeting monthly activity costs for each month of 2013. Each successive month, the budgeted cost-driver rate decreases by 0.4% relative to the preceding month. So, for example, February's budgeted cost-driver rate is 0.996 times January's budgeted cost-driver rate, and March's budgeted cost-driver rate is 0.996 times the budgeted February rate. Jiffy Mart assumes that the budgeted amount of cost-driver usage remains the same each month.

Required

1. What is the total budgeted cost for each activity and the total budgeted indirect cost for March 2013?
2. What are the benefits of using a Kaizen approach to budgeting? What are the limitations of this approach, and how might Jiffy Mart management overcome them?

12-20 Responsibility and controllability. Consider each of the following independent situations for Tropical Hot Tubs. Tropical manufactures and sells hot tubs. The company also contracts to service both its own and other brands of hot tubs. Tropical has a manufacturing plant, a supply warehouse that supplies both the manufacturing plant and the service technicians (who often need parts to repair hot tubs), and 10 service vans. The service technicians drive to customer sites to service the hot tubs. Tropical owns the vans, pays for the gas, and supplies hot tub parts, but the technicians own their own tools.

1. In the manufacturing plant, the production manager is not happy with the motors that the purchasing manager has been purchasing. In May, the production manager stops requesting motors from the supply warehouse and starts purchasing them directly from a different motor manufacturer. Actual materials costs in May are higher than budgeted.
2. Overhead costs in the manufacturing plant for June are much higher than budgeted. Investigation reveals a utility rate hike in effect that was not figured into the budget.
3. Gasoline costs for each van are budgeted based on the service area of the van and the amount of driving expected for the month. The driver of van 3 routinely has monthly gasoline costs exceeding the budget for van 3. After investigating, the service manager finds that the driver has been driving the van for personal use.
4. Cascades Resort and Spa, one of Tropical's hot tub service customers, calls the service people only for emergencies and not for routine maintenance. Thus, the materials and labor costs for these service calls exceeds the monthly budgeted costs for a contract customer.
5. Tropical's service technicians are paid an hourly wage, with overtime pay if they exceed 40 hours per week, excluding driving time. Fred Friendly, one of the technicians, frequently exceeds 40 hours per week. Service customers are happy with Fred's work, but the service manager talks to him constantly about working more quickly. Fred's overtime causes the actual costs of service to exceed the budget almost every month.
6. The cost of gasoline has increased by 50% this year, which caused the actual gasoline costs to greatly exceed the budgeted costs for the service vans.

Required

For each situation described, determine where (that is, with whom) (a) responsibility and (b) controllability lie. Suggest ways to solve the problem or to improve the situation.

12-21 Responsibility, controllability, and stretch targets. Consider each of the following independent situations for Happy Tours, a company owned by Jason Haslett, which sells motor coach tours to schools and other groups. Happy Tours owns a fleet of 10 motor coaches, and employs 12 drivers, 1 maintenance technician, 3 sales representatives, and an office manager. Happy Tours pays for all fuel and maintenance on the coaches. Drivers are paid $0.50 per mile while in transit, plus $15 per hour while idle (time spent waiting while tour groups are visiting their destinations). The maintenance technician and office manager are both full-time salaried employees. The sales representatives work on straight commission.

1. When the office manager receives calls from potential customers, she is instructed to handle the contracts herself. Recently, however, the number of contracts written up by the office manager has declined. At the same time, one of the sales representatives has experienced a significant increase in contracts. The other two representatives believe that the office manager has been colluding with the third representative to send him the prospective customers.
2. One of the motor coach drivers seems to be reaching his destinations more quickly than any of the other drivers, and is reporting longer idle time.
3. Fuel costs have increased significantly in recent months. Driving the motor coaches at 60 miles per hour on the highway consumes significantly less fuel than driving them at 65 miles per hour.
4. Regular preventive maintenance of the motor coaches has been proven to improve fuel efficiency and reduce overall operating costs by averting costly repairs. During busy months, however, it is difficult for the maintenance technician to complete all of the maintenance tasks within his 40-hour work week.
5. Jason Haslett has read about stretch targets, and he believes that a change in the compensation structure of the sales representatives may improve sales. Rather than a straight commission of 10% of sales, he is considering a system where each representative is given a monthly goal of 50 contracts. If the goal is met, the representative is paid a 12% commission. If the goal is not met, the commission falls to 8%. Currently, each sales representative averages 45 contracts per month.

For situations 1–4, discuss which employee has responsibility for the related costs, and the extent to which costs are controllable and by whom. What are the risks or costs to the company? What can be done to solve the problem or improve the situation? For situation 5, describe the potential benefits and costs of establishing stretch targets.

Required

12-22 Cash flow analysis, sensitivity analysis. Game Depot is a retail store selling video games. Sales are uniform for most of the year, but pick up in June and December, both because new releases come out and because consumers purchase games in anticipation of summer or winter holidays. Game Depot also sells and repairs game systems. The forecast of sales and service revenue for the March–June 2013 is as follows:

Sales and Service Revenue Budget March–June 2013			
Month	Expected Sales Revenue	Expected Service Revenue	Total Revenue
March	$ 9,000	$1,500	$10,500
April	11,000	2,000	13,000
May	12,400	2,800	15,200
June	19,400	5,200	24,600

Almost all the service revenue is paid for by bank credit card, so Game Depot budgets this as 100% bank card revenue. The bank cards charge an average fee of 3% of the total. Half of the sales revenue is also paid for by bank credit card, for which the fee is also 3% on average. About 10% of the sales are paid in cash, and the rest (the remaining 40%) are carried on a store account. Although the store tries to give store credit only to the best customers, it still averages about 2% for uncollectible accounts; 90% of store accounts are paid in the month following the purchase, and 8% are paid 2 months after purchase.

Required

1. Calculate the cash that Game Depot expects to collect in May and in June 2013. Show calculations for each month.
2. Game Depot has budgeted expenditures for May of $8,700 for the purchase of games and game systems, $2,800 for rent and utilities and other costs, and $2,000 in wages for the two part-time employees.
   a. Given your answer to requirement 1, will Game Depot be able to cover its payments for May?
   b. The projections for May are a budget. Assume (independently for each situation) that May revenues might also be 5% less and 10% less, and that costs might be 8% higher. Under each of those three scenarios, show the total net cash for May and the amount Game Depot would have to borrow if cash receipts are less than cash payments. Assume the beginning cash balance for May is $200.
3. Why do Game Depot's managers prepare a cash budget in addition to the revenue, expenses, and operating income budget? Has preparing the cash budget been helpful? Explain briefly.
4. Suppose the costs for May are as described in requirement 2, but the expected cash receipts for May are $12,400 and beginning cash balance is $200. Game Depot has the opportunity to purchase the games and game systems on account in May, but the supplier offers the company credit terms of 2/10 net 30, which means if Game Depot pays within 10 days (in May) it will get a 2% discount on the price of the merchandise. Game Depot can borrow money at a rate of 24%. Should Game Depot take the purchase discount?

Problems

12-23 Budget schedules for a manufacturer. Lame Specialties manufactures, among other things, woolen blankets for the athletic teams of the two local high schools. The company sews the blankets from fabric and sews on a logo patch purchased from the licensed logo store site. The teams are as follows:

- Knights, with red blankets and the Knights logo
- Raiders, with black blankets and the Raider logo

Also, the black blankets are slightly larger than the red blankets.

The budgeted direct-cost inputs for each product in 2013 are as follows:

	Knights Blanket	Raiders Blanket
Red wool fabric	4 yards	0 yards
Black wool fabric	0	5
Knight logo patches	1	0
Raider logo patches	0	1
Direct manufacturing labor	3 hours	4 hours

Unit data pertaining to the direct materials for March 2013 are as follows:

Actual Beginning Direct Materials Inventory (3/1/2013)		
	Knights Blanket	Raiders Blanket
Red wool fabric	35 yards	0 yards
Black wool fabric	0	15
Knight logo patches	45	0
Raider logo patches	0	60

Target Ending Direct Materials Inventory (3/31/2013)		
	Knights Blanket	Raiders Blanket
Red wool fabric	25 yards	0 yards
Black wool fabric	0	25
Knight logo patches	25	0
Raider logo patches	0	25

Unit cost data for direct-cost inputs pertaining to February 2013 and March 2013 are as follows:

	February 2013 (actual)	March 2013 (budgeted)
Red wool fabric (per yard)	$ 9	$10
Black wool fabric (per yard)	12	11
Knight logo patches (per patch)	7	7
Raider logo patches (per patch)	6	8
Manufacturing labor cost per hour	26	27

Manufacturing overhead (both variable and fixed) is allocated to each blanket on the basis of budgeted direct manufacturing labor-hours per blanket. The budgeted variable manufacturing overhead rate for March 2013 is $16 per direct manufacturing labor-hour. The budgeted fixed manufacturing overhead for March 2013 is $14,640. Both variable and fixed manufacturing overhead costs are allocated to each unit of finished goods.

Data relating to finished goods inventory for March 2013 are as follows:

	Knights Blankets	Raiders Blankets
Beginning inventory in units	12	17
Beginning inventory in dollars (cost)	$1,440	$2,550
Target ending inventory in units	22	27

Budgeted sales for March 2013 are 130 units of the Knights blankets and 190 units of the Raiders blankets. The budgeted selling prices per unit in March 2013 are $229 for the Knights blankets and $296 for the Raiders blankets. Assume the following in your answer:

- Work-in-process inventories are negligible and ignored.
- Direct materials inventory and finished goods inventory are costed using the FIFO method.
- Unit costs of direct materials purchased and finished goods are constant in March 2013.

Required

1. Prepare the following budgets for March 2013:
   a. Revenues budget
   b. Production budget in units
   c. Direct material usage budget and direct material purchases budget
   d. Direct manufacturing labor budget
   e. Manufacturing overhead budget
   f. Ending inventories budget (direct materials and finished goods)
   g. Cost of goods sold budget

2. Suppose Lame Specialties decides to incorporate continuous improvement into its budgeting process. Describe two areas where it could incorporate continuous improvement into the budget schedules in requirement 1.

12-24 Budgeted costs, kaizen improvements. Trendy T-Shirt Factory manufactures plain white and solid-colored T-shirts. Inputs include the following:

	Price	Quantity	Cost per unit of output
Fabric	$ 7 per yard	1 yard per unit	$7 per unit
Labor	$14 per DMLH	0.25 DMLH per unit	$3.50 per unit

Additionally, the colored T-shirts require 3 ounces of dye per shirt at a cost of $0.40 per ounce. The shirts sell for $14 each for white and $18 each for colors. The company expects to sell 12,000 white T-shirts and 60,000 colored T-shirts uniformly over the year.

Trendy has the opportunity to switch from using the dye it currently uses to using an environmentally friendly dye that costs $1.25 per ounce. The company would still need 3 ounces of dye per shirt. Trendy is reluctant to change because of the increase in costs (and decrease in profit) but the Environmental Protection Agency has threatened to fine the company $120,000 if it continues to use the harmful but less expensive dye.

Required

1. Given the preceding information, would Trendy be better off financially by switching to the environmentally friendly dye? (Assume all other costs would remain the same.)
2. Assume Trendy chooses to be environmentally responsible regardless of cost, and it switches to the new dye. The production manager suggests trying Kaizen costing. If Trendy can reduce fabric and labor costs each by 1% per month, how close will it be at the end of 12 months to the profit it would have earned before switching to the more expensive dye? (Round to the nearest dollar for calculating cost reductions.)
3. Refer to requirement 2. How could the reduction in material and labor costs be accomplished? Are there any problems with this plan?

12-25 Revenue and production budgets. (CPA, adapted) The Saadi Corporation manufactures and sells two products: Thingone and Thingtwo. In July 2012, Saadi's budget department gathered the following data to prepare budgets for 2013:

2013 Projected Sales		
Product	Units	Price
Thingone	63,000	$174
Thingtwo	47,000	$260

2013 Inventories in Units		
	Expected Target	
Product	January 1, 2013	December 31, 2013
Thingone	27,000	32,000
Thingtwo	7,000	8,000

The following direct materials are used in the two products:

		Amount Used per Unit	
Direct Material	Unit	Thingone	Thingtwo
A	pound	6	7
B	pound	4	5
C	each	0	3

Projected data for 2013 for direct materials are:

Direct Material	Anticipated Purchase Price	Expected Inventories January 1, 2013	Target Inventories December 31, 2013
A	$15	36,000 lb.	41,000 lb.
B	5	32,000 lb.	35,000 lb.
C	3	10,000 units	12,000 units

Projected direct manufacturing labor requirements and rates for 2013 are:

Product	Hours per Unit	Rate per Hour
Thingone	4	$15
Thingtwo	5	20

Manufacturing overhead is allocated at the rate of $24 per direct manufacturing labor-hour.

Required Based on the preceding projections and budget requirements for Thingone and Thingtwo, prepare the following budgets for 2013:

1. Revenues budget (in dollars)
2. What questions might the CEO ask the marketing manager when reviewing the revenues budget? Explain briefly.
3. Production budget (in units)
4. Direct material purchases budget (in quantities)
5. Direct material purchases budget (in dollars)
6. Direct manufacturing labor budget (in dollars)
7. Budgeted finished goods inventory at December 31, 2013 (in dollars)
8. What questions might the CEO ask the production manager when reviewing the production, direct materials, and direct manufacturing labor budgets?
9. How does preparing a budget help Saadi Corporation's top management better manage the company?

12-26 Budgeted income statement. (CMA, adapted) Videocom Company is a manufacturer of videoconferencing products. Maintaining the videoconferencing equipment is an important area of customer satisfaction. A recent downturn in the computer industry has caused the videoconferencing equipment segment to suffer, leading to a decline in Videocom's financial performance. The following income statement shows results for 2012:

Videocom Company Income Statement for the Year Ended December 31, 2012 (in thousands)		
Revenues		
Equipment	$6,500	
Maintenance contracts	1,800	
Total revenues		$8,300
Cost of goods sold		4,700
Gross margin		3,600
Operating costs		
Marketing	680	
Distribution	100	
Customer maintenance	1,500	
Administration	940	
Total operating costs		3,220
Operating income		$ 380

Videocom's management team is preparing the 2013 budget and is studying the following information:

1. Selling prices of equipment are expected to increase by 15% as the economic recovery begins. The selling price of each maintenance contract is expected to remain unchanged from 2012.
2. Equipment sales in units are expected to increase by 8%, with a corresponding 8% growth in units of maintenance contracts.
3. Cost of each unit sold is expected to increase by 4% to pay for the necessary technology and quality improvements.
4. Marketing costs are expected to increase by $290,000, but administration costs are expected to remain at 2012 levels.
5. Distribution costs vary in proportion to the number of units of equipment sold.
6. Two maintenance technicians are to be hired at a total cost of $190,000, which covers wages and related travel costs. The objective is to improve customer service and shorten response time.
7. There is no beginning or ending inventory of equipment.

Required

1. Prepare a budgeted income statement for the year ending December 31, 2013.
2. How well does the budget align with Videocom's strategy?
3. What questions might the CEO ask the management team when reviewing the budget?
4. How does preparing the budget help Videocom's management team better manage the company?

12-27 Responsibility in a restaurant. Paula Beane owns a restaurant franchise that is part of a chain of "southern homestyle" restaurants. One of the chain's popular breakfast items is biscuits and gravy. Central Warehouse makes and freezes the biscuit dough, which it then sells to the franchise stores where it is thawed and baked in the individual stores by the cook. Each franchise also has a purchasing agent who orders the biscuits (and other items) based on expected demand. In March 2013, one of the freezers in Central Warehouse breaks down and biscuit production is reduced by 25% for 3 days. During those 3 days, Paula's franchise runs out of biscuits but demand does not slow down. Paula's franchise cook, Betty Baker, sends one of the kitchen helpers to the local grocery store to buy refrigerated ready-to-bake biscuits. Although the customers are kept happy, the refrigerated biscuits cost Paula's franchise three times the cost of the Central Warehouse frozen biscuits, and the franchise loses money on this item for those 3 days. Paula is angry with the purchasing agent for not ordering enough biscuits to avoid running out of stock and with Betty for spending too much money on the replacement biscuits.

Required

Who is responsible for the cost of the biscuits? At what level is the cost controllable? Do you agree that Paula should be angry with the purchasing agent? With Betty? Why or why not?

12-28 Comprehensive problem with ABC costing. Animal Gear Company makes two pet carriers, the Cat-allac and the Dog-eriffic. They are both made of plastic with metal doors, but the Cat-allac is smaller. Information for the two products for the month of April is given in the following tables:

Input Prices

Direct materials	
Plastic	$ 5 per pound
Metal	$ 4 per pound
Direct manufacturing labor	$10 per direct manufacturing labor-hour

Input Quantities per Unit of Output

	Cat-allac	Dog-eriffic
Direct materials		
Plastic	4 pounds	6 pounds
Metal	0.5 pounds	1 pound
Direct manufacturing labor-hours	3 hours	5 hours
Machine-hours (MH)	11 MH	19 MH

Inventory Information, Direct Materials

	Plastic	Metal
Beginning inventory	290 pounds	70 pounds
Target ending inventory	410 pounds	65 pounds
Cost of beginning inventory	$1,102	$217

Animal Gear accounts for direct materials using a FIFO cost flow assumption.

Sales and Inventory Information, Finished Goods		
	Cat-allac	Dog-eriffic
Expected sales in units	530	225
Selling price	$ 205	$ 310
Target ending inventory in units	30	10
Beginning inventory in units	10	25
Beginning inventory in dollars	$1,000	$4,650

Animal Gear uses a FIFO cost flow assumption for finished goods inventory.

Animal Gear uses an activity-based costing system and classifies overhead into three activity pools: Setup, Processing, and Inspection. Activity rates for these activities are $105 per setup-hour, $10 per machine-hour, and $15 per inspection-hour, respectively. Other information follows:

Cost Driver Information		
	Cat-allac	Dog-eriffic
Number of units per batch	25	9
Setup time per batch	1.50 hours	1.75 hours
Inspection time per batch	0.5 hour	0.7 hour

Nonmanufacturing fixed costs for March equal $32,000, half of which are salaries. Salaries are expected to increase 5% in April. The only variable nonmanufacturing cost is sales commission, equal to 1% of sales revenue.

Required Prepare the following for April:

1. Revenues budget
2. Production budget in units
3. Direct material usage budget and direct material purchases budget
4. Direct manufacturing labor cost budget
5. Manufacturing overhead cost budgets for each of the three activities
6. Budgeted unit cost of ending finished goods inventory and ending inventories budget
7. Cost of goods sold budget
8. Nonmanufacturing costs budget
9. Budgeted income statement (ignore income taxes)
10. What questions might the CEO ask the management team when reviewing the budget?
11. How does preparing the budget help Animal Gear's management team better manage the company?

12-29 Cash budget (continuation of 12-28). Refer to the information in Problem 12-28.

Assume the following: Animal Gear (AG) does not make any sales on credit. AG sells only to the public, and accepts cash and credit cards; 90% of its sales are to customers using credit cards, for which AG gets the cash right away, less a 2% transaction fee.

Purchases of materials are on account. AG pays for half the purchases in the period of the purchase, and the other half in the following period. At the end of March, AG owes suppliers $8,000.

AG plans to replace a machine in April at a net cash cost of $13,000.

Labor, other manufacturing costs, and nonmanufacturing costs are paid in cash in the month incurred except of course depreciation, which is not a cash flow. $25,000 of the manufacturing cost and $10,000 of the nonmanufacturing cost for April is depreciation.

AG currently has a $2,000 loan at an annual interest rate of 24%. The interest is paid at the end of each month. If AG has more than $10,000 cash at the end of April it will pay back the loan. AG owes $5,000 in income taxes that need to be remitted in April. AG has cash of $5,900 on hand at the end of March.

Required

1. Prepare a cash budget for April for Animal Gear.
2. Why do Animal Gear's managers prepare a cash budget in addition to the revenue, expenses, and operating income budget?

12-30 Comprehensive operating budget. Sleds, Inc., manufactures and sells snowboards. Sleds manufactures a single model, the Pipex. In the summer of 2012, Sleds' management accountant gathered the following data to prepare budgets for 2013:

Materials and Labor Requirements

Direct materials	
Wood	7 board feet (b.f.) per snowboard
Fiberglass	6 yards per snowboard
Direct manufacturing labor	6 hours per snowboard

Sleds' management expects to sell 1,275 snowboards during 2013 at an estimated retail price of $550 per board. Furthermore, the CEO expects 2013 beginning inventory of 500 snowboards and would like to end 2013 with 700 snowboards in stock.

Direct Materials Inventories		
	Beginning Inventory 1/1/2013	Ending Inventory 12/31/2013
Wood	2,010 b.f.	1,510 b.f.
Fiberglass	1,010 yards	2,500 yards

Variable manufacturing overhead is $10 per direct manufacturing labor-hour. There are also $70,800 in fixed manufacturing overhead costs budgeted for 2013. Sleds combines both variable and fixed manufacturing overhead into a single rate based on direct manufacturing labor-hours. Variable marketing costs are allocated at the rate of $260 per sales visit. The marketing plan calls for 35 sales visits during 2013. Finally, there are $32,400 in fixed nonmanufacturing costs budgeted for 2013.

Other data include:

	2012 Unit Price	2013 Unit Price
Wood	$29.00 per b.f.	$31.00 per b.f.
Fiberglass	$ 5.00 per yard	$10.00 per yard
Direct manufacturing labor	$25.00 per hour	$26.00 per hour

The inventoriable unit cost for ending finished goods inventory on December 31, 2012, is $440.00. Assume Sleds uses a FIFO inventory method for both direct materials and finished goods. Ignore work in process in your calculations.

Required

1. Prepare the 2013 revenues budget (in dollars).
2. Prepare the 2013 production budget (in units).
3. Prepare the direct material usage and purchases budgets for 2013.
4. Prepare a direct manufacturing labor budget for 2013.
5. Prepare a manufacturing overhead budget for 2013.
6. What is the budgeted manufacturing overhead rate for 2013?
7. What is the budgeted manufacturing overhead cost per output unit in 2013?
8. Calculate the cost of a snowboard manufactured in 2013.
9. Prepare an ending inventory budget for both direct materials and finished goods for 2013.
10. Prepare a cost of goods sold budget for 2013.
11. Prepare the budgeted income statement for Sleds, Inc., for the year ending December 31, 2013.
12. What questions might the CEO ask the management team when reviewing the budget? Should the CEO set stretch targets? Explain briefly.
13. How does preparing the budget help Sleds' management team better manage the company?

12-31 Cash budgeting. Retail outlets purchase snowboards from Sleds, Inc., throughout the year. However, in anticipation of late summer and early fall purchases, outlets ramp up inventories from May through August. Outlets are billed when boards are ordered. Invoices are payable within 60 days. From past experience, Sleds' accountant projects 10% of invoices will be paid in the month invoiced, 55% will be paid in the following month, and 35% of invoices will be paid 2 months after the month of invoice. The average selling price per snowboard is $550.

To meet demand, Sleds increases production from April through July because the snowboards are produced a month prior to their projected sale. Direct materials are purchased in the month of production and are paid for during the following month (terms are payment in full within 30 days of the invoice date). During this period there is no production for inventory, and no materials are purchased for inventory.

Direct manufacturing labor and manufacturing overhead are paid monthly. Variable manufacturing overhead is incurred at the rate of $10 per direct manufacturing labor-hour. Variable marketing costs are driven by the number of sales visits. However, there are no sales visits during the months studied. Sleds, Inc., also incurs fixed manufacturing overhead costs of $5,900 per month and fixed nonmanufacturing overhead costs of $2,700 per month.

Projected Sales	
May, 90 units	August, 110 units
June, 140 units	September, 60 units
July, 170 units	October, 50 units

Direct Materials and Direct Manufacturing Labor Utilization and Cost			
	Units per Board	Price per Unit	Unit
Wood	7	$31	board feet
Fiberglass	6	10	yard
Direct manufacturing labor	6	26	hour

The beginning cash balance for July 1, 2013, is $10,000. On October 1, 2012, Sleds had a cash crunch and borrowed $25,000 on a 6% 1-year note with interest payable monthly. The note is due October 1, 2013.

Required

1. Prepare a cash budget for the months of July through September 2013. Show supporting schedules for the calculation of receivables and payables.
2. Will Sleds be in a position to pay off the $25,000 1-year note that is due on October 1, 2013? If not, what actions would you recommend to Sleds' management?
3. Suppose Sleds is interested in maintaining a minimum cash balance of $11,000. Will the company be able to maintain such a balance during all 3 months analyzed? If not, suggest a suitable cash management strategy.
4. Why do Sleds' managers prepare a cash budget in addition to the revenue, expenses, and operating income budget?

12-32 Cash budgeting. On December 1, 2012, the Itallem Wholesale Co. is attempting to project cash receipts and disbursements through January 31, 2013. On this latter date, a note will be payable in the amount of $106,000. This amount was borrowed in September to carry the company through the seasonal peak in November and December.

Selected general ledger balances on December 1 are:

Cash	$99,000	
Inventory	102,000	
Accounts payable		86,000

Sales terms call for a 3% discount if payment is made within the first 10 days of the month after sale, with the balance due by the end of the month after sale. Experience has shown that 40% of the billings will be collected within the discount period, 25% by the end of the month after purchase, and 20% in the following month. The remaining 15% will be uncollectible. There are no cash sales.

The average selling price of the company's products is $160 per unit. Actual and projected sales are:

October actual	$ 286,000
November actual	560,000
December estimated	512,000
January estimated	560,000
February estimated	304,000
Total estimated for year ending June 30, 2013	$3,040,000

All purchases are payable within 15 days. Approximately 60% of the purchases in a month are paid that month, and the rest the following month. The average unit purchase cost is $120. Target ending inventories are 560 units plus 15% of the next month's unit sales.

Total budgeted marketing, distribution, and customer-service costs for the year are $660,000. Of this amount, $150,000 are considered fixed (and include depreciation of $39,600). The remainder varies with sales. Both fixed and variable marketing, distribution, and customer-service costs are paid as incurred.

Required

1. Prepare a cash budget for December 2012 and January 2013. Supply supporting schedules for collections of receivables; payments for merchandise; and marketing, distribution, and customer-service costs.
2. Why do Itallem's managers prepare a cash budget in addition to the operating income budget?

12-33 Comprehensive problem; ABC manufacturing, two products. Hazlett, Inc., operates at capacity and makes plastic combs and hairbrushes. Although the combs and brushes are a matching set, they are sold individually and so the sales mix is not 1:1. Hazlett's management is planning its annual budget for fiscal year 2013. Here is information for 2013:

Input Prices	
Direct materials	
Plastic	$ 0.30 per ounce
Bristles	$ 0.75 per bunch
Direct manufacturing labor	$18 per direct manufacturing labor-hour

Input Quantities per Unit of Output		
	Combs	Brushes
Direct materials		
Plastic	5 ounces	8 ounces
Bristles	—	16 bunches
Direct manufacturing labor	0.05 hours	0.2 hours
Machine-hours (MH)	0.025 MH	0.1 MH

Inventory Information, Direct Materials		
	Plastic	Bristles
Beginning inventory	1,600 ounces	1,820 bunches
Target ending inventory	1,766 ounces	2,272 bunches
Cost of beginning inventory	$456	$1,419

Hazlett accounts for direct materials using a FIFO cost flow.

Sales and Inventory Information, Finished Goods		
	Combs	Brushes
Expected sales in units	12,000	14,000
Selling price	$ 9	$ 30
Target ending inventory in units	1,200	1,400
Beginning inventory in units	600	1,200
Beginning inventory in dollars	$ 2,700	$27,180

Hazlett uses a FIFO cost flow assumption for finished goods inventory.

Combs are manufactured in batches of 200, and brushes are manufactured in batches of 100. It takes 20 minutes to set up for a batch of combs, and 1 hour to set up for a batch of brushes.

Hazlett uses activity-based costing and has classified all overhead costs as shown in the following table. Budgeted fixed overhead costs vary with capacity. Hazlett operates at capacity so budgeted fixed overhead cost per unit equals the budgeted fixed overhead costs divided by the budgeted quantities of the cost allocation base.

Cost Type	Budgeted Variable	Budgeted Fixed	Cost Driver/Allocation Base
Manufacturing			
Materials handling	$17,235	$22,500	Number of ounces of plastic used
Setup	10,245	16,650	Setup-hours
Processing	11,640	30,000	Machine-hours
Inspection	10,500	1,560	Number of units produced

Cost Type	Budgeted Variable	Budgeted Fixed	Cost Driver/Allocation Base
Nonmanufacturing			
Marketing	$21,150	$90,000	Sales revenue
Distribution	0	1,170	Number of deliveries

Delivery trucks transport units sold in delivery sizes of 1,000 combs or 1,000 brushes.

Required Do the following for the year 2013:

1. Prepare the revenues budget.
2. Use the revenue budget to
   a. find the budgeted allocation rate for marketing costs.
   b. find the budgeted number of deliveries and allocation rate for distribution costs.
3. Prepare the production budget in units.
4. Use the production budget to
   a. find the budgeted number of setups, setup-hours, and the allocation rate for setup costs.
   b. find the budgeted total machine-hours and the allocation rate for processing costs.
   c. find the budgeted total units produced and the allocation rate for inspection costs.
5. Prepare the direct material usage budget and the direct material purchases budgets in both units and dollars; round to whole dollars.
6. Use the direct material usage budget to find the budgeted allocation rate for materials-handling costs.
7. Prepare the direct manufacturing labor cost budget.
8. Prepare the manufacturing overhead cost budget for materials handling, setup, processing, and inspection costs.
9. Prepare the budgeted unit cost of ending finished goods inventory and ending inventories budget.
10. Prepare the cost of goods sold budget.
11. Prepare the nonmanufacturing overhead costs budget for marketing and distribution.
12. Prepare a budgeted income statement (ignore income taxes).
13. What questions might the CEO ask the management team when reviewing the budget?
14. How does preparing the budget help Hazlett's management team better manage the company?

12-34 Budgeting and ethics. Jayzee Company manufactures a variety of products in a variety of departments, and evaluates departments and departmental managers by comparing actual cost and output relative to the budget. Departmental managers help create the budgets, and usually provide information about input quantities for materials, labor, and overhead costs.

Kurt Jackson is the manager of the department that produces product Z. Kurt has estimated these inputs for product Z:

Input	Budget Quantity per Unit of Output
Direct material	8 pounds
Direct manufacturing labor	30 minutes
Machine time	24 minutes

The department produces about 100 units of product Z each day. Kurt's department always gets excellent evaluations, sometimes exceeding budgeted production quantities. For each 100 units of product Z produced, the company uses, on average, about 48 hours of direct manufacturing labor (eight people working 6 hours each), 790 pounds of material, and 39.5 machine-hours.

Top management of Jayzee Company has decided to implement budget standards that will challenge the workers in each department, and it has asked Kurt to design more challenging input standards for product Z. Kurt provides top management with the following input quantities:

Input	Budget Quantity per Unit of Output
Direct material	7.9 pounds
Direct manufacturing labor	29 minutes
Machine time	23.6 minutes

Discuss the following:

Required

1. Are these budget standards challenging for the department that produces product Z?
2. Why do you suppose Kurt picked these particular standards?
3. What steps can Jayzee Company's top management take to make sure Kurt's standards really meet the goals of the firm?

12-35 Human aspects of budgeting in a service firm. Vidal Sanson owns three upscale hair salons: Bristles I, II, and III. Each of the salons has a manager and 10 stylists who rent space in the salons as independent contractors and who pay a fee of 10% of each week's revenue to the salon as rent. In exchange they get to use the facility and utilities, but must bring their own equipment.

The manager of each salon schedules each customer appointment to last an hour, and then allows the stylist 10 minutes between appointments to clean up, rest, and prepare for the next appointment. The salons are open from 10:00 a.m. to 6:00 p.m., so each stylist can serve seven customers per day. Stylists each work 5 days a week on a staggered schedule, so the salon is open 7 days a week. Everyone works on Saturdays, but some stylists have Sunday and Monday off, some have Tuesday and Wednesday off, and some have Thursday and Friday off.

Vidal Sanson knows that utility costs are rising. Vidal wants to increase revenues to cover at least some part of rising utility costs, so Vidal tells each of the managers to find a way to increase productivity in the salons so that the stylists will pay more to the salons. Vidal does not want to increase the rental fee above 10% of revenue for fear the stylists will leave. And each salon has only 10 stations, so Vidal feels each salon cannot hire more than 10 full-time stylists.

The manager of Bristles I attacks the problem by simply telling the stylists that, from now on, customers will be scheduled for 40-minute appointments and breaks will be 5 minutes. This will allow each stylist to add one more customer per day.

The manager of Bristles II asks the stylists on a voluntary basis to work one extra hour per day, from 10:00 a.m. to 7:00 p.m., to add an additional customer per stylist per day.

The manager of Bristles III sits down with the stylists and discusses the issue. After considering shortening the appointment and break times, or lengthening the hours of operation, one of the stylists says, "I know we rent stations in your store, but I am willing to share my station. You could hire an 11th stylist, who will simply work at whatever station is vacant during our days off. Since we use our own equipment, this will not be a problem for me as long as there is a secure place I can leave my equipment on my days off." Most of the other stylists agree that this is a good solution.

Required

1. Which manager's style do you think is most effective? Why?
2. How do you think the stylists will react to the managers of salons I and II? If the stylists are displeased, how can they indicate their displeasure?
3. In Bristles III, if the stylists did not want to share their stations with another party, how else could they find a way to increase revenues?
4. Refer again to the action that the manager of Bristles I has chosen. How does this action relate to the concept of stretch targets?

12-36 Comprehensive budgeting problem; activity-based costing, operating and financial budgets. Tyva makes a very popular undyed cloth sandal in one style, but in Regular and Deluxe. The Regular sandals have cloth soles and the Deluxe sandals have cloth-covered wooden soles. Tyva is preparing its budget for June 2013 and has estimated sales based on past experience.

Other information for the month of June follows:

Input Prices

Direct materials	
Cloth	$5.25 per yard
Wood	$7.50 per board foot
Direct manufacturing labor	$15 per direct manufacturing labor-hour

Input Quantities per Unit of Output (per pair of sandals)		
	Regular	Deluxe
Direct materials		
Cloth	1.3 yards	1.5 yards
Wood	0	2 b.f.
Direct manufacturing labor-hours (DMLH)	5 hours	7 hours
Setup-hours per batch	2 hours	3 hours

Inventory Information, Direct Materials		
	Cloth	Wood
Beginning inventory	610 yards	800 b.f.
Target ending inventory	386 yards	295 b.f.
Cost of beginning inventory	$3,219	$6,060

Tyva accounts for direct materials using a FIFO cost flow assumption.

Sales and Inventory Information, Finished Goods		
	Regular	Deluxe
Expected sales in units (pairs of sandals)	2,000	3,000
Selling price	$ 120	$ 195
Target ending inventory in units	400	600
Beginning inventory in units	250	650
Beginning inventory in dollars	$23,250	$92,625

Tyva uses a FIFO cost flow assumption for finished goods inventory.

All the sandals are made in batches of 50 pairs of sandals. Tyva incurs manufacturing overhead costs, marketing and general administration, and shipping costs. Besides materials and labor, manufacturing costs include setup, processing, and inspection costs. Tyva ships 40 pairs of sandals per shipment. Tyva uses activity-based costing and has classified all overhead costs for the month of June as shown in the following chart:

Cost type	Denominator Activity	Rate
Manufacturing		
Setup	Setup-hours	$18 per setup-hour
Processing	Direct manufacturing labor-hours	$1.80 per DMLH
Inspection	Number of pairs of sandals	$1.35 per pair
Nonmanufacturing		
Marketing and general administration	Sales revenue	8%
Shipping	Number of shipments	$15 per shipment

Required

1. Prepare each of the following for June:
   a. Revenues budget
   b. Production budget in units
   c. Direct material usage budget and direct material purchases budget in both units and dollars; round to dollars
   d. Direct manufacturing labor cost budget
   e. Manufacturing overhead cost budgets for processing and setup activities
   f. Budgeted unit cost of ending finished goods inventory and ending inventories budget
   g. Cost of goods sold budget
   h. Marketing and general administration costs budget

2. Tyva's balance sheet for May 31 follows.

Tyva Balance Sheet as of May 31		
Assets		
Cash		$ 9,435
Accounts receivable	$324,000	
Less: Allowance for bad debts	16,200	307,800
Inventories		
Direct materials		9,279
Finished goods		115,875
Fixed assets	$870,000	
Less: Accumulated depreciation	136,335	733,665
Total assets		$1,176,054
Liabilities and Equity		
Accounts payable		$ 15,600
Taxes payable		10,800
Interest payable		750
Long-term debt		150,000
Common stock		300,000
Retained earnings		698,904
Total liabilities and equity		$1,176,054

Use the balance sheet and the following information to prepare a cash budget for Tyva for June. Round to dollars.

- All sales are on account; 60% are collected in the month of the sale, 38% are collected the following month, and 2% are never collected and written off as bad debts.
- All purchases of materials are on account. Tyva pays for 80% of purchases in the month of purchase and 20% in the following month.
- All other costs are paid in the month incurred, including the declaration and payment of a $15,000 cash dividend in June.
- Tyva is making monthly interest payments of 0.5% (6% per year) on a $150,000 long-term loan.
- Tyva plans to pay the $10,800 of taxes owed as of May 31 in the month of June. Income tax expense for June is zero.
- 30% of processing, setup, and inspection costs and 10% of marketing and general administration and shipping costs are depreciation.

3. Prepare a budgeted income statement for June.

4. What questions might the CEO ask the management team when reviewing the budget?

5. How does preparing the budget help Tyva's management team better manage the company?

Case

Western Pants

Western Pants, Inc. is one of America's oldest clothing firms. Founded in the mid-nineteenth century, the firm successfully weathered lean years and the Great Depression largely as the result of the market durability of its dominant, and at times only, product—blue denim jeans. Until 1950, the firm had never seriously marketed other products or even additional types of trousers. A significant change in marketing strategy in the 1950s altered that course, which Western's management had revered for 100 years. Aggressive new managers decided at that time that Western's well-established name could and should be used to market other lines of pants. Consumers welcomed initial offerings in a men's casual trouser. The company produced different patterns of this basic style and stylish, tailored variations of the same casual motif almost yearly.

Alert managerial planning in the early 1960s enabled Western to become the first pants manufacturer to establish itself in the revolutionary "wash and wear" field. Further refinement of this process broadened the weave and fabric types that could be tailored into fashionable trousers and still survive enough machine wash and dry cycles to satisfy Western's rigid quality-control standards.

With the advent of "mod" clothing and the generally casual yet stylish garb that became acceptable attire at semiformal affairs, pants became fashion attire, rather than the mere clothing staples they had been in years past. Western quickly gained a foothold in the bell-bottom and flare market, and from there grew with the "leg look" to its present position as the free world's largest clothing manufacturer.

Today Western, in addition to its still remarkably popular blue denim jeans, offers a complete line of casual trousers, an extensive array of "dress and fashion jeans" for both men and boys, and a complete line of pants for women. Last year the firm sold approximately 70 million pairs of pants.

Production

For the last twenty years, Western Pants has been in a somewhat unusual and enviable market position. In each of those years, it has sold virtually all its production and often had to begin rationing its clothing to established customers or refusing orders from new customers as early as six months prior to the close of the production year. Whereas most business ventures face limited demand and, in the long run, excess production, Western, whose sales have doubled each five years during that twenty year period, has had to face excess and growing demand with limited although rapidly growing production capacity.

The firm has established 33 plants in its 150 year history. These production units vary somewhat in output capacity, but the average is roughly 20,000 pairs of trousers per week. With the exception of two or three plants that usually produce only blue denim jeans during the entire production year, Western's plants produce various styles of pants for all of Western's departments (see Western Pants Exhibit 1).

The firm has for some years augmented its own productive capacity by contractual agreements with independent manufacturers of pants. At the present time, there are nearly 20 such contractors producing all lines of Western's pants (including blue jeans). Last year, contractors produced about one-third of the total volume in units sold by Western.

The Budgeting and Responsibility Accounting System

"We treat all our plants pretty much as cost centers (see Western Pants Exhibit 1)," Mr. Wicks, Western's vice president for production and operations, commented. "Of course, we exercise no control whatever over the contractors. We just pay them the agreed price per pair of pants. Our own operations at each plant have been examined thoroughly by industrial engineers. You know, time-motion studies and all. We've updated this information consistently for over ten years. I'm quite proud of the way we've been able to tie our budgeted hours down. Over the years, we've even been

Source: Horngren/Datar, CASES IN COST ACCOUNTING, (c) 1994. Printed and electronically reproduced by permission of Pearson Education, Inc., Upper Saddle River, New Jersey.

Western Pants Exhibit 1

Organization Chart: Western Pants Inc.

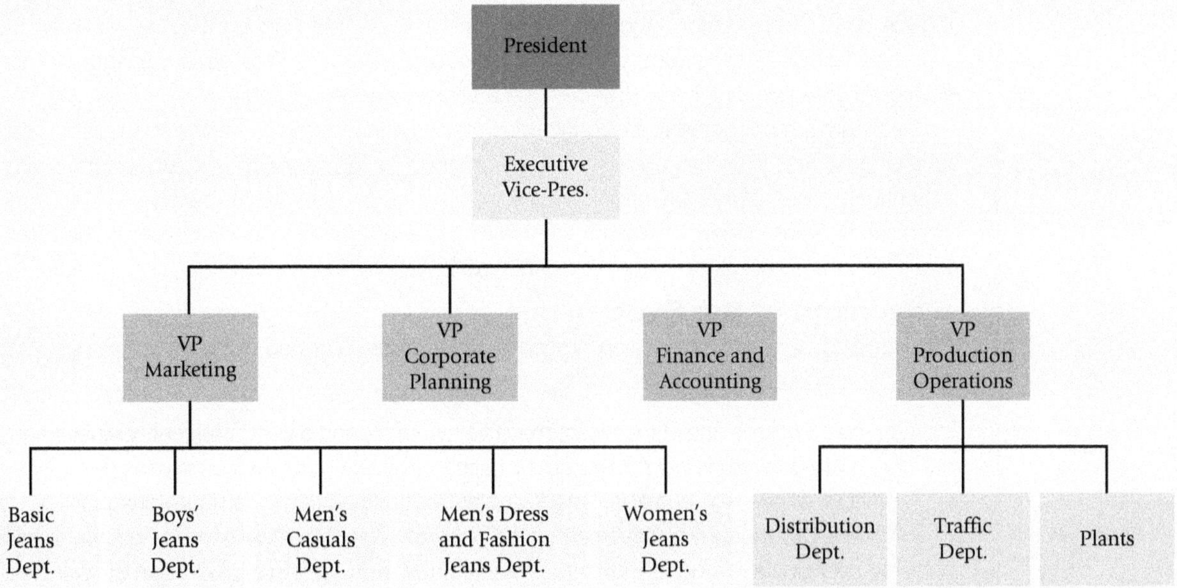

able to develop learning curves that tell us how long after a product switchover it will take production to reach the budgeted time per unit for the new style. We know the rate at which total production time per unit reaches the budgeted time for every basic style of pants that Western makes!

We use this information for budgeting a plant's costs. The marketing staff figure out how many pants of each style it wants produced each year and passes that information on to us. We divvy up the total production among plants pretty much by eyeballing the total amounts for each style of pants. We like to put one plant to work for a whole year on one style of pants, if that's possible. It saves time losses from startups and changeovers. We can sell all we make, you know, so we like to keep plants working at peak efficiency. Unfortunately, marketing always manages to come up with a lot of midyear changes, so this objective winds up like a lot of other good intentions in life. You know what they say about the road to Hell! Anyhow, it's still a game plan we like to stick to, and two or three plants making the basic blue jeans accomplish it every year.

The budgeting operation begins with me and my staff determining what a plant's quota for each month should be for one year ahead of time. We do this mostly by looking at what past performance at a plant has been. Of course, we add a little to this. We expect people to improve around here. These yearly budgets are updated at the end of each month in the light of the previous month's production. Budget figures incidentally, are in units of production. If a plant manager beats this budget figure, we feel he's done well. If he can't meet the quota, his people haven't been working at what the engineers feel is a very reasonable level of speed and efficiency. Or possibly absenteeism, a big problem in all our plants, has been excessively high. Or turnover, another big problem, has been unacceptably high. At any rate when the quota hasn't been made, we want to know why, and we want to get the problem corrected as quickly as possible.

Given the number of pants that a plant actually produces in a month, we can determine, by using the budgeted numbers I was boasting about earlier, the number of labor hours each operation should have accumulated during the month. We measure this figure against the hours we actually paid for to determine how a plant performed as a cost center. As you might guess, we don't like unfavorable variances here anymore than shortfalls in a plant manager's performance against quota.

We watch the plant performance figures monthly. If a plant manager meets his quota and his cost variances are OK, we let him know that we are pleased. I almost always call them myself and relay my satisfaction, or, if they haven't done well, my concern. I think this kind of prompt feedback is important. We also look for other things in evaluating a plant manager. Has he or she maintained good community relations? Are his or her people happy? The family that owns almost all of Western's stock is very concerned about this."

A Christmas bonus constitutes the meat of Western's reward system. Mr. Wicks and his two chief assistants subjectively rate a plant manager's performance for the year on a one to five scale. Western's top management at the close of each year determines a bonus base by evaluating the firms overall performance and profit for the year. That bonus base has recently been as high as $12,000. The performance rating for each member of Western's management team is multiplied by this bonus base to determine a given manager's bonus.

Western's management group includes many finance and marketing specialists. The case writer noted that these personnel, who are located at the corporate headquarters, were consistently awarded higher ratings by their supervisors than were plant managers. This difference consistently approached a full point. Last year, the average rating in the corporate headquarters was 3.85; the average for plant managers was 2.92.

Evaluation of the System

Mia Packard, a recent accounting graduate, gave some informed opinions regarding Western's production operation and its budgeting procedures.

> "Mr. Wicks is one of the nicest men I've ever met, and a very intelligent businessman. But I really don't think that the system he uses to evaluate his plant managers is good for the firm as a whole. Not long ago, I made a plant visit as part of my company orientation program, and I accidentally discovered that the plant manager 'hoarded' some of the pants produced over quota in a good month to protect himself against future production deficiencies. That plant manager was really upset that I stumbled onto his storehouse. He insisted that all the other managers did the same thing and begged me not to tell Mr. Wicks. This seems like precisely the wrong kind of behavior in a firm that usually has to turn away orders! Yet I believe the quota system that is one of Western's tools for evaluating plant performance encourages this type of behavior. I don't think I could prove this, but I suspect that most plant managers aren't really pushing for maximum production. If they do increase output, their quotas are going to go up, and yet they won't receive any immediate monetary rewards to compensate for the increase in their responsibilities or requirements. If I were a plant manager, I wouldn't want my production exceeding quota until the end of the year.
>
> Also, Mr. Wicks came up to the vice presidency through the ranks. He was a plant manager himself once—a very good plant manager. But he has a tendency to feel that everyone should run a plant the way he did. For example, in Mr. Wick's plant there were eleven workers for every supervisor or member of the office and administrative staff. Since then, Mr. Wicks has elevated this supervision ratio to some sort of sacred index of leadership efficiency. All plant managers shoot for it, and as a result, usually understaff their offices. As a result, we can't get timely and accurate reports from plants. There simply aren't enough people in the offices out there to generate the information we desperately need when we need it.
>
> Another thing—some of the plants have been built in the last five years or so and have much newer equipment, yet there's no difference in the budgeted hours calculated for these plants and the older ones. This puts the managers of older plants at a terrific disadvantage. Their sewing machines break down more often, require maintenance, and probably aren't as easy to work with."

Required

1. Describe the steps and the process of developing cost budgets for operations within a plant at Western Pants?
2. For what purposes do managers at Western Pants use budgets?
3. With respect to plant operations, what decisions are made by headquarters and what decisions are made by plant managers? Do you regard plant managers as cost centers or profit centers?
4. What problems at the plants result from the budgeting system and why?
5. What changes in Western's budgeting and responsibility accounting system would you recommend?

Flexible Budgets, Cost Variances, and Management Control

13

Learning Objectives

1. Explain static budgets and static-budget variances
2. Develop flexible budgets and compute flexible-budget variances and sales-volume variances
3. Compute price variances and efficiency variances for direct-cost categories
4. Plan for variable and fixed overhead costs and calculate budgeted variable and fixed overhead cost rates
5. Partition the variable overhead flexible-budget variance into variable overhead efficiency and spending variances
6. Compute the fixed overhead flexible-budget (or spending) variance and the fixed overhead production-volume variance
7. Show how the variance analysis approach reconciles the actual results for a period with the results expected for that period
8. Understand how managers use variances

Every organization, regardless of its profitability or growth, has to step back and take a hard look at its spending decisions. And when customers are affected by a recession, the need for managers to employ budgeting and variance analysis tools for cost control becomes especially critical. By studying variances, managers can focus on where specific performances have fallen short and use the information they learn to make corrective adjustments and achieve significant savings for their companies.

For a retailer such as Starbucks, an intricate understanding of direct costs is essential in order to make each high-quality beverage at the lowest possible cost. Companies such as DuPont, International Paper, and U.S. Steel, which invest heavily in capital equipment, or Amazon.com and Yahoo!, which invest heavily in software, have a similar need to control their overhead costs. Understanding the behavior of costs, planning for them, performing variance analysis, and acting appropriately on the results are critical functions for managers.

In Chapter 12, you saw how budgets help managers with their planning function. We now explain how budgets, specifically flexible budgets, are used to compute variances, which assist managers in their control function. Flexible budgets and variances enable managers to make meaningful comparisons of actual results against planned performance and gain insights into why they differ. Variance analysis supports the critical final function in the five-step decision-making process by making it possible for managers to *evaluate performance and learn* after decisions are implemented. The Chapter at a Glance below outlines how this chapter explains this evaluation process.

Chapter at a Glance

- Variances provide managers with a framework for correctly assessing current performance and help them take corrective actions to ensure that decisions are implemented correctly. They also enable managers to generate more informed predictions about the future.
- Cost variances are most informative when calculated relative to the flexible budget, which adjusts the master budget for the actual level of output during the period.
- For variable cost categories, flexible budget variances are typically partitioned into two parts: (1) the portion caused by unexpected shifts in input prices and (2) the part that results from unexpected changes in the efficiency with which inputs are processed.

- In a standard-costing system, managers apply costs to output produced by multiplying the standard prices or overhead rates by the standard quantities of inputs or drivers allowed for actual outputs produced. This simplifies the accounting and also enables managers to evaluate performance and take corrective action when these standards are subsequently compared to the actual costs incurred.
- The difference between the costs applied in a standard-costing system and the actual costs incurred by the firm equals the flexible budget variance. For fixed overhead alone, the difference also includes the production-volume variance, which alerts managers to changes in capacity utilization relative to the level anticipated at the start of the period.
- Managers use standards to identify deviations from desired outcomes. They set standards based on engineering studies, continuous improvement goals, or by benchmarking against peer or "best practice" organizations.
- Firms often supplement variance information with nonfinancial performance measures that provide more timely feedback on individual aspects of a manager's and/or employee's performance, thus enabling faster learning and the ability to take corrective action sooner.

Learning Objective 1

Explain static budgets

... the master budget based on output planned at start of period

and static budget variances

... the difference between actual results and the corresponding budget amounts in the static budget

Static Budgets and Variances

A **variance** is the difference between actual results and expected performance. The expected performance is also called **budgeted performance,** which is a point of reference for making comparisons.

The Use of Variances

Variances bring together the planning and control functions of management. They assist managers in implementing their strategies by enabling *management by exception.* **Management by exception** is the practice of focusing management attention on areas that are not operating as expected (such as a large shortfall in sales of a product) and devoting less time to areas operating as expected. In other words, by highlighting the areas that have deviated most from expectations, variances enable managers to focus their efforts on the most critical areas of the design, engineering, production, or customer experience process. Consider scrap and rework costs at a Maytag appliances plant. If actual costs are much higher than originally budgeted, the variances will guide managers to seek explanations and to take early corrective action, ensuring that future operations result in less scrap and rework. Sometimes a large positive variance may occur, such as a significant decrease in manufacturing costs of a product. Managers will try to understand the reasons for this decrease (better operator training or changes in manufacturing methods, for example), so these practices can be appropriately continued and transferred to other divisions within the organization.

Variances are also used in performance evaluation and to motivate managers. Production-line managers at Maytag may have quarterly efficiency incentives linked to achieving a budgeted amount of operating costs.

Sometimes variances suggest that the company should consider a change in strategy. For example, large negative variances caused by excessive defect rates for a new product may suggest a flawed product design. Managers may then want to investigate the product design and potentially change the mix of products being offered.

Variance analysis contributes in many ways to making the five-step decision-making process more effective. It allows managers to evaluate performance and learn by providing a framework for correctly assessing current performance. In turn, managers take corrective actions to ensure that their employees correctly implement their decisions and attain previously budgeted results. Variances also enable managers to generate more informed predictions about the future, and thereby improve the quality of the five-step decision-making process.

The benefits of variance analysis are not restricted to companies. In today's difficult economic environment, where many constituents are contending with the recession, public officials have realized that it is important to use variance monitoring to help stabilize tax and fee increases. For example, the city of Scottsdale, Arizona, monitors the taxes and fees it collects against expenditures monthly. Why? One of the city's goals is to keep its water-usage rates stable, with incremental increases from year to year that users can afford instead of less frequent but larger increases. By monitoring the extent to which water revenues are meeting current expenses and obligations, while simultaneously building up funds for future infrastructure projects, the city can avoid sudden spikes in the rate it charges to customers.[1]

How important is variance analysis? A survey by the United Kingdom's Chartered Institute of Management Accountants in July 2009 found that variance analysis was easily the most popular costing tool in practice across organizations of all sizes.

Static Budgets and Static-Budget Variances

We take a closer look at variances by examining one company's accounting system. Note as you study the exhibits in this chapter that "level" followed by a number denotes the amount of detail shown by a variance analysis. Level 1 reports the least detail, level 2 offers more information; and so on.

Consider Webb Company, a firm that manufactures and sells jackets that require tailoring and many other hand operations. Webb sells exclusively to distributors, who in turn sell to independent clothing stores and retail chains. For simplicity, we assume the following:

1. Webb's only costs are in the manufacturing function; Webb incurs no costs in other value-chain functions, such as marketing and distribution.
2. All units manufactured in April 2013 are sold in April 2013, so all direct materials are purchased and used in the same budget period.
3. There is no direct materials inventory at either the beginning or the end of the period. No work-in-process or finished goods inventories exist at either the beginning or the end of the period.

Webb has three variable-cost categories. The budgeted variable cost per jacket for each category is:

Cost Category	Variable Cost per Jacket
Direct material costs	$60
Direct manufacturing labor costs	16
Variable manufacturing overhead costs	12
Total variable costs	$88

The *number of units manufactured* is the cost driver for direct materials, direct manufacturing labor, and variable manufacturing overhead. The relevant range for the cost driver is from 0 to 12,000 jackets. Budgeted and actual data for April 2013 are:

Budgeted fixed costs for production between 0 and 12,000 jackets	$276,000	
Budgeted selling price	$ 120	per jacket
Budgeted production and sales	12,000	jackets
Actual production and sales	10,000	jackets

The **static budget,** or master budget, is based on the level of output planned at the start of the budget period. The master budget is called a static budget because the budget for the period is developed around a single (static) planned output level. Exhibit 13-1, column 3, presents the static budget for Webb Company for April 2013 that was prepared at the end of 2012. For each line item in the income statement, Exhibit 13-1, column 1, displays data for the actual April results. For example, actual revenues are $1,250,000, and the actual selling price is $1,250,000 ÷ 10,000 jackets = $125 per jacket—compared with the budgeted selling price of $120 per jacket. Similarly, actual direct material costs are $621,600, and the direct material cost per jacket is $621,600 ÷ 10,000 = $62.16 per jacket—compared with the budgeted direct material cost per jacket of $60. We describe potential reasons and explanations for these differences as we discuss different variances throughout the chapter.

[1] For an excellent discussion and other related examples from governmental settings, see S. Kavanagh and C. Swanson, "Tactical Financial Management: Cash Flow and Budgetary Variance Analysis," *Government Finance Review* (October 1, 2009).

Exhibit 13-1

Static Budget–Based Variance Analysis for Webb Company for April 2013[a]

Level 1 Analysis

	Actual Results (1)	Static-Budget Variances (2) = (1) – (3)	Static Budget (3)
Units sold	10,000	2,000 U	12,000
Revenues	$ 1,250,000	$190,000 U	$1,440,000
Variable costs			
Direct materials	621,600	98,400 F	720,000
Direct manufacturing labor	198,000	6,000 U	192,000
Variable manufacturing overhead	130,500	13,500 F	144,000
Total variable costs	950,100	105,900 F	1,056,000
Contribution margin	299,900	84,100 U	384,000
Fixed costs	285,000	9,000 U	276,000
Operating income	$ 14,900	$ 93,100 U	$ 108,000

$ 93,100 U
Static-budget variance

[a]F = favorable effect on operating income; U = unfavorable effect on operating income.

The **static-budget variance** (see Exhibit 13-1, column 2) is the difference between the actual result and the corresponding budgeted amount in the static budget.

A **favorable variance,** denoted "F" in this book, has the effect, when considered in isolation, of increasing operating income relative to the budgeted amount. For revenue items, F means actual revenues exceed budgeted revenues. For cost items, F means actual costs are less than budgeted costs. An **unfavorable variance,** denoted "U" in this book, has the effect, when viewed in isolation, of decreasing operating income relative to the budgeted amount. Unfavorable variances are also called *adverse variances* in some countries, such as the United Kingdom.

The unfavorable static-budget variance for operating income of $93,100 in Exhibit 13-1 is calculated by subtracting static-budget operating income of $108,000 from actual operating income of $14,900:

$$\begin{array}{c}\text{Static-budget}\\ \text{variance for}\\ \text{operating income}\end{array} = \begin{array}{c}\text{Actual}\\ \text{result}\end{array} - \begin{array}{c}\text{Static-budget}\\ \text{amount}\end{array}$$

$$= \$14{,}900 - \$108{,}000$$

$$= \$93{,}100 \text{ U.}$$

The analysis in Exhibit 13-1 provides managers with additional information on the static-budget variance for operating income of $93,100 U. The more detailed breakdown indicates how the line items that comprise operating income, revenues, individual variable costs and fixed costs, add up to the static-budget variance of $93,100.

Remember, Webb produced and sold only 10,000 jackets, although managers anticipated an output of 12,000 jackets in the static budget. *Managers want to know how much of the static-budget variance is because of inaccurate forecasting of output units sold and how much is due to Webb's performance in manufacturing and selling 10,000 jackets.* Managers, therefore, create a *flexible budget,* which enables a more in-depth understanding of deviations from the static budget.

Keys to Success

Managers use detailed variance analysis to understand why actual results differ from the static budget developed at the start of the budget period. This helps managers to evaluate performance and motivate employees, as well as to take corrective action to ensure that actual outcomes meet or exceed the preset targets.

Flexible Budgets

Learning Objective 2

Develop flexible budgets

... proportionately increase variable costs; keep fixed costs the same

and compute flexible-budget variances

... each flexible-budget variance is the difference between an actual result and a flexible-budget amount

and sales-volume variances

... each sales-volume variance is the difference between a flexible-budget amount and a static-budget amount

A **flexible budget** calculates budgeted revenues and budgeted costs based on the *actual output in the budget period.* The flexible budget is prepared at the end of the period (April 2013 for Webb), after managers note the actual output of 10,000 jackets. The flexible budget is the *hypothetical* budget that Webb would have prepared at the start of the budget period if it had correctly forecast the actual output of 10,000 jackets. In other words, the flexible budget is not the plan Webb initially had in mind for April 2013 (remember Webb planned for an output of 12,000 jackets). Rather, it is the budget Webb *would have* put together for April if it knew in advance that the output for the month would be 10,000 jackets. In preparing the flexible budget, note that:

- The budgeted selling price is the same $120 per jacket used in preparing the static budget.
- The budgeted unit variable cost is the same $88 per jacket used in the static budget.
- The budgeted *total* fixed costs are the same static-budget amount of $276,000. Why? Because the 10,000 jackets produced falls within the relevant range of 0 to 12,000 jackets. Therefore, Webb's managers would have budgeted the same amount of fixed costs, $276,000, whether they anticipated making 10,000 or 12,000 jackets.

The *only* difference between the static budget and the flexible budget is that the static budget is prepared for the planned output of 12,000 jackets, whereas the flexible budget is based on the actual output of 10,000 jackets. The static budget is being "flexed," or adjusted, from 12,000 jackets to 10,000 jackets.

Webb develops its flexible budget in three steps:

Step 1: Identify the Actual Quantity of Output. In April 2013, Webb produced and sold 10,000 jackets.

Step 2: Calculate the Flexible Budget for Revenues Based on Budgeted Selling Price and Actual Quantity of Output.

$$\text{Flexible-budget revenues} = \$120 \text{ per jacket} \times 10{,}000 \text{ jackets}$$
$$= \$1{,}200{,}000$$

Step 3: Calculate the Flexible Budget for Costs Based on Budgeted Variable Cost per Output Unit, Actual Quantity of Output, and Budgeted Fixed Costs.

Flexible-budget variable costs	
Direct materials, $60 per jacket × 10,000 jackets	$ 600,000
Direct manufacturing labor, $16 per jacket × 10,000 jackets	160,000
Variable manufacturing overhead, $12 per jacket × 10,000 jackets	120,000
Total flexible-budget variable costs	880,000
Flexible-budget fixed costs	276,000
Flexible-budget total costs	$1,156,000

These three steps enable Webb to prepare a flexible budget, as shown in Exhibit 13-2, column 3.[2] The flexible budget allows for a more detailed analysis of the $93,100 unfavorable static-budget variance for operating income.

Exhibit 13-2 shows the flexible budget–based variance analysis for Webb, which subdivides the $93,100 unfavorable static-budget variance for operating income into two parts: a flexible-budget variance of $29,100 U and a *sales-volume variance* of $64,000 U. The **sales-volume variance** is the difference between a flexible-budget amount and the corresponding static-budget amount. The **flexible-budget variance** is the difference between an actual result and the corresponding flexible-budget amount.

[2] The flexible budget for 10,000 jackets assumes that all costs are either completely variable or completely fixed for the number of jackets produced. If that is not the case, for example, if variable costs are nonlinear or fixed costs are step costs, then the flexible budget would incorporate those factors in arriving at the best estimate of the expected cost of making 10,000 jackets.

Exhibit 13-2

Level 2 Flexible Budget–Based Variance Analysis for Webb Company for April 2013[a]

Level 2 Analysis

	Actual Results (1)	Flexible-Budget Variances (2) = (1) – (3)	Flexible Budget (3)	Sales-Volume Variances (4) = (3) – (5)	Static Budget (5)
Units sold	10,000	0	10,000	2,000 U	12,000
Revenues	$1,250,000	$50,000 F	$1,200,000	$240,000 U	$1,440,000
Variable costs					
Direct materials	621,600	21,600 U	600,000	120,000 F	720,000
Direct manufacturing labor	198,000	38,000 U	160,000	32,000 F	192,000
Variable manufacturing overhead	130,500	10,500 U	120,000	24,000 F	144,000
Total variable costs	950,100	70,100 U	880,000	176,000 F	1,056,000
Contribution margin	299,900	20,100 U	320,000	64,000 U	384,000
Fixed manufacturing costs	285,000	9,000 U	276,000	0	276,000
Operating income	$ 14,900	$29,100 U	$ 44,000	$ 64,000 U	$ 108,000

Level 2: $29,100 U Flexible-budget variance; $ 64,000 U Sales-volume variance

Level 1: $93,100 U Static-budget variance

[a]F = favorable effect on operating income; U = unfavorable effect on operating income.

Sales-Volume Variances

Keep in mind that the flexible-budget amounts in column 3 in Exhibit 13-2 and the static-budget amounts in column 5 are both computed using budgeted selling prices, budgeted variable cost per jacket, and budgeted fixed costs. The difference between the static-budget and the flexible-budget amounts is called the sales-volume variance because it arises *solely* from the difference between the 10,000 actual quantity (or volume) of jackets sold and the 12,000 quantity of jackets expected to be sold in the static budget.

$$\text{Sales-volume variance for operating income} = \text{Flexible-budget amount} - \text{Static-budget amount}$$
$$= \$44{,}000 - \$108{,}000$$
$$= \$64{,}000\text{ U}$$

The sales-volume variance in operating income for Webb measures the change in budgeted contribution margin because Webb sold only 10,000 jackets rather than the budgeted 12,000.

$$\text{Sales-volume variance for operating income} = \left(\text{Budgeted contribution margin per unit}\right) \times \left(\text{Actual units sold} - \text{Static-budget units sold}\right)$$
$$= \left(\text{Budgeted selling price} - \text{Budgeted variable cost per unit}\right) \times \left(\text{Actual units sold} - \text{Static-budget units sold}\right)$$
$$= (\$120\text{ per jacket} - \$88\text{ per jacket}) \times (10{,}000\text{ jackets} - 12{,}000\text{ jackets})$$
$$= \$32\text{ per jacket} \times (-2{,}000\text{ jackets})$$
$$= \$64{,}000\text{ U}$$

Exhibit 13-2, column 4, shows the components of this overall variance by identifying the sales-volume variance for each of the line items in the income statement. Webb's managers determine that the unfavorable sales-volume variance in operating income could be because of one or more of the following reasons:

1. The overall demand for jackets is not growing at the rate that managers anticipated.
2. Competitors are taking away market share from Webb.
3. Webb did not adapt quickly to changes in customer preferences and tastes.
4. Budgeted sales targets were set without careful analysis of market conditions.
5. Quality problems developed that led to customer dissatisfaction with Webb's jackets.

How Webb responds to the unfavorable sales-volume variance will be influenced by what management believes to be the cause of the variance. For example, if Webb's managers believe the unfavorable sales-volume variance was caused by market-related reasons (reasons 1, 2, 3, or 4), the sales manager would be in the best position to explain what happened and to suggest corrective actions that may be needed, such as sales promotions or market studies. If, however, managers believe the unfavorable sales-volume variance was caused by quality problems (reason 5), the production manager would be in the best position to analyze the causes and to suggest strategies for improvement, such as changes in the manufacturing process or investments in new machines.

The static-budget variances compared actual revenues and costs for 10,000 jackets against budgeted revenues and costs for 12,000 jackets. A portion of this difference, the sales-volume variance, reflects the effects of inaccurate forecasting of output units sold. By removing this component from the static-budget variance, managers can compare actual revenues earned and costs incurred for April 2013 against the flexible budget (the revenues and costs Webb would have budgeted for the 10,000 jackets actually produced and sold). *These flexible-budget variances are a better measure of operating performance than static-budget variances because they compare actual revenues to budgeted revenues and actual costs to budgeted costs for the same 10,000 jackets of output.*

Flexible-Budget Variances

The first three columns in Exhibit 13-2 compare actual results with flexible-budget amounts. Flexible-budget variances are in column 2 for each line item in the income statement:

$$\text{Flexible-budget variance} = \text{Actual result} - \text{Flexible-budget amount}$$

The operating income line in Exhibit 13-2 shows the flexible-budget variance is \$29,100 U (\$14,900 − \$44,000). The \$29,100 U arises because actual selling price, actual variable cost per unit, and actual fixed costs differ from their budgeted amounts. The actual results and budgeted amounts for the selling price and variable cost per unit are:

	Actual Result	Budgeted Amount
Selling price	\$125.00 (\$1,250,000 ÷ 10,000 jackets)	\$120.00 (\$1,200,000 ÷ 10,000 jackets)
Variable cost per jacket	\$95.01 (\$950,100 ÷ 10,000 jackets)	\$88.00 (\$880,000 ÷ 10,000 jackets)

The flexible-budget variance for revenues is called the **selling-price variance** because it arises solely from the difference between the actual selling price and the budgeted selling price:

$$\begin{aligned}\text{Selling-price variance} &= \left(\text{Actual selling price} - \text{Budgeted selling price}\right) \times \text{Actual units sold}\\ &= (\$125 \text{ per jacket} - \$120 \text{ per jacket}) \times 10{,}000 \text{ jackets}\\ &= \$50{,}000 \text{ F}\end{aligned}$$

Webb has a favorable selling-price variance because the \$125 actual selling price exceeds the \$120 budgeted amount, which increases operating income. Marketing managers are generally in the best position to understand and explain the reason for this selling price difference. For example, was the difference due to better quality? Or was it due to an overall increase in market prices? Webb's managers concluded it was due to a general increase in prices.

The flexible-budget variance for total variable costs is unfavorable (\$70,100 U) for the actual output of 10,000 jackets, due to one or both of the following:

- Webb used greater quantities of inputs (such as direct manufacturing labor-hours) compared to the budgeted quantities of inputs.

- Webb incurred higher prices per unit for the inputs (such as the wage rate per direct manufacturing labor-hour) compared to the budgeted prices per unit of the inputs.

Higher input quantities and/or higher input prices relative to the budgeted amounts could be the result of (1) Webb deciding to produce a better product than what was planned or (2) the result of inefficiencies in Webb's manufacturing and purchasing, or both. *You should always think of variance analysis as providing suggestions for further investigation rather than as establishing conclusive evidence of good or bad performance.*

The actual fixed costs of $285,000 are $9,000 more than the budgeted amount of $276,000. This unfavorable flexible-budget variance reflects unexpected increases in the cost of fixed indirect resources, such as factory rent or supervisory salaries.

Keys to Success

Managers develop flexible budgets in order to separate the change in profits due to deviations in output (sales-volume variance) from those that reflect actual operating performance (flexible-budget variance). Managers should view flexible-budget variances as providing suggestions for further investigation rather than as conclusive evidence of good or bad performance.

Learning Objective 3

Compute price variances

. . . each price variance is the difference between an actual input price and a budgeted input price

and efficiency variances

. . . each efficiency variance is the difference between an actual input quantity and a budgeted input quantity for actual output

for direct-cost categories

Price Variances and Efficiency Variances for Direct-Cost Inputs

To gain further insight into why a flexible-budget variance arose, managers find it useful to subdivide the flexible-budget variance for direct-cost inputs into two more detailed variances:

1. A price variance that reflects the difference between an actual input price and a budgeted input price
2. An efficiency variance that reflects the difference between an actual input quantity and a budgeted input quantity

The information available from these variances helps managers to better understand past performance and take corrective actions to implement more effective future strategies. Managers generally have more control over efficiency variances than price variances because the quantity of inputs used is primarily affected by factors inside the company (such as the efficiency with which operations are performed), whereas changes in the price of materials or in wage rates may be largely dictated by market forces outside the company (see Concepts in Action: Starbucks Reduces Direct-Cost Variances to Brew a Turnaround).

Obtaining Budgeted Input Prices and Budgeted Input Quantities

To calculate price and efficiency variances, Webb needs to obtain budgeted input prices and budgeted input quantities. Webb's managers have three main sources for this information: (1) past data, (2) data from similar companies, and (3) standards.

1. **Actual input data from past periods.** Most companies have past data on actual input prices and actual input quantities. These historical data could be analyzed for trends or patterns (using some of the techniques discussed in Chapter 8) to obtain estimates of budgeted prices and quantities.

   Advantages: They represent quantities and prices that are real, rather than hypothetical, and can serve as benchmarks for continuous improvement. Another advantage is that past data are typically available at low cost.

   Disadvantages: Past data can include inefficiencies such as wastage of direct materials. They also do not incorporate any changes expected for the budget period.

Concepts in Action: Starbucks Reduces Direct-Cost Variances to Brew a Turnaround

Source: Dorothy Alexander/Alamy

Along with coffee, Starbucks brewed profitable growth for many years. But when consumers tightened their purse strings amid the 2007–2009 recession, Starbucks' profit margins were under attack. With Starbucks' profitability depending on making each beverage at the lowest possible costs, an intricate understanding of direct costs is critical. In each Starbucks store, the two key direct costs are materials and labor.

Materials costs at Starbucks include coffee beans, milk, syrups, pastries, paper cups, and lids. To reduce budgeted costs for materials, Starbucks focused on two key inputs: coffee and milk. For coffee, Starbucks sought to avoid waste by no longer brewing decaffeinated and darker coffee blends in the afternoon and evening, when store traffic is slower. With milk prices rising, the company switched to 2% milk, which is healthier and costs less, and redoubled efforts to reduce spoilage. Labor costs, which cost 24% of company revenue annually, were another area of variance focus. Many stores employed fewer baristas. In other stores, Starbucks adopted many "lean" production techniques by making its drink-making processes more efficient.

The company took additional steps to align labor costs with its pricing. Each year, Starbucks gradually lifted prices on its drinks and introduced VIA packaged coffee and other non-labor-intensive items into its stores. Starbucks' focus on reducing variances paid off. From fiscal year 2008 to 2010, despite inflation, the company reduced its store operating expenses by $193 million, or 5.2%. Continued focus on direct-cost variances will be critical to the company's future success in any economic climate.

Sources: Based on Annie Gasparro, "Starbucks to raise prices," *Wall Street Journal* (January 4, 2012); Starbucks Corporation, 2011 Annual Report (Seattle, WA: Starbucks Corporation, 2012); Janet Adamy, "Starbucks brews up new cost cuts by putting lid on afternoon decaf," *Wall Street Journal* (January 28, 2009); Janet Adamy, "New Starbucks brew attracts customers, flak," *Wall Street Journal* (July 1, 2008); Craig Harris, "Starbucks slips; lattes rise," *Seattle Post Intelligencer* (July 23, 2007); Julie Jargon, "Starbucks growth revives, perked by Via," *Wall Street Journal* (January 21, 2010); Julie Jargon, "Latest Starbucks buzzword: 'Lean' Japanese techniques," *Wall Street Journal* (August 4, 2009); David Kesmodel, "Starbucks sees demand stirring again," *Wall Street Journal* (November 6, 2009).

2. **Data from other companies that have similar processes.** Another possibility is to use information from peer companies or companies that have similar processes as a benchmark.

   Advantages: The budget numbers represent competitive benchmarks from other companies. For example, Baptist Healthcare System in Louisville, Kentucky, maintains detailed flexible budgets and benchmarks its labor performance against hospitals that provide similar types of services and volumes and are in the upper quartile of a national benchmark.

   Disadvantages: Input-price and input-quantity data from other companies are often not available or may not be comparable to a particular company's situation. Consider American Apparel, which makes over 1 million articles of clothing a week. At its sole factory, in Los Angeles, workers receive hourly wages, piece rates, and medical benefits well in excess of those paid by its competitors, virtually all of whom are offshore and have significantly lower production costs.

3. **Standards developed by Webb.** A **standard** is a carefully determined price, cost, or quantity that is used as a benchmark for judging performance. Standards are usually expressed on a per-unit basis. Consider how Webb determines its direct manufacturing labor standards. Webb conducts engineering studies to obtain a detailed breakdown of the steps required to make a jacket. Each step is assigned a standard time based on work performed by a *skilled* worker using equipment operating in an *efficient* manner.

Advantages: Standard times (1) aim to exclude past inefficiencies and (2) take into account changes expected to occur in the budget period. An example of the second advantage is the decision to lease new, faster, and more accurate sewing machines. Similarly, Webb determines the standard quantity of square yards of cloth required by a skilled operator to make each jacket. *Disdvantages:* Since they are not based on achieved benchmarks, standards might be infeasible and lead to unhappiness among workers.

The term "standard" refers to many different things:

- A **standard input** is a carefully determined quantity of input, such as square yards of cloth or direct manufacturing labor-hours, required for one unit of output, such as a jacket.
- A **standard price** is a carefully determined price that a company expects to pay for a unit of input. In the Webb example, the standard wage rate that Webb expects to pay its operators is an example of a standard price of a direct manufacturing labor-hour.
- A **standard cost** is a carefully determined cost of a unit of output, such as the standard direct manufacturing labor cost of a jacket at Webb.

$$\frac{\text{Standard cost per output unit for}}{\text{each variable direct-cost input}} = \frac{\text{Standard input allowed}}{\text{for one output unit}} \times \frac{\text{Standard price}}{\text{per input unit}}$$

Standard direct material cost per jacket: 2 square yards of cloth input allowed per output unit (jacket) manufactured, at $30 standard price per square yard

$$\text{Standard direct material cost per jacket} = 2 \text{ square yards} \times \$30 \text{ per square yard} = \$60$$

Standard direct manufacturing labor cost per jacket: 0.8 manufacturing labor-hour of input allowed per output unit manufactured, at $20 standard price per hour

$$\text{Standard direct manufacturing labor cost per jacket} = 0.8 \text{ labor-hour} \times \$20 \text{ per labor-hour} = \$16$$

How are the words *budget* and *standard* related? Budget is the broader term. To clarify, budgeted input prices, input quantities, and costs need *not* be based on standards. As we saw previously, they could be based on past data or competitive benchmarks, for example. However, when standards *are* used to obtain budgeted input quantities and prices, the words *standard* and *budget* are used interchangeably. The standard cost of each input required for one unit of output is determined by the standard quantity of the input required for one unit of output and the standard price per input unit. See how the standard-cost computations shown previously for direct materials and direct manufacturing labor result in the budgeted direct material cost per jacket of $60 and the budgeted direct manufacturing labor cost of $16 referred to earlier (page 537).

In its standard-costing system, Webb uses standards that are attainable through efficient operations but that allow for normal disruptions. An alternative is to set more challenging standards that are more difficult to attain. As we discussed in Chapter 12, managers sometimes set challenging standards in order to increase motivation and performance. If, however, workers regard standards as essentially unachievable, it can increase frustration and hurt performance.

Data for Calculating Webb's Price Variances and Efficiency Variances

Consider Webb's two direct-cost categories. The actual cost for each of these categories for the 10,000 jackets manufactured and sold in April 2013 is:

Direct Materials Purchased and Used[3]

1. Square yards of cloth input purchased and used	22,200
2. Actual price incurred per square yard	$ 28
3. Direct material costs (22,200 × $28) [shown in Exhibit 13-2, column 1]	$621,600

Direct Manufacturing Labor

1. Direct manufacturing labor-hours	9,000
2. Actual price incurred per direct manufacturing labor-hour	$ 22
3. Direct manufacturing labor costs (9,000 × $22) [shown in Exhibit 13-2, column 1]	$198,000

[3] The Problem for Self-Study (pages 564–566) relaxes the assumption that the quantity of direct materials used equals the quantity of direct materials purchased.

Let's use the Webb Company data to illustrate the price variance and the efficiency variance for direct-cost inputs.

A **price variance** is the difference between actual price and budgeted price, multiplied by actual input quantity, such as direct materials purchased. A price variance is sometimes called a **rate variance,** especially when referring to a price variance for direct manufacturing labor. An **efficiency variance** is the difference between actual input quantity used, such as square yards of cloth of direct materials, and budgeted input quantity allowed for actual output, multiplied by budgeted price. An efficiency variance is sometimes called a **usage variance.** Let's explore price and efficiency variances in greater detail so we can see how managers use these variances to improve their future performance.

Price Variances

The formula for computing the price variance is:

$$\text{Price variance} = \left(\text{Actual price of input} - \text{Budgeted price of input}\right) \times \text{Actual quantity of input}$$

Price variances for Webb's two direct-cost categories are as follows:

Direct-Cost Category	(Actual price of input − Budgeted price of input)	×	Actual quantity of input	=	Price variance
Direct materials	($28 per sq. yard − $30 per sq. yard)	×	22,200 square yards	=	$44,400 F
Direct manufacturing labor	($22 per hour − $20 per hour)	×	9,000 hours	=	$18,000 U

The direct materials price variance is favorable because the actual price of cloth is less than the budgeted price, resulting in an increase in operating income. The direct manufacturing labor price variance is unfavorable because the actual wage rate paid to labor is more than the budgeted rate, resulting in a decrease in operating income.

Managers should always consider a broad range of possible causes for a price variance. For example, Webb's favorable direct materials price variance could be due to one or more of the following:

- Webb's purchasing manager negotiated the direct materials prices more skillfully than was planned for in the budget.
- The purchasing manager changed to a lower-price supplier.
- Webb's purchasing manager ordered larger quantities than the quantities budgeted, thereby obtaining quantity discounts.
- Direct material prices decreased unexpectedly because of, say, industry oversupply.
- Budgeted purchase prices of direct materials were set too high without careful analysis of market conditions.
- The purchasing manager received favorable prices because he was willing to accept unfavorable terms on factors other than prices (such as lower-quality material).

Webb's managers' responses to a direct materials price variance depend on what is believed to be the cause of the variance. Assume Webb's managers attribute the favorable price variance to the purchasing manager's ordering in larger quantities than budgeted, thereby receiving quantity discounts. The managers could then examine if purchasing in these larger quantities resulted in higher storage costs. If the increase in storage and inventory holding costs exceeds the quantity discounts, purchasing in larger quantities is not beneficial. Some companies have reduced their materials storage areas to prevent their purchasing managers from ordering in larger quantities (see Chapter 10).

Keys to Success

Firms calculate price variances to estimate the impact on profits of actual input prices for labor or materials being different than expected. This allows senior management to evaluate the performance of purchasing managers (for materials) or personnel managers (for labor) with regard to the prices paid for inputs.

Efficiency Variance

For any actual level of output, the efficiency variance is the difference between actual quantity of input used and the budgeted quantity of input allowed for that output level, multiplied by the budgeted input price:

$$\text{Efficiency variance} = \left(\begin{array}{c}\text{Actual}\\ \text{quantity of}\\ \text{input used}\end{array} - \begin{array}{c}\text{Budgeted quantity}\\ \text{of input allowed}\\ \text{for actual output}\end{array}\right) \times \begin{array}{c}\text{Budgeted price}\\ \text{of input}\end{array}$$

The idea here is that a company is inefficient if it uses a larger quantity of input than the budgeted quantity for its actual level of output; the company is efficient if it uses a smaller quantity of input than was budgeted for that output level.

The efficiency variances for each of Webb's direct-cost categories are:

Direct-Cost Category	(Actual quantity of input used − Budgeted quantity of input allowed for actual output)	×	Budgeted price of input	=	Efficiency variance
Direct materials	[22,200 sq. yards − (10,000 units × 2 sq. yards/unit)]	×	$30 per sq. yard		
	= (22,200 sq. yards − 20,000 sq. yards)	×	$30 per sq. yard	=	$66,000 U
Direct manufacturing labor	[9,000 hours − (10,000 units × 0.8 hour/unit)]	×	$20 per hour		
	= (9,000 hours − 8,000 hours)	×	$20 per hour	=	20,000 U

The two manufacturing efficiency variances, (1) direct materials efficiency variance and (2) direct manufacturing labor efficiency variance, are each unfavorable because more input was used than was budgeted for the actual output, resulting in a decrease in operating income.

As with price variances, there is a broad range of possible causes for these efficiency variances. For example, Webb's unfavorable efficiency variance for direct manufacturing labor could be because of one or more of the following:

- Webb's personnel manager hired underskilled workers.
- Webb's production scheduler inefficiently scheduled work, resulting in more manufacturing labor time than budgeted being used per jacket.
- Webb's maintenance department did not properly maintain machines, resulting in more manufacturing labor time than budgeted being used per jacket.
- Budgeted time standards were set too tight without careful analysis of the operating conditions and the employees' skills.

Suppose Webb's managers determine that the unfavorable variance is due to poor machine maintenance. Webb may then establish a team consisting of plant engineers and machine operators to develop a maintenance schedule that will reduce future breakdowns and thereby prevent adverse effects on labor time and product quality.

Keys to Success

Firms calculate efficiency variances to estimate the impact on profits of actual input usage for labor or materials being different than expected. This enables managers to evaluate the operational performance of the firm in terms of the efficiency with which inputs are used, and to take corrective steps by adjusting production processes or upgrading the skill level or training of the workforce.

Exhibit 13-3 provides an alternative way to calculate price and efficiency variances and illustrates how the price variance and the efficiency variance subdivide the flexible-budget variance. Consider direct materials. The direct materials flexible-budget variance of $21,600 U is the difference between actual costs incurred (actual input quantity × actual price) of $621,600 shown in

Exhibit 13-3

Columnar Presentation of Variance Analysis: Direct Costs for Webb Company for April 2013[a]

Level 3 Analysis

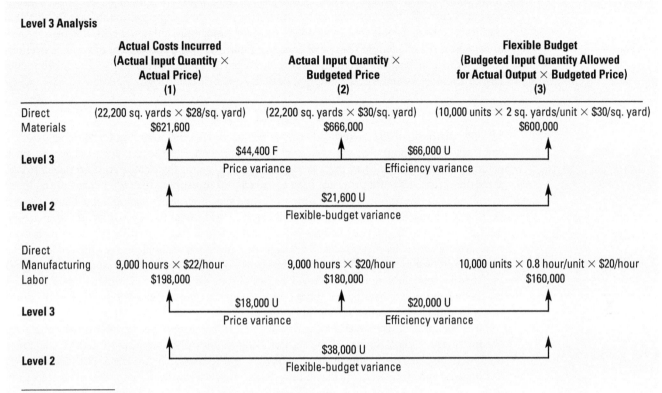

	Actual Costs Incurred (Actual Input Quantity × Actual Price) (1)		Actual Input Quantity × Budgeted Price (2)		Flexible Budget (Budgeted Input Quantity Allowed for Actual Output × Budgeted Price) (3)
Direct Materials	(22,200 sq. yards × $28/sq. yard) $621,600		(22,200 sq. yards × $30/sq. yard) $666,000		(10,000 units × 2 sq. yards/unit × $30/sq. yard) $600,000
Level 3		$44,400 F Price variance		$66,000 U Efficiency variance	
Level 2			$21,600 U Flexible-budget variance		
Direct Manufacturing Labor	9,000 hours × $22/hour $198,000		9,000 hours × $20/hour $180,000		10,000 units × 0.8 hour/unit × $20/hour $160,000
Level 3		$18,000 U Price variance		$20,000 U Efficiency variance	
Level 2			$38,000 U Flexible-budget variance		

[a]F = favorable effect on operating income; U = unfavorable effect on operating income.

column 1 and the flexible budget (budgeted input quantity allowed for actual output × budgeted price) of $600,000 shown in column 3. Column 2 (actual input quantity × budgeted price) is inserted between column 1 and column 3. The difference between columns 1 and 2 is the price variance of $44,400 F. This price variance occurs because the same actual input quantity (22,200 sq. yds.) is multiplied by *actual price* ($28) in column 1 and *budgeted price* ($30) in column 2. The difference between columns 2 and 3 is the efficiency variance of $66,000 U because the same budgeted price ($30) is multiplied by *actual input quantity* (22,200 sq. yds.) in column 2 and *budgeted input quantity allowed for actual output* (20,000 sq. yds.) in column 3. The sum of the direct materials price variance, $44,400 F, and the direct materials efficiency variance, $66,000 U, equals the direct materials flexible budget variance, $21,600 U.

We next use the Webb Company example again to illustrate the planning and control of variable and fixed overhead costs.

Planning Overhead Costs and Calculating Overhead Rates

Learning Objective 4

Plan for variable and fixed overhead costs

. . . plan to undertake only essential activities, and to perform them efficiently

and calculate budgeted variable and fixed overhead cost rates

. . . budgeted costs divided by budgeted quantity of cost-allocation base

Recall our assumption that Webb's only costs are *manufacturing* costs. In addition to direct materials and direct manufacturing labor, Webb also incurs variable and fixed manufacturing overhead costs. In this chapter, we refer to variable and fixed manufacturing overhead costs simply as variable and fixed overhead costs. Variable overhead costs for Webb include energy, machine maintenance, engineering support, and indirect materials. Fixed overhead costs include plant leasing costs, depreciation on plant equipment, and the salaries of the plant managers.

Planning Variable Overhead Costs

To effectively plan variable overhead costs for a product or service, managers must focus attention on the activities that create a superior product or service for their customers and eliminate activities that do not add value. Webb's managers examine how each of their variable overhead costs relates to delivering a superior product or service to customers. For example, customers expect Webb's jackets to last, so managers at Webb consider high-quality sewing to be an essential activity. Therefore, maintenance activities for sewing machines, which are included in Webb's variable overhead costs, are also essential activities for which management must plan. Such maintenance should also be done in a cost-effective way, such as by scheduling periodic equipment maintenance rather than waiting for sewing machines to break down. For many companies today, it is critical to plan for ways to become more efficient in the use of energy, a rapidly growing component of variable overhead costs. Webb installs smart meters in order to monitor energy use in real time and steer production operations away from peak consumption periods.

Planning Fixed Overhead Costs

Effective planning of fixed overhead costs is similar to effective planning for variable overhead costs; managers should plan only essential activities and aim to execute them efficiently. But in planning fixed overhead costs, there is one more strategic issue that managers must take into consideration: choosing the appropriate level of capacity or investment that will benefit the company in the long run. Consider Webb's leasing of sewing machines, each having a fixed cost per year. Leasing more machines than necessary will result in additional fixed leasing costs on machines not fully used during the year. Leasing insufficient machine capacity will result in an inability to meet demand, lost sales of jackets, and unhappy customers. For example, AT&T did not foresee the widespread consumer use of iPhones for data downloads and applications, so it did not upgrade its network's capability. As a result, AT&T had to impose limits on how their customers could use the iPhone. Because of insufficient space on its network, in December 2009, AT&T had the lowest customer satisfaction ratings among all major carriers.

The planning of fixed overhead costs differs from the planning of variable overhead costs in one important respect: timing. At the start of a budget period, management will have made most of the decisions that determine the level of fixed overhead costs to be incurred. But, it's the day-to-day, ongoing operating decisions that mainly determine the level of variable overhead costs incurred in that period. In hospitals, for example, variable overhead, which includes disposable supplies, unit doses of medication, suture packets, and medical waste disposal costs, is a function of the number and nature of procedures carried out, as well as the practice patterns of the physicians. However, the majority of the cost of providing hospital service is related to buildings, equipment, and salaried labor, which are fixed overhead items, unrelated to the volume of activity.[4]

Standard Costing

We now discuss the development of standards for Webb's manufacturing overhead costs. **Standard costing** is a costing system that (1) traces direct costs to output produced by multiplying the standard prices or rates by the standard quantities of inputs allowed for actual outputs produced and (2) allocates overhead costs on the basis of the standard overhead-cost rates times the standard quantities of the allocation bases allowed for the actual outputs produced.

The standard cost of Webb's jackets can be computed at the start of the budget period. This feature of standard costing simplifies record keeping because no record is needed of the actual overhead costs or of the actual quantities of the cost-allocation bases used for making the jackets. What managers *do* need are the standard overhead cost rates for variable and fixed overhead. Webb's management accountants calculate these cost rates based on the planned amounts of variable and fixed overhead and the standard quantities of the allocation bases. This information comes from managers via the budgeting process described in Chapter 12. Note that once managers set standards, the costs of using standard costing are low relative to the costs of using actual costing or normal costing.

Developing Budgeted Variable Overhead Rates

Budgeted variable overhead cost-allocation rates can be developed in four steps. Throughout the chapter, we use the broader term "budgeted rate" rather than "standard rate" to be consistent with the term used in describing normal costing in earlier chapters. In standard costing, the budgeted rates are standard rates.

---

[4] Free-standing surgery centers have thrived because they have an economic advantage of lower fixed overhead when compared to a traditional hospital. For an enlightening summary of costing issues in health care, see A. Macario, "What Does One Minute of Operating Room Time Cost?", Stanford University School of Medicine (2009).

Step 1: Choose the Period to Be Used for the Budget. Webb uses a 12-month budget period for the reasons listed in Chapter 4 (pages 119–120).

Step 2: Select the Cost-Allocation Bases to Use in Allocating Variable Overhead Costs to Output Produced. Webb's operating managers select machine-hours as the cost-allocation base because they believe that machine-hours is the only cost driver of variable overhead. Based on an engineering study, Webb estimates it will take 0.40 of a machine-hour per actual output unit. For its budgeted output of 144,000 jackets in 2013, Webb budgets 57,600 (0.40 × 144,000) machine-hours.

Step 3: Identify the Variable Overhead Costs Associated with Each Cost-Allocation Base. Webb groups all of its variable overhead costs, including costs of energy, machine maintenance, engineering support, indirect materials, and indirect manufacturing labor in a single cost pool. Webb's total budgeted variable overhead costs for 2013 are $1,728,000.

Step 4: Compute the Rate per Unit of Each Cost-Allocation Base Used to Allocate Variable Overhead Costs to Output Produced. Dividing the amount in Step 3 ($1,728,000) by the amount in Step 2 (57,600 machine-hours), Webb estimates a rate of $30 per standard machine-hour for allocating its variable overhead costs.

In standard costing, the variable overhead rate per unit of the cost-allocation base ($30 per machine-hour for Webb) is generally expressed as a standard rate per output unit. Webb's managers calculate the budgeted variable overhead cost rate per output unit as follows:

$$\begin{aligned}\begin{array}{c}\text{Budgeted variable}\\ \text{overhead cost rate}\\ \text{per output unit}\end{array} &= \begin{array}{c}\text{Budgeted input}\\ \text{allowed per}\\ \text{output unit}\end{array} \times \begin{array}{c}\text{Budgeted variable}\\ \text{overhead cost rate}\\ \text{per input unit}\end{array}\\ &= 0.40 \text{ hour per jacket} \times \$30 \text{ per hour}\\ &= \$12 \text{ per jacket}\end{aligned}$$

The $12-per-jacket rate is the budgeted variable overhead cost rate in both the static budget for 2013 and in the monthly performance reports it prepares during 2013.

The $12-per-jacket rate represents the amount by which managers expect Webb's variable overhead costs to change for output units for planning and control purposes. Accordingly, as the number of jackets manufactured increases, variable overhead costs are allocated to output units (for the inventory costing purpose) at the same rate of $12 per jacket. Of course, this presents an overall picture of total variable overhead costs, which in reality consist of many items, including energy, repairs, indirect labor, and so on. Managers help control variable overhead costs by budgeting each line item and then investigating possible causes for any significant variances.

Developing Budgeted Fixed Overhead Rates

Fixed overhead costs are, by definition, a lump sum of costs that remains unchanged in total for a given period, despite wide changes in the level of total activity or volume related to those overhead costs. Fixed costs are included in flexible budgets, but they remain the same total amount within the relevant range of activity regardless of the output level chosen to "flex" the variable costs and revenues. Recall from Exhibit 13-2 (page 540) and the steps in developing a flexible budget that the fixed-cost amount is the same $276,000 in the static budget and in the flexible budget. Do not assume, however, that fixed overhead costs can never be changed. Managers can reduce fixed overhead costs by selling equipment or by laying off employees. But they are fixed in the sense that, unlike variable costs such as direct material costs, fixed costs do not *automatically* increase or decrease with the level of activity within the relevant range.

The process of developing the budgeted fixed overhead rate is the same as that detailed earlier for calculating the budgeted variable overhead rate. The four steps are as follows:

Step 1: Choose the Period to Use for the Budget. As with variable overhead costs, the budget period for fixed overhead costs is typically 12 months.

Step 2: Select the Cost-Allocation Bases to Use in Allocating Fixed Overhead Costs to Output Produced. Webb uses machine-hours as the only cost-allocation base for fixed overhead costs. Why? Because Webb's managers believe that, in the long run, fixed overhead costs will increase or decrease to the levels needed to support the amount of machine-hours. Therefore, in the long run, the amount of machine-hours used is the only cost driver of fixed overhead costs. The number of machine-hours is the denominator in the budgeted fixed overhead rate computation and is called the **denominator level.** For simplicity, we assume Webb expects to operate at capacity in fiscal year 2013, with a budgeted usage of 57,600 machine-hours for a budgeted output of 144,000 jackets.[5]

Step 3: Identify the Fixed Overhead Costs Associated with Each Cost-Allocation Base. Because Webb's managers identify only a single cost-allocation base—machine-hours—to allocate fixed overhead costs, they group all such costs into a single cost pool. Costs in this pool include depreciation on plant and equipment, plant and equipment leasing costs, and the plant manager's salary. The fixed overhead budget for 2013 is $3,312,000.

Step 4: Compute the Rate per Unit of Each Cost-Allocation Base Used to Allocate Fixed Overhead Costs to Output Produced. Dividing the $3,312,000 from Step 3 by the 57,600 machine-hours from Step 2, managers estimate a fixed overhead cost rate of $57.50 per machine-hour:

$$\begin{array}{c}\text{Budgeted fixed}\\\text{overhead cost per}\\\text{unit of cost-allocation}\\\text{base}\end{array} = \frac{\text{Budgeted total costs in fixed overhead cost pool}}{\text{Budgeted total quantity of cost-allocation base}} = \frac{\$3{,}312{,}000}{57{,}600} = \$57.50 \text{ per machine-hour}$$

In standard costing, the $57.50 fixed overhead cost per machine-hour is usually expressed as a standard cost per output unit. Recall that Webb's engineering study estimates that it will take 0.40 machine-hour per output unit, and managers can now calculate the budgeted fixed overhead cost per output unit as:

$$\begin{array}{c}\text{Budgeted fixed}\\\text{overhead cost per}\\\text{output unit}\end{array} = \begin{array}{c}\text{Budgeted quantity of}\\\text{cost-allocation}\\\text{base allowed per}\\\text{output unit}\end{array} \times \begin{array}{c}\text{Budgeted fixed}\\\text{overhead cost}\\\text{per unit of}\\\text{cost-allocation base}\end{array}$$

$$= 0.40 \text{ of a machine-hour per jacket} \times \$57.50 \text{ per machine-hour}$$

$$= \$23.00 \text{ per jacket}$$

When preparing monthly budgets for 2013, Webb divides the $3,312,000 annual total fixed costs into 12 equal monthly amounts of $276,000.

Keys to Success

The plans and information provided by managers in the budgeting process form the basis for calculating budgeted variable and fixed overhead rates, which are then used to allocate overhead costs to output during the period.

Learning Objective 5

Compute the variable overhead flexible-budget variance,

. . . difference between actual variable overhead costs and flexible-budget variable overhead amounts

the variable overhead efficiency variance,

. . . difference between actual quantity of cost-allocation base and budgeted quantity of cost-allocation base

and the variable overhead spending variance

. . . difference between actual variable overhead cost rate and budgeted variable overhead cost rate

Variable Overhead Cost Variances

We now illustrate how managers use the budgeted variable overhead rate to compute Webb's variable overhead cost variances. The following data are for April 2013, when Webb produced and sold 10,000 jackets:

	Actual Result	Flexible-Budget Amount
1. Output units (jackets)	10,000	10,000
2. Machine-hours per output unit	0.45	0.40
3. Machine-hours (1 × 2)	4,500	4,000
4. Variable overhead costs	$130,500	$120,000
5. Variable overhead costs per machine-hour (4 ÷ 3)	$ 29.00	$ 30.00
6. Variable overhead costs per output unit (4 ÷ 1)	$ 13.05	$ 12.00

As in the case of direct-cost inputs, the flexible budget enables Webb's managers to highlight the differences between actual costs and actual quantities versus budgeted costs and budgeted quantities for the actual output level of 10,000 jackets.

[5] Because Webb plans its capacity over multiple periods, anticipated demand in 2013 could be such that budgeted output for 2013 is less than capacity. Companies vary in the denominator levels they choose; some may choose budgeted output and others may choose capacity. In either case, the basic approach and analysis presented in this chapter is unchanged.

Flexible-Budget Analysis

The **variable overhead flexible-budget variance** measures the difference between actual variable overhead costs incurred and flexible-budget variable overhead amounts.

$$\begin{aligned}\text{Variable overhead flexible-budget variance} &= \text{Actual costs incurred} - \text{Flexible-budget amount}\\ &= \$130{,}500 - \$120{,}000\\ &= \$10{,}500\text{ U}\end{aligned}$$

This $10,500 unfavorable flexible-budget variance means Webb's actual variable overhead exceeded the flexible-budget amount by $10,500 for the 10,000 jackets actually produced and sold. Webb's managers would want to know why actual costs exceeded the flexible-budget amount. Did Webb use more machine-hours than planned to produce the 10,000 jackets? If so, was it because workers were less skilled than expected in using machines? Or did Webb spend more on variable overhead costs, such as maintenance?

Just as we illustrated earlier with the flexible-budget variance for direct-cost items, Webb's managers can get further insight into the reason for the $10,500 unfavorable variance by subdividing it into the efficiency variance and spending variance.

Variable Overhead Efficiency Variance

The **variable overhead efficiency variance** is the difference between actual quantity of the cost-allocation base used and budgeted quantity of the cost-allocation base that should have been used to produce actual output, multiplied by budgeted variable overhead cost per unit of the cost-allocation base.

$$\begin{aligned}\text{Variable overhead efficiency variance} &= \left(\begin{array}{c}\text{Actual quantity of variable overhead}\\\text{cost-allocation base used for actual output}\end{array} - \begin{array}{c}\text{Budgeted quantity of variable overhead}\\\text{cost-allocation base allowed for actual output}\end{array}\right) \times \begin{array}{c}\text{Budgeted variable overhead cost per unit}\\\text{of cost-allocation base}\end{array}\\ &= (4{,}500\text{ hours} - 0.40\text{ hr./unit} \times 10{,}000\text{ units}) \times \$30\text{ per hour}\\ &= (4{,}500\text{ hours} - 4{,}000\text{ hours}) \times \$30\text{ per hour}\\ &= \$15{,}000\text{ U}\end{aligned}$$

Columns 2 and 3 in Exhibit 13-4 depict the variable overhead efficiency variance. Note the variance arises solely because of the difference between actual quantity (4,500 hours) and budgeted quantity (4,000 hours) of the cost-allocation base. The variable overhead efficiency variance is computed the

Exhibit 13-4

Columnar Presentation of Variable Overhead Variance Analysis: Webb Company for April 2013[a]

	Actual Costs Incurred: Actual Input Quantity × Actual Rate (1)		**Actual Input Quantity × Budgeted Rate (2)**		**Flexible Budget: Budgeted Input Quantity Allowed for Actual Output × Budgeted Rate (3)**
					(0.40 hour/unit × 10,000 units × $30/hour)
	(4,500 hours × $29/hour)		(4,500 hours × $30/hour)		4,000 hours × $30/hour
	$130,500		$135,000		$120,000
Level 3		$4,500 F Spending variance		$15,000 U Efficiency variance	
Level 2			$10,500 U Flexible-budget variance		

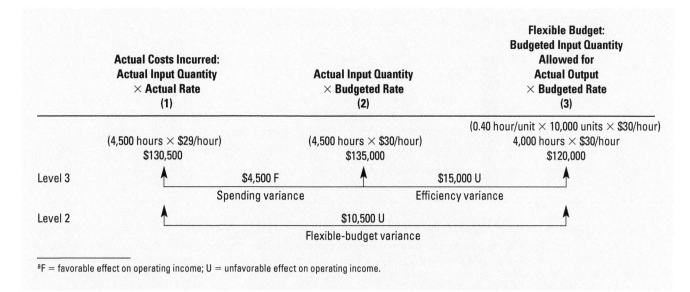

[a]F = favorable effect on operating income; U = unfavorable effect on operating income.

same way as the efficiency variance for direct-cost items (page 546). However, the interpretation of the variance is quite different. Efficiency variances for direct-cost items are based on differences between actual inputs used and budgeted inputs allowed for actual output produced. For example, a forensic laboratory (the kind popularized by television shows such as *CSI* and *Dexter*) would calculate a direct labor efficiency variance based on whether the lab used more or fewer hours than the standard hours allowed for the actual number of DNA tests. In contrast, the efficiency variance for variable overhead cost is based on the efficiency with which the *cost-allocation base* is used. Webb's unfavorable variable overhead efficiency variance of $15,000 means that the actual machine-hours (the cost-allocation base) of 4,500 hours turned out to be higher than the budgeted machine-hours of 4,000 hours allowed to manufacture 10,000 jackets.

The following table shows possible causes for Webb's actual machine-hours exceeding budgeted machine-hours and management's potential responses to each of these causes.

Possible Causes for Exceeding Budget	Potential Management Responses
1. Workers were less skilled than expected in using machines.	1. Encourage the human resources department to implement better employee-hiring practices and training procedures.
2. Production scheduler inefficiently scheduled jobs, resulting in more machine-hours used than budgeted.	2. Improve plant operations by installing production scheduling software.
3. Machines were not maintained in good operating condition.	3. Ensure preventive maintenance is done on all machines.
4. Webb's sales staff promised a distributor a rush delivery, which resulted in more machine-hours used than budgeted.	4. Coordinate production schedules with sales staff and distributors and share information with them.
5. Budgeted machine time standards were set too tight.	5. Commit more resources to develop appropriate standards.

Management would assess the cause(s) of the $15,000 U variance in April 2013 and respond accordingly. Note how, depending on the cause(s) of the variance, corrective actions may need to be taken not just in manufacturing but also in other business functions of the value chain, such as sales and distribution.

Webb's managers discovered that one reason for actual machine-hours exceeding budgeted machine-hours was the use of underskilled workers. As a result, Webb is initiating steps to improve hiring and training practices. Another reason machines operated below budgeted efficiency levels in April 2013 was insufficient maintenance performed in the prior 2 months. Further study revealed that a former plant manager delayed maintenance in a presumed attempt to meet monthly budget cost targets. As we discussed in Chapter 12, *managers should not be focused on meeting short-run budget targets if they are likely to result in harmful long-run consequences.* If the risks of machine breakdown because of the delayed maintenance are substantial, the plant manager's actions were both dangerous and unethical. Webb is now strengthening its internal maintenance procedures so that failure to do monthly maintenance will raise a "red flag" that must be immediately explained to management. Webb is also attempting to educate managers to the harmful effects of fixating on near-term goals, and taking a hard look at its own evaluation practices to determine if they were implicitly pressuring managers into such actions.

Keys to Success

Managers use the variable overhead efficiency variance to understand the impact on income of the efficiency with which the cost driver for variable overhead is consumed. The measure captures the actual use of the driver relative to the amount budgeted to be used for the actual output level.

Variable Overhead Spending Variance

The **variable overhead spending variance** is the difference between actual variable overhead cost per unit of the cost-allocation base and budgeted variable overhead cost per unit of the cost-allocation base, multiplied by the actual quantity of variable overhead cost-allocation base used.

$$\begin{aligned}\begin{matrix}\text{Variable}\\ \text{overhead}\\ \text{spending}\\ \text{variance}\end{matrix} &= \left(\begin{matrix}\text{Actual variable}\\ \text{overhead cost per unit}\\ \text{of cost-allocation base}\end{matrix} - \begin{matrix}\text{Budgeted variable}\\ \text{overhead cost per unit}\\ \text{of cost-allocation base}\end{matrix}\right) \times \begin{matrix}\text{Actual quantity of}\\ \text{variable overhead}\\ \text{cost-allocation base}\\ \text{used}\end{matrix}\\ &= (\$29 \text{ per machine-hour} - \$30 \text{ per machine-hour}) \times 4{,}500 \text{ machine-hours}\\ &= (-\$1 \text{ per machine-hour} \times 4{,}500 \text{ machine-hours})\\ &= \$4{,}500 \text{ F}\end{aligned}$$

Since Webb operated in April 2013 with a lower-than-budgeted variable overhead cost per machine-hour, there is a favorable variable overhead spending variance. Columns 1 and 2 in Exhibit 13-4 depict this variance.

To understand the favorable variable overhead spending variance and its implications, Webb's managers need to recognize why *actual* variable overhead cost per unit of the cost-allocation base ($29 per machine-hour) is *lower* than the *budgeted* variable overhead cost per unit of the cost-allocation base ($30 per machine-hour).

Overall, Webb used 4,500 machine-hours, which is 12.5% greater than the flexible-budget amount of 4,000 machine hours. However, actual variable overhead costs of $130,500 are only 8.75% greater than the flexible-budget amount of $120,000. Thus, relative to the flexible budget, the percentage increase in actual variable overhead costs is *less* than the percentage increase in machine-hours. Consequently, actual variable overhead cost per machine-hour is lower than the budgeted amount, resulting in a favorable variable overhead spending variance.

Recall that variable overhead costs include costs of energy, machine maintenance, indirect materials, and indirect labor. Two possible reasons why the percentage increase in actual variable overhead costs is less than the percentage increase in machine-hours are:

1. Actual prices of individual inputs included in variable overhead costs, such as the price of energy, indirect materials, or indirect labor, are lower than budgeted prices of these inputs. For example, the actual price of electricity may only be $0.09 per kilowatt-hour, compared with a price of $0.10 per kilowatt-hour in the flexible budget.
2. Relative to the flexible budget, the percentage increase in the actual usage of individual items in the variable overhead-cost pool is less than the percentage increase in machine-hours. Compared with the flexible-budget amount of 30,000 kilowatt-hours, suppose the machines' actual energy use is 32,400 kilowatt-hours, or 8% higher. The fact that this is a smaller percentage increase than the 12.5% increase in machine-hours (4,500 actual machine-hours vs. a flexible budget of 4,000 machine hours) will lead to a favorable variable overhead spending variance, which can be partially or completely traced to the efficient use of energy and other variable overhead items.

As part of the last stage of the five-step decision-making process, Webb's managers will need to examine the signals provided by the variable overhead variances to *evaluate performance and learn*. By understanding the reasons for these variances, Webb can take appropriate actions and make more precise predictions in order to achieve improved results in future periods.

For example, Webb's managers must examine why actual prices of variable overhead cost items are different from budgeted prices. The price effects could be the result of skillful negotiation on the part of the purchasing manager, oversupply in the market, or lower quality of inputs such as indirect materials. Webb's response depends on what is believed to be the cause of the variance. If the concerns are about quality, for instance, Webb may want to put in place new quality management systems.

Similarly, Webb's managers should understand the possible causes for the efficiency with which variable overhead resources are used. These causes include skill levels of workers, maintenance of machines, and the efficiency of the manufacturing process. Webb's managers discovered that Webb used fewer supervision resources per machine-hour because of manufacturing process improvements. As a result, they began organizing cross-functional teams to see if more process improvements could be achieved.

We emphasize that a manager should not always view a favorable variable overhead spending variance as desirable. For example, the variable overhead spending variance would be favorable if Webb purchased lower-priced, poor-quality indirect materials, hired less-talented supervisors, or performed less machine maintenance. These decisions, however, are likely to hurt product quality and harm the long-run prospects of the business.

We next demonstrate the value of calculating fixed overhead cost variances.

Keys to Success

Managers use the variable overhead spending variance to understand the effect on income of differences between the budgeted variable overhead rate and the actual variable overhead cost per unit of the cost driver. The variance captures both the unexpected changes in price as well as the efficiency of use of variable overhead items such as energy and indirect materials.

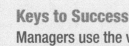

Learning Objective 6

Compute the fixed overhead flexible-budget variance,

. . . difference between actual fixed overhead costs and flexible-budget fixed overhead amounts

the fixed overhead spending variance,

. . . same as above

and the fixed overhead production-volume variance

. . . difference between budgeted fixed overhead and fixed overhead allocated on the basis of actual output produced

Fixed Overhead Cost Variances

The flexible-budget amount for a fixed-cost item is also the amount included in the static budget prepared at the start of the period. No adjustment is required for differences between actual output and budgeted output for fixed costs because fixed costs are unaffected by changes in the output level within the relevant range. At the start of 2013, Webb's managers budgeted fixed overhead costs to be $276,000 per month. The actual amount for April 2013 turned out to be $285,000. The **fixed overhead flexible-budget variance** is the difference between actual fixed overhead costs and fixed overhead costs in the flexible budget:

$$\begin{aligned}\text{Fixed overhead flexible-budget variance} &= \text{Actual costs incurred} - \text{Flexible-budget amount}\\ &= \$285{,}000 - \$276{,}000\\ &= \$9{,}000\text{ U}\end{aligned}$$

The variance is unfavorable because $285,000 actual fixed overhead costs exceed the $276,000 budgeted for April 2013, which decreases that month's operating income by $9,000.

Managers subdivided the variable overhead flexible-budget variance described earlier in this chapter into a spending variance and an efficiency variance. There is no efficiency variance for fixed overhead costs because a given lump sum of fixed overhead costs will be unaffected by how efficiently machine-hours are used to produce output in a given budget period. As we will see later in this chapter, this does not mean that a company cannot be efficient or inefficient in its use of fixed-overhead-cost resources. As Exhibit 13-5 shows, because there is no efficiency variance, the **fixed overhead spending variance** is the same amount as the fixed overhead flexible-budget variance:

$$\begin{aligned}\text{Fixed overhead spending variance} &= \text{Actual costs incurred} - \text{Flexible-budget amount}\\ &= \$285{,}000 - \$276{,}000\\ &= \$9{,}000\text{ U}\end{aligned}$$

Reasons for the unfavorable spending variance could be higher plant-leasing costs, higher depreciation on plant and equipment, or higher administrative costs, such as a higher-than-budgeted salary paid to the plant manager. Webb's managers investigated this variance and found that there was a $9,000 per month unexpected increase in its equipment-leasing costs. However, management concluded that the new lease rates were competitive with lease rates available elsewhere. If this were not the case, management would look to lease equipment from other suppliers.

Keys to Success

The fixed overhead spending variance informs managers of the difference between actual spending on fixed overhead and the planned amount of spending in the master budget. This highlights to managers the sources of unexpected changes in resources expended to acquire capacity.

Exhibit 13-5

Columnar Presentation of Fixed Overhead Variance Analysis: Webb Company for April 2013[a]

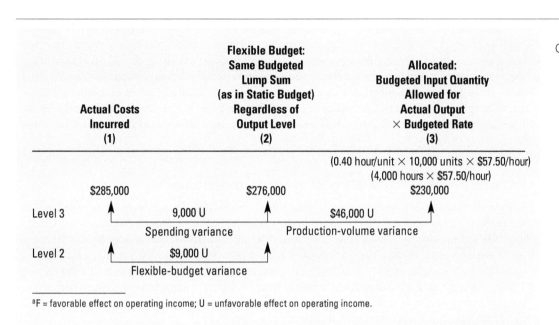

	Actual Costs Incurred (1)	Flexible Budget: Same Budgeted Lump Sum (as in Static Budget) Regardless of Output Level (2)	Allocated: Budgeted Input Quantity Allowed for Actual Output × Budgeted Rate (3)
			(0.40 hour/unit × 10,000 units × \$57.50/hour)
			(4,000 hours × \$57.50/hour)
	\$285,000	\$276,000	\$230,000

Level 3: (1) to (2): 9,000 U Spending variance; (2) to (3): \$46,000 U Production-volume variance

Level 2: (1) to (2): \$9,000 U Flexible-budget variance

[a]F = favorable effect on operating income; U = unfavorable effect on operating income.

Production-Volume Variance

We now examine a variance, the production-volume variance, which arises only for fixed costs. Recall that at the start of the year, Webb's managers calculated a budgeted fixed overhead rate of \$57.50 per machine hour. Under standard costing, Webb's budgeted fixed overhead costs are allocated to actual output produced during the period at the rate of \$57.50 per standard machine-hour, equivalent to a rate of \$23 per jacket (0.40 machine-hour per jacket × \$57.50 per machine-hour). If Webb produces 1,000 jackets, \$23,000 (\$23 per jacket × 1,000 jackets) out of April's budgeted fixed overhead costs of \$276,000 will be allocated to the jackets. If Webb produces 10,000 jackets, \$230,000 (\$23 per jacket × 10,000 jackets) will be allocated. Only if Webb produces 12,000 jackets (i.e., operates at capacity) will all \$276,000 (\$23 per jacket × 12,000 jackets) of the budgeted fixed overhead cost be allocated to the jacket output. The key point here is that even though Webb budgets fixed overhead costs to be \$276,000, it does not necessarily allocate all these costs to output. The reason is that Webb budgets \$276,000 of fixed costs to support its planned production of 12,000 jackets. If Webb produces fewer than 12,000 jackets, it only allocates the budgeted cost of capacity actually needed and used to produce the jackets.

The **production-volume variance,** also referred to as the **denominator-level variance,** is the difference between budgeted fixed overhead and fixed overhead allocated on the basis of actual output produced. The allocated fixed overhead can be expressed in terms of allocation-base units (machine-hours for Webb) or in terms of the budgeted fixed cost per unit:

$$
\begin{aligned}
\text{Production-volume variance} &= \text{Budgeted fixed overhead} - \text{Fixed overhead allocated for actual output units produced} \\
&= \$276{,}000 - (0.40 \text{ hour per jacket} \times \$57.50 \text{ per hour} \times 10{,}000 \text{ jackets}) \\
&= \$276{,}000 - (\$23 \text{ per jacket} \times 10{,}000 \text{ jackets}) \\
&= \$276{,}000 - \$230{,}000 \\
&= \$46{,}000 \text{ U}
\end{aligned}
$$

As shown in Exhibit 13-5, the budgeted fixed overhead (\$276,000) will be the lump sum shown in the static budget and also in any flexible budget within the relevant range. Fixed overhead allocated (\$230,000) is the amount of fixed overhead costs allocated under standard costing. It is calculated by multiplying the number of output units produced during the budget period (10,000 units) by the budgeted cost per output unit (\$23). Every output unit that Webb manufactures will increase the fixed overhead allocated to products by \$23. That is, for purposes of allocating fixed overhead costs to jackets, these costs are viewed *as if* they had a variable-cost behavior pattern. The \$46,000 U production-volume variance can therefore be thought of as \$23 per jacket × 2,000 jackets that were *not* produced (12,000 jackets planned – 10,000 jackets produced). We explore possible causes for the unfavorable production-volume variance and its management implications in the following section.

Managers should always be careful to distinguish the true behavior of fixed costs from the manner in which fixed costs are assigned to products. In particular, while fixed costs are unitized and allocated for inventory costing purposes as described above, managers should be wary of using the same unitized fixed overhead costs for planning and control purposes. When forecasting fixed costs, managers should concentrate on total lump-sum costs. Similarly, when managers are looking to assign costs for control purposes or identify the best way to use capacity resources that are fixed in the short run, recall from Chapters 2 and 9 that the use of unitized fixed costs often leads to incorrect decisions.

Interpreting the Production-Volume Variance

Lump-sum fixed costs represent costs of acquiring capacity that do not decrease automatically if the resources needed turn out to be less than the resources acquired. Sometimes costs are fixed for a specific time period for contractual reasons, such as an annual lease contract for a plant. At other times, costs are fixed because the firm needs to acquire capacity or dispose of it in fixed increments, or lumps. For example, suppose that acquiring a sewing machine gives Webb the ability to produce 1,000 jackets. Then, if it is not possible to buy or lease a fraction of a machine, Webb can add capacity only in increments of 1,000 jackets. That is, Webb may choose capacity levels of 10,000, 11,000, or 12,000 jackets, but nothing in between.

Webb's management would want to analyze why this overcapacity occurred. Is demand weak? Should Webb reevaluate its product and marketing strategies? Is there a quality problem? Or did Webb make a strategic mistake by acquiring too much capacity? The causes of the $46,000 unfavorable production-volume variance will drive the actions Webb's managers will take in response to this variance.

In contrast, a favorable production-volume variance indicates an overallocation of fixed overhead costs. That is, the overhead costs allocated to the actual output produced exceed the budgeted fixed overhead costs of $276,000. The favorable production-volume variance comprises the fixed costs allocated in excess of $276,000.

Be careful when drawing conclusions regarding a company's decisions about capacity planning and usage from the type (i.e., favorable, F, or unfavorable, U) or the magnitude associated with a production-volume variance. To interpret the $46,000 unfavorable variance, Webb should consider why it sold only 10,000 jackets in April. Suppose a new competitor had gained market share by pricing below Webb's selling price. To sell the budgeted 12,000 jackets, Webb might have had to reduce its own selling price on all 12,000 jackets. Suppose it decided that selling 10,000 jackets at a higher price yielded higher operating income than selling 12,000 jackets at a lower price. The production-volume variance does not take into account such information. The failure of the production-volume variance to consider such information is why Webb should not interpret the $46,000 U amount as the total economic cost of selling 2,000 jackets fewer than the 12,000 jackets budgeted. If, however, Webb's managers anticipate they will not need capacity beyond 10,000 jackets, they may reduce the excess capacity, say, by canceling the lease on some of the machines.

Companies plan their plant capacity strategically on the basis of market information about how much capacity they will need over some future time horizon. For 2013, Webb's budgeted quantity of output is equal to the maximum capacity of the plant for that budget period. Actual demand (and quantity produced) turned out to be below the budgeted quantity of output, so Webb reports an unfavorable production-volume variance for April 2013. However, it would be incorrect to conclude that Webb's management made a poor planning decision regarding plant capacity. Demand for Webb's jackets might be highly uncertain. Given this uncertainty and the cost of not having sufficient capacity to meet sudden demand surges (including lost contribution margins as well as reduced repeat business), Webb's management may have made a wise choice in planning 2013 plant capacity. Of course, if demand is unlikely to pick up again, Webb's managers may look to cancel the lease on some of the machines or to sublease the machines to other parties with the goal of reducing the unfavorable production-volume variance.

Managers must always explore the "why" of a variance before concluding that the label of unfavorable or favorable necessarily indicates, respectively, poor or good management performance. Understanding the reasons for a variance also helps managers decide on future courses of action. Should Webb's managers try to reduce capacity, increase sales, or do nothing? Based on their analysis of the situation, Webb's managers decided to reduce some capacity but continued to maintain some excess capacity to accommodate unexpected surges in demand. Concepts in Action: Variance

Analysis and Standard Costing Help Sandoz Manage Its Overhead Costs highlights another example of managers using variances, and the reasons behind them, to help guide their decisions.

Concepts in Action: Variance Analysis and Standard Costing Help Sandoz Manage Its Overhead Costs

In the United States, the importance of generic pharmaceuticals is growing dramatically. Sandoz, a $9.5 billion subsidiary of Swiss-based Novartis AG, is one of the largest generic drug developers. Market pricing pressure means that Sandoz operates on razor-thin margins. As a result, the company must tackle the challenge of accounting for overhead costs. Sandoz uses standard costing and variance analysis to manage its overhead costs.

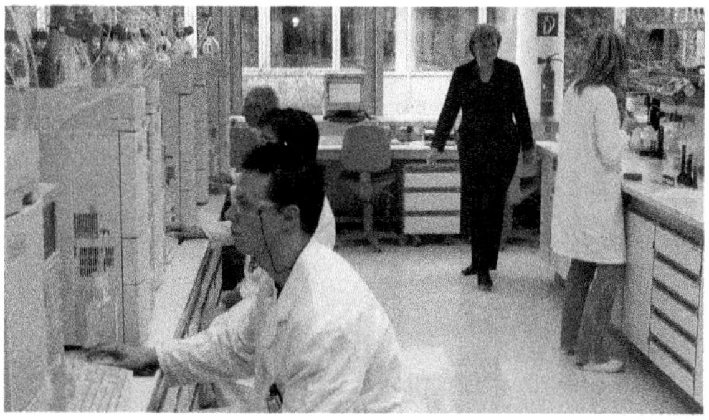

Source: Arnd Wiegmann/Reuters

Each year, Sandoz prepares an overhead budget based on a detailed production plan, planned overhead spending, and other factors. Sandoz then uses activity-based costing to assign budgeted overhead costs to different work centers (mixing, blending, tableting, testing, and packaging). Finally, overhead costs are assigned to products based on the activity levels required by each product at each work center. The resulting standard product cost is used in profitability analysis and as a basis for pricing decisions. The two main focal points in Sandoz's performance analyses are overhead absorption analysis and manufacturing overhead variance analysis.

Each month, Sandoz uses absorption analysis to compare actual production and actual costs to the standard costs of processed inventory. The monthly analysis evaluates two key trends:

1. Are costs in line with the budget? If not, the reasons are examined and the accountable managers are notified.
2. Are production volume and product mix conforming to plan? If not, Sandoz reviews and adjusts machine capacities and the absorption trend. Plant management uses absorption analysis to determine if it is on budget and has an appropriate capacity level to efficiently satisfy the needs of its customers.

Managers examine manufacturing overhead variances at the work-center level. These variances help managers (1) determine when equipment is not running as expected, which leads to repair or replacement; (2) identify inefficiencies in processing and setup and cleaning times, which leads to more efficient ways to use equipment; and (3) review and improve the standards themselves. Management reviews current and future capacity use on a monthly basis, using standard hours entered into the plan's enterprise resource planning system. The standards are a useful tool in identifying capacity constraints and future capital needs. These efforts result in better pricing and product mix decisions, lower waste, process improvements, and efficient capacity choices for Sandoz, all of which contribute to overall profitability.

Sources: Based on conversations with, and documents prepared by, Eric Evans and Erich Erchr (of Sandoz), 2004; Novartis International AG. 2012. 2011 Annual Report. Basel, Switzerland: Novartis International AG.

Keys to Success

The fixed overhead production volume variance shows managers the impact on income of fixed overhead resources being utilized at higher or lower levels of capacity than budgeted. This information helps managers choose whether the firm should acquire additional capacity or reduce it in future periods, as well as to decide on ways to use the capacity better, such as running promotions to increase sales or reassigning production from work areas that are closer to full utilization.

Learning Objective 7

Show how the variance analysis approach reconciles the actual results for a period with the results expected for that period

. . . the variance analysis approach identifies price and efficiency variances for direct-cost inputs, spending and efficiency variances for variable overhead costs, and spending and production-volume variances for fixed overhead costs

Integrated Analysis of Variances

As our discussion indicates, the variance calculations for variable overhead and fixed overhead differ:

- Variable overhead has no production-volume variance.
- Fixed overhead has no efficiency variance.

Exhibit 13-6 presents an integrated summary of the variable overhead variances and the fixed overhead variances computed using standard costs for April 2013. Panel A shows the variances for variable overhead, while Panel B contains the fixed overhead variances. As you study Exhibit 13-6, note how the columns in Panels A and B are aligned to measure the different variances. In both Panels A and B,

- the difference between columns 1 and 2 measures the spending variance.
- the difference between columns 2 and 3 measures the efficiency variance (if applicable).
- the difference between columns 3 and 4 measures the production-volume variance (if applicable).

Panel A contains an efficiency variance; Panel B has no efficiency variance for fixed overhead. As discussed earlier, a lump-sum amount of fixed costs will be unaffected by the degree of operating efficiency in a given budget period.

Panel A does not have a production-volume variance because the amount of variable overhead allocated is always the same as the flexible-budget amount. Variable costs never have any unused capacity. When production and sales decline from 12,000 jackets to 10,000 jackets, budgeted variable overhead costs proportionately decline. Fixed costs are different. Panel B has a production-volume variance because Webb's managers had to acquire the fixed manufacturing overhead resources they had committed to when planning production of 12,000 jackets, even though they produced only 10,000 jackets and did not use some of the capacity.

As we have discussed earlier, the variances identified by Webb are not necessarily independent of each other. For example, Webb may purchase lower-quality machine fluids (leading to a favorable variable overhead spending variance), which results in the machines taking longer to operate than budgeted (causing an unfavorable variable overhead efficiency variance) and producing less than budgeted output (causing an unfavorable production-volume variance).

Detailed variance analyses are most common in large, complex businesses, such as General Electric and Disney, because it is impossible for those managers to keep track of all that is happening within their areas of responsibility. The detailed analyses help managers identify and focus on the areas not operating as expected. Managers of small businesses understand their operations better based on personal observations and nonfinancial measures. They find less value in doing the additional measurements required for comprehensive variance analyses. For example, to simplify their costing systems, small companies may not distinguish variable overhead incurred from fixed overhead incurred because making this distinction is often not clear-cut. As we saw in Chapters 2 and 8, many costs such as supervision, quality control, and materials handling have both variable- and fixed-cost components that may be difficult to separate. Managers may therefore use a less detailed analysis that *combines* the variable overhead and fixed overhead into a single total overhead.

Returning to Exhibit 13-6, note that the sum of the flexible budget and production volume variances for variable and fixed overhead yields an overall overhead variance figure of $65,500. This single **total-overhead variance** equals the total amount of underallocated (or underapplied) overhead costs. (Recall our discussion of underallocated overhead costs in normal costing from Chapter 4, pages 134–137.) Similarly, the sum of the flexible-budget variances for direct materials and direct labor (see Exhibit 13-3) is $59,600 U ($21,600 U + $38,000 U). The total of these two amounts, $125,100 U, is the difference between the costs applied to manufactured units in a standard-costing system and the actual costs incurred. As in a normal costing system, this underallocation is disposed of at the end of the period using some combination of writeoffs to Cost of Goods Sold and proration among Cost of Goods Sold, Work-in-Process, and Finished Goods balances.

Summary of Variances

As we complete our study of variance analysis for Webb Company, it is helpful to step back to see the "big picture" and to link the accounting and performance evaluation functions of standard costing. Exhibit 13-1, page 538, first identified a static-budget variance of $93,100 U as the difference between the static budget operating income of $108,000 and the actual operating income of

Exhibit 13-6

Columnar Presentation of Integrated Variance Analysis: Webb Company for April 2013[a]

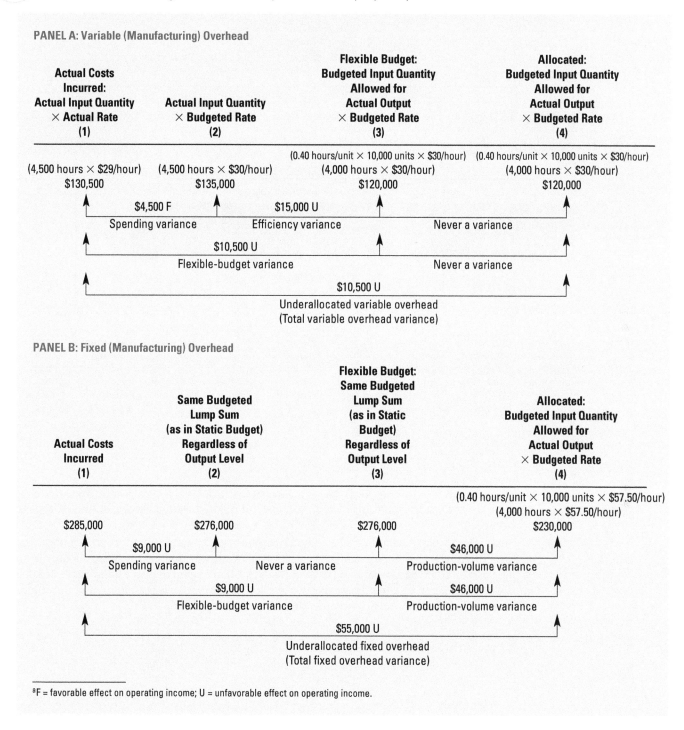

PANEL A: Variable (Manufacturing) Overhead

Actual Costs Incurred: Actual Input Quantity × Actual Rate (1)	Actual Input Quantity × Budgeted Rate (2)	Flexible Budget: Budgeted Input Quantity Allowed for Actual Output × Budgeted Rate (3)	Allocated: Budgeted Input Quantity Allowed for Actual Output × Budgeted Rate (4)
		(0.40 hours/unit × 10,000 units × $30/hour)	(0.40 hours/unit × 10,000 units × $30/hour)
(4,500 hours × $29/hour)	(4,500 hours × $30/hour)	(4,000 hours × $30/hour)	(4,000 hours × $30/hour)
$130,500	$135,000	$120,000	$120,000

(1)–(2): $4,500 F Spending variance; (2)–(3): $15,000 U Efficiency variance; (3)–(4): Never a variance

(1)–(3): $10,500 U Flexible-budget variance; (3)–(4): Never a variance

(1)–(4): $10,500 U Underallocated variable overhead (Total variable overhead variance)

PANEL B: Fixed (Manufacturing) Overhead

Actual Costs Incurred (1)	Same Budgeted Lump Sum (as in Static Budget) Regardless of Output Level (2)	Flexible Budget: Same Budgeted Lump Sum (as in Static Budget) Regardless of Output Level (3)	Allocated: Budgeted Input Quantity Allowed for Actual Output × Budgeted Rate (4)
			(0.40 hours/unit × 10,000 units × $57.50/hour)
			(4,000 hours × $57.50/hour)
$285,000	$276,000	$276,000	$230,000

(1)–(2): $9,000 U Spending variance; (2)–(3): Never a variance; (3)–(4): $46,000 U Production-volume variance

(1)–(3): $9,000 U Flexible-budget variance; (3)–(4): $46,000 U Production-volume variance

(1)–(4): $55,000 U Underallocated fixed overhead (Total fixed overhead variance)

[a]F = favorable effect on operating income; U = unfavorable effect on operating income.

$14,900. Exhibit 13-2, page 540, then subdivided the static-budget variance of $93,100 U into a flexible-budget variance of $29,100 U and a sales-volume variance of $64,000 U. Subsequently, we presented more detailed variances that subdivided, whenever possible, individual flexible-budget variances for selling price, direct materials, direct manufacturing labor, and variable overhead. For fixed overhead, we noted that the flexible-budget variance ($9,000 U) is the same as the spending variance ($9,000 U). Where does the production-volume variance belong then?

The production-volume variance forms part of sales-volume variance. Recall that the sales-volume variance of $64,000 U indicates to managers the lost contribution margin from selling 2,000 fewer jackets. This loss has two components. First, in standard costing, fixed overhead cost

Exhibit 13-7

Summary of Levels 1, 2, and 3 Variance Analysis

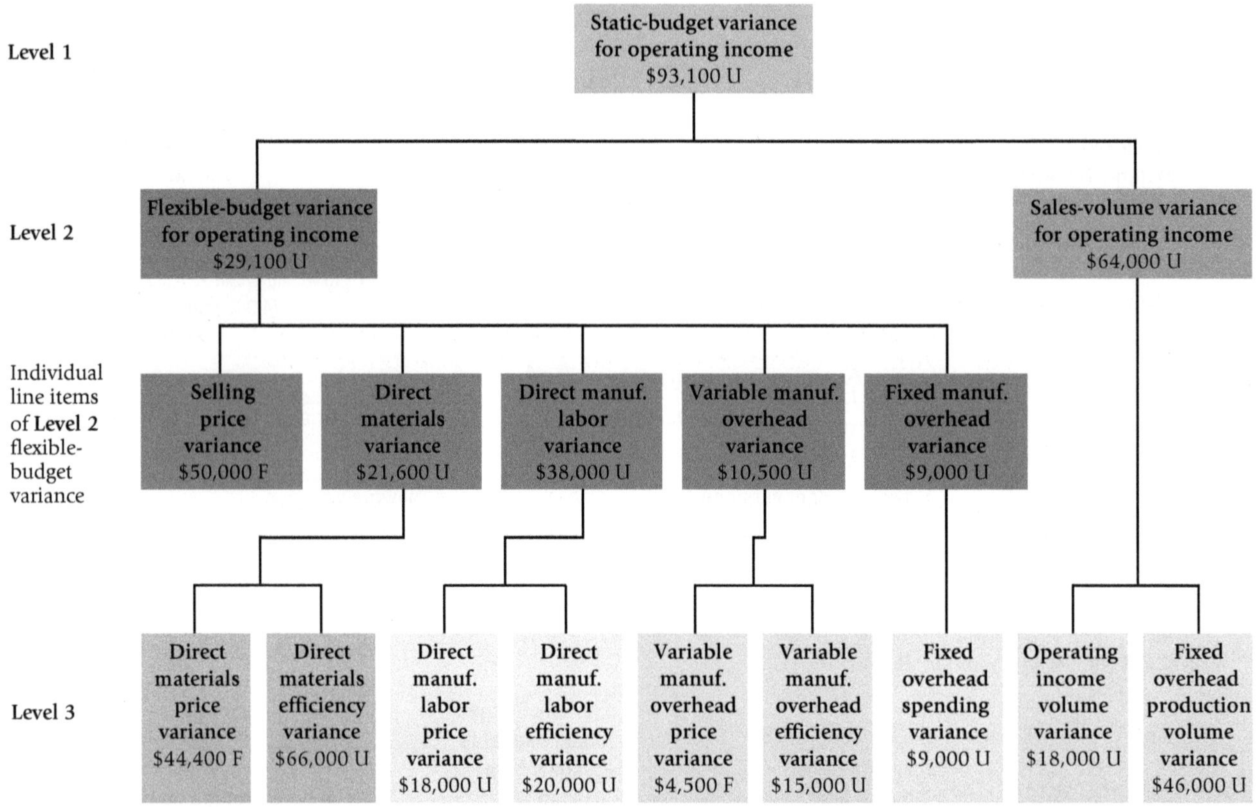

is treated as if it is a variable cost. The static-budget operating income of $108,000 for 12,000 jackets equates to $9 in income per jacket. The shortfall of 2,000 jackets thus produces a shortfall in income of $18,000 U (2,000 units × $9). This amount is the **operating-income volume variance.** It equals the static-budget operating income per unit multiplied by the difference between the budgeted and actual level of output. The second component of the sales-volume variance reflects the fact that managers have made commitments to fixed overhead resources that were not utilized to the expected extent because output fell below budget. This is captured by the unfavorable $46,000 production-volume variance. In summary, the sales-volume variance is comprised of operating-income volume and production-volume variances, as follows:

	Operating-income volume variance	$18,000 U
(+)	Production-volume variance	46,000 U
Equals	Sales-volume variance	$64,000 U

We can now provide a summary (see Exhibit 13-7) that formally disaggregates the static-budget variance of $93,100 U into its components. Note how the variances at each higher level provide disaggregated and more detailed information for evaluating performance.

We next describe how managers make use of variance information.

Learning Objective 8

Understand how managers use variances

. . . managers use variances to improve future performance

How Managers Use Variances

Managers use variances to evaluate performance after decisions are implemented, to trigger organization learning, and to make continuous improvements. Variances serve as an early warning system to alert managers to existing problems or to opportunities. Variance analysis enables managers to evaluate the effectiveness of the actions and performance of personnel in the current period, as well as to fine-tune strategies for achieving improved performance in the future. To make sure that managers interpret variances correctly and make appropriate decisions based on them, managers need to recognize that variances can have multiple causes.

Multiple Causes of Variances

Managers must not interpret variances in isolation of each other. The causes of variances in one part of the value chain can be the result of decisions made in another part of the value chain. Consider an unfavorable direct materials efficiency variance on Webb's production line. Possible operational causes of this variance across the value chain of the company are:

1. Poor design of products or processes
2. Poor work on the production line because of underskilled workers or faulty machines
3. Inappropriate assignment of labor or machines to specific jobs
4. Congestion due to scheduling a large number of rush orders from Webb's sales representatives
5. Webb's suppliers not manufacturing cloth materials of uniformly high quality

Item 5 offers an even broader reason for the cause of the unfavorable direct materials efficiency variance by considering inefficiencies in the supply chain of companies—in this case, by the cloth suppliers for Webb's jackets. Whenever possible, managers must attempt to understand the root causes of the variances.

When to Investigate Variances

Managers must realize that a standard is not a single measure but rather a range of possible acceptable input quantities, costs, output quantities, or prices. Consequently, they should expect small variances to arise. A variance within an acceptable range is considered to be an "in-control occurrence" and calls for no investigation or action by managers. So, when would managers need to investigate variances?

Frequently, managers investigate variances based on subjective judgments or rules of thumb. For critical items, such as product defects, even a small variance may prompt investigations and actions. For other items, such as direct material costs, labor costs, and repair costs, companies generally have rules such as "investigate all variances exceeding $5,000 or 25% of the budgeted cost, whichever is lower." The idea is that a 4% variance in direct material costs of $1 million—a $40,000 variance—deserves more attention than a 20% variance in repair costs of $10,000—a $2,000 variance. Variance analysis is subject to the same cost–benefit test as all other phases of a management control system.

Performance Measurement Using Variances

Managers often use variance analysis when evaluating the performance of their subordinates. Two attributes of performance are commonly evaluated:

1. **Effectiveness:** the degree to which a predetermined objective or target is met, such as sales, market share, and customer satisfaction ratings of Starbucks' VIA® Ready Brew line of instant coffees.
2. **Efficiency:** the relative amount of inputs used to achieve a given output level. For example, the smaller the quantity of Arabica beans used to make a given number of VIA packets or the greater the number of VIA packets made from a given quantity of beans, the greater the efficiency.

As we discussed earlier, managers must be sure they understand the causes of a variance before using it for performance evaluation. Suppose a Webb purchasing manager has just negotiated a deal that results in a favorable price variance for direct materials. The deal could have achieved a favorable variance for any or all of the following reasons:

1. The purchasing manager bargained effectively with suppliers.
2. The purchasing manager secured a discount for buying in bulk with fewer purchase orders. (However, buying larger quantities than necessary for the short run resulted in excessive inventory.)
3. The purchasing manager accepted a bid from the lowest-priced supplier after only minimal effort to check quality amid concerns about the supplier's materials.

If the purchasing manager's performance is evaluated solely on price variances, then the evaluation will be positive. Reason 1 would support this favorable conclusion: The purchasing manager bargained effectively. Reasons 2 and 3 have short-run gains, buying in bulk or making only minimal effort to check the supplier's quality-monitoring procedures. However, these short-run gains could be offset by higher inventory storage costs or higher inspection costs and defect rates on Webb's production line, leading to unfavorable direct manufacturing labor and direct materials efficiency variances. Webb may ultimately lose more money because of reasons 2 and 3 than it gains from the favorable price variance.

The bottom line is that managers should not automatically interpret a favorable variance as "good news."

Managers benefit from variance analysis because it highlights individual aspects of performance. However, if any single performance measure (e.g., a labor efficiency variance or a consumer rating report) receives excessive emphasis, managers will tend to make decisions that will cause the particular performance measure to look good. These actions may conflict with the company's overall goals, inhibiting the goals from being achieved. This faulty perspective on performance usually arises when top management designs a performance evaluation and reward system that does not emphasize total company objectives.

Organization Learning

The goal of variance analysis is for managers to understand why variances arise, to learn, and to improve future performance. For instance, to reduce the unfavorable direct materials efficiency variance, Webb's managers may seek improvements in product design, in the commitment of workers to do the job right the first time, and in the quality of supplied materials, among other improvements. Sometimes an unfavorable direct materials efficiency variance may signal a need to change product strategy, perhaps because the product cannot be made at a low enough cost. Variance analysis should not be a tool to "play the blame game" (i.e., seeking a person to blame for every unfavorable variance). Rather, variance analysis should help managers learn about what happened and how to perform better in the future.

Managers need to strike a delicate balance between the two uses of variances we have discussed: performance evaluation and organization learning. Variance analysis is helpful for performance evaluation, but an overemphasis on performance evaluation and meeting individual variance targets can undermine learning and continuous improvement. Why? Because achieving the standard becomes an end in and of itself. As a result, managers will seek targets that are easy to attain rather than targets that are challenging and that require creativity and resourcefulness. For example, if performance evaluation is overemphasized, Webb's manufacturing manager will prefer an easy standard that allows workers ample time to manufacture a jacket; he will then have little incentive to improve processes and methods to reduce manufacturing time and cost.

An overemphasis on performance evaluation may also cause managers to take actions to achieve the budget and avoid an unfavorable variance, even if such actions could hurt the company in the long run. For example, the manufacturing manager may push workers to produce jackets within the time allowed, even if this action could lead to poorer quality jackets being produced, which could later hurt revenues. Such negative effects are less likely to occur if managers see variance analysis as a way of promoting organization learning.

Keys to Success

It is critical that managers use variance analysis as a means for learning and improvement rather than as a way to punish those who do not reach targets. Placing too much emphasis on achieving standards will lead to the setting of poor targets, and to gaming and dysfunctional behavior aimed at meeting benchmarks that could have potentially negative long-run consequences.

Continuous Improvement

Managers can also use variance analysis to create a virtuous cycle of continuous improvement. How? By repeatedly identifying causes of variances, initiating corrective actions, and evaluating results of actions. Improvement opportunities are often easier to identify when the company first produces the products. Once managers identify easy opportunities, much more ingenuity may be required to identify successive improvement opportunities. Some companies use kaizen budgeting (Chapter 12, page 506) to specifically target reductions in budgeted costs over successive periods. The advantage of kaizen budgeting is that it makes continuous improvement goals explicit.

Financial and Nonfinancial Performance Measures

Almost all companies use a combination of financial and nonfinancial performance measures for planning and control rather than relying exclusively on either type of measure. To control a production process, supervisors cannot wait for an accounting report with variances reported in dollars. Instead, timely nonfinancial performance measures are frequently used for control purposes in such situations. For example, a Nissan plant compiles data such as defect rates and production-schedule attainment and broadcasts them in ticker-tape fashion on screens throughout the plant.

In Webb's cutting room, cloth is laid out and cut into pieces, which are then matched and assembled. Managers exercise control in the cutting room by observing workers and by focusing on *nonfinancial measures,* such as number of square yards of cloth used to produce 1,000 jackets or percentage of jackets started and completed without requiring any rework. Webb production workers find these nonfinancial measures easy to understand. At the same time, Webb production managers will also use *financial measures* to evaluate the overall cost efficiency with which operations are being run and to help guide decisions about, say, changing the mix of inputs used in manufacturing jackets. Financial measures are often critical in a company because they indicate the economic impact of diverse physical activities. This knowledge allows managers to make tradeoffs, such as increasing the costs of one physical activity (say, cutting) to reduce the costs of another physical measure (say, defects).

Similarly, Webb would likely find the following nonfinancial measures helpful in planning and controlling its overhead costs:

1. Quantity of actual indirect materials used per machine-hour, relative to quantity of budgeted indirect materials used per machine-hour
2. Actual energy used per machine-hour, relative to budgeted energy used per machine-hour
3. Actual machine-hours per jacket, relative to budgeted machine-hours per jacket

These performance measures, like the financial variances discussed in this chapter, can be described as signals to direct managers' attention to problems. These nonfinancial performance measures probably would be reported daily or hourly on the production floor. The overhead variances we discussed in this chapter capture the financial effects of items such as the three factors listed, which in many cases first appear as nonfinancial performance measures. An interesting example along these lines comes from Japan, where some companies have introduced budgeted-to-actual variance analysis and internal trading systems among group units as a means to rein in their CO_2 emissions. The goal is to raise employee awareness of emissions reduction in preparation for the anticipated future costs of greenhouse-gas reduction plans being drawn up by the Japanese government.

Finally, both financial and nonfinancial performance measures are used to evaluate the performance of managers. Exclusive reliance on either is always too simplistic because each gives a different perspective on performance. Nonfinancial measures (such as those described previously) provide feedback on individual aspects of a manager's performance, whereas financial measures evaluate the overall effect of and the tradeoffs among different nonfinancial performance measures.

Cost Variances in Nonmanufacturing Settings

Our Webb Company example examines variable manufacturing overhead costs and fixed manufacturing overhead costs. Managers can also use variance analysis to examine the overhead costs of the nonmanufacturing areas of the company and to make decisions about (1) pricing, (2) managing costs, and (3) product mix. For example, managers in industries in which distribution costs are high, such as automobiles, consumer durables, cement, and steel, may use standard costing to give reliable and timely information on variable distribution overhead spending variances and efficiency variances.

Some labor-intensive service-sector companies, such as McDonald's, use standard costs to control labor costs. Consider companies in other service-sector industries such as airlines, hospitals, hotels, and railroads. The measures of output these companies commonly use are passenger-miles flown, patient-days provided, room-days occupied, and ton-miles of freight hauled, respectively. Few costs can be traced to these outputs in a cost-effective way. The majority of costs are fixed overhead costs, such as the costs of equipment, buildings, and staff. Using capacity effectively is the key to profitability, and fixed overhead variances can help managers in this task. Retail businesses, such as Kmart, also have high capacity–related fixed costs (lease and occupancy costs). In the case of Kmart, sales declines resulted in unused capacity and unfavorable fixed-cost variances. Kmart reduced fixed costs by closing some of its stores, but it also had to file for Chapter 11 bankruptcy in January 2002.

Impact of Information Technology on Variances

Modern information technology promotes the increased use of standard-costing systems for product costing and control. Companies such as Dell and Sandoz store standard prices and standard quantities in their computer systems. A bar code scanner records the receipt of materials, immediately costing each material using its stored standard price. The receipt of materials is then matched with the purchase order to record accounts payable and to isolate the direct materials price variance.

The direct materials efficiency variance is calculated as output is completed by comparing the standard quantity of direct materials that should have been used with the computerized request for direct materials submitted by an operator on the production floor. Labor variances are calculated as employees log into production-floor terminals and punch in their employee numbers, start and end times, and the quantity of product they helped produce. Managers use this instantaneous feedback from variances to initiate immediate corrective action, as needed.

Technology has helped many companies improve their performance:

- Total quality management systems help companies in both the manufacturing and service industries to control costs. Companies as diverse as Disney, Federal Express, and Kentucky Fried Chicken have well-developed quality management programs that focus on simplifying processes and monitoring them continuously, as well as the use of information technology to enable reduced waste and faster service.
- Computer-integrated manufacturing (CIM) systems help companies such as Toyota use flexible budgeting and standard costing to manage activities such as materials handling and setups.
- Enterprise resource planning (ERP) systems, as described in Chapter 10, have made it easy for companies to keep track of standard, average, and actual costs for inventory items and to make real-time assessments of variances. Managers in companies such as Caterpillar, Heineken, and Porsche use variance information to identify areas of the firm's manufacturing or purchasing process that most need attention.

Keys to Success

Managers have developed and used information technology, including ERP systems, to promote a greater use of standard-costing systems and variance analysis at a significantly lower cost to the company.

Problem for Self-Study

David James is a manager at Doorknob Design Company (DDC), which manufactures expensive brass doorknobs. DDC uses two direct cost categories: direct materials and direct manufacturing labor. The business analysts at DDC feel that manufacturing overhead is most closely related to material usage. Therefore, DDC allocates manufacturing overhead to production based on pounds of materials used.

At the beginning of 2013, DDC budgeted annual production of 400,000 doorknobs and adopted the following standards for each doorknob:

	Input	Cost/Doorknob
Direct materials (brass)	0.3 lb. @ $10/lb.	$ 3.00
Direct manufacturing labor	1.2 hours @ $20/hour	24.00
Manufacturing overhead		
Variable	$6/lb. × 0.3 lb.	1.80
Fixed	$15/lb. × 0.3 lb.	4.50
Standard cost per doorknob		$33.30

Actual results for April 2013 were:

Production	35,000 doorknobs
Direct materials purchased	12,000 lb. at $11/lb.
Direct materials used	10,450 lb.
Direct manufacturing labor	38,500 hours for $808,500
Variable manufacturing overhead	$64,150
Fixed manufacturing overhead	$152,000

Required

1. For the month of April, compute the following variances, indicating whether each is favorable (F) or unfavorable (U):
   a. Direct materials price variance (based on purchases)

b. Direct materials efficiency variance (based on usage)
c. Direct manufacturing labor price variance
d. Direct manufacturing labor efficiency variance
e. Variable manufacturing overhead spending variance
f. Variable manufacturing overhead efficiency variance
g. Production-volume variance
h. Fixed manufacturing overhead spending variance

2. Can James use any of the variances to help explain any of the other variances? Give examples.

Solution

1. See Exhibit 13-8. Note, in particular, the two sets of computations in column 2 for direct materials: the $120,000 for direct materials purchased and the $104,500 for direct materials used. The direct materials price variance is calculated on purchases so that managers responsible

Exhibit 13-8

Columnar Presentation of Integrated Variance Anaysis: Doorknob Design Company (DDC) for April 2013[a]

	Actual Costs Incurred: Actual Input Quantity × Actual Rate	**Actual Input Quantity × Budgeted Price: Purchases**	**Actual Input Quantity × Budgeted Price: Usage**	**Flexible Budget: Budgeted Input Quantity Allowed for Actual Output × Budgeted Price**
Direct Materials	(12,000 × $11) $132,000	(12,000 × $10) $120,000	(10,450 × $10) $104,500	(0.3 × 35,000 × $10) $105,000

$12,000 U — a. Price variance; $500 F — b. Efficiency variance

Direct Manufacturing Labor	$808,500	(38,500 × $20) $770,000	(1.2 × 35,000 × $20) $840,000

$38,500 U — c. Price variance; $70,000 F — d. Efficiency variance

	Actual Costs Incurred	**Actual Input Quantity × Budgeted Rate**	**Flexible Budget: Budgeted Input Quantity Allowed for Actual Output × Budgeted Rate**	**Allocated: (Budgeted Input Quantity Allowed for Actual Output × Budgeted Rate)**
Variable Manufacturing Overhead	$64,150	(10,450 × $6) $62,700	(0.3 × 35,000 × $6) $63,000	(0.3 × 35,000 × $6) $63,000
Fixed Manufacturing Overhead	$152,000	$150,000*	$150,000	(0.3 × 35,000 × $15) $157,500

Variable manufacturing overhead: $1,450U — e. Spending variance; $300 F — f. Efficiency variance; Never a variance

Fixed manufacturing overhead: $2,000 U — g. Spending variance; Never a variance; $7,500 F — h. Production volume variance

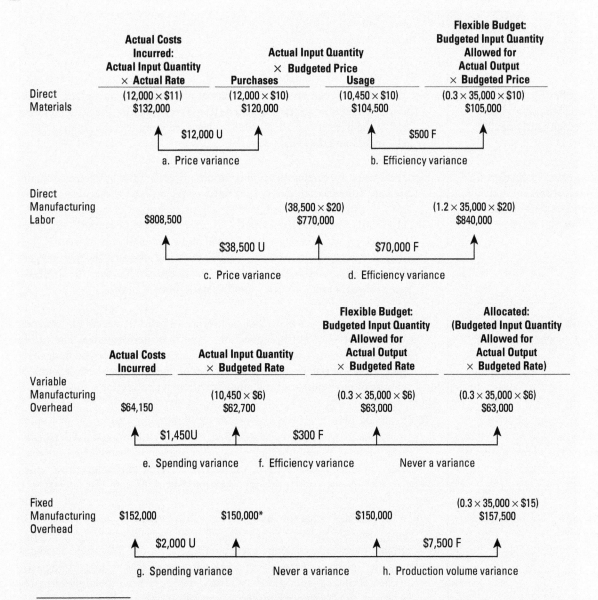

[a]F = favorable effect on operating income; U = unfavorable effect on operating income.
*Denominator level (Annual) in pounds of material: 400,000 x .3 = 120,000 pounds
Annual budgeted fixed overhead: 120,000 x $15/lb = $1,800,000
Monthly budgeted FOH: $1,800,000 / 12 = $150,000

for the purchase can immediately identify and isolate reasons for the variance and initiate any desired corrective action. The efficiency variance is the responsibility of the production manager, so this variance is identified only at the time materials are used.

2. The direct materials price variance indicates that DDC paid more for brass than they had planned. If this is because they purchased higher-quality brass, it may explain why they used less brass than expected (leading to a favorable material efficiency variance). In turn, since DDC managers assigned variable manufacturing overhead based on pounds of materials used, they saw a favorable variable overhead efficiency variance. The purchase of better-quality brass may also explain why it took less labor time to produce the doorknobs than expected (the favorable direct labor efficiency variance). Finally, the unfavorable direct labor price variance could imply that the workers who were hired were more experienced than expected, which could also be related to the positive direct material and direct labor efficiency variances.

Decision Points

The following question-and-answer format summarizes the chapter's learning objectives. Each decision presents a key question related to a learning objective. The guidelines are the answer to that question.

Decision	Guidelines
1. How does a flexible budget differ from a static budget, and why should companies use flexible budgets?	A static budget is based on the level of output planned at the start of the budget period. A flexible budget is adjusted (flexed) to recognize the actual output level of the budget period. Flexible budgets are more useful to managers to help understand the causes of variances.
2. How can managers develop a flexible budget and compute the flexible-budget variance and the sales-volume variance?	Managers use a three-step procedure to develop a flexible budget. When all costs are either variable in output units or fixed, these three steps require only information about budgeted selling price, budgeted variable cost per output unit, budgeted fixed costs, and actual quantity of output units. The static-budget variance can be subdivided into a flexible-budget variance (the difference between an actual result and the corresponding flexible-budget amount) and a sales-volume variance (the difference between the flexible-budget amount and the corresponding static-budget amount).
3. Why should a company calculate price and efficiency variances?	The computation of price and efficiency variances helps managers understand two different—but not independent—aspects of performance. The price variance focuses on the difference between actual input price and budgeted input price. The efficiency variance focuses on the difference between actual quantity of input and budgeted quantity of input allowed for actual output.
4. How do companies plan for overhead costs, and how do they calculate budgeted overhead cost rates?	To effectively plan overhead costs, managers must plan to undertake only essential activities, and to perform them efficiently. Planning fixed overhead costs also involves making choices regarding capacity. The budgeted variable (fixed) overhead cost rate is calculated by dividing the budgeted variable (fixed) overhead costs by the denominator level of the cost-allocation base.
5. What variances can be calculated for variable overhead?	When the flexible budget for variable overhead is developed, an overhead efficiency variance and an overhead spending variance can be computed. The variable overhead efficiency variance focuses on the difference between the actual quantity of the cost-allocation base used relative to the budgeted quantity of the cost-allocation base. The variable overhead spending variance focuses on the difference between the actual variable overhead cost per unit of the cost-allocation base relative to the budgeted variable overhead cost per unit of the cost-allocation base.

Decision	Guidelines
6. What variances can be calculated for fixed overhead?	For fixed overhead, the static and flexible budgets coincide. The difference between the budgeted and actual amount of fixed overhead is the flexible-budget variance, also referred to as the spending variance. The production-volume variance measures the difference between budgeted fixed overhead and fixed overhead allocated on the basis of actual output produced.
7. What is the most detailed way for a company to reconcile actual earnings results with the budgeted earnings for the period?	A comprehensive variance analysis presents price and efficiency variances for direct materials and direct labor, spending and efficiency variances for variable overhead costs, and spending and production-volume variances for fixed overhead costs. By analyzing these variances together, managers can reconcile the actual costs with the amount of costs allocated to output produced during a period.
8. How do managers use variances?	Managers use variances for control, decision implementation, performance evaluation, organization learning, and continuous improvement. When using variances for these purposes, managers consider several variances together rather than focusing only on an individual variance.

Terms to Learn

This chapter and the Glossary at the end of the book contain definitions of the following important terms:

budgeted performance (p. 536)
denominator level (p. 549)
denominator-level variance (p. 555)
effectiveness (p. 561)
efficiency (p. 561)
efficiency variance (p. 545)
favorable variance (p. 538)
fixed overhead flexible-budget variance (p. 554)
fixed overhead spending variance (p. 554)
flexible budget (p. 539)
flexible-budget variance (p. 539)
management by exception (p. 536)
operating-income volume variance (p. 560)
price variance (p. 545)
production-volume variance (p. 555)
rate variance (p. 545)
sales-volume variance (p. 539)
selling-price variance (p. 541)
standard (p. 543)
standard cost (p. 544)
standard costing (p. 548)
standard input (p. 544)
standard price (p. 544)
static budget (p. 537)
static-budget variance (p. 538)
total-overhead variance (p. 558)
unfavorable variance (p. 538)
usage variance (p. 545)
variable overhead efficiency variance (p. 551)
variable overhead flexible-budget variance (p. 551)
variable overhead spending variance (p. 552)
variance (p. 536)

Assignment Material

Questions

13-1 Distinguish between a favorable variance and an unfavorable variance.

13-2 Why might managers find a flexible-budget analysis more informative than a static-budget analysis?

13-3 List three causes of a favorable direct materials price variance.

13-4 Describe three reasons for an unfavorable direct manufacturing labor efficiency variance.

13-5 Comment on the following statement made by a plant manager: "Meetings with my plant accountant are frustrating. All he wants to do is pin the blame on someone for the many variances he reports."

13-6 How does the planning of fixed overhead costs differ from the planning of variable overhead costs?

13-7 What are the factors that affect the spending variance for variable manufacturing overhead?

13-8 Assume variable manufacturing overhead is allocated using machine-hours. Give three possible reasons for a favorable variable overhead efficiency variance.

13-9 What are the steps in developing a budgeted fixed overhead rate?

13-10 "Overhead variances should be viewed as interdependent rather than independent." Give an example.

Exercises

13-11 Flexible budget. Connolly Enterprises manufactures tires for the Formula I motor racing circuit. For August 2013, it budgeted to manufacture and sell 3,500 tires at a variable cost of $75 per tire and total fixed costs of $56,500. The budgeted selling price was $112 per tire. Actual results in August 2013 were 3,400 tires manufactured and sold at a selling price of $113 per tire. The actual total variable costs were $278,800 and the actual total fixed costs were $51,500.

Required

1. Prepare a performance report (akin to Exhibit 13-2, page 540) that uses a flexible budget and a static budget.
2. Comment on the results in requirement 1.

13-12 Flexible budget. Harvin Company's budgeted prices for direct materials, direct manufacturing labor, and direct marketing (distribution) labor per attaché case are $37, $9, and $13, respectively. The president is pleased with the following performance report:

	Actual Costs	Static Budget	Variance
Direct materials	$373,000	$407,000	$34,000 F
Direct manufacturing labor	97,200	99,000	1,800 F
Direct marketing (distribution) labor	133,000	143,000	10,000 F

Actual output was 9,800 attaché cases. Assume all three direct-cost items shown are variable costs.

Required

Is the president's pleasure justified? Prepare a revised performance report that uses a flexible budget and a static budget.

13-13 Flexible-budget preparation and analysis. Check It Off Printers, Inc., produces luxury checkbooks with three checks and stubs per page. Each checkbook is designed for an individual customer and is ordered through the customer's bank. The company's operating budget for September 2013 included these data:

Number of checkbooks	13,000
Selling price per book	$ 21
Variable cost per book	$ 6
Fixed costs for the month	$125,000

The actual results for September 2013 were as follows:

Number of checkbooks produced and sold	9,500
Average selling price per book	$ 23
Variable cost per book	$ 4
Fixed costs for the month	$132,000

The executive vice president of the company observed that the operating income for September was much lower than anticipated, despite a higher-than-budgeted selling price and a lower-than-budgeted variable cost per unit. As the manager responsible for the checkbook unit, you have been asked to provide explanations for the disappointing September results.

Check It Off develops its flexible budget on the basis of budgeted per-output-unit revenue and per-output-unit variable costs without detailed analysis of budgeted inputs.

Required

1. Prepare a static budget–based variance analysis of the September performance.
2. Prepare a flexible budget–based variance analysis of the September performance.
3. Why might Check It Off find the flexible budget–based variance analysis more informative than the static budget–based variance analysis? Explain your answer.

13-14 Flexible budget, working backward. The Putnam Company produces engine parts for car manufacturers. A new accountant intern at Putnam has accidentally deleted the company's variance analysis calculations for the year ended December 31, 2012. The following table is what remains of the data:

	A	B	C	D	E	F
1	Performance Report, Year Ended December 31, 2012					
2						
3		Actual Results	Flexible-Budget Variances	Flexible Budget	Sales-Volume Variances	Static Budget
4	Units sold	100,000				95,000
5	Revenues (sales)	$716,000				$389,500
6	Variable costs	485,000				209,000
7	Contribution margin	231,000				180,500
8	Fixed costs	145,500				95,000
9	Operating income	$ 85,500				$ 85,500

Required

1. Calculate all the required variances. (If your work is accurate, you will find that the total static-budget variance is $0.)
2. What are the actual and budgeted selling prices? What are the actual and budgeted variable costs per unit?
3. Review the variances you have calculated and discuss possible causes and potential problems. What is the important lesson learned here?

13-15 Materials and manufacturing labor variances. Consider the following data collected for Country Homes, Inc.:

	Direct Materials	Direct Manufacturing Labor
Cost incurred: Actual inputs × actual prices	$204,000	$93,000
Actual inputs × standard prices	207,000	87,000
Standard inputs allowed for actual output × standard prices	217,000	82,000

Required

Compute the price, efficiency, and flexible-budget variances for direct materials and direct manufacturing labor.

13-16 Direct materials and direct manufacturing labor variances. AmyDee, Inc., designs and manufactures T-shirts. It sells its T-shirts to brand-name clothes retailers in lots of one dozen. AmyDee's May 2012 static budget and actual results for direct inputs are as follows:

Static Budget	
Number of T-shirt lots (1 lot = 1 dozen)	450
Per Lot of T-shirts	
Direct materials	14 meters at $1.80 per meter = $25.20
Direct manufacturing labor	2.20 hours at $7.70 per hour = $16.94
Actual Results	
Number of T-shirt lots sold	500
Total Direct Inputs	
Direct materials	7,600 meters at $2.05 per meter = $15,580
Direct manufacturing labor	1,050 hours at $7.80 per hour = $8,190

AmyDee has a policy of analyzing all input variances when they add up to more than 10% of the total cost of materials and labor in the flexible budget, and this is true in May 2012. The production manager discusses the sources of the variances: "A new type of material was purchased in May. This led to faster cutting and sewing, but the workers used more material than usual as they learned to work with it. For now, the standards are fine."

Required

1. Calculate the direct materials and direct manufacturing labor price and efficiency variances in May 2012. What is the total flexible-budget variance for both inputs (direct materials and direct manufacturing labor) combined? What percentage is this variance of the total cost of direct materials and direct manufacturing labor in the flexible budget?
2. Amy Young, the CEO, is concerned about the input variances. However, she likes the quality and feel of the new material and agrees to use it for one more year. In May 2013, AmyDee again produces 500 lots of T-shirts. Relative to May 2012, 2% less direct material is used, the direct material price is down 5%, and 2% less direct manufacturing labor is used. The labor price has remained the same as in May 2012. Calculate the direct materials and direct manufacturing labor price and efficiency variances in May 2013. What is the total flexible-budget variance for both inputs (direct materials and direct manufacturing labor) combined? What percentage is this variance of the total cost of direct materials and direct manufacturing labor in the flexible budget?
3. Comment on the May 2013 results. Would you continue the "experiment" of using the new material?

13-17 Price and efficiency variances. The Seneca Corporation manufactures lamps. It has set up the following standards per finished unit for direct materials and direct manufacturing labor:

Direct materials: 10 lb. at $5.40 per lb.	$54.00
Direct manufacturing labor: 0.5 hour at $29 per hour	14.50

The number of finished units budgeted for January 2013 was 9,760; 9,600 units were actually produced. Actual results in January 2013 were:

Direct materials: 95,500 lbs. used	
Direct manufacturing labor: 4,700 hours	$143,350

Assume that there was no beginning inventory of either direct materials or finished units.

During the month, materials purchased amounted to 97,600 lb., at a total cost of $536,800. Input price variances are isolated upon purchase. Input-efficiency variances are isolated at the time of usage.

Required

1. Compute the January 2013 price and efficiency variances of direct materials and direct manufacturing labor.
2. Comment on the January 2013 price and efficiency variances of Seneca Corporation.
3. Why might Seneca calculate direct materials price variances and direct materials efficiency variances with reference to different points in time?

13-18 Continuous improvement (continuation of 13-17). The Seneca Corporation sets monthly standard costs using a continuous-improvement approach. In January 2013, the standard direct material cost is $54 per unit and the standard direct manufacturing labor cost is $14.50 per unit. Due to more efficient operations, the standard quantities for February 2013 are set at 0.980 of the standard quantities for January. In March 2013, the standard quantities are set at 0.990 of the standard quantities for February 2013. Assume the same information for March 2013 as in Exercise 13-17, except for these revised standard quantities.

Required

1. Compute the March 2013 standard quantities for direct materials and direct manufacturing labor (to three decimal places).
2. Compute the March 2013 price and efficiency variances for direct materials and direct manufacturing labor (round to the nearest dollar).

13-19 Materials and manufacturing labor variances, standard costs. Dawson, Inc., is a privately held furniture manufacturer. For August 2012, Dawson had the following standards for one of its products, a wicker chair:

	Standards per Chair
Direct materials	2 square yards of input at $5.50 per square yard
Direct manufacturing labor	0.5 hour of input at $10.80 per hour

The following data were compiled regarding *actual performance:* actual output units (chairs) produced, 2,600; square yards of input purchased and used, 4,700; price per square yard, $5.80; direct manufacturing labor costs, $9,660; actual hours of input, 920; labor price per hour, $10.50.

Required

1. Show computations of price and efficiency variances for direct materials and direct manufacturing labor. Give a plausible explanation of why each variance occurred.
2. Suppose 7,000 square yards of materials were purchased (at $5.80 per square yard), even though only 4,700 square yards were used. Suppose further that variances are identified at their most timely control point; accordingly, direct materials price variances are isolated and traced at the time of purchase to the purchasing department rather than to the production department. Compute the direct materials price and efficiency variances under this approach.

13-20 Variable manufacturing overhead, variance analysis. Grand Clothing is a manufacturer of designer suits. The cost of each suit is the sum of three variable costs (direct material costs, direct manufacturing labor costs, and manufacturing overhead costs) and one fixed-cost category (manufacturing overhead costs). Variable manufacturing overhead cost is allocated to each suit on the basis of budgeted direct manufacturing labor-hours per suit. For June 2013 each suit is budgeted to take 4 labor-hours. Budgeted variable manufacturing overhead cost per labor-hour is $14. The budgeted number of suits to be manufactured in June 2013 is 1,020.

Actual variable manufacturing costs in June 2013 were $67,650 for 1,000 suits started and completed. There were no beginning or ending inventories of suits. Actual direct manufacturing labor-hours for June were 4,510.

Required

1. Compute the flexible-budget variance, the spending variance, and the efficiency variance for variable manufacturing overhead.
2. Comment on the results.

13-21 Fixed manufacturing overhead, variance analysis (continuation of 13-20). Grand Clothing allocates fixed manufacturing overhead to each suit using budgeted direct manufacturing labor-hours per suit. Data pertaining to fixed manufacturing overhead costs for June 2013 are budgeted, $61,200, and actual, $63,900.

Required

1. Compute the spending variance for fixed manufacturing overhead. Comment on the results.
2. Compute the production-volume variance for June 2013. What inferences can Grand Clothing draw from this variance?

13-22 Variable manufacturing overhead variance analysis. The Whole Bread Company bakes baguettes for distribution to upscale grocery stores. The company has two direct-cost categories: direct materials and direct manufacturing labor. Variable manufacturing overhead is allocated to products on the basis of standard direct manufacturing labor-hours. Following is some budget data for the Whole Bread Company:

Direct manufacturing labor use	0.02 hours per baguette
Variable manufacturing overhead	$10.00 per direct manufacturing labor-hour

The Whole Bread Company provides the following additional data for the year ended December 31, 2012:

Planned (budgeted) output	3,000,000	baguettes
Actual production	2,400,000	baguettes
Direct manufacturing labor	42,000	hours
Actual variable manufacturing overhead	$558,600	

Required

1. What is the denominator level used for allocating variable manufacturing overhead? (That is, for how many direct manufacturing labor-hours is Whole Bread budgeting?)
2. Prepare a variance analysis of variable manufacturing overhead. Use Exhibit 13-6 (page 559) for reference.
3. Discuss the variances you have calculated and give possible explanations for them.

13-23 Fixed manufacturing overhead variance analysis (continuation of 13-22). The Whole Bread Company also allocates fixed manufacturing overhead to products on the basis of standard direct manufacturing labor-hours. For 2012, fixed manufacturing overhead was budgeted at $3.00 per direct manufacturing labor-hour. Actual fixed manufacturing overhead incurred during the year was $284,000.

Required

1. Prepare a variance analysis of fixed manufacturing overhead cost. Use Exhibit 13-6 (page 559) as a guide.
2. Is fixed overhead underallocated or overallocated? By what amount?
3. Comment on your results. Discuss the variances and explain what may be driving them.

13-24 Manufacturing overhead, variance analysis. The Gustafs Corporation is a manufacturer of centrifuges. Fixed and variable manufacturing overheads are allocated to each centrifuge using budgeted assembly-hours. Budgeted assembly time is 2 hours per unit. The following table shows the budgeted amounts and actual results related to overhead for June 2013.

	A–E	F	G
1	The Gustafs Corporation (June 2013)	Actual Results	Static Budget
2	Number of centrifuges assembled and sold	220	190
3	Hours of assembly time	330	
4	Variable manufacturing overhead cost per hour of assembly time		$32.00
5	Variable manufacturing overhead costs	$10,981	
6	Fixed manufacturing overhead costs	$18,910	$17,480

Required

1. Prepare an analysis of all variable manufacturing overhead and fixed manufacturing overhead variances using the columnar approach in Exhibit 13-6 (page 559).
2. How does the planning and control of variable manufacturing overhead costs differ from the planning and control of fixed manufacturing overhead costs?

13-25 Straightforward overhead variance analysis. The Ramirez Company uses standard costing in its manufacturing plant for auto parts. The standard cost of a particular auto part, based on a denominator level of 4,100 output units per year, included 5 machine-hours of variable manufacturing overhead at $7 per hour and 5 machine-hours of fixed manufacturing overhead at $13 per hour. Actual output produced was 4,500 units. Variable manufacturing overhead incurred was $255,000. Fixed manufacturing overhead incurred was $385,000. Actual machine-hours were 29,000.

Required

1. Prepare an analysis of all variable manufacturing overhead and fixed manufacturing overhead variances, using the integrated variance analysis in Exhibit 13-6 (page 559).
2. Describe how individual fixed manufacturing overhead items are controlled from day to day.
3. Discuss possible causes of the fixed manufacturing overhead variances.

13-26 Straightforward coverage of manufacturing overhead, standard-costing system. The Mongolia division of a Canadian telecommunications company uses standard costing for its machine-paced production of telephone equipment. Data regarding production during June are:

Variable manufacturing overhead costs incurred	$541,690
Variable manufacturing overhead cost rate	$7 per standard machine-hour
Fixed manufacturing overhead costs incurred	$146,300
Fixed manufacturing overhead costs budgeted	$138,000
Denominator level in machine-hours	69,000
Standard machine-hour allowed per unit of output	1.2
Units of output	65,100
Actual machine-hours used	76,300
Ending work-in-process inventory	0

Required

1. Prepare an analysis of all manufacturing overhead variances. Use the variance analysis framework illustrated in Exhibit 13-6 (page 559).
2. Describe how individual variable manufacturing overhead items are controlled from day to day.
3. Discuss possible causes of the variable manufacturing overhead variances.

13-27 Overhead variances, service sector. Easy Meals Now (EMN) operates a meal home-delivery service. It has agreements with 20 restaurants to pick up and deliver meals to customers who phone or fax orders to EMN. EMN allocates variable and fixed overhead costs on the basis of delivery time. EMN's owner, Don King, obtains the following information for May 2013 overhead costs:

	A	B	C
1	Easy Meals Now (May 2013)	Actual Results	Static Budget
2	Output units (number of deliveries)	8,600	12,000
3	Hours per delivery		0.70
4	Hours of delivery time	5,640	
5	Variable overhead cost per hour of delivery time		$ 1.75
6	Variable overhead costs	$10,716	
7	Fixed overhead costs	$39,200	$33,600

Required

1. Compute spending and efficiency variances for EMN's variable overhead in May 2013.
2. Compute the spending variance and production-volume variance for EMN's fixed overhead in May 2013.
3. Comment on EMN's overhead variances and suggest how Don King might manage EMN's variable overhead differently from its fixed overhead costs.

Problems

13-28 Flexible budget, direct materials, and direct manufacturing labor variances. Palermo Statuary manufactures bust statues of famous historical figures. All statues are the same size. Each unit requires the same amount of resources. The following information is from the static budget for 2013:

Expected production and sales	6,300 units
Total fixed costs	$1,350,000

Standard quantities, standard prices, and standard unit costs follow for direct materials and direct manufacturing labor:

	Standard Quantity	Standard Price	Standard Unit Cost
Direct materials	14 pounds	$12 per pound	$168
Direct manufacturing labor	3.1 hours	$40 per hour	$124

During 2013, actual number of units produced and sold was 4,800. Actual cost of direct materials used was $813,750, based on 62,500 pounds purchased at $13.02 per pound. Direct manufacturing labor-hours actually used were 17,500, at the rate of $33.48 per hour. As a result, actual direct manufacturing labor costs were $585,900. Actual fixed costs were $1,160,000. There were no beginning or ending inventories.

Required

1. Calculate the sales-volume variance and flexible-budget variance for operating income.
2. Compute price and efficiency variances for direct materials and direct manufacturing labor.

13-29 Variance analysis, nonmanufacturing setting. Stevie McQueen has run Zippy Car Detailing for the past 10 years. His static budget and actual results for June 2013 are provided next. Stevie has one employee who has been with him for all 10 years that he has been in business. In addition, at any given time he also employs two other less experienced workers. It usually takes each employee 2 hours to detail a vehicle, regardless of his or her experience. Stevie pays his experienced employee $30 per vehicle and the other two employees $15 per vehicle. There were no wage increases in June.

Zippy Car Detailing Actual and Budgeted Income Statements for the Month Ended June 30, 2013		
	Budget	Actual
Cars detailed	240	280
Revenue	$40,800	$54,600
Variable costs		
Costs of supplies	1,320	2,120
Labor	5,760	6,750
Total variable costs	7,080	8,870
Contribution margin	33,720	45,730
Fixed costs	9,700	9,700
Operating income	$24,020	$36,030

Required

1. How many cars, on average, did Stevie budget for each employee? How many cars did each employee actually detail?
2. Prepare a flexible budget for June 2013.
3. Compute the sales price variance and the labor efficiency variance for each labor type.
4. What information, in addition to that provided in the income statements, should Stevie gather in order to improve operational efficiency?

13-30 Comprehensive variance analysis, responsibility issues. (CMA, adapted) Ultra, Inc., manufactures a full line of well-known sunglass frames and lenses. Ultra uses a standard-costing system to set attainable standards for direct materials, labor, and overhead costs. Ultra reviews and revises standards annually, as necessary. Department managers, whose evaluations and bonuses are affected by their department's performance, are held responsible to explain variances in their department performance reports.

Recently, the manufacturing variances in the Bravo prestige line of sunglasses have caused some concern. For no apparent reason, unfavorable materials and labor variances have occurred. At the monthly staff meeting, Stuart Forman, manager of the Bravo line, will be expected to explain his variances and suggest ways of improving performance. Forman will be asked to explain the following performance report for 2012:

	Actual Results	Static-Budget Amounts
Units sold	7,350	7,800
Revenues	$573,300	$585,000
Variable manufacturing costs	338,982	250,380
Fixed manufacturing costs	100,000	111,000
Gross margin	134,318	223,620

Forman collected the following information:

Three items comprised the standard variable manufacturing costs in 2012:

- Direct materials: Frames. Static budget cost of $53,820. The standard input for 2012 is 3.00 ounces per unit.
- Direct materials: Lenses. Static budget costs of $93,600. The standard input for 2012 is 4.00 ounces per unit.
- Direct manufacturing labor: Static budget costs of $102,960. The standard input for 2012 is 1.10 hours per unit.

Assume there are no variable manufacturing overhead costs.

The actual variable manufacturing costs in 2012 were:

- Direct materials: Frames. Actual costs of $64,680. Actual ounces used were 4.40 ounces per unit.
- Direct materials: Lenses. Actual costs of $145,530. Actual ounces used were 6.00 ounces per unit.
- Direct manufacturing labor: Actual costs of $128,772. The actual labor rate was $14.60 per hour.

Required

1. Prepare a report that includes the following:

   a. Selling-price variance

b. Sales-volume variance and flexible-budget variance for operating income in the format of the analysis in Exhibit 13-2

c. Price and efficiency variances for the following:

- Direct materials: frames
- Direct materials: lenses
- Direct manufacturing labor

2. Give three possible explanations for each of the three price and efficiency variances at Ultra in requirement 1c.

13-31 Possible causes for price and efficiency variances. You are a student preparing for a job interview with a *Fortune* 100 consumer products manufacturer. You are applying for a job in the finance department. This company is known for its rigorous case-based interview process. One of the students who successfully obtained a job with them upon graduation last year advised you to "know your variances cold!" When you inquired further, she told you that she had been asked to pretend that she was investigating wage and materials variances. Per her advice, you have been studying the causes and consequences of variances. You are excited when you walk in and find that the first case deals with variance analysis. You are given the following data for May for a detergent bottling plant located in Mexico:

Actual	
Bottles filled	300,000
Direct materials used in production	6,200,000 oz.
Actual direct material cost	2,108,000 pesos
Actual direct manufacturing labor-hours	22,000 hours
Actual direct manufacturing labor cost	663,740 pesos

Standards	
Purchase price of direct materials	0.33 pesos/oz
Bottle size	15 oz.
Wage rate	29.15 pesos/hour
Bottles per minute	0.50

Please respond to the following questions as if you were in an interview situation:

Required

1. Calculate the materials efficiency and price variance and the wage and labor efficiency variances for the month of May.
2. You are given the following context: "Union organizers are targeting our detergent bottling plant in Puebla, Mexico, for a union." Can you provide a better explanation for the variances that you have calculated on the basis of this information?

13-32 Material cost variances, use of variances for performance evaluation. Katharine Rouse is the owner of Groovy Bikes, a company that produces high-quality cross-country bicycles. Groovy Bikes participates in a supply chain that consists of suppliers, manufacturers, distributors, and elite bicycle shops. For several years Groovy Bikes has purchased titanium from suppliers in the supply chain. Groovy Bikes uses titanium for the bicycle frames because it is stronger and lighter than other metals and therefore increases the quality of the bicycle. Earlier this year, Groovy Bikes hired Michael Anderson, a recent graduate from State University, as purchasing manager. Michael believed that he could reduce costs if he purchased titanium from an online marketplace at a lower price.

Groovy Bikes established the following standards based on the company's experience with previous suppliers. The standards are as follows:

Cost of titanium	$17 per pound
Titanium used per bicycle	8 lbs.

Actual results for the first month using the online supplier of titanium are:

Bicycles produced	300
Titanium purchased	3,400 lbs. for $54,400
Titanium used in production	2,900 lbs.

Required

1. Compute the direct materials price and efficiency variances.
2. What factors can explain the variances identified in requirement 1? Could any other variances be affected?
3. Was switching suppliers a good idea for Groovy Bikes? Explain why or why not.
4. Should Michael Anderson's performance evaluation be based solely on price variances? Should the production manager's evaluation be based solely on efficiency variances? Why is it important for Katharine Rouse to understand the causes of a variance before she evaluates performance?
5. Other than performance evaluation, what reasons are there for calculating variances?
6. What future problems could result if Groovy Bikes purchased lower-quality titanium from the online marketplace?

13-33 Flexible budgets, integrated variance analysis. (CMA, adapted) Clarke Products uses standard costing. It allocates manufacturing overhead (both variable and fixed) to products on the basis of standard direct manufacturing labor-hours (DLH). Clarke develops its manufacturing overhead rate from the current annual budget. The manufacturing overhead budget for 2013 is based on budgeted output of 636,000 units, requiring 3,816,000 DLH. The company is able to schedule production uniformly throughout the year.

A total of 74,000 output units requiring 318,000 DLH was produced during May 2013. Manufacturing overhead (MOH) costs incurred for May amounted to $340,200. The actual costs, compared with the annual budget and 1/12 of the annual budget, are:

	Annual Manufacturing Overhead Budget for 2013				
	Total Amount	Per Output Unit	Per DLH Input Unit	Monthly MOH Budget for May 2013	Actual MOH Costs for May 2013
Variable MOH					
Indirect manufacturing labor	$ 381,600	$0.60	$0.10	$ 31,800	$ 31,800
Supplies	763,200	1.20	0.20	63,600	113,000
Fixed MOH					
Supervision	610,560	0.96	0.16	50,880	42,000
Utilities	457,920	0.72	0.12	38,160	58,000
Depreciation	1,144,800	1.80	0.30	95,400	95,400
Total	$3,358,080	$5.28	$0.88	$279,840	$340,200

Required

Calculate the following amounts for Clarke Products for May 2013:

1. Total manufacturing overhead costs allocated
2. Variable manufacturing overhead spending variance
3. Fixed manufacturing overhead spending variance
4. Variable manufacturing overhead efficiency variance
5. Production-volume variance

Be sure to identify each variance as favorable (F) or unfavorable (U).

13-34 Direct manufacturing labor and variable manufacturing overhead variances. Linda Grace's Art Supply Company produces various types of paints. Actual direct manufacturing labor-hours in the factory that produces paint have been higher than budgeted hours for the last few months and the owner, Linda G. Martin, is concerned about the effect this has had on the company's cost overruns. Because variable manufacturing overhead is allocated to units produced using direct manufacturing labor-hours, Linda feels that the mismanagement of labor will have a twofold effect on company profitability. Following are the relevant budgeted and actual results for the second quarter of 2013.

	Budget Information	Actual Results
Paint set production	23,000	38,000
Direct manuf. labor-hours per paint set	2 hours	2.4 hours
Direct manufacturing labor rate	$8/hour	$10.20/hour
Variable manufacturing overhead rate	$24/hour	$17.95/hour

Required

1. Calculate the direct manufacturing labor price and efficiency variances and indicate whether each is favorable (F) or unfavorable (U).
2. Calculate the variable manufacturing overhead spending and efficiency variances and indicate whether each is favorable (F) or unfavorable (U).
3. For both direct manufacturing labor and variable manufacturing overhead, do the price/spending variances help Linda explain the efficiency variances?
4. Is Linda correct in her assertion that the mismanagement of labor has a twofold effect on cost overruns? Why might the variable manufacturing overhead efficiency variance not be an accurate representation of the effect of labor overruns on variable manufacturing overhead costs?

13-35 Production-volume variance analysis and sales volume variance. Beata Floral Creations, Inc., makes jewelry in the shape of flowers. Each piece is handmade and takes an average of 1.5 hours to produce because of the intricate design and scrollwork. Beata uses direct labor hours to allocate the overhead cost to production. Fixed overhead costs, including rent, depreciation, supervisory salaries, and other production expenses are budgeted at $9,000 per month. These costs are incurred for a facility large enough to produce 1,000 pieces of jewelry a month.

During the month of February, Beata produced 600 pieces of jewelry and actual fixed costs were $9,200.

Required

1. Calculate the fixed overhead spending variance and indicate whether it is favorable (F) or unfavorable (U).
2. If Beata uses direct labor hours available at capacity to calculate the budgeted fixed overhead rate, what is the production-volume variance? Indicate whether it is favorable (F) or unfavorable (U).
3. An unfavorable production-volume variance is a measure of the underallocation of fixed overhead cost caused by production levels at less than capacity. It therefore could be interpreted as the economic cost of unused capacity. Why would Beata be willing to incur this cost? Your answer should consider separately the following two unrelated factors:
   a. Demand could vary from month to month while available capacity remains constant.
   b. Beata would not want to produce at capacity unless it could sell all the units produced. What does Beata need to do to raise demand and what effect would this have on profit?
4. Beata's budgeted variable cost per unit is $25 and it expects to sell its jewelry for $55 apiece. Compute the sales-volume variance and reconcile it with the production-volume variance calculated in requirement 2. What does each concept measure?

13-36 Review of Chapter 13. (CPA, adapted) The Blazon Manufacturing Company's costing system has two direct-cost categories: direct materials and direct manufacturing labor. Manufacturing overhead (both variable and fixed) is allocated to products on the basis of standard direct manufacturing labor-hours (DLH). At the beginning of 2013, Blazon adopted the following standards for its manufacturing costs:

	Input	Cost per Output Unit
Direct materials	4 lbs. at $5 per lb.	$ 20.00
Direct manufacturing labor	4 hours at $14 per hour	56.00
Manufacturing overhead		
Variable	$5 per DLH	20.00
Fixed	$9 per DLH	36.00
Standard manufacturing cost per output unit		$132.00

The denominator level for total manufacturing overhead per month in 2013 is 39,000 direct manufacturing labor-hours. Blazon's flexible budget for January 2013 was based on this denominator level. The records for January indicated the following:

Direct materials purchased	37,000 lb. at $4.90 per lb.
Direct materials used	34,000 lb.
Direct manufacturing labor	31,600 hours at $14.10 per hour
Total actual manufacturing overhead (variable and fixed)	$650,000
Actual production	8,400 output units

Required

1. Prepare a schedule of total standard manufacturing costs for the 8,400 output units in January 2013.

2. For the month of January 2013, compute the following variances, indicating whether each is favorable (F) or unfavorable (U):
   a. Direct materials price variance, based on purchases
   b. Direct materials efficiency variance
   c. Direct manufacturing labor price variance
   d. Direct manufacturing labor efficiency variance
   e. Total manufacturing overhead spending variance
   f. Variable manufacturing overhead efficiency variance
   g. Production-volume variance

13-37 Nonfinancial variances. Best Friend Canine Products produces high-quality dog food distributed only through veterinary offices. To ensure that the food is of the highest quality and has taste appeal, Best Friend has a rigorous inspection process. For quality control purposes, Best Friend has a standard based on the pounds of food inspected per hour and the number of pounds that pass or fail the inspection.

Best Friend expects that for every 11,000 pounds of food produced, 1,100 pounds of food will be inspected. Inspection of 1,100 pounds of dog food should take 1 hour. Best Friend also expects that 5% of the food inspected will fail the inspection. During the month of May, Best Friend produced 2,310,000 pounds of food and inspected 220,000 pounds of food in 205 hours. Of the 220,000 pounds of food inspected, 11,800 pounds of food failed to pass the inspection.

Required

1. Compute two variances that help determine whether the time spent on inspections was more or less than expected. (Follow a format similar to the one used for the variable overhead spending and efficiency variances, but without prices.)
2. Compute two variances that can be used to evaluate the percentage of the food that fails the inspection.

13-38 Overhead variances, ethics. Schmidt Company uses standard costing. The company has two manufacturing plants, one in Colorado and the other in Michigan. For the Colorado plant, Schmidt has budgeted annual output of 4,000,000 units. Standard labor-hours per unit are 0.25, and the variable overhead rate for the Colorado plant is $3.25 per direct labor-hour. Fixed overhead for the Colorado plant is budgeted at $2,500,000 for the year.

For the Michigan plant, Schmidt has budgeted annual output of 4,200,000 units with standard labor-hours also 0.25 per unit. However, the variable overhead rate for the Michigan plant is $3 per hour, and the budgeted fixed overhead for the year is only $2,310,000.

Firm management has always used variance analysis as a performance measure for the two plants, and has compared the results of the two plants.

Jim Johnson has just been hired as a new controller for Schmidt. Jim is good friends with the Michigan plant manager and wants him to get a favorable review. Jim suggests allocating the firm's budgeted common fixed costs of $3,150,000 to the two plants, but on the basis of one-third to the Michigan plant and two-thirds to the Colorado plant. His explanation for this allocation base is that Colorado is a more expensive state than Michigan.

At the end of the year, the Colorado plant reported the following actual results: output of 3,900,000 using 1,014,000 labor-hours in total, at a cost of $3,244,800 in variable overhead and $2,520,000 in fixed overhead. Actual results for the Michigan plant are an output of 4,350,000 units using 1,218,000 labor-hours with a variable cost of $3,775,800 and fixed overhead cost of $2,400,000. The actual common fixed costs for the year were $3,126,000.

Required

1. Compute the budgeted fixed cost per labor-hour for the fixed overhead separately for each plant:
   a. Excluding allocated common fixed costs
   b. Including allocated common fixed costs
2. Compute the variable overhead spending variance and the variable overhead efficiency variance separately for each plant.
3. Compute the fixed overhead spending and volume variances for each plant:
   a. Excluding allocated common fixed costs
   b. Including allocated common fixed costs
4. Did Jim Johnson's attempt to make the Michigan plant look better than the Colorado plant by allocating common fixed costs work? Why or why not?
5. Should common fixed costs be allocated in general when variances are used as performance measures? Why or why not?
6. What do you think of Jim Johnson's behavior overall?

Case

Software Associates

Robert S. Kaplan

Susan, I have just seen the quarterly P&L. It's great that we exceeded our billed hours and revenue targets. But why, with higher revenues, is our bottom line less than half of what we had budgeted. Can we have a meeting tomorrow morning at 8 AM so you can explain this discrepancy to me?

—Richard Norton, CEO of Software Associates

Norton, the founder and CEO of Software Associates called Susan Jenkins, CFO of Software Associates, after skimming the second quarter profit and loss statement (see Software Associates Exhibit 1). Jenkins had been preparing to go home but now anticipated a long evening ahead to prepare for the next morning's meeting.

Assignment Question 1: Prepare a variance analysis report based on the information in Software Associates Exhibit 1. Would this be sufficient to explain the profit shortfall to Norton at the 8 AM meeting?

History

Richard Norton had founded Software Associates ten years ago to perform system integration projects for clients. While initially set up to operate in client-server environments, Norton had been nimble enough to make the transition to Web applications, and his company had continued to grow and prosper during the rapid technological evolution of the 1990s.

Annual revenues exceeded $12 million, and profit margins were usually between 15% and 20%. Currently, Software Associates offered two types of services to clients. The Solutions business helped clients rapidly develop targeted information management strategies, and then mobilized business and technology resources to deliver software solutions. Typical services included IT strategy and management, IT architecture and design, information management, and data warehousing. The Contract business offered clients experienced software engineers, programmers, and consultants, on a short-term project basis, to help the clients implement their own IT tools and solutions. This service enabled clients to implement major IT projects without having to hire expensive, experienced software personnel.

Preparing the Budget

Each quarter Norton and Jenkins prepared a detailed budget for the next three months, based on the annual plan, and recent operating experience and information from the market. Norton knew that in his fast-paced business, he could not manage with just an annual budget. He wanted to

Software Associates Exhibit 1

Software Associates Income Statement, Q2, 2000

	Actual	Budget
Revenues	$3,264,000	$3,231,900
Expenses	2,967,610	2,625,550
Operating profit	$ 296,390	$ 606,350
Profit percentage	9.1%	18.8%

continually scan the environment and industry trends before locking into a hiring plan, an operating plan, and a budget for a period. For the quarterly budget, Jenkins estimated consulting revenues by multiplying together the expected number of full-time-equivalent (FTE) consultants at the firm, the number of hours available (450 per quarter) per FTE, the expected billing percentage (the ratio of hours billed to total hours available), and the average hourly billing rate. She calculated consultant expenses by multiplying the average compensation (including fringe benefits) per consultant by the number of FTE consultants. She then estimated operating expenses such as advertising, administrative support, education and training, information systems, occupancy, office expense, postage and telecommunications. Software Associates Exhibit 2 contains the budget and the actual financial results for the second quarter of 2000.

Assignment Question 2: Prepare a variance analysis report based on the information in Software Associates Exhibit 2.

Expense Analysis

Jenkins knew that the budgeted operating expenses were neither entirely variable nor entirely fixed during the quarter. Some expenses varied during the quarter based on the number of consultants hired and working, while other were "fixed," independent of the number of consultants on board. Obviously, consultant expense varied with the number of consultants hired. Occupancy expenses, however, were fixed through the quarter unless she authorized the acquisition or rental of additional space. Expenses such as computing and telecommunications had both fixed and variable components. Because of the profit shortfall in Q2 2000, Jenkins knew that she had better be prepared to explain to Norton why expenses had exceeded the budgeted amounts. During the evening, she spent several hours studying the operating expense categories, eventually preparing Software Associates Exhibit 3, which showed budgeted operating expenses by category and her judgment about their degree of variability. She also listed the actual operating expenses for the period on the exhibit.

Assignment Question 3: Prepare a spending and volume variance analysis of operating expenses based on the additional information supplied in Software Associates Exhibit 3.

Billing Percentage

Jenkins wondered why if the actual number of consultants was nearly 8% higher than budgeted (see Software Associates Exhibit 2), revenues had increased only 1%. Were consultants becoming less productive? She knew that a key operating statistic for consulting organizations was the percentage of time billed.

Software Associates Exhibit 2

Budget and Actual Income Statement: Q2 2000

	Actual	Budget
Revenues	$3,264,000	$3,231,900
Less:		
Consultants' salaries and fringes	$2,029,050	$1,748,250
Operating expenses	938,560	877,300
Total expenses	$2,967,610	$2,625,550
Operating profit	$ 296,390	$ 606,350
Profit %	9.1%	18.8%
Operating Statistics		
Number of consultants (FTE)	113	105
Hours supplied	50,850	47,250
Hours billed	39,000	35,910
Average billing rate	$83.69	$90.00

Software Associates Exhibit 3

Expense Items: Budget Q2 2000

	Actual	Budget	% Variable
Advertising and promotion	$ 22,100	$ 15,100	0%
Administrative and support staff	225,000	191,250	80
Information systems	126,200	120,000	80
Depreciation	23,400	22,700	0
Dues and subscriptions	11,800	13,100	80
Education and training	36,200	38,900	80
Equipment leases	23,500	22,440	25
Insurance	33,600	32,200	0
Professional services	39,500	34,700	0
Office expense	42,100	36,550	100
Office supplies	86,200	89,600	80
Postage	27,300	24,700	80
Rent—real estate	117,260	117,260	0
Telephone	40,000	38,500	100
Travel and entertainment	57,800	56,300	100
Utilities	26,600	24,000	25
Total	$938,560	$877,300	

Assignment Question 4: Prepare an analysis of the revenue change, separating the volume effect (increase in number of consultants) from the productivity effect (billing percentage).

Lines of Business

Jenkins was, by now, getting quite tired and was looking forward to returning home to catch a few hours of sleep. As she prepared to leave, however, she realized that Software Associates Exhibits 1 and 2 only reported on the aggregate financial performance of the firm. She knew that its two lines of business, Contract and Solutions, had quite different operating characteristics. Typically Richard Norton didn't want to get too involved in the details of these different business lines. But perhaps some of the decline in profit margin and lower revenue per consultant could be attributed to operating results within each of the two lines of business. Jenkins reluctantly returned to her desk and started to gather more detailed information about the Contracting and Solution business lines. Several hours later, she had produced the data shown in Software Associates Exhibit 4.

Assignment Question 5: Prepare an analysis of actual versus budgeted revenues, consultant expenses, and margins using the additional information supplied in Software Associates Exhibit 4.

Additional Analysis

Jenkins was finally driving home at 2 AM. She felt well equipped for the meeting the next morning but wondered about other forms of analysis she might have done if she had more time. For example, Norton had been quite pleased with the growth in revenues and billed hours. But was that due to good work by the firm, or had the overall consulting industry grown faster than expected during the quarter. In other words, was Software Associates increasing or decreasing its share of software consulting business? Also, Jenkins had assumed that operating expenses varied only with the number of consultants. She pondered whether the consultants from the Solutions business required more support than did the consultants in the Contract business.

Software Associates Exhibit 4

Line of Business Budget and Actual Operating Statistics: Q2 2000

	Contract	Solutions	Total
Actual			
Number of consultants (FTE)	64	49	113
Billed hours	24,000	15,000	39,000
Billed revenues	$1,344,000	$1,920,000	$3,264,000
Hours supplied	28,800	22,050	50,850
Consultant costs	$1,036,800	$ 992,250	$2,029,050
Budget			
Number of consultants (FTE)	56	49	105
Billed hours	20,160	15,750	35,910
Billed revenues	$1,088,640	$2,143,260	$3,231,900
Hours supplied	25,200	22,050	47,250
Consultant costs	$ 756,000	$ 992,250	$1,748,250

Also, did support expenses vary with the number of consultants, of either type, or with the number of hours they worked or billed? Within each business line, she had used an average billing and cost rate per consultant. Would she get additional insights by looking at the mix of consultants used within each business or even on each job to understand better the economics of the business. She resolved to think more about these issues in the upcoming quarter, but her most urgent task was to get some sleep before presenting her analysis to Richard Norton in a few hours.

Strategy, Balanced Scorecard, and Strategic Profitability Analysis

14

Learning Objectives

1. Recognize which of two generic strategies a company is using
2. Understand what comprises reengineering
3. Understand the four perspectives of the balanced scorecard
4. Analyze changes in operating income to evaluate strategy
5. Identify unused capacity and how to manage it

Olive Garden wants to know.

So do Barnes and Noble, PepsiCo, and L.L. Bean. Even your local car dealer and transit authority are curious. They all want to know how well they are doing and how they score against the measures they strive to meet. The balanced scorecard can help them answer this question by evaluating key performance measures. Many companies have successfully used the balanced scorecard approach to measure their progress.

This chapter focuses on how management accounting information helps companies implement and evaluate their strategies. Strategy drives the operations of a company and guides managers' short-run and long-run decisions. The Chapter at a Glance presents a summary of the key ideas in this chapter.

Chapter at a Glance

- Strategy describes how an organization creates value for customers while differentiating itself from its competitors. Companies typically choose from two basic strategies: *product differentiation*—offering a unique and superior product (or service) relative to competitors' products for which customers are willing to pay a higher price, and *cost leadership*—offering a product similar to competitors but at a lower price because of lower costs.
- To achieve competitive advantage through either product differentiation or cost leadership, companies reengineer—rethink and redesign—their business activities to improve performance on product design, cost, quality, and speed of service.
- The balanced scorecard uses financial and nonfinancial measures to evaluate how a company is doing with its short-run and long-run strategic goals.
- The links in the scorecard work as follows: enhancing learning and growth (employee and information-systems capabilities) improves internal-business processes (innovation, quality, product delivery and efficiency) that boosts customer satisfaction and market share and generates superior, sustainable financial performance.
- A company can evaluate the success of its product-differentiation or cost-leadership strategy by subdividing changes in operating income into growth, price-recovery, and productivity components. The growth component isolates the effect on operating income from selling more or fewer units, the price-recovery component from changes in input and output prices, and the productivity component from efficient use of inputs.
- An important way companies reduce costs is by reducing unused capacity.

Learning Objective 1

Recognize which of two generic strategies a company is using

. . . product differentiation or cost leadership

What Is Strategy?

Strategy specifies how an organization matches its own capabilities with the opportunities in the marketplace to accomplish its objectives. In other words, strategy describes how an organization can create value for its customers while differentiating itself from its competitors. For example, Walmart, the retail giant, creates value for its customers by locating stores in suburban and rural areas, and by offering low prices, a wide range of product categories, and few choices within each product category. Consistent with this strategy, Walmart has developed the capability to keep costs down by aggressively negotiating low prices with its suppliers in exchange for high volumes and by maintaining a no-frills, cost-conscious environment.

In formulating its strategy, an organization must first thoroughly understand its industry. Industry analysis focuses on five forces: (1) competitors, (2) potential entrants into the market, (3) equivalent products, (4) bargaining power of customers, and (5) bargaining power of input suppliers.[1] The collective effect of these forces shapes an organization's profit potential. In general, profit potential decreases with greater competition, stronger potential entrants, products that are similar, and more demanding customers and suppliers. Below, we illustrate these five forces for Chipset, Inc., maker of linear integrated circuit devices (LICDs) used in modems and communication networks. Chipset produces a single specialized product, CX1, a standard, high-performance microchip, that can be used in multiple applications. Chipset designed CX1 after extensive market research and input from its customer base.

1. **Competitors.** The CX1 model faces severe competition based on price, timely delivery, and quality. Companies in the industry have high fixed costs and persistent pressures to reduce selling prices and utilize capacity fully. Price reductions spur growth because it makes LICDs a cost-effective option in new applications such as digital subscriber lines (DSLs).
2. **Potential entrants into the market.** The small profit margins and high capital costs discourage new entrants. Moreover, incumbent companies such as Chipset have experience lowering costs and building close relationships with customers and suppliers.
3. **Equivalent products.** Chipset tailors CX1 to customer needs and lowers prices by continuously improving CX1's design and processes to reduce production costs. This reduces the risk of equivalent products or new technologies replacing CX1.
4. **Bargaining power of customers.** Customers, such as EarthLink and Verizon, negotiate aggressively with Chipset and its competitors to keep prices down because they buy large quantities of product.
5. **Bargaining power of input suppliers.** To produce CX1, Chipset requires high-quality materials (such as silicon wafers, pins for connectivity, and plastic or ceramic packaging) and skilled engineers, technicians, and manufacturing labor. The skill sets that suppliers and employees bring gives them bargaining power to demand higher prices and wages.

In summary, strong competition and the bargaining powers of customers and suppliers put significant pressure on Chipset's selling prices. To respond to these challenges, Chipset must choose from one of two basic strategies: *differentiating its product* or *achieving cost leadership.*

Product differentiation is an organization's ability to offer products or services its customers perceive to be superior and unique relative to the products or services of its competitors. Apple Inc. has successfully differentiated its products in the consumer electronics industry, as have Johnson & Johnson in the pharmaceutical industry and Coca-Cola in the soft drink industry. These companies have achieved differentiation through innovative product R&D, careful development and promotion of their brands, and the rapid push of products to market. Managers use differentiation to increase brand loyalty and charge higher prices.

Cost leadership is an organization's ability to achieve lower costs relative to competitors through productivity and efficiency improvements, elimination of waste, and tight cost control. Cost leaders in their respective industries include Walmart (consumer retailing), Home Depot and Lowe's (building products), Texas Instruments (consumer electronics), and Emerson Electric (electric motors). These companies provide products and services that are similar to—not differentiated from—their competitors, but at a lower cost to the customer. Lower selling prices, rather than unique products or services, provide a competitive advantage for these cost leaders.

[1] M. Porter, *Competitive Strategy* (New York: Free Press, 1980); M. Porter, *Competitive Advantage* (New York: Free Press, 1985); and M. Porter, "What Is Strategy?" *Harvard Business Review* (November–December 1996): 61–78.

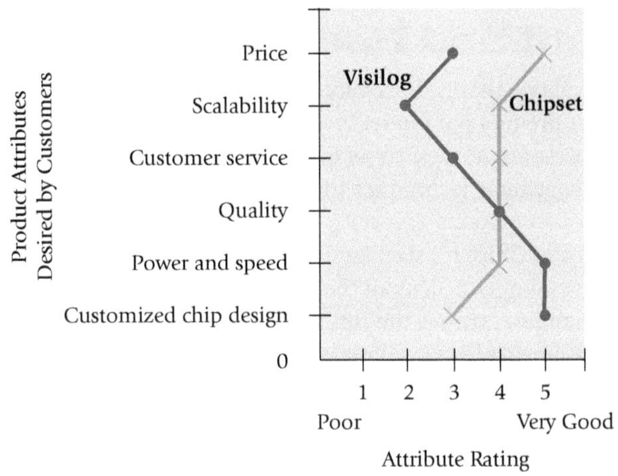

Exhibit 14-1
Customer Preference Map for LICDs

To evaluate the success of its strategy, a company must trace the sources of its profitability to product differentiation or cost leadership. For example, an analysis of Porsche's profitability shows that the increase in its profitability is due to successful implementation of its product-differentiation strategy. Product differentiation enabled Porsche to increase its profit margins and grow sales. Changes in Home Depot's profitability are closely tied to its success in cost leadership through productivity and quality improvements.

What strategy should Chipset follow? In order to make this decision, Chipset managers develop the customer preference map shown in Exhibit 14-1. The y-axis describes various attributes of the product desired by customers. The x-axis describes how well Chipset and its competitor, Visilog, which follows a product-differentiation strategy, do along various attributes desired by customers from 1 (poor) to 5 (very good). The map highlights the tradeoffs in any strategy. It shows the advantages CX1 enjoys in terms of price, scalability,[2] and customer service. Visilog's chips, however, are faster and more powerful, and are customized for various applications such as different types of modems and communication networks.

CX1 is somewhat differentiated from competing products. Differentiating CX1 further would be costly, but Chipset may be able to charge a higher price. Conversely, reducing the cost of manufacturing CX1 would allow Chipset to lower prices, spur growth, and increase market share. The scalability of CX1 makes it an effective solution for meeting varying customer needs. Also, consistent with its strategy, Chipset has, over the years, recruited an engineering staff that is more skilled at making product and process improvements than at creatively designing new products and technologies. The market benefit from lowering prices by improving manufacturing efficiency through process improvements leads Chipset to choose a cost-leadership strategy.

To achieve its cost-leadership strategy, Chipset must improve its own internal capabilities. It must enhance quality and reengineer processes to downsize and eliminate excess capacity. At the same time, Chipset's management team does not want to make cuts in personnel that would hurt company morale and hinder future growth. We explore these actions in the next section.

Keys to Success

Managers design product differentiation strategies to achieve higher profits because customers are willing to pay higher prices for products or services that they perceive to be superior and unique. Managers adopt cost leadership strategies to achieve lower costs through greater productivity and efficiency, less waste, and tight control over costs.

[2] The ability to achieve different performance levels by altering the number of CX1 units in a product.

Learning Objective 2

Understand what comprises reengineering

. . . redesigning business processes to improve performance by reducing cost and improving quality

Building Internal Capabilities: Quality Improvement and Reengineering at Chipset

To improve product quality—that is, to reduce defect rates and improve manufacturing yields—Chipset must maintain process parameters within tight ranges based on real-time data about manufacturing-process parameters, such as temperature and pressure. Chipset must also train workers in quality-management techniques to identify the root causes of defects and actions to improve quality.

The second element of Chipset's strategy is to reengineer its order-delivery process. Some of Chipset's customers have complained about the lengthening time span between ordering products and receiving them. **Reengineering** is the fundamental rethinking and redesign of business processes to achieve improvements in critical measures of performance, such as cost, quality, service, speed, and customer satisfaction.[3] To illustrate reengineering, consider the order-delivery system at Chipset in 2011. When Chipset received an order from a customer, a copy was sent to manufacturing, where a production scheduler began planning the manufacturing of the ordered products. Frequently, a considerable amount of time elapsed before equipment became available for production to begin. After manufacturing was complete, CX1 chips moved to the shipping department, which matched the quantities of CX1 to be shipped against customer orders. Often, completed CX1 chips stayed in inventory until a truck became available for shipment. If the quantity to be shipped was less than the number of chips requested by the customer, a special shipment was made for the balance of the chips. Shipping documents moved to the billing department for issuing invoices. Special staff in the accounting department followed up with customers for payments.

The many transfers of CX1 chips and information across departments (sales, manufacturing, shipping, billing, and accounting) to satisfy a customer's order created delays. Moreover, no single individual was responsible for fulfilling a customer order. To respond to these challenges, Chipset formed a cross-functional team in late 2011 and implemented a reengineered order-delivery process in 2012.

Under the new system, a customer-relationship manager, responsible for each customer, negotiates long-term contracts specifying quantities and prices. The customer-relationship manager works closely with the customer and with manufacturing to specify delivery schedules for CX1 one month in advance of shipment and sends the schedule of customer orders and delivery dates electronically to manufacturing. Completed chips are shipped directly from the manufacturing plant to customer sites. Each shipment automatically triggers an electronic invoice and customers electronically transfer funds to Chipset's bank. Companies, such as AT&T, Banca di America e di Italia, Cigna Insurance, Cisco, PepsiCo, and Siemens Nixdorf, have benefited significantly by reengineering their processes across design, production, and marketing (just as in the Chipset example). Reengineering has limited benefits when reengineering efforts focus on only a single activity such as shipping or invoicing rather than the entire order-delivery process. To be successful, reengineering efforts must focus on an entire process, change roles and responsibilities, eliminate unnecessary activities and tasks, use information technology, and develop employee skills.

Take another look at Exhibit 14-1 and note the interrelatedness and consistency in Chipset's strategy. To help meet customer preferences for price, quality, and customer service, Chipset decides on a cost-leadership strategy. And to achieve cost leadership, Chipset builds internal capabilities by reengineering its processes. Chipset's next challenge is to effectively implement its strategy.

Keys to Success

Reengineering aids managers in rethinking business practices and improving performance on measures such as costs, quality, service, speed, and customer satisfaction.

---

[3] See M. Hammer and J. Champy, *Reengineering the Corporation: A Manifesto for Business Revolution* (New York: Harper, 1993); E. Ruhli, C. Treichler, and S. Schmidt, "From Business Reengineering to Management Reengineering—A European Study," *Management International Review* (1995): 361–371; and K. Sandberg, "Reengineering Tries a Comeback—This Time for Growth, Not Just for Cost Savings," *Harvard Management Update* (November 2001).

Strategy Implementation and the Balanced Scorecard

Learning Objective 3

Understand the four perspectives of the balanced scorecard

. . . financial, customer, internal business process, and learning and growth

Many organizations, such as Allstate Insurance, Bank of Montreal, British Petroleum, and Dow Chemical, have introduced a *balanced scorecard* approach to track progress and manage the implementation of their strategies.

The Balanced Scorecard

The **balanced scorecard** translates an organization's mission and strategy into a set of performance measures that provides the framework for implementing its strategy.[4] Not only does the balanced scorecard focus on achieving financial objectives, it also highlights the nonfinancial objectives that an organization must achieve to meet and sustain its financial objectives. The scorecard measures an organization's performance from four perspectives:

1. Financial: the profits and value created for shareholders
2. Customer: the success of the company in its target market
3. Internal business processes: the internal operations that create value for customers
4. Learning and growth: the people and system capabilities that support operations

The measures that a company uses to track performance depends on its strategy. This tool is called a "balanced scorecard" because it balances the use of financial and nonfinancial performance measures to evaluate short-run and long-run performance in a single report. The balanced scorecard reduces managers' emphasis on short-run financial performance, such as quarterly earnings, because the key strategic nonfinancial and operational indicators, such as product quality and customer satisfaction, measure changes that a company is making for the long run. The financial benefits of these long-run changes may not show up immediately in short-run earnings; however, strong improvement in nonfinancial measures usually indicates the creation of future economic value. For example, an increase in customer satisfaction, as measured by customer surveys and repeat purchases, signals a strong likelihood of higher sales and income in the future. By balancing the mix of financial and nonfinancial measures, the balanced scorecard broadens management's attention to short-run *and* long-run performance. *Never lose sight of the key point. In for-profit companies, the primary goal of the balanced scorecard is to sustain long-run financial performance. Nonfinancial measures simply serve as leading indicators for the hard-to-measure long-run financial performance.*

Strategy Maps and the Balanced Scorecard

In this section, we use the Chipset example to develop strategy maps and the four perspectives of the balanced scorecard. The objectives and measures Chipset's managers choose for each perspective relates to the action plans for furthering Chipset's cost-leadership strategy: *improving quality* and *reengineering processes.*

Strategy Maps. A useful first step in designing a balanced scorecard is a *strategy map.* A **strategy map** is a diagram that describes how an organization creates value by connecting strategic objectives in explicit cause-and-effect relationships with each other in the financial, customer, internal business process, and learning and growth perspectives. Exhibit 14-2 presents Chipset's strategy map. Follow the arrows to see how a strategic objective affects other strategic objectives. For example, empowering the workforce helps align employee and organization goals and improves processes, which improves manufacturing quality and productivity, reduces customer delivery time, meets specified delivery dates, and improves post-sales service, all of which increase customer satisfaction. Improving manufacturing quality and productivity grows operating income directly

[4] See R. S. Kaplan and D. P. Norton, *The Balanced Scorecard* (Boston: Harvard Business School Press, 1996); R. S. Kaplan and D. P. Norton, *The Strategy-Focused Organization: How Balanced Scorecard Companies Thrive in the New Business Environment* (Boston: Harvard Business School Press, 2001); R. S. Kaplan and D. P. Norton, *Strategy Maps: Converting Intangible Assets into Tangible Outcomes* (Boston: Harvard Business School Press, 2004); and R. S. Kaplan and D. P. Norton, *Alignment: Using the Balanced Scorecard to Create Corporate Synergies* (Boston: Harvard Business School Press, 2006).

For simplicity, this chapter, and much of the literature, emphasizes long-run financial objectives as the primary goal of for-profit companies. For-profit companies interested in long-run financial, environmental, and social objectives adapt the balanced scorecard to implement all three objectives.

Exhibit 14-2

Strategy Map for Chipset, Inc., for 2012

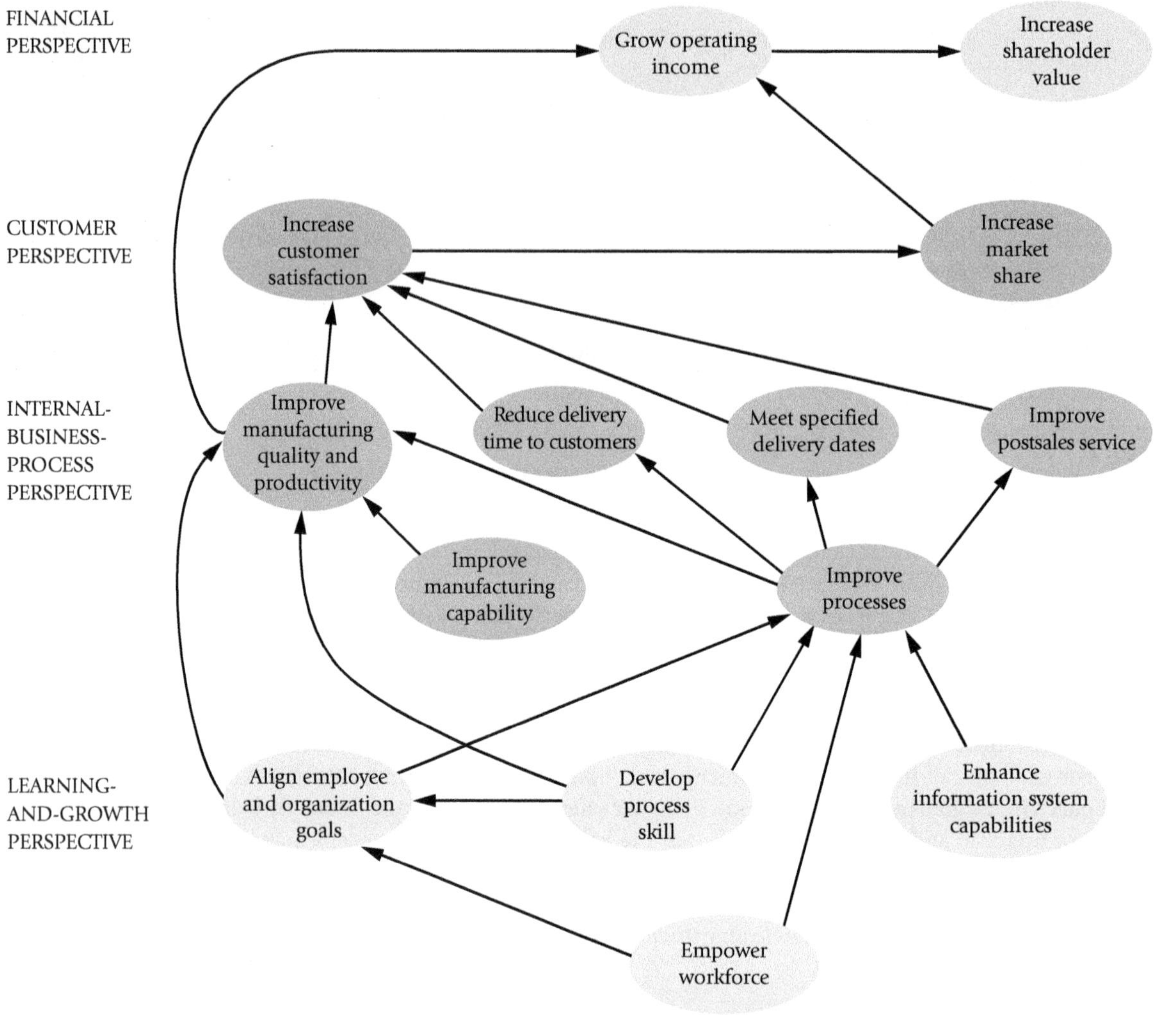

and also increases customer satisfaction that, in turn, increases market share, operating income, and shareholder value.

To compete successfully, Chipset invests in its employees, implements new technology and process controls, improves quality, and reengineers processes. The strategy map helps Chipset evaluate whether these activities are generating financial returns.

Chipset could include many other cause-and-effect relationships in the strategy map in Exhibit 14-2. But, Chipset, like other companies implementing the balanced scorecard, focuses on only those relationships that it believes to be the most significant so that the scorecard does not become unwieldy and difficult to understand.

Chipset uses the strategy map from Exhibit 14-2 to build the balanced scorecard presented in Exhibit 14-3. The scorecard highlights the four perspectives of performance: financial, customer, internal business process, and learning and growth. The first column presents the strategic objectives from the strategy map in Exhibit 14-2. At the beginning of 2012, the company's managers specify the strategic objectives, measures, initiatives (the actions necessary to achieve the objectives), and target performance (the first four columns in Exhibit 14-3).

Chipset wants to use the balanced scorecard targets to drive the organization to higher levels of performance. Managers therefore set targets at a level of performance that is achievable, yet distinctly better than competitors. Chipset's managers complete the fifth column, reporting actual performance at the end of 2012. This column compares Chipset's performance relative to target.

Four Perspectives of the Balanced Scorecard. We next describe the perspectives in general terms and illustrate each perspective using the measures chosen by Chipset in the context of its strategy.

Exhibit 14-3

The Balanced Scorecard for Chipset, Inc., for 2012

Strategic Objectives	Measures	Initiatives	Target Performance	Actual Performance
Financial Perspective				
Grow operating income	Operating income from productivity gain	Manage costs and unused capacity	$1,850,000	$1,912,500
Increase shareholder value	Operating income from growth	Build strong customer relationships	$2,500,000	$2,820,000
	Revenue growth		9%	10%[a]
Customer Perspective				
Increase market share	Market share in communication-networks segment	Identify future needs of customers	6%	7%
Increase customer satisfaction	Number of new customers	Identify new target-customer segments	1	1[b]
	Customer-satisfaction ratings	Increase customer focus of sales organization	90% of customers give top two ratings	87% of customers give top two ratings
Internal-Business-Process Perspective				
Improve postsales service	Service response time	Improve customer-service process	Within 4 hours	Within 3 hours
Improve manufacturing quality and productivity	Yield	Identify root causes of problems and improve quality	78%	79.3%
Reduce delivery time to customers	Order-delivery time	Reengineer order-delivery process	30 days	30 days
Meet specified delivery dates	On-time delivery	Reengineer order-delivery process	92%	90%
Improve processes	Number of major improvements in manufacturing and business processes	Organize teams from manufacturing and sales to modify processes	5	5
Improve manufacturing capability	Percentage of processes with advanced controls	Organize R&D/manufacturing teams to implement advanced controls	75%	75%
Learning-and-Growth Perspective				
Align employee and organization goals	Employee-satisfaction ratings	Employee participation and suggestions program to build teamwork	80% of employees give top two ratings	88% of employees give top two ratings
Empower workforce	Percentage of line workers empowered to manage processes	Have supervisors act as coaches rather than decision makers	85%	90%
Develop process skill	Percentage of employees trained in process and quality management	Employee training programs	90%	92%
Enhance information-system capabilities	Percentage of manufacturing processes with real-time feedback	Improve online and offline data gathering	80%	80%

[a](Revenues in 2012 – Revenues in 2011) ÷ Revenues in 2011 = ($25,300,000 – $23,000,000) ÷ $23,000,000 = 10%.

[b]Number of customers increased from seven to eight in 2012.

1. **Financial perspective.** This perspective evaluates the profitability of the strategy and the creation of shareholder value. Because Chipset's key strategic initiatives are cost reduction relative to competitors' costs and sales growth, the financial perspective focuses on how much operating income results from reducing costs and selling more units of CX1.
2. **Customer perspective.** This perspective identifies targeted customer and market segments and measures the company's success in these segments. To monitor its customer objectives, Chipset's managers use market research to determine market share in the communication-networks segment, and information about the number of new customers and customer-satisfaction ratings from its customer management systems.
3. **Internal-business-process perspective.** This perspective focuses on internal operations that create value for customers that, in turn, help achieve financial performance. Managers at Chipset determine internal-business-process improvement targets after benchmarking against its main competitors using information from published financial statements, prevailing prices, customers, suppliers, former employees, industry experts, and financial analysts. The internal-business-process perspective comprises three subprocesses:
   - **Innovation process:** Creating products, services, and processes that will meet the needs of customers. This is a very important process for companies that follow a product-differentiation strategy and must constantly design and develop innovative new products to remain competitive in the marketplace. Chipset's innovation focuses on improving its manufacturing capability and process controls to lower costs and improve quality. Chipset measures innovation by the number of improvements in manufacturing processes and percentage of processes with advanced controls.
   - **Operations process:** Producing and delivering existing products and services that will meet the needs of customers. Chipset's strategic initiatives are (a) improving manufacturing quality, (b) reducing delivery time to customers, and (c) meeting specified delivery dates so it measures yield, order-delivery time, and on-time deliveries.
   - **Postsales-service process:** Providing service and support to the customer after the sale of a product or service. Chipset monitors how quickly and accurately it is responding to customer-service requests.
4. **Learning-and-growth perspective.** This perspective identifies the people and information capabilities necessary for an organization to learn, improve, and grow. These capabilities help achieve superior internal processes that in turn create value for customers and shareholders. Chipset's learning and growth perspective emphasizes three capabilities:
   - Information-system capabilities, measured by the percentage of manufacturing processes with real-time feedback
   - Employee capabilities, measured by the percentage of employees trained in process and quality management
   - Motivation, measured by employee satisfaction and the percentage of manufacturing and sales employees (line employees) empowered to manage processes

The arrows in Exhibit 14-3 indicate the *broad* cause-and-effect linkages: how gains in the learning-and-growth perspective lead to improvements in internal business processes, which lead to higher customer satisfaction and market share, and finally lead to superior financial performance. Note how the scorecard describes elements of Chipset's strategy implementation. Worker training and empowerment improve employee satisfaction and lead to manufacturing and business-process improvements that improve quality and reduce delivery time. The end result of worker training and empowerment is increased customer satisfaction and higher market share. Exhibit 14-3 indicates that Chipset's actions have been successful from a financial perspective. Chipset has earned significant operating income from executing its cost-leadership strategy, and that strategy has also led to growth.

To sustain long-run financial performance, a company must strengthen all links across its different balanced scorecard perspectives. For example, Southwest Airlines' high employee satisfaction levels (learning and growth perspective) lead to greater efficiency and customer responsiveness (internal-business process perspective) that enhances customer satisfaction (customer perspective) and boosts profits and return on investment (financial perspective).

A major benefit of the balanced scorecard is that it promotes causal thinking as described in the previous paragraph—where improvement in one activity causes an improvement in another. Think of the balanced scorecard as a *linked scorecard* or a *causal scorecard.* Managers must search for empirical evidence (rather than rely on intuition alone) to test the validity and strength of the various connections. A causal scorecard enables a company to focus on the key drivers that steer the implementation of the strategy. Without convincing links, the scorecard loses much of its value.

Implementing a Balanced Scorecard

To successfully implement a balanced scorecard, subordinate managers and executives require commitment and leadership from top management. At Chipset, the team building the balanced scorecard (headed by the vice president of strategic planning) conducted interviews with senior managers; probed executives about customers, competitors, and technological developments; and sought proposals for balanced scorecard objectives across the four perspectives. The team then met to discuss the responses and to build a prioritized list of objectives.

In a meeting with all senior managers, the team sought to achieve consensus on the scorecard objectives. The vice president of strategic management then divided senior management into four groups, with each group responsible for one of the perspectives. In addition, each group broadened the base of inputs by including representatives from the next-lower levels of management and key functional managers. The groups identified measures for each objective and the sources of information for each measure. The groups then met to finalize scorecard objectives, measures, targets, and the initiatives to achieve the targets.

Managers at Chipset (like managers at Citibank, Exxon-Mobil, and Infosys) made sure that employees understood the scorecard and the scorecard process. The final balanced scorecard was communicated to all employees. Sharing the scorecard allowed engineers and operating personnel, for example, to understand the reasons for customer satisfaction and dissatisfaction and to make suggestions for improving internal processes directly aimed at satisfying customers and implementing Chipset's strategy. Too often, scorecards are seen by only a select group of managers. By limiting the scorecard's exposure, Chipset would lose the opportunity for widespread organization engagement and alignment.

Chipset also encourages each department to develop its own scorecard that ties into Chipset's main scorecard described in Exhibit 14-3. For example, the quality control department's scorecard has measures that its department managers use to improve yield—number of quality circles, statistical process control charts, Pareto diagrams, and root-cause analyses (see Chapter 10, pages 400–402 for more details). Department scorecards help align the actions of each department to implement Chipset's strategy.

Companies frequently use balanced scorecards to evaluate and reward managerial performance and to influence managerial behavior (see Concepts in Action: Balanced Scorecard Helps Infosys Transform into a Leading Consultancy). Using the balanced scorecard for performance evaluation widens the performance management lens and motivates managers to give greater attention to nonfinancial drivers of performance. Surveys indicate, however, that companies continue to assign more weight to the financial perspective (55%) than to the other perspectives—customer (19%), internal business process (12%), and learning and growth (14%). Companies cite several reasons for the relatively smaller weight on nonfinancial measures: difficulty evaluating the relative importance of nonfinancial measures; challenges in measuring and quantifying qualitative, nonfinancial data; and difficulty in compensating managers despite poor financial performance (see Chapter 16 for a more detailed discussion of performance evaluation). More and more companies in the manufacturing, merchandising, and service sectors are giving greater weight to nonfinancial measures when promoting employees because they believe that nonfinancial measures (such as customer satisfaction, process improvements, and employee motivation) better assess a manager's potential to succeed at senior levels of management. As this trend continues, operating managers will put more weight on nonfinancial factors when making decisions even though these factors carry smaller weights when determining their annual compensation. For the balanced scorecard to be effective, however, managers must view it as fairly assessing and rewarding all important aspects of a manager's performance and promotion prospects.

Different Strategies Lead to Different Scorecards

Recall Chipset's competitor Visilog, which follows a product-differentiation strategy by designing custom chips for modems and communication networks. Visilog designs its balanced scorecard to fit its strategy. For example, in the financial perspective, Visilog evaluates how much of its operating income comes from charging premium prices for its products. In the customer perspective, Visilog measures the percentage of its revenues from new products and new customers. In the internal-business-process perspective, Visilog measures the number of new products introduced and new product development time. In the learning-and-growth perspective, Visilog measures the

Concepts in Action: Balanced Scorecard Helps Infosys Transform into a Leading Consultancy

In the early 2000s, Infosys Technologies was in transition. The Bangalore-based company was a market leader in information technology outsourcing, but it needed to expand to meet increased client demand. Infosys invested in many new areas, including business process outsourcing, project management, and management consulting. To develop an integrated management structure that would help align these new, diverse initiatives, Infosys turned to the balanced scorecard to help formulate and monitor its strategy.

Source: Jagadeesh NV/EPA/Newscom

The executive team used the scorecard to guide discussions about customers, employees, and new products and services during its meetings. The continual process of adaptation, execution, and management that the balanced scorecard fostered helped the team respond to, and even anticipate, its clients' evolving needs. Eventually, use of the scorecard for performance measurement spread to the rest of the organization, with monetary incentives linked to the company's performance along the different dimensions. Over time, the balanced scorecard helped steer the transformation of Infosys from a technology outsourcer to a leading business consultancy, with sales growing from $120 million in 1999 to more than $6.8 billion in 2011.

Sources: Based on F. Asis Martinez-Jerez, Robert S. Kaplan, and Katherine Miller, "Infosys's relationship scorecard: Measuring transformational partnerships," Harvard Business School Case No. 9-109-006 (Boston: Harvard Business School Publishing, 2011); Infosys Limited, "Infosys—About the Company," Infosys Limited website, accessed March 2012.

development of advanced manufacturing capabilities to produce custom chips. Visilog also uses some of the measures described in Chipset's balanced scorecard in Exhibit 14-3. For example, revenue growth, customer satisfaction ratings, order-delivery time, on-time delivery, percentage of frontline workers empowered to manage processes, and employee-satisfaction ratings are also important measures under the product-differentiation strategy. The goal is to align the balanced scorecard with company strategy.[5] Exhibit 14-4 presents some common measures found on company scorecards in the service, retail, and manufacturing sectors.

Features of a Good Balanced Scorecard

A well-designed balanced scorecard has several features:

1. **It tells the story of a company's strategy, articulating a sequence of cause-and-effect relationships—the links among the various perspectives that align implementation of the strategy.** In for-profit companies, each measure in the scorecard is part of a cause-and-effect chain leading to financial outcomes. Not-for-profit organizations design the cause-and-effect chain to achieve their strategic service objectives—for example, reducing the number of people in poverty or raising high school graduation rates.
2. **The balanced scorecard helps to communicate the strategy to all members of the organization by translating the strategy into a coherent and linked set of understandable and measurable operational targets.** Guided by the scorecard, managers and employees take actions and make decisions to achieve the company's strategy. Companies that have distinct strategic business units (SBUs)—such as consumer products and pharmaceuticals at Johnson & Johnson—develop their balanced scorecards at the SBU level. Each SBU has its own unique

[5] For simplicity, we have presented the balanced scorecard in the context of companies that have followed either a cost-leadership or a product-differentiation strategy. Of course, a company may have some products for which cost leadership is critical and other products for which product differentiation is important. The company will then develop separate scorecards to implement the different product strategies. In still other contexts, product differentiation may be of primary importance, but some cost leadership must also be achieved. The balanced scorecard would then include measures for product differentiation and cost leadership.

Exhibit 14-4

Frequently Cited Balanced Scorecard Measures

Financial Perspective
Income measures: Operating income, gross margin percentage
Revenue and cost measures: Revenue growth, revenues from new products, cost reductions in key areas
Income and investment measures: Economic value added[a] (EVA®), return on investment
Customer Perspective
Market share, customer satisfaction, customer-retention percentage, time taken to fulfill customers' requests, number of customer complaints
Internal-Business-Process Perspective
Innovation Process: Operating capabilities, number of new products or services, new-product development times, and number of new patents
Operations Process: Yield, defect rates, time taken to deliver product to customers, percentage of on-time deliveries, average time taken to respond to orders, setup time, manufacturing downtime
Postsales Service Process: Time taken to replace or repair defective products, hours of customer training for using the product
Learning-and-Growth Perspective
Employee measures: Employee education and skill levels, employee-satisfaction ratings, employee turnover rates, percentage of employee suggestions implemented, percentage of compensation based on individual and team incentives
Technology measures: Information system availability, percentage of processes with advanced controls

[a]This measure is described in Chapter 16.

strategy and implementation goals; building separate scorecards allows each SBU to choose measures that help implement its distinctive strategy.

3. **In for-profit companies, the balanced scorecard must motivate managers to take actions that eventually result in improvements in financial performance.** Managers sometimes tend to focus too much on innovation, quality, and customer satisfaction as ends in themselves. For example, Xerox spent heavily to increase customer satisfaction without a resulting financial payoff because higher levels of satisfaction did not translate into customer loyalty and higher sales. Some companies use statistical methods, such as regression analysis, to test the anticipated cause-and-effect relationships among nonfinancial measures and financial performance. The data for this analysis can come from either time-series data (collected over time) or cross-sectional data (collected, for example, across multiple stores of a retail chain). In the Chipset example, improvements in nonfinancial factors have, in fact, already led to improvements in financial factors.
4. **The balanced scorecard limits the number of measures, identifying only the most critical ones.** Chipset's scorecard, for example, has 16 measures, between three and six measures for each perspective. Limiting the number of measures focuses managers' attention on those that most affect strategy implementation. Using too many measures makes it difficult for managers to process relevant information.
5. **The balanced scorecard highlights less-than-optimal tradeoffs that managers may make when they fail to consider operational and financial measures together.** For example, a company whose strategy is innovation and product differentiation could achieve superior short-run financial performance by reducing spending on R&D. A good balanced scorecard would signal that the short-run financial performance might have been achieved by taking actions that hurt future financial performance because a leading indicator of that performance, R&D spending and R&D output, has declined.

Pitfalls in Implementing a Balanced Scorecard

Pitfalls to avoid in implementing a balanced scorecard include the following:

1. **Managers should not assume the cause-and-effect linkages are precise.** These linkages are merely hypotheses. Over time, a company must gather evidence of the strength and timing of the linkages among the nonfinancial and financial measures. With experience, organizations should alter their scorecards to include those nonfinancial strategic objectives and measures that are the best leading indicators (the causes) of financial performance (a lagging indicator or the effect). Understanding that the scorecard evolves over time helps managers avoid unproductively spending time and money trying to design the "perfect" scorecard at the outset. Moreover, as the business environment and strategy change over time, the measures in the scorecard also need to change.

2. **Managers should not seek improvements across all of the measures all of the time.** For example, strive for quality and on-time performance but not beyond the point at which further improvement in these objectives is so costly that it is inconsistent with long-run profit maximization. Cost–benefit considerations should always be central when designing a balanced scorecard.
3. **Managers should not use only objective measures in the balanced scorecard.** Chipset's balanced scorecard includes both objective measures (such as operating income from cost leadership, market share, and manufacturing yield) and subjective measures (such as customer- and employee-satisfaction ratings). When using subjective measures, however, managers must be careful that the benefits of this potentially rich information are not lost by using measures that are inaccurate or that can be easily manipulated.
4. **Despite challenges of measurement, top management should not ignore nonfinancial measures when evaluating managers and other employees.** Managers tend to focus on the measures used to reward their performance. Excluding nonfinancial measures (such as customer satisfaction or product quality) when evaluating performance will reduce their significance and importance to managers.

Evaluating the Success of Strategy and Implementation

To evaluate how successful Chipset's strategy and its implementation have been, its management compares the target- and actual-performance columns in the balanced scorecard (Exhibit 14-3). Chipset met most targets set on the basis of competitor benchmarks in 2012 itself because improvements in Chipset's learning and growth perspective quickly rippled through to the financial perspective. While Chipset will continue to make improvements to achieve the targets it did not meet, managers were satisfied that the strategic initiatives that Chipset identified and measured for learning and growth resulted in improvements in internal business processes, customer measures, and financial performance.

How would Chipset know if it had problems in strategy implementation? If it did not meet its targets on the two perspectives that are more internally focused: learning and growth and internal business processes.

What if Chipset performed well on learning and growth and internal business processes, but customer measures and financial performance in this year and the next still did not improve? Chipset's managers would then conclude that Chipset did a good job of implementation, as the various internal nonfinancial measures it targeted improved, but that its strategy was faulty because there was no effect on customers or on long-run financial performance and value creation. In this case, management had failed to identify the correct causal links and did a good job implementing the wrong strategy! Management would then reevaluate the strategy and the factors that drive it.

Keys to Success

The "balance" in the balanced scorecard is between financial and nonfinancial performance measures. A good balanced scorecard helps managers link strategy with the results that matter for the organization's success, measure only the most critical yardsticks for performance, and show where tradeoffs might have to be made. In developing the scorecard, managers should avoid assuming cause-and-effect relationships, make only cost-effective improvements, and not overlook nonfinancial and subjective measures.

Learning Objective 4

Analyze changes in operating income to evaluate strategy

. . . growth, price recovery, and productivity

Strategic Analysis of Operating Income

As we have discussed, Chipset performed well on its various nonfinancial measures, and operating income over this year and the next also increased. Chipset's managers might be tempted to declare the strategy a success but, in fact, they cannot conclude with any confidence that Chipset successfully formulated and implemented its intended strategy. That's because operating income could have increased simply because the entire market expanded or a competitor declared bankruptcy. Alternatively, a company that has chosen a cost-leadership strategy, like Chipset, may find that its operating-income increase actually resulted from some degree of product differentiation. *To evaluate the success of a strategy, managers and management accountants need to link strategy to the sources of operating-income increases.* These are the kinds of details that top management and boards of directors routinely discuss in their meetings when evaluating performance. Managers who have mastered the strategic analysis of operating income changes gain an understanding of the levers of strategy and strategy implementation that help them deliver sustained operating performance.

For Chipset managers to conclude that they were successful in implementing their strategy, they must demonstrate that improvements in the company's financial performance and operating income over time resulted from achieving targeted cost savings and growth in market share. Fortunately, the top two rows of Chipset's balanced scorecard in Exhibit 14-3 show that operating-income gains from productivity ($1,912,500) and growth ($2,820,000) exceeded targets. (The next section of this chapter describes how these numbers were calculated.) Because its strategy has been successful, Chipset's management can be more confident that the gains will be sustained in subsequent years.

Chipset's management accountants subdivide changes in operating income into components that can be identified with product differentiation, cost leadership, and growth. Managers look to growth because successful product differentiation or cost leadership generally increases market share and helps a company to grow. Subdividing the change in operating income to evaluate the success of a strategy is conceptually similar to the variance analysis discussed in Chapter 13. One difference, however, is that management accountants compare actual operating performance over *two different periods,* not actual to budgeted numbers in the *same time period* as in variance analysis.[6]

We next explain how the change in operating income from one period to *any* future period can be subdivided into product differentiation, cost leadership, and growth components.[7] We illustrate the analysis using data from 2011 and 2012 because Chipset implemented key elements of its strategy in late 2011 and early 2012 and expects the financial consequences of these strategies to occur in 2012. Suppose the financial consequences of these strategies had been expected to affect operating income in only 2013. Then we could just as easily have compared 2011 to 2013. If necessary, we could also have compared 2011 to 2012 and 2013 taken together.

Chipset's data for 2011 and 2012 are:

	2011	2012
1. Units of CX1 produced and sold	1,000,000	1,150,000
2. Selling price	$23	$22
3. Direct materials (square centimeters of silicon wafers)	3,000,000	2,900,000
4. Direct material cost per square centimeter	$1.40	$1.50
5. Manufacturing processing capacity (in square centimeters of silicon wafer)	3,750,000	3,500,000
6. Conversion costs (all manufacturing costs other than direct material costs)	$16,050,000	$15,225,000
7. Conversion cost per unit of capacity (row 6 ÷ row 5)	$4.28	$4.35

Chipset managers obtain the following additional information:

1. Conversion costs (labor and overhead costs) for each year depend on production processing capacity defined in terms of the quantity of square centimeters of silicon wafers that Chipset can process. These costs do not vary with the actual quantity of silicon wafers processed.
2. Chipset incurs no R&D costs. Its marketing, sales, and customer-service costs are small relative to the other costs. Chipset has fewer than 10 customers, each purchasing roughly the same quantities of CX1. Because of the highly technical nature of the product, Chipset uses a cross-functional team for its marketing, sales, and customer-service activities. This cross-functional approach ensures that, although marketing, sales, and customer-service costs are small, the entire Chipset organization, including manufacturing engineers, remains focused on increasing customer satisfaction and market share. (The Problem for Self-Study at the end of this chapter describes a situation in which marketing, sales, and customer-service costs are significant.)

[6] Other examples of focusing on actual performance over two periods rather than comparisons of actuals with budgets can be found in J. Hope and R. Fraser, *Beyond Budgeting* (Boston: Harvard Business School Press, 2003).

[7] For other details, see R. Banker, S. Datar, and R. Kaplan, "Productivity Measurement and Management Accounting," *Journal of Accounting, Auditing and Finance* (1989): 528–554; and A. Hayzens and J. Reeve, "Examining the Relationships in Productivity Accounting," *Management Accounting Quarterly* (2000): 32–39.

3. Chipset's asset structure is very similar in 2011 and 2012.
4. Operating income for each year is as follows:

	2011	2012
Revenues		
($23 per unit × 1,000,000 units; $22 per unit × 1,150,000 units)	$23,000,000	$25,300,000
Costs		
Direct material costs		
($1.40/sq. cm. × 3,000,000 sq. cm.; $1.50/sq. cm. × 2,900,000 sq. cm.)	4,200,000	4,350,000
Conversion costs		
($4.28/sq. cm. × 3,750,000 sq. cm.; $4.35/sq. cm. × 3,500,000 sq. cm.)	16,050,000	15,225,000
Total costs	20,250,000	19,575,000
Operating income	$ 2,750,000	$ 5,725,000
Change in operating income	$2,975,000 F	

The goal of Chipset's managers is to evaluate how much of the $2,975,000 increase in operating income was caused by the successful implementation of the company's cost-leadership strategy. To do this, management accountants start by analyzing three main factors: (1) growth, (2) price recovery, and (3) productivity.

The **growth component** measures the change in operating income attributable solely to the change in the quantity of output sold between 2011 and 2012. The **price-recovery component** measures the change in operating income attributable solely to changes in Chipset's prices of inputs and outputs between 2011 and 2012. The price-recovery component measures change in output price compared with changes in input prices. A company that has successfully pursued a strategy of product differentiation will be able to increase its output price faster than the increase in its input prices, boosting profit margins and operating income: The company will show a large positive price-recovery component.

The **productivity component** measures the change in costs attributable to a change in the quantity of inputs used in 2012 relative to the quantity of inputs that would have been used in 2011 to produce the 2012 output. The productivity component measures the amount by which operating income increases by using inputs efficiently to lower costs. A company that has successfully pursued a strategy of cost leadership will be able to produce a given quantity of output with a lower cost of inputs and will show a large positive productivity component. Given Chipset's strategy of cost leadership, managers expect the increase in operating income to be attributable to the productivity and growth components, not to price recovery. We now examine these three components in detail.

Growth Component of Change in Operating Income

The growth component of the change in operating income measures the increase in revenues minus the increase in costs from selling more units of CX1 in 2012 (1,150,000 units) than in 2011 (1,000,000 units), *assuming nothing else has changed.*

Revenue Effect of Growth

$$\text{Revenue effect of growth} = \left(\begin{array}{c}\text{Actual units of}\\ \text{output sold}\\ \text{in 2012}\end{array} - \begin{array}{c}\text{Actual units of}\\ \text{output sold}\\ \text{in 2011}\end{array}\right) \times \begin{array}{c}\text{Selling}\\ \text{price}\\ \text{in 2011}\end{array}$$

$$= (1{,}150{,}000 \text{ units} - 1{,}000{,}000 \text{ units}) \times \$23 \text{ per unit}$$

$$= \$3{,}450{,}000 \text{ F}$$

This component is favorable (F) because the increase in output sold in 2012 increases operating income. Components that decrease operating income are unfavorable (U).

Note that Chipset uses the 2011 price of CX1 and focuses only on the increase in units sold between 2011 and 2012 because the revenue effect of growth component measures how much revenues would have changed in 2011 if Chipset had sold 1,150,000 units instead of 1,000,000 units.

Cost Effect of Growth. The cost effect of growth measures how much costs would have changed in 2011 if Chipset had produced 1,150,000 units of CX1 instead of 1,000,000 units. To measure the cost effect of growth, Chipset's managers distinguish variable costs such as direct material costs from fixed costs such as conversion costs because as units produced (and sold) increase, variable costs increase proportionately but fixed costs, generally, do not change.

$$\begin{matrix}\text{Cost effect of}\\ \text{growth for}\\ \text{variable costs}\end{matrix} = \left(\begin{matrix}\text{Units of input}\\ \text{required to}\\ \text{produce 2012}\\ \text{output in 2011}\end{matrix} - \begin{matrix}\text{Actual units of}\\ \text{input used}\\ \text{to produce}\\ \text{2011 output}\end{matrix}\right) \times \begin{matrix}\text{Input}\\ \text{price}\\ \text{in 2011}\end{matrix}$$

$$\begin{matrix}\text{Cost effect of}\\ \text{growth for}\\ \text{direct materials}\end{matrix} = \left(3{,}000{,}000 \text{ sq. cm.} \times \frac{1{,}150{,}000 \text{ units}}{1{,}000{,}000 \text{ units}} - 3{,}000{,}000 \text{ sq. cm.}\right) \times \$1.40 \text{ per sq. cm.}$$

$$= (3{,}450{,}000 \text{ sq. cm.} - 3{,}000{,}000 \text{ sq. cm.}) \times \$1.40 \text{ per sq. cm.} = \$630{,}000 \text{ U}$$

The units of input required to produce 2012 output in 2011 can also be calculated as follows:

$$\text{Units of input per unit of output in 2011} = \frac{3{,}000{,}000 \text{ sq. cm.}}{1{,}000{,}000 \text{ units}} = 3 \text{ sq. cm./unit}$$

Units of input required to produce 2012 output of 1,150,000 units in 2011 = 3 sq. cm. per unit × 1,150,000 units = 3,450,000 sq. cm.

$$\begin{matrix}\text{Cost effect of}\\ \text{growth for}\\ \text{fixed costs}\end{matrix} = \left(\begin{matrix}\text{Actual units of capacity in}\\ \text{2011 because adequate capacity}\\ \text{exists to produce 2012 output in 2011}\end{matrix} - \begin{matrix}\text{Actual units}\\ \text{of capacity}\\ \text{in 2011}\end{matrix}\right) \times \begin{matrix}\text{Price per}\\ \text{unit of}\\ \text{capacity}\\ \text{in 2011}\end{matrix}$$

$$\begin{matrix}\text{Cost effect of}\\ \text{growth for}\\ \text{conversion costs}\end{matrix} = (3{,}750{,}000 \text{ sq. cm.} - 3{,}750{,}000 \text{ sq. cm.}) \times \$4.28 \text{ per sq. cm.} = \$0$$

Conversion costs are fixed costs at a given level of capacity. Chipset has manufacturing capacity to process 3,750,000 square centimeters of silicon wafers in 2011 at a cost of $4.28 per square centimeter (rows 5 and 7 of data on page 595). To produce 1,150,000 units of output in 2011, Chipset needs to process 3,450,000 square centimeters of direct materials, which is less than the available capacity of 3,750,000 sq. cm. Throughout this chapter, we assume adequate capacity exists in the current year (2011) to produce next year's (2012) output. Under this assumption, the cost effect of growth for capacity-related fixed costs is, by definition, $0. Had 2011 capacity been inadequate to produce 2012 output in 2011, we would need to calculate the additional capacity required to produce 2012 output in 2011. These calculations are beyond the scope of the book.

In summary, the net increase in operating income attributable to growth equals the following:

Revenue effect of growth		$3,450,000 F
Cost effect of growth		
Direct material costs	$630,000 U	
Conversion costs	0	630,000 U
Change in operating income due to growth		$2,820,000 F

Price-Recovery Component of Change in Operating Income

Assuming that the 2011 relationship between inputs and outputs continued in 2012, the price-recovery component of the change in operating income measures solely the effect of price changes on revenues and costs to produce and sell the 1,150,000 units of CX1 in 2012.

Revenue Effect of Price Recovery

$$\begin{matrix}\text{Revenue effect of}\\ \text{price recovery}\end{matrix} = \left(\begin{matrix}\text{Selling price}\\ \text{in 2012}\end{matrix} - \begin{matrix}\text{Selling price}\\ \text{in 2011}\end{matrix}\right) \times \begin{matrix}\text{Actual units}\\ \text{of output}\\ \text{sold in 2012}\end{matrix}$$

$$= (\$22 \text{ per unit} - \$23 \text{ per unit}) \times 1{,}150{,}000 \text{ units}$$

$$= \$1{,}150{,}000 \text{ U}$$

Note that the calculation focuses on revenue changes caused by changes in the selling price of CX1 between 2011 and 2012.

Cost Effect of Price Recovery. Chipset's management accountants calculate the cost effects of price recovery separately for variable costs and for fixed costs, just as they did when calculating the cost effect of growth.

$$\begin{matrix}\text{Cost effect of}\\\text{price recovery for}\\\text{variable costs}\end{matrix} = \left(\begin{matrix}\text{Input price}\\\text{in 2012}\end{matrix} - \begin{matrix}\text{Input price}\\\text{in 2011}\end{matrix}\right) \times \begin{matrix}\text{Units of input}\\\text{required to}\\\text{produce 2012}\\\text{output in 2011}\end{matrix}$$

$$\begin{matrix}\text{Cost effect of}\\\text{price recovery for}\\\text{direct materials}\end{matrix} = (\$1.50 \text{ per sq. cm.} - \$1.40 \text{ per sq. cm.}) \times 3{,}450{,}000 \text{ sq.} = \$345{,}000\text{ U}$$

Recall that the direct materials of 3,450,000 square centimeters required to produce 2012 output in 2011 had already been calculated when computing the cost effect of growth (page 597).

$$\begin{matrix}\text{Cost effect of}\\\text{price recovery for}\\\text{fixed costs}\end{matrix} = \left(\begin{matrix}\text{Price per}\\\text{unit of}\\\text{capacity}\\\text{in 2012}\end{matrix} - \begin{matrix}\text{Price per}\\\text{unit of}\\\text{capacity}\\\text{in 2011}\end{matrix}\right) \times \begin{matrix}\text{Actual units of capacity in}\\\text{2011 (because adequate}\\\text{capacity exists to produce}\\\text{2012 output in 2011)}\end{matrix}$$

Cost effect of price recovery for fixed costs is as follows:

$$\text{Conversion costs: } (\$4.35 \text{ per sq. cm.} - \$4.28 \text{ per sq. cm.}) \times 3{,}750{,}000 \text{ sq. cm.} = \$262{,}500\text{ U}$$

Recall that the detailed analyses of capacities were presented when computing the cost effect of growth (page 597).

In summary, the net decrease in operating income attributable to price recovery equals the following:

Revenue effect of price recovery		$1,150,000 U
Cost effect of price recovery		
Direct material costs	$345,000 U	
Conversion costs	262,500 U	607,500 U
Change in operating income due to price recovery		$1,757,500 U

The price-recovery analysis indicates that, even as the prices of its inputs increased, the selling prices of CX1 decreased and Chipset could not pass on input-price increases to its customers.

Productivity Component of Change in Operating Income

The productivity component of the change in operating income uses 2012 input prices to measure how costs have decreased as a result of using fewer inputs, a better mix of inputs, and/or less capacity to produce 2012 output, compared with the inputs and capacity that would have been used to produce this output in 2011.

The productivity-component calculations use 2012 prices and output. That's because the productivity component isolates the change in costs between 2011 and 2012 caused solely by the change in the quantities, mix, and/or capacities of inputs.[8]

[8] Note that the productivity-component calculation uses actual 2012 input prices, whereas its counterpart, the efficiency variance in Chapter 12, uses budgeted prices. (In effect, the budgeted prices correspond to 2011 prices.) Year 2012 prices are used in the productivity calculation because Chipset wants its managers to choose input quantities to minimize costs in 2012 based on currently prevailing prices. If 2011 prices had been used in the productivity calculation, managers would choose input quantities based on irrelevant input prices that prevailed a year ago! Why does using budgeted prices in Chapter 13 not pose a similar problem? Because, unlike 2011 prices that describe what happened a year ago, budgeted prices represent prices that are expected to prevail in the current period. Moreover, budgeted prices can be changed, if necessary, to bring them in line with actual current-period prices.

$$\begin{array}{c}\text{Cost effect of}\\ \text{productivity for}\\ \text{variable costs}\end{array} = \left(\begin{array}{c}\text{Actual units of}\\ \text{input used}\\ \text{to produce}\\ \text{2012 output}\end{array} - \begin{array}{c}\text{Units of input}\\ \text{required to}\\ \text{produce 2012}\\ \text{output in 2011}\end{array}\right) \times \begin{array}{c}\text{Input}\\ \text{price}\\ \text{in 2012}\end{array}$$

Using the 2012 data given on page 595 and the calculation of units of input required to produce 2012 output in 2011 when discussing the cost effects of growth (page 597),

$$\begin{array}{l}\text{Cost effect of}\\ \text{productivity for}\\ \text{direct materials}\end{array} = (2{,}900{,}000 \text{ sq. cm.} - 3{,}450{,}000 \text{ sq. cm.}) \times \$1.50 \text{ per sq. cm.}$$

$$= 550{,}000 \text{ sq. cm.} \times \$1.50 \text{ per sq. cm.} = \$825{,}000 \text{ F}$$

Chipset's quality and yield improvements reduced the quantity of direct materials needed to produce output in 2012 relative to 2011.

$$\begin{array}{c}\text{Cost effect of}\\ \text{productivity for}\\ \text{fixed costs}\end{array} = \left(\begin{array}{c}\text{Actual units of}\\ \text{capacity}\\ \text{in 2012}\end{array} - \begin{array}{c}\text{Actual units of capacity in}\\ \text{2011 because adequate}\\ \text{capacity exists to produce}\\ \text{2012 output in 2011}\end{array}\right) \times \begin{array}{c}\text{Price per}\\ \text{unit of}\\ \text{capacity}\\ \text{in 2012}\end{array}$$

To calculate the cost effect of productivity for fixed costs, we use the 2012 data given on page 595, and the analyses of capacity required to produce 2012 output in 2011 when discussing the cost effect of growth (page 597).

Cost effects of productivity for fixed costs are:

$$\text{Conversion costs: } (3{,}500{,}000 \text{ sq. cm} - 3{,}750{,}000 \text{ sq. cm.}) \times \$4.35 \text{ per sq. cm.} = \$1{,}087{,}500 \text{ F}$$

Chipset's managers decreased manufacturing capacity in 2012 to 3,500,000 square centimeters by selling off old equipment and laying off workers.

In summary, the net increase in operating income attributable to productivity equals:

Cost effect of productivity	
Direct material costs	$ 825,000 F
Conversion costs	1,087,500 F
Change in operating income due to productivity	$1,912,500 F

The productivity component indicates that Chipset was able to increase operating income by improving quality and productivity and eliminating capacity to reduce costs. Note that the productivity component focuses exclusively on costs, so there is no revenue effect for this component.

Exhibit 14-5 summarizes the growth, price-recovery, and productivity components of the changes in operating income. Generally, companies that have been successful at cost leadership will show favorable productivity and growth components. Companies that have successfully

Exhibit 14-5

Strategic Analysis of Profitability

	Income Statement Amounts in 2011 (1)	Revenue and Cost Effects of Growth Component in 2012 (2)	Revenue and Cost Effects of Price-Recovery Component in 2012 (3)	Cost Effect of Productivity Component in 2012 (4)	Income Statement Amounts in 2012 (5) = (1) + (2) + (3) + (4)
Revenues	$23,000,000	$3,450,000 F	$1,150,000 U	—	$25,300,000
Costs	20,250,000	630,000 U	607,500 U	$1,912,000 F	19,575,000
Operating income	$ 2,750,000	$2,820,000 F	$1,757,500 U	$1,912,500 F	$ 5,725,000

$2,975,000 F

Change in operating income

differentiated their products will show favorable price-recovery and growth components. In Chipset's case, consistent with its strategy and its implementation, productivity contributed $1,912,500 to the increase in operating income, and growth contributed $2,820,000. Price recovery contributed a $1,757,500 decrease in operating income, however, because, even as input prices increased, the selling price of CX1 decreased. Had Chipset been able to differentiate its product and charge a higher price, the price-recovery effects might have been less unfavorable or perhaps even favorable. As a result, Chipset's managers plan to evaluate some modest changes in product features that might help differentiate CX1 somewhat more from competing products.

Further Analysis of Growth, Price-Recovery, and Productivity Components

As in all variance and profit analysis, Chipset's managers may want to further analyze the change in operating income. For example, Chipset's growth might have been helped by an increase in industry market size. Therefore, at least part of the increase in operating income may be attributable to favorable economic conditions in the industry rather than to any successful implementation of strategy. Some of the growth might relate to the management decision to decrease selling price, made possible by the productivity gains. In this case, the increase in operating income from cost leadership must include operating income from productivity-related growth in market share in addition to the productivity gain. These analyses are beyond the scope of this book. Concepts in Action: Operating Income Analysis Reveals Strategic Flaws at Best Buy describes how an analysis of its operating income helped Best Buy change its strategy to compete with Amazon.

Applying the Five-Step Decision-Making Framework to Strategy

We next briefly describe how the five-step decision-making framework, introduced in Chapter 1, is also useful in making decisions about strategy.

Concepts in Action: Operating Income Analysis Reveals Strategic Flaws at Best Buy

Source: Bonnie Kamin/PhotoEdit, Inc.

In 2008, Best Buy was the undisputed king of electronics retailing after its largest competitor, Circuit City, went bankrupt. Without another bricks-and-mortar competitor, Best Buy reaffirmed its previously successful strategy of aggressive "big-box" store expansion. From 2008 to 2011, Best Buy added 346 new stores across the United States, increasing capacity by 35 percent and growing annual revenue by $10 billion.

By 2011, however, an analysis of the company's operating income revealed strategic flaws. Though revenue was growing, operating income was flat from 2008 to 2011. Meanwhile, same-store sales were declining and selling, general, and administrative expenses were rising. These numbers reveal that e-commerce was eroding Best Buy's performance. While the company pursued strategic differentiation through customer experience and add-on services, many consumers were drawn to the low prices of Amazon and other online retailers to buy flat-screen televisions, computers, and digital cameras—three of Best Buy's largest categories. To respond to this challenge, Best Buy ramped up spending on advertising and its e-commerce capabilities, which increased its overall costs.

To turn the company around, Best Buy (1) announced plans to shrink its square footage by 10% and open smaller stores focused on selling smartphones; (2) further expand its online presence to compete better with Amazon; and (3) sell more services through its "Geek Squad" customer-support business.

Sources: Based on Miguel Bustillo, "Best Buy to Shrink 'Big Box' Store Strategy," *The Wall Street Journal* (April 15, 2011); Andria Cheng, "Best Buy to Scale Back Big-Box Strategy," *MarketWatch* (April 14, 2012); Best Buy, Inc. Form 10-K. Best Buy, Inc., Richfield, MN: 2011.

1. *Identify the problem and uncertainties.* Chipset's strategy choice depends on resolving two uncertainties: (1) whether Chipset can add value to its customers that its competitors cannot copy and (2) whether Chipset can develop the necessary internal capabilities to add this value.
2. *Obtain information.* Chipset's managers develop customer preference maps to identify various product attributes desired by customers and the competitive advantage or disadvantage it has on each attribute relative to competitors. The managers also gather data on Chipset's internal capabilities. How good is Chipset in designing and developing innovative new products? How good are its process and marketing capabilities?
3. *Make predictions about the future.* Chipset's managers conclude that they will not be able to develop innovative new products in a cost-effective way. They believe that Chipset's strength lies in improving quality, reengineering processes, reducing costs, and delivering products faster to customers.
4. *Make decisions by choosing among alternatives.* Chipset's management decides to follow a cost-leadership rather than a product-differentiation strategy. It decides to introduce a balanced scorecard to align and measure its quality improvement and process reengineering efforts.
5. *Implement the decision, evaluate performance, and learn.* On its balanced scorecard, Chipset's managers compare actual and targeted performance and evaluate possible cause-and-effect relationships. They learn, for example, that increasing the percentage of processes with advanced controls improves yield. As a result, just as they had anticipated, productivity and growth initiatives result in increases in operating income in 2012. The one change Chipset's managers plan for 2013 is to make modest changes in product features that might help differentiate CX1 somewhat from competing products. In this way, feedback and learning help in the development of future strategies and implementation plans.

Keys to Success

Managers evaluate the success of product-differentiation or cost-leadership strategies by subdividing changes in operating income into growth, price-recovery, and productivity components.

Downsizing and the Management of Processing Capacity

Learning Objective 5

Identify unused capacity

. . . capacity available minus capacity used for engineered costs but difficult to determine for discretionary costs

and how to manage it

. . . downsize to reduce capacity

As we saw in our discussion of the productivity component (page 598), fixed costs are tied to capacity. Unlike variable costs, fixed costs do not change automatically with changes in activity level (for example, fixed conversion costs do not change with changes in the quantity of silicon wafers started into production). How then can managers reduce capacity-based fixed costs? By measuring and managing *unused capacity.* **Unused capacity** is the amount of productive capacity available over and above the productive capacity employed to meet customer demand in the current period. To understand unused capacity, it is necessary to distinguish *engineered costs* from *discretionary costs.*

Engineered and Discretionary Costs

Engineered costs result from a cause-and-effect relationship between the cost driver—output—and the (direct or indirect) resources used to produce that output. Engineered costs have a detailed, physically observable, and repetitive relationship with output. In the Chipset example, direct material costs are *direct engineered costs.* Conversion costs are an example of *indirect engineered costs.* Consider 2012. The output of 1,150,000 units of CX1 and the efficiency with which inputs are converted into outputs result in 2,900,000 square centimeters of silicon wafers being started into production. Manufacturing-conversion-cost resources used equal $12,615,000 ($4.35 per sq. cm. × 2,900,000 sq. cm.), but actual conversion costs ($15,225,000) are higher because Chipset has manufacturing capacity to process 3,500,000 square centimeters of silicon wafers ($4.35 per sq. cm. × 3,500,000 sq. cm. = $15,225,000). Although these costs are fixed in the short run, over the long run there is a cause-and-effect relationship between output and manufacturing capacity required (and conversion costs needed). In the long run, Chipset will try to match its capacity to its needs.

In general, cost leadership requires careful attention be paid to engineered costs and managing capacity. Companies such as General Motors and United Airlines have struggled to achieve profitability because of the difficulties they have had in managing capacity-related engineered costs.

Discretionary costs have two important features: (1) They arise from periodic (usually annual) decisions regarding the maximum amount to be incurred and (2) they have no measurable cause-and-effect relationship between output and resources used. There is often a delay between when a resource is acquired and when it is used. Examples of discretionary costs include advertising, executive training, R&D, and corporate-staff department costs such as legal, human resources, and public relations. Unlike engineered costs, the relationship between discretionary costs and output is a "black box" because it is nonrepetitive and nonroutine. A noteworthy aspect of discretionary costs is that managers are seldom confident that the "correct" amounts are being spent. The founder of Lever Brothers, an international consumer-products company, once noted, "Half the money I spend on advertising is wasted; the trouble is, I don't know which half!"[9]

Identifying Unused Capacity for Engineered and Discretionary Overhead Costs

Identifying unused capacity is very different for engineered costs compared to discretionary costs. Consider engineered conversion costs.

At the start of 2012, Chipset had capacity to process 3,750,000 square centimeters of silicon wafers. Quality and productivity improvements made during 2012 enabled Chipset to produce 1,150,000 units of CX1 by processing 2,900,000 square centimeters of silicon wafers. Unused manufacturing capacity is 850,000 (3,750,000 − 2,900,000) square centimeters of silicon-wafer processing capacity at the beginning of 2012 when Chipset makes its capacity decisions for the year. At the 2012 conversion cost of $4.35 per square centimeter,

$$\begin{aligned}\text{Cost of unused capacity} &= \text{Cost of capacity at the beginning of the year} - \text{Manufacturing resources used during the year}\\ &= (3{,}750{,}000 \text{ sq. cm.} \times \$4.35 \text{ per sq. cm.}) - (2{,}900{,}000 \text{ sq. cm.} \times \$4.35 \text{ per sq. cm.})\\ &= \$16{,}312{,}500 - \$12{,}615{,}000 = \$3{,}697{,}500\end{aligned}$$

The absence of a cause-and-effect relationship makes identifying unused capacity for discretionary costs difficult. For example, management cannot determine the R&D resources used for the actual output produced. And without a measure of capacity used, it is not possible to compute unused capacity.

Managing Unused Capacity

What actions can Chipset management take when it identifies unused capacity? In general, it has two alternatives: eliminate unused capacity or grow output to utilize the unused capacity.

In recent years, many companies have *downsized* in an attempt to eliminate unused capacity. **Downsizing** (also called **rightsizing**) is an integrated approach of configuring processes, products, and people to match costs to the activities that need to be performed to operate effectively and efficiently in the present and future. Companies such as AT&T, Delta Airlines, Ford Motor Company, and IBM have downsized to focus on their core businesses and have instituted organization changes to increase efficiency, reduce costs, and improve quality. However, downsizing often means eliminating jobs, which can adversely affect employee morale and the culture of a company.

Consider Chipset's alternatives for dealing with unused manufacturing capacity. Because it needed to process 2,900,000 square centimeters of silicon wafers in 2012, the company could have reduced capacity to 3,000,000 square centimeters (Chipset can add or reduce

[9] Managers also describe some costs as infrastructure costs—costs that arise from having property, plant, and equipment and a functioning organization. Examples are depreciation, long-run lease rental, and the acquisition of long-run technical capabilities. These costs are generally fixed costs because they are committed to and acquired before they are used. Infrastructure costs can be engineered or discretionary. For instance, manufacturing-overhead cost incurred at Chipset to acquire manufacturing capacity is an infrastructure cost that is an example of an engineered cost. In the long run, there is a cause-and-effect relationship between output and manufacturing-overhead costs needed to produce that output. R&D cost incurred to acquire technical capability is an infrastructure cost that is an example of a discretionary cost. There is no measurable cause-and-effect relationship between output and R&D cost incurred.

manufacturing capacity in increments of 250,000 sq. cm.), resulting in cost savings of $3,262,500 [(3,750,000 sq. cm. − 3,000,000 sq. cm.) × $4.35 per sq. cm.]. Chipset's strategy, however, is not just to reduce costs but also to grow its business. So in early 2012, Chipset reduces its manufacturing capacity by only 250,000 square centimeters—from 3,750,000 square centimeters to 3,500,000 square centimeters—saving $1,087,500 ($4.35 per sq. cm. × 250,000 sq. cm.). It retains some extra capacity for future growth. By avoiding greater reductions in capacity, it also maintains the morale of its skilled and capable workforce. The success of this strategy will depend on Chipset achieving the future growth it has projected.

Identifying unused capacity for discretionary costs, such as R&D costs, is difficult, so downsizing or otherwise managing this unused capacity is also difficult. Management must exercise considerable judgment in deciding the level of R&D costs that would generate the needed product and process improvements. Unlike engineered costs, there is no clear-cut way to know whether management is spending too much (or too little) on R&D.

Keys to Success

Managers recognize that an important form of productivity improvement is eliminating excess, unused capacity for engineered costs (such as manufacturing costs). It is more difficult for managers to identify and manage unused capacity in the case of discretionary costs, such as R&D costs.

Problem for Self-Study

Following a strategy of product differentiation, Westwood Corporation makes a high-end kitchen range hood, KE8. Westwood's data for 2011 and 2012 are:

	2011	2012
1. Units of KE8 produced and sold	40,000	42,000
2. Selling price	$100	$110
3. Direct materials (square feet)	120,000	123,000
4. Direct material cost per square foot	$10	$11
5. Manufacturing capacity for KE8	50,000 units	50,000 units
6. Conversion costs	$1,000,000	$1,100,000
7. Conversion cost per unit of capacity (row 6 ÷ row 5)	$20	$22
8. Selling and customer-service capacity	30 customers	29 customers
9. Selling and customer-service costs	$720,000	$725,000
10. Cost per customer of selling and customer-service capacity (row 9 ÷ row 8)	$24,000	$25,000

In 2012, Westwood produced no defective units and reduced direct material usage per unit of KE8. Conversion costs in each year are tied to manufacturing capacity. Selling and customer service costs are related to the number of customers that the selling and service functions are designed to support. Westwood had 23 customers (wholesalers) in 2011 and 25 customers in 2012.

Required

1. Describe briefly the elements you would include in Westwood's balanced scorecard.
2. Calculate the growth, price-recovery, and productivity components that explain the change in operating income from 2011 to 2012.
3. How successful has Westwood been in implementing its strategy? Explain.

Solution

1. The balanced scorecard should describe Westwood's product-differentiation strategy. Elements that should be included in its balanced scorecard are as follows:
   - **Financial perspective.** Increase in operating income from higher margins on KE8 and from growth
   - **Customer perspective.** Customer satisfaction and market share in the high-end market
   - **Internal-business-process perspective.** New product features, development time for new products, improvements in manufacturing processes, manufacturing quality, order-delivery time, and on-time delivery
   - **Learning-and-growth perspective.** Number of employees in product development, percentage of employees trained in process and quality management, and employee satisfaction ratings
2. Operating income for each year is:

	2011	2012
Revenues		
($100 per unit × 40,000 units; $110 per unit × 42,000 units)	$4,000,000	$4,620,000
Costs		
Direct material costs		
($10 per sq. ft. × 120,000 sq. ft.; $11 per sq. ft. × 123,000 sq. ft.)	1,200,000	1,353,000
Conversion costs		
($20 per unit × 50,000 units; $22 per unit × 50,000 units)	1,000,000	1,100,000
Selling and customer-service cost		
($24,000 per customer × 30 customers; $25,000 per customer × 29 customers)	720,000	725,000
Total costs	2,920,000	3,178,000
Operating income	$1,080,000	$1,442,000
Change in operating income	$362,000 F	

Growth Component of Operating Income Change

$$\text{Revenue effect of growth} = \left(\begin{array}{c}\text{Actual units of}\\ \text{output sold}\\ \text{in 2012}\end{array} - \begin{array}{c}\text{Actual units of}\\ \text{output sold}\\ \text{in 2011}\end{array}\right) \times \begin{array}{c}\text{Selling}\\ \text{price}\\ \text{in 2011}\end{array}$$

$$= (42{,}000 \text{ units} - 40{,}000 \text{ units}) \times \$100 \text{ per unit} = \$200{,}000 \text{ F}$$

$$\begin{array}{c}\text{Cost effect}\\ \text{of growth for}\\ \text{variable costs}\end{array} = \left(\begin{array}{c}\text{Units of input}\\ \text{required to produce}\\ \text{2012 output in 2011}\end{array} - \begin{array}{c}\text{Actual units of input}\\ \text{used to produce}\\ \text{2011 output}\end{array}\right) \times \begin{array}{c}\text{Input}\\ \text{price}\\ \text{in 2011}\end{array}$$

$$\begin{array}{c}\text{Cost effect}\\ \text{of growth for}\\ \text{direct materials}\end{array} = \left(120{,}000 \text{ sq. ft.} \times \frac{42{,}000 \text{ units}}{40{,}000 \text{ units}} - 120{,}000 \text{ sq. ft.}\right) \times \$10 \text{ per sq. ft.}$$

$$= (126{,}000 \text{ sq. ft.} - 120{,}000 \text{ sq. ft.}) \times \$10 \text{ per sq. ft.} = \$60{,}000 \text{ U}$$

$$\begin{array}{c}\text{Cost effect}\\ \text{of growth for}\\ \text{fixed costs}\end{array} = \left(\begin{array}{c}\text{Actual units of capacity in}\\ \text{2011 because adequate capacity}\\ \text{exists to produce 2012 output in 2011}\end{array} - \begin{array}{c}\text{Actual units}\\ \text{of capacity}\\ \text{in 2011}\end{array}\right) \times \begin{array}{c}\text{Price per}\\ \text{unit of}\\ \text{capacity}\\ \text{in 2011}\end{array}$$

Cost effects of growth for fixed costs are:

Conversion costs: (50,000 units − 50,000 units) × $20 per unit = $0

Selling and customer-service costs: (30 customers − 30 customers) × $24,000 per customer = $0

In summary, the net increase in operating income attributable to growth equals:

Revenue effect of growth		$200,000 F
Cost effect of growth		
Direct material costs	$60,000 U	
Conversion costs	0	
Selling and customer-service costs	0	60,000 U
Change in operating income due to growth		$140,000 F

Price-Recovery Component of Operating-Income Change

$$\text{Revenue effect of price recovery} = \left(\text{Selling price in 2012} - \text{Selling price in 2011}\right) \times \text{Actual units of output sold in 2012}$$

$$= (\$110 \text{ per unit} - \$100 \text{ per unit}) \times 42{,}000 \text{ units} = \$420{,}000 \text{ F}$$

$$\text{Cost effect of price recovery for variable costs} = \left(\text{Input price in 2012} - \text{Input price in 2011}\right) \times \text{Units of input required to produce 2012 output in 2011}$$

Direct material costs: ($11 per sq. ft. − $10 per sq. ft.) × 126,000 sq. ft. = $126,000 U

$$\text{Cost effect of price recovery for fixed costs} = \left(\text{Price per unit of capacity in 2012} - \text{Price per unit of capacity in 2011}\right) \times \text{Actual units of capacity in 2011 because adequate capacity exists to produce 2012 output in 2011}$$

Cost effects of price recovery for fixed costs are:

Conversion costs: ($22 per unit − 20 per unit) × 50,000 units = $100,000 U

Selling and cust.-service costs: ($25,000 per cust. − $24,000 per cust.) × 30 customers = $30,000 U

In summary, the net increase in operating income attributable to price recovery equals:

Revenue effect of price recovery		$420,000 F
Cost effect of price recovery		
Direct material costs	$126,000 U	
Conversion costs	100,000 U	
Selling and customer-service costs	30,000 U	256,000 U
Change in operating income due to price recovery		$164,000 F

Productivity Component of Operating-Income Change

$$\text{Cost effect of productivity for variable costs} = \left(\text{Actual units of input used to produce 2012 output} - \text{Units of input required to produce 2012 output in 2011}\right) \times \text{Input price in 2012}$$

$$\text{Cost effect of productivity for direct materials} = (123{,}000 \text{ sq. ft.} - 126{,}000 \text{ sq. ft.}) \times \$11 \text{ per sq. ft.} = \$33{,}000 \text{ F}$$

$$\text{Cost effect of productivity for fixed costs} = \left(\text{Actual units of capacity in 2012} - \text{Actual units of capacity in 2011 because adequate capacity exists to produce 2012 output in 2011}\right) \times \text{Price per unit of capacity in 2012}$$

Cost effects of productivity for fixed costs are:

Conversion costs: (50,000 units − 50,000 units) × $22 per unit = $0

Selling and customer-service costs: (29 customers − 30 customers) × $25,000/customer = $25,000 F

In summary, the net increase in operating income attributable to productivity equals:

Cost effect of productivity:	
Direct material costs	$33,000 F
Conversion costs	0
Selling and customer-service costs	25,000 F
Change in operating income due to productivity	$58,000 F

A summary of the change in operating income between 2011 and 2012 follows.

	Income Statement Amounts in 2011 (1)	Revenue and Cost Effects of Growth Component in 2012 (2)	Revenue and Cost Effects of Price-Recovery Component in 2012 (3)	Cost Effect of Productivity Component in 2012 (4)	Income Statement Amounts in 2012 (5) = (1) + (2) + (3) + (4)
Revenue	$4,000,000	$200,000 F	$420,000 F	—	$4,620,000
Costs	2,920,000	60,000 U	256,000 U	$58,000 F	3,178,000
Operating income	$1,080,000	$140,000 F	$164,000 F	$58,000 F	$1,442,000
			362,000 F		
			Change in operating income		

3. The analysis of operating income indicates that a significant amount of the increase in operating income resulted from Westwood's successful implementation of its product-differentiation strategy (operating income attributable to price recovery, $164,000 F). The company was able to continue to charge a premium price for KE8 while increasing sales (operating income attributable to growth, 140,000 F). Westwood was also able to earn additional operating income from improving its productivity (operating income attributable to productivity, $58,000 F).

Decision Points

The following question-and-answer format summarizes the chapter's learning objectives. Each decision presents a key question related to a learning objective. The guidelines are the answer to that question.

Decision	Guidelines
1. What are two generic strategies a company can use?	Two generic strategies are product differentiation and cost leadership. Product differentiation is offering products and services that are perceived by customers as being superior and unique. Cost leadership is achieving low costs relative to competitors. A company chooses its strategy based on an understanding of customer preferences and its own internal capabilities, while differentiating itself from its competitors.
2. What is reengineering?	Reengineering is the rethinking of business processes, such as the order-delivery process, to improve critical performance measures such as cost, quality, and customer satisfaction.
3. How can an organization translate its strategy into a set of performance measures?	An organization can develop a balanced scorecard that provides the framework for a strategic measurement and management system. The balanced scorecard measures performance from four perspectives: (1) financial, (2) customer, (3) internal business processes, and (4) learning and growth. To build their balanced scorecards, organizations often create strategy maps to represent the cause-and-effect relationships across various strategic objectives.

Decision	Guidelines
4. How can a company analyze changes in operating income to evaluate the success of its strategy?	To evaluate the success of its strategy, a company can subdivide the change in operating income into growth, price-recovery, and productivity components. The growth component measures the change in revenues and costs from selling more or less units, assuming nothing else has changed. The price-recovery component measures changes in revenues and costs solely as a result of changes in the prices of outputs and inputs. The productivity component measures the decrease in costs from using fewer inputs, a better mix of inputs, and reducing capacity. If a company is successful in implementing its strategy, changes in components of operating income align closely with strategy.
5. How can a company identify and manage unused capacity?	A company must first distinguish engineered costs from discretionary costs. Engineered costs result from a cause-and-effect relationship between output and the resources needed to produce that output. Discretionary costs arise from periodic (usually annual) management decisions regarding the amount of cost to be incurred. Discretionary costs are not tied to a cause-and-effect relationship between inputs and outputs. Identifying unused capacity is easier for engineered costs and more difficult for discretionary costs. Downsizing is an approach to managing unused capacity that matches costs to the activities that need to be performed to operate effectively.

Terms to Learn

This chapter and the Glossary at the end of the book contain definitions of the following important terms:

balanced scorecard (p. 587)
cost leadership (p. 584)
discretionary costs (p. 602)
downsizing (p. 602)
engineered costs (p. 601)
growth component (p. 596)
price-recovery component (p. 596)
product differentiation (p. 584)
productivity component (p. 596)
reengineering (p. 586)
rightsizing (p. 602)
strategy map (p. 587)
unused capacity (p. 601)

Assignment Material

Questions

14-1 Describe the five key forces to consider when analyzing an industry.

14-2 Describe two generic strategies.

14-3 What is a customer preference map and why do managers use it?

14-4 What is a strategy map?

14-5 What are four key perspectives in the balanced scorecard?

14-6 Describe three features of a good balanced scorecard.

14-7 What are three important pitfalls to avoid when implementing a balanced scorecard?

14-8 Describe three key components in conducting a strategic analysis of operating income.

14-9 "The price recovery component is the most important component of a strategic analysis of operating income." Do you agree? Explain briefly.

14-10 "It is easy to manage unused capacity for engineered costs relative to discretionary costs." Do you agree? Explain briefly.

Exercises

14-11 Balanced scorecard. RT Sports manufactures industrial-size insulated coolers. It competes and plans to grow by selling high-quality coolers at a low price and by delivering them to customers quickly after receiving customers' orders. There are many other manufacturers who produce similar coolers. RT Sports believes that continuously improving its manufacturing processes and having satisfied employees are critical to implementing its strategy in 2013.

Required

1. Is RT Sports' 2013 strategy one of product differentiation or cost leadership? Explain briefly.
2. Dryer Corporation, a competitor of RT Sports, manufactures insulated coolers with more sizes and color combinations than RT Sports at a higher price. Dryer's coolers are of high quality but require more time to produce and so have longer delivery times. Draw a simple customer preference map as in Exhibit 14-1 for RT Sports and Dryer using the attributes of price, delivery time, quality, and design.
3. Draw a strategy map as in Exhibit 14-2 with two strategic objectives you would expect to see under each balanced scorecard perspective.
4. For each strategic objective indicate a measure you would expect to see in RT Sports' balanced scorecard for 2013.

14-12 Analysis of growth, price-recovery, and productivity components (continuation of 14-11). An analysis of RT Sports' operating-income changes between 2012 and 2013 shows the following:

Operating income for 2012	$2,350,000
Add growth component	95,000
Deduct price-recovery component	(87,000)
Add productivity component	225,000
Operating income for 2013	$2,583,000

The industry market size for insulated coolers did not grow in 2013, input prices did not change, and RT Sports reduced the prices of its coolers.

Required

1. Was RT Sports' gain in operating income in 2013 consistent with the strategy you identified in requirement 1 of Exercise 14-11?
2. Explain the productivity component. In general, does it represent savings in only variable costs, only fixed costs, or both variable and fixed costs?

14-13 Balanced scorecard. Kimmo Company manufactures and sells snow skis. It competes and plans to grow by customizing high-quality skis and offering the customer a pleasant experience in their store. Because Kimmo custom fits and designs the skis, customers pay a higher price. Kimmo's customers also understand that the delivery time will be 2–3 weeks. There are other ski manufacturers, but few who offer custom fitting and graphics. Kimmo believes that tailoring the experience for the customer is critical to its success in 2013.

Required

1. Is Kimmo's 2013 strategy one of product differentiation or cost leadership? Explain briefly.
2. Sammi Corporation, a competitor of Kimmo's, also manufactures quality skis and offers them at a lower price. Sammi does not customize the skis, but customers can pick up their skis the day they are purchased. Draw a simple customer preference map as in Exhibit 14-1 for Kimmo and Sammi using the attributes of price, delivery time, quality, and design.
3. Draw a strategy map as in Exhibit 14-2 with two strategic objectives you would expect to see under each balanced scorecard perspective.
4. For each strategic objective indicate a measure you would expect to see in Kimmo's balanced scorecard for 2013.

14-14 Analysis of growth, price-recovery, and productivity components (continuation of 14-13). An analysis of Kimmo's operating-income changes between 2012 and 2013 shows the following:

Operating income for 2012	$755,000
Add growth component	35,000
Add price-recovery component	170,000
Deduct productivity component	(45,000)
Operating income for 2013	$915,000

The industry market size for skis did not grow in 2013, input prices did not change, and Kimmo was able to increase the price of its skis.

Required

1. Was Kimmo's gain in operating income in 2013 consistent with the strategy you identified in requirement 1 in Exercise 14-13?
2. Explain the price recovery component.

14-15 Strategy, balanced scorecard, merchandising operation. Raneiro & Sons buys T-shirts in bulk, applies its own trendsetting silk-screen designs, and then sells the T-shirts to a number of retailers. Raneiro wants to be known for its trendsetting designs, and it wants every teenager to be seen in a distinctive Raneiro T-shirt. Raneiro presents the following data for its first 2 years of operations, 2011 and 2012.

	2011	2012
1. Number of T-shirts purchased	213,060	253,000
2. Number of T-shirts discarded	12,060	14,500
3. Number of T-shirts sold (row 1 − row 2)	201,000	238,500
4. Average selling price	$28.00	$29.00
5. Average cost per T-shirt	$13.00	$11.00
6. Administrative capacity (number of customers)	4,300	4,050
7. Administrative costs	$1,419,000	$1,377,000
8. Administrative cost per customer (row 7 ÷ row 6)	$330	$340

Administrative costs depend on the number of customers that Raneiro has created capacity to support, not on the actual number of customers served. Raneiro had 3,900 customers in 2011 and 3,800 customers in 2012.

Required

1. Is Raneiro's strategy one of product differentiation or cost leadership? Explain briefly.
2. Describe briefly the key measures Raneiro should include in its balanced scorecard and the reasons it should do so.

14-16 Strategic analysis of operating income (continuation of 14-15). Refer to Exercise 14-15.

Required

1. Calculate Raneiro's operating income in both 2011 and 2012.
2. Calculate the growth, price-recovery, and productivity components that explain the change in operating income from 2011 to 2012.
3. Comment on your answers in requirement 2. What does each of these components indicate?

14-17 Identifying and managing unused capacity (continuation of 14-15). Refer to Exercise 14-15.

Required

1. Calculate the amount and cost of unused administrative capacity at the beginning of 2012 based on the actual number of customers Raneiro served in 2012.
2. Suppose Raneiro can only add or reduce administrative capacity in increments of 250 customers. What is the maximum amount of costs that Raneiro can save in 2012 by downsizing administrative capacity?
3. What factors, other than cost, should Raneiro consider before it downsizes administrative capacity?

14-18 Strategy, balanced scorecard. Melissa Corporation makes a special-purpose machine, D4H, used in the textile industry. Melissa has designed the D4H machine for 2012 to be distinct from its competitors. It has been generally regarded as a superior machine. Melissa presents the following data for 2011 and 2012.

		2011	2012
1.	Units of D4H produced and sold	270	290
2.	Selling price	$36,000	$38,000
3.	Direct materials (kilograms)	285,000	290,000
4.	Direct material cost per kilogram	$8.00	$8.25
5.	Manufacturing capacity in units of D4H	300	300
6.	Total conversion costs	$2,100,000	$2,175,000
7.	Conversion cost per unit of capacity (row 6 ÷ row 5)	$7,000	$7,250
8.	Selling and customer-service capacity	125 customers	120 customers
9.	Total selling and customer-service costs	$1,225,000	$1,164,000
10.	Selling and customer-service capacity cost per customer (row 9 ÷ row 8)	$9,800	$9,700

Melissa produces no defective machines, but it wants to reduce direct materials usage per D4H machine in 2012. Conversion costs in each year depend on production capacity defined in terms of D4H units that can be produced, not the actual units produced. Selling and customer-service costs depend on the number of customers that Melissa can support, not the actual number of customers it serves. Melissa had 77 customers in 2011 and 82 customers in 2012.

Required

1. Is Melissa's strategy one of product differentiation or cost leadership? Explain briefly.
2. Describe briefly key measures that you would include in Melissa's balanced scorecard and the reasons for doing so.

14-19 Strategic analysis of operating income (continuation of 14-18). Refer to Exercise 14-18.

Required

1. Calculate the operating income of Melissa Corporation in 2011 and 2012.
2. Calculate the growth, price-recovery, and productivity components that explain the change in operating income from 2011 to 2012.
3. Comment on your answer in requirement 2. What do these components indicate?

14-20 Identifying and managing unused capacity (continuation of 14-18). Refer to Exercise 14-18.

Required

1. Calculate the amount and cost of (a) unused manufacturing capacity and (b) unused selling and customer-service capacity at the beginning of 2012 based on actual production and actual number of customers served in 2012.
2. Suppose Melissa can add or reduce its manufacturing capacity in increments of 10 units. What is the maximum amount of costs that Melissa could save in 2012 by downsizing manufacturing capacity?
3. Melissa, in fact, does not eliminate any of its unused manufacturing capacity. Why might Melissa not downsize?

14-21 Strategy, balanced scorecard, service company. Northland Corporation is a small information-systems consulting firm that specializes in helping companies implement standard sales-management software. The market for Northland's services is very competitive. To compete successfully, Northland must deliver quality service at a low cost. Northland presents the following data for 2011 and 2012.

		2011	2012
1.	Number of jobs billed	40	55
2.	Selling price per job	$45,000	$42,000
3.	Software-implementation labor-hours	25,000	28,000
4.	Cost per software-implementation labor-hour	$58	$60
5.	Software-implementation support capacity (number of jobs it can do)	70	70
6.	Total cost of software-implementation support	$224,000	$252,000
7.	Software-implementation support-capacity cost per job (row 6 ÷ row 5)	$3,200	$3,600

Software-implementation labor-hour costs are variable costs. Software-implementation support costs for each year depend on the software-implementation support capacity Northland chooses to maintain each year (that is, the number of jobs it can do each year). Software-implementation support costs do not vary with the actual number of jobs done that year.

Required

1. Is Northland Corporation's strategy one of product differentiation or cost leadership? Explain briefly.
2. Describe key measures you would include in Northland's balanced scorecard and your reasons for doing so.

14-22 Strategic analysis of operating income (continuation of 14-21). Refer to Exercise 14-21.

Required

1. Calculate the operating income of Northland Corporation in 2011 and 2012.
2. Calculate the growth, price-recovery, and productivity components that explain the change in operating income from 2011 to 2012.
3. Comment on your answer in requirement 2. What do these components indicate?

14-23 Identifying and managing unused capacity (continuation of 14-21). Refer to Exercise 14-21.

Required

1. Calculate the amount and cost of unused software-implementation support capacity at the beginning of 2012, based on the number of jobs actually done in 2012.
2. Suppose Northland can add or reduce its software-implementation support capacity in increments of 10 units. What is the maximum amount of costs that Northland could save in 2012 by downsizing software-implementation support capacity?
3. Northland, in fact, does not eliminate any of its unused software-implementation support capacity. Why might Northland not downsize?

Problems

14-24 Balanced scorecard and strategy. Scott Company manufactures a DVD player called the Maxus. The company sells the player to discount stores throughout the country. This player is significantly less expensive than similar products sold by Scott's competitors, but the Maxus offers just DVD playback, compared with DVD and Blu-ray playback offered by competitor Nomad Manufacturing. Furthermore, the Maxus has experienced production problems that have resulted in significant rework costs. Nomad's model has an excellent reputation for quality but is considerably more expensive.

Required

1. Draw a simple customer preference map for Scott and Nomad using the attributes of price, quality, and playback features. Use the format of Exhibit 14-1.
2. Is Scott's current strategy that of product differentiation or cost leadership?
3. Scott would like to improve quality and decrease costs by improving processes and training workers to reduce rework. Scott's managers believe the increased quality will increase sales. Draw a strategy map as in Exhibit 14-2 describing the cause-and-effect relationships among the strategic objectives you would expect to see in Scott's balanced scorecard.
4. For each strategic objective, suggest a measure you would recommend in Scott's balanced scorecard.

14-25 Strategic analysis of operating income (continuation of 14-24). Refer to Problem 14-24. As a result of the actions taken, quality has significantly improved in 2012 while rework and unit costs of the Maxus have decreased. Scott has reduced manufacturing capacity because capacity is no longer needed to support rework. Scott has also lowered the Maxus' selling price to gain market share and unit sales have increased. Information about the current period (2012) and last period (2011) follows.

	2011	2012
1. Units of Maxus produced and sold	8,000	11,000
2. Selling price	$95	$80
3. Direct materials used (kits*)	10,000	11,000
4. Direct material cost per kit*	$32	$32
5. Manufacturing capacity in units	14,000	13,000

continued

	2011	2012
6. Total conversion costs	$280,000	$260,000
7. Conversion cost per unit of capacity (row 6 ÷ row 5)	$20	$20
8. Selling and customer-service capacity	90 customers	90 customers
9. Total selling and customer-service costs	$13,500	$16,200
10. Selling and customer-service capacity cost per customer (row 9 ÷ row 8)	$150	$180

*A kit comprises all the major components needed to produce a DVD player.

Conversion costs in each year depend on production capacity defined in terms of units of Maxus that can be produced, not the actual units produced. Selling and customer-service costs depend on the number of customers that Scott can support, not the actual number of customers it serves. Scott has 70 customers in 2011 and 80 customers in 2012.

Required

1. Calculate operating income of Scott Company for 2011 and 2012.
2. Calculate the growth, price-recovery, and productivity components that explain the change in operating income from 2011 to 2012.
3. Comment on your answer in requirement 2. What do these components indicate?

14-26 Identifying and managing unused capacity (continuation of 14-25) Refer to the information for Scott Company in Problem 14-25.

Required

1. Calculate the amount and cost of (a) unused manufacturing capacity and (b) unused selling and customer-service capacity at the beginning of 2012 based on actual production and actual number of customers served in 2012.
2. Suppose Scott can add or reduce its selling and customer-service capacity in increments of five customers. What is the maximum amount of costs that Scott could save in 2012 by downsizing selling and customer-service capacity?
3. Scott, in fact, does not eliminate any of its unused selling and customer-service capacity. Why might Scott not downsize?

14-27 Balanced scorecard. Following is a random-order listing of perspectives, strategic objectives, and performance measures for the balanced scorecard.

Perspectives	Performance Measures
Internal business process	Percentage of defective-product units
Customer	Return on assets
Learning and growth	Number of patents
Financial	Employee turnover rate
Strategic Objectives	Net income
Acquire new customers	Customer profitability
Increase shareholder value	Percentage of processes with real-time feedback
Retain customers	Return on sales
Improve manufacturing quality	Average job-related training-hours per employee
Develop profitable customers	Return on equity
Increase proprietary products	Percentage of on-time deliveries by suppliers
Increase information-system capabilities	Product cost per unit
Enhance employee skills	Profit per salesperson
On-time delivery by suppliers	Percentage of error-free invoices
Increase profit generated by each salesperson	Customer cost per unit
Introduce new products	Earnings per share
Minimize invoice-error rate	Number of new customers
	Percentage of customers retained

For each perspective, select those strategic objectives from the list that best relate to it. For each strategic objective, select the most appropriate performance measure(s) from the list.

Required

14-28 Balanced scorecard. (R. Kaplan, adapted) Petrocal, Inc., refines gasoline and sells it through its own Petrocal gas stations. On the basis of market research, Petrocal determines that 60% of the overall gasoline market consists of "service-oriented customers," medium- to high-income individuals who are willing to pay a higher price for gas if the gas stations can provide excellent customer service, such as a clean facility, a convenience store, friendly employees, a quick turnaround, the ability to pay by credit card, and high-octane premium gasoline. The remaining 40% of the overall market are "price shoppers" who look to buy the cheapest gasoline available. Petrocal's strategy is to focus on the 60% of service-oriented customers. Petrocal's balanced scorecard for 2012 follows. For brevity, the initiatives taken under each objective are omitted.

Objectives	Measures	Target Performance	Actual Performance
Financial Perspective			
Increase shareholder value	Operating-income changes from price recovery	$90,000,000	$95,000,000
	Operating-income changes from growth	$65,000,000	$67,000,000
Customer Perspective			
Increase market share	Market share of overall gasoline market	10%	9.8%
Internal-Business-Process Perspective			
Improve gasoline quality	Quality index	94 points	95 points
Improve refinery performance	Refinery-reliability index (%)	91%	91%
Ensure gasoline availability	Product-availability index (%)	99%	100%
Learning-and-Growth Perspective			
Increase refinery process capability	Percentage of refinery processes with advanced controls	88%	90%

Required

1. Was Petrocal successful in implementing its strategy in 2012? Explain your answer.
2. Would you have included some measure of employee satisfaction and employee training in the learning-and-growth perspective? Are these objectives critical to Petrocal for implementing its strategy? Why or why not? Explain briefly.
3. Explain how Petrocal did not achieve its target market share in the total gasoline market but still exceeded its financial targets. Is "market share of overall gasoline market" the correct measure of market share? Explain briefly.
4. Is there a cause-and-effect linkage between improvements in the measures in the internal-business-process perspective and the measure in the customer perspective? That is, would you add other measures to the internal-business-process perspective or the customer perspective? Why or why not? Explain briefly.
5. Do you agree with Petrocal's decision not to include measures of changes in operating income from productivity improvements under the financial perspective of the balanced scorecard? Explain briefly.

14-29 Balanced scorecard. Vic Corporation manufactures various types of color laser printers in a highly automated facility with high fixed costs. The market for laser printers is competitive. The various color laser printers on the market are comparable in terms of features and price. Vic believes that satisfying customers with products of high quality at low costs is key to achieving its target profitability. For 2012, Vic plans to achieve higher quality and lower costs by improving yields and reducing defects in its manufacturing operations. Vic will train workers and encourage and empower them to take the necessary actions. Currently, a significant amount of Vic's capacity is used to produce products that are defective and cannot be sold. Vic expects that higher yields will reduce the capacity that Vic needs to manufacture products. Vic does not anticipate that improving manufacturing will automatically lead to lower costs because Vic has high fixed costs. To reduce fixed costs per unit, Vic could lay off employees and sell equipment, or it could use the capacity to produce and sell more of its current products or improved models of its current products.

Vic's balanced scorecard (initiatives omitted) for the just-completed fiscal year 2012 follows.

Objectives	Measures	Target Performance	Actual Performance
Financial Perspective			
Increase shareholder value	Operating-income changes from productivity improvements	$1,000,000	$400,000
	Operating-income changes from growth	$1,500,000	$600,000
Customer Perspective			
Increase market share	Market share in color laser printers	5%	4.6%
Internal-Business-Process Perspective			
Improve manufacturing quality	Yield	82%	85%
Reduce delivery time to customers	Order-delivery time	25 days	22 days
Learning-and-Growth Perspective			
Develop process skills	Percentage of employees trained in process and quality management	90%	92%
Enhance information-system capabilities	Percentage of manufacturing processes with real-time feedback	85%	87%

Required

1. Was Vic successful in implementing its strategy in 2012? Explain.
2. Is Vic's balanced scorecard useful in helping the company understand why it did not reach its target market share in 2012? If it is, explain why. If it is not, explain what other measures you might want to add under the customer perspective and why.
3. Would you have included some measure of employee satisfaction in the learning-and-growth perspective and new-product development in the internal-business-process perspective? That is, do you think employee satisfaction and development of new products are critical for Vic to implement its strategy? Why or why not? Explain briefly.
4. What problems, if any, do you see in Vic improving quality and significantly downsizing to eliminate unused capacity?

14-30 Balanced scorecard. Cerebral Chocolates makes custom-labeled, high-quality, specialty candy bars for special events and advertising purposes. The company employs several chocolatiers who were trained in Germany. The company offers many varieties of chocolate, including milk chocolate, semi-sweet, white, and dark chocolate. They also offer a variety of ingredients, such as coffee, berries, and fresh mint. The real appeal for the company's product, however, is its custom labeling. Customers can order labels for special occasions (for example, wedding invitation labels) or business purposes (for example, business card labels). The company's balanced scorecard for 2012 follows. For brevity, the initiatives taken under each objective are omitted.

Objectives	Measures	Target Performance	Actual Performance
Financial Perspective			
Increase shareholder value	Operating-income changes from price recovery	$500,000	$750,000
	Operating-income changes from growth	$100,000	$125,000
Customer Perspective			
Increase market share	Market share of overall candy bar market	8%	7.8%
Increase the number of new product offerings	Number of new product offerings	5	7
Internal-Business-Process Perspective			
Reduce time to customer	Average design time	3 days	3 days
Increase quality	Internal quality rating (10-point scale)	7 points	8 points
Learning-and-Growth Perspective			
Increase number of professional chocolatiers	Number of chocolatiers	5	6

Required

1. Was Cerebral successful in implementing its strategy in 2012? Explain your answer.
2. Would you have included some measure of customer satisfaction in the customer perspective? Are these objectives critical to Cerebral for implementing its strategy? Why or why not? Explain briefly.

3. Explain how Cerebral did not achieve its target market share in the candy bar market but still exceeded its financial targets. Is "market share of overall candy bar market" a good measure of market share for Cerebral? Explain briefly.
4. Do you agree with Cerebral's decision not to include measures of changes in operating income from productivity improvements under the financial perspective of the balanced scorecard? Explain briefly.

14-31 Balanced scorecard. Rocky Plain Company provides cable and Internet services in the greater Denver area. There are many competitors that provide similar services. Rocky Plain believes that the key to financial success is to offer a quality service at the lowest cost. Rocky Plain currently spends a significant amount of hours on installation and post-installation support. This is one area that the company has targeted for cost reduction. Rocky Plain's balanced scorecard for 2012 follows.

Objectives	Measures	Target Performance	Actual Performance
Financial Perspective			
Increase shareholder value	Operating-income changes from productivity	$1,200,000	$400,000
	Operating-income changes from growth	$260,000	$125,000
Customer Perspective			
Increase customer satisfaction	Positive customer survey responses	70%	65%
Internal-Business-Process Perspective			
Develop innovative services	Research and development costs as a percentage of revenue	12%	15%
Increase installation efficiency	Installation time per customer	5 hours	4.5 hours
Learning-and-Growth Perspective			
Increase employee competence	Number of annual training hours per employee	10	11
Increase leadership skills	Number of leadership workshops offered	2	1

Required

1. Was Rocky Plain successful in implementing its strategy in 2012? Explain.
2. Do you agree with Rocky Plain's decision to include measures of developing innovative services (research and development costs) in the internal-business-process perspective of the balanced scorecard? Explain briefly.
3. Is there a cause-and-effect linkage between the measures in the internal-business-process perspective and the customer perspective? That is, would you add other measures to the internal-business-process perspective or the customer perspective? Why or why not? Explain briefly.

14-32 Balanced scorecard. SmoothAir is a no-frills airline that services the Midwest. Its mission is to be the only short-haul, low-fare, high-frequency, point-to-point carrier in the Midwest. However, there are several large commercial carriers offering air transportation, and SmoothAir knows that it cannot compete with them based on the services those carriers provide. SmoothAir has chosen to reduce costs by not offering many inflight services, such as food and entertainment options. Instead, the company is dedicated to providing the highest quality transportation at the lowest fare. SmoothAir's balanced scorecard measures (and actual results) for 2012 follow:

Objectives	Measures	Target Performance	Actual Performance
Financial Perspective			
Increase shareholder value	Operating-income changes from productivity	$1,200,000	$1,400,000
	Operating-income changes from price recovery	$450,000	$600,000
	Operating-income changes from growth	$500,000	$660,000
Customer Perspective			
Increase the number of on-time arrivals	FAA on-time arrival ranking	1st in industry	2nd in industry
Internal-Business-Process Perspective			
Reduce turnaround time	On-ground time	<25 minutes	30 minutes
Learning-and-Growth Perspective			
Align ground crews	% of ground crew stockholders	70%	68%

Required

1. What is SmoothAir's strategy? Was SmoothAir successful in implementing its strategy in 2012? Explain your answer.
2. Based on the strategy identified in requirement 1 above, what role does the price-recovery component play in explaining the success of SmoothAir?
3. Would you have included customer-service measures in the customer perspective? Why or why not? Explain briefly.
4. Would you have included some measure of employee satisfaction and employee training in the learning-and-growth perspective? Would you consider this objective critical to SmoothAir for implementing its strategy? Why or why not? Explain briefly.

14-33 Strategic analysis of operating income. Kelton Company sells women's clothing. Kelton's strategy is to offer a wide selection of clothes and excellent customer service and to charge a premium price. Kelton presents the following data for 2011 and 2012. For simplicity, assume that each customer purchases one piece of clothing.

	2011	2012
1. Pieces of clothing purchased and sold	50,000	50,000
2. Average selling price	$32	$31.50
3. Average cost per piece of clothing	$15	$16.50
4. Selling and customer-service capacity	62,000 customers	52,000 customers
5. Selling and customer-service costs	$403,000	$291,200
6. Selling and customer-service capacity cost per customer (row 5 ÷ row 4)	$6.50 per customer	$5.60 per customer
7. Purchasing and administrative capacity	780 designs	620 designs
8. Purchasing and administrative costs	$62,400	$40,300
9. Purchasing and administrative capacity cost per distinct design (row 8 ÷ row 7)	$80 per design	$65 per design

Total selling and customer-service costs depend on the number of customers that Kelton has created capacity to support, not the actual number of customers that Kelton serves. Total purchasing and administrative costs depend on purchasing and administrative capacity that Kelton has created (defined in terms of the number of distinct clothing designs that Kelton can purchase and administer). Purchasing and administrative costs do not depend on the actual number of distinct clothing designs purchased. Kelton purchased 710 distinct designs in 2011 and 580 distinct designs in 2012.

At the start of 2011, Kelton planned to increase operating income by 10% over operating income in 2012.

Required

1. Is Kelton's strategy one of product differentiation or cost leadership? Explain.
2. Calculate Kelton's operating income in 2011 and 2012.
3. Calculate the growth, price-recovery, and productivity components of changes in operating income between 2011 and 2012.
4. Does the strategic analysis of operating income indicate Kelton was successful in implementing its strategy in 2012? Explain.

Case

TWA Parts (A)[1]

V. G. Narayanan
Lisa Brem

Ellen Bright, CEO of TWA Parts (TWAP), looked at the two balanced scorecards before her. One, from the luxury division, showed strong financial results; while the other, from the economy division, reported disappointing financial performance but good progress in achieving the targets for its nonfinancial goals. She wondered what feedback she should give the heads of each division about their progress in implementing their strategies.

TWAP, a $6.6 billion subsidiary of a U.S. diversified manufacturing company, was a Tier 1 manufacturer of original and after-market parts for automobile producers in the United States and abroad. TWAP had been directly affected by the downturn in the auto industry. Major customers, including Chrysler and General Motors, were on the brink of insolvency, and even robust car makers, such as Toyota and Honda, were selling many fewer cars amidst the global recession. TWAP manufactured two core product lines—electronics and interiors—in four customer-centered divisions: luxury, economy, mid-priced, and truck. TWAP served three geographic markets: North America, Europe, and Asia. Bright believed she had to make radical changes in strategy and then implement the new strategy flawlessly in order to take advantage of opportunities in international markets, particularly emerging markets, such as China.

The Executive Staff Meeting: Defining a Strategy

In December 2008, Bright prepared for a high-level strategy meeting. Attending the meeting were Aaron Eckhard, the president of the luxury division; Kim Kwon, the president of the economy division; the chief financial officer; and the vice presidents of marketing, manufacturing, and research and development. After presenting a report that showed the product level financials (TWA Parts Exhibit 1), Bright summarized her position:

TWA Parts Exhibit 1
TWAP Selected Financial Data, by Customer Division (in $USM), FYE 2008

Product Category	Economy Small to Midsized Cars/ SUVs/CUVs	Moderately Priced Cars/ SUVs/CUVs	Luxury (all segments)	Truck (all segments)	Total
Revenue	$2,255	$ 745	$2,939	$ 742	$6,681
COGS	2,100	899	2,560	801	6,360
SGA	135	244	171	128	678
Operating Income	$ 20	$(398)	$ 208	$(187)	$ (357)

Source: Casewriters.

[1]This case borrows heavily from an earlier case: Robert Kaplan, "Domestic Auto Parts," HBS No. 105-078 (Boston: Harvard Business School Publishing, 2005) and its accompanying teaching note: HBS No. 107-087 (Boston: Harvard Business School Publishing, 2007), as well as Professor Kaplan's accumulated published works on strategy maps and the balanced scorecard. The authors wish to thank Professor Kaplan for his guidance, ideas, and direction in developing this case. This case is also the abridged version of "Trans World Auto Parts (A)," HBS No.110-027.

The case was prepared by V.G. Narayanan as the basis for class discussion rather than to illustrate either effective or ineffective handling of an administrative situation.

TWA Parts Exhibit 2

TWAP Customer Division Value Proposition, December 2008

End-User [or "Consumer"] Defined Attributes (in ranking of importance to end-user)	Midsize	Luxury	Economy
First most important	Comfort	Innovation	Low cost
Second most important	Low cost	Performance	Fuel economy
Third most important	Quality	High quality	Quality
Customer (OEM) Defined Attributes (in ranking of importance to OEM)			
First most important	Price	New product innovation	Price
Second most important	Customer service	Product design	Product quality
Third most important	On-time delivery	Technical expertise	JIT/lean

Source: Casewriters.

The best course of action for us would be to close down the mid-priced and truck divisions, which are losing money, and go after the segments that give us the potential for the most profit. Those segments are the luxury car makers (mostly serviced from plants in Europe) and the economy car makers. Now, I realize that plants in both the United States and Asia serve a high proportion of economy car makers, but I feel strongly that TWAP should focus its resources on Asia, since it is a growing market with great potential. We will close down the plants in the United States, leaving the majority of the facilities in Europe and Asia intact. I believe we can grow our top line by selling more products to our customers in profitable segments and win over new customers in new markets, primarily in Asia. Of course, the luxury and economy divisions have very different customers and customer value propositions (see TWA Parts Exhibit 2).

Based on a competitive analysis conducted by an outside market research firm and an internal analysis of our core competencies, we've decided to differentiate ourselves in the economy division by producing high-quality car parts with the lowest lifetime price. All of our major competitors in the economy segment focus their strategy on producing parts with the lowest initial price. We will differentiate ourselves by instead producing high-quality parts that will be known in the industry for durability and low maintenance cost. We must make sure that we clearly communicate our value position to auto makers who have built a reputation for durable, high-quality cars in the economy segment.

In the luxury division, our strategy will be to produce the most innovative, quality parts in the market. While our major competitors are pursuing a customer integration strategy, we believe that if we focus our efforts on producing the most innovative and technologically superior car parts in the industry, then luxury original equipment manufacturers (OEMs) will come knocking at our door.

I'd like to hear from each of you about how your division will help us achieve both our financial goals and our market strategy. Let's start off with you, Joe.

Joe Nathan, Bright's newly hired CFO, shared his data with the group:

I designed a simple model to pinpoint the critical economic drivers needed to reach our goal of an 8% return on capital employed (ROCE) and positive cash flow by 2011. We forecasted only $4.5 billion in sales in 2009. That means, to cut our negative ROCE from −15% to −7% in one year, we need to reduce our cost of goods sold (COGS) from 95% to 90% in 2009, then to 83% over the next two years. We need to better

> utilize our capital assets, both current and new—currently we are operating at 65% on old assets—and we must get to 90% utilization on an upgraded and downsized asset base. Finally, we need to get to the lowest cost quartile to compete.

Aaron Eckhard, the luxury division president, chimed in:

> We have always been a leader in product innovation, something our customers continue to value. The innovative products we designed for our high-end customers five years ago have started to filter down to the rest of our customer divisions. Satellite radio and Bluetooth capability, for example, are now becoming options for the economy segments.

Bright asked Michael Milton, vice president of manufacturing, for his perspective. Milton said:

> Because of the uncertainty in the market, the OEM's production schedules are all over the map, making it nearly impossible to anticipate their volumes, which in turn makes any capacity utilization target extremely difficult to make. In addition, our raw material costs are so unpredictable that it's hard to keep COGS under control. But we need to coordinate supplier management, manufacturing, and product delivery so we can effectively and efficiently get products to the customer. We need to be on time and on spec and reduce raw material costs by consolidating our product lines, increasing capacity utilization in the remaining plants, and redesigning our products to reduce their materials costs without sacrificing product quality or functionality.
>
> We also need to balance our focus on cost cutting with the need to make investments in process improvements and new and upgraded equipment to meet the needs of the luxury car manufacturers. Unscheduled downtime and the inability to make fast product switchovers on the manufacturing floor are killing us. Upgraded capital and preventive maintenance will both reduce our costs and help deliver consistently on time and on spec.

Kim Kwon, president of the economy division, added his thoughts:

> We must master just-in-time (JIT) and lean processes in order to gain and retain the economy car OEM customers in Asia. Every single employee must be trained in these processes.

Rita Richardson, vice president of research and development, responded to the challenge to produce state-of-the-art, technologically sophisticated products:

> If we are to compete in the luxury segment, we certainly need to bring to market new and improved products in partnership with our leading customers. In Europe, they want us to move faster—we have to come up with new designs and product innovations to keep up with new regulations on emissions and safety standards and customer needs. To reduce new product development time, we need to invest in new CAD/CAM software, acquire and train skilled design engineers, scientists, and technicians, invest in prototyping equipment, and strip our competitors' products to reverse engineer those technologies, and acquire those capabilities.

Stewart, VP of marketing, added:

> We must be much more aggressive in signing new customers in Asia and respond better to the evolving needs of our customer base. Our OEM customers are looking to partner more closely with their suppliers to build fully assembled systems that they can use for final assembly. Finally, we need to showcase the enhanced R&D capability that Rita is talking about by working more closely with our customers to design the products they want and to anticipate changes in production schedules.

Milton replied:

> Yes, I agree that we should work more closely with our customers but I think we're getting ahead of ourselves here with all this commitment to R&D. We have to do the basic things right by focusing on efficiencies and quality control at all our plants before we can move to innovation and new customers. We don't have unlimited resources.

Richardson rebutted:

> If you wait on R&D until you have all the factories working flawlessly, we'll be so far behind that we'll never catch up.

Bright interrupted the argument by saying:

> We have to be able to be competitive in all these dimensions, but each division will emphasize its own value proposition and an implementation plan and measurements that can keep us on track. We know our overarching strategy is to target the economy and luxury segments with low-cost/high-quality products and enhanced product innovation. We know our financial goals are to increase cash flow and ROCE; our customer goals are to increase market share in Europe and Asia. We know we have to improve our internal processes and our employee competency levels to accomplish this. Now we need to decide how to craft implementation plans for each division that will help us reach our goals. I'm very intrigued by the idea of a strategy map and balanced scorecard (BSC). To create a good BSC, we need to think hard about cause-and-effect relationships between the four perspectives. How exactly will utilizing IT, for example, help with product development? These linkages will provide the foundation for the programs we implement to reach our strategic goals. We must never forget that all of the nonfinancial goals have to be linked to our financial goals.

The Balanced Scorecard

During the next several weeks, Ron Royerson, the vice president of strategic development, led a small project team to conduct interviews with the corporate VPs and division managers about their customers, competitors, quality initiatives, suppliers, and internal processes.

After several long days and weekend retreats, the team was able to complete strategy maps, balanced scorecards, targets, and action plans for the luxury and economy divisions (see TWA Parts Exhibits 3a and 3b for the luxury division, and TWA Parts Exhibits 4a and 4b for the economy division).

Eckhard described his experience crafting the scorecard:

> I was quite concerned that we should not bite off more than we could chew. I wanted to focus on just a few important measures that would help us reach our financial targets. Also, I am a great believer that you can effectively focus only on a few things at a time. It may be a cliché, but less is more.

Kwon explained why his division had developed a more extensive scorecard:

> There were many cause-and-effect linkages that would become crucial levers for changing behavior and thus enabling our organization to meet our goals. When a pilot flies a plane, he doesn't just worry about altitude; he has to be concerned with airspeed, fuel levels, trajectories, and weather conditions. Like the pilot, we believed that we had to simultaneously manage many factors if we wanted to reach our destination.

Eckhard and Kwon both knew that the COO position was vacant and they were both being considered for the job. The division manager with the better performance based on the balanced scorecard was more likely to get the job.

TWA Parts Exhibit 3a

TWAP Luxury Division Strategy Map, FY 2009

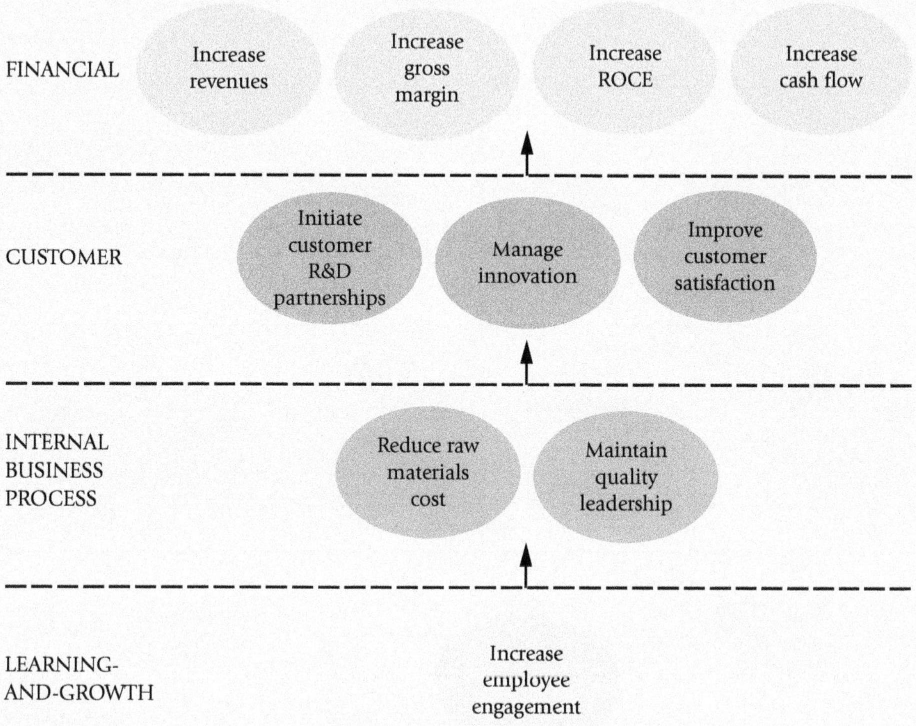

Source: Casewriters.

TWA Parts Exhibit 3b

TWAP Luxury Division Balanced Scorecard, Action Plan, and Results Metrics for Six Months Ending June 30, 2009 (budget figures are for a three-year budget)

Balanced Scorecard			Action Plan		Actual Performance
Objectives	**Measures**	**Target**	**Initiative**	**Budget**	
		Financial Perspective			
Increased ROCE	• ROCE	• −7%			• 4%
Increase cash flow	• Year-to-date (YTD) cash flow from operating activities	• −$12M			• $8M
Increase revenue	• YTD revenue	• 1.3B			• 1.2B
Increase gross margin	• Gross margin %	• 14%			• 15%
		Customer Perspective			
Improve customer satisfaction	• Global market share	• 5%	"Innovation" campaign	$50M	• 5%
Manage innovation	• Customer survey: % of customers who consider TWAP "excellent" at innovation, product design, & technical expertise	• 85%	Customer attitudes survey	$2.5M	• 83%
	• Number of new products introduced	• 50	New product launch	$50M	• 50
Initiate customer R&D partnerships	• Number of customers with whom TWAP partners to research and develop new products	• 20	Partnership initiative	$10M	• 10
		Internal Business Process Perspective			
Reduce raw materials cost	• Cost of raw materials (% of revenue)	• 65%	Supplier optimization program	$5M	• 60%
Maintain quality leadership	• Reduce defect rates (per 1 million parts)	• 3 PPM	TQM initiative	$10M	• 5 PPM
		Learning and Growth Perspective			
Increase employee engagement	• % of employees "very satisfied" with the resources they have to do their job (annual survey).	• 80%	Employee engagement and satisfaction ratings	$25M	• 62%
	• % of employees "very satisfied" with the training they received in the past 12 months.	• 80%			• 65%

Source: Casewriters.

TWA Parts Exhibit 4a

TWAP Economy Division Strategy Map, FY 2009

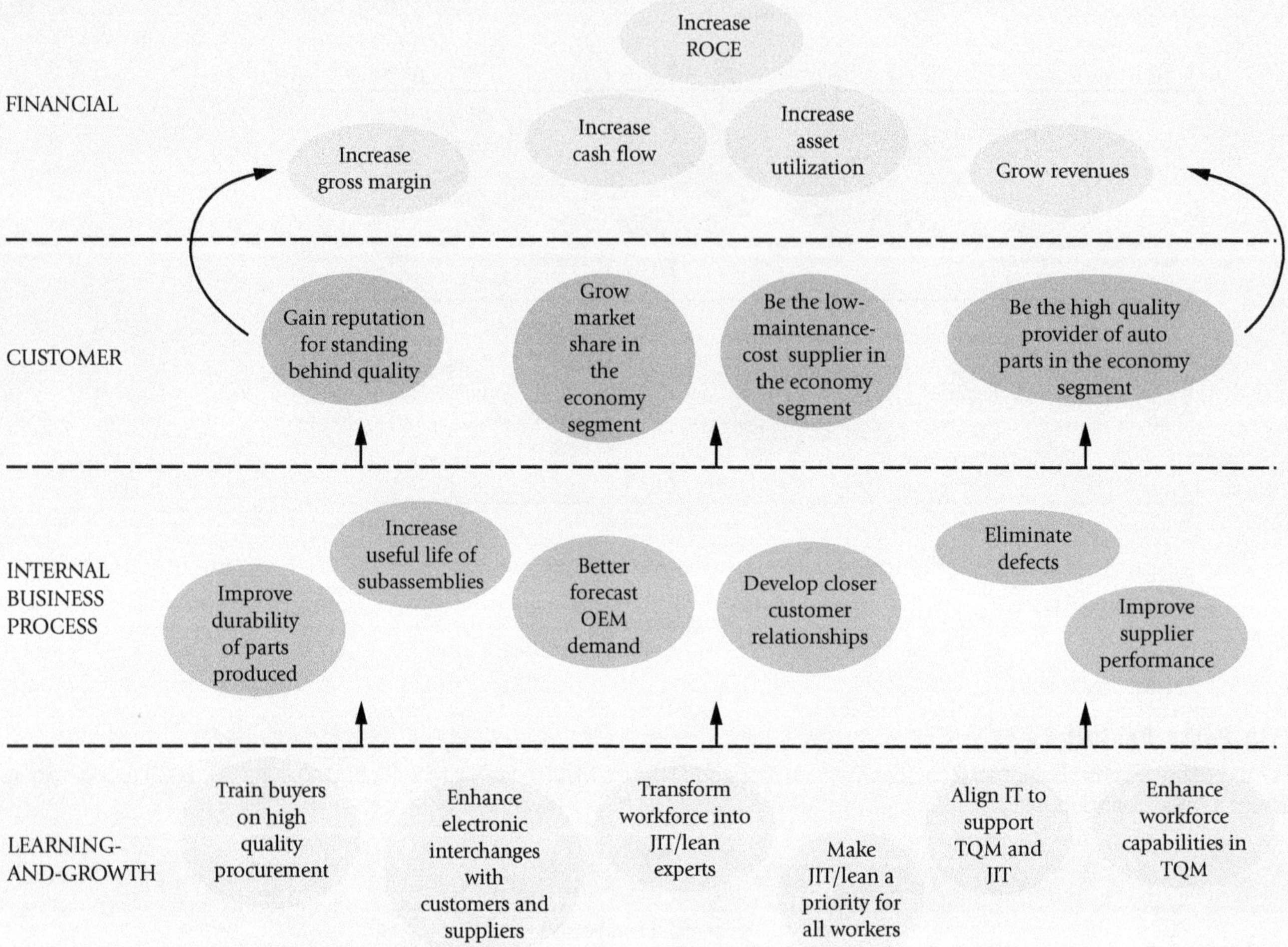

Source: Casewriters.

Six Months Later—Summer 2009

In July 2009, Bright reviewed the BSC results (see TWA Parts Exhibits 3b and 4b). She was pleased to see that Eckhard had surpassed his cash flow and profit targets. She noticed that the luxury division's quality indicators had dropped slightly, but it continued to rate highly on innovation. Overall, Eckhard and his division had done a wonderful job exceeding their financial goals, adding to the company's overall financial health, and allowed TWAP to report better results from the prior year. They were also close to target on most of their customer initiatives. On the other hand, the economy division had not attained its financial targets. Bright was particularly puzzled at the economy division's results because it had been so successful in the learning and process dimensions. Nevertheless, the division managers had positioned themselves to take advantage of anticipated growth in the economy segment, which would contribute to TWAP's long-term financial performance.

As she sat back she thought to herself: "The more I look at these results, the more confused I become. I can't decide which division has performed better."

Required

1. Describe the business strategy of each division.
2. Comment on the strategy maps and balanced scorecards of the luxury car division and the economy car division. What would you change in the strategy maps and balanced scorecards of each division?
3. Which division manager prepared a better strategy map and balanced scorecard?
4. Which division manager performed better? Explain.

TWA Parts Exhibit 4b

TWAP Economy Division Balanced Scorecard, Action Plan, and Results Metrics for Six Months Ending June 30, 2009 (budget figures are for a three-year budget)

Balanced Scorecard			Action Plan		
Objectives	**Measures**	**Target**	**Initiative**	**Budget**	**Actual**
		Financial Perspective			
Increase ROCE	• ROCE	• −7%			• −12%
Increase cash flow	• YTD cash flow from operating activities	• −$12M			• −$14M
Increase gross margin	• Gross margin %	• 6%			• 4%
Grow revenues	• YTD revenue	• $1B			• $0.9B
Increase asset utilization	• Asset turnover ratio	• 1.25			• 1.23
		Customer Perspective			
Grow market share in economy segment	• Global market share in economy segment	• 6%	"Lowest Lifetime Cost/Highest Quality" campaign	$50M	• 5.9%
Be the low-maintenance-cost supplier in the economy segment	• Customer survey: % customers in economy segment that rate TWAP as having lowest maintenance costs.	• 80%	"Low Maintenance Cost" Campaign	$3.5M	• 75%
Gain reputation for standing behind quality	• % of customers who rank company guarantee as "best in class"	• 75%	"No Questions Asked" Replacement Policy	$75M	• 70%
Be the high-quality provider of auto parts in the economy segment	• Customer survey: % customers in economy segment that view TWAP as being "excellent" in quality attributes	• 80%	Customer attitudes survey	$2.5M	• 79%
		Internal Business Process Perspective			
Improve durability of parts produced	• % of parts with top rating for durability	• 65%	R&D Initiative: Wear Resistant Parts	$ 5M	• 63%
	• % of parts that "fail in the field"	• 7%	Low Field Failure Rate Initiative	$ 5M	• 7%
Better forecast OEM demand	• Stock outs • Inventory carrying costs (% reduction)	• 4% • 35%	TWAP liaison onsite at customer	$ 1M	• 2% • 35%
Increase useful life of subassemblies	• % of subassemblies passing 10-year life tests	• 75%	Joint TQM/R&D program for longer useful life of subassemblies	$40M	• 75%
Develop closer customer relationships	• # of customers with which TWAP has preferred supplier status	• 50	TWAP status review	$ 1M	• 60
Eliminate defects	• Reduce defect rates (parts per million)	• 5 PPM	TQM, lean/kaizen	$10M	• 4 PPM
Improve supplier base and supplier performance	• % of suppliers with an A rating • Reduce avg. delivery time (days)	• 75% • 26	Supplier optimization program	$ 5M	• 78% • 25
		Learning and Growth Perspective			
Enhance workforce capabilities in Total Quality Management (TQM)	• % of employees certified in TQM capabilities	• 50%	TQM training	$25M	• 53%
	• # of TQM engineers hired	• 60	TQM hiring program	$ 2M	• 65
Transform workforce into JIT/lean experts	• % of employees receiving JIT & Kaizen training	• 50%	Kaizen/JIT training	$25M	• 52%
	• # of JIT/lean process engineers hired	• 60	JIT/lean hiring program	$ 2M	• 64
Make JIT/lean a priority for all workers	• % of worker pay dependent upon JIT/lean measures	• 5%	Incentive restructuring	$ 2M	• 5%
Align information technology to support TQM and JIT	• % increase in IT spending	• 20%	Upgrade forecasting & supplier data base systems	$40M	• 20%
	• % of employees who rate information availability "appropriate and adequate" for their process improvement objectives	• 40%	Employee engagement survey	$ 2M	• 45%
Enhance electronic interchanges with customers and suppliers	• % of orders received and placed through streamlined/EDI process	• 90%	EDI Implementation and Roll-out Program	$ 5M	• 95%
Train buyers on high-quality procurement	• % of buyers trained in high-quality procurement processes	• 20%	Hiring & training programs	$50M	• 25%

Source: Casewriters.

15 Transfer Pricing

Learning Objectives

1. Describe a management control system and its three key properties
2. Describe the benefits and costs of decentralization
3. Explain transfer prices and the four criteria managers use to evaluate them
4. Calculate transfer prices using three methods
5. Illustrate how market-based transfer prices promote goal congruence in perfectly competitive markets
6. Understand how to avoid making suboptimal decisions when transfer prices are based on full cost plus a markup
7. Describe the range of feasible transfer prices when there is unused capacity and alternative methods for arriving at the eventual hybrid price
8. Apply a general guideline for determining a minimum transfer price
9. Understand how taxes affect transfer pricing at multinational corporations

Transfer pricing is the price one subunit of a company charges for the services it provides another subunit of the same company. At Ford, for example, automotive components, vehicles, and assembly services are bought and sold internally across segments. For many pharmaceutical companies, such as Merck, intellectual property patents are usually held by foreign subsidiaries, making the transfer price to these subsidiaries a critical factor in how much income is recognized in various tax jurisdictions. Top management uses transfer prices (1) to focus managers' attention on the performance of their own subunits and (2) to plan and coordinate the actions of different subunits to maximize the company's income as a whole. While transfer pricing is productive, it can also be contentious because managers of different subunits often have very different preferences about how transfer prices should be set. For example, some managers prefer the prices be based on market prices. Others prefer the prices be based on costs alone. Controversy also arises when multinational corporations seek to reduce their overall income tax burden by charging high transfer prices from units located in countries with low tax rates.

This chapter develops the links among strategy, organization structure, management control systems, and accounting information. We discuss the costs and benefits of decentralization. As the Chapter at a Glance highlights, we also describe the many ways in which transfer prices can be determined and the factors managers consider when determining the right set of prices to maximize a firm's overall profitability.

Chapter at a Glance

- Management control is a means of gathering and using information to aid and coordinate the planning and control decisions throughout an organization and to guide the behavior of its managers and other employees.
- Effective management control should be aligned with an organization's strategies and goals, support the responsibilities assigned to individual managers, and adequately motivate managers and other employees.
- A key decision for an organization is the extent to which it is decentralized, a structure that provides autonomy for managers at lower levels to make decisions on their own.
- Decentralization empowers subunit managers and enables better and more timely decision making. The cost of decentralization is that it leads to duplication of activities across subunits and may lead to subunit managers acting in their own unit's interest and not that of the firm as a whole.
- A transfer price is the internal price charged by one subunit (department or division) for a product or service supplied to another subunit of the same organization.
- Choosing an appropriate transfer price is essential for adequate measurement of the performance of subunits, as well as to ensure overall goal congruence.

- Managers can set transfer prices based on either prevailing market prices, the cost of providing the product or service, or negotiations between the transacting parties.
- If perfect markets exist for the transferred product, market-based transfer prices provide appropriate incentives for managers.
- Cost-based transfer pricing methods are widely used. If prices are determined based on fully allocated costs, goal incongruence is possible for sourcing decisions.
- In general, the transfer price must equal at least the sum of the incremental cost per unit incurred up to the point of transfer and the opportunity cost per unit to the selling division.
- When goods are transferred across countries, transfer prices play an important function in minimizing a firm's overall tax burden. In addition, managers must choose transfer prices carefully to balance considerations of customs duties and tariffs, as well as restrictions on currency repatriations and dividend payouts.

Management Control Systems

Learning Objective 1

Describe a management control system

. . . gathers information for planning and control decisions

and its three key properties

. . . aligns with strategy, supports organizational responsibility of managers, and motivates employees

A **management control system** is a means of gathering and using information to aid and coordinate planning and control decisions throughout an organization and to guide the behavior of its managers and other employees. Some companies design their management control system around the concept of the balanced scorecard. For example, ExxonMobil's management control system contains financial and nonfinancial information in each of the four perspectives of the balanced scorecard (see Chapter 14 for details). Well-designed management control systems use information both from within the company, such as net income and employee satisfaction, and from outside the company, such as stock price and customer satisfaction.

Formal and Informal Systems

Management control systems consist of formal and informal control systems. The formal management control system of a company includes explicit rules, procedures, performance measures, and incentive plans that guide the behavior of its managers and other employees. The formal control system is comprised of several systems, such as:

- The management accounting systems, which provide information regarding costs, revenues, and income
- The human resources systems, which provide information on recruiting, training, absenteeism, and accidents
- The quality systems, which provide information on yield, defective products, and late deliveries to customers

The informal management control system includes shared values, loyalties, and mutual commitments among members of the organization, company culture, and the unwritten norms about acceptable behavior for managers and other employees. Examples of company slogans that reinforce values and loyalties are "At Ford, Quality Is Job 1" and "At Home Depot, Low Prices Are Just the Beginning."

Effective Management Control

To be effective, management control systems should be closely aligned with the organization's strategies and goals. Two possible strategies at ExxonMobil are (1) providing innovative products and services to increase market share in key customer segments (by targeting customers who are willing to pay more for faster service, better facilities, and well-stocked convenience stores) and (2) reducing costs and targeting price-sensitive customers. Suppose ExxonMobil decides to pursue the former strategy. The management control system must then reinforce this goal, and ExxonMobil should tie managers' rewards to achieving the targeted measures.

Management control systems should also be designed to support the organizational responsibilities of individual managers. Different levels of management at ExxonMobil need different kinds of information to perform their tasks. For example, top management needs stock-price information to evaluate how much shareholder value the company has created. Stock price, however, is less important for line managers supervising individual oil refineries. Those managers are more concerned with obtaining information about on-time delivery of gasoline, equipment downtime, product quality, number of days lost to accidents and environmental problems, cost per gallon of gasoline, and employee satisfaction. Similarly, marketing managers are more concerned with information about service at gas stations, customer satisfaction, and market share.

Effective management control systems should also motivate managers and other employees. **Motivation** is the desire to attain a selected goal (the *goal-congruence* aspect) combined with the resulting pursuit of that goal (the *effort* aspect).

Goal congruence exists when individuals and groups work toward achieving the organization's goals—that is, managers working in their own best interest take actions that align with the overall goals of top management. Suppose the goal of ExxonMobil's top management is to maximize operating income. If the management control system evaluates the refinery manager *only* on the basis of costs, the manager may be tempted to make decisions that minimize cost but overlook product quality or timely delivery to retail stations. This oversight probably won't maximize the operating income of the company as a whole. In this case, the management control system will not achieve goal congruence.

Effort is the extent to which managers strive or endeavor to achieve a goal. Effort goes beyond physical exertion, such as a worker producing at a faster rate, to include mental actions as well. For example, effort includes the diligence or acumen with which a manager gathers and analyzes data before authorizing a new investment. It is impossible to directly observe or reward effort. As a result, management control systems motivate employees to exert effort by rewarding them for the achievement of observable goals, such as profit targets or stock returns. This system induces managers to exert effort because higher levels of effort increase the likelihood of the company achieving its goals. The rewards can be monetary (such as cash, shares of company stock, use of a company car, or membership in a club) or nonmonetary (such as a better job title, greater responsibility, or authority over a larger number of employees). Management control systems must fit an organization's structure. An organization whose structure is decentralized has additional issues to consider for its management control system to be effective.

Keys to Success

Effective management control should be aligned with an organization's strategies and goals, support the organizational responsibilities of individual managers, and motivate managers and other employees.

Learning Objective 2

Describe the benefits of decentralization

. . . responsiveness to customers, faster decision making, management development

and the costs of decentralization

. . . loss of control, duplication of activities

Decentralization

Until the mid-20th century, many firms were organized in a centralized, hierarchical fashion. **Centralization** is an organizational structure in which power is concentrated at the top and there is relatively little freedom for managers at the lower levels to make decisions. Perhaps the most famous example of a highly centralized structure is the Soviet Union, prior to its collapse in the late 1980s.

Today, organizations are far more decentralized and many companies have pushed decision-making authority down to subunit managers. **Decentralization** is an organizational structure that gives managers at lower levels the freedom to make decisions. **Autonomy** is the degree of freedom to make decisions. The greater the freedom, the greater the autonomy. As we discuss the issues of decentralization and autonomy, we use the term "subunit" to refer to any part of an organization. A subunit may be a large division, such as the refining division of ExxonMobil, or a small group, such as a two-person advertising department of a local clothing chain.

Examples of firms with decentralized structures include Nucor, the U.S. steel giant, which allows substantial operational autonomy to the general managers of its plants, and Tesco, Britain's largest retailer, which offers great latitude to its store managers. Of course, no firm is completely decentralized. At Nucor headquarters in North Carolina, management still retains responsibility for overall strategic planning, company financing, setting base salary levels and bonus targets, and purchase of steel scrap. How much decentralization is optimal? Companies try to choose the degree of decentralization that maximizes benefits over costs. We next discuss the key benefits and costs of decentralization.

Benefits of Decentralization

Supporters of decentralizing decision making and granting responsibilities to managers of subunits advocate the following benefits:

1. **Creates greater responsiveness to the needs of a subunit's customers, suppliers, and employees.** Managers cannot make good decisions without good information. Compared with top managers, subunit managers are better informed about their customers, competitors, suppliers, and employees, as well as about local factors that affect performance, such as ways to decrease costs, improve quality, and be responsive to customers. Eastman Kodak reports that two advantages of decentralization are an "increase in the company's knowledge of the marketplace and improved service to customers."
2. **Leads to gains from faster decision making by subunit managers.** Decentralization speeds decision making, creating a competitive advantage over centralized organizations. Centralization slows decision making because responsibility for decisions creeps upward through layer after layer of management. Interlake Mecalux, a leader in the provision of storage products and material-handling solutions, cites this benefit of decentralization: "We have distributed decision-making powers more broadly to the cutting edge of product and market opportunity." Interlake's storage system solutions must often be customized to fit the needs of customers. Delegating decision making to the sales force allows Interlake to respond faster to changing customer requirements.
3. **Increases motivation of subunit managers.** Subunit managers are more motivated and committed when they can exercise initiative. Hawei & Hawei, a Chinese multinational networking and telecommunications company, is highly decentralized and maintains that "Decentralization = Creativity = Productivity."
4. **Assists management development and learning.** Giving managers more responsibility helps develop an experienced pool of management talent to fill higher-level management positions. The company also learns which people are unlikely to be successful top managers. According to Tektronix, an electronics company based in Oregon, "Decentralized units provide a training ground for general managers and a visible field of combat where product champions can fight for their ideas."
5. **Sharpens the focus of subunit managers, broadens the reach of top management.** In a decentralized setting, the manager of a subunit has a concentrated focus. The head of Yahoo Japan, for example, can develop country-specific knowledge and expertise (local advertising trends, cultural norms, and payment forms) and focus attention on maximizing Yahoo's profits in Japan. At the same time, this relieves Yahoo's top management in Sunnyvale, California, from the burden of controlling day-to-day operating decisions in Japan. The American managers can now spend more time and effort on strategic planning for the entire organization.

Costs of Decentralization

Advocates of more centralized decision making point to the following costs of decentralizing decision making:

1. **Leads to suboptimal decision making.** This cost arises because top management has given up control over decision making. If the subunit managers do not have the necessary expertise or talent to handle this responsibility, the company, as a whole, is worse off.

   Even if subunit managers are sufficiently skilled, **suboptimal decision making**—also called **incongruent decision making** or **dysfunctional decision making**—occurs when a decision's benefit to one subunit is more than offset by the costs to the organization as a whole. This is most prevalent when the subunits in the company are highly interdependent, such as when the end product of one subunit is used or sold by another subunit. For example, suppose that Nintendo's marketing group receives an order for additional Wii consoles in Australia following the release of some unexpectedly popular new games. A manufacturing manager in Japan who is evaluated on the basis of costs may be unwilling to arrange this rush order since altering production schedules invariably increases manufacturing costs. From Nintendo's viewpoint, however, not supplying the consoles is a problem, both because the Australian customers are willing to pay a premium price and because the current shipment is expected to stimulate orders for other Nintendo games and consoles in the future.

2. **Focuses managers' attention on the subunit rather than the company as a whole.** Individual subunit managers may regard themselves as competing with managers of other subunits in the same company as if they were external rivals. This pushes them to view the relative performance of the subunit as more important than the goals of the company. Consequently, managers may be unwilling to assist when another subunit faces an emergency (as in the Nintendo example) or share important information. The 2010 Congressional hearings on the recall of Toyota vehicles revealed that it was common for Toyota's Japan unit to not share information about engineering problems or reported defects between its United States, Asian, and European operations. Toyota has since asserted that it will change this dysfunctional behavior.
3. **Results in duplication of output.** If subunits provide similar products or services, their internal competition could lead to failure in the external markets because divisions may find it easier to steal market share from one another by mimicking each other's successful products rather than from outside firms. Eventually, this leads to confusion in the minds of customers and the loss of each division's distinctive strengths. A classic example is General Motors, which has had to wind down its Oldsmobile, Pontiac, and Saturn divisions and end up in bankruptcy reorganization. Similarly, Condé Nast Publishing's initially distinct food magazines, *Bon Appétit* and *Gourmet,* eventually ended up chasing the same readers and advertisers, to the detriment of both. *Gourmet* magazine stopped publication in November 2009.[1]
4. **Results in duplication of activities.** Even if the subunits operate in distinct markets, several individual subunits of the company may undertake the same activity separately. In a highly decentralized company, each subunit may have personnel to carry out staff functions such as human resources or information technology. Centralizing these functions helps to streamline and use fewer resources for these activities and eliminates wasteful duplication. For example, ABB of Switzerland, a global leader in power and automation technology, is decentralized but has generated significant cost savings by centralizing its sourcing decisions across business units for parts, such as pipe pumps and fittings, as well as engineering and construction services. Having subunits share services such as information technology and human resources is becoming popular with companies because it saves 30–40% of the cost of having each subunit purchase such services on its own.

Comparison of Benefits and Costs

To choose an organizational structure that will implement a company's strategy, top managers must compare the benefits and costs of decentralization, often on a function-by-function basis. Surveys of U.S. and European companies report that the decisions made most frequently at the decentralized level are related to product mix and product advertising. In these areas, subunit managers develop their own operating plans and performance reports and make faster decisions based on local information. Decisions related to the type and source of long-term financing and income taxes are made least frequently at the decentralized level. Corporate managers have better information about financing terms in different markets and can obtain the best terms. Centralizing income tax strategies allows the organization to trade off and manage income in a subunit with losses in others. The benefits of decentralization are generally greater when companies face uncertainties in their environments, require detailed local knowledge for performing various jobs, and have few interdependencies among divisions.

Decentralization in Multinational Companies

Multinational companies—companies that operate in multiple countries—are often decentralized because centralized control of a company with subunits around the world is often physically and practically impossible. Also, language, customs, cultures, business practices, rules, laws, and regulations vary significantly across countries. Decentralization enables managers in different countries to make decisions that exploit their knowledge of local business and political conditions and enables them to deal with uncertainties in their individual environments. For example, Philips, a global

[1] For an intriguing comparison of the failure of decentralization in these disparate settings, see Jack Shafer's article, "How Condé Nast is Like General Motors: The Magazine Empire as Car Wreck," *Slate* (October 5, 2009), www.slate.com/id/2231177/.

electronics company headquartered in the Netherlands, delegates marketing and pricing decisions for its television business in the Indian and Singaporean markets to the managers in those countries. Multinational corporations often rotate managers between foreign locations and corporate headquarters. Job rotation combined with decentralization helps develop the ability of managers to operate in the global environment.

There are drawbacks to decentralizing multinational companies. One of the most important is the lack of control and the resulting risks. Barings PLC, a British investment banking firm, went bankrupt in 1995 and had to be sold when one of its traders in Singapore caused the firm to lose more than £1 billion on unauthorized trades that were not detected until after the trades were made. Similarly, in October 2011, a trader working for UBS, Switzerland's largest bank, in London apparently circumvented the bank's risk controls and engaged in unauthorized trading that resulted in a $2.3 billion loss. The chief executive and the co-chiefs of global equities of UBS have since resigned because of the scandal. Multinational corporations that implement decentralized decision making usually design their management control systems to measure and monitor division performance. Information and communications technology helps the flow of information for reporting and control.

Choices About Responsibility Centers

Recall (from Chapter 12) that a responsibility center is a segment or subunit of the organization whose manager is accountable for a specified set of activities. To measure the performance of subunits in centralized or decentralized companies, the management control system uses one or a mix of the four types of responsibility centers:

1. **Cost center**—the manager is accountable for costs only.
2. **Revenue center**—the manager is accountable for revenues only.
3. **Profit center**—the manager is accountable for revenues and costs.
4. **Investment center**—the manager is accountable for investments, revenues, and costs.

Centralization or decentralization is not mentioned in the descriptions of these centers because each type of responsibility center can be found in either centralized or decentralized companies.

A common misconception is that *profit center*—and, in some cases, *investment center*—is a synonym for a decentralized subunit, and *cost center* is a synonym for a centralized subunit. *Profit centers can be coupled with a highly centralized organization, and cost centers can be coupled with a highly decentralized organization.* For example, managers in a division organized as a profit center may have little freedom in making decisions. They may need to obtain approval from corporate headquarters to introduce new products and services or to make expenditures over some preset limit. When Michael Eisner ran Walt Disney Company, the giant media and entertainment conglomerate, from 1984 until 2005, the strategic-planning division applied so much scrutiny to business proposals that managers were reluctant to even pitch new ideas.[2] In other companies, divisions such as Information Technology may be organized as cost centers, but their managers may have great latitude with regard to capital expenditures and the purchase of materials and services. In short, the labels "profit center" and "cost center" are independent of the degree of centralization or decentralization in a company. In the next several sections, we describe performance measures for business units operating within a decentralized organizational structure.

Keys to Success

Decentralization empowers subunit managers and enables faster and more responsive local decision making by managers. However, decentralization also results in duplication of activities and services and, in the absence of appropriate controls, may lead to subunit managers acting in the interest of their subunit and not that of the organization as a whole.

[2] When Robert Iger replaced Eisner as CEO in 2005, one of his first acts was to disassemble the strategic-planning division, thereby giving more authority to Disney's business units (parks and resorts, consumer products, and media networks).

Learning Objective 3

Explain transfer prices

. . . price one subunit charges another for product

and the four criteria managers use to evaluate them

. . . goal congruence, management effort, subunit performance evaluation, and subunit autonomy

Transfer Pricing

In decentralized organizations, much of the decision-making power resides in the individual subunits. Often, the subunits interact by supplying goods or services to one another. In these cases, top management uses *transfer prices* to coordinate the actions of the subunits and to evaluate the performance of their managers.

A **transfer price** is the price one subunit (department or division) charges for a product or service supplied to another subunit of the same organization. If, for example, a car manufacturer like BMW or Ford has a separate division that manufactures engines, the transfer price is the price the engine division charges when it transfers engines to the car assembly division. The transfer price creates revenues for the selling subunit (the engine division in our example) and costs for the buying subunit (the assembly division in our example), affecting each subunit's operating income. These operating incomes can be used to evaluate subunits' performances and to motivate their managers. The product or service transferred between subunits of an organization is called an **intermediate product.** The receiving subunit (the assembly division in the engine example) may work on the product further or the product may be transferred from production to marketing and sold directly to an external customer.

In one sense, transfer pricing is a curious phenomenon. Activities within an organization are clearly nonmarket in nature because products and services are not bought and sold as they are in open-market transactions. Yet, establishing prices for transfers among subunits of a company has a distinctly market flavor. The rationale for transfer prices is that when subunit managers (such as the manager of the engine division) make decisions, they need only focus on how their decisions will affect their subunit's performance without evaluating how their decisions affect company-wide performance. In this sense, transfer prices ease the subunit managers' information-processing and decision-making tasks. In a well-designed transfer-pricing system, a manager focuses on maximizing subunit performance (the performance of the engine division) and in so doing optimizes the performance of the company as a whole.

Criteria for Evaluating Transfer Prices

As in all management control systems, transfer prices should help achieve a company's strategies and goals and fit its organization structure. Transfer pricing should meet four key criteria:

1. Promote goal congruence, so that division managers acting in their own interest will take actions that are aligned with the objectives of top management.
2. Induce managers to exert a high level of effort. Subunits selling a product or service should be motivated to hold down their costs; subunits buying the product or service should be motivated to acquire and use inputs efficiently.
3. Help top management evaluate the performance of individual subunits.
4. Preserve a high degree of subunit autonomy in decision making if top management favors a high degree of decentralization. That is, a subunit manager seeking to maximize the operating income of the subunit should have the freedom to transact with other subunits of the company (on the basis of transfer prices) or to transact with external parties.

Keys to Success

With a well-designed transfer price, each divisional manager makes the best decision for his or her subunit, while simultaneously maximizing the profits of the firm.

Learning Objective 4

Calculate transfer prices using three methods

. . . (a) market-based, (b) cost-based, or (c) hybrid, each of which yields different operating incomes for the subunits

Calculating Transfer Prices

There are three broad categories of methods that top management can use for determining transfer prices:

1. **Market-based transfer prices.** Top management may choose to use the price of a similar product or service publicly listed in, say, a trade association Web site. Also, top management may select, for the internal price, the external price that a subunit charges to outside customers.

2. **Cost-based transfer prices.** Top management may choose a transfer price based on the cost of producing the product in question. Examples include variable production cost, variable and fixed production costs, and full cost of the product. Full cost of the product includes all production costs plus costs from other business functions (R&D, design, marketing, distribution, and customer service). The cost used in cost-based transfer prices can be actual cost or budgeted cost. Sometimes, the cost-based transfer price includes a markup or profit margin that represents a return on subunit investment.
3. **Hybrid transfer prices.** Hybrid transfer prices take into account both cost and market information. Top management may administer such prices, for example, by specifying a transfer price that is an average of the cost of producing and transporting the product internally and the market price for comparable products. At other times, a hybrid transfer price may take the form where the revenue recognized by the selling unit is different from the cost recognized by the buying unit. The most common form of hybrid price arises via negotiation—the subunit managers are asked to negotiate the transfer price between them and to decide whether to transact internally or deal with external parties. Information regarding costs and prices plays a critical role in this bargaining process. Negotiated transfer prices are often employed when market prices are volatile.

Under what circumstances should top management use each of these options? To answer this question, we next demonstrate how each of the three transfer-pricing methods works and highlight the differences among them. We examine transfer pricing at Horizon Petroleum against the four criteria of promoting goal congruence, motivating management effort, evaluating subunit performance, and preserving subunit autonomy.

An Illustration of Transfer Pricing

Horizon Petroleum has two divisions, each operating as a profit center. The transportation division purchases crude oil in Matamoros, Mexico, and transports it from Matamoros to Houston, Texas. The refining division processes crude oil into gasoline. For simplicity, we assume gasoline is the only salable product the Houston refinery makes and that it takes two barrels of crude oil to yield one barrel of gasoline.

Variable costs in each division are associated with a single cost driver: barrels of crude oil transported by the transportation division, and barrels of gasoline produced by the refining division. The fixed cost per unit is based on the budgeted annual fixed costs and the total amount of crude oil that can be transported by the transportation division and the budgeted annual fixed costs and total amount of gasoline that can be produced by the refining division. Horizon Petroleum reports all costs and revenues of its non-U.S. operations in U.S. dollars using the prevailing exchange rate.

- The transportation division has obtained rights to certain oil fields in the Matamoros area. It has a long-term contract to purchase crude oil produced from these fields at $72 per barrel. The division transports the oil to Houston and then "sells" it to the refining division. The pipeline from Matamoros to Houston has the capacity to carry 40,000 barrels of crude oil per day.
- The refining division has been operating at capacity (30,000 barrels of crude oil a day) using oil supplied by Horizon's transportation division (an average of 10,000 barrels per day) and oil bought from another producer and delivered to the Houston refinery (an average of 20,000 barrels per day at $85 per barrel).
- The refining division sells the gasoline it produces to outside parties at $190 per barrel.

Exhibit 15-1 summarizes Horizon Petroleum's variable and fixed costs per barrel of crude oil in the transportation division and variable and fixed costs per barrel of gasoline in the refining division, the external market prices of buying crude oil, and the external market price of selling gasoline. What's missing in the exhibit is the actual transfer price from the transportation division to the refining division. This transfer price will vary depending on the transfer-pricing method used. Transfer prices from the transportation division to the refining division under each of the three methods are:

1. Market-based transfer price of $85 per barrel of crude oil based on the competitive market price in Houston.
2. Cost-based transfer prices at, say, 105% of full cost, where full cost is the cost of the crude oil purchased in Matamoros plus the transportation division's variable and fixed costs (from Exhibit 15-1): 1.05 × ($72 + $1 + $3) = $79.80.

Exhibit 15-1

Operating Data for Horizon Petroleum

	A	B	C	D	E	F	G	H
1								
2				**Transportation Division**				
3	Contract price per barrel of crude oil supplied in Matamoros =	$72	→	Variable cost per barrel of crude oil	$1			
4				Fixed cost per barrel of crude oil	3			
5				Full cost per barrel of crude oil	$4			
6				↓				
7								
8				Barrels of crude oil transferred				
9				↓				
10								
11				**Refining Division**				
12	Market price per barrel of crude oil supplied to Houston refinery =	$85	→	Variable cost per barrel of gasoline	$ 8	→	Market price per barrel of gasoline sold to external parties =	$190
13				Fixed cost per barrel of gasoline	6			
14				Full cost per barrel of gasoline	$14			
15								

3. Hybrid transfer price of, say, $82 per barrel of crude oil, which is between the market-based and cost-based transfer prices. We describe later in this section the various ways in which managers can determine hybrid prices.

Exhibit 15-2 presents division operating incomes per 100 barrels of crude oil purchased under each transfer-pricing method. Transfer prices create income for the selling division and corresponding costs for the buying division that cancel out when division results are consolidated for the company as a whole. The exhibit assumes all three transfer-pricing methods yield transfer prices that are in a range that does not cause division managers to change the business relationships shown in Exhibit 15-1. That is, Horizon Petroleum's total operating income from purchasing, transporting, and refining the 100 barrels of crude oil and selling the 50 barrels of gasoline is the same, $1,200, *regardless of the internal transfer prices used.*

$$\text{Operating income} = \text{Revenues} - \begin{array}{c}\text{Cost of crude}\\ \text{oil purchases}\\ \text{in Matamoros}\end{array} - \begin{array}{c}\text{Transportation}\\ \text{division}\\ \text{costs}\end{array} - \begin{array}{c}\text{Refining}\\ \text{division}\\ \text{costs}\end{array}$$

$$= (\$190 \times 50 \text{ barrels of gasoline}) - (\$72 \times 100 \text{ barrels of crude oil})$$

$$- (\$4 \times 100 \text{ barrels of crude oil}) - (\$14 \times 50 \text{ barrels of gasoline})$$

$$= \$9{,}500 - \$7{,}200 - \$400 - \$700 = \$1{,}200$$

Note that under all three methods, summing the two division operating incomes equals Horizon Petroleum's total operating income of $1,200. By keeping total operating income the same, we focus attention on the effects of different transfer-pricing methods on the operating income of each division. Subsequent sections of this chapter show that different transfer-pricing methods can cause managers to take different actions leading to different total operating incomes.

Consider the two methods in the first two columns in Exhibit 15-2. The operating income of the transportation division is $520 more ($900 − $380) if transfer prices are based on market prices rather than on 105% of full cost. The operating income of the refining division is $520 more ($820 − $300) if transfer prices are based on 105% of full cost rather than market prices. If the transportation division's sole criterion were to maximize its own division operating income, it would favor transfer prices at market prices. In contrast, the refining division would prefer transfer prices at 105% of full cost to maximize its own division operating income. The hybrid transfer price of $82 is between the 105% of full cost and market-based transfer prices. It splits the $1,200 of operating income equally between the divisions, and could arise as a result of negotiations between the transportation and refining division managers.

It's not surprising that subunit managers, especially those whose compensation or promotion directly depends on subunit operating income, take considerable interest in setting transfer

Exhibit 15-2

Division Operating Income of Horizon Petroleum for 100 Barrels of Crude Oil Under Alternative Transfer-Pricing Methods

	A	B	C	D	E	F	G	H
1	**Production and Sales Data**							
2	Barrels of crude oil transferred =	100						
3	Barrels of gasoline sold =	50						
4								
5		**Internal Transfers at**			**Internal Transfers at**			
6		**Market Price =**			**105% of Full Cost =**		**Hybrid Price =**	
7		**$85 per Barrel**			**$79.80 per Barrel**		**$82 per Barrel**	
8	**Transportation Division**							
9	Revenues, $85, $79.80, $82 × 100 barrels of crude oil	$8,500			$7,980		$8,200	
10	Costs							
11	Crude oil purchase costs, $72 × 100 barrels of crude oil	7,200			7,200		7,200	
12	Division variable costs, $1 × 100 barrels of crude oil	100			100		100	
13	Division fixed costs, $3 × 100 barrels of crude oil	300			300		300	
14	Total division costs	7,600			7,600		7,600	
15	Division operating income	$ 900			$ 380		$ 600	
16								
17	**Refining Division**							
18	Revenues, $190 × 50 barrels of gasoline	$9,500			$9,500		$9,500	
19	Costs							
20	Transferred-in costs, $85, $79.80, $82							
21	× 100 barrels of crude oil	8,500	←		7,980	←	8,200	←
22	Division variable costs, $8 × 50 barrels of gasoline	400			400		400	
23	Division fixed costs, $6 × 50 barrels of gasoline	300			300		300	
24	Total division costs	9,200			8,680		8,900	
25	Division operating income	$ 300			$ 820		$ 600	
26	Operating income of both divisions together	$1,200			$1,200		$1,200	

prices. To reduce the excessive focus of subunit managers on their own subunits, many companies compensate subunit managers on the basis of both subunit and company-wide operating incomes.

We next examine market-based, cost-based, and hybrid transfer prices in more detail. We show how the choice of transfer-pricing method combined with managers' sourcing decisions can determine the size of the company-wide operating-income pie itself.

Keys to Success

Subunit managers care deeply about transfer pricing since different methods result in varying levels of subunit incomes, and thereby affect the managers' performance evaluation and compensation levels.

Learning Objective 5

Illustrate how market-based transfer prices promote goal congruence in perfectly competitive markets

. . . division managers transacting internally are motivated to take the same actions as if they were transacting externally

Market-Based Transfer Prices

Transferring products or services at market prices generally leads to optimal decisions when three conditions are satisfied: (1) The market for the intermediate product is perfectly competitive, (2) interdependencies of subunits are minimal, and (3) there are no additional costs or benefits to the company as a whole from buying or selling in the external market instead of transacting internally.

Perfectly Competitive Market

A **perfectly competitive market** exists when there is a homogeneous product with buying prices equal to selling prices and no individual buyers or sellers can affect those prices by their own actions. By using market-based transfer prices in perfectly competitive markets, a company can

(1) promote goal congruence, (2) motivate management effort, (3) evaluate subunit performance, and (4) preserve subunit autonomy.

Consider Horizon Petroleum again. Assume there is a perfectly competitive market for crude oil in the Houston area. As a result, the transportation division can sell and the refining division can buy as much crude oil as each wants at $85 per barrel. Horizon would prefer its managers to buy or sell crude oil internally. Think about the decisions that Horizon's division managers would make if each had the autonomy to sell or buy crude oil externally. If the transfer price between Horizon's transportation and refining divisions is set below $85, the manager of the transportation division will be motivated to sell all crude oil to external buyers in the Houston area at $85 per barrel. If the transfer price is set above $85, the manager of the refining division will be motivated to purchase all crude oil requirements from external suppliers. Only an $85 transfer price will motivate the transportation division and the refining division to buy and sell internally. That's because neither division profits by buying or selling in the external market.

Suppose Horizon evaluates division managers on the basis of their individual division's operating income. The transportation division will sell, either internally or externally, as much crude oil as it can profitably transport, and the refining division will buy, either internally or externally, as much crude oil as it can profitably refine. An $85-per-barrel transfer price achieves goal congruence—the actions that maximize each division's operating income are also the actions that maximize operating income of Horizon Petroleum as a whole. Furthermore, because the transfer price is not based on costs, it motivates each division manager to exert management effort to maximize his or her own division's operating income. Market prices also serve to evaluate the economic viability and profitability of each division individually. For example, Koch Industries, the second-largest private company in the United States, uses market-based pricing for all internal transfers. As CFO Steve Feilmeier notes, "We believe that the alternative for any given asset should always be considered in order to best optimize the profitability of the asset. If you simply transfer price between two different divisions at cost, then you may be subsidizing your whole operation and not know it." Returning to our Horizon example, suppose that under market-based transfer prices, the refining division consistently shows small or negative profits. Then Horizon may consider shutting down the refining division and simply transport and sell the oil to other refineries in the Houston area.

Distress Prices

When supply outstrips demand, market prices may drop well below their historical averages. If the drop in prices is expected to be temporary, these low market prices are sometimes called "distress prices." Deciding whether a current market price is a distress price is often difficult. Prior to the worldwide spike in commodity prices in the 2006–2008 period, the market prices of several mineral and agricultural commodities, including nickel, uranium, and wheat, stayed for many years at what people initially believed were temporary distress levels!

Which transfer price should managers use to judge performance if distress prices prevail? Some companies use the distress prices themselves, but others use long-run average prices, or "normal" market prices. In the short run, the manager of the selling subunit should supply the product or service at the distress price as long as it exceeds the *incremental costs* of supplying the product or service. If the distress price is used as the transfer price, the selling division will show a loss because the distress price will not exceed the *full cost* of the division. If the long-run average market price is used, forcing the manager to buy internally at a price above the current market price will hurt the buying division's short-run operating income. But the long-run average market price will provide a better measure of the long-run profitability and viability of the supplier division. Of course, if the price remains low in the long run, the company should use the low market price as the transfer price. If this price is lower than the variable and fixed costs that can be saved if manufacturing facilities are shut down, the production facilities of the selling subunit should be sold, and the buying subunit should purchase the product from an external supplier.

Imperfect Competition

If markets are not perfectly competitive, selling prices affect the quantity of product sold. Consider an auto dealer, for example. In order to move more new or used cars off the lot, the dealer has to reduce the price of the vehicles. A similar situation applies to industries ranging from toilet paper and toothpaste to software. Faced with an imperfectly competitive market, the manager of the selling division will choose a price and quantity combination for the intermediate product that maximizes the division's operating income. If the transfer price is set at this price, the buying division may find that acquiring the product is too costly and results in a loss. The division may decide not to purchase the product. Yet, from the point of view of the company as a whole, it may well be that profits are maximized if the selling division transfers the product to the buying division for further processing and sale. For this reason, when the market for the intermediate good is imperfectly competitive, the transfer price must generally be set below the external market price (but above the selling division's variable cost) in order to induce efficient transfers.[3]

Keys to Success

In competitive markets, it is efficient to set the transfer prices equal to the market price of the intermediate goods. Under imperfect competition, the transfer price should be set at a suitable *discount* to the external price in order to induce the manager of the buying division to seek internal transfers.

Cost-Based Transfer Prices

Learning Objective 6

Understand how to avoid making suboptimal decisions when transfer prices are based on full cost plus a markup

. . . buying divisions should not regard the fixed costs and the markup as variable costs

Cost-based transfer prices are helpful when market prices are unavailable, inappropriate, or too costly to obtain, such as when markets are not perfectly competitive, when the product is specialized, or when the internal product is different from the products available externally in terms of quality and customer service.

Full-Cost Bases

In practice, many companies use transfer prices based on full cost. To approximate market prices, cost-based transfer prices are sometimes set at full cost plus a margin. These transfer prices, however, can lead to suboptimal decisions. Suppose Horizon Petroleum makes internal transfers at 105% of full cost. Recall that the refining division purchases, on average, 20,000 barrels of crude oil per day from a local Houston supplier, who delivers the crude oil to the refinery at a price of $85 per barrel. To reduce crude oil costs, the refining division has located an independent producer in Matamoros—Gulfmex Corporation—that is willing to sell 20,000 barrels of crude oil per day at $79 per barrel, delivered to Horizon's pipeline in Matamoros. Given Horizon's organization structure, the transportation division would purchase the 20,000 barrels of crude oil in Matamoros from Gulfmex, transport it to Houston, and then sell it to the refining division. The pipeline has unused capacity and can ship the 20,000 barrels per day at its variable cost of $1 per barrel without affecting the shipment of the 10,000 barrels of crude oil per day acquired under its existing long-term contract arrangement. Will Horizon Petroleum incur lower costs by purchasing crude oil from Gulfmex in Matamoros or by purchasing crude oil from the Houston supplier? Will the refining division show lower crude oil purchasing costs by acquiring oil from Gulfmex or by acquiring oil from its current Houston supplier?

The following analysis shows that Horizon Petroleum's operating income would be maximized by purchasing oil from Gulfmex. The analysis compares the incremental costs in both divisions under the two alternatives. The analysis assumes the fixed costs of the transportation division will

[3] Consider a firm where division S produces the intermediate product. S has a capacity of 15 units and a variable cost per unit of $2. The imperfect competition is illustrated in a downward-sloping demand curve for the intermediate product—if S wants to sell Q units, it has to lower the market price to $P = 20 - Q$. The division's profit function is therefore given by $Q \times (20 - Q) - 2Q = 18Q - Q^2$. Simple calculus reveals that it is optimal for S to sell 9 units of the intermediate product at a price of $11, thereby making a profit of $81. Now, suppose that division B in the same firm can take the intermediate product, incur an additional variable cost of $4, and sell it in the external market for $12. Since S has surplus capacity (it only uses 9 of its 15 units of capacity), it is clearly in the firm's interest to have S make additional units and transfer them to B. The firm makes an incremental profit of $12 − $2 − $4 = $6 for each transferred unit. However, if the transfer price for the intermediate product were set equal to the market price of $11, B would reject the transaction since it would lose money on it ($12 − $11 − $4 = −$3 per unit).

To resolve this conflict, the transfer price should be set at a suitable *discount* to the external price in order to induce the buying division to seek internal transfers. In our example, the selling price must be greater than S's variable cost of $2, but less than B's contribution margin of $8. That is, the transfer price has to be discounted relative to the market price ($11) by a minimum of $3. We explore the issue of feasible transfer pricing ranges further in the section on hybrid transfer prices.

be the same regardless of the alternative chosen. That is, the transportation division cannot save any of its fixed costs if it does not transport Gulfmex's 20,000 barrels of crude oil per day.

- **Alternative 1:** Buy 20,000 barrels from the Houston supplier at \$85 per barrel. Total costs to Horizon Petroleum are 20,000 barrels × \$85 per barrel = \$1,700,000.
- **Alternative 2:** Buy 20,000 barrels in Matamoros at \$79 per barrel and transport them to Houston at a variable cost of \$1 per barrel. Total costs to Horizon Petroleum are 20,000 barrels × (\$79 + \$1) per barrel = \$1,600,000.

There is a reduction in total costs to Horizon Petroleum of \$100,000 (\$1,700,000 − \$1,600,000) by acquiring oil from Gulfmex.

Suppose the transportation division's transfer price to the refining division is 105% of full cost. The refining division will see its reported division costs increase if the crude oil is purchased from Gulfmex:

$$\text{Transfer price} = 1.05 \times \left(\begin{array}{c}\text{Purchase price}\\ \text{from}\\ \text{Gulfmex}\end{array} + \begin{array}{c}\text{Variable cost per unit}\\ \text{of transportation}\\ \text{division}\end{array} + \begin{array}{c}\text{Fixed cost per unit}\\ \text{of transportation}\\ \text{division}\end{array} \right)$$

$$= 1.05 \times (\$79 + \$1 + \$3) = 1.05 \times \$83 = \$87.15 \text{ per barrel}$$

- **Alternative 1:** Buy 20,000 barrels from Houston supplier at \$85 per barrel. Total costs to refining division are 20,000 barrels × \$85 per barrel = \$1,700,000.
- **Alternative 2:** Buy 20,000 barrels from the transportation division of Horizon Petroleum that were purchased from Gulfmex. Total costs to refining division are 20,000 barrels × \$87.15 per barrel = \$1,743,000.

As a profit center, the refining division can maximize its short-run division operating income by purchasing from the Houston supplier.

The refining division looks at each barrel that it obtains from the transportation division as a variable cost of \$87.15 per barrel; if 10 barrels are transferred, it costs the refining division \$871.50; if 100 barrels are transferred, it costs \$8,715. However, the true variable cost per barrel is \$80 (\$79 to purchase the oil from Gulfmex plus \$1 to transport it to Houston). The remaining \$7.15 (\$87.15 − \$80) per barrel is the transportation division's fixed cost and markup. *The full cost plus a markup transfer-pricing method causes the refining division to regard the fixed cost (and the 5% markup) of the transportation division as a variable cost and leads to goal incongruence.*

Should Horizon's top management interfere and force the refining division to buy from the transportation division? Top management interference would undercut the philosophy of decentralization, so Horizon's top management would probably view the decision by the refining division to purchase crude oil from external suppliers as an inevitable cost of decentralization and not intervene. Of course, some interference may occasionally be necessary to prevent costly blunders. But recurring interference and constraints would simply transform Horizon from a decentralized company into a centralized company.

What transfer price will promote goal congruence for both the transportation and refining divisions? The minimum transfer price is \$80 per barrel. A transfer price below \$80 does not provide the transportation division with an incentive to purchase crude oil from Gulfmex in Matamoros because it is below the transportation division's incremental costs. The maximum transfer price is \$85 per barrel. A transfer price above \$85 will cause the refining division to purchase crude oil from the external market in Houston rather than from the transportation division. A transfer price between the minimum and maximum transfer prices of \$80 and \$85 will promote goal congruence: Each division will increase its own reported operating income while increasing Horizon Petroleum's operating income if the refining division purchases crude oil from Gulfmex in Matamoros.

In the absence of a market-based transfer price, senior management at Horizon Petroleum has difficulty determining the profitability of the investment made in the transportation division and, in turn, whether Horizon should keep or sell the pipeline. Furthermore, if the transfer price had been based on the actual costs of the transportation division, it would provide the division with no incentive to control costs. That's because all cost inefficiencies of the transportation division would get passed along as part of the actual full-cost transfer price. In fact, every additional dollar of cost arising from wastefulness in the transportation division would generate an additional 5 cents in profit for the division under the "105% of full cost" rule!

Surveys by accounting firms and researchers indicate that, despite the limitations, managers generally prefer to use full-cost transfer pricing because (1) they represent relevant costs for long-run decisions, (2) they facilitate external pricing based on variable and fixed costs, and (3) they are the least costly to administer. However, full-cost transfer pricing does raise many issues. How are each subunit's indirect costs allocated to products? Have the correct activities, cost pools, and cost-allocation bases been identified? Should the chosen fixed-cost rates be actual or budgeted? The issues here are similar to those that arise in allocating fixed costs, which were introduced in Chapter 4. Many companies determine the transfer price based on budgeted rates and capacity because it overcomes the problem of inefficiencies in actual costs and costs of unused capacity getting passed along to the buying division.

Keys to Success

There is a risk of suboptimal decisions when transfer prices are based on full cost plus a markup because the buying division manager perceives the cost of each transferred unit to be higher than the true (variable) cost from the firm's standpoint.

Variable-Cost Bases

Transferring 20,000 barrels of crude oil from the transportation division to the refining division at the variable cost of $80 per barrel achieves goal congruence, as shown in the preceding section. The refining division would buy from the transportation division because the transportation division's variable cost is less than the $85 price charged by external suppliers. Setting the transfer price equal to the variable cost has other benefits. Knowledge of the variable cost per barrel of crude oil is very helpful to the refining division for many decisions such as the short-run pricing decisions discussed in Chapter 9. However, at the $80-per-barrel transfer price, the transportation division would record an operating loss, and the refining division would show large profits because it would be charged only for the variable costs of the transportation division. One approach to addressing this problem is to have the refining division make a lump-sum transfer payment to cover fixed costs and generate some operating income for the transportation division while the transportation division continues to make transfers at variable cost. The fixed payment is the price the refining division pays for using the capacity of the transportation division. The company can then use income earned by each division to evaluate the performance of each division and its manager.

Hybrid Transfer Prices

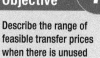

Learning Objective 7

Describe the range of feasible transfer prices when there is unused capacity

. . . from variable cost to market price of the product transferred

and alternative methods for arriving at the eventual hybrid price

. . . proration, negotiation between divisions, and dual pricing

Consider again Horizon Petroleum. As we saw earlier, the transportation division has unused capacity it can use to transport crude oil from Matamoros to Houston at an incremental cost of $80 per barrel. Horizon Petroleum, as a whole, maximizes operating income if the refining division purchases crude oil from the transportation division rather than from the Houston market (incremental cost per barrel of $80 vs. price per barrel of $85). Both divisions would be interested in transacting with each other (and the firm achieves goal congruence) if the transfer price is between $80 and $85.

For any internal transaction, there is generally a minimum transfer price the selling division will not go below, based on its cost structure. In the Horizon Petroleum example, the minimum price acceptable to the transportation division is $80. There is also a maximum price the buying division will not wish to exceed, given by the lower of two quantities—the eventual contribution it generates from an internal transaction and the price of purchasing a comparable intermediate product from an outside party. For the refining division, each barrel of gasoline sold to external parties generates $182 in contribution (the $190 price less the $8 variable cost of refining). Since it takes two barrels of crude oil to generate a barrel of gasoline, this is equivalent to a contribution of $91 per barrel of crude. For any price higher than $91, the refining division would lose money for each barrel of crude it takes from the transportation division. On the other hand, the refining division can purchase crude oil on the open market for $85 rather than having it transported internally. The maximum feasible transfer price is thus the lower of $91 and $85, or $85 in this instance. We saw previously that a transfer price between the minimum price ($80) and the maximum ($85) would promote goal congruence. We now describe three different ways in which firms attempt to determine the specific transfer price within these bounds.

Prorating the Difference Between Maximum and Minimum Transfer Prices

One approach that Horizon Petroleum could pursue is to choose a transfer price that splits, on some fair basis, the $5 difference between the $85-per-barrel market-based maximum price the refining division is willing to pay and the $80-per-barrel variable cost-based minimum price the transportation division wants to receive. An easy solution is to split the difference equally, resulting in a transfer price of $82.50. However, this solution ignores the relative costs incurred by the two divisions and might lead to disparate profit margins on the work contributed by each division to the final product. As an alternative approach, Horizon Petroleum could allocate the $5 difference on the basis of the variable costs of the two divisions. Using the data in Exhibit 15-1 (page 632), variable costs are:

Transportation division's variable costs to transport 100 barrels of crude oil ($1 × 100)	$100
Refining division's variable costs to refine 100 barrels of crude oil and produce 50 barrels of gasoline ($8 × 50)	400
Total variable costs	$500

Of the $5 difference, the transportation division gets to keep ($100 ÷ $500) × $5.00 = $1.00 and the refining division gets to keep ($400 ÷ $500) × $5.00 = $4.00. That is, the transfer price is $81 per barrel of crude oil ($79 purchase cost + $1 variable cost + $1 the transportation division gets to keep). In effect, this approach results in a budgeted variable-cost-plus transfer price. The "plus" indicates the setting of a transfer price above variable cost.

To decide on the $1 and $4 allocations of the $5 incremental benefit to total company operating income per barrel, the divisions must share information about their variable costs. In effect, neither division operates (at least for this transaction) in a totally decentralized manner. Furthermore, each division has an incentive to overstate its variable costs to receive a more-favorable transfer price. In the preceding example, suppose the transportation division claims a cost of $2 per barrel to ship crude oil from Gulfmex to Houston. This increased cost raises the variable cost-based minimum price to $79 + $2 = $81 per barrel; the maximum price remains $85. Of the $4 difference between the minimum and maximum, the transportation division now gets to keep ($200 ÷ ($200 + $400)) × $4.00 = $1.33, resulting in a higher transfer price of $82.33. The refining division similarly benefits from asserting that its variable cost to refine 100 barrels of crude oil is greater than $400. As a consequence, proration methods either require a high degree of trust and information exchange among divisions or include provisions for objective audits of cost information in order to be successful.

Negotiated Pricing

Negotiated pricing is the most common hybrid method. Under this method, top management does not administer a specific split of the eventual profits across the transacting divisions. Rather, the eventual transfer price results from a bargaining process between the selling and buying subunits. In the Horizon Petroleum case, for example, the transportation division and the refining division would be free to negotiate a price that is mutually acceptable to both.

As described earlier, the minimum and maximum feasible transfer prices are $80 and $85, respectively, per barrel of crude oil. Where between $80 and $85 will the transfer price per barrel be set? Under a negotiated transfer price, the answer depends on several things: the bargaining strengths of the two divisions; information the transportation division has about the price minus incremental marketing costs of supplying crude oil to outside refineries; and the information the refining division has about its other available sources of crude oil. Negotiations become particularly sensitive because Horizon Petroleum can now evaluate each division's performance on the basis of division operating income. The price negotiated by the two divisions will, in general, have no specific relationship to either costs or market price. But cost and price information is often the starting point in the negotiation process.

Consider the following situation: Suppose the refining division receives an order to supply specially processed gasoline. The incremental cost to purchase and supply crude oil is still $80 per barrel. However, suppose the refining division will profit from this order only if the transportation division can supply crude oil at a price not exceeding $82 per barrel.[4] In this case, the transfer price that would benefit both divisions must be greater than $80 but less than $82. Negotiations would allow the two divisions to achieve an acceptable transfer price. By contrast, a rule-based transfer price, such as a market-based price of $85 or 105% of the full-cost-based price of $87.15, would result in Horizon passing up a profitable opportunity.

A negotiated transfer price strongly preserves division autonomy. It also has the advantage that each division manager is motivated to put forth effort to increase division operating income. Surveys have found that approximately 15–20% of firms set transfer prices based on negotiation among divisions. The key reason cited by firms that do not use negotiated prices is the cost of the bargaining process, that is, the time and energy spent by managers haggling over transfer prices.

Keys to Success

A hybrid price is determined within the range of feasible prices by either a prespecified sharing rule or by allowing division managers to negotiate among themselves.

Dual Pricing

There is seldom a single transfer price that simultaneously meets the criteria of promoting goal congruence, motivating management effort, evaluating subunit performance, and preserving subunit autonomy. As a result, some companies choose **dual pricing,** using two separate transfer-pricing methods to price each transfer from one subunit to another. An example of dual pricing arises when the selling division receives a full-cost-based price and the buying division pays the market price for the internally transferred products. Assume Horizon Petroleum purchases crude oil from Gulfmex in Matamoros at $79 per barrel. Here is one way managers can record the transfer between the transportation division and the refining division:

1. Charge the refining division (the buying division) with the market-based transfer price of $85 per barrel of crude oil.
2. Credit the transportation division (the selling division) with the 105%-of-full-cost transfer price of $87.15 per barrel of crude oil.
3. Charge a corporate account for the $2.15 ($87.15 − $85) per barrel difference between the two transfer prices.

The dual-pricing system promotes goal congruence because it makes the refining division no worse off if it purchases the crude oil from the transportation division rather than from the external supplier at $85 per barrel. The transportation division receives a corporate subsidy. In dual pricing, the operating income for Horizon Petroleum as a whole is less than the sum of the operating incomes of the divisions.

Dual pricing is not widely used in practice even though it reduces the goal incongruence associated with a pure cost-based transfer-pricing method. One concern with dual pricing is that it leads to problems and disputes about which price should be used when computing the taxable income of subunits located in different tax jurisdictions, such as in our example, where the transportation division is taxed in Mexico while the refining division is taxed in the United States. A second concern is that dual pricing insulates managers from the realities of the marketplace because costs, not market prices, affect the revenues of the supplying division.

Keys to Success

Dual pricing is the practice of recording different prices for the buying and selling division for the same transaction.

[4] For example, suppose a barrel of specially processed gasoline could be sold for $200 but also required a higher variable cost of refining of $36 per barrel. In this setting, the incremental contribution to the refining division is $164 per barrel of gasoline, which implies that it will pay at most $82 for a barrel of crude oil (since two barrels of crude are required for one barrel of gasoline).

Exhibit 15-3

Comparison of Different Transfer-Pricing Methods

Criteria	Market-Based	Cost-Based	Negotiated
Achieves goal congruence	Yes, when markets are competitive	Often, but not always	Yes
Motivates management effort	Yes	Yes, when based on budgeted costs; less incentive to control costs if transfers are based on actual costs	Yes
Useful for evaluating subunit performance	Yes, when markets are competitive	Difficult unless transfer price exceeds full cost and even then is somewhat arbitrary	Yes, but transfer prices are affected by bargaining strengths of the buying and selling divisions
Preserves subunit autonomy	Yes, when markets are competitive	No, because it is rule-based	Yes, because it is based on negotiations between subunits
Other factors	Market may not exist, or markets may be imperfect or in distress	Useful for determining full cost of products and services; easy to implement	Bargaining and negotiations take time and may need to be reviewed repeatedly as conditions change

Learning Objective 8

Apply a general guideline for determining a minimum transfer price

. . . incremental cost plus opportunity cost of supplying division

A General Guideline for Transfer-Pricing Situations

Exhibit 15-3 summarizes the properties of market-based, cost-based, and negotiated transfer-pricing methods using the criteria described in this chapter. As the exhibit indicates, it is difficult for a transfer-pricing method to meet all criteria. Managers must simultaneously consider (1) market conditions, (2) the goal of the transfer-pricing system, and (3) the criteria of promoting goal congruence, motivating management effort, evaluating subunit performance, and preserving subunit autonomy (if desired). The transfer price a company will eventually choose depends on the economic circumstances and the decision at hand. Surveys of company practice by Ernst & Young as well as those sponsored by the Institute of Management Accountants indicate that the full-cost-based transfer price is generally the most frequently used transfer-pricing method around the world, followed by market-based transfer price and negotiated transfer price.[5]

Our discussion so far highlights that, barring settings in which a perfectly competitive market exists for the intermediate product, there is generally a range of possible transfer prices that would induce goal congruence. We now provide a general guideline for determining the minimum price in that range. The following formula is a helpful first step in setting the minimum transfer price in many situations:

$$\text{Minimum transfer price} = \begin{array}{c}\text{Incremental cost}\\ \text{per unit}\\ \text{incurred up}\\ \text{to the point of transfer}\end{array} + \begin{array}{c}\text{Opportunity cost}\\ \text{per unit}\\ \text{to the selling subunit}\end{array}$$

Incremental cost in this context means the additional cost of producing and transferring the product or service. Opportunity cost here is the maximum contribution margin forgone by the selling subunit if the product or service is transferred internally. For example, if the selling subunit is operating at capacity, the opportunity cost of transferring a unit internally rather than selling it externally is equal to the market price minus variable cost. That's because by transferring a unit internally, the subunit forgoes the contribution margin it could have obtained by selling the unit

[5] See, for example, *Current Trends and Corporate Cases in Transfer Pricing*, by Roger Tang with IMA Foundation for Applied Research, Institute of Management Accountants (Westport, CT: Quorum Books, 2002).

in the external market. We distinguish incremental cost from opportunity cost because financial accounting systems record incremental cost but do not record opportunity cost. The guideline measures a *minimum* transfer price because it represents the selling unit's cost of transferring the product. We illustrate the general guideline in some specific situations using data from Horizon Petroleum.

1. **A perfectly competitive market for the intermediate product exists and the selling division has no unused capacity.** If the market for crude oil in Houston is perfectly competitive, the transportation division can sell all the crude oil it transports to the external market at \$85 per barrel, and it will have no unused capacity. The transportation division's incremental cost (as shown in Exhibit 15-1, page 632) is \$73 per barrel (purchase cost of \$72 per barrel + variable transportation cost of \$1 per barrel) for oil purchased under the long-term contract or \$80 per barrel (purchase cost of \$79 + variable transportation cost of \$1) for oil purchased at current market prices from Gulfmex. The transportation division's opportunity cost per barrel of transferring the oil internally is the contribution margin per barrel forgone by not selling the crude oil in the external market: \$12 for oil purchased under the long-term contract (market price, \$85 − variable cost, \$73) and \$5 for oil purchased from Gulfmex (market price, \$85 − variable cost, \$80). In either case,

$$\frac{\text{Minimum transfer price}}{\text{per barrel}} = \frac{\text{Incremental cost}}{\text{per barrel}} + \frac{\text{Opportunity cost}}{\text{per barrel}}$$

$$= \$73 + \$12 = \$85$$

or

$$= \$80 + \$5 = \$85$$

2. **An intermediate market exists that is not perfectly competitive and the selling division has unused capacity.** In markets that are not perfectly competitive, companies can increase capacity utilization only by decreasing prices. Unused capacity exists because decreasing prices is often not worthwhile because it decreases operating income.

   If the transportation division at Horizon Petroleum has unused capacity, its opportunity cost of transferring the oil internally is zero because the division does not forgo any external sales or contribution margin from internal transfers. In this case,

$$\frac{\text{Minimum transfer price}}{\text{per barrel}} = \frac{\text{Incremental cost}}{\text{per barrel}} = \begin{array}{c}\text{\$73 per barrel for oil purchased under the}\\ \text{long-term contract or \$80 per barrel for}\\ \text{oil purchased from Gulfmex in Matamoros}\end{array}$$

   In general, when markets are not perfectly competitive, the potential to influence demand and operating income through prices complicates the measurement of opportunity costs. The transfer price depends on constantly changing levels of supply and demand. There is not just one transfer price. Rather, the transfer prices for various quantities supplied and demanded depend on the incremental costs and opportunity costs of the units transferred.

3. **No market exists for the intermediate product.** This situation would occur for the Horizon Petroleum case if the crude oil transported by the transportation division could be used only by the Houston refinery (due to, say, its high tar content) and would not be wanted by external parties. Here, the opportunity cost of supplying crude oil internally is zero because the inability to sell crude oil externally means no contribution margin is forgone. For the transportation division of Horizon Petroleum, the minimum transfer price under the general guideline is the incremental cost per barrel (either \$73 or \$80). As in the previous case, any transfer price between the incremental cost and \$85 will achieve goal congruence.

Keys to Success

With competitive markets, top management must use the market price as the transfer price; in all other cases, the sum of the incremental and opportunity costs of the selling division is the minimum of the range of feasible prices that will induce goal congruence.

Learning Objective 9

Understand how taxes affect transfer pricing at multinational corporations

. . . set transfer prices to minimize tax payments to the extent permitted by tax authorities

Multinational Transfer Pricing and Tax Considerations

Transfer pricing is an important accounting priority for managers around the world. A 2010 Ernst & Young survey of multinational enterprises in 25 countries found that 74% of parent firms and 76% of subsidiary respondents believed that transfer pricing was "absolutely critical" or "very important" to their organizations. The reason is that parent companies can save large sums of money in taxes if they choose an appropriate transfer pricing policy. Consider Google, which has a 90% market share of UK Internet searches and earned £6 billion in advertising revenues in the United Kingdom from 2004 to 2010. Yet, despite a UK corporate income tax rate of 28%, Google UK paid just £8 million in taxes during that time. How is that possible? To start, Google has licensed the offshore rights to its intellectual property to Google Ireland Holdings, an Irish company whose management is centered in Bermuda, thereby exempting it from Irish taxes. When Google earns revenue from a customer in Britain, that amount is credited to a different Irish entity, Google Ireland Limited, located in Dublin. About 88% of Google's non-U.S. revenues flow through this entity. However, the entity records a minimal amount of pretax profit because it pays a royalty fee to the Bermuda/Irish company for the use of Google's intellectual property. Rather than pay the amount directly, which would trigger an Irish withholding tax, the money is routed through Google Netherlands Holdings BV (Amsterdam), a company that has no employees.[6] These techniques are estimated to have saved Google about $1 billion a year. Other companies that are built on intellectual property have used similar transfer pricing practices, including Facebook, Microsoft, and Forest Laboratories. Such profit-shifting arrangements are estimated to save companies as much as $60 billion annually.[7]

Transfer prices affect not just income taxes but also payroll taxes, customs duties, tariffs, sales taxes, value-added taxes, environment-related taxes, and other government levies. Our aim here is to highlight tax factors, and in particular income taxes, as important considerations for managers when determining transfer prices.

Transfer Pricing for Tax Minimization

Consider the Horizon Petroleum data in Exhibit 15-2 (page 633). Assume that the transportation division based in Mexico pays Mexican income taxes at 30% of operating income and that the refining division based in the United States pays income taxes at 20% of operating income. Horizon Petroleum would minimize its total income tax payments with the 105%-of-full-cost transfer-pricing method, as shown in the following table, because this method minimizes income reported in Mexico, where income is taxed at a higher rate than in the United States.

	Operating Income for 100 Barrels of Crude Oil			Income Tax on 100 Barrels of Crude Oil		
Transfer-Pricing Method	Transportation Division (Mexico) (1)	Refining Division (United States) (2)	Total (3) = (1) + (2)	Transportation Division (Mexico) (4) = 0.30 × (1)	Refining Division (United States) (5) = 0.20 × (2)	Total (6) = (4) + (5)
Market price	$900	$300	$1,200	$270	$60	$330
105% of full costs	380	820	1,200	114	164	278
Hybrid price	600	600	1,200	180	120	300

[6] This arrangement, which involves transfers between two Irish entities via the Netherlands, is referred to by tax planners as "Double Irish" or "Dutch Sandwich"; see http://www.businessweek.com/technology/google-tax-cut/google-terminal.html. For a detailed description of Apple's use of this structure, see http://www.nytimes.com/interactive/2012/04/28/business/Double-Irish-With-A-Dutch-Sandwich.html?ref=business.

[7] It is important to understand that U.S. companies pay no taxes to the IRS until the profits are repatriated back to the United States. As a result, the incentive for top management is to keep and reinvest cash overseas rather than in the United States. For example, as of March 2012, Apple had $64 billion in cash overseas. According to Apple CFO Peter Oppenheimer, "We think that the current tax laws provide a considerable economic disincentive to U.S. companies that might otherwise repatriate."

Income tax considerations raise additional issues. Tax issues may conflict with other objectives top management hopes to achieve via transfer pricing. Suppose the market for crude oil in Houston is perfectly competitive. In this case, the market-based transfer price achieves goal congruence, provides incentives for management effort, and helps Horizon to evaluate the economic profitability of the transportation division. But this transfer price is costly from the perspective of income taxes. To minimize income taxes, Horizon would favor using 105% of full cost for tax reporting. Tax laws in the United States and Mexico, however, constrain this option. In particular, the Mexican tax authorities, aware of Horizon's incentives to minimize income taxes by reducing the income reported in Mexico, would challenge any attempts to shift income to the refining division through an unreasonably low transfer price (see Concepts in Action: Transfer-Pricing Dispute Temporarily Stops the Flow of Fiji Water).

Section 482 of the U.S. Internal Revenue Code governs taxation of multinational transfer pricing. Section 482 requires that transfer prices between a company and its foreign division or subsidiary, for both tangible and intangible property, equal the price that an outside third party would charge in a comparable transaction. Regulations related to Section 482 recognize that transfer prices can be market-based or cost-plus-based, where the plus represents margins on comparable transactions.[8]

If the market for crude oil in Houston is perfectly competitive, Horizon would be required to calculate taxes using the market price of $85 for transfers from the transportation division to the

Concepts in Action: Transfer-Pricing Dispute Temporarily Stops the Flow of Fiji Water

From 2008 until 2010, Fiji Water, LLC, a U.S.-based company, was engaged in a fierce transfer-pricing dispute with the government of the Fiji Islands, where its water bottling plant is located. While Fiji Water is produced in the Fiji Islands, all other activities in the company's value chain—importing, distributing, and retailing—occur in the 40 countries where Fiji Water is sold. Over time, the Fiji Islands government became concerned that Fiji Water was engaging in transfer-price manipulations, selling the water shipments produced in the Fiji Islands at a very low price to the company's U.S. headquarters.

Source: John Nordell/The Image Works

As a result, the Fiji Islands Revenue and Customs Authority (FIRCA) halted Fuji Water exports in January 2008 and accused Fiji Water of transfer-price manipulations. FIRCA's chief executive, Jitoko Tikolevu, said, "The wholly U.S.-owned Fijian subsidiary sold its water exclusively to its U.S. parent at the declared rate, in Fiji, of $4 a carton. In the U.S., though, the same company then sold it for up to $50 a carton." Fiji Water immediately filed a lawsuit against FIRCA with the High Court of Fiji arguing that on a global basis it sold each carton of water for $20 – $28, and it did not make a profit due to "heavy investments in assets, employees, and marketing necessary to aggressively grow a successful branded product."

The transfer-pricing dispute between FICRA and Fiji Water was not permanently resolved due to political instability in Fiji. While Fiji Water maintained its previous transfer price of $4 for water produced at its bottling plant in the Fiji Islands, the Fijian government implemented a new 15-cents-per-liter excise tax on water extracted by Fiji Water. While the company disputed the new tax, in late 2010 the company agreed to pay the new levy. As this high-profile case demonstrates, transfer pricing formulas and taxation details remain a contentious issue for governments and countries around the globe.

Sources: Based on Robert Matau, "Fiji Water explains saga." *Fiji Times* (February 9, 2008); James McMaster and Jan Novak. "Fiji Water and corporate social responsibility—Green makeover or 'green-washing'?" The University of Western Ontario Richard Ivey School of Business No. 909A08 (London, Ontario: Ivey Publishing, 2009); Paul Chapman, "Fiji Water reopens Pacific bottling plant," *The Telegraph* (December 1, 2010).

[8] J. Styron, "Transfer Pricing and Tax Planning: Opportunities for US Corporations Operating Abroad," *CPA Journal Online* (November 2007); R. Feinschreiber (Ed.), *Transfer Pricing Handbook,* 3rd ed. (New York: Wiley, 2002).

refining division. Horizon might successfully argue that the transfer price should be set below the market price because the transportation division incurs no marketing and distribution costs when selling crude oil to the refining division. For example, if marketing and distribution costs equal \$2 per barrel, Horizon could set the transfer price at \$83 (\$85 − \$2) per barrel, the selling price net of marketing and distribution costs. Under the U.S. Internal Revenue Code, Horizon could obtain advanced approval of the transfer-pricing arrangements from the tax authorities, called an *advance pricing agreement (APA)*. The APA is a binding agreement for a specified number of years. The goal of the APA program is to avoid costly transfer-pricing disputes between taxpayers and tax authorities. As of the end of 2011, the APA program had completed 1,015 APAs since inception and had pending requests for another 258 new APAs. In 2011 alone, there were 42 APAs executed, of which 34 were bilateral agreements with other tax treaty countries. Walmart, for example, signed the first bilateral APA between the United States and China in 2007.

The recent global recession has pushed governments around the world to impose tighter trading rules and more aggressively pursue tax revenues. The number of countries that have imposed transfer-pricing regulations approximately quadrupled from 1995 to 2007, according to a 2008 KPMG report. Officials in China, where foreign businesses enjoyed favorable treatment until recently, has issued new rules requiring multinationals to submit extensive transfer-pricing documentation. Countries such as India, Canada, Turkey, and Greece have brought greater scrutiny to bear on transfer pricing, focusing in particular on intellectual-property values, costs of back-office functions, and losses of any type. In the United States, the Obama administration proposed plans in 2009 to shrink a "tax gap" the IRS estimates may be as high as \$345 billion by restricting or closing several widely used tax loopholes. While the plan does not directly address transfer-pricing practice, the IRS has become more aggressive with enforcement. The agency added 1,200 people to its international staff in 2009, and the 2010 budget called for hiring another 800. In 2011, the IRS named its first director of transfer pricing and, in early 2012, raised inquiries or disputes with a variety of technology firms, including Amazon, Adobe, Juniper Networks, and Yahoo. With Amazon, the IRS has proposed a \$1.5 billion tax increase related to transfer pricing for the period 2005–2012. In 2006, the IRS won the largest settlement ever in a transfer-pricing dispute, getting GlaxoSmithKline, a UK-based pharmaceutical and healthcare company, to pay \$3.4 billion to cover back taxes and interest for the period 1989–2005. Of course, the IRS is not always successful in its claims, as illustrated by Concepts in Action: Symantec Wins \$545 Million Opinion in Transfer-Pricing Dispute with the IRS.

Transfer Prices Designed for Multiple Objectives

We have seen that top management uses transfer-pricing policy to meet a variety of objectives. At times it is infeasible for one price to satisfy all of the objectives, such as minimizing income taxes, achieving goal congruence, and motivating management effort. As a result, a company may choose to keep one set of accounting records for tax reporting and a second set for internal management reporting. Of course, it is costly to maintain two sets of books. Companies such as Case New Holland, a world leader in the agricultural and construction equipment business, also oppose it on the principle that statutory and internal reporting systems must reflect the same information. However, a survey by the AnswerThink Consulting Group of large companies (more than \$2 billion in revenues) found that 77% of companies considered to follow "best practices" used separate reporting systems to track internal pricing information, compared with about 25% of companies outside that group. Microsoft, for example, believes in "delinking" transfer pricing and employs an internal measurement system (Microsoft Accounting Principles, or MAPs) that uses a separate set of company-designed rules and accounts.[9] A key aspect of management control at Microsoft is the desire to hold local managers accountable for product profitability and to establish appropriate sales and marketing spending levels for every product line. To establish these sales and spending levels, the firm creates a profitability statement for every product in every region, and allocates G&A and R&D costs across sales divisions in ways that aren't necessarily the most tax-efficient.

Even if a company does not have such formal separated reporting systems, top management can still informally adjust transfer prices to satisfy the tradeoff between tax minimization and incentive provision. Consider a multinational firm that makes semiconductor products that it sells through its sales organization in a higher-tax country. To minimize taxes, the parent sets a high transfer price, thereby lowering the operating income of the foreign sales organization. It would be inappropriate to penalize the country sales manager for this low income since the sales organization

[9] For further details, see I. Springsteel, "Separate but Unequal," *CFO Magazine* (August 1999).

Concepts in Action: Symantec Wins $545 Million Opinion in Transfer-Pricing Dispute with the IRS

Source: Tony Avelar/Bloomberg via Getty Images

Symantec Corp., a large U.S. software company, won a court decision in 2009, saving it $545 million in contested back taxes. The Internal Revenue Service (IRS) was seeking back taxes it alleged were owed by Veritas Software Corp., a company Symantec acquired in 2005. The dispute was over the company's formula for "transfer pricing," a complex set of rules determining how companies set prices, fees, and cost-allocation arrangements between their operations in different tax jurisdictions.

At issue were the fees and cost-allocation arrangements between Veritas and its Irish subsidiary, which was granted rights to conduct research and development on various intangibles (such as computer programs and manufacturing process technologies) related to data-storage software and related devices. Under the agreement, Veritas Ireland paid $160 million for this grant of rights from 1999 to 2001. Based on a discounted cash flow analysis, the IRS contended that the true value of the transferred rights was closer to $1.675 billion. As a consequence, the IRS claimed that the transaction artificially increased the income of Veritas Ireland at the expense of income in the U.S. parent corporation, consequently lowering the company's U.S. tax bills.

Veritas, however, maintained that it acted appropriately. Veritas testified that the $160 million figure was based on royalty rates it had received from original equipment manufacturers for rights to incorporate the company's U.S. software and technologies into an operating system, with adjustments made for purposes of comparability. At trial, the United States Tax Court supported this position and called the IRS's valuation of the intangibles "arbitrary, capricious, and unreasonable." While Symantec was victorious in this case, the company was unsuccessful in another recent transfer-pricing case in India that dealt with the use of comparable data and multiyear data.

Sources: Based on Cabell Chinnis, et al., "Tax court upends IRS's billion dollar buy-in valuation adjustment in 'Veritas,'" Mondaq Business Briefing (December 17, 2009); John Letzing, "Symantec wins $545M opinion in tax case," Dow Jones News Service (December 11, 2009); Anonymous "Indian Revenue opportunism rules out multiple year data," *Transfer Pricing Week* (August 17, 2011).

has no say in determining the transfer price. As an alternative, the company can evaluate the sales manager on the direct contribution (revenues minus marketing costs) incurred in the country. That is, the transfer price incurred to acquire the semiconductor products is omitted for performance-evaluation purposes. Of course, this is not a perfect solution. By ignoring the cost of acquiring the products, the sales manager has incentives to overspend on local marketing relative to what would be optimal from the firm's overall perspective. If the dysfunctional effects of this are suitably large, corporate managers must then step in, evaluate the numbers and situation, and dictate specific operational guidelines and goals for the manager. More generally, adoption of a tax-compliant transfer-pricing policy creates a need for nonfinancial performance indicators (such as production yields, shipments, customer response times, or segment sales) at lower management levels in order to better evaluate and reward performance.[10]

Additional Issues in Transfer Pricing: Tariffs and Customs Duties

Additional factors that arise in multinational transfer pricing include tariffs and customs duties governments levy on imports of products into a country. The issues here are similar to income tax considerations: Companies will have incentives to lower transfer prices for products imported into a country to reduce tariffs and customs duties charged on those products.

[10] Cools et al., "Management control in the transfer pricing tax compliant multinational enterprise," *Accounting, Organizations and Society* (August 2008), provides an illustrative case study of this issue in the context of a semiconductor product division of a multinational firm.

In addition to the motivations for choosing transfer prices already described, multinational transfer prices are sometimes influenced by restrictions that some countries place on dividend- or income-related payments to parties outside their national borders. By increasing the prices of goods or services transferred into divisions in these countries, companies can seek to increase the cash paid out of these countries without violating dividend- or income-related restrictions.

> **Keys to Success**
> **In multinational settings, top management must choose transfer prices carefully to balance tax minimization considerations (income taxes, tariffs, and duties), currency repatriation issues, and the evaluation of divisional managerial performance.**

Problem for Self-Study

The Pillercat Corporation is a highly decentralized company. Each division manager has full authority for sourcing decisions and selling decisions. The machining division of Pillercat has been the major supplier of the 2,000 crankshafts that the tractor division needs each year.

The tractor division, however, has just announced that it plans to purchase all its crankshafts in the forthcoming year from two external suppliers at $200 per crankshaft. The machining division of Pillercat recently increased its selling price for the forthcoming year to $220 per unit (from $200 per unit in the current year).

Juan Gomez, manager of the machining division, feels that the 10% price increase is justified. The increase results from a higher depreciation charge on some new specialized equipment used to manufacture crankshafts and an increase in labor costs. Gomez wants the president of Pillercat Corporation to force the tractor division to buy all its crankshafts from the machining division at the price of $220. The following table summarizes the key data.

	A	B
1	Number of crankshafts purchased by tractor division	2,000
2	External supplier's market price per crankshaft	$ 200
3	Variable cost per crankshaft in machining division	$ 190
4	Fixed cost per crankshaft in machining division	$ 20

Required

1. Compute the advantage or disadvantage in terms of annual operating income to the Pillercat Corporation as a whole if the tractor division buys crankshafts internally from the machining division under each of the following cases:
   a. The machining division has no alternative use for the facilities used to manufacture crankshafts.
   b. The machining division can use the facilities for other production operations, which will result in annual cash operating savings of $29,000.
   c. The machining division has no alternative use for its facilities, and the external supplier drops the price to $185 per crankshaft.
2. As the president of Pillercat, how would you respond to Juan Gomez's request that you force the tractor division to purchase all of its crankshafts from the machining division? Would your response differ according to the three cases described in requirement 1? Explain.

Solution

1. Computations for the tractor division buying crankshafts internally for 1 year under cases **a**, **b**, and **c** are as follows:

	A	B	C	D
1			Case	
2		a	b	c
3	Number of crankshafts purchased by tractor division	2,000	2,000	2,000
4	External supplier's market price per crankshaft	$ 200	$ 200	$ 185
5	Variable cost per crankshaft in machining division	$ 190	$ 190	$ 190
6	Opportunity costs of the machining division supplying crankshafts to the tractor division	-	$ 29,000	-
7				
8	Total purchase costs if buying from an external supplier			
9	(2,000 shafts × $200, $200, $185 per shaft)	$400,000	$400,000	$370,000
10	Incremental cost of buying from the machining division			
11	(2,000 shafts × $190 per shaft)	380,000	380,000	380,000
12	Total opportunity costs of the machining division	-	29,000	-
13	Total relevant costs	380,000	409,000	380,000
14	Annual operating income advantage (disadvantage) to			
15	Pillercat of buying from the machining division	$ 20,000	$ (9,000)	$ (10,000)

The general guideline that was introduced in the chapter (page 640) as a first step in setting a transfer price can be used to highlight the alternatives:

	A	B	C	D	E	F	G
1	Case	Incremental Cost per Unit Incurred to Point of Transfer	+	Opportunity Cost per Unit to the Supplying Division	=	Transfer Price	External Market Price
2	a	$190	+	$0	=	$190.00	$200
3	b	$190	+	$14.50[a]	=	$204.50	$200
4	c	$190	+	$0	=	$190.00	$185
5							
6–7	[a]Opportunity cost per unit	=	Total opportunity costs	÷	Number of crankshafts	= $29,000 ÷ 2,000 = $14.50	

Comparing transfer price to external-market price, the tractor division will maximize annual operating income of Pillercat Corporation as a whole by purchasing from the machining division in case **a** and by purchasing from the external supplier in cases **b** and **c.**

2. Pillercat Corporation is a highly decentralized company. If no forced transfer were made, the tractor division would use an external supplier, a decision that would be in the best interest of the company as a whole in cases **b** and **c** of requirement 1 but not in case **a.**

   Suppose in case **a** the machining division refuses to meet the price of $200. This decision means that the company will be $20,000 worse off in the short run. Should top management interfere and force a transfer at $200? This interference would undercut the philosophy of decentralization. Many top managers would not interfere because they would view the $20,000 as an inevitable cost of a suboptimal decision that can occur under decentralization. But how high must this cost be before managers are tempted to interfere? $30,000? $40,000?

   Any top management interference with lower-level decision making weakens decentralization. Of course, Pillercat's management may occasionally interfere to prevent costly mistakes. But recurring interference and constraints would hurt Pillercat's attempts to operate as a decentralized company.

Decision Points

The following question-and-answer format summarizes the chapter's learning objectives. Each decision presents a key question related to a learning objective. The guidelines are the answer to that question.

Decision	Guidelines
1. What is a management control system and how should it be designed?	A management control system is a means of gathering and using information to aid and coordinate the planning and control decisions throughout the organization and to guide the behavior of managers and other employees. Effective management control systems (a) are closely aligned to the organization's strategy, (b) support the organizational responsibilities of individual managers, and (c) motivate managers and other employees to give effort to achieve the organization's goals.
2. What are the benefits and costs of decentralization?	The benefits of decentralization include (a) greater responsiveness to local needs, (b) gains from faster decision making, (c) increased motivation of subunit managers, (d) greater management development and learning, and (e) sharpened focus of subunit managers. The costs of decentralization include (a) suboptimal decision making, (b) excessive focus on the subunit rather than the company as a whole, (c) increased costs of information gathering, and (d) duplication of activities.
3. What are transfer prices, and what criteria do managers use to evaluate them?	A transfer price is the price one subunit charges for a product or service supplied to another subunit of the same organization. Transfer prices seek to (a) promote goal congruence, (b) motivate management effort, (c) help evaluate subunit performance, and (d) preserve subunit autonomy (if desired).
4. What are three alternative methods of calculating transfer prices?	Transfer prices can be (a) market-based, (b) cost-based, or (c) hybrid. Different transfer-pricing methods produce different revenues and costs for individual subunits, and so, different operating incomes for the subunits.
5. Under what market conditions do market-based transfer prices promote goal congruence?	In perfectly competitive markets, there is no unused capacity, and division managers can buy and sell as much of a product or service as they want at the market price. In such settings, using the market price as the transfer price motivates division managers to transact internally and to take exactly the same actions as they would if they were transacting in the external market.
6. What problems can arise when a firm uses full cost plus a markup as the transfer price?	A transfer price based on full cost plus a markup may lead to suboptimal decisions because it leads the buying division to regard the fixed costs and the markup of the selling division as a variable cost. The buying division may then purchase products from an external supplier expecting savings in costs that, in fact, will not occur.
7. Within a range of feasible transfer prices, what are alternative ways for firms to arrive at the eventual hybrid price?	When there is unused capacity, the transfer-price range lies between the minimum price at which the selling division is willing to sell (its variable cost per unit) and the maximum price the buying division is willing to pay (the lower of its contribution or the price at which the product is available from external suppliers). Methods for arriving at a price in this range include proration (such as splitting the difference equally or on the basis of relative variable costs), negotiation between divisions, and dual pricing.
8. What is the general guideline for determining a minimum transfer price?	The general guideline states that the minimum transfer price equals the incremental cost per unit incurred up to the point of transfer plus the opportunity cost per unit to the selling division resulting from transferring products or services internally.
9. How do income-tax considerations affect transfer pricing in multinationals?	Transfer prices can reduce income tax payments by reporting more income in low-tax-rate countries and less income in high-tax-rate countries. However, tax regulations of different countries restrict the transfer prices that companies can use.

Terms to Learn

This chapter and the Glossary at the end of the book contain definitions of the following important terms:

autonomy (p. 626)
centralization (p. 626)
decentralization (p. 626)
dual pricing (p. 639)
dysfunctional decision making (p. 627)
effort (p. 626)
goal congruence (p. 626)
incongruent decision making (p. 627)
intermediate product (p. 630)
management control system (p. 625)
motivation (p. 626)
perfectly competitive market (p. 633)
suboptimal decision making (p. 627)
transfer price (p. 630)

Assignment Material

Questions

15-1 Describe three criteria you would use to evaluate whether a management control system is effective.

15-2 Name three benefits and two costs of decentralization.

15-3 What properties should transfer-pricing systems have?

15-4 "All transfer-pricing methods give the same division operating income." Do you agree? Explain.

15-5 Under what conditions is a market-based transfer price optimal?

15-6 What is one potential limitation of full-cost-based transfer prices?

15-7 "Cost and price information play no role in negotiated transfer prices." Do you agree? Explain.

15-8 "Under the general guideline for transfer pricing, the minimum transfer price will vary depending on whether the supplying division has unused capacity or not." Do you agree? Explain.

15-9 How should managers consider income-tax issues when choosing a transfer-pricing method?

15-10 What issues other than taxes are important when setting transfer prices for multinational companies?

Exercises

15-11 Evaluating management control systems, balanced scorecard. Experience Parks Inc. (EPI) operates 12 theme parks throughout the United States. The company's slogan is "Feel the Excitement," and its mission is to offer an exciting theme-park experience to visitors of all ages. EPI's corporate strategy supports this mission by stressing the importance of sparkling clean surroundings, efficient crowd management, and, above all, cheerful employees. Of course, improved shareholder value drives this strategy.

Required

1. Assume that EPI uses a balanced scorecard approach (see Chapter 14) to formulate its management control system. List three measures that EPI might use to evaluate each of the four balanced-scorecard perspectives: financial perspective, customer perspective, internal-business-process perspective, and learning-and-growth perspective.
2. How would the management controls related to financial and customer perspectives at EPI differ between the following three managers: a souvenir shop manager, a park general manager, and the corporation's CEO?

15-12 Cost centers, profit centers, decentralization. Dormer Corporation manufactures windows with wood and metal frames. Dormer has three departments: glass, wood, and metal. The glass department makes the window glass and sends it to either the wood or metal department where the glass is framed. The window is then sold. Upper management sets the production schedules for the three departments and evaluates them on output quantity, cost variances, and product quality.

Required

1. Are the three departments cost centers, revenue centers, or profit centers?
2. Are the three departments centralized or decentralized?
3. Can a centralized department be a profit center? Why or why not?

15-13 Benefits and costs of decentralization. Branca Markets, a chain of traditional supermarkets, is interested in gaining access to the organic and health food retail market by acquiring a regional company in that sector. Branca intends to operate the newly acquired stores independently from its supermarkets.

One of the prospects is Fresh Source, a chain of 20 stores in the mid-Atlantic. Buying for all 20 stores is done by the company's central office. Store managers must follow strict guidelines for all aspects of store management in an attempt to maintain consistency among stores. Store managers are evaluated on the basis of achieving profit goals developed by the central office.

The other prospect is Singing Moon, a chain of 30 stores in the Northeast. Singing Moon managers are given significant flexibility in product offerings, allowing them to negotiate purchases with local organic farmers. Store managers are rewarded for exceeding self-developed return on investment goals with company stock options. Some managers have become significant shareholders in the company, and have even decided on their own to open additional store locations to improve market penetration. However, the increased autonomy has led to competition and price cutting among Singing Moon stores within the same geographic market, resulting in lower margins.

Required

1. Would you describe Fresh Source as having a centralized or a decentralized structure? Explain.
2. Would you describe Singing Moon as having a centralized or a decentralized structure? Discuss some of the benefits and costs of that type of structure.
3. Would stores in each chain be considered cost centers, revenue centers, profit centers, or investment centers? How does that tie into the evaluation of store managers?
4. Assume that Branca chooses to acquire Singing Moon. What steps can Branca take to improve goal congruence between store managers and the larger company?

15-14 Multinational transfer pricing, effect of alternative transfer-pricing methods, global income-tax minimization. User Able Computer, Inc., with headquarters in San Francisco, manufactures and sells desktop computers. User Able has three divisions, each of which is located in a different country:

a. China division—manufactures memory devices and keyboards
b. South Korea division—assembles desktop computers using locally manufactured parts, along with memory devices and keyboards from the China division
c. U.S. division—packages and distributes desktop computers

Each division is run as a profit center. The costs for the work done in each division for a single desktop computer are as follows:

China division: Variable cost = 875 yuan
Fixed cost = 1,575 yuan
South Korea division: Variable cost = 375,000 won
Fixed cost = 525,000 won
U.S. division: Variable cost = $75
Fixed cost = $175

- Chinese income-tax rate on the China division's operating income: 32%
- South Korean income-tax rate on the South Korea division's operating income: 24%
- U.S. income-tax rate on the U.S. division's operating income: 40%

Each desktop computer is sold to retail outlets in the United States for $3,400. Assume that the current foreign exchange rates are:

7 yuan = $1 U.S.
1,500 won = $1 U.S.

Both the China and the South Korea divisions sell part of their production under a private label. The China division sells the comparable memory/keyboard package used in each User Able desktop computer to a Chinese manufacturer for 2,800 yuan. The South Korea division sells the comparable desktop computer to a South Korean distributor for 1,725,000 won.

Required

1. Calculate the after-tax operating income per unit (in dollars) earned by each division under the following transfer-pricing methods: (a) market price, (b) 200% of full cost, and (c) 300% of variable cost. (Costs transferred in from prior divisions are included in the computation of the cost-based transfer prices but income taxes are excluded.)
2. Which transfer-pricing method(s) will maximize the after-tax operating income per unit of User Able Computer?

15-15 Transfer-pricing methods, goal congruence. Calgary Lumber has a raw lumber division and a finished lumber division. The variable costs are:

- Raw lumber division: $130 per 100 board-feet of raw lumber
- Finished lumber division: $155 per 100 board-feet of finished lumber

Assume that there is no board-feet loss in processing raw lumber into finished lumber. Raw lumber can be sold at $255 per 100 board-feet. Finished lumber can be sold at $330 per 100 board-feet.

Required

1. Should Calgary Lumber process raw lumber into its finished form? Show your calculations.
2. Assume that internal transfers are made at 150% of variable cost. Will each division maximize its division operating-income contribution by adopting the action that is in the best interest of Calgary Lumber as a whole? Explain.
3. Assume that internal transfers are made at market prices. Will each division maximize its division operating-income contribution by adopting the action that is in the best interest of Calgary Lumber as a whole? Explain.

15-16 Effect of alternative transfer-pricing methods on division operating income. (CMA, adapted) Aken Corporation has two divisions. The mining division makes toldine, which is then transferred to the metals division. The toldine is further processed by the metals division and is sold to customers at a price of $180 per unit. The mining division is currently required by Aken to transfer its total yearly output of 235,000 units of toldine to the metals division at 125% of full manufacturing cost. Unlimited quantities of toldine can be purchased and sold on the outside market at $75 per unit.

The following table gives the manufacturing cost per unit in the mining and metals divisions for 2013:

	Mining Division	Metals Division
Direct material cost	$18	$12
Direct manufacturing labor cost	20	26
Manufacturing overhead cost	30[a]	40[b]
Total manufacturing cost per unit	$68	$78

[a]Manufacturing overhead costs in the mining division are 30% fixed and 70% variable.
[b]Manufacturing overhead costs in the metals division are 65% fixed and 35% variable.

Required

1. Calculate the operating incomes for the mining and metals divisions for the 235,000 units of toldine transferred under the following transfer-pricing methods: (a) market price and (b) 125% of full manufacturing cost.
2. Suppose Aken rewards each division manager with a bonus, calculated as 1% of division operating income (if positive). What is the amount of bonus each division manager will receive under the transfer-pricing methods in requirement 1? Which transfer-pricing method will each division manager prefer to use?
3. What arguments would Bryce Jones, manager of the metals division, make to support the transfer-pricing method that he prefers?

15-17 Transfer pricing, general guideline, goal congruence. (CMA, adapted). Fermi Motors, Inc., operates as a decentralized multidivision company. The Vevo division of Fermi Motors purchases most of its airbags from the airbag division. The airbag division's incremental cost for manufacturing the airbags is $200 per unit. The airbag division is currently working at 75% of capacity. The current market price of the airbags is $225 per unit.

Required

1. Using the general guideline presented in the chapter, what is the minimum price at which the airbag division would sell airbags to the Vevo division?
2. Suppose that Fermi Motors requires that whenever divisions with unused capacity sell products internally, they must do so at the incremental cost. Evaluate this transfer-pricing policy using the criteria of goal congruence, evaluating division performance, motivating management effort, and preserving division autonomy.

3. If the two divisions were to negotiate a transfer price, what is the range of possible transfer prices? Evaluate this negotiated transfer-pricing policy using the criteria of goal congruence, evaluating division performance, motivating management effort, and preserving division autonomy.
4. Instead of allowing negotiation, suppose that Fermi specifies a hybrid transfer price that "splits the difference" between the minimum and maximum prices from the divisions' standpoint. What would be the resulting transfer price for airbags?

15-18 Multinational transfer pricing, global tax minimization. The Questron Company manufactures telecommunications equipment at its plant in Scranton, Pennsylvania. The company has marketing divisions throughout the world. A Questron marketing division in Hamburg, Germany, imports 100,000 broadband routers from the United States. The following information is available:

U.S. income tax rate on the U.S. division's operating income	35%
German income tax rate on the German division's operating income	40%
German import duty	15%
Variable manufacturing cost per router	$275
Full manufacturing cost per router	$400
Selling price (net of marketing and distribution costs) in Germany	$575

Suppose the United States and German tax authorities only allow transfer prices that are between the full manufacturing cost per unit of $400 and a market price of $475, based on comparable imports into Germany. The German import duty is charged on the price at which the product is transferred into Germany. Any import duty paid to the German authorities is a deductible expense for calculating German income taxes.

Required

1. Calculate the after-tax operating income earned by the United States and German divisions from transferring 100,000 broadband routers (a) at full manufacturing cost per unit and (b) at market price of comparable imports. (Income taxes are not included in the computation of the cost-based transfer prices.)
2. Which transfer price should the Questron Company select to minimize the total of company import duties and income taxes? Remember that the transfer price must be between the full manufacturing cost per unit of $400 and the market price of $475 of comparable imports into Germany. Explain your reasoning.

15-19 Multinational transfer pricing, goal congruence (continuation of 15-18). Suppose that the U.S. division could sell as many broadband routers as it makes at $450 per unit in the U.S. market, net of all marketing and distribution costs.

Required

1. From the viewpoint of the Questron Company as a whole, would after-tax operating income be maximized if it sold the 100,000 routers in the United States or in Germany? Show your computations.
2. Suppose division managers act autonomously to maximize their division's after-tax operating income. Will the transfer price calculated in requirement 2 in Exercise 15-18 result in the U.S. division manager taking the actions determined to be optimal in requirement 1 of this exercise? Explain.
3. What is the minimum transfer price that the U.S. division manager would agree to? Does this transfer price result in the Questron Company as a whole paying more import duty and taxes than the answer to requirement 2 in Exercise 15-18? If so, by how much?

15-20 Transfer-pricing dispute. The Michael-Brown Corporation, a manufacturer of tractors and other heavy farm equipment, is organized along decentralized product lines, with each manufacturing division operating as a separate profit center. Each division manager has been delegated full authority on all decisions involving the sale of that division's output both to outsiders and to other divisions of Michael-Brown. Division C has in the past always purchased its requirement of a particular tractor-engine component from division A. However, when informed that division A is increasing its selling price to $155, division C's manager decides to purchase the engine component from external suppliers.

Division C can purchase the component for $145 per unit in the open market. Division A insists that, because of the recent installation of some highly specialized equipment and the resulting high depreciation charges, it will not be able to earn an adequate return on its investment unless it raises its price. Division A's manager appeals to top management of Michael-Brown for support in the dispute with division C and supplies the following operating data:

C's annual purchases of the tractor-engine component	1,500 units
A's variable cost per unit of the tractor-engine component	$115
A's fixed cost per unit of the tractor-engine component	$ 25

Required

1. Assume that there are no alternative uses for internal facilities of division A. Determine whether the company as a whole will benefit if division C purchases the component from external suppliers for $145 per unit. How should the transfer price for the component be set so that division managers acting in their own divisions' best interests take actions that are also in the best interest of the company as a whole?
2. Assume that internal facilities of division A would not otherwise be idle. By not producing the 1,500 units for division C, division A's equipment and other facilities would be used for other production operations that would result in annual cash-operating savings of $24,000. Should division C purchase from external suppliers? Show your computations.
3. Assume that there are no alternative uses for division A's internal facilities and that the price from outsiders drops $35. Should division C purchase from external suppliers? How should the transfer price for the component be set so that division managers acting in their own divisions' best interests take actions that are also in the best interest of the company as a whole?

15-21 Transfer-pricing problem (continuation of 15-20). Refer to Exercise 15-20. Assume that division A can sell the 1,500 units to other customers at $158 per unit, with a variable marketing cost of $3 per unit.

Required

Determine whether Michael-Brown will benefit if division C purchases the 1,500 units from external suppliers at $145 per unit. Show your computations.

15-22 Ethics, transfer pricing. The Stevens Division of Wertheim Industries manufactures component R25, which it transfers to Parker Division at 150% of variable cost. The variable cost of R25 is $18 per unit. Jim Laker, head of the Stevens Division, calls Sarah Tanner, his accountant, into his office. Laker says, "I am not sure about the fixed- and variable-cost distinctions you are making. I think the variable cost is higher than $18 per unit."

Tanner knows that showing a higher variable cost will increase the Stevens Division's profits and lead to higher bonuses for Laker and other division employees. However, Tanner is uncomfortable about making any changes because she has used the same method to classify costs as either fixed or variable over the last few years. Nevertheless, Tanner recognizes that fixed- and variable-cost distinctions are not always clear-cut.

Required

1. Calculate Stevens Division's contribution margin from transferring 10,000 units of R25 (a) if the variable cost is $18 per unit, and (b) if the variable cost is $22 per unit.
2. Evaluate whether Laker's suggestion to Tanner regarding variable costs is ethical. Would it be ethical for Tanner to revise the variable cost per unit? What steps should Tanner take to resolve the situation?

15-23 General guideline, transfer pricing. The Clover Company manufactures and sells television sets. Its assembly division (AD) buys television screens from the screen division (SD) and assembles the TV sets. The SD, which is operating at capacity, incurs an incremental manufacturing cost of $90 per screen. The SD can sell all its output to the outside market at a price of $135 per screen, after incurring a variable marketing and distribution cost of $6 per screen. If the AD purchases screens from outside suppliers at a price of $135 per screen, it will incur a variable purchasing cost of $2 per screen. Clover's division managers can act autonomously to maximize their own division's operating income.

Required

1. What is the minimum transfer price at which the SD manager would be willing to sell screens to the AD?
2. What is the maximum transfer price at which the AD manager would be willing to purchase screens from the SD?
3. Now suppose that the SD can sell only 85% of its output capacity of 5,000 screens per month on the open market. Capacity cannot be reduced in the short run. The AD can assemble and sell more than 5,000 TV sets per month.
   a. What is the minimum transfer price at which the SD manager would be willing to sell screens to the AD?
   b. From the point of view of Clover's management, how much of the SD output should be transferred to the AD?
   c. If Clover mandates the SD and AD managers to "split the difference" on the minimum and maximum transfer prices they would be willing to negotiate over, what would be the resulting transfer price? Does this price achieve the outcome desired in requirement 3b?

Problems

15-24 Pertinent transfer price. Mod Wheel, Inc., has two divisions, A and B, that manufacture expensive bicycles. Division A produces the bicycle frame and division B assembles the rest of the bicycle onto the frame. There is a market for both the subassembly and the final product. Each division has been designated as a profit center. The transfer price for the subassembly has been set at the long-run average market price. The following data are available for each division:

Selling price for final product	$340
Long-run average selling price for intermediate product	250
Incremental cost per unit for completion in division B	130
Incremental cost per unit in division A	140

The manager of division B has made the following calculation:

Selling price for final product		$340
Transferred-in cost per unit (market)	$250	
Incremental cost per unit for completion	130	380
Contribution (loss) on product		$(40)

Required

1. Should transfers be made to division B if there is no unused capacity in division A? Is the market price the correct transfer price? Show your computations.
2. Assume that division A's maximum capacity for this product is 2,000 units per month and sales to the intermediate market are now 1,200 units. Should 800 units be transferred to division B? At what transfer price? Assume that for a variety of reasons, division A will maintain the $250 selling price indefinitely. That is, division A is not considering lowering the price to outsider buyers even if idle capacity exists.
3. Suppose division A quoted a transfer price of $210 for up to 800 units. What would be the contribution to the company as a whole if a transfer were made? As manager of division B, would you be inclined to buy at $210? Explain.

15-25 Pricing in imperfect markets (continuation of 15-24). Refer to Problem 15-24.

Required

1. Suppose the manager of division A has the option of (a) cutting the external price to $242, with the certainty that sales will rise to 2,000 units or (b) maintaining the external price of $250 for the 1,200 units and transferring the 800 units to division B at a price that would produce the same operating income for division A. What transfer price would produce the same operating income for division A? Is that price consistent with that recommended by the general guideline in the chapter so that the resulting decision would be desirable for the company as a whole?
2. Suppose that if the selling price for the intermediate product were dropped to $242, sales to external parties could be increased to 1,600 units. Division B wants to acquire as many as 800 units if the transfer price is acceptable. For simplicity, assume that there is no external market for the final 400 units of division A's capacity.
   a. Using the general guideline, what is (are) the minimum transfer price(s) that should lead to the correct economic decision? Ignore performance-evaluation considerations.
   b. Compare the total contributions under the alternatives to show why the transfer price(s) recommended lead(s) to the optimal economic decision.

15-26 Effect of alternative transfer-pricing methods on division operating income. Cran Health Products is a cranberry cooperative that operates two divisions, a harvesting division and a processing division. Currently, all of harvesting's output is converted into cranberry juice by the processing division, and the juice is sold to large beverage companies that produce cranberry juice blends. The processing division has a yield of 500 gallons of juice per 1,000 pounds of cranberries. Cost and market price data for the two divisions are:

	A	B	C	D	E
1	**Harvesting Division**			**Processing Division**	
2	Variable cost per pound of cranberries	$0.06		Variable processing cost per gallon of juice produced	$0.35
3	Fixed cost per pound of cranberries	$0.34		Fixed cost per gallon of juice produced	$0.37
4	Selling price per pound of cranberries in outside market	$0.58		Selling price per gallon of juice	$2.40

Required

1. Compute Cran Health's operating income from harvesting 440,000 pounds of cranberries during June 2013 and processing them into juice.
2. Cran Health rewards its division managers with a bonus equal to 6% of operating income. Compute the bonus earned by each division manager in June 2013 for each of the following transfer pricing methods:
   a. 175% of full cost
   b. Market price
3. Which transfer-pricing method will each division manager prefer? How might Cran Health resolve any conflicts that may arise on the issue of transfer pricing?

15-27 Goal-congruence problems with cost-plus transfer-pricing methods, dual-pricing system (continuation of 15-26). Assume that Pat Borges, CEO of Cran Health, had mandated a transfer price equal to 175% of full cost. Now he decides to decentralize some management decisions and distributes a memo that states the following: "Effective immediately, each division of Cran Health is free to make its own decisions regarding the purchase of direct materials and the sale of finished products."

Required

1. Give an example of a goal-congruence problem that will arise if Cran Health continues to use a transfer price of 175% of full cost and Borges's decentralization policy is adopted.
2. Borges feels that a dual transfer-pricing policy will improve goal congruence. He suggests that transfers out of the harvesting division be made at 175% of full cost and transfers into the processing division be made at market price. Compute the operating income of each division under this dual transfer-pricing method when 440,000 pounds of cranberries are harvested during June 2013 and processed into juice.
3. Why is the sum of the division operating incomes computed in requirement 2 different from Cran Health's operating income from harvesting and processing 440,000 pounds of cranberries?
4. Suggest two problems that may arise if Cran Health implements the dual transfer prices described in requirement 2.

15-28 Multinational transfer pricing, global tax minimization. Express Grow Inc., based in Lincoln, Nebraska, has two divisions:

- North Germany mining division, which mines potash in northern Germany
- U.S. processing division, which uses potash in manufacturing top-grade fertilizer

The processing division's yield is 50%: It takes 2 tons of raw potash to produce 1 ton of top-grade fertilizer. Although all of the mining division's output of 12,000 tons of potash is sent for processing in the United States, there is also an active market for potash in Germany. The foreign exchange rate is 0.80 Euro = $1 U.S. The following information is known about the two divisions:

	A	F	G
1	**North Germany Mining Division**		
2	Variable cost per ton of raw potash	72	EURO
3	Fixed cost per ton of raw potash	112	EURO
4	Market price per ton of raw potash	296	EURO
5	Tax rate	30%	
6			
7	**U.S. Processing Division**		
8	Variable cost per ton of fertilizer	48	U.S. dollars
9	Fixed cost per ton of fertilizer	120	U.S. dollars
10	Market price per ton of fertilizer	1,150	U.S. dollars
11	Tax rate	35%	

Required

1. Compute the annual pretax operating income, in U.S. dollars, of each division under the following transfer-pricing methods: (a) 150% of full cost and (b) market price.
2. Compute the after-tax operating income, in U.S. dollars, for each division under the transfer-pricing methods in requirement 1. (Income taxes are not included in the computation of cost-based transfer price, and Express Grow does not pay U.S. income tax on income already taxed in Germany.)

3. If the two division managers are compensated based on after-tax division operating income, which transfer-pricing method will each prefer? Which transfer-pricing method will maximize the total after-tax operating income of Express Grow?
4. In addition to tax minimization, what other factors might Express Grow consider in choosing a transfer-pricing method?

15-29 International transfer pricing, taxes, goal congruence. Castor, a division of Gemini Corporation, is located in the United States. Its effective income tax rate is 30%. Another division of Gemini, Pollux, is located in Canada, where the income tax rate is 40%. Pollux manufactures, among other things, an intermediate product for Castor called IP-2013. Pollux operates at capacity and makes 15,000 units of IP-2013 for Castor each period, at a variable cost of $56 per unit. Assume that there are no outside customers for IP-2013. Because the IP-2013 must be shipped from Canada to the United States, it costs Pollux an additional $8 per unit to ship the IP-2013 to Castor. There are no direct fixed costs for IP-2013. Pollux also manufactures other products.

A product similar to IP-2013 that Castor could use as a substitute is available in the United States for $77 per unit.

Required

1. What is the minimum and maximum transfer price that would be acceptable to Castor and Pollux for IP-2013, and why?
2. What transfer price would minimize income taxes for Gemini Corporation as a whole? Would Pollux and Castor want to be evaluated on operating income using this transfer price?
3. Suppose Gemini uses the transfer price from requirement 2, and each division is evaluated on its own after-tax division operating income. Now suppose Pollux has an opportunity to sell 8,000 units of IP-2013 to an outside customer for $62 each. Pollux will not incur shipping costs because the customer is nearby and offers to pay for shipping. Assume that if Pollux accepts the special order, Castor will have to buy 8,000 units of the substitute product in the United States at $77 per unit.
   a. Will accepting the special order maximize after-tax operating income for Gemini Corporation as a whole?
   b. Will Castor want Pollux to accept this special order? Why or why not?
   c. Will Pollux want to accept this special order? Explain.
   d. Suppose Gemini Corporation wants to operate in a decentralized manner. What transfer price should Gemini set for IP-2013 so that each division acting in its own best interest takes actions for the special order that are in the best interests of Gemini Corporation as a whole?

15-30 Transfer pricing, goal congruence. The Beatz Corporation makes and sells 20,000 multisystem music players each year. Its assembly division purchases components from other divisions of Beatz or from external suppliers and assembles the multisystem music players. In particular, the assembly division can purchase the CD player from the compact disc division of Beatz or from Youku Corporation. Youku agrees to meet all of Beatz's quality requirements and is currently negotiating with the assembly division to supply 20,000 CD players at a price between $44 and $52 per CD player.

A critical component of the CD player is the head mechanism that reads the disc. To ensure the quality of its multisystem music players, Beatz requires that if Youku wins the contract to supply CD players, it must purchase the head mechanism from Beatz's compact disc division for $24 each.

The compact disc division can manufacture at most 22,000 CD players annually. It also manufactures as many additional head mechanisms as can be sold. The incremental cost of manufacturing the head mechanism is $18 per unit. The incremental cost of manufacturing a CD player (including the cost of the head mechanism) is $30 per unit, and any number of CD players can be sold for $45 each in the external market.

Required

1. What are the incremental costs minus revenues from sales to external buyers for the company as a whole if the compact disc division transfers 20,000 CD players to the assembly division and sells the remaining 2,000 CD players on the external market?
2. What are the incremental costs minus revenues from sales to external buyers for the company as a whole if the compact disc division sells 22,000 CD players on the external market and the assembly division accepts Youku's offer at (a) $44 per CD player or (b) $52 per CD player?
3. What is the minimum transfer price per CD player at which the compact disc division would be willing to transfer 20,000 CD players to the assembly division?
4. Suppose that the transfer price is set to the minimum computed in requirement 3 plus $2, and the division managers at Beatz are free to make their own profit-maximizing sourcing and selling decisions. Now, Youku offers 20,000 CD players for $52 each.

a. What decisions will the managers of the compact disc division and assembly division make?

b. Are these decisions optimal for Beatz as a whole?

c. Based on this exercise, at what price would you recommend the transfer price be set?

15-31 Transfer pricing, goal congruence, ethics. HookLine Industries manufactures cardboard containers (boxes) made from recycled paper products. The company operates two divisions: paper recycling and box manufacturing. Each division operates as a decentralized entity. The recycling division is free to sell recycled paper to outside buyers, and the box manufacturing division is free to purchase recycled paper from other sources. Currently, however, the recycling division sells all of its output to the manufacturing division, and the manufacturing division does not purchase materials from any outside suppliers.

The recycled paper is transferred from the recycling division to the manufacturing division at 110% of full cost. The recycling division purchases recyclable paper products for $0.075 per pound. The recycling division uses 100 pounds of recyclable paper products to produce one roll of recycled paper. The division's other variable costs equal $6.35 per roll, and fixed costs at a monthly production level of 10,000 rolls are $2.15 per roll. During the most recent month, 10,000 rolls of recycled paper were transferred between the two divisions. The recycling division's capacity is 15,000 rolls.

Due to increased demand, the manufacturing division expects to use 12,000 rolls of paper next month. Sinker Corporation has offered to sell 2,000 rolls of recycled paper next month to the manufacturing division for $17.00 per roll.

Required

1. Calculate the transfer price per roll of recycled paper. Assuming that each division is considered a profit center, would the manufacturing manager choose to purchase 2,000 rolls next month from Sinker Corporation?
2. Is the purchase in the best interest of HookLine Industries? Show your calculations. What is the cause of this goal incongruence?
3. The manufacturing division manager suggests that $17.00 is now the market price for recycled paper rolls, and that this should be the new transfer price. HookLine's corporate management tends to agree. The paper recycling manager is suspicious. Sinker's prices have always been considerably higher than $17.00 per roll. Why the sudden price cut? After further investigation by the recycling division manager, it is revealed that the $17.00 per roll price was a one-time-only offer made to the manufacturing division due to excess inventory at Sinker. Future orders would be priced at $18.50 per roll. Comment on the validity of the $17.00 per roll market price and the ethics of the manufacturing manager. Would changing the transfer price to $17.00 matter to HookLine Industries?

15-32 Transfer pricing, utilization of capacity. (J. Patell, adapted) Shome Inc. consists of a semiconductor division and a process-control division, each of which operates as an independent profit center. The semiconductor division employs craftsmen who produce two different electronic components: the new high-performance Xcel chip and an older product called the Dcel chip. These two products have the following cost characteristics:

	Xcel-chip	Dcel-chip
Direct materials	$ 10	$ 8
Direct manufacturing labor, 4 hours × $25; 2 hours × $25	100	50

Due to the high skill level necessary for the craftsmen, the semiconductor division's capacity is set at 55,000 hours per year.

Maximum demand for the Xcel chip is 13,750 units annually, at a price of $130 per chip. There is unlimited demand for the Dcel chip at $65 per chip.

The process-control division produces only one product, a process-control unit, with the following cost structure:

- Direct materials (circuit board): $80
- Direct manufacturing labor (3.5 hours × $10): $35

The current market price for the control unit is $125 per unit.

A joint research project has just revealed that a single Xcel chip could be substituted for the circuit board currently used to make the process-control unit. Direct labor cost of the process-control unit would be unchanged. The improved process-control unit could be sold for $185.

Required

1. Calculate the contribution margin per direct-labor hour of selling Xcel chip and Dcel chip. If no transfers of Xcel chip are made to the process-control division, how many Xcel chips and Dcel chips should the semiconductor division manufacture and sell? What would be the division's annual contribution margin? Show your computations.
2. The process-control division expects to sell 1,250 process-control units this year. From the viewpoint of Shome Inc. as a whole, should 1,250 Xcel chips be transferred to the process-control division to replace circuit boards? Show your computations.
3. What transfer price, or range of prices, would ensure goal congruence among the division managers? Show your calculations.
4. If labor capacity in the semiconductor division were 60,000 hours instead of 55,000, would your answer to requirement 3 differ? Show your calculations.

15-33 Transfer pricing, perfect and imperfect markets. Malkin Company has three divisions (R, S, and T), organized as decentralized profit centers. Division R produces the basic chemical Randine (in multiples of 1,000 pounds) and transfers it to Divisions S and T. Division S processes Randine into the final product Syntex, and Division T processes Randine into the final product Termix. No material is lost during processing.

Division R has no fixed costs. The variable cost per pound of Randine is $0.18. Division R has a capacity limit of 10,000 pounds. Divisions S and T have capacity limits of 4,000 and 6,000 pounds, respectively. Divisions S and T sell their final product in separate markets. The company keeps no inventories of any kind.

The *cumulative* net revenues (i.e., total revenues (−) total processing costs) for divisions S and T at various output levels are summarized below.

Division S				
Pounds of Randine Processed in S	1,000	2,000	3,000	4,000
Total Net Revenues ($) from Sale of Syntex	$ 500	$ 850	$1,100	$1,200

Division T						
Pounds of Randine Processed in T	1,000	2,000	3,000	4,000	5,000	6,000
Total Net Revenues ($) from Sale of Termix	$ 600	$1,200	$1,800	$2,100	$2,250	$2,350

Required

1. Suppose there is no external market for Randine. What quantity of Randine should the Malkin Company produce to maximize overall income? How should this quantity be allocated between the two processing divisions?
2. What range of transfer prices will motivate Divisions S and T to demand the quantities that maximize overall income (as determined in requirement 1), as well as motivate Division R to produce the sum of those quantities?
3. Suppose that Division R can sell any quantity of Randine in a perfectly competitive market for $0.33 a pound. To maximize Malkin's income, how many pounds of Randine should Division R transfer to Divisions S and T, and how much should it sell in the external market?
4. What range of transfer prices will result in Divisions R, S, and T taking the actions determined as optimal in requirement 3? Explain your answer.

15-34 Goal congruence, income taxes, different market conditions. The Fresno Corporation makes water pumps. The Engine Division makes the engines and supplies them to the Assembly Division, where the pumps are assembled. Fresno is a profitable corporation that attributes much of its success to its decentralized structure. Each division manager is compensated on the basis of division operating income.

The Assembly Division currently acquires all its engines from the Engine Division. The Assembly Division manager could purchase similar engines in the market for $400 each. The Engine Division is currently operating at 80% of its capacity of 4,000 units and has the following costs:

Direct materials ($125 per unit × 3,200 units)	$400,000
Direct manufacturing labor ($50 per unit × 3,200 units)	160,000
Variable manufacturing overhead ($25 per unit × 3,200 units)	80,000
Fixed manufacturing overhead costs	520,000

All the Engine Division's 3,200 units are currently transferred to the Assembly Division. No engines are sold in the external market.

The Engine Division has just received an order for 2,000 units at $375 per engine that would utilize half the capacity of the plant. The order must either be taken in full or rejected. The order is for a slightly different engine than what the Engine Division currently makes. To produce the new engine would require a direct material cost per unit of $100, a direct manufacturing labor cost per unit of $40, and a variable manufacturing overhead cost per unit of $25.

Required

1. From the viewpoint of the Fresno Corporation as a whole, should the Engine Division accept the order for the 2,000 units? Show your computations.
2. What range of transfer prices will result in achieving the actions determined to be optimal in requirement 1 if division managers act in a decentralized manner?
3. The manager of the Assembly Division has proposed a transfer price for the engines equal to the full cost of the engines, including an allocation of overhead cost. The Engine Division allocates overhead cost to engines on the basis of the total capacity of the plant used to manufacture the engines.
   a. Calculate the transfer price for the engines transferred to the Assembly Division under this arrangement.
   b. Do you think the transfer price calculated in requirement 3a will result in achieving the actions determined to be optimal in requirement 1 if division managers act in a decentralized manner?
   c. Comment in general on one advantage and one disadvantage of using full cost of the producing division as the basis for setting transfer prices.
4. Now consider the effect of income taxes.
   a. Suppose the Assembly Division is located in a state that imposes a 10% tax on income earned within its boundaries and the Engine Division is located in a state that imposes no tax on income earned within its boundaries. What transfer price would be chosen by Fresno Corporation to minimize state income taxes for the company as a whole? Assume that only transfer prices greater than or equal to full manufacturing cost and less than or equal to the market price of "substantially similar" engines are acceptable to the tax authorities.
   b. Suppose that the Fresno Corporation announces the transfer price computed in requirement 4a to price all transfers between the Engine and Assembly divisions. Each division manager then acts autonomously to maximize division operating income. Will division managers acting in a decentralized manner achieve the actions determined to be optimal in requirement 1? Explain.
5. Consider your response to requirements 1–4 and assume the Engine Division will continue to have opportunities for outside business as described in requirement 1. What transfer-pricing policy would you recommend Fresno use, and why? Would you continue to evaluate division performance on the basis of division operating incomes? Explain.

Case

Shuman Automobiles, Inc.

Clark Shuman, owner and general manager of an automobile dealership, was nearing retirement and wanted to begin relinquishing his personal control over the business's operations. (See Shuman Automobiles, Inc. Exhibit 1 for current financial statements.) The reputation he had established in the community led him to believe that the recent growth in his business would continue. His long-standing policy of emphasizing new-car sales as the principal business of the dealership had paid off, in Shuman's opinion. This, combined with close attention to customer relations so that a

Shuman Automobiles, Inc. Exhibit 1

SHUMAN AUTOMOBILES, INC.
Income Statement
For the Year Ended December 31

Sales of new cars		$6,879,371	
Cost of new-car sales*	$6,221,522		
Sales remuneration	137,470	6,358,992	
		520,379	
Allowances on trade†		154,140	
New-car gross profit			$366,239
Sales of used cars		3,052,253	
Cost of used-car sales*	$2,623,100		
Sales remuneration	92,815		
		2,715,915	
		336,338	
Allowances on trade†		56,010	
Used-car gross profit			280,328
			646,567
Service sales to customers		980,722	
Cost of work*		726,461	
		254,261	
Service work on reconditioning:			
Charge	238,183		
Cost*	245,915	(7,732)	
Service work gross profit			246,529
Dealership gross profit			893,096
General and administrative expenses			345,078
Income before taxes			$548,018

* These amounts include all costs assignable directly to the department, but exclude allocated general dealership overhead.
† Allowances on trade represent the excess of amounts allowed on cars taken in trade over their appraised value.

Source: Reprinted by permission of Harvard Business School

Harvard Business School case 9-177-033
The case was prepared by J. Reece as the basis for class discussion rather than to illustrate either effective or ineffective handling of an administrative situation.

substantial amount of repeat business was generated, had increased the company's sales to a new high level. Therefore, he wanted to make organizational changes to cope with the new situation, especially given his desire to withdraw from any day-to-day managerial responsibilities.

Accordingly, Shuman divided up the business into three departments: new-car sales, used-car sales, and the service department. He then appointed three of his most trusted employees managers of the new departments: Janet Moyer, new-car sales; Paul Fiedler, used-car sales: and Nate Bianci, service department. All of these people had been with the dealership for several years.

Each manager was told to run her or his department as if it were an independent business. In order to give the new managers an incentive, their remuneration was to be calculated as a straight percentage of their department's gross profit.

Soon after taking over as manager of new-car sales, Janet Moyer had to settle upon the amount to offer a particular customer who wanted to trade his old car as a part of the purchase price of a new one with a list price of $14,400. Before closing the sale, Moyer had to decide the amount she would offer the customer for the trade-in value of the old car. She knew that if no trade-in were involved, she would deduct about 8 percent from the list price of this model new car to be competitive with several other dealers in the area. However, she also wanted to make sure that she did not lose out on the sale by offering too low a trade-in allowance.

During her conversation with the customer, it had become apparent that the customer had an inflated view of the worth of his old car, a far from uncommon event. In this case, it probably meant that Moyer had to be prepared to make some sacrifices to close the sale. The new car had been in stock for some time, and the model was not selling very well, so she was rather anxious to make the sale if this could be done profitably.

In order to establish the trade-in value of the car, the used-car manager, Fiedler, accompanied Moyer and the customer out to the parking lot to examine the car. In the course of his appraisal, Fiedler estimated the car would require reconditioning work costing about $840, after which the car would retail for about $7,100. On a wholesale basis, he could either buy or sell such a car, after reconditioning, for about $6,100. The retail automobile dealer's handbook of used-car prices, the "Blue Book," gave a cash buying price range of $5,500 to $5,800 for the trade-in model in good condition. This range represented the distribution of cash prices paid by automobile dealers for the model of car in the area in the past month. Fiedler estimated that he could get about $5,000 for the car "as is" (that is, without any work being done to it) at next week's regional used car auction.

The new-car department manager had the right to buy any trade-in at any price she thought appropriate, but then it was her responsibility to dispose of the car. She had the alternative of either trying to persuade the used-car manager to take over the car and accepting the used-car manager's appraisal price, or she herself could sell the car through wholesale channels or at auction. Whatever course Moyer adopted, it was her primary responsibility to make a profit for the dealership on the new cars she sold, without affecting her performance through excessive allowances on trade-ins. This primary goal, Moyer said, had to be "balanced against the need to satisfy the customers and move the new cars out of inventory—and there is only a narrow line between allowing enough on a used car and allowing too much."

After weighing all these factors, with particular emphasis on the personality of the customer, Moyer decided to allow $6,500 for the used car, provided the customer agreed to pay the list price for the new car. After a certain amount of haggling, during which the customer came down from a higher figure and Moyer came up from a lower one, the $6,500 allowance was agreed upon. The necessary papers were signed, and the customer drove off.

Moyer returned to the office and explained the situation to Joanne Brunner, who had recently joined the dealership as accountant. After listening with interest to Moyer's explanation of the sale, Brunner set about recording the sale in the accounting records of the business. As soon as she saw that the new car had been purchased from the manufacturer for $12,240, she was uncertain as to the value she should place on the trade-in vehicle. Since the new car's list price was $14,400 and it had cost $12,240, Brunner reasoned that the gross margin on the new-car sale was $2,160. Yet Moyer had allowed $6,500 for the old car, which needed $840 of repairs and could be sold retail for $7,100 or wholesale for $6,100. Did this mean that the new-car sale involved a loss?

Brunner was not at all sure she knew the answer to this question. Also, she was uncertain about the value she should place on the used car for inventory valuation purposes. Brunner decided that she would put down a valuation of $6,500, and then await instructions from her superiors.

When Fiedler, the used-car manager, found out what Brunner had done, he stated forcefully that he would not accept $6,500 as the valuation of the used car. He commented as follows:

> My used-car department has to get rid of that used car, unless Janet (Moyer) agrees to take it over herself. I would certainly never have allowed the customer $6,500 for that old tub. I wouldn't have given anymore than $5,260, which is the wholesale price less the cost of repairs. My department has to make a profit too, you know. My own income depends on the gross profit I show on the sale of used cars, and I won't stand for having my income hurt because Janet is too generous toward her customers!

Brunner replied that she had not meant to cause trouble but had simply recorded the car at what seemed to be its cost of acquisition, because she had been taught that this was the best accounting practice. Whatever response Fiedler was about to make to this comment was cut off by the arrival of Clark Shuman, the general manager, and Nate Bianci, the service department manager. Shuman picked up the phone and called Janet Moyer, asking her to come over right away.

"All right, Nate," said Shuman, "now that we are all here, would you tell them what you just told me?"

Bianci said, "Clark, the trouble is with this trade-in. Janet and Paul were right in thinking that the repairs they thought necessary would cost about $840. Unfortunately, they failed to notice that the rear axle is cracked; it will have to be replaced before we can retail the car. This will probably use up parts and labor costing about $640.

"Beside this," Bianci continued, "there is another thing that is bothering me a good deal more. Under the accounting system we've been using, I can't charge as much on an internal job as I would for the same job performed for an outside customer. As you can see from my department statement (Shuman Automobiles, Inc. Exhibit 2), I lost almost $8,000 on internal work last year. On a reconditioning job like this, which costs out at $1,480, I don't even break even. If I did work costing $1,480 for an outside customer, I would be able to charge about $2,000 for the job. The Blue Book gives a range of $1,960 to $2,040 for the work this car needs, and I have always aimed for about the middle of the Blue Book range.[1] That would give my department a gross profit of $520, and my own income is now based on that gross profit. Since a large proportion of the work of my department is the reconditioning of trade-ins for resale, I figure that I should be able to make the same charge for repairing a trade-in as I would get for an outside repair job."

Fiedler and Moyer both started to talk at once at this point. Fiedler managed to edge out Moyer: "This axle business is unfortunate, all right; but it's very hard to spot a cracked axle. Nate is likely to be just as lucky the other way next time. He has to take the rough with the smooth. It's up to him to get the cars ready for me to sell."

Moyer, after agreeing that the failure to spot the axle was unfortunate, added: "This error is hardly my fault, however. Anyway, it's ridiculous that the service department should make a profit on jobs it does for the rest of the dealership. The company can't make money when its left hand sells to its right."

At this point, Clark Shuman was getting a little confused about the situation. He thought there was a little truth in everything that had been said, but he was not sure how much. It was evident to him that some action was called for, both to sort out the present problem and to prevent its recurrence. He instructed Ms. Brunner, the accountant, to "work out how much we are really going to make on this whole deal," and then retired to his office to consider how best to get his managers to make a profit for the dealership.

A week after the events described above, Clark Shuman was still far from sure what action to take to motivate his managers to make a profit for the business. During the week, Bianci had

[1] In addition to the monthly Blue Book for used-car prices, there was a monthly Blue Book that gave the range of charges for various classes of repair work, based on the actual charges made and reported by vehicle repair shops in the area.

Shuman Automobiles, Inc. Exhibit 2

SHUMAN AUTOMOBILES, INC. Analysis of Service Department Expenses For the Year Ended December 31	Customer Jobs	Reconditioning Jobs	Total
Number of jobs	3,780	468	4,248
Direct labor	$302,116	$ 98,820	$ 400,936
Supplies	103,966	32,755	136,721
Department overhead	84,592	27,670	112,262
	490,684	159,245	649,919
Parts	235,787	86,670	322,457
	726,461	245,915	972,376
Charges made for jobs to customers or other departments	980,722	238,183	1,218,905
Gross profit (loss)	$245,261	$ (7,732)	246,529
General overhead proportion			140,868
Departmental profit for the year			$ 105,661

reported to him that the repairs to the used car had cost $1,594, of which $741 represented the cost of those repairs that had been spotted at the time of purchase, and the remaining $853 the cost of supplying and fitting a replacement for the cracked axle. To support his own case for a higher allowance on reconditioning jobs, Bianci had looked through the duplicate customer invoices over the last few months and had found examples of similar (but not identical) work to that which had been done on the trade-in car. The amounts of these invoices averaged $2,042, and the average of the costs assigned to these jobs was $1,512. (General overhead was not assigned to individual jobs.) In addition, Bianci had obtained from Ms. Brunner the cost analysis shown in Shuman Automobiles, Inc. Exhibit 2. Bianci told Shuman that this was a fairly typical distribution of the service department's expenses.

Questions

1. Suppose the new-car deal is consummated, with the repaired used car being retailed for $7,100, the repairs costing Shuman $1,594. Assume that all sales personnel are on salary (no commissions) and that general overhead costs are fixed. What is the dealership incremental gross profit on the total transaction (i.e., new and repaired-used cars sold)?
2. Assume each department (new, used, service) is treated as a profit center, as described in the case. Also assume in *a–c* that it is known with certainty *beforehand* that the repairs will cost $1,594.
   a. In your opinion, at what value should this trade-in (unrepaired) be transferred from the new-car department to the used-car department? Why?
   b. In your opinion, how much should the service department be able to charge the used-car department for the repairs on this trade-in car? Why?
   c. Given your responses to *a* and *b,* what will be each department's incremental gross profit on this deal?
3. Is there a strategy in this instance that would give the dealership more profit than the one assumed above (i.e., repairing and retailing this trade-in used car)? Explain. In answering *this* question, assume the service department operates at capacity.
4. Do you feel the three-profit-center approach is appropriate for Shuman? If so, explain why, including an explanation of how this is better than other specific alternatives. If not, propose a better alternative and explain why it is better than three profit centers and any other alternatives you have considered.

16 Performance Measurement and Compensation

Learning Objectives

1. Select financial and nonfinancial performance measures to use in a balanced scorecard
2. Examine accounting-based measures for evaluating business unit performance, including return on investment (ROI), residual income (RI), and economic value added (EVA®)
3. Analyze how companies choose the details of their key performance measures
4. Understand the choice of performance targets and the design of feedback mechanisms
5. Explain the difficulties of comparing the performance of divisions operating in different countries
6. Understand the roles of salaries and incentives when rewarding managers
7. Describe the four levers of control and why they are necessary

When you complete this course, you'll receive a grade that represents a measure of your performance in it. Your grade will likely consist of three elements: homework, exams, and class participation. Do some of these elements better prove your knowledge of the material than others? Would the relative weights your instructor places on the various elements when determining your final grade influence how much effort you expend to improve performance on the different elements? Would it be fair if you received a good grade regardless of your performance? Such questions come up in corporate situations repeatedly in the context of linking managers' compensation to their performance and that of the organization. The consequences of failing to tie pay to performance can be dramatic. The financial crisis of 2007–2009 has been linked to the fact that managers at a variety of financial services firms were rewarded for taking on excessive amounts of risk. For example, chief executive Martin Sullivan of insurance giant American International Group (AIG) continued to receive performance bonuses despite pushing his firm to the brink of bankruptcy. By failing to link pay to performance, the AIG board of directors rewarded behavior that eventually led to a government takeover of the firm in 2008.

Companies measure performance and reward managers to motivate them to achieve company strategies and goals. If the measures are inappropriate or not connected to sustained performance, managers may improve their performance evaluations and increase compensation without achieving company goals. As the Chapter at a Glance highlights, this chapter discusses the general design, implementation, and uses of performance measures, part of the final step in the decision-making process.

Chapter at a Glance

- Internal financial measures based on accounting numbers are the most widely used performance measures for the intermediate-to-long time horizon. Examples of such measures are return on investment, residual income, and return on sales.
- Return on investment captures the income generated as a function of investment, but its use as a performance measure may lead to goal incongruence. Residual income and economic value added are other measurement options that are more likely to lead to goal congruence.
- Companies need to make many decisions when designing accounting-based measures for subunit managers, including the timeframe over which measures are computed, the definition of key terms such as "investment," and the calculation of particular components of each measure.
- Companies should customize target levels and feedback processes to the nature of the subunit, as well as the available set of information systems and performance measures.

- To compare the performance of subunit managers across countries, top management must adjust for differences in operating conditions, and account for disparities in movements of price levels and currency exchange rates.
- To prevent unethical and fraudulent behavior, companies must balance the push for performance resulting from quantitative metrics with other levers of control, such as standards of behavior, codes of conduct, statements of mission and core values, and a process of active discussion and debate.

Financial and Nonfinancial Performance Measures

Learning Objective 1

Select financial performance measures

. . . such as return on investment, residual income

and nonfinancial performance measures to use in a balanced scorecard

. . . such as customer satisfaction, number of defects

As we saw earlier (in Chapter 14), many organizations are increasingly presenting financial and nonfinancial performance measures for their subunits in a single report called the *balanced scorecard*. Different organizations stress different measures in their scorecards, but the measures are always derived from a company's strategy. Consider the case of Hospitality Inns, a chain of hotels. Hospitality Inns' strategy is to provide excellent customer service and to charge a higher room rate than its competitors. Hospitality Inns uses the following measures in its balanced scorecard:

1. **Financial perspective**—stock price, net income, return on sales, return on investment, and economic value added
2. **Customer perspective**—market share in different geographic locations, customer satisfaction, and average number of repeat visits
3. **Internal-business-process perspective**—customer-service time for making reservations and for check-in and restaurants; cleanliness of hotel and room; quality of room service; time taken to clean rooms; quality of restaurant experience; number of new services provided to customers (wireless Internet, video games); time taken to plan and build new hotels
4. **Learning-and-growth perspective**—employee education and skill levels, employee satisfaction, employee turnover, hours of employee training, and availability of information systems

As in all balanced-scorecard implementations, the goal is to make improvements in the learning-and-growth perspective that will lead to improvements in the internal-business-process perspective that, in turn, will result in improvements in the customer and financial perspectives. Hospitality Inns also uses balanced-scorecard measures to evaluate and reward the performance of its managers.

Some performance measures, such as the time it takes to plan and build new hotels, have a long time horizon. Other measures, such as time taken to check in or quality of room service, have a short time horizon. In this chapter, we focus on *organization subunits'* most widely-used performance measures that cover an intermediate-to-long time horizon. These are internal financial measures based on accounting numbers routinely reported by organizations. In later sections, we describe why companies use both financial and nonfinancial measures to evaluate performance.

Designing accounting-based performance measures requires several steps:

Step 1: Choose Performance Measures That Align with Top Management's Financial Goals. For example, is operating income, net income, return on assets, or revenues the best measure of a subunit's financial performance?

Step 2: Choose the Details of Each Performance Measure in Step 1. Once a firm has chosen a specific performance measure, it must make a variety of decisions about the precise way in which various components of the measure are to be calculated. For example, if the chosen performance measure is return on assets, should it be calculated for one year or for a multiyear period? Should assets be defined as total assets or net assets (total assets minus total liabilities)? Should assets be measured at historical cost or current cost?

Step 3: Choose a Target Level of Performance and Feedback Mechanism for Each Performance Measure in Step 1. For example, should all subunits have identical targets, such as the same required rate of return on assets? Should performance reports be sent to top management daily, weekly, or monthly?

Managers don't need to perform these steps sequentially. The issues considered in each step are interdependent, and top management will often proceed through these steps several times before deciding on one or more accounting-based performance measure. The answers to the questions raised at each step depend on top management's beliefs about how well each alternative measure fulfills the behavioral criteria of promoting goal congruence, motivating management effort, evaluating subunit performance, and preserving subunit autonomy (see Chapter 15).

Learning Objective 2

Examine accounting-based measures for evaluating business unit performance, including return on investment (ROI),

. . . return on sales times investment turnover

residual income (RI),

. . . income minus a dollar amount for required return on investment

and economic value added (EVA®)

. . . a variation of residual income

Accounting-Based Measures for Business Units

Companies commonly use four measures to evaluate the economic performance of their subunits. We illustrate these measures for Hospitality Inns.

Hospitality Inns owns and operates three hotels, one each in San Francisco, Chicago, and New Orleans. Exhibit 16-1 summarizes data for each hotel for 2012. At present, Hospitality Inns does not allocate the total long-term debt of the company to the three separate hotels. The exhibit indicates that the New Orleans hotel generates the highest operating income, \$510,000, compared with Chicago's \$300,000 and San Francisco's \$240,000. But does this comparison mean the New Orleans hotel is the most "successful"? The main weakness of comparing operating incomes alone is that it ignores differences in *the size of the investment* in each hotel. **Investment** refers to the resources or assets used to generate income. It is not sufficient to compare operating incomes alone. The real question is whether a division generates sufficient operating income relative to the investment made to earn it.

Three of the approaches to measuring performance include a measure of investment: return on investment, residual income, and economic value added. A fourth approach, return on sales, does not measure investment.

Return on Investment

Return on investment (ROI) is an accounting measure of income divided by an accounting measure of investment:

$$\text{Return on investment} = \frac{\text{Income}}{\text{Investment}}$$

Return on investment is the most popular approach to measure performance. ROI is popular for two reasons: (1) it blends all the ingredients of profitability—revenues, costs, and investment—into a single percentage and (2) it can be compared with the rate of return on opportunities elsewhere,

Exhibit 16-1

Financial Data for Hospitality Inns for 2012 (in thousands)

	A	B	C	D	E
1		San Francisco Hotel	Chicago Hotel	New Orleans Hotel	Total
2	Hotel revenues	\$1,200,000	\$1,400,000	\$3,185,000	\$5,785,000
3	Hotel variable costs	310,000	375,000	995,000	1,680,000
4	Hotel fixed costs	650,000	725,000	1,680,000	3,055,000
5	Hotel operating income	\$ 240,000	\$ 300,000	\$ 510,000	1,050,000
6	Interest costs on long-term debt at 10%				450,000
7	Income before income taxes				600,000
8	Income taxes at 30%				180,000
9	Net income				\$ 420,000
10	Net book value at the end of 2012:				
11	Current assets	\$ 400,000	\$ 500,000	\$ 660,000	\$1,560,000
12	Long-term assets	600,000	1,500,000	2,340,000	4,440,000
13	Total assets	\$1,000,000	\$2,000,000	\$3,000,000	\$6,000,000
14	Current liabilities	\$ 50,000	\$ 150,000	\$ 300,000	\$ 500,000
15	Long-term debt				4,500,000
16	Stockholders' equity				1,000,000
17	Total liabilities and stockholders' equity				\$6,000,000
18					

inside or outside the company. As with any single performance measure, however, managers should use ROI cautiously and in conjunction with other measures.

ROI is also called the *accounting rate of return* or the *accrual accounting rate of return* (Chapter 11, pages 455–456). Managers usually use the term "ROI" when evaluating the performance of an organization's subunit and the term "accrual accounting rate of return" when using an ROI measure to evaluate a project. Companies vary in the way they define income in the numerator and investment in the denominator of the ROI calculation. Some companies use operating income for the numerator; others prefer to calculate ROI on an after-tax basis and use net income. Some companies use total assets in the denominator; others prefer to focus on only those assets financed by long-term debt and stockholders' equity and use total assets minus current liabilities.

Consider the ROIs of each of the three Hospitality hotels in Exhibit 16-1. For our calculations, we use the operating income of each hotel for the numerator and total assets of each hotel for the denominator.

Using these ROI figures, the San Francisco hotel appears to make the best use of its total assets.

Hotel	Operating Income	÷	Total Assets	=	ROI
San Francisco	$240,000	÷	$1,000,000	=	24%
Chicago	$300,000	÷	$2,000,000	=	15%
New Orleans	$510,000	÷	$3,000,000	=	17%

Each hotel manager can increase ROI by increasing revenues or decreasing costs (each of which increases the numerator), or by decreasing investment (which decreases the denominator). A hotel manager can increase ROI even when operating income decreases by reducing total assets by a greater percentage. Suppose, for example, that operating income of the Chicago hotel decreases by 4% from $300,000 to $288,000 [$300,000 × (1 − 0.04)] and total assets decrease by 10% from $2,000,000 to $1,800,000 [$2,000,000 × (1 − 0.10)]. The ROI of the Chicago hotel would then increase from 15% to 16% ($288,000 ÷ $1,800,000).

ROI can provide more insight into performance when it is represented as two components:

$$\frac{\text{Income}}{\text{Investment}} = \frac{\text{Income}}{\text{Revenues}} \times \frac{\text{Revenues}}{\text{Investment}}$$

which is also written as

$$ROI = \text{Return on sales} \times \text{Investment turnover}$$

This approach is known as the *DuPont method of profitability analysis.* The DuPont method recognizes the two basic ingredients in profit-making: increasing income per dollar of revenues and using assets to generate more revenues. An improvement in either ingredient without changing the other increases ROI.

Assume that top management at Hospitality Inns adopts a 30% target ROI for the San Francisco hotel. How can this return be attained? Below we illustrate the DuPont method for the San Francisco hotel and three ways for that hotel's managers to increase its ROI from 24% to 30%.

	Operating Income (1)	Revenues (2)	Total Assets (3)	Operating Income / Revenues (4) = (1) ÷ (2)	×	Revenues / Total Assets (5) = (2) ÷ (3)	=	Operating Income / Total Assets (6) = (4) × (5)
Current ROI	$240,000	$1,200,000	$1,000,000	20%	×	1.2	=	24%
Alternatives								
A. Decrease assets (such as receivables), keeping revenues and operating income per dollar of revenue constant	$240,000	$1,200,000	$ 800,000	20%	×	1.5	=	30%

continued

	Operating Income (1)	Revenues (2)	Total Assets (3)	Operating Income / Revenues (4) = (1) ÷ (2)	×	Revenues / Total Assets (5) = (2) ÷ (3)	=	Operating Income / Total Assets (6) = (4) × (5)
B. Increase revenues (via higher occupancy rate), keeping assets and operating income per dollar of revenue constant	$300,000	$1,500,000	$1,000,000	20%	×	1.5	=	30%
C. Decrease costs (via, say, efficient maintenance) to increase operating income per dollar of revenue, keeping revenue and assets constant	$300,000	$1,200,000	$1,000,000	25%	×	1.2	=	30%

Other alternatives, such as increasing the selling price per room, could increase both the revenues per dollar of total assets and the operating income per dollar of revenues. ROI makes clear the benefits managers can obtain by reducing their investment in current or long-term assets. Some managers know the need to boost revenues or to control costs, but they pay less attention to reducing their investment base. Reducing the investment base involves decreasing idle cash, managing credit judiciously, determining proper inventory levels, and spending carefully on long-term assets.

Residual Income

Residual income (RI) is an accounting measure of income minus a charge for required return on an accounting measure of investment.

$$\text{Residual income } (RI) = \text{Income} - (\text{Required rate of return} \times \text{Investment})$$

Required rate of return multiplied by the investment is the *imputed cost of the investment.* The **imputed cost** of the investment is a cost recognized in particular situations but not recorded in financial accounting systems because it is an opportunity cost. The imputed cost for Hospitality Inns refers to the return the company could have obtained by making an alternative investment with similar risk characteristics.

Assume each hotel faces similar risks, and that Hospitality Inns has a required rate of return of 12%. The RI for each hotel is calculated as the operating income minus the required rate of return of 12% of total assets:

Hotel	Operating Income	−	(Required Rate of Return	×	Investment)	=	Residual Income
San Francisco	$240,000	−	(12%	×	$1,000,000)	=	$120,000
Chicago	$300,000	−	(12%	×	$2,000,000)	=	$ 60,000
New Orleans	$510,000	−	(12%	×	$3,000,000)	=	$150,000

Note that the New Orleans hotel has the best RI. In general, RI is influenced by size—for a given level of performance, larger divisions generate higher RI.

Some companies favor the RI measure because managers will concentrate on maximizing an absolute amount, such as dollars of RI, rather than a percentage, such as ROI. The objective of maximizing RI means that as long as a subunit earns a return in excess of the required return for investments, that subunit should continue to invest.

The objective of maximizing ROI may induce managers of highly profitable subunits to reject projects that, from the viewpoint of the company as a whole, should be accepted. Suppose Hospitality Inns is considering upgrading room features and furnishings at the San Francisco hotel. The upgrade will increase operating income of the San Francisco hotel by $70,000 and increase its total assets by \$400,000. The ROI for the expansion is 17.5% (\$70,000 ÷ \$400,000), which is attractive to Hospitality Inns because it exceeds the required rate of return of 12%. By making this expansion, however, the San Francisco hotel's ROI will decrease:

$$\text{Pre-upgrade } ROI = \frac{\$240{,}000}{\$1{,}000{,}000} = 0.24, \text{ or } 24\%$$

$$\text{Post-upgrade } ROI = \frac{\$240{,}000 + \$70{,}000}{\$1{,}000{,}000 + \$400{,}000} = \frac{\$310{,}000}{\$1{,}400{,}000} = 0.221, \text{ or } 22.1\%$$

The annual bonus paid to the San Francisco manager may decrease if ROI affects the bonus calculation and the upgrading option is selected. Consequently, the manager may shun the expansion. In contrast, if the annual bonus is a function of RI, the San Francisco manager will favor the expansion:

$$\text{Pre-upgrade } RI = \$240{,}000 - (0.12 \times \$1{,}000{,}000) = \$120{,}000$$
$$\text{Post-upgrade } RI = \$310{,}000 - (0.12 \times \$1{,}400{,}000) = \$142{,}000$$

Goal congruence (ensuring that subunit managers work toward achieving the company's goals) is thus more likely using RI rather than ROI as a measure of the subunit manager's performance.

To see that this is a general result, observe that the post-upgrade ROI is a weighted average of the pre-upgrade ROI and the ROI of the project under consideration. Therefore, whenever a new project has a return higher than the required rate of return (12% in our example) but below the current ROI of the division (24% in our example), the division manager is tempted to reject it even though it is a project the shareholders would like to pursue.[1] On the other hand, RI is a measure that aggregates linearly, that is, the post-upgrade RI always equals the pre-upgrade RI plus the RI of the project under consideration. To verify this in the preceding example, observe that the project's RI is \$70,000 − 12% × \$400,000 = \$22,000, which is the difference between the post-upgrade and pre-upgrade RI amounts. As a result, a manager who is evaluated on residual income will choose a new project only if it has a positive RI. But this is exactly the criterion shareholders want the manager to employ; in other words, RI achieves goal congruence.

Economic Value Added[2]

Many companies use *economic value added,* a specific type of RI calculation. **Economic value added (EVA®)** equals after-tax operating income *minus* the (after-tax) weighted-average cost of capital *multiplied* by total assets minus current liabilities.

$$\text{Economic value added (EVA)} = \text{After-tax operating income} - \left[\text{Weighted-average cost of capital} \times \left(\text{Total assets} - \text{Current liabilities}\right)\right]$$

EVA substitutes the following numbers in the RI calculations: (1) income equal to after-tax operating income, (2) required rate of return equal to the (after-tax) weighted-average cost of capital, and (3) investment equal to total assets minus current liabilities.[3]

We use the Hospitality Inns data in Exhibit 16-1 to illustrate the basic EVA calculations. The weighted-average cost of capital (WACC) equals the *after-tax* average cost of all the long-term funds Hospitality Inns uses. The company has two sources of long-term funds: (a) long-term debt with a market value and book value of \$4.5 million issued at an interest rate of 10% and (b) equity capital that also has a market value of \$4.5 million (but a book value of \$1 million).[4] Because interest costs are tax-deductible and the income-tax rate is 30%, the after-tax cost of debt financing is

---

[1] Similarly, the manager of an underperforming division with an ROI of, say, 7% may wish to accept projects with returns between 7% and 12% even though these opportunities do not meet the shareholders' required rate of return.

[2] S. O'Byrne and D. Young, *EVA and Value-Based Management: A Practical Guide to Implementation* (New York: McGraw-Hill, 2000); J. Stein, J. Shiely, and I. Ross, *The EVA Challenge: Implementing Value Added Change in an Organization* (New York: Wiley, 2001).

[3] When implementing EVA, companies make several adjustments to the operating income and asset numbers reported under Generally Accepted Accounting Principles (GAAP). For example, when calculating EVA, costs such as R&D, restructuring costs, and leases that have long-run benefits are recorded as assets (which are then amortized), rather than as current operating costs. The goal of these adjustments is to obtain a better representation of the economic assets, particularly intangible assets, used to earn income. Of course, the specific adjustments applicable to a company will depend on its individual circumstances.

[4] The market value of Hospitality Inns' equity exceeds book value because book value, based on historical cost, does not measure the current value of the company's assets and because various intangible assets, such as the company's brand name, are not shown at current value in the balance sheet under GAAP.

$0.10 \times (1 - \text{Tax rate}) = 0.10 \times (1 - 0.30) = 0.10 \times 0.70 = 0.07$, or 7%. The cost of equity capital is the opportunity cost to investors of not investing their capital in another investment that is similar in risk to Hospitality Inns. Hospitality Inns' cost of equity capital is 14%.[5] The WACC computation, which uses market values of debt and equity, is:

$$WACC = \frac{(7\% \times \text{Market value of debt}) + (14\% \times \text{Market value of equity})}{\text{Market value of debt} + \text{Market value of equity}}$$

$$= \frac{(0.07 \times \$4{,}500{,}000) + (0.14 \times \$4{,}500{,}000)}{\$4{,}500{,}000 + \$4{,}500{,}000}$$

$$= \frac{\$945{,}000}{\$9{,}000{,}000} = 0.105, \text{ or } 10.5\%$$

The company applies the same WACC to all its hotels because each hotel faces similar risks.

Total assets minus current liabilities (see Exhibit 16-1) can also be computed as follows:

$$\begin{aligned}\text{Total assets} - \text{Current liabilities} &= \text{Long-term assets} + \text{Current assets} - \text{Current liabilities}\\ &= \text{Long-term assets} + \text{Working capital}\end{aligned}$$

where

$$\text{Working capital} = \text{Current assets} - \text{Current liabilities}$$

After-tax hotel operating income is:

$$\text{Hotel operating income} \times (1 - \text{Tax rate}) = \text{Hotel operating income} \times (1 - 0.30) = \text{Hotel operating income} \times 0.70$$

EVA calculations for Hospitality Inns are:

Hotel	After-Tax Operating Income	−	[WACC × (Total Assets − Current Liabilities)]	=	EVA
San Francisco	$240,000 × 0.70	−	[10.50% × ($1,000,000 − $50,000)]	=	$68,250
Chicago	$300,000 × 0.70	−	[10.50% × ($2,000,000 − $150,000)]	=	$15,750
New Orleans	$510,000 × 0.70	−	[10.50% × ($3,000,000 − $300,000)]	=	$73,500

The New Orleans hotel has the highest EVA. Economic value added, like residual income, charges managers for the cost of their investments in long-term assets and working capital. Value is created only if after-tax operating income exceeds the cost of investing the capital. To improve EVA, managers can, for example, (a) earn more after-tax operating income with the same capital, (b) use less capital to earn the same after-tax operating income, or (c) invest capital in high-return projects.[6]

Managers in companies such as Briggs and Stratton, Coca-Cola, CSX, Equifax, and FMC use the estimated impact on EVA to guide their decisions. Division managers find EVA helpful because it allows them to incorporate the cost of capital, which is generally only available at the company-wide level, into decisions at the division level. Comparing the actual EVA achieved to the estimated EVA is useful for evaluating performance and providing feedback to managers about performance. CSX, a railroad company, credits EVA for decisions such as to run trains with three locomotives instead of four and to schedule arrivals just in time for unloading rather than having trains arrive at their destination several hours in advance. The result? Higher income because of lower fuel costs and lower capital investments in locomotives.

---

[5] In practice, the most common method of calculating the cost of equity capital is by applying the capital asset pricing model (CAPM). For details, see J. Berk and P. DeMarzo, *Corporate Finance*, 2nd ed. (Upper Saddle River, NJ: Prentice Hall, 2010).

[6] Observe that the sum of the divisional after-tax operating incomes used in the EVA calculation, ($240,000 + $300,000 + $510,000) × 0.7 = $735,000, exceeds the firm's net income of $420,000. The difference is due to the firm's after-tax interest expense on its long-term debt, which amounts to $450,000 × 0.7 = $315,000. Because the EVA measure includes a charge for the weighted average cost of capital, which includes the after-tax cost of debt, the income figure used in computing EVA should reflect the after-tax profit before interest payments on debt are considered. After-tax operating income (often referred to in practice as NOPAT, or net operating profit after taxes) is thus the relevant measure of divisional profit for EVA calculations.

Return on Sales

The income-to-revenues ratio (or sales ratio), often called *return on sales* (*ROS*), is a frequently used financial performance measure. As we have seen, ROS is one component of ROI in the DuPont method of profitability analysis. To calculate ROS for each of Hospitality's hotels, we divide operating income by revenues:

Hotel	Operating Income	÷	Revenues (Sales)	=	ROS
San Francisco	$240,000	÷	$1,200,000	=	20.0%
Chicago	$300,000	÷	$1,400,000	=	21.4%
New Orleans	$510,000	÷	$3,185,000	=	16.0%

The Chicago hotel has the highest ROS, but its performance is rated worse than the other hotels using measures such as ROI, RI, and EVA.

Comparing Performance Measures

The following table summarizes the performance of each hotel and ranks it (in parentheses) under each of the four performance measures:

Hotel	ROI	RI	EVA	ROS
San Francisco	24% (1)	$120,000 (2)	$68,250 (2)	20.0% (2)
Chicago	15% (3)	$ 60,000 (3)	$15,750 (3)	21.4% (1)
New Orleans	17% (2)	$150,000 (1)	$73,500 (1)	16.0% (3)

The RI and EVA rankings are the same. They differ from the ROI and ROS rankings. Consider the ROI and RI rankings for the San Francisco and New Orleans hotels. The New Orleans hotel has a smaller ROI. Although its operating income is only slightly more than twice the operating income of the San Francisco hotel—$510,000 versus $240,000—its total assets are three times as large—$3 million versus $1 million. The New Orleans hotel has a higher RI because it earns a higher income after covering the required rate of return on investment of 12%. The high ROI of the San Francisco hotel indicates that its assets are being used efficiently. Even though each dollar invested in the New Orleans hotel does not give the same return as the San Francisco hotel, this large investment creates considerable value because its return exceeds the required rate of return. The Chicago hotel has the highest ROS but the lowest ROI. The high ROS indicates that the Chicago hotel has the lowest cost structure per dollar of revenues of all of Hospitality Inns' hotels. Chicago has a low ROI because it generates very low revenues per dollar of assets invested. Is any method better than the others for measuring performance? No, because each evaluates a different aspect of performance.

ROS measures how effectively companies manage costs. To evaluate overall aggregate performance, ROI, RI, or EVA measures are more appropriate than ROS because they consider both income and investment. ROI indicates which investment yields the highest return. RI and EVA measures overcome some of the goal-congruence problems of ROI. Some managers favor EVA because of the accounting adjustments related to the capitalization of investments in intangibles. Other managers favor RI because it is easier to calculate and because, in most cases, it leads to the same conclusions as EVA. Generally, companies use multiple financial measures to evaluate performance.

Keys to Success

Managers can increase ROI or RI by increasing revenues, decreasing costs, and decreasing investment. RI and its variant, EVA, are more likely than ROI to promote goal congruence. EVA necessitates accounting adjustments that can make it difficult for managers to implement.

Learning Objective 3

Analyze how companies choose the details of their key performance measures

. . . choice of time horizon, alternative definitions, and measurement of assets

Choosing the Details of the Performance Measures

It is not sufficient for a company to identify the set of performance measures it wishes to use. The company has to determine how to compute the measures. These range from decisions regarding the timeframe over which the measures are computed, to the definition of key terms such as "investment" and the calculation of particular components of each performance measure.

Alternative Time Horizons

An important element in designing accounting-based performance measures is choosing the time horizon of the performance measures. The ROI, RI, EVA, and ROS calculations represent the results for a single period, 1 year in our example. Managers could take actions that cause short-run increases in these measures but that conflict with the long-run interest of the company. For example, managers may curtail R&D and plant maintenance in the last 3 months of a fiscal year to achieve a target level of annual operating income. For this reason, many companies evaluate subunits on the basis of ROI, RI, EVA, and ROS over multiple years.

Another reason to evaluate subunits over multiple years is that the benefits of actions taken in the current period may not show up in short-run performance measures, such as the current year's ROI or RI. For example, an investment in a new hotel may adversely affect ROI and RI in the short run but benefit ROI and RI in the long run.

A multiyear analysis highlights another advantage of the RI measure: Net present value of all cash flows over the life of an investment equals net present value of the RIs.[7] This characteristic means that if managers use the net present value method to make investment decisions (as advocated in Chapter 11), then using multiyear RI to evaluate managers' performances achieves goal congruence.

Another way to motivate managers to take a long-run perspective is by compensating them on the basis of changes in the market price of the company's stock because stock prices incorporate the expected future effects of current decisions.

Alternative Definitions of Investment

Companies use a variety of definitions for measuring investment in divisions. Four common alternative definitions used in the construction of accounting-based performance measures are:

1. **Total assets available**—includes all assets, regardless of their intended purpose.
2. **Total assets employed**—total assets available minus the sum of idle assets and assets purchased for future expansion. For example, if the New Orleans hotel in Exhibit 16-1 has unused land set aside for potential expansion, total assets employed by the hotel would exclude the cost of that land.
3. **Total assets employed minus current liabilities**—total assets employed, excluding assets financed by short-term creditors. One drawback of defining investment in this way is that it may encourage subunit managers to use an excessive amount of short-term debt because short-term debt reduces the amount of investment.

[7] This equivalence, often referred to as the "conservation property" of residual income, was originally articulated by Gabriel Preinreich in 1938. To see the equivalence, suppose the $400,000 investment in the San Francisco hotel increases operating income by $70,000 per year as follows: increase in operating cash flows of $150,000 each year for 5 years minus depreciation of $80,000 ($400,000 ÷ 5) per year, assuming straight-line depreciation and $0 terminal disposal value. Depreciation reduces the investment amount by $80,000 each year. Assuming a required rate of return of 12%, net present values of cash flows and residual incomes are:

Year	0	1	2	3	4	5	Net Present Value
(1) Cash flow	−$400,000	$150,000	$150,000	$150,000	$150,000	$150,000	
(2) Present value of $1 discounted at 12%	1	0.89286	0.79719	0.71178	0.63552	0.56743	
(3) Present value: (1) × (2)	−$400,000	$133,929	$119,578	$106,767	$ 95,328	$ 85,114	$140,716
(4) Operating income		$ 70,000	$ 70,000	$ 70,000	$ 70,000	$ 70,000	
(5) Assets at start of year		$400,000	$320,000	$240,000	$160,000	$ 80,000	
(6) Capital charge: (5) × 12%		$ 48,000	$ 38,400	$ 28,800	$ 19,200	$ 9,600	
(7) Residual income: (4) − (6)		$ 22,000	$ 31,600	$ 41,200	$ 50,800	$ 60,400	
(8) Present value of RI: (7) × (2)		$ 19,643	$ 25,191	$ 29,325	$ 32,284	$ 34,273	$140,716

4. **Stockholders' equity**—calculated by assigning liabilities among subunits and deducting these amounts from the total assets of each subunit. One drawback of this method is that it combines operating decisions made by hotel managers with financing decisions made by top management.

Companies that use ROI or RI generally define investment as the total assets available. When top management directs a subunit manager to carry extra or idle assets, total assets employed (used) can be more informative than total assets available. Companies that adopt EVA define investment as total assets employed minus current liabilities. The most common rationale for using this definition is that the subunit manager often influences decisions on current liabilities of the subunit.

Alternative Asset Measurements

To design accounting-based performance measures, we must consider different ways to measure assets included in the investment calculations. Should assets be measured at historical cost or current cost? Should gross book value (that is, original cost) or net book value (that is, original cost minus accumulated depreciation) be used for depreciable assets?

Current Cost. **Current cost** is the cost of purchasing an asset today identical to the one currently held, or the cost of purchasing an asset that provides services like the one currently held if an identical asset cannot be purchased. Of course, measuring assets at current costs will result in different ROIs than the ROIs calculated on the basis of historical costs.

We illustrate the current-cost ROI calculations using the data for Hospitality Inns (Exhibit 16-1) and then compare current-cost-based ROIs and historical-cost-based ROIs. Assume the following information about the long-term assets of each hotel:

	San Francisco	Chicago	New Orleans
Age of facility in years (at end of 2012)	8	4	2
Gross book value (original cost)	$1,400,000	$2,100,000	$2,730,000
Accumulated depreciation	$ 800,000	$ 600,000	$ 390,000
Net book value (at end of 2012)	$ 600,000	$1,500,000	$2,340,000
Depreciation for 2012	$ 100,000	$ 150,000	$ 195,000

Hospitality Inns assumes a 14-year estimated useful life, zero terminal disposal value for the physical facilities, and straight-line depreciation.

An index of construction costs indicating how the cost of construction has changed over the 8-year period that Hospitality Inns has been operating (2004 year-end = 100) is:

Year	2005	2006	2007	2008	2009	2010	2011	2012
Construction cost index	110	122	136	144	152	160	174	180

Earlier in this chapter, we computed an ROI of 24% for San Francisco, 15% for Chicago, and 17% for New Orleans (page 667). One possible explanation of the high ROI for the San Francisco hotel is that its long-term assets are expressed in 2004 construction-price levels—prices that prevailed 8 years ago—and the long-term assets for the Chicago and New Orleans hotels are expressed in terms of higher, more recent construction-price levels, which depress ROIs for these two hotels.

Exhibit 16-2 illustrates a step-by-step approach for incorporating current-cost estimates of long-term assets and depreciation expense into the ROI calculation. We make these calculations to approximate what it would cost today to obtain assets that would produce the same expected operating income that the subunits currently earn. (Similar adjustments to represent the current costs of capital employed and depreciation expense can also be made in the RI and EVA calculations.) The current-cost adjustment reduces the ROI of the San Francisco hotel by more than half.

	Historical-Cost ROI	Current-Cost ROI
San Francisco	24%	10.8%
Chicago	15%	11.1%
New Orleans	17%	14.7%

Exhibit 16-2

ROI for Hospitality Inns: Computed Using Current-Cost Estimates as of the End of 2012 for Depreciation Expense and Long-Term Assets

Home Insert Page Layout Formulas Data Review View

	A	B	C	D	E	F	G	H	I	J
1	**Step 1:** Restate long-term assets from gross book value at historical cost to gross book value at current cost as of the end of 2012.									
2		**Gross book value of long-term assets at historical cost**	×	**(Construction cost index in 2012**	÷	**Construction cost index in year of construction)**	=	**Gross book value of long-term assets at current cost at end of 2012**		
3	San Francisco	$1,400,000	×	(180	÷	100)	=	$2,520,000		
4	Chicago	$2,100,000	×	(180	÷	144)	=	$2,625,000		
5	New Orleans	$2,730,000	×	(180	÷	160)	=	$3,071,250		
6										
7	**Step 2:** Derive net book value of long-term assets at current cost as of the end of 2012. (Assume estimated useful life of each hotel is 14 years.)									
8		**Gross book value of long-term assets at current cost at end of 2012**	×	**(Estimated remaining useful life**	÷	**Estimated total useful life)**	=	**Net book value of long-term assets at current cost at end of 2012**		
9	San Francisco	$2,520,000	×	(6	÷	14)	=	$1,080,000		
10	Chicago	$2,625,000	×	(10	÷	14)	=	$1,875,000		
11	New Orleans	$3,071,250	×	(12	÷	14)	=	$2,632,500		
12										
13	**Step 3:** Compute current cost of total assets in 2012. (Assume current assets of each hotel are expressed in 2012 dollars.)									
14		**Current assets at end of 2012 (from Exhibit 16-1)**	+	**Long-term assets from Step 2**	=	**Current cost of total assets at end of 2012**				
15	San Francisco	$400,000	+	$1,080,000	=	$1,480,000				
16	Chicago	$500,000	+	$1,875,000	=	$2,375,000				
17	New Orleans	$660,000	+	$2,632,500	=	$3,292,500				
18										
19	**Step 4:** Compute current-cost depreciation expense in 2012 dollars.									
20		**Gross book value of long-term assets at current cost at end of 2012 (from Step 1)**	÷	**Estimated total useful life**	=	**Current-cost depreciation expense in 2012 dollars**				
21	San Francisco	$2,520,000	÷	14	=	$180,000				
22	Chicago	$2,625,000	÷	14	=	$187,500				
23	New Orleans	$3,071,250	÷	14	=	$219,375				
24										
25	**Step 5:** Compute 2012 operating income using 2012 current-cost depreciation expense.									
26		**Historical-cost operating income**	−	**(Current-cost depreciation expense in 2012 dollars (from Step 4)**	−	**Historical-cost depreciation expense)**	=	**Operating income for 2012 using current-cost depreciation expense in 2012 dollars**		
27	San Francisco	$240,000	−	($180,000	−	$100,000)	=	$160,000		
28	Chicago	$300,000	−	($187,500	−	$150,000)	=	$262,500		
29	New Orleans	$510,000	−	($219,375	−	$195,000)	=	$485,625		
30										
31	**Step 6:** Compute ROI using current-cost estimates for long-term assets and depreciation expense.									
32		**Operating income for 2012 using current-cost depreciation expense in 2012 dollars (from Step 5)**	÷	**Current cost of total assets at end of 2012 (from Step 3)**	=	**ROI using current-cost estimate**				
33	San Francisco	$160,000	÷	$1,480,000	=	10.8%				
34	Chicago	$262,500	÷	$2,375,000	=	11.1%				
35	New Orleans	$485,625	÷	$3,292,500	=	14.7%				

Adjusting assets to recognize current costs negates differences in the investment base caused solely by differences in construction-price levels. Compared with historical-cost ROI, current-cost ROI better measures the current economic returns from the investment. If Hospitality Inns were to invest in a new hotel today, investing in one like the New Orleans hotel offers the best ROI.

Current cost estimates may be difficult to obtain for some assets. Why? Because the estimate requires a company to consider, in addition to increases in price levels, technological advances and processes that could reduce the current cost of assets needed to earn today's operating income.

Long-Term Assets. Gross or Net Book Value? Managers often use historical cost of assets to calculate ROI. There has been much discussion about whether managers should use gross book value or net book value of assets. Using the data in Exhibit 16-1 (page 666), we calculate ROI using net and gross book values of plant and equipment:

	Operating Income (from Exhibit 16-1) (1)	Net Book Value of Total Assets (from Exhibit 16-1) (2)	Accumulated Depreciation (from page 673) (3)	Gross Book Value of Total Assets (4) = (2) + (3)	2012 ROI Using Net Book Value of Total Assets (calculated earlier) (5) = (1) ÷ (2)	2012 ROI Using Gross Book Value of Total Assets (6) = (1) ÷ (4)
San Francisco	$240,000	$1,000,000	$800,000	$1,800,000	24%	13.3%
Chicago	$300,000	$2,000,000	$600,000	$2,600,000	15%	11.5%
New Orleans	$510,000	$3,000,000	$390,000	$3,390,000	17%	15.0%

Using gross book value, the 13.3% ROI of the older San Francisco hotel is lower than the 15.0% ROI of the newer New Orleans hotel. Those who favor using gross book value claim it enables more accurate comparisons of ROI across subunits. For example, when using gross-book-value calculations, the return on the original plant-and-equipment investment is higher for the newer New Orleans hotel than for the older San Francisco hotel. This difference probably reflects the decline in earning power of the San Francisco hotel. Using the net book value masks this decline in earning power because the constantly decreasing investment base results in a higher ROI for the San Francisco hotel—24% in this example. This higher rate may mislead decision makers into thinking that the earning power of the San Francisco hotel has not decreased.

The proponents of using net book value as an investment base maintain that it is less confusing because (1) it is consistent with the amount of total assets shown in the conventional balance sheet and (2) it is consistent with income computations that include deductions for depreciation expense. Surveys report net book value to be the dominant measure of assets used by companies for internal performance evaluation.

Keys to Success

Designing accounting-based measures for subunit managers requires they make decisions about (1) the time-frame over which to compute each measure, (2) the definition of key terms such as "investment," and (3) the calculation of particular components of each performance measure.

Target Levels of Performance and Feedback

Learning Objective 4

Understand the choice of performance targets and the design of feedback mechanisms

. . . carefully crafted budgets and sufficient feedback for timely corrective action

Now that we have covered the different types of measures and how to choose them, we turn our attention to how managers set and measure target levels of performance.

Choosing Target Levels of Performance

Historical-cost-based accounting measures are usually inadequate for evaluating economic returns on new investments and, in some cases, create disincentives for expansion. Despite these problems, managers can use historical-cost ROIs to evaluate current performance by establishing *target* ROIs. For Hospitality Inns, we need to recognize that the hotels were built in different years, which means they were built at different construction-price levels. Top management could adjust the target historical-cost-based ROIs accordingly, say, by setting San Francisco's ROI at 26%, Chicago's at 18%, and New Orleans' at 19%.

Companies frequently overlook this useful alternative of comparing actual results with target or budgeted performance. *Companies should tailor and negotiate a budget to a particular subunit, a particular accounting system, and a particular performance measure while keeping in mind historical cost accounting pitfalls.* For example, many problems of asset valuation and income measurement can be resolved if top management can persuade subunit managers to focus on what is attainable in the forthcoming budget period—whether ROI, RI, or EVA is used and whether the financial measures are based on historical cost or some other measure, such as current cost.

A popular way to establish targets is to set continuous improvement targets. If a company is using EVA as a performance measure, top management can evaluate operations on year-to-year changes in EVA, rather than on absolute measures of EVA. Evaluating performance on the basis of *improvements* in EVA makes the initial method of calculating EVA less important.

In establishing targets for financial performance measures, companies using the balanced scorecard simultaneously determine targets in the customer, internal-business-process, and learning-and-growth perspectives. For example, Hospitality Inns will establish targets for employee training and employee satisfaction, customer-service time for reservations and check-in, quality of room service, and customer satisfaction that each hotel must reach to achieve its ROI and EVA targets.

Choosing the Timing of Feedback

A final critical step in designing accounting-based performance measures is the timing of feedback, which depends largely on (1) how critical the information is for the success of the organization, (2) the specific level of management receiving the feedback, and (3) the sophistication of the organization's information technology. For example, hotel managers responsible for room sales want information on the number of rooms sold (rented) on a daily or weekly basis because a large percentage of hotel costs are fixed costs. Achieving high room sales and taking quick action to reverse any declining sales trends are critical to the financial success of each hotel. Supplying managers with daily information about room sales is much easier if Hospitality Inns has a computerized room-reservation and check-in system. Top management, however, may look at information about daily room sales only on a monthly basis. In some instances, for example, because of concern about the low revenues-to-total-assets ratio of the Chicago hotel, management may want the information weekly.

The timing of feedback for measures in the balanced scorecard varies. For example, human resources managers at each hotel measure employee satisfaction annually because satisfaction is best measured over a longer horizon. However, housekeeping department managers measure the quality of room service over much shorter time horizons, such as a week, because poor levels of performance in these areas for even a short period of time can harm a hotel's reputation for a long period. Moreover, managers can detect and resolve housekeeping problems over a short time period.

> **Keys to Success**
> Companies should tailor budgets and the timing of feedback to managers and employees to the nature of the subunit, the accounting system in place, and the particular performance measure being used for evaluation.

Learning Objective 5

Explain the difficulties of comparing the performance of divisions operating in different countries

. . . adjustments needed for differences in inflation rates and changes in exchange rates

Performance Measurement in Multinational Companies

Our discussion so far has focused on performance evaluation of different divisions of a company operating within a single country. We next discuss the additional difficulties created when managers compare the performance of divisions of a company operating in different countries. Several issues arise:[8]

- The economic, legal, political, social, and cultural environments differ significantly across countries. Operating a division in an open economy like Singapore is very different from

[8] See M. Z. Iqbal, *International Accounting—A Global Perspective* (Cincinnati, OH: South-Western College Publishing, 2002).

navigating a closed economy such as Venezuela with its controlled prices and the constant threat of nationalization.

- Governments in some countries may limit selling prices of, and impose controls on, a company's products. For example, some countries in Asia, Latin America, and Eastern Europe impose tariffs and customs duties to restrict imports of certain goods.
- Availability of materials and skilled labor, as well as costs of materials, labor, and infrastructure (power, transportation, and communication), may also differ significantly across countries. Companies operating in Indonesia, for example, must spend 30% of their total production costs on transportation, whereas such costs account for just 12% of total spending in China.
- Divisions operating in different countries account for their performance in different currencies. Issues of inflation and fluctuations in foreign-currency exchange rates affect performance measures. Fast-growing economies such as Paraguay, Nigeria, and Vietnam suffer from double-digit inflation, which dampens the performance of divisions in those countries when measured in dollar terms.

As a result of these differences, adjustments need to be made to compare performance measures across countries.

Calculating the Foreign Division's ROI in the Foreign Currency

Suppose Hospitality Inns invests in a hotel in Mexico City. The investment consists mainly of the costs of buildings and furnishings. Also assume the following:

- The exchange rate at the time of Hospitality's investment on December 31, 2011, is 10 pesos = \$1.
- During 2012, the Mexican peso suffers a steady decline in its value. The exchange rate on December 31, 2012, is 15 pesos = \$1.
- The average exchange rate during 2012 is $[(10 + 15) \div 2] = 12.5$ pesos = \$1.
- The investment (total assets) in the Mexico City hotel is 30,000,000 pesos.
- The operating income of the Mexico City hotel in 2012 is 6,000,000 pesos.

What is the historical-cost-based ROI for the Mexico City hotel in 2012?

To answer this question, Hospitality Inns' managers first have to determine if they should calculate the ROI in pesos or in dollars. If they calculate the ROI in dollars, what exchange rate should they use? The managers may also be interested in how the ROI of Hospitality Inns Mexico City (HIMC) compares with the ROI of Hospitality Inns New Orleans (HINO), which is also a relatively new hotel of approximately the same size. The answers to these questions yield information that will be helpful when making future investment decisions.

$$\text{HIMC's } ROI \text{ (calculated using pesos)} = \frac{\text{Operating income}}{\text{Total assets}} = \frac{6{,}000{,}000 \text{ pesos}}{30{,}000{,}000 \text{ pesos}} = 0.20, \text{ or } 20\%$$

HIMC's ROI of 20% is higher than HINO's ROI of 17% (page 667). Does this mean that HIMC outperformed HINO based on the ROI criterion? Not necessarily. That's because HIMC operates in a very different economic environment than HINO.

The peso has declined in value relative to the dollar in 2012. This decline has led to higher inflation in Mexico than in the United States. As a result of the higher inflation in Mexico, HIMC will charge higher prices for its hotel rooms, which will increase HIMC's operating income and lead to a higher ROI. Inflation clouds the real economic returns on an asset and makes historical-cost-based ROI higher. Differences in inflation rates between the two countries make a direct comparison of HIMC's peso-denominated ROI with HINO's dollar-denominated ROI misleading.

Calculating the Foreign Division's ROI in U.S. Dollars

One way to make a comparison of historical-cost-based ROIs more meaningful is to restate HIMC's performance in U.S. dollars. But what exchange rate should the managers use to make the comparison meaningful? Assume operating income was earned evenly throughout 2012. Hospitality Inns' managers should use the average exchange rate of 12.5 pesos = \$1 to convert operating income from pesos to dollars: 6,000,000 pesos ÷ 12.5 pesos per dollar = $480,000. The effect of dividing the operating income in pesos by the higher pesos-to-dollar exchange rate prevailing during 2012, rather than the 10 pesos = $1 exchange rate prevailing on December 31, 2011, is that any increase in operating income in pesos as a result of inflation during 2012 is eliminated when converting back to dollars.

At what rate should HIMC's total assets of 30,000,000 pesos be converted? The 10 pesos = $1 exchange rate prevailing when the assets were acquired on December 31, 2011, because HIMC's assets are recorded in pesos at the December 31, 2011, cost, and the assets are not revalued as a result of inflation in Mexico in 2012. Because subsequent inflation does not affect the cost of assets in HIMC's financial accounting records, managers should use the exchange rate prevailing when the assets were acquired to convert the assets into dollars. Using exchange rates after December 31, 2011, would be incorrect because these exchange rates incorporate the higher inflation in Mexico in 2012. Total assets are converted to 30,000,000 pesos ÷ 10 pesos per dollar = $3,000,000.

Then,

$$\text{HIMC's } ROI \text{ (calculated using dollars)} = \frac{\text{Operating income}}{\text{Total assets}} = \frac{\$480{,}000}{\$3{,}000{,}000} = 0.16, \text{ or } 16\%$$

As we have discussed, these adjustments make the historical-cost-based ROIs of the Mexico City and New Orleans hotels comparable because they negate the effects of any differences in inflation rates between the two countries. HIMC's ROI of 16% is less than HINO's ROI of 17%.

Residual income calculated in pesos suffers from the same problems as ROI calculated using pesos. Calculating HIMC's RI in dollars adjusts for changes in exchange rates and makes for more meaningful comparisons with Hospitality's other hotels:

$$\begin{aligned}\text{HIMC's } RI &= \$480{,}000 - (0.12 \times \$3{,}000{,}000)\\ &= \$480{,}000 - \$360{,}000 = \$120{,}000\end{aligned}$$

which is also less than HINO's RI of $150,000. In interpreting HIMC's and HINO's ROI and RI, keep in mind that they are historical-cost-based calculations. They do, however, pertain to relatively new hotels.

Keys to Success

To compare the performance of subunit managers in different countries, top management must take into account differences in operating conditions, as well as make adjustments to account for variations in inflation and currency exchange rates.

Learning Objective 6

Understand the roles of salaries and incentives when rewarding managers

. . . balancing risk and performance-based rewards

Distinction Between Managers and Organization Units[9]

Our focus has been on how to evaluate the performance of a subunit of a company, such as a division. However, is evaluating the performance of a subunit manager the same as evaluating the performance of the subunit? If the subunit performed well, does it mean the manager performed well? In this section, we argue that a company should distinguish between the performance evaluation of a *manager* and the performance evaluation of that manager's *subunit*. For example, companies often put the most skillful division manager in charge of the division producing the poorest economic return in an attempt to improve it. The division may take years to show improvement. Furthermore, the manager's efforts may result merely in bringing the division up to a minimum acceptable ROI. The division may continue to be a poor performer in comparison with other divisions, but it would be a mistake to conclude from the poor performance of the division that the manager is performing poorly. The division's performance may be adversely affected by economic conditions, such as a recession, over which the manager has no control.

As another example, consider again the Hospitality Inns Mexico City (HIMC) hotel. Suppose, despite the high inflation in Mexico, HIMC could not increase room prices because of price-control

[9] The presentations here draw (in part) from teaching notes prepared by S. Huddart, N. Melumad, and S. Reichelstein.

regulations imposed by the government. HIMC's performance in dollar terms would be very poor because of the decline in the value of the peso. But should top management conclude from HIMC's poor performance that the HIMC manager performed poorly? Probably not. The poor performance of HIMC is largely the result of regulatory factors beyond the manager's control.

In the following sections, we show the basic principles for evaluating the performance of an individual subunit manager. These principles apply to managers at all organization levels. Later sections consider examples at the individual-worker level and the top-management level. We illustrate these principles using the RI performance measure.

The Basic Tradeoff: Creating Incentives versus Imposing Risk

How companies measure and evaluate the performance of managers and other employees affects their rewards. Compensation arrangements range from a flat salary with no direct performance-based incentive (or bonus), as in the case of many government employees, to rewards based solely on performance, as in the case of real estate agents who are compensated only via commissions paid on the properties they sell. Most managers' total compensation includes some combination of salary and performance-based incentive. In designing compensation arrangements, we need to consider the *tradeoff between creating incentives and imposing risk.* We illustrate this tradeoff in the context of our Hospitality Inns example.

Indra Chungi owns the Hospitality Inns chain of hotels. Roger Brett manages the Hospitality Inns San Francisco (HISF) hotel. Assume Chungi uses RI to measure performance. To improve RI, Chungi would like Brett to increase sales, control costs, provide prompt and courteous customer service, and reduce working capital. But even if Brett did all those things, high RI is not guaranteed. HISF's RI is affected by many factors beyond Chungi's and Brett's control, such as a recession in the San Francisco economy, an earthquake that might negatively affect HISF, or even road construction near competing hotels, which would drive customers to HISF. Uncontrollable factors make HISF's profitability uncertain and, therefore, risky.

As an entrepreneur, Chungi expects to bear risk. But Brett does not like being subject to risk. One way of "insuring" Brett against risk is to pay Brett a flat salary, regardless of the actual amount of RI earned. Chungi would then bear all the risk. This arrangement creates a problem, however, because Brett's effort is difficult to monitor. The absence of performance-based compensation means that Brett has no direct incentive to work harder or to undertake extra physical and mental effort beyond what is necessary to retain his job or to uphold his own personal values.

Moral hazard describes a situation in which an employee prefers to exert less effort (or to report distorted information) compared with the effort (or accurate information) the owner desires because the owner cannot accurately monitor and enforce the employee's effort (or validity of the reported information).[10] In some repetitive jobs, such as in electronic assembly, a supervisor can monitor the workers' actions, and the moral-hazard problem may not arise. However, a manager's job is to gather and interpret information and to exercise judgment on the basis of the information obtained. Monitoring a manager's effort is more difficult.

Paying no salary and rewarding Brett *only* on the basis of some performance measure—RI in our example—raises different concerns. In this case, Brett would be motivated to strive to increase RI because his rewards would increase with increases in RI. But compensating Brett on RI also subjects him to risk because HISF's RI depends not only on Brett's effort, but also on factors such as local economic conditions over which Brett has no control.

Brett does not like being subject to risk. To compensate Brett for taking risk, Chungi must pay him extra compensation. That is, using performance-based bonuses will cost Chungi more money, *on average,* than paying Brett a flat salary. Why "on average"? Because Chungi's compensation payment to Brett will vary with RI outcomes. When averaged over these outcomes, the RI-based compensation will cost Chungi more than paying Brett a flat salary. The motivation for having some salary and some performance-based bonus in compensation arrangements is to balance the benefit of incentives against the extra cost of imposing risk on the manager.

[10] The term *moral hazard* originated in insurance contracts to represent situations in which insurance coverage caused insured parties to take less care of their properties than they might otherwise. One response to moral hazard in insurance contracts is the system of deductibles (that is, the insured parties pay for damages below a specified amount).

Intensity of Incentives and Financial and Nonfinancial Measurements

What affects the intensity of incentives? That is, how large should the incentive component of a manager's compensation be relative to the salary component? To answer these questions, we need to understand how much the performance measure is affected by actions the manager takes to further the owner's objectives.

Preferred performance measures are those that are sensitive to or that change significantly with the manager's performance. They do not change much with changes in factors that are beyond the manager's control. Sensitive performance measures motivate the manager as well as limit the manager's exposure to risk, reducing the cost of providing incentives. Less-sensitive performance measures are not affected by the manager's performance and fail to induce the manager to improve. The more that owners have sensitive performance measures available to them, the more they can rely on incentive compensation for their managers.

The salary component of compensation dominates when performance measures that are sensitive to managers' actions are not available. This is the case, for example, for some corporate staff and government employees. A high salary component, however, does not mean incentives are completely absent. Promotions and salary increases do depend on some overall measure of performance, but the incentives are less direct. The incentive component of compensation is high when sensitive performance measures are available and when monitoring the employee's effort is difficult, such as in real estate agencies.

In evaluating Brett, Chungi uses measures from multiple perspectives of the balanced scorecard because nonfinancial measures on the balanced scorecard—employee satisfaction and the time taken for check-in, cleaning rooms, and providing room service—are more sensitive to Brett's actions. Financial measures such as RI are less sensitive to Brett's actions because they are affected by external factors such as local economic conditions beyond Brett's control. Residual income may be a very good measure of the economic viability of the hotel, but it is only a partial measure of Brett's performance.

Another reason for using nonfinancial measures in the balanced scorecard is that these measures follow Hospitality Inns' strategy and are drivers of future performance. Evaluating managers on these nonfinancial measures motivates them to take actions that will sustain long-run performance. Therefore, evaluating performance in all four perspectives of the balanced scorecard promotes both short- and long-run actions.

Benchmarks and Relative Performance Evaluation

Owners often use financial and nonfinancial benchmarks to evaluate performance. Benchmarks representing "best practice" may be available inside or outside an organization. For HISF, benchmarks could be from similar hotels, either within or outside the Hospitality Inns chain. Suppose Brett has responsibility for revenues, costs, and investments. In evaluating Brett's performance, Chungi would want to use as a benchmark a hotel of a similar size influenced by the same uncontrollable factors, such as location, demographic trends, or economic conditions, which affect HISF. If all these factors were the same, *differences* in performances of the two hotels would occur only because of differences in the two managers' performances. Benchmarking, which is also called *relative performance evaluation,* filters out the effects of the common uncontrollable factors.

Can the performance of two managers responsible for running similar operations within a company be benchmarked against each other? Yes, but this approach could create a problem: The use of these benchmarks may reduce incentives for these managers to help one another because a manager's performance-evaluation measure improves either by doing a better job or as a result of the other manager doing poorly. When managers do not cooperate, the company suffers. In this case, using internal benchmarks for performance evaluation may not lead to goal congruence (see also Concepts in Action: Avoiding Performance Measurement Silos at Staples).

Performance Measures at the Individual Activity Level

There are two issues when evaluating performance at the individual-activity level: (1) designing performance measures for activities that require multiple tasks and (2) designing performance measures for activities done in teams.

Concepts in Action: Avoiding Performance-Measurement Silos at Staples

To effectively measure company performance, organizations should not allow hierarchical boundaries and concerns to dictate performance metrics. While it is natural for organizations to measure managers on the performance of their functional departments, measuring too narrowly leads to suboptimization and conflict within companies. To improve company-wide performance, organizations need to understand and measure the key drivers of success and profitability.

Source: Jeff Greenberg/Alamy

At Staples, the $25 billion office-supply retailer, the leading performance measurement metric is customer satisfaction. Highly satisfied Staples customers are more profitable than other customers, and they are more likely to recommend the company to other potential customers. Previously, Staples' leaders focused on departmental or functional expense metrics (for example, warehouse operating expense as a percent of sales). As a result, many functional managers built careers as expert cost managers, but it created an environment where many individuals could be "successful" reaching their numbers while Staples only succeeded marginally.

To overcome this performance-measurement problem, Staples created incentives for functional managers to provide enhanced service to customers, even if it means exceeding their budget targets. The company was able to demonstrate how investments in service translated into faster sales growth of higher-margin products. As a result, the company rewarded managers who "failed" in the expense measures related to their own units but who, in doing so, delivered substantially more profits in other shared measures. The effects have been impressive: Staples' sales have grown by 29 percent, or $5.6 billion, in the last 5 years.

Sources: Based on Michael Hammer, "The Seven Deadly Sins of Performance Measurement and How To Avoid Them." *MIT Sloan Management Review* 48 (Spring 2007): 19-28; Staples, Inc. 2011 Annual Report. Framingham, Massachusetts: Staples, Inc., 2012.

Performing Multiple Tasks. Most employees perform more than one task as part of their jobs. Marketing representatives sell products, provide customer support, and gather market information. Manufacturing workers are responsible for both the quantity and quality of their output. Employers want employees to allocate their time and effort intelligently among various tasks or aspects of their jobs.

Consider mechanics at an auto repair shop. Their jobs have two distinct aspects: (1) repair work—performing more repair work generates more revenues for the shop—and (2) customer satisfaction—the higher the quality of the job, the more likely the customer will be pleased. If the employer wants an employee to focus on both aspects, then the employer must measure and compensate performance on both aspects.

Suppose that the employer can easily measure the quantity, but not the quality, of auto repairs. If the employer rewards workers on a by-the-job rate, which pays workers only on the basis of the number of repairs actually performed, mechanics will likely increase the number of repairs they make and quality will likely suffer. Sears Auto Center experienced this problem when it introduced by-the-job rates for its mechanics. To resolve the problem, Sears' managers took three steps to motivate workers to balance both quantity and quality: (1) They dropped the by-the-job rate system and paid mechanics an hourly salary, a step that deemphasized the quantity of repairs. Management determined mechanics' bonuses, promotions, and pay increases on the basis of an assessment of each mechanic's overall performance regarding quantity and quality of repairs. (2) Sears evaluated employees, in part, using data such as customer-satisfaction surveys, the number of dissatisfied customers, and the number of customer complaints. (3) Finally, Sears used staff from an independent outside agency to randomly monitor whether the repairs performed were of high quality.

Team-Based Compensation Arrangements. Many manufacturing, marketing, and design problems can be resolved when employees with multiple skills, knowledge, experiences, and perceptions pool their talents. A team achieves better results than individual employees acting alone.[11] Companies reward individuals on a team based on team performance. Such team-based incentives encourage individuals to help one another as they strive toward a common goal.

The specific forms of team-based compensation vary across companies. Colgate-Palmolive rewards teams on the basis of each team's performance. Novartis, a Swiss pharmaceutical company, rewards teams on company-wide performance; a certain amount of team-based bonuses are paid only if the company reaches certain goals. To encourage the development of team skills, Eastman Chemical Company rewards team members using a checklist of team skills, such as communication and willingness to help one another. Whether team-based compensation is desirable depends, to a large extent, on the culture and management style of a particular organization. For example, one criticism of team-based compensation is that incentives for individual employees to excel are diminished, harming overall performance. Another problem is how to manage team members who are not productive contributors to the team's success but who, nevertheless, share in the team's rewards.

Executive Performance Measures and Compensation

The principles of performance evaluation described in the previous sections also apply to executive compensation plans. These plans are based on both financial and nonfinancial performance measures and consist of a mix of (1) base salary; (2) annual incentives, such as a cash bonus based on achieving a target annual RI; (3) long-run incentives, such as grants of stock options (described later in this section) that must be held for several years; and (4) other benefits, such as medical benefits, pension plans, and life insurance.

Well-designed plans use a compensation mix that balances risk (the effect of uncontrollable factors on the performance measure and, therefore, compensation) with short-run and long-run incentives to achieve the organization's goals. For example, evaluating performance on the basis of annual EVA sharpens an executive's short-run focus. And using EVA and stock option plans over, say, 5 years motivates the executive to take a long-run view as well.

Stock options give executives the right to buy company stock at a specified price (called the exercise price) within a specified period. Suppose that on September 16, 2012, Hospitality Inns gave its CEO the option to buy 200,000 shares of the company's stock at any time before June 30, 2020, at the September 16, 2012, market price of $49 per share. Let's say Hospitality Inns' stock price rises to $69 per share on March 24, 2018, and the CEO exercises his options on all 200,000 shares. The CEO would earn $20 ($69 − $49) per share on 200,000 shares, or $4 million. If Hospitality Inns' stock price stays below $49 during the entire period, the CEO will simply forgo his right to buy the shares. By linking CEO compensation to increases in the company's stock price, the stock option plan motivates the CEO to improve the company's long-run performance and stock price (see also Concepts in Action: Government Bailouts, Record Profits, and the Wall Street Compensation Dilemma).[12]

The Securities and Exchange Commission (SEC) requires detailed disclosures of the compensation arrangements of top-level executives. In complying with these rules in 2011, Starwood Hotels and Resorts, for example, disclosed a compensation table showing the salaries, bonuses, stock options, other stock awards, and other compensation earned by its top five executives during the 2008, 2009, and 2010 fiscal years. Starwood, whose brands include Sheraton, Westin, and the W Hotels, also disclosed the peer companies that it uses to set executive pay and conduct performance comparisons. These companies include competitors in the hotel and hospitality industry (such as Host, Marriott, and Wyndham), as well as companies with similar revenues in other industries relevant to key talent recruitment needs (including Colgate-Palmolive, Nike, and Starbucks). Investors use this information to evaluate the relationship between compensation and performance across companies generally, and across companies operating in similar industries.

The SEC rules also require companies to disclose the principles underlying their executive compensation plans and the performance criteria—such as profitability, revenue growth, and market share—used in determining compensation. In its financial statements, Starwood described some of these principles as promoting the company's competitive position, providing a balanced

[11] *Teams That Click: The Results-Driven Manager Series* (Boston: Harvard Business School Press, 2004).

[12] Although stock options can improve incentives by linking CEO pay to improvements in stock price, they have been criticized for promoting improper or illegal activities by CEOs to increase the options' value. See J. Fox, "Sleazy CEOs Have Even More Options Tricks," www.money.cnn.com/2006/11/13/magazines/fortune/options_scandals.fortune/index.htm (accessed August 12, 2012).

Concepts in Action: Government Bailouts, Record Profits, and the Wall Street Compensation Dilemma

Source: Dan Herrick/ZUMA Wire Service/Alamy

After requiring a government bailout in 2008, Wall Street firms paid out billions of dollars in bonuses to their employees from 2009 until 2011. As a result, many in the public were furious, given Wall Street's role in triggering the recent economic crisis. After losing $42.8 billion in 2008, Wall Street firms recorded $102.5 billion in 2009–2011 profits. These results begged a serious question for managers at investment banks and Washington, D.C., policymakers: After requiring public support in 2008, just how big should bankers' paydays be going forward?

Highly paid executives on Wall Street are usually investment bankers or the top executives of the firms that employ them. Wall Street firms traditionally paid their investment bankers a share of the total revenue garnered by their unit. While this system worked for many years, many argued it led to bankers taking the excessive risks that pushed the U.S. financial system to the brink of collapse.

In recent years, some changes were made to Wall Street bonuses to help soothe public infuriation. Bonus pools, or the amount of revenues allocated to bonuses, were reduced and firms introduced more long-term compensation into the bonus mix. At Goldman Sachs, for example, top executives received no cash bonuses in 2009, and instead received shares in the company that must be held for 5 years. In 2010, however, Goldman Sachs partners had their salaries tripled and firm-wide bonuses reached $15.3 billion.

With continued public scrutiny and the birth of the Occupy Wall Street movement, the debate over investment banker compensation will remain a hot-button issue on Wall Street, Main Street, and in Washington, D.C., for years to come.

Sources: Based on Michael Corkery, "Goldman bows to pressure, makes changes to compensation." *Wall Street Journal* "Deal Journal" blog, December 10, 2009; Douglas J. Elliott, "Wall Street Pay: A Primer." Washington, DC: The Brookings Institution 2010; Matt Phillips, "Goldman: Employees don't mind record low pay ratios." *Wall Street Journal* "MarketBeat" blog, February 3, 2010; Adam Shell, "Despite recession, average Wall Street bonus leaps 25%" USA, February 24, 2010; *Wall Street Journal;* Sam Gustin, "Average Wall Street Bonus Dips to $120k After Bad 2011." USA, March 1, 2012, *Time;* Liz Rappaport, "Goldman Boosts Pay of Partners." USA, January 29, 2011, *Wall Street Journal;* Jill Treanor, "Goldman Sachs bankers to receive $15.3bn in pay and bonuses." UK, January 19, 2011, *The Guardian.*

approach to incentivizing and retaining employees, and aligning senior management's interests with those of shareholders. Starwood uses earnings per share and EBITDA as performance criteria to determine annual incentives for all of its executives. In addition, each executive has an individual scorecard of financial and nonfinancial performance measures. The company's board of directors develops the overall strategic direction of the company. The board then establishes individual and strategic goals for executives that support the overall company goals and are tailored to each executive's area of control.

Keys to Success

Companies should structure compensation for managers to balance the benefit of incentives to achieve an organization's goals against the extra cost of imposing risk on the manager. This involves the use of performance metrics that are sensitive to managerial actions, not overly affected by factors outside the manager's control, and that do not cause the manager to overemphasize a subset of his/her tasks.

Learning Objective 7

Describe the four levers of control and why they are necessary

. . . boundary, belief, and interactive control systems counterbalance diagnostic control systems

Strategy and Levers of Control[13]

This chapter has emphasized the role of quantitative financial and nonfinancial performance-evaluation measures that companies use to implement their strategies. These measures, such as ROI, RI, EVA, customer satisfaction, and employee satisfaction, monitor critical performance variables that help managers track progress toward achieving a company's strategic goals. Because these measures help diagnose whether a company is performing to expectations, they are collectively called **diagnostic control systems.** Companies motivate managers to achieve goals by holding them accountable for and by rewarding them for meeting these goals. The concern, however, is that the pressure to perform may cause managers to cut corners and misreport numbers to make their performance look better than it is, as happened at companies such as Enron, WorldCom, Tyco, and Health South. To prevent unethical and outright fraudulent behavior, companies need to balance the push for performance resulting from diagnostic control systems, the first of four levers of control, with three other levers: *boundary systems, belief systems,* and *interactive control systems.*

Boundary Systems

Boundary systems describe standards of behavior and codes of conduct expected of all employees, especially actions that are off-limits. Ethical behavior on the part of managers is paramount. In particular, numbers that subunit managers report should not be tainted by "cooking the books." They should be free of, for example, overstated assets, understated liabilities, fictitious revenues, and understated costs.

Codes of business conduct signal appropriate and inappropriate individual behaviors. The following are excerpts from Caterpillar's "Worldwide Code of Conduct":

> While we conduct our business within the framework of applicable laws and regulations, for us, mere compliance with the law is not enough. We strive for more than that. . . . We must not engage in activities that create, or even appear to create, conflict between our personal interests and the interests of the company. (Source: Based on LACP 2010 Vision Awards Annual Reports Competition.)

Division managers often cite enormous pressure from top management "to make the budget" as excuses or rationalizations for not adhering to legal or ethical accounting policies and procedures. A healthy amount of motivational pressure is desirable, as long as the "tone from the top" and the code of conduct simultaneously communicate the absolute need for all managers to behave ethically at all times. Managers should train employees to behave ethically. They should promptly and severely reprimand unethical conduct, regardless of the benefits that might accrue to the company from unethical actions. Some companies, such as Lockheed-Martin, emphasize ethical behavior by routinely evaluating employees against a business code of ethics.

Many organizations also set explicit boundaries precluding actions that harm the environment. Environmental violations, such as water and air pollution, carry heavy fines and prison terms under the laws of the United States and other countries. But in many companies, environmental responsibilities extend beyond legal requirements.

Socially responsible companies set aggressive environmental goals and measure and report their performance against them. German, Swiss, Dutch, and Scandinavian companies report on environmental performance as part of a larger set of social responsibility disclosures (such as employee welfare and community development activities). Some companies, such as DuPont, make environmental performance a line item on every employee's salary appraisal report. Duke Power Company appraises employees on their performance in reducing solid waste, cutting emissions and discharges, and implementing environmental plans. The result? Duke Power has met all of its environmental goals.

Belief Systems

Belief systems articulate the mission, purpose, and core values of a company. They describe the accepted norms and patterns of behavior expected of all managers and other employees when interacting with one another, shareholders, customers, and communities. For example, Johnson & Johnson describes its values and norms in a credo statement that is intended to inspire all managers and other employees to do their best.[14] Belief systems play to employees' *intrinsic motivation,* the

[13] For a more detailed discussion, see R. Simons, *Levers of Control: How Managers Use Innovative Control Systems to Drive Strategic Renewal* (Boston: Harvard Business School Press, 1995).

[14] A full statement of the credo can be accessed at www.jnj.com/connect/about-jnj/jnj-credo/.

desire to achieve self-satisfaction from good performance regardless of external rewards such as bonuses or promotion. Intrinsic motivation comes from being given greater responsibility, doing interesting and creative work, having pride in doing that work, establishing commitment to the organization, and developing personal bonds with coworkers. High intrinsic motivation enhances performance because managers and workers have a sense of achievement in doing something important, feel satisfied with their jobs, and see opportunities for personal growth.

Interactive Control Systems

Interactive control systems are formal information systems that managers use to focus the company's attention and learning on key strategic issues. Managers use interactive control systems to create an ongoing dialogue around these key issues and to personally involve themselves in the decision-making activities of subordinates. An excessive focus on diagnostic control systems and critical performance variables can cause an organization to ignore emerging threats and opportunities—changes in technology, customer preferences, regulations, and industry competition that can undercut a business. Interactive control systems help prevent this problem by highlighting and tracking strategic uncertainties that businesses face, such as the emergence of digital imaging in the case of Kodak and Fujifilm, airline deregulation in the case of American Airlines, and the shift in customer preferences for mini- and microcomputers in the case of IBM. The key to this control lever is frequent face-to-face communications regarding these critical uncertainties. The result is ongoing discussion and debate about assumptions and action plans. New strategies emerge from the dialogue and debate surrounding the interactive process. Interactive control systems force busy managers to step back from the actions needed to manage the business today and to shift their focus forward to positioning the organization for the opportunities and threats of tomorrow.

Measuring and rewarding managers for achieving critical performance variables is an important driver of corporate performance. But companies must balance these diagnostic control systems with other levers of control—boundary systems, belief systems, and interactive control systems—to ensure that proper business ethics, inspirational values, and attention to future threats and opportunities are not sacrificed while achieving business results.

Keys to Success

To prevent unethical and fraudulent behavior, companies must balance the push for performance resulting from diagnostic control systems with three other levers of control: *boundary systems* (standards of behavior and codes of conduct), *belief systems* (mission and core values), and *interactive control systems* (ongoing discussion and debate).

Problem for Self-Study

The baseball division of Home Run Sports manufactures and sells baseballs. Assume production equals sales. Budgeted data for February 2013 are:

Current assets	$ 400,000
Long-term assets	600,000
Total assets	$1,000,000
Production output	200,000 baseballs per month
Target ROI (Operating income ÷ Total assets)	30%
Fixed costs	$400,000 per month
Variable cost	$4 per baseball

Required

1. Compute the minimum selling price per baseball necessary to achieve the target ROI of 30%.
2. Using the selling price from requirement 1, separate the target ROI into its two components using the DuPont method.

3. Compute the RI of the baseball division for February 2013 using the selling price from requirement 1. Home Run Sports uses a required rate of return of 12% on total division assets when computing division RI.
4. In addition to her salary, Amanda Kelly, the division manager, receives 3% of the monthly RI of the baseball division as a bonus. Compute Kelly's bonus. Why do you think Kelly is rewarded using both salary and a performance-based bonus? Kelly does not like bearing risk.

Solution

1.

$$\text{Target operating income} = 30\% \text{ of } \$1{,}000{,}000 \text{ of total assets}$$
$$= \$300{,}000$$
$$\text{Let } P = \text{Selling price}$$
$$\text{Revenues} - \text{Variable costs} - \text{Fixed costs} = \text{Operating income}$$
$$200{,}000P - (200{,}000 \times \$4) - \$400{,}000 = \$300{,}000$$
$$200{,}000P = \$300{,}000 + \$800{,}000 + \$400{,}000$$
$$= \$1{,}500{,}000$$
$$P = \$7.50 \text{ per baseball}$$

Proof:	Revenues, 200,000 baseballs × $7.50/baseball	$1,500,000
	Variable costs, 200,000 baseballs × $4/baseball	800,000
	Contribution margin	700,000
	Fixed costs	400,000
	Operating income	$300,000

2. The DuPont method describes ROI as the product of two components: return on sales (income ÷ revenues) and investment turnover (revenues ÷ investment).

$$\frac{\text{Income}}{\text{Revenues}} \times \frac{\text{Revenues}}{\text{Investment}} = \frac{\text{Income}}{\text{Investment}}$$
$$\frac{\$300{,}000}{\$1{,}500{,}000} \times \frac{\$1{,}500{,}000}{\$1{,}000{,}000} = \frac{\$300{,}000}{\$1{,}000{,}000}$$
$$0.2 \times 1.5 = 0.30, \text{ or } 30\%$$

3.
$$RI = \text{Operating income} - \text{Required return on investment}$$
$$= \$300{,}000 - (0.12 \times \$1{,}000{,}000)$$
$$= \$300{,}000 - \$120{,}000$$
$$= \$180{,}000$$

4.
$$\text{Kelly's bonus} = 3\% \text{ of } RI$$
$$= 0.03 \times \$180{,}000 = \$5{,}400$$

The baseball division's RI is affected by many factors, such as general economic conditions, beyond Kelly's control. These uncontrollable factors make the baseball division's profitability uncertain and risky. Because Kelly does not like bearing risk, paying her a flat salary, regardless of RI, would shield her from this risk. But there is a moral-hazard problem with this compensation arrangement. Because Kelly's effort is difficult to monitor, the absence of performance-based compensation will provide her with no incentive to undertake extra physical and mental effort beyond what is necessary to retain her job or to uphold her personal values.

Paying no salary and rewarding Kelly only on the basis of RI provides her with incentives to work hard but also subjects her to excessive risk because of uncontrollable factors that will affect RI and, in turn, Kelly's compensation. A compensation arrangement based only on RI would be more costly for Home Run Sports because it would have to compensate Kelly for taking on uncontrollable risk. A compensation arrangement that consists of both a salary and an RI-based performance bonus balances the benefits of incentives against the extra costs of imposing uncontrollable risk.

Decision Points

The following question-and-answer format summarizes the chapter's learning objectives. Each decision presents a key question related to a learning objective. The guidelines are the answer to that question.

Decision	Guidelines
1. What financial and nonfinancial performance measures do companies use in their balanced scorecards?	Financial measures such as return on investment and residual income measure aspects of both managerial performance and organization-subunit performance. In many cases, financial measures are supplemented with nonfinancial measures of performance from the customer, internal-business-process, and learning-and-growth perspectives of the balanced scorecard—for example, customer satisfaction, quality of products and services, and employee satisfaction.
2. What are the relative merits of return on investment (ROI), residual income (RI), and economic-value added (EVA) as performance measures for subunit managers?	Return on investment is the product of two components: income divided by revenues (return on sales) and revenues divided by investment (investment turnover). Managers can increase ROI by increasing revenues, decreasing costs, and decreasing investment. However, ROI may induce managers of highly profitable divisions to reject projects that are in the firm's best interest because accepting the project reduces divisional ROI. Residual income is income minus a dollar amount of required return on investment. RI is more likely than ROI to promote goal congruence. Evaluating managers on RI is also consistent with the use of discounted cash flow to choose long-term projects. Economic value added is a variation of the RI calculation. EVA equals after-tax operating income minus the product of (after-tax) weighted-average cost of capital and total assets minus current liabilities.
3. Over what timeframe should companies measure performance, and what are the alternative choices for calculating the components of each performance measure?	A multiyear perspective induces managers to consider the long-term consequences of their actions and prevents a myopic focus on short-run profits. When constructing accounting-based performance measures, firms must first decide on a definition of investment. They must also choose whether to measure assets included in the investment calculations at historical cost or current cost, and whether to calculate depreciable assets at gross or net book value.
4. What targets should companies use and when should they give feedback to managers about their performance relative to these targets?	Companies should tailor a budget to a particular subunit, a particular accounting system, and a particular performance measure. In general, companies can overcome problems of asset valuation and income measurement in a performance measure by emphasizing budgets and targets that stress continuous improvement. Timely feedback is critical to enable managers to implement actions that correct deviations from target performance.
5. How can companies compare the performance of divisions operating in different countries?	Comparing the performance of divisions operating in different countries is difficult because of legal, political, social, economic, and currency differences. ROI and RI calculations for subunits operating in different countries need to be adjusted for differences in inflation between the two countries and changes in exchange rates.
6. Why are managers compensated based on a mix of salary and incentives?	Companies create incentives by rewarding managers on the basis of performance. But managers face risks because factors beyond their control may also affect their performance. Owners choose a mix of salary and incentive compensation to trade off the incentive benefit against the cost of imposing risk.
7. What are the four levers of control, and why does a company need to implement them?	The four levers of control are diagnostic control systems, boundary systems, belief systems, and interactive control systems. Implementing the four levers of control helps a company simultaneously strive for performance, behave ethically, inspire employees, and respond to strategic threats and opportunities.

Terms to Learn

This chapter and the Glossary at the end of the book contain definitions of the following important terms:

belief systems (p. 684)
boundary systems (p. 684)
current cost (p. 673)
diagnostic control systems (p. 684)
economic value added (EVA®) (p. 669)
imputed cost (p. 668)
interactive control systems (p. 685)
investment (p. 666)
moral hazard (p. 679)
residual income (RI) (p. 668)
return on investment (ROI) (p. 666)

Assignment Material

Questions

16-1 What are the three steps in designing accounting-based performance measures?

16-2 What factors affecting ROI does the DuPont method of profitability analysis highlight?

16-3 "RI is not identical to ROI, although both measures incorporate income and investment into their computations." Do you agree?

16-4 Describe EVA.

16-5 What special problems arise when managers evaluate performance in multinational companies?

16-6 Why is it important to distinguish between the performance of a manager and the performance of the organization subunit for which the manager is responsible? Give an example.

16-7 "Managers should be rewarded only on the basis of their performance measures. They should be paid no salary." Do you agree? Explain.

16-8 Explain the role of benchmarking in evaluating managers.

16-9 Explain the incentive problems that can arise when employees must perform multiple tasks as part of their jobs.

16-10 Describe the four levers of control.

Exercises

16-11 ROI, comparisons of three companies. (CMA, adapted) Return on investment is often expressed as follows:

$$\frac{\text{Income}}{\text{Investment}} = \frac{\text{Income}}{\text{Revenues}} \times \frac{\text{Revenues}}{\text{Investment}}$$

Required

1. What are the advantages of breaking down the computation into two separate components?
2. Fill in the following blanks:

	Companies in Same Industry		
	A	B	C
Revenues	$500,000	$200,000	?
Income	$150,000	$ 60,000	?
Investment	$250,000	?	$1,000,000
Income as a percentage of revenues	?	?	3%
Investment turnover	?	?	2.0
ROI	?	6%	?

After filling in the blanks, comment on the relative performance of these companies as thoroughly as the data permit.

16-12 Analysis of return on invested assets, comparison of two divisions, DuPont method. Beyond Learning, Inc., has two divisions: Test Preparation and Language Arts. Results (in millions) for the past 3 years are partially displayed here:

	A	B	C	D	E	F	G
1–3		Operating Income	Operating Revenues	Total Assets	Operating Income/ Operating Revenues	Operating Revenues/ Total Assets	Operating Income/ Total Assets
4	Test Preparation Division						
5	2011	$ 660	$ 7,500	$ 1,875	?	?	?
6	2012	780	?	?	8.0%	?	41.6%
7	2013	1,160	?	?	12.5%	4	?
8	Language Arts Division						
9	2011	$ 620	$ 2,480	$ 1,550	?	?	?
10	2012	?	3,500	2,500	21%	?	?
11	2013	?	?	2,500	?	2	23%
12	Beyond Learning, Inc.						
13	2011	$ 1,280	$ 9,980	$ 3,425	?	?	?
14	2012	?	?	?	?	?	?
15	2013	?	?	?	?	?	?

Required

1. Complete the table by filling in the blanks.
2. Use the DuPont method of profitability analysis to explain changes in the operating-income-to-total-assets ratios over the 2011–2013 period for each division and for Beyond Learning as a whole. Comment on the results.

16-13 ROI and RI. (D. Kleespie, adapted) The New Athletics Company produces a wide variety of outdoor sports equipment. Its newest division, Golf Technology, manufactures and sells a single product—AccuDriver, a golf club that uses global positioning satellite technology to improve the accuracy of golfers' shots. The demand for AccuDriver is relatively insensitive to price changes. The following data are available for Golf Technology, which is an investment center for New Athletics:

Total annual fixed costs	$28,000,000
Variable cost per AccuDriver	$ 350
Number of AccuDrivers sold each year	160,000
Average operating assets invested in the division	$44,000,000

Required

1. Compute Golf Technology's ROI if the selling price of AccuDrivers is $570 per club.
2. If management requires an ROI of at least 30% from the division, what is the minimum selling price that the Golf Technology Division should charge per AccuDriver club?
3. Assume that New Athletics judges the performance of its investment centers on the basis of RI rather than ROI. What is the minimum selling price that Golf Technology should charge per AccuDriver if the company's required rate of return is 22%?

16-14 ROI and RI with manufacturing costs. Fabulous Motor Company makes electric cars and has only two products, Simplegreen and Fabulousgreen. To produce Simplegreen, Fabulous Motor employed assets of $14,600,000 at the beginning of the period, and $27,300,000 of assets at the end of the period. Other costs to manufacture Simplegreen include the following:

Direct materials	$1,000 per unit
Setup	$1,800 per setup-hour
Production	$580 per machine-hour

General administration and selling costs total $8,460,000 for the period. In the current period, Fabulous Motor produced 8,000 Simplegreen cars using 7,000 setup-hours and 178,600 machine-hours. Fabulous Motor sold these cars for $17,000 each.

Required

1. Assuming that Fabulous Motor defines investment as average assets during the period, what is the return on investment for the Simplegreen division?
2. Calculate the residual income for Simplegreen if Fabulous Motor has a required rate of return of 13% on investments.

16-15 Financial and nonfinancial performance measures, goal congruence. (CMA, adapted) Precision Equipment specializes in the manufacture of medical equipment, a field that has become increasingly competitive. Approximately 2 years ago, Pedro Mendez, president of Precision, decided to revise the bonus plan (based, at the time, entirely on operating income) to encourage division managers to focus on areas that were important to customers and that added value without increasing cost. In addition to a profitability incentive, the revised plan includes incentives for reduced rework costs, reduced sales returns, and on-time deliveries. The company calculates and rewards bonuses semiannually on the following basis: A base bonus is calculated at 2% of operating income; this amount is then adjusted as:

a. (i) Reduced by excess of rework costs over and above 2% of operating income
   (ii) No adjustment if rework costs are less than or equal to 2% of operating income

b. (i) Increased by $4,000 if more than 98% of deliveries are on time, and by $1,500 if 96–98% of deliveries are on time
   (ii) No adjustment if on-time deliveries are below 96%

c. (i) Increased by $2,500 if sales returns are less than or equal to 1.5% of sales
   (ii) Decreased by 50% of excess of sales returns over 1.5% of sales

Note: If the calculation of the bonus results in a negative amount for a particular period, the manager simply receives no bonus, and the negative amount is not carried forward to the next period.

Results for Precision's Central division and Western division for 2013, the first year under the new bonus plan, follow. In 2012, under the old bonus plan, the Central division manager earned a bonus of $20,295 and the Western division manager, a bonus of $15,830.

	Central Division		Western Division	
	January 1, 2013, to June 30, 2013	July 1, 2013, to Dec. 31, 2013	January 1, 2013, to June 30, 2013	July 1, 2013, to Dec. 31, 2013
Revenues	$3,150,000	$3,300,000	$2,137,500	$2,175,000
Operating income	$346,500	$330,000	$256,500	$304,500
On-time delivery	95.4%	97.3%	98.2%	94.6%
Rework costs	$8,625	$8,250	$4,500	$6,000
Sales returns	$63,000	$52,500	$33,560	$31,875

Required

1. Why did Mendez need to introduce these new performance measures? That is, why does Mendez need to use these performance measures in addition to the operating-income numbers for the period?
2. Calculate the bonus earned by each manager for each 6-month period and for 2013.
3. What effect did the change in the bonus plan have on each manager's behavior? Did the new bonus plan achieve what Mendez wanted? What changes, if any, would you make to the new bonus plan?

16-16 Goal incongruence and ROI. McCall Corporation manufactures furniture in several divisions, including the Patio Furniture division. The manager of the Patio Furniture division plans to retire in 2 years. The manager receives a bonus based on the division's ROI, which is currently 15%.

One of the machines the Patio Furniture division uses to manufacture furniture is rather old, and the manager must decide whether to replace it. The new machine would cost $35,000 and would last 10 years. It would have no salvage value. The old machine is fully depreciated and has no trade-in value. McCall uses straight-line depreciation for all assets. The new machine, being new and more efficient, would save the company $7,000 per year in cash operating costs. The only difference between cash flow and net income is depreciation. The internal rate of return of the project is approximately 15%. McCall Corporation's weighted average cost of capital is 8%. McCall is not subject to any income taxes.

Required

1. Should McCall Corporation replace the machine? Why or why not?
2. Assume that "investment" is defined as average net long-term assets after depreciation. Compute the project's ROI for each of its first 5 years. If the Patio Furniture manager is interested in maximizing his bonus, would he replace the machine before he retires? Why or why not?
3. What can McCall do to entice the manager to replace the machine before retiring?

16-17 ROI, RI, EVA. Accelerate Auto Company operates a new car division (that sells high-performance sports cars) and a performance parts division (that sells performance improvement parts for family cars). Some division financial measures for 2012 are:

	A	B	C
1		New Car Division	Performance Parts Division
2	Total assets	$ 40,000,000	$ 31,562,500
3	Current liabilities	$ 6,100,000	$ 8,300,000
4	Operating income	$ 2,600,000	$ 2,525,000
5	Required rate of return	9%	9%

Required

1. Calculate ROI for each division using operating income as a measure of income and total assets as a measure of investment.
2. Calculate residual income (RI) for each division using operating income as a measure of income and total assets minus current liabilities as a measure of investment.
3. William Abraham, the New Car Division manager, argues that the performance parts division has "loaded up on a lot of short-term debt" to boost its RI. Calculate an alternative RI for each division that is not sensitive to the amount of short-term debt taken on by the performance parts division. Comment on the result.
4. Accelerate Auto Company, whose tax rate is 35%, has two sources of funds: long-term debt with a market value of $19,000,000 at an interest rate of 10%, and equity capital with a market value of $9,000,000 and a cost of equity of 14%. Applying the same weighted-average cost of capital (WACC) to each division, calculate EVA for each division.
5. Use your preceding calculations to comment on the relative performance of each division.

16-18 ROI, RI, measurement of assets. (CMA, adapted) Cole Corporation recently announced a bonus plan to be awarded to the manager of the most profitable division. The three division managers are to choose whether ROI or RI will be used to measure profitability. In addition, they must decide whether investment will be measured using gross book value or net book value of assets. Cole defines income as operating income and investment as total assets. The following information is available for the year just ended:

Division	Gross Book Value of Assets	Accumulated Depreciation	Operating Income
Fowler	$2,103,000	$1,100,000	$220,500
Baldwin	1,360,000	786,000	156,000
Ulster	826,000	531,000	99,900

Cole uses a required rate of return of 9% on investment to calculate RI.

Required

Each division manager has selected a method of bonus calculation that ranks his or her division number one. Identify the method for calculating profitability that each manager selected, supporting your answer with appropriate calculations. Comment on the strengths and weaknesses of the methods chosen by each manager.

16-19 Multinational performance measurement, ROI, RI. The Pioneer Corporation manufactures similar products in the United States and Norway. The U.S. and Norwegian operations are organized as decentralized divisions. The following information is available for 2012; ROI is calculated as operating income divided by total assets:

	U.S. Division	Norwegian Division
Operating income	?	7,560,000 kroner
Total assets	$8,000,000	54,000,000 kroner
ROI	14.0%	?

Both investments were made on December 31, 2011. The exchange rate at the time of Pioneer's investment in Norway on December 31, 2011, was 6 kroner = $1. During 2012, the Norwegian kroner decreased steadily in value so that the exchange rate on December 31, 2012, is 8 kroner = $1. The average exchange rate during 2012 is $[(6 + 8) \div 2] = 7$ kroner = $1.

Required

1. a. Calculate the U.S. division's operating income for 2012.
   b. Calculate the Norwegian division's ROI for 2012 in kroner.
2. Top management wants to know which division earned a better ROI in 2012. What would you tell them? Explain your answer.
3. Which division do you think had the better RI performance? Explain your answer. The required rate of return on investment (calculated in U.S. dollars) is 13%.

16-20 ROI, RI, EVA, and performance evaluation. Cora Manufacturing makes fashion products and competes on the basis of quality and leading-edge designs. The company has $2,500,000 invested in assets in its clothing manufacturing division. After-tax operating income from sales of clothing this year is $550,000. The cosmetics division has $11,000,000 invested in assets and an after-tax operating income this year of $1,650,000. Income for the clothing division has grown steadily over the last few years. The weighted-average cost of capital for Cora is 8% and the previous period's after-tax return on investment for each division was 13%. The CEO of Cora has told the manager of each division that the division that "performs best" this year will get a bonus.

Required

1. Calculate the ROI and residual income (using the weighted-average cost of capital) for each division of Cora Manufacturing, and briefly explain which manager will get the bonus. What are the advantages and disadvantages of each measure?
2. The CEO of Cora Manufacturing has recently heard of another measure similar to residual income called EVA. The CEO has the accountant calculate EVA adjusted incomes of clothing and cosmetics, and finds that the adjusted after-tax operating incomes are $401,400 and $2,067,200, respectively. Also, the clothing division has $270,000 of current liabilities, while the cosmetics division has only $120,000 of current liabilities. Using the preceding information, calculate EVA and discuss which division manager will get the bonus.
3. What nonfinancial measures could Cora use to evaluate divisional performances?

16-21 Risk sharing, incentives, benchmarking, multiple tasks. The Peterson division of MACO sells car batteries. MACO's corporate management gives Peterson management considerable operating and investment autonomy in running the division. MACO is considering how it should compensate Ben Starks, the general manager of the Peterson division. Proposal 1 calls for paying Starks a fixed salary. Proposal 2 calls for paying Starks no salary and compensating him only on the basis of the division's ROI, calculated based on operating income before any bonus payments. Proposal 3 calls for paying Starks some salary and some bonus based on ROI. Assume that Starks does not like bearing risk.

Required

1. Evaluate the three proposals, specifying the advantages and disadvantages of each.
2. Suppose that MACO competes against Crown Industries in the car battery business. Crown is approximately the same size as the Peterson division and operates in a business environment that is similar to Peterson's. The top management of MACO is considering evaluating Starks on the basis of Peterson's ROI minus Crown's ROI. Starks complains that this approach is unfair because the performance of another company, over which he has no control, is included in his performance-evaluation measure. Is Starks's complaint valid? Why or why not?
3. Now suppose that Starks has no authority for making capital-investment decisions. Corporate management makes these decisions. Is ROI a good performance measure to use to evaluate Starks? Is ROI a good measure to evaluate the economic viability of the Peterson division? Explain.
4. Peterson's salespeople are responsible for selling and providing customer service and support. Sales are easy to measure. Although customer service is important to Peterson in the long run, it has not yet implemented customer-service measures. Starks wants to compensate his sales force only on the basis of sales commissions paid for each unit of product sold. He cites two advantages to this plan: (a) It creates strong incentives for the sales force to work hard and (b) the company pays salespeople only when the company itself is earning revenues. Do you like his plan? Why or why not?

Problems

16-22 Residual income and EVA, timing issues. Doorharmony Company makes doorbells. It has a weighted average cost of capital of 8% and total assets of $5,450,000. Doorharmony has current liabilities of $600,000. Its operating income for the year was $640,000. Doorharmony does not have to pay any income taxes. One of the expenses for accounting purposes was a $150,000 advertising campaign. The entire amount was deducted this year, although the Doorharmony CEO believes the beneficial effects of this advertising will last 4 years.

Required

1. Calculate residual income (using the weighted-average cost of capital), assuming Doorharmony defines investment as total assets.

2. Calculate EVA for the year. Adjust both the assets and operating income for advertising assuming that for the purposes of economic value added the advertising is capitalized and amortized on a straight-line basis over 4 years.
3. Discuss the difference between the outcomes of requirements 1 and 2. Which measure would you recommend?

16-23 ROI performance measures based on historical cost and current cost. Natural Bounty Corporation operates three divisions that process and bottle natural fruit juices. The historical-cost accounting system reports the following information for 2012:

	Passion Fruit Division	Kiwi Fruit Division	Mango Fruit Division
Revenues	$900,000	$1,600,000	$2,500,000
Operating costs (excluding plant depreciation)	550,000	830,000	900,000
Plant depreciation	80,000	180,000	270,000
Operating income	$270,000	$ 590,000	$1,330,000
Current assets	$475,000	$ 520,000	$ 700,000
Long-term assets—plant	160,000	1,260,000	2,700,000
Total assets	$635,000	$1,780,000	$3,400,000

Natural Bounty estimates the useful life of each plant to be 12 years, with no terminal disposal value. The company uses the straight-line depreciation method. At the end of 2012, the Passion Fruit plant is 10 years old, the Kiwi Fruit plant is 5 years old, and the Mango Fruit plant is 2 years old. An index of construction costs over the 10-year period that Natural Bounty has been operating (2002 year-end = 100) is:

2002	2007	2010	2012
100	130	180	190

Given the high turnover of current assets, management believes that the historical-cost and current-cost measures of current assets are approximately the same.

Required

1. Compute the ROI ratio (operating income to total assets) of each division using historical-cost measures. Comment on the results.
2. Use the approach in Exhibit 16-2 (page 674) to compute the ROI of each division, incorporating current-cost estimates as of 2012 for depreciation expense and long-term assets. Comment on the results.
3. What advantages might arise from using current-cost asset measures as compared with historical-cost measures for evaluating the performance of the managers of the three divisions?

16-24 ROI, measurement alternatives for performance measures Appleton's operates casual dining restaurants in three regions: St. Louis, Memphis, and New Orleans. Each geographic market is considered a separate division. The St. Louis division is made up of four restaurants, each built in early 2003. The Memphis division is made up of three restaurants, each built in January 2007. The New Orleans division is the newest, consisting of three restaurants built 4 years ago. Division managers at Appleton's are evaluated on the basis of ROI. The following information refers to the three divisions at the end of 2013:

	A	B	C	D	E
1		St. Louis	Memphis	New Orleans	Total
2	Division revenues	$17,336,000	$12,050,000	$10,890,000	$40,276,000
3	Division expenses	15,890,000	11,042,000	9,958,000	36,890,000
4	Division operating income	1,446,000	1,008,000	932,000	3,386,000
5	Gross book value of long-term assets	9,000,000	7,500,000	8,100,000	24,600,000
6	Accumulated depreciation	6,600,000	3,500,000	2,160,000	12,260,000
7	Current assets	1,999,600	1,536,400	1,649,200	5,185,200
8	Depreciation expense	600,000	500,000	540,000	1,640,000
9	Construction cost index for year of construction	100	110	118	

Required

1. Calculate ROI for each division using net book value of total assets.
2. Compute ROI using current-cost estimates for long-term assets and depreciation expense. Construction cost index for 2013 is 122. Estimated useful life of operational assets is 15 years.
3. How does the choice of long-term asset valuation affect management decisions about new capital investments? Why might this choice be more significant to the St. Louis division manager than to the New Orleans division manager?

16-25 ROI, RI, and multinational firms. Versa Corporation has a division in the United States and another in France. The investment in the French assets was made when the exchange rate was $1.30 per euro. The average exchange rate for the year was $1.40 per euro. The exchange rate at the end of the fiscal year was $1.45 per euro. Income and investment for the two divisions are:

	United States	France
Investment in assets	$10,900,000	7,600,000 euro
Income for current year	$1,362,500	972,800 euro

Required

1. The required return for Versa is 12%. Calculate ROI and RI for the two divisions. For the French division, calculate these measures using both dollars and euro. Which division is doing better?
2. What are the advantages and disadvantages of translating the French division information from euro to dollars?

16-26 Multinational firms, differing risk, comparison of profit, ROI and RI. Zeiss Multinational, Inc., has divisions in the United States, Germany, and New Zealand. The U.S. division is the oldest and most established of the three, and has a cost of capital of 6.5%. The German division was started 3 years ago when the exchange rate for the euro was 1 euro = $1.40. The German division is a large and powerful division of Zeiss, Inc., with a cost of capital of 10%. The New Zealand division was started this year, when the exchange rate was 1 New Zealand Dollar (NZD) = $0.75. Its cost of capital is 13%. Average exchange rates for the current year are 1 euro = $1.50 and 1 NZD = $0.60. Other information for the three divisions includes:

	United States	Germany	New Zealand
Long-term assets	$24,214,700	11,897,321 euro	7,343,744 NZD
Operating revenues	$23,362,940	6,250,000 euros	5,718,750 NZD
Operating expenses	$18,520,000	4,200,000 euros	4,250,000 NZD
Income-tax rate	40%	35%	25%

Required

1. Translate the German and New Zealand information into dollars to make the divisions comparable. Find the after-tax operating income for each division and compare the profits.
2. Calculate ROI using after-tax operating income. Compare among divisions.
3. Use after-tax operating income and the individual cost of capital of each division to calculate residual income and compare.
4. Redo requirement 2 using pretax operating income instead of net income. Why is there a big difference, and what does it mean for performance evaluation?

16-27 ROI, RI, DuPont method, investment decisions, balanced scorecard. World Information Group has two major divisions: print and Internet. Summary financial data (in millions) for 2011 and 2012 are:

Home Insert Page Layout Formulas Data Review View

	A	B	C	D	E	F	G	H	I
1		Operating Income			Revenues			Total Assets	
2		2011	2012		2011	2012		2011	2012
3	Print	$3,780	$5,850		$18,700	$18,800		$18,450	$22,500
4	Internet	560	754		25,100	26,000		11,250	13,000

The annual bonuses of the two division managers are based on division ROI (defined as operating income divided by total assets). If a division reports an increase in ROI from the previous year, its management is automatically eligible for a bonus; however, the management of a division reporting a decline in ROI has to present an explanation to the World Information Group board and is unlikely to get any bonus.

Carol Mays, manager of the print division, is considering a proposal to invest $1,550 million in a new computerized news reporting and printing system. It is estimated that the new system's state-of-the-art graphics and ability to quickly incorporate late-breaking news into papers will increase 2013 division operating income by $310 million. World Information Group uses a 16% required rate of return on investment for each division.

Required

1. Use the DuPont method of profitability analysis to explain differences in 2012 ROIs between the two divisions. Use 2012 total assets as the investment base.
2. Why might Mays be less than enthusiastic about accepting the investment proposal for the new system, despite her belief in the benefits of the new technology?
3. Brett Gostkowski, CEO of World Information Group, is considering a proposal to base division executive compensation on division RI.
   a. Compute the 2012 RI of each division.
   b. Would adoption of an RI measure reduce Mays's reluctance to adopt the new computerized system investment proposal?
4. Gostkowski is concerned that the focus on annual ROI could have an adverse long-run effect on World Information Group's customers. What other measurements, if any, do you recommend that Gostkowski use? Explain briefly.

16-28 Division managers' compensation, levers of control (continuation of 16-27). Brett Gostkowski seeks your advice on revising the existing bonus plan for division managers of World Information Group. Assume division managers do not like bearing risk. Gostkowski is considering three ideas:

- Make each division manager's compensation depend on division RI.
- Make each division manager's compensation depend on company-wide RI.
- Use benchmarking and compensate division managers on the basis of their division's RI minus the RI of the other division.

Required

1. Evaluate Gostkowski's three ideas using performance-evaluation concepts described in this chapter. Indicate the benefits and drawbacks of each proposal.
2. Gostkowski is concerned that the pressure for short-run performance may cause managers to cut corners. What systems might Gostkowski introduce to avoid this problem? Explain briefly.
3. Gostkowski is also concerned that the pressure for short-run performance might cause managers to ignore emerging threats and opportunities. What system might Gostkowski introduce to prevent this problem? Explain briefly.

16-29 Executive compensation, balanced scorecard. Mercantile Bank recently introduced a new bonus plan for its business unit executives. The company believes that current profitability and customer satisfaction levels are equally important to the bank's long-term success. As a result, the new plan awards a bonus equal to 1% of salary for each 1% increase in business unit net income or 1% increase in the business unit's customer satisfaction index. For example, increasing net income from $3 million to $3.3 million (or 10% from its initial value) leads to a bonus of 10% of salary, while increasing the business unit's customer satisfaction index from 70 to 73.5 (or 5% from its initial value) leads to a bonus of 5% of salary. There is no bonus penalty when net income or customer satisfaction declines. In 2012 and 2013, Mercantile Bank's three business units reported the following performance results:

	Retail Banking		Business Banking		Credit Cards	
	2012	2013	2012	2013	2012	2013
Net income	$3,600,000	$3,912,000	$3,800,000	$3,940,000	$3,550,000	$3,499,000
Customer satisfaction	73	75.48	68	75.9	67	78.88

Required

1. Compute the bonus as a percent of salary earned by each business unit executive in 2013.
2. What factors might explain the differences between improvement rates for net income and those for customer satisfaction in the three units? Are increases in customer satisfaction likely to result in increased net income right away?
3. Mercantile Bank's board of directors is concerned that the 2013 bonus awards may not actually reflect the executives' overall performance. In particular, the bank is concerned that executives can earn large bonuses by doing well on one performance dimension but underperforming on the other. What changes can it make to the bonus plan to prevent this from happening in the future? Explain briefly.

16-30 Ethics, manager's performance evaluation. (A. Spero, adapted) Stanford Semiconductors manufactures specialized chips that sell for $50 each. Stanford's manufacturing costs consist of variable cost of $6 per chip and fixed costs of $16,000,000. Stanford also incurs $1,800,000 in fixed marketing costs each year.

Stanford calculates operating income using absorption costing—that is, Stanford calculates manufacturing cost per unit by dividing total manufacturing costs by actual production. Stanford costs all units in inventory at this rate and expenses the costs in the income statement at the time when the units in inventory are sold. Next year, 2014, appears to be a difficult year for Stanford. It expects to sell only 400,000 units. The demand for these chips fluctuates considerably, so Stanford usually holds minimal inventory.

Required

1. Calculate Stanford's operating income in 2014 (a) if Stanford manufactures 400,000 units and (b) if it manufactures 500,000 units.
2. Would it be unethical for Randy Franklin, general manager of Stanford Semiconductors, to produce more units than can be sold in order to show better operating results? Franklin's compensation has a bonus component based on operating income. Explain your answer.
3. Would it be unethical for Franklin to ask distributors to buy more product than they need? Stanford follows the industry practice of booking sales when products are shipped to distributors. Explain your answer.

16-31 Ethics, levers of control. Best Moulding is a large manufacturer of wood picture frame moulding. The company operates distribution centers in Dallas and Philadelphia. The distribution centers cut frames to size (called "chops") and ship them to custom picture framers. Because of the exacting standards and natural flaws of wood picture frame moulding, the company typically produces a large amount of waste in cutting chops. In recent years, the company's average yield has been 78% of length moulding. The remaining 22% is sent to a wood recycler. Best's performance-evaluation system pays its distribution center managers substantial bonuses if the company achieves annual budgeted profit numbers. In the last quarter of 2013, Stuart Brown, Best's controller, noted a significant increase in yield percentage of the Dallas distribution center, from 76% to 87%. This increase resulted in a 6% increase in the center's profits.

During a recent trip to the Dallas center, Brown wandered into the moulding warehouse. He noticed that much of the scrap moulding was being returned to the inventory bins rather than being placed in the discard pile. Upon further inspection, he determined that the moulding was in fact unusable. When he asked one of the workers, he was told that the center's manager had directed workers to stop scrapping all but the very shortest pieces. This practice resulted in the center overreporting both yield and ending inventory. The overstatement of Dallas inventory will have a significant impact on Best's financial statements.

Required

1. What should Brown do? You may want to refer to the *IMA Statement of Ethical Professional Practice,* pages 17–18.
2. Which lever of control is Best emphasizing? What changes, if any, should be made?

16-32 RI, EVA, measurement alternatives, goal congruence. Renewal Resorts, Inc., operates health spas in Key West, Florida; Phoenix, Arizona; and Carmel, California. The Key West spa was the company's first and opened in 1986. The Phoenix spa opened in 1999, and the Carmel spa opened in 2008. Renewal Resorts has previously evaluated divisions based on RI, but the company is considering changing to an EVA approach. All spas are assumed to face similar risks. Data for 2012 are:

Home Insert Page Layout Formulas Data Review View

	A	B	C	D	E
1		**Key West Spa**	**Phoenix Spa**	**Carmel Spa**	**Total**
2	Revenues	$4,100,000	$4,380,000	$3,230,000	$11,710,000
3	Variable costs	1,600,000	1,630,000	955,000	4,185,000
4	Fixed costs	1,280,000	1,560,000	980,000	3,820,000
5	Operating income	1,220,000	1,190,000	1,295,000	3,705,000
6	Interest costs on long-term debt at 8%	368,000	416,000	440,000	1,224,000
5	Income before taxes at 35%	852,000	774,000	855,000	2,481,000
6	Net income	553,800	503,100	555,750	1,612,650
7					
8	Net book value at 2012 year-end:				
9	Current assets	$1,280,000	$ 850,000	$ 600,000	$ 2,730,000
10	Long-term assets	4,875,000	5,462,000	6,835,000	17,172,000
11	Total assets	6,155,000	6,312,000	7,435,000	19,902,000
12	Current liabilities	330,000	265,000	84,000	679,000
13	Long-term debt	4,600,000	5,200,000	5,500,000	15,300,000
14	Stockholders' equity	1,225,000	847,000	1,851,000	3,923,000
15	Total liabilities and stockholders' equity	6,155,000	6,312,000	7,435,000	19,902,000
16					
17	Market value of debt	$4,600,000	$5,200,000	$5,500,000	$15,300,000
18	Market value of equity	2,400,000	2,660,000	2,590,000	7,650,000
19	Cost of equity capital				14%
20	Required rate of return				11%
21	Accumulated depreciation on long-term assets	2,220,000	1,510,000	220,000	

Required

1. Calculate RI for each of the spas based on operating income and using total assets as the measure of investment. Suppose that the Key West spa is considering adding a new group of saunas from Finland that will cost $225,000. The saunas are expected to bring in operating income of $22,000. What effect would this project have on the RI of the Key West spa? Based on RI, would the Key West manager accept or reject this project? Why? Without resorting to calculations, would the other managers accept or reject the project? Why?
2. Why might Renewal Resorts want to use EVA instead of RI for evaluating the performance of the three spas?
3. Refer back to the original data. Calculate the WACC for Renewal Resorts.
4. Refer back to the original data. Calculate EVA for each of the spas, using net book value of long-term assets. Calculate EVA again, this time using gross book value of long-term assets. Comment on the differences between the two methods.
5. How does the selection of asset measurement method affect goal congruence?

Case

Enager Industries, Inc.

> I don't get it. I've got a new product proposal that can't help but make money, and top management turns thumbs down. No matter how we price this new item, we expect to make $390,000 on it pretax. That would contribute over ten cents per share to our earnings after taxes, which is more than the 10-cent earnings-per-share increase last year that the president made such a big thing about in the shareholders' annual report. It just doesn't make sense for the president to be touting EPS while his subordinates are rejecting profitable projects like this one.

The speaker was Sarah McNeil, product development manager of the Consumer Products Division of Enager Industries, Inc. Enager was a relatively young company, which had grown rapidly to its current sales level of over $222 million. (See Enager Industries, Inc. Exhibits 1 and 2 for financial data.)

Enager had three divisions, Consumer Products, Industrial Products, and Professional Services, each of which accounted for about one third of total sales. Consumer Products, the oldest division, designed, manufactured, and marketed a line of houseware items, primarily for use in the kitchen. The Industrial Products Division built one-of-a-kind machine tools to customer specifications; i.e., it was a large "job shop," with the typical job taking several months to complete. The Professional Services Division, the newest of the three, had been added to Enager by acquiring a large firm that provided land planning, landscape architecture, structural architecture, and consulting engineering services. This division had grown rapidly in part because of its capability to perform environmental impact studies, as required by law on many new land development projects.

Enager Industries, Inc. Exhibit 1

Income Statements ($000, except shares and earnings per share figures)

	Year Ended December 31	
	Last Year	This Year
Sales	$ 212,193	$ 222,675
Cost of sales	162,327	168,771
Gross Margin	$ 49,866	$ 53,904
Other Expenses:		
Development	$ 12,096	$ 12,024
Selling and general	19,521	20,538
Interest	1,728	2,928
Total	$ 33,345	$ 35,490
Income before taxes	$ 16,521	$ 18,414
Income tax expense	5,617	6,261
Net Income	$ 10,904	$ 12,153
Shares outstanding	1,500,000	1,650,000
Earnings per share	$ 7.27	$ 7.37

Source: This case was prepared by Professor James S. Reece. It is intended as a basis for class discussion and not to illustrate either effective or ineffective handling of an administrative situation.

Enager Industries, Inc. Exhibit 2

Balance Sheets ($000)

Assets	As of December 31 Last Year	This Year
Current assets:		
Cash & temporary investments	$ 4,212	$ 4,407
Accounts receivable	41,064	46,821
Inventories	66,486	76,401
Total current assets	$111,762	$127,629
Plant & equipment:		
Original cost	111,978	137,208
Accumulated depreciation	38,073	47,937
Net	$ 73,905	$ 89,271
Investments & other assets	6,429	9,357
Total Assets	$192,096	$226,257
Liabilities and Owners Equity		
Current liabilities		
Accounts payable	$ 29,160	$ 36,858
Taxes payable	3,630	3,135
Current portion of long-term debt	0	4,902
Total current liabilities	$ 32,790	$ 44,895
Deferred income taxes	1,677	2,955
Long-term debt	37,866	46,344
Total liabilities	$ 72,333	$ 94,194
Common stock	52,104	58,536
Retained earnings	67,659	73,527
Total owners' equity	$119,763	$132,063
Total liabilities and owners' equity	$192,096	$226,257

Because of the differing nature of their activities, each division was treated as an essentially independent company. There were only a few corporate-level managers and staff people, whose job was to coordinate the activities of the three divisions. One aspect of this coordination was that all new project proposals requiring investment in excess of $1,500,000 had to be reviewed by the corporate vice president of finance, Henry Hubbard. It was Hubbard who had recently rejected McNeil's new product proposal, the essentials of which are shown in Enager Industries, Inc. Exhibit 3.

Performance Evaluation

Historically, each division had been treated as a profit center, with an annual division profit budget negotiated between the president and the division's general manager. At that time, Enager's president, Carl Randall, had become concerned about high interest rates and their impact on the company's profitability. At the urging of Mr. Hubbard, Mr. Randall had decided to begin treating each division as an investment center so as to be able to relate each division's profit to the assets it used to generate its profits.

Starting two years ago, each division began to be measured based on its return on assets, which was defined to be its net income divided by its total assets. Net income for a division was calculated by taking its income before taxes and subtracting its share of corporate administrative expenses (allocated on the basis of divisional revenues) and its share of income tax expense (the

Enager Industries, Inc. Exhibit 3

Financial Data from New Product Proposal

1.	Projected asset investment:*		
	Cash		$ 150,000
	Accounts receivable		450,000
	Inventories		900,000
	Plant and equipment†		1,500,000
	Total		$3,000,000
2.	Cost data:		
	Variable cost per unit		$ 9.00
	Differential fixed costs (per year)‡		$ 510,000
3.	Price/market estimates (per year):		
	Unit Price	Unit Sales	Breakeven Volume
	$18.00	100,000	56,667 units
	21.00	75,000	42,500
	24.00	60,000	34,000

*Assumes 100,000 units' sales.
†Annual capacity of 120,000 units.
‡Includes straight-line depreciation on new plant and equipment.

tax rate applied to the division's income after subtracting the allocated corporate administrative expenses). Although Mr. Hubbard realized there were other ways to define a division's income, he and Mr. Randall preferred this method since it ". . . made the sum of the [divisional] parts equal to the [corporate] whole."

Similarly, Enager's total assets were subdivided among the three divisions. Since each division operated in physically separate facilities, it was easy to attribute most assets, including receivables, to the appropriate division. The corporate-office assets, including the centrally controlled cash account, were allocated to the divisions on the basis of divisional revenue. All fixed assets were recorded at their balance sheet values, that is, original cost less accumulated straight-line depreciation.

Thus, the sum of the assets for the three divisions was equal to the amount shown on the corporate balance sheet ($226,257 as of December 31 of the current year).

Two years ago, Enager had a return on assets (net income divided by total year-end assets) of 5.2 percent. According to Mr. Hubbard, this corresponded to a "gross return" of 9.3 percent; he defined gross return as earnings *before* interest and taxes (EBIT) divided by total year-end assets. Mr. Hubbard felt that a company like Enager should have a gross EBIT return on assets of at least 12 percent, especially given the interest rates the corporation had to pay on its recent borrowings. He therefore instructed each division manager to try to earn a gross return of 12 percent. In order to help pull the return up to this level, Mr. Hubbard decided that new investment proposals would have to show a return of at least 15 percent in order to be approved.

Results of the Last Two Years

Messrs. Hubbard and Randall were moderately pleased with the results following the change to investment centers, especially since that year was a particularly difficult one for some of Enager's competitors. Enager had managed to increase its return on assets from 5.2 to 5.7 percent, and its gross return from 9.3 to 9.5 percent.

Despite these improvements, Mr. Randall had put pressure on the general manager of the Industrial Products Division to improve its return on assets, suggesting that this division was not "carrying its share of the load." The division manager had taken exception to this comment, saying the division could get a higher return "if we had a lot of old machines the way Consumer

Enager Industries, Inc.
Exhibit 4
Calculation of Gross Return on Assets for Most Recent Year

Division	Sales	EBIT	W/C	Fixed Assets	Allocations	Total Assets	Gross ROA
Consumer Products	74.3	10.8	60.8	34.6	4.6	100.0	10.8%
Industrial Products	74.2	7.2	44.4	54.7	4.6	103.7	6.9%
Professional Services	74.2	3.3	18.0	0.0	4.6	22.6	14.6%
Total	222.7	21.3	123.2	89.3	13.8	226.3	9.4%

Products does." Mr. Randall had responded that he did not understand the relevance of this remark, adding, "I don't see why the return on an old asset should be higher than that on a new asset, just because the old one cost less."

The current year's results both disappointed and puzzled Mr. Randall. Return on assets fell from 5.7 to 5.4 percent, and gross return dropped from 9.5 to 9.4 percent, At the same time, return on sales (net income divided by sales) rose from 5.1 to 5.5 percent, and return on owners' equity increased, from 9.1 to 9.2 percent. The Professional Services Division easily exceeded the 12 percent gross return target; Consumer Products gross return on assets was 10.8 percent, and Industrial Products return was 6.9 percent (see Enager Industries, Inc. Exhibit 4). These results prompted Mr. Randall to say the following to Mr. Hubbard:

> You know, Henry, I've been a marketer most of my career, but until recently I thought I understood the notion of return on investment. Now I see our profit margin was up and our earnings per share were up; yet two of your return on investment figures were down, one—return on invested capital—held constant, and return on owners' equity went up. I just don't understand these discrepancies.
>
> Moreover, there seems to be a lot more tension among our managers the last two years. The general manger of Professional Services seems to be doing a good job, and she seems pleased with the praise I've given her. But the general manager of Industrial Products looks daggers at me every time we meet. And last week, when I was eating lunch with the division manager at Consumer Products, the product development manager came over to our table and expressed her frustration about your rejecting a new product proposal of hers the other day
>
> I'm wondering if I should follow up on the idea that Karen Kraus in personnel brought back from that two-day organization development workshop she attended over at the university. She thinks we ought to have a one-day offsite "retreat" of all the corporate and divisional managers to talk over this entire return on investment matter.

Assignment

1. Why was McNeil's new product proposal rejected? Should it have been?
2. Prepare a cash flow statement for the most recent year. Using it in conjunction with the comparative income statements and balance sheets, what conclusions do you draw about Enager Industries financial health?
3. Evaluate the manner in which Messrs. Randall and Hubbard have implemented their investment center concept. What pitfalls did they apparently not anticipate?
4. What, if anything, should Mr. Randall do now with regard to his investment center approach?

Appendix

Notes on Compound Interest and Interest Tables

Interest is the cost of using money. It is the rental charge for funds, just as renting a building and equipment entails a rental charge. When the funds are used for a period of time, it is necessary to recognize interest as a cost of using the borrowed ("rented") funds. This requirement applies even if the funds represent ownership capital and if interest does not entail an outlay of cash. Why must interest be considered? Because the selection of one alternative automatically commits a given amount of funds that could otherwise be invested in some other alternative.

Interest is generally important, even when short-term projects are under consideration. Interest looms correspondingly larger when long-run plans are studied. The rate of interest has significant enough impact to influence decisions regarding borrowing and investing funds. For example, \$100,000 invested now and compounded annually for 10 years at 8% will accumulate to \$215,900; at 20%, the \$100,000 will accumulate to \$619,200.

Interest Tables

Many computer programs and pocket calculators are available that handle computations involving the time value of money. You may also turn to the following four basic tables to compute interest.

Table 1—Future Amount of \$1

Table 1 shows how much \$1 invested now will accumulate in a given number of periods at a given compounded interest rate per period. Consider investing \$1,000 now for three years at 8% compound interest. A tabular presentation of how this \$1,000 would accumulate to \$1,259.70 follows:

Year	Interest per Year	Cumulative Interest Called Compound Interest	Total at End of Year
0	\$—	\$—	\$1,000.00
1	80.00 (0.08 × \$1,000)	80.00	1,080.00
2	86.40 (0.08 × \$1,080)	166.40	1,166.40
3	93.30 (0.08 × \$1,166.40)	259.70	1,259.70

This tabular presentation is a series of computations that could appear as follows, where S is the future amount and the subscripts 1, 2, and 3 indicate the number of time periods.

$$S_1 = \$1{,}000(1.08)^1 = \$1{,}080$$

$$S_2 = \$1{,}080(1.08) = \$1{,}000(1.08)^2 = \$1{,}166.40$$

$$S_3 = \$1{,}166.40 \times (1.08) = \$1{,}000(1.08)^3 = \$1{,}259.70$$

The formula for the "amount of \$$P$", often called the "future value of \$$P$" or "future amount of \$$P$", can be written as follows:

$$S = P(1 + r)^n$$

S is the future value amount; P is the present value, r is the rate of interest; and n is the number of time periods.

When $P = \$1{,}000$, $n = 3$, $r = 0.08$, $S = \$1{,}000(1 + .08)^3 = \$1{,}259.70$

Fortunately, tables make key computations readily available. A facility in selecting the *proper* table will minimize computations. Check the accuracy of the preceding answer using Table 1, page 705.

Table 2—Present Value of $1

In the previous example, if $1,000 compounded at 8% per year will accumulate to $1,259.70 in three years, then $1,000 must be the present value of $1,259.70 due at the end of three years. The formula for the present value can be derived by reversing the process of *accumulation* (finding the future amount) that we just finished.

If

$$S = P(1 + r)^n$$

then

$$P = \frac{S}{(1 + r)^n}$$

In our example, $S = \$1{,}259.70$, $n = 3$, $r = 0.08$, so

$$P = \frac{\$1{,}259.70}{(1.08)^3} = \$1{,}000$$

Use Table 2, p. 706, to check this calculation.

When accumulating, we advance or roll forward in time. The difference between our original amount and our accumulated amount is called *compound interest.* When discounting, we retreat or roll back in time. The difference between the future amount and the present value is called *compound discount.* Note the following formulas:

$$\text{Compound interest} = P[(1 + r)^n - 1]$$

In our example, $P = \$1{,}000$, $n = 3$, $r = 0.08$, so

$$\text{Compound interest} = \$1{,}000[(1.08)^3 - 1] = \$259.70$$

$$\text{Compound discount} = S\left[1 - \frac{1}{(1 + r)^n}\right]$$

In our example, $S = \$1{,}259.70$, $n = 3$, $r = 0.08$, so

$$\text{Compound discount} = \$1{,}259.70\left[1 - \frac{1}{(1.08)^3}\right] = \$259.70$$

Table 3—Amount of Annuity of $1

An (ordinary) *annuity* is a series of equal payments (receipts) to be paid (or received) at the end of successive periods of equal length. Assume that $1,000 is invested at the end of each of 3 years at 8%:

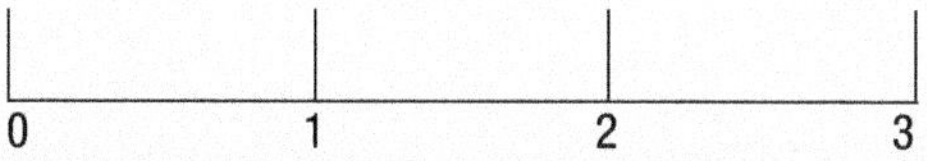

End of Year	Amount
1st payment	$1,000.00 ⟶ $1,080.00 ⟶ $1,166.40, which is $\$1{,}000(1.08)^2$
2nd payment	$1,000.00 ⟶ 1,080.00, which is $\$1{,}000(1.08)^1$
3rd payment	1,000.00
Accumulation (future amount)	$3,246.40

The preceding arithmetic may be expressed algebraically as the amount of an ordinary annuity of $1,000 for 3 years $= \$1{,}000(1 + r)^2 + \$1{,}000(1 + r)^1 + \$1{,}000$.

We can develop the general formula for S_n, the amount of an ordinary annuity of $1, by using the preceding example as a basis where $n = 3$ and $r = 0.08$:

1. $S_3 = 1 + (1 + r)^1 + (1 + r)^2$
2. Substitute: $S_3 = 1 + (1.08)^1 + (1.08)^2$
3. Multiply (2) by $(1 + r)$: $(1.08)S_3 = (1.08)^1 + (1.08)^2 + (1.08)^3$
4. Subtract (2) from (3): Note that all terms on the right-hand side are removed except $(1.08)^3$ in equation (3) and 1 in equation (2). $1.08S_3 - S_3 = (1.08)^3 - 1$

5. Factor (4): $S_3(1.08 - 1) = (1.08)^3 - 1$

6. Divide (5) by (1.08 − 1): $S_3 = \dfrac{(1.08)^3 - 1}{1.08 - 1} = \dfrac{(1.08)^3 - 1}{.08} = \dfrac{0.2597}{0.08} = 3.246$

7. The general formula for the amount of an ordinary annuity of $1 becomes: $S_n = \dfrac{(1 + r)^n - 1}{r}$ or $\dfrac{\text{Compound interest}}{\text{Rate}}$

This formula is the basis for Table 3, p. 707. Check the answer in the table.

Table 4—Present Value of an Ordinary Annuity of $1

Using the same example as for Table 3, we can show how the formula of P_n, *the present value of an ordinary annuity*, is developed.

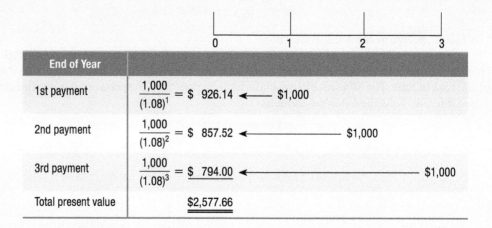

End of Year		0	1	2	3
1st payment	$\dfrac{1{,}000}{(1.08)^1}$ = $ 926.14	←	$1,000		
2nd payment	$\dfrac{1{,}000}{(1.08)^2}$ = $ 857.52	←		$1,000	
3rd payment	$\dfrac{1{,}000}{(1.08)^3}$ = $ 794.00	←			$1,000
Total present value	$2,577.66				

We can develop the general formula for P_n by using the preceding example as a basis where $n = 3$ and $r = 0.08$:

1. $P_3 = \dfrac{1}{1 + r} + \dfrac{1}{(1 + r)^2} + \dfrac{1}{(1 + r)^3}$

2. Substitute: $P_3 = \dfrac{1}{1.08} + \dfrac{1}{(1.08)^2} + \dfrac{1}{(1.08)^3}$

3. Multiply by $\dfrac{1}{1.08}$: $P_3\dfrac{1}{1.08} = \dfrac{1}{(1.08)^2} + \dfrac{1}{(1.08)^3} + \dfrac{1}{(1.08)^4}$

4. Subtract (3) from (2): $P_3 - P_3\dfrac{1}{1.08} = \dfrac{1}{1.08} - \dfrac{1}{(1.08)^4}$

5. Factor (4): $P_3\left(1 - \dfrac{1}{(1.08)}\right) = \dfrac{1}{1.08}\left[1 - \dfrac{1}{(1.08)^3}\right]$

6. or $P_3\left(\dfrac{.08}{1.08}\right) = \dfrac{1}{1.08}\left[1 - \dfrac{1}{(1.08)^3}\right]$

7. Multiply by $\dfrac{1.08}{.08}$: $P_3 = \dfrac{1}{.08}\left[1 - \dfrac{1}{(1.08)^3}\right] = \dfrac{.2062}{.08} = 2.577$

The general formula for the present value of an annuity of $1.00 is as follows:

$$P_n = \frac{1}{r}\left[1 - \frac{1}{(1 + r)^n}\right] = \frac{\text{Compound discount}}{\text{Rate}}$$

The formula is the basis for Table 4, page 708. Check the answer in the table. The present value tables, Tables 2 and 4, are used most frequently in capital budgeting.

The tables for annuities are not essential. With Tables 1 and 2, compound interest and compound discount can readily be computed. It is simply a matter of dividing either of these by the rate to get values equivalent to those shown in Tables 3 and 4.

Table 1 Compound Amount of $1.00 (The Future Value of $1.00)
$S = P(1 + r)^n$. In this table $P = \$1.00$

Periods	2%	4%	6%	8%	10%	12%	14%	16%	18%	20%	22%	24%	26%	28%	30%	32%	40%	Periods
1	1.020	1.040	1.060	1.080	1.100	1.120	1.140	1.160	1.180	1.200	1.220	1.240	1.260	1.280	1.300	1.320	1.400	1
2	1.040	1.082	1.124	1.166	1.210	1.254	1.300	1.346	1.392	1.440	1.488	1.538	1.588	1.638	1.690	1.742	1.960	2
3	1.061	1.125	1.191	1.260	1.331	1.405	1.482	1.561	1.643	1.728	1.816	1.907	2.000	2.097	2.197	2.300	2.744	3
4	1.082	1.170	1.262	1.360	1.464	1.574	1.689	1.811	1.939	2.074	2.215	2.364	2.520	2.684	2.856	3.036	3.842	4
5	1.104	1.217	1.338	1.469	1.611	1.762	1.925	2.100	2.288	2.488	2.703	2.932	3.176	3.436	3.713	4.007	5.378	5
6	1.126	1.265	1.419	1.587	1.772	1.974	2.195	2.436	2.700	2.986	3.297	3.635	4.002	4.398	4.827	5.290	7.530	6
7	1.149	1.316	1.504	1.714	1.949	2.211	2.502	2.826	3.185	3.583	4.023	4.508	5.042	5.629	6.275	6.983	10.541	7
8	1.172	1.369	1.594	1.851	2.144	2.476	2.853	3.278	3.759	4.300	4.908	5.590	6.353	7.206	8.157	9.217	14.758	8
9	1.195	1.423	1.689	1.999	2.358	2.773	3.252	3.803	4.435	5.160	5.987	6.931	8.005	9.223	10.604	12.166	20.661	9
10	1.219	1.480	1.791	2.159	2.594	3.106	3.707	4.411	5.234	6.192	7.305	8.594	10.086	11.806	13.786	16.060	28.925	10
11	1.243	1.539	1.898	2.332	2.853	3.479	4.226	5.117	6.176	7.430	8.912	10.657	12.708	15.112	17.922	21.199	40.496	11
12	1.268	1.601	2.012	2.518	3.138	3.896	4.818	5.936	7.288	8.916	10.872	13.215	16.012	19.343	23.298	27.983	56.694	12
13	1.294	1.665	2.133	2.720	3.452	4.363	5.492	6.886	8.599	10.699	13.264	16.386	20.175	24.759	30.288	36.937	79.371	13
14	1.319	1.732	2.261	2.937	3.797	4.887	6.261	7.988	10.147	12.839	16.182	20.319	25.421	31.691	39.374	48.757	111.120	14
15	1.346	1.801	2.397	3.172	4.177	5.474	7.138	9.266	11.974	15.407	19.742	25.196	32.030	40.565	51.186	64.359	155.568	15
16	1.373	1.873	2.540	3.426	4.595	6.130	8.137	10.748	14.129	18.488	24.086	31.243	40.358	51.923	66.542	84.954	217.795	16
17	1.400	1.948	2.693	3.700	5.054	6.866	9.276	12.468	16.672	22.186	29.384	38.741	50.851	66.461	86.504	112.139	304.913	17
18	1.428	2.026	2.854	3.996	5.560	7.690	10.575	14.463	19.673	26.623	35.849	48.039	64.072	85.071	112.455	148.024	426.879	18
19	1.457	2.107	3.026	4.316	6.116	8.613	12.056	16.777	23.214	31.948	43.736	59.568	80.731	108.890	146.192	195.391	597.630	19
20	1.486	2.191	3.207	4.661	6.727	9.646	13.743	19.461	27.393	38.338	53.358	73.864	101.721	139.380	190.050	257.916	836.683	20
21	1.516	2.279	3.400	5.034	7.400	10.804	15.668	22.574	32.324	46.005	65.096	91.592	128.169	178.406	247.065	340.449	1171.356	21
22	1.546	2.370	3.604	5.437	8.140	12.100	17.861	26.186	38.142	55.206	79.418	113.574	161.492	228.360	321.184	449.393	1639.898	22
23	1.577	2.465	3.820	5.871	8.954	13.552	20.362	30.376	45.008	66.247	96.889	140.831	203.480	292.300	417.539	593.199	2295.857	23
24	1.608	2.563	4.049	6.341	9.850	15.179	23.212	35.236	53.109	79.497	118.205	174.631	256.385	374.144	542.801	783.023	3214.200	24
25	1.641	2.666	4.292	6.848	10.835	17.000	26.462	40.874	62.669	95.396	144.210	216.542	323.045	478.905	705.641	1033.590	4499.880	25
26	1.673	2.772	4.549	7.396	11.918	19.040	30.167	47.414	73.949	114.475	175.936	268.512	407.037	612.998	917.333	1364.339	6299.831	26
27	1.707	2.883	4.822	7.988	13.110	21.325	34.390	55.000	87.260	137.371	214.642	332.955	512.867	784.638	1192.533	1800.927	8819.764	27
28	1.741	2.999	5.112	8.627	14.421	23.884	39.204	63.800	102.967	164.845	261.864	412.864	646.212	1004.336	1550.293	2377.224	12347.670	28
29	1.776	3.119	5.418	9.317	15.863	26.750	44.693	74.009	121.501	197.814	319.474	511.952	814.228	1285.550	2015.381	3137.935	17286.737	29
30	1.811	3.243	5.743	10.063	17.449	29.960	50.950	85.850	143.371	237.376	389.758	634.820	1025.927	1645.505	2619.996	4142.075	24201.432	30
35	2.000	3.946	7.686	14.785	28.102	52.800	98.100	180.314	327.997	590.668	1053.402	1861.054	3258.135	5653.911	9727.860	16599.217	130161.112	35
40	2.208	4.801	10.286	21.725	45.259	93.051	188.884	378.721	750.378	1469.772	2847.038	5455.913	10347.175	19426.689	36118.865	66520.767	700037.697	40

Table 2 ***(Place a clip on this page for easy reference.)***
Present Value of $1.00

$$P = \frac{S}{(1+r)^n}$$. **In this table S = $1.00.**

Periods	2%	4%	6%	8%	10%	12%	14%	16%	18%	20%	22%	24%	26%	28%	30%	32%	40%	Periods
1	0.980	0.962	0.943	0.926	0.909	0.893	0.877	0.862	0.847	0.833	0.820	0.806	0.794	0.781	0.769	0.758	0.714	1
2	0.961	0.925	0.890	0.857	0.826	0.797	0.769	0.743	0.718	0.694	0.672	0.650	0.630	0.610	0.592	0.574	0.510	2
3	0.942	0.889	0.840	0.794	0.751	0.712	0.675	0.641	0.609	0.579	0.551	0.524	0.500	0.477	0.455	0.435	0.364	3
4	0.924	0.855	0.792	0.735	0.683	0.636	0.592	0.552	0.516	0.482	0.451	0.423	0.397	0.373	0.350	0.329	0.260	4
5	0.906	0.822	0.747	0.681	0.621	0.567	0.519	0.476	0.437	0.402	0.370	0.341	0.315	0.291	0.269	0.250	0.186	5
6	0.888	0.790	0.705	0.630	0.564	0.507	0.456	0.410	0.370	0.335	0.303	0.275	0.250	0.227	0.207	0.189	0.133	6
7	0.871	0.760	0.665	0.583	0.513	0.452	0.400	0.354	0.314	0.279	0.249	0.222	0.198	0.178	0.159	0.143	0.095	7
8	0.853	0.731	0.627	0.540	0.467	0.404	0.351	0.305	0.266	0.233	0.204	0.179	0.157	0.139	0.123	0.108	0.068	8
9	0.837	0.703	0.592	0.500	0.424	0.361	0.308	0.263	0.225	0.194	0.167	0.144	0.125	0.108	0.094	0.082	0.048	9
10	0.820	0.676	0.558	0.463	0.386	0.322	0.270	0.227	0.191	0.162	0.137	0.116	0.099	0.085	0.073	0.062	0.035	10
11	0.804	0.650	0.527	0.429	0.350	0.287	0.237	0.195	0.162	0.135	0.112	0.094	0.079	0.066	0.056	0.047	0.025	11
12	0.788	0.625	0.497	0.397	0.319	0.257	0.208	0.168	0.137	0.112	0.092	0.076	0.062	0.052	0.043	0.036	0.018	12
13	0.773	0.601	0.469	0.368	0.290	0.229	0.182	0.145	0.116	0.093	0.075	0.061	0.050	0.040	0.033	0.027	0.013	13
14	0.758	0.577	0.442	0.340	0.263	0.205	0.160	0.125	0.099	0.078	0.062	0.049	0.039	0.032	0.025	0.021	0.009	14
15	0.743	0.555	0.417	0.315	0.239	0.183	0.140	0.108	0.084	0.065	0.051	0.040	0.031	0.025	0.020	0.016	0.006	15
16	0.728	0.534	0.394	0.292	0.218	0.163	0.123	0.093	0.071	0.054	0.042	0.032	0.025	0.019	0.015	0.012	0.005	16
17	0.714	0.513	0.371	0.270	0.198	0.146	0.108	0.080	0.060	0.045	0.034	0.026	0.020	0.015	0.012	0.009	0.003	17
18	0.700	0.494	0.350	0.250	0.180	0.130	0.095	0.069	0.051	0.038	0.028	0.021	0.016	0.012	0.009	0.007	0.002	18
19	0.686	0.475	0.331	0.232	0.164	0.116	0.083	0.060	0.043	0.031	0.023	0.017	0.012	0.009	0.007	0.005	0.002	19
20	0.673	0.456	0.312	0.215	0.149	0.104	0.073	0.051	0.037	0.026	0.019	0.014	0.010	0.007	0.005	0.004	0.001	20
21	0.660	0.439	0.294	0.199	0.135	0.093	0.064	0.044	0.031	0.022	0.015	0.011	0.008	0.006	0.004	0.003	0.001	21
22	0.647	0.422	0.278	0.184	0.123	0.083	0.056	0.038	0.026	0.018	0.013	0.009	0.006	0.004	0.003	0.002	0.001	22
23	0.634	0.406	0.262	0.170	0.112	0.074	0.049	0.033	0.022	0.015	0.010	0.007	0.005	0.003	0.002	0.002	0.000	23
24	0.622	0.390	0.247	0.158	0.102	0.066	0.043	0.028	0.019	0.013	0.008	0.006	0.004	0.003	0.002	0.001	0.000	24
25	0.610	0.375	0.233	0.146	0.092	0.059	0.038	0.024	0.016	0.010	0.007	0.005	0.003	0.002	0.001	0.001	0.000	25
26	0.598	0.361	0.220	0.135	0.084	0.053	0.033	0.021	0.014	0.009	0.006	0.004	0.002	0.002	0.001	0.001	0.000	26
27	0.586	0.347	0.207	0.125	0.076	0.047	0.029	0.018	0.011	0.007	0.005	0.003	0.002	0.001	0.001	0.001	0.000	27
28	0.574	0.333	0.196	0.116	0.069	0.042	0.026	0.016	0.010	0.006	0.004	0.002	0.002	0.001	0.001	0.000	0.000	28
29	0.563	0.321	0.185	0.107	0.063	0.037	0.022	0.014	0.008	0.005	0.003	0.002	0.001	0.001	0.000	0.000	0.000	29
30	0.552	0.308	0.174	0.099	0.057	0.033	0.020	0.012	0.007	0.004	0.003	0.002	0.001	0.001	0.000	0.000	0.000	30
35	0.500	0.253	0.130	0.068	0.036	0.019	0.010	0.006	0.003	0.002	0.001	0.001	0.000	0.000	0.000	0.000	0.000	35
40	0.453	0.208	0.097	0.046	0.022	0.011	0.005	0.003	0.001	0.001	0.000	0.000	0.000	0.000	0.000	0.000	0.000	40

Table 3 Compound Amount of Annuity of $1.00 in Arrears* (Future Value of Annuity)

$$S_n = \frac{(1+r)^n - 1}{r}$$

Periods	2%	4%	6%	8%	10%	12%	14%	16%	18%	20%	22%	24%	26%	28%	30%	32%	40%	Periods
1	1.000	1.000	1.000	1.000	1.000	1.000	1.000	1.000	1.000	1.000	1.000	1.000	1.000	1.000	1.000	1.000	1.000	1
2	2.020	2.040	2.060	2.080	2.100	2.120	2.140	2.160	2.180	2.200	2.220	2.240	2.260	2.280	2.300	2.320	2.400	2
3	3.060	3.122	3.184	3.246	3.310	3.374	3.440	3.506	3.572	3.640	3.708	3.778	3.848	3.918	3.990	4.062	4.360	3
4	4.122	4.246	4.375	4.506	4.641	4.779	4.921	5.066	5.215	5.368	5.524	5.684	5.848	6.016	6.187	6.362	7.104	4
5	5.204	5.416	5.637	5.867	6.105	6.353	6.610	6.877	7.154	7.442	7.740	8.048	8.368	8.700	9.043	9.398	10.946	5
6	6.308	6.633	6.975	7.336	7.716	8.115	8.536	8.977	9.442	9.930	10.442	10.980	11.544	12.136	12.756	13.406	16.324	6
7	7.434	7.898	8.394	8.923	9.487	10.089	10.730	11.414	12.142	12.916	13.740	14.615	15.546	16.534	17.583	18.696	23.853	7
8	8.583	9.214	9.897	10.637	11.436	12.300	13.233	14.240	15.327	16.499	17.762	19.123	20.588	22.163	23.858	25.678	34.395	8
9	9.755	10.583	11.491	12.488	13.579	14.776	16.085	17.519	19.086	20.799	22.670	24.712	26.940	29.369	32.015	34.895	49.153	9
10	10.950	12.006	13.181	14.487	15.937	17.549	19.337	21.321	23.521	25.959	28.657	31.643	34.945	38.593	42.619	47.062	69.814	10
11	12.169	13.486	14.972	16.645	18.531	20.655	23.045	25.733	28.755	32.150	35.962	40.238	45.031	50.398	56.405	63.122	98.739	11
12	13.412	15.026	16.870	18.977	21.384	24.133	27.271	30.850	34.931	39.581	44.874	50.895	57.739	65.510	74.327	84.320	139.235	12
13	14.680	16.627	18.882	21.495	24.523	28.029	32.089	36.786	42.219	48.497	55.746	64.110	73.751	84.853	97.625	112.303	195.929	13
14	15.974	18.292	21.015	24.215	27.975	32.393	37.581	43.672	50.818	59.196	69.010	80.496	93.926	109.612	127.913	149.240	275.300	14
15	17.293	20.024	23.276	27.152	31.772	37.280	43.842	51.660	60.965	72.035	85.192	100.815	119.347	141.303	167.286	197.997	386.420	15
16	18.639	21.825	25.673	30.324	35.950	42.753	50.980	60.925	72.939	87.442	104.935	126.011	151.377	181.868	218.472	262.356	541.988	16
17	20.012	23.698	28.213	33.750	40.545	48.884	59.118	71.673	87.068	105.931	129.020	157.253	191.735	233.791	285.014	347.309	759.784	17
18	21.412	25.645	30.906	37.450	45.599	55.750	68.394	84.141	103.740	128.117	158.405	195.994	242.585	300.252	371.518	459.449	1064.697	18
19	22.841	27.671	33.760	41.446	51.159	63.440	78.969	98.603	123.414	154.740	194.254	244.033	306.658	385.323	483.973	607.472	1491.576	19
20	24.297	29.778	36.786	45.762	57.275	72.052	91.025	115.380	146.628	186.688	237.989	303.601	387.389	494.213	630.165	802.863	2089.206	20
21	25.783	31.969	39.993	50.423	64.002	81.699	104.768	134.841	174.021	225.026	291.347	377.465	489.110	633.593	820.215	1060.779	2925.889	21
22	27.299	34.248	43.392	55.457	71.403	92.503	120.436	157.415	206.345	271.031	356.443	469.056	617.278	811.999	1067.280	1401.229	4097.245	22
23	28.845	36.618	46.996	60.893	79.543	104.603	138.297	183.601	244.487	326.237	435.861	582.630	778.771	1040.358	1388.464	1850.622	5737.142	23
24	30.422	39.083	50.816	66.765	88.497	118.155	158.659	213.978	289.494	392.484	532.750	723.461	982.251	1332.659	1806.003	2443.821	8032.999	24
25	32.030	41.646	54.865	73.106	98.347	133.334	181.871	249.214	342.603	471.981	650.955	898.092	1238.636	1706.803	2348.803	3226.844	11247.199	25
26	33.671	44.312	59.156	79.954	109.182	150.334	208.333	290.088	405.272	567.377	795.165	1114.634	1561.682	2185.708	3054.444	4260.434	15747.079	26
27	35.344	47.084	63.706	87.351	121.100	169.374	238.499	337.502	479.221	681.853	971.102	1383.146	1968.719	2798.706	3971.778	5624.772	22046.910	27
28	37.051	49.968	68.528	95.339	134.210	190.699	272.889	392.503	566.481	819.223	1185.744	1716.101	2481.586	3583.344	5164.311	7425.699	30866.674	28
29	38.792	52.966	73.640	103.966	148.631	214.583	312.094	456.303	669.447	984.068	1447.608	2128.965	3127.798	4587.680	6714.604	9802.923	43214.343	29
30	40.568	56.085	79.058	113.263	164.494	241.333	356.787	530.312	790.948	1181.882	1767.081	2640.916	3942.026	5873.231	8729.985	12940.859	60501.081	30
35	49.994	73.652	111.435	172.317	271.024	431.663	693.573	1120.713	1816.652	2948.341	4783.645	7750.225	12527.442	20188.966	32422.868	51869.427	325400.279	35
40	60.402	95.026	154.762	259.057	442.593	767.091	1342.025	2360.757	4163.213	7343.858	12936.535	22728.803	39792.982	69377.460	120392.883	207874.272	1750091.741	40

*Payments (or receipts) at the end of each period.

Table 4 ***(Place a clip on this page for easy reference.)***
Present Value of Annuity $1.00 in Arrears*

$$P_n = \frac{1}{r}\left[1 - \frac{1}{(1+r)^n}\right]$$

Periods	2%	4%	6%	8%	10%	12%	14%	16%	18%	20%	22%	24%	26%	28%	30%	32%	40%	Periods
1	0.980	0.962	0.943	0.926	0.909	0.893	0.877	0.862	0.847	0.833	0.820	0.806	0.794	0.781	0.769	0.758	0.714	1
2	1.942	1.886	1.833	1.783	1.736	1.690	1.647	1.605	1.566	1.528	1.492	1.457	1.424	1.392	1.361	1.331	1.224	2
3	2.884	2.775	2.673	2.577	2.487	2.402	2.322	2.246	2.174	2.106	2.042	1.981	1.923	1.868	1.816	1.766	1.589	3
4	3.808	3.630	3.465	3.312	3.170	3.037	2.914	2.798	2.690	2.589	2.494	2.404	2.320	2.241	2.166	2.096	1.849	4
5	4.713	4.452	4.212	3.993	3.791	3.605	3.433	3.274	3.127	2.991	2.864	2.745	2.635	2.532	2.436	2.345	2.035	5
6	5.601	5.242	4.917	4.623	4.355	4.111	3.889	3.685	3.498	3.326	3.167	3.020	2.885	2.759	2.643	2.534	2.168	6
7	6.472	6.002	5.582	5.206	4.868	4.564	4.288	4.039	3.812	3.605	3.416	3.242	3.083	2.937	2.802	2.677	2.263	7
8	7.325	6.733	6.210	5.747	5.335	4.968	4.639	4.344	4.078	3.837	3.619	3.421	3.241	3.076	2.925	2.786	2.331	8
9	8.162	7.435	6.802	6.247	5.759	5.328	4.946	4.607	4.303	4.031	3.786	3.566	3.366	3.184	3.019	2.868	2.379	9
10	8.983	8.111	7.360	6.710	6.145	5.650	5.216	4.833	4.494	4.192	3.923	3.682	3.465	3.269	3.092	2.930	2.414	10
11	9.787	8.760	7.887	7.139	6.495	5.938	5.453	5.029	4.656	4.327	4.035	3.776	3.543	3.335	3.147	2.978	2.438	11
12	10.575	9.385	8.384	7.536	6.814	6.194	5.660	5.197	4.793	4.439	4.127	3.851	3.606	3.387	3.190	3.013	2.456	12
13	11.348	9.986	8.853	7.904	7.103	6.424	5.842	5.342	4.910	4.533	4.203	3.912	3.656	3.427	3.223	3.040	2.469	13
14	12.106	10.563	9.295	8.244	7.367	6.628	6.002	5.468	5.008	4.611	4.265	3.962	3.695	3.459	3.249	3.061	2.478	14
15	12.849	11.118	9.712	8.559	7.606	6.811	6.142	5.575	5.092	4.675	4.315	4.001	3.726	3.483	3.268	3.076	2.484	15
16	13.578	11.652	10.106	8.851	7.824	6.974	6.265	5.668	5.162	4.730	4.357	4.033	3.751	3.503	3.283	3.088	2.489	16
17	14.292	12.166	10.477	9.122	8.022	7.120	6.373	5.749	5.222	4.775	4.391	4.059	3.771	3.518	3.295	3.097	2.492	17
18	14.992	12.659	10.828	9.372	8.201	7.250	6.467	5.818	5.273	4.812	4.419	4.080	3.786	3.529	3.304	3.104	2.494	18
19	15.678	13.134	11.158	9.604	8.365	7.366	6.550	5.877	5.316	4.843	4.442	4.097	3.799	3.539	3.311	3.109	2.496	19
20	16.351	13.590	11.470	9.818	8.514	7.469	6.623	5.929	5.353	4.870	4.460	4.110	3.808	3.546	3.316	3.113	2.497	20
21	17.011	14.029	11.764	10.017	8.649	7.562	6.687	5.973	5.384	4.891	4.476	4.121	3.816	3.551	3.320	3.116	2.498	21
22	17.658	14.451	12.042	10.201	8.772	7.645	6.743	6.011	5.410	4.909	4.488	4.130	3.822	3.556	3.323	3.118	2.498	22
23	18.292	14.857	12.303	10.371	8.883	7.718	6.792	6.044	5.432	4.925	4.499	4.137	3.827	3.559	3.325	3.120	2.499	23
24	18.914	15.247	12.550	10.529	8.985	7.784	6.835	6.073	5.451	4.937	4.507	4.143	3.831	3.562	3.327	3.121	2.499	24
25	19.523	15.622	12.783	10.675	9.077	7.843	6.873	6.097	5.467	4.948	4.514	4.147	3.834	3.564	3.329	3.122	2.499	25
26	20.121	15.983	13.003	10.810	9.161	7.896	6.906	6.118	5.480	4.956	4.520	4.151	3.837	3.566	3.330	3.123	2.500	26
27	20.707	16.330	13.211	10.935	9.237	7.943	6.935	6.136	5.492	4.964	4.524	4.154	3.839	3.567	3.331	3.123	2.500	27
28	21.281	16.663	13.406	11.051	9.307	7.984	6.961	6.152	5.502	4.970	4.528	4.157	3.840	3.568	3.331	3.124	2.500	28
29	21.844	16.984	13.591	11.158	9.370	8.022	6.983	6.166	5.510	4.975	4.531	4.159	3.841	3.569	3.332	3.124	2.500	29
30	22.396	17.292	13.765	11.258	9.427	8.055	7.003	6.177	5.517	4.979	4.534	4.160	3.842	3.569	3.332	3.124	2.500	30
35	24.999	18.665	14.498	11.655	9.644	8.176	7.070	6.215	5.539	4.992	4.541	4.164	3.845	3.571	3.333	3.125	2.500	35
40	27.355	19.793	15.046	11.925	9.779	8.244	7.105	6.233	5.548	4.997	4.544	4.166	3.846	3.571	3.333	3.125	2.500	40

*Payments (or receipts) at the end of each period.

Field-Based Assignments and Experiential Learning

Introduction

In recent years, critics of management education have pointed to a persistent knowing–doing gap. Textbooks and lectures teach students theories, frameworks, and tools but do not expose them to the challenges of applying these ideas in practice. For example, coursework and cases help students learn about fixed and variable costs and their application in cost-volume-profit (CVP) analysis, or about cost drivers and their application in activity-based costing (ABC), but the classroom pedagogy does not help students learn how to identify fixed costs, variable costs, and cost drivers in real organizations. Students can learn to identify costs and cost drivers only through experiential learning. Working on real world-based projects substantially increases students' understanding of managerial accounting concepts. Students also begin to appreciate that management accounting is an integrative course touching all parts of the value chain from design to post-sales service.

This appendix provides guidelines for doing field-based assignments designed to help you apply various concepts, tools, and techniques discussed in the book to real world settings. These assignments have been used for the past five years to help students learn about management accounting in practice. In turn, organizations have valued students' contributions toward improving operations, costing, and product pricing.[1]

Basic Preparation and General Tips for Obtaining Information

1. Identify organizations, either through your own research or from faculty recommendations, where you and your team can make between two and four short visits during the course. You must be able to understand the basic workings of the organization relatively easily. Hotels, restaurants, small-scale manufacturing units, service units, hospitals, dairies, retail outlets, car dealerships, workshops, or garment shops may be good candidates for this project. A large organization could also work if you focus on a particular department or production subunit.
    - **a.** Please keep in mind that in doing this project, you will encounter problems with extracting information, find that information is not easily available within the organization, experience challenges communicating the exact nature of the information you need, and sense inertia and lack of knowledge among people in the organization. The real challenges in management accounting are not computational but data insufficiency, unavailability, and interpretation. It is important to learn how to address these challenges. Be confident that you will be able to estimate, seek, and develop information for cost analysis.
    - **b.** On behalf of the school, your instructor may need to issue a formal letter addressed to the organization introducing the project and requesting support.
2. You and your team should establish a good understanding of the operating process, context, and environment. While interacting with operating personnel, be sure to confirm that your understanding of processes is correct. Often, you may need to estimate costs based on this understanding.

---

[1] The authors thank Keyur Thaker, Associate Professor, IIM Indore for many insightful discussions and for sharing his ideas about experiential learning in management accounting.

3. Operations personnel may not understand you because your terminology and language is straight out of the textbook. Learning to speak the language that shop floor and operations people understand and assuming their perspective will help you communicate with employees.
4. Many times the people working in the organization may not have cost information readily available. This is the norm in many organizations. When individuals in an organization are unable to answer your questions, either because data are not readily available or because they do not know the answer, be sure to think about how you can work with them to obtain the necessary data. For example, you can take the available inputs and develop the estimates yourself based on your understanding of the process, the causal links, and the methods and techniques of management accounting.
5. Organizations may not define costs in the way and in the terms given in the textbook. Gain an understanding of the nature of the cost, cost terms, and purpose, and then decide how best to map the cost to the definitions used in the textbook. For example, some organizations may define direct costs and variable costs differently from the definitions used in the book.
6. Whenever possible, avoid asking direct questions such as, "What is the indirect cost of a product?" Instead, break down the problem. For example, enquire about the cost of processes needed to produce the product and how much time the product spends at each process.
7. As you develop cost information, make cost estimates, and assign costs, share your work and thought processes with individuals in the organization for verification and correction.
8. People in the organization are busy; they may not find any value in interacting with you and your team. In the final analysis, it is your hard work, commitment, and preparedness that make the difference. If managers are convinced that sharing information can lead to useful analysis, you will have a better chance of getting their help.

The field project will be performed in different phases or chunks. We next describe the basic phases of the project. The phases relate to particular groups of chapters. Your instructor may choose to assign all or only a few of the tasks described in each phase. Your instructor may also decide to assign one or more phases separately or assign multiple phases at once.

Phase I
Understanding the Context
Text Chapters: 1, 2, and 3

Key Objectives

The focus of the first phase is to understand the organization, products, operations, and processes. The tasks are (1) identify and develop a list of different costs, (2) estimate costs for a typical period, and (3) if possible, classify them. Try to understand the organization and role of management accounting. What cost information are managers in the organization looking for? Refrain from seeking cost information directly at this stage.

Potential Tasks

1. Prepare an overview of the organization, structure, products, services, departments, etc.
2. What kinds of information do different managers need from the management accounting function? How satisfied are the managers with the information they are getting and what additional information or analysis would they like? Classify the activities performed by managers and management accountants as planning and control activities.

3a. Describe the activities in each area of the value chain.

3b. Identify important costs for each activity in the value chain.

4. Classify costs as fixed, variable, direct, and indirect. Cost classification in several instances may not be based on what you see. For example, an organization may classify what appears to be a direct cost as an indirect cost because it is impossible to trace the cost to the cost object in an economically feasible way or because the information is simply not available.

5a. Perform cost-volume-profit (CVP) analysis and calculate the breakeven point. You may need to make assumptions about cost behaviors. Develop and challenge the assumptions needed to perform CVP and breakeven analysis.

5b. Perform "what if" analysis. That is, how would CVP and breakeven analysis be affected if a variable cost were treated as a fixed cost or vice versa or if the variable or fixed costs were greater or smaller than the amounts estimated.

Preparation

Read the assigned textbook chapters and develop a detailed check list of information you would like to obtain. Remember that no one in the company or organization will spoon-feed you. The better you understand the operations and activites, the better you can identify costs and classify them. Be clear about the information you need. Be sure to speak in a language that practitioners understand. You will not be able to communicate and obtain the information you need if you cannot explain what you need in terms that practitioners can understand.

Sources of Information

The following sources of information are often helpful: (1) Direct interactions with managers and management accountants; (2) personal observations; (3) cost and accounting records; and (4) independent investigation of market prices of inputs and outputs.

Phase II
Collecting and Developing Cost Information
Text Chapters: 4, 5, 6, and 7

Key Objectives

1. Identify the product costing environment and use absorption costing
2. Understand the nuances of the existing costing system.
3. Analyze allocation of overhead cost using activity-based costing.

Potential Tasks

1. Understand and describe the present costing system. Is it a job, process, or batch costing system? Identify cost objects, for example, products or jobs.

2a. Draw a diagram as in Exhibit 6-1 to represent the cost system by identifying direct and indirect cost categories and the cost allocation bases for the indirect costs. Talk to management to ascertain the rationale for the present system.

2b. Develop a basic cost sheet for different products or jobs. Determine the direct and indirect costs of products and jobs.

2c. Explore the relationship of the present costing system with pricing. Is pricing cost-based or market based? Try to understand how pricing or product–mix decisions are made using the present costing system and if the system is not used, why it is not used.

2d. Calculate product profitability for a representative set of products or jobs based on the present costing system.

3a. Evaluate whether the present costing system reasonably accurately calculates the cost of products or jobs? How do you know? Which products, if any, are undercosted or overcosted?

3b. Identify the cost hierarchy categories for the various overhead cost pools, for example, unit, batch, product-sustaining, or facility-sustaining.

3c. Refine the cost systems using activity-based costing (ABC).

3d. How could you use ABC for pricing decisions and to improve operations and reduce costs?

3e. How could you use ABC information to determine customer profitability?

Preparation

Read the assigned textbook chapters and develop a detailed check list of information you would like to obtain. Remember that the better you understand the operations and activites, the better you can identify costs and classify them. Be clear about the information you need. Be sure to speak in a language that practitioners understand. You will not be able to communicate and obtain the information you need if you cannot explain what you need in terms that practitioners can understand.

Develop a rough sketch and templates of the information you need. You may even fill it with your estimates.

Sources of Information

The following sources of information are often helpful: (1) Direct interactions with managers, industrial engineering staff, supervisors, foremen, others familiar with different functions of the business, and management accountants; (2) personal observations; (3) cost and accounting records; (4) independent investigation of market prices of inputs and outputs; and (5) time-and-motion studies.

If cost estimates are not available in dollar terms, make physical estimates, for example in kilograms or hours, and use current market rates to estimate costs. Share your estimates with individuals in the organization who can help you develop better estimates.

Make things work. Develop a prototype with many assumptions and keep on improving it. Don't expect to arrive at a perfect estimate right away.

You will learn that the more information you unearth and gather, the better the cost estimates that you can make. You will also realize, however, that obtaining the true cost of a product or job is nearly impossible. For example, you can estimate fairly accurate product costs if you carefully allocate indirect costs using two or three good cost-allocation bases. You can obtain even more accurate product costs by computing activity-based costs based on cost hierarchies, tracing larger number of costs directly, and allocating indirect costs using cost drivers. Estimating activity-based costs requires involvement and information from people close to the operations. Even so, activity-based cost estimates also require assumptions because of information deficiency and are never fully accurate. Designing cost systems requires judgment, balancing the benefits of greater accuracy when making decisions against the costs of obtaining information.

Phase III
Cost Information for Decision Making
Text Chapters: 8, 9, 10, and 11

Key Objectives

1. The focus of this phase is to identify decisions that managers make and to determine and obtain the information they need to make those decisions.
2. Assess the difficulties that organizations and decision makers face when using the prevalent cost accounting information.

Potential Tasks

1. List various decisions for which managers need information, such as pricing, special order, make or buy, quantities to be produced, machine replacement, and capital investment.
2. Understand the relevant revenues and relevant costs of the decision. Develop the information you would need to calculate the relevant revenues and relevant costs. Do not forget to consider opportunity costs. If required, make assumptions.
3. Understand and measure the different costs of quality. What nonfinancial measures would you use to improve quality?
4. Consider a capital investment decision. Develop the relevant revenues and relevant costs for this decision. Are there other strategic considerations or nonfinancial information that would help in making the decision?

Preparation

Read the assigned textbook chapters and develop a detailed check list of information you would like to obtain. Remember that the better you understand the operations and activites, the better you can identify relevant revenues and relevant costs. Be clear about the information you need. Be sure to speak in a language that practitioners understand. You will not be able to communicate and obtain the information you need if you cannot explain what you need in terms that practitioners can understand.

Try to identify the possible decisions you plan to study in Phase III while working on Phase II. Suggest a decision that is valuable to the company.

Sources of Information

The following sources of information are often helpful: (1) Direct interactions with managers, industrial engineering staff, supervisors, foremen, others familiar with different functions of the business, and management accountants; (2) personal observations; (3) cost and accounting records; and (4) independent investigation of market prices of inputs and outputs,

Phase IV
Analysis of Strategic Costs and Management Control (all aspects may not be feasible)
Text Chapters: 12, 13, 14, 15, and 16

Key Objectives

The objective of this phase is to understand and analyze important aspects of management control, especially responsibility centers, the budgeting process, variances relative to the budget, balanced scorecard, transfer pricing, and performance management.

Potential Tasks

1. Chart the responsibility centers and key result areas.
2. Enquire into different aspects of budgeting and planning. What role do managers of various operating departments play in the budgeting process?
3. How does the company analyze performance against budget? What kind of variance analyses does the organization perform? Calculate and interpret different variances based on the budgeted numbers. What actions does it motivate?
4. Describe the organization's strategy and how the organization implements strategy. Does the organization use any performance management system such as a balanced scorecard? If it uses a balanced scorecard, evaluate it. If it does not, develop a balanced scorecard for the organization.
5. How are people in the organization compensated? Describe the compensation system across various levels of the organization. Evaluate the system and indicate how it might be improved.
6. Do various subunits in the organization send goods and services to one another? If so, what do managers think about the way in which the accounting system records these transactions?

Preparation

Read the assigned textbook chapters and develop a detailed check list of information you would like to obtain. The better you understand the operations and activites, the better you can identify responsibility centers and understand the budgeting and performance evaluation processes. Be sure to speak in a language that practitioners understand. You will not be able to communicate and obtain the information you need if you cannot explain what you need in terms that practitioners can understand.

Sources of Information

The following sources of information are often helpful: (1) Direct interactions with managers, industrial engineering staff, supervisors, foremen, others familiar with different functions of the business, and management accountants; (2) personal observations; (3) cost and accounting records; and (4) independent investigation of market prices of inputs and outputs.

Glossary

A

absorption costing Method of inventory costing that measures the cost of all manufacturing resources, whether variable or fixed, necessary to produce inventory. (p. 52)

account analysis method Estimates cost functions by classifying various cost accounts as variable, fixed, or mixed in regard to the identified level of activity. (p. 310)

accrual accounting rate-of-return (AARR) method Divides the average annual (accrual accounting) income of a project by a measure of the investment in it. (p. 455)

activity Event, task, or unit of work with a specified purpose. (p. 213)

activity-based budgeting (ABB) Focuses on the budgeted cost of the activities necessary to produce and sell products and services. (p. 494)

activity-based costing (ABC) Refines a costing system by identifying individual activities as the fundamental cost objects. (p. 213)

activity-based management (ABM) Method of management decision making that uses activity-based costing information to improve customer satisfaction and profitability. (p. 224)

actual cost Cost incurred (a historical or past cost). (p. 29)

actual costing Traces direct costs to a cost object based on the actual direct-cost rates multiplied by the actual quantities of the direct-cost inputs and allocates indirect costs to the cost object based on the actual indirect-cost rates multiplied by the actual quantities of the cost allocation bases. (p. 119)

actual indirect-cost rate Actual total indirect costs in a cost pool divided by the actual total quantity of the cost-allocation base for that cost pool. (p. 127)

adjusted allocation-rate approach Restates all overhead entries in the general ledger and job-cost records to represent actual cost rates rather than budgeted cost rates. (p. 135)

appraisal costs Costs incurred to detect which of the individual units of products do not conform to specifications. (p. 397)

artificial costs A support department's own costs plus any interdepartmental cost allocations. Also called *complete reciprocated costs*. (p. 149)

autonomy Degree of freedom to make decisions. (p. 626)

average cost Total cost divided by the related number of units. Also called *unit cost*. (p. 36)

average waiting time Average amount of time that an order waits in line before the machine is set up and the order is processed. (p. 423)

B

balanced scorecard Translates an organization's mission and strategy into a set of performance measures that provides the framework for implementing its strategy. (p. 587)

batch-level costs Costs of activities related to a group of units of a product or service rather than each individual unit of product or service. (p. 216)

belief systems Articulate the mission, purpose, and core values of a company and describe the accepted norms and patterns of behavior expected of all managers and other employees when interacting with one another, shareholders, customers, and communities. (p. 684)

book value Original cost minus accumulated depreciation of an asset. (p. 364)

bottleneck An operation where the work to be performed approaches or exceeds the capacity available to do it. (p. 421)

boundary systems Describe standards of behavior and codes of conduct expected of all employees, especially actions that are off-limits. (p. 684)

breakeven point (BEP) Quantity of output sold at which total revenues equal total costs. (p. 82)

budget Quantitative expression of a proposed plan of action by management and an aid to coordinating what needs to be done to execute that plan. (p. 9)

budgetary slack Practice of underestimating budgeted revenues, or overestimating budgeted costs, to make budgeted targets more easy to achieve. (p. 504)

budgeted cost Predicted or forecasted cost (future cost). (p. 29)

budgeted indirect-cost rate Budgeted annual indirect costs in a cost pool divided by the budgeted annual quantity of the cost allocation base. (p. 121)

budgeted performance Expected performance, which is a point of reference to compare actual results. (p. 536)

business function costs Sum of all costs (variable and fixed) in a particular business function of the value chain. (p. 345)

C

capital budgeting Process of making long-run planning decisions for investments in projects. (p. 445)

carrying costs Costs that arise while holding goods in inventory. (p. 406)

cash budget Schedule of expected cash receipts and disbursements. (p. 510)

cause-and-effect diagram Identifies potential causes of defects using a diagram that resembles the bone structure of a fish (therefore also called a *fishbone diagram*). (p. 401)

centralization Organizational structure in which power is concentrated at the top with relatively little freedom for managers at lower levels to make decisions. (p. 626)

chief financial officer (CFO) Executive responsible for overseeing the financial operations of an organization. Also called *finance director*. (p. 13)

choice criterion Objective that can be quantified in a decision model. (p. 99)

collusive pricing Occurs when companies in an industry conspire in their pricing and production decisions to achieve a price above the competitive price and so restrain trade, which is a violation of antitrust laws. (p. 280)

common cost Cost of operating a facility, department, activity, or similar cost object that two or more users share. (p. 191)

complete reciprocated costs A support department's own costs plus any interdepartmental cost allocations. Also called *artificial costs*. (p. 149)

conference method Estimates cost functions on the basis of analysis and opinions about costs and their drivers gathered from various departments of a company. (p. 309)

conformance quality Performance of a product or service relative to its design and product specifications. (p. 396)

constant Component of total cost that does not vary with changes in the level of the activity. Also called *intercept*. (p. 304)

constraint Mathematical inequality or equality that must be satisfied by the variables in a mathematical model. (p. 373)

continuous budget Budget that is always available for a specified future period; created by continually adding a month, quarter, or year to the period that just ended. Also called *rolling budget* or *rolling forecast*. (p. 488)

contribution income statement Income statement that groups costs into variable costs and fixed costs to highlight contribution margin. (p. 78)

contribution margin Difference between total revenues and total variable costs. (p. 56, 78)

contribution margin per unit Selling price minus variable cost per unit. (p. 78)

contribution margin percentage Contribution margin per unit divided by selling price. Also called *contribution margin ratio*. (p. 79)

contribution margin ratio Contribution margin per unit divided by selling price. Also called *contribution margin percentage*. (p. 79)

control Term that comprises taking actions that implement planning decisions, deciding how to evaluate performance, and providing feedback and learning to help future decision making. (p. 9)

control chart Graph of a series of successive observations of a particular step, procedure, or operation taken at regular intervals of time. Each observation is plotted relative to specified ranges that represent the limits within which observations are expected to fall. (p. 400)

controllability Degree of influence that a specific manager has over costs, revenues, or related items for which he or she is responsible. (p. 503)

controllable cost Any cost that is primarily subject to the influence of a given responsibility center manager for a given period. (p. 503)

controller Financial executive primarily responsible for management accounting and financial accounting. Also called *chief accounting officer*. (p. 13)

conversion costs All manufacturing costs, other than direct material costs, that represent costs incurred to convert direct materials into finished goods. (p. 45)

cost Resource sacrificed or forgone to achieve a specific objective. (p. 29)

cost accumulation Collection of cost data in some organized way by means of an accounting system. (p. 29)

cost allocation Assignment of indirect costs to a particular cost object. (p. 30)

cost-allocation base Systematic way to link an indirect cost or group of indirect costs to a cost object. (p. 116)

cost-application base Systematic way to link an indirect cost or group of indirect costs to a cost object when the cost object is a job, product, or customer. (p. 116)

cost assignment General term that encompasses both (1) tracing direct costs to a cost object and (2) allocating indirect costs to a cost object. (p. 30)

cost–benefit approach Guideline that helps managers provide the most value to their companies in strategic and operational decision making. This approach dictates that managers should spend resources if the expected benefits to the company exceed the expected costs. (p. 12)

cost center Responsibility center in which the manager is accountable for costs only. (p. 502)

cost driver Variable, such as the level of activity or volume, that causally affects costs over a given time span. (p. 33)

cost estimation Measures a relationship based on data from past costs and the related level of an activity. (p. 307)

cost function Mathematical description of how a cost changes with changes in the level of an activity relating to that cost. (p. 303)

cost hierarchy Categorizes various activity cost pools on the basis of the different types of cost drivers, cost-allocation bases, or different degrees of difficulty in determining cause-and-effect (or benefits-received) relationships. (p. 216)

cost incurrence Describes when a resource is consumed (or benefit forgone) to meet a specific objective. (p. 261)

cost leadership Ability of an organization to achieve lower costs relative to competitors through productivity and efficiency improvements, elimination of waste, and tight cost control. (p. 584)

cost management The approaches and activities of managers to use resources to increase value to customers and to achieve organizational goals. (p. 2)

cost object Anything for which a measurement of costs is desired. (p. 29)

cost of capital Minimum acceptable annual rate of return on an investment. Also called *discount rate*, *hurdle rate*, *opportunity cost of capital*, or *required rate of return*. (p. 447)

cost of goods manufactured Cost of goods brought to completion, whether they were started before or during the current accounting period. (p. 42)

costs of quality (COQ) Costs incurred to prevent the production of a low-quality product or the costs arising as a result of such products. (p. 397)

cost pool Grouping of individual indirect cost items. (p. 116)

cost predictions Forecasts of future costs. (p. 307)

cost tracing Describes the assignment of direct costs to a particular cost object. (p. 30)

cost–volume–profit (CVP) analysis Studies the behavior and relationship among cost, volume, and profit as changes occur in the number of units sold, the selling price, the variable cost per unit, or the fixed costs of a product. (p. 77)

current cost Cost of purchasing an asset today identical to the one currently held, or the cost of purchasing an asset that provides services like the one currently held if an identical asset cannot be purchased. (p. 673)

customer-cost hierarchy Categorizes costs related to customers into different cost pools on the basis of different types of cost drivers, or cost-allocation bases, or different degrees of difficulty in determining cause-and-effect or benefits-received relationships. (p. 268)

customer life-cycle costs Costs that focus on the total costs incurred by a customer to acquire, use, maintain, and dispose of a product or service; influence the prices a company can charge for its products. (p. 278)

customer-profitability analysis Reporting and assessment of revenues earned from customers and the costs incurred to earn those revenues. (p. 267)

customer relationship management (CRM) Strategy that integrates people and technology in all business functions to deepen relationships with customers, partners, and distributors. (p. 5)

customer-response time How long it takes from the time a customer places an order for a product or service to the time the product or service is delivered to the customer. (p. 420)

customer service Business function that provides after-sales service to customers. (p. 5)

D

decentralization Organizational structure that gives managers at lower levels the freedom to make decisions. (p. 626)

decision model Formal method of making a choice that often involves both quantitative and qualitative analyses. (p. 342)

decision table Summary of the alternative actions, events, outcomes, and probabilities of events in a decision model. (p. 100)

degree of operating leverage Contribution margin divided by operating income; helps managers calculate the effect of sales fluctuations on operating income. (p. 91)

denominator level The denominator in a budgeted fixed overhead rate computation. (p. 549)

denominator-level variance Difference between budgeted fixed overhead and fixed overhead allocated on the basis of actual output produced. Also called *production-volume variance*. (p. 555)

dependent variable Cost to be predicted and managed; step in estimating a cost function using quantitative analysis of a past cost relationship. (p. 311)

design of products and processes Business function that details planning, engineering, and testing of products and processes. (p. 4)

design quality How closely the characteristics of a product or service meet the needs and wants of customers. (p. 396)

designed-in costs Costs that have not yet been incurred but will be incurred in the future based on decisions that have already been made. Also called *locked-in costs*. (p. 261)

diagnostic control systems Measures that help diagnose whether a company is performing to expectations. (p. 684)

differential cost Difference in total cost between two alternatives. (p. 350)

differential revenue Difference in total revenue between two alternatives. (p. 350)

direct costs of a cost object Costs related to a particular cost object that can be traced to it in an economically feasible (cost-effective) way. (p. 30)

direct manufacturing labor costs Costs that include the compensation of all manufacturing labor that can be traced to the cost object (work in process and then finished goods) in an economically feasible way. (p. 38)

direct material costs Acquisition costs of all materials that eventually become part of the cost object (work in process and then finished goods) and that can be traced to the cost object in an economically feasible way. (p. 38)

direct materials inventory Direct materials in stock and awaiting use in the manufacturing process. (p. 38)

direct method Allocates each support department's costs to operating departments only. (p. 145)

discount rate Minimum acceptable annual rate of return on an investment. Also called *cost of capital*, *hurdle rate*, *opportunity cost of capital*, or *required rate of return*. (p. 447)

discounted cash flow (DCF) method Measures all expected future cash inflows and outflows of a project discounted back to the present point in time. (p. 447)

discounted payback method Calculates the amount of time required for the discounted expected future cash flows to recoup the net initial investment in a project. (p. 454)

discretionary costs Costs that arise from periodic (usually annual) decisions regarding the maximum amount to be incurred and have no measurable cause-and-effect relationship between output and resources used. (p. 602)

distribution Business function that processes orders and ships products or services to customers. (p. 4)

downsizing Integrated approach of configuring processes, products, and people to match costs to the activities that need to be performed to operate effectively and efficiently in the present and future. Also called *rightsizing*. (p. 602)

dual pricing Practice that uses two separate transfer-pricing methods to price each transfer from one subunit to another. (p. 639)

dumping When a non-U.S. company sells a product in the United States at a price below the market value in the country where it is produced, and this lower price materially injures or threatens to materially injure an industry in the United States, which is a violation of antitrust laws. (p. 280)

dysfunctional decision making Occurs when a decision's benefit to one subunit is more than offset by the costs to the organization as a whole. Also called *incongruent decision making* or *suboptimal decision making*. (p. 627)

E

economic order quantity (EOQ) Decision model that, under a given set of assumptions, calculates the optimal quantity of inventory to order. (p. 406)

economic value added (EVA®) Equals after-tax operating income minus the (after-tax) weighted-average cost of capital multiplied by total assets minus current liabilities. (p. 669)

effectiveness Degree to which a predetermined objective or target is met. (p. 561)

efficiency Relative amount of inputs used to achieve a given output level. (p. 561)

efficiency variance Difference between actual input quantity used and budgeted input quantity allowed for actual output multiplied by budgeted price. Also called *usage variance*. (p. 545)

effort Extent to which managers strive or endeavor to achieve a goal. (p. 626)

engineered costs Result from a cause-and-effect relationship between the cost driver—output—and the (direct or indirect) resources used to produce that output. (p. 601)

enterprise resource planning (ERP) System that comprises an integrated set of software modules covering accounting, distribution, manufacturing, purchasing, human resources, and other functions. (p. 416)

equivalent units Derived amount of output units that (1) combines the quantity of each input (factor of production) in units completed and in incomplete units of work in process and (2) converts the quantity of input into the amount of completed output units that could be produced with that quantity of input. (p. 175)

event Possible relevant occurrence in a decision model. (p. 99)

expected monetary value Expected value when outcomes are measured in monetary terms. (p. 101)

expected value Weighted average of outcomes, with the probability of each outcome serving as the weight. (p. 101)

experience curve Function that measures the decline in cost per unit in various business functions of the value chain as the amount of these activities increases. (p. 306)

external failure costs Costs incurred on defective products after they have been shipped to customers. (p. 397)

F

facility-sustaining costs Costs of activities that cannot be traced to individual products or services but that support the organization as a whole. (p. 217)

factory overhead costs All manufacturing costs that are related to the cost object (work in process and then finished goods) but cannot be traced to that cost object in an economically feasible way. Also called *indirect manufacturing costs* or *manufacturing overhead costs*. (p. 38)

favorable variance Increases operating income relative to the budgeted amount. (p. 538)

finance director Executive responsible for overseeing the financial operations of an organization. Also called *chief financial officer*. (p. 13)

financial accounting Form of accounting that reports financial information to external parties such as investors, government agencies, banks, and suppliers; measures and records business transactions and provides financial statements that are based on generally accepted accounting principles (GAAP). (p. 2)

financial budget Part of the master budget that is made up of the capital expenditures budget, the cash budget, the budgeted balance sheet, and the budgeted statement of cash flows. (p. 489)

financial planning models Mathematical representations of the relationships among operating activities, financing activities, and other factors that affect the master budget. (p. 449)

finished goods inventory Goods completed but not yet sold. (p. 38)

first-in, first-out (FIFO) process-costing method (1) Assigns the cost of the previous accounting period's equivalent units in beginning work-in-process inventory to the first units completed and transferred out of the process, and (2) assigns the cost of equivalent units worked on during the *current* period first to complete beginning inventory, next to start and complete new units, and finally to units in ending work-in-process inventory. (p. 182)

fixed cost Cost that remains unchanged in total for a given time period, despite wide changes in the related level of total activity or volume. (p. 31)

fixed overhead flexible-budget variance Difference between actual fixed overhead costs and fixed overhead costs in a flexible budget. (p. 554)

fixed overhead spending variance Same amount as the fixed overhead flexible-budget variance. Difference between actual fixed overhead costs and fixed overhead costs in a flexible budget. (p. 554)

flexible budget Calculates budgeted revenues and budgeted costs based on the actual output in the budget period. (p. 539)

flexible-budget variance Difference between an actual result and the corresponding flexible-budget amount.(p. 539)

full costs of the product Sum of all variable and fixed costs in all business functions of the value chain (R&D, design, production, marketing, distribution, and customer service). (p. 345)

G

goal congruence Exists when individuals and groups work toward achieving an organization's goals. (p. 626)

gross margin percentage Gross margin divided by revenues. (p. 97)

growth component Measures the change in operating income attributable solely to the change in the quantity of output sold in a given time period. (p. 596)

H

high–low method Simplest form of quantitative analysis to estimate a cost function using only the highest and lowest observed values of the cost driver within the relevant range and their respective costs. (p. 313)

hurdle rate Minimum acceptable annual rate of return on an investment. Also called *cost of capital*, *discount rate*, *opportunity cost of capital*, or *required rate of return*. (p. 447)

hybrid-costing system Blends characteristics from both job-costing and process-costing systems. (p. 187)

I

idle time Wages paid for unproductive time caused by lack of orders, machine or computer breakdowns, work delays, poor scheduling, and the like. (p. 46)

imputed cost Cost recognized in particular situations but not recorded in financial accounting systems because it is an opportunity cost. (p. 668)

incongruent decision making Occurs when a decision's benefit to one subunit is more than offset by the costs to the organization as a whole. Also called *dysfunctional decision making* or *suboptimal decision making*. (p. 627)

incremental cost Additional total cost incurred for an activity. (p. 350)

incremental cost-allocation method Method that ranks the individual users of a cost object in the order of users most responsible for the common cost and then uses this ranking to allocate cost among those users. (p. 191)

incremental revenue Additional total revenue from an activity. (p. 350)

independent variable Level of activity or cost driver used to predict the dependent variable (costs) in a cost estimation or prediction model; step in estimating a cost function using quantitative analysis of a past cost relationship. (p. 311)

indirect costs of a cost object Costs related to a particular cost object but cannot be traced to it in an economically feasible (cost-effective) way. (p. 30)

indirect manufacturing costs All manufacturing costs that are related to the cost object (work in process and then finished goods) but cannot be traced to that cost object in an economically feasible way. Also called *factory overhead costs* or *manufacturing overhead costs*. (p. 38)

industrial engineering method Estimates cost functions by analyzing the relationship between inputs and outputs in physical terms. Also called *work-measurement method*. (p. 309)

inflation Decline in the general purchasing power of a monetary unit, such as dollars. (p. 468)

insourcing Producing the same goods or providing the same services within an organization. (p. 348)

interactive control systems Formal information systems that managers use to focus a company's attention and learning on key strategic issues. (p. 685)

intercept Component of total cost that does not vary with changes in the level of the activity. Also called *constant*. (p. 304)

intermediate product Product or service transferred between subunits of an organization. (p. 630)

internal failure costs Costs incurred on defective products before they are shipped to customers. (p. 397)

internal rate-of-return (IRR) method Calculates the discount rate at which an investment's present value of all expected cash inflows equals the present value of its expected cash outflows. (p. 449)

inventoriable costs All costs of a product that are considered as assets in the balance sheet when they are incurred and that become cost of goods sold only when the product is sold. (p. 38)

investment Resources or assets used to generate income. (p. 666)

investment center Responsibility center in which the manager is accountable for investments, revenues, and costs. (p. 502)

J

job In a job-costing system, a unit or multiple units of a distinct product or service. (p. 117)

job-cost record Records and accumulates all the costs assigned to a specific job, starting when work begins. Also called a *job-cost sheet*. (p. 121)

job-cost sheet Records and accumulates all the costs assigned to a specific job, starting when work begins. Also called a *job-cost record*. (p. 121)

job-costing system System in which the cost object is a unit or multiple units of a distinct product or service. (p. 117)

joint costs Costs of a production process that yields multiple products simultaneously. (p. 190)

just-in-time (JIT) production "Demand-pull" manufacturing system that manufactures each component in a production line as soon as, and only when, needed by the next step in the production line. Also called *lean production*. (p. 414)

just-in-time (JIT) purchasing Purchase of materials (or goods) so that they are delivered just as needed for production (or sales). (p. 410)

K

kaizen budgeting Incorporates continuous improvement anticipated during the budget period into the budget numbers. (p. 506)

L

labor-time sheet Source document that contains information about the amount of labor time spent on a specific job in a specific department or on other activities. (p. 122)

lean accounting Costing method that supports creating value for customers by costing value streams, as distinguished from individual products or departments, thereby eliminating waste in the accounting process. (p. 417)

lean production "Demand-pull" manufacturing system that manufactures each component in a production line as soon as, and only when, needed by the next step in the production line. Also called *just-in-time production*. (p. 414)

learning Strategy that involves examining past performance and systematically exploring alternative ways to make better-informed decisions and plans in the future; leads to changes in goals, strategies, the ways decision alternatives are identified, and the range of information collected when making predictions, and sometimes can lead to changes in managers. (p. 10)

learning curve Function that measures how labor-hours per unit decline as units of production increase because workers are learning and becoming better at their jobs. (p. 306)

life-cycle budgeting Estimates the revenues and business function costs across the entire value chain from a product's initial R&D to its final customer service and support. (p. 276)

life-cycle costing Tracks and accumulates business function costs across the entire value chain from a product's initial R&D to its final customer service and support. (p. 276)

line management Type of management that is directly responsible for achieving the goals of the organization. Examples are production, marketing, and distribution management. (p. 13)

linear cost function Graphically, total cost versus the level of a single activity related to that cost is a straight line within a relevant range. (p. 303)

linear programming (LP) Optimization technique used to maximize the objective function when there are multiple constraints. (p. 373)

locked-in costs Costs that have not yet been incurred but will be incurred in the future based on decisions that have already been made. Also called *designed-in costs*. (p. 261)

M

make-or-buy decisions Decisions about whether a producer of goods or services will insource or outsource. (p. 348)

management accounting Form of accounting that measures, analyzes, and reports financial and nonfinancial information that helps managers make decisions to fulfill the goals of an organization. (p. 20)

management by exception Practice that focuses management attention on areas that are not operating as expected and devotes less time to areas operating as expected. (p. 536)

management control system Means of gathering and using information to aid and coordinate planning and control decisions throughout an organization and to guide the behavior of its managers and other employees. (p. 625)

manufacturing cells Groupings of all the different types of equipment used to make a given product. (p. 414)

manufacturing cycle efficiency (MCE) Value-added manufacturing time divided by manufacturing cycle time. (p. 421)

manufacturing cycle time How long it takes from the time an order is received by manufacturing to the time a finished good is produced. Also called *manufacturing lead time*. (p. 420)

manufacturing lead time How long it takes from the time an order is received by manufacturing to the time a finished good is produced. Also called *manufacturing cycle time*. (p. 420)

manufacturing overhead allocated Amount of manufacturing overhead costs allocated to individual jobs based on the budgeted rate multiplied by actual quantity used of the allocation base. Also called *manufacturing overhead applied*. (p. 132)

manufacturing overhead applied Amount of manufacturing overhead costs allocated to individual jobs based on the budgeted rate multiplied by actual quantity used of the allocation base. Also called *manufacturing overhead allocated*. (p. 132)

manufacturing overhead costs All manufacturing costs that are related to the cost object (work in process and then finished goods) but cannot be traced to that cost object in an economically feasible way. Also called *factory overhead costs* or *indirect manufacturing costs*. (p. 38)

manufacturing-sector companies Companies that purchase materials and components and convert them into various finished goods. (p. 37)

margin of safety Aspect of sensitivity analysis that answers the "what-if" question of how far budgeted revenues can fall below budget before the breakeven point is reached. (p. 89)

marketing Business function that promotes and sells products or services to customers or prospective customers. (p. 4)

master budget Expresses management's operating and financial plans for a specified period, usually a fiscal year, including a set of budgeted financial statements. (p. 485)

materials requirements planning (MRP) "Push-through" system that manufactures finished goods for inventory on the basis of demand forecasts. (p. 413)

materials-requisition record Basic source document that contains information about the cost of direct materials used on a specific job and in a specific department. (p. 121)

merchandising-sector companies Companies that purchase and then sell tangible products without changing their basic form. (p. 37)

mixed cost Cost that has both fixed and variable elements. Also called *semivariable cost*. (p. 304)

moral hazard Describes a situation in which an employee prefers to exert less effort (or to report distorted information) compared with the effort (or accurate information) the owner desires because the owner cannot accurately monitor and enforce the employee's effort (or validity of the reported information). (p. 679)

motivation Desire to attain a selected goal combined with the resulting pursuit of that goal. (p. 626)

multiple regression Analysis that estimates the relationship between the dependent variable and two or more independent variables.(p. 315)

N

net income Operating income plus nonoperating revenues (such as interest revenue) minus nonoperating costs (such as interest cost) minus income taxes. (p. 85)

net present value (NPV) method Calculates the expected monetary gain or loss from a project by discounting all expected future cash inflows and outflows back to the present point in time using the required rate of return. (p. 447)

nominal rate of return Rate of return demanded to cover investment risk and the decline in general purchasing power of the monetary unit as a result of expected inflation. (p. 468)

nonlinear cost function Total cost (based on the level of a single activity) graphically displayed is not a straight line within a relevant range. (p. 305)

non-value-added cost Cost that, if eliminated, would not reduce the actual or perceived value or utility (usefulness) customers gain from using the product or service. (p. 260)

normal costing Costing system that (1) traces direct costs to a cost object by using the actual direct-cost rates multiplied by the actual quantities of the direct-cost inputs and (2) allocates indirect costs based on the budgeted indirect-cost rates multiplied by the actual quantities of the cost-allocation bases. (p. 121)

O

objective function Expresses the objective or goal to be maximized or minimized. (p. 372)

on-time performance Delivery of a product or service by the time it is scheduled to be delivered. (p. 421)

one-time-only special order Type of decision that affects output levels that involves accepting or rejecting special orders when there is idle production capacity and the special orders have no long-run implications. (p. 344)

operating budget The budgeted income statement and its supporting budget schedules. (p. 489)

operating department Adds value to a product or service made or done by a company. Also called *production department*. (p. 143)

operating income Equals total revenues from operations minus cost of goods sold and operating (period) costs (excluding interest expense and income taxes) or, equivalently, gross margin minus period costs. (p. 42)

operating-income volume variance Equals the static budget operating income per unit multiplied by the difference between the budgeted and actual level of output. (p. 560)

operating leverage Describes the effects that fixed costs have on changes in operating income as changes occur in units sold and contribution margin. (p. 91)

operation Standardized method or technique that is performed repetitively, often on different materials, resulting in different finished goods. (p. 187)

operation-costing system Hybrid costing system applied to batches of similar, but not identical, products. Within each operation, all product units use identical amounts of the operation's resources. (p. 188)

opportunity cost Contribution to operating income that is forgone by not using a limited resource in its next-best alternative use. (p. 353)

opportunity cost of capital Minimum acceptable annual rate of return on an investment. Also called *cost of capital*, *discount rate*, *hurdle rate*, or *required rate of return*. (p. 447)

ordering costs Costs that arise in preparing and issuing purchase orders; receiving and inspecting the items included in the orders; and matching invoices received, purchase orders, and delivery records to make payments. (p. 406)

organization structure Arrangement of lines of responsibility within an organization. (p. 502)

outcome Specifies the predicted economic results of various possible combinations of actions and events. (p. 100)

output unit–level costs Costs of activities performed on each individual unit of a product or service. (p. 216)

outsourcing Purchasing goods and services from outside vendors. (p. 348)

overabsorbed indirect costs When the allocated amount of indirect costs in an accounting period is greater than the actual (incurred) amount. Also called *overallocated indirect costs* or *overapplied indirect costs*. (p. 134)

overallocated indirect costs When the allocated amount of indirect costs in an accounting period is greater than the actual (incurred) amount. Also called *overabsorbed indirect costs* or *overapplied indirect costs*. (p. 134)

overapplied indirect costs When the allocated amount of indirect costs in an accounting period is greater than the actual (incurred) amount. Also called *overabsorbed indirect costs* or *overallocated indirect costs*. (p. 134)

overtime premium Wage rate paid to workers (for both direct labor and indirect labor) in excess of their straight-time wage rates. (p. 46)

P

Pareto diagram Chart that indicates how frequently each type of a defect occurs, ordered from the most frequent to the least frequent. (p. 400)

payback method Measures the time it will take to recoup, in the form of expected future cash flows, the net initial investment in a project. (p. 452)

peak-load pricing Practice of charging a higher price for the same product or service when demand approaches the physical limit of the capacity to produce that product or service. (p. 279)

perfectly competitive market Scenario of a homogeneous product with buying prices equal to selling prices and no individual buyers or sellers affecting those prices by their own actions. (p. 633)

period costs All costs in the income statement other than cost of goods sold. (p. 39)

planning Process that selects organization goals and strategies, predicts results under various alternative ways of achieving those goals, decides how to attain the desired goals, and communicates the goals and how to achieve them to the entire organization. (p. 9)

predatory pricing Practice of deliberately pricing below costs in an effort to drive competitors out of the market and restrict supply, and then raising prices rather than enlarging demand, which is a violation of antitrust laws. (p. 279)

prevention costs Costs incurred to prevent the production of products that do not conform to specifications. (p. 397)

price discount Reduction in selling price below list selling price to encourage customers to purchase more quantities. (p. 267)

price discrimination Practice of charging different customers different prices for the same product or service. (p. 278)

price-recovery component Measures the change in operating income attributable solely to changes in prices of inputs and outputs in a given time period. (p. 596)

price variance Difference between actual price and budgeted price, multiplied by actual input quantity. Also called *rate variance*. (p. 545)

prime costs All direct manufacturing costs. (p. 43)

pro forma statements Another term for budgeted financial statements. (p. 485)

probability Likelihood or chance that an event will occur. (p. 100)

probability distribution Likelihood, or probability, that each mutually exclusive and collectively exhaustive set of events will occur. (p. 100)

process-costing system System in which the cost object is masses of identical or similar units of a product or service. (p. 117)

product cost Sum of the costs assigned to a product for a specific purpose. (p. 47)

product-cost cross-subsidization Practice of undercosting (overcosting) one product, then overcosting (undercosting) at least one other product. (p. 207)

product differentiation Ability of an organization to offer products or services its customers perceive to be superior and unique relative to the products or services of its competitors. (p. 584)

product life cycle Spans the time from initial R&D on a product to when customer service and support is no longer offered for that product. (p. 276)

product-mix decisions Decisions managers make about which products to sell and in what quantities. (p. 356)

product overcosting Scenario in which a product consumes a low level of resources per unit but is reported to have a high cost per unit. (p. 207)

product-sustaining costs Costs of activities undertaken to support individual products regardless of the number of units or batches in which the units are produced. (p. 216)

product undercosting Scenario in which a product consumes a high level of resources per unit but is reported to have a low cost per unit. (p. 207)

production Business function that procures, transports, stores, coordinates, and assembles resources to produce a product or deliver a service. (p. 4)

production department Adds value to a product or service made or done by a company. Also called *operating department*. (p. 143)

production-volume variance Difference between budgeted fixed overhead and fixed overhead allocated on the basis of actual output produced. Also called *denominator-level variance*. (p. 555)

productivity component Measures the change in costs attributable to a change in the quantity of inputs used in the current year relative to the quantity of inputs that would have been used in the prior year to produce the current year's output. (p. 596)

profit center Responsibility center in which the manager is accountable for revenues and costs. (p. 502)

proration Spreads underallocated overhead or overallocated overhead among ending work-in-process inventory, finished goods inventory, and cost of goods sold. (p. 135)

purchase-order lead time Time between placing an order and its delivery. (p. 406)

purchasing costs Costs of goods acquired from suppliers, including incoming freight costs. (p. 406)

PV graph Method that shows how changes in the quantity of units sold affect operating income. (p. 84)

Q

qualitative factors Outcomes that are difficult to measure accurately in numerical terms. (p. 344)

quality Total features and characteristics of a product or a service made or performed according to specifications to satisfy customers at the time of purchase and during use. (p. 396)

quantitative factors Outcomes that are measured in numerical terms. (p. 343)

R

rate variance Difference between actual price and budgeted price, multiplied by actual input quantity. Also called *price variance*. (p. 545)

real rate of return Rate of return demanded to cover investment risk if there is no inflation. (p. 468)

reciprocal method Allocates support-department costs to operating departments by fully recognizing the mutual services provided among all support departments. (p. 147)

reengineering Fundamental rethinking and redesign of business processes to achieve improvements in critical measures of performance. (p. 586)

refined costing system Costing system that reduces the use of broad averages for assigning the cost of resources to cost objects and provides better measurement of the costs of indirect resources used by different cost objects, no matter how differently various cost objects use indirect resources. (p. 212)

regression analysis Statistical method that measures the average amount of change in the dependent variable associated with a unit change in one or more independent variables. (p. 315)

relevant costs Expected future costs that differ among the alternative courses of action being considered. (p. 342)

relevant range Band or range of normal activity level or volume in which there is a specific relationship between the level of activity or volume and the cost in question. (p. 34)

relevant revenues Expected future revenues that differ among the alternative courses of action being considered. (p. 342)

reorder point Quantity level of inventory on hand that triggers a new purchase order. (p. 408)

required rate of return (RRR) Minimum acceptable annual rate of return on an investment. Also called *cost of capital*, *discount rate*, *hurdle rate*, or *opportunity cost of capital*. (p. 447)

research and development (R&D) Business function that generates and experiments with ideas related to new products, services, or processes. (p. 4)

residual income (RI) Accounting measure of income minus charge for required return on an accounting measure of investment. (p. 668)

residual term Measures the distance between actual cost and estimated cost for each observation of the cost driver. (p. 316)

responsibility accounting System that measures the plans, budgets, actions, and actual results of each responsibility center. (p. 502)

responsibility center Part, segment, or subunit of an organization whose manager is accountable for a specified set of activities. (p. 502)

return on investment (ROI) Accounting measure of income divided by accounting measure of investment. (p. 666)

revenue Inflow of assets (usually cash or accounts receivable) received for products or services customers purchase. (p. 38)

revenue center Responsibility center in which the manager is accountable for revenues only. (p. 502)

revenue driver Variable, such as volume, that causally affects revenues. (p. 82)

rightsizing Integrated approach of configuring processes, products, and people to match costs to the activities that need to be performed to operate effectively and efficiently in the present and future. Also called *downsizing*. (p. 602)

rolling budget Budget that is always available for a specified future period; created by continually adding a month, quarter, or year to the period that just ended. Also called *continuous budget* or *rolling forecast*. (p. 488)

rolling forecast Budget that is always available for a specified future period; created by continually adding a month, quarter, or year to the period that just ended. Also called *continuous budget* or *rolling budget*. (p. 488)

S

safety stock Inventory held at all times regardless of the quantity of inventory ordered. (p. 409)

sales mix Quantities (or proportion) of various products (or services) that constitute total unit sales of a company. (p. 92)

sales-volume variance Difference between a flexible-budget amount and the corresponding static-budget amount. (p. 539)

selling-price variance Difference between the actual selling price and the budgeted selling price multiplied by the actual units sold. (p. 541)

semivariable cost Cost that has both fixed and variable elements. Also called *mixed cost*. (p. 304)

sensitivity analysis "What-if" technique that managers use to examine how an outcome will change if the original predicted data are not achieved or if an underlying assumption changes. (p. 87)

separable costs All costs—manufacturing, marketing, distribution, and so on—incurred beyond the splitoff point that are assignable to each of the specific products identified at the splitoff point. (p. 191)

sequential allocation method Allocates support-department costs to other support departments and to operating departments in a sequential manner that partially recognizes the mutual services provided among all support departments. Also called the *step-down method*. (p. 146)

service department Provides the services that assist other internal departments in a company. Also called *support department*. (p. 143)

service-sector companies Companies that provide services (intangible products) to their customers. (p. 37)

service-sustaining costs Costs of activities undertaken to support individual services regardless of the number of units or batches in which the units are produced. (p. 216)

shrinkage costs Costs that result from theft by outsiders, embezzlement by employees, misclassifications, and clerical errors. (p. 406)

simple regression Analysis that estimates the relationship between the dependent variable and one independent variable. (p. 315)

slope coefficient Amount by which total cost changes when a one-unit change occurs in the level of activity. (p. 304)

source document Original record that supports journal entries in an accounting system. (p. 121)

splitoff point Juncture in a joint production process when two or more products become separately identifiable. (p. 191)

staff management Type of management that provides advice, support, and assistance to line management. Examples are management accountants and information technology and human-resources management. (p. 13)

stand-alone cost-allocation method Determines the weights for cost allocation by considering each user of the cost as a separate entity. (p. 191)

standard Carefully determined price, cost, or quantity that is used as a benchmark for judging performance; usually expressed on a per-unit basis. (p. 543)

standard cost Carefully determined cost of a unit of output. (p. 544)

standard costing System that (1) traces direct costs to output produced by multiplying the standard prices or rates by the standard quantities of inputs allowed for actual outputs produced and (2) allocates overhead costs on the basis of the standard overhead-cost rates times the standard quantities of the allocation bases allowed for the actual outputs produced. (p. 548)

standard input Carefully determined quantity of input required for one unit of output. (p. 544)

standard price Carefully determined price that a company expects to pay for a unit of input. (p. 544)

static budget Budget that is based on the level of output planned at the start of the budget period. (p. 537)

static-budget variance Difference between the actual result and the corresponding budgeted amount in the static budget. (p. 538)

step cost function Cost function in which the cost remains the same over various ranges of the level of activity, but the cost increases by discrete amounts—that is, increases in steps—as the level of activity increases from one range to the next. (p. 305)

step-down method Allocates support-department costs to other support departments and to operating departments in a sequential manner that partially recognizes the mutual services provided among all support departments. Also called the *sequential allocation method*. (p. 146)

stockout costs Costs that arise when a company runs out of a particular item for which there is customer demand. (p. 406)

strategic cost management Describes cost management that specifically focuses on strategic issues. (p. 3)

strategy How an organization matches its own capabilities with the opportunities in the marketplace to accomplish its objectives. (p. 3)

strategy map Diagram that describes how an organization creates value by connecting strategic objectives in explicit cause-and-effect relationships with each other in the financial, customer, internal business process, and learning and growth perspectives. (p. 587)

suboptimal decision making Occurs when a decision's benefit to one subunit is more than offset by the costs to the organization as a whole. Also called *dysfunctional decision making* or *incongruent decision making*. (p. 627)

sunk costs Past costs that are unavoidable and cannot be changed no matter what action is taken. (p. 343)

supply chain Term that describes the flow of goods, services, and information from the initial sources of materials and services to the delivery of products to consumers, regardless of whether those activities occur in the same organization or in other organizations. (p. 6)

support department Provides the services that assist other internal departments in a company. Also called *service department*. (p. 143)

sustainability Development and implementation of strategies to achieve long-term financial, social, and environmental performance. (p. 8)

T

target cost per unit Estimated long-run cost per unit of a product or service that enables the company to achieve its target operating income per unit when selling at the target price. Equal to target price minus target operating income per unit. (p. 260)

target operating income per unit Operating income that a company aims to earn per unit of a product or service sold. (p. 259)

target price Estimated price for a product or service that potential customers are willing to pay. (p. 260)

target rate of return on investment Target annual operating income divided by invested capital. (p. 265)

theory of constraints (TOC) Describes methods to maximize operating income when faced with some bottleneck and some nonbottleneck operations. (p. 357)

throughput margin Revenues minus the direct material costs of the goods sold. (p. 357)

time driver Any factor that causes a change in the speed of an activity when the factor changes. (p. 421)

time value of money Key feature of the discounted cash flow method that means that a dollar (or any other monetary unit) received today is worth more than a dollar received at any future time. (p. 447)

total-overhead variance Equals the total amount of underallocated (or underapplied) overhead costs. (p. 558)

total quality management (TQM) Integrative philosophy of management for continuously improving the quality of products and processes, with the goal of delivering products and services that exceed customer expectations; the responsibility of everyone throughout the value chain. (p. 6)

transfer price Price one subunit (department or division) charges for a product or service supplied to another subunit of the same organization. (p. 630)

U

uncertainty Possibility that an actual amount will deviate from an expected amount. (p. 90)

underabsorbed indirect costs When the allocated amount of indirect costs in an accounting period is less than the actual (incurred) amount. Also called *underallocated indirect costs* or *underapplied indirect costs*. (p. 134)

underallocated indirect costs When the allocated amount of indirect costs in an accounting period is less than the actual (incurred) amount. Also called *underabsorbed indirect costs* or *underapplied indirect costs*. (p. 134)

underapplied indirect costs When the allocated amount of indirect costs in an accounting period is less than the actual (incurred) amount. Also called *underabsorbed indirect costs* or *underallocated indirect costs*. (p. 134)

unfavorable variance Decreases operating income relative to the budgeted amount. (p. 538)

unit cost Cost calculated by dividing total cost by the related number of units. Also called *average cost*. (p. 36)

unused capacity Amount of productive capacity available over and above the productive capacity employed to meet customer demand in the current period. (p. 601)

usage variance Difference between actual input quantity used and budgeted input quantity allowed for actual output multiplied by budgeted price. Also called *efficiency variance*. (p. 545)

V

value-added cost Cost that, if eliminated, would reduce the actual or perceived value or utility (usefulness) customers experience from using the product or service. (p. 260)

value chain Sequence of business functions in which customer usefulness is added to products. (p. 4)

value engineering Systematic evaluation of all aspects of the value chain, with the objective of reducing costs and achieving a quality level that satisfies customers. (p. 260)

value stream All value-added activities needed to design, manufacture, and deliver a given product or product line to customers. (p. 417)

variable cost Cost that changes in total in proportion to changes in the related level of total activity or volume. (p. 31)

variable costing Method of inventory costing in which fixed manufacturing costs are excluded from inventoriable costs and are treated instead as costs of the period in which they are incurred. (p. 56)

variable overhead efficiency variance Difference between actual quantity of the cost-allocation base used and budgeted quantity of the cost-allocation base that should have been used to produce actual output, multiplied by budgeted variable overhead cost per unit of the cost-allocation base. (p. 551)

variable overhead flexible-budget variance Difference between actual variable overhead costs incurred and flexible-budget variable overhead amounts. (p. 551)

variable overhead spending variance Difference between actual variable overhead cost per unit of the cost-allocation base and budgeted variable overhead cost per unit of the cost-allocation base, multiplied by the actual quantity of variable overhead cost-allocation base used. (p. 552)

variance Difference between actual results and expected performance. (p. 536)

W

weighted-average process-costing method Calculates cost per equivalent unit of all work done to date (regardless of the accounting period in which it was done) and assigns this cost to equivalent units completed and transferred out of the process and to equivalent units in ending work-in-process inventory. (p. 179)

whale curve Chart of cumulative customer-level operating income that shows a backward-bend at the point where customers start to become unprofitable, thus resembling a humpback whale. (p. 272)

work-in-process inventory Goods partially worked on but not yet completed. Also called *work in progress*. (p. 38)

work in progress Goods partially worked on but not yet completed. Also called *work-in-process inventory*. (p. 38)

work-measurement method Estimates cost functions by analyzing the relationship between inputs and outputs in physical terms. Also called *industrial engineering method*. (p. 309)

Index

Author

Company

Q

R

S